UNDERSTANDING
THE
CONSTITUTION

UNDERSTANDING
THE
CONSTITUTION

CONSTANTINOS E. SCAROS, JD, MA

SERVED AS DEAN OF CRIMINAL JUSTICE
KATHARINE GIBBS SCHOOL
NEW YORK, NEW YORK

JONES AND BARTLETT PUBLISHERS
Sudbury, Massachusetts
BOSTON   TORONTO   LONDON   SINGAPORE

World Headquarters
Jones and Bartlett Publishers
40 Tall Pine Drive
Sudbury, MA 01776
978-443-5000
info@jbpub.com
www.jbpub.com

Jones and Bartlett Publishers
Canada
6339 Ormindale Way
Mississauga, Ontario L5V 1J2
Canada

Jones and Bartlett Publishers
International
Barb House, Barb Mews
London W6 7PA
United Kingdom

Jones and Bartlett's books and products are available through most bookstores and online booksellers. To contact Jones and Bartlett Publishers directly, call 800-832-0034, fax 978-443-8000, or visit our website, www.jbpub.com.

Substantial discounts on bulk quantities of Jones and Bartlett's publications are available to corporations, professional associations, and other qualified organizations. For details and specific discount information, contact the special sales department at Jones and Bartlett via the above contact information or send an email to specialsales@jbpub.com.

This publication is designed to provide accurate and authoritative information in regard to the Subject Matter covered. It is sold with the understanding that the publisher is not engaged in rendering legal, accounting, or other professional service. If legal advice or other expert assistance is required, the service of a competent professional person should be sought.

Production Credits
Publisher, Higher Education: Cathleen Sether
Acquisitions Editor: Sean Connelly
Associate Editor: Megan R. Turner
Senior Production Editor: Renée Sekerak
Associate Marketing Manager: Jessica Cormier
Manufacturing and Inventory Control Supervisor: Amy Bacus
Composition: Glyph International
Cover and Title Page Design: Scott Moden
Photo and Permissions Associate: Emily Howard
Cover Images: George Washington Statue © stephane106/ShutterStock, Inc.; U.S. Capitol Building © Johnny Kuo/ShutterStock, Inc.; U.S. Capitol Rotunda © Pete Hoffman/ShutterStock, Inc.; James Madison Statue on the campus of James Madison University, Harrisonburg, VA. Courtesy of Photography Services, James Madison University
Printing and Binding: Courier Westford
Cover Printing: Courier Westford

Library of Congress Cataloging-in-Publication Data
Scaros, Constantinos E.
  Understanding the constitution/Constantinos E. Scaros.
    p. cm.
  Includes bibliographic references and index.
  ISBN 978-0-7637-5811-0 (alk. paper)
  1. Constitutional law—United States. I. Title.
  KF4550.S238 2010
  342.7302—dc22
                                        2010000577

6048

Printed in the United States of America
14 13 12 11 10   10 9 8 7 6 5 4 3 2 1

To my wife, Anna, with love.

CONTENTS

So what's the big deal about the Constitution, anyway? Isn't it just an old document printed on that antique-looking paper written by those men who wore those funny white wigs? Sure, it makes sense that we might want to learn a little bit about it, just like we knew that in the old days, people rode around on horses and buggies, and before that there were dinosaurs. Just like these things have nothing to do with modern life, neither does the Constitution, right? No.

The Constitution is important not only because of its *historical* importance—it is the document on which our nation's government was founded—but also because of its value in our everyday lives, here and now! To say that the Constitution is an old document that has nothing to do with modern-day life would be like saying that just because George Washington's heart, lungs, and brain were necessary to keep him alive then, those body parts are not vital to keep us alive now, because that was a long time ago and things were different then. The human body is still the human body and human behavior has not changed all that much, either. In fact, the more you learn about the past, the more you will realize that it is not as different from the present as you might expect. Teenagers had crushes on one another in the 1700s too, except back then they did not daydream about their heartthrob while listening to music on an iPod. Families still gather for holiday dinners, church services, and celebrations. Family dynamics are not all that different nowadays, even though the outfits we wear have changed dramatically. Some of the nasty behavior has endured as well, unfortunately. During colonial times, people committed murder, abused alcohol and drugs, engaged in adultery, and stole from their neighbors, although they no longer get tarred and feathered for such acts and they are not accused of witchcraft and stoned to death.

The Constitution then, is a living, breathing story about America's past and present, and is the premier guide for its immediate and long-range future. As remarkable a document as it is— and it is quite incredible—it truly was written by a group of men wearing white wigs (which was the fashion at the time), known as the Framers, Founders, or Founding Fathers (we will use those terms interchangeably). As brilliant as those men were, it is doubtful that any of them could imagine a world today filled with cars, airplanes, nuclear weapons, cell phones, and the Internet, when the Constitution was written in 1787. As marvelous a document as they created, it falls short of perfection, nonetheless. Moreover, none of those men are alive today to explain to us exactly what they meant in instances when we are not 100% clear. So, who is it that decides what those men in the funny white wigs meant? Another small group,

made up of men and women, wearing black robes. They are the Justices of the United States Supreme Court.

A useful way to understand the Constitution and its effect in the world you live in is to think of it as the blueprint of our society. We will revisit that concept throughout the book.

Before we move on, let's be clear on a few terms:

America: The word "America" throughout this book means the United States. It does not mean Canada or Mexico, nor any of the Central or South American countries. Of course, all of those countries are part of America too, but the word "America" is often synonymous with the United States. For instance, when people refer to the American dream, the American way of life, or something being as American as apple pie, they are talking about the United States. Accordingly, we will use the terms America and United States interchangeably.

Us and We: To that end, when I talk about "us" or "we," I mean you—the reader and me—the author. Also, I talk about the collective "we" as Americans. Of course, I wrote this book to be read by my fellow human beings all over the world, and I welcome people to read it throughout the far reaches of the globe. However, as it was primarily written for college students studying in the United States, when I speak of the collective "we," I am speaking as an American to other Americans. Nonetheless, "we" the Constitutional scholars— which is just a fancy way of saying those of us learning about the Constitution—hail from every nation on earth.

This book will help you become a Constitutional scholar. The "Introduction" begins with a walk through the Constitution, explaining its various parts. By reading the Constitution right away, you will appreciate each chapter even more, and in turn benefit from each chapter's focus on a particular Constitutional topic.

Chapter 1 questions whether we really live in a democracy and whether we really have the right to vote. The true answer might surprise you! Chapter 2 takes us back in time to learn how the Constitution came to be. As a young nation, the United States appeared to be doomed, until the Constitution saved it and allowed it to grow into a large and powerful nation.

Chapter 3 addresses our system of government in detail, which helps us to make sense of how our laws work. Chapter 4 discusses our religious freedoms and restrictions. We all hear of a separation of church and state, yet Congress begins its daily session with a prayer. Chapter 5 is about our freedoms of speech and expression. To what extent are we permitted to speak, write, or express ourselves?

Chapters 6 through 12 deal with some of the most controversial Constitutional issues today: abortion, affirmative action, civil liberties and security, crime and punishment, double jeopardy, eminent domain, and the right to keep and bear arms. Many people have opinions on these topics, but not everyone understands them as well as they should. The key to mastering these issues is to understand the Constitution, and that is what this book will help you do.

Also, you will notice that each chapter of the book will contain some "Questions for Review," a more detailed and thought-provoking question under the heading "Constitutionally Speaking," and one or more United States Supreme Court cases that are relevant to one or more of the subject matters covered in that chapter. Incidentally, many of the cases were decided during times when the English language sounded a bit different than it does today and long before computers and automated spell-checking programs were invented. For historical accuracy, the cases appear here in their original language, mistakes and all. These additional learning tools will help you to understand the chapter material even better and each chapter will serve as a building block toward your overall knowledge of the Constitution.

Before we begin, there are two more things to consider: understanding the Constitution is not a one-time task. It is a lifelong process, but a wonderful one. Finally, the good news is that it is a lot easier than you might think, precisely because the Constitution deals with issues that affect you, and that inevitably, you will find irresistible to discuss and debate.

Many thanks to my family, friends, and colleagues, for whom I am very grateful, and to my students, whom I not only teach but from whom I learn.

Thanks also to those who reviewed my manuscript: Brian K. McDuffie, Florida State College at Jacksonville; Mike Ardis, Pensacola Junior College; Pamella A. Seay, Florida Gulf Coast University; Kerry L. Muehlenbeck, Mesa Community College; and Johnnie Dumas Myers, Savannah State University.

Special thanks to the folks at Jones and Bartlett for their wonderful support throughout this entire project.

Last, but not least, to my parents, Emmanuel and Anthousa Scaros, for the love and support that they have always given me, and to my wife, Anna, for making my life wonderful.

A Walk through the Constitution

The United States of America is considered to be the most influential country on earth—politically, economically, and militarily, and is often referred to as the only remaining superpower in the world. Accordingly, one who is not familiar with the U.S. Constitution, the document from which all of our country's other laws stem, might think that it is an extremely lengthy piece of writing, maybe even hundreds of pages long. But most of you, or even all of you, probably already know that it is really quite short. You have probably seen it in the back of many textbooks, and realize that if you read it from beginning to end it would probably take you less than an hour.

How then, is such an evidently brief writing, the legal foundation of the most powerful country in the world, are there seemingly endless debates about what it means? How can something so small wield such power and create such controversy? That is exactly what we are going to learn in this book. Not just what the Constitution is, but also what it means. And in some cases, you will discover some reasons why the debates will continue.

Many other textbooks contain the Constitution hidden in the back pages. However, because this book *is* about the Constitution, it is placed here, front and center, so that you may read it *before* you read anything else in this book.

So, set aside a little time and read it. Certainly, the most important document in our nation's history is worth spending an afternoon to get to know. But it will not even take you nearly that long.

Let's begin with a little walk through the Constitution. When you are done, we will meet up again and pick up the discussion in Chapter 1.

President Barack Obama has written that the Constitution's words seem so perfect, that it is easy to believe that they were divinely inspired.

A Walk through the Constitution

Considering that the United States Constitution is the document on which the government of the most powerful nation in the world is founded, it is rather surprising to learn that it is only a few pages long! Its brevity results both in frustration and awe, as for many there is a struggle to understand what the Founding Fathers meant, and appreciation of its magnificence.

The Preamble

The Constitution begins with an introduction, known as the *Preamble*, which sets forth its purpose, that the people of the United States, in order to improve their system of government, have established the Constitution.

The Articles

There are seven sections in the Constitution, known as Articles. Articles I, II, and III describe the three branches of government—legislative, executive, and judicial—respectively. Essentially, the first three Articles are the heart of the Constitution. Article IV is about the relationship of the individual states to the federal government, and provides for "full faith and credit" measures whereby one state will respect the acts (such as the judicial decisions) of another. Article V addresses the amending process, Article VI establishes the Constitution as the law of the land, and Article VII is about the ratification process.

The Amendments

Following the seven Articles are the 27 Amendments to the Constitution. The first 10—collectively known as the Bill of Rights—were ratified all at once, in 1791, just 4 years after the Constitution itself was adopted. The remaining 17 were ratified between 1798 and 1992. Seventeen changes in 194 years averages about 1 change every 11 years, and changes have become more frequent.

During the 18th century, 1787 (from its inception) to 1799, the Constitution was changed 11 times. Discounting the Bill of Rights, there was only one additional change. There were just four new Amendments in the 19th century, but 12 were instituted in the 20th century.

Overall, 27 changes to the Constitution do not seem to be all that many, considering everything our country has been through: the Civil War—the end of slavery, railroad expansion into the West, institution of national and state parks, World War I, women's right to vote, World War II, the inventions of the automobile, airplane, television, and computer; the Civil Rights and feminist movements; the Korean and Vietnam wars; vast and diverse immigration from all over the world; landing on the moon; Three Mile Island and the environmental movement; and 9/11. Nonetheless, it has been changed often enough that we can all anticipate experiencing more changes to it in our lifetimes, which is why it is important for us to understand it well.

Remember, this was written well over 200 years ago, so you might find some words that appear peculiar. Surprisingly, the language has not changed all that much. And so, without further delay, here is the Constitution of the United States of America.

We the People of the United States, in Order to form a more perfect Union, establish Justice, insure domestic Tranquility, provide for the common defence, promote the general Welfare, and secure the Blessings of Liberty to ourselves and our Posterity, do ordain and establish this Constitution for the United States of America.

Article

Section 1.

All legislative Powers herein granted shall be vested in a Congress of the United States, which shall consist of a Senate and House of Representatives.

Section 2.

The House of Representatives shall be composed of Members chosen every second Year by the People of the several States, and the Electors in each State shall have the Qualifications requisite for Electors of the most numerous Branch of the State Legislature.

No Person shall be a Representative who shall not have attained to the age of twenty five Years, and been seven Years a Citizen of the United States, and who shall not, when elected, be an Inhabitant of that State in which he shall be chosen.

Representatives and direct Taxes shall be apportioned among the several States which may be included within this Union, according to their respective Numbers, which shall be determined by adding to the whole Number of free Persons, including those bound to Service for a Term of Years, and excluding Indians not taxed, three fifths of all other Persons. The actual Enumeration shall be made within three Years after the first Meeting of the Congress of the United States, and within every subsequent Term of ten Years, in such Manner as they shall by Law direct. The Number of Representatives shall not exceed one for every thirty Thousand, but each State shall have at Least one Representative; and until such enumeration shall be made, the State of New Hampshire shall be entitled to chuse three, Massachusetts eight, Rhode-Island and Providence Plantations one, Connecticut five, New-York six, New Jersey four, Pennsylvania eight, Delaware one, Maryland six, Virginia ten, North Carolina five, South Carolina five, and Georgia three.

When vacancies happen in the Representation from any State, the Executive Authority thereof shall issue Writs of Election to fill such Vacancies.

The House of Representatives shall chuse their Speaker and other Officers; and shall have the sole Power of Impeachment.

Section 3.

The Senate of the United States shall be composed of two Senators from each State, chosen by the Legislature thereof, for six Years; and each Senator shall have one Vote.

Immediately after they shall be assembled in Consequence of the first Election, they shall be divided as equally as may be into three Classes. The Seats of the Senators of the first Class shall be vacated at the Expiration of the second Year, of the second Class at the Expiration of the fourth Year, and the third Class at the Expiration of the sixth Year, so that one third may be chosen every second Year; and if Vacancies happen by Resignation, or otherwise, during the Recess of the Legislature of any State, the Executive thereof may make temporary Appointments until the next Meeting of the Legislature, which shall then fill such Vacancies.

No Person shall be a Senator who shall not have attained to the Age of thirty Years, and been nine Years a Citizen of the United States and who shall not, when elected, be an Inhabitant of that State for which he shall be chosen.

The Vice President of the United States shall be President of the Senate, but shall have no Vote, unless they be equally divided.

The Senate shall chuse their other Officers, and also a President pro tempore, in the Absence of the Vice President, or when he shall exercise the Office of President of the United States.

The Senate shall have the sole Power to try all Impeachments. When sitting for that Purpose, they shall be on Oath or Affirmation. When the President of the United States is tried, the Chief Justice shall preside: And no Person shall be convicted without the Concurrence of two thirds of the Members present.

Judgment in Cases of Impeachment shall not extend further than to removal from Office, and disqualification to hold and enjoy any Office of Honor, Trust or Profit under the United States: but the Party convicted shall nevertheless be liable and subject to Indictment, Trial, Judgment and Punishment, according to Law.

Section 4.

The Times, Places and Manner of holding Elections for Senators and Representatives, shall be prescribed in each State by the Legislature thereof; but the Congress may at any time by Law make or alter such Regulations, except as to the Places of chusing Senators.

The Congress shall assemble at least once in every Year, and such Meeting shall be on the first Monday in December, unless they shall by Law appoint a different Day.

Section 5.

Each House shall be the Judge of the Elections, Returns and Qualifications of its own Members, and a Majority of each shall constitute a Quorum to do Business; but a smaller Number may adjourn from day to day, and may be authorized to compel the Attendance of absent Members, in such Manner, and under such Penalties as each House may provide.

Each House may determine the Rules of its Proceedings, punish its Members for disorderly Behaviour, and, with the Concurrence of two thirds, expel a Member.

Each House shall keep a Journal of its Proceedings, and from time to time publish the same, excepting such Parts as may in their Judgment require Secrecy; and the Yeas and Nays of the Members of either House on any question shall, at the Desire of one fifth of those Present, be entered on the Journal.

Neither House, during the Session of Congress, shall, without the Consent of the other, adjourn for more than three days, nor to any other Place than that in which the two Houses shall be sitting.

Section 6.

The Senators and Representatives shall receive a Compensation for their Services, to be ascertained by Law, and paid out of the Treasury of the United States. They shall in all Cases, except Treason, Felony and Breach of the Peace, be privileged from Arrest during their Attendance at the Session of their respective Houses, and in going to and returning from the same; and for any Speech or Debate in either House, they shall not be questioned in any other Place.

No Senator or Representative shall, during the Time for which he was elected, be appointed to any civil Office under the Authority of the United States, which shall have been created, or the Emoluments whereof shall have been encreased during such time: and no Person holding any Office under the United States, shall be a Member of either House during his Continuance in Office.

Section 7.

All Bills for raising Revenue shall originate in the House of Representatives; but the Senate may propose or concur with Amendments as on other Bills.

Every Bill which shall have passed the House of Representatives and the Senate, shall, before it become a Law, be presented to the President of the United States; if he approve he shall sign it, but if not he shall return it, with his Objections to that House in which it shall have originated, who shall enter the Objections at large on their Journal, and proceed to reconsider it. If after such Reconsideration two thirds of that House shall agree to pass the Bill, it shall be sent, together with the Objections, to the other House, by which it shall likewise be reconsidered, and if approved by two thirds of that House, it shall become a Law. But in all such Cases the Votes of both Houses shall be determined by Yeas and Nays, and the Names of the Persons voting for and against the Bill shall be entered on the Journal of each House respectively. If any Bill shall not be returned by the President within ten Days (Sundays excepted) after it shall have been presented to him, the Same shall be a Law, in like Manner as if he had signed it, unless the Congress by their Adjournment prevent its Return, in which Case it shall not be a Law.

Every Order, Resolution, or Vote to which the Concurrence of the Senate and House of Representatives may be necessary (except on a question of Adjournment) shall be presented to the President of the United States; and before the Same shall take Effect, shall be approved by him, or being disapproved by him, shall be repassed by two thirds of the Senate and House of Representatives, according to the Rules and Limitations prescribed in the Case of a Bill.

Section 8.

The Congress shall have Power To lay and collect Taxes, Duties, Imposts and Excises, to pay the Debts and provide for the common Defence and general Welfare of the United States; but all Duties, Imposts and Excises shall be uniform throughout the United States;

To borrow Money on the credit of the United States;

To regulate Commerce with foreign Nations, and among the several States, and with the Indian Tribes;

To establish an uniform Rule of Naturalization, and uniform Laws on the subject of Bankruptcies throughout the United States;

To coin Money, regulate the Value thereof, and of foreign Coin, and fix the Standard of Weights and Measures;

To provide for the Punishment of counterfeiting the Securities and current Coin of the United States;

To establish Post Offices and post Roads;

To promote the Progress of Science and useful Arts, by securing for limited Times to Authors and Inventors the exclusive Right to their respective Writings and Discoveries;

To constitute Tribunals inferior to the supreme Court;

To define and punish Piracies and Felonies committed on the high Seas, and Offences against the Law of Nations;

To declare War, grant Letters of Marque and Reprisal, and make Rules concerning Captures on Land and Water;

To raise and support Armies, but no Appropriation of Money to that Use shall be for a longer Term than two Years;

To provide and maintain a Navy;

To make Rules for the Government and Regulation of the land and naval Forces;

To provide for calling forth the Militia to execute the Laws of the Union, suppress Insurrections and repel Invasions;

To provide for organizing, arming, and disciplining, the Militia, and for governing such Part of them as may be employed in the Service of the United States, reserving to the States respectively, the Appointment of the Officers, and the Authority of training the Militia according to the discipline prescribed by Congress;

To exercise exclusive Legislation in all Cases whatsoever, over such District (not exceeding ten Miles square) as may, by Cession of particular States, and the Acceptance of Congress, become the Seat of the Government of the United States, and to exercise like Authority over all Places purchased by the Consent of the Legislature of the State in which the Same shall be, for the Erection of Forts, Magazines, Arsenals, dock-Yards, and other needful Buildings;—And

To make all Laws which shall be necessary and proper for carrying into Execution the foregoing Powers, and all other Powers vested by this Constitution in the Government of the United States, or in any Department or Officer thereof.

Section 9.

The Migration or Importation of such Persons as any of the States now existing shall think proper to admit, shall not be prohibited by the Congress prior to the Year one thousand eight hundred and eight, but a Tax or duty may be imposed on such Importation, not exceeding ten dollars for each Person.

The Privilege of the Writ of Habeas Corpus shall not be suspended, unless when in Cases of Rebellion or Invasion the public Safety may require it.

No Bill of Attainder or ex post facto Law shall be passed.

No Capitation, or other direct, Tax shall be laid, unless in Proportion to the Census or Enumeration herein before directed to be taken.

No Tax or Duty shall be laid on Articles exported from any State.

No Preference shall be given by any Regulation of Commerce or Revenue to the Ports of one State over those of another: nor shall Vessels bound to, or from, one State, be obliged to enter, clear or pay Duties in another.

No Money shall be drawn from the Treasury, but in Consequence of Appropriations made by Law; and a regular Statement and Account of Receipts and Expenditures of all public Money shall be published from time to time.

No Title of Nobility shall be granted by the United States: And no Person holding any Office of Profit or Trust under them, shall, without the Consent of the Congress, accept of any present, Emolument, Office, or Title, of any kind whatever, from any King, Prince, or foreign State.

Section 10.

No State shall enter into any Treaty, Alliance, or Confederation; grant Letters of Marque and Reprisal; coin Money; emit Bills of Credit; make any Thing but gold and silver Coin a Tender in Payment of Debts; pass any Bill of Attainder, ex post facto Law, or Law impairing the Obligation of Contracts, or grant any Title of Nobility.

No State shall, without the Consent of the Congress, lay any Imposts or Duties on Imports or Exports, except what may be absolutely necessary for executing it's inspection Laws: and the net Produce of all Duties and Imposts, laid by any State on Imports or Exports, shall be for the Use of the Treasury of the United States; and all such Laws shall be subject to the Revision and Controul of the Congress.

No State shall, without the Consent of Congress, lay any Duty of Tonnage, keep Troops, or Ships of War in time of Peace, enter into any Agreement or Compact with another State, or with a foreign Power, or engage in War, unless actually invaded, or in such imminent Danger as will not admit of delay.

Article II
Section 1.

The executive Power shall be vested in a President of the United States of America. He shall hold his Office during the Term of four Years, and, together with the Vice President, chosen for the same Term, be elected, as follows:

Each State shall appoint, in such Manner as the Legislature thereof may direct, a Number of Electors, equal to the whole Number of Senators and Representatives to which the State may be entitled in the Congress: but no Senator or Representative, or Person holding an Office of Trust or Profit under the United States, shall be appointed an Elector.

The Electors shall meet in their respective States, and vote by Ballot for two Persons, of whom one at least shall not be an Inhabitant of the same State with themselves. And they shall make a List of all the Persons voted for, and of the Number of Votes for each; which List they shall sign and certify, and transmit sealed to the Seat of the Government of the United States, directed to the President of the Senate. The President of the Senate shall, in the Presence of the Senate and House of Representatives, open all the Certificates, and the Votes shall then be counted. The Person having the greatest Number of Votes shall be the President, if such Number be a Majority of the whole Number of Electors appointed; and if there be more than one who have such Majority, and have an equal Number of Votes, then the House of Representatives shall immediately chuse by Ballot one of them for President; and if no Person have a Majority, then from the five highest on the List the said House shall in like Manner chuse the President. But in chusing the President, the Votes shall be taken by States, the

Representation from each State having one Vote; A quorum for this Purpose shall consist of a Member or Members from two thirds of the States, and a Majority of all the States shall be necessary to a Choice. In every Case, after the Choice of the President, the Person having the greatest Number of Votes of the Electors shall be the Vice President. But if there should remain two or more who have equal Votes, the Senate shall chuse from them by Ballot the Vice President.

The Congress may determine the Time of chusing the Electors, and the Day on which they shall give their Votes; which Day shall be the same throughout the United States.

No Person except a natural born Citizen, or a Citizen of the United States, at the time of the Adoption of this Constitution, shall be eligible to the Office of President; neither shall any Person be eligible to that Office who shall not have attained to the Age of thirty five Years, and been fourteen Years a Resident within the United States.

In Case of the Removal of the President from Office, or of his Death, Resignation, or Inability to discharge the Powers and Duties of the said Office, the Same shall devolve on the Vice President, and the Congress may by Law provide for the Case of Removal, Death, Resignation or Inability, both of the President and Vice President, declaring what Officer shall then act as President, and such Officer shall act accordingly, until the Disability be removed, or a President shall be elected.

The President shall, at stated Times, receive for his Services, a Compensation, which shall neither be encreased nor diminished during the Period for which he shall have been elected, and he shall not receive within that Period any other Emolument from the United States, or any of them.

Before he enter on the Execution of his Office, he shall take the following Oath or Affirmation:—"I do solemnly swear (or affirm) that I will faithfully execute the Office of President of the United States, and will to the best of my Ability, preserve, protect and defend the Constitution of the United States."

Section 2.

The President shall be Commander in Chief of the Army and Navy of the United States, and of the Militia of the several States, when called into the actual Service of the United States; he may require the Opinion, in writing, of the principal Officer in each of the executive Departments, upon any Subject relating to the Duties of their respective Offices, and he shall have Power to grant Reprieves and Pardons for Offences against the United States, except in Cases of Impeachment.

He shall have Power, by and with the Advice and Consent of the Senate, to make Treaties, provided two thirds of the Senators present concur; and he shall nominate, and by and with the Advice and Consent of the Senate, shall appoint Ambassadors, other public Ministers and Consuls, Judges of the supreme Court, and all other Officers of the United States, whose Appointments are not herein otherwise provided for, and which shall be established by Law: but the Congress may by Law vest the Appointment of such inferior Officers, as they think proper, in the President alone, in the Courts of Law, or in the Heads of Departments.

The President shall have Power to fill up all Vacancies that may happen during the Recess of the Senate, by granting Commissions which shall expire at the End of their next Session.

Section 3.

He shall from time to time give to the Congress Information of the State of the Union, and recommend to their Consideration such Measures as he shall judge necessary and expedient; he may, on extraordinary Occasions, convene both Houses, or either of them, and in Case of Disagreement between them, with Respect to the Time of Adjournment, he may adjourn them to such Time as he shall think proper; he shall receive Ambassadors and other public Ministers; he shall take Care that the Laws be faithfully executed, and shall Commission all the Officers of the United States.

Section 4.

The President, Vice President and all civil Officers of the United States, shall be removed from Office on Impeachment for, and Conviction of, Treason, Bribery, or other high Crimes and Misdemeanors.

Article III

Section 1.

The judicial Power of the United States, shall be vested in one supreme Court, and in such inferior Courts as the Congress may from time to time ordain and establish. The Judges, both of the supreme and inferior Courts, shall hold their Offices during good Behaviour, and shall, at stated Times, receive for their Services, a Compensation, which shall not be diminished during their Continuance in Office.

Section 2.

The judicial Power shall extend to all Cases, in Law and Equity, arising under this Constitution, the Laws of the United States, and Treaties made, or which shall be made, under their Authority;—to all Cases affecting Ambassadors, other public Ministers and Consuls;—to all Cases of admiralty and maritime Jurisdiction;—to Controversies to which the United States shall be a Party;—to Controversies between two or more States;—between a State and Citizens of another State;—between Citizens of different States;—between Citizens of the same State claiming Lands under Grants of different States, and between a State, or the Citizens thereof, and foreign States, Citizens or Subjects.

In all Cases affecting Ambassadors, other public Ministers and Consuls, and those in which a State shall be Party, the supreme Court shall have original Jurisdiction. In all the other Cases before mentioned, the supreme Court shall have appellate Jurisdiction, both as to Law and Fact, with such Exceptions, and under such Regulations as the Congress shall make.

The Trial of all Crimes, except in Cases of Impeachment, shall be by Jury; and such Trial shall be held in the State where the said Crimes shall have been committed; but when not committed within any State, the Trial shall be at such Place or Places as the Congress may by Law have directed.

Section 3.

Treason against the United States, shall consist only in levying War against them, or in adhering to their Enemies, giving them Aid and Comfort. No Person shall be convicted of Treason unless on the Testimony of two Witnesses to the same overt Act, or on Confession in open Court.

The Congress shall have Power to declare the Punishment of Treason, but no Attainder of Treason shall work Corruption of Blood, or Forfeiture except during the Life of the Person attainted.

Article IV

Section 1.

Full Faith and Credit shall be given in each State to the public Acts, Records, and judicial Proceedings of every other State. And the Congress may by general Laws prescribe the Manner in which such Acts, Records, and Proceedings shall be proved, and the Effect thereof.

Section 2.

The Citizens of each State shall be entitled to all Privileges and Immunities of Citizens in the several States.

A Person charged in any State with Treason, Felony, or other Crime, who shall flee from Justice, and be found in another State, shall on Demand of the executive Authority of the State from which he fled, be delivered up, to be removed to the State having Jurisdiction of the Crime.

No Person held to Service or Labour in one State, under the Laws thereof, escaping into another, shall, in Consequence of any Law or Regulation therein, be discharged from such Service or Labour, but shall be delivered up on Claim of the Party to whom such Service or Labour may be due.

Section 3.

New States may be admitted by the Congress into this Union; but no new States shall be formed or erected within the Jurisdiction of any other State; nor any State be formed by the Junction of two or more States, or Parts of States, without the Consent of the Legislatures of the States concerned as well as of the Congress.

The Congress shall have Power to dispose of and make all needful Rules and Regulations respecting the Territory or other Property belonging to the United States; and nothing in this Constitution shall be so construed as to Prejudice any Claims of the United States, or of any particular State.

Section 4.

The United States shall guarantee to every State in this Union a Republican Form of Government, and shall protect each of them against Invasion; and on Application of the Legislature, or of the Executive (when the Legislature cannot be convened) against domestic Violence.

Article V

The Congress, whenever two thirds of both Houses shall deem it necessary, shall propose Amendments to this Constitution, or, on the Application of the Legislatures of two thirds of the several States, shall call a Convention for proposing Amendments, which, in either Case, shall be valid to all Intents and Purposes, as Part of this Constitution, when ratified by the Legislatures of three fourths of the several States, or by Conventions in three fourths thereof, as the one or the other Mode of Ratification may be proposed by the Congress; Provided that no Amendment which may be made prior to the Year One thousand eight hundred and eight shall in any Manner affect the first and fourth Clauses in the Ninth Section of the first Article; and that no State, without its Consent, shall be deprived of its equal Suffrage in the Senate.

Article VI

All Debts contracted and Engagements entered into, before the Adoption of this Constitution, shall be as valid against the United States under this Constitution, as under the Confederation.

This Constitution, and the Laws of the United States which shall be made in Pursuance thereof; and all Treaties made, or which shall be made, under the Authority of the United States, shall be the supreme Law of the Land; and the Judges in every State shall be bound thereby, any Thing in the Constitution or Laws of any State to the Contrary notwith-standing.

The Senators and Representatives before mentioned, and the Members of the several State Legislatures, and all executive and judicial Officers, both of the United States and of the several States, shall be bound by Oath or Affirmation, to support this Constitution; but no religious Test shall ever be required as a Qualification to any Office or public Trust under the United States.

Article VII

The Ratification of the Conventions of nine States, shall be sufficient for the Establishment of this Constitution between the States so ratifying the Same.

Done in Convention by the Unanimous Consent of the States present the Seventeenth Day of September in the Year of our Lord one thousand seven hundred and Eighty seven and of the Independence of the United States of America the Twelfth

In witness whereof We have hereunto subscribed our Names,

George Washington—President and deputy from Virginia
New Hampshire: John Langdon, Nicholas Gilman
Massachusetts: Nathaniel Gorham, Rufus King
Connecticut: William Samuel Johnson, Roger Sherman
New York: Alexander Hamilton
New Jersey: William Livingston, David Brearly, William Paterson, Jonathan Dayton
Pennsylvania: Benjamin Franklin, Thomas Mifflin, Robert Morris, George Clymer, Thomas FitzSimons, Jared Ingersoll, James Wilson, Gouverneur Morris
Delaware: George Read, Gunning Bedford, Jr., John Dickinson, Richard Bassett, Jacob Broom
Maryland: James McHenry, Daniel of Saint Thomas Jenifer, Daniel Carroll
Virginia: John Blair, James Madison, Jr.

North Carolina: William Blount, Richard Dobbs Spaight, Hugh Williamson

South Carolina: John Rutledge, Charles Cotesworth Pinckney, Charles Pinckney, Pierce Butler

Georgia: William Few, Abraham Baldwin

Amendment I

Congress shall make no law respecting an establishment of religion, or prohibiting the free exercise thereof; or abridging the freedom of speech, or of the press; or the right of the people peaceably to assemble, and to petition the Government for a redress of grievances.

Amendment II

A well regulated Militia, being necessary to the security of a free State, the right of the people to keep and bear Arms, shall not be infringed.

Amendment III

No Soldier shall, in time of peace be quartered in any house, without the consent of the Owner, nor in time of war, but in a manner to be prescribed by law.

Amendment IV

The right of the people to be secure in their persons, houses, papers, and effects, against unreasonable searches and seizures, shall not be violated, and no Warrants shall issue, but upon probable cause, supported by Oath or affirmation, and particularly describing the place to be searched, and the persons or things to be seized.

Amendment V

No person shall be held to answer for a capital, or otherwise infamous crime, unless on a presentment or indictment of a Grand Jury, except in cases arising in the land or naval forces, or in the Militia, when in actual service in time of War or public danger; nor shall any person be subject for the same offence to be twice put in jeopardy of life or limb; nor shall be compelled in any criminal case to be a witness against himself, nor be deprived of life, liberty, or property, without due process of law; nor shall private property be taken for public use, without just compensation.

Amendment VI

In all criminal prosecutions, the accused shall enjoy the right to a speedy and public trial, by an impartial jury of the State and district wherein the crime shall have been committed, which district shall have been previously ascertained by law, and to be informed of the nature and cause of the accusation; to be confronted with the witnesses against him; to have compulsory process for obtaining witnesses in his favor, and to have the Assistance of Counsel for his defence.

Amendment VII

In Suits at common law, where the value in controversy shall exceed twenty dollars, the right of trial by jury shall be preserved, and no fact tried by a jury, shall be otherwise re-examined in any Court of the United States, than according to the rules of the common law.

Amendment VIII

Excessive bail shall not be required, nor excessive fines imposed, nor cruel and unusual punishments inflicted.

Amendment IX

The enumeration in the Constitution, of certain rights, shall not be construed to deny or disparage others retained by the people.

Amendment X

The powers not delegated to the United States by the Constitution, nor prohibited by it to the States, are reserved to the States respectively, or to the people.

Amendment XI

The Judicial power of the United States shall not be construed to extend to any suit in law or equity, commenced or prosecuted against one of the United States by Citizens of another State, or by Citizens or Subjects of any Foreign State.

Ratification was completed on February 7, 1795.

Amendment XII

The Electors shall meet in their respective states, and vote by ballot for President and Vice President, one of whom, at least, shall not be an inhabitant of the same state with themselves; they shall name in their ballots the person voted for as President, and in distinct ballots the person voted for as Vice President, and they shall make distinct lists of all persons voted for as President, and of all persons voted for as Vice President, and of the number of votes for each, which lists they shall sign and certify, and transmit sealed to the seat of the government of the United States, directed to the President of the Senate;—The President of the Senate shall, in the presence of the Senate and House of Representatives, open all the certificates and the votes shall then be counted;—The person having the greatest number of votes for President, shall be the President, if such number be a majority of the whole number of Electors appointed; and if no person have such majority, then from the persons having the highest numbers not exceeding three on the list of those voted for as President, the House of Representatives shall choose immediately, by ballot, the President. But in choosing the President, the votes shall be taken by states, the representation from each state having one vote; a quorum for this purpose shall consist of a member or members from two-thirds of the states, and a majority of all the states shall be necessary to a choice. And if the House of Representatives shall not choose a President whenever the right of choice shall devolve upon them, before the fourth day of March next following, then the Vice President shall act as President, as in the case of the death or other constitutional disability of the President. —The person having the greatest number of votes as Vice President, shall be the

Vice President, if such number be a majority of the whole number of Electors appointed, and if no person have a majority, then from the two highest numbers on the list, the Senate shall choose the Vice President; a quorum for the purpose shall consist of two-thirds of the whole number of Senators, and a majority of the whole number shall be necessary to a choice. But no person constitutionally ineligible to the office of President shall be eligible to that of Vice President of the United States.

Proposal and Ratification The twelfth amendment to the Constitution of the United States was proposed to the legislatures of the several States by the Eighth Congress, on the 9th of December, 1803, in lieu of the original third paragraph of the first section of the second article; and was declared in a proclamation of the Secretary of State, dated the 25th of September, 1804, to have been ratified by the legislatures of 13 of the 17 States. The dates of ratification were: North Carolina, December 21, 1803; Maryland, December 24, 1803; Kentucky, December 27, 1803; Ohio, December 30, 1803; Pennsylvania, January 5, 1804; Vermont, January 30, 1804; Virginia, February 3, 1804; New York, February 10, 1804; New Jersey, February 22, 1804; Rhode Island, March 12, 1804; South Carolina, May 15, 1804; Georgia, May 19, 1804; New Hampshire, June 15, 1804.

Ratification was completed on June 15, 1804.

Amendment XIII

Section 1.
Neither slavery nor involuntary servitude, except as a punishment for crime whereof the party shall have been duly convicted, shall exist within the United States, or any place subject to their jurisdiction.

Section 2.
Congress shall have power to enforce this article by appropriate legislation.

Proposal and Ratification

Ratification was completed on December 6, 1865.

Amendment XIV

Section 1.
All persons born or naturalized in the United States, and subject to the jurisdiction thereof, are citizens of the United States and of the State wherein they reside. No State shall make or enforce any law which shall abridge the privileges or immunities of citizens of the United States; nor shall any State deprive any person of life, liberty, or property, without due process of law; nor deny to any person within its jurisdiction the equal protection of the laws.

Section 2.
Representatives shall be apportioned among the several States according to their respective numbers, counting the whole number of persons in each State, excluding Indians not taxed. But when the right to vote at any election for the choice of electors for President and Vice President of the United States, Representatives in Congress, the Executive and Judicial officers of a State, or the members of the Legislature thereof, is denied to any of the male inhabitants of such State, being twenty-one years of age, and citizens of the United States, or in any way abridged, except for participation in rebellion, or other crime, the basis of representation therein shall be reduced in the proportion which the number of such male citizens shall bear to the whole number of male citizens twenty-one years of age in such State.

Section 3.
No person shall be a Senator or Representative in Congress, or elector of President and Vice President, or hold any office, civil or military, under the United States, or under any State, who, having previously taken an oath, as a member of Congress, or as an officer of the United States, or as a member of any State legislature, or as an executive or judicial officer of any State, to support the Constitution of the United States, shall have engaged in insurrection or rebellion against the same, or given aid or comfort to the enemies thereof. But Congress may by a vote of two-thirds of each House, remove such disability.

Section 4.
The validity of the public debt of the United States, authorized by law, including debts incurred for payment of pensions and bounties for services in suppressing insurrection or rebellion, shall not be questioned. But neither the United States nor any State shall assume or pay any debt or obligation incurred in aid of insurrection or rebellion against the United States, or any claim for the loss or emancipation of any slave; but all such debts, obligations and claims shall be held illegal and void.

Section 5.
The Congress shall have power to enforce, by appropriate legislation, the provisions of this article.

Amendment XV

Section 1.
The right of citizens of the United States to vote shall not be denied or abridged by the United States or by any State on account of race, color, or previous condition of servitude.

Section 2.
The Congress shall have power to enforce this article by appropriate legislation.

Amendment XVI

The Congress shall have power to lay and collect taxes on incomes, from whatever source derived, without apportionment among the several States, and without regard to any census or enumeration.

Amendment XVII

The Senate of the United States shall be composed of two Senators from each State, elected by the people thereof, for six years; and each Senator shall have one vote. The electors in each State shall have the qualifications requisite for electors of the most numerous branch of the State legislatures.

When vacancies happen in the representation of any State in the Senate, the executive authority of such State shall issue writs of election to fill such vacancies: Provided, That the legislature of any State may empower the executive thereof to make temporary appointments until the people fill the vacancies by election as the legislature may direct.

This amendment shall not be so construed as to affect the election or term of any Senator chosen before it becomes valid as part of the Constitution.

Amendment XVIII

Section 1.
After one year from the ratification of this article the manufacture, sale, or transportation of intoxicating liquors within, the importation thereof into, or the exportation thereof from the United States and all territory subject to the jurisdiction thereof for beverage purposes is hereby prohibited.

Section 2.
The Congress and the several States shall have concurrent power to enforce this article by appropriate legislation.

Section 3.
This article shall be inoperative unless it shall have been ratified as an amendment to the Constitution by the legislatures of the several States, as provided in the Constitution, within seven years from the date of the submission hereof to the States by the Congress.

Amendment XIX

The right of citizens of the United States to vote shall not be denied or abridged by the United States or by any State on account of sex.

Congress shall have power to enforce this article by appropriate legislation.

Amendment XX

Section 1.
The terms of the President and Vice President shall end at noon on the 20th day of January, and the terms of Senators and Representatives at noon on the 3d day of January, of the years in which such terms would have ended if this article had not been ratified; and the terms of their successors shall then begin.

Section 2.
The Congress shall assemble at least once in every year, and such meeting shall begin at noon on the 3d day of January, unless they shall by law appoint a different day.

Section 3.
If, at the time fixed for the beginning of the term of the President, the President elect shall have died, the Vice President elect shall become President. If a President shall not have been chosen before the time fixed for the beginning of his term, or if the President elect shall have failed to qualify, then the Vice President elect shall act as President until a President shall have qualified; and the Congress may by law provide for the case wherein neither a President elect nor a Vice President elect shall have qualified, declaring who shall then act as President, or the manner in which one who is to act shall be selected, and such person shall act accordingly until a President or Vice President shall have qualified.

Section 4.
The Congress may by law provide for the case of the death of any of the persons from whom the House of Representatives may choose a President whenever the right of choice shall have devolved upon them, and for the case of the death of any of the persons from whom the Senate may choose a Vice President whenever the right of choice shall have devolved upon them.

Section 5.
Sections 1 and 2 shall take effect on the 15th day of October following the ratification of this article.

Section 6.
This article shall be inoperative unless it shall have been ratified as an amendment to the Constitution by the legislatures of three-fourths of the several States within seven years from the date of its submission.

Amendment XXI

Section 1.
The eighteenth article of amendment to the Constitution of the United States is hereby repealed.

Section 2.
The transportation or importation into any State, Territory, or possession of the United States for delivery or use therein of intoxicating liquors, in violation of the laws thereof, is hereby prohibited.

Section 3.
This article shall be inoperative unless it shall have been ratified as an amendment to the Constitution by conventions in the several States, as provided in the Constitution, within seven years from the date of the submission hereof to the States by the Congress.

Amendment XXII

Section 1.
No person shall be elected to the office of the President more than twice, and no person who has held the office of President, or acted as President, for more than two years of a term to which some other person was elected President shall be elected to the office of the President more than once. But this article shall not apply to any person holding the office of President when this article was proposed by the Congress, and shall not prevent any person who may be holding the office of President, or acting as President, during the term within which this article becomes operative from holding the office of President or acting as President during the remainder of such term.

Section 2.
This article shall be inoperative unless it shall have been ratified as an amendment to the Constitution by the legislatures

of three-fourths of the several states within seven years from the date of its submission to the states by the Congress.

Amendment XXIII

Section 1.
The District constituting the seat of government of the United States shall appoint in such manner as the Congress may direct:

A number of electors of President and Vice President equal to the whole number of Senators and Representatives in Congress to which the District would be entitled if it were a state, but in no event more than the least populous state; they shall be in addition to those appointed by the states, but they shall be considered, for the purposes of the election of President and Vice President, to be electors appointed by a state; and they shall meet in the District and perform such duties as provided by the twelfth article of amendment.

Section 2.
The Congress shall have power to enforce this article by appropriate legislation.

Amendment XXIV

Section 1.
The right of citizens of the United States to vote in any primary or other election for President or Vice President, for electors for President or Vice President, or for Senator or Representative in Congress, shall not be denied or abridged by the United States or any state by reason of failure to pay any poll tax or other tax.

Section 2.
The Congress shall have power to enforce this article by appropriate legislation.

Amendment XXV

Section 1.
In case of the removal of the President from office or of his death or resignation, the Vice President shall become President.

Section 2.
Whenever there is a vacancy in the office of the Vice President, the President shall nominate a Vice President who shall take office upon confirmation by a majority vote of both Houses of Congress.

Section 3.
Whenever the President transmits to the President pro tempore of the Senate and the Speaker of the House of Representatives his written declaration that he is unable to discharge the powers and duties of his office, and until he transmits to them a written declaration to the contrary, such powers and duties shall be discharged by the Vice President as Acting President.

Section 4.
Whenever the Vice President and a majority of either the principal officers of the executive departments or of such other body as Congress may by law provide, transmit to the President pro tempore of the Senate and the Speaker of the House of Representatives their written declaration that the President is unable to discharge the powers and duties of his office, the Vice President shall immediately assume the powers and duties of the office as Acting President.

Thereafter, when the President transmits to the President pro tempore of the Senate and the Speaker of the House of Representatives his written declaration that no inability exists, he shall resume the powers and duties of his office unless the Vice President and a majority of either the principal officers of the executive department or of such other body as Congress may by law provide, transmit within four days to the President pro tempore of the Senate and the Speaker of the House of Representatives their written declaration that the President is unable to discharge the powers and duties of his office. Thereupon Congress shall decide the issue, assembling within forty-eight hours for that purpose if not in session. If the Congress, within twenty-one days after receipt of the latter written declaration, or, if Congress is not in session, within twenty-one days after Congress is required to assemble, determines by two-thirds vote of both Houses that the President is unable to discharge the powers and duties of his office, the Vice President shall continue to discharge the same as Acting President; otherwise, the President shall resume the powers and duties of his office.

Amendment XXVI

Section 1.
The right of citizens of the United States, who are 18 years of age or older, to vote, shall not be denied or abridged by the United States or any state on account of age.

Section 2.
The Congress shall have the power to enforce this article by appropriate legislation.

Amendment XXVII

No law varying the compensation for the services of the Senators and Representatives shall take effect until an election of Representatives shall have intervened.

Constantinos E. Scaros has been a college professor and administrator for more than 17 years. He is also a political columnist and an attorney. This is his fifth book; he has also written books on the introduction to law, torts, immigration, and college success.

Do We Really Live in a Democracy, and Do We Really Have the Right to Vote?

Chapter Objectives

In this chapter you will learn . . .

- The differences between a democracy and a republic
- What the Constitution really says about the right to vote
- The process of electing the president of the United States
- What happens when state law conflicts with federal law
- The importance of case law

Introduction

Surely, you have heard the United States referred to as a democracy. Phrases such as, "after all, this is a democracy, isn't it?" and "we do live in a democracy, don't we?" are as common in describing the United States as referring to it as a "free country" (more on that later). Accordingly, you might be surprised to learn that, actually, the United States is really *not* a democracy, nor was it ever intended to be.

"Democratic republic" is a far more accurate description of our system of government than is "democracy." But, before we move beyond that phrase, let us define it by asking, what is a democracy and what is a republic?

Democracy

A democracy is a system of government in which all of the people rule. If the United States were a democracy in the purest sense of the word, then every American citizen would have the ability to vote on every issue, and the choice that received the most votes would prevail. By 2005, the U.S. population had grown to 300 million people. Imagine how long it would take 300 million people to vote on anything! Why, if you were to even count to 300 million, it would take you over 3 years—and that is counting every second and every minute of every day, month, and year, with no time for sleep, or even to have a snack! In other words, it would be impossible for anything to ever be accomplished in a nation of 300 million people if everyone had the opportunity to vote on every issue.

Of course, not everyone is eligible to vote anyway. For instance, as the Twenty-Sixth Amendment states, only

those U.S. citizens who are at least 18 years old may vote. Eliminating minors and noncitizens might reduce the total number of eligible voters to 200 million, but that would hardly make things any easier. So, we can all agree that we do not live in a system of *pure democracy*, and that such a system would not work in a country so large. But what about a *representative democracy*; isn't that what we have here? That sounds a little more along the lines of our system of government. After all, we elect our representatives, and, hopefully, they will vote as we would expect them to, and so that is democracy at work—or maybe not.

You see, a democracy is based on the system of majority rule. So, let's see if this system of democracy works here. To illustrate, let's take a look at the First Amendment, which states (among other things) that Congress shall make no law respecting the establishment of religion. (By the way, we'll discuss Congress and the freedom of religion in more detail later—but let's continue with our example.) Considering that the vast majority of Americans are Christians, let's suppose that Congress decided to pass a law declaring Christianity as the official religion in the United States. As long as a majority voted in favor of that law, it would be enacted, right? Wrong. Because it would directly violate the Constitution, and it takes a whole lot more than majority rule to change the Constitution. That is a prime example of why the United States of America is *not* a democracy.

Republic

If the United States is not a democracy, then what is it? It is a *republic*, which is a representative form of government. In other words, it is a system of government whereby the power belongs to the people, but that power is exercised through their elected representatives. Unlike a democracy, not only are decisions not made by all of the people, but not all decisions are made by majority rule.

At this point, you might be thinking, "republic sounds a whole lot like democracy, so what's the difference?" The difference is that a democracy *may* have direct or representative participation (in other words, either you or your senator may make the law), whereas a republic *must* have representative democracy (your senator may make the law, but you may not). A second difference is that in a democracy, the majority rules. In a republic, that is not *necessarily* the case, although it often is. And in the

United States, because the majority often prevails, we tend to refer to our nation as a *democratic republic*.

The United States Is a Republic, First and Foremost

In that sense, the word *democratic* is the adjective, which describes the word *republic*, which is the noun. Republic is the more powerful word. A democratic republic is a republic that has democratic tendencies, whereas a republican democracy is a democracy that has republic traits. Still not sure? Consider this example. If you live in New York City, the weather in the wintertime might be 20°F or even lower on a typical day. But, suppose that during a particular winter the temperature is much warmer, reaching an average of 50°F nearly every day. You might be tempted to say that it is a *summery* winter. Conversely, you might spend the summer in New York when the temperature typically reaches the 80s, and sometimes the 90s. But during this particular summer, the temperature barely reaches above 70°F. In that case, you might describe it as a *wintery* summer. In either case, the first word is the less powerful one. A summery winter is still winter, and a wintery summer is still summer. No matter how you look at it, the weather in the wintery summer is still warmer than during the summery winter. Similarly, a democratic-republic is still more of a republic than a democracy.

If we can accept that the United States is a republic, not a democracy, the next question might be, does it really matter? As we will find out, it matters a whole lot, because we need to be clear about this notion as it is an important key in our adventure of understanding the Constitution.

The Right to Vote

There are many misconceptions about American history that, when repeated over and over again, are simply assumed to be true, but in fact are quite inaccurate. Among these is the notion that you, me, or anyone else has a Constitutional right to vote for, say, the president of the United States, or a politician from your congressional district seeking a seat in the House of Representatives. Along those lines, some might say, "Well, when Abraham Lincoln freed the slaves, the Fifteenth Amendment granted black men the right to vote." Notice the word *men*, because one might continue to say, "and the Nineteenth Amendment granted women the right to vote." It does not matter. Both statements are incorrect.

Let's begin with the Fifteenth Amendment. Read it carefully. Does it say anything like "black men hereby are granted the right to vote?" No, it says nothing of the kind. Instead, it says that the right to vote *may not be denied* based on race or color. Let's consider Charlie, a white man, and Joe, a black man: If both of them went to vote on Election Day, and the local officials let Charlie in but told Joe "you cannot vote because you are black," that would be a clear violation of Joe's Constitutional rights. Not because Joe has any right to vote, but because his right to vote *may not be denied* based on race. In other words, if the election official told both Charlie and Joe, "excuse me, gentlemen, neither

of you can vote, because we passed a law that states that only college graduates have the right to vote, and neither of you is a college graduate." Or, "neither of you may vote because you have to write a book about American history before you are granted that right." In these cases, Joe would not be protected by the Constitution because he is being denied the opportunity to vote based on a factor *other* than race. He cannot turn to the Fifteenth Amendment for help.

Now, let's take a look at the Nineteenth Amendment. It states that the right to vote *may not be denied* based on sex (in other words, gender). So, if David and Sally went to vote and Sally was denied the opportunity *because* she is a woman, that would be a clear violation of her Constitutional rights. But if she was denied because, say, she needs to visit our nation's capital, Washington, D.C., before she would be eligible (and the same would be true for David and for everyone else, too, male or female), then her right to vote would not be denied based on her gender. The Nineteenth Amendment would not help her cause any more than the Fifteenth Amendment would help Joe in the example above.

Let's take a look at one more Amendment, the one we mentioned earlier, the Twenty-Sixth. This time, let's consider Judy, who is an 18-year-old Asian woman. Suppose that the local election official denies her the right to vote, stating that she must be 21. "If you're not old enough to legally drink a beer, I say you're not old enough to vote," snarled the official. That is a clear violation of Judy's Constitutional right according to the Twenty-Sixth Amendment, which guarantees that the right to vote will not be denied based on age for anyone 18 years or older. Also, the election official could not deny her the vote because she is Asian, or because she is a woman, as those would violate the Fifteenth and Nineteenth Amendments, respectively. But if the election official denied her the right to vote because she does not speak at least three foreign languages, then Judy would have no Constitutional recourse; she could not turn to the Constitution for help.

The Fourteenth Amendment

When faced with the shocking reality that nothing in the Constitution guarantees our right to vote, some point to the Fourteenth Amendment for the answer. That Amendment, best known for its Section 1, in which it guarantees all Americans equal protection under the law, contains provisions regarding voting in Section 2, as follows: if any male American citizen 21 years or older, who has not participated in a crime, is denied the right to vote, then the state that denies him will lose Representatives (House members) proportionately to the number of such individuals to whom it denies that right. Sounds confusing, right? Here's the simple version, in two steps:

1. Let's take the state of Massachusetts, which has 10 Representatives, as an example. If Massachusetts denied the right to vote to 30% of its American citizen noncriminal males who are 21 or old**er**, then Massachusetts would lose 30% of its Representatives (3 in total), thereby reducing its total number of Representatives from ten to seven.

2. The Fourteenth Amendment was ratified in 1868; since then, women and all persons 18 years or older were guaranteed the right to vote by the Nineteenth and Twenty-Sixth Amendments, respectively. Therefore, if any of them were denied the right to vote, they would be part of the equation determining the reduction in Representatives as well.

The important point here is that the Fourteenth Amendment creates a severe penalty for denial of the right to vote, but does not expressly forbid it.

In fact, all of these examples help to illustrate that there is nothing in the Constitution that specifically guarantees anyone the right to vote. The only thing that is guaranteed is that the right to vote *may not be denied* on the basis of race, color, gender, and age. That makes a big difference, legally.

Technical Versus Practical Reality: Your Right to Vote Is on Solid Ground

The examples above might seem a bit troubling, especially if you can envision your state's legislature granting the right to vote to only those who can, say: (1) type 90 words per minute; (2) play the trombone; (3) slam dunk a basketball; and (4) fly an airplane. If you cannot do all four things, you cannot vote. Well, don't panic. Just because the Constitution cannot automatically strike down such laws, it does not mean they would get very far.

First, those laws actually would have to be passed by the particular state legislature. Can you imagine *any* state legislature creating such absurd requirements regarding the right to vote? But even if the requirements did not seem preposterous, the American people undoubtedly would not sit still for it. They would likely demand, at that point, a Constitutional Amendment that would once and for all establish a guarantee to vote.

Moreover, the stiff penalty imposed by the Fourteenth Amendment would make it even more unlikely that a state would deny any noncriminal American citizen age 18 or older the right to vote.

Nonetheless, just because there is no real threat of that happening does not mean that we have that right spelled out anywhere in the Constitution—we do not.

Let us now move on and talk a little more about the Constitution's sheer power. If you have the Constitution on your side, no other law, rule, or regulation can touch you.

The Supremacy Clause

The Constitution is the most powerful legal bodyguard you can have. Article Six clearly states that the Constitution is the supreme law of the land, and no state law *to the contrary* shall be binding. This language, known as the Supremacy Clause, guarantees that if there is a conflict between the Constitution and any other law (for example, a state or local law), the Constitution will always prevail. Of course, that does not mean that a state law cannot be *different* from the Constitution; it simply means that it cannot directly conflict with it.

For instance, the Fourth Amendment guarantees the right to a jury trial in criminal cases. If a particular state *also* guaranteed jury trials in civil cases, that law would be

different from what is written in the Constitution, but the two laws would not conflict. All the Constitution discusses is a guarantee of a jury criminal trial. The state law does not deny that, it merely *adds* to the rights. That is perfectly fine. However, if the state explicitly *denied* a right to criminal trial by jury, then that would be unconstitutional; a direct violation of the Supremacy Clause.

Returning to our examples about Joe, Sally, and Judy, suppose that the state in which they lived passed laws that denied them the right to vote based on race, gender, and age. Those laws would be struck down as unconstitutional; the Constitution would have served as their Guardian Angel. What if, however, their state passed a law that stated, "only those who have served in the U.S. military for a minimum of 4 years shall be eligible to vote." Suppose that none of those three individuals, not to mention millions of inhabitants in their state, would qualify. Could these disaffected citizens turn to the Constitution for help? It does not appear that they could, considering there is no language in the Constitution that either guarantees the right to vote, or explicitly states that the vote shall not be denied based on military service or lack thereof.

Electing the President of the United States

The 2000 presidential election, whose major candidates were incumbent Vice President Al Gore, the Democratic Party nominee, versus Texas Governor George W. Bush, the

George W. Bush and Al Gore. Bush defeated Gore in the close and controversial 2000 presidential election.

Republican. The election was arguably the most exciting, nerve-wracking, vindicating, and frustrating—depending on one's perspective—of our lifetimes. Even the 1960 election, which was about five times closer in terms of total vote count, was not surrounded by such drama. By examining the 2000 election, we can gain a better understanding of the voting process.

On the evening of November 7, 2000, it appeared that George W. Bush had won the election to become the 43rd president of the United States. But, one of the many unusual characteristics of that election was that his opponent, Al Gore, actually received more votes. The final tally was Gore: 51,003,926 and Bush: 50,460,110. That final total, however, was not tallied and did not become official until well over a month later, when the United States Supreme Court confirmed that Bush had in fact won. Without even addressing the controversy surrounding the recounting of votes, causing the Supreme Court to become involved and deciding the outcome in mid-December, let's examine the results on election night. Gore had received over 500,000 more votes than Bush. In an election that yielded over 100 million votes, 500,000 is not a very large number. Nonetheless, Gore received more votes. Why, then was he not declared the winner? Because Bush received more *electoral* votes: 271 to 266, to be exact. Accordingly, even though Gore received more votes than Bush, that fact is not good enough to be elected president. And this is further evidence that we *don't* really live in a democracy. Now, let's take a look at the whole *electoral* voting process.

The Electoral College

"The masses are asses." That is what Alexander Hamilton—one of the most prominent and, arguably, one of, if not *the* most brilliant of the Founding Fathers—said in support of his plan to prevent ordinary citizens from having too direct a role in the election process. It is not as if Hamilton had disdain for common, everyday folks; he simply did not think they were properly qualified to be entrusted with such a solemn and monumental decision.

Hamilton was the principal author of *The Federalist Papers*, which were a collection of anonymous letters written to New York newspapers, urging the adoption of the Constitution. Hamilton's *Federalist* system included the election of the president of the United States by electors. So, what does that really mean?

Electors are selected by their respective states, and by the District of Columbia (Washington, D.C.). Each state has as many electors as it has Senators and Representatives, and D.C., which has neither of each, has three total electors. Accordingly, the total number of electors is 538 (which is the total of 100 U.S. Senators, 435 U.S. Representatives, and 3 D.C. electors). On Election Day, the people vote directly for these electors, who have pledged to vote for a particular presidential candidate. Consider this example. Assume that it is 1984, and Larry would like to vote for Ronald Reagan for president. Larry will not simply go to the voting booth and vote for Reagan on Election Day. Instead, he will vote for Reagan's elector—let's call her Martha. Martha, in turn, has pledged that if she is "elected," she will cast her vote for Reagan.

Why this extra step? Why does Martha have to be involved at all? Why can't Larry simply vote for Reagan directly? Returning to Hamilton's "masses are asses" notion, the Founding Fathers feared that the general public might be caught up in some sweeping movement and decide to vote irresponsibly. In other words, the Founding Fathers believed, to some extent, that the people could not always be trusted to make a responsible decision.

For instance, suppose that famous National Football League (NFL) quarterback Peyton Manning felt strongly about nuclear weapons in the hands of foreign leaders, and he took a month-long trip to visit some of those countries. In speaking with their leaders, he returned to the United States with some promising news: the leaders were all very accommodating and promised him that negotiations would continue, and that they might even consider dismantling their nuclear weapons programs under the right circumstances.

Suppose, then, that this story made the front page of every newspaper in the country, and that the people were swept up with Manningmania! Suddenly, Manning became the front-runner in all polls, and was elected president of the United States!

With all due respect to Manning (because, after all, we could not definitively say whether he would be a great president, an awful one, or fall somewhere in between), it would be quite impulsive to vote for him based on one trip abroad that might potentially yield some good results, based on some inconclusive, unsubstantiated information. In other words, leaving it up to the American people's whims might lead to some catastrophic decisions.

Although our Constitution is based on the principle of "we the people," that policy is tempered by the concern that the people, if left unchecked, might be swept up by some impulse and, elect, say, the winner of the *American Idol* or *Survivor* television show as the next president of the United States.

Breaking the Piggy Bank and Sharing the Loot!

Imagine if every man, woman, and child in the United States divided up all the money in the country, that everyone would have about a hundred thousand dollars! That sounds like a pretty good deal, doesn't it? Of course, if everyone "broke the national piggy bank" and took the cash, there would not be any money to run the country: no money for the military, or to pay the president, or Congress. No money to pay judges, or FBI or CIA agents, or to launch rockets to the moon or to other points in outer space.

Some people might support the following statement: "So what? Let's divide the money! The president and Congress are doing a terrible job anyway. Why pay them? As far as the military goes, give peace a chance! We have been fighting all of these wars and where has that gotten us? Let's just lay down our arms and make love, not war. As for the Federal Bureau of Investigation (FBI) and the Central Intelligence Agency (CIA), they investigate criminals and terrorists. Well, if we have no military, then terrorists will leave us alone. And if everyone has a hundred thousand dollars, they will not need to commit any crimes, so we will not need a federal agency to stop crime. And as far as outer space, what's the big deal? No need to explore there, let's just keep the money!"

Do you see the potential of a "take the money and run" mentality? That is exactly why we do not live in a democracy. Because, if we did, the people could simply get tired of the government and decide to do away with it.

Getting back to the Electoral College, that is precisely why we have electors: to keep the people from doing something impulsive. So, how is it that someone can win an election by gaining more electoral votes than popular (one person, one vote) votes? Let's take a look.

In 2000, George W. Bush carried 30 states to Al Gore's 21 (plus Washington, D.C.). However, as we said before, Gore received more individual votes. Why then, did Bush win and Gore lose? Because *United States* means just that: in some ways, we are not one big country, but rather 50 small ones (states), united by a common bond in some ways. Perhaps this example might help to appreciate the distinction.

Many of you may be baseball fans, though some of you might know nothing about the game. So, here is a quick lesson: The object in baseball is to score *runs* (baseball's version of "points"), and the team with the most runs wins the game. Each year, the best team in each league (the American League and the National League) plays against each other in the World Series. Whichever team wins four games first, wins; this means that the teams might play up to seven games (the maximum number of games it would take so that one team wins at least four games).

Suppose that the two teams in the next World Series are the Texas Rangers from the American League and the New York Mets from the National League. Now, take a look at the games and see who wins (**Table 1-1**).

The Mets won the World Series, four games to three. They won games one, three, five, and seven, whereas the Rangers won games two, four, and six. However, if you look at the total runs scored in the entire series, the Rangers scored 38 runs while the Mets only scored 22. Why, then, did the Mets win? Because they won more *games*, even though they scored fewer total *runs*. Similarly, Bush won more *states*, whereas Gore won more *votes*.

To this point we have determined that: (1) Americans do not have a Constitutional right to vote; and (2) at least for the office of the president of the United States, the people vote for electors who, in turn, vote for president.

Again, just because the Constitution does not *guarantee* the right to vote, that does not mean that individual states cannot guarantee that right in their own state constitutions. After all, as long as a state law *does not directly conflict* with the Constitution, then it is fine. And the Constitution

certainly does not expressly *deny* anyone the right to vote, so a state law expressly granting voting rights would not be contradictory.

Regarding our voting for electors rather than for the president, from a practical perspective, it is basically the same thing. In other words, though it is technically possible, it is realistically extremely improbable in this day and age that electors will change their votes and decide to elect, say, the actor Martin Sheen as president at the very last minute (because they like the job he did playing the role of president on the TV show *West Wing*). There would be a better chance of you being injured on your way to the voting booth because you were attacked by a giraffe that had escaped from the zoo and was running down the street.

Before we move to the cases at the end of the chapter, which include the one about the 2000 presidential election, let's have a quick overview about how to read and understand a court *opinion* (decision).

The Importance of Case Law

As we will discuss later, case law is vital to understanding the Constitution. Law is generally made in one of two ways: either by the legislative branch of government, or by the courts, as a result of interpreting the law already in existence. As for the Constitution, which requires a long and difficult process to amend, law is usually established by an interpretation by the United States Supreme Court, the highest court in the country.

When a legal dispute usually winds up in court, it is at the *trial* level, where *questions of fact* are decided (such as: did the driver run the red light, did the defendant rob the grocery store, and so forth). A person who brings a lawsuit is the *plaintiff*, and the person against whom the lawsuit is brought is the *defendant*. If either the plaintiff or the defendant loses at trial, he or she has the right to *appeal* the decision to a higher court. At that point, the person bringing the appeal is known as the *petitioner*, and the person against whom the appeal is brought is the *respondent*. The petitioner and respondent are also referred to as the appellant and appellee, respectively.

Cases decided on appeal are known as *opinions*, and they are helpful to study because they resolve *questions of law* (such as, does a woman have a right to an abortion, may a minor who committed murder be sentenced to death, and so forth). Unlike questions of fact, which are really limited to a particular case (for example, just because one defendant set fire to a barn does not mean another defendant 5 years later did the same thing), questions of law are blueprints for all of us to follow.

Table 1-1							
Scores for the World Series							
	Game 1	Game 2	Game 3	Game 4	Game 5	Game 6	Game 7
Rangers	2	10	4	9	1	6	6
Mets	3	1	5	2	2	2	7

Not all judges (or Justices, in the case of the Supreme Court) always agree on the decision, which is why many cases contain multiple opinions.

First, let's take a look at the judgment. It is either a *majority* or a *plurality* opinion. A majority is any number greater than 50%. In the case of the Supreme Court, which is comprised of nine Justices, the number would be five. A plurality consists of the highest number, even though it may not be a majority. For instance, if four Justices decided one way, three another way, and two yet another way, the opinion in which four took part would prevail, though it would be a plurality opinion, not a majority one.

A *dissenting* opinion is one that flatly disagrees with the reasoning of the prevailing (majority or plurality) opinion.

A *concurring* opinion is one that agrees with the prevailing opinion (judgment), but for different reasons, or focuses on something that the judgment did not mention extensively, if at all. Consider the following example, to illustrate:

The National Television Association (NTA) was going to issue an award for the best police TV drama of all time. In a snub to more modern police shows, the NTA selected three finalists, all shows from the 1970s: *Kojak*, *Mod Squad*, and *Starsky & Hutch*. The final decision was left to a panel of nine judges. Here is how they voted:

- Four judges voted for *Starsky & Hutch*, because it combined good plots, action-packed scenes, and good humor.
- Two other judges also voted for *Starsky & Hutch*, but advised that a different program should have been nominated, *Columbo*. *Columbo* was labeled more a mystery drama than a police show, but the two concurring judges disagreed, and elaborated on how great *Columbo* was as a police show.
- Finally, three other judges disagreed completely, and voted for *Kojak*. They disagreed with the other six judges that *Starsky & Hutch* was a better show, citing the socially relevant storylines that rendered *Kojak* superior.

The decision by the six judges would stand and the winner would be *Starsky & Hutch*, as the best TV police drama of all time. Because there were nine judges, however, the decision was a majority, because the two concurring judges joined with the four who rendered the judgment, to make six in total.

The three judges who voted for *Kojak* formed the dissenting opinion, because they flatly disagreed with the decision.

The two concurring judges who voted for *Starsky & Hutch* were not in dissent, because they agreed with the decision, but they pointed out that *Columbo* should have been nominated as well.

Does that clear things up a bit? There is the judgment, the dissent opposes it, and the concurring agrees with it, but for different reasons.

One final word about reading cases: read them slowly and carefully. At first, you may have to read a case two or three times to fully understand it. There are a lot of Latin terms sprinkled throughout them, and many other cases are cited, which throw in volume numbers and page numbers mixed in with the text, often disrupting a flowing

Starsky & Hutch: **A great police television drama in the 1970s. Was *Columbo* better?**

reading pattern. If at first you find reading cases to be frustrating, don't worry as soon enough it will come as natural to you as tying your shoelaces.

Conclusion: Our Vote Does Count!

We have spent the entire chapter talking about how we do not really live in a democracy, how we do not really have a Constitutional right to vote, and that, even to the extent to which we are allowed to vote, we do not elect the president of the United States directly. If the previous sentence were a summary of our American way of life, then it would seem that we really do not have much say in it at all. In reality, however, our ability to shape our own lives is not nearly as bleak.

The American People: The Most Powerful Political Force in the World

Individually, none of us is particularly powerful. And that is not even limited to ordinary citizens; it is also true of the mayor of our town, the governor of our state, or the president of the entire country. This is a good thing because, after all, this nation was designed to be a republic, not a dictatorship. But all together, we, the people, are the most powerful political force on earth. We continue to live in the world's most powerful nation, and, ultimately, what we say goes. If we the people are not happy with our electors, we can demand that different ones are appointed. And if Congress does not change the laws, we can vote those members out and elect new ones.

Even though there are limitations that prevent a sweeping wave of impulse from grasping the general public's imagination and resulting in reckless political consequences, ultimately, it is what we, the people, say that counts. Accordingly, a democracy does not mean that we do not have the power to decide how to live our lives. Rather, it means that we live in a republic, which safeguards the power of the people into political representatives who are, directly or indirectly, elected by the American people.

Later in the book we will discuss this incredible power that we, the American people, possess, and how to make better use of it. We will begin to consider our elected representatives—the mayor, the governor, the president, all of the members of Congress, and many others—as folks who work for us, not the other way around.

As for whether our individual vote "counts," consider this example. As we mentioned before, the 2000 presidential election was incredibly close. George W. Bush won by the slimmest of electoral margins, and he won Florida by only a few hundred votes. Those who were rooting for Bush all along were certainly glad to have gone to the polls to vote for him, and those who preferred Gore but chose not to vote surely must have kicked themselves for not doing so. Then there's Ralph Nader, who also ran for president as a third-party candidate, on the Green Party ticket. He received almost 100,000 votes. Had some voters chosen to vote for Bush or Gore instead, or if some Bush or Gore voters had voted for Nader or for another minor party candidate instead, the result might have been different.

In Chapter Two, we will learn about how and why the Constitution was written in the first place.

Questions for Review

1. What is a democracy?
2. What is a republic?
3. What is the difference between a democratic republic and a republican democracy?
4. Does the Constitution guarantee Americans the right to vote?
5. What does the Fifteenth Amendment say about the right to vote?
6. What does the Nineteenth Amendment say about the right to vote?
7. What does the Twenty-Sixth Amendment say about the right to vote?
8. What does the Fourteenth Amendment say about the right to vote?
9. What is the Supremacy Clause?
10. What is the Electoral College?

Constitutionally Speaking

The president of the United States is not directly elected by the American people, and must win a majority of electoral votes. Whether or not he or she wins the most actual individual votes does not matter. Moreover, the major political parties, Democratic and Republican, select their nominees through state-by-state primaries, on different days over the period of several months.

If the system were to change, and all Americans would vote for president directly, both in the primaries, on a single National Primary Day, and on general Election Day, what would be the advantages and disadvantages of changing to that type of system rather than leaving things the way they are?

Constitutional Cases

We discussed the controversial 2000 presidential election, in which George W. Bush ultimately emerged victorious over Al Gore. Below is the case, *Bush v. Gore*, which declared the election over and put a stop to the recount process.

The second case, *Williams v. Mississippi*, addresses the issue of voting rights for newly freed slaves following the end of the Civil War.

Bush v. Gore, 531 U.S. 98 (2000), *Per Curiam.*

I

On December 8, 2000, the Supreme Court of Florida ordered that the Circuit Court of Leon County tabulate by hand 9,000 ballots in Miami-Dade County. It also ordered the inclusion in the certified vote totals of 215 votes identified in Palm Beach County and 168 votes identified in Miami-Dade County for Vice President Albert Gore, Jr., and Senator Joseph Lieberman, Democratic Candidates for President and Vice President. The Supreme Court noted that petitioner Governor George W. Bush asserted that the net gain for Vice President Gore in Palm Beach County was 176 votes, and directed the Circuit Court to resolve that dispute on remand. ___ So. 2d, at ___ (slip op., at 4, n. 6). The court

(Continues)

(Continued)

further held that relief would require manual recounts in all Florida counties where so-called "undervotes" had not been subject to manual tabulation. The court ordered all manual recounts to begin at once. Governor Bush and Richard Cheney, Republican Candidates for the Presidency and Vice Presidency, filed an emergency application for a stay of this mandate. On December 9, we granted the application, treated the application as a petition for a writ of certiorari, and granted certiorari. *Post*, p. ___.

The proceedings leading to the present controversy are discussed in some detail in our opinion in *Bush* v. *Palm Beach County Canvassing Bd., ante*, p. ____ (*per curiam*) (*Bush I*). On November 8, 2000, the day following the Presidential election, the Florida Division of Elections reported that petitioner, Governor Bush, had received 2,909,135 votes, and respondent, Vice President Gore, had received 2,907,351 votes, a margin of 1,784 for Governor Bush. Because Governor Bush's margin of victory was less than "one-half of a percent . . . of the votes cast," an automatic machine recount was conducted under §102.141(4) of the election code, the results of which showed Governor Bush still winning the race but by a diminished margin. Vice President Gore then sought manual recounts in Volusia, Palm Beach, Broward, and Miami-Dade Counties, pursuant to Florida's election protest provisions. Fla. Stat. §102.166 (2000). A dispute arose concerning the deadline for local county canvassing boards to submit their returns to the Secretary of State (Secretary). The Secretary declined to waive the November 14 deadline imposed by statute. §§102.111, 102.112. The Florida Supreme Court, however, set the deadline at November 26. We granted certiorari and vacated the Florida Supreme Court's decision, finding considerable uncertainty as to the grounds on which it was based. *Bush I, ante*, at ___—___ (slip. op., at 6–7). On December 11, the Florida Supreme Court issued a decision on remand reinstating that date. ___ So. 2d ___, ___ (slip op. at 30–31).

On November 26, the Florida Elections Canvassing Commission certified the results of the election and declared Governor Bush the winner of Florida's 25 electoral votes. On November 27, Vice President Gore, pursuant to Florida's contest provisions, filed a complaint in Leon County Circuit Court contesting the certification. Fla. Stat. §102.168 (2000). He sought relief pursuant to §102.168(3)(c), which provides that "[r]eceipt of a number of illegal votes or rejection of a number of legal votes sufficient to change or place in doubt the result of the election" shall be grounds for a contest. The Circuit Court denied relief, stating that Vice President Gore failed to meet his burden of proof. He appealed to the First District Court of Appeal, which certified the matter to the Florida Supreme Court.

Accepting jurisdiction, the Florida Supreme Court affirmed in part and reversed in part. *Gore* v. *Harris*, ___ So. 2d. ____ (2000). The court held that the Circuit Court had been correct to reject Vice President Gore's challenge to the results certified in Nassau County and his challenge to the Palm Beach County Canvassing Board's determination that 3,300 ballots cast in that county were not, in the statutory phrase, "legal votes."

The Supreme Court held that Vice President Gore had satisfied his burden of proof under §102.168(3)(c) with respect to his challenge to Miami-Dade County's failure to tabulate, by manual count, 9,000 ballots on which the machines had failed to detect a vote for President ("undervotes"). ___ So. 2d., at ___ (slip. op., at 22–23). Noting the closeness of the election, the Court explained that "[o]n this record, there can be no question that there are legal votes within the 9,000 uncounted votes sufficient to place the results of this election in doubt." *Id.*, at ___ (slip. op., at 35). A "legal vote," as determined by the Supreme Court, is "one in which there is a 'clear indication of the intent of the voter.'" *Id.*, at ____ (slip op., at 25). The court therefore ordered a hand recount of the 9,000 ballots in Miami-Dade County. Observing that the contest provisions vest broad discretion in the circuit judge to "provide any relief appropriate under such circumstances," Fla. Stat. §102.168(8) (2000), the Supreme Court further held that the Circuit Court could order "the Supervisor of Elections and the Canvassing Boards, as well as the necessary public officials, in all counties that have not conducted a manual recount or tabulation of the undervotes . . . to do so forthwith, said tabulation to take place in the individual counties where the ballots are located." ____ So. 2d, at ____ (slip. op., at 38).

The Supreme Court also determined that both Palm Beach County and Miami-Dade County, in their earlier manual recounts, had identified a net gain of 215 and 168 legal votes for Vice President Gore. *Id.*, at ___ (slip. op., at 33–34). Rejecting the Circuit Court's conclusion that Palm Beach County lacked the authority to include the 215 net votes submitted past the November 26 deadline, the Supreme Court explained that the deadline was not intended to exclude votes identified after that date through ongoing manual recounts. As to Miami-Dade County, the Court concluded that although the 168 votes identified were the result of a partial recount, they were "legal votes [that] could change the outcome of the election." *Id.*, at (slip op., at 34). The Supreme Court therefore directed the Circuit Court to include those totals in the certified results, subject to resolution of the actual vote total from the Miami-Dade partial recount.

The petition presents the following questions: whether the Florida Supreme Court established new standards for resolving Presidential election contests, thereby violating Art. II, §1, cl. 2, of the United States Constitution and failing to comply with *3 U.S.C. §5* and whether the use of standardless manual recounts violates the Equal Protection and Due Process Clauses. With respect to the equal protection question, we find a violation of the Equal Protection Clause.

II

A

The closeness of this election, and the multitude of legal challenges which have followed in its wake, have brought into sharp focus a common, if heretofore unnoticed, phenomenon. Nationwide statistics reveal that an estimated 2% of ballots cast do not register a vote for President for whatever reason, including deliberately choosing no candidate at all or some voter error, such as voting for two candidates or insufficiently marking a ballot. See Ho, More Than 2M Ballots Uncounted, *AP Online* (Nov. 28, 2000); Kelley, Balloting Problems Not Rare But Only In A Very Close Election Do Mistakes And Mismarking Make A Difference, *Omaha World-Herald* (Nov. 15, 2000). In certifying election results, the votes eligible for inclusion in the certification are the votes meeting the properly established legal requirements.

This case has shown that punch card balloting machines can produce an unfortunate number of ballots which are not punched in a clean, complete way by the voter. After the current counting, it is likely legislative bodies nationwide will examine ways to improve the mechanisms and machinery for voting.

B

The individual citizen has no federal constitutional right to vote for electors for the President of the United States unless and until the state legislature chooses a statewide election as the means to implement its power to appoint members of the Electoral College. U.S. Const., Art. II, §1. This is the source for the statement in *McPherson v. Blacker, 146 U.S. 1, 35 (1892)*, that the State legislature's power to select the manner for appointing electors is plenary; it may, if it so chooses, select the electors itself, which indeed was the manner used by State legislatures in several States for many years after the Framing of our Constitution. *Id.*, at 28–33. History has now favored the voter, and in each of the several States the citizens themselves vote for Presidential electors. When the state legislature vests the right to vote for President in its people, the right to vote as the legislature has prescribed is fundamental; and one source of its fundamental nature lies in the equal weight accorded to each vote and the equal dignity owed to each voter. The State, of course, after granting the franchise in the special context of Article II, can take back the power to appoint electors. See *id.*, at 35 ("[T]here is no doubt of the right of the legislature to resume the power at any time, for it can neither be taken away nor abdicated") (quoting S. Rep. No. 395, 43d Cong., 1st Sess.).

The right to vote is protected in more than the initial allocation of the franchise. Equal protection applies as well to the manner of its exercise. Having once granted the right to vote on equal terms, the State may not, by later arbitrary and disparate treatment, value one person's vote over that of another. See, *e.g., Harper v. Virginia Bd. of Elections, 383 U.S. 663, 665 (1966)* ("[O]nce the franchise is granted to the electorate, lines may not be drawn which are inconsistent with the Equal Protection Clause of the *Fourteenth Amendment*"). It must be remembered that "the right of suffrage can be denied by a debasement or dilution of the weight of a citizen's vote just as effectively as by wholly prohibiting the free exercise of the franchise." *Reynolds v. Sims, 377 U.S. 533, 555 (1964)*.

There is no difference between the two sides of the present controversy on these basic propositions. Respondents say that the very purpose of vindicating the right to vote justifies the recount procedures now at issue. The question before us, however, is whether the recount procedures the Florida Supreme Court has adopted are consistent with its obligation to avoid arbitrary and disparate treatment of the members of its electorate.

(*Continues*)

Much of the controversy seems to revolve around ballot cards designed to be perforated by a stylus but which, either through error or deliberate omission, have not been perforated with sufficient precision for a machine to count them. In some cases a piece of the card—a chad—is hanging, say by two corners. In other cases there is no separation at all, just an indentation.

The Florida Supreme Court has ordered that the intent of the voter be discerned from such ballots. For purposes of resolving the equal protection challenge, it is not necessary to decide whether the Florida Supreme Court had the authority under the legislative scheme for resolving election disputes to define what a legal vote is and to mandate a manual recount implementing that definition. The recount mechanisms implemented in response to the decisions of the Florida Supreme Court do not satisfy the minimum requirement for nonarbitrary treatment of voters necessary to secure the fundamental right. Florida's basic command for the count of legally cast votes is to consider the "intent of the voter." *Gore v. Harris,* ___ So. 2d, at ___ (slip op., at 39). This is unobjectionable as an abstract proposition and a starting principle. The problem inheres in the absence of specific standards to ensure its equal application. The formulation of uniform rules to determine intent based on these recurring circumstances is practicable and, we conclude, necessary.

The law does not refrain from searching for the intent of the actor in a multitude of circumstances; and in some cases the general command to ascertain intent is not susceptible to much further refinement. In this instance, however, the question is not whether to believe a witness but how to interpret the marks or holes or scratches on an inanimate object, a piece of cardboard or paper which, it is said, might not have registered as a vote during the machine count. The factfinder confronts a thing, not a person. The search for intent can be confined by specific rules designed to ensure uniform treatment.

The want of those rules here has led to unequal evaluation of ballots in various respects. See *Gore v. Harris,* ___ So. 2d, at ___ (slip op., at 51) (Wells, J., dissenting) ("Should a county canvassing board count or not count a 'dimpled chad' where the voter is able to successfully dislodge the chad in every other contest on that ballot? Here, the county canvassing boards disagree"). As seems to have been acknowledged at oral argument, the standards for accepting or rejecting contested ballots might vary not only from county to county but indeed within a single county from one recount team to another.

The record provides some examples. A monitor in Miami-Dade County testified at trial that he observed that three members of the county canvassing board applied different standards in defining a legal vote. 3 Tr. 497, 499 (Dec. 3, 2000). And testimony at trial also revealed that at least one county changed its evaluative standards during the counting process. Palm Beach County, for example, began the process with a 1990 guideline which precluded counting completely attached chads, switched to a rule that considered a vote to be legal if any light could be seen through a chad, changed back to the 1990 rule, and then abandoned any pretense of a *per se* rule, only to have a court order that the county consider dimpled chads legal. This is not a process with sufficient guarantees of equal treatment.

An early case in our one person, one vote jurisprudence arose when a State accorded arbitrary and disparate treatment to voters in its different counties. *Gray v. Sanders, 372 U.S. 368* (1963). The Court found a constitutional violation. We relied on these principles in the context of the Presidential selection process in *Moore v. Ogilvie, 394 U.S. 814* (1969), where we invalidated a county-based procedure that diluted the influence of citizens in larger counties in the nominating process. There we observed that "[t]he idea that one group can be granted greater voting strength than another is hostile to the one man, one vote basis of our representative government." *Id.,* at 819.

The State Supreme Court ratified this uneven treatment. It mandated that the recount totals from two counties, Miami-Dade and Palm Beach, be included in the certified total. The court also appeared to hold *sub silentio* that the recount totals from Broward County, which were not completed until after the original November 14 certification by the Secretary of State, were to be considered part of the new certified vote totals even though the county certification was not contested by Vice President Gore. Yet each of the counties used varying standards to determine what was a legal vote. Broward County used a more forgiving standard than Palm Beach County, and uncovered almost three times as many new votes, a result markedly disproportionate to the difference in population between the counties.

In addition, the recounts in these three counties were not limited to so-called undervotes but extended to all of the ballots. The distinction has real consequences. A manual recount of all ballots identifies not only those ballots which show no vote but also those which contain more than one, the so-called overvotes. Neither category will be counted by the machine. This is not a trivial concern. At oral argument, respondents estimated there are as many as 110,000 overvotes statewide. As a result, the citizen whose ballot was not read by a machine because he failed to vote for a candidate in a way readable by a machine may still have his vote counted in a manual recount; on the other hand, the citizen who marks two candidates in a way discernable by the machine will not have the same opportunity to have his vote count, even if a manual examination of the ballot would reveal the requisite indicia of intent. Furthermore, the citizen who marks two candidates, only one of which is discernable by the machine, will have his vote counted even though it should have been read as an invalid ballot. The State Supreme Court's inclusion of vote counts based on these variant standards exemplifies concerns with the remedial processes that were under way.

That brings the analysis to yet a further equal protection problem. The votes certified by the court included a partial total from one county, Miami-Dade. The Florida Supreme Court's decision thus gives no assurance that the recounts included in a final certification must be complete. Indeed, it is respondent's submission that it would be consistent with the rules of the recount procedures to include whatever partial counts are done by the time of final certification, and we interpret the Florida Supreme Court's decision to permit this. See ____ So. 2d, at ____, n. 21 (slip op., at 37, n. 21) (noting "practical difficulties" may control outcome of election, but certifying partial Miami-Dade total nonetheless). This accommodation no doubt results from the truncated contest period established by the Florida Supreme Court in *Bush I*, at respondents' own urging. The press of time does not diminish the constitutional concern. A desire for speed is not a general excuse for ignoring equal protection guarantees.

In addition to these difficulties the actual process by which the votes were to be counted under the Florida Supreme Court's decision raises further concerns. That order did not specify who would recount the ballots. The county canvassing boards were forced to pull together ad hoc teams comprised of judges from various Circuits who had no previous training in handling and interpreting ballots. Furthermore, while others were permitted to observe, they were prohibited from objecting during the recount.

The recount process, in its features here described, is inconsistent with the minimum procedures necessary to protect the fundamental right of each voter in the special instance of a statewide recount under the authority of a single state judicial officer. Our consideration is limited to the present circumstances, for the problem of equal protection in election processes generally presents many complexities.

The question before the Court is not whether local entities, in the exercise of their expertise, may develop different systems for implementing elections. Instead, we are presented with a situation where a state court with the power to assure uniformity has ordered a statewide recount with minimal procedural safeguards. When a court orders a statewide remedy, there must be at least some assurance that the rudimentary requirements of equal treatment and fundamental fairness are satisfied.

Given the Court's assessment that the recount process underway was probably being conducted in an unconstitutional manner, the Court stayed the order directing the recount so it could hear this case and render an expedited decision. The contest provision, as it was mandated by the State Supreme Court, is not well calculated to sustain the confidence that all citizens must have in the outcome of elections. The State has not shown that its procedures include the necessary safeguards. The problem, for instance, of the estimated 110,000 overvotes has not been addressed, although Chief Justice Wells called attention to the concern in his dissenting opinion. See ____ So. 2d, at ____, n. 26 (slip op., at 45, n. 26).

Upon due consideration of the difficulties identified to this point, it is obvious that the recount cannot be conducted in compliance with the requirements of equal protection and due process without substantial additional work. It would require not only the adoption (after opportunity for argument) of adequate statewide standards for determining what is a legal vote, and practicable procedures to implement them, but also orderly judicial review of any disputed matters that might arise. In addition, the Secretary of State has advised that the recount of only a portion of the ballots requires that the vote tabulation equipment be used to screen out undervotes, a function for which the machines were not designed. If a recount of overvotes were also required, perhaps even a second screening would be necessary. Use of the equipment for this purpose, and any new software developed for it, would have to be evaluated for accuracy by the Secretary of State, as required by Fla. Stat. §101.015 (2000).

The Supreme Court of Florida has said that the legislature intended the State's electors to "participat[e] fully in the federal electoral process," as provided in *3 U.S.C. §5.* ____ So. 2d, at ____

(Continues)

(*Continued*)

(slip op. at 27); see also *Palm Beach Canvassing Bd. v. Harris*, 2000 WL 1725434, *13 (Fla. 2000). That statute, in turn, requires that any controversy or contest that is designed to lead to a conclusive selection of electors be completed by December 12. That date is upon us, and there is no recount procedure in place under the State Supreme Court's order that comports with minimal constitutional standards. Because it is evident that any recount seeking to meet the December 12 date will be unconstitutional for the reasons we have discussed, we reverse the judgment of the Supreme Court of Florida ordering a recount to proceed.

Seven Justices of the Court agree that there are constitutional problems with the recount ordered by the Florida Supreme Court that demand a remedy. See post, at 6 (Souter, J., dissenting); *post*, at 2, 15 (Breyer, J., dissenting). The only disagreement is as to the remedy. Because the Florida Supreme Court has said that the Florida Legislature intended to obtain the safe-harbor benefits of *3 U.S.C. §5* Justice Breyer's proposed remedy—remanding to the Florida Supreme Court for its ordering of a constitutionally proper contest until December 18—contemplates action in violation of the Florida election code, and hence could not be part of an "appropriate" order authorized by Fla. Stat. §102.168(8) (2000).

* * *

None are more conscious of the vital limits on judicial authority than are the members of this Court, and none stand more in admiration of the Constitution's design to leave the selection of the President to the people, through their legislatures, and to the political sphere. When contending parties invoke the process of the courts, however, it becomes our unsought responsibility to resolve the federal and constitutional issues the judicial system has been forced to confront.

The judgment of the Supreme Court of Florida is reversed, and the case is remanded for further proceedings not inconsistent with this opinion.

Pursuant to this Court's Rule 45.2, the Clerk is directed to issue the mandate in this case forthwith.

It is so ordered.

Chief Justice Rehnquist, with whom Justice Scalia and Justice Thomas join, concurring.

We join the *per curiam* opinion. We write separately because we believe there are additional grounds that require us to reverse the Florida Supreme Court's decision.

I

We deal here not with an ordinary election, but with an election for the President of the United States. In *Burroughs v. United States, 290 U.S. 534, 545 (1934)*, we said:

> "While presidential electors are not officers or agents of the federal government (*In re Green*, 134 U.S. 377, 379), they exercise federal functions under, and discharge duties in virtue of authority conferred by, the Constitution of the United States. The President is vested with the executive power of the nation. The importance of his election and the vital character of its relationship to and effect upon the welfare and safety of the whole people cannot be too strongly stated."

Likewise, in *Anderson v. Celebrezze, 460 U.S. 780, 794–795 (1983)* (footnote omitted), we said: "[I]n the context of a Presidential election, state-imposed restrictions implicate a uniquely important national interest. For the President and the Vice President of the United States are the only elected officials who represent all the voters in the Nation."

In most cases, comity and respect for federalism compel us to defer to the decisions of state courts on issues of state law. That practice reflects our understanding that the decisions of state courts are definitive pronouncements of the will of the States as sovereigns. Cf. *Erie R. Co. v. Tompkins, 304 U.S. 64 (1938)*. Of course, in ordinary cases, the distribution of powers among the branches of a State's government raises no questions of federal constitutional law, subject to the requirement that the government be republican in character. See U.S. Const., Art. IV, §4. But there are a few exceptional cases in which the Constitution imposes a duty or confers a power on a particular branch of a State's government. This is one of them. Article II, §1, cl. 2, provides that "[e]ach State shall appoint, in such Manner as the *Legislature* thereof may direct," electors for President and Vice President. (Emphasis added.) Thus, the text of the election law itself, and not just its interpretation by the courts of the States, takes on independent significance.

In *McPherson v. Blacker, 146 U.S. 1* (1892), we explained that Art. II, §1, cl. 2, "convey[s] the broadest power of determination" and "leaves it to the legislature exclusively to define the method" of appointment. *Id.*, at 27. A significant departure from the legislative scheme for appointing Presidential electors presents a federal constitutional question.

3 U.S.C. §5 informs our application of Art. II, §1, cl. 2, to the Florida statutory scheme, which, as the Florida Supreme Court acknowledged, took that statute into account. Section 5 provides that the State's selection of electors "shall be conclusive, and shall govern in the counting of the electoral votes" if the electors are chosen under laws enacted prior to election day, and if the selection process is completed six days prior to the meeting of the electoral college. As we noted in *Bush v. Palm Beach County Canvassing Bd., ante*, at 6.

> "Since §5 contains a principle of federal law that would assure finality of the State's determination if made pursuant to a state law in effect before the election, a legislative wish to take advantage of the 'safe harbor' would counsel against any construction of the Election Code that Congress might deem to be a change in the law."

If we are to respect the legislature's Article II powers, therefore, we must ensure that postelection state-court actions do not frustrate the legislative desire to attain the "safe harbor" provided by §5.

In Florida, the legislature has chosen to hold statewide elections to appoint the State's 25 electors. Importantly, the legislature has delegated the authority to run the elections and to oversee election disputes to the Secretary of State (Secretary), Fla. Stat. §97.012(1) (2000), and to state circuit courts, §§102.168(1), 102.168(8). Isolated sections of the code may well admit of more than one interpretation, but the general coherence of the legislative scheme may not be altered by judicial interpretation so as to wholly change the statutorily provided apportionment of responsibility among these various bodies. In any election but a Presidential election, the Florida Supreme Court can give as little or as much deference to Florida's executives as it chooses, so far as Article II is concerned, and this Court will have no cause to question the court's actions. But, with respect to a Presidential election, the court must be both mindful of the legislature's role under Article II in choosing the manner of appointing electors and deferential to those bodies expressly empowered by the legislature to carry out its constitutional mandate.

In order to determine whether a state court has infringed upon the legislature's authority, we necessarily must examine the law of the State as it existed prior to the action of the court. Though we generally defer to state courts on the interpretation of state law—see, *e.g., Mullaney v. Wilbur, 421 U.S. 684* (1975)—there are of course areas in which the Constitution requires this Court to undertake an independent, if still deferential, analysis of state law.

For example, in *NAACP v. Alabama ex rel. Patterson, 357 U.S. 449* (1958), it was argued that we were without jurisdiction because the petitioner had not pursued the correct appellate remedy in Alabama's state courts. Petitioners had sought a state-law writ of certiorari in the Alabama Supreme Court when a writ of mandamus, according to that court, was proper. We found this state-law ground inadequate to defeat our jurisdiction because we were "unable to reconcile the procedural holding of the Alabama Supreme Court" with prior Alabama precedent. *Id.*, at 456. The purported state-law ground was so novel, in our independent estimation, that "petitioner could not fairly be deemed to have been apprised of its existence." *Id.*, at 457.

Six years later we decided *Bouie v. City of Columbia, 378 U.S. 347* (1964), in which the state court had held, contrary to precedent, that the state trespass law applied to black sit-in demonstrators who had consent to enter private property but were then asked to leave. Relying upon *NAACP*, we concluded that the South Carolina Supreme Court's interpretation of a state penal statute had impermissibly broadened the scope of that statute beyond what a fair reading provided, in violation of due process. See 378 U.S., at 361–362. What we would do in the present case is precisely parallel: Hold that the Florida Supreme Court's interpretation of the Florida election laws impermissibly distorted them beyond what a fair reading required, in violation of Article II.[1]

This inquiry does not imply a disrespect for state *courts* but rather a respect for the constitutionally prescribed role of state *legislatures*. To attach definitive weight to the pronouncement of a state court, when the very question at issue is whether the court has actually departed from the statutory meaning, would be to abdicate our responsibility to enforce the explicit requirements of Article II.

(Continues)

(*Continued*)

II

Acting pursuant to its constitutional grant of authority, the Florida Legislature has created a detailed, if not perfectly crafted, statutory scheme that provides for appointment of Presidential electors by direct election. Fla. Stat. §103.011 (2000). Under the statute, "[v]otes cast for the actual candidates for President and Vice President shall be counted as votes cast for the presidential electors supporting such candidates." *Ibid.* The legislature has designated the Secretary of State as the "chief election officer," with the responsibility to "[o]btain and maintain uniformity in the application, operation, and interpretation of the election laws." §97.012. The state legislature has delegated to county canvassing boards the duties of administering elections. §102.141. Those boards are responsible for providing results to the state Elections Canvassing Commission, comprising the Governor, the Secretary of State, and the Director of the Division of Elections. §102.111. Cf. *Boardman v. Esteva*, 323 So. 2d 259, 268, n. 5 (1975) ("The election process . . . is committed to the executive branch of government through duly designated officials all charged with specific duties. . . . [The] judgments [of these officials] are entitled to be regarded by the courts as presumptively correct . . .").

After the election has taken place, the canvassing boards receive returns from precincts, count the votes, and in the event that a candidate was defeated by .5% or less, conduct a mandatory recount. Fla. Stat. §102.141(4) (2000). The county canvassing boards must file certified election returns with the Department of State by 5 p.m. on the seventh day following the election. §102.112(1). The Elections Canvassing Commission must then certify the results of the election. §102.111(1).

The state legislature has also provided mechanisms both for protesting election returns and for contesting certified election results. Section 102.166 governs protests. Any protest must be filed prior to the certification of election results by the county canvassing board. §102.166(4)(b). Once a protest has been filed, "the county canvassing board may authorize a manual recount." §102.166(4)(c). If a sample recount conducted pursuant to §102.166(5) "indicates an error in the vote tabulation which could affect the outcome of the election," the county canvassing board is instructed to: "(a) Correct the error and recount the remaining precincts with the vote tabulation system; (b) Request the Department of State to verify the tabulation software; or (c) Manually recount all ballots," §102.166(5). In the event a canvassing board chooses to conduct a manual recount of all ballots, §102.166(7) prescribes procedures for such a recount.

Contests to the certification of an election, on the other hand, are controlled by §102.168. The grounds for contesting an election include "[r]eceipt of a number of illegal votes or rejection of a number of legal votes sufficient to change or place in doubt the result of the election." §102.168(3)(c). Any contest must be filed in the appropriate Florida circuit court, Fla. Stat. §102.168(1), and the canvassing board or election board is the proper party defendant, §102.168(4). Section 102.168(8) provides that "[t]he circuit judge to whom the contest is presented may fashion such orders as he or she deems necessary to ensure that each allegation in the complaint is investigated, examined, or checked, to prevent or correct any alleged wrong, and to provide any relief appropriate under such circumstances." In Presidential elections, the contest period necessarily terminates on the date set by 3 *U.S.C.* §5 for concluding the State's "final determination" of election controversies."

In its first decision, *Palm Beach Canvassing Bd. v. Harris*, ___ So. 2d, ___ (Nov. 21, 2000) (*Harris I*), the Florida Supreme Court extended the 7-day statutory certification deadline established by the legislature.[2] This modification of the code, by lengthening the protest period, necessarily shortened the contest period for Presidential elections. Underlying the extension of the certification deadline and the shortchanging of the contest period was, presumably, the clear implication that certification was a matter of significance: The certified winner would enjoy presumptive validity, making a contest proceeding by the losing candidate an uphill battle. In its latest opinion, however, the court empties certification of virtually all legal consequence during the contest, and in doing so departs from the provisions enacted by the Florida Legislature.

The court determined that canvassing boards' decisions regarding whether to recount ballots past the certification deadline (even the certification deadline established by *Harris I*) are to be reviewed *de novo*, although the election code clearly vests discretion whether to recount in the boards, and sets strict deadlines subject to the Secretary's rejection of late tallies and monetary fines for tardiness. See Fla. Stat. §102.112 (2000). Moreover, the Florida court held that all late vote tallies arriving during the contest period should be automatically included in the certification regardless of the certification deadline (even the certification deadline established by *Harris I*), thus virtually eliminating both the deadline and the Secretary's discretion to disregard recounts that violate it.[3]

Moreover, the court's interpretation of "legal vote," and hence its decision to order a contest-period recount, plainly departed from the legislative scheme. Florida statutory law cannot reasonably be thought to *require* the counting of improperly marked ballots. Each Florida precinct before election day provides instructions on how properly to cast a vote, §101.46; each polling place on election day contains a working model of the voting machine it uses, §101.5611; and each voting booth contains a sample ballot, §101.46. In precincts using punch-card ballots, voters are instructed to punch out the ballot cleanly:

AFTER VOTING, CHECK YOUR BALLOT CARD TO BE SURE YOUR VOTING SELECTIONS ARE CLEARLY AND CLEANLY PUNCHED AND THERE ARE NO CHIPS LEFT HANGING ON THE BACK OF THE CARD.

Instructions to Voters, quoted in *Touchston v. McDermott*, 2000 WL 1781942, *6 & n. 19 (CA11) (Tjoflat, J., dissenting). No reasonable person would call it "an error in the vote tabulation," Fla. Stat. §102.166(5), or a "rejection of legal votes," Fla. Stat. §102.168(3)(c),[4] when electronic or electromechanical equipment performs precisely in the manner designed, and fails to count those ballots that are not marked in the manner that these voting instructions explicitly and prominently specify. The scheme that the Florida Supreme Court's opinion attributes to the legislature is one in which machines are *required* to be "capable of correctly counting votes," §101.5606(4), but which nonetheless regularly produces elections in which legal votes are predictably *not* tabulated, so that in close elections manual recounts are regularly required. This is of course absurd. The Secretary of State, who is authorized by law to issue binding interpretations of the election code, §§97.012, 106.23, rejected this peculiar reading of the statutes. See DE 00–13 (opinion of the Division of Elections). The Florida Supreme Court, although it must defer to the Secretary's interpretations, see *Krivanek v. Take Back Tampa Political Committee*, 625 So. 2d 840, 844 (Fla. 1993), rejected her reasonable interpretation and embraced the peculiar one. See *Palm Beach County Canvassing Board v. Harris*, No. SC00–2346 (Dec. 11, 2000) (*Harris III*).

But as we indicated in our remand of the earlier case, in a Presidential election the clearly expressed intent of the legislature must prevail. And there is no basis for reading the Florida statutes as requiring the counting of improperly marked ballots, as an examination of the Florida Supreme Court's textual analysis shows. We will not parse that analysis here, except to note that the principal provision of the election code on which it relied, §101.5614(5), was, as the Chief Justice pointed out in his dissent from *Harris II*, entirely irrelevant. See *Gore v. Harris*, No. SC00–2431, slip op., at 50 (Dec. 8, 2000). The State's Attorney General (who was supporting the Gore challenge) confirmed in oral argument here that never before the present election had a manual recount been conducted on the basis of the contention that "undervotes" should have been examined to determine voter intent. Tr. of Oral Arg. in *Bush v. Palm Beach County Canvassing Bd.*, 39–40 (Dec. 1, 2000); cf. *Broward County Canvassing Board v. Hogan*, 607 So. 2d 508, 509 (Fla. Ct. App. 1992) (denial of recount for failure to count ballots with "hanging paper chads"). For the court to step away from this established practice, prescribed by the Secretary of State, the state official charged by the legislature with "responsibility to . . . [o]btain and maintain uniformity in the application, operation, and interpretation of the election laws," §97.012(1), was to depart from the legislative scheme.

III

The scope and nature of the remedy ordered by the Florida Supreme Court jeopardizes the "legislative wish" to take advantage of the safe harbor provided by *3 U.S.C. §5*. *Bush v. Palm Beach County Canvassing Bd., ante*, at 6. December 12, 2000, is the last date for a final determination of the Florida electors that will satisfy §5. Yet in the late afternoon of December 8th—four days before this deadline—the Supreme Court of Florida ordered recounts of tens of thousands of so-called "undervotes" spread through 64 of the State's 67 counties. This was done in a search for elusive—perhaps delusive—certainty as to the exact count of 6 million votes. But no one claims that these ballots have not previously been tabulated; they were initially read by voting machines at the time of the election, and thereafter reread by virtue of Florida's automatic recount provision. No one claims there was any fraud in the election. The Supreme Court of Florida ordered this additional recount under the provision of the election code giving the circuit judge the authority to provide relief that is "appropriate under such circumstances." Fla. Stat. §102.168(8) (2000).

(Continues)

(Continued)

Surely when the Florida Legislature empowered the courts of the State to grant "appropriate" relief, it must have meant relief that would have become final by the cut-off date of 3 *U.S.C.* §5. In light of the inevitable legal challenges and ensuing appeals to the Supreme Court of Florida and petitions for certiorari to this Court, the entire recounting process could not possibly be completed by that date. Whereas the majority in the Supreme Court of Florida stated its confidence that "the remaining undervotes in these counties can be [counted] within the required time frame," ___ So. 2d. at ___, n. 22 (slip op., at 38, n. 22), it made no assertion that the seemingly inevitable appeals could be disposed of in that time. Although the Florida Supreme Court has on occasion taken over a year to resolve disputes over local elections, see, *e.g., Beckstrom v. Volusia County Canvassing Bd.*, 707 So. 2d 720 (1998) (resolving contest of sheriff's race 16 months after the election), it has heard and decided the appeals in the present case with great promptness. But the federal deadlines for the Presidential election simply do not permit even such a shortened process.

As the dissent noted:

"In [the four days remaining], all questionable ballots must be reviewed by the judicial officer appointed to discern the intent of the voter in a process open to the public. Fairness dictates that a provision be made for either party to object to how a particular ballot is counted. Additionally, this short time period must allow for judicial review. I respectfully submit this cannot be completed without taking Florida's presidential electors outside the safe harbor provision, creating the very real possibility of disenfranchising those nearly 6 million voters who are able to correctly cast their ballots on election day." ___ So. 2d, at ___ (slip op., at 55) (Wells, C. J., dissenting).

The other dissenters echoed this concern: "[T]he majority is departing from the essential requirements of the law by providing a remedy which is impossible to achieve and which will ultimately lead to chaos." *Id.*, at ___ (slip op., at 67) (Harding, J., dissenting, Shaw, J. concurring).

Given all these factors, and in light of the legislative intent identified by the Florida Supreme Court to bring Florida within the "safe harbor" provision of 3 *U.S.C.* §5 the remedy prescribed by the Supreme Court of Florida cannot be deemed an "appropriate" one as of December 8. It significantly departed from the statutory framework in place on November 7, and authorized open-ended further proceedings which could not be completed by December 12, thereby preventing a final determination by that date.

For these reasons, in addition to those given in the *per curiam*, we would reverse.

Notes

1. Similarly, our jurisprudence requires us to analyze the "background principles" of state property law to determine whether there has been a taking of property in violation of the Takings Clause. That constitutional guarantee would, of course, afford no protection against state power if our inquiry could be concluded by a state supreme court holding that state property law accorded the plaintiff no rights. See *Lucas v. South Carolina Coastal Council, 505 U.S.* 1003 (1992). In one of our oldest cases, we similarly made an independent evaluation of state law in order to protect federal treaty guarantees. In *Fairfax's Devisee v. Hunter's Lessee*, 7 Cranch 603 (1813), we disagreed with the Supreme Court of Appeals of Virginia that a 1782 state law had extinguished the property interests of one Denny Fairfax, so that a 1789 ejectment order against Fairfax supported by a 1785 state law did not constitute a future confiscation under the 1783 peace treaty with Great Britain. See *id.*, at 623; *Hunter v. Fairfax's Devisee*, 1 Munf. 218 (Va. 1809).
2. We vacated that decision and remanded that case; the Florida Supreme Court reissued the same judgment with a new opinion on December 11, 2000, ___ So. 2d, ___.
3. Specifically, the Florida Supreme Court ordered the Circuit Court to include in the certified vote totals those votes identified for Vice President Gore in Palm Beach County and Miami-Dade County.
4. It is inconceivable that what constitutes a vote that must be counted under the "error in the vote tabulation" language of the protest phase is different from what constitutes a vote that must be counted under the "legal votes" language of the contest phase.

Justice Stevens, with whom Justice Ginsburg and Justice Breyer join, dissenting.
The Constitution assigns to the States the primary responsibility for determining the manner of selecting the Presidential electors. See Art. II, §1, cl. 2. When questions arise about the meaning of state laws, including election laws, it is our settled practice to accept the opinions of the highest

courts of the States as providing the final answers. On rare occasions, however, either federal statutes or the Federal Constitution may require federal judicial intervention in state elections. This is not such an occasion.

The federal questions that ultimately emerged in this case are not substantial. Article II provides that "[e]ach *State* shall appoint, in such Manner as the Legislature *thereof* may direct, a Number of Electors." *Ibid.* (emphasis added). It does not create state legislatures out of whole cloth, but rather takes them as they come—as creatures born of, and constrained by, their state constitutions. Lest there be any doubt, we stated over 100 years ago in *McPherson v. Blacker, 146 U.S. 1*, 25 (1892), that "[w]hat is forbidden or required to be done by a State" in the Article II context "is forbidden or required of the legislative power under state constitutions as they exist." In the same vein, we also observed that "[t]he [State's] legislative power is the supreme authority except as limited by the constitution of the State." *Ibid.*; cf. *Smiley v. Holm, 285 U.S. 355*, 367 (1932).[5] The legislative power in Florida is subject to judicial review pursuant to Article V of the Florida Constitution, and nothing in Article II of the Federal Constitution frees the state legislature from the constraints in the state constitution that created it. Moreover, the Florida Legislature's own decision to employ a unitary code for all elections indicates that it intended the Florida Supreme Court to play the same role in Presidential elections that it has historically played in resolving electoral disputes. The Florida Supreme Court's exercise of appellate jurisdiction therefore was wholly consistent with, and indeed contemplated by, the grant of authority in Article II.

It hardly needs stating that Congress, pursuant to *3 U.S.C. §5* did not impose any affirmative duties upon the States that their governmental branches could "violate." Rather, §5 provides a safe harbor for States to select electors in contested elections "by judicial or other methods" established by laws prior to the election day. Section 5, like Article II, assumes the involvement of the state judiciary in interpreting state election laws and resolving election disputes under those laws. Neither §5 nor Article II grants federal judges any special authority to substitute their views for those of the state judiciary on matters of state law.

Nor are petitioners correct in asserting that the failure of the Florida Supreme Court to specify in detail the precise manner in which the "intent of the voter," Fla. Stat. §101.5614(5) (Supp. 2001), is to be determined rises to the level of a constitutional violation.[6] We found such a violation when individual votes within the same State were weighted unequally, see, *e.g., Reynolds v. Sims, 377 U.S. 533*, 568 (1964), but we have never before called into question the substantive standard by which a State determines that a vote has been legally cast. And there is no reason to think that the guidance provided to the factfinders, specifically the various canvassing boards, by the "intent of the voter" standard is any less sufficient—or will lead to results any less uniform—than, for example, the "beyond a reasonable doubt" standard employed everyday by ordinary citizens in courtrooms across this country.[7]

Admittedly, the use of differing substandards for determining voter intent in different counties employing similar voting systems may raise serious concerns. Those concerns are alleviated—if not eliminated—by the fact that a single impartial magistrate will ultimately adjudicate all objections arising from the recount process. Of course, as a general matter, "[t]he interpretation of constitutional principles must not be too literal. We must remember that the machinery of government would not work if it were not allowed a little play in its joints." *Bain Peanut Co. of Tex. v. Pinson, 282 U.S. 499*, 501 (1931) (Holmes, J.). If it were otherwise, Florida's decision to leave to each county the determination of what balloting system to employ—despite enormous differences in accuracy[8]—might run afoul of equal protection. So, too, might the similar decisions of the vast majority of state legislatures to delegate to local authorities certain decisions with respect to voting systems and ballot design.

Even assuming that aspects of the remedial scheme might ultimately be found to violate the Equal Protection Clause, I could not subscribe to the majority's disposition of the case. As the majority explicitly holds, once a state legislature determines to select electors through a popular vote, the right to have one's vote counted is of constitutional stature. As the majority further acknowledges, Florida law holds that all ballots that reveal the intent of the voter constitute valid votes. Recognizing these principles, the majority nonetheless orders the termination of the contest proceeding before all such votes have been tabulated. Under their own reasoning, the appropriate course of action would be to remand to allow more specific procedures for implementing the legislature's uniform general standard to be established.

In the interest of finality, however, the majority effectively orders the disenfranchisement of an unknown number of voters whose ballots reveal their intent—and are therefore legal votes under state

(*Continues*)

law—but were for some reason rejected by ballot-counting machines. It does so on the basis of the deadlines set forth in Title 3 of the United States Code. *Ante*, at 11. But, as I have already noted, those provisions merely provide rules of decision for Congress to follow when selecting among conflicting slates of electors. *Supra*, at 2. They do not prohibit a State from counting what the majority concedes to be legal votes until a bona fide winner is determined. Indeed, in 1960, Hawaii appointed two slates of electors and Congress chose to count the one appointed on January 4, 1961, well after the Title 3 deadlines. See Josephson & Ross, Repairing the Electoral College, 22 J. Legis. 145, 166, n. 154 (1996).[9] Thus, nothing prevents the majority, even if it properly found an equal protection violation, from ordering relief appropriate to remedy that violation without depriving Florida voters of their right to have their votes counted. As the majority notes, "[a] desire for speed is not a general excuse for ignoring equal protection guarantees." *Ante*, at 10.

Finally, neither in this case, nor in its earlier opinion in *Palm Beach County Canvassing Bd. v. Harris*, 2000 WL 1725434 (Fla., Nov. 21, 2000), did the Florida Supreme Court make any substantive change in Florida electoral law.[10] Its decisions were rooted in long-established precedent and were consistent with the relevant statutory provisions, taken as a whole. It did what courts do[11]—it decided the case before it in light of the legislature's intent to leave no legally cast vote uncounted. In so doing, it relied on the sufficiency of the general "intent of the voter" standard articulated by the state legislature, coupled with a procedure for ultimate review by an impartial judge, to resolve the concern about disparate evaluations of contested ballots. If we assume—as I do—that the members of that court and the judges who would have carried out its mandate are impartial, its decision does not even raise a colorable federal question.

What must underlie petitioners' entire federal assault on the Florida election procedures is an unstated lack of confidence in the impartiality and capacity of the state judges who would make the critical decisions if the vote count were to proceed. Otherwise, their position is wholly without merit. The endorsement of that position by the majority of this Court can only lend credence to the most cynical appraisal of the work of judges throughout the land. It is confidence in the men and women who administer the judicial system that is the true backbone of the rule of law. Time will one day heal the wound to that confidence that will be inflicted by today's decision. One thing, however, is certain. Although we may never know with complete certainty the identity of the winner of this year's Presidential election, the identity of the loser is perfectly clear. It is the Nation's confidence in the judge as an impartial guardian of the rule of law.

I respectfully dissent.

Notes

5. "Wherever the term 'legislature' is used in the Constitution it is necessary to consider the nature of the particular action in view." 285 U.S., at 367. It is perfectly clear that the meaning of the words "Manner" and "Legislature" as used in Article II, §1, parallels the usage in Article I, §4, rather than the language in Article V. *U.S. Term Limits, Inc. v. Thornton, 514 U.S. 779, 805 (1995).* Article I, §4, and Article II, §1, both call upon legislatures to act in a lawmaking capacity whereas Article V simply calls on the legislative body to deliberate upon a binary decision. As a result, petitioners' reliance on *Leser v. Garnett, 258 U.S. 130 (1922),* and *Hawke v. Smith (No. 1), 253 U.S. 221 (1920),* is misplaced.

6. The Florida statutory standard is consistent with the practice of the majority of States, which apply either an "intent of the voter" standard or an "impossible to determine the elector's choice" standard in ballot recounts. The following States use an "intent of the voter" standard: Ariz. Rev. Stat. Ann. §16—645(A) (Supp. 2000) (standard for canvassing write-in votes); Conn. Gen. Stat. §9—150a(j) (1999) (standard for absentee ballots, including three conclusive presumptions); Ind. Code §3—12—1—1 (1992); Me. Rev. Stat. Ann., Tit. 21—A, §1(13) (1993); Md. Ann. Code, Art. 33, §11—302(d) (2000 Supp.) (standard for absentee ballots); Mass. Gen. Laws §70E (1991) (applying standard to Presidential primaries); Mich. Comp. Laws §168.799a(3) (Supp. 2000); Mo. Rev. Stat. §115.453(3) (Cum. Supp. 1998) (looking to voter's intent where there is substantial compliance with statutory requirements); Tex. Elec. Code Ann. §65.009(c) (1986); Utah Code Ann. §20A—4—104(5)(b) (Supp. 2000) (standard for write-in votes), §20A—4—105(6)(a) (standard for mechanical ballots); Vt. Stat. Ann., Tit. 17, §2587(a) (1982); Va. Code Ann. §24.2—644(A) (2000); Wash. Rev. Code §29.62.180(1) (Supp. 2001) (standard for write-in votes); Wyo. Stat. Ann. §22—14—104 (1999). The following States employ a standard in which a vote is counted unless it is "impossible

to determine the elector's [or voter's] choice": Ala. Code §11—46—44(c) (1992), Ala. Code §17—13—2 (1995); Ariz. Rev. Stat. Ann. §16—610 (1996) (standard for rejecting ballot); Cal. Elec. Code Ann. §15154(c) (West Supp. 2000); Colo. Rev. Stat. §1—7—309(1) (1999) (standard for paper ballots), §1—7—508(2) (standard for electronic ballots); Del. Code Ann., Tit. 15, §4972(4) (1999); Idaho Code §34—1203 (1981); Ill. Comp. Stat., ch. 10, §5/7—51 (1993) (standard for primaries), *id.*, ch. 10, §5/17—16 (1993) (standard for general elections); Iowa Code §49.98 (1999); Me. Rev. Stat. Ann., Tit. 21—A §§696(2)(B), (4) (Supp. 2000); Minn. Stat. §204C.22(1) (1992); Mont. Code Ann. §13—15—202 (1997) (not counting votes if "elector's choice cannot be determined"); Nev. Rev. Stat. §293.367(d) (1995); N.Y. Elec. Law §9—112(6) (McKinney 1998); N. C. Gen. Stat. §§163—169(b), 163—170 (1999); N.D. Cent. Code §16.1—15—01(1) (Supp. 1999); Ohio Rev. Code Ann. §3505.28 (1994); 26 Okla. Stat., Tit. 26, §7—127(6) (1997); Ore. Rev. Stat. §254.505(1) (1991); S. C. Code Ann. §7—13—1120 (1977); S.D. Codified Laws §12—20—7 (1995); Tenn. Code Ann. §2—7—133(b) (1994); W. Va. Code §3—6—5(g) (1999).

7. Cf. *Victor v. Nebraska, 511 U.S. 1, 5* (1994) ("The beyond a reasonable doubt standard is a requirement of due process, but the Constitution neither prohibits trial courts from defining reasonable doubt nor requires them to do so").

8. The percentage of nonvotes in this election in counties using a punch-card system was 3.92%; in contrast, the rate of error under the more modern optical-scan systems was only 1.43%. *Siegel v. LePore*, No. 00—15981, 2000 WL 1781946, *31, *32, *43 (charts C and F) (CA11, Dec. 6, 2000). Put in other terms, for every 10,000 votes cast, punch-card systems result in 250 more nonvotes than optical-scan systems. A total of 3,718,305 votes were cast under punch-card systems, and 2,353,811 votes were cast under optical-scan systems. *Ibid.*

9. Republican electors were certified by the Acting Governor on November 28, 1960. A recount was ordered to begin on December 13, 1960. Both Democratic and Republican electors met on the appointed day to cast their votes. On January 4, 1961, the newly elected Governor certified the Democratic electors. The certification was received by Congress on January 6, the day the electoral votes were counted. Josephson & Ross, 22 J. Legis., at 166, n. 154.

10. When, for example, it resolved the previously unanswered question whether the word "shall" in Fla. Stat. §102.111 or the word "may" in §102.112 governs the scope of the Secretary of State's authority to ignore untimely election returns, it did not "change the law." Like any other judicial interpretation of a statute, its opinion was an authoritative interpretation of what the statute's relevant provisions have meant since they were enacted. *Rivers v. Roadway Express, Inc., 511 U.S. 298, 312—313* (1994).

11. "It is emphatically the province and duty of the judicial department to say what the law is." *Marbury v. Madison., 1 Cranch 137, 177* (1803).

Justice Souter, with whom Justice Breyer joins and with whom Justice Stevens and Justice Ginsburg join with regard to all but Part C, dissenting.

The Court should not have reviewed either *Bush v. Palm Beach County Canvassing Bd., ante*, p. ____ (*per curiam*), or this case, and should not have stopped Florida's attempt to recount all undervote ballots, see *ante* at ____, by issuing a stay of the Florida Supreme Court's orders during the period of this review, see *Bush v. Gore, post* at ____ (slip op., at 1). If this Court had allowed the State to follow the course indicated by the opinions of its own Supreme Court, it is entirely possible that there would ultimately have been no issue requiring our review, and political tension could have worked itself out in the Congress following the procedure provided in *3 U.S.C. §15*. The case being before us, however, its resolution by the majority is another erroneous decision.

As will be clear, I am in substantial agreement with the dissenting opinions of Justice Stevens, Justice Ginsburg and Justice Breyer. I write separately only to say how straightforward the issues before us really are.

There are three issues: whether the State Supreme Court's interpretation of the statute providing for a contest of the state election results somehow violates *3 U.S.C. §5*; whether that court's construction of the state statutory provisions governing contests impermissibly changes a state law from what the State's legislature has provided, in violation of Article II, §1, cl. 2, of the national Constitution; and whether the manner of interpreting markings on disputed ballots failing to cause machines to register votes for President (the undervote ballots) violates the equal protection or due process guaranteed by the *Fourteenth Amendment*. None of these issues is difficult to describe or to resolve.

(Continues)

(*Continued*)

A

The *3 U.S.C. §5* issue is not serious. That provision sets certain conditions for treating a State's certification of Presidential electors as conclusive in the event that a dispute over recognizing those electors must be resolved in the Congress under *3 U.S.C. §15*. Conclusiveness requires selection under a legal scheme in place before the election, with results determined at least six days before the date set for casting electoral votes. But no State is required to conform to §5 if it cannot do that (for whatever reason); the sanction for failing to satisfy the conditions of §5 is simply loss of what has been called its "safe harbor." And even that determination is to be made, if made anywhere, in the Congress.

B

The second matter here goes to the State Supreme Court's interpretation of certain terms in the state statute governing election "contests," Fla. Stat. §102.168 (2000); there is no question here about the state court's interpretation of the related provisions dealing with the antecedent process of "protesting" particular vote counts, §102.166, which was involved in the previous case, *Bush v. Palm Beach County Canvassing Board*. The issue is whether the judgment of the state supreme court has displaced the state legislature's provisions for election contests: is the law as declared by the court different from the provisions made by the legislature, to which the national Constitution commits responsibility for determining how each State's Presidential electors are chosen? See U.S. Const., Art. II, §1, cl. 2. Bush does not, of course, claim that any judicial act interpreting a statute of uncertain meaning is enough to displace the legislative provision and violate Article II; statutes require interpretation, which does not without more affect the legislative character of a statute within the meaning of the Constitution. Brief for Petitioners 48, n. 22, in *Bush v. Palm Beach County Canvassing Bd., et al.*, 531 U.S. ___ (2000). What Bush does argue, as I understand the contention, is that the interpretation of §102.168 was so unreasonable as to transcend the accepted bounds of statutory interpretation, to the point of being a nonjudicial act and producing new law untethered to the legislative act in question.

The starting point for evaluating the claim that the Florida Supreme Court's interpretation effectively rewrote §102.168 must be the language of the provision on which Gore relies to show his right to raise this contest: that the previously certified result in Bush's favor was produced by "rejection of a number of legal votes sufficient to change or place in doubt the result of the election." Fla. Stat. §102.168(3)(c) (2000). None of the state court's interpretations is unreasonable to the point of displacing the legislative enactment quoted. As I will note below, other interpretations were of course possible, and some might have been better than those adopted by the Florida court's majority; the two dissents from the majority opinion of that court and various briefs submitted to us set out alternatives. But the majority view is in each instance within the bounds of reasonable interpretation, and the law as declared is consistent with Article II.

1. The statute does not define a "legal vote," the rejection of which may affect the election. The State Supreme Court was therefore required to define it, and in doing that the court looked to another election statute, §101.5614(5), dealing with damaged or defective ballots, which contains a provision that no vote shall be disregarded "if there is a clear indication of the intent of the voter as determined by a canvassing board." The court read that objective of looking to the voter's intent as indicating that the legislature probably meant "legal vote" to mean a vote recorded on a ballot indicating what the voter intended. *Gore v. Harris*, ___ So. 2d ___ (slip op., at 23–25) (Dec. 8, 2000). It is perfectly true that the majority might have chosen a different reading. See, *e.g.*, Brief for Respondent Harris et al. 10 (defining "legal votes" as "votes properly executed in accordance with the instructions provided to all registered voters in advance of the election and in the polling places"). But even so, there is no constitutional violation in following the majority view; Article II is unconcerned with mere disagreements about interpretive merits.

2. The Florida court next interpreted "rejection" to determine what act in the counting process may be attacked in a contest. Again, the statute does not define the term. The court majority read the word to mean simply a failure to count. ____ So. 2d, at___ (slip op., at 26–27). That reading is certainly within the bounds of common sense, given the objective to give effect to a voter's intent if that can be determined. A different reading, of course, is possible. The majority might have concluded that "rejection" should refer to machine malfunction, or that a ballot should not be treated as "reject[ed]" in the absence of wrongdoing by election officials, lest

contests be so easy to claim that every election will end up in one. Cf. *id.*, at ____ (slip op., at 48) (Wells, C. J., dissenting). There is, however, nothing nonjudicial in the Florida majority's more hospitable reading.

3. The same is true about the court majority's understanding of the phrase "votes sufficient to change or place in doubt" the result of the election in Florida. The court held that if the uncounted ballots were so numerous that it was reasonably possible that they contained enough "legal" votes to swing the election, this contest would be authorized by the statute.[12] While the majority might have thought (as the trial judge did) that a probability, not a possibility, should be necessary to justify a contest, that reading is not required by the statute's text, which says nothing about probability. Whatever people of good will and good sense may argue about the merits of the Florida court's reading, there is no warrant for saying that it transcends the limits of reasonable statutory interpretation to the point of supplanting the statute enacted by the "legislature" within the meaning of Article II.

In sum, the interpretations by the Florida court raise no substantial question under Article II. That court engaged in permissible construction in determining that Gore had instituted a contest authorized by the state statute, and it proceeded to direct the trial judge to deal with that contest in the exercise of the discretionary powers generously conferred by Fla. Stat. §102.168(8) (2000), to "fashion such orders as he or she deems necessary to ensure that each allegation in the complaint is investigated, examined, or checked, to prevent or correct any alleged wrong, and to provide any relief appropriate under such circumstances." As Justice Ginsburg has persuasively explained in her own dissenting opinion, our customary respect for state interpretations of state law counsels against rejection of the Florida court's determinations in this case.

C

It is only on the third issue before us that there is a meritorious argument for relief, as this Court's *Per Curiam* opinion recognizes. It is an issue that might well have been dealt with adequately by the Florida courts if the state proceedings had not been interrupted, and if not disposed of at the state level it could have been considered by the Congress in any electoral vote dispute. But because the course of state proceedings has been interrupted, time is short, and the issue is before us, I think it sensible for the Court to address it.

Petitioners have raised an equal protection claim (or, alternatively, a due process claim, see generally *Logan v. Zimmerman Brush Co., 455 U.S. 422 (1982)*), in the charge that unjustifiably disparate standards are applied in different electoral jurisdictions to otherwise identical facts. It is true that the Equal Protection Clause does not forbid the use of a variety of voting mechanisms within a jurisdiction, even though different mechanisms will have different levels of effectiveness in recording voters' intentions; local variety can be justified by concerns about cost, the potential value of innovation, and so on. But evidence in the record here suggests that a different order of disparity obtains under rules for determining a voter's intent that have been applied (and could continue to be applied) to identical types of ballots used in identical brands of machines and exhibiting identical physical characteristics (such as "hanging" or "dimpled" chads). See, *e.g.*, Tr., at 238–242 (Dec. 2–3, 2000) (testimony of Palm Beach County Canvassing Board Chairman Judge Charles Burton describing varying standards applied to imperfectly punched ballots in Palm Beach County during precertification manual recount); *id.*, at 497–500 (similarly describing varying standards applied in Miami-Dade County); Tr. of Hearing 8–10 (Dec. 8, 2000) (soliciting from county canvassing boards proposed protocols for determining voters' intent but declining to provide a precise, uniform standard). I can conceive of no legitimate state interest served by these differing treatments of the expressions of voters' fundamental rights. The differences appear wholly arbitrary.

In deciding what to do about this, we should take account of the fact that electoral votes are due to be cast in six days. I would therefore remand the case to the courts of Florida with instructions to establish uniform standards for evaluating the several types of ballots that have prompted differing treatments, to be applied within and among counties when passing on such identical ballots in any further recounting (or successive recounting) that the courts might order.

Unlike the majority, I see no warrant for this Court to assume that Florida could not possibly comply with this requirement before the date set for the meeting of electors, December 18. Although one of the dissenting justices of the State Supreme Court estimated that disparate standards potentially affected 170,000 votes, *Gore v. Harris, supra*, ____ So. 2d, at ____ (slip op., at 66), the

(Continues)

number at issue is significantly smaller. The 170,000 figure apparently represents all uncounted votes, both undervotes (those for which no Presidential choice was recorded by a machine) and overvotes (those rejected because of votes for more than one candidate). Tr. of Oral Arg. 61–62. But as Justice Breyer has pointed out, no showing has been made of legal overvotes uncounted, and counsel for Gore made an uncontradicted representation to the Court that the statewide total of undervotes is about 60,000. *Id.*, at 62. To recount these manually would be a tall order, but before this Court stayed the effort to do that the courts of Florida were ready to do their best to get that job done. There is no justification for denying the State the opportunity to try to count all disputed ballots now.

I respectfully dissent.

Note

12. When the Florida court ruled, the totals for Bush and Gore were then less than 1,000 votes apart. One dissent pegged the number of uncounted votes in question at 170,000. *Gore v. Harris, supra,* __ So. 2d __, (slip op., at 66) (opinion of Harding, J.). Gore's counsel represented to us that the relevant figure is approximately 60,000, Tr. of Oral Arg. 62, the number of ballots in which no vote for President was recorded by the machines.

Justice Ginsburg, with whom Justice Stevens joins, and with whom Justice Souter and Justice Breyer join as to Part I, dissenting.

I

The Chief Justice acknowledges that provisions of Florida's Election Code "may well admit of more than one interpretation." *Ante*, at 3. But instead of respecting the state high court's province to say what the State's Election Code means, The Chief Justice maintains that Florida's Supreme Court has veered so far from the ordinary practice of judicial review that what it did cannot properly be called judging. My colleagues have offered a reasonable construction of Florida's law. Their construction coincides with the view of one of Florida's seven Supreme Court justices. *Gore v. Harris*, __ So. 2d __, __ (Fla. 2000) (slip op., at 45–55) (Wells, C. J., dissenting); *Palm Beach County Canvassing Bd. v. Harris*, __ So. 2d __, __ (Fla. 2000) (slip op., at 34) (on remand) (confirming, 6–1, the construction of Florida law advanced in *Gore*). I might join The Chief Justice were it my commission to interpret Florida law. But disagreement with the Florida court's interpretation of its own State's law does not warrant the conclusion that the justices of that court have legislated. There is no cause here to believe that the members of Florida's high court have done less than "their mortal best to discharge their oath of office," *Sumner v. Mata, 449 U.S. 539,* 549 (1981), and no cause to upset their reasoned interpretation of Florida law.

This Court more than occasionally affirms statutory, and even constitutional, interpretations with which it disagrees. For example, when reviewing challenges to administrative agencies' interpretations of laws they implement, we defer to the agencies unless their interpretation violates "the unambiguously expressed intent of Congress." *Chevron U.S.A. Inc. v. Natural Resources Defense Council, Inc., 467 U.S. 837,* 843 (1984). We do so in the face of the declaration in Article I of the United States Constitution that "All legislative Powers herein granted shall be vested in a Congress of the United States." Surely the Constitution does not call upon us to pay more respect to a federal administrative agency's construction of federal law than to a state high court's interpretation of its own state's law. And not uncommonly, we let stand state-court interpretations of *federal* law with which we might disagree. Notably, in the habeas context, the Court adheres to the view that "there is 'no intrinsic reason why the fact that a man is a federal judge should make him more competent, or conscientious, or learned with respect to [federal law] than his neighbor in the state courthouse.'" *Stone v. Powell, 428 U.S. 465,* 494, n. 35 (1976) (quoting Bator, Finality in Criminal Law and Federal Habeas Corpus For State Prisoners, 76 *Harv. L. Rev.* 441, 509 (1963)); see *O'Dell v. Netherland, 521 U.S. 151,* 156 (1997) ("[T]he *Teague* doctrine validates reasonable, good-faith interpretations of existing precedents made by state courts even though they are shown to be contrary to later decisions.") (citing *Butler v. McKellar, 494 U.S. 407,* 414 (1990)); O'Connor, Trends in the Relationship between the Federal and State Courts from the Perspective of a State Court Judge, 22 *Wm. & Mary L. Rev.* 801, 813 (1981) ("There is no reason to assume that state court judges cannot and will not provide a 'hospitable forum' in litigating federal constitutional questions.").

No doubt there are cases in which the proper application of federal law may hinge on interpretations of state law. Unavoidably, this Court must sometimes examine state law in order to protect federal rights. But we have dealt with such cases ever mindful of the full measure of respect we owe to interpretations of state law by a State's highest court. In the Contract Clause case, *General Motors Corp. v. Romein, 503 U.S. 181* (1992), for example, we said that although "ultimately we are bound to decide for ourselves whether a contract was made," the Court "accord[s] respectful consideration and great weight to the views of the State's highest court." *Id.*, at 187 (citation omitted). And in *Central Union Telephone Co. v. Edwardsville, 269 U.S. 190* (1925), we upheld the Illinois Supreme Court's interpretation of a state waiver rule, even though that interpretation resulted in the forfeiture of federal constitutional rights. Refusing to supplant Illinois law with a federal definition of waiver, we explained that the state court's declaration "should bind us unless so unfair or unreasonable in its application to those asserting a federal right as to obstruct it." *Id.*, at 195. [13]

In deferring to state courts on matters of state law, we appropriately recognize that this Court acts as an "'outside[r]' lacking the common exposure to local law which comes from sitting in the jurisdiction." *Lehman Brothers v. Schein, 416 U.S. 386*, 391 (1974). That recognition has sometimes prompted us to resolve doubts about the meaning of state law by certifying issues to a State's highest court, even when federal rights are at stake. Cf. *Arizonans for Official English v. Arizona, 520 U.S. 43*, 79 (1997) ("Warnings against premature adjudication of constitutional questions bear heightened attention when a federal court is asked to invalidate a State's law, for the federal tribunal risks friction-generating error when it endeavors to construe a novel state Act not yet reviewed by the State's highest court."). Notwithstanding our authority to decide issues of state law underlying federal claims, we have used the certification devise to afford state high courts an opportunity to inform us on matters of their own State's law because such restraint "helps build a cooperative judicial federalism." *Lehman Brothers*, 416 U.S., at 391.

Just last term, in *Fiore v. White, 528 U.S. 23* (1999), we took advantage of Pennsylvania's certification procedure. In that case, a state prisoner brought a federal habeas action claiming that the State had failed to prove an essential element of his charged offense in violation of the Due Process Clause. *Id.*, at 25–26. Instead of resolving the state-law question on which the federal claim depended, we certified the question to the Pennsylvania Supreme Court for that court to "help determine the proper state-law predicate for our determination of the federal constitutional questions raised." *Id.*, at 29; *id.*, at 28 (asking the Pennsylvania Supreme Court whether its recent interpretation of the statute under which Fiore was convicted "was always the statute's meaning, even at the time of Fiore's trial"). The Chief Justice's willingness to *reverse* the Florida Supreme Court's interpretation of Florida law in this case is at least in tension with our reluctance in *Fiore* even to interpret Pennsylvania law before seeking instruction from the Pennsylvania Supreme Court. I would have thought the "cautious approach" we counsel when federal courts address matters of state law, *Arizonans*, 520 U.S., at 77, and our commitment to "build[ing] cooperative judicial federalism," *Lehman Brothers*, 416 U.S., at 391, demanded greater restraint.

Rarely has this Court rejected outright an interpretation of state law by a state high court. *Fairfax's Devisee v. Hunter's Lessee*, 7 Cranch 603 (1813), *NAACP v. Alabama ex rel. Patterson, 357 U.S. 449* (1958), and *Bouie v. City of Columbia, 378 U.S. 347* (1964), cited by The Chief Justice, are three such rare instances. See *ante*, at 4, 5, and n. 2. But those cases are embedded in historical contexts hardly comparable to the situation here. *Fairfax's Devisee*, which held that the Virginia Court of Appeals had misconstrued its own forfeiture laws to deprive a British subject of lands secured to him by federal treaties, occurred amidst vociferous States' rights attacks on the Marshall Court. G. Gunther & K. Sullivan, *Constitutional Law*, 61–62 (13th ed. 1997). The Virginia court refused to obey this Court's *Fairfax's Devisee* mandate to enter judgment for the British subject's successor in interest. That refusal led to the Court's pathmarking decision in *Martin v. Hunter's Lessee*, 1 Wheat. 304 (1816). *Patterson*, a case decided three months after *Cooper v. Aaron, 358 U.S. 1* (1958), in the face of Southern resistance to the civil rights movement, held that the Alabama Supreme Court had irregularly applied its own procedural rules to deny review of a contempt order against the NAACP arising from its refusal to disclose membership lists. We said that "our jurisdiction is not defeated if the nonfederal ground relied on by the state court is without any fair or substantial support." 357 U.S., at 455. *Bouie*, stemming from a lunch counter "sit-in" at the height of the civil rights movement, held that the South Carolina Supreme Court's construction of its trespass laws—criminalizing conduct not covered by the text of an otherwise clear statute—was "unforeseeable" and thus violated due process when applied retroactively to the petitioners. 378 U.S., at 350, 354.

(Continues)

(*Continued*)

The Chief Justice's casual citation of these cases might lead one to believe they are part of a larger collection of cases in which we said that the Constitution impelled us to train a skeptical eye on a state court's portrayal of state law. But one would be hard pressed, I think, to find additional cases that fit the mold. As Justice Breyer convincingly explains, see *post*, at 5–9 (dissenting opinion), this case involves nothing close to the kind of recalcitrance by a state high court that warrants extraordinary action by this Court. The Florida Supreme Court concluded that counting every legal vote was the overriding concern of the Florida Legislature when it enacted the State's Election Code. The court surely should not be bracketed with state high courts of the Jim Crow South.

The Chief Justice says that Article II, by providing that state legislatures shall direct the manner of appointing electors, authorizes federal superintendence over the relationship between state courts and state legislatures, and licenses a departure from the usual deference we give to state court interpretations of state law. *Ante*, at 5 ("To attach definitive weight to the pronouncement of a state court, when the very question at issue is whether the court has actually departed from the statutory meaning, would be to abdicate our responsibility to enforce the explicit requirements of Article II."). The Framers of our Constitution, however, understood that in a republican government, the judiciary would construe the legislature's enactments. See U.S. Const., Art. III; *The Federalist* No. 78 (A. Hamilton). In light of the constitutional guarantee to States of a "Republican Form of Government," U.S. Const., Art. IV, §4, Article II can hardly be read to invite this Court to disrupt a State's republican regime. Yet The Chief Justice today would reach out to do just that. By holding that Article II requires our revision of a state court's construction of state laws in order to protect one organ of the State from another, The Chief Justice contradicts the basic principle that a State may organize itself as it sees fit. See, *e.g.*, *Gregory v. Ashcroft, 501 U.S. 452, 460* (1991) ("Through the structure of its government, and the character of those who exercise government authority, a State defines itself as a sovereign."); *Highland Farms Dairy, Inc. v. Agnew, 300 U.S. 608, 612* (1937) ("How power shall be distributed by a state among its governmental organs is commonly, if not always, a question for the state itself.").[14] Article II does not call for the scrutiny undertaken by this Court.

The extraordinary setting of this case has obscured the ordinary principle that dictates its proper resolution: Federal courts defer to state high courts' interpretations of their state's own law. This principle reflects the core of federalism, on which all agree. "The Framers split the atom of sovereignty. It was the genius of their idea that our citizens would have two political capacities, one state and one federal, each protected from incursion by the other." *Saenz v. Roe, 526 U.S. 489, 504,* n. 17 (1999) (citing *U.S. Term Limits, Inc. v. Thornton, 514 U.S. 779, 838* (1995) (Kennedy, J., concurring)). The Chief Justice's solicitude for the Florida Legislature comes at the expense of the more fundamental solicitude we owe to the legislature's sovereign. U.S. Const., Art. II, §1, cl. 2 ("Each *State* shall appoint, in such Manner as the Legislature *thereof* may direct," the electors for President and Vice President) (emphasis added); *ante*, at 1–2 (Stevens, J., dissenting).[15] Were the other members of this Court as mindful as they generally are of our system of dual sovereignty, they would affirm the judgment of the Florida Supreme Court.

II

I agree with Justice Stevens that petitioners have not presented a substantial equal protection claim. Ideally, perfection would be the appropriate standard for judging the recount. But we live in an imperfect world, one in which thousands of votes have not been counted. I cannot agree that the recount adopted by the Florida court, flawed as it may be, would yield a result any less fair or precise than the certification that preceded that recount. See, *e.g.*, *McDonald v. Board of Election Comm'rs of Chicago, 394 U.S. 802, 807* (1969) (even in the context of the right to vote, the state is permitted to reform "'one step at a time'") (quoting *Williamson v. Lee Optical of Oklahoma, Inc., 348 U.S. 483, 489* (1955)).

Even if there were an equal protection violation, I would agree with Justice Stevens, Justice Souter, and Justice Breyer that the Court's concern about "the December 12 deadline," *ante*, at 12, is misplaced. Time is short in part because of the Court's entry of a stay on December 9, several hours after an able circuit judge in Leon County had begun to superintend the recount process. More fundamentally, the Court's reluctance to let the recount go forward—despite its suggestion that "[t]he search for intent can be confined by specific rules designed to ensure uniform treatment," *ante*, at 8—ultimately turns on its own judgment about the practical realities of implementing a recount, not the judgment of those much closer to the process.

Equally important, as Justice Breyer explains, *post*, at 12 (dissenting opinion), the December 12 "deadline" for bringing Florida's electoral votes into *3 U.S.C. §5*'s safe harbor lacks the significance the Court assigns it. Were that date to pass, Florida would still be entitled to deliver electoral votes Congress *must* count unless both Houses find that the votes "ha[d] not been . . . regularly given." *3 U.S.C. §15*. The statute identifies other significant dates. See, *e.g.*, §7 (specifying December 18 as the date electors "shall meet and give their votes"); §12 (specifying "the fourth Wednesday in December"—this year, December 27—as the date on which Congress, if it has not received a State's electoral votes, shall request the state secretary of state to send a certified return immediately). But none of these dates has ultimate significance in light of Congress' detailed provisions for determining, on "the sixth day of January," the validity of electoral votes. §15.

The Court assumes that time will not permit "orderly judicial review of any disputed matters that might arise." *Ante*, at 12. But no one has doubted the good faith and diligence with which Florida election officials, attorneys for all sides of this controversy, and the courts of law have performed their duties. Notably, the Florida Supreme Court has produced two substantial opinions within 29 hours of oral argument. In sum, the Court's conclusion that a constitutionally adequate recount is impractical is a prophecy the Court's own judgment will not allow to be tested. Such an untested prophecy should not decide the Presidency of the United States.

I dissent.

Notes

13. See also *Lucas v. South Carolina Coastal Council, 505 U.S. 1003*, 1032, n. 18 (1992) (South Carolina could defend a regulatory taking "if an *objectively reasonable application* of relevant precedents [by its courts] would exclude . . . beneficial uses in the circumstances in which the land is presently found"); *Bishop v. Wood, 426 U.S. 341*, 344–345 (1976) (deciding whether North Carolina had created a property interest cognizable under the Due Process Clause by reference to state law as interpreted by the North Carolina Supreme Court). Similarly, in *Gurley v. Rhoden, 421 U.S. 200* (1975), a gasoline retailer claimed that due process entitled him to deduct a state gasoline excise tax in computing the amount of his sales subject to a state sales tax, on the grounds that the legal incidence of the excise tax fell on his customers and that he acted merely as a collector of the tax. The Mississippi Supreme Court held that the legal incidence of the excise tax fell on petitioner. Observing that "a State's highest court is the final judicial arbiter of the meaning of state statutes," we said that "[w]hen a state court has made its own definitive determination as to the operating incidence, . . . [w]e give this finding great weight in determining the natural effect of a statute, and if it is consistent with the statute's reasonable interpretation it will be deemed conclusive." *Id.*, at 208.

14. Even in the rare case in which a State's "manner" of making and construing laws might implicate a structural constraint, Congress, not this Court, is likely the proper governmental entity to enforce that constraint. See U.S. Const., amend. XII; *3 U.S.C. §1–15*; cf. *Ohio ex rel. Davis v. Hildebrant, 241 U.S. 565*, 569 (1916) (treating as a nonjusticiable political question whether use of a referendum to override a congressional districting plan enacted by the state legislature violates Art. I, §4); *Luther v. Borden*, 7 How. 1, 42 (1849).

15. "[B]ecause the Framers recognized that state power and identity were essential parts of the federal balance, see The Federalist No. 39, the Constitution is solicitous of the prerogatives of the States, even in an otherwise sovereign federal province. The Constitution . . . grants States certain powers over the times, places, and manner of federal elections (subject to congressional revision), Art. I, §4, cl. 1 . . ., and allows States to appoint electors for the President, Art. II, §1, cl. 2." *U.S. Term Limits, Inc. v. Thornton, 514 U.S. 779*, 841–842 (1995) (Kennedy, J., concurring).

Justice Breyer, with whom Justice Stevens and Justice Ginsburg join except as to Part I—A—1, and with whom Justice Souter joins as to Part I, dissenting.

The Court was wrong to take this case. It was wrong to grant a stay. It should now vacate that stay and permit the Florida Supreme Court to decide whether the recount should resume.

(Continues)

(*Continued*)

I

The political implications of this case for the country are momentous. But the federal legal questions presented, with one exception, are insubstantial.

A

1

The majority raises three Equal Protection problems with the Florida Supreme Court's recount order: first, the failure to include overvotes in the manual recount; second, the fact that *all* ballots, rather than simply the undervotes, were recounted in some, but not all, counties; and third, the absence of a uniform, specific standard to guide the recounts. As far as the first issue is concerned, petitioners presented no evidence, to this Court or to any Florida court, that a manual recount of overvotes would identify additional legal votes. The same is true of the second, and, in addition, the majority's reasoning would seem to invalidate any state provision for a manual recount of individual counties in a statewide election.

The majority's third concern does implicate principles of fundamental fairness. The majority concludes that the Equal Protection Clause requires that a manual recount be governed not only by the uniform general standard of the "clear intent of the voter," but also by uniform subsidiary standards (for example, a uniform determination whether indented, but not perforated, "undervotes" should count). The opinion points out that the Florida Supreme Court ordered the inclusion of Broward County's undercounted "legal votes" even though those votes included ballots that were not perforated but simply "dimpled," while newly recounted ballots from other counties will likely include only votes determined to be "legal" on the basis of a stricter standard. In light of our previous remand, the Florida Supreme Court may have been reluctant to adopt a more specific standard than that provided for by the legislature for fear of exceeding its authority under Article II. However, since the use of different standards could favor one or the other of the candidates, since time was, and is, too short to permit the lower courts to iron out significant differences through ordinary judicial review, and since the relevant distinction was embodied in the order of the State's highest court, I agree that, in these very special circumstances, basic principles of fairness may well have counseled the adoption of a uniform standard to address the problem. In light of the majority's disposition, I need not decide whether, or the extent to which, as a remedial matter, the Constitution would place limits upon the content of the uniform standard.

2

Nonetheless, there is no justification for the majority's remedy, which is simply to reverse the lower court and halt the recount entirely. An appropriate remedy would be, instead, to remand this case with instructions that, even at this late date, would permit the Florida Supreme Court to require recounting *all* undercounted votes in Florida, including those from Broward, Volusia, Palm Beach, and Miami-Dade Counties, whether or not previously recounted prior to the end of the protest period, and to do so in accordance with a single-uniform substandard.

The majority justifies stopping the recount entirely on the ground that there is no more time. In particular, the majority relies on the lack of time for the Secretary to review and approve equipment needed to separate undervotes. But the majority reaches this conclusion in the absence of *any* record evidence that the recount could not have been completed in the time allowed by the Florida Supreme Court. The majority finds facts outside of the record on matters that state courts are in a far better position to address. Of course, it is too late for any such recount to take place by December 12, the date by which election disputes must be decided if a State is to take advantage of the safe harbor provisions of *3 U.S.C. §5*. Whether there is time to conduct a recount prior to December 18, when the electors are scheduled to meet, is a matter for the state courts to determine. And whether, under Florida law, Florida could or could not take further action is obviously a matter for Florida courts, not this Court, to decide. See *ante*, at 13 (*per curiam*).

By halting the manual recount, and thus ensuring that the uncounted legal votes will not be counted under any standard, this Court crafts a remedy out of proportion to the asserted harm. And that remedy harms the very fairness interests the Court is attempting to protect. The manual recount would itself redress a problem of unequal treatment of ballots. As Justice Stevens points out, see *ante*, at 4 and n. 4 (Stevens, J., dissenting opinion), the ballots of voters in counties that use punch-card systems are more likely to be disqualified than those in counties using optical-scanning systems. According to recent news reports, variations in the undervote rate are even more pronounced. See Fessenden, No-Vote Rates Higher in Punch Card Count, N. Y. Times, Dec. 1, 2000, p. A29 (reporting that 0.3% of ballots cast in 30 Florida counties using optical-scanning systems registered no Presidential vote, in comparison to 1.53% in the 15 counties using Votomatic punch-card ballots). Thus, in a system that allows counties to use different types of voting systems, voters already arrive at the polls with an unequal chance that their votes will be counted. I do not see how the fact that this results from counties' selection of different voting machines rather than a court order makes the outcome any more fair. Nor do I understand why the Florida Supreme Court's recount order, which helps to redress this inequity, must be entirely prohibited based on a deficiency that could easily be remedied.

B

The remainder of petitioners' claims, which are the focus of the Chief Justice's concurrence, raise no significant federal questions. I cannot agree that the Chief Justice's unusual review of state law in this case, see *ante*, at 5–8 (Ginsburg, J., dissenting opinion), is justified by reference either to Art. II, §1, or to *3 U.S.C. §5*. Moreover, even were such review proper, the conclusion that the Florida Supreme Court's decision contravenes federal law is untenable.

While conceding that, in most cases, "comity and respect for federalism compel us to defer to the decisions of state courts on issues of state law," the concurrence relies on some combination of Art. II, §1, and *3 U.S.C. §5* to justify the majority's conclusion that this case is one of the few in which we may lay that fundamental principle aside. *Ante*, at 2 (Opinion of Rehnquist, C. J. The concurrence's primary foundation for this conclusion rests on an appeal to plain text: Art. II, §1's grant of the power to appoint Presidential electors to the State "Legislature." *Ibid.* But neither the text of Article II itself nor the only case the concurrence cites that interprets Article II, *McPherson v. Blacker, 146 U.S. 1* (1892), leads to the conclusion that Article II grants unlimited power to the legislature, devoid of any state constitutional limitations, to select the manner of appointing electors. See *id.*, at 41 (specifically referring to state constitutional provision in upholding state law regarding selection of electors). Nor, as Justice Stevens points out, have we interpreted the Federal constitutional provision most analogous to Art. II, §1—Art. I, §4—in the strained manner put forth in the concurrence. *Ante*, at 1–2 and n. 1 (dissenting opinion).

The concurrence's treatment of §5 as "inform[ing]" its interpretation of Article II, §1, cl. 2, *ante*, at 3 (Rehnquist, C. J., concurring), is no more convincing. The Chief Justice contends that our opinion in *Bush v. Palm Beach County Canvassing Bd., ante*, p. ____, (*per curiam*) (*Bush I*), in which we stated that "a legislative wish to take advantage of [§5] would counsel against" a construction of Florida law that Congress might deem to be a change in law, *id.*, (slip op. at 6), now means that *this Court* "must ensure that postelection state court actions do not frustrate the legislative desire to attain the 'safe harbor' provided by §5." *Ante*, at 3. However, §5 is part of the rules that govern Congress' recognition of slates of electors. Nowhere in *Bush I* did we establish that *this Court* had the authority to enforce §5. Nor did we suggest that the permissive "counsel against" could be transformed into the mandatory "must ensure." And nowhere did we intimate, as the concurrence does here, that a state court decision that threatens the safe harbor provision of §5 does so in violation of Article II. The concurrence's logic turns the presumption that legislatures would wish to take advantage of §5's "safe harbor" provision into a mandate that trumps other statutory provisions and overrides the intent that the legislature *did* express.

But, in any event, the concurrence, having conducted its review, now reaches the wrong conclusion. It says that "the Florida Supreme Court's interpretation of the Florida election laws impermissibly distorted them beyond what a fair reading required, in violation of Article II." *Ante*, at 4–5 (Rehnquist, C. J, concurring). But what precisely is the distortion? Apparently, it has three elements. First, the Florida court, in its earlier opinion, changed the election certification date from November 14 to November 26. Second, the Florida court ordered a manual recount of "undercounted" ballots that could not have been fully completed by the December 12 "safe harbor" deadline. Third, the Florida court, in the opinion now under review, failed to give adequate deference to the determinations of canvassing boards and the Secretary.

To characterize the first element as a "distortion," however, requires the concurrence to second-guess the way in which the state court resolved a plain conflict in the language of different statutes.

(Continues)

(Continued)

Compare Fla. Stat. §102.166 (2001) (foreseeing manual recounts during the protest period) with §102.111 (setting what is arguably too short a deadline for manual recounts to be conducted); compare §102.112(1) (stating that the Secretary "may" ignore late returns) with §102.111(1) (stating that the Secretary "shall" ignore late returns). In any event, that issue no longer has any practical importance and cannot justify the reversal of the different Florida court decision before us now.

To characterize the second element as a "distortion" requires the concurrence to overlook the fact that the inability of the Florida courts to conduct the recount on time is, in significant part, a problem of the Court's own making. The Florida Supreme Court thought that the recount could be completed on time, and, within hours, the Florida Circuit Court was moving in an orderly fashion to meet the deadline. This Court improvidently entered a stay. As a result, we will never know whether the recount could have been completed.

Nor can one characterize the third element as "impermissibl[e] distort[ing]" once one understands that there are two sides to the opinion's argument that the Florida Supreme Court "virtually eliminated the Secretary's discretion." *Ante*, at 9 (Rehnquist, C. J, concurring). The Florida statute in question was amended in 1999 to provide that the "grounds for contesting an election" include the "rejection of a number of legal votes sufficient to . . . place in doubt the result of the election." Fla. Stat. §§102.168(3), (3)(c) (2000). And the parties have argued about the proper meaning of the statute's term "legal vote." The Secretary has claimed that a "legal vote" is a vote "properly executed in accordance with the instructions provided to all registered voters." Brief for Respondent Harris et al. 10. On that interpretation, punchcard ballots for which the machines cannot register a vote are not "legal" votes. *Id.*, at 14. The Florida Supreme Court did not accept her definition. But it had a reason. Its reason was that a different provision of Florida election laws (a provision that addresses damaged or defective ballots) says that no vote shall be disregarded "if there is a clear indication of the intent of the voter as determined by the canvassing board" (adding that ballots should not be counted "if it is impossible to determine the elector's choice"). Fla. Stat. §101.5614(5) (2000). Given this statutory language, certain roughly analogous judicial precedent, *e.g., Darby v. State ex rel. McCollough*, 75 So. 411 (Fla. 1917) (*per curiam*), and somewhat similar determinations by courts throughout the nation, see cases cited *infra,* at 9, the Florida Supreme Court concluded that the term "legal vote" means a vote recorded on a ballot that clearly reflects what the voter intended. *Gore v. Harris,* ___ So. 2d ___, ___ (2000) (slip op., at 19). That conclusion differs from the conclusion of the Secretary. But nothing in Florida law requires the Florida Supreme Court to accept as determinative the Secretary's view on such a matter. Nor can one say that the Court's ultimate determination is so unreasonable as to amount to a constitutionally "impermissible distort[ion]" of Florida law.

The Florida Supreme Court, applying this definition, decided, on the basis of the record, that respondents had shown that the ballots undercounted by the voting machines contained enough "legal votes" to place "the results" of the election "in doubt." Since only a few hundred votes separated the candidates, and since the "undercounted" ballots numbered tens of thousands, it is difficult to see how anyone could find this conclusion unreasonable—however strict the standard used to measure the voter's "clear intent." Nor did this conclusion "strip" canvassing boards of their discretion. The boards retain their traditional discretionary authority during the protest period. And during the contest period, as the court stated, "the Canvassing Board's actions [during the protest period] may constitute evidence that a ballot does or does not qualify as a legal vote." *Id.*, at *13. Whether a local county canvassing board's discretionary judgment during the protest period not to conduct a manual recount will be set aside during a contest period depends upon whether a candidate provides additional evidence that the rejected votes contain enough "legal votes" to place the outcome of the race in doubt. To limit the local canvassing board's discretion in this way is not to eliminate that discretion. At the least, one could reasonably so believe.

The statute goes on to provide the Florida circuit judge with authority to "fashion such orders as he or she deems necessary to ensure that each allegation . . . is *investigated, examined, or checked, . . .* and to provide any relief appropriate." Fla. Stat. §102.168(8) (2000) (emphasis added). The Florida Supreme Court did just that. One might reasonably disagree with the Florida Supreme Court's interpretation of these, or other, words in the statute. But I do not see how one could call its plain language interpretation of a 1999 statutory change so misguided as no longer to qualify as judicial interpretation or as a usurpation of the authority of the State legislature. Indeed, other state courts have interpreted roughly similar state statutes in similar ways. See, *e.g., In re Election of U.S. Representative for Second Congressional Dist.*, 231 Conn. 602, 621, 653 A. 2d 79, 90–91 (1994) ("Whatever the process used to vote and to count votes, differences in technology should not furnish a basis for disregarding the bedrock principle that the purpose of the voting process is to ascertain the intent of the voters"); *Brown v. Carr*, 130 W. Va. 401, 460, 43 S. E.2d 401, 404–405 (1947) ("[W]hether a ballot shall be counted . . . depends on the intent of the voter . . . Courts decry any resort to technical rules in reaching a conclusion as to the intent of the voter").

I repeat, where is the "impermissible" distortion?

II

Despite the reminder that this case involves "an election for the President of the United States," *ante*, at 1 (Rehnquist, C. J., concurring), no preeminent legal concern, or practical concern related to legal questions, required this Court to hear this case, let alone to issue a stay that stopped Florida's recount process in its tracks. With one exception, petitioners' claims do not ask us to vindicate a constitutional provision designed to protect a basic human right. See, *e.g.*, *Brown v. Board of Education*, 347 U.S. 483 (1954). Petitioners invoke fundamental fairness, namely, the need for procedural fairness, including finality. But with the one "equal protection" exception, they rely upon law that focuses, not upon that basic need, but upon the constitutional allocation of power. Respondents invoke a competing fundamental consideration—the need to determine the voter's true intent. But they look to state law, not to federal constitutional law, to protect that interest. Neither side claims electoral fraud, dishonesty, or the like. And the more fundamental equal protection claim might have been left to the state court to resolve if and when it was discovered to have mattered. It could still be resolved through a remand conditioned upon issuance of a uniform standard; it does not require reversing the Florida Supreme Court.

Of course, the selection of the President is of fundamental national importance. But that importance is political, not legal. And this Court should resist the temptation unnecessarily to resolve tangential legal disputes, where doing so threatens to determine the outcome of the election.

The Constitution and federal statutes themselves make clear that restraint is appropriate. They set forth a road map of how to resolve disputes about electors, even after an election as close as this one. That road map foresees resolution of electoral disputes by *state* courts. See *3 U.S.C. §5* (providing that, where a "State shall have provided, by laws enacted prior to [election day], for its final determination of any controversy or contest concerning the appointment of . . . electors . . . by *judicial* or other methods," the subsequently chosen electors enter a safe harbor free from congressional challenge). But it nowhere provides for involvement by the United States Supreme Court.

To the contrary, the *Twelfth Amendment commits* to Congress the authority and responsibility to count electoral votes. A federal statute, the Electoral Count Act, enacted after the close 1876 Hayes-Tilden Presidential election, specifies that, after States have tried to resolve disputes (through "judicial" or other means), Congress is the body primarily authorized to resolve remaining disputes. See Electoral Count Act of 1887, 24 Stat. 373, *3 U.S.C. §5* 6, and 15.

The legislative history of the Act makes clear its intent to commit the power to resolve such disputes to Congress, rather than the courts:

> "The two Houses are, by the Constitution, authorized to make the count of electoral votes. They can only count legal votes, and in doing so must determine, from the best evidence to be had, what are legal votes. . . .
> The power to determine rests with the two Houses, and there is no other constitutional tribunal." H. Rep. No. 1638, 49th Cong., 1st Sess., 2 (1886) (report submitted by Rep. Caldwell, Select Committee on the Election of President and Vice-President).

The Member of Congress who introduced the Act added:

> "The power to judge of the legality of the votes is a necessary consequent of the power to count. The existence of this power is of absolute necessity to the preservation of the Government. The interests of all the States in their relations to each other in the Federal Union demand that the ultimate tribunal to decide upon the election of President should be a constituent body, in which the States in their federal relationships and the people in their sovereign capacity should be represented." 18 Cong. Rec. 30 (1886).
> "Under the Constitution who else could decide? Who is nearer to the State in determining a question of vital importance to the whole union of States than the constituent body upon whom the Constitution has devolved the duty to count the vote?" *Id.*, at 31.

(Continues)

The Act goes on to set out rules for the congressional determination of disputes about those votes. If, for example, a state submits a single slate of electors, Congress must count those votes unless both Houses agree that the votes "have not been . . . regularly given." *3 U.S.C. §15.* If, as occurred in 1876, one or more states submits two sets of electors, then Congress must determine whether a slate has entered the safe harbor of §5, in which case its votes will have "conclusive" effect. *Ibid.* If, as also occurred in 1876, there is controversy about "which of two or more of such State authorities . . . is the lawful tribunal" authorized to appoint electors, then each House shall determine separately which votes are "supported by the decision of such State so authorized by its law." *Ibid.* If the two Houses of Congress agree, the votes they have approved will be counted. If they disagree, then "the votes of the electors whose appointment shall have been certified by the executive of the State, under the seal thereof, shall be counted." *Ibid.*

Given this detailed, comprehensive scheme for counting electoral votes, there is no reason to believe that federal law either foresees or requires resolution of such a political issue by this Court. Nor, for that matter, is there any reason to that think the Constitution's Framers would have reached a different conclusion. Madison, at least, believed that allowing the judiciary to choose the presidential electors "was out of the question." Madison, July 25, 1787 (reprinted in 5 Elliot's Debates on the Federal Constitution 363 (2d ed. 1876)).

The decision by both the Constitution's Framers and the 1886 Congress to minimize this Court's role in resolving close federal presidential elections is as wise as it is clear. However awkward or difficult it may be for Congress to resolve difficult electoral disputes, Congress, being a political body, expresses the people's will far more accurately than does an unelected Court. And the people's will is what elections are about.

Moreover, Congress was fully aware of the danger that would arise should it ask judges, unarmed with appropriate legal standards, to resolve a hotly contested Presidential election contest. Just after the 1876 Presidential election, Florida, South Carolina, and Louisiana each sent two slates of electors to Washington. Without these States, Tilden, the Democrat, had 184 electoral votes, one short of the number required to win the Presidency. With those States, Hayes, his Republican opponent, would have had 185. In order to choose between the two slates of electors, Congress decided to appoint an electoral commission composed of five Senators, five Representatives, and five Supreme Court Justices. Initially the Commission was to be evenly divided between Republicans and Democrats, with Justice David Davis, an Independent, to possess the decisive vote. However, when at the last minute the Illinois Legislature elected Justice Davis to the United States Senate, the final position on the Commission was filled by Supreme Court Justice Joseph P. Bradley.

The Commission divided along partisan lines, and the responsibility to cast the deciding vote fell to Justice Bradley. He decided to accept the votes by the Republican electors, and thereby awarded the Presidency to Hayes.

Justice Bradley immediately became the subject of vociferous attacks. Bradley was accused of accepting bribes, of being captured by railroad interests, and of an eleventh-hour change in position after a night in which his house "was surrounded by the carriages" of Republican partisans and railroad officials. C. Woodward, Reunion and Reaction 159–160 (1966). Many years later, Professor Bickel concluded that Bradley was honest and impartial. He thought that " 'the great question' for Bradley was, in fact, whether Congress was entitled to go behind election returns or had to accept them as certified by state authorities," an "issue of principle." The Least Dangerous Branch 185 (1962). Nonetheless, Bickel points out, the legal question upon which Justice Bradley's decision turned was not very important in the contemporaneous political context. He says that "in the circumstances the issue of principle was trivial, it was overwhelmed by all that hung in the balance, and it should not have been decisive." *Ibid.*

For present purposes, the relevance of this history lies in the fact that the participation in the work of the electoral commission by five Justices, including Justice Bradley, did not lend that process legitimacy. Nor did it assure the public that the process had worked fairly, guided by the law. Rather, it simply embroiled Members of the Court in partisan conflict, thereby undermining respect for the judicial process. And the Congress that later enacted the Electoral Count Act knew it.

This history may help to explain why I think it not only legally wrong, but also most unfortunate, for the Court simply to have terminated the Florida recount. Those who caution judicial restraint in resolving political disputes have described the quintessential case for that restraint as a case marked, among other things, by the "strangeness of the issue," its "intractability to principled resolution," its "sheer momentousness, . . . which tends to unbalance judicial judgment," and "the inner vulnerability, the self-doubt of an institution which is electorally irresponsible and has no earth to draw strength from." Bickel, *supra*, at 184. Those characteristics mark this case.

At the same time, as I have said, the Court is not acting to vindicate a fundamental constitutional principle, such as the need to protect a basic human liberty. No other strong reason to act is present. Congressional statutes tend to obviate the need. And, above all, in this highly politicized matter, the appearance of a split decision runs the risk of undermining the public's confidence in the Court itself. That confidence is a public treasure. It has been built slowly over many years, some of which were marked by a Civil War and the tragedy of segregation. It is a vitally necessary ingredient of any successful effort to protect basic liberty and, indeed, the rule of law itself. We run no risk of returning to the days when a President (responding to this Court's efforts to protect the Cherokee Indians) might have said, "John Marshall has made his decision; now let him enforce it!" Loth, Chief Justice John Marshall and The Growth of the American Republic 365 (1948). But we do risk a self-inflicted wound—a wound that may harm not just the Court, but the Nation.

I fear that in order to bring this agonizingly long election process to a definitive conclusion, we have not adequately attended to that necessary "check upon our own exercise of power," "our own sense of self-restraint." *United States* v. *Butler,* 297 *U.S. 1*, 79 (1936) (Stone, J., dissenting). Justice Brandeis once said of the Court, "The most important thing we do is not doing." Bickel, *supra*, at 71. What it does today, the Court should have left undone. I would repair the damage done as best we now can, by permitting the Florida recount to continue under uniform standards.

I respectfully dissent.

Williams v. State of Mississippi, 170 U.S. 213 (1898)

At June term, 1896, of the circuit court of Washington county, Miss., the plaintiff in error was indicted by a grand jury composed entirely of white men for the crime of murder. On the 15th day of June he made a motion to quash the indictment, which was in substance as follows, omitting repetitions, and retaining the language of the motion as nearly as possible:

Now comes the defendant in this cause, Henry Williams by name, and moves the circuit court of Washington county, Miss., to quash the indictment herein filed, and upon [170 U.S. 213, 214] which it is proposed to try him for the alleged offense of murder[16]: Because the laws by which the grand jury was selected, organized, summoned, and charged, which presented the said indictment, are unconstitutional and repugnant to the spirit and letter of the constitution of the United States of America, fourteenth amendment thereof, in this: that the constitution prescribes the qualifications of electors, and that, to be a juror, one must be an elector; that the constitution also requires that those offering to vote shall produce to the election officers satisfactory evidence that they have paid their taxes; that the legislature is to provide means for enforcing the constitution, and, in the exercise of this authority, enacted section 3643, also section 3644 of 1892, which respectively provide that the election commissioners shall appoint three election managers, and that the latter shall be judges of the qualifications of electors, and are required 'to examine on oath any person duly registered and offering to vote touching his qualifications as an elector.' And then the motion states that 'the registration roll is not *prima facie* evidence of an elector's right to vote, but the list of those persons having been passed upon by the various district election managers of the county to compose the registration book of voters as named in section 2358 of said Code of 1892, and that there was no registration books of voters prepared for the guidance of said officers of said county at the time said grand jury was drawn.' It is further alleged that there is no statute of the state providing for the procurement of any registration books of voters of said county, and (it is alleged in detail) the terms of the constitution and the section of the Code mentioned, and the discretion given to the officers, 'is but a scheme on the part of the framers of that constitution to abridge the suffrage of the colored electors in the state of Mississippi on account of the previous condition of servitude by granting a discretion to the said officers as mentioned in the several sections of the constitution of the state and

(Continues)

(*Continued*)

the statute of the state adopted under the said constitution. The use of said discretion can be and has been used in the said Washington county to the end complained of.' After some detail to the [170 U.S. 213, 215] same effect, it is further alleged: 'That the constitutional convention was composed of 134 members, only one of whom was a negro. That under prior laws there were 190,000 colored voters and 69,000 white voters. The makers of the new constitution arbitrarily refused to submit it to the voters of the state for approval, but ordered it adopted, and an election to be held immediately under it, which election was held under the election ordinances of the said Constitution in November, 1891, and the legislature assembled in 1892, and enacted the statutes complained of, for the purpose to discriminate aforesaid, and but for that the 'defendant's race would have been represented impartially on the grand jury which presented this indictment,' and hence he is deprived of the equal protection of the laws of the state. It is further alleged that the state has not reduced its representation in congress, and generally for the reasons aforesaid, and because the indictment should have been returned under the constitution of 1869 and statute of 1889, it is null and void. The motion concludes as follows: 'Further, the defendant is a citizen of the United States, and, for the many reasons herein named, asks that the indictment be quashed, and he be recognized to appear at the next term of the court.'

This motion was accompanied by four affidavits, subscribed and sworn to before the clerk of the court, on June 15, 1896, to wit:

1. An affidavit of the defendant, 'who, being duly sworn, deposes and says that the facts set forth in the foregoing motion are true to the best of his knowledge, of the language of the constitution and the statute of the state mentioned in said motion, and upon information and belief as to the other facts, and that the affiant verily believes the information to be reliable and true.'

2. Another affidavit of the defendant, 'who, being first duly sworn, deposes and says that he has heard the motion to quash the indictment herein read, and that he thoroughly understands the same, and that the facts therein stated are true, to the best of his knowledge and belief. As to the existence of the several sections of the state constitution, and the [170 U.S. 213, 216] several sections of the state statute, mentioned in said motion to quash, further affiant states that the facts stated in said motion, touching the manner and method peculiar of the said election, by which the delegates to said constitutional convention were elected, and the purpose for which said objectionable provisions were enacted, and the fact that the said discretion complained of as aforesaid has abridged the suffrage of the number mentioned therein, for the purpose named therein, all such material allegations are true, to the best of affiant's knowledge and belief, and the fact of the race and color of the prisoner in this cause, and that race and color of the voters of the state whose elective franchise is abridged as alleged therein, and the fact that they who are discriminated against, as aforesaid, are citizens of the United States, and that prior to the adoption of the said constitution and said statute the said state was represented in congress by seven representatives in the lower house, and two senators, and that since the adoption of the said objectionable laws there has been no reduction of said representation in congress. All allegations herein, as stated in said motion aforesaid, are true, to the best of affiant's knowledge and belief.'

3. An affidavit of John H. Dixon, 'who, being duly sworn, deposes and says that he had heard the motion to quash the indictment filed in the Henry Williams Case, and thoroughly understands the same, and that he has also heard the affidavit sworn to by said Henry Williams carefully read to him, and thoroughly understands the same. And in the same manner the facts are sworn to in the said affidavit, and the same facts alleged therein upon information and belief are hereby adopted as in all things the sworn allegations of affiant, and the facts alleged therein, as upon knowledge and belief, are made hereby the allegations of affiant upon his knowledge and belief.'

4. An affidavit of C. J. Jones, 'who, being duly sworn, deposes and says that he has read carefully the affidavit filed in the John Dixon Case sworn to by him (said C. J. Jones), and that he, said affiant, thoroughly understands the same, and adopts the said allegations therein as his deposition in [170 U.S. 213, 217] this case upon hearing this motion to quash the indictment herein, and that said allegations are in all things correct and true as therein alleged.'

The motion was denied, and the defendant excepted. A motion was then made to remove the cause to the United States circuit court, based substantially on the same grounds as the motion to quash the indictment. This was also denied, and an exception reserved.

The accused was tried by a jury composed entirely of white men, and convicted. A motion for a new trial was denied, and the accused sentenced to be hanged. An appeal to the Supreme Court was taken, and the judgment of the court below was affirmed.

The following are the assignments of error:

1. The trial court erred in denying motion to quash the indictment, and petitioned for removal.
2. The trial court erred in denying motion for new trial, and pronouncing death penalty under the verdict.
3. The supreme court erred in affirming the judgment of the trial court.

The sections of the constitution of Mississippi and the laws referred to in the motion of the plaintiff in error are printed in the margin. 1 [170 U.S. 213, 218] Cornelius J. Jones, for plaintiff in error.

C. B. Mitchell, for defendant in error. [170 U.S. 213, 219].

Mr. Justice McKENNA, after stating the case, delivered the opinion of the court.

The question presented is, are the provisions of the constitution of the state of Mississippi and the laws enacted to enforce the same repugnant to the fourteenth amendment of the constitution of the United States? That amendment and its effect upon the rights of the colored race have been considered by this court in a number of cases, and it has been uniformly held that the constitution of the United States, as amended, forbids, so far as civil and political rights are concerned, discriminations by the general government or by the states against any citizen because of his race; but it has also been held, in a very recent case, to justify a removal from a state court to a federal court of a cause in which such rights are alleged to be denied, that such denial must be the result of the constitution or laws of the state, not of the administration of them. Nor can the conduct of a criminal trial in a state court be reviewed by this court unless the trial is had under some statute repugnant to the constitution of the United [170 U.S. 213, 220] States, or was so conducted as to deprive the accused of some right or immunity secured to him by that instrument. Upon this general subject, this court, in Gibson v. Mississippi, 162 U.S. 566, 581, 16 S. Sup. Ct. 906, after referring to previous cases, said: 'But those cases were held to have also decided that the fourteenth amendment was broader than the provisions of section 641 of the Revised Statutes; that, since that section authorized the removal of a criminal prosecution before trial, it did not embrace a case in which a right is denied by judicial action during a trial, or in the sentence, or in the mode o executing the sentence; that for such denials arising from judicial action after a trial commenced, the remedy lay in the revisory power of the higher courts of the state, and ultimately in the power of review which this court may exercise over their judgments whenever rights, privileges, or immunities claimed under the constitution or laws of the United States are withheld or violated; and that the denial or inability to enforce in the judicial tribunals of the states rights secured by any law providing for the equal civil rights of citizens of the United States to which section 641 refers, and on account of which a criminal prosecution may be removed from a state court, is primarily, if not exclusively, a denial of such rights, or an inability to enforce them resulting from the constitution or laws of the state, rather than a denial first made manifest at or during the trial of the case.'

It is not asserted by plaintiff in error that either the constitution of the state or its laws discriminate in terms against the negro race, either as to the elective franchise or the privilege or duty of sitting on juries. These results, if we understand plaintiff in error, are alleged to be effected by the powers vested in certain administrative officers.

Plaintiff in error says:

'Section 241 of the constitution of 1890 prescribes the qualifications for electors; that residence in the state for two years, one year in the precinct of the applicant, must be effected; that he is twenty-one years or over of age, having paid all taxes legally due of him for two years prior to 1st day of February of the year he offers to vote, not having [170 U.S. 213, 221] been convicted of theft, arson, rape, receiving money or goods under false pretenses, bigamy, embezzlement.

'Section 242 of the constitution provides the mode of registration; that the legislature shall provide by law for registration of all persons entitled to vote at any election, and that all persons offering to register shall take the oath; that they are not disqualified for voting by reason of any of the crimes named in the constitution of this state; that they will truly answer all questions propounded to them concerning their antecedents so far as they relate to the applicant's right to vote, and also as to their residence before their citizenship in the district in which such application for registration is made. The court readily sees the scheme. If the applicant swears, as he must do, that he is not disqualified by reason of the crimes specified, and that he has effected the required residence, what right has he to answer all questions as to his former residence? Section 244 of the constitution requires that the applicant for registration, after January, 1892, shall be able to read any section of the constitution, or he shall be able to understand the same (being any section of the organic law), or give a reasonable

(Continues)

interpretation thereof. Now, we submit that these provisions vest in the administrative officers the full power, under section 242, to ask all sorts of vain, impertinent questions; and it is with that officer to say whether the questions relate to the applicant's right to vote. This officer can reject whomsoever he chooses, and register whomsoever he chooses, for he is vested by the constitution with that power. Under section 244 it is left with the administrative officer to determine whether the applicant reads, understands, or interprets the section of the constitution designated. The officer is the sole judge of the examination of the applicant, and, even though the applicant be qualified, it is left with the officer to so determine; and the said officer can refuse him registration.'

To make the possible dereliction of the officers the dereliction of the constitution and laws, the remarks of the supreme court of the state are quoted by plaintiff in error as to their intent. The constitution provides for the payment of a poll [170 U.S. 213, 222] tax, and by a section of the Code its payment cannot be compelled by a seizure and sale of property. We gather from the brief of counsel that its payment is a condition of the right to vote, and, in a case to test whether its payment was or was not optional (*Ratcliff v. Beal*, 20 South. 865), the supreme court of the state said: 'Within the field of permissible action under the limitations imposed by the federal constitution, the convention swept the field of expedients, to obstruct the exercise of suffrage by the negro race.' And further the court said, speaking of the negro race: 'By reason of its previous condition of servitude and dependencies, this race had acquired or accentuated certain peculiarities of habit, of temperament, and of character, which clearly distinguished it as a race from the whites; a patient, docile people, but careless, landless, migratory within narrow limits, without forethought, and its criminal members given to furtive offenses, rather than the robust crimes of the whites. Restrained by the federal constitution from discriminating against the negro race, the convention discriminates against its characteristics, and the offenses to which its criminal members are prone.' But nothing tangible can be deduced from this. If weakness were to be taken advantage of, it was to be done 'within the field of permissible action under the limitations imposed by the federal constitution,' and the means of it were the alleged characteristics of the negro race, not the administration of the law by officers of the state. Besides, the operation of the constitution and laws is not limited by their language or effects to one race. They reach weak and vicious white men as well as weak and vicious black men, and whatever is sinister in their intention, if anything, can be prevented by both races by the exertion of that duty which voluntarily pays taxes and refrains from crime.

It cannot be said, therefore, that the denial of the equal protection of the laws arises primarily from the constitution and laws of Mississippi; nor is there any sufficient allegation of an evil and discriminating administration of them. The only allegation is '. . . by granting a discretion to the said officers, as mentioned in the several sections of the constitution [170 U.S. 213, 223] of the state, and the statute of the state adopted under the said constitution, the use of which discretion can be and has been used by said officers in the said Washington county to the end here complained of, to wit, the abridgment of the elective franchise of the colored voters of Washington county; that such citizens are denied the right to be selected as jurors to serve in the circuit court of the county; and that this denial to them of the right to equal protection and benefits of the laws of the state of Mississippi on account of their color and race, resulting from the exercise of the discretion partial to the white citizens, is in accordance with the purpose and intent of the framers of the present constitution of said state. . . .'

It will be observed that there is nothing direct and definite in this allegation either as to means or time as affecting the proceedings against the accused. There is no charge against the officers to whom is submitted the selection of grand or petit jurors, or those who procure the lists of the jurors. There is an allegation of the purpose of the convention to disfranchise citizens of the colored race; but with this we have no concern, unless the purpose is executed by the constitution or laws or by those who administer them. If it is done in the latter way, how or by what means should be shown. We gather from the statements of the motion that certain officers are invested with discretion in making up lists of electors, and that this discretion can be and has been exercised against the colored race, and from these lists jurors are selected. The supreme court of Mississippi, however, decided, in a case presenting the same questions as the one at bar, 'that jurors are not selected from or with reference to any lists furnished by such election officers.' *Dixo v. Mississippi* (Nov. 9, 1896) 20 South. 839.

We do not think that this case is brought within the ruling in *Yick Wo v. Hopkins*, 118 U.S. 356, 6 Sup. Ct. 1064. In that case the ordinances passed on discriminated against laundries conducted in wooden buildings. For the conduct of these the consent of the board of supervisors was required, and not for the conduct of laundries in brick or stone buildings. It was [170 U.S. 213, 224] admitted that there were about 320 laundries in the city and county of San Francisco, of which 240 were owned and conducted by subjects of China, and, of the whole number, 310 were constructed of wood, the same material that constitutes nine-tenths of the houses of the city, and that the capital invested was not less than $200,000.

It was alleged that 150 Chinamen were arrested, and not one of the persons who were conducting the other 80 laundries, and who were not Chinamen. It was also admitted 'that petitioner and 200 of his countrymen similarly situated petitioned the board of supervisors for permission to continue their business in the various houses which they had been occupying and using for laundries for more than twenty years, and such petitions were denied, and all the petitions of those who were not Chinese, with one exception of Mrs. Mary Meagles, were granted.'

The ordinances were attacked as being void on their face, and as being within the prohibition of the fourteenth amendment, but, even if not so, that they were void by reason of their administration. Both contentions were sustained.

Mr. Justice Matthews said that the ordinance drawn in question 'does not describe a rule and conditions for the regulation of the use of property for laundry purposes, to which all similarly situated may conform. It allows without restriction the use for such purposes of buildings of brick or stone, but as to wooden buildings, constituting all those in previous use, divides the owners or occupiers into two classes, not having respect to their personal character and qualifications for the business, nor the situation and nature and adaptation of the buildings themselves, but merely by an arbitrary line, on one side of which are those who are permitted to pursue their industry by the mere will and consent of the supervisors, and on the other those from whom that consent is withheld, at their mere will and pleasure.' The ordinances, therefore, were on their face repugnant to the fourteenth amendment. The court, however, went further, and said: 'This conclusion and the reasoning on which it is based are deductions from the face of the ordinance, as to its [170 U.S. 213, 225] necessary tendency and ultimate actual operation. In the present cases we are not obliged to reason from the probable to the actual, and pass upon the validity of the ordinances complained of as tried merely by the opportunities which their terms afford of unequal and unjust discrimination in their administration. For the cases present, the ordinances in actual operation, and the facts shown, establish an administration directed so exclusively against a particular class of persons as to warrant and require the conclusion that, whatever may have been the intent of the ordinances as adopted, they are applied by the public authorities charged with their administration, and thus representing the state itself, with a mind so unequal and oppressive as to amount to a practical denial by the state of that equal protection of the laws which is secured to the petitioners, as to all other persons, by the broad and benign provisions of the fourteenth amendment to the constitution of the United States. Though the law itself be fair on its face and impartial in appearance, yet, if it is applied and administered by public authority with an evil eye and an unequal hand, so as practically to make unjust and illegal discriminations between persons in similar circumstances, material to their rights, the denial of equal justice is still within the prohibition of the constitution. This principle of interpretation has been sanctioned in *Henderson v. Mayor of New York*, 92 U.S. 259; *Chy Lung v. Freeman, Id.* 275; *Ex parte Virginia*, 100 U.S. 339; *Neal v. Delaware*, 103 U.S. 370; and *Soon Hing v. Crowley*, 113 U.S. 703, 5 Sup. Ct. 730.'

This comment is not applicable to the constitution of Mississippi and its statutes. They do not on their face discriminate between the races, and it has not been shown that their actual administration was evil; only that evil was possible under them.

If follows, therefore, that the judgment must be affirmed.

Note

16. The three sections of article 12 of the constitution of the state of Mississippi above referred to read as follows:

> 'Sec. 241. Every male inhabitant of this state except idiots, insane persons and Indians not taxed, who is a citizen of the United States, twenty-one years old and upwards, who has resided in this state two years, and one year in the election district, or in the incorporated city or town in which he offers to vote, and who is duly registered as provided in this article, and who has never been convicted of bribery, burglary, theft, arson, obtaining money or goods under false pretenses, perjury, forgery, embezzlement or bigamy, and who has paid, on or before the 1st day of February of the year in which he shall offer to vote all taxes which may have been legally required of him,

(Continues)

(Continued)

and which he has had an opportunity of paying according to law for the two preceding years, and who shall produce to the officer holding the election satisfactory evidence that he has paid said taxes, is declared to be a qualified elector; but any minister of the gospel in charge of an organized church shall be entitled to vote after six months' residence in the election district, if otherwise qualified.'

'Sec. 242. The legislature shall provide by law for the registration of all persons entitled to vote at any election, and all persons offering to register shall take the following oath or affirmation: 'I, _____, do solemnly swear (or affirm) that I am twenty-one years old (or I will be before the next election in this county) and that I will have resided in this state two years and _____ election district of _____ county one year next preceding the ensuing election (or if it be stated in the oath that the person proposing to register is a minister of the gospel in charge of an organized church, then it will be sufficient to aver therein two years' residence in the state and six months in said election district) and am now in good faith a resident of the same, and that I am not disqualified from voting by reason of having been convicted of any crime named in the constitution of this state as a disqualification to be an elector; that I will truly answer all questions propounded to me concerning my antecedents so far as they relate to my right to vote, and also as to my residence before my citizenship in this district; that I will faithfully support the constitution of the United States and of the state of Mississippi, and will bear true faith and allegiance to the same. So held me God.' In registering voters in cities and towns not wholly in one election district the name of such city or town may be substituted in the oath for the election district. Any willful and corrupt false statement in said affidavit, or in answer to any material question propounded as herein authorized shall be perjury.

'Sec. 244. On and after the first day of January, A. D. 1892, every elector shall, in addition to the foregoing qualifications, be able to read any section of the constitution of this state; or he shall be able to understand the same when read to him, or give a reasonable interpretation thereof. A new registration shall be made before the next ensuing election after January the first, A. D. 1892.'

Section 264 of article 14 of the constitution of the state of Mississippi, above referred to, reads as follows:

'Sec. 264. No person shall be a grand or petit juror unless a qualified elector and able to read and write; but the want of any such qualification in any juror shall not vitiate any indictment or verdict. The legislature shall provide by law for procuring a list of persons so qualified, and the drawing therefrom of grand and petit jurors for each term of the circuit court.'

The three sections of the Code of 1892 of the State of Mississippi above referred to read as follows:

'Sec. 2358. How List of Jurors Procured. The board of supervisors at the first meeting in each year, or a subsequent meeting if not done at the first, shall select and make a list of persons to serve as jurors in the circuit court for the next two terms to be held more than thirty days afterwards, and as a guide in making the list, they shall use the registration books of voters; and it shall select and list the names of qualified persons of good intelligence, sound judgment and fair character, and shall take them as nearly as it conveniently can from the several election districts in proportion to the number of the qualified persons in each, excluding all who have served on the regular panel within two years, if there be not a deficiency of jurors.'

'Sec. 3643. Managers of Election Appointed. Prior to every election the commissioners of election shall appoint three persons for each election district to be managers of the election, who shall not all be of the same political party, if suitable persons of different political parties can be had in the district, and if any person appointed shall fail to attend and serve, the managers present, if any, may designate one to fill his place, and if the commissioners of election fail to make the appointments, or in case of the failure of all those appointed to attend and serve, any three qualified electors present when the polls should be opened may act as managers.'

'Sec. 3644. Duties and Powers of Managers. The managers shall take care that the election is conducted fairly and agreeably to law, and they shall be judges of the qualifications of electors and may examine on oath any person duly registered and offering to vote touching his qualifications as an elector, which oath any of the managers may administer.'

The Articles of Confederation—The First U.S. Government

Chapter Objectives

In this chapter you will learn . . .

- That George Washington was not really the first U.S. president
- Whether Christopher Columbus really discovered America
- That the first United States government failed and had to be reorganized
- That the Constitution was based on *The Federalist Papers*
- That the Constitution was ratified as a compromise

Introduction

If someone were to ask you: who was the first president of the United States, you would confidently reply, George Washington, right? Well, what if you were to find out that George Washington was *not* really the first president? In fact, what if you found out that he was not even the second, third, or fourth? Technically, George Washington was the *eighth* president of the United States! So, who came before him?

Was it Thomas Jefferson? No, he became president after Washington.
Abraham Lincoln? No, he became president *much* later.
Paul Revere? No, he was never president.

Aaaah, it must have been Benjamin Franklin! No, he was never president, either.

So, who were these seven men who preceded George Washington? Well, the first one was John Hanson. Aha! The guy who signed the Declaration of Independence! No, that was John *Hancock*. So who was this John Hanson person? Before we answer that, let's take a look at the other six presidents who preceded Washington: Elias Boudinot, Thomas Mifflin, Richard Henry Lee, Nathan Gordman, Arthur St. Clair, and Cyrus Griffin.

Chances are that you do not know who *any* of those presidents were, and, in that respect, you are certainly not alone. They are not mentioned in most history books, especially the books that you probably read while studying history in school. And when we think about famous Americans during the colonial and revolutionary times, we refer to Washington, Jefferson, Franklin, and several others, but *none* of the first seven presidents! Why, then, do we know so much about George Washington, but very little about the presidents who came before him? In order to find out, let's begin with a quick history of America.

Did Christopher Columbus Discover America?

Over the past few years, there has been a great deal of controversy surrounding Christopher Columbus' discovery of America. Emphatically, some who are itching to rewrite history declare: "Christopher Columbus *did not* discover America!" Clearly, they are wrong. If their argument was that Christopher Columbus was not the *first* person to discover the land that became America, then they are correct. But to *discover* something does not necessarily mean being the first person to do so. Consider these examples:

1. Ralph *discovered* that the Italian restaurant in his neighborhood made excellent ravioli.
2. Paula *discovered* that sleeping on a heating pad made her back feel much better in the morning.
3. Marilyn *discovered* America when she first visited in 1995.

All three of these people made discoveries, yet none of them was the *first* to do so. Similarly, Christopher Columbus was not the first person to discover America; he discovered it in 1492. A bunch of people had discovered it earlier, and hundreds of millions have discovered it since that time. Why, then, do we point to Columbus' discovery?

The Importance of Columbus' Discovery

The reason we celebrate Columbus Day every year, as opposed to other discoverers of America, is because Columbus' discovery paved the way for the settlements that eventually led to the formation of the United States of America. It does not matter whether he was the first, second, fifth, eighth, or 3,894th person to discover America. What *does* matter is that *his* discovery was the one that counted in terms of colonial settlements—mostly from England, France, and Spain—that eventually resulted in the creation of the United States of America.

Millions of people have discovered America over the centuries. But Christopher Columbus' discovery was particularly important.

From Columbus to the Constitution

If we were to study the entire saga of this land—from Columbus' settlement to the formation of the Constitution—in great detail, that would be an entire book of its own, if not several of them! Instead, let's take just a brief look at what happened over that 300-year period.

Various countries began to send colonists to settle in the New World. It was a great trade-off for both parties; the settlers were able to enjoy a combination of adventure, profit, and religious freedom. You see, here in the United States, we are permitted to worship in whatever way we choose and to whomever we choose, or decide that we do not want to be religious at all (more about that later in Chapter Four). That is not the case in some other countries, and it certainly was not the case in various European nations back in the 1700s.

Additionally, the land on which the United States sits is one of massive proportion, indeed! Imagine all of that land readily available to anyone who simply ran and jumped on it and said, "mine!" This provided great economic opportunity for anyone who had the financial resources to send workers here to work the land. As the saying goes, the workers had the opportunity to "make the pie" for the owners, but who then gave the workers "a slice of the pie?"

Colonial life was not all rosy, however. Those living in the colonies from different countries had territorial and cultural disputes not only among each other, but also with multiple Native American Indian nations, whose inhabitants had been displaced by the settlers. At that time,

the British colonists were extremely dependent upon and loyal to their Mother Country: Great Britain. Much like a small child who needs the guidance and protection of its parents, the colonists relied on Britain for that support. As Britain eventually became the dominant colonial nation in the New World, thus greatly reducing if not altogether eliminating any threat to the colonists from other nations, things began to change.

The colonists no longer behaved like loyal, affectionate toddlers. Instead, they acted more like rebellious teenagers, demanding various rights that their parent was not providing. As a result, they decided to break apart from Great Britain and become their own nation, simply by saying that's what they would do!

In fact, the Declaration of Independence is simply a fancy way to state, "we say we're free!" Think about it in modern-day terms. Suppose that you and nine of your friends decide to take over an office building and you declare, "This building is now our country. It is our property, and we can do whatever we want here!" Well, in that case, what would probably happen next is that the security guard would have all of you removed. If you managed to overpower the guard, the police might be called in to do the job. If, astonishingly, the ten of you overpowered the entire police department, then perhaps the National Guard would be called in, followed by the entire U.S. military! And, if, by some incredible miracle, the ten of you managed to overpower *all* of those forces, to the point where they simply stopped fighting and agreed to your terms, then guess what: the ten of you would, indeed, be your own nation!

Of course, the chances of ten individuals overpowering the entire United States Armed Forces is about as likely as an elephant growing wings and flying like a bird. Nonetheless, that is what it would take to gain independence. And in the case of the colonists, the odds might not have been quite that extreme, but they were extreme nonetheless, and the result was rather miraculous in its own right.

You see, Great Britain was the most powerful force in the world. Yet the colonies were barely even united. This was not a case of 13 colonies meshing together wonderfully. Instead, many colonies were reluctant to join forces with one another, and many individuals inside the colonies were either loyal to Great Britain and did not want to rebel, or simply did not want to risk life and limb to do so. Then again, some simply did not care either way; they just wanted to go about their lives and political issues and injustices did not really concern them.

When Great Britain received the news that the colonies had formed their own nation, the United States of America, they sent in troops to squash the revolution. The better part of the fighting was not over until 5 years later. In the meantime, the fledgling young nation had to be governed. During the Revolutionary War, also known as the War for Independence, the United States was governed by the Second Continental Congress (the First was the one that was formed to declare independence in the first place).

In 1781, once the fighting was over upon Great Britain's surrender, the United States was truly free! But now what? No longer under the protection of the most powerful nation in the world, the 13 colonies found themselves in quite a dilemma. Do they return to being independent and risk being attacked by any number of nations, or do they stay together and give up the blessings of not being confined to a group?

The Articles of Confederation

The first government actually formed after the United States was truly independent was established by the Articles of Confederation, in 1781. We do not really hear a whole lot about that government, and for good reason: it failed after 6 short years of operation. Its successor, the U.S. Constitution, has lasted quite long. Born in 1787, it is still going strong. Accordingly, it is understandable why we know some things about the Constitution, but next to nothing about the Articles. In order to better understand the government that we have in place now, it is wise to take a look at the one that came beforehand.

Essentially, the Articles contained many of the same provisions (and much of the same language) found in the Constitution, but there were some notable differences. Let's take a look at the Preamble and all 13 articles of the Articles, highlight the key points of each, and compare and contrast them with the Constitution.

Preamble

The Articles' Preamble merely lists the names of the 13 states that joined together in a *perpetual union*. They are 12 of the original 13 states that also joined together under the Constitution to form the new government (New Hampshire later joined the 12 to form the Constitution). In alphabetical order they are: Connecticut, Delaware, Georgia, Maryland, Massachusetts (referred to in the Articles as Massachusetts Bay), New Jersey, New York, North Carolina, Pennsylvania, Rhode Island (referred to as Rhode Island and the Providence Plantations), South Carolina, and Virginia.

Article I

The name of the *confederacy* shall be: The United States of America.

(*Note:* the use of the word *confederacy* in the Articles has no relation to the Confederacy, or Confederate States of America, which was formed when the Southern States seceded from the Union and formed their own country during the American Civil War).

Article II

Other than rights specifically granted to Congress in these Articles, each state retains its own sovereignty and freedom. The Constitution's Tenth Amendment states something similar. "The powers not delegated to the United States by the Constitution, nor prohibited by it to the states, are reserved to the states. . . ." The question then, is to what extent the federal government was stronger than the states, or vice versa, in both documents.

Article III

The states hereby unite for their common defense, against attacks for whatever reason, for their liberty, and for their general welfare.

Article IV

All free inhabitants of every state shall have the same privileges in any other state. Excepted are vagabonds and fugitives from justice. Notably, this is the first distinction of rights held by those who were free as opposed to those who were enslaved.

Article V

Delegates from each state shall be sent to Congress, no less than two and no more than seven from each state. No delegate may serve more than 3 years during any 6-year period, and each state shall have one vote.

Article VI

No state may wage wars or execute foreign policy without the consent of Congress, nor shall any two states enter into any alliance without Congressional approval.

Article VII

When an army is raised for the common defense, soldiers under the rank of colonel shall be appointed by the legislatures of their respective states, and it shall be that state's responsibility to fill any vacancies. This Article was one of the primary reasons why the Articles ultimately failed. Essentially, it leaves the responsibility of maintaining a common military to each individual state.

Suppose that nowadays, each state had the responsibility of supplying forces to prevent any terrorist attacks from occurring on U.S. soil. States such as California and New York, for example, might have greater reason to be concerned about such attacks, as both of those states house large, powerful cities, which can be perceived as likely targets. But what about states such as Arkansas, Vermont, and Wyoming? Of course, anything is possible, but is it likely that those states would be the victims of a terrorist attack? If not, then why would the taxpayers of those states be willing to foot the bill for a cause that is unlikely to affect them? Would they do it out of sheer patriotism? Maybe, though they might argue that their contribution should be minimal as compared with the proportions paid by their counterparts in states more likely to be attacked.

Similarly, looking back at the geographical breakdown of the 12 U.S. states, a state such as North Carolina was shielded by other states and unlikely to be the victim of a border attack, such as Georgia. Accordingly, North Carolina might not have been particularly zealous in establishing and maintaining a formidable military.

Article VIII

Contributions to the common defense shall be made by each state, proportionate to the amount of its land. Thus, a state with a large land size might not be particularly happy with this type of arrangement, particularly if it is not likely to be a victim of a terrorist attack. Today, that would mean a state such as Montana would pay nearly 19 times more in military taxes than a small state like New Jersey. Population was not taken into account for this tax.

Article IX

This Article, the longest of the 13, contains various provisions whereby Congress shall have ultimate power in waging war, coining money, and deciding disputes among two or more states. However, as some of the provisions required 9 of the 12 states to agree, it made it very difficult for an effective national government to exercise its authority and influence the direction of the nation.

Article X

In the absence of Congress, nine states would be necessary to act as Congress would. Again, this requirement made it difficult for policy to be implemented absent almost unanimous agreement.

Article XI

This Article provides that Canada may be admitted into the United States if it so chose, but that any other territory that wished to gain admission would have to be assented to by nine states.

Article XII

The United States will pay off all of its debts.

Article XIII

All states shall obey Articles, fully ratify them, and so forth.

Taken as a whole, the Articles were not wholly inconsistent to the notions that were made part of the U.S. Constitution. The main differences were that in the Articles the states had too much veto power, which made it difficult for national policy to be effective.

The First Seven Presidents

Getting back to our trivia question about the seven men who were president of the United States *before* George Washington, each of them served a one-year term under the Articles. We never really got to the part about why we do not really know anything about them. For the same reasons that we do not really know too much about most of the people who discovered America before Columbus: because they did not really matter a whole lot, at least, not in terms of American history.

Similarly, the seven presidents under the Articles of Confederation did not have nearly the amount of power and influence as the presidents under the Constitution. They were largely administrative figureheads rather than leaders of a nation. Accordingly, they did not do a whole lot in their capacity as president to merit noteworthiness and to be embedded into our memories.

Another reason why John Hanson and the six presidents who followed him are not household words is because the government under the Articles was a failure. As the

George Washington, the Father of Our Country, technically was not the first U.S. President.

Constitution became the new law of the land, upon which the new form of government was founded, there was still a great deal of concern about whether it would succeed. Nowadays, well over 200 years since the Constitution was ratified, we have long been in a state of relief, knowing that our *second* U.S. government, the Constitution, was the one that lasted.

But what about the first few years after the Constitution took effect? What if in 1789, or 1792, or 1795, a textbook about American history was written? Would it include information about the Articles? Maybe some small mention, but it would probably focus on the *new and improved* American government, the Constitution. If the Articles had been given considerable attention, then the Constitution might be viewed as destined to fail, too.

Accordingly, the first seven presidents of the United States are a mere afterthought in American history. Because the Articles were unsuccessful, and because their presidents' tenures were uneventful, most children and adults nationwide consider their first president to have been George Washington.

The Federalists

The road from the Articles to the Constitution was not as simple as changing the name and a few words here and there. It took a Constitutional Convention to ratify the document that would become the most important in our nation's history. And, in great part, the delegates at that Convention were swayed by a series of articles sent to various New York newspapers, titled *The Federalist* and modernly referred to as *The Federalist Papers*. The three authors were, in order of number of contributions, Alexander Hamilton, James Madison, and John Jay. At the time, they wrote anonymously, using the name Publius.

The type of government they proposed—a strong federal one—inspired the name Federalists to indicate those who espoused that ideology.

Alexander Hamilton

The biography of Alexander Hamilton is one of the most fascinating stories in American history. In fact, it would be difficult to find a fictional tale more compelling. Hamilton was born in the West Indies, which today would render him ineligible to run for President of the United States, because Article Two of the Constitution prohibits anyone who is not a natural-born U.S. citizen to become president. However, there is a stipulation that anyone who was a U.S. citizen *when the Constitution was ratified*, which Hamilton was, would be eligible. Why, then, did such an important and influential American statesman not run for president? Two main reasons: first, he was a polarizing figure. Many idolized him and considered him among the greatest of the Founding Fathers, if not *the* greatest. Others, however, chastised him for being abrasive and elitist. The second reason is that he was an illegitimate child, a very difficult stigma to overcome in politics.

In any event, Hamilton was a brilliant thinker who won George Washington's favor, both militarily and politically. He was instrumental in propelling *The Federalist Papers* to the forefront of Constitutional discussion. Indeed, much of Hamilton's mark has been embedded on our current system of government.

Amazingly, Hamilton's life was cut short when he was killed in a duel by Aaron Burr, who was Vice President of the United States at the time. But that's a whole other story.

James Madison

Often referred to as the father of the Constitution, James Madison eventually parted ways with his *Federalist Papers* coauthor, Hamilton, and instead became Thomas Jefferson's protégé and, eventually, President of the United States. Where Hamilton was polarizing, Madison was conciliatory. It was Madison's ability to bring disputing parties together toward the common cause of forming a new government that was instrumental in the ratification of the Constitution.

John Jay

John Jay wrote the fewest of *The Federalist Papers*, but that was not really by choice. You see, Jay was injured in a politically-motivated physical attack. Between that and the Burr–Hamilton duel, you can imagine how intense and violent things were back then in comparison to, say, today's political battles, which are usually reduced to verbal attacks in the media and in campaign commercials.

In any event, Jay went on to become the first Chief Justice of the U.S. Supreme Court.

Some of the Key Federalist Papers

There were 85 *Federalist Papers* in all: Hamilton wrote 51 of them, Madison 29, and Jay 5. Let's take a look at some of the more notable ones.

The Federalist Number 1

In the first of the *Papers*, Hamilton called upon his fellow Americans to support a new Constitution, resist opposition to it, all the while respecting and encouraging the moderation that will evolve from clashing intellectual differences. In a series of papers, he proposed to discuss the usefulness of a successful federal government, the insufficiency of the Articles to preserve the Union, and the need to preserve the republican form of government, liberty, and property.

The Federalist Numbers 2 and 6 through 9

In the second *Paper*, Jay cited many reasons why the nation ought to remain united, including geographical and cultural unity, and that severing the nation would be a risk to liberty. In the *Federalists* 3, 4, and 5, Jay continued his argument about why a fragmented nation would invite foreign attack. Hamilton, in Numbers 6 through 9, echoed those same concerns with respect to attacks by individual or groups of states against one another.

The Federalist Number 10

This is the first *Paper* that Madison authored, and is one of the most important of them all. Madison explained that a pure democracy would result in violent chaos, as there would be no safeguards against the trampling of the rights of the minority. Moreover, he conveyed how a republic is superior to a democracy, because a large republic will have more qualified people whose talent will be pooled together, and it will be more conspicuous, thus reducing the chance for corruption.

The Federalist Number 17

In the *Federalist* 17, Hamilton continued his advocacy for a strong central government, insisting that state and local governments would not lose their effectiveness if commerce, finance, and foreign policy are federally controlled.

The Federalist Numbers 23, 29, and 46

Two more Hamilton writings supported a strong and energetic national government. Number 29, in particular, discussed the need for a strong national military, though state militias equipped with local civilians would prevent the federal military from spiraling out of control. In *Federalist* 46, Madison specifically wrote that America is unique because it arms its citizens and its militias to prevent federal authority from overstepping its bounds. We discuss more about the right to bear arms in Chapter 10.

The Federalist Numbers 67 through 74

Hamilton spent a great deal of time advocating for a president, something that was lacking in the Articles. He dissuaded fears that the president would be like a king, and explained, in great detail, how a president's powers would be significantly fewer. Moreover, Hamilton discussed the concept of electors, and how they were ideally suited to choose the president, because that would be their only function. In *Federalists* 71 and 72, Hamilton discussed the notion of term limits, explaining why they would exclude worthy candidates from seeking reelection. Finally, Hamilton advocated for a 4-year presidential term, arguing that it is just the right amount of time for a president to establish his agenda.

The Federalist Numbers 84 and 85

Hamilton concluded *The Federalist Papers* with a discussion about a Bill of Rights. More specifically, that he was not in favor of such a notion. He believed that a Bill of Rights would weaken government, and was confident that the Constitution itself was a bill of rights, because the people retained the power. Finally, he added that the Constitution could always be amended later on, if the people were not completely satisfied with it.

Ratification

Although many of Hamilton's ideas were tempered considerably at the Convention, he and his fellow federalists were instrumental in implementing their agenda. Hamilton himself, though perpetually opinionated, was willing to compromise significantly in order to achieve ratification.

On June 21, 1788, 9 of the 13 states had ratified, in this order: Delaware, Pennsylvania, New Jersey, Georgia, Connecticut, Massachusetts, Maryland, South Carolina, and New Hampshire. Nine were enough to secure ratification, and the other four states ratified afterward: Virginia a few days later, New York a month later, Rhode Island 2 years later, and the last holdout, Vermont, on January 10, 1791.

Therefore, the Constitution was unanimously approved, and has been the law of our land ever since.

Conclusion

It took two tries, then, not just one, for the United States to figure out what government worked best. The result was the Constitution, which is a compromise in itself of a strong central government balanced with individual state rights.

In Chapter three we discuss the essence of our Constitutional government, which is divided into two tiers, each with three branches.

Questions for Review

1. Who were the six presidents of the United States before George Washington?
2. Why do most history books ignore the presidents before George Washington?
3. What were the Articles of Confederation?
4. Did Christopher Columbus discover America?
5. What were *The Federalist Papers*?
6. Who was Alexander Hamilton?
7. Who was James Madison?
8. Who was John Jay?
9. When was the Constitution ratified?
10. Which nine states ratified the Constitution originally, rendering it the law of the land?

Constitutionally Speaking

When the Constitution was established, there was an intense debate between the Federalists, who preferred a strong national government, and the Antifederalists, who believed that far more authority ought to rest with the individual states.

But that was the 18th Century, and now we are in the 21st. How should our government operate nowadays: should most of the decisions come from Congress and the president in Washington, D.C., or should they be left up to the state and local governments? Which do you think would result in a more effective system, and why?

James Madison's Preface to the Constitutional Convention

This is the preface to the Constitutional Convention, by James Madison, who was one of the authors of *The Federalist Papers*, is called the father of our Constitution, and was the fourth president of the United States.

As the weakness and wants of man naturally lead to an association of individuals, under a common authority whereby each may have the protection of the whole against danger from without, and enjoy in safety within, the advantages of social intercourse, and an exchange of the necessaries & comforts of life: in like manner feeble communities, independent of each other, have resorted to a Union, less intimate, but with common Councils, for the common safety against powerful neighbors, and for the preservation of justice and peace among themselves. Ancient history furnishes examples of these confederal associations, tho' with a very imperfect account, of their structure, and of the attributes and functions of the presiding Authority. There are examples of modern date also, some of them still existing, the modifications and transactions of which are sufficiently known.

It remained for the British Colonies, now United States, of North America, to add to those examples, one of a more interesting character than any of them: which led to a system without a example ancient or modern, a system founded on popular rights, and so combining, a federal form with the forms of individual Republics, as may enable each to supply the defects of the other and obtain the advantages of both.

Whilst the Colonies enjoyed the protection of the parent Country as it was called, against foreign danger; and were secured by its superintending controul, against conflicts among themselves, they continued independent of each other, under a common, tho' limited dependence, on the parental Authority. When however the growth of the offspring in strength and in wealth, awakened the jealousy and tempted the avidity of the parent, into schemes of usurpation & exaction, the obligation was felt by the former of uniting their counsels and efforts to avert the impending calamity.

As early as the year 1754, indications having been given of a design in the British Government to levy contributions on the Colonies, without their consent; a meeting of Colonial deputies took place at Albany, which attempted to introduce a compromising substitute, that might at once satisfy the British requisitions, and save their own rights from violation. The attempt had no other effect, than by bringing these rights into a more conspicuous view, to invigorate the attachment to them, on one side; and to nourish the haughty & encroaching spirit on the other.

In 1774, the progress made by G.B. in the open assertion of her pretensions and in the apprehended purpose of otherwise maintaining them than by Legislative enactments and declarations, had been such that the Colonies did not hesitate to assemble, by their deputies, in a formal Congress, authorized to oppose to the British innovations whatever measures might be found best adapted to the occasion; without however losing sight of an eventual reconciliation.

The dissuasive measures of that Congress, being without effect, another Congress was held in 1775, whose pacific efforts to bring about a change in the views of the other party, being equally unavailing, and the commencement of actual hostilities having at length put an end to all hope of reconciliation; the Congress finding moreover that the popular voice began to call for an entire & perpetual dissolution of the political ties which had connected them with G.B., proceeded on the memorable 4th of July, 1776 to declare the 13 Colonies, Independent States.

During the discussions of this solemn Act, a Committee consisting of a member from each colony had been appointed to prepare & digest a form of Confederation, for the future management of the common interests, which had hitherto been left to the discretion of Congress, guided by the exigences of the contest, and by the known intentions or occasional instructions of the Colonial Legislatures.

It appears that as early as the 21st of July 1775, a plan entitled "Articles of Confederation & perpetual Union of the Colonies" had been sketched by Docr Franklin, the plan being on that day submitted by him to Congress; and tho' not copied into their Journals remaining on their files in his handwriting. But notwithstanding the term "perpetual" observed in the title, the articles provided expressly for the event of a return of the Colonies to a connection with G. Britain.

This sketch became a basis for the plan reported by the Come on the 12 of July, now also remaining on the files of Congress, in the handwriting of Mr Dickinson. The plan, tho' dated after the Declaration of Independence, was probably drawn up before that event; since the name of Colonies, not States is used throughout the draught. The plan reported, was debated and amended from time to time, till the 17th of November 1777, when it was agreed to by Congress, and proposed to the Legislatures of the States, with an explanatory and recommendatory letter. The ratifications of these by their Delegates in Congs duly authorized took place at successive dates; but were not compleated till March 1. 1781, when Maryland who had made it a prerequisite that the vacant lands acquired from the British Crown should be a Common fund, yielded to the persuasion that a final & formal establishment of the federal Union & Govt would make a favorable impression not only on other foreign Nations, but on G.B. herself.

The great difficulty experienced in so framing the fedl system as to obtain the unanimity required for its due sanction, may be inferred from the long interval, and recurring discussions, between the commencement and completion of the work; from the changes made during its progress; from the language of Congs when proposing it to the States, wch dwelt on the impracticability of devising a system acceptable to all of them; from the reluctant assent given by some; and the various alterations proposed by others; and by a tardiness in others again which produced a special address to them from Congs enforcing the duty of sacrificing local considerations and favorite opinions to the public safety, and the necessary harmony: Nor was the assent of some of the States finally yielded without strong protests against particular articles, and a reliance on future amendments removing their objections.

It is to be recollected, no doubt, that these delays might be occasioned in some degree, by an occupation of the public Councils both general & local, with the deliberations and measures, essential to a Revolutionary struggle; But there must have been a balance for these causes, in the obvious motives to hasten the establishment of a regular and efficient Govt; and in the tendency of the crisis to repress opinions and pretensions, which might be inflexible in another state of things.

The principal difficulties which embarrassed the progress, and retarded the completion of the plan of Confederation, may be traced to (1) the natural repugnance of the parties to a relinquishment of power; (2) a natural jealousy of its abuse in other hands than their own; (3) the rule of suffrage among parties

(Continues)

unequal in size, but equal in sovereignty; (4) the ratio of contributions in money and in troops, among parties, whose inequality in size did not correspond with that of their wealth, or of their military or free population; and (5) the selection and definition of the powers, at once necessary to the federal head, and safe to the several members.

To these sources of difficulty, incident to the formation of all such Confederacies, were added two others one of a temporary, the other of a permanent nature. The first was the case of the Crown lands, so called because they had been held by the British Crown, and being ungranted to individuals when its authority ceased, were considered by the States within whose charters or asserted limits they lay, as devolving on them; whilst it was contended by the others, that being wrested from the dethroned authority, by the equal exertion of all, they resulted of right and in equity to the benefit of all. The lands being of vast extent and of growing value, were the occasion of much discussion & heart-burning; & proved the most obstinate of the impediments to an earlier consummation of the plan of federal Govt. The State of Maryland the last that acceded to it held out as already noticed, till March 1, 1781, and then yielded only to the hope that by giving a stable & authoritative character to the Confederation, a successful termination of the Contest might be accelerated. The dispute was happily compromised by successive surrenders of portions of the territory by the States having exclusive claims to it, and acceptances of them by Congress.

The other source of dissatisfaction was the peculiar situation of some of the States, which having no convenient ports for foreign commerce, were subject to be taxed by their neighbors, thro whose ports, their commerce was carried on. New Jersey, placed between Phila & N. York, was likened to a cask tapped at both ends; and N. Carolina, between Virga & S. Carolina to a patient bleeding at both arms. The Articles Of Confederation provided no remedy for the complaint: which produced a strong protest on the part of N. Jersey: and never ceased to be a source of dissatisfaction & discord until the new Constitution, superseded the old.

But the radical infirmity of the "arts Of Confederation" was the dependence of Congs on the voluntary and simultaneous compliance with its Requisitions, by so many independant Communities, each consulting more or less its particular interests & convenience and distrusting the compliance of the others. Whilst the paper emissions of Congs continued to circulate they were employed as a sinew of war, like gold & silver. When that ceased to be the case, the fatal defect of the political System was felt in its alarming force. The war was merely kept alive and brought to a successful conclusion by such foreign aids and temporary expedients as could be applied; a hope prevailing with many, and a wish with all, that a state of peace, and the sources of prosperity opened by it, would give to the Confederacy in practice, the efficiency which had been inferred from its theory.

The close of the war however brought no cure for the public embarrassments. The States relieved from the pressure of foreign danger, and flushed with the enjoyment of independent and sovereign power; [instead of a diminished disposition to part with it,] persevered in omissions and in measures incompatible with thier relations to the Federal Govt and with those among themselves.

Having served as a member of Congs through the period between Mar. 1780 & the arrival of peace in 1783, I had become intimately acquainted with the public distresses and the causes of them. I had observed the successful opposition to every attempt to procure a remedy by new grants of power to Congs. I had found moreover that despair of success hung over the compromising provision of April 1783 for the public necessities which had been so elaborately planned, and so impressively recommended to the States. Sympathizing, under this aspect of affairs, in the alarm of the friends of free Govt, at the threatened danger of an abortive result to the great & perhaps last experiment in its favour, I could not be insensible to the obligation to co-operate as far as I could in averting the calamity. With this view I acceded to the desire of my fellow Citizens of the County that I should be one of its representatives in the Legislature, hoping that I might there best contribute to inculcate the critical posture to which the Revolutionary cause was reduced, and the merit of a leading agency of the State in bringing about a rescue of the Union and the blessings of liberty a staked on it, from an impending catastrophe.

It required but little time after taking my seat in the House of Delegates in May 1784 to discover that, however favorable the general disposition of the State might be towards the Confederacy the Legislature retained the aversion of its predecessors to transfers of power from the State to the Govt of the Union; notwithstanding the urgent demands of the Federal Treasury; the glaring inadequacy of the authorized mode of supplying it, the rapid growth of anarchy in the Fedl System, and the animosity kindled among the States by their conflicting regulations.

The temper of the Legislature & the wayward course of its proceedings may be gathered from the Journals of its Sessions in the years 1784 & 1785.

The failure however of the varied propositions in the Legislature for enlarging the powers of Congress, the continued failure of the efforts of Congs to obtain from them the means of providing for the debts of the Revolution; and of countervailing the commercial laws of G.B., a source of much irritation & agst which the separate efforts of the States were found worse than abortive; these Considerations with the lights thrown on the whole subject, by the free & full discussion it had undergone led to an general acquiescence in the Resoln passed, on the 21 of Jany 1786, which proposed & invited a meeting of Deputies from all the States to "insert the Resol (See Journal.)"

The resolution had been brought forward some weeks before on the failure of a proposed grant of power to Congress to collect a revenue from commerce, which had been abandoned by its friends in consequence of material alterations made in the grant by a Committee of the whole. The Resolution tho introduced by Mr Tyler an influencial member, who having never served in Congress, had more the ear of the House than those whose services there exposed them to an imputable bias, was so little acceptable that it was not then persisted in. Being now revived by him, on the last day of the Session, and being the alternative of adjourning without any effort for the crisis in the affairs of the Union, it obtained a general vote; less however with some of its friends from a confidence in the success of the experiment than from a hope that it might prove a step to a more comprehensive & adequate provision for the wants of the Confederacy.

It happened also that Commissioners who had been appointed by Virga & Maryd to settle the jurisdiction on waters dividing the two States had, apart from their official reports recommended a uniformity in the regulations of the 2 States on several subjects & particularly on those having relation to foreign trade. It apeared at the same time that Maryd had deemed a concurrence of her neighbors Pena & Delaware indispensable in such a case, who for like reasons would require that of their neighbors. So apt and forceable an illustration of the necessity of a uniformity throughout all the States could not but favour the passage of a Resolution which proposed a Convention having that for its object.

The commissioners appointed by the Legisl: & who attended the Convention were E. Randolph the Attorney of the State, St. Geo: Tucker & J. M. The designation of the time & place for its meeting to be proposed and communicated to the States having been left to the Comrs they named for the time early September and for the place the City of Annapolis avoiding the residence of Congs and large Commercial Cities as liable to suspicions of an extraneous influence.

Altho the invited Meeting appeared to be generally favored, five States only assembled; some failing to make appointments, and some of the individuals appointed not hastening their attendance, the result in both cases being ascribed mainly, to a belief that the time had not arrived for such a political reform, as might be expected from a further experience of its necessity.

But in the interval between the proposal of the Convention and the time of its meeting, such had been the advance of public opinion in the desired direction, stimulated as it had been by the effect of the contemplated object, of the meeting, in turning the genal attention to the Critical State of things, and in calling forth the sentiments and exertions of the most enlightened & influencial patriots, that the Convention thin as it was did not scruple to decline the limited task assigned to it and to recommend to the States a Convention with powers adequate to the occasion. Nor was it unnoticed that the commission of the N. Jersey Deputation, had extended its object to a general provision for the exigencies of the Union. A recommendation for this enlarged purpose was accordingly reported by a Come to whom the subject had been referred. It was drafted by Col H. and finally agreed to unanimously in the following form. Insert it.

The recommendation was well recd by the Legislature of Virga which happened to be the first that acted on it, and the example of her compliance was made as conciliatory and impressive as possible. The Legislature were unanimous or very nearly so on the occasion and as a proof of the magnitude & solemnity attached to it, they placed Genl W. at the head of the Deputation from the State; and as a proof of the deep interest he felt in the case he overstepped the obstacles to his acceptance of the appointment.

The law complying with the recommendation from Annapolis was in the terms following:

A resort to a General Convention to remodel the Confederacy, was not a new idea. It had entered at an early date into the conversations and speculations of the most reflecting & foreseeing observers of the inadequacy of the powers allowed to Congress. In a pamphlet published in May 81 at the seat of Congs Pelatiah Webster an able tho' not conspicuous Citizen, after discussing the fiscal system of the U. States, and suggesting among other remedial provisions including a national Bank remarks that "the Authority of Congs at present is very inadequate to the performance of their duties; and this indicates the necessity of their calling a Continental Convention for the express purpose of ascertaining, defining, enlarging, and limiting, the duties & powers of their Constitution."

(Continues)

(Continued)

On the 1. day of Apl 1783, Col. Hamilton, in a debate in Congs observed that

He alluded probably to [see Life of Schuyler in Longacre. It does not appear however that his expectation had been fulfilled].

In a letter to J. M. from R. H. Lee then President of Congs dated Novr 26, 1784 He says

The answer of J. M. remarks

In 1785, Noah Webster whose pol. & other valuable writings had made him known to the public, in one of his publications of American policy brought into view the same resort for supplying the defects of the Fedl System [see his life in Longacre].

The proposed & expected Convention at Annapolis the first of a general character that appears to have been realized, & the state of the public mind awakened by it had attracted the particular attention of Congs and favored the idea there of a Convention with fuller powers for amending the Confederacy.

It does not appear that in any of these cases, the reformed system was to be otherwise sanctioned than by the Legislative authy of the States; nor whether or how far, a change was to be made in the structure of the Depository of Federal powers.

The act of Virga providing for the Convention at Philada, was succeeded by appointments from other States as their Legislatures were assembled, the appointments being selections from the most experienced & highest standing Citizens. Rh. I. was the only exception to a compliance with the recommendation from Annapolis, well known to have been swayed by an obdurate adherence to an advantage which her position gave her of taxing her neighbors thro' their consumption of imported supplies, an advantage which it was foreseen would be taken from her by a revisal of the "Articles of Confederation."

As the pub. mind had been ripened for a salutary Reform of the pol. System, in the interval between the proposal & the meeting, of Comrs at Annapolis, the interval between the last event, and the meeting of Deps at Phila had continued to develop more & more the necessity & the extent of a Systematic provision for the preservation and Govt of the Union; among the ripening incidents was the Insurrection of Shays, in Massts against her Govt; which was with difficulty suppressed, notwithstanding the influence on the insurgents of an apprehended interposition of the Fedl troops.

At the date of the Convention, the aspect & retrospect of the pol: condition of the U.S. could not but fill the pub. mind with a gloom which was relieved only by a hope that so select a Body would devise an adequate remedy for the existing and prospective evils so impressively demanding it.

It was seen that the public debt rendered so sacred by the cause in which it had been incurred remained without any provision for its payment. The reiterated and elaborate efforts of Cong. to procure from the States a more adequate power to raise the means of payment had failed. The effect of the ordinary requisitions of Congress had only displayed the inefficiency of the authy making them: none of the States having duly complied with them, some having failed altogether or nearly so; and in one instance, that of N. Jersey a compliance was expressly refused; nor was more yielded to the expostulations of members of Congs deputed to her Legislature, than a mere repeal of the law, without a compliance. [see letter of Grayson to J. M.]

The want of authy in Congs to regulate Commerce had produced in Foreign nations particularly G.B. a monopolizing policy injurious to the trade of the U.S. and destructive to their navigation; the imbecilicity and anticipated dissolution of the Confederacy extinguishg all apprehensions of a Countervailing policy on the part of the U. States.

The same want of a general power over Commerce, led to an exercise of the power separately, by the States, wch not only proved abortive, but engendered rival, conflicting and angry regulations. Besides the vain attempts to supply their respective treasuries by imposts, which turned their commerce into the neighbouring ports, and to coerce a relaxation of the British monopoly of the W. Inds navigation, which was attempted by Virga [see the Journal of the States having ports for foreign commerce, taxed & irritated the adjoining States, trading thro' them, as N.Y. Pena Virga & S. Carolina. Some of the States, as Connecticut, taxed imports as from Massts higher than imports even from G.B. of wch Massts complained to Virga and doubtless to other States. [See letter of J. M. In sundry instances as of N.Y. N.J. Pa & Maryd [see] the navigation laws treated the Citizens other States as aliens.

In certain cases the authy of the Confederacy was disregarded, as in violations not only of the Treaty of peace; but of Treaties with France & Holland, which were complained of to Congs.

In other cases the Fedl Authy was violated by Treaties & wars with Indians, as by Geo: by troops raised & kept up witht the consent of Congs as by Massts by compacts witht the consent of Congs as between Pena and N. Jersey, and between Virga & Maryd. From the Legisl: Journals of Virga it appears, that a vote refusing to apply for a sanction of Congs was followed by a vote agst the communication of the Compact to Congs.

In the internal administration of the States a violation of Contracts had become familiar in the form of depreciated paper made a legal tender, of property substituted for money, of Instalment laws, and of the occlusions of the Courts of Justice; although evident that all such interferences affected the rights of other States, relatively creditor, as well as Citizens Creditors within the State.

Among the defects which had been severely felt was that of a uniformity in cases requiring it, as laws of naturalization, bankruptcy, a Coercive authority operating on individuals and a guaranty of the internal tranquillity of the States.

As natural consequences of this distracted and disheartening condition of the union, the Fedl Authy had ceased to be respected abroad, and dispositions shown there, particularly in G.B., to take advantage of its imbecility, and to speculate on its approaching downfall; at home it had lost all confidence & credit; the unstable and unjust career of the States had also forfeited the respect & confidence essential to order and good Govt, involving the general decay and confidence & credit between man & man. It was found moreover, that those least partial to popular Govt, or most distrustful of its efficacy were yielding to anticipations, that from an increase of the confusion a Govt might result more congenial with their taste or their opinions; whilst those most devoted to the principles and forms of Republics, were alarmed for the cause of liberty itself, at stake in the American Experiment, and anxious for a system that wd avoid the inefficacy of a mere confederacy without passing into the opposite extreme of a consolidated govt it was known that there were individuals who had betrayed a bias toward Monarchy [see Knox to G W & him to Jay] (Marshall's life) and there had always been some not unfavorable to a partition of the Union into several Confederacies; either from a better chance of figuring on a Sectional Theatre, or that the Sections would require stronger Govts, or by their hostile conflicts lead to a monarchical consolidation. The idea of a dismemberment had recently made its appearance in the Newspapers.

Such were the defects, the deformities, the diseases and the ominous prospects, for which the Convention were to provide a remedy, and which ought never to be overlooked in expounding & appreciating the Constitutional Charter the remedy that was provided.

As a sketch on paper, the earliest perhaps of a Constitutional Govt for the Union [organized into the regular Departments with physical means operating on individuals] to be sanctioned by the people of the States, acting in their original & sovereign character, was contained in a letter of Apl. 8. 1787 from J. M. to Govr Randolph, a copy of the letter is here inserted.

The feature in the letter which vested in the general Authy. a negative on the laws of the States, was suggested by the negative in the head of the British Empire, which prevented collisions between the parts & the whole, and between the parts themselves. It was supposed that the substitution, of an elective and responsible authority for an hereditary and irresponsible one, would avoid the appearance even of a departure from the principle of Republicanism. But altho' the subject was so viewed in the Convention, and the votes on it were more than once equally divided, it was finally & justly abandoned see note for __ for this erasure substitute the amendt marked * for this page [as, apart from other objections, it was not practicable among so many states, increasing in number, and enacting, each of them, so many laws instead of the proposed negative, the objects of it were left as finally provided for in the Constitution.]

On the arrival of the Virginia Deputies at Phila it occurred to them that from the early and prominent part taken by that State in bringing about the Convention some initiative step might be expected from them. The Resolutions introduced by Governor Randolph were the result of a Consultation on the subject; with an understanding that they left all the Deputies entirely open to the lights of discussion, and free to concur in any alterations or modifications which their reflections and judgments might approve. The Resolutions as the Journals shew became the basis on which the proceedings of the Convention commenced, and to the developments, variations and modifications of which the plan of Govt proposed by the Convention may be traced.

The curiosity I had felt during my researches into the History of the most distinguished Confederacies, particularly those of antiquity, and the deficiency I found in the means of satisfying it more especially in what related to the process, the principles, the reasons, & the anticipations, which prevailed in the formation of them, determined me to preserve as far as I could an exact account of what might pass in the Convention whilst executing its trust, with the magnitude of which I was duly impressed, as I was with the gratification promised to future curiosity by an authentic exhibition of the objects, the opinions & the reasonings from which the new System of Govt was to receive its peculiar structure & organization. Nor was I unaware of the value of such a contribution to the fund of materials for the History of a Constitution on which would be staked the happiness of a people great even in its infancy, and possibly the cause of Liberty throught the world.

(Continues)

(Continued)

In pursuance of the task I had assumed I chose a seat in front of the presiding member, with the other members on my right & left hands. In this favorable position for hearing all that passed, I noted in terms legible & in abbreviations & marks intelligible to myself what was read from the Chair or spoken by the members; and losing not a moment unnecessarily between the adjournment & reassembling of the Convention I was enabled to write out my daily notes [see page 18 during the session or within a few finishing days after its close—see pa. 18 in the extent and form preserved in my own hand on my files.]

In the labour & correctness of doing this, I was not a little aided by practice & by a familiarity with the style and the train of observation & reasoning which characterized the principal speakers. It happened, also that I was not absent a single day, nor more than a cassual fraction of an hour in any day, so that I could not have lost a single speech, unless a very short one. Insert the Remark on the _____ slip of paper marked A.

[It may be proper to remark, that, with a very few exceptions, the speeches were neither furnished, nor revised, nor sanctioned, by the speakers, but written out from my notes, aided by the freshness of my recollections. A further remark may be proper, that views of the subject might occasionally be presented in the speeches and proceedings, with a latent reference to a compromise on some middle ground, by mutual concessions. The exceptions alluded to were, –first, the sketch furnished by Mr. Randolph of his speech on the introduction of his propositions, on the twenty-ninth day of May; secondly, the speech of Mr. Hamilton, who happened to call on me when putting the last hand to it, and who acknowledged its fidelity, without suggesting more than a very few verbal alterations which were made; thirdly, the speech of Gouverneur Morris on the second day of May, which was communicated to him on a like occasion, and who acquiesced in it without even a verbal change. The correctness of his language and the distinctness of his enunciation were particularly favorable to a reporter. The speeches of Doctor Franklin, excepting a few brief ones, were copied from the written ones read to the Convention by his colleague, Mr. Wilson, it being inconvenient to the Doctor to remain long on his feet.]

Of the ability & intelligence of those who composed the Convention, the debates & proceedings may be a test; as the character of the work which was the offspring of their deliberations must be tested by the experience of the future, added to that of the nearly half century which has passed.

But whatever may be the judgment pronounced on the competency of the architects of the Constitution, or whatever may be the destiny, of the edifice prepared by them, I feel it a duty to express my profound & solemn conviction, derived from my intimate opportunity of observing & appreciating the views of the Convention, collectively & individually, that there never was an assembly of men, charged with a great & arduous trust, who were more pure in their motives, or more exclusively or anxiously [devoted to the object committed to them, than were the members of the Federal Convention of 1787, to the object of devising and proposing a constitutional system which would best supply the defects of that which it was to replace, and best secure the permanent liberty and happiness of their country.]

AMERICAN COURT CASES UNDER THE ARTICLES OF CONFEDERATION

Here is a rare glimpse at some cases decided by the U.S. Supreme Court during the days of the Articles of Confederation, before the Constitution was established. As compared to subsequent Supreme Court opinions, these early ones were rather brief.

Shrider's Lessee v. Morgan, 1 U.S. 68 (1782)

In this cause, M'Kean C. S. said, that he had ruled it in a case at Lancaster, that the lessor of the plaintiff shall not be obliged to show his title further back, than from the person who last died seized, first showing the estate to be out of the Proprietaries, or the commonwealth.

It was objected by Lewis and Clymer, that a sheriff's deed of sale of lands, under a writ of venditioni exponas, not being recorded in the Rolls Office, according to the Act of Assembly of 1774, could not be read in evidence. Sed mon allocatur: Because it was acknowledged [*Shrider's Lessee v. Morgan* 1 U.S. 68 (1782)] in court, and the registring of it in the Prothonotary's office (as is always done) is a sufficient recording within the act.

Sergeant and Ingersol opposed the reading a deed in evidence, upon this ground: that by the1 act of assembly last mentioned, all deeds not recorded in the Rolls Office, according to the particular directions of that act, are declared void as against subsequent purchasers, and therefore, though this deed was dated before the sheriff's deed, under which the defendant claimed, 'et as it was not recorded till afterwards, they insisted it was void, and could be no evidence at all. Sed non allocatur: And M'Kean C. S. said, we cannot hinder the reading of a deed under seal, but what use will be made of it is another thing: and he cited the case of *Ford v. Lord Grey* 6. Alod. 44.2.

Kennedy v. Fury, 1 U.S. 72 (1783)

A conveyance was made to A. in trust for B. and B. brought an ejectment on his own demise. Blair contended that the demise ought to have been laid in the name of A. in-as-much as the legal estate was in him.

But by Atlee Justice, (M'Kean C. J. being absent) the demise by B. is well enough. We have no Court of Equity here; and, therefore, unless the cestui que trust could bring an ejectment in his own name, he would be without remedy, in the case of an obstinate trustee.

Leib v. Bolton, 1 U.S. 82 (1784)

A motion was made, the 10th of November, on the part of the defendant, to set aside the return of the jury of inquiry, on affidavit of irregular proceedings; and the Court granted a rule to show cause & c.

And now two of the jurors attended and deposed, that Leib's book, supported by his own oath, had been admitted as evidence of the delivery of a quantity of leather by Leib, to the order of Bolton, in part discharge of an agreement between them. But being asked, whether they founded their inquest in any degree upon that evidence, they said it was founded upon that, and concurrent testimony.

In support of the motion it was contended, that, though the admission of books in the manner above stated, had been customary; yet that the custom ought not to be carried farther than to prove work done, or wares delivered; that the purpose for which they had been introduced, on the present occasion, arose upon a collateral point, to establish a sett off in diminution of the damages, and that it was, therefore, irregular to admit them. With respect to the concurrent testimony mentioned by the jurors, it was said, that as neither the nature, or effect of it, appeared to the Court, it might have been even more improper than the allowance of the books as evidence; but that, in all events, the inquest ought to be set aside, as what did appear, shows it to have been raised so far upon an erroneous foundation.

But, BY THE COURT: We will not set aside the verdicts of juries of inquiry; nor the reports of referrees, upon frivolous grounds. Nor, will we examine into the effect of any particular piece of evidence upon the minds of the jury; for, unless it appears, that there was no proper evidence before them, we must presume that they had sufficient grounds for their inquest.

The Rule discharged.

Wharton v. Morris, 1 U.S. 125 (1785)

Debt upon a bond. Plea, payment, with leave to give the special matter in evidence.

The case was this: The plaintiffs, copartners; fold to Pleasants, Shore & Co. merchants in Virginia, a considerable quanitity of tobacco in March 1778, when the Pennsylvania scale of depreciation, estimates continental money at the rate of five for one. Articles of agreement were executed between the vendors and the purchasers, in which Plesants, Shore & Co. covenanted to procure Willing, Morris, and Inglis, merchants of Philadelphia, as sureties for the payment of the tobacco; and, accordingly, a bond for that purpose was afterwards executed by those gentlemen, in the penalty of L12,000 on condition to be void, if Pleasants & Co. should pay the sum agreed upon (that is L7 per cent.) 'on the thirtieth of September 1782 in lawful current money of Pennsylvania.' It appeared that Inglis, one of the defendants, had offered to pay the value of the tobacco, at the time of the sale, with interest; but this was refused by the plaintiffs; and no payment or tender, being made upon the 30th of September 1782, they brought the present action upon the bond. [125-Continued.]

The evidence was brief, consisting only of the articles of agreement, the bond, a deposition of the offer made by Inglis, and testimony that the usual price of tobacco, during many years preceeding the war, was about 20s per Cwt.

Wilcocks, Sergeant, and Lewis, for the plaintiffs, contended that this transaction was a fair and lawful wager on the part of Wharton, & Co. in confidence that the continental money would recover its original value; and that on the other hand they ran a considerable risque; as, if it depreciated, they would have been bound to take it, provided it continued a legal currency. But the act which repealed the

(Continues)

tender law destroyed its currency; so that on the 30th September 1782, when the bond became due and payable, the only lawful current money of Pennsylvania, was coin, of gold or silver; and that by the terms of the bond ought to be paid.

Governeur Morris, Wilson and Ingersol, for the defendants, denied that the transaction was founded in a wager; and contended that the plaintiffs had set up a hard and unconscionable demand: for, they instited, that the lawful current money, expressed in the bond, meant what was current at the time of its execution; and they declared the readiness of the defendants either to pay at the rate established by the scale of depreciation, or according to the real value of the tobacco, with interest from the date of the sale.

McKean, Chief Justice delivered a circumstantial and learned charge to the Jury. He said, that the want of a Court with equitable powers, like those of the Chancery in England, had long been felt in Pennsylvania. The institution of such a Court, he observed, had once been agitated here; but the houses of Assembly, antecedent to the revolution, successfully opposed it; because they were apprehensive of encreasing, by that means, the power and influence [Page 1 U.S. 125, 126] of the Governor, who claimed it as a right to be Chancellor. For this reason, many inconveniences have been suffered. No adequate remedy is provided for a breach of trust; no relief can be obtained in cases of covenants with a penalty & c. This defect of jurisdiction, has necessarily obliged the Court upon such occasions, to refer the question to the jury, under an equitable and consciencious interpretation of the agreement of the parties; and it is upon that ground, the jury must consider and decide the present cause.

His Honor, having recapitulated the evidence, concluded with the following observations.

The bond is made payable in current money of Pennsylvania; but, I would ask, what is the current money of Pennsylvania? For my part, I know of none, that can properly be so called, for current and lawful are synonymous. In Great Britain, the King by his proclamation may render any species of coin a lawful currency. But here, it can only be done by an act of assembly; and except in the temporary laws for supporting the former emissions of paper-money, there is no pretence that the legislature has ever interfered upon this subject. The expressions in the 2 Sect. of the act of the 27th January, 1777, cannot be construed to make the Spanish milled dollars a legal tender, as they are only mentioned by words of referrence; but that which was declared to be a lawful tender, and consequently, became the legal currency of the land, was the money emitted under the authority of Congress.

To that species of money, therefore, the bond must be taken to relate; and the jury will either reduce the penalty to gold or silver, according to the scale of depreciation; or, if they think it more equitable, they will find a verdict for the value of the tobacco, and give the plaintiffs legal interest from the day of sale.

The jury adopted the latter opinion, and found for the plaintiffs with £.3,600 damages and 6d. costs.

Hollingsworth v. Leiper, 1 U.S. 161 (1786)

A rule had been obtained to show cause, why the report of Referrees should not be set aside, on the ground of their having heard a witness interested in the event of the suit; and, after argument, THE PRESIDENT pronounced the decision of the Court.

SHIPPEN, President.

The determination of causes by referrees under a rule of Court, has become so frequent and useful a practice, and is attended with so many advantages towards the summary administration of justice, that is would be extremely mischievous to shake their reports by captious objections, where the substantial rules of justice are not violated. The merits of the cause are solely submitted to them, as judges of the parties own chusing, and are not afterward; enquired into by the Court, unless there should appear a plain mistake of the law or fact.

Page 1 U.S. 161, 162

As to the forms of their proceeding, both parties should have an opportunity of being heard, and that in the presence of each other, that they may be enabled to apply their testimony to the allegations. The witnesses, on both sides, are likewise, to give their evidence in the presence of the parties, that they may have an opportunity of cross examining them. No surprise is permitted, such as refusing the parties a reasonable time to bring forward their witnesses, or refusing to hear them when they are brought. These rules, or similar ones, are founded in natural justice, and are absolutely necessary for the due administration of justice in every form whatever.

As to the kind of evidence which the referrees may hear, there always has been, and must necessarily be, in this kind of tribunal, a very great latitude. The parties, generally unassisted by counsel, are permitted to relate their own stories, and confront each other; their witnesses are heard even without an oath, unless the contrary is stipulated, or the referrees require it. Books and papers are inspected and examined by them, without regard to their being such as would be strictly evidence in a Court of Law. And this practice being known to both parties before they agree to the reference, and the advantages arising from it, being mutual, there seems no just reason to complain of it.

In public trials in Courts of law, the judges sit to superintend the evidence, and no interested witnesses are, in general, permitted to give evidence to the jury; but referrees occupy the office both of judge and jurymen; their discretion, therefore, must necessarily be much relied on, and as they are generally unacquainted with the artificial rules of law, they must be guided principally by their own reason. If we were once to set aside a report, because the referrees had heard an interested witness, we should open a door for such a variety of objections, that scarcely a single report would stand the test. Papers not formally or legally proved, or hearsay evidence admitted, would be as fatal to reports, as the admission of interested witnesses, being equal violations of the rules of evidence.

Gerard v. La Coste, 1 U.S. 194 (1787)

This case came before the Court on a special verdict, and, after argument, the following judgment was pronounced by the President.

Shippen, President.

This action is brought against the acceptors of an inland Bill of Exchange, made payable to Bass and Soyer and indorsed by them, after the Acceptance, to the Plaintiff for a valuable consideration. The Bill is payable to Bass and Soyer, without the usual words 'or order' 'or assigns,' or any other words of negotiability. The question is, whether this is a Bill of Exchange, which, by the law merchant, is indorsable over, so as to enable the indorsee to maintain an action on it against the acceptors, in his own name.

The Court has taken some time to consider the case, not so much from their own doubts, as because it is said eminent Lawyers, as well as Judges, in America, have entertained different opinions concerning it. There is certainly no precise form of words necessary to constitute a Bill of Exchange, yet from the earliest time to the present, merchants have agreed upon nearly the same form, which contains few or no superfluous words, terms of negotiability usually appearing to make a part of it. It is indeed generally for the benefit of trade that Bills of Exchange, especially foreign ones, should be assignable; but when they are so, it must appear to be a part of the contract, and the power to assign must be contained in the Bill itself.

Page 1 U.S. 194, 195

The drawer is the lawgiver, and directs the payment as he pleases; the receiver knows the terms, acquiesces in them, and must conform. There have doubtless been many draughts made payable to the party himself, without more, generally perhaps to prevent their negotiability: Whether these draughts can properly be called Bills of Exchange, even between the parties themselves, seems to have been left in some doubt by the modern Judges. Certainly there are draughts, in the nature of Bills of Exchange, which are not strictly such, as those issuing out of a contingent fund; these, (say the Judges in 2 Black. Rep. 1140.) do not operate as Bills of Exchange, but, when accepted, are binding between the parties. The question, however, here, is not whether this would be a good Bill of Exchange between the drawer, payee, and acceptor, but whether it is indorsable. *Marius's Advice* is an old book of good authority; in page 141 he mentions expresly such a Bill of Exchange as the present, and the effect of it, and he says, that the Bill not being payable to a man or his Assigns, or Order, an assignment of it will not avail, but the money must be paid to the man himself. In 1 Salkeld 125, it is said, that it is by force of the words, 'or order' in the Bill itself, that authority is given to the party to assign it by indorsement. In 3 Salk. 67 it is ruled, that where a Bill is drawn payable to a man, 'or order,' it is within the custom of merchants; and such a Bill may be negotiated and assigned by custom and the Contract of the Parties. And in 1 Salk. 133 it is expressly said by the Court, that the words 'or to his order,' give the authority to assign the Bill by indorsement, and that without those words the Drawer was not answerable to the indorsee, although the Indorser might. An argument of some plausibility is drawn in favor of the Plaintiff from the fimilarity of Promissory Notes to Bills of Exchange. The statute of 3 & 4 of Ann appears to have two objects; one to enable the person to whom the Note is made payable, to sue the drawer upon the Note as an instrument (which he could not do before that Act) and the other to enable the Indorsee to maintain an action in his own name against the drawer. The words in this Act which describe the Note on which an action will lie for the Payee, are said to be the same as those on which the action will lie for the indorsee, namely, that it shall be a Note payable to any person, or his Order; and it appearing by adjudged cases, that an action will lie for the Payee although the words 'or order' are not in the note, it follows (it is contended) that an

(Continues)

(*Continued*)

action will also lie for the Indorsee, without those words. If the Letter of the Act was strictly adhered to, certainly neither the Payee, nor Indorsee, could support an action on a Note, which did not contain such words of negotiability as are mentioned in the Act; yet the construction of the Judges has been, that the original payee may support an action on a Note not made assignable in terms. The foundation of this construction does not fully appear in the cases, but it was probably thought consonant to the Spirit [Page 1 U.S. 194, 196] of the Act, as the words 'or order' could have no effect, and might be supposed immaterial, in a suit brought by the payee himself against the maker of the Note. But to extend this construction to the case of an Indorsement, without any authority to make it appearing on the face of the Note, would have been to violate not only the Letter but the Spirit of the Act. Consequently no such case any where appears. On the contrary, wherever the Judges speak of the effect of an indorsement, they always suppose the Note itself to have been originally made indorsable. The case of *Moore versus Manning* in Com. Rep. 311. was the case of a Promissory Note originally payable to one and his Order; it was assigned without the words 'or order' in the indorsment; the question was, whether the assignee could assign it again: The Chief Justice, at first, inclined that he could not, but it was afterwards resolved by the whole Court, that if the Bill was originally assignable, 'as it will be (say the Court) if it be payable to one and his Order,' then to whomsoever it is assigned, he has all the interest in the Bill, and may assign it as he pleases. Here the whole stress of the determination is laid upon what were the original terms of the Bill, if it was made payable to one and his Order, it was assignable, even by an indorsee without the word 'order' in the indorsment; it follows, therefore, that if the Bill was not originally payable to order, it was not assignable at all. The same point is determined, for the same reasons, in the case of *Edie & Laird v. the East India Company*, in 1 Black. R. 29, where Lord Mansfield says, 'the main foundation is to consider what the Bill was in its origin; if in its original creation it was a negotiable draught, it carries the power to assign it.' In a similar case, cited in Buller's nisi prius 390, the Court held, that as the Note was in its original creation indorsable, it would be so in the hands of the indorsee, though not so expressed in the indorsment.

These cases leave no room to doubt what have been the sentiments of the Courts in England upon the subject. To make Bills, or Notes, assignable, the power to assign them must appear in the instruments themselves; and then, the custom of merchants, in the case of Bills of Exchange, and the Act of Parliament, in the case of Notes, operating upon the Contract of the Parties, will make them assignable.

In the case before us, no such contract appears in the Bill. The acceptance was an engagement to pay according to the terms of the Bill to Bass & Soyer; a subsequent indorsment, not authorized by the Bill, cannot vary or enlarge that engagement, so as to subject the acceptor, by the law merchant, to an action at the suit of the indorsee.

Judgment for the Defendant.

Our Two-Tier, Three-Branch System of Government

Chapter Objectives

In this chapter you will learn . . .

- How the government is divided into federal and state levels
- How the three branches of government work together
- What term limits are and why they exist
- Why the president must be a natural-born U.S. citizen
- The history of the major American political parties

Introduction

In the last chapter we learned about the Articles of Confederation and the long road to the Constitution. We even learned that, technically, George Washington was not the first president of the United States after all. *The Federalist Papers* paved the way for the Constitution to be ratified in 1788 in Philadelphia.

Just so that we are clear about the dates, the Constitution was adopted in 1787 by the Founding Fathers (also referred to as the Founders or the Framers), and was actually *ratified* (established as official) in 1788. Now, let's take a closer look at it.

Two Tiers of Government: Federal and State

As we discussed in Chapter Two, the original 13 states were not particularly interested in uniting as a nation, because that meant giving up much of their individuality. Even though the Founding Fathers eventually agreed to ratify the Constitution, they reached a consensus based on a compromise: namely, that there would be a strong national government, but that the states would retain a great deal of their power and independence.

States' rights were further fortified by the Tenth Amendment, which states that: **The powers not delegated to the United States by the Constitution, nor prohibited by it to the States, are reserved to the States respectively, or to the people.** In other words, although the Constitution includes a good amount of law, there is a whole lot more that is not included. There is no mention in the Constitution about whether murder is against the law,

whether children are required to attend school, or how much sales tax will be charged on a purchase. These laws, then, are to be made by the states.

In some cases, states may choose to delegate laws not *enumerated* in the Constitution to local governments, such as town councils. For instance, a law that prohibits playing loud music after 10 PM is more likely to be a town ordinance than a state law. And, certainly, there is nothing in the Constitution about not playing the radio past a certain hour!

The Supremacy Clause

In Chapter One, we began to discuss the Supremacy Clause. Now, let's take a look at it in greater detail. Article VI, Section 2 establishes the Constitution as the Supreme Law of the Land, superior to any state or local laws that contradict it. For example, the Twenty-Sixth Amendment states that U.S. citizens who are 18 years or older may not be denied the right to vote because of age. However, if a particular state were to require that all of its citizens reach age 21 to be eligible to vote, that would be unconstitutional. That is because such a law would directly contradict the Constitution.

A different scenario, however, might allow a state law to exist even if it were different from the Constitution. For instance, the Seventh Amendment states that any dispute of $20 or more would require a jury trial.

A courtroom trial may consist of a trial by jury, whereas the decision (let's say, if the defendant is guilty of kidnapping) is reached by the jury based on directions from the judge, or one in which the decision is reached by the judge.

Granted, $20 seems like a tiny sum of money for which to sue in the first place; that anyone would sue in court for a dispute of less than $20 seems silly. However, keep in mind that the Seventeenth Amendment was ratified in 1791. At the time, spending the night in a posh New York hotel, seeing a show (a live show—they did not have movies back then), and having dinner for two, might have cost about a dollar or two. Don't forget, the entire island of Manhattan was purchased by Dutch settlers for a sum that many claim was equivalent to 24 dollars!

Nonetheless, suppose that people nowadays really did sue for measly amounts such as $20. If, say, the state of Ohio required that all lawsuits brought there for $10 or higher must be jury trials, then that would be fine. You see, that law does not *contradict* the Constitution: the requirement that all disputes higher than $20 require a jury trial remains satisfied. That it also would be required in Ohio for trials from $10 to $19.99 would not be an issue of dispute.

Three Branches: Legislative, Executive, and Judicial

Although Hamilton and the other Federalists favored a strong chief executive, and the rest of the Framers realized that one of the Articles' principal failures was a lack thereof, there was a strong desire to prevent one branch of government from becoming too powerful. After all, it had only been a few years since the colonists declared their independence from a government they considered to have been oppressive, even tyrannical; the last thing they wanted was to relive such a nightmare.

Accordingly, the Framers decided on a three-branch system of government, as articulated in the Constitution's first three Articles: legislative, executive, and judicial. Let's take a look at each of the three branches.

Article I: The Legislative Branch

All legislative powers arise from the Congress of the United States, which is comprised two chambers, or houses: the Senate and the House of Representatives. Two senators are elected from each state; as there are 50 states in the nation, there are one hundred total United States senators. The number of representatives elected from each state depends on that state's population. Based on population results from the 2000 Census, the most populous state in the nation remains California, which has 53 representatives. The seven least populous states—Alaska, Delaware, Montana, North Dakota, South Dakota, Vermont, and Wyoming—each have only one.

The Bicameral Compromise

The very essence of Congress, a *bicameral* (two-house) system, was based on yet another compromise. Some of the Founders believed that representation should be based on a state's population; after all, the bigger the state, the more people would be affected by legislation. On the other hand, others were concerned that the larger states would dominate national politics. For these reasons, the compromise was reached so that one house (the Senate) would be equally portioned, whereas the other house (the House of Representatives) would be based on population.

Qualifications

Representatives, also referred to as Congressmen or Congresswomen (notwithstanding that Senators are members of Congress, too) must be at least 25 years old, U.S. citizens for at least 7 years, and residents of the state to which they are elected at the time they take office.

Senators must be at least 30 years old, U.S. citizens for at least 9 years, and residents of the state to which they are elected at the time they take office.

Elections and Terms

The House of Representatives was (and is) often referred to as "the people's house" because the people elected their representatives directly. Senators, however, were appointed by the legislature of the state in which they ran for office. Nowadays, when you vote in your state's Senate races, you cast your vote directly. Originally, the people would depend on their state's legislature to make such appointments. That you are able to now vote for senators directly is courtesy of the Seventeenth Amendment, which was ratified in 1913.

Representatives are elected to a 2-year term, and senators to a 6-year term. Representatives, thus, are elected every 2 years, whereas one-third of Senators are elected in every 2-year cycle. Let's look at the following example, to illustrate: In 1980, the entire House of Representatives was up for reelection, as was one-third of the Senate (for the sake of this example, let's call it Part 1). Accordingly, the 1980 Representatives would remain in office until 1982, and the Part 1 Senators until 1986. In 1982, the entire House would be up for reelection again, as would Part 2 (another third) of the Senate. The House term would be up in 1984, and the Part 2 Senators would complete their term in 1988. In 1984, the House again would be up for reelection as would Part 3 (the remaining third) of the Senate. The victorious Representatives in the 1984 election would hold their seat until the end of 1986, and the Part 3 Senators until 1990.

Term Limits

Term limits dictate how many terms an elected official is permitted to hold office. There has been a great deal of debate about imposing term limits on members of Congress (both Representatives and Senators). From the origin of the Constitution, all members of Congress have had an opportunity to be reelected to an unlimited number of terms.

To date, the Representative who has been elected to the highest number of terms is Jamie L. Whitten, who served as a Congressman from Mississippi from November 1941 to January 1995, a staggering 54 years. To put it in historical context, he took office shortly before the attack on

The U.S. Capitol Building, in Washington, D.C., where Congress makes the nation's laws.

Pearl Harbor and retired at the midpoint of President Bill Clinton's first term!

The longest-serving Senator is Robert C. Byrd from West Virginia, who has served since 1959. He broke the record held by Strom Thurmond of South Carolina, who had served a little over 46 years and retired at the age of 100. In case you were wondering, Thurmond was the oldest serving U.S. Senator ever, indeed!

Although Whitten, Byrd, and Thurmond are not typical examples, it is common for Representatives and Senators to serve multiple terms. Some argue that allowing them to run for reelection without limitation hampers our electoral process because it provides an unfair advantage to those in office. The advantage, many contend, extends beyond name recognition: conceivably, those already in power can do favors for others in order to ensure their support and, in turn, continue to be reelected.

The other side of the argument is that term limits would force everyone—those running for office and those voting for them—to stop serving before they, or the people, so choose. It would force great leaders to retire prematurely. Besides, many will argue, what better form of term limit is there than new elections? If the people are not happy with a particular candidate, they vote him or her out of office. That is the term limit.

What Is Congress Permitted to Do?

Think about it: if Congress is the branch of government that has the ability to make laws, just what types of laws can it make? Initially, you might say, "well, they can make laws about anything, can't they?" The short response to that statement would be, "*anything* covers a whole lot of ground!"

Actually, Congress has the power to make all laws *necessary and proper* to enforce all of its powers enumerated in the Constitution and all other aspects of the Constitution. That does not mean that Congress has the authority to make laws about anything and everything. This goes back to the notion that our government is a *limited* one, not an absolute one. Part of the reason that the people of the states were able to agree on this system of government was because basic fundamental principles of liberty were retained by the people.

Nonetheless, Article I, Section 8 of the Constitution specifically enumerates the things that Congress is supposed to do:

- Collect taxes
- Provide for the common defense
- Provide for the general welfare
- Borrow money
- Regulate commerce with foreign nations, domestic states, and Indian tribes
- Establish federal immigration and bankruptcy laws
- Coin money and fix the standard of weights and measures
- Punish those who counterfeit money
- Establish post offices and postal roads
- Promote the arts and sciences by issuing patents and copyrights to authors and inventors for their original ideas

- Constitute tribunals (similar to trials), though inferior to the Supreme Court
- Define and punish piracies and other felonies committed on the high seas
- Declare war and make rules concerning prisoners of war
- Raise and support an army and a navy and regulate them
- Provide a mechanism by which the militia is called forth in time of national need
- Oversee militia operations insofar as the militia is called into the service of the United States
- Make all laws necessary and proper to carry out these initiatives and all others set forth in the Constitution

Federalists, Antifederalists, Republicans, Democrats, and the Size of Government

The list above, which enumerates what Congress is empowered to do, certainly does not seem like a long one if placed next to a theoretical list of "Congress can do everything." However, there is one segment, the "necessary and proper" clause, which is known as the catch-all. In other words, although the list of things that Congress is empowered to do is rather short and very specific, there is the very broad clause that permits Congress to make any other laws that are necessary and proper to carry out anything set forth in the Constitution. Taken together with the charges that Congress is to "provide for the common defense" and "promote the general welfare," it would seem that Congress can do just about anything!

That is precisely the argument that many have made since the creation of our government. Simply put, a Congress that can make laws about everything under the sun constitutes a *big government*. By contrast, if Congress is limited to a few, specific things, leaving the rest of the laws to be made by individual states, then that is *small government*.

History of American Political Parties

If we trace the roots of our modern major political parties, the Republicans and the Democrats, they are loosely connected to the Federalists and the Antifederalists, respectively. In the first presidential election, when the Constitution was first ratified in 1788, George Washington ran unopposed. Although John Adams (and others) ran for "president" as well, they really did not oppose Washington. Rather, they were running for vice president. At the time, the person who received the second-highest number of votes would have become vice president. Consider this modern-day example.

In the election of 2004, George W. Bush, a Republican, ran against John Kerry, a Democrat. Bush's running mate (for Vice President) was Dick Cheney, and Kerry's running mate was John Edwards. Bush won the election and so he and Cheney became (actually remained, as they were already in office) president and vice president, respectively. In the days of Washington, however, the person who received the second-highest number of votes would become vice president.

Had that law remained in effect in 2004, Bush would have been elected president, and his vice president would have been his opponent, John Kerry. Imagine that!

In any event, Washington served as president for two terms and then decided to retire from politics (at the time, presidents could run for an unlimited number of terms, but we will talk about that a little later). He is often listed in some books as a Federalist, though he never officially belonged to the Federalist Party or to any other political party. In fact, in his famous Farewell Address to the nation, Washington warned against the formation of political parties, believing that they would be more destructive than constructive. As beloved a leader as Washington was, his words did not have a lasting effect on his successors. No sooner than his retirement did Adams, a Federalist, run for president (in 1796) in a bitterly disputed election against Thomas Jefferson, of the newly formed Democratic-Republican Party.

Adams defeated Jefferson in that election, but Jefferson returned the favor 4 years later, in 1800. The Federalists never won another presidential election and soon faded away. By 1828, the Democratic-Republican Party—which saw a second victory by Jefferson, then two terms by James Madison, two by James Monroe, and one by John Quincy Adams (who, unlike his father, did not run under the Federalist banner)—had split into two new parties, ideologically: the Democratic Party, which propelled Andrew Jackson to victory in that year, and the Whig Party.

The Whigs also faded away by 1860, giving way to the Republican Party, whose candidate, Abraham Lincoln, won the election. The modern-day Democratic and Republican Parties, then, can be traced directly to those who produced the Jackson and Lincoln presidencies, respectively. Less directly, they are linked to the Jefferson Antifederalists and the Adams Federalists, respectively.

The analysis becomes tricky when considering that, modernly, Republicans are famous for advocating small government, whereas Democrats tend to favor big government; the opposite was true in the days of Jefferson and Adams. Then again, that trend has changed time and time again, and may change again in the years to come.

In any event, the concept of big government versus small government can be explained in the following example. Suppose that you have $100 and you want to buy various items, such as groceries, shampoo, toothpaste, and so forth. Consider the following options about how to do that:

1. You may go shopping yourself;
2. You may ask your neighbor to shop for you; or
3. You may ask your cousin to shop for you.

Suppose that if you did your own shopping, you would spend the $100 and come home with a medium-sized bag of items. Instead, suppose that you gave the $100 to your neighbor, who is an excellent bargain shopper and was able to buy twice as many items as you did that were just as good in quality for the same $100. Finally, suppose that, rather than doing the shopping yourself or asking your neighbor to do it for you, you gave the $100 to your cousin, who carelessly bought overpriced items and came home with only half of what you would have bought.

Essentially, those who favor big government believe that the government can spend their money and take care of them better than they can fare for themselves. They believe the government is a good shopper, much like your neighbor. Those who prefer small government, however, believe that the government will squander the people's money, and that the people are better off keeping more of their own money and taking care of themselves. They view the government as being a bad shopper, like your cousin.

Big government proponents refer to the "necessary and proper" clause to argue that Congress has far-reaching legislative powers, even if those are not specifically enumerated. By contrast, small government advocates emphasize that the Founders specifically listed the things that Congress was empowered to do, and intentionally limited Congress to just those items.

Now that we have gone through a basic overview of the legislative branch of government, let's take a look at the second of the three branches: the executive.

Article II: The Executive Branch

If you recall from our earlier discussion, the Federalists pressed the issue that at the core of the new government ought to be a strong chief executive. The Framers as a whole agreed, and so the very significant executive branch was described in Article II of the Constitution.

In order to qualify for the presidency, a person must be at least 35 years old, must have been a resident of the United States for at least 14 years, and must be a natural-born citizen (or a citizen at the time the Constitution was ratified).

Natural-Born Citizenship Requirement

If we compare the requirement that the president of the United States must be a natural-born citizen (except for those citizens at the time when the Constitution was ratified, which is no longer practically relevant, as there is no one still alive from 1787 to run), as opposed to the requirements for members of Congress, you see that there are two types of American citizens: those who are *natural born* (born in the United States, or with some exception, such as being born on a U.S. military base overseas), and *naturalized* (i.e., those who became citizens through the immigration process). Accordingly, whereas a Representative or a Senator may have been born in another country—Germany, Thailand, Zambia, or another—and later became an American citizen, that person would not qualify to be president.

Why do you suppose that such a requirement is placed on the president? Well, unlike members of Congress, of which there are many (535 to be exact), there is only one president. Accordingly, the Founders considered it very important that the president be a natural-born citizen so as not to have a conflict with one's native country. For instance, imagine someone born in Iraq who moved to the United States at age 24, became an American citizen, has lived here for 40 years, and now wants to run for president. That person would not qualify, as there might be a fear that he or she might have a soft spot for the country in which he or she was born and raised. In the case of

Iraq, a country with which the United States went to war in the late 20th and early 21st Centuries, the level of concern among the American people might be particularly high.

Of course, that reasoning is far from perfect. For instance, the person in question could be a patriotic American to the core, with absolutely no emotional ties to Iraq or to any country other than the "good ol' USA." Conversely, a natural-born American citizen who has lived in another country for several years, or who has a spouse or family members from that country, might have some deep-seated favoritism for that country and yet be eligible to become president.

A few years ago, there was talk about proposing a Constitutional amendment that would repeal that natural-born requirement. That incentive arose when Arnold Schwartzenegger, the popular movie star, became governor of California. Schwartzenegger, a U.S. citizen who was born in Austria, is not eligible to become president. Because of his easygoing manner and popular appeal, Schwartzenegger drew early acclaim from many who likened him to another actor-turned-politician who became governor of California and then went on to become president: Ronald Reagan. The comparisons to Reagan faded rather quickly, and the movement was squelched. Nonetheless, as we learned from the great historian, Thucydides, history tends to repeat itself. Therefore, it is very likely that at some point in the future, another foreign-born naturalized citizen will emerge with whom the American public will become so enchanted that they will take up the cause once again. As we will discover throughout this book, amendments to the Constitution usually have an interesting story behind them.

Presidential Term Limits

Unlike members of Congress, the president is elected to a four-year term and may only be *elected* to two terms of office. That was not always the case, however. Let us begin by examining the two ways by which a person can become president of the United States: by election, or by hierarchy. You see, the conventional way of becoming president is to win an election. However, a person who is Vice President of the United States may become president if the president dies or becomes incapacitated (i.e., is unable to carry out the duties office).

Our first eight presidents (*Note:* unless otherwise noted, we will now refer to "presidents" as those under the Constitution, beginning with George Washington—not John Hanson or any of the other fellows under the Articles of Confederation) served without having died or having been incapacitated. But our ninth president, William Henry Harrison, died just one month after taking office. The story is too interesting to ignore, so here is a brief version: Harrison was 68 years old when he was inaugurated, which made him the oldest president ever to take office not only at the time, but also until 1980, when Ronald Reagan broke the record by a year (Reagan was 69).

Not only was Harrison, in 1841, the oldest person to become president, but he was also the first to belong to the Whig Party. His political opponents, not happy about having a Whig in the White House, made an issue about his age. To defy his critics and display his vigor, Harrison delivered his inaugural address, a particularly long one and on a particularly cold day, outdoors without wearing an overcoat. Sadly, his bravado cost him his life, as he developed pneumonia and died a month later. His vice president, John Tyler, became president at that point.

All subsequent presidents, from James Polk to Herbert Hoover, served a maximum of two terms (some served a full two, some served less, but none served more) until 1932, when Franklin Roosevelt was elected to his first of *four* presidential terms. His last term began in 1945 and, as you can imagine, his supporters were thrilled and his critics were incensed, that Roosevelt had already been in office for 12 years and had just been elected to 4 more. However, health problems, no doubt worsened by the stress of having to manage the country through World War II, led to Roosevelt's death that April, at age 63 and only a few months into his fourth term.

Roosevelt's critics believed that four terms (16 years) is simply too much time for one person to occupy the highest office in the land. Accordingly, the Twenty-Second Amendment was ratified in 1951, which states that no person may be *elected* to more than two terms, and any person who has served *more than two years* of another president's term may only be elected to one term. For example, let's consider George H.W. Bush, our 41st president, who was elected in 1988 and lost to Bill Clinton in 1992 in a reelection bid. Bush was a one-term president who, if he ever wanted to come out of retirement, would be eligible to run for one additional term.

Next, let's consider Gerald Ford, who, as vice president became president when President Richard Nixon resigned in August 1974. Ford completed Nixon's term and was replaced on January 20, 1977, by Jimmy Carter, who defeated Ford in his reelection bid in 1976. Suppose that

Franklin Roosevelt was President longer than anyone else, having served for more than 12 years.

William Henry Harrison served the shortest time, a mere 32 days.

Ford was still alive and wanted to run for president again: for how many terms could he be elected?

A. None
B. One
C. Two
D. More than two

Answer D is obviously wrong, as we just discussed how the Twenty-Second Amendment prevents anyone from being elected to more than two terms. That leaves options A, B, or C (none, one, or two). Most people will dismiss answer A, because, they know that Ford was not *elected* to any terms. That means the correct answer is C, that he could have been elected to a full two terms, right? Wrong. Actually, the correct answer is B. Had Ford decided to run again, he could have been elected to just one more term. Why? Because Ford had served *more than two years* of Nixon's term, and was thereby restricted from running for two terms under the Twenty-Second Amendment.

Electors

As we discussed in Chapter One, the president is elected by electors and not directly by the people. Accordingly, when you cast your vote for president, you are really voting for an elector. Traditionally, electors then cast their votes for the person to whom they have pledged them.

Practically, if electors were to cast their votes for someone else, there would be such outrage that the Electoral College (as the body of electors is called) would be dismantled. Of course, in order for that to happen, a new Constitutional amendment would have to be created.

Presidential Powers

The president is the Commander in Chief of the armed forces and of the militia of the states *when called into the actual service of the United States*. With the approval of the Senate, the president may appoint ambassadors, Supreme Court Justices, and other officials. The president may be impeached and removed from office if convicted of treason, bribery, or other high crimes and misdemeanors.

Commander over the Entire Military

Technically, Article II of the Constitution authorizes the president as commander in chief over the *army and the navy*. Also technically, the other two branches of our military, the Air Force and the Marines, neither of which existed at the time of ratification, are subbranches of the Army and Navy, respectively. Accordingly, the president is in full command of the Air Force and the Marines, too. Nonetheless, if either or both of those were separate branches, then it would require an interpretation of Article II to determine that the Founders wrote *army and navy* because that was the full extent of the military, and they really meant the entire military. Of course, someone can make the argument that someone else other than the president should be in charge of the Air Force and the Marines. That argument, however, probably would not carry much weight. If it did, though, then it might require an amendment for clarification.

Hurricane Katrina and the National Guard

In 2005, New Orleans and other American cities along the Gulf Coast were struck by a particularly powerful hurricane, Katrina. President George W. Bush was heavily criticized for not calling on the National Guard to intervene earlier than he did. Whether or not President Bush reacted to the crisis in a timely manner is another issue altogether, but regarding the National Guard, it was up to the governor or Louisiana to respond to the crisis.

The National Guard, referred to as the *militia* in the Constitution, can only be called into service by the president when it involves a national matter. Hurricanes and other natural disasters do not fall into that category. In those cases, it is up to the governor(s) of the state(s) in question to call upon the National Guard, as its members are assigned to individual states. In the case of war, however, the president may in fact call the National Guard into action, as that constitutes being "in the service of the United States."

Impeachment

Impeachment is the process of charging certain elected officials (such as the president) with an offense for which, if convicted, could result in removal from office. To date, only two presidents have been impeached: Andrew Johnson and Bill Clinton. A third, Richard Nixon, resigned prior to being impeached, which was almost certain to occur. In fact,

Nixon's conviction was rather likely, too. Let's take a quick look at all three situations.

Andrew Johnson became president after Abraham Lincoln was assassinated. In addition to being one of the famous presidents of all time, Lincoln was also the first to be assassinated. Johnson, who was Lincoln's Vice President, did not belong to the same political party. Although Lincoln ran for president several decades after the Twelfth Amendment had provided that the president and vice president would be elected separately, thus prompting political parties to run tickets with presidential and vice presidential running mates, Republican Lincoln chose Democrat Johnson in 1864 (as Lincoln ran for reelection) in order to balance the ticket at the volatile time of the Civil War. It was an attempt to unify the bitterly divided nation.

In any event, after Johnson became president, he had a very difficult relationship with the predominantly Republican Congress. In 1868, Congress impeached Johnson for violating the Tenure of Office Act, a law that Congress had passed, which Johnson believed to have been unconstitutional. As the Constitution dictates, Johnson was impeached by the House of Representatives, which required a simple majority, and would stand trial in the Senate. The Senate trial is to be presided over by the Chief Justice of the Supreme Court, and, a two-thirds majority is needed to convict. Johnson escaped conviction by one vote. His presidency was weakened and he is perpetually remembered as one of our worst presidents. Ironically, however, the Supreme Court, several years later, declared that Congress had overstepped its bounds on the Tenure of Office Act, thus vindicating Johnson. Not much is made of that fact, however, which is another striking example of the power of public perception.

One of the biggest misconceptions about Clinton's impeachment is why he was impeached. Simply put, *he was not impeached because he had an affair with his intern, Monica Lewinsky*. Rather, he was impeached because he lied about that matter under oath. That is *perjury*, which is a crime, and, as such, sufficient grounds for impeachment. Granted, conventional wisdom suggests that there was a great deal of political motivation behind the impeachment. Nonetheless, Clinton was impeached for perjury, not for adultery. He was acquitted by a comfortable margin and, unlike Johnson, Clinton's presidency did not suffer a tremendous setback; he left office with particularly high approval ratings.

Nixon faced near-certain impeachment in 1974 for his involvement in the Watergate scandal. Watergate was named after the Watergate Hotel, where the Democratic National Committee's headquarters were situated, into whose offices some men linked to Nixon's White House were caught breaking and entering. Although Nixon was not suspected of orchestrating the break-in, it was strongly believed that he intentionally tried to cover up the evidence, which is an *obstruction of justice*, an impeachable offense. Rather than face impeachment and conviction, both of which were far more likely than not, Nixon became the first (and, to date, only) president to resign from office.

There had been some talk of impeaching President George W. Bush, but there was never any plausible case to be made. It was simply a matter of a president's political opponents being outraged over his policies and screaming "impeach!" That has been going on since John Adams was elected in 1796. In fact, even arguably our most beloved President (no, not Lincoln, who was actually despised by more people at the time of his presidency than any other president you can imagine, never mind that he is lauded as one of the all-time greats nowadays!), George Washington, was accused of "ruining our country," and by Thomas Jefferson no less!

Threats of impeachment have come and gone and probably will continue to do so with many presidencies. But only two presidents have been impeached and Nixon would have been an almost certain third.

Article III: The Judicial Branch

The third branch of government is the judicial branch, which enforces the laws, and which is vested in the U.S. Supreme Court, the highest court in the land.

The judges that sit on the high Court are called Justices. There are nine of them, appointed by the president but approved by the Senate, and they are appointed for life.

Much of our discussion in the forthcoming chapters deals with interpretations about the Constitution that the Justices have made over the years. As successful as the Founding Fathers were in creating a document that has lasted over two centuries and is still going strong, some of the language was so unclear that it has been interpreted in radically different ways during all this time. Many of the Supreme Court's critics contend that the entire process of appointment and confirmation of Justices is overly political, and they often tend to label any decision with which they disagree as illegitimate. Consider, for instance, two important cases: *Roe v. Wade*, which we will discuss in Chapter Six, and *Bush v. Gore*, which we already talked about in Chapter One. *Roe* was about a woman's right to have an abortion, and the *Bush* case determined the outcome of the 2000 presidential election. For every angry pro-life advocate who screams that *Roe* was the worst decision in American judicial history, there is a Bush-basher who proclaims that Bush lost the election and became president only because his cronies on the Supreme Court gave it to him.

Conclusion

The more you understand the Constitution, the more you can analyze its modern-day interpretations by the nine men and women wearing the black robes, and render a scholarly assessment of their determinations.

Throughout the book, we will continue to see how the issue of checks and balances unfolds, so that no one branch of government can become too powerful. We are now ready for our series of discussions on a number of controversial Constitutional issues, beginning in Chapter Four with religion.

Questions for Review

1. What are the two tiers of our government?
2. What are the three branches of our government?
3. What does the Tenth Amendment state?

4. What is the Supremacy Clause?
5. What are the requirements to be elected as a representative?
6. What are the requirements to be elected as a senator?
7. What are the requirements to be elected as president?
8. What is the difference between a natural-born citizen and a naturalized citizen?
9. What does the Twenty-Second Amendment state about presidential term limits?
10. What is the process by which a person becomes a Justice on the U.S. Supreme Court?

Constitutionally Speaking

Suppose that two politicians, Smith and Walters, would like to become president of the United States. Smith was born in the United States, but when he was 2 months old, his family moved to China. Smith grew up in China and became fully immersed in the Chinese language and customs. He lived in China until he was 48 years old, and has just celebrated the 15th anniversary of his return to the United States. Since returning to America, Smith became very interested in the American way of life, learned the English language very well, and decided to enter politics. Having been elected mayor of his town, and then to Congress from his district, he has now set his sights on the presidency.

Walters was born in France, but was legally adopted by an American couple and brought to the United States when he was 6 months old, where he has lived his entire life. He is now 60 years old. Walters majored in political science in college and went on to become a U.S. Senator, a position he has held for the past 12 years. He is now seeking the presidency as well.

Which of these politicians has the legal right to become president: Smith, Walters, both, or neither?

In your opinion, which of these politicians *should* have the legal right to become president: Smith, Walters, both, or neither?

Constitutional Cases

In looking at our system of checks and balances, whereby one branch of government does not become too powerful, the case of *Marbury v. Madison* established the power of the Supreme Court to review actions taken by the other two branches. Prior to *Marbury* is President George Washington's Farewell Address to the nation upon his retirement from public life in 1796. Note Washington's words of advice carefully, and think about how much of that advice is practiced today.

George Washington's Farewell Address

Friends and Citizens:

The period for a new election of a citizen to administer the executive government of the United States being not far distant, and the time actually arrived when your thoughts must be employed in designating the person who is to be clothed with that important trust, it appears to me proper, especially as it may conduce to a more distinct expression of the public voice, that I should now apprise you of the resolution I have formed, to decline being considered among the number of those out of whom a choice is to be made.

I beg you, at the same time, to do me the justice to be assured that this resolution has not been taken without a strict regard to all the considerations appertaining to the relation which binds a dutiful citizen to his country; and that in withdrawing the tender of service, which silence in my situation might imply, I am influenced by no diminution of zeal for your future interest, no deficiency of grateful respect for your past kindness, but am supported by a full conviction that the step is compatible with both.

The acceptance of, and continuance hitherto in, the office to which your suffrages have twice called me have been a uniform sacrifice of inclination to the opinion of duty and to a deference for what appeared to be your desire. I constantly hoped that it would have been much earlier in my power, consistently with motives which I was not at liberty to disregard, to return to that retirement from which I had been reluctantly drawn. The strength of my inclination to do this, previous to the last election, had even led to the preparation of an address to declare it to you; but mature reflection on the then perplexed and critical posture of our affairs with foreign nations, and the unanimous advice of persons entitled to my confidence, impelled me to abandon the idea.

I rejoice that the state of your concerns, external as well as internal, no longer renders the pursuit of inclination incompatible with the sentiment of duty or propriety, and am persuaded, whatever partiality may be retained for my services, that, in the present circumstances of our country, you will not disapprove my determination to retire.

The impressions with which I first undertook the arduous trust were explained on the proper occasion. In the discharge of this trust, I will only say that I have, with good intentions, contributed towards the organization and administration of the government the best exertions of which a very fallible judgment was capable. Not unconscious in the outset of the inferiority of my qualifications, experience in my own eyes, perhaps still more in the eyes of others, has strengthened the motives to diffidence of myself; and every day the increasing weight of years admonishes me more and more that the shade of retirement is as necessary to me as it will be welcome. Satisfied that if any circumstances have given peculiar value to my services, they were temporary, I have the consolation to believe that, while choice and prudence invite me to quit the political scene, patriotism does not forbid it.

In looking forward to the moment which is intended to terminate the career of my public life, my feelings do not permit me to suspend the deep acknowledgment of that debt of gratitude which I owe to my beloved country for the many honors it has conferred upon me; still more for the steadfast confidence with which it has supported me; and for the opportunities I have thence enjoyed of manifesting my inviolable attachment, by services faithful and persevering, though in usefulness unequal to my zeal. If benefits have resulted to our country from these services, let it always be remembered to your praise, and as an instructive example in our annals, that under circumstances in which the passions, agitated in every direction, were liable to mislead, amidst appearances sometimes dubious, vicissitudes of fortune often discouraging, in situations in which not unfrequently want of success has countenanced the spirit of criticism, the constancy of your support was the essential prop of the efforts, and a guarantee of the plans by which they were effected. Profoundly penetrated with this idea, I shall carry it with me to my grave, as a strong incitement to unceasing vows that heaven may continue to you the choicest tokens of its beneficence; that your union and brotherly affection may be perpetual; that the free Constitution, which is the work of your hands, may be sacredly maintained; that its administration in every department may be stamped with wisdom and virtue; that, in fine, the happiness of the people of these States, under the auspices of liberty, may be made complete by so careful a preservation and so prudent a use of this blessing as will acquire to them the glory of recommending it to the applause, the affection, and adoption of every nation which is yet a stranger to it.

Here, perhaps, I ought to stop. But a solicitude for your welfare, which cannot end but with my life, and the apprehension of danger, natural to that solicitude, urge me, on an occasion like the present, to offer to your solemn contemplation, and to recommend to your frequent review, some sentiments which are the result of much reflection, of no inconsiderable observation, and which appear to me all-important to the permanency of your felicity as a people. These will be offered to you with the more freedom, as you can only see in them the disinterested warnings of a parting friend, who can possibly have no personal motive to bias his counsel. Nor can I forget, as an encouragement to it, your indulgent reception of my sentiments on a former and not dissimilar occasion.

Interwoven as is the love of liberty with every ligament of your hearts, no recommendation of mine is necessary to fortify or confirm the attachment.

The unity of government which constitutes you one people is also now dear to you. It is justly so, for it is a main pillar in the edifice of your real independence, the support of your tranquility at home, your peace abroad; of your safety; of your prosperity; of that very liberty which you so highly prize. But as it is easy to foresee that, from different causes and from different quarters, much pains will be taken, many artifices employed to weaken in your minds the conviction of this truth; as this is the point in your political fortress against which the batteries of internal and external enemies will be most constantly and actively (though often covertly and insidiously) directed, it is of infinite moment that you should properly estimate the immense value of your national union to your collective and individual happiness; that you should cherish a cordial, habitual, and immovable attachment to it; accustoming yourselves to think and speak of it as of the palladium of your political safety and prosperity; watching for its preservation with jealous anxiety; discountenancing whatever may suggest even a suspicion that it can in any event be abandoned; and indignantly frowning upon the first dawning of every attempt to alienate any portion of our country from the rest, or to enfeeble the sacred ties which now link together the various parts.

For this you have every inducement of sympathy and interest. Citizens, by birth or choice, of a common country, that country has a right to concentrate your affections. The name of American, which belongs to you in your national capacity, must always exalt the just pride of patriotism more than any appellation derived from local discriminations. With slight shades of difference, you have the same religion, manners, habits, and political principles. You have in a common cause fought and triumphed together; the independence and liberty you possess are the work of joint counsels, and joint efforts of common dangers, sufferings, and successes.

But these considerations, however powerfully they address themselves to your sensibility, are greatly outweighed by those which apply more immediately to your interest. Here every portion of our country finds the most commanding motives for carefully guarding and preserving the union of the whole.

(Continues)

The North, in an unrestrained intercourse with the South, protected by the equal laws of a common government, finds in the productions of the latter great additional resources of maritime and commercial enterprise and precious materials of manufacturing industry. The South, in the same intercourse, benefiting by the agency of the North, sees its agriculture grow and its commerce expand. Turning partly into its own channels the seamen of the North, it finds its particular navigation invigorated; and, while it contributes, in different ways, to nourish and increase the general mass of the national navigation, it looks forward to the protection of a maritime strength, to which itself is unequally adapted. The East, in a like intercourse with the West, already finds, and in the progressive improvement of interior communications by land and water, will more and more find a valuable vent for the commodities which it brings from abroad, or manufactures at home. The West derives from the East supplies requisite to its growth and comfort, and, what is perhaps of still greater consequence, it must of necessity owe the secure enjoyment of indispensable outlets for its own productions to the weight, influence, and the future maritime strength of the Atlantic side of the Union, directed by an indissoluble community of interest as one nation. Any other tenure by which the West can hold this essential advantage, whether derived from its own separate strength, or from an apostate and unnatural connection with any foreign power, must be intrinsically precarious.

While, then, every part of our country thus feels an immediate and particular interest in union, all the parts combined cannot fail to find in the united mass of means and efforts greater strength, greater resource, proportionably greater security from external danger, a less frequent interruption of their peace by foreign nations; and, what is of inestimable value, they must derive from union an exemption from those broils and wars between themselves, which so frequently afflict neighboring countries not tied together by the same governments, which their own rival ships alone would be sufficient to produce, but which opposite foreign alliances, attachments, and intrigues would stimulate and embitter. Hence, likewise, they will avoid the necessity of those overgrown military establishments which, under any form of government, are inauspicious to liberty, and which are to be regarded as particularly hostile to republican liberty. In this sense it is that your union ought to be considered as a main prop of your liberty, and that the love of the one ought to endear to you the preservation of the other.

These considerations speak a persuasive language to every reflecting and virtuous mind, and exhibit the continuance of the Union as a primary object of patriotic desire. Is there a doubt whether a common government can embrace so large a sphere? Let experience solve it. To listen to mere speculation in such a case were criminal. We are authorized to hope that a proper organization of the whole with the auxiliary agency of governments for the respective subdivisions, will afford a happy issue to the experiment. It is well worth a fair and full experiment. With such powerful and obvious motives to union, affecting all parts of our country, while experience shall not have demonstrated its impracticability, there will always be reason to distrust the patriotism of those who in any quarter may endeavor to weaken its bands.

In contemplating the causes which may disturb our Union, it occurs as matter of serious concern that any ground should have been furnished for characterizing parties by geographical discriminations, Northern and Southern, Atlantic and Western; whence designing men may endeavor to excite a belief that there is a real difference of local interests and views. One of the expedients of party to acquire influence within particular districts is to misrepresent the opinions and aims of other districts. You cannot shield yourselves too much against the jealousies and heartburnings which spring from these misrepresentations; they tend to render alien to each other those who ought to be bound together by fraternal affection. The inhabitants of our Western country have lately had a useful lesson on this head; they have seen, in the negotiation by the Executive, and in the unanimous ratification by the Senate, of the treaty with Spain, and in the universal satisfaction at that event, throughout the United States, a decisive proof how unfounded were the suspicions propagated among them of a policy in the General Government and in the Atlantic States unfriendly to their interests in regard to the Mississippi; they have been witnesses to the formation of two treaties, that with Great Britain, and that with Spain, which secure to them everything they could desire, in respect to our foreign relations, towards confirming their prosperity. Will it not be their wisdom to rely for the preservation of these advantages on the Union by which they were procured? Will they not henceforth be deaf to those advisers, if such there are, who would sever them from their brethren and connect them with aliens?

To the efficacy and permanency of your Union, a government for the whole is indispensable. No alliance, however strict, between the parts can be an adequate substitute; they must inevitably experience the infractions and interruptions which all alliances in all times have experienced. Sensible of this momentous truth, you have improved upon your first essay, by the adoption of a constitution of government better calculated than your former for an intimate union, and for the efficacious management of your common concerns. This government, the offspring of our own choice, uninfluenced and unawed, adopted upon full investigation and mature deliberation, completely free in its principles, in the distribution of its powers, uniting security with energy, and containing within itself a provision for its own amendment, has a just claim to your confidence and your support. Respect for its authority, compliance with its laws, acquiescence in its measures, are duties enjoined by the fundamental maxims of true liberty. The basis of our political systems is the right of the people to make and to alter their constitutions of government. But the **Constitution** which at any time exists, till changed by an explicit and authentic act of the whole people, is sacredly obligatory upon all. The very idea of the power and the right of the people to establish government presupposes the duty of every individual to obey the established government.

All obstructions to the execution of the laws, all combinations and associations, under whatever plausible character, with the real design to direct, control, counteract, or awe the regular deliberation and action of the constituted authorities, are destructive of this fundamental principle, and of fatal tendency. They serve to organize faction, to give it an artificial and extraordinary force; to put, in the place of the delegated will of the nation the will of a party, often a small but artful and enterprising minority of the community; and, according to the alternate triumphs of different parties, to make the public administration the mirror of the ill-concerted and incongruous projects of faction, rather than the organ of consistent and wholesome plans digested by common counsels and modified by mutual interests.

However combinations or associations of the above description may now and then answer popular ends, they are likely, in the course of time and things, to become potent engines, by which cunning, ambitious, and unprincipled men will be enabled to subvert the power of the people and to usurp for themselves the reins of government, destroying afterwards the very engines which have lifted them to unjust dominion.

Towards the preservation of your government, and the permanency of your present happy state, it is requisite, not only that you steadily discountenance irregular oppositions to its acknowledged authority, but also that you resist with care the spirit of innovation upon its principles, however specious the pretexts. One method of assault may be to effect, in the forms of the **Constitution**, alterations which will impair the energy of the system, and thus to undermine what cannot be directly overthrown. In all the changes to which you may be invited, remember that time and habit are at least as necessary to fix the true character of governments as of other human institutions; that experience is the surest standard by which to test the real tendency of the existing constitution of a country; that facility in changes, upon the credit of mere hypothesis and opinion, exposes to perpetual change, from the endless variety of hypothesis and opinion; and remember, especially, that for the efficient management of your common interests, in a country so extensive as ours, a government of as much vigor as is consistent with the perfect security of liberty is indispensable. Liberty itself will find in such a government, with powers properly distributed and adjusted, its surest guardian. It is, indeed, little else than a name, where the government is too feeble to withstand the enterprises of faction, to confine each member of the society within the limits prescribed by the laws, and to maintain all in the secure and tranquil enjoyment of the rights of person and property.

I have already intimated to you the danger of parties in the State, with particular reference to the founding of them on geographical discriminations. Let me now take a more comprehensive view, and warn you in the most solemn manner against the baneful effects of the spirit of party generally.

This spirit, unfortunately, is inseparable from our nature, having its root in the strongest passions of the human mind. It exists under different shapes in all governments, more or less stifled, controlled, or repressed; but, in those of the popular form, it is seen in its greatest rankness, and is truly their worst enemy.

The alternate domination of one faction over another, sharpened by the spirit of revenge, natural to party dissension, which in different ages and countries has perpetrated the most horrid enormities, is itself a frightful despotism. But this leads at length to a more formal and permanent despotism. The disorders and miseries which result gradually incline the minds of men to seek security and repose in the absolute power of an individual; and sooner or later the chief of some prevailing faction, more able or more fortunate than his competitors, turns this disposition to the purposes of his own elevation, on the ruins of public liberty.

Without looking forward to an extremity of this kind (which nevertheless ought not to be entirely out of sight), the common and continual mischiefs of the spirit of party are sufficient to make it the interest and duty of a wise people to discourage and restrain it.

(Continues)

It serves always to distract the public councils and enfeeble the public administration. It agitates the community with ill-founded jealousies and false alarms, kindles the animosity of one part against another, foments occasionally riot and insurrection. It opens the door to foreign influence and corruption, which finds a facilitated access to the government itself through the channels of party passions. Thus the policy and the will of one country are subjected to the policy and will of another.

There is an opinion that parties in free countries are useful checks upon the administration of the government and serve to keep alive the spirit of liberty. This within certain limits is probably true; and in governments of a monarchical cast, patriotism may look with indulgence, if not with favor, upon the spirit of party. But in those of the popular character, in governments purely elective, it is a spirit not to be encouraged. From their natural tendency, it is certain there will always be enough of that spirit for every salutary purpose. And there being constant danger of excess, the effort ought to be by force of public opinion, to mitigate and assuage it. A fire not to be quenched, it demands a uniform vigilance to prevent its bursting into a flame, lest, instead of warming, it should consume.

It is important, likewise, that the habits of thinking in a free country should inspire caution in those entrusted with its administration, to confine themselves within their respective constitutional spheres, avoiding in the exercise of the powers of one department to encroach upon another. The spirit of encroachment tends to consolidate the powers of all the departments in one, and thus to create, whatever the form of government, a real despotism. A just estimate of that love of power, and proneness to abuse it, which predominates in the human heart, is sufficient to satisfy us of the truth of this position. The necessity of reciprocal checks in the exercise of political power, by dividing and distributing it into different depositaries, and constituting each the guardian of the public weal against invasions by the others, has been evinced by experiments ancient and modern; some of them in our country and under our own eyes. To preserve them must be as necessary as to institute them. If, in the opinion of the people, the distribution or modification of the constitutional powers be in any particular wrong, let it be corrected by an amendment in the way which the **Constitution** designates. But let there be no change by usurpation; for though this, in one instance, may be the instrument of good, it is the customary weapon by which free governments are destroyed. The precedent must always greatly overbalance in permanent evil any partial or transient benefit, which the use can at any time yield.

Of all the dispositions and habits which lead to political prosperity, religion and morality are indispensable supports. In vain would that man claim the tribute of patriotism, who should labor to subvert these great pillars of human happiness, these firmest props of the duties of men and citizens. The mere politician, equally with the pious man, ought to respect and to cherish them. A volume could not trace all their connections with private and public felicity. Let it simply be asked: Where is the security for property, for reputation, for life, if the sense of religious obligation desert the oaths which are the instruments of investigation in courts of justice? And let us with caution indulge the supposition that morality can be maintained without religion. Whatever may be conceded to the influence of refined education on minds of peculiar structure, reason and experience both forbid us to expect that national morality can prevail in exclusion of religious principle.

It is substantially true that virtue or morality is a necessary spring of popular government. The rule, indeed, extends with more or less force to every species of free government. Who that is a sincere friend to it can look with indifference upon attempts to shake the foundation of the fabric?

Promote then, as an object of primary importance, institutions for the general diffusion of knowledge. In proportion as the structure of a government gives force to public opinion, it is essential that public opinion should be enlightened.

As a very important source of strength and security, cherish public credit. One method of preserving it is to use it as sparingly as possible, avoiding occasions of expense by cultivating peace, but remembering also that timely disbursements to prepare for danger frequently prevent much greater disbursements to repel it, avoiding likewise the accumulation of debt, not only by shunning occasions of expense, but by vigorous exertion in time of peace to discharge the debts which unavoidable wars may have occasioned, not ungenerously throwing upon posterity the burden which we ourselves ought to bear. The execution of these maxims belongs to your representatives, but it is necessary that public opinion should co-operate. To facilitate to them the performance of their duty, it is essential that you should practically bear in mind that towards the payment of debts there must be revenue; that to have revenue there must be taxes; that no taxes can be devised which are not more or less inconvenient and unpleasant; that the intrinsic embarrassment, inseparable from the selection of the proper objects (which is always a choice of difficulties), ought to be a decisive motive for a candid construction of the conduct of the government in making it, and for a spirit of acquiescence in the measures for obtaining revenue, which the public exigencies may at any time dictate.

Observe good faith and justice towards all nations; cultivate peace and harmony with all. Religion and morality enjoin this conduct; and can it be, that good policy does not equally enjoin it. It will be worthy of a free, enlightened, and at no distant period, a great nation, to give to mankind the magnanimous and too novel example of a people always guided by an exalted justice and benevolence. Who can doubt that, in the course of time and things, the fruits of such a plan would richly repay any temporary advantages which might be lost by a steady adherence to it? Can it be that Providence has not connected the permanent felicity of a nation with its virtue? The experiment, at least, is recommended by every sentiment which ennobles human nature. Alas! Is it rendered impossible by its vices?

In the execution of such a plan, nothing is more essential than that permanent, inveterate antipathies against particular nations, and passionate attachments for others, should be excluded; and that, in place of them, just and amicable feelings towards all should be cultivated. The nation which indulges towards another a habitual hatred or a habitual fondness is in some degree a slave. It is a slave to its animosity or to its affection, either of which is sufficient to lead it astray from its duty and its interest. Antipathy in one nation against another disposes each more readily to offer insult and injury, to lay hold of slight causes of umbrage, and to be haughty and intractable, when accidental or trifling occasions of dispute occur. Hence, frequent collisions, obstinate, envenomed, and bloody contests. The nation, prompted by ill-will and resentment, sometimes impels to war the government, contrary to the best calculations of policy. The government sometimes participates in the national propensity, and adopts through passion what reason would reject; at other times it makes the animosity of the nation subservient to projects of hostility instigated by pride, ambition, and other sinister and pernicious motives. The peace often, sometimes perhaps the liberty, of nations, has been the victim.

So likewise, a passionate attachment of one nation for another produces a variety of evils. Sympathy for the favorite nation, facilitating the illusion of an imaginary common interest in cases where no real common interest exists, and infusing into one the enmities of the other, betrays the former into a participation in the quarrels and wars of the latter without adequate inducement or justification. It leads also to concessions to the favorite nation of privileges denied to others which is apt doubly to injure the nation making the concessions; by unnecessarily parting with what ought to have been retained, and by exciting jealousy, ill-will, and a disposition to retaliate, in the parties from whom equal privileges are withheld. And it gives to ambitious, corrupted, or deluded citizens (who devote themselves to the favorite nation), facility to betray or sacrifice the interests of their own country, without odium, sometimes even with popularity; gilding, with the appearances of a virtuous sense of obligation, a commendable deference for public opinion, or a laudable zeal for public good, the base or foolish compliances of ambition, corruption, or infatuation.

As avenues to foreign influence in innumerable ways, such attachments are particularly alarming to the truly enlightened and independent patriot. How many opportunities do they afford to tamper with domestic factions, to practice the arts of seduction, to mislead public opinion, to influence or awe the public councils? Such an attachment of a small or weak towards a great and powerful nation dooms the former to be the satellite of the latter.

Against the insidious wiles of foreign influence (I conjure you to believe me, fellow-citizens) the jealousy of a free people ought to be constantly awake, since history and experience prove that foreign influence is one of the most baneful foes of republican government. But that jealousy to be useful must be impartial; else it becomes the instrument of the very influence to be avoided, instead of a defense against it. Excessive partiality for one foreign nation and excessive dislike of another cause those whom they actuate to see danger only on one side, and serve to veil and even second the arts of influence on the other. Real patriots who may resist the intrigues of the favorite are liable to become suspected and odious, while its tools and dupes usurp the applause and confidence of the people, to surrender their interests.

The great rule of conduct for us in regard to foreign nations is in extending our commercial relations, to have with them as little political connection as possible. So far as we have already formed engagements, let them be fulfilled with perfect good faith. Here let us stop. Europe has a set of primary interests which to us have none; or a very remote relation. Hence she must be engaged in frequent controversies, the causes of which are essentially foreign to our concerns. Hence, therefore, it must be unwise in us to implicate ourselves by artificial ties in the ordinary vicissitudes of her politics, or the ordinary combinations and collisions of her friendships or enmities.

(Continues)

(*Continued*)

Our detached and distant situation invites and enables us to pursue a different course. If we remain one people under an efficient government. the period is not far off when we may defy material injury from external annoyance; when we may take such an attitude as will cause the neutrality we may at any time resolve upon to be scrupulously respected; when belligerent nations, under the impossibility of making acquisitions upon us, will not lightly hazard the giving us provocation; when we may choose peace or war, as our interest, guided by justice, shall counsel.

Why forego the advantages of so peculiar a situation? Why quit our own to stand upon foreign ground? Why, by interweaving our destiny with that of any part of Europe, entangle our peace and prosperity in the toils of European ambition, rivalship, interest, humor or caprice?

It is our true policy to steer clear of permanent alliances with any portion of the foreign world; so far, I mean, as we are now at liberty to do it; for let me not be understood as capable of patronizing infidelity to existing engagements. I hold the maxim no less applicable to public than to private affairs, that honesty is always the best policy. I repeat it, therefore, let those engagements be observed in their genuine sense. But, in my opinion, it is unnecessary and would be unwise to extend them.

Taking care always to keep ourselves by suitable establishments on a respectable defensive posture, we may safely trust to temporary alliances for extraordinary emergencies.

Harmony, liberal intercourse with all nations, are recommended by policy, humanity, and interest. But even our commercial policy should hold an equal and impartial hand; neither seeking nor granting exclusive favors or preferences; consulting the natural course of things; diffusing and diversifying by gentle means the streams of commerce, but forcing nothing; establishing (with powers so disposed, in order to give trade a stable course, to define the rights of our merchants, and to enable the government to support them) conventional rules of intercourse, the best that present circumstances and mutual opinion will permit, but temporary, and liable to be from time to time abandoned or varied, as experience and circumstances shall dictate; constantly keeping in view that it is folly in one nation to look for disinterested favors from another; that it must pay with a portion of its independence for whatever it may accept under that character; that, by such acceptance, it may place itself in the condition of having given equivalents for nominal favors, and yet of being reproached with ingratitude for not giving more. There can be no greater error than to expect or calculate upon real favors from nation to nation. It is an illusion, which experience must cure, which a just pride ought to discard.

In offering to you, my countrymen, these counsels of an old and affectionate friend, I dare not hope they will make the strong and lasting impression I could wish; that they will control the usual current of the passions, or prevent our nation from running the course which has hitherto marked the destiny of nations. But, if I may even flatter myself that they may be productive of some partial benefit, some occasional good; that they may now and then recur to moderate the fury of party spirit, to warn against the mischiefs of foreign intrigue, to guard against the impostures of pretended patriotism; this hope will be a full recompense for the solicitude for your welfare, by which they have been dictated.

How far in the discharge of my official duties I have been guided by the principles which have been delineated, the public records and other evidences of my conduct must witness to you and to the world. To myself, the assurance of my own conscience is, that I have at least believed myself to be guided by them.

In relation to the still subsisting war in Europe, my proclamation of the twenty-second of April, 1793, is the index of my plan. Sanctioned by your approving voice, and by that of your representatives in both houses of Congress, the spirit of that measure has continually governed me, uninfluenced by any attempts to deter or divert me from it.

After deliberate examination, with the aid of the best lights I could obtain, I was well satisfied that our country, under all the circumstances of the case, had a right to take, and was bound in duty and interest to take, a neutral position. Having taken it, I determined, as far as should depend upon me, to maintain it, with moderation, perseverance, and firmness.

The considerations which respect the right to hold this con duct, it is not necessary on this occasion to detail. I will only observe that, according to my understanding of the matter, that right, so far from being denied by any of the belligerent powers, has been virtually admitted by all.

The duty of holding a neutral conduct may be inferred, without anything more, from the obligation which justice and humanity impose on every nation, in cases in which it is free to act, to maintain inviolate the relations of peace and amity towards other nations.

The inducements of interest for observing that conduct will best be referred to your own reflections and experience. With me a predominant motive has been to endeavor to gain time to our country to settle and mature its yet recent institutions, and to progress without interruption to that degree of strength and consistency which is necessary to give it, humanly speaking, the command of its own fortunes.

Though, in reviewing the incidents of my administration, I am unconscious of intentional error, I am nevertheless too sensible of my defects not to think it probable that I may have committed many errors. Whatever they may be, I fervently beseech the Almighty to avert or mitigate the evils to which they may tend. I shall also carry with me the hope that my country will never cease to view them with indulgence; and that, after forty five years of my life dedicated to its service with an upright zeal, the faults of incompetent abilities will be consigned to oblivion, as myself must soon be to the mansions of rest.

Relying on its kindness in this as in other things, and actuated by that fervent love towards it, which is so natural to a man who views in it the native soil of himself and his progenitors for several generations, I anticipate with pleasing expectation that retreat in which I promise myself to realize, without alloy, the sweet enjoyment of partaking, in the midst of my fellow-citizens, the benign influence of good laws under a free government, the ever-favorite object of my heart, and the happy reward, as I trust, of our mutual cares, labors, and dangers.

Geo. Washington

Marbury v. Madison, 5 U.S. 137 (1803)

Mr. Chief Justice MARSHALL delivered the opinion of the Court.

At the last term, on the affidavits then read and filed with the clerk, a rule was granted in this case requiring the Secretary of State to show cause why a mandamus [p154] should not issue directing him to deliver to William Marbury his commission as a justice of the peace for the county of Washington, in the District of Columbia.

No cause has been shown, and the present motion is for a mandamus. The peculiar delicacy of this case, the novelty of some of its circumstances, and the real difficulty attending the points which occur in it require a complete exposition of the principles on which the opinion to be given by the Court is founded.

These principles have been, on the side of the applicant, very ably argued at the bar. In rendering the opinion of the Court, there will be some departure in form, though not in substance, from the points stated in that argument.

In the order in which the Court has viewed this subject, the following questions have been considered and decided.

1. Has the applicant a right to the commission he demands?
2. If he has a right, and that right has been violated, do the laws of his country afford him a remedy?
3. If they do afford him a remedy, is it a mandamus issuing from this court?

The first object of inquiry is:

1. Has the applicant a right to the commission he demands?

His right originates in an act of Congress passed in February, 1801, concerning the District of Columbia.

After dividing the district into two counties, the eleventh section of this law enacts,

that there shall be appointed in and for each of the said counties such number of discreet persons to be justices of the peace as the President of the United States shall, from time to time, think expedient, to continue in office for five years. [p155]

It appears from the affidavits that, in compliance with this law, a commission for William Marbury as a justice of peace for the County of Washington was signed by John Adams, then President of the United States, after which the seal of the United States was affixed to it, but the commission has never reached the person for whom it was made out.

In order to determine whether he is entitled to this commission, it becomes necessary to inquire whether he has been appointed to the office. For if he has been appointed, the law continues him in

(Continues)

office for five years, and he is entitled to the possession of those evidences of office, which, being completed, became his property.

The second section of the second article of the Constitution declares,

> The President shall nominate, and, by and with the advice and consent of the Senate, shall appoint ambassadors, other public ministers and consuls, and all other officers of the United States, whose appointments are not otherwise provided for.

The third section declares, that "He shall commission all the officers of the United States."

An act of Congress directs the Secretary of State to keep the seal of the United States,

> to make out and record, and affix the said seal to all civil commissions to officers of the United States to be appointed by the President, by and with the consent of the Senate, or by the President alone; provided that the said seal shall not be affixed to any commission before the same shall have been signed by the President of the United States.

These are the clauses of the Constitution and laws of the United States which affect this part of the case. They seem to contemplate three distinct operations:

1. The nomination. This is the sole act of the President, and is completely voluntary.
2. The appointment. This is also the act of the President, and is also a voluntary act, though it can only be performed by and with the advice and consent of the Senate. [p156]
3. The commission. To grant a commission to a person appointed might perhaps be deemed a duty enjoined by the Constitution. "He shall," says that instrument, "commission all the officers of the United States."

The acts of appointing to office and commissioning the person appointed can scarcely be considered as one and the same, since the power to perform them is given in two separate and distinct sections of the Constitution. The distinction between the appointment and the commission will be rendered more apparent by adverting to that provision in the second section of the second article of the Constitution which authorises Congress

> to vest by law the appointment of such inferior officers as they think proper in the President alone, in the Courts of law, or in the heads of departments;

thus contemplating cases where the law may direct the President to commission an officer appointed by the Courts or by the heads of departments. In such a case, to issue a commission would be apparently a duty distinct from the appointment, the performance of which perhaps could not legally be refused.

Although that clause of the Constitution which requires the President to commission all the officers of the United States may never have been applied to officers appointed otherwise than by himself, yet it would be difficult to deny the legislative power to apply it to such cases. Of consequence, the constitutional distinction between the appointment to an office and the commission of an officer who has been appointed remains the same as if in practice the President had commissioned officers appointed by an authority other than his own.

It follows too from the existence of this distinction that, if an appointment was to be evidenced by any public act other than the commission, the performance of such public act would create the officer, and if he was not removable at the will of the President, would either give him a right to his commission or enable him to perform the duties without it.

These observations are premised solely for the purpose of rendering more intelligible those which apply more directly to the particular case under consideration. [p157]

This is an appointment made by the President, by and with the advice and consent of the Senate, and is evidenced by no act but the commission itself. In such a case, therefore, the commission and the appointment seem inseparable, it being almost impossible to show an appointment otherwise than by proving the existence of a commission; still, the commission is not necessarily the appointment; though conclusive evidence of it.

But at what stage does it amount to this conclusive evidence?

The answer to this question seems an obvious one. The appointment, being the sole act of the President, must be completely evidenced when it is shown that he has done everything to be performed by him.

Should the commission, instead of being evidence of an appointment, even be considered as constituting the appointment itself, still it would be made when the last act to be done by the President was performed, or, at furthest, when the commission was complete.

The last act to be done by the President is the signature of the commission. He has then acted on the advice and consent of the Senate to his own nomination. The time for deliberation has then passed. He has decided. His judgment, on the advice and consent of the Senate concurring with his nomination, has been made, and the officer is appointed. This appointment is evidenced by an open, unequivocal act, and, being the last act required from the person making it, necessarily excludes the idea of its being, so far as it respects the appointment, an inchoate and incomplete transaction.

Some point of time must be taken when the power of the Executive over an officer, not removable at his will, must cease. That point of time must be when the constitutional power of appointment has been exercised. And this power has been exercised when the last act required from the person possessing the power has been performed. This last act is the signature of the commission. This idea seems to have prevailed with the Legislature when the act passed converting the Department [p158] of Foreign Affairs into the Department of State. By that act, it is enacted that the Secretary of State shall keep the seal of the United States,

and shall make out and record, and shall affix the said seal to all civil commissions to officers of the United States, to be appointed by the President: . . . provided that the said seal shall not be affixed to any commission before the same shall have been signed by the President of the United States, nor to any other instrument or act without the special warrant of the President therefore.

The signature is a warrant for affixing the great seal to the commission, and the great seal is only to be affixed to an instrument which is complete. It attests, by an act supposed to be of public notoriety, the verity of the Presidential signature.

It is never to be affixed till the commission is signed, because the signature, which gives force and effect to the commission, is conclusive evidence that the appointment is made.

The commission being signed, the subsequent duty of the Secretary of State is prescribed by law, and not to be guided by the will of the President. He is to affix the seal of the United States to the commission, and is to record it.

This is not a proceeding which may be varied if the judgment of the Executive shall suggest one more eligible, but is a precise course accurately marked out by law, and is to be strictly pursued. It is the duty of the Secretary of State to conform to the law, and in this he is an officer of the United States, bound to obey the laws. He acts, in this respect, as has been very properly stated at the bar, under the authority of law, and not by the instructions of the President. It is a ministerial act which the law enjoins on a particular officer for a particular purpose.

If it should be supposed that the solemnity of affixing the seal is necessary not only to the validity of the commission, but even to the completion of an appointment, still, when the seal is affixed, the appointment is made, and [p159] the commission is valid. No other solemnity is required by law; no other act is to be performed on the part of government. All that the Executive can do to invest the person with his office is done, and unless the appointment be then made, the Executive cannot make one without the cooperation of others.

After searching anxiously for the principles on which a contrary opinion may be supported, none has been found which appear of sufficient force to maintain the opposite doctrine.

Such as the imagination of the Court could suggest have been very deliberately examined, and after allowing them all the weight which it appears possible to give them, they do not shake the opinion which has been formed.

In considering this question, it has been conjectured that the commission may have been assimilated to a deed to the validity of which delivery is essential.

This idea is founded on the supposition that the commission is not merely evidence of an appointment, but is itself the actual appointment—a supposition by no means unquestionable. But, for the purpose of examining this objection fairly, let it be conceded that the principle claimed for its support is established.

The appointment being, under the Constitution, to be made by the President personally, the delivery of the deed of appointment, if necessary to its completion, must be made by the President also. It is not necessary that the livery should be made personally to the grantee of the office; it never is so made. The law

(Continues)

(*Continued*)

would seem to contemplate that it should be made to the Secretary of State, since it directs the secretary to affix the seal to the commission after it shall have been signed by the President. If then the act of livery be necessary to give validity to the commission, it has been delivered when executed and given to the Secretary for the purpose of being sealed, recorded, and transmitted to the party.

But in all cases of letters patent, certain solemnities are required by law, which solemnities are the evidences [p160] of the validity of the instrument. A formal delivery to the person is not among them. In cases of commissions, the sign manual of the President and the seal of the United States are those solemnities. This objection therefore does not touch the case.

It has also occurred as possible, and barely possible, that the transmission of the commission and the acceptance thereof might be deemed necessary to complete the right of the plaintiff.

The transmission of the commission is a practice directed by convenience, but not by law. It cannot therefore be necessary to constitute the appointment, which must precede it and which is the mere act of the President. If the Executive required that every person appointed to an office should himself take means to procure his commission, the appointment would not be the less valid on that account. The appointment is the sole act of the President; the transmission of the commission is the sole act of the officer to whom that duty is assigned, and may be accelerated or retarded by circumstances which can have no influence on the appointment. A commission is transmitted to a person already appointed, not to a person to be appointed or not, as the letter enclosing the commission should happen to get into the post office and reach him in safety, or to miscarry.

It may have some tendency to elucidate this point to inquire whether the possession of the original commission be indispensably necessary to authorize a person appointed to any office to perform the duties of that office. If it was necessary, then a loss of the commission would lose the office. Not only negligence, but accident or fraud, fire or theft might deprive an individual of his office. In such a case, I presume it could not be doubted but that a copy from the record of the Office of the Secretary of State would be, to every intent and purpose, equal to the original. The act of Congress has expressly made it so. To give that copy validity, it would not be necessary to prove that the original had been transmitted and afterwards lost. The copy would be complete evidence that the original had existed, and that the appointment had been made, but not that the original had been transmitted. If indeed it should appear that [p161] the original had been mislaid in the Office of State, that circumstance would not affect the operation of the copy. When all the requisites have been performed which authorize a recording officer to record any instrument whatever, and the order for that purpose has been given, the instrument is in law considered as recorded, although the manual labour of inserting it in a book kept for that purpose may not have been performed.

In the case of commissions, the law orders the Secretary of State to record them. When, therefore, they are signed and sealed, the order for their being recorded is given, and, whether inserted in the book or not, they are in law recorded.

A copy of this record is declared equal to the original, and the fees to be paid by a person requiring a copy are ascertained by law. Can a keeper of a public record erase therefrom a commission which has been recorded? Or can he refuse a copy thereof to a person demanding it on the terms prescribed by law?

Such a copy would, equally with the original, authorize the justice of peace to proceed in the performance of his duty, because it would, equally with the original, attest his appointment.

If the transmission of a commission be not considered as necessary to give validity to an appointment, still less is its acceptance. The appointment is the sole act of the President; the acceptance is the sole act of the officer, and is, in plain common sense, posterior to the appointment. As he may resign, so may he refuse to accept; but neither the one nor the other is capable of rendering the appointment a nonentity.

That this is the understanding of the government is apparent from the whole tenor of its conduct.

A commission bears date, and the salary of the officer commences from his appointment, not from the transmission or acceptance of his commission. When a person appointed to any office refuses to accept that office, the successor is nominated in the place of the person who [p162] has declined to accept, and not in the place of the person who had been previously in office and had created the original vacancy.

It is therefore decidedly the opinion of the Court that, when a commission has been signed by the President, the appointment is made, and that the commission is complete when the seal of the United States has been affixed to it by the Secretary of State.

Where an officer is removable at the will of the Executive, the circumstance which completes his appointment is of no concern, because the act is at any time revocable, and the commission may be arrested if still in the office. But when the officer is not removable at the will of the Executive, the appointment is not revocable, and cannot be annulled. It has conferred legal rights which cannot be resumed.

The discretion of the Executive is to be exercised until the appointment has been made. But having once made the appointment, his power over the office is terminated in all cases, where by law the officer is not removable by him. The right to the office is then in the person appointed, and he has the absolute, unconditional power of accepting or rejecting it.

Mr. Marbury, then, since his commission was signed by the President and sealed by the Secretary of State, was appointed, and as the law creating the office gave the officer a right to hold for five years independent of the Executive, the appointment was not revocable, but vested in the officer legal rights which are protected by the laws of his country.

To withhold the commission, therefore, is an act deemed by the Court not warranted by law, but violative of a vested legal right.

This brings us to the second inquiry, which is:

2. If he has a right, and that right has been violated, do the laws of his country afford him a remedy? [p163]

The very essence of civil liberty certainly consists in the right of every individual to claim the protection of the laws whenever he receives an injury. One of the first duties of government is to afford that protection. In Great Britain, the King himself is sued in the respectful form of a petition, and he never fails to comply with the judgment of his court.

In the third volume of his Commentaries, page 23, Blackstone states two cases in which a remedy is afforded by mere operation of law.

"In all other cases," he says,

it is a general and indisputable rule that where there is a legal right, there is also a legal remedy by suit or action at law whenever that right is invaded.

And afterwards, page 109 of the same volume, he says,

I am next to consider such injuries as are cognizable by the Courts of common law. And herein I shall for the present only remark that all possible injuries whatsoever that did not fall within the exclusive cognizance of either the ecclesiastical, military, or maritime tribunals are, for that very reason, within the cognizance of the common law courts of justice, for it is a settled and invariable principle in the laws of England that every right, when withheld, must have a remedy, and every injury its proper redress.

The Government of the United States has been emphatically termed a government of laws, and not of men. It will certainly cease to deserve this high appellation if the laws furnish no remedy for the violation of a vested legal right.

If this obloquy is to be cast on the jurisprudence of our country, it must arise from the peculiar character of the case.

It behooves us, then, to inquire whether there be in its composition any ingredient which shall exempt from legal investigation or exclude the injured party from legal redress. In pursuing this inquiry, the first question which presents itself is whether this can be arranged [p164] with that class of cases which come under the description of *damnum absque injuria*—a loss without an injury.

This description of cases never has been considered, and, it is believed, never can be considered, as comprehending offices of trust, of honour or of profit. The office of justice of peace in the District of Columbia is such an office; it is therefore worthy of the attention and guardianship of the laws. It has received that attention and guardianship. It has been created by special act of Congress, and has been secured, so far as the laws can give security to the person appointed to fill it, for five years. It is not then on account of the worthlessness of the thing pursued that the injured party can be alleged to be without remedy.

Is it in the nature of the transaction? Is the act of delivering or withholding a commission to be considered as a mere political act belonging to the Executive department alone, for the performance of which entire confidence is placed by our Constitution in the Supreme Executive, and for any misconduct respecting which the injured individual has no remedy?

That there may be such cases is not to be questioned, but that every act of duty to be performed in any of the great departments of government constitutes such a case is not to be admitted.

By the act concerning invalids, passed in June, 1794, the Secretary at War is ordered to place on the pension list all persons whose names are contained in a report previously made by him to Congress. If he

(Continues)

should refuse to do so, would the wounded veteran be without remedy? Is it to be contended that where the law, in precise terms, directs the performance of an act in which an individual is interested, the law is incapable of securing obedience to its mandate? Is it on account of the character of the person against whom the complaint is made? Is it to be contended that the heads of departments are not amenable to the laws of their country?

Whatever the practice on particular occasions may be, the theory of this principle will certainly never be maintained. [p165] No act of the Legislature confers so extraordinary a privilege, nor can it derive countenance from the doctrines of the common law. After stating that personal injury from the King to a subject is presumed to be impossible, *Blackstone*, Vol. III. p. 255, says,

> but injuries to the rights of property can scarcely be committed by the Crown without the intervention of its officers, for whom, the law, in matters of right, entertains no respect or delicacy, but furnishes various methods of detecting the errors and misconduct of those agents by whom the King has been deceived and induced to do a temporary injustice.

By the act passed in 1796, authorizing the sale of the lands above the mouth of Kentucky river, the purchaser, on paying his purchase money, becomes completely entitled to the property purchased, and, on producing to the Secretary of State the receipt of the treasurer upon a certificate required by the law, the President of the United States is authorized to grant him a patent. It is further enacted that all patents shall be countersigned by the Secretary of State, and recorded in his office. If the Secretary of State should choose to withhold this patent, or, the patent being lost, should refuse a copy of it, can it be imagined that the law furnishes to the injured person no remedy?

It is not believed that any person whatever would attempt to maintain such a proposition.

It follows, then, that the question whether the legality of an act of the head of a department be examinable in a court of justice or not must always depend on the nature of that act.

If some acts be examinable and others not, there must be some rule of law to guide the Court in the exercise of its jurisdiction.

In some instances, there may be difficulty in applying the rule to particular cases; but there cannot, it is believed, be much difficulty in laying down the rule.

By the Constitution of the United States, the President is invested with certain important political powers, in the [p166] exercise of which he is to use his own discretion, and is accountable only to his country in his political character and to his own conscience. To aid him in the performance of these duties, he is authorized to appoint certain officers, who act by his authority and in conformity with his orders.

In such cases, their acts are his acts; and whatever opinion may be entertained of the manner in which executive discretion may be used, still there exists, and can exist, no power to control that discretion. The subjects are political. They respect the nation, not individual rights, and, being entrusted to the Executive, the decision of the Executive is conclusive. The application of this remark will be perceived by adverting to the act of Congress for establishing the Department of Foreign Affairs. This officer, as his duties were prescribed by that act, is to conform precisely to the will of the President. He is the mere organ by whom that will is communicated. The acts of such an officer, as an officer, can never be examinable by the Courts.

But when the Legislature proceeds to impose on that officer other duties; when he is directed peremptorily to perform certain acts; when the rights of individuals are dependent on the performance of those acts; he is so far the officer of the law, is amenable to the laws for his conduct, and cannot at his discretion, sport away the vested rights of others.

The conclusion from this reasoning is that, where the heads of departments are the political or confidential agents of the Executive, merely to execute the will of the President, or rather to act in cases in which the Executive possesses a constitutional or legal discretion, nothing can be more perfectly clear than that their acts are only politically examinable. But where a specific duty is assigned by law, and individual rights depend upon the performance of that duty, it seems equally clear that the individual who considers himself injured has a right to resort to the laws of his country for a remedy.

If this be the rule, let us inquire how it applies to the case under the consideration of the Court. [p167]

The power of nominating to the Senate, and the power of appointing the person nominated, are political powers, to be exercised by the President according to his own discretion. When he has made an appointment, he has exercised his whole power, and his discretion has been completely applied to the case. If, by law, the officer be removable at the will of the President, then a new appointment may be immediately made, and the rights of the officer are terminated. But as a fact which has existed cannot be made never to have existed, the appointment cannot be annihilated, and consequently, if the officer is by law not removable at the will of the President, the rights he has acquired are protected by the law, and are not resumable by the President. They cannot be extinguished by Executive authority, and he has the privilege of asserting them in like manner as if they had been derived from any other source.

The question whether a right has vested or not is, in its nature, judicial, and must be tried by the judicial authority. If, for example, Mr. Marbury had taken the oaths of a magistrate and proceeded to act as one, in consequence of which a suit had been instituted against him in which his defence had depended on his being a magistrate; the validity of his appointment must have been determined by judicial authority.

So, if he conceives that, by virtue of his appointment, he has a legal right either to the commission which has been made out for him or to a copy of that commission, it is equally a question examinable in a court, and the decision of the Court upon it must depend on the opinion entertained of his appointment.

That question has been discussed, and the opinion is that the latest point of time which can be taken as that at which the appointment was complete and evidenced was when, after the signature of the President, the seal of the United States was affixed to the commission.

It is then the opinion of the Court:

1. That, by signing the commission of Mr. Marbury, the President of the United States appointed him a justice [p168] of peace for the County of Washington in the District of Columbia, and that the seal of the United States, affixed thereto by the Secretary of State, is conclusive testimony of the verity of the signature, and of the completion of the appointment, and that the appointment conferred on him a legal right to the office for the space of five years.

2. That, having this legal title to the office, he has a consequent right to the commission, a refusal to deliver which is a plain violation of that right, for which the laws of his country afford him a remedy.
   It remains to be inquired whether,

3. He is entitled to the remedy for which he applies. This depends on:

   1. The nature of the writ applied for, and
   2. The power of this court.

1. The nature of the writ.
Blackstone, in the third volume of his Commentaries, page 110, defines a mandamus to be

a command issuing in the King's name from the Court of King's Bench, and directed to any person, corporation, or inferior court of judicature within the King's dominions requiring them to do some particular thing therein specified which appertains to their office and duty, and which the Court of King's Bench has previously determined, or at least supposes, to be consonant to right and justice.

Lord Mansfield, in 3 Burrows, 1266, in the case of *The King v. Baker et al.*, states with much precision and explicitness the cases in which this writ may be used.
"Whenever," says that very able judge,

there is a right to execute an office, perform a service, or exercise a franchise (more especially if it be in a matter of public concern or attended with profit), and a person is kept out of possession, or dispossessed of such right, and [p169] has no other specific legal remedy, this court ought to assist by mandamus, upon reasons of justice, as the writ expresses, and upon reasons of public policy, to preserve peace, order and good government.

In the same case, he says,

this writ ought to be used upon all occasions where the law has established no specific remedy, and where in justice and good government there ought to be one.

In addition to the authorities now particularly cited, many others were relied on at the bar which show how far the practice has conformed to the general doctrines that have been just quoted.

(Continues)

(Continued)

This writ, if awarded, would be directed to an officer of government, and its mandate to him would be, to use the words of Blackstone,

> to do a particular thing therein specified, which appertains to his office and duty and which the Court has previously determined or at least supposes to be consonant to right and justice.

Or, in the words of Lord Mansfield, the applicant, in this case, has a right to execute an office of public concern, and is kept out of possession of that right.

These circumstances certainly concur in this case.

Still, to render the mandamus a proper remedy, the officer to whom it is to be directed must be one to whom, on legal principles, such writ may be directed, and the person applying for it must be without any other specific and legal remedy.

2. With respect to the officer to whom it would be directed. The intimate political relation, subsisting between the President of the United States and the heads of departments, necessarily renders any legal investigation of the acts of one of those high officers peculiarly irksome, as well as delicate, and excites some hesitation with respect to the propriety of entering into such investigation. Impressions are often received without much reflection or examination, and it is not wonderful that, in such a case as this, the assertion by an individual of his legal claims in a court of justice, to which claims it is the duty of that court to attend, should, at first view, be considered [p170] by some as an attempt to intrude into the cabinet and to intermeddle with the prerogatives of the Executive.

It is scarcely necessary for the Court to disclaim all pretensions to such a jurisdiction. An extravagance so absurd and excessive could not have been entertained for a moment. The province of the Court is solely to decide on the rights of individuals, not to inquire how the Executive or Executive officers perform duties in which they have a discretion. Questions, in their nature political or which are, by the Constitution and laws, submitted to the Executive, can never be made in this court.

But, if this be not such a question; if so far from being an intrusion into the secrets of the cabinet, it respects a paper which, according to law, is upon record, and to a copy of which the law gives a right, on the payment of ten cents; if it be no intermeddling with a subject over which the Executive can be considered as having exercised any control; what is there in the exalted station of the officer which shall bar a citizen from asserting in a court of justice his legal rights, or shall forbid a court to listen to the claim or to issue a mandamus directing the performance of a duty not depending on Executive discretion, but on particular acts of Congress and the general principles of law?

If one of the heads of departments commits any illegal act under colour of his office by which an individual sustains an injury, it cannot be pretended that his office alone exempts him from being sued in the ordinary mode of proceeding, and being compelled to obey the judgment of the law. How then can his office exempt him from this particular mode of deciding on the legality of his conduct if the case be such a case as would, were any other individual the party complained of, authorize the process?

It is not by the office of the person to whom the writ is directed, but the nature of the thing to be done, that the propriety or impropriety of issuing a mandamus is to be determined. Where the head of a department acts in a case in which Executive discretion is to be exercised, in which he is the mere organ of Executive will, it is [p171] again repeated, that any application to a court to control, in any respect, his conduct, would be rejected without hesitation.

But where he is directed by law to do a certain act affecting the absolute rights of individuals, in the performance of which he is not placed under the particular direction of the President, and the performance of which the President cannot lawfully forbid, and therefore is never presumed to have forbidden—as for example, to record a commission, or a patent for land, which has received all the legal solemnities; or to give a copy of such record—in such cases, it is not perceived on what ground the Courts of the country are further excused from the duty of giving judgment that right to be done to an injured individual than if the same services were to be performed by a person not the head of a department.

This opinion seems not now for the first time to be taken up in this country.

It must be well recollected that, in 1792, an act passed, directing the secretary at war to place on the pension list such disabled officers and soldiers as should be reported to him by the Circuit Courts, which act, so far as the duty was imposed on the Courts, was deemed unconstitutional; but some of the judges, thinking that the law might be executed by them in the character of commissioners, proceeded to act and to report in that character.

This law being deemed unconstitutional at the circuits, was repealed, and a different system was established; but the question whether those persons who had been reported by the judges, as commissioners, were entitled, in consequence of that report, to be placed on the pension list was a legal question, properly determinable in the Courts, although the act of placing such persons on the list was to be performed by the head of a department.

That this question might be properly settled, Congress passed an act in February, 1793, making it the duty of the Secretary of War, in conjunction with the Attorney General, to take such measures as might be necessary to obtain an adjudication of the Supreme Court of the United [p172] States on the validity of any such rights, claimed under the act aforesaid.

After the passage of this act, a mandamus was moved for, to be directed to the Secretary of War, commanding him to place on the pension list a person stating himself to be on the report of the judges.

There is, therefore, much reason to believe that this mode of trying the legal right of the complainant was deemed by the head of a department, and by the highest law officer of the United States, the most proper which could be selected for the purpose.

When the subject was brought before the Court, the decision was not that a mandamus would not lie to the head of a department directing him to perform an act enjoined by law, in the performance of which an individual had a vested interest, but that a mandamus ought not to issue in that case— the decision necessarily to be made if the report of the commissioners did not confer on the applicant a legal right.

The judgment in that case is understood to have decided the merits of all claims of that description, and the persons, on the report of the commissioners, found it necessary to pursue the mode prescribed by the law subsequent to that which had been deemed unconstitutional in order to place themselves on the pension list.

The doctrine, therefore, now advanced is by no means a novel one.

It is true that the mandamus now moved for is not for the performance of an act expressly enjoined by statute.

It is to deliver a commission, on which subjects the acts of Congress are silent. This difference is not considered as affecting the case. It has already been stated that the applicant has, to that commission, a vested legal right of which the Executive cannot deprive him. He has been appointed to an office from which he is not removable at the will of the Executive, and, being so [p173] appointed, he has a right to the commission which the Secretary has received from the President for his use. The act of Congress does not, indeed, order the Secretary of State to send it to him, but it is placed in his hands for the person entitled to it, and cannot be more lawfully withheld by him than by another person.

It was at first doubted whether the action of detinue was not a specific legal remedy for the commission which has been withheld from Mr. Marbury, in which case a mandamus would be improper. But this doubt has yielded to the consideration that the judgment in detinue is for the thing itself, or its value. The value of a public office not to be sold is incapable of being ascertained, and the applicant has a right to the office itself, or to nothing. He will obtain the office by obtaining the commission or a copy of it from the record.

This, then, is a plain case of a mandamus, either to deliver the commission or a copy of it from the record, and it only remains to be inquired:

Whether it can issue from this Court.

The act to establish the judicial courts of the United States authorizes the Supreme Court

to issue writs of mandamus, in cases warranted by the principles and usages of law, to any courts appointed, or persons holding office, under the authority of the United States.

The Secretary of State, being a person, holding an office under the authority of the United States, is precisely within the letter of the description, and if this Court is not authorized to issue a writ of mandamus to such an officer, it must be because the law is unconstitutional, and therefore absolutely incapable of conferring the authority and assigning the duties which its words purport to confer and assign.

The Constitution vests the whole judicial power of the United States in one Supreme Court, and such inferior courts as Congress shall, from time to time, ordain and establish. This power is expressly extended to all cases arising under the laws of the United States; and consequently, in some form, may be exercised over the present [p174] case, because the right claimed is given by a law of the United States.

In the distribution of this power. it is declared that

The Supreme Court shall have original jurisdiction in all cases affecting ambassadors, other public ministers and consuls, and those in which a state shall be a party. In all other cases, the Supreme Court shall have appellate jurisdiction.

(Continues)

(Continued)

It has been insisted at the bar, that, as the original grant of jurisdiction to the Supreme and inferior courts is general, and the clause assigning original jurisdiction to the Supreme Court contains no negative or restrictive words, the power remains to the Legislature to assign original jurisdiction to that Court in other cases than those specified in the article which has been recited, provided those cases belong to the judicial power of the United States.

If it had been intended to leave it in the discretion of the Legislature to apportion the judicial power between the Supreme and inferior courts according to the will of that body, it would certainly have been useless to have proceeded further than to have defined the judicial power and the tribunals in which it should be vested. The subsequent part of the section is mere surplusage—is entirely without meaning—if such is to be the construction. If Congress remains at liberty to give this court appellate jurisdiction where the Constitution has declared their jurisdiction shall be original, and original jurisdiction where the Constitution has declared it shall be appellate, the distribution of jurisdiction made in the Constitution, is form without substance.

Affirmative words are often, in their operation, negative of other objects than those affirmed, and, in this case, a negative or exclusive sense must be given to them or they have no operation at all.

It cannot be presumed that any clause in the Constitution is intended to be without effect, and therefore such construction is inadmissible unless the words require it. [p175]

If the solicitude of the Convention respecting our peace with foreign powers induced a provision that the Supreme Court should take original jurisdiction in cases which might be supposed to affect them, yet the clause would have proceeded no further than to provide for such cases if no further restriction on the powers of Congress had been intended. That they should have appellate jurisdiction in all other cases, with such exceptions as Congress might make, is no restriction unless the words be deemed exclusive of original jurisdiction.

When an instrument organizing fundamentally a judicial system divides it into one Supreme and so many inferior courts as the Legislature may ordain and establish, then enumerates its powers, and proceeds so far to distribute them as to define the jurisdiction of the Supreme Court by declaring the cases in which it shall take original jurisdiction, and that in others it shall take appellate jurisdiction, the plain import of the words seems to be that, in one class of cases, its jurisdiction is original, and not appellate; in the other, it is appellate, and not original. If any other construction would render the clause inoperative, that is an additional reason for rejecting such other construction, and for adhering to the obvious meaning.

To enable this court then to issue a mandamus, it must be shown to be an exercise of appellate jurisdiction, or to be necessary to enable them to exercise appellate jurisdiction.

It has been stated at the bar that the appellate jurisdiction may be exercised in a variety of forms, and that, if it be the will of the Legislature that a mandamus should be used for that purpose, that will must be obeyed. This is true; yet the jurisdiction must be appellate, not original.

It is the essential criterion of appellate jurisdiction that it revises and corrects the proceedings in a cause already instituted, and does not create that case. Although, therefore, a mandamus may be directed to courts, yet to issue such a writ to an officer for the delivery of a paper is, in effect, the same as to sustain an original action for that paper, and therefore seems not to belong to [p176] appellate, but to original jurisdiction. Neither is it necessary in such a case as this to enable the Court to exercise its appellate jurisdiction.

The authority, therefore, given to the Supreme Court by the act establishing the judicial courts of the United States to issue writs of mandamus to public officers appears not to be warranted by the Constitution, and it becomes necessary to inquire whether a jurisdiction so conferred can be exercised.

The question whether an act repugnant to the Constitution can become the law of the land is a question deeply interesting to the United States, but, happily, not of an intricacy proportioned to its interest. It seems only necessary to recognise certain principles, supposed to have been long and well established, to decide it.

That the people have an original right to establish for their future government such principles as, in their opinion, shall most conduce to their own happiness is the basis on which the whole American fabric has been erected. The exercise of this original right is a very great exertion; nor can it nor ought it to be frequently repeated. The principles, therefore, so established are deemed fundamental. And as the authority from which they proceed, is supreme, and can seldom act, they are designed to be permanent.

This original and supreme will organizes the government and assigns to different departments their respective powers. It may either stop here or establish certain limits not to be transcended by those departments.

The Government of the United States is of the latter description. The powers of the Legislature are defined and limited; and that those limits may not be mistaken or forgotten, the Constitution is written. To what purpose are powers limited, and to what purpose is that limitation committed to writing, if these limits may at any time be passed by those intended to be restrained? The distinction between a government with limited and unlimited powers is abolished if those limits do not confine the persons on whom they are imposed, and if acts prohibited [p177] and acts allowed are of equal obligation. It is a proposition too plain to be contested that the Constitution controls any legislative act repugnant to it, or that the Legislature may alter the Constitution by an ordinary act.

Between these alternatives there is no middle ground. The Constitution is either a superior, paramount law, unchangeable by ordinary means, or it is on a level with ordinary legislative acts, and, like other acts, is alterable when the legislature shall please to alter it.

If the former part of the alternative be true, then a legislative act contrary to the Constitution is not law; if the latter part be true, then written Constitutions are absurd attempts on the part of the people to limit a power in its own nature illimitable.

Certainly all those who have framed written Constitutions contemplate them as forming the fundamental and paramount law of the nation, and consequently the theory of every such government must be that an act of the Legislature repugnant to the Constitution is void.

This theory is essentially attached to a written Constitution, and is consequently to be considered by this Court as one of the fundamental principles of our society. It is not, therefore, to be lost sight of in the further consideration of this subject.

If an act of the Legislature repugnant to the Constitution is void, does it, notwithstanding its invalidity, bind the Courts and oblige them to give it effect? Or, in other words, though it be not law, does it constitute a rule as operative as if it was a law? This would be to overthrow in fact what was established in theory, and would seem, at first view, an absurdity too gross to be insisted on. It shall, however, receive a more attentive consideration.

It is emphatically the province and duty of the Judicial Department to say what the law is. Those who apply the rule to particular cases must, of necessity, expound and interpret that rule. If two laws conflict with each other, the Courts must decide on the operation of each. [p178]

So, if a law be in opposition to the Constitution, if both the law and the Constitution apply to a particular case, so that the Court must either decide that case conformably to the law, disregarding the Constitution, or conformably to the Constitution, disregarding the law, the Court must determine which of these conflicting rules governs the case. This is of the very essence of judicial duty.

If, then, the Courts are to regard the Constitution, and the Constitution is superior to any ordinary act of the Legislature, the Constitution, and not such ordinary act, must govern the case to which they both apply.

Those, then, who controvert the principle that the Constitution is to be considered in court as a paramount law are reduced to the necessity of maintaining that courts must close their eyes on the Constitution, and see only the law.

This doctrine would subvert the very foundation of all written Constitutions. It would declare that an act which, according to the principles and theory of our government, is entirely void, is yet, in practice, completely obligatory. It would declare that, if the Legislature shall do what is expressly forbidden, such act, notwithstanding the express prohibition, is in reality effectual. It would be giving to the Legislature a practical and real omnipotence with the same breath which professes to restrict their powers within narrow limits. It is prescribing limits, and declaring that those limits may be passed at pleasure.

That it thus reduces to nothing what we have deemed the greatest improvement on political institutions—a written Constitution, would of itself be sufficient, in America where written Constitutions have been viewed with so much reverence, for rejecting the construction. But the peculiar expressions of the Constitution of the United States furnish additional arguments in favour of its rejection.

The judicial power of the United States is extended to all cases arising under the Constitution. [p179]

Could it be the intention of those who gave this power to say that, in using it, the Constitution should not be looked into? That a case arising under the Constitution should be decided without examining the instrument under which it arises?

This is too extravagant to be maintained.

In some cases then, the Constitution must be looked into by the judges. And if they can open it at all, what part of it are they forbidden to read or to obey?

(Continues)

(Continued)

There are many other parts of the Constitution which serve to illustrate this subject.

It is declared that "no tax or duty shall be laid on articles exported from any State." Suppose a duty on the export of cotton, of tobacco, or of flour, and a suit instituted to recover it. Ought judgment to be rendered in such a case? Ought the judges to close their eyes on the Constitution, and only see the law?

The Constitution declares that "no bill of attainder or *ex post facto* law shall be passed."

If, however, such a bill should be passed and a person should be prosecuted under it, must the Court condemn to death those victims whom the Constitution endeavours to preserve?

"No person," says the Constitution, "shall be convicted of treason unless on the testimony of two witnesses to the same overt act, or on confession in open court."

Here, the language of the Constitution is addressed especially to the Courts. It prescribes, directly for them, a rule of evidence not to be departed from. If the Legislature should change that rule, and declare one witness, or a confession out of court, sufficient for conviction, must the constitutional principle yield to the legislative act?

From these and many other selections which might be made, it is apparent that the framers of the Constitution [p180] contemplated that instrument as a rule for the government of courts, as well as of the Legislature.

Why otherwise does it direct the judges to take an oath to support it? This oath certainly applies in an especial manner to their conduct in their official character. How immoral to impose it on them if they were to be used as the instruments, and the knowing instruments, for violating what they swear to support!

The oath of office, too, imposed by the Legislature, is completely demonstrative of the legislative opinion on this subject. It is in these words:

> I do solemnly swear that I will administer justice without respect to persons, and do equal right to the poor and to the rich; and that I will faithfully and impartially discharge all the duties incumbent on me as according to the best of my abilities and understanding, agreeably to the Constitution and laws of the United States.

Why does a judge swear to discharge his duties agreeably to the Constitution of the United States if that Constitution forms no rule for his government? If it is closed upon him and cannot be inspected by him?

If such be the real state of things, this is worse than solemn mockery. To prescribe or to take this oath becomes equally a crime.

It is also not entirely unworthy of observation that, in declaring what shall be the supreme law of the land, the Constitution itself is first mentioned, and not the laws of the United States generally, but those only which shall be made in pursuance of the Constitution, have that rank.

Thus, the particular phraseology of the Constitution of the United States confirms and strengthens the principle, supposed to be essential to all written Constitutions, that a law repugnant to the Constitution is void, and that courts, as well as other departments, are bound by that instrument.

The rule must be discharged.

Freedom of Religion, Freedom from Religion

Chapter Objectives

In this chapter you will learn . . .

- Whether the First Amendment differs from the Fourth in terms of Congress' role
- The history of prayer in public schools
- Why God is referred to in the Pledge of Allegiance
- That Congress begins its session each day with a prayer
- Why a nativity scene is different from *Frosty the Snowman* in terms of displays on public property

Introduction

In Chapter 2 we discussed why colonial settlers immigrated to this New World. One reason was to gain religious freedom. There is no doubt that the United States provides such freedom for everyone. All Americans are free to worship in whatever way they choose, belong to whichever religion they choose, or choose to not worship at all. Beyond that, however, the answers are not as evident. Are children allowed to pray in school? Is their teacher allowed to wear a religious symbol, or to speak about God? Can tax dollars be used to support church programs? In order to answer these questions and to better understand the issues, let's turn to the very beginning of the Bill of Rights: the First Amendment.

The First Amendment

The First Amendment to the Constitution states:

Congress shall make no law respecting an establishment of religion, or prohibiting the free exercise thereof; or abridging the freedom of speech, or of the press; or the right of the people peaceably to assemble, and to petition the Government for a redress of grievances.

The first portion of the Amendment, written here in **bold**, is the part that specifically pertains to religion. It is important to include the entire Amendment, but for reasons that we will discuss later. For now, let's take a look at the bold sentence: Congress shall make no law respecting an establishment of religion, or prohibiting the free exercise thereof.

Comparing the First and Fourth Amendments

Let us compare this for a moment with the Fourth Amendment, which states:

The right of the people to be secure in their persons, houses, papers, and effects, against unreasonable searches and seizures, shall not be violated, and no Warrants shall issue, but upon probable cause, supported by Oath or affirmation, and particularly describing the place to be searched, and the persons or things to be seized.

A reasonable summary of the First Amendment would be that it is about preserving the freedoms of religion, speech, the press, assembly, and being able to formally request legal justice from the government. The Fourth Amendment can be summarized as preserving people's rights against unreasonable searches and seizures, and against search warrants not based on probable cause and/or missing specific details about the time and place of a search, and the persons and items to be seized.

Taken together, these two Amendments seem to be quite similar. After all, they were both made part of the Constitution in 1791, along with eight others, with which they were collectively known as the Bill of Rights: the first ten Amendments to the Constitution. It then seems logical that the First Amendment might protect ideas (such as religion, speech, and so forth), whereas the Fourth Amendment protects privacy. And it would seem likely that the other Amendments, at least those other eight also ratified in 1791, would protect other freedoms. In fact, a reading of those Amendments would confirm that notion. However, there is a major difference between the First Amendment and the Fourth as well as any of the others: it is the only Amendment that prohibits Congress, specifically and exclusively, from doing something.

Congress Shall Make No Law . . .

The very first word of the First Amendment is Congress. It is *Congress* that shall make no law respecting an establishment of religion or prohibiting the free exercise thereof. The Fourth Amendment, by comparison, does not mention the word *Congress*. It seems that if, say, the state of Rhode Island decided to create a law respecting the establishment of religion (such as, establishing the Episcopal Church as the official church of that state), or one that prohibits the free exercise thereof (for example, prevented any religious group other than Episcopalians to gather to worship), that would not be a First Amendment violation! Why not? Because Rhode Island is not *Congress*.

However, if Rhode Island passed a law that gave police officers the right to enter someone's home without a search warrant, or with a warrant not issued based on probable cause (more on what probable cause is, later), then that would be a Fourth Amendment violation. Why? Because the Fourth Amendment says there cannot be such a violation, period, whereas the First Amendment specifically prohibits *Congress* from committing such a violation.

It is possible, of course, for someone to present the argument that the Founders wrote *Congress* but really meant state governments, or the people. Another argument might be that the Founders inserted the phrase, "Congress shall make no law . . ." in the First Amendment, implying that it would apply to the entire Bill of Rights. These are prime examples of the debate about *legislative intent*: what the legislators (in this case, the Founders) intended to mean by their words.

For example, suppose that Brian, an Oregon police officer, was interested in preventing drug deals from taking place in a particular neighborhood. He could randomly knock on doors, enter the homes, and search the residents' bedrooms, closets, wallets, purses, and so on, without violating their Constitutional rights. After all, it would be the Oregon legislature, not Congress, who would have established that law. However, in reality, Brian would not have the right to conduct such searches in Oregon or in any other state because the Fourth Amendment guarantees all of the people's rights to be protected against unreasonable searches and seizures. Accordingly, no law—whether federal, state, or local—could grant authorization to the contrary.

To further illustrate the difference, consider another Amendment, the Fifth, which was ratified at the same time as was the First. The Fifth Amendment states that no person . . . *shall be deprived of life, liberty, or property without due process of law.* Again, it specifically states that "no person shall . . ." rather than that Congress shall make no such law. As a result, no one is allowed to take anyone else's life, liberty, or property, for whatever purpose and by whatever use of force, unless such action is consistent with the law. Had the language read that "Congress shall make no law," then, again, it would be possible for, say, the state of Oklahoma to permit its residents to, say, steal property from one another if there was no state law.

Congress, then, shall make no law establishing religion or prohibiting the free exercise thereof. Congress cannot establish, for example, Christianity as the nation's official religion, nor can it prevent a religious group from attending worship services.

God in the Classroom

Let us turn our attention to prayer in public schools, for it was not too long ago (only a few decades) that children all across America began their day of school with a prayer. But in 1962, in the case *Engel v. Vitale*, the U.S Supreme Court declared that any *state-composed* prayer, even if nondenominational, was unconstitutional because it violated the First Amendment.

The facts of that case are as follows.

The Board of Education in New Hyde Park, New York, directed that the following prayer would be said out loud in class each morning. "Almighty God, we acknowledge our dependence upon Thee, and we beg Thy blessings upon us, our parents, our teachers, and our Country."

Even though the prayer itself was not specific to a particular religion or religious denomination, and that no child was *required* to recite the prayer (for instance, children could have opted to silently pray another prayer or remain silent altogether), the Supreme Court determined that a union of government and religion tends to destroy government and degrade religion. The Court held that this requirement, though made by New York State and not by Congress, nonetheless violated the students' Constitutional rights insofar as being a law that established religion.

In 1970, the Supreme Court expanded its basis for determining the constitutionality of statutes related to prayer in *Lemon v. Kurtzman*. The *Lemon* case concerned both a Pennsylvania and a Rhode Island statute, each of which used state funds to supplement teachers' salaries at nonpublic schools, most of which were religious (in both cases, Catholic). The Court struck down both statutes as unconstitutional, and established a three-pronged test regarding government vis-à-vis the Establishment Clause:

1. The purpose of the statute must be secular.
2. The statute's primary effect must be to neither advance nor inhibit religion.
3. The statute must not create a condition of excessive government entanglement with religion, because, among other reasons, there should not be political division along religious lines.

Let's take a look at some examples to better illustrate the *Lemon* test. Suppose that Wyoming enacted a statute that required Bible study in literature class in all of its public high schools, and that the primary purpose of that act was to examine the Bible as a piece of literary work. In other words, the Bible would be read and analyzed no differently than would Shakespeare or Greek mythology. In that case, a strong argument could be made that the purpose of the statute is secular.

Next, suppose that the purpose of this statute was to familiarize students with various philosophical movements throughout history, including Communism, Fascism, Narcissism, and existentialism. Judaism and Christianity, then, would be looked at in context of other intellectual schools of thought. In that case, it could be argued that, because the scope of reference to the Bible would be neither supportive nor critical, students would not necessarily be more or less likely to accept or reject the bible as a result of having studied it in that context.

Finally, if the lesson plans were clear and consistent from instructor to instructor, and from class to class, then, presumably, Wyoming's Board of Education would be satisfied and would not have to monitor the lessons to any greater extent than it would monitor, say, a math course, and there probably would not be a great deal of divisive political controversy in the state as a result of that statute.

That example might pass the *Lemon* test, though it is a difficult test to pass; not one that many actual state statutes can satisfy. Before we move on to the next point, let's take a look at a more recent Supreme Court decision in which the Court applied that test. In *Santa Fe Independent School District v. Doe*, decided in 2000, the Supreme Court held that voluntary student-led prayers at public high school football games did not pass the *Lemon* test. The holding reinforced the long-held notion that the Fourteenth Amendment extended to the states the restriction on Congress not to make any law establishing or prohibiting religion. The Justices considered the voluntary prayer in a public forum to have been a form of social pressure that improperly coerced those present to participate in a religious act.

The dissenting Justices vigorously attacked the majority for what they considered a hostile opinion on all things religious in public life, and questioned whether this type of activity even has anything to do with the Establishment Clause, referring to George Washington's proclamation, backed by the very Congress that enacted the Bill of Rights, of a public day of thanksgiving and prayer, to be observed by acknowledgement of the Almighty God. The *Santa Fe* case, decided in 2000, reflects the continuing and unresolved debate about this issue.

The Pledge of Allegiance

Every morning all across America, schoolchildren hear their teachers' words, prompting them to stand and salute the flag: "Okay, class, please stand, salute, and pledge." With that command, the children begin reciting the Pledge of Allegiance. "I pledge allegiance to the flag of the United States of America, and to the Republic for which it stands, one Nation, under God, indivisible, with liberty and justice for all." The pledge, originally written by Francis Bellamy in 1892, was used in schools across the country upon the proclamation by President Benjamin Harrison. The words "flag of the United States of America" were added years later, replacing the simpler phrase, "my flag," in order to confirm to immigrants that the pledge was intended toward the American flag and not the flag of their native countries.

On Flag Day (June 14), 1954, President Dwight D. Eisenhower signed a bill that included the words "under God" in the pledge. Until that time, those words were not a part of it. President Eisenhower's rationale was to remind Americans that as mighty as our nation might be, we ought to be humbled in realizing that there is an even higher and mightier authority, God, who governs us.

Consistent with the Supreme Court's numerous rulings, it would seem that the phrase "under God" in itself would not be considered to be a violation of the Establishment Clause. Instead, it would be more of an affirmation of our

President Eisenhower led the effort to include the words "under God" in the Pledge of Allegiance.

history than an attempt to establish religion. For instance, it would not be wholly different from schoolchildren reciting the history of Thanksgiving Day and making references to God.

God on Display

What if no actual prayer was recited, but religious symbols were displayed in classrooms, school hallways, or in other public buildings? Consider the case *Lynch v. Donnely*, decided in 1984. Each year, Pawtucket, Rhode Island, displayed Christmas symbols in a public park, including Santa Claus, a reindeer, a Christmas tree, and a nativity scene. The number of symbols that depicted the holiday side of Christmas outweighed any direct religious references. The Court concluded that the display did not violate any of the three tests in *Lemon*. First, the primary purpose was a secular one: to celebrate the tradition of the Christmas season, which in American culture is not necessarily tied to the religious significance. After all, *Frosty the Snowman* has nothing to do with the birth of Jesus Christ. Second, any advancement of religion was deemed to have been indirect, remote, and incidental. A nativity scene display, mixed in with an array of nonreligious Christmas symbols, did not amount to the Town of Pawtucket demanding, coercing, or even suggesting to any of its citizens that Christianity was the city's official religion. Finally, because the display was established and maintained by the town itself, there was no administrative entanglement with any religious organizations.

Although five Justices formed the majority that gave rise to the *Lynch* decision, a five to four majority is a slim one, indeed. The four dissenters argued that the display was in considerable part motivated by those who advocate keeping Christ in Christmas. Moreover, the dissenters reasoned that the primary effect of the display was to demonstrate how the township was in favor of that notion, too. Finally, they believed that the entire issue caused deep political division in Pawtucket.

The case of *Allegheny County v. American Civil Liberties Union*, decided in 1989, resulted in a somewhat different decision than *Lynch*, but the logic was fairly consistent: A nativity scene at the Allegheny County Courthouse in Pittsburgh, Pennsylvania, was not accompanied by nonreligious Christmas holiday symbols, and had been placed there by a private group, rather than by the government itself. Those two distinctions prompted the Court to rule differently. However, the same Justices held that an 18-foot Hanukkah menorah in a public place did not violate the Establishment Clause because: (1) the menorah was placed next to a Christmas tree, which is not a religious symbol, and (2) the tree was 45-feet tall, which dwarfed the menorah in comparison.

A third case, *Capitol Square Review Board v. Pinette*, decided in 1995, permitted the Ku Klux Klan to display a cross in a public park. The four-Justice plurality reasoned that the Klan is a private group, not the government, and because the park had long been accessible to private groups' expressive acts, this act did not fall within the scope of the Establishment Clause; it was not the government who was displaying the cross.

The Reasonable Observer Test

In *Pinette* as well as in other cases, the Court considered the *reasonable observer test*, which meant that if a person who understood the history and context of a particular forum believed that the government was responsible for a particular religious display, then the display was unconstitutional, *even if the government was not actually responsible for it.*

The Free Exercise Clause

To this point we have discussed the Establishment Clause portion of the First Amendment. Now, let us turn our attention to the Free Exercise Clause, namely, that Congress may not make a law that prohibits the free exercise of religion.

Generally, the Free Exercise Clause becomes an issue when the government prohibits activities that are essential to a particular religious belief, or requires activities that directly oppose a particular religious belief.

For example, suppose that the state of Kentucky passes a law that makes it illegal to kill an ant, although killing ants might be an essential component of a particular religion's ritual. Next, suppose that the state of Missouri requires all restaurant employees to wash their hands before handling food, but that such action directly violates the beliefs of another religion. Both of those activities would bring the Free Exercise Clause into question: would followers of those religions be permitted to kill ants in

Kentucky, or to handle food with unwashed hands in Missouri?

To better understand these questions, let's turn to some cases for the answers.

In *Bob Jones University v. United States*, decided in 1983, the Supreme Court supported the Internal Revenue Service's denial of tax exempt status to Bob Jones University on the basis that the university admitted only White applicants. The university, which is Christian, holds the belief that the Bible forbids interracial marriage, and even interracial dating. By admitting nonwhites and whites to the same campus, the university feared that such interracial commingling would take place, thus contradicting its strongly held religious convictions. Nonetheless, the Court found that there was a compelling state interest in preventing racial discrimination, even when practiced by a private institution, that such interest superseded the university's right to exercise their religious beliefs in that capacity.

The *Bob Jones* case is a classic example of a *compelling state interest*, in this case, racial discrimination, whereby individual rights have to take a back seat to prevent the deprivation of others' rights. Though a private university ought to have the right to practice its religious beliefs, it may not do so at the expense of an entire race of people. Constitutional rights, then, are not absolute.

In a more recent case, *Church of the Lukumi Babalu Aye, Inc. v. Hialeah*, the Supreme Court's decision depicted that, sometimes, not only the rights of people, but the rights of animals as well, sometimes outweigh the right to practice one's religion. Nonetheless, in *Lukumi*, which was decided in 1993, practitioners of Santeria were not denied the right to sacrifice animals in furtherance of that faith. The reason that the Court ruled in their favor was because it found that the city ordinance of Hialeah, Florida, was specifically enacted to stop the Santeria practice, even though the ordinance did not make a direct reference to Santeria but, instead, made it unlawful to sacrifice an animal for religious practice. The Court found that because the ordinance was targeted against Santeria, upholding the ordinance would amount to a violation of the Free Exercise Clause.

And in *Sherbert v. Verner*, decided in 1963, the Court found that Sherbert, a Seventh Day Adventist who was denied unemployment benefits in South Carolina because he refused to accept jobs that required work on Saturdays, was denied his Constitutional rights under the Free Exercise Clause. The Court reasoned that Sherbert was forced to choose between his religious practice—which required him not to work on Saturdays—and receiving unemployment benefits.

Moreover, the Court in *Sherbert* pointed out that no similar condition was placed on Sunday worshippers. For instance, a beneficiary who turned down a job that required Sunday work because of worship commitments would not have been disqualified from receiving benefits. Accordingly, the rationale was discriminatory against Seventh Day Adventists (and all others whose day of worship was not Sunday).

Each of these cases requires us to examine a different issue. *Bob Jones* was about a private college being able to discriminate based on race; *Lukumi* determined whether an ordinance could be designed to discriminate against a particular religion; and *Sherbert* considered discriminatory application of statutory benefits, favoring followers of some religions over others.

The Court has been fairly consistent regarding the Free Exercise Clause: Though there are numerous other cases on the subject, we can draw the following conclusions by summarizing the Court's holdings simply in those three: Freedom of religion is not absolute, and cannot intrude upon other civil rights (such as, the right to not be subjected to discrimination based on race). An exception would exist if the law in question was either specifically designed to discriminate against a particular religion, or even if the effect was discriminatory, if not the intent.

God in Other Public Places

Given all that we have learned about religion and the First Amendment to this point, some of the following information might seem to be surprising. Let's take a look at each item, one by one, and make sense of it.

In God We Trust

Reach into your pocket or open up your wallet and take out some money: a dollar bill, a five dollar bill, a ten, a twenty, or maybe a penny, a nickel, a dime, or a quarter. Each of these types of currency contains the words "In God We Trust" on it. That phrase is actually our country's official national motto. It became our official motto in 1956, when it was signed into law by President Eisenhower. The following year, the motto appeared on paper money, but it was embossed onto coins long before that time. In fact, "In God We Trust" first appeared on American coins during the time of the Civil War.

How, then, is our national motto not a violation of the First Amendment? The same rationale as with the Pledge of Allegiance applies: it is more about our country's history than it is an establishment of religion.

So Help Me God

In courtrooms across America, witnesses are sworn in every day by affirming that they "swear to tell the truth,

The U.S. Dollar, as all other currency, contains the words "In God We Trust."

the whole truth, and nothing but the truth, so help me God." Why is that permitted, if courtrooms are government buildings? Because the reason for inducing a sworn statement is not to promote religion, but to rely on each individual's own sense of conscience not to lie in God's name, because that person might feel a sense of betrayal to God as a result.

After all, even hardened criminals often feel completely justified regarding the crimes they commit. Many think it perfectly acceptable even to take another human life! But lie in God's name, that's where some of them draw the line. After all, the overwhelming majority of Americans profess to believing in God, and so the courts have a legitimate reason for requiring that oath: in order to generate truthful testimony.

The same can be said of elected officials, even the president of the United States, who solemnly swears "that I will faithfully execute the office of President of the United States and will, to the best of my ability, preserve, protect, and defend the Constitution of the United States, so help me God." The president-elect (that is what the president is called before officially taking office) has the option to *affirm* rather than *swear*. To date, none of the presidents have exercised that option.

Prayer in Congress

Congress itself, the epitome of government, begins its sessions each day with a prayer. That is the most difficult of all of the examples presented here to this point to reconcile, and a reminder that sometimes, traditional customs are the exceptions to policy.

Religion in 21st Century America

Early in the 21st Century, religion remains an integral part of American life, and most Americans seem happy with the *status quo*. Even the staunchest believers probably would not want to see religion forced into anyone's life, though many would prefer to see prayer reinstated in public schools, or at least a few minutes of silence to encourage people to silently pray.

As for our politicians, the presidency of George W. Bush is most vivid in our minds. An outspoken unabashed Christian, President Bush urged an increase in faith-based charities. Although he recognized that government cannot excessively tangle with religion, faith-based charities are private entities.

Moreover, most polls show that the overwhelming majority of Americans would not be comfortable voting for an atheist. Faith remains a very powerful force in American life.

Conclusion

Where, then, does this leave us with respect to religion? Does government have the right to establish it? No. Does it have the right to prohibit its free exercise? No again. In other words, constitutionally, government has no role regarding religion.

However, phrases such as "under God," "so help me God," and the singing of "God Bless America" at public school events do not constitute religion. Neither do Christmas trees, *Frosty the Snowman*, nor *Rudolph the Red-Nosed Reindeer*.

As we discussed earlier, laws are often shaped by the judicial branch just as much as by its legislative and executive counterparts. Accordingly, it is important to keep a close watch on this Supreme Court, as every Supreme Court, to determine whether there is a chance that some of the cases we have been talking about in this chapter would be overturned.

In Chapter Five, we will discuss two other concepts that stem from the First Amendment: freedom of speech and freedom of expression.

Questions for Review

1. Which body of government does the First Amendment refer to regarding religion?
2. Provide an example of how the government might establish religion.
3. Provide an example of how the government might prohibit the free exercise of religion.
4. What is the rationale for prohibiting state governments from establishing religion in their respective states?
5. Why would an icon of Jesus Christ be prohibited from being displayed on a public high school wall, whereas a picture of Santa Claus would not?
6. When children in public schools recite the Pledge of Allegiance, which makes reference to God, how is this not a First Amendment violation?
7. What is the reasonable observer test regarding religion and the First Amendment?
8. How can a private university be prevented from discriminatory admissions policies, when such policies are consistent with its own faith?
9. Give an example of how when a private religious group is permitted to practice its faith even when some of the acts violate a particular law.
10. If government is not supposed to establish religion, then why does "In God We Trust" appear on our coins and paper money?

Constitutionally Speaking

Consider these two scenarios: In the first, any American can openly speak, pray, perform religious rituals, or otherwise engage in the practice of religion anyplace, anytime. That includes teachers in the classroom, judges on the bench, and police officers while in uniform. In the second scenario, none of those people would be allowed to mention anything about religion or God in a school, courthouse, or other public building, or read the Bible or other religious book there either, and schools, offices, and banks would no longer be closed on Christmas Day.

Think about those two scenarios. Does either one sound reasonable to you? Do both sound reasonable? Which do you think is the better alternative? Are we better off now, being somewhere in the middle? And, if we really are in the middle of those two, are we closer to one than the other?

Constitutional Cases

Here are two cases that will help you to further expand your knowledge about religion and the Constitution. *Reynolds v. United States* is about a man who claimed that it was his religious duty to be married to two women at the same time. *Marsh v. Chambers* deals with whether a state legislature could open its proceedings with a prayer.

Reynolds v. United States, 98 U.S. 145 (1878)

ERROR to the Supreme Court of the Territory of Utah.

This is an indictment found in the District Court for the third judicial district of the Territory of Utah, charging George Reynolds with bigamy, in violation of sect. 5352 of the Revised Statutes, which, omitting its exceptions, is as follows:

'Every person having a husband or wife living, who marries another, whether married or single, in a Territory, or other place over which the United States have exclusive jurisdiction, is guilty of bigamy, and shall be punished by a fine of not more than $500, and by imprisonment for a term of not more than five years.'

The prisoner pleaded in abatement that the indictment was not found by a legal grand jury, because fifteen persons, and no more, were impaneled and sworn to serve as a grand jury at the term of the court during which the indictment was found, whereas sect. 808 of the Revised Statutes of the United States enacts that every grand jury impaneled before any District or Circuit Court shall consist of not less than sixteen persons.

An act of the legislature of Utah of Feb. 18, 1870, provides that the court shall impanel fifteen men to serve as a grand jury. Compiled Laws of Utah, ed. of 1876, p. 357, sect. 4.

The court overruled the plea, on the ground that the territorial enactment governed.

The prisoner then pleaded not guilty. Several jurors were examined on their *voire dire* by the district attorney. Among them was Eli Ransohoff, who, in answer to the question, 'Have you formed or expressed an opinion as to the guilt or innocence of the prisoner at the bar?' said, 'I have expressed an opinion by reading the papers with the reports of the trial.'

Q. 'Would that opinion influence your verdict in hearing the evidence?'
A. 'I don't think it would.'
By the defendant: 'You stated that you had formed some opinion by reading the reports of the previous trial?'
A. 'Yes.'
Q. 'Is that an impression which still remains upon your mind?' [98 U.S. 145, 147]
A. 'No; I don't think it does: I only glanced over it, as everybody else does.'
Q. 'Do you think you could try the case wholly uninfluenced by any thing?'
A. 'Yes.'
Charles Read, called as a juror, was asked by the district attorney, 'Have you formed or expressed any opinion as to the guilt or innocence of this charge?'
A. 'I believe I have formed an opinion.'
By the court: 'Have you formed and expressed an opinion?'
A. 'No, sir; I believe not.'
Q. 'You say you have formed an opinion?'
A. 'I have.'
Q. 'Is that based upon evidence?'
A. 'Nothing produced in court.'
Q. 'Would that opinion influence your verdict?'
A. 'I don't think it would.'
By defendant: 'I understood you to say that you had formed an opinion, but not expressed it.'
A. 'I don't know that I have expressed an opinion: I have formed one.'
Q. 'Do you now entertain that opinion?'
A. 'I do.'

The defendant challenged each of these jurors for cause. The court overruled the challenge, and permitted them to be sworn. The defendant excepted.

The court also, when Homer Brown was called as a juror, allowed the district attorney to ask him the following questions: Q. 'Are you living in polygamy?' A. 'I would rather not answer that.' The court instructed the witness that he must answer the question, unless it would criminate him. By the district attorney: 'You understand the conditions upon which you refuse?' A. 'Yes, sir.' Q. 'Have you such an opinion that you could not find a verdict for the commission of that crime?' A. 'I have no opinion on it in this particular case. I think under the evidence and the law I could render a verdict accordingly.' Whereupon the United States challenged the said Brown for favor, which challenge was sustained by the court, and the defendant excepted. [98 U.S. 145, 148] John W. Snell, also a juror, was asked by the district attorney on *voire dire*: Q. 'Are you living in polygamy?' A. 'I decline to answer that question.' Q. 'On what ground?' A. 'It might criminate myself; but I am only a fornicator.' Whereupon Snell was challenged by the United States for cause, which challenge was sustained, and the defendant excepted.

After the trial commenced, the district attorney, after proving that the defendant had been married on a certain day to Mary Ann Tuddenham, offered to prove his subsequent marriage to one Amelia Jane Schofield during the lifetime of said Mary. He thereupon called one Pratt, the deputy marshal, and showed him a subpoena for witnesses in this case, and among other names thereon was the name of Mary Jane Schobold, but no such name as Amelia Jane Schofield. He testified that this subpoena was placed in his hands to be served.

Q. 'Did you see Mr. Reynolds when you went to see Miss Schofield?'
A. 'Yes, sir.'
Q. 'Who did you inquire for?'
A. 'I inquired for Mary Jane Schofield, to the best of my knowledge. I will state this, that I inserted the name in the subpoena, and intended it for the name of the woman examined in this case at the former term of the court, and inquired for Mary Jane Schofield, or Mrs. Reynolds, I do not recollect certainly which.'

(Continues)

(*Continued*)

Q. 'State the reply.'
A. 'He said she was not at home.'
Q. 'Did he say any thing further.'
A. 'I asked him then where I could find her. I said, 'Where is she? And he said, 'You will have to find out.''
Q. 'Did he know you to be a deputy marshal?'
A. 'Yes, sir.'
Q. 'Did you tell him what your business was as deputy marshal?'
A. 'I don't remember now: I don't think I did.'
Q. 'What else did he say?' [98 U.S. 145, 149]
A. 'He said, just as I was leaving, as I understood it, that she did not appear in this case.'

The court then ordered a subpoena to issue for Amelia Jane Schofield, returnable instanter.

Upon the following day, at ten o'clock A.M., the said subpoena for the said witness having issued about nine o'clock P.M. of the day before, the said Arthur Pratt was again called upon, and testified as follows:

Q. (By district attorney.) 'State whether you are the officer that had subpoena in your hands.' (Exhibiting subpoena last issued, as above set forth.)
A. 'Yes, sir.'
Q. 'State to the court what efforts you have made to serve it.'
A. 'I went to the residence of Mr. Reynolds, and a lady was there, his first wife, and she told me that this woman was not there; that that was the only home that she had, but that she hadn't been there for two or three weeks. I went again this morning, and she was not there.'
Q. 'Do you know any thing about her home, where she resides?'
A. 'I know where I found her before.'
Q. 'Where?'
A. 'At the same place.'
Q. 'You are the deputy marshal that executed the process of the court?'
A. 'Yes, sir.'
Q. 'Repeat what Mr. Reynolds said to you when you went with the former subpoena introduced last evening.'
A. 'I will state that I put her name on the subpoena myself. I know the party, and am well acquainted with her, and I intended it for the same party that I subpoenaed before in this case. He said that she was not in, and that I could get a search-warrant if I wanted to search the house. I said, 'Will you tell me where she is?' He said, 'No; that will be for you to find out.' He said, just as I was leaving the house, I don't remember exactly what it was, but my best recollection is that he said she would not appear in this case.' [98 U.S. 145, 150]
Q. 'Can't you state that more particularly?'
A. 'I can't give you the exact words, but I can say that was the purport of them.'
Q. 'Give the words as nearly as you can.'
A. 'Just as I said, I think those were his words.'

The district attorney then offered to prove what Amelia Jane Schofield had testified to on a trial of another indictment charging the prisoner with bigamy in marrying her; to which the prisoner objected, on the ground that a sufficient foundation had not been laid for the introduction of the evidence.

A. S. Patterson, having been sworn, read, and other witnesses stated, said Amelia's testimony on the former trial, tending to show her marriage with the defendant. The defendant excepted to the admission of the evidence.

The court, in summing up to the jury, declined to instruct them, as requested by the prisoner, that if they found that he had married in pursuance of and conformity with what he believed at the time to be a religious duty, their verdict should be 'not guilty,' but instructed them that if he, under the influence of a religious belief that it was right, had 'deliberately married a second time, having a first wife living, the want of consciousness of evil intent—the want of understanding on his part that he was committing crime—did not excuse him, but the law inexorably, in such cases, implies criminal intent.'

The court also said, 'I think it not improper, in the discharge of your duties in this case, that you should consider what are to be the consequences to the innocent victims of this delusion. As this contest goes on, they multiply, and there are pure-minded women and there are innocent children, innocent in a sense even beyond the degree of the innocence of childhood itself. These are to be the sufferers; and as jurors fail to do their duty, and as these cases come up in the Territory, just so do these victims multiply and spread themselves over the land.'

To the refusal of the court to charge as requested, and to the charge as given, the prisoner excepted. The jury found him guilty, as charged in the indictment; and the judgment that he be imprisoned at hard labor for a term of two years, and pay [98 U.S. 145, 151] a fine of $500, rendered by the District Court, having been affirmed by the Supreme Court of the Territory, he sued out this writ of error.

The assignments of error are set out in the opinion of the court.

Mr. George W. Biddle and Mr. Ben Sheeks for the plaintiff in error.

First, The jury was improperly drawn. Two of the jurors were challenged for cause by the defendant below, because they admitted that they had formed, and still entertained, an opinion upon the guilt or innocence of the prisoner. The holding by a juror of any opinions which would disqualify him from rendering a verdict in accordance with the law of the land, is a valid objection to his serving.

An opinion based merely upon a hypothetical case, as that 'if so and so is true, the prisoner is guilty,' is not always sufficient; but where the opinion is as to the actual fact of guilt or innocence, it is a disqualification, according to all the authorities. Burr's Trial, 414, 415; *United States v. Wilson*, 1 Baldw. 83; *Ex parte* Vermilyea, 6 Cow. (N.Y.) 563; *The People v. Mather*, 4 Wend. (N.Y.) 238; *Cancemi v. People*, 16 N. Y. 502; *Fouts v. The State*, 11 Ohio St. 472; *Neely v. The People*, 23 Ill. 685; *Schoeffler v. The State*, 3 Wis. 831; *Trimble v. The State*, 2 Greene (Iowa), 404; *Commonwealth v. Lesher*, 17 Serg. & R. (Pa.) 155; *Staup v. Commonwealth*, 74 Pa. St. 458; Armistead's Case, 11 Leigh (Va.), 658; *Stewart v. The State*, 13 Ark. 740.

It was clearly erroneous for the prosecution to ask several of the jurymen, upon *voire dire*, whether they were living in polygamy; questions which tend to disgrace the person questioned, or to render him amenable to a criminal prosecution, have never been allowed to be put to a juror. Anonymous, Salk. 153; Bacon, Abr., tit. Juries, 12(f); 7 Dane, Abr. 334; *Hudson v. The State*, 1 Blackf. (Ind.) 319.

Second, The proof of what the witness, Amelia Jane Schofield, testified to in a former trial, under another indictment, should not have been admitted. The constitutional right of a prisoner to confront the witness and cross-examine him is not to be abrogated, unless it be shown that the witness is dead, or [98 U.S. 145, 152] out of the jurisdiction of the court; or that, having been summoned, he appears to have been kept away by the adverse party on the trial. It appeared not only that no such person as Amelia Jane Schofield had been subpoenaed, but that no subpoena had ever been taken out for her. An unserved subpoena with the name of Mary Jane Schobold was shown. At nine o'clock in the evening, during the trial, a new subpoena was issued; and on the following morning, with no attempt to serve it beyond going to the prisoner's usual residence and inquiring for her, the witness Patterson was allowed to read from a paper what purported to be statements made by Amelia Jane Schofield on a former trial. No proof was offered as to the genuineness of the paper or its origin, nor did the witness testify to its contents of his own knowledge. This is in the teeth of the ruling in *United States v. Wood* (3 Wash. 440), and the rule laid down in all the American authorities. *Richardson v. Stewart*, 2 Serg. & R. (Pa.) 84; *Chess v. Chess*, 17 id. 409; *Huidekopper v. Cotton*, 3 Watts (Pa.) 56; *Powell v. Waters*, 17 Johns. (N.Y.) 176; *Cary v. Sprague*, 12 Wend. (N.Y.) 45; *The People v. Newman*, 5 Hill (N.Y.), 295; *Brogy v. The Commonwealth*, 10 Gratt. (Va.) 722; *Bergen v. The People*, 17 Ill. 426; *Dupree v. The State*, 33 Ala. 380.

Third, As to the constitutionality of the Poland Bill. Rev. Stat., sect. 5352. Undoubtedly Congress, under art. 4, sect. 3, of the Constitution, which gives 'power to dispose of and make all needful rules and regulations respecting the territory or other property belonging to the United States,' and under the decisions of this court upon it, may legislate over such territory, and regulate the form of its local government. But its legislation can be neither exclusive nor arbitrary. The power of this government to obtain and hold territory over which it might legislate, without restriction, would be inconsistent with its own existence in its present form. There is always an excess of power exercised when the Federal government attempts to provide for more than the assertion and preservation of its rights over such territory, and interferes by positive enactment with the social and domestic life of its inhabitants and their internal police. The offence prohibited by sect. 5352 is not a *malum in se*; it is not prohibited by the decalogue; and, if it be said [98 U.S. 145, 153] that its prohibition is to be found in the teachings of the New Testament, we know that a majority of the people of this Territory deny that the Christian law contains any such prohibition.

(Continues)

(Continued)

The Attorney-General and The Solicitor-General, contra.

MR. CHIEF JUSTICE WAITE delivered the opinion of the court.

The assignments of error, when grouped, present the following questions:

1. Was the indictment bad because found by a grand jury of less than sixteen persons?
2. Were the challenges of certain petit jurors by the accused improperly overruled?
3. Were the challenges of certain other jurors by the government improperly sustained?
4. Was the testimony of Amelia Jane Schofield, given at a former trial for the same offence, but under another indictment, improperly admitted in evidence?
5. Should the accused have been acquitted if he married the second time, because he believed it to be his religious duty?
6. Did the court err in that part of the charge which directed the attention of the jury to the consequences of polygamy?

These questions will be considered in their order.

1. As to the grand jury.

The indictment was found in the District Court of the third judicial district of the Territory. The act of Congress 'in relation to courts and judicial officers in the Territory of Utah,' approved June 23, 1874 (18 Stat. 253), while regulating the qualifications of jurors in the Territory, and prescribing the mode of preparing the lists from which grand and petit jurors are to be drawn, as well as the manner of drawing, makes no provision in respect to the number of persons of which a grand jury shall consist. Sect. 808, Revised Statutes, requires that a grand jury impaneled before any district or circuit court of the United States shall consist of not less than sixteen nor more than twenty-three persons, while a statute of the Territory limits the number in the district courts of the Territory [98 U.S. 145, 154] to fifteen. Comp. Laws Utah, 1876, 357. The grand jury which found this indictment consisted of only fifteen persons, and the question to be determined is, whether the section of the Revised Statutes referred to or the statute of the Territory governs the case.

By sect. 1910 of the Revised Statutes the district courts of the Territory have the same jurisdiction in all cases arising under the Constitution and laws of the United States as is vested in the circuit and district courts of the United States; but this does not make them circuit and district courts of the United States. We have often so decided. *American Insurance Co. v. Canter*, 1 Pet. 511; *Benner et al. v. Porter*, 9 How. 235; *Clinton v. Englebrecht*, 13 Wall. 434. They are courts of the Territories, invested for some purposes with the powers of the courts of the United States. Writs of error and appeals lie from them to the Supreme Court of the Territory, and from that court as a territorial court to this in some cases.

Sect. 808 was not designed to regulate the impaneling of grand juries in all courts where offenders against the laws of the United States could be tried, but only in the circuit and district courts. This leaves the territorial courts free to act in obedience to the requirements of the territorial laws in force for the time being. *Clinton v. Englebrecht*, supra; *Hornbuckle v. Toombs*, 18 Wall. 648. As Congress may at any time assume control of the matter, there is but little danger to be anticipated from improvident territorial legislation in this particular. We are therefore of the opinion that the court below no more erred in sustaining this indictment than it did at a former term, at the instance of this same plaintiff in error, in adjudging another bad which was found against him for the same offence by a grand jury composed of twenty-three persons. 1 Utah, 226.

2. As to the challenges by the accused.

By the Constitution of the United States (Amend. VI.), the accused was entitled to a trial by an impartial jury. A juror to be impartial must, to use the language of Lord Coke, 'be indifferent as he stands unsworn.' Co. Litt. 155 b. Lord Coke also says that a principal cause of challenge is 'so called because, if it be found true, it standeth sufficient of itself, without [98 U.S. 145, 155] leaving any thing to the conscience or discretion of the triers' (id. 156 b); or, as stated in Bacon's Abridgment, 'it is grounded on such a manifest presumption of partiality, that, if found to be true, it unquestionably sets aside the . . . juror.' Bac. Abr., tit. Juries, E. 1. 'If the truth of the matter alleged is admitted, the law pronounces the judgment; but if denied, it must be made out by proof to the satisfaction of the court or the triers.' Id. E. 12. To make out the existence of the fact, the juror who is challenged may be examined on his *voire dire*, and asked any questions that do not tend to his infamy or disgrace.

All of the challenges by the accused were for principal cause. It is good ground for such a challenge that a juror has formed an opinion as to the issue to be tried. The courts are not agreed as to the knowledge upon which the opinion must rest in order to render the juror incompetent, or whether the opinion must be accompanied by malice or ill-will; but all unite in holding that it must be founded on some evidence, and be more than a mere impression. Some say it must be positive (Gabbet, *Criminal Law*, 391); others, that it must be decided and substantial (Armistead's Case, 11 Leigh (Va.), 659; Wormley's Case, 10 Gratt. (Va.) 658; *Neely v. The People*, 13 Ill. 685); others, fixed (*State v. Benton*, 2 Dev. & B. (N.C.) L. 196); and, still others, deliberate and settled (*Staup v. Commonwealth*, 74 Pa. St. 458; *Curley v. Commonwealth*, 84 id. 151). All concede, however, that, if hypothetical only, the partiality is not so manifest as to necessarily set the juror aside. Mr. Chief Justice Marshall, in Burr's Trial (1 Burr's Trial, 416), states the rule to be that 'light impressions, which may fairly be presumed to yield to the testimony that may be offered, which may leave the mind open to a fair consideration of the testimony, constitute no sufficient objection to a juror; but that those strong and deep impressions which close the mind against the testimony that may be offered in opposition to them, which will combat that testimony and resist its force, do constitute a sufficient objection to him.' The theory of the law is that a juror who has formed an opinion cannot be impartial. Every opinion which he may entertain need not necessarily have that effect. In these days of newspaper enterprise and universal education, every case of public interest is almost, as a matter of necessity, [98 U.S. 145, 156] brought to the attention of all the intelligent people in the vicinity, and scarcely any one can be found among those best fitted for jurors who has not read or heard of it, and who has not some impression or some opinion in respect to its merits. It is clear, therefore, that upon the trial of the issue of fact raised by a challenge for such cause the court will practically be called upon to determine whether the nature and strength of the opinion formed are such as in law necessarily to raise the presumption of partiality. The question thus presented is one of mixed law and fact, and to be tried, as far as the facts are concerned, like any other issue of that character, upon the evidence. The finding of the trial court upon that issue ought not to be set aside by a reviewing court, unless the error is manifest. No less stringent rules should be applied by the reviewing court in such a case than those which govern in the consideration of motions for new trial because the verdict is against the evidence. It must be made clearly to appear that upon the evidence the court ought to have found the juror had formed such an opinion that he could not in law be deemed impartial. The case must be one in which it is manifest the law left nothing to the 'conscience or discretion' of the court.

The challenge in this case most relied upon in the argument here is that of Charles Read. He was sworn on his *voire dire*; and his evidence, 1 taken as a whole, shows that he 'believed' he had formed an opinion which he had never expressed, but which he did not think would influence his verdict on hearing the testimony. We cannot think this is such a manifestation of partiality as to leave nothing to the 'conscience or discretion' of the triers. The reading of the evidence leaves the impression that the juror had some hypothetical opinion about the case, but it falls far short of raising a manifest presumption of partiality. In considering such questions in a reviewing court, we ought not to be unmindful of the fact we have so often observed in our experience, that jurors not unfrequently seek to excuse themselves on the ground of having formed an opinion, when, on examination, it turns out that no real disqualification exists. In such cases the manner of the [98 U.S. 145, 157] juror while testifying is oftentimes more indicative of the real character of his opinion than his words. That is seen below, but cannot always be spread upon the record. Care should, therefore, be taken in the reviewing court not to reverse the ruling below upon such a question of fact, except in a clear case. The affirmative of the issue is upon the challenger. Unless he shows the actual existence of such an opinion in the mind of the juror as will raise the presumption of partiality, the juror need not necessarily be set aside, and it will not be error in the court to refuse to do so. Such a case, in our opinion, was not made out upon the challenge of Read. The fact that he had not expressed his opinion is important only as tending to show that he had not formed one which disqualified him. If a positive and decided opinion had been formed, he would have been incompetent even though it had not been expressed. Under these circumstances, it is unnecessary to consider the case of Ransohoff, for it was confessedly not as strong as that of Read.

3. As to the challenges by the government.

The questions raised upon these assignments of error are not whether the district attorney should have been permitted to interrogate the jurors while under examination upon their *voire dire* as to the fact of their living in polygamy. No objection was made below to the questions, but only to the ruling of the court upon the challenges after the testimony taken in answer to the questions was in. From the testimony it is apparent that all the jurors to whom the challenges related were or had been living in polygamy. It needs no argument to show that such a jury could not have gone into the box entirely free from bias and prejudice, and that if the challenge was not good for principal cause, it

(Continues)

was for favor. A judgment will not be reversed simply because a challenge good for favor was sustained in form for cause. As the jurors were incompetent and properly excluded, it matters not here upon what form of challenge they were set aside. In one case the challenge was for favor. In the courts of the United States all challenges are tried by the court without the aid of triers (Rev. Stat. sect. 819), and we are not advised that the practice in the territorial courts of Utah is different. [98 U.S. 145, 158] 4. As to the admission of evidence to prove what was sworn to by Amelia Jane Schofield on a former trial of the accused for the same offence but under a different indictment.

The Constitution gives the accused the right to a trial at which he should be confronted with the witnesses against him; but if a witness is absent by his own wrongful procurement, he cannot complain if competent evidence is admitted to supply the place of that which he has kept away. The Constitution does not guarantee an accused person against the legitimate consequences of his own wrongful acts. It grants him the privilege of being confronted with the witnesses against him; but if he voluntarily keeps the witnesses away, he cannot insist on his privilege. If, therefore, when absent by his procurement, their evidence is supplied in some lawful way, he is in no condition to assert that his constitutional rights have been violated.

In Lord Morley's Case (6 State Trials, 770), as long ago as the year 1666, it was resolved in the House of Lords 'that in case oath should be made that any witness, who had been examined by the coroner and was then absent, was detained by the means or procurement of the prisoner, and the opinion of the judges asked whether such examination might be read, we should answer, that if their lordships were satisfied by the evidence they had heard that the witness was detained by means or procurement of the prisoner, then the examination might be read; but whether he was detained by means or procurement of the prisoner was matter of fact, of which we were not the judges, but their lordships.' This resolution was followed in Harrison's Case (12 id. 851), and seems to have been recognized as the law in England ever since. In *Regina v. Scaife* (17 Ad. & El. N.S. 242), all the judges agreed that if the prisoner had resorted to a contrivance to keep a witness out of the way, the deposition of the witness, taken before a magistrate and in the presence of the prisoner, might be read. Other cases to the same effect are to be found, and in this country the ruling has been in the same way. *Drayton v. Wells*, 1 Nott & M. (S.C.) 409; *Williams v. The State*, 19 Ga. 403. So that now, in the leading text-books, it is laid down that if a witness is kept away by the adverse party, [98 U.S. 145, 159] his testimony, taken on a former trial between the same parties upon the same issues, may be given in evidence. 1 Greenl. Evid., sect. 163; 1 Taylor, Evid., sect. 446. Mr. Wharton (1 Whart. Evid., sect. 178) seemingly limits the rule somewhat, and confines it to cases where the witness has been corruptly kept away by the party against whom he is to be called, but in reality his statement is the same as that of the others; for in all it is implied that the witness must have been wrongfully kept away. The rule has its foundation in the maxim that no one shall be permitted to take advantage of his own wrong; and, consequently, if there has not been, in legal contemplation, a wrong committed, the way has not been opened for the introduction of the testimony. We are content with this long-established usage, which, so far as we have been able to discover, has rarely been departed from. It is the outgrowth of a maxim based on the principles of common honesty, and, if properly administered, can harm no one.

Such being the rule, the question becomes practically one of fact, to be settled as a preliminary to the admission of secondary evidence. In this respect it is like the preliminary question of the proof of loss of a written instrument, before secondary evidence of the contents of the instrument can be admitted. In Lord Morley's Case (supra), it would seem to have been considered a question for the trial court alone, and not subject to review on error or appeal; but without deeming it necessary in this case to go so far as that, we have no hesitation in saying that the finding of the court below is, at least, to have the effect of a verdict of a jury upon a question of fact, and should not be disturbed unless the error is manifest.

The testimony shows that the absent witness was the alleged second wife of the accused; that she had testified on a former trial for the same offence under another indictment; that she had no home, except with the accused; that at some time before the trial a subpoena had been issued for her, but by mistake she was named as Mary Jane Schobold; that an officer who knew the witness personally went to the house of the accused to serve the subpoena, and on his arrival inquired for her, either by the name of Mary Jane Schofield or Mrs. Reynolds; that he was tole by the accused she was not at home; [98 U.S. 145, 160] that he then said, 'Will you tell me where she is?' that the reply was 'No; that will be for you to find out;' that the officer then remarked she was making him considerable trouble, and that she would get into trouble herself; and the accused replied, 'Oh, no; she won't, till the subpoena is served upon her,' and then, after some further conversation, that 'She does not appear in this case.'

It being discovered after the trial commenced that a wrong name had been inserted in the subpoena, a new subpoena was issued with the right name, at nine o'clock in the evening. With this the officer went again to the house, and there found a person known as the first wife of the accused. He was told by her that the witness was not there, and had not been for three weeks. He went again the next morning, and not finding her, or being able to ascertain where she was by inquiring in the neighborhood, made return of that fact to the court. At ten o'clock that morning the case was again called; and the foregoing facts being made to appear, the court ruled that evidence of what the witness had sworn to at the former trial was admissible.

In this we see no error. The accused was himself personally present in court when the showing was made, and had full opportunity to account for the absence of the witness, if he would, or to deny under oath that he had kept her away. Clearly, enough had been proven to cast the burden upon him of showing that he had not been instrumental in concealing or keeping the witness away. Having the means of making the necessary explanation, and having every inducement to do so if he would, the presumption is that he considered it better to rely upon the weakness of the case made against him than to attempt to develop the strength of his own. Upon the testimony as it stood, it is clear to our minds that the judgment should not be reversed because secondary evidence was admitted.

This brings us to the consideration of what the former testimony was, and the evidence by which it was proven to the jury.

It was testimony given on a former trial of the same person for the same offence, but under another indictment. It was [98 U.S. 145, 161] substantially testimony given at another time in the same cause. The accused was present at the time the testimony was given, and had full opportunity of cross-examination. This brings the case clearly within the well-established rules. The cases are fully cited in 1 Whart. Evid., sect. 177.

The objection to the reading by Mr. Patterson of what was sworn to on the former trial does not seem to have been because the paper from which he read was not a true record of the evidence as given, but because the foundation for admitting the secondary evidence had not been laid. This objection, as has already been seen, was not well taken.

5. As to the defence of religious belief or duty.

On the trial, the plaintiff in error, the accused, proved that at the time of his alleged second marriage he was, and for many years before had been, a member of the Church of Jesus Christ of Latter-Day Saints, commonly called the Mormon Church, and a believer in its doctrines; that it was an accepted doctrine of that church 'that it was the duty of male members of said church, circumstances permitting, to practise polygamy; . . . that this duty was enjoined by different books which the members of said church believed to be of divine origin, and among others the Holy Bible, and also that the members of the church believed that the practice of polygamy was directly enjoined upon the male members thereof by the Almighty God, in a revelation to Joseph Smith, the founder and prophet of said church; that the failing or refusing to practise polygamy by such male members of said church, when circumstances would admit, would be punished, and that the penalty for such failure and refusal would be damnation in the life to come.' He also proved 'that he had received permission from the recognized authorities in said church to enter into polygamous marriage; . . . that Daniel H. Wells, one having authority in said church to perform the marriage ceremony, married the said defendant on or about the time the crime is alleged to have been committed, to some woman by the name of Schofield, and that such marriage ceremony was performed under and pursuant to the doctrines of said church.'

Upon this proof he asked the court to instruct the jury that if they found from the evidence that he 'was married as [98 U.S. 145, 162] charged—if he was married—in pursuance of and in conformity with what he believed at the time to be a religious duty, that the verdict must be 'not guilty.'' This request was refused, and the court did charge 'that there must have been a criminal intent, but that if the defendant, under the influence of a religious belief that it was right, under an inspiration, if you please, that it was right, deliberately married a second time, having a first wife living, the want of consciousness of evil intent—the want of understanding on his part that he was committing a crime—did not excuse him; but the law inexorably in such case implies the criminal intent.'

Upon this charge and refusal to charge the question is raised, whether religious belief can be accepted as a justification of an overt act made criminal by the law of the land. The inquiry is not as

(Continues)

to the power of Congress to prescribe criminal laws for the Territories, but as to the guilt of one who knowingly violates a law which has been properly enacted, if he entertains a religious belief that the law is wrong.

Congress cannot pass a law for the government of the Territories which shall prohibit the free exercise of religion. The first amendment to the Constitution expressly forbids such legislation. Religious freedom is guaranteed everywhere throughout the United States, so far as congressional interference is concerned. The question to be determined is, whether the law now under consideration comes within this prohibition.

The word 'religion' is not defined in the Constitution. We must go elsewhere, therefore, to ascertain its meaning, and nowhere more appropriately, we think, than to the history of the times in the midst of which the provision was adopted. The precise point of the inquiry is, what is the religious freedom which has been guaranteed.

Before the adoption of the Constitution, attempts were made in some of the colonies and States to legislate not only in respect to the establishment of religion, but in respect to its doctrines and precepts as well. The people were taxed, against their will, for the support of religion, and sometimes for the support of particular sects to whose tenets they could not and did not subscribe. Punishments were prescribed for a failure to attend upon public worship, and sometimes for entertaining [98 U.S. 145, 163] heretical opinions. The controversy upon this general subject was animated in many of the States, but seemed at last to culminate in Virginia. In 1784, the House of Delegates of that State having under consideration 'a bill establishing provision for teachers of the Christian religion,' postponed it until the next session, and directed that the bill should be published and distributed, and that the people be requested 'to signify their opinion respecting the adoption of such a bill at the next session of assembly.'

This brought out a determined opposition. Amongst others, Mr. Madison prepared a 'Memorial and Remonstrance,' which was widely circulated and signed, and in which he demonstrated 'that religion, or the duty we owe the Creator,' was not within the cognizance of civil government. Semple's Virginia Baptists, Appendix. At the next session the proposed bill was not only defeated, but another, 'for establishing religious freedom,' drafted by Mr. Jefferson, was passed. 1 Jeff. Works, 45; 2 Howison, *Hist. of Va.* 298. In the preamble of this act (12 Hening's Stat. 84) religious freedom is defined; and after a recital 'that to suffer the civil magistrate to intrude his powers into the field of opinion, and to restrain the profession or propagation of principles on supposition of their ill tendency, is a dangerous fallacy which at once destroys all religious liberty,' it is declared 'that it is time enough for the rightful purposes of civil government for its officers to interfere when principles break out into overt acts against peace and good order.' In these two sentences is found the true distinction between what properly belongs to the church and what to the State.

In a little more than a year after the passage of this statute the convention met which prepared the Constitution of the United States.' Of this convention Mr. Jefferson was not a member, he being then absent as minister to France. As soon as he saw the draft of the Constitution proposed for adoption, he, in a letter to a friend, expressed his disappointment at the absence of an express declaration insuring the freedom of religion (2 *Jeff. Works*, 355), but was willing to accept it as it was, trusting that the good sense and honest intentions of the people would bring about the necessary alterations. [98 U.S. 145, 164] 1 *Jeff. Works*, 79. Five of the States, while adopting the Constitution, proposed amendments. Three—New Hampshire, New York, and Virginia—included in one form or another a declaration of religious freedom in the changes they desired to have made, as did also North Carolina, where the convention at first declined to ratify the Constitution until the proposed amendments were acted upon. Accordingly, at the first session of the first Congress the amendment now under consideration was proposed with others by Mr. Madison. It met the views of the advocates of religious freedom, and was adopted. Mr. Jefferson afterwards, in reply to an address to him by a committee of the Danbury Baptist Association (8 id. 113), took occasion to say: 'Believing with you that religion is a matter which lies solely between man and his God; that he owes account to none other for his faith or his worship; that the legislative powers of the government reach actions only, and not opinions, I contemplate with sovereign reverence that act of the whole American people which declared that their legislature should 'make no law respecting an establishment of religion or prohibiting the free exercise thereof,' thus building a wall of separation between church and State. Adhering to this expression of the supreme will of the nation in behalf of the rights of conscience, I shall see with sincere satisfaction the progress of those sentiments which tend to restore man to all his natural rights, convinced he has no natural right in opposition to his social duties.' Coming as this does from an acknowledged leader of the advocates of the measure, it may be accepted almost as an authoritative declaration of the scope and effect of the amendment thus secured. Congress was deprived of all legislative power over mere opinion, but was left free to reach actions which were in violation of social duties or subversive of good order.

Polygamy has always been odious among the northern and western nations of Europe, and, until the establishment of the Mormon Church, was almost exclusively a feature of the life of Asiatic and of African people. At common law, the second marriage was always void (2 Kent, Com. 79), and from the earliest history of England polygamy has been treated as an offence against society. After the establishment of the ecclesiastical [98 U.S. 145, 165] courts, and until the time of James I., it was punished through the instrumentality of those tribunals, not merely because ecclesiastical rights had been violated, but because upon the separation of the ecclesiastical courts from the civil the ecclesiastical were supposed to be the most appropriate for the trial of matrimonial causes and offences against the rights of marriage, just as they were for testamentary causes and the settlement of the estates of deceased persons.

By the statute of 1 James I. (c. 11), the offence, if committed in England or Wales, was made punishable in the civil courts, and the penalty was death. As this statute was limited in its operation to England and Wales, it was at a very early period re-enacted, generally with some modifications, in all the colonies. In connection with the case we are now considering, it is a significant fact that on the 8th of December, 1788, after the passage of the act establishing religious freedom, and after the convention of Virginia had recommended as an amendment to the Constitution of the United States the declaration in a bill of rights that 'all men have an equal, natural, and unalienable right to the free exercise of religion, according to the dictates of conscience,' the legislature of that State substantially enacted the statute of James I., death penalty included, because, as recited in the preamble, 'it hath been doubted whether bigamy or poligamy be punishable by the laws of this Commonwealth.' 12 Hening's Stat. 691. From that day to this we think it may safely be said there never has been a time in any State of the Union when polygamy has not been an offence against society, cognizable by the civil courts and punishable with more or less severity. In the face of all this evidence, it is impossible to believe that the constitutional guaranty of religious freedom was intended to prohibit legislation in respect to this most important feature of social life. Marriage, while from its very nature a sacred obligation, is nevertheless, in most civilized nations, a civil contract, and usually regulated by law. Upon it society may be said to be built, and out of its fruits spring social relations and social obligations and duties, with which government is necessarily required to deal. In fact, according as monogamous or polygamous marriages are allowed, do we find the principles on which the government of [98 U.S. 145, 166] the people, to a greater or less extent, rests. Professor Lieber says, polygamy leads to the patriarchal principle, and which, when applied to large communities, fetters the people in stationary despotism, while that principle cannot long exist in connection with monogamy. Chancellor Kent observes that this remark is equally striking and profound. 2 Kent, Com. 81, note (e). An exceptional colony of polygamists under an exceptional leadership may sometimes exist for a time without appearing to disturb the social condition of the people who surround it; but there cannot be a doubt that, unless restricted by some form of constitution, it is within the legitimate scope of the power of every civil government to determine whether polygamy or monogamy shall be the law of social life under its dominion.

In our opinion, the statute immediately under consideration is within the legislative power of Congress. It is constitutional and valid as prescribing a rule of action for all those residing in the Territories, and in places over which the United States have exclusive control. This being so, the only question which remains is, whether those who make polygamy a part of their religion are excepted from the operation of the statute. If they are, then those who do not make polygamy a part of their religious belief may be found guilty and punished, while those who do, must be acquitted and go free. This would be introducing a new element into criminal law. Laws are made for the government of actions, and while they cannot interfere with mere religious belief and opinions, they may with practices. Suppose one believed that human sacrifices were a necessary part of religious worship, would it be seriously contended that the civil government under which he lived could not interfere to prevent a sacrifice? Or if a wife religiously believed it was her duty to burn herself upon the funeral pile of her dead husband, would it be beyond the power of the civil government to prevent her carrying her belief into practice?

(Continues)

(*Continued*)

So here, as a law of the organization of society under the exclusive dominion of the United States, it is provided that plural marriages shall not be allowed. Can a man excuse his practices to the contrary because of his religious belief? [98 U.S. 145, 167]. To permit this would be to make the professed doctrines of religious belief superior to the law of the land, and in effect to permit every citizen to become a law unto himself. Government could exist only in name under such circumstances.

A criminal intent is generally an element of crime, but every man is presumed to intend the necessary and legitimate consequences of what he knowingly does. Here the accused knew he had been once married, and that his first wife was living. He also knew that his second marriage was forbidden by law. When, therefore, he married the second time, he is presumed to have intended to break the law. And the breaking of the law is the crime. Every act necessary to constitute the crime was knowingly done, and the crime was therefore knowingly committed. Ignorance of a fact may sometimes be taken as evidence of a want of criminal intent, but not ignorance of the law. The only defence of the accused in this case is his belief that the law ought not to have been enacted. It matters not that his belief was a part of his professed religion: it was still belief, and belief only.

In *Regina v. Wagstaff* (10 Cox Crim. Cases, 531), the parents of a sick child, who omitted to call in medical attendance because of their religious belief that what they did for its cure would be effective, were held not to be guilty of manslaughter, while it was said the contrary would have been the result if the child had actually been starved to death by the parents, under the notion that it was their religious duty to abstain from giving it food. But when the offence consists of a positive act which is knowingly done, it would be dangerous to hold that the offender might escape punishment because he religiously believed the law which he had broken ought never to have been made. No case, we believe, can be found that has gone so far.

6. As to that part of the charge which directed the attention of the jury to the consequences of polygamy.

The passage complained of is as follows: 'I think it not improper, in the discharge of your duties in this case, that you should consider what are to be the consequences to the innocent victims of this delusion. As this contest goes on, they multiply, [98 U.S. 145, 168] and there are pure-minded women and there are innocent children, innocent in a sense even beyond the degree of the innocence of childhood itself. These are to be the sufferers; and as jurors fail to do their duty, and as these cases come up in the Territory of Utah, just so do these victims multiply and spread themselves over the land.'

While every appeal by the court to the passions or the prejudices of a jury should be promptly rebuked, and while it is the imperative duty of a reviewing court to take care that wrong is not done in this way, we see no just cause for complaint in this case. Congress, in 1862 (12 Stat. 501), saw fit to make bigamy a crime in the Territories. This was done because of the evil consequences that were supposed to flow from plural marriages. All the court did was to call the attention of the jury to the peculiar character of the crime for which the accused was on trial, and to remind them of the duty they had to perform. There was no appeal to the passions, no instigation of prejudice. Upon the showing made by the accused himself, he was guilty of a violation of the law under which he had been indicted: and the effort of the court seems to have been not to withdraw the minds of the jury from the issue to be tried, but to bring them to it; not to make them partial, but to keep them impartial.

Upon a careful consideration of the whole case, we are satisfied that no error was committed by the court below.

Judgment affirmed.

MR. JUSTICE FIELD.

I concur with the majority of the court on the several points decided except one, that which relates to the admission of the testimony of Amelia Jane Schofield given on a former trial upon a different indictment. I do not think that a sufficient foundation was laid for its introduction. The authorities cited by the Chief Justice to sustain its admissibility seem to me to establish conclusively the exact reverse.

NOTE. At a subsequent day of the term a petition for a rehearing having been filed, MR. CHIEF JUSTICE WAITE delivered the opinion of the court.

Since our judgment in this case was announced, a petition for rehearing has been filed, in which our attention is called to the fact that the sentence of the [98 U.S. 145, 169] court below requires the imprisonment to be at hard labor, when the act of Congress under which the indictment was found provides for punishment by imprisonment only. This was not assigned for error on the former hearing, and we might on that account decline to consider it now; but as the irregularity is one which appears on the face of the record, we vacate our former judgment of affirmance, and reverse the judgment of the court below for the purpose of correcting the only error which appears in the record, to wit, in the form of the sentence. The cause is remanded, with instructions to cause the sentence of the District Court to be set aside and a new one entered on the verdict in all respects like that before imposed, except so far as it requires the imprisonment to be at hard labor.

Marsh v. Chambers, 463 U.S. 783 (1983)

The Nebraska Legislature begins each of its sessions with a prayer by a chaplain paid by the State with the legislature's approval. Respondent member of the Nebraska Legislature brought an action in Federal District Court, claiming that the legislature's chaplaincy practice violates the Establishment Clause of the First Amendment, and seeking injunctive relief. The District Court held that the Establishment Clause was not breached by the prayer but was violated by paying the chaplain from public funds, and accordingly enjoined the use of such funds to pay the chaplain. The Court of Appeals held that the whole chaplaincy practice violated the Establishment Clause, and accordingly prohibited the State from engaging in any aspect of the practice.

Held:

The Nebraska Legislature's chaplaincy practice does not violate the Establishment Clause. Pp. 786–795.

(a) The practice of opening sessions of Congress with prayer has continued without interruption for almost 200 years ever since the First Congress drafted the First Amendment, and a similar practice has been followed for more than a century in Nebraska and many other states. While historical patterns, standing alone, cannot justify contemporary violations of constitutional guarantees, historical evidence in the context of this case sheds light not only on what the drafters of the First Amendment intended the Establishment Clause to mean but also on how they thought that Clause applied to the chaplaincy practice authorized by the First Congress. In applying the First Amendment to the states through the Fourteenth Amendment, it would be incongruous to interpret the Clause as imposing more stringent First Amendment limits on the states than the draftsmen imposed on the Federal Government. In light of the history, there can be no doubt that the practice of opening legislative sessions with prayer has become part of the fabric of our society. To invoke divine guidance on a public body entrusted with making the laws is not, in these circumstances, a violation of the Establishment Clause; it is simply a tolerable acknowledgment of beliefs widely held among the people of this country. Pp. 786–792.

(b) Weighed against the historical background, the facts that a clergyman of only one denomination has been selected by the Nebraska Legislature [463 U.S. 783, 784] for 16 years, that the chaplain is paid at public expense, and that the prayers are in the Judeo-Christian tradition do not serve to invalidate Nebraska's practice. Pp. 792–795.

675 F.2d 228, reversed.

BURGER, C. J., delivered the opinion of the Court, in which WHITE, BLACKMUN, POWELL, REHNQUIST, and O'CONNOR, J.J., joined. BRENNAN, J., filed a dissenting opinion, in which MARSHALL, J., joined, post, p. 795. STEVENS, J., filed a dissenting opinion, post, p. 822.

Shanler D. Cronk, Assistant Attorney General of Nebraska, argued the cause for petitioners. With him on the briefs was Paul L. Douglas, Attorney General.

Herbert J. Friedman argued the cause for respondent. With him on the brief were Stephen L. Pevar, Burt Neuborne, and Charles S. Sims.*

---

*Solicitor General Lee, Assistant Attorney General McGrath, Deputy Solicitor General Geller, Kathryn A. Oberly, Leonard Schaitman, and Michael Jay Singer filed a brief for the United States as *amicus curiae* urging reversal.

(Continues)

Briefs of *amici curiae* urging affirmance were filed by Nathan Z. Dershowitz and Marc D. Stern for the American Jewish Congress; by David J. Eiseman, Justin J. Finger, and Jeffrey P. Sinensky for the Anti-Defamation League of B'nai B'rith; and by Thomas P. Gies for Jon Garth Murray et al.

Lanny M. Proffer filed a brief for the National Conference of State Legislatures as amicus curiae.

CHIEF JUSTICE BURGER delivered the opinion of the Court.

The question presented is whether the Nebraska Legislature's practice of opening each legislative day with a prayer by a chaplain paid by the State violates the Establishment Clause of the First Amendment.

I

The Nebraska Legislature begins each of its sessions with a prayer offered by a chaplain who is chosen biennially by the Executive Board of the Legislative Council and paid out of [463 U.S. 783, 785] public funds.[1] Robert E. Palmer, a Presbyterian minister, has served as chaplain since 1965 at a salary of $319.75 per month for each month the legislature is in session.

Ernest Chambers is a member of the Nebraska Legislature and a taxpayer of Nebraska. Claiming that the Nebraska Legislature's chaplaincy practice violates the Establishment Clause of the First Amendment, he brought this action under 42 U.S.C. 1983, seeking to enjoin enforcement of the practice.[2] After denying a motion to dismiss on the ground of legislative immunity, the District Court held that the Establishment Clause was not breached by the prayers, but was violated by paying the chaplain from public funds. 504 F. Supp. 585 (Neb. 1980). It therefore enjoined the legislature from using public funds to pay the chaplain; it declined to enjoin the policy of beginning sessions with prayers. Cross-appeals were taken.[3]

The Court of Appeals for the Eighth Circuit rejected arguments that the case should be dismissed on Tenth Amendment, legislative immunity, standing, or federalism grounds. On the merits of the chaplaincy issue, the court refused to treat respondent's challenges as separable issues as the District Court had done. Instead, the Court of Appeals assessed the practice as a whole because "[p]arsing out [the] [463 U.S. 783, 786] elements" would lead to "an incongruous result." 675 F.2d 228, 233 (1982).

Applying the three-part test of *Lemon v. Kurtzman*, 403 U.S. 602, 612–613 (1971), as set out in *Committee for Public Education & Religious Liberty v. Nyquist*, 413 U.S. 756, 773 (1973), the court held that the chaplaincy practice violated all three elements of the test: the purpose and primary effect of selecting the same minister for 16 years and publishing his prayers was to promote a particular religious expression; use of state money for compensation and publication led to entanglement. 675 F.2d, at 234–235. Accordingly, the Court of Appeals modified the District Court's injunction and prohibited the State from engaging in any aspect of its established chaplaincy practice.

We granted *certiorari* limited to the challenge to the practice of opening sessions with prayers by a state-employed clergyman, 459 U.S. 966 (1982), and we reverse.[4]

II

The opening of sessions of legislative and other deliberative public bodies with prayer is deeply embedded in the history and tradition of this country. From colonial times through the founding of the Republic and ever since, the practice of legislative prayer has coexisted with the principles of disestablishment and religious freedom. In the very courtrooms in which the United States District Judge and later three Circuit Judges heard and decided this case, the proceedings opened with an announcement that concluded, "God save the United States and this Honorable Court." The same invocation occurs at all sessions of this Court. [463 U.S. 783, 787].

The tradition in many of the Colonies was, of course, linked to an established church,[5] but the Continental Congress, beginning in 1774, adopted the traditional procedure of opening its sessions with a prayer offered by a paid chaplain. See, e.g., 1 J. Continental Cong. 26 (1774); 2 id., at 12 (1775); 5 id., at 530 (1776); 6 id., at 887 (1776); 27 id., at 683 (1784). See also 1 A. Stokes, *Church and State in the United States*, 448–450 (1950). Although prayers were not offered during the Constitutional Convention,[6] the First Congress, as one of [463 U.S. 783, 788] its early items of business, adopted the policy of selecting a chaplain to open each session with prayer. Thus, on April 7, 1789, the Senate appointed a committee "to take under consideration the manner of electing Chaplains." *S. Jour.*, 1st Cong., 1st Sess., 10 (1820 ed.). On April 9, 1789, a similar committee was appointed by the House of Representatives. On April 25, 1789, the Senate elected its first chaplain, id., at 16; the House followed suit on May 1, 1789, *H. R. Jour.*, 1st Cong., 1st Sess., 26 (1826 ed.).

A statute providing for the payment of these chaplains was enacted into law on September 22, 1789.[7] 2 *Annals of Cong.* 2180; 4, 1 Stat. 71.[8]

On September 25, 1789, three days after Congress authorized the appointment of paid chaplains, final agreement was reached on the language of the Bill of Rights, *S. Jour.*, supra, at 88; *H. R. Jour.*, *supra*, at 121.[9] Clearly the men who wrote the First Amendment Religion Clauses did not view paid legislative chaplains and opening prayers as a violation of that Amendment, for the practice of opening sessions with prayer has continued without interruption ever since that early session of Congress.[10] It has also been followed consistently [463 U.S. 783, 789] in most of the states,[11] including Nebraska, where the institution of opening legislative sessions with prayer was adopted even before the State attained statehood. Neb. [463 U.S. 783, 790] Jour. of Council, General Assembly, 1st Sess., 16 (Jan. 22, 1855).

Standing alone, historical patterns cannot justify contemporary violations of constitutional guarantees, but there is far more here than simply historical patterns. In this context, historical evidence sheds light not only on what the draftsmen intended the Establishment Clause to mean, but also on how they thought that Clause applied to the practice authorized by the First Congress their actions reveal their intent. An Act

> "passed by the first Congress assembled under the Constitution, many of whose members had taken part in framing that instrument, . . . is contemporaneous and weighty evidence of its true meaning." *Wisconsin v. Pelican Ins. Co.*, 127 U.S. 265, 297 (1888).

In *Walz v. Tax Comm'n*, 397 U.S. 664, 678 (1970), we considered the weight to be accorded to history:

> "It is obviously correct that no one acquires a vested or protected right in violation of the Constitution by long use, even when that span of time covers our entire national existence and indeed predates it. Yet an unbroken practice . . . is not something to be lightly cast aside."

No more is Nebraska's practice of over a century, consistent with two centuries of national practice, to be cast aside. It can hardly be thought that in the same week Members of the First Congress voted to appoint and to pay a chaplain for each House and also voted to approve the draft of the First Amendment for submission to the states, they intended the Establishment Clause of the Amendment to forbid what they had just declared acceptable. In applying the First Amendment to the states through the Fourteenth Amendment, *Cantwell v. Connecticut*, 310 U.S. 296 (1940), it would be incongruous to interpret that Clause as imposing more stringent [463 U.S. 783, 791] First Amendment limits on the states than the draftsmen imposed on the Federal Government.

This unique history leads us to accept the interpretation of the First Amendment draftsmen who saw no real threat to the Establishment Clause arising from a practice of prayer similar to that now challenged. We conclude that legislative prayer presents no more potential for establishment than the provision of school transportation, *Everson v. Board of Education*, 330 U.S. 1 (1947), beneficial grants for higher education, *Tilton v. Richardson*, 403 U.S. 672 (1971), or tax exemptions for religious organizations, Walz, *supra*.

Respondent cites JUSTICE BRENNAN's concurring opinion in *Abington School Dist. v. Schempp*, 374 U.S. 203, 237 (1963), and argues that we should not rely too heavily on "the advice of the Founding Fathers" because the messages of history often tend to be ambiguous and not relevant to a society far more heterogeneous than that of the Framers, id., at 240. Respondent also points out that John Jay and John Rutledge opposed the motion to begin the first session of the Continental Congress with prayer. Brief for Respondent 60.[12]

We do not agree that evidence of opposition to a measure weakens the force of the historical argument; indeed it infuses it with power by demonstrating that the subject was considered carefully and the action not taken thoughtlessly, by force of long tradition and without regard to the problems posed by a pluralistic society. Jay and Rutledge specifically grounded their objection on the fact that the delegates to the Congress "were so divided in religious sentiments . . . that [they] could not join in the same act of worship." Their objection [463 U.S. 783, 792] was met by Samuel Adams, who stated that "he was no bigot, and could hear a prayer from a gentleman of piety and virtue, who was at the same time a friend to his country." C. Adams, *Familiar Letters of John Adams and his Wife, Abigail Adams, during the Revolution*, 37–38, reprinted in Stokes, at 449.

(Continues)

(*Continued*)

This interchange emphasizes that the delegates did not consider opening prayers as a proselytizing activity or as symbolically placing the government's "official seal of approval on one religious view," cf. 675 F.2d, at 234. Rather, the Founding Fathers looked at invocations as "conduct whose . . . effect . . . harmonize[d] with the tenets of some or all religions." *McGowan v. Maryland*, 366 U.S. 420, 442 (1961). The Establishment Clause does not always bar a state from regulating conduct simply because it "harmonizes with religious canons." Id., at 462 (Frankfurter, J., concurring). Here, the individual claiming injury by the practice is an adult, presumably not readily susceptible to "religious indoctrination," see Tilton, *supra*, at 686; *Colo v. Treasurer & Receiver General*, 378 Mass. 550, 559, 392 N. E. 2d 1195, 1200 (1979), or peer pressure, compare Abington, *supra*, at 290 (BRENNAN, J., concurring).

In light of the unambiguous and unbroken history of more than 200 years, there can be no doubt that the practice of opening legislative sessions with prayer has become part of the fabric of our society. To invoke Divine guidance on a public body entrusted with making the laws is not, in these circumstances, an "establishment" of religion or a step toward establishment; it is simply a tolerable acknowledgment of beliefs widely held among the people of this country. As Justice Douglas observed, "[w]e are a religious people whose institutions presuppose a Supreme Being." *Zorach v. Clauson*, 343 U.S. 306, 313 (1952).

III

We turn then to the question of whether any features of the Nebraska practice violate the Establishment Clause. [463 U.S. 783, 793] Beyond the bare fact that a prayer is offered, three points have been made: first, that a clergyman of only one denomination—Presbyterian—has been selected for 16 years[13]; second, that the chaplain is paid at public expense; and third, that the prayers are in the Judeo-Christian tradition.[14] Weighed against the historical background, these factors do not serve to invalidate Nebraska's practice.[15]

The Court of Appeals was concerned that Palmer's long tenure has the effect of giving preference to his religious views. We cannot, any more than Members of the Congresses of this century, perceive any suggestion that choosing a clergyman of one denomination advances the beliefs of a particular church. To the contrary, the evidence indicates that Palmer was reappointed because his performance and personal qualities were acceptable to the body appointing him.[16] Palmer was not the only clergyman heard by the legislature; guest chaplains have officiated at the request of various legislators and as substitutes during Palmer's absences. Tr. of Oral Arg. 10. Absent proof that the chaplain's reappointment stemmed from an impermissible motive, we conclude [463 U.S. 783, 794] that his long tenure does not in itself conflict with the Establishment Clause.[17]

Nor is the compensation of the chaplain from public funds a reason to invalidate the Nebraska Legislature's chaplaincy; remuneration is grounded in historic practice initiated, as we noted earlier, *supra*, at 788, by the same Congress that drafted the Establishment Clause of the First Amendment. The Continental Congress paid its chaplain, see, e.g., 6 J. Continental Cong. 887 (1776), as did some of the states, see, e.g., Debates of the Convention of Virginia 470 (June 26, 1788). Currently, many state legislatures and the United States Congress provide compensation for their chaplains, Brief for National Conference of State Legislatures as *Amicus Curiae* 3; 2 U.S.C. 61d and 84-2 (1982 ed.); H. R. Res. 7, 96th Cong., 1st Sess. (1979).[18] Nebraska has paid its chaplain for well over a century, see 1867 Neb. Laws 85, 2–4 (June 21, 1867), reprinted in Neb. Gen. Stat. 459 (1873). The content of the prayer is not of concern to judges where, as here, there is no indication that the prayer opportunity has been exploited to proselytize or advance any one, [463 U.S. 783, 795] or to disparage any other, faith or belief. That being so, it is not for us to embark on a sensitive evaluation or to parse the content of a particular prayer.

We do not doubt the sincerity of those, who like respondent, believe that to have prayer in this context risks the beginning of the establishment the Founding Fathers feared. But this concern is not well founded, for as Justice Goldberg aptly observed in his concurring opinion in *Abington*, 374 U.S., at 308:

"It is of course true that great consequences can grow from small beginnings, but the measure of constitutional adjudication is the ability and willingness to distinguish between real threat and mere shadow."

The unbroken practice for two centuries in the National Congress and for more than a century in Nebraska and in many other states gives abundant assurance that there is no real threat "while this Court sits," *Panhandle Oil Co. v. Mississippi ex rel. Knox,* 277 U.S. 218, 223 (1928) (Holmes, J., dissenting).

The judgment of the Court of Appeals is
Reversed.

Notes

1. Rules of the Nebraska Unicameral, Rules 1, 2, and 21. These prayers are recorded in the *Legislative Journal* and, upon the vote of the legislature, collected from time to time into prayerbooks, which are published at public expense. In 1975, 200 copies were printed; prayerbooks were also published in 1978 (200 copies), and 1979 (100 copies). In total, publication costs amounted to $458.56.

2. Respondent named as defendants State Treasurer Frank Marsh, Chaplain Palmer, and the members of the Executive Board of the Legislative Council in their official capacity. All appear as petitioners before us.

3. The District Court also enjoined the State from using public funds to publish the prayers, holding that this practice violated the Establishment Clause. Petitioners have represented to us that they did not challenge this facet of the District Court's decision, Tr. of Oral Arg. 19–20. Accordingly, no issue as to publishing these prayers is before us.

4. Petitioners also sought review of their Tenth Amendment, federalism, and immunity claims. They did not, however, challenge the Court of Appeals' decision as to standing and we agree that Chambers, as a member of the legislature and as a taxpayer whose taxes are used to fund the chaplaincy, has standing to assert this claim.

5. The practice in Colonies with established churches is, of course, not dispositive of the legislative prayer question. The history of Virginia is instructive, however, because that Colony took the lead in defining religious rights. In 1776, the Virginia Convention adopted a Declaration of Rights that included, as Article 16, a guarantee of religious liberty that is considered the precursor of both the Free Exercise and Establishment Clauses. 1 B. Schwartz, *The Bill of Rights: A Documentary History,* 231–236 (1971); S. Cobb, *The Rise of Religious Liberty in America,* 491–492 (1970). Virginia was also among the first to disestablish its church. Both before and after disestablishment, however, Virginia followed the practice of opening legislative session with prayer. See, e.g., J. House of Burgesses 34 (Nov. 20, 1712); Debates of the Convention of Virginia 470 (June 2, 1788) (ratification convention); J. House of Delegates of Va. 3 (June 24, 1788) (state legislature).

   Rhode Island's experience mirrored that of Virginia. That Colony was founded by Roger Williams, who was among the first of his era to espouse the principle of religious freedom. Cobb, *supra,* at 426. As early as 1641, its legislature provided for liberty of conscience. Id., at 430. Yet the sessions of its ratification convention, like Virginia's, began with prayers, see W. Staples, *Rhode Island in the Continental Congress,* 1765–1790, p. 668 (1870) (reprinting May 26, 1790, minutes of the convention).

6. History suggests that this may simply have been an oversight. At one point, Benjamin Franklin suggested that, "henceforth prayers imploring the assistance of Heaven, and its blessings on our deliberations, be held in this Assembly every morning before we proceed to business." 1 M. Farrand, *Records of the Federal Convention of 1787,* p. 452 (1911). His proposal was rejected not because the Convention was opposed to prayer, but because it was thought that a midstream adoption of the policy would highlight prior omissions and because "[t]he Convention had no funds." Ibid.; see also Stokes, at 455–456.

7. The statute provided:

   "[T]here shall be allowed to each chaplain of Congress . . . five hundred dollars per annum during the session of Congress."

   This salary compares favorably with the Congressmen's own salaries of $6 for each day of attendance, 1 Stat. 70–71.

8. It bears note that James Madison, one of the principal advocates of religious freedom in the Colonies and a drafter of the Establishment Clause, see, e.g., Cobb, *supra* n. 5, at 495–497; Stokes, at 537–552, was one of those appointed to undertake this task by the House of Representatives, *H. R. Jour.,* at 11–12; Stokes, at 541–549, and voted for the bill authorizing payment of the chaplains, 1 *Annals of Cong.* 891 (1789).

(Continues)

9. Interestingly, September 25, 1789, was also the day that the House resolved to request the President to set aside a Thanksgiving Day to acknowledge "the many signal favors of Almighty God," *H. R. Jour.*, at 123. See also *S. Jour.*, at 88.

10. The chaplaincy was challenged in the 1850s by "sundry petitions praying Congress to abolish the office of chaplain," S. Rep. No. 376, 32d Cong., 2d Sess., 1 (1853). After consideration by the Senate Committee on the [463 U.S. 783, 789] Judiciary, the Senate decided that the practice did not violate the Establishment Clause, reasoning that a rule permitting Congress to elect chaplains is not a law establishing a national church and that the chaplaincy was no different from Sunday Closing Laws, which the Senate thought clearly constitutional. In addition, the Senate reasoned that since prayer was said by the very Congress that adopted the Bill of Rights, the Founding Fathers could not have intended the First Amendment to forbid legislative prayer or viewed prayer as a step toward an established church. Id., at 2–4. In any event, the 35th Congress abandoned the practice of electing chaplains in favor of inviting local clergy to officiate, see *Cong. Globe*, 35th Cong., 1st Sess., 14, 27–28 (1857). Elected chaplains were reinstituted by the 36th Congress, *Cong. Globe*, 36th Cong., 1st Sess., 162 (1859); id., at 1016 (1860).

11. See *Brief for National Conference of State Legislatures as* Amicus Curiae. Although most state legislatures begin their sessions with prayer, most do not have a formal rule requiring this procedure. But see, e.g., Alaska Legislature Uniform Rules 11 and 17 (1981) (providing for opening invocation); Ark. Rule of Senate 18 (1983); *Colo. Legislator's Handbook*, H. R. Rule 44 (1982); Idaho Rules of H. R. and Joint Rules 2 and 4 (1982); Ind. H. R. Rule 10 (1983); Kan. Rule of Senate 4 (1983); Kan. Rule of H. R. 103 (1983); Ky. General Assembly H. Res. 2 (1982); La. Rules of Order, Senate Rule 10.1 (1983); La. Rules of Order, H. R. Rule 8.1 (1982); Me. Senate and House Register, Rule of H. R. 4 (1983); Md. Senate and House of Delegates Rules 1 (1982 and 1983); Mo. Rules of Legislature, Joint Rule 1–1 (1983); N.H. *Manual for the General Court of N.H.*, Rule of H. R. 52(a) (1981); N.D. Senate and H. R. Rules 101 and 301 (1983); Ore. Rule of Senate 4.01 (1983); Ore. Rule of H. R. 4.01 (1983) (opening session only); 104 Pa. Code 11.11 (1983), 107 Pa. Code 21.17 (1983); S.D. *Official Directory and Rules of Senate and H. R.*, Joint Rule of the Senate and House 4–1 (1983); Tenn. Permanent Rules of Order of the Senate 1 and 6 (1981–1982) (provides for admission into Senate chamber of the "Chaplain of the Day"); Tex. Rule of H. R. 2, 6 (1983); Utah Rules of Senate and H. R. 4.04 (1983); *Va. Manual of Senate and House of Delegates*, Rule of Senate 21(a) (1982) (session opens with "period of devotions"); Wash. Permanent Rule of H. R. 15 (1983); Wyo. Rule of Senate 4-1 (1983); Wyo. Rule of H. R. 2-1 (1983). See also P. Mason, *Manual of Legislative Procedure* 586(2) (1979).

12. It also could be noted that objections to prayer were raised, apparently successfully, in Pennsylvania while ratification of the Constitution was debated, *Penn. Herald*, Nov. 24, 1787, and that in the 1820s Madison expressed doubts concerning the chaplaincy practice. See L. Pfeffer, *Church, State, and Freedom*, 248–249 (rev. ed. 1967), citing Fleet, Madison's "Detached Memoranda," 3 *Wm. & Mary Quarterly* 534, 558–559 (1946).

13. In comparison, the First Congress provided for the appointment of two chaplains of different denominations who would alternate between the two Chambers on a weekly basis, *S. Jour.*, 1st Cong., 1st Sess., 12 (1820 ed.); *H. R. Jour.*, 1st Cong., 1st Sess., 16 (1826 ed.).

14. Palmer characterizes his prayers as "nonsectarian," "Judeo Christian," and with "elements of the American civil religion." App. 75 and 87 (deposition of Robert E. Palmer). Although some of his earlier prayers were often explicitly Christian, Palmer removed all references to Christ after a 1980 complaint from a Jewish legislator. Id., at 49.

15. It is also claimed that Nebraska's practice of collecting the prayers into books violates the First Amendment. Because the State did not appeal the District Court order enjoining further publications, see n. 3, *supra*, this issue is not before us and we express no opinion on it.

16. Nebraska's practice is consistent with the manner in which the First Congress viewed its chaplains. Reports contemporaneous with the elections reported only the chaplains' names, and not their religions or church affiliations, see, e.g., 2 *Gazette of the U.S.* 18 (Apr. 25, 1789); 5 id., at 18 (Apr. 27, 1789) (listing nominees for Chaplain of the House); 6 id., at 23 (May 1, 1789). See also *S. Rep.* 376, *supra* n. 10, at 3.

17. We note that Dr. Edward L. R. Elson served as Chaplain of the Senate of the United States from January 1969 to February 1981, a period of 12 years; Dr. Frederick Brown Harris served from February 1949 to January 1969, a period of 20 years. *Senate Library, Chaplains of the Federal Government* (rev. ed. 1982).

18. The states' practices differ widely. Like Nebraska, several states choose a chaplain who serves for the entire legislative session. In other states, the prayer is offered by a different clergyman each day. Under either system, some states pay their chaplains and others do not. For States providing for compensation statutorily or by resolution, see, e.g., Cal. Gov't Code Ann. 9170, 9171, 9320 (West 1980), and S. Res. No. 6, 1983–1984 Sess.; Colo. H. R. J., 54th Gen. Assembly, 1st Sess., 17–19 (Jan. 5, 1983); Conn. Gen. Stat. Ann. 2–9 (1983–1984); Ga. H. R. Res. No. 3, 1(e) (1983); Ga. S. Res. No. 3, 1(c) (1983); Iowa Code 2.11 (1983); Mo. Rev. Stat. 21.150 (1978); Nev. Rev. Stat. 218.200 (1981); N.J. Stat. Ann. 52:11–2 (West 1970); N.M. Const., Art. IV, 9; Okla. Stat. Ann., Tit. 74, 291.12 and 292.1 (West Supp. 1982–1983); Vt. Stat. Ann., Tit. 2, 19 (Supp. 1982); Wis. Stat. Ann. 13.125 (West Supp. 1982).

JUSTICE BRENNAN, with whom JUSTICE MARSHALL joins, dissenting.

The Court today has written a narrow and, on the whole, careful opinion. In effect, the Court holds that officially sponsored legislative prayer, primarily on account of its "unique history," *ante*, at 791, is generally exempted from the First Amendment's prohibition against "an establishment of religion." The Court's opinion is consistent with dictum in at least one of our prior decisions,[19] and its limited rationale should pose little threat to the overall fate of the Establishment Clause. Moreover, disagreement with the Court [463 U.S. 783, 796] requires that I confront the fact that some 20 years ago, in a concurring opinion in one of the cases striking down official prayer and ceremonial Bible reading in the public schools, I came very close to endorsing essentially the result reached by the Court today.[20] Nevertheless, after much reflection, I have come to the conclusion that I was wrong then and that the Court is wrong today. I now believe that the practice of official invocational prayer, as it exists in Nebraska and most other state legislatures, is unconstitutional. It is contrary to the doctrine as well the underlying purposes of the Establishment Clause, and it is not saved either by its history or by any of the other considerations suggested in the Court's opinion.

I respectfully dissent.

I

The Court makes no pretense of subjecting Nebraska's practice of legislative prayer to any of the formal "tests" that have traditionally structured our inquiry under the Establishment Clause. That it fails to do so is, in a sense, a good thing, for it simply confirms that the Court is carving out an exception to the Establishment Clause rather than reshaping Establishment Clause doctrine to accommodate legislative prayer. For my purposes, however, I must begin by demonstrating what should be obvious: that, if the Court were to judge legislative prayer through the unsentimental eye of our settled doctrine, it would have to strike it down as a clear violation of the Establishment Clause.

The most commonly cited formulation of prevailing Establishment Clause doctrine is found in *Lemon v. Kurtzman*, 403 U.S. 602 (1971): [463 U.S. 783, 797]

> "Every analysis in this area must begin with consideration of the cumulative criteria developed by the Court over many years. Three such tests may be gleaned from our cases. First, the statute [at issue] must have a secular legislative purpose; second, its principal or primary effect must be one that neither advances nor inhibits religion; finally, the statute must not foster 'an excessive government entanglement with religion.'" Id., at 612–613 (citations omitted).[21]

That the "purpose" of legislative prayer is pre-eminently religious rather than secular seems to me to be self-evident.[22] "To invoke Divine guidance on a public body entrusted with making the laws," *ante*, at 792, is nothing but a religious act. Moreover, whatever secular functions legislative prayer might play—formally opening the legislative session, getting the members of the body to quiet down, and imbuing them with a sense of seriousness and high purpose—could so plainly be performed in a purely nonreligious fashion that to claim a secular purpose for the prayer is an insult to the perfectly [463 U.S. 783, 798] honorable individuals who instituted and continue the practice.

The "primary effect" of legislative prayer is also clearly religious. As we said in the context of officially sponsored prayers in the public schools, "prescribing a particular form of religious worship,"

(Continues)

even if the individuals involved have the choice not to participate, places "indirect coercive pressure upon religious minorities to conform to the prevailing officially approved religion. . . ." *Engel v. Vitale*, 370 U.S. 421, 431 (1962).[23] More importantly, invocations in Nebraska's legislative halls explicitly link religious belief and observance to the power and prestige of the State. "[T]he mere appearance of a joint exercise of legislative authority by Church and State provides a significant symbolic benefit to religion in the minds of some by reason of the power conferred." *Larkin v. Grendel's Den, Inc.*, 459 U.S. 116, 125–126 (1982).[24] See *Abington School Dist. v. Schempp*, 374 U.S. 203, 224 (1963).

Finally, there can be no doubt that the practice of legislative prayer leads to excessive "entanglement" between the State and religion. Lemon pointed out that "entanglement" can take two forms: First, a state statute or program might involve the state impermissibly in monitoring and overseeing [463 U.S. 783, 799] religious affairs. 403 U.S., at 614–622.[25] In the case of legislative prayer, the process of choosing a "suitable" chaplain, whether on a permanent or rotating basis, and insuring that the chaplain limits himself or herself to "suitable" prayers, involves precisely the sort of supervision that agencies of government should if at all possible avoid.[26]

Second, excessive "entanglement" might arise out of "the divisive political potential" of a state statute or program. 403 U.S., at 622.

> "Ordinarily political debate and division, however vigorous or even partisan, are normal and healthy manifestations of our democratic system of government, but political division along religious lines was one of the principal evils against which the First Amendment was intended to protect. The potential divisiveness of such conflict is a threat to the normal political process." Ibid. (citations omitted).

In this case, this second aspect of entanglement is also clear. The controversy between Senator Chambers and his colleagues, which had reached the stage of difficulty and rancor long before this lawsuit was brought, has split the Nebraska [463 U.S. 783, 800] Legislature precisely on issues of religion and religious conformity. App. 21–24. The record in this case also reports a series of instances, involving legislators other than Senator Chambers, in which invocations by Reverend Palmer and others led to controversy along religious lines.[27] And in general, the history of legislative prayer has been far more eventful—and divisive—than a hasty reading of the Court's opinion might indicate.[28]

In sum, I have no doubt that, if any group of law students were asked to apply the principles of Lemon to the question [463 U.S. 783, 801] of legislative prayer, they would nearly unanimously find the practice to be unconstitutional.[29]

II

The path of formal doctrine, however, can only imperfectly capture the nature and importance of the issues at stake in this case. A more adequate analysis must therefore take [463 U.S. 783, 802] into account the underlying function of the Establishment Clause, and the forces that have shaped its doctrine.

A

Most of the provisions of the Bill of Rights, even if they are not generally enforceable in the absence of state action, nevertheless arise out of moral intuitions applicable to individuals as well as governments. The Establishment Clause, however, is quite different. It is, to its core, nothing less and nothing more than a statement about the proper role of government in the society that we have shaped for ourselves in this land.

The Establishment Clause embodies a judgment, born of a long and turbulent history, that, in our society, religion "must be a private matter for the individual, the family, and the institutions of private choice . . ." *Lemon v. Kurtzman*, 403 U.S., at 625.

"Government in our democracy, state and national, must be neutral in matters of religious theory, doctrine, and practice. It may not be hostile to any religion or to the advocacy of no-religion; and it may not aid, foster, or promote one religion or religious theory against another or even against the militant opposite. The First Amendment mandates governmental neutrality between religion and religion, and between religion and non-religion." *Epperson v. Arkansas*, 393 U.S. 97, 103–104 (1968) (footnote omitted).

"In the words of Jefferson, the clause against establishment of religion by law was intended to erect 'a wall of separation between church and State.'" *Everson v. Board of Education*, 330 U.S. 1, 16 (1947), quoting *Reynolds v. United States*, 98 U.S. 145, 164 (1879).[30] [463 U.S. 783, 803]

The principles of "separation" and "neutrality" implicit in the Establishment Clause serve many purposes. Four of these are particularly relevant here.

The first, which is most closely related to the more general conceptions of liberty found in the remainder of the First Amendment, is to guarantee the individual right to conscience.[31] The right to conscience, in the religious sphere, is not only implicated when the government engages in direct or indirect coercion. It is also implicated when the government requires individuals to support the practices of a faith with which they do not agree.

"'[T]o compel a man to furnish contributions of money for the propagation of [religious] opinions which he disbelieves, is sinful and tyrannical; . . . even . . . forcing him to support this or that teacher of his own religious persuasion, is depriving him of the comfortable liberty of giving his contributions to the particular pastor, whose morals he would make his pattern . . .'" *Everson v. Board of Education*, *supra*, at 13, quoting Virginia Bill for Religious Liberty, 12 Hening, Statutes of Virginia 84 (1823).

The second purpose of separation and neutrality is to keep the state from interfering in the essential autonomy of religious life, either by taking upon itself the decision of religious [463 U.S. 783, 804] issues,[32] or by unduly involving itself in the supervision of religious institutions or officials.[33]

The third purpose of separation and neutrality is to prevent the trivialization and degradation of religion by too close an attachment to the organs of government. The Establishment Clause "stands as an expression of principle on the part of the Founders of our Constitution that religion is too personal, too sacred, too holy, to permit its 'unhallowed perversion' by a civil magistrate." *Engel v. Vitale*, 370 U.S., at 432, quoting *Memorial and Remonstrance against Religious Assessments*, 2 Writings of Madison 187. See also Schempp, 374 U.S., at 221–222; id., at 283–287 (BRENNAN, J., concurring).[34] [463 U.S. 783, 805].

Finally, the principles of separation and neutrality help assure that essentially religious issues, precisely because of their importance and sensitivity, not become the occasion for battle in the political arena. See *Lemon*, 403 U.S., at 622–624; *Board of Education v. Allen*, 392 U.S. 236, 249 (Harlan, J., concurring); Engel, *supra*, at 429–430. With regard to most issues, the government may be influenced by partisan argument and may act as a partisan itself. In each case, there will be winners and losers in the political battle, and the losers' most common recourse is the right to dissent and the right to fight the battle again another day. With regard to matters that are essentially religious, however, the Establishment Clause seeks that there should be no political battles, and that no American should at any point feel alienated [463 U.S. 783, 806] from his government because that government has declared or acted upon some "official" or "authorized" point of view on a matter of religion.[35]

B

The imperatives of separation and neutrality are not limited to the relationship of government to religious institutions or denominations, but extend as well to the relationship of government to religious beliefs and practices. In *Torcaso v. Watkins*, 367 U.S. 488 (1961), for example, we struck down a state provision requiring a religious oath as a qualification to hold office, not only because it violated principles of free exercise of religion, but also because it violated the principles of nonestablishment of religion. And, of course, in the pair of cases that hang over this one like a reproachful set of parents, we held that official prayer and prescribed Bible reading in the public schools represent a serious encroachment on the Establishment Clause. Schempp, *supra*; Engel, *supra*. As we said in Engel, "[i]t is neither sacrilegious nor anti-religious to say that each separate government in this country should stay out of the business of writing or sanctioning official prayers and leave that purely religious function to the people themselves and to those the people choose to look to for religious guidance." 370 U.S., at 435 (footnote omitted).

Nor should it be thought that this view of the Establishment Clause is a recent concoction of an overreaching judiciary. [463 U.S. 783, 807]. Even before the First Amendment was written, the Framers of the Constitution broke with the practice of the Articles of Confederation and many state constitutions, and did not invoke the name of God in the document. This "omission of a reference to the Deity was not inadvertent; nor did it remain unnoticed."[36] Moreover, Thomas Jefferson and

(Continues)

(Continued)

Andrew Jackson, during their respective terms as President, both refused on Establishment Clause grounds to declare national days of thanksgiving or fasting.[37] And James Madison, writing subsequent to his own Presidency on essentially the very issue we face today, stated:

> "Is the appointment of Chaplains to the two Houses of Congress consistent with the Constitution, and with the pure principle of religious freedom?
>
> "In strictness, the answer on both points must be in the negative. The Constitution of the U.S. forbids everything like an establishment of a national religion. The law appointing Chaplains establishes a religious worship for the national representatives, to be performed by Ministers of religion, elected by a majority of [463 U.S. 783, 808] them; and these are to be paid out of the national taxes. Does not this involve the principle of a national establishment, applicable to a provision for a religious worship for the Constituent as well as of the representative Body, approved by the majority, and conducted by Ministers of religion paid by the entire nation." Fleet, Madison's "Detached Memoranda," 3 *Wm. & Mary Quarterly* 534, 558 (1946).

C

Legislative prayer clearly violates the principles of neutrality and separation that are embedded within the Establishment Clause. It is contrary to the fundamental message of Engel and Schempp. It intrudes on the right to conscience by forcing some legislators either to participate in a "prayer opportunity," *ante*, at 794, with which they are in basic disagreement, or to make their disagreement a matter of public comment by declining to participate. It forces all residents of the State to support a religious exercise that may be contrary to their own beliefs. It requires the State to commit itself on fundamental theological issues.[38] It has the potential for degrading religion by allowing a religious call to worship to be intermeshed with a secular call to order. And it injects religion into the political sphere by creating the potential that each and every selection of a chaplain, or consideration of a particular prayer, or even reconsideration of the practice itself, will provoke a political battle along religious lines and ultimately alienate some religiously identified group of citizens.[39] [463 U.S. 783, 809].

D

One response to the foregoing account, of course, is that "neutrality" and "separation" do not exhaust the full meaning of the Establishment Clause as it has developed in our cases. It is indeed true that there are certain tensions inherent in the First Amendment itself, or inherent in the role of religion and religious belief in any free society, that have shaped the doctrine of the Establishment Clause, and required us to deviate from an absolute adherence to separation and neutrality. Nevertheless, these considerations, although very important, are also quite specific, and where none of them is present, the Establishment Clause gives us no warrant simply to look the other way and treat an unconstitutional practice as if it were constitutional. Because the Court occasionally suggests that some of these considerations might apply here, it becomes important that I briefly identify the most prominent of them and explain why they do not in fact have any relevance to legislative prayer.

(1)

A number of our cases have recognized that religious institutions and religious practices may, in certain contexts, receive the benefit of government programs and policies generally available, on the basis of some secular criterion, to a wide class of similarly situated nonreligious beneficiaries,[40] and the precise cataloging of those contexts is not necessarily an easy task. I need not tarry long here, however, because the provision for a daily official invocation by a nonmember officer of [463 U.S. 783, 810] a legislative body could by no stretch of the imagination appear anywhere in that catalog.

(2)

Conversely, our cases have recognized that religion can encompass a broad, if not total, spectrum of concerns, overlapping considerably with the range of secular concerns, and that not every governmental act which coincides with or conflicts with a particular religious belief is for that reason an establishment of religion. See, e.g., *McGowan v. Maryland*, 366 U.S. 420, 431–445 (1961) (Sunday Laws); *Harris v. McRae*, 448 U.S. 297, 319–320 (1980) (abortion restrictions). The Court seems to suggest at one point that the practice of legislative prayer may be excused on this ground, *ante*, at 792, but I cannot really believe that it takes this position seriously.[41] The practice of legislative prayer is nothing like the statutes we considered in *McGowan and Harris v. McRae*; prayer is not merely "conduct whose . . . effect . . . harmonize[s] with the tenets of some or all religions," *McGowan, supra*, at 442; prayer is fundamentally and necessarily religious. "It is prayer which distinguishes religious phenomena from all those which resemble them or lie near to them, from the moral sense, for instance, or aesthetic feeling."[42] Accord, Engel, 370 U.S., at 424.

(3)

We have also recognized that government cannot, without adopting a decidedly anti-religious point of view, be forbidden [463 U.S. 783, 811] to recognize the religious beliefs and practices of the American people as an aspect of our history and culture.[43] Certainly, bona fide classes in comparative religion can be offered in the public schools.[44] And certainly, the text of Abraham Lincoln's Second Inaugural Address which is inscribed on a wall of the Lincoln Memorial need not be purged of its profound theological content. The practice of offering invocations at legislative sessions cannot, however, simply be dismissed as "a tolerable acknowledgment of beliefs widely held among the people of this country." *Ante*, at 792 (emphasis added). "Prayer is religion in act."[45] "Praying means to take hold of a word, the end, so to speak, of a line that leads to God."[46] Reverend Palmer and other members of the clergy who offer invocations at legislative sessions are not museum pieces put on display once a day for the edification of the legislature. Rather, they are engaged by the legislature to lead it—as a body—in an act of religious worship. If upholding the practice requires denial of this fact, I suspect that many supporters of legislative prayer would feel that they had been handed a pyrrhic victory.

(4)

Our cases have recognized that the purposes of the Establishment Clause can sometimes conflict. For example, in *Walz v. Tax Comm'n*, 397 U.S. 664 (1970), we upheld tax exemptions for religious institutions in part because subjecting those institutions to taxation might foster serious administrative entanglement. Id., at 674–676. Here, however, no [463 U.S. 783, 812] such tension exists; the State can vindicate all the purposes of the Establishment Clause by abolishing legislative prayer.

(5)

Finally, our cases recognize that, in one important respect, the Constitution is not neutral on the subject of religion: Under the Free Exercise Clause, religiously motivated claims of conscience may give rise to constitutional rights that other strongly held beliefs do not. See n. 13, *supra*. Moreover, even when the government is not compelled to do so by the Free Exercise Clause, it may to some extent act to facilitate the opportunities of individuals to practice their religion.[47] See Schempp, 374 U.S., at 299 (BRENNAN, J., concurring) ("hostility, not neutrality, would characterize the refusal to provide chaplains and places of worship for prisoners and soldiers cut off by the State from all civilian opportunities for public communion"). This is not, however, a case in which a State is accommodating individual religious interests. We are not faced here with the right of the legislature to allow its members to offer prayers during the course of [463 U.S. 783, 813] general legislative debate. We are certainly not faced with the right of legislators to form voluntary groups for prayer or worship. We are not even faced with the right of the State to employ members of the clergy to minister to the private religious needs of individual legislators. Rather, we are faced here with the regularized practice of conducting official prayers, on behalf of the entire legislature, as part of the order of business constituting the formal opening of every single session of the legislative term. If this is free exercise, the Establishment Clause has no meaning whatsoever.

III

With the exception of the few lapses I have already noted, each of which is commendably qualified so as to be limited to the facts of this case, the Court says almost nothing contrary to the above analysis. Instead, it holds that "the practice of opening legislative sessions with prayer has become part of the fabric of our society," *ante*, at 792, and chooses not to interfere. I sympathize with

(Continues)

(Continued)

the Court's reluctance to strike down a practice so prevalent and so ingrained as legislative prayer. I am, however, unconvinced by the Court's arguments, and cannot shake my conviction that legislative prayer violates both the letter and the spirit of the Establishment Clause.

A

The Court's main argument for carving out an exception sustaining legislative prayer is historical. The Court cannot—and does not—purport to find a pattern of "undeviating acceptance," Walz, *supra*, at 681 (BRENNAN, J., concurring), of legislative prayer. See *ante*, at 791, and n. 12; n. 10, *supra*. It also disclaims exclusive reliance on the mere longevity of legislative prayer. *Ante*, at 790. The Court does, however, point out that, only three days before the First Congress reached agreement on the final wording of the Bill of Rights, it authorized the appointment of paid chaplains for [463 U.S. 783, 814] its own proceedings, *ante*, at 788, and the Court argues that in light of this "unique history," *ante*, at 791, the actions of Congress reveal its intent as to the meaning of the Establishment Clause, *ante*, at 788–790. I agree that historical practice is "of considerable import in the interpretation of abstract constitutional language," Walz, 397 U.S., at 681 (BRENNAN, J., concurring). This is a case, however, in which—absent the Court's invocation of history—there would be no question that the practice at issue was unconstitutional. And despite the surface appeal of the Court's argument, there are at least three reasons why specific historical practice should not in this case override that clear constitutional imperative.[48]

First, it is significant that the Court's historical argument does not rely on the legislative history of the Establishment Clause itself. Indeed, that formal history is profoundly unilluminating on this and most other subjects. Rather, the Court assumes that the Framers of the Establishment Clause would not have themselves authorized a practice that they thought violated the guarantees contained in the Clause. *Ante*, at 790. This assumption, however, is questionable. Legislators, influenced by the passions and exigencies of the moment, the pressure of constituents and colleagues, and the press of business, do not always pass sober constitutional judgment on every piece of legislation they enact,[49] and this [463 U.S. 783, 815] must be assumed to be as true of the Members of the First Congress as any other. Indeed, the fact that James Madison, who voted for the bill authorizing the payment of the first congressional chaplains, *ante*, at 788, n. 8, later expressed the view that the practice was unconstitutional, see *supra*, at 807–808, is instructive on precisely this point. Madison's later views may not have represented so much a change of mind as a change of role, from a Member of Congress engaged in the hurly-burly of legislative activity to a detached observer engaged in unpressured reflection. Since the latter role is precisely the one with which this Court is charged, I am not at all sure that Madison's later writings should be any less influential in our deliberations than his earlier vote.

Second, the Court's analysis treats the First Amendment simply as an Act of Congress, as to whose meaning the intent of Congress is the single touchstone. Both the Constitution and its Amendments, however, became supreme law only by virtue of their ratification by the States, and the understanding of the States should be as relevant to our analysis as the understanding of Congress.[50] See *Richardson v. Ramirez*, 418 U.S. 24, 43 (1974); *Maxwell v. Dow*, 176 U.S. 581, 602 (1900).[51] This observation is especially compelling in considering [463 U.S. 783, 816] the meaning of the Bill of Rights. The first ten Amendments were not enacted because the Members of the First Congress came up with a bright idea one morning; rather, their enactment was forced upon Congress by a number of the States as a condition for their ratification of the original Constitution.[52] To treat any practice authorized by the First Congress as presumptively consistent with the Bill of Rights is therefore somewhat akin to treating any action of a party to a contract as presumptively consistent with the terms of the contract. The latter proposition, if it were accepted, would of course resolve many of the heretofore perplexing issues in contract law.

Finally, and most importantly, the argument tendered by the Court is misguided because the Constitution is not a static document whose meaning on every detail is fixed for all time by the life experience of the Framers. We have recognized in a wide variety of constitutional contexts that the practices that were in place at the time any particular guarantee was enacted into the Constitution do not necessarily fix forever the meaning of that guarantee.[53] To be truly faithful to the Framers, "our use of the history of their time must limit itself to broad purposes, not specific practices." *Abington School Dist. v. Schempp*, 374 U.S., at 241 (BRENNAN, J., concurring). Our primary task must be to translate "the majestic generalities of the Bill of Rights, conceived as part of the pattern of liberal government in the eighteenth century, into concrete restraints on officials dealing with the [463 U.S. 783, 817] problems of the twentieth century . . ." *West Virginia Bd. of Education v. Barnette*, 319 U.S. 624, 639 (1943).

The inherent adaptability of the Constitution and its amendments is particularly important with respect to the Establishment Clause. "[O]ur religious composition makes us a vastly more diverse people than were our forefathers. . . . In the face of such profound changes, practices which may have been objectionable to no one in the time of Jefferson and Madison may today be highly offensive to many persons, the deeply devout and the nonbelievers alike." Schempp, *supra*, at 240–241 (BRENNAN, J., concurring). Cf. *McDaniel v. Paty*, 435 U.S. 618, 628 (1978) (plurality opinion). President John Adams issued during his Presidency a number of official proclamations calling on all Americans to engage in Christian prayer.[54] Justice Story, in his treatise on the Constitution, contended that the "real object" of the First Amendment "was, not to countenance, much less to advance Mahometanism, or Judaism, or infidelity, by prostrating Christianity; but to exclude all rivalry among Christian sects . . ."[55] Whatever deference Adams' actions and Story's views might once have deserved in this Court, the Establishment Clause must now be read in a very different light. Similarly, the Members of the First Congress should be treated, not as sacred figures whose every action must be emulated, but as the authors of a document meant to last for the ages. Indeed, a proper respect for the Framers themselves forbids us to give so static and lifeless a meaning to their work. To my mind, the Court's focus here on a narrow piece of history is, in a fundamental sense, a betrayal of the lessons of history. [463 U.S. 783, 818].

B

Of course, the Court does not rely entirely on the practice of the First Congress in order to validate legislative prayer. There is another theme which, although implicit, also pervades the Court's opinion. It is exemplified by the Court's comparison of legislative prayer with the formulaic recitation of "God save the United States and this Honorable Court." *Ante*, at 786. It is also exemplified by the Court's apparent conclusion that legislative prayer is, at worst, a "'mere shadow'" on the Establishment Clause rather than a "'real threat'" to it. *Ante*, at 795, quoting Schempp, *supra*, at 308 (Goldberg, J., concurring). Simply put, the Court seems to regard legislative prayer as at most a *de minimis* violation, somehow unworthy of our attention. I frankly do not know what should be the proper disposition of features of our public life such as "God save the United States and this Honorable Court," "In God We Trust," "One Nation Under God," and the like. I might well adhere to the view expressed in Schempp that such mottos are consistent with the Establishment Clause, not because their import is *de minimis*, but because they have lost any true religious significance. 374 U.S. at 303–304 (BRENNAN, J., concurring). Legislative invocations, however, are very different.

First of all, as JUSTICE STEVENS' dissent so effectively highlights, legislative prayer, unlike mottos with fixed wordings, can easily turn narrowly and obviously sectarian.[56] I agree with the Court that the federal judiciary should not sit as a board of censors on individual prayers, but to may mind the better way of avoiding that task is by striking down all official legislative invocations. [463 U.S. 783, 819].

More fundamentally, however, any practice of legislative prayer, even if it might look "nonsectarian" to nine Justices of the Supreme Court, will inevitably and continuously involve the State in one or another religious debate.[57] Prayer is serious business—serious theological business—and it is not a mere "acknowledgment of beliefs widely held among the people of this country" for the State to immerse itself in that business.[58] Some religious individuals or groups find it theologically problematic to engage in joint religious exercises predominantly influenced by faiths not their own.[59] Some might object even to the attempt to fashion a "nonsectarian" prayer.[60] Some would find it impossible to participate in any "prayer opportunity," *ante*, at 794, marked by [463 U.S. 783, 820] Trinitarian references.[61] Some would find a prayer not invoking the name of Christ to represent a flawed view of the relationship between human beings and God.[62] Some might find any petitionary prayer to be improper.[63] Some might find any prayer that lacked a petitionary element to be deficient.[64] Some might be troubled by what they consider shallow public prayer,[65] or nonspontaneous prayer,[66] or prayer without adequate spiritual preparation or concentration.[67] Some might, of course, have theological objections to any prayer sponsored by an organ of government.[68] Some [463 U.S. 783, 821] might object on theological grounds to the level of political neutrality generally expected of government-sponsored invocational prayer.[69] And some might object on

(Continues)

theological grounds to the Court's requirement, *ante*, at 794, that prayer, even though religious, not be proselytizing.[70] If these problems arose in the context of a religious objection to some otherwise decidedly secular activity, then whatever remedy there is would have to be found in the Free Exercise Clause. See n. 13, *supra*. But, in this case, we are faced with potential religious objections to an activity at the very center of religious life, and it is simply beyond the competence of government, and inconsistent with our conceptions of liberty, for the State to take upon itself the role of ecclesiastical arbiter.

IV

The argument is made occasionally that a strict separation of religion and state robs the Nation of its spiritual identity. I believe quite the contrary. It may be true that individuals cannot be "neutral" on the question of religion.[71] But the judgment of the Establishment Clause is that neutrality by the organs of government on questions of religion is both possible and imperative. Alexis de Tocqueville wrote the following concerning his travels through this land in the early 1830s:

"The religious atmosphere of the country was the first thing that struck me on arrival in the United States . . ."

"In France I had seen the spirits of religion and of freedom almost always marching in opposite directions. In America I found them intimately linked together in joint reign over the same land." [463 U.S. 783, 822]

"My longing to understand the reason for this phenomenon increased daily."

"To find this out, I questioned the faithful of all communions; I particularly sought the society of clergymen, who are the depositaries of the various creeds and have a personal interest in their survival . . . I expressed my astonishment and revealed my doubts to each of them; I found that they all agreed with each other except about details; all thought that the main reason for the quiet sway of religion over their country was the complete separation of church and state. I have no hesitation in stating that throughout my stay in America I met nobody, lay or cleric, who did not agree about that." *Democracy in America*, 295 (G. Lawrence trans., J. Mayer ed., 1969).

More recent history has only confirmed De Tocqueville's observations.[72] If the Court had struck down legislative prayer today, it would likely have stimulated a furious reaction. But it would also, I am convinced, have invigorated both the "spirit of religion" and the "spirit of freedom."

I respectfully dissent.

Notes

19. *Zorach v. Clauson*, 343 U.S. 306, 312–313 (1952); cf. *Abington School Dist. v. Schempp*, 374 U.S. 203, 213 (1963).

20. "The saying of invocational prayers in legislative chambers, state or federal, and the appointment of legislative chaplains, might well represent no involvements of the kind prohibited by the Establishment Clause. Legislators, federal and state, are mature adults who may presumably absent themselves from such public and ceremonial exercises without incurring any penalty, direct or indirect." *Schempp, supra*, at 299–300 (BRENNAN, J., concurring) (footnote omitted).

21. See, e.g., *Larkin v. Grendel's Den, Inc.*, 459 U.S. 116, 123 (1982); *Widmar v. Vincent*, 454 U.S. 263, 271 (1981); *Wolman v. Walter*, 433 U.S. 229, 236 (1977); *Committee for Public Education & Religious Liberty v. Nyquist*, 413 U.S. 756, 772–773 (1973).

22. See *Stone v. Graham*, 449 U.S. 39, 41 (1980) (finding "pre-eminent purpose" of state statute requiring posting of Ten Commandments in each public school classroom to be "plainly religious in nature," despite legislative recitations of "supposed secular purpose"); *Epperson v. Arkansas*, 393 U.S. 97, 107–109 (1968) (state "anti-evolution" statute clearly religious in purpose); cf. *Schempp, supra*, at 223–224 (public school exercise consisting of Bible reading and recitation of Lord's Prayer).

As Reverend Palmer put the matter: "I would say that I strive to relate the Senators and their helpers to the divine." Palmer Deposition, at 28. "[M]y purpose is to provide an opportunity for Senators to be drawn closer to their understanding of God as they understand God. In order that the divine wisdom might be theirs as they conduct their business for the day." Id., at 46. Cf. *Prayers of the Chaplain of the Massachusetts Senate, 1963–1968*, p. 58 (1969) (hereinafter *Massachusetts Senate Prayers*) ("Save this moment, O God, from merely being a gesture to custom").

23. Cf. *Stone v. Graham, supra,* at 42.

The Court argues that legislators are adults, "presumably not readily susceptible to . . . peer pressure." *Ante,* at 792. I made a similar observation in my concurring opinion in Schempp. See n. 2, *supra.* Quite apart from the debatable constitutional significance of this argument, see Schempp, 374 U.S., at 224–225; *Engel v. Vitale,* 370 U.S., at 430, I am now most uncertain as to whether it is even factually correct: Legislators, by virtue of their instinct for political survival, are often loath to assert in public religious views that their constituents might perceive as hostile or nonconforming. See generally P. Blanshard, *God and Man in Washington,* 94–106 (1960).

24. As I point out *infra,* at 803–804, 808, official religious exercises may also be of significant symbolic detriment to religion.

25. See *Larkin v. Grendel's Den, Inc., supra,* at 125, n. 9; *Walz v. Tax Comm'n,* 397 U.S. 664, 674–676 (1970).

26. In Lemon, we struck down certain state statutes providing aid to sectarian schools, in part because "the program requires the government to examine the school's records in order to determine how much of the total expenditures is attributable to secular education and how much to religious activity." 403 U.S., at 620. In this case, by the admission of the very government officials involved, supervising the practice of legislative prayer requires those officials to determine if particular members of the clergy and particular prayers are "too explicitly Christian," App. 49 (testimony of Rev. Palmer) or consistent with "the various religious preferences that the Senators may or may not have," id., at 48 (same), or likely to "inject some kind of a religious dogma" into the proceedings, id., at 68 (testimony of Frank Lewis, Chairman of the Nebraska Legislature Executive Board).

27. See id., at 49 (testimony of Rev. Palmer) (discussing objections raised by some Senators to Christological references in certain of his prayers and in a prayer offered by a guest member of the clergy).

28. As the Court points out, the practice of legislative prayers in Congress gave rise to serious controversy at points in the 19th century. *Ante,* at 788–789, n. 10. Opposition to the practice in that period arose "both on the part of certain radicals and of some rather extreme Protestant sects. These have been inspired by very different motives but have united in opposing government chaplaincies as breaking down the line of demarcation between Church and State. The sectarians felt that religion had nothing to do with the State, while the radicals felt that the State had nothing to do with religion." 3 A. Stokes, Church and State in the United States 130 (1950) (hereinafter Stokes). See also id., at 133–134. Similar controversies arose in the States. See Report of the Select Committee of the New York State Assembly on the Several Memorials Against Appointing Chaplains to the Legislature (1832) (recommending that practice be abolished), reprinted in J. Blau, *Cornerstones of Religious Freedom in America,* 141–156 (1949).

In more recent years, particular prayers and particular chaplains in the state legislatures have periodically led to serious political divisiveness along religious lines. See, e.g., *The Oregonian,* Apr. 1, 1983, p. C8 ("Despite protests from at least one representative, a follower of an Indian guru was allowed to give the prayer at the start of Thursday's [Oregon] House [of Representatives] session. Shortly before Ma Anand Sheela began the invocation, about a half-dozen representatives walked off the House floor in apparent protest of the prayer"); *Cal. Senate Jour.,* 37th Sess., 171–173, 307–308 (1907) (discussing request by a State Senator that State Senate Chaplain not use the name of Christ in legislative prayer, and response by one local clergyman claiming that the legislator who made the request had committed a "crowning infamy" and that his "words were those of an irreverent and godless man"). See also *infra,* at 805–806, 808, 818–821.

29. The Lemon tests do not, of course, exhaust the set of formal doctrines that can be brought to bear on the issues before us today. Last Term, for example, we made clear that a state program that discriminated among religious faiths, and not merely in favor of all religious faiths, "must be invalidated unless it is justified by a compelling governmental interest, cf. *Widmar v. Vincent,* 454 U.S. 263, 269–270 (1981), and unless it is closely fitted to further that interest, *Murdock v. Pennsylvania,* 319 U.S. 105, 116–117 (1943)." *Larson v. Valente,* 456 U.S. 228, 247 (1982). In this case, the appointment of a single chaplain for 16 years, and the evident impossibility of a Buddhist monk or Sioux Indian religious worker being appointed for a similar period, App. 69–70, see post, p. 822 (STEVENS, J., dissenting), might well justify application of the Larson test. Moreover, given the pains that petitioners have gone through to emphasize the "ceremonial" function of legislative prayer, Brief for Petitioners 16, and given the case with which a similar "ceremonial" function could be performed without the necessity for prayer, cf. *supra,* at 797–798, I have little doubt that the Nebraska practice, at least, would fail the Larson test.

(Continues)

(Continued)

In addition, I still find compelling the Establishment Clause test that I articulated in Schempp:

"What the Framers meant to foreclose, and what our decisions under the Establishment Clause have forbidden, are those involvements of religious with secular institutions which (a) serve the essentially religious activities of religious institutions; (b) employ the organs of government for essentially religious purposes; or (c) use essentially religious means to serve governmental ends, where secular means would suffice." 374 U.S., at 294–295.

See *Roemer v. Maryland Board of Public Works*, 426 U.S. 736, 770–771 (1976) (BRENNAN, J., dissenting); *Hunt v. McNair*, 413 U.S. 734, 750 (1973) (BRENNAN, J., dissenting); *Lemon v. Kurtzman*, 403 U.S., at 643 (BRENNAN, J., concurring); *Walz v. Tax Comm'n*, 397 U.S., at 680–681 (BRENNAN, J., concurring). For reasons similar to those I have already articulated, I believe that the Nebraska practice of legislative prayer, as well as most other comparable practices, would fail at least the second and third elements of this test.

30. See also, e.g., *Larkin v. Grendel's Den, Inc.*, 459 U.S., at 122–123; *Stone v. Graham*, 449 U.S., at 42; *Abington School Dist. v. Schempp*, 374 U.S., at 214–225; id., at 232–234, 243–253 (BRENNAN, J., concurring).

31. See, e.g., *Larson v. Valente*, supra, at 244–247; Schempp, supra, at 222; *Torcaso v. Watkins*, 367 U.S. 488, 490, 494–496 (1961); *McDaniel v. Paty*, 435 U.S. 618, 636 (1978) (BRENNAN, J., concurring in judgment).

The Free Exercise Clause serves a similar function, though often in a quite different way. In particular, we have held that, under certain circumstances, an otherwise constitutional law may not be applied as against persons for whom the law creates a burden on religious belief or practice. See, e.g., *Thomas v. Review Bd. of Indiana Employment Security Division*, 450 U.S. 707 (1981); *Wisconsin v. Yoder*, 406 U.S. 205 (1972); *Sherbert v. Verner*, 374 U.S. 398 (1963).

32. See, e.g., *Presbyterian Church v. Mary Elizabeth Blue Hull Memorial Presbyterian Church*, 393 U.S. 440 (1969); *United States v. Ballard*, 322 U.S. 78 (1944).

33. See *Lemon v. Kurtzman*, 403 U.S., at 614–622; *NLRB v. Catholic Bishop of Chicago*, 440 U.S. 490, 501–504 (1979).

This and the remaining purposes that I discuss cannot be reduced simply to a question of individual liberty. A court, for example, will refuse to decide an essentially religious issue even if the issue is otherwise properly before the court, and even if it is asked to decide it.

34. Consider, in addition to the formal authorities cited in text, the following words by a leading Methodist clergyman:

"[Some propose] to reassert religious values by posting the Ten Commandments on every school-house wall, by erecting cardboard nativity shrines on every corner, by writing God's name on our money, and by using His Holy Name in political oratory. Is this not the ultimate in profanity? . . .

"What is the result of all this display of holy things in public places? Does it make the market-place more holy? Does it improve people? Does it change their character or motives? On the contrary, the sacred symbols are thereby cheapened and degraded. The effect is often that of a television commercial on a captive audience—boredom and resentment." Kelley, Beyond Separation of Church and State, 5 *J. Church & State* 181, 190–191 (1963).

Consider also this condensed version of words first written in 1954 by one observer of the American scene:

"The manifestations of religion in Washington have become pretty thick. We have had opening prayers, Bible breakfasts, [and so on]; now we have [463 U.S. 783, 805] added . . . a change in the Pledge of Allegiance. The Pledge, which has served well enough in times more pious than ours, has now had its rhythm upset but its anti-Communist spirituality improved by the insertion of the phrase 'under God.' . . . A bill has been introduced directing the post office to cancel mail with the slogan 'Pray for Peace.' (The devout, in place of daily devotions, can just read what is stuck and stamped all over the letters in their mail.) . . .

"To note all this in a deflationary tone is not to say that religion and politics don't mix. Politicians should develop deeper religious convictions, and religious folk should develop wiser political convictions; both need to relate political duties to religious faith—but not in an unqualified and public way that confuses the absolute and emotional loyalties of religion with the relative and shifting loyalties of politics . . . .

"All religious affirmations are in danger of standing in contradiction to the life that is lived under them, but none more so than these general, inoffensive, and externalized ones which are put together for public purposes." W. Miller, *Piety Along the Potomac*, 41–46 (1964).

See also, e.g., Prayer in Public Schools and Buildings—Federal Court Jurisdiction, Hearings before the Subcommittee on Courts, Civil Liberties, and the Administration of Justice of the House Committee on the Judiciary, 96th Cong., 2d Sess., 46–47 (1980) (testimony of M. William Howard, President of the National Council of the Churches of Christ in the U.S.A.) (hereinafter Hearings); cf. Fox, The National Day of Prayer, 29 *Theology Today* 258 (1972).

35. It is sometimes argued that to apply the Establishment Clause alienates those who wish to see a tighter bond between religion and state. This is obviously true. (I would vigorously deny, however, any claim that the Establishment Clause disfavors the much broader class of persons for whom religion is a necessary and important part of life. See *supra*, at 803–804; *infra*, at 821–822.) But I would submit that even this dissatisfaction is tempered by the knowledge that society is adhering to a fixed rule of neutrality rather than rejecting a particular expression of religious belief.

36. Pfeffer, The Deity in American Constitutional History, 23 *J. Church & State* 215, 217 (1981). See also 1 Stokes 523.

37. See L. Pfeffer, *Church, State, and Freedom*, 266 (rev. ed. 1967) (hereinafter Pfeffer). Jefferson expressed his views as follows:

"'I consider the government of the United States as interdicted by the Constitution from intermeddling with religious institutions, their doctrines, discipline, or exercises. [I]t is only proposed that I should recommend not prescribe a day of fasting and prayer. [But] I do not believe it is for the interest of religion to invite the civil magistrate to direct its exercises, its discipline, or its doctrine . . . Fasting and prayer are religious exercises; the enjoining of them an act of discipline. Every religious society has a right to determine for itself the times for these exercises, and the objects proper for them, according to their own particular tenets; and the right can never be safer than in their hands, where the Constitution has deposited it.'" Ibid., quoting 11 *Jefferson's Writings* 428–430 (Monticello ed. 1905).

38. See also *infra*, at 819–821.

39. In light of the discussion in text, I am inclined to agree with the Court that the Nebraska practice of legislative prayer is not significantly more troubling than that found in other States. For example, appointing one chaplain for 16 years may give the impression of "establishing" one particular religion, but the constant attention to the selection process which would be the result of shorter terms might well increase the opportunity for [463 U.S. 783, 809] religious discord and entanglement. The lesson I draw from all this, however, is that any regular practice of official invocational prayer must be deemed unconstitutional.

40. See, e.g., *Everson v. Board of Education*, 330 U.S. 1 (1947) (transportation of students to and from school); *Walz v. Tax Comm'n*, 397 U.S. 664 (1970) (charitable tax exemptions).

41. The Court does sensibly, if not respectfully, ascribe this view to the Founding Fathers rather than to itself. See *ante*, at 792.

42. A. Sabatier, *Outlines of a Philosophy of Religion*, 25–26 (T. Seed trans., 1957 ed.). See also, e.g., W. James, *The Varieties of Religious Experience*, 352–353 (New American Library ed., 1958); F. Heiler, *Prayer*, xiii–xvi (S. McComb trans., 1958 ed.).

43. See Schempp, 374 U.S., at 300–304 (BRENNAN, J., concurring); Illinois ex rel. *McCollum v. Board of Education*, 333 U.S. 203, 235–236 (1948) (Jackson, J., concurring).

44. See Schempp, *supra*, at 225.

45. Sabatier, *supra*, at 25 (emphasis added).

46. A. Heschel, *Man's Quest for God*, 30 (1954).

47. Justice Douglas' famous observation that "[w]e are a religious people whose institutions presuppose a Supreme Being," *Zorach v. Clauson*, 343 U.S., at 313 , see *ante*, at 792, arose in precisely such a context. Indeed, a more complete quotation from the paragraph in which that statement appears is instructive here:

"We are a religious people whose institutions presuppose a Supreme Being. We guarantee the freedom to worship as one chooses. We make room for as wide a variety of beliefs and creeds as the spiritual needs of man deem necessary. We sponsor an attitude on the part of government that shows no partiality to any one group and that lets each flourish according to the zeal of its adherents and the appeal of its dogma . . . The government must be neutral when it comes to competition between sects. It may not thrust any sect on any person. It may not make a religious observance compulsory. It may not coerce anyone to attend church, to observe a religious holiday, or to take religious instruction. But it can close its doors or suspend its operations as to those who want to repair to their religious sanctuary for worship or instruction. No more than that is undertaken here." 343 U.S., at 313–314.

(*Continues*)

48. Indeed, the sort of historical argument made by the Court should be advanced with some hesitation in light of certain other skeletons in the congressional closet. See, e.g., An Act for the Punishment of certain Crimes against the United States, 16, 1 Stat. 116 (1790) (enacted by the First Congress and requiring that persons convicted of certain theft offenses "be publicly whipped, not exceeding thirty-nine stripes"); Act of July 23, 1866, 14 Stat. 216 (reaffirming the racial segregation of the public schools in the District of Columbia; enacted exactly one week after Congress proposed Fourteenth Amendment to the States).

49. See generally D. Morgan, *Congress and the Constitution* (1966); E. Eidenberg & R. Morey, *An Act of Congress* (1969); cf. C. Miller, *The Supreme Court and the Uses of History*, 61–64 (1969).

One commentator has pointed out that the chaplaincy established by the First Congress was "a carry-over from the days of the Continental Congress, [463 U.S. 783, 815] which . . . exercised plenary jurisdiction in matters of religion; and ceremonial practices such as [this] are not easily dislodged after becoming so firmly established." Pfeffer 170.

50. As a practical matter, "we know practically nothing about what went on in the state legislatures" during the process of ratifying the Bill of Rights. 2 B. Schwartz, *The Bill of Rights: A Documentary History*, 1171 (1971). Moreover, looking to state practices is, as the Court admits, *ante*, at 787, n. 5, of dubious relevance because the Establishment Clause did not originally apply to the States. Nevertheless, these difficulties give us no warrant to give controlling weight on the constitutionality of a specific practice to the collateral acts of the Members of Congress who proposed the Bill of Rights to the States.

51. See also 1 J. Story, *Commentaries on the Constitution*, 406 (1st ed., 1833); Fleet, Madison's "Detached Memoranda," 3 *Wm. & Mary Quarterly* 534, 544 (1946); Wofford, The Blinding Light: The Uses of History in Constitutional Interpretation, 31 *U. Chi. L. Rev.* 502, 508–509 (1964).

52. See generally 1 Annals of Cong. 431–433, 662, 730 (1789); *Barron v. Mayor and City Council of Baltimore*, 7 Pet. 243, 250 (1833); E. Dumbauld, *The Bill of Rights and What it Means Today*, 10–34 (1957); 2 Schwartz, *supra*, at 697–980, 983–984.

53. See, e.g., *Frontiero v. Richardson*, 411 U.S. 677 (1973) (gender discrimination); *Brown v. Board of Education*, 347 U.S. 483 (1954) (race discrimination); *Colgrove v. Battin*, 413 U.S. 149, 155–158 (1973) (jury trial); *Trop v. Dulles*, 356 U.S. 86, 101 (1958) (cruel and unusual punishment); *Katz v. United States*, 389 U.S. 347 (1967) (search and seizure).

54. See Pfeffer 266; 1 Stokes 513.

55. 3 Story, *supra*, 1871. Cf. *Church of Holy Trinity v. United States*, 143 U.S. 457, 470–471 (1892); *Vidal v. Girard's Executors*, 2 How. 127, 197–199 (1844).

56. Indeed, the prayers said by Reverend Palmer in the Nebraska Legislature are relatively "nonsectarian" in comparison with some other examples. See, e.g., *Massachusetts Senate Prayers*, 11, 14–17, 71–73, 108; *Invocations by Rev. Fred S. Holloman, Chaplain of the Kansas Senate*, 1980–1982 Legislative Sessions, pp. 40–41, 46–47, 101–102, 106–107.

57. See generally Cahn, On Government and Prayer, 37 *N.Y. U. L. Rev.* 981 (1962); Hearings, at 47 (testimony of M. Howard) ("there is simply no such thing as 'nonsectarian' prayer . . .").

Cf. *N.Y. Times*, Sept. 4, 1982, p. 8, col. 2 ("Mr. [Jerry] Falwell [founder of the organization "Moral Majority"] is quoted as telling a meeting of the Religious Newswriters Association in New Orleans that because members of the Moral Majority represented a variety of denominations, 'if we ever opened a Moral Majority meeting with prayer, silent or otherwise, we would disintegrate'").

58. I put to one side, not because of its irrelevance, but because of its obviousness, the fact that any official prayer will pose difficulties both for nonreligious persons and for religious persons whose faith does not include the institution of prayer, see, e.g., H. Smith, *The Religions of Man* 138 (Perennial Library ed. 1965) (discussing Theravada Buddhism).

59. See, e.g., Hearings, at 46–47 (testimony of M. Howard) ("We are told that [school] prayers could be 'nonsectarian,' or that they could be offered from various religious traditions in rotation. I believe such a solution is least acceptable to those most fervently devoted to their own religion"); S. Freehof, *Modern Reform Responsa*, 71 (1971) (ecumenical services not objectionable in principle, but they should not take place too frequently); J. Bancroft, *Communication in Religious Worship with Non-Catholics* (1943).

60. See, e.g., Hearings, at 47 (testimony of M. Howard) (nonsectarian prayer, even if were possible, would likely be "offensive to devout members of all religions").

61. See, e.g., S. Freehof, *Reform Responsa*, 115 (1960).

62. See, e.g., D. Bloesch, *The Struggle of Prayer*, 36–37 (1980) (hereinafter Bloesch) ("Because our Savior plays such a crucial role in the life of prayer, we should always pray having in mind his salvation and intercession. We should pray not only in the spirit of Christ but also in the name of Christ . . . To pray in his name means that we recognize that our prayers cannot penetrate the tribunal of God unless they are presented to the Father by the Son, our one Savior and Redeemer"); cf. Fischer, The Role of Christ in Christian Prayer, 41 *Encounter* 153, 155–156 (1980).

   As the Court points out, Reverend Palmer eliminated the Christological references in his prayers after receiving complaints from some of the State Senators. *Ante*, at 793, n. 14. Suppose, however, that Reverend Palmer had said that he could not in good conscience omit some references. Should he have been dismissed? And, if so, what would have been the implications of that action under both the Establishment and the Free Exercise Clauses?

63. See, e.g., *Meister Eckhart*, 88-89 (R. Blakney trans. 1941); T. Merton, *Contemplative Prayer* (1971); J. Williams, *What Americans Believe and How They Worship*, 412–413 (3d ed. 1969) (hereinafter Williams) (discussing Christian Science belief that only proper prayer is prayer of communion).

64. See, e.g., Bloesch 72–73; Stump, Petitionary Prayer, 16 *Am. Philosophical Q.* 81 (1979); Wells, Prayer: Rebelling Against the Status Quo, *Christianity Today*, Nov. 2, 1979, pp. 32–34.

65. See, e.g., Matthew 6:6 ("But thou, when thou prayest, enter into thy closet, and when thou hast shut thy door, pray to thy Father which is in secret; and thy Father which seeth in secret shall reward thee openly").

66. See, e.g., Williams 274–275 (discussing traditional Quaker practice).

67. See, e.g., Heschel, *supra* n. 28, at 53; Heiler, *supra* n. 24, at 283–285.

68. See, e.g., Williams 256; 3 Stokes 133–134; Hearings, at 65–66 (statement of Baptist Joint Committee on Public Affairs).

69. See, e.g., R. Niebuhr, *Faith and Politics*, 100 (R. Stone ed. 1968) ("A genuinely prophetic religion speaks a word of judgment against every ruler and every nation, even against good rulers and good nations").

70. See, e.g., Bloesch 159 ("World evangelization is to be numbered among the primary goals in prayer, since the proclaiming of the gospel is what gives glory to God").

71. See W. James, *The Will to Believe*, 1–31 (1st ed. 1897).

72. See generally J. Murray, *We Hold These Truths*, 73–74 (1960) (American religion "has benefited . . . by the maintenance, even in exaggerated form, of the distinction between church and state"); Martin, *Revived Dogma and New Cult*, 111 Daedalus 53, 54–55 (1982) (The "icy thinness of religion in the cold airs of Northwest Europe and in the vapors of Protestant England is highly significant, because it represents a fundamental difference in the Protestant world between North America and the original exporting countries. In all those countries with stable monarchies and Protestant state churches, [religious] institutional vitality is low. In North America, lacking either monarchy or state church, it is high" [footnote omitted]).

JUSTICE STEVENS, dissenting.

In a democratically elected legislature, the religious beliefs of the chaplain tend to reflect the faith of the majority of the [463 U.S. 783, 823] lawmakers' constituents. Prayers may be said by a Catholic priest in the Massachusetts Legislature and by a Presbyterian minister in the Nebraska Legislature, but I would not expect to find a Jehovah's Witness or a disciple of Mary Baker Eddy or the Reverend Moon serving as the official chaplain in any state legislature. Regardless of the motivation of the majority that exercises the power to appoint the chaplain,[73] it seems plain to me that the designation of a member of one religious faith to serve as the sole official chaplain of a state legislature for a period of 16 years constitutes the preference of one faith over another in violation of the Establishment Clause of the First Amendment.

The Court declines to "embark on a sensitive evaluation or to parse the content of a particular prayer." *Ante*, at 795. Perhaps it does so because it would be unable to explain away the clearly sectarian content of some of the prayers given by Nebraska's chaplain.[74] Or perhaps the Court is unwilling to [463 U.S. 783, 824] acknowledge that the tenure of the chaplain must inevitably be conditioned on the acceptability of that content to the silent majority.

I would affirm the judgment of the Court of Appeals.

(Continues)

(*Continued*)

Notes

73. The Court holds that a chaplain's 16-year tenure is constitutional as long as there is no proof that his reappointment "stemmed from an impermissible motive." *Ante*, at 793. Thus, once again, the Court makes the subjective motivation of legislators the decisive criterion for judging the constitutionality of a state legislative practice. Cf. *Rogers v. Lodge*, 458 U.S. 613 (1982), and *City of Mobile v. Bolden*, 446 U.S. 55 (1980). Although that sort of standard maximizes the power of federal judges to review state action, it is not conducive to the evenhanded administration of the law. See 458 U.S., at 642–650 (STEVENS, J., dissenting); 446 U.S., at 91–94 (STEVENS, J., concurring in judgment).

74. On March 20, 1978, for example, Chaplain Palmer gave the following invocation:

"Father in heaven, the suffering and death of your son brought life to the whole world moving our hearts to praise your glory. The power of the cross reveals your concern for the world and the wonder of Christ crucified.

"The days of his life-giving death and glorious resurrection are approaching. This is the hour when he triumphed over Satan's pride; the time when we celebrate the great event of our redemption. [463 U.S. 783, 824]

"We are reminded of the price he paid when we pray with the Psalmist:

"'My God, my God, why have you forsaken me, far from my prayer, from the words of my cry?

"'O my God, I cry out by day, and you answer not; by night, and there is no relief for me.

"'Yet you are enthroned in the Holy Place, O glory of Israel!

"'In you our fathers trusted; they trusted, and you delivered them.

"'To you they cried, and they escaped; in you they trusted, and they were not put to shame.

"'But I am a worm, not a man; the scorn of men, despised by the people.

"'All who see me scoff at me; they mock me with parted lips, they wag their heads:

"'He relied on the Lord; let Him deliver him, let Him rescue him, if He loves him.' Amen." App. 103–104. [463 U.S. 783, 825]

Freedom of Speech and Freedom of Expression

Chapter Objectives

In this chapter you will learn . . .

- Whether freedom of speech is absolute
- What defamation, libel, and slander are
- The differences between content-based and content-neutral speech
- The famous "Seven Dirty Words" case
- Whether it is legal to burn the American flag

Introduction

In Chapter 4 we examined the controversial subject of religion as it pertains to government involvement. Now, we will examine another hotly debated issue: the freedom to speak or express anything about anything. We ask: is that guaranteed under the Constitution? If not, should it be? If it is, should that legislation be overturned?

The First Amendment

Let us turn, once again, to the First Amendment as our first stop in this chapter's Constitutional journey. In pertinent part, the First Amendment reads: Congress shall make no law . . . abridging the freedom of speech, or of the press.

Freedom of Speech and Freedom of the Press

Freedom of speech and freedom of the press go hand-in-hand in the language of the First Amendment, and that seems to make sense. After all, it would seem illogical if a person were allowed to express an opinion verbally but not express that opinion in a letter to a newspaper editor that would be published. The opposite is also true: someone permitted to express his or her opinion in the newspaper would not be denied the right to make a speech regarding that same opinion. The same applies to other forms of speech, such as nonverbal gestures, holding up signs (such as, during demonstrations) and omissions of acts.

Are these freedoms, as guaranteed absolute? Absolutely not! In fact, here are five examples of communication that are not protected by the First Amendment.

1. Yelling "fire" in a crowded theater.
2. Writing a letter to the newspaper falsely accusing someone of having committed a crime.
3. Vandalizing the White House in order to protest the president's policies.
4. Threatening to physically harm another person.
5. Walking on a public street while completely nude, as a protest against the use of animals for commercialized clothing purposes.

Let's take a look at each of these examples, one by one.

Yelling "Fire" in a Crowded Theater

One of the most famous Supreme Court cases that, among other things, relates to freedom of speech, uses the example of falsely yelling "fire" in a crowded theater as not being a form of protected speech under the First Amendment. *Schenck v. United States*, decided in 1919, was actually about whether certain leaflets denouncing the United States' involvement in World War I were protected speech (more on that later). Nonetheless, the Court used the example that falsely yelling "fire" in a crowded theater is not protected speech.

That is a classic example of why freedom of speech is not absolute. The right of an individual to say exactly what he or she wants to say does not outweigh public safety. If, say, someone did yell "fire" in a crowded theater simply for his or her own amusement, numerous people might get hurt—or even killed—as they scurried for the exits. Public safety, then, supersedes personal whim.

Falsely Accusing Someone of Having Committed a Crime

One might argue that freedom of speech allows a person to say or write anything at all. We are about to discuss why that is not the case. In fact, there are laws designed against harming another person's reputation. You see, allowing one person to do something may cause some type of harm or detriment to another.

For example, granting someone the freedom to speak or write falsely about another may damage that other person's reputation. To further illustrate, let's take a look at the impact of false statements (or writings).

Defamation

Defamation is intentionally or negligently making a false statement about another person, which is heard or read by a third person and reasonably interpreted to be true, and thereby harms or tends to harm the reputation of the person about whom the statement was made. If the statement is made about a public figure, it is defamatory only if there is actual malice.

Most of the laws that are made in our country are made by the states, not by the federal government. Each state, then, has its own laws regarding defamation. Let's take a look at some examples, of defamation, to illustrate.

1. John lies to the teacher, falsely claiming that David cheated on the test.
2. Bill carelessly spreads false rumors that Jenny is pregnant, because he heard someone else say that Penny is pregnant and got the two women confused.
3. Paula writes a letter to the local newspaper, falsely accusing Steven, who is the mayor of the town, of stealing from the public trust fund. Paula's motive is to discredit Steven so that he will be forced to resign.

Each of these examples is an example of defamation. The only difference is that in the cases of John and Bill, the defamation is verbal, which is known as *slander*. In Paula's case, the defamation is written, which is known as *libel*.

Libel Versus Slander: Is One More Serious Than the Other?

Does it really matter if a false statement is made verbally rather than written or recorded? Think about it. If someone were to make a false statement about you that might cause you embarrassment and harm to your reputation, which would be worse: if the statement were made verbally in a room full of people or if it were published in a magazine? As bad as it might be for a room full of people to hear, the printed word lasts a lot longer. In fact, not only could the magazine circulate to far more people than the number who would fill a room, but it could be saved and read by people in 20, 50, even 100 years from now!

For that reason, and all other things being equal, it is both illegal and morally wrong to commit slander, but even worse (with possibly worse legal consequences) to commit libel.

Misunderstanding Versus Actual Malice

In Chapter 9 we will examine crime and punishment in greater detail, and distinguish between accidental and purposeful acts that violate the law. For now, let us simply focus on defamatory statements. If the victim of defamation is not a public figure, then the defamer is liable even if the false statement was an honest mistake. When the person is in the public eye, however, the false statement will be considered defamatory only if the defamer knew that it was false and made it with malicious intent.

In the famous case *New York Times v. Sullivan*, decided in 1964, the Supreme Court emphatically defended the concept of "robust debate" as it applies to public figures. It held that if there is no actual malice, then defamation cannot apply to a public figure simply based on factual error.

Essentially, the *Sullivan* case (which appears in its entirety at the end of this chapter) related to a story that the *New York Times* newspaper wrote about the Montgomery Police Department regarding their treatment of civil rights activist Dr. Martin Luther King, Jr. and his associates. There was no evidence to support that the story, which contained factual errors, was written maliciously against the Montgomery Police. Accordingly, because the department is a public entity, a great deal more leeway is afforded to those who speak out against it.

The judgment was unanimous, and though all of the Justices agreed, some went even further regarding the right to criticize public officials, believing that the "actual malice" requirement should not even exist, because it would be difficult to both prove and disprove.

In any event, John, Bill, and Paula have one thing in common: none of them is legally permitted to make those false statements. Accordingly, freedom of speech is not absolute.

Types of Speech

Regarding the government's interest in curbing the freedom of speech, there are two main types of speech that it seeks to curb: content-based and content-neutral. Let's take a look at each. Content-based speech is speech where the actual content is what the government is trying to prevent from being uttered or written. Content-neutral speech is not about the content, but about its effect on people. Consider these examples, to illustrate.

Suppose that the state of Kansas prohibits the sale of magazines containing nude photographs and related articles from being sold within 500 yards of any school containing students under the age of 18. In this case, the rationale would be to prevent minors from being exposed to content intended for adults. Accordingly, it is content-based speech that the government seeks to curb.

Instead, suppose that Kansas prohibited the sale of all magazines within 500 yards of schools containing minor students because it would be a tempting distraction that would cause students to leave school early and spend all of their time at the newsstand. In this case, it is not the actual content of the magazine—which could be about sports, fashion, or politics—but it is about the distraction that magazines of any kind might cause. That type of speech, therefore, is content-neutral.

Content-Based Speech and the Marketplace of Ideas

In *Abrams v. United States*, decided in 1919, the Supreme Court discussed the concept of the "marketplace of ideas," and that when ideas, left undisturbed within that marketplace, will naturally compete with one another. In *Abrams*, the Court supported the Sedition Act of 1918, which, in amending the Espionage Act of 1917, made it illegal to criticize the federal government during time of war. The Act was passed during World War I with the strong support of President Woodrow Wilson, who believed that negative criticism of the government during time of war was a danger to morale. It also gave the Postmaster General (and in turn, the U.S. Post Office) the right to refuse to deliver any mail that might contain such negative criticism.

A dissent by Oliver Wendell Holmes, one of the most famous Supreme Court Justices of all, argued for the inclusion of unpopular ideas, as they should be tested in the "marketplace." Holmes also contended that the government should only regulate speech if there is a clear and present danger. In *Abrams*, Holmes argued, the issue at hand involved the printing of leaflets that he dismissed as silly and insignificant, certainly not likely to invite danger.

The *Abrams* case appears in whole at the end of this chapter, and it is an interesting case to read, word for word. Meanwhile, let's consider the concept of testing the truth in the marketplace of ideas.

Suppose that Marvin creates his own political party and speaks out against how are society functions. He does not advocate the overthrow of the American government, because he believes in a peaceful transfer of power. However, he would like to persuade the American people to do away with income taxes altogether, and to reduce the federal, state, and local governments by 90%. In other words, schools, highways, police departments, fire departments, utilities, and even the armed forces, would be in private hands. Some are alarmed at Marvin's radical approach and even more disturbed because he gains a sizeable following in a very short period of time. Nonetheless, Marvin remains free to share his ideas with anyone and everyone.

As Marvin's ideas are "tested" in the "marketplace of ideas," it is likely that they will not prevail. In fact, it is likely that most Americans, when they realize that the government will have absolutely no authority over matters of national security would probably dismiss Marvin's ideas as being too outrageous. In this sense, rather than stifling Marvin's freedom of speech, the content would be allowed to compete in the marketplace of ideas and, as free market competition dictates, the most popular ideas would triumph.

Protesting War

In 2003, Congress voted to give President George W. Bush the authority to use military force on Iraq, if he deemed such action necessary. Based on intelligence received from the United States' ally, the United Kingdom, Bush believed that Iraqi dictator Saddam Hussein possessed or was very close to possessing weapons of mass destruction (WMDs), which he could sell to terrorists who, in turn, could conceivably use against the United States. That year, the United States invaded Iraq, ousted Hussein, and assisted the Iraqis in establishing a democracy.

Things did not go quite as well as were expected, however. Pockets of insurgency emerged and terrorists embarked upon Iraq, relishing in the opportunity to wreak havoc on the American troops. Accordingly, Iraq remained a political and military mess several years into the conflict, and, once the United States admitted that it relied upon faulty intelligence and that there were no WMDs, support for the war quickly dwindled. Even Bush's staunchest supporters began to acknowledge that either the war was a mistake to begin with, or that we were not using the correct strategy necessary to win. Bush's critics had a far worse

take on things: that Bush was a murderer and a war criminal, a liar because he knew there were no WMDs to begin with, and caused thousands of American deaths by waging war on a nation that was harmless to us only to acquire Iraq's oil, and to avenge a personal family vendetta against Hussein.

These multiple schools of thought, taken together, accounted for a rapid decline of popular support for the war. However, the difference between the early 20th Century and the early 21st Century is that back then, criticism against the war was highly regulated; nowadays, speaking out against war is almost commonplace. Now that we have covered content-based speech, let's turn to speech that is content-neutral.

Many who thought that President Bush (top) considered criticism against the war unpatriotic might have been surprised to learn that under President Wilson (bottom), it was downright illegal.

Content-Neutral Speech

What if the speech itself is content-neutral? In a public forum (such as a park or a public street), the government must demonstrate that its interest in banning the expression is narrowly tailored to achieve a significant government interest. For instance, suppose that Ron and nine of his friends went to the local park after dark and played basketball under the lights. The ten youths were loud in their playing—laughing and carrying on quite a bit—and disturbed the neighbors who lived nearby.

In an effort to stop the noise, the town passed a law that stated: Groups of more than five people are not permitted in this park. That law probably would not meet the test, as it is not narrowly tailored. A family of six could not go to the park together. Neither could large groups of friends or a class on a field trip. Baseball games, which have nine to a team, could not take place. And neither could many basketball games, for that matter. A better law might state that the park closes at 8 P.M. That way, the neighborhood could remain quiet at night and large groups of people could enjoy the park by day. The original version is what is known as a law that is overbroad.

Hate Speech

Given all that we have discussed to this point, it would seem that certain types of speech, such as telling someone, "have a nice day," is protected, whereas telling someone to "go jump in a lake and drown" would be prohibited, right? Not necessarily. You see, certain types of speech, even the worst kind—hate speech—is afforded some sort of Constitutional protection. It greatly depends on time, place, and manner restrictions.

If Justice Holmes' dissent in *Abrams* were to be followed, that would mean that hate speech could only be prohibited if there was a clear and present danger. As long as it was not apparent that danger was imminent, then all hate speech would be protected. But in *Brandenburg v. Ohio*, decided in 1969, the Court widened the criteria by which some speech would not be protected. The facts of *Brandenburg* are that the leader of an Ohio chapter of the Ku Klux Klan invited a television station to tape the Klan's rally. The rally's speeches included derogatory remarks made against blacks and Jews, and a threat of "revengeance" if the president and Congress continued to suppress the white race. The Klan's group leader, Brandenburg, was convicted for violating a statute that prohibited gathering to advocate criminal activity.

The Court reversed the conviction, holding that a conviction could only be upheld if the advocacy was for imminent lawless action and was likely to produce such action. For example, if the Klan had specified that criminal action against government officials would be taken and even specified a place and time, and if appeared likely to have the effect of motivating those who heard it to actually take such action, then that type of rally could be banned.

The *Brandenburg* decision, which was unanimous, somewhat narrows the type of speech that can be protected, as compared to the clear and present danger test. *Brandenburg* established that there does not have to be an actual clear and present danger, only that any speech advocating for imminent lawlessness and likely to produce that result satisfied the requirement necessary to ban it.

Concurring opinions in *Brandenburg* advocated for virtually limitless protection of speech except during time of war. In any event, the part regarding derogatory comments made against blacks and Jews was protected, because however distasteful one person or millions of people, might find certain remarks, it is extremely difficult to curb the speaker's right to utter them.

The Court has remained rather consistent about hateful and threatening speech since *Brandenburg*. For example, in 1982, the Court in *NAACP v. Claiborne Hardware Co.* defended a group of blacks who were boycotting white merchants when they stated that if blacks violated their boycott, they would be disciplined by their own people. The Court determined that the remarks did not constitute incitement. As in *Brandenburg*, there were no dissenting opinions in *Claiborne*, nor was there any consideration of banning the speech solely because it was hateful.

Obscenity

Now that we have studied the Court's opinions about defamatory, hateful, and dangerous types of speech, what about words, photographs, or even live displays that are considered obscene? Why would a person not be able to walk around nude on a public street, or pin up a centerfold of a nude model from a magazine in a public display, yet paintings and statues of nude men and women fill the walls and halls of art museums? In order to make more sense of the standard of obscenity, let's take a look at what the Supreme Court has said about it.

Actually, the Supreme Court has not had a very easy time trying to define obscenity: Justice Potter Stewart famously wrote in *Jacobellis v. Ohio*, decided in 1964, that he could not pinpoint what the exact definition of obscenity ought to be, but that "I know it when I see it." He also believed that the First Amendment protects all obscenity except for hard-core pornography.

The 1973 Supreme Court case, *Miller v. California*, established the modern-day standard of obscenity. Marvin Miller operated a large mail-order business in California, distributing leaflets through the mail that contained sexually explicit images. A restaurant manager and his mother found these unsolicited leaflets in their mail and complained to the police. Miller was arrested and convicted, and lost on appeal. The Supreme Court then established the following standard regarding material that does not receive First Amendment protection.

1. The average person, based on local community standards (not national standards), must conclude that the material as a whole appeals to the *prurient* (lustful) interest.
2. The material describes sexual or *excretory* functions (i.e., "going to the bathroom") in a patently offensive way.
3. The work as a whole must lack any serious literary, artistic, political, or scientific value.

Let's look at the standard a little closer.

Local Community Standards

The United States is often referred to as multicultural, and it certainly is, but in more than just one way. Quite often, multicultural refers to the United States immigrants who hail from various countries, thereby bringing incorporating some of their own culture into the country. In addition to multiple cultures from other lands, there are also multiple *American* cultures within one country. The culture of New York City, for instance, is a whole lot different from the culture of Billings, Montana, which, again, is entirely different from the culture of Tarpon Springs, Florida. Accordingly, what might be considered obscene in one place might be considered perfectly acceptable in another.

The standard, then, to define obscenity is a local one, to be determined based on the values of the particular community, not the nation as a whole.

Offensive Sexual or Excretory Functions

A photograph of a nude body or a person urinating or having a bowel movement might be perfectly appropriate in a medical book, but inappropriate if the person is engaging in a sexual act or defecating on a public street. These are more examples of why Constitutional law is not absolute; it often depends on the circumstances.

Lacking in Literary, Artistic, Political, or Scientific Value

Words or images that might otherwise be considered obscene would warrant First Amendment protection nonetheless if they possessed some sort of socially redeeming value, in terms of literature, art, politics, or science. That is why a nude painting hanging in a museum is perfectly acceptable, or why profane words in literary context are permitted.

The dissenting Justices in *Miller* were critical of the decision, arguing that the Court's three-pronged test essentially amends the Constitution (which, as we have discussed before, is not taken very lightly!).

Indecency: The Seven Dirty Words Case

At first glance you might wonder, "what's the difference between obscenity and indecency?" The short version of the answer is, according to the Supreme Court, not a whole lot, except that indecency is less severe.

FCC v. Pacifica Foundation, decided in 1978, is commonly known as the "Seven Dirty Words" case. Comedian George Carlin was doing his "Seven Dirty Words" routine on a radio station owned by Pacifica Foundation, and a father complained to the Federal Communications Commission (FCC) because his son, a minor, was exposed to the broadcast.

The Court held that the material was indecent, but not obscene, and therefore did not categorically prohibit its airing. However, it found that there was a compelling interest to shield minors from such profane language, and so it left the decision up to the FCC to determine its own standards of decency.

Dissenting Justices pointed out that when a speech is offensive in the form of a radio broadcast, the individual who stumbles upon it has the choice to simply turn it off.

Of course, this does not take care of the problem of shielding minors from such offensive language, but the counterargument is that it is the responsibility of the parents, not the government, to monitor their minor children's activities (so as not to let them stumble upon such broadcasts).

The First Amendment and the Internet

Congress passed the Communications Decency Act of 1996 (DCA) in order to regulate pornographic material on the Internet, and mainly to prevent it from falling into the hands of children. But in the following year, the Court in *ACLU v. Reno* declared that the Internet was afforded full Constitutional protection as a communications media, no different than the press, and thus the main thrust would be targeted against obscenity and child pornography. The parts that would criminalize any adult knowingly conveying information of a sexual nature to any minor were considered largely unenforceable.

Concurring Justices hoped for better technology that would allow for an adult zone on the Internet, which could then be better regulated like other types of media.

The *Reno* case is a classic example of the Court dealing with an issue that our Founding Fathers, in all their brilliance, could not have possibly imagined: the Internet.

Flag Burning

Suppose that you are walking along and you see some person setting fire to the American flag. Should that be against the law? Your gut reaction might go in one of two directions.

1. For shame! How can anyone set fire to the American flag? That's a disgrace and that person should be in jail!
2. Precisely *because* this is America, this person has the right to burn the flag, even if it is something that I find so distasteful.

Your point of view might be somewhere in-between, or may be based on a more practical notion, such as, "Isn't it dangerous to burn something that large in public?" In any event, flag burning is a serious issue that has been debated in the halls of Congress as well as throughout America. As with many Constitutional issues, the Founders did not explicitly permit or prohibit it; the Constitution itself is silent on the topic. But in 1989, the U.S. Supreme Court, in *Texas v. Johnson*, addressed the issue. The *Johnson* Court held that flag burning was protected under the First Amendment.

Specifically, Gregory Lee Johnson participated in a demonstration in Dallas, Texas, in 1984, the site of the Republican National Convention that year. Johnson was protesting the policies of President Ronald Reagan and of certain Dallas companies. When someone handed him an American flag, he poured kerosene on it and set it on fire. During the burning, various protestors shouted, "red, white, and blue, we spit on you!" Some people were so offended at that display, and one person took the ashes of the burned flag and buried them in his backyard. Johnson was convicted, but the Texas Court of Appeals overturned the conviction. The Supreme Court, in affirming the Court of

Which is more important: Freedom of expression, or preservation of the American flag?

Appeals' decision, declared that flag burning, although not verbal, is a form of expressive conduct equivalent to speech, and thus protected by the First Amendment.

The dissenting Justices argued that the American flag is in a category all its own: it is not merely an idea and bears no political point of view. It is a national symbol that is revered by so many and should be afforded such special protection that even the First Amendment cannot supersede it. Essentially, the majority agreed with everything except that last sentence.

The following year, the Court reaffirmed its *Johnson* holding in *United States v. Eichman*, with the Justices making the same arguments, for and against, that they had made the year before.

Conclusion

As we have learned in this chapter, the freedoms of speech and expression are plenty, and are a big part of what makes the United States a particularly free country, as compared to many other ones. But we also learned that these freedoms are not absolute: we cannot yell "fire" in a crowded theater, indeed! Our rights to make a particular statement or engage in some type of specific conduct, are

balanced against our fellow Americans' rights not to have to see or hear what we do. So, who wins? We, or they? It all depends on the situation.

In Chapter Six, we will continue our trend of exploring exciting and controversial Constitutional issues. Next up for discussion and debate: abortion.

Questions for Review

1. Explain the example of yelling "fire" in a crowded theater and why it is against the law.
2. What is defamation?
3. What is libel?
4. What is slander?
5. Why is libel often more damaging than slander?
6. What is content-based speech?
7. What is content-neutral speech?
8. What is "prurient" interest?
9. What is an example of sexual material that would offer scientific value?
10. Is nonverbal expression protected under the First Amendment?

Constitutionally Speaking

Alex buys an American flag from a flag store, takes it home, and sets it on fire in the privacy of his own backyard on the Fourth of July in protest of the United States. Timothy draws an American flag on a piece of paper and admires it for awhile. A few weeks later, when he is cleaning off his desk, he thinks of the drawing as clutter, tears it up, and throws it in the wastebasket. Wendy buys an American flag t-shirt from a local department store and wears it to a Memorial Day parade. After a few weeks, she realizes that she will not really wear it again and decides to use it as a rag. She washes her car and scrubs the floor with it. Wendy's American flag shirt is now dirty and torn.

Do Alex, Timothy, and Wendy have a right to do what each of them did? Does any of them have more or less of a right than the other two? Explain.

Constitutional Cases

The Sedition Act of 1918 appears below, followed by two cases we talked about in this chapter: *New York Times v. Sullivan* and *Abrams v. U.S.*

SEDITION ACT OF 1918

Whoever, when the United States is at war, shall willfully make or convey false reports or false statements with intent to interfere with the operation or success of the military or naval forces of the United States, or to promote the success of its enemies, or shall willfully make or convey false reports or false statements, or say or do anything except by way of bona fide and not disloyal advice to an investor or investors, with intent to obstruct the sale by the United States of bonds or other securities of the United States or the making of loans by or to the United States, and whoever when the United States is at war, shall willfully cause or attempt to cause, or incite or attempt to incite, insubordination, disloyalty, mutiny, or refusal of duty, in the military or naval forces of the United States, or shall willfully obstruct or attempt to obstruct the recruiting or enlistment services of the United States, and whoever, when the United States is at war, shall willfully utter, print, write or publish any disloyal, profane, scurrilous, or abusive language about the form of government of the United States or the Constitution of the United States, or the military or naval forces of the United States, or the flag of the United States, or the uniform of the Army or Navy of the United States into contempt, scorn, contumely, or disrepute, or shall willfully utter, print, write, or publish any language intended to incite, provoke, or encourage resistance to the United States, or to promote the cause of its enemies, or shall willfully display the flag of any foreign enemy, or shall willfully by utterance, writing, printing, publication, or language spoken, urge, incite, or advocate any curtailment of production in this country of any thing or things, product or products, necessary or essential to the prosecution of the war in which the United States may be engaged, with intent by such curtailment to cripple or hinder the United States in the prosecution of war, and whoever shall willfully advocate, teach, defend, or suggest the doing of any of the acts or things in this section enumerated, and whoever shall by word or act support or favor the cause of any country with which the United States is at war or by word or act oppose the cause of the United States therein, shall be punished by a fine of not more than $10,000 or the imprisonment for not more than 20 years, or both: Provided, that any employee or official of the United States Government who commits any disloyal act or utters any unpatriotic or disloyal language, or who, in an abusive and violent manner criticizes the Army or Navy or the flag of the United States shall be at once dismissed from the service.

When the United States is at war, the Postmaster General may, upon evidence satisfactory to him that any person or concern is using the mails in violation of any of the provisions of this Act, instruct the postmaster at any post office at which mail is received addressed to such person or concern to return to the postmaster at the office at which they were originally mailed all letters or other matter so addressed, with the words "Mail to this address undeliverable under Espionage Act" plainly written or stamped upon the outside thereof, and all such letters or other matter so returned to such postmasters shall be by them returned to the senders thereof under such regulations as the Postmaster General may prescribe.

New York Times Co. v. Sullivan, 376 U.S. 254 (1964)

Syllabus

Respondent, an elected official in Montgomery, Alabama, brought suit in a state court alleging that he had been libeled by an advertisement in corporate petitioner's newspaper, the text of which appeared over the names of the four individual petitioners and many others. The advertisement included statements, some of which were false, about police action allegedly directed against students who participated in a civil rights demonstration and against a leader of the civil rights movement; respondent claimed the statements referred to him because his duties included supervision of the police department. The trial judge instructed the jury that such statements were "libelous *per se*," legal injury being implied without proof of actual damages, and that, for the purpose of compensatory damages, malice was presumed, so that such damages could be awarded against petitioners if the statements were found to have been published by them and to have related to respondent. As to punitive damages, the judge instructed that mere negligence was not evidence of actual malice, and would not justify an award of punitive damages; he refused to instruct that actual intent to harm or recklessness had to be found before punitive damages could be awarded, or that a verdict for respondent should differentiate between compensatory and punitive damages. The jury found for respondent, and the State Supreme Court affirmed.

Held: A State cannot, under the First and Fourteenth Amendments, award damages to a public official for defamatory falsehood relating to his official conduct unless he proves "actual malice"—that the statement was made with knowledge of its falsity or with reckless disregard of whether it was true or false. Pp. 376 U. S. 265–292.

(a) Application by state courts of a rule of law, whether statutory or not, to award a judgment in a civil action, is "state action" under the Fourteenth Amendment. P. 376 U.S. 265.

(*Continues*)

(Continued)

(b) Expression does not lose constitutional protection to which it would otherwise be entitled because it appears in the form of a paid advertisement. Pp. 376 U.S. 265–266.

(c) Factual error, content defamatory of official reputation, or both, are insufficient to warrant an award of damages for false statements unless "actual malice"—knowledge that statements are false or in reckless disregard of the truth—is alleged and proved. Pp. 376 U.S. 279–283.

(d) State court judgment entered upon a general verdict which does not differentiate between punitive damages, as to which, under state law, actual malice must be proved, and general damages, as to which it is "presumed," precludes any determination as to the basis of the verdict, and requires reversal, where presumption of malice is inconsistent with federal constitutional requirements. Pp. 376 U.S. 284.

(e) The evidence was constitutionally insufficient to support the judgment for respondent, since it failed to support a finding that the statements were made with actual malice or that they related to respondent. Pp. 376 U.S. 285–292.

273 Ala. 656, 144 So.2d 25, reversed and remanded.

MR. JUSTICE BRENNAN delivered the opinion of the Court.

We are required in this case to determine for the first time the extent to which the constitutional protections for speech and press limit a State's power to award damages in a libel action brought by a public official against critics of his official conduct.

Respondent L. B. Sullivan is one of the three elected Commissioners of the City of Montgomery, Alabama. He testified that he was "Commissioner of Public Affairs, and the duties are supervision of the Police Department, Fire Department, Department of Cemetery and Department of Scales."

He brought this civil libel action against the four individual petitioners, who are Negroes and Alabama clergymen, and against petitioner the New York Times Company, a New York corporation which publishes the *New York Times*, a daily newspaper. A jury in the Circuit Court of Montgomery County awarded him damages of $500,000, the full amount claimed, against all the petitioners, and the Supreme Court of Alabama affirmed. 273 Ala. 656, 144 So.2d 25.

Respondent's complaint alleged that he had been libeled by statements in a full-page advertisement that was carried in the *New York Times* on March 29, 1960.[1] Entitled "Heed Their Rising Voices," the advertisement began by stating that,

"As the whole world knows by now, thousands of Southern Negro students are engaged in widespread nonviolent demonstrations in positive affirmation of the right to live in human dignity as guaranteed by the U.S. Constitution and the Bill of Rights."

It went on to charge that, "in their efforts to uphold these guarantees, they are being met by an unprecedented wave of terror by those who would deny and negate that document which the whole world looks upon as setting the pattern for modern freedom. . . ."

Succeeding paragraphs purported to illustrate the "wave of terror" by describing certain alleged events. The text concluded with an appeal for funds for three purposes: support of the student movement, "the struggle for the right to vote," and the legal defense of Dr. Martin Luther King, Jr., leader of the movement, against a perjury indictment then pending in Montgomery.

The text appeared over the names of 64 persons, many widely known for their activities in public affairs, religion, trade unions, and the performing arts. Below these names, and under a line reading "We in the south who are struggling daily for dignity and freedom warmly endorse this appeal," appeared the names of the four individual petitioners and of 16 other persons, all but two of whom were identified as clergymen in various Southern cities. The advertisement was signed at the bottom of the page by the "Committee to Defend Martin Luther King and the Struggle for Freedom in the South," and the officers of the Committee were listed.

Of the 10 paragraphs of text in the advertisement, the third and a portion of the sixth were the basis of respondent's claim of libel. They read as follows:

Third paragraph:

"In Montgomery, Alabama, after students sang 'My Country, 'Tis of Thee' on the State Capitol steps, their leaders were expelled from school, and truckloads of police armed with shotguns and teargas ringed the Alabama State College Campus. When the entire student body protested to state authorities by refusing to reregister, their dining hall was padlocked in an attempt to starve them into submission."

Sixth paragraph:

"Again and again, the Southern violators have answered Dr. King's peaceful protests with intimidation and violence. They have bombed his home, almost killing his wife and child. They have assaulted his person. They have arrested him seven times—for 'speeding,' 'loitering' and similar 'offenses.' And now they have charged him with 'perjury'—a *felony* under which they could imprison him for *ten years*. . . ."

Although neither of these statements mentions respondent by name, he contended that the word "police" in the third paragraph referred to him as the Montgomery Commissioner who supervised the Police Department, so that he was being accused of "ringing" the campus with police. He further claimed that the paragraph would be read as imputing to the police, and hence to him, the padlocking of the dining hall in order to starve the students into submission.[2] As to the sixth paragraph, he contended that, since arrests are ordinarily made by the police, the statement "They have arrested [Dr. King] seven times" would be read as referring to him; he further contended that the "They" who did the arresting would be equated with the "They" who committed the other described acts and with the "Southern violators." Thus, he argued, the paragraph would be read as accusing the Montgomery police, and hence him, of answering Dr. King's protests with "intimidation and violence," bombing his home, assaulting his person, and charging him with perjury. Respondent and six other Montgomery residents testified that they read some or all of the statements as referring to him in his capacity as Commissioner.

It is uncontroverted that some of the statements contained in the two paragraphs were not accurate descriptions of events which occurred in Montgomery. Although Negro students staged a demonstration on the State Capitol steps, they sang the National Anthem and not "My Country, 'Tis of Thee." Although nine students were expelled by the State Board of Education, this was not for leading the demonstration at the Capitol, but for demanding service at a lunch counter in the Montgomery County Courthouse on another day. Not the entire student body, but most of it, had protested the expulsion, not by refusing to register, but by boycotting classes on a single day; virtually all the students did register for the ensuing semester. The campus dining hall was not padlocked on any occasion, and the only students who may have been barred from eating there were the few who had neither signed a preregistration application nor requested temporary meal tickets. Although the police were deployed near the campus in large numbers on three occasions, they did not at any time "ring" the campus, and they were not called to the campus in connection with the demonstration on the State Capitol steps, as the third paragraph implied. Dr. King had not been arrested seven times, but only four, and although he claimed to have been assaulted some years earlier in connection with his arrest for loitering outside a courtroom, one of the officers who made the arrest denied that there was such an assault.

On the premise that the charges in the sixth paragraph could be read as referring to him, respondent was allowed to prove that he had not participated in the events described. Although Dr. King's home had, in fact, been bombed twice when his wife and child were there, both of these occasions antedated respondent's tenure as Commissioner, and the police were not only not implicated in the bombings, but had made every effort to apprehend those who were. Three of Dr. King's four arrests took place before respondent became Commissioner. Although Dr. King had, in fact, been indicted (he was subsequently acquitted) on two counts of perjury, each of which carried a possible 5-year sentence, respondent had nothing to do with procuring the indictment.

Respondent made no effort to prove that he suffered actual pecuniary loss as a result of the alleged libel.[3] One of his witnesses, a former employer, testified that, if he had believed the statements, he doubted whether he "would want to be associated with anybody who would be a party to such things that are stated in that ad," and that he would not reemploy respondent if he believed "that he allowed the Police Department to do the things that the paper say he did." But neither this witness nor any of the others testified that he had actually believed the statements in their supposed reference to respondent. The cost of the advertisement was approximately $4,800, and it was published by the *Times* upon an order from a New York advertising agency acting for the signatory Committee. The agency submitted the advertisement with a letter from A. Philip Randolph, Chairman of the Committee, certifying that the persons whose names appeared on the advertisement had given their permission. Mr. Randolph was known to the *Times*' Advertising Acceptability Department as a responsible person, and, in accepting the letter as sufficient proof of authorization, it followed its established practice. There was testimony that the copy of the advertisement which accompanied the letter listed only the 64 names

(Continues)

appearing under the text, and that the statement, "We in the south . . . warmly endorse this appeal," and the list of names thereunder, which included those of the individual petitioners, were subsequently added when the first proof of the advertisement was received. Each of the individual petitioners testified that he had not authorized the use of his name, and that he had been unaware of its use until receipt of respondent's demand for a retraction. The manager of the Advertising Acceptability [P. 376, U.S. 261] Department testified that he had approved the advertisement for publication because he knew nothing to cause him to believe that anything in it was false, and because it bore the endorsement of "a number of people who are well known and whose reputation" he "had no reason to question." Neither he nor anyone else at the *Times* made an effort to confirm the accuracy of the advertisement, either by checking it against recent *Times* news stories relating to some of the described events or by any other means.

Alabama law denies a public officer recovery of punitive damages in a libel action brought on account of a publication concerning his official conduct unless he first makes a written demand for a public retraction and the defendant fails or refuses to comply. Alabama Code, Tit. 7, §914. Respondent served such a demand upon each of the petitioners. None of the individual petitioners responded to the demand, primarily because each took the position that he had not authorized the use of his name on the advertisement, and therefore had not published the statements that respondent alleged had libeled him. The *Times* did not publish a retraction in response to the demand, but wrote respondent a letter stating, among other things, that "we . . . are somewhat puzzled as to how you think the statements in any way reflect on you," and "you might, if you desire, let us know in what respect you claim that the statements in the advertisement reflect on you." Respondent filed this suit a few days later without answering the letter. The *Times* did, however, subsequently publish a retraction of the advertisement upon the demand of Governor John Patterson of Alabama, who asserted that the publication charged him with

"grave misconduct and . . . improper actions and omissions as Governor of Alabama and Ex-Officio Chairman of the State Board of Education of Alabama."

When asked to explain why there had been a retraction for the Governor but not for respondent, the Secretary of the *Times* testified:

"We did that because we didn't want anything that was published by *The Times* to be a reflection on the State of Alabama, and the Governor was, as far as we could see, the embodiment of the State of Alabama and the proper representative of the State, and, furthermore, we had by that time learned more of the actual facts which the and purported to recite and, finally, the ad did refer to the action of the State authorities and the Board of Education, presumably of which the Governor is the ex-officio chairman. . . ."

On the other hand, he testified that he did not think that "any of the language in there referred to Mr. Sullivan."

The trial judge submitted the case to the jury under instructions that the statements in the advertisement were "libelous *per se*," and were not privileged, so that petitioners might be held liable if the jury found that they had published the advertisement and that the statements were made "of and concerning" respondent. The jury was instructed that, because the statements were libelous *per se*, "the law . . . implies legal injury from the bare fact of publication itself," "falsity and malice are presumed," "general damages need not be alleged or proved, but are presumed," and "punitive damages may be awarded by the jury even though the amount of actual damages is neither found nor shown." An award of punitive damages—as distinguished from "general" damages, which are compensatory in nature—apparently requires proof of actual malice under Alabama law, and the judge charged that "mere negligence or carelessness is not evidence of actual malice or malice in fact, and does not justify an award of exemplary or punitive damages."

He refused to charge, however, that the jury must be "convinced" of malice, in the sense of "actual intent" to harm or "gross negligence and recklessness," to make such an award, and he also refused to require that a verdict for respondent differentiate between compensatory and punitive damages. The judge rejected petitioners' contention that his rulings abridged the freedoms of speech and of the press that are guaranteed by the First and Fourteenth Amendments.

In affirming the judgment, the Supreme Court of Alabama sustained the trial judge's rulings and instructions in all respects. 273 Ala. 656, 144 So.2d 25. It held that, "where the words published tend to injure a person libeled by them in his reputation, profession, trade or business, or charge him with an indictable offense, or tend to bring the individual into public contempt,"

they are "libelous *per se*"; that "the matter complained of is, under the above doctrine, libelous *per se*, if it was published of and concerning the plaintiff," and that it was actionable without "proof of pecuniary injury . . . such injury being implied." *Id.* at 673, 676, 144 So.2d at 37, 41. It approved the trial court's ruling that the jury could find the statements to have been made "of and concerning" respondent, stating:

"We think it common knowledge that the average person knows that municipal agents, such as police and firemen, and others, are under the control and direction of the city governing body, and, more particularly, under the direction and control of a single commissioner. In measuring the performance or deficiencies of such groups, praise or criticism is usually attached to the official in complete control of the body." *Id.* at 674–675, 144 So.2d at 39.

In sustaining the trial court's determination that the verdict was not excessive, the court said that malice could be inferred from the *Times*' "irresponsibility" in printing the advertisement while

"the *Times*, in its own files, had articles already published which would have demonstrated the falsity of the allegations in the advertisement";

from the *Times*' failure to retract for respondent while retracting for the Governor, whereas the falsity of some of the allegations was then known to the *Times* and "the matter contained in the advertisement was equally false as to both parties," and from the testimony of the *Times*' Secretary that, apart from the statement that the dining hall was padlocked, he thought the two paragraphs were "substantially correct." *Id.* at 686–687, 144 So.2d at 50–51. The court reaffirmed a statement in an earlier opinion that "There is no legal measure of damages in cases of this character." *Id.* at 686, 144 So.2d at 50. It rejected petitioners' constitutional contentions with the brief statements that "The First Amendment of the U.S. Constitution does not protect libelous publications," and "The Fourteenth Amendment is directed against State action, and not private action." *Id.* at 676, 144 So.2d at 40.

Because of the importance of the constitutional issues involved, we granted the separate petitions for *certiorari* of the individual petitioners and of the *Times*. 371 U.S. 946. We reverse the judgment. We hold that the rule of law applied by the Alabama courts is constitutionally deficient for failure to provide the safeguards for freedom of speech and of the press that are required by the First and Fourteenth Amendments in a libel action brought by a public official against critics of his official conduct.[4] We further hold that, under the proper safeguards, the evidence presented in this case is constitutionally insufficient to support the judgment for respondent.

I

We may dispose at the outset of two grounds asserted to insulate the judgment of the Alabama courts from constitutional scrutiny. The first is the proposition relied on by the State Supreme Court—that "The Fourteenth Amendment is directed against State action, and not private action." That proposition has no application to this case. Although this is a civil lawsuit between private parties, the Alabama courts have applied a state rule of law which petitioners claim to impose invalid restrictions on their constitutional freedoms of speech and press. It matters not that that law has been applied in a civil action and that it is common law only, though supplemented by statute. See, e.g., Alabama Code, Tit. 7, §§908–917. The test is not the form in which state power has been applied but, whatever the form, whether such power has, in fact, been exercised. *See Ex parte Virginia*, 100 U.S. 339, 100 U.S. 346–347; *American Federation of Labor v. Swing.* 312 U.S. 321.

The second contention is that the constitutional guarantees of freedom of speech and of the press are inapplicable here, at least so far as the *Times* is concerned, because the allegedly libelous statements were published as part of a paid, "commercial" advertisement. The argument relies on *Valentine v. Chrestensen*, 316 U.S. 52, where the Court held that a city ordinance forbidding street distribution of commercial and business advertising matter did not abridge the First Amendment freedoms, even as applied to a handbill having a commercial message on one side but a protest against certain official

(Continues)

action, on the other. The reliance is wholly misplaced. The Court in *Chrestensen* reaffirmed the constitutional protection for "the freedom of communicating information and disseminating opinion"; its holding was based upon the factual conclusions that the handbill was "purely commercial advertising" and that the protest against official action had been added only to evade the ordinance.

The publication here was not a "commercial" advertisement in the sense in which the word was used in *Chrestensen*. It communicated information, expressed opinion, recited grievances, protested claimed abuses, and sought financial support on behalf of a movement whose existence and objectives are matters of the highest public interest and concern. See *NAACP v. Button*, 371 U.S. 415, 371 U.S. 435. That the *Times* was paid for publishing the advertisement is as immaterial in this connection as is the fact that newspapers and books are sold. *Smith v. California*, 361 U.S. 147, 361 U.S. 150; cf. *Bantam Books, Inc. v. Sullivan*, 372 U.S. 58, 372 U.S. 64, n. 6. Any other conclusion would discourage newspapers from carrying "editorial advertisements" of this type, and so might shut off an important outlet for the promulgation of information and ideas by persons who do not themselves have access to publishing facilities—who wish to exercise their freedom of speech even though they are not members of the press. Cf. *Lovell v. Griffin*, 303 U.S. 444, 303 U.S. 452; *Schneider v. State*, 308 U.S. 147, 308 U.S. 164. The effect would be to shackle the First Amendment in its attempt to secure "the widest possible dissemination of information from diverse and antagonistic sources." *Associated Press v. United States*, 326 U.S. 1, 326 U.S. 20. To avoid placing such a handicap upon the freedoms of expression, we hold that, if the allegedly libelous statements would otherwise be constitutionally protected from the present judgment, they do not forfeit that protection because they were published in the form of a paid advertisement.[5]

II

Under Alabama law, as applied in this case, a publication is "libelous *per se*" if the words "tend to injure a person . . . in his reputation" or to "bring [him] into public contempt"; the trial court stated that the standard was met if the words are such as to "injure him in his public office, or impute misconduct to him in his office, or want of official integrity, or want of fidelity to a public trust. . . ." The jury must find that the words were published "of and concerning" the plaintiff, but, where the plaintiff is a public official, his place in the governmental hierarchy is sufficient evidence to support a finding that his reputation has been affected by statements that reflect upon the agency of which he is in charge. Once "libel *per se*" has been established, the defendant has no defense as to stated facts unless he can persuade the jury that they were true in all their particulars. *Alabama Ride Co. v. Vance*, 235 Ala. 263, 178 So. 438 (1938); *Johnson Publishing Co. v. Davis*, 271 Ala. 474, 494 495, 124 So.2d 441, 457–458 (1960). His privilege of "fair comment" for expressions of opinion depends on the truth of the facts upon which the comment is based. *Parsons v. Age-Herald Publishing Co.*, 181 Ala. 439, 450, 61 So. 345, 350 (1913). Unless he can discharge the burden of proving truth, general damages are presumed, and may be awarded without proof of pecuniary injury. A showing of actual malice is apparently a prerequisite to recovery of punitive damages, and the defendant may, in any event, forestall a punitive award by a retraction meeting the statutory requirements. Good motives and belief in truth do not negate an inference of malice, but are relevant only in mitigation of punitive damages if the jury chooses to accord them weight. *Johnson Publishing Co. v. Davis, supra*, 271 Ala., at 495, 124 So.2d at 458.

The question before us is whether this rule of liability, as applied to an action brought by a public official against critics of his official conduct, abridges the freedom of speech and of the press that is guaranteed by the First and Fourteenth Amendments.

Respondent relies heavily, as did the Alabama courts, on statements of this Court to the effect that the Constitution does not protect libelous publications.[6] Those statements do not foreclose our inquiry here. None of the cases sustained the use of libel laws to impose sanctions upon expression critical of the official conduct of public officials. The dictum in *Pennekamp v. Florida*, 328 U. S. 331, 328 U.S. 348–349, that "when the statements amount to defamation, a judge has such remedy in damages for libel as do other public servants," implied no view as to what remedy might constitutionally be afforded to public officials. In *Beauharnais v. Illinois*, 343 U.S. 250, the Court sustained an Illinois criminal libel statute as applied to a publication held to be both defamatory of a racial group and "liable to cause violence and disorder." But the Court was careful to note that it "retains and exercises authority to nullify action which encroaches on freedom of utterance under the guise of punishing libel"; for "public men are, as it were, public property," and "discussion cannot be denied, and the right, as well as the duty, of criticism must not be stifled." *Id.* at 343 U.S. 263–264, and n. 18. In the only previous case that did present the question of constitutional limitations upon the power to award damages for libel of a public official, the Court was equally divided and the question was not decided. *Schenectady Union Pub. Co. v. Sweeney*, 316 U.S. 642.

In deciding the question now, we are compelled by neither precedent nor policy to give any more weight to the epithet "libel" than we have to other "mere labels" of state law. *NAACP v. Button*, 371 U.S. 415, 371 U.S. 429. Like insurrection,[7] contempt,[8] advocacy of unlawful acts,[9] breach of the peace,[10] obscenity,[11] solicitation of legal business,[12] and the various other formulae for the repression of expression that have been challenged in this Court, libel can claim no talismanic immunity from constitutional limitations. It must be measured by standards that satisfy the First Amendment.

The general proposition that freedom of expression upon public questions is secured by the First Amendment has long been settled by our decisions. The constitutional safeguard, we have said, "was fashioned to assure unfettered interchange of ideas for the bringing about of political and social changes desired by the people." *Roth v. United States*, 354 U.S. 476, 354 U.S. 484.

"The maintenance of the opportunity for free political discussion to the end that government may be responsive to the will of the people and that changes may be obtained by lawful means, an opportunity essential to the security of the Republic, is a fundamental principle of our constitutional system."

Stromberg v. California, 283 U.S. 359, 283 U.S. 369. "[I]t is a prized American privilege to speak one's mind, although not always with perfect good taste, on all public institutions," *Bridges v. California*, 314 U.S. 252, 314 U.S. 270, and this opportunity is to be afforded for "vigorous advocacy" no less than "abstract discussion." *NAACP v. Button*, 371 U.S. 415, 371 U.S. 429.

The First Amendment, said Judge Learned Hand, "presupposes that right conclusions are more likely to be gathered out of a multitude of tongues than through any kind of authoritative selection. To many, this is, and always will be, folly, but we have staked upon it our all."

United States v. Associated Press, 52 F.Supp. 362, 372 (D.C.S.D.N.Y.1943). Mr. Justice Brandeis, in his concurring opinion in *Whitney v. California*, 274 U.S. 357, 274 U.S. 375–376, gave the principle its classic formulation:

"Those who won our independence believed . . . that public discussion is a political duty, and that this should be a fundamental principle of the American government. They recognized the risks to which all human institutions are subject. But they knew that order cannot be secured merely through fear of punishment for its infraction; that it is hazardous to discourage thought, hope and imagination; that fear breeds repression; that repression breeds hate; that hate menaces stable government; that the path of safety lies in the opportunity to discuss freely supposed grievances and proposed remedies, and that the fitting remedy for evil counsels is good ones. Believing in the power of reason as applied through public discussion, they eschewed silence coerced by law—the argument of force in its worst form. Recognizing the occasional tyrannies of governing majorities, they amended the Constitution so that free speech and assembly should be guaranteed."

Thus, we consider this case against the background of a profound national commitment to the principle that debate on public issues should be uninhibited, robust, and wide-open, and that it may well include vehement, caustic, and sometimes unpleasantly sharp attacks on government and public officials. See *Terminiello v. Chicago*, 337 U.S. 1, 337 U.S. 4; *De Jonge v. Oregon*, 299 U.S. 353.

299 U.S. 365. The present advertisement, as an expression of grievance and protest on one of the major public issues of our time, would seem clearly to qualify for the constitutional protection. The question is whether it forfeits that protection by the falsity of some of its factual statements and by its alleged defamation of respondent.

Authoritative interpretations of the First Amendment guarantees have consistently refused to recognize an exception for any test of truth—whether administered by judges, juries, or administrative officials—and especially one that puts the burden of proving truth on the speaker. Cf. *Speiser v. Randall*, 357 U.S. 513, 357 U.S. 525–526. The constitutional protection does not turn upon "the truth, popularity, or social utility of the ideas and beliefs which are offered." *NAACP v. Button*, 371 U.S. 415, 371 U.S. 445. As Madison said, "Some degree of abuse is inseparable from the proper use of every thing, and in no

(Continues)

instance is this more true than in that of the press." 4 Elliot's Debates on the Federal Constitution (1876), p. 571. In *Cantwell v. Connecticut*, 310 U.S. 296, 310 U.S. 310, the Court declared:

> "In the realm of religious faith, and in that of political belief, sharp differences arise. In both fields, the tenets of one man may seem the rankest error to his neighbor. To persuade others to his own point of view, the pleader, as we know, at times resorts to exaggeration, to vilification of men who have been, or are, prominent in church or state, and even to false statement. But the people of this nation have ordained, in the light of history, that, in spite of the probability of excesses and abuses, these liberties are, in the long view, essential to enlightened opinion and right conduct on the part of the citizens of a democracy."

That erroneous statement is inevitable in free debate, and that it must be protected if the freedoms of expression are to have the "breathing space" that they "need . . . to survive," *NAACP v. Button*, 371 U.S. 415, 371 U.S. 433, was also recognized by the Court of Appeals for the District of Columbia Circuit in *Sweeney v. Patterson*, 76 U.S.App.D.C. 23, 24, 128 F.2d 457, 458 (1942), *cert. denied*, 317 U.S. 678. Judge Edgerton spoke for a unanimous court which affirmed the dismissal of a Congressman's libel suit based upon a newspaper article charging him with anti-Semitism in opposing a judicial appointment. He said:

> "Cases which impose liability for erroneous reports of the political conduct of officials reflect the obsolete doctrine that the governed must not criticize their governors. . . . The interest of the public here outweighs the interest of appellant or any other individual. The protection of the public requires not merely discussion, but information. Political conduct and views which some respectable people approve, and others condemn, are constantly imputed to Congressmen. Errors of fact, particularly in regard to a man's mental states and processes, are inevitable. . . . Whatever is added to the field of libel is taken from the field of free debate."[13]

Injury to official reputation affords no more warrant for repressing speech that would otherwise be free than does factual error. Where judicial officers are involved, this Court has held that concern for the dignity and reputation of the courts does not justify the punishment as criminal contempt of criticism of the judge or his decision. *Bridges v. California*, 314 U.S. 252. This is true even though the utterance contains "half-truths" and "misinformation." *Pennekamp v. Florida*, 328 U.S. 331, 328 U.S. 342, 328 U.S. 343, n. 5, 328 U.S. 345. Such repression can be justified, if at all, only by a clear and present danger of the obstruction of justice. *See also Craig v. Harney*, 331 U.S. 367; *Wood v. Georgia*, 370 U.S. 375. If judges are to be treated as "men of fortitude, able to thrive in a hardy climate," *Craig v. Harney, supra*, 331 U.S. at 331 U.S. 376, surely the same must be true of other government officials, such as elected city commissioners.[14] Criticism of their official conduct does not lose its constitutional protection merely because it is effective criticism, and hence diminishes their official reputations.

If neither factual error nor defamatory content suffices to remove the constitutional shield from criticism of official conduct, the combination of the two elements is no less inadequate. This is the lesson to be drawn from the great controversy over the Sedition Act of 1798, 1 Stat. 596, which first crystallized a national awareness of the central meaning of the First Amendment. *See* Levy, *Legacy of Suppression* (1960), at 258 *et seq.*; Smith, *Freedom's Fetters* (1956), at 426, 431, and *passim*. That statute made it a crime, punishable by a $5,000 fine and 5 years in prison, "if any person shall write, print, utter or publish . . . any false, scandalous and malicious writing or writings against the government of the United States, or either house of the Congress . . . or the President . . . with intent to defame . . . or to bring them, or either of them, into contempt or disrepute; or to excite against them, or either or any of them, the hatred of the good people of the United States."

The Act allowed the defendant the defense of truth, and provided that the jury were to be judges both of the law and the facts. Despite these qualifications, the Act was vigorously condemned as unconstitutional in an attack joined in by Jefferson and Madison. In the famous Virginia Resolutions of 1798, the General Assembly of Virginia resolved that it

> "doth particularly protest against the palpable and alarming infractions of the Constitution in the two late cases of the 'Alien and Sedition Acts,' passed at the last session of Congress . . . [The Sedition Act] exercises . . . a power not delegated by the Constitution, but, on the contrary, expressly and positively forbidden by one of the amendments thereto—a power which, more than any other, ought to produce universal alarm because it is leveled against the right of freely examining public characters and measures, and of free communication among the people thereon, which has ever been justly deemed the only effectual guardian of every other right."

4 Elliot's Debates, *supra*, pp. 553–554. Madison prepared the *Report* in support of the protest. His premise was that the Constitution created a form of government under which "The people, not the government, possess the absolute sovereignty." The structure of the government dispersed power in reflection of the people's distrust of concentrated power, and of power itself at all levels. This form of government was "altogether different" from the British form, under which the Crown was sovereign and the people were subjects. "Is it not natural and necessary, under such different circumstances," he asked, "that a different degree of freedom in the use of the press should be contemplated?" *Id.*, pp. 569–570. Earlier, in a debate in the House of Representatives, Madison had said:

"If we advert to the nature of Republican Government, we shall find that the censorial power is in the people over the Government, and not in the Government over the people."

4 Annals of Congress, p. 934 (1794). Of the exercise of that power by the press, his *Report* said:

"In every state, probably, in the Union, the press has exerted a freedom in canvassing the merits and measures of public men, of every description, which has not been confined to the strict limits of the common law. On this footing, the freedom of the press has stood; on this foundation it yet stands. . . ."

4 Elliot's Debates, *supra,* p. 570. The right of free public discussion of the stewardship of public officials was thus, in Madison's view, a fundamental principle of the American form of government.[15]

Although the Sedition Act was never tested in this Court,[16] the attack upon its validity has carried the day in the court of history. Fines levied in its prosecution were repaid by Act of Congress on the ground that it was unconstitutional. *See, e.g.,* Act of July 4, 1840, c. 45, 6 Stat. 802, accompanied by H.R. Rep. No. 86, 26th Cong., 1st Sess. (1840). Calhoun, reporting to the Senate on February 4, 1836, assumed that its invalidity was a matter "which no one now doubts." Report with Senate bill No. 122, 24th Cong., 1st Sess., p. 3. Jefferson, as President, pardoned those who had been convicted and sentenced under the Act and remitted their fines, stating:

"I discharged every person under punishment or prosecution under the sedition law because I considered, and now consider, that law to be a nullity, as absolute and as palpable as if Congress had ordered us to fall down and worship a golden image."

Letter to Mrs. Adams, July 22, 1804, 4 *Jefferson's Works* (Washington ed.), pp. 555, 556. The invalidity of the Act has also been assumed by Justices of this Court. *See* Holmes, J., dissenting and joined by Brandeis, J., in *Abrams v. United States,* 250 U.S. 616, 250 U.S. 630; Jackson, J., dissenting in *Beauharnais v. Illinois,* 343 U.S. 250, 343 U.S. 288–289; Douglas, *The Right of the People* (1958), p. 47. *See also* Cooley, *Constitutional Limitations* (8th ed., Carrington, 1927), pp. 899–900; Chafee, *Free Speech in the United States* (1942), pp. 27–28. These views reflect a broad consensus that the Act, because of the restraint it imposed upon criticism of government and public officials, was inconsistent with the First Amendment.

There is no force in respondent's argument that the constitutional limitations implicit in the history of the Sedition Act apply only to Congress, and not to the States. It is true that the First Amendment was originally addressed only to action by the Federal Government, and that Jefferson, for one, while denying the power of Congress "to controul the freedom of the press," recognized such a power in the States. *See* the 1804 Letter to Abigail Adams quoted in *Dennis v. United States,* 341 U.S. 494, 341 U.S. 522, n. 4 (concurring opinion). But this distinction was eliminated with the adoption of the Fourteenth Amendment and the application to the States of the First Amendment's restrictions. See, e.g., *Gitlow v. New York,* 268 U.S. 652, 268 U.S. 666; *Schneider v. State,* 308 U.S. 147, 308 U.S. 160; *Bridges v. California,* 314 U.S. 252, 314 U.S. 268; *Edwards v. South Carolina,* 372 U.S. 229, 372 U.S. 235.

What a State may not constitutionally bring about by means of a criminal statute is likewise beyond the reach of its civil law of libel.[17] The fear of damage awards under a rule such as that invoked by the Alabama courts here may be markedly more inhibiting than the fear of prosecution under a criminal statute. See *City of Chicago v. Tribune Co.,* 307 Ill. 595, 607, 139 N.E. 86, 90 (1923). Alabama, for example, has a criminal libel law which subjects to prosecution "any person who speaks, writes, or prints of and concerning another any accusation falsely and maliciously importing the commission by such person of a felony, or any other indictable offense involving moral turpitude," and which allows as punishment upon conviction a fine not exceeding $500 and a prison sentence of 6 months.

(Continues)

(Continued)

Alabama Code, Tit. 14, §350. Presumably, a person charged with violation of this statute enjoys ordinary criminal law safeguards such as the requirements of an indictment and of proof beyond a reasonable doubt. These safeguards are not available to the defendant in a civil action. The judgment awarded in this case—without the need for any proof of actual pecuniary loss—was one thousand times greater than the maximum fine provided by the Alabama criminal statute, and one hundred times greater than that provided by the Sedition Act.

And since there is no double jeopardy limitation applicable to civil lawsuits, this is not the only judgment that may be awarded against petitioners for the same publication.[18] Whether or not a newspaper can survive a succession of such judgments, the pall of fear and timidity imposed upon those who would give voice to public criticism is an atmosphere in which the First Amendment freedoms cannot survive. Plainly the Alabama law of civil libel is

"a form of regulation that creates hazards to protected freedoms markedly greater than those that attend reliance upon the criminal law." *Bantam Books, Inc. v. Sullivan,* 372 U.S. 58, 372 U.S. 70.

The state rule of law is not saved by its allowance of the defense of truth. A defense for erroneous statements honestly made is no less essential here than was the requirement of proof of guilty knowledge which, in *Smith v. California*, 361 U.S. 147, we held indispensable to a valid conviction of a bookseller for possessing obscene writings for sale. We said:

"For, if the bookseller is criminally liable without knowledge of the contents, . . . He will tend to restrict the books he sells to those he has inspected, and thus the State will have imposed a restriction upon the distribution of constitutionally protected, as well as obscene, literature. . . . And the bookseller's burden would become the public's burden, for, by restricting him, the public's access to reading matter would be restricted. . . . [H]is timidity in the face of his absolute criminal liability thus would tend to restrict the public's access to forms of the printed word which the State could not constitutionally suppress directly. The bookseller's self-censorship, compelled by the State, would be a censorship affecting the whole public, hardly less virulent for being privately administered. Through it, the distribution of all books, both obscene and not obscene, would be impeded." (361 U.S. 361 U.S. 147, 361 U.S. 153–154.)

A rule compelling the critic of official conduct to guarantee the truth of all his factual assertions— and to do so on pain of libel judgments virtually unlimited in amount—leads to a comparable "self-censorship." Allowance of the defense of truth, with the burden of proving it on the defendant, does not mean that only false speech will be deterred.[19] Even courts accepting this defense as an adequate safeguard have recognized the difficulties of adducing legal proofs that the alleged libel was true in all its factual particulars. See, e.g., *Post Publishing Co. v. Hallam*, 59 F.5d 0, 540 (C.A. 6th Cir. 1893); see also Noel, Defamation of Public Officers and Candidates, 49 *Col. L. Rev.* 875, 892 (1949). Under such a rule, would-be critics of official conduct may be deterred from voicing their criticism, even though it is believed to be true and even though it is, in fact, true, because of doubt whether it can be proved in court or fear of the expense of having to do so. They tend to make only statements which "steer far wider of the unlawful zone." *Speiser v. Randall, supra*, 357 U.S. at 357 U.S. 526. The rule thus dampens the vigor and limits the variety of public debate. It is inconsistent with the First and Fourteenth Amendments. The constitutional guarantees require, we think, a federal rule that prohibits a public official from recovering damages for a defamatory falsehood relating to his official conduct unless he proves that the statement was made with "actual malice"—that is, with knowledge that it was false or with reckless disregard of whether it was false or not. An oft-cited statement of a like rule, which has been adopted by a number of state courts,[20] is found in the Kansas case of *Coleman v. MacLennan*, 78 Kan. 711, 98 P. 281 (1908). The State Attorney General, a candidate for reelection and a member of the commission charged with the management and control of the state school fund, sued a newspaper publisher for alleged libel in an article purporting to state facts relating to his official conduct in connection with a school-fund transaction. The defendant pleaded privilege and the trial judge, over the plaintiff's objection, instructed the jury that

"where an article is published and circulated among voters for the sole purpose of giving what the defendant believes to be truthful information concerning a candidate for public office and for the purpose of enabling such voters to cast their ballot more intelligently, and the whole thing is done in good faith and without malice, the article is privileged, although the principal matters contained in the article may be untrue, in fact, and derogatory to the character of the plaintiff, and in such a case the burden is on the plaintiff to show actual malice in the publication of the article."

In answer to a special question, the jury found that the plaintiff had not proved actual malice, and a general verdict was returned for the defendant. On appeal, the Supreme Court of Kansas, in an opinion by Justice Burch, reasoned as follows (78 Kan., at 724, 98 P. at 286):

"It is of the utmost consequence that the people should discuss the character and qualifications of candidates for their suffrages. The importance to the state and to society of such discussions is so vast, and the advantages derived are so great, that they more than counterbalance the inconvenience of private persons whose conduct may be involved, and occasional injury to the reputations of individuals must yield to the public welfare, although at times such injury may be great. The public benefit from publicity is so great, and the chance of injury to private character so small, that such discussion must be privileged."

The court thus sustained the trial court's instruction as a correct statement of the law, saying:

"In such a case the occasion gives rise to a privilege, qualified to this extent: any one claiming to be defamed by the communication must show actual malice or go remediless. This privilege extends to a great variety of subjects, and includes matters of public concern, public men, and candidates for office." 78 Kan. at 723, 98 P. at 285.

Such a privilege for criticism of official conduct[21] is appropriately analogous to the protection accorded a public official when he is sued for libel by a private citizen. In *Barr v. Matteo*, 360 U.S. 564, 360 U.S. 575, this Court held the utterance of a federal official to be absolutely privileged if made "within the outer perimeter" of his duties. The States accord the same immunity to statements of their highest officers, although some differentiate their lesser officials and qualify the privilege they enjoy.[22] But all hold that all officials are protected unless actual malice can be proved. The reason for the official privilege is said to be that the threat of damage suits would otherwise "inhibit the fearless, vigorous, and effective administration of policies of government" and "dampen the ardor of all but the most resolute, or the most irresponsible, in the unflinching discharge of their duties." *Barr v. Matteo, supra*, 360 U.S. at 360 U.S. 571. Analogous considerations support the privilege for the citizen-critic of government. It is as much his duty to criticize as it is the official's duty to administer. *See Whitney v. California*, 274 U.S. 357, 274 U.S. 375 (concurring opinion of Mr. Justice Brandeis), quoted *supra*, p. 376 U.S. 270. As Madison said, *see supra* p. 376 U.S. 275, "the censorial power is in the people over the Government, and not in the Government over the people." It would give public servants an unjustified preference over the public they serve, if critics of official conduct did not have a fair equivalent of the immunity granted to the officials themselves.

We conclude that such a privilege is required by the First and Fourteenth Amendments.

III

We hold today that the Constitution delimits a State's power to award damages for libel in actions brought by public officials against critics of their official conduct. Since this is such an action,[23] the rule requiring proof of actual malice is applicable. While Alabama law apparently requires proof of actual malice for an award of punitive damages,[24] where general damages are concerned malice is "presumed." Such a presumption is inconsistent with the federal rule. "The power to create presumptions is not a means of escape from constitutional restrictions," *Bailey v. Alabama*, 219 U.S. 219, 219 U.S. 239, "the showing of malice required for the forfeiture of the privilege is not presumed but is a matter for proof by the plaintiff . . ." *Lawrence v. Fox,* 357 Mich. 134, 146, 97 N.W.2d 719, 725 (1959).[25] Since the trial judge did not instruct the jury to differentiate between general and punitive damages, it may be that the verdict was wholly an award of one or the other. But it is impossible to know, in view of the general verdict returned. Because of this uncertainty, the judgment must be reversed and the case remanded. *Stromberg v. California*, 283 U.S. 359, 283 U.S. 367–368; *Williams v. North Carolina*, 317 U.S. 287, 317 U.S. 291–292; see *Yates v. United States*, 354 U.S. 298, 354 U.S. 311–312; *Cramer v. United States*, 325 U.S. 1, 325 U.S. 36, n. 45.

Since respondent may seek a new trial, we deem that considerations of effective judicial administration require us to review the evidence in the present record to determine whether it could constitutionally support a judgment for respondent. This Court's duty is not limited to the elaboration of

(Continues)

constitutional principles; we must also in proper cases review the evidence to make certain that those principles have been constitutionally applied. This is such a case, particularly since the question is one of alleged trespass across "the line between speech unconditionally guaranteed and speech which may legitimately be regulated." *Speiser v. Randall*, 357 U.S. 513, 357 U.S. 525. In cases where that line must be drawn, the rule is that we

> "examine for ourselves the statements in issue and the circumstances under which they were made to see . . . whether they are of a character which the principles of the First Amendment, as adopted by the Due Process Clause of the Fourteenth Amendment, protect."

Pennekamp v. Florida, 328 U.S. 331, 328 U.S. 335; see also *One, Inc. v. Olesen*, 355 U.S. 371; *Sunshine Book Co. v. Summerfield*, 355 U.S. 372. We must "make an independent examination of the whole record," *Edwards v. South Carolina*, 372 U.S. 229, 372 U.S. 235, so as to assure ourselves that the judgment does not constitute a forbidden intrusion on the field of free expression.[26]

Applying these standards, we consider that the proof presented to show actual malice lacks the convincing clarity which the constitutional standard demands, and hence that it would not constitutionally sustain the judgment for respondent under the proper rule of law. The case of the individual petitioners requires little discussion. Even assuming that they could constitutionally be found to have authorized the use of their names on the advertisement, there was no evidence whatever that they were aware of any erroneous statements or were in any way reckless in that regard. The judgment against them is thus without constitutional support.

As to the *Times*, we similarly conclude that the facts do not support a finding of actual malice. The statement by the *Times*' Secretary that, apart from the padlocking allegation, he thought the advertisement was "substantially correct," affords no constitutional warrant for the Alabama Supreme Court's conclusion that it was a

> "cavalier ignoring of the falsity of the advertisement [from which] the jury could not have but been impressed with the bad faith of The Times, and its maliciousness inferable therefrom."

The statement does not indicate malice at the time of the publication; even if the advertisement was not "substantially correct"—although respondent's own proofs tend to show that it was—that opinion was at least a reasonable one, and there was no evidence to impeach the witness' good faith in holding it. The *Times*' failure to retract upon respondent's demand, although it later retracted upon the demand of Governor Patterson, is likewise not adequate evidence of malice for constitutional purposes. Whether or not a failure to retract may ever constitute such evidence, there are two reasons why it does not here. First, the letter written by the *Times* reflected a reasonable doubt on its part as to whether the advertisement could reasonably be taken to refer to respondent at all. Second, it was not a final refusal, since it asked for an explanation on this point—a request that respondent chose to ignore. Nor does the retraction upon the demand of the Governor supply the necessary proof. It may be doubted that a failure to retract, which is not itself evidence of malice, can retroactively become such by virtue of a retraction subsequently made to another party. But, in any event, that did not happen here, since the explanation given by the *Times*' Secretary for the distinction drawn between respondent and the Governor was a reasonable one, the good faith of which was not impeached.

Finally, there is evidence that the *Times* published the advertisement without checking its accuracy against the news stories in the *Times*' own files. The mere presence of the stories in the files does not, of course, establish that the *Times* "knew" the advertisement was false, since the state of mind required for actual malice would have to be brought home to the persons in the *Times*' organization having responsibility for the publication of the advertisement. With respect to the failure of those persons to make the check, the record shows that they relied upon their knowledge of the good reputation of many of those whose names were listed as sponsors of the advertisement, and upon the letter from A. Philip Randolph, known to them as a responsible individual, certifying that the use of the names was authorized. There was testimony that the persons handling the advertisement saw nothing in it that would render it unacceptable under the *Times*' policy of rejecting advertisements containing "attacks of a personal character"[27]; their failure to reject it on this ground was not unreasonable. We think the evidence against the *Times* supports, at most, a finding of negligence in failing to discover the misstatements, and is constitutionally insufficient to show the recklessness that is required for a finding of actual malice. Cf. *Charles Parker Co. v. Silver City Crystal Co.*, 142 Conn. 605, 618, 116 A.2d 440, 446 (1955); *Phoenix Newspapers, Inc. v. Choisser*, 82 Ariz. 271, 277–278, 312 P.2d 150, 154–155 (1957).

We also think the evidence was constitutionally defective in another respect: it was incapable of supporting the jury's finding that the allegedly libelous statements were made "of and concerning" respondent. Respondent relies on the words of the advertisement and the testimony of six witnesses to establish a connection between it and himself. Thus, in his brief to this Court, he states:

> "The reference to respondent as police commissioner is clear from the ad. In addition, the jury heard the testimony of a newspaper editor . . .; a real estate and insurance man . . .; the sales manager of a men's clothing store . . .; a food equipment man . . .; a service station operator . . ., and the operator of a truck line for whom respondent had formerly worked. . . . Each of these witnesses stated that he associated the statements with respondent. . . ."

(Citations to record omitted.) There was no reference to respondent in the advertisement, either by name or official position. A number of the allegedly libelous statements—the charges that the dining hall was padlocked and that Dr. King's home was bombed, his person assaulted, and a perjury prosecution instituted against him—did not even concern the police; despite the ingenuity of the arguments which would attach this significance to the word "They," it is plain that these statements could not reasonably be read as accusing respondent of personal involvement in the acts in question. The statements upon which respondent principally relies as referring to him are the two allegations that did concern the police or police functions: that "truckloads of police . . . ringed the Alabama State College Campus" after the demonstration on the State Capitol steps, and that Dr. King had been "arrested . . . seven times." These statements were false only in that the police had been "deployed near" the campus, but had not actually "ringed" it, and had not gone there in connection with the State Capitol demonstration, and in that Dr. King had been arrested only four times. The ruling that these discrepancies between what was true and what was asserted were sufficient to injure respondent's reputation may itself raise constitutional problems, but we need not consider them here. Although the statements may be taken as referring to the police, they did not, on their face, make even an oblique reference to respondent as an individual. Support for the asserted reference must, therefore, be sought in the testimony of respondent's witnesses. But none of them suggested any basis for the belief that respondent himself was attacked in the advertisement beyond the bare fact that he was in overall charge of the Police Department and thus bore official responsibility for police conduct; to the extent that some of the witnesses thought respondent to have been charged with ordering or approving the conduct or otherwise being personally involved in it, they based this notion not on any statements in the advertisement, and not on any evidence that he had, in fact, been so involved, but solely on the unsupported assumption that, because of his official position, he must have been.[28] This reliance on the bare fact of respondent's official position[29] was made explicit by the Supreme Court of Alabama. That court, in holding that the trial court "did not err in overruling the demurrer [of the *Times*] in the aspect that the libelous matter was not of and concerning the [plaintiff]," based its ruling on the proposition that:

> "We think it common knowledge that the average person knows that municipal agents, such as police and firemen, and others, are under the control and direction of the city governing body, and more particularly under the direction and control of a single commissioner. In measuring the performance or deficiencies of such groups, praise or criticism is usually attached to the official in complete control of the body." 273 Ala., at 674–675, 144 So.2d at 39.

This proposition has disquieting implications for criticism of governmental conduct. For good reason,

> "no court of last resort in this country has ever held, or even suggested, that prosecutions for libel on government have any place in the American system of jurisprudence." *City of Chicago v. Tribune Co.*, 307 Ill. 595, 601, 139 N.E. 86, 88 (1923).

The present proposition would sidestep this obstacle by transmuting criticism of government, however impersonal it may seem on its face, into personal criticism, and hence potential libel, of the officials of whom the government is composed. There is no legal alchemy by which a State may thus create the cause of action that would otherwise be denied for a publication which, as respondent himself

(Continues)

said of the advertisement, "reflects not only on me but on the other Commissioners and the community." Raising as it does the possibility that a good faith critic of government will be penalized for his criticism, the proposition relied on by the Alabama courts strikes at the very center of the constitutionally protected area of free expression.[30] We hold that such a proposition may not constitutionally be utilized to establish that an otherwise impersonal attack on governmental operations was a libel of an official responsible for those operations. Since it was relied on exclusively here, and there was no other evidence to connect the statements with respondent, the evidence was constitutionally insufficient to support a finding that the statements referred to respondent.

The judgment of the Supreme Court of Alabama is reversed, and the case is remanded to that court for further proceedings not inconsistent with this opinion.

Reversed and remanded.

Notes

1. A copy of the advertisement is printed in the Appendix [omitted].
2. Respondent did not consider the charge of expelling the students to be applicable to him, since "that responsibility rests with the State Department of Education."
3. Approximately 394 copies of the edition of the *Times* containing the advertisement were circulated in Alabama. Of these, about 35 copies were distributed in Montgomery County. The total circulation of the *Times* for that day was approximately 650,000 copies.
4. Since we sustain the contentions of all the petitioners under the First Amendment's guarantees of freedom of speech and of the press as applied to the States by the Fourteenth Amendment, we do not decide the questions presented by the other claims of violation of the Fourteenth Amendment. The individual petitioners contend that the judgment against them offends the Due Process Clause because there was no evidence to show that they had published or authorized the publication of the alleged libel, and that the Due Process and Equal Protection Clauses were violated by racial segregation and racial bias in the courtroom. The *Times* contends that the assumption of jurisdiction over its corporate person by the Alabama courts overreaches the territorial limits of the Due Process Clause. The latter claim is foreclosed from our review by the ruling of the Alabama courts that the *Times* entered a general appearance in the action, and thus waived its jurisdictional objection; we cannot say that this ruling lacks "fair or substantial support" in prior Alabama decisions. *See Thompson v. Wilson*, 224 Ala. 299, 140 So. 439 (1932); *compare NAACP v. Alabama*, 357 U.S. 449, 357 U.S. 454–458.
5. *See* American Law Institute, Restatement of Torts, §593, Comment *b* (1938).
6. *Konigsberg v. State Bar of California*, 366 U.S. 36, 366 U.S. 49, and n. 10; *Times Film Corp. v. City of Chicago*, 365 U.S. 43, 365 U.S. 48; *Roth v. United States*, 354 U.S. 476, 354 U.S. 486–487; *Beauharnais v. Illinois*, 343 U.S. 250, 343 U.S. 266; *Pennekamp v. Florida*, 328 U.S. 331, 328 U.S. 348–349; *Chaplinsky v. New Hampshire*, 315 U.S. 568, 315 U.S. 572; *Near v. Minnesota*, 283 U.S. 697, 283 U.S. 715.
7. *Herndon v. Lowry*, 301 U.S. 242.
8. *Bridges v. California*, 314 U.S. 252; *Pennekamp v. Florida*, 328 U.S. 331.
9. *De Jonge v. Oregon*, 299 U.S. 353.
10. *Edwards v. South Carolina*, 372 U.S. 229.
11. *Roth v. United States*, 354 U.S. 476.
12. *NAACP v. Button*, 371 U.S. 415.
13. *See also* Mill, *On Liberty* (Oxford: Blackwell, 1947), at 47:

    ". . . [T]o argue sophistically, to suppress facts or arguments, to misstate the elements of the case, or misrepresent the opposite opinion . . ., all this, even to the most aggravated degree, is so continually done in perfect good faith by persons who are not considered, and in many other respects may not deserve to be considered, ignorant or incompetent that it is rarely possible, on adequate grounds, conscientiously to stamp the misrepresentation as morally culpable, and still less could law presume to interfere with this kind of controversial misconduct."

14. The climate in which public officials operate, especially during a political campaign, has been described by one commentator in the following terms:

---

*Together with No. 40, *Abernathy et al. v. Sullivan*, also on certiorari to the same court, argued January 7, 1964.

"Charges of gross incompetence, disregard of the public interest, communist sympathies, and the like usually have filled the air, and hints of bribery, embezzlement, and other criminal conduct are not infrequent." Noel, *Defamation of Public Officers and Candidates*, 49 Col.L.Rev. 875 (1949).

For a similar description written 60 years earlier, *see* Chase, *Criticism of Public Officers and Candidates for Office*, 23 Am.L.Rev. 346 (1889).

15. The Report on the Virginia Resolutions further stated:

"[I]t is manifestly impossible to punish the intent to bring those who administer the government into disrepute or contempt, without striking at the right of freely discussing public characters and measures, . . . which, again, is equivalent to a protection of those who administer the government, if they should at any time deserve the contempt or hatred of the people, against being exposed to it by free animadversions on their characters and conduct. Nor can there be a doubt . . . that a government thus entrenched in penal statutes against the just and natural effects of a culpable administration will easily evade the responsibility which is essential to a faithful discharge of its duty."

"Let it be recollected, lastly, that the right of electing the members of the government constitutes more particularly the essence of a free and responsible government. The value and efficacy of this right depends on the knowledge of the comparative merits and demerits of the candidates for public trust, and on the equal freedom, consequently, of examining and discussing these merits and demerits of the candidates respectively." 4 Elliot's Debates, *supra*, p. 575.

16. The Act expired, by its terms, in 1801.

17. Cf. *Farmers Union v. WDAY*, 360 U.S. 525, 360 U.S. 535.

18. The *Times* states that four other libel suits based on the advertisement have been filed against it by others who have served as Montgomery City Commissioners and by the Governor of Alabama; that another $500,000 verdict has been awarded in the only one of these cases that has yet gone to trial, and that the damages sought in the other three total $2,000,000.

19. Even a false statement may be deemed to make a valuable contribution to public debate, since it brings about "the clearer perception and livelier impression of truth, produced by its collision with error." Mill, *On Liberty* (Oxford: Blackwell, 1947), at 15; *see also* Milton, Areopagitia, in *Prose Works* (Yale, 1959), Vol. II, at 561.

20. *E.g., Ponder v. Cobb*, 257 N.C. 281, 299, 126 S.E.2d 67, 80 (1962); *Lawrence v. Fox*, 357 Mich. 134, 146, 97 N.W.2d 719, 725 (1959); *Stice v. Beacon Newspaper Corp.*, 185 Kan. 61, 65–67, 340 P.2d 396, 400–401 (1959); *Bailey v. Charleston Mail Assn.*, 126 W. Va. 292, 307, 27 S.E.2d 837, 844 (1943); *Salinger v. Cowles*, 195 Iowa 873, 889, 191 N.W. 167, 174 (1922); *Snively v. Record Publishing Co.*, 185 Cal. 565, 571–576, 198 P. 1 (1921); *McLean v. Merriman*, 42 S.D. 394, 175 N.W. 878 (1920). Applying the same rule to candidates for public office, see, e.g., *Phoenix Newspapers v. Choisser*, 82 Ariz. 271, 276–277, 312 P.2d 150, 154 (1957); *Friedell v. Blakely Printing Co.*, 163 Minn. 226, 230, 203 N.W. 974, 975 (1925). And see *Chagnon v. Union-Leader Corp.*, 103 N.H. 426, 438, 174 A.2d 825, 833 (1961), *cert. denied*, 369 U.S. 830.

The consensus of scholarly opinion apparently favors the rule that is here adopted. E.g., Harper and James, Torts, §5.26, at 449–450 (1956); Noel, Defamation of Public Officers and Candidates, 49 *Col. L. Rev.* 875, 891–895, 897, 903 (1949); Hallen, Fair Comment, 8 *Tex.L.Rev.* 41, 61 (1929); Smith, Charges Against Candidates, 18 *Mich. L. Rev.* 1, 115 (1919); Chase, Criticism of Public Officers and Candidates for Office, 23 *Am.L.Rev.* 346, 367–371 (1889); Cooley, *Constitutional Limitations* (7th ed., Lane, 1903), at 604, 616–628. But see, e.g., American Law Institute, Restatement of Torts, §598, Comment *a* (1938) (reversing the position taken in Tentative Draft 13, §1041(2) (1936)); Veeder, Freedom of Public Discussion, 23 *Harv.L.Rev.* 413, 419 (1910).

21. The privilege immunizing honest misstatements of fact is often referred to as a "conditional" privilege, to distinguish it from the "absolute" privilege recognized in judicial, legislative, administrative and executive proceedings. See, e.g., Prosser, Torts (2d ed., 1955), §95.

22. *See* 1 Harper and James, Torts, §5.23, at 429–430 (1956); Prosser, Torts (2d ed., 1955), at 612–613; American Law Institute, Restatement of Torts (1938), §591.

23. We have no occasion here to determine how far down into the lower ranks of government employees the "public official" designation would extend for purposes of this rule, or otherwise to specify categories of persons who would or would not be included. Cf. *Barr v. Matteo*, 360 U.S. 564, 360 U.S. 573–575. Nor need we here determine the boundaries of the "official conduct" concept. It is enough for the present case that respondent's position as an elected city commissioner clearly made him a public official, and that the allegations in the advertisement concerned what was allegedly his official conduct

(Continues)

as Commissioner in charge of the Police Department. As to the statements alleging the assaulting of Dr. King and the bombing of his home, it is immaterial that they might not be considered to involve respondent's official conduct if he himself had been accused of perpetrating the assault and the bombing. Respondent does not claim that the statements charged him personally with these acts; his contention is that the advertisement connects him with them only in his official capacity as the Commissioner supervising the police, on the theory that the police might be equated with the "They" who did the bombing and assaulting. Thus, if these allegations can be read as referring to respondent at all, they must be read as describing his performance of his official duties.

24. *Johnson Publishing Co. v. Davis*, 271 Ala. 474, 487, 124 So.2d 441, 450 (1960). Thus, the trial judge here instructed the jury that

> "mere negligence or carelessness is not evidence of actual malice or malice, in fact, and does not justify an award of exemplary or punitive damages in an action for libel."

The court refused, however, to give the following instruction which had been requested by the *Times*:

> "I charge you . . . that punitive damages, as the name indicates, are designed to punish the defendant, the New York Times Company, a corporation, and the other defendants in this case, . . . and I further charge you that such punitive damages may be awarded only in the event that you, the jury, are convinced by a fair preponderance of the evidence that the defendant . . . was motivated by personal ill will, that is actual intent to do the plaintiff harm, or that the defendant . . . was guilty of gross negligence and recklessness, and not of just ordinary negligence or carelessness in publishing the matter complained of so as to indicate a wanton disregard of plaintiff's rights."

The trial court's error in failing to require any finding of actual malice for an award of general damages makes it unnecessary for us to consider the sufficiency under the federal standard of the instructions regarding actual malice that were given as to punitive damages.

25. *Accord, Coleman v. MacLennan, supra*, 78 Kan., at 741, 98 P. at 292; *Gough v. Tribune-Journal Co.*, 75 Idaho 502, 510, 275 P.2d 663, 668 (1954).

26. The Seventh Amendment does not, as respondent contends, preclude such an examination by this Court. That Amendment, providing that "no fact tried by a jury shall be otherwise reexamined in any Court of the United States than according to the rules of the common law," is applicable to state cases coming here. *Chicago, B. & Q. R. Co. v. Chicago*, 166 U.S. 226, 166 U.S. 242–243; cf. *76 U.S. Murray*, 9 Wall. 274. But its ban on reexamination of facts does not preclude us from determining whether governing rules of federal law have been properly applied to the facts.

"[T]his Court will review the finding of facts by a State court . . . where a conclusion of law as to a Federal right and a finding of fact are so intermingled as to make it necessary, in order to pass upon the Federal question, to analyze the facts." *Fiske v. Kansas*, 274 U.S. 380, 274 U.S. 385–386. See also *Haynes v. Washington*, 373 U.S. 503, 373 U.S. 515–516.

27. The Times has set forth in a booklet its "Advertising Acceptability Standards." Listed among the classes of advertising that the newspaper does not accept are advertisements that are "fraudulent or deceptive," that are "ambiguous in wording and . . . may mislead," and that contain "attacks of a personal character." In replying to respondent's interrogatories before the trial, the Secretary of the *Times* stated that,

> "as the advertisement made no attacks of a personal character upon any individual and otherwise met the advertising acceptability standards promulgated,"

it had been approved for publication.

28. Respondent's own testimony was that,

> "as Commissioner of Public Affairs, it is part of my duty to supervise the Police Department, and I certainly feel like it [a statement] is associated with me when it describes police activities."

He thought that, "by virtue of being Police Commissioner and Commissioner of Public Affairs," he was charged with "any activity on the part of the Police Department." "When it describes police action, certainly I feel it reflects on me as an individual." He added that "[i]t is my feeling that it reflects not only on me, but on the other Commissioners and the community."

Grover C. Hall testified that, to him, the third paragraph of the advertisement called to mind "the City government—the Commissioners," and that,

"now that you ask it, I would naturally think a little more about the police Commissioner, because his responsibility is exclusively with the constabulary."

It was "the phrase about starvation" that led to the association; "the other didn't hit me with any particular force."

Arnold D. Blackwell testified that the third paragraph was associated in his mind with "the Police Commissioner and the police force. The people on the police force." If he had believed the statement about the padlocking of the dining hall, he would have thought

"that the people on our police force or the heads of our police force were acting without their jurisdiction, and would not be competent for the position."

"I would assume that the Commissioner had ordered the police force to do that, and therefore it would be his responsibility."

Harry W. Kaminsky associated the statement about "truckloads of police" with respondent, "because he is the Police Commissioner." He thought that the reference to arrests in the sixth paragraph

"implicates the Police Department, I think, or the authorities that would do that—arrest folks for speeding and loitering and such as that."

Asked whether he would associate with respondent a newspaper report that the police had "beat somebody up or assaulted them on the streets of Montgomery," he replied:

"I still say he is the Police Commissioner and those men are working directly under him, and therefore I would think that he would have something to do with it."

In general, he said, "I look at Mr. Sullivan when I see the Police Department."

H. M. Price, Sr., testified that he associated the first sentence of the third paragraph with respondent because:

"I would just automatically consider that the Police Commissioner in Montgomery would have to put his approval on those kind of things as an individual."

William M. Parker, Jr., testified that he associated the statements in the two paragraphs with "the Commissioners of the City of Montgomery," and, since respondent "was the Police Commissioner," he "thought of him first." He told the examining counsel: "I think, if you were the Police Commissioner, I would have thought it was speaking of you."

Horace W. White, respondent's former employer, testified that the statement about "truckloads of police" made him think of respondent "as being the head of the Police Department." Asked whether he read the statement as charging respondent himself with ringing the campus or having shotguns and tear gas, he replied: "Well, I thought of his department being charged with it, yes, sir. He is the head of the Police Department, as I understand it." He further said that the reason he would have been unwilling to reemploy respondent if he had believed the advertisement was "the fact that he allowed the Police Department to do the things that the paper say he did."

29. Compare *Ponder v. Cobb*, 257 N.C. 281, 126 S.E.2d 67 (1962).
30. Insofar as the proposition means only that the statements about police conduct libeled respondent by implicitly criticizing his ability to run the Police Department, recovery is also precluded in this case by the doctrine of fair comment. See American Law Institute, Restatement of Torts (1938), §607. Since the Fourteenth Amendment requires recognition of the conditional privilege for honest misstatements of fact, it follows that a defense of fair comment must be afforded for honest expression of opinion based upon privileged, as well as true, statements of fact. Both defenses are, of course, defeasible if the public official proves actual malice, as was not done here.

MR. JUSTICE BLACK, with whom MR. JUSTICE DOUGLAS joins, concurring.

I concur in reversing this half-million-dollar judgment against the New York Times Company and the four individual defendants. In reversing, the Court holds that

"the Constitution delimits a State's power to award damages for libel in actions brought by public officials against critics of their official conduct." *Ante*, p. 376 U.S. 283.

(Continues)

(*Continued*)

I base my vote to reverse on the belief that the First and Fourteenth Amendments not merely "delimit" a State's power to award damages to "public officials against critics of their official conduct," but completely prohibit a State from exercising such a power. The Court goes on to hold that a State can subject such critics to damages if "actual malice" can be proved against them. "Malice," even as defined by the Court, is an elusive, abstract concept, hard to prove and hard to disprove. The requirement that malice be proved provides, at best, an evanescent protection for the right critically to discuss public affairs, and certainly does not measure up to the sturdy safeguard embodied in the First Amendment. Unlike the Court, therefore, I vote to reverse exclusively on the ground that the *Times* and the individual defendants had an absolute, unconditional constitutional right to publish in the *Times* advertisement their criticisms of the Montgomery agencies and officials. I do not base my vote to reverse on any failure to prove that these individual defendants signed the advertisement or that their criticism of the Police Department was aimed at the plaintiff Sullivan, who was then the Montgomery City Commissioner having supervision of the city's police; for present purposes, I assume these things were proved. Nor is my reason for reversal the size of the half-million-dollar judgment, large as it is. If Alabama has constitutional power to use its civil libel law to impose damages on the press for criticizing the way public officials perform or fail to perform their duties, I know of no provision in the Federal Constitution which either expressly or impliedly bars the State from fixing the amount of damages.

The half-million-dollar verdict does give dramatic proof, however, that state libel laws threaten the very existence of an American press virile enough to publish unpopular views on public affairs and bold enough to criticize the conduct of public officials. The factual background of this case emphasizes the imminence and enormity of that threat. One of the acute and highly emotional issues in this country arises out of efforts of many people, even including some public officials, to continue state-commanded segregation of races in the public schools and other public places despite our several holdings that such a state practice is forbidden by the Fourteenth Amendment. Montgomery is one of the localities in which widespread hostility to desegregation has been manifested. This hostility has sometimes extended itself to persons who favor desegregation, particularly to so-called "outside agitators," a term which can be made to fit papers like the *Times*, which is published in New York. The scarcity of testimony to show that Commissioner Sullivan suffered any actual damages at all suggests that these feelings of hostility had at least as much to do with rendition of this half-million-dollar verdict as did an appraisal of damages. Viewed realistically, this record lends support to an inference that, instead of being damaged, Commissioner Sullivan's political, social, and financial prestige has likely been enhanced by the *Times'* publication. Moreover, a second half-million-dollar libel verdict against the *Times* based on the same advertisement has already been awarded to another Commissioner. There, a jury again gave the full amount claimed. There is no reason to believe that there are not more such huge verdicts lurking just around the corner for the *Times* or any other newspaper or broadcaster which might dare to criticize public officials. In fact, briefs before us show that, in Alabama, there are now pending eleven libel suits by local and state officials against the *Times* seeking $5,600,000, and five such suits against the Columbia Broadcasting System seeking $1,700,000. Moreover, this technique for harassing and punishing a free press—now that it has been shown to be possible—is by no means limited to cases with racial overtones; it can be used in other fields where public feelings may make, local as well as out-of-state, newspapers easy prey for libel verdict seekers.

In my opinion, the Federal Constitution has dealt with this deadly danger to the press in the only way possible without leaving the free press open to destruction—by granting the press an absolute immunity for criticism of the way public officials do their public duty. *Compare Barr v. Matteo,* 360 U.S. 564. Stopgap measures like those the Court adopts are, in my judgment, not enough. This record certainly does not indicate that any different verdict would have been rendered here whatever the Court had charged the jury about "malice," "truth," "good motives," "justifiable ends," or any other legal formulas which, in theory, would protect the press. Nor does the record indicate that any of these legalistic words would have caused the courts below to set aside or to reduce the half-million-dollar verdict in any amount.

I agree with the Court that the Fourteenth Amendment made the First applicable to the States.[31] This means to me that, since the adoption of the Fourteenth Amendment, a State has no more power than the Federal Government to use a civil libel law or any other law to impose damages for merely discussing public affairs and criticizing public officials. The power of the United States to do that is, in my judgment, precisely nil. Such was the general view held when the First Amendment was adopted, and ever since.[32] Congress never has sought to challenge this viewpoint by passing any civil libel law. It did pass the Sedition Act in 1798,[33] which made it a crime—"seditious libel"—to criticize federal officials or the

Federal Government. As the Court's opinion correctly points out, however, *ante,* pp. 376 U.S. 273–276, that Act came to an ignominious end and, by common consent, has generally been treated as having been a wholly unjustifiable and much to be regretted violation of the First Amendment. Since the First Amendment is now made applicable to the States by the Fourteenth, it no more permits the States to impose damages for libel than it does the Federal Government.

We would, I think, more faithfully interpret the First Amendment by holding that, at the very least, it leaves the people and the press free to criticize officials and discuss public affairs with impunity. This Nation of ours elects many of its important officials; so do the States, the municipalities, the counties, and even many precincts. These officials are responsible to the people for the way they perform their duties. While our Court has held that some kinds of speech and writings, such as "obscenity," *Roth v. United States,* 354 U.S. 476, and "fighting words," *Chaplinsky v. New Hampshire,* 315 U.S. 568, are not expression within the protection of the First Amendment,[34] freedom to discuss public affairs and public officials is unquestionably, as the Court today holds, the kind of speech the First Amendment was primarily designed to keep within the area of free discussion. To punish the exercise of this right to discuss public affairs or to penalize it through libel judgments is to abridge or shut off discussion of the very kind most needed. This Nation, I suspect, can live in peace without libel suits based on public discussions of public affairs and public officials. But I doubt that a country can live in freedom where its people can be made to suffer physically or financially for criticizing their government, its actions, or its officials.

"For a representative democracy ceases to exist the moment that the public functionaries are by any means absolved from their responsibility to their constituents, and this happens whenever the constituent can be restrained in any manner from speaking, writing, or publishing his opinions upon any public measure, or upon the conduct of those who may advise or execute it."[35]

An unconditional right to say what one pleases about public affairs is what I consider to be the minimum guarantee of the First Amendment.[36]

I regret that the Court has stopped short of this holding indispensable to preserve our free press from destruction.

Notes

31. See cases collected in *Speiser v. Randall,* 357 U.S. 513, 357 U.S. 530 (concurring opinion).

32. See, e.g., 1 Tucker, *Blackstone's Commentaries* (1803), 297–299 (editor's appendix). St. George Tucker, a distinguished Virginia jurist, took part in the Annapolis Convention of 1786, sat on both state and federal courts, and was widely known for his writings on judicial and constitutional subjects.

33. Act of July 14, 1798, 1 Stat. 596.

34. But see *Smith v. California,* 361 U.S. 147, 361 U.S. 155 (concurring opinion); *Roth v. United States,* 354 U.S. 476, 354 U.S. 508 (dissenting opinion).

35. 1 Tucker, *Blackstone's Commentaries* (1803), 297 (editor's appendix); cf. Brant, Seditious Libel: Myth and Reality, 39 *N.Y.U.L. Rev.* 1.

36. Cf. Meiklejohn, *Free Speech and Its Relation to Self-Government* (1948).

MR. JUSTICE GOLDBERG, with whom MR. JUSTICE DOUGLAS joins, concurring in the result.

The Court today announces a constitutional standard which prohibits

"a public official from recovering damages for a defamatory falsehood relating to his official conduct unless he proves that the statement was made with 'actual malice'—that is, with knowledge that it was false or with reckless disregard of whether it was false or not."

Ante at 376 U.S. 279–280. The Court thus rules that the Constitution gives citizens and newspapers a "conditional privilege" immunizing nonmalicious misstatements of fact regarding the official conduct of a government officer. The impressive array of history[37] and precedent marshaled by the Court, however, confirms my belief that the Constitution affords greater protection than that provided by the Court's standard to citizen and press in exercising the right of public criticism.

In my view, the First and Fourteenth Amendments to the Constitution afford to the citizen and to the press an absolute, unconditional privilege to criticize official conduct despite the harm which

(Continues)

may flow from excesses and abuses. The prized American right "to speak one's mind," cf. *Bridges v. California*, 314 U.S. 252, 314 U.S. 270, about public officials and affairs needs "breathing space to survive," *NAACP v. Button*, 371 U.S. 415, 371 U.S. 433. The right should not depend upon a probing by the jury of the motivation[38] of the citizen or press. The theory of our Constitution is that every citizen may speak his mind and every newspaper express its view on matters of public concern, and may not be barred from speaking or publishing because those in control of government think that what is said or written is unwise, unfair, false, or malicious. In a democratic society, one who assumes to act for the citizens in an executive, legislative, or judicial capacity must expect that his official acts will be commented upon and criticized. Such criticism cannot, in my opinion, be muzzled or deterred by the courts at the instance of public officials under the label of libel.

It has been recognized that "prosecutions for libel on government have [no] place in the American system of jurisprudence." *City of Chicago v. Tribune Co.*, 307 Ill. 595, 601, 139 N.E. 86, 88. I fully agree. Government, however, is not an abstraction; it is made up of individuals—of governors responsible to the governed. In a democratic society, where men are free by ballots to remove those in power, any statement critical of governmental action is necessarily "of and concerning" the governors, and any statement critical of the governors' official conduct is necessarily "of and concerning" the government. If the rule that libel on government has no place in our Constitution is to have real meaning, then libel on the official conduct of the governors likewise can have no place in our Constitution.

We must recognize that we are writing upon a clean slate.[39] As the Court notes, although there have been "statements of this Court to the effect that the Constitution does not protect libelous publications . . ., [n]one of the cases sustained the use of libel laws to impose sanctions upon expression critical of the official conduct of public officials."

Ante at 376 U.S. 268. We should be particularly careful, therefore, adequately to protect the liberties which are embodied in the First and Fourteenth Amendments. It may be urged that deliberately and maliciously false statements have no conceivable value as free speech. That argument, however, is not responsive to the real issue presented by this case, which is whether that freedom of speech which all agree is constitutionally protected can be effectively safeguarded by a rule allowing the imposition of liability upon a jury's evaluation of the speaker's state of mind. If individual citizens may be held liable in damages for strong words, which a jury finds false and maliciously motivated, there can be little doubt that public debate and advocacy will be constrained. And if newspapers, publishing advertisements dealing with public issues, thereby risk liability, there can also be little doubt that the ability of minority groups to secure publication of their views on public affairs and to seek support for their causes will be greatly diminished. Cf. *Farmers Educational & Coop. Union v. WDAY, Inc.*, 360 U.S. 525, 360 U.S. 530. The opinion of the Court conclusively demonstrates the chilling effect of the Alabama libel laws on First Amendment freedoms in the area of race relations. The American Colonists were not willing, nor should we be, to take the risk that "[m]en who injure and oppress the people under their administration [and] provoke them to cry out and complain" will also be empowered to "make that very complaint the foundation for new oppressions and prosecutions." The Trial of John Peter Zenger, 17 Howell's St. Tr. 675, 721–722 (1735) (argument of counsel to the jury). To impose liability for critical, albeit erroneous or even malicious, comments on official conduct would effectively resurrect "the obsolete doctrine that the governed must not criticize their governors." Cf. *Sweeney v. Patterson*, 76 U.S.App.D.C. 23, 24, 128 F.2d 457, 458.

Our national experience teaches that repressions breed hate, and "that hate menaces stable government." *Whitney v. California*, 274 U.S. 357, 274 U.S. 375 (Brandeis, J., concurring). We should be ever mindful of the wise counsel of Chief Justice Hughes:

> "[I]mperative is the need to preserve inviolate the constitutional rights of free speech, free press and free assembly in order to maintain the opportunity for free political discussion, to the end that government may be responsive to the will of the people and that changes, if desired, may be obtained by peaceful means. Therein lies the security of the Republic, the very foundation of constitutional government." *De Jonge v. Oregon*, 299 U.S. 353, 299 U.S. 365.

This is not to say that the Constitution protects defamatory statements directed against the private conduct of a public official or private citizen. Freedom of press and of speech insures that government will respond to the will of the people, and that changes may be obtained by peaceful means. Purely private defamation has little to do with the political ends of a self-governing society. The imposition of liability for private defamation does not abridge the freedom of public speech or any other freedom protected by the First Amendment.[40] This, of course, cannot be said

"where public officials are concerned, or where public matters are involved. . . . [O]ne main function of the First Amendment is to ensure ample opportunity for the people to determine and resolve public issues. Where public matters are involved, the doubts should be resolved in favor of freedom of expression, rather than against it." Douglas, *The Right of the People* (1958), p. 41.

In many jurisdictions, legislators, judges and executive officers are clothed with absolute immunity against liability for defamatory words uttered in the discharge of their public duties. See, e.g., *Barr v. Matteo*, 360 U.S. 564; *City of Chicago v. Tribune Co.*, 307 Ill., at 610, 139 N.E. at 91. Judge Learned Hand ably summarized the policies underlying the rule:

"It does indeed go without saying that an official who is, in fact, guilty of using his powers to vent his spleen upon others, or for any other personal motive not connected with the public good, should not escape liability for the injuries he may so cause; and, if it were possible in practice to confine such complaints to the guilty, it would be monstrous to deny recovery. The justification for doing so is that it is impossible to know whether the claim is well founded until the

Page 376 U.S. 303

case has been tried, and that to submit all officials, the innocent as well as the guilty, to the burden of a trial and to the inevitable danger of its outcome would dampen the ardor of all but the most resolute, or the most irresponsible, in the unflinching discharge of their duties. Again and again, the public interest calls for action which may turn out to be founded on a mistake, in the face of which an official may later find himself hard put to it to satisfy a jury of his good faith. There must indeed be means of punishing public officers who have been truant to their duties; but that is quite another matter from exposing such as have been honestly mistaken to suit by anyone who has suffered from their errors. As is so often the case, the answer must be found in a balance between the evils inevitable in either alternative. In this instance, it has been thought in the end better to leave unredressed the wrongs done by dishonest officers than to subject those who try to do their duty to the constant dread of retaliation. . . ."

"The decisions have, indeed, always imposed as a limitation upon the immunity that the official's act must have been within the scope of his powers, and it can be argued that official powers, since they exist only for the public good, never cover occasions where the public good is not their aim, and hence that to exercise a power dishonestly is necessarily to overstep its bounds. A moment's reflection shows, however, that that cannot be the meaning of the limitation without defeating the whole doctrine. What is meant by saying that the officer must be acting within his power cannot be more than that the occasion must be such as would have justified the act, if he had been using his power for any of the purposes on whose account it was vested in him. . . ." *Gregoire v. Biddle*, 177 F.2d 579, 581.

If the government official should be immune from libel actions, so that his ardor to serve the public will not be dampened and "fearless, vigorous, and effective administration of policies of government" not be inhibited, *Barr v. Matteo, supra,* at 360 U.S. 571, then the citizen and the press should likewise be immune from libel actions for their criticism of official conduct. Their ardor as citizens will thus not be dampened, and they will be free "to applaud or to criticize the way public employees do their jobs, from the least to the most important."[41] If liability can attach to political criticism because it damages the reputation of a public official as a public official, then no critical citizen can safely utter anything but faint praise about the government or its officials. The vigorous criticism by press and citizen of the conduct of the government of the day by the officials of the day will soon yield to silence if officials in control of government agencies, instead of answering criticisms, can resort to friendly juries to forestall criticism of their official conduct.[42]

The conclusion that the Constitution affords the citizen and the press an absolute privilege for criticism of official conduct does not leave the public official without defenses against unsubstantiated opinions or deliberate misstatements.

"Under our system of government, counterargument and education are the weapons available to expose these matters, not abridgment . . . of free speech. . . ." *Wood v. Georgia*, 370 U.S. 375, 370 U.S. 389. The public official certainly has equal, if not greater, access than most private citizens to media of

(Continues)

(Continued)

communication. In any event, despite the possibility that some excesses and abuses may go unremedied, we must recognize that

> "the people of this nation have ordained, in the light of history, that, in spite of the probability of excesses and abuses, [certain] liberties are, in the long view, essential to enlightened opinion and right conduct on the part of the citizens of a democracy." *Cantwell v. Connecticut*, 310 U.S. 296, 310 U.S. 310.

As Mr. Justice Brandeis correctly observed, "sunlight is the most powerful of all disinfectants."[43]
For these reasons, I strongly believe that the Constitution accords citizens and press an unconditional freedom to criticize official conduct. It necessarily follows that, in a case such as this, where all agree that the allegedly defamatory statements related to official conduct, the judgments for libel cannot constitutionally be sustained.

Notes

37. I fully agree with the Court that the attack upon the validity of the Sedition Act of 1798, 1 Stat. 596, "has carried the day in the court of history," *ante* at 376 U.S. 276, and that the Act would today be declared unconstitutional. It should be pointed out, however, that the Sedition Act proscribed writings which were "false, scandalous *and malicious.*" (Emphasis added.) For prosecutions under the Sedition Act charging malice, *see, e.g.*, Trial of Matthew Lyon (1798), in Wharton, *State Trials of the United States* (1849), p. 333; Trial of Thomas Cooper (1800), in *id.* at 659; Trial of Anthony Haswell (1800), in *id.* at 684; Trial of James Thompson Callender (1800), in *id.* at 688.

38. The requirement of proving actual malice or reckless disregard may, in the mind of the jury, add little to the requirement of proving falsity, a requirement which the Court recognizes not to be an adequate safeguard. The thought suggested by Mr. Justice Jackson in *United States v. Ballard*, 322 U.S. 78, 322 U.S. 92–93, is relevant here:

> "[A]s a matter of either practice or philosophy, I do not see how we can separate an issue as to what is believed from considerations as to what is believable. The most convincing proof that one believes his statements is to show that they have been true in his experience. Likewise, that one knowingly falsified is best proved by showing that what he said happened never did happen."
>
> *See* note 376 U.S. 4, *infra.*

39. It was not until *Gitlow v. New York*, 268 U.S. 652, decided in 1925, that it was intimated that the freedom of speech guaranteed by the First Amendment was applicable to the States by reason of the Fourteenth Amendment. Other intimations followed. *See Whitney v. California*, 274 U.S. 357; *Fiske v. Kansas*, 274 U.S. 380. In 1931, Chief Justice Hughes, speaking for the Court in *Stromberg v. California*, 283 U.S. 359, 283 U.S. 368, declared:

> "It has been determined that the conception of liberty under the due process clause of the Fourteenth Amendment embraces the right of free speech."

Thus, we deal with a constitutional principle enunciated less than four decades ago, and consider for the first time the application of that principle to issues arising in libel cases brought by state officials.

40. In most cases, as in the case at bar, there will be little difficulty in distinguishing defamatory speech relating to private conduct from that relating to official conduct. I recognize, of course, that there will be a gray area. The difficulties of applying a public–private standard are, however, certainly of a different genre from those attending the differentiation between a malicious and nonmalicious state of mind. If the constitutional standard is to be shaped by a concept of malice, the speaker takes the risk not only that the jury will inaccurately determine his state of mind, but also that the jury will fail properly to apply the constitutional standard set by the elusive concept of malice. See 376 U.S. *supra.*

41. MR. JUSTICE BLACK, concurring in *Barr v. Matteo*, 360 U.S. 564, 360 U.S. 577, observed that:

> "The effective functioning of a free government like ours depends largely on the force of an informed public opinion. This calls for the widest possible understanding of the quality of government service rendered by all elective or appointed public officials or employees. Such an informed understanding depends, of course, on the freedom people have to applaud or to criticize the way public employees do their jobs, from the least to the most important."

42. *See* notes 2 4 *supra.*
43. *See* Freund, *The Supreme Court of the United States* (1949), p. 61.

Abrams v. United States, 250 U.S. 616 (1919)

Mr. Justice CLARKE delivered the opinion of the Court.

On a single indictment, containing four counts, the five plaintiffs in error, hereinafter designated the defendants, were convicted of conspiring to violate provisions of the [250 U.S. 616, 617] Espionage Act of Congress (section 3, title I, of Act June 15, 1917, c. 30, 40 Stat. 219, as amended by Act May 16, 1918, c. 75, 40 Stat. 553 [Comp. St. 1918, 10212c]).

Each of the first three counts charged the defendants with conspiring, when the United States was at war with the Imperial Government of Germany, to unlawfully utter, print, write and publish: In the first count, 'disloyal, scurrilous and abusive language about the form of government of the United States;' in the second count, language 'intended to bring the form of government of the United States into contempt, scorn, contumely, and disrepute;' and in the third count, language 'intended to incite, provoke and encourage resistance to the United States in said war.' The charge in the fourth count was that the defendants conspired 'when the United States was at war with the Imperial German Government, . . . unlawfully and willfully, by utterance, writing, printing and publication to urge, incite and advocate curtailment of production of things and products, to wit, ordnance and ammunition, necessary and essential to the prosecution of the war.' The offenses were charged in the language of the act of Congress.

It was charged in each count of the indictment that it was a part of the conspiracy that the defendants would attempt to accomplish their unlawful purpose by printing, writing and distributing in the city of New York many copies of a leaflet or circular, printed in the English language, and of another printed in the Yiddish language, copies of which, properly identified, were attached to the indictment.

All of the five defendants were born in Russia. They were intelligent, had considerable schooling, and at the time they were arrested they had lived in the United States terms varying from five to ten years, but none of them had applied for naturalization. Four of them testified as witnesses in their own behalf, and of these three frankly avowed that they were 'rebels,' 'revolutionists,' [250 U.S. 616, 618] 'anarchists,' that they did not believe in government in any form, and they declared that they had no interest whatever in the government of the United States. The fourth defendant testified that he was a 'Socialist' and believed in 'a proper kind of government, not capitalistic,' but in his classification the government of the United States was 'capitalistic.'

It was admitted on the trial that the defendants had united to print and distribute the described circulars and that 5,000 of them had been printed and distributed about the 22nd day of August, 1918. The group had a meeting place in New York City, in rooms rented by defendant Abrams, under an assumed name, and there the subject of printing the circulars was discussed about two weeks before the defendants were arrested. The defendant Abrams, although not a printer, on July 27, 1918, purchased the printing outfit with which the circulars were printed, and installed it in a basement room where the work was done at night. The circulars were distributed, some by throwing them from a window of a building where one of the defendants was employed and others secretly, in New York City.

The defendants pleaded 'not guilty,' and the case of the government consisted in showing the facts we have stated, and in introducing in evidence copies of the two printed circulars attached to the indictment, a sheet entitled 'Revolutionists Unite for Action,' written by the defendant Lipman, and found on him when he was arrested, and another paper, found at the headquarters of the group, and for which Abrams assumed responsibility.

Thus the conspiracy and the doing of the overt acts charged were largely admitted and were fully established.

On the record thus described it is argued, somewhat faintly, that the acts charged against the defendants were not unlawful because within the protection of that freedom [250 U.S. 616, 619] of speech and of the press which is guaranteed by the First Amendment to the Constitution of the United States, and that the entire Espionage Act is unconstitutional because in conflict with that amendment.

This contention is sufficiently discussed and is definitely negatived in *Schenck v. United States* and *Baer v. United States*, 249 U.S. 47, 39 Sup. Ct. 247, and in *Frohwerk v. United States*, 249 U.S. 204, 39 Sup. Ct. 249.

The claim chiefly elaborated upon by the defendants in the oral argument and in their brief is that there is no substantial evidence in the record to support the judgment upon the verdict of guilty and

(Continues)

that the motion of the defendants for an instructed verdict in their favor was erroneously denied. A question of law is thus presented, which calls for an examination of the record, not for the purpose of weighing conflicting testimony, but only to determine whether there was some evidence, competent and substantial, before the jury, fairly tending to sustain the verdict. *Troxell, Administrator v. Delaware, Lackawanna & Western R.R. Co.*, 227 U.S. 434, 442, 33 S. Sup. Ct. 274; *Lancaster v. Collins*, 115 U.S. 222, 225, 6 S. Sup. Ct. 33; *Chicago & North Western Ry. Co. v. Ohle*, 117 U.S. 123, 129 , 6 S. Sup. Ct. 632. We shall not need to consider the sufficiency, under the rule just stated, of the evidence introduced as to all of the counts of the indictment, for, since the sentence imposed did not exceed that which might lawfully have been imposed under any single count, the judgment upon the verdict of the jury must be affirmed if the evidence is sufficient to sustain any one of the counts. *Evans v. United States*, 153 U.S. 608, 14 Sup. Ct. 939; *Claassen v. United States*, 142 U.S. 140, 12 Sup. Ct. 169; *Debs v. United States*, 249 U.S. 211, 216, 39 S. Sup. Ct. 252.

The first of the two articles attached to the indictment is conspicuously headed, 'The Hypocrisy of the United States and her Allies.' After denouncing President Wilson as a hypocrite and a coward because troops were sent into Russia, it proceeds to assail our government in general, saying: [250 U.S. 616, 620] 'His [the President's] shameful, cowardly silence about the intervention in Russia reveals the hypocrisy of the plutocratic gang in Washington and vicinity.'

It continues:

'He [the President] is too much of a coward to come out openly and say: 'We capitalistic nations cannot afford to have a proletarian republic in Russia.''

Among the capitalistic nations Abrams testified the United States was included. Growing more inflammatory as it proceeds, the circular culminates in:

'The Russian Revolution cries: Workers of the World! Awake! Rise! Put down your enemy and mine!'
  'Yes friends, there is only one enemy of the workers of the world and that is CAPITALISM.'

This is clearly an appeal to the 'workers' of this country to arise and put down by force the government of the United States which they characterize as their 'hypocritical,' 'cowardly' and 'capitalistic' enemy.

It concludes:

'Awake! Awake, you Workers of the World!
  REVOLUTIONISTS.'

The second of the articles was printed in the Yiddish language and in the translation is headed, 'Workers-Wake Up.' After referring to 'his Majesty, Mr. Wilson, and the rest of the gang, dogs of all colors!' it continues:

'Workers, Russian emigrants, you who had the least belief in the honesty of our government,'

—which defendants admitted referred to the United States government—

'must now throw away all confidence, must spit in the face the false, hypocritic, military propaganda which has fooled you so relentlessly, calling forth your sympathy, your help, to the prosecution of the war.'

The purpose of this obviously was to persuade the persons to whom it was addressed to turn a deaf ear to patriotic [250 U.S. 616, 621] appeals in behalf of the government of the United States, and to cease to render it assistance in the prosecution of the war.

It goes on:

'With the money which you have loaned, or are going to loan them, they will make bullets not only for the Germans, but also for the Workers Soviets of Russia. Workers in the ammunition factories, you are producing bullets, bayonets, cannon, to murder not only the Germans, but also your dearest, best, who are in Russia and are fighting for freedom.'

It will not do to say, as is now argued, that the only intent of these defendants was to prevent injury to the Russian cause. Men must be held to have intended, and to be accountable for, the effects which their acts were likely to produce. Even if their primary purpose and intent was to aid the cause of the Russian Revolution, the plan of action which they adopted necessarily involved, before it could be realized, defeat of the war program of the United States, for the obvious effect of this appeal, if it should become effective, as they hoped it might, would be to persuade persons of character such as those whom they regarded themselves as addressing, not to aid government loans and not to work in ammunition factories, where their work would produce 'bullets, bayonets, cannon' and other munitions of war, the use of which would cause the 'murder' of Germans and Russians.

Again, the spirit becomes more bitter as it proceeds to declare that—

'America and her Allies have betrayed [the Workers]. Their robberish aims are clear to all men. The destruction of the Russian Revolution, that is the politics of the march to Russia.

'Workers, our reply to the barbaric intervention has to be a general strike! An open challenge only will let the government know that not only the Russian Worker fights for [250 U.S. 616, 622] freedom, but also here in America lives the spirit of Revolution.'

This is not an attempt to bring about a change of administration by candid discussion, for no matter what may have incited the outbreak on the part of the defendant anarchists, the manifest purpose of such a publication was to create an attempt to defeat the war plans of the government of the United States, by bringing upon the country the paralysis of a general strike, thereby arresting the production of all munitions and other things essential to the conduct of the war.

This purpose is emphasized in the next paragraph, which reads:

'Do not let the government scare you with their wild punishment in prisons, hanging and shooting. We must not and will not betray the splendid fighters of Russia. Workers, up to fight.'

After more of the same kind, the circular concludes:

'Woe unto those who will be in the way of progress. Let solidarity live!'
It is signed, 'The Rebels.'

That the interpretation we have put upon these articles, circulated in the greatest port of our land, from which great numbers of soldiers were at the time taking ship daily, and in which great quantities of war supplies of every kind were at the time being manufactured for transportation overseas, is not only the fair interpretation of them, but that it is the meaning which their authors consciously intended should be conveyed by them to others is further shown by the additional writings found in the meeting place of the defendant group and on the person of one of them. One of these circulars is headed: 'Revolutionists! Unite for Action!'

After denouncing the President as 'Our Kaiser' and the hypocrisy of the United States and her Allies, this article concludes: [250 U.S. 616, 623] 'Socialists, Anarchists, Industrial Workers of the World, Socialists, Labor party men and other revolutionary organizations Unite for Action and let us save the Workers' Republic of Russia!

'Know you lovers of freedom that in order to save the Russian revolution, we must keep the armies of the allied countries busy at home.'

Thus was again avowed the purpose to throw the country into a state of revolution, if possible, and to thereby frustrate the military program of the government.

The remaining article, after denouncing the President for what is characterized as hostility to the Russian revolution, continues:

'We, the toilers of America, who believe in real liberty, shall pledge ourselves, in case the United States will participate in that bloody conspiracy against Russia, to create so great a disturbance that the autocrats of America shall be compelled to keep their armies at home, and not be able to spare any for Russia.'

It concludes with this definite threat of armed rebellion:

'If they will use arms against the Russian people to enforce their standard of order, so will we use arms, and they shall never see the ruin of the Russian Revolution.'

(Continues)

These excerpts sufficiently show, that while the immediate occasion for this particular outbreak of lawlessness, on the part of the defendant alien anarchists, may have been resentment caused by our government sending troops into Russia as a strategic operation against the Germans on the eastern battle front, yet the plain purpose of their propaganda was to excite, at the supreme crisis of the war, disaffection, sedition, riots, and, as they hoped, revolution, in this country for the purpose of embarrassing and if possible defeating the military plans of the government in Europe. A technical distinction may perhaps be taken between disloyal and abusive language applied to the form of our government or language intended to bring the form [250 U.S. 616, 624] of our government into contempt and disrepute, and language of like character and intended to produce like results directed against the President and Congress, the agencies through which that form of government must function in time of war. But it is not necessary to a decision of this case to consider whether such distinction is vital or merely formal, for the language of these circulars was obviously intended to provoke and to encourage resistance to the United States in the war, as the third count runs, and, the defendants, in terms, plainly urged and advocated a resort to a general strike of workers in ammunition factories for the purpose of curtailing the production of ordnance and munitions necessary and essential to the prosecution of the war as is charged in the fourth count. Thus it is clear not only that some evidence but that much persuasive evidence was before the jury tending to prove that the defendants were guilty as charged in both the third and fourth counts of the indictment and under the long established rule of law hereinbefore stated the judgment of the District Court must be AFFIRMED.

Mr. Justice HOLMES, dissenting.

This indictment is founded wholly upon the publication of two leaflets which I shall describe in a moment. The first count charges a conspiracy pending the war with Germany to publish abusive language about the form of government of the United States, laying the preparation and publishing of the first leaflet as overt acts. The second count charges a conspiracy pending the war to publish language intended to bring the form of government into contempt, laying the preparation and publishing of the two leaflets as overt acts. The third count alleges a conspiracy to encourage resistance to the United States in the same war and to attempt to effectuate the purpose by publishing the same leaflets. The fourth count lays a conspiracy [250 U.S. 616, 625] to incite curtailment of production of things necessary to the prosecution of the war and to attempt to accomplish it by publishing the second leaflet to which I have referred.

The first of these leaflets says that the President's cowardly silence about the intervention in Russia reveals the hypocrisy of the plutocratic gang in Washington. It intimates that 'German militarism combined with allied capitalism to crush the Russian revolution'—goes on that the tyrants of the world fight each other until they see a common enemy—working class enlightenment, when they combine to crush it; and that now militarism and capitalism combined, though not openly, to crush the Russian revolution. It says that there is only one enemy of the workers of the world and that is capitalism; that it is a crime for workers of America, etc., to fight the workers' republic of Russia, and ends 'Awake! Awake, you workers of the world! Revolutionists.' A note adds 'It is absurd to call us pro-German. We hate and despise German militarism more than do you hypocritical tyrants. We have more reason for denouncing German militarism than has the coward of the White House.'

The other leaflet, headed 'Workers-Wake Up,' with abusive language says that America together with the Allies will march for Russia to help the Czecko-Slovaks in their struggle against the Bolsheviki, and that his time the hypocrites shall not fool the Russian emigrants and friends of Russia in America. It tells the Russian emigrants that they now must spit in the face of the false military propaganda by which their sympathy and help to the prosecution of the war have been called forth and says that with the money they have lent or are going to lend 'they will make bullets not only for the Germans but also for the Workers Soviets of Russia,' and further, 'Workers in the ammunition factories, you are producing bullets, bayonets, cannon to murder not only the Germans, [250 U.S. 616, 626] but also your dearest, best, who are in Russia fighting for freedom.' It then appeals to the same Russian emigrants at some length not to consent to the 'inquisitionary expedition in Russia,' and says that the destruction of the Russian revolution is 'the politics of the march on Russia.' The leaflet winds up by saying 'Workers, our reply to this barbaric intervention has to be a general strike!' and after a few words on the spirit of revolution, exhortations not to be afraid, and some usual tall talk ends 'Woe unto those who will be in the way of progress. Let solidarity live! The Rebels.'

No argument seems to be necessary to show that these pronunciamentos in no way attack the form of government of the United States, or that they do not support either of the first two counts. What little I have to say about the third count may be postponed until I have considered the fourth. With regard to that it seems too plain to be denied that the suggestion to workers in the ammunition factories that they are producing bullets to murder their dearest, and the further advocacy of a general strike, both in the second leaflet, do urge curtailment of production of things necessary to the prosecution of the war within the meaning of the Act of May 16, 1918, c. 75, 40 Stat. 553, amending section 3 of the earlier Act of 1917 (Comp. St. 10212c). But to make the conduct criminal that statute requires that it should be 'with intent by such curtailment to cripple or hinder the United States in the prosecution of the war.' It seems to me that no such intent is proved.

I am aware of course that the word 'intent' as vaguely used in ordinary legal discussion means no more than knowledge at the time of the act that the consequences said to be intended will ensue. Even less than that will satisfy the general principle of civil and criminal liability. A man may have to pay damages, may be sent to prison, at common law might be hanged, if at the time of his act [250 U.S. 616, 627] he knew facts from which common experience showed that the consequences would follow, whether he individually could foresee them or not. But, when words are used exactly, a deed is not done with intent to produce a consequence unless that consequence is the aim of the deed. It may be obvious, and obvious to the actor, that the consequence will follow, and he may be liable for it even if he regrets it, but he does not do the act with intent to produce it unless the aim to produce it is the proximate motive of the specific act, although there may be some deeper motive behind.

It seems to me that this statute must be taken to use its words in a strict and accurate sense. They would be absurd in any other. A patriot might think that we were wasting money on aeroplanes, or making more cannon of a certain kind than we needed, and might advocate curtailment with success, yet even if it turned out that the curtailment hindered and was thought by other minds to have been obviously likely to hinder the United States in the prosecution of the war, no one would hold such conduct a crime. I admit that my illustration does not answer all that might be said but it is enough to show what I think and to let me pass to a more important aspect of the case. I refer to the First Amendment to the Constitution that Congress shall make no law abridging the freedom of speech.

I never have seen any reason to doubt that the questions of law that alone were before this Court in the Cases of Schenck (249 U.S. 47, 29 Sup. Ct. 247) Frohwerk (249 U.S. 204, 39 Sup. Ct. 249), and Debs (249 U.S. 211, 39 Sup. Ct. 252), were rightly decided. I do not doubt for a moment that by the same reasoning that would justify punishing persuasion to murder, the United States constitutionally may punish speech that produces or is intended to produce a clear and imminent danger that it will bring about forthwith certain substantive evils that the United States constitutionally may seek to prevent. The power undoubtedly is [250 U.S. 616, 628] greater in time of war than in time of peace because war opens dangers that do not exist at other times.

But as against dangers peculiar to war, as against others, the principle of the right to free speech is always the same. It is only the present danger of immediate evil or an intent to bring it about that warrants Congress in setting a limit to the expression of opinion where private rights are not concerned. Congress certainly cannot forbid all effort to change the mind of the country. Now nobody can suppose that the surreptitious publishing of a silly leaflet by an unknown man, without more, would present any immediate danger that its opinions would hinder the success of the government arms or have any appreciable tendency to do so. Publishing those opinions for the very purpose of obstructing, however, might indicate a greater danger and at any rate would have the quality of an attempt. So I assume that the second leaflet if published for the purposes alleged in the fourth count might be punishable. But it seems pretty clear to me that nothing less than that would bring these papers within the scope of this law. An actual intent in the sense that I have explained is necessary to constitute an attempt, where a further act of the same individual is required to complete the substantive crime, for reasons given in *Swift & Co. v. United States*, 196 U.S. 375, 396, 25 S. Sup. Ct. 276. It is necessary where the success of the attempt depends upon others because if that intent is not present the actor's aim may be accomplished without bringing about the evils sought to be checked. An intent to prevent interference with the revolution in Russia might have been satisfied without any hindrance to carrying on the war in which we were engaged.

I do not see how anyone can find the intent required by the statute in any of the defendant's words. The second leaflet is the only one that affords even a foundation for the charge, and there, without invoking the hatred of German militarism expressed in the former one, it is evident [250 U.S. 616, 629] from the beginning to the end that the only object of the paper is to help Russia and stop

(Continues)

American intervention there against the popular government—not to impede the United States in the war that it was carrying on. To say that two phrases taken literally might import a suggestion of conduct that would have interference with the war as an indirect and probably undesired effect seems to me by no means enough to show an attempt to produce that effect.

I return for a moment to the third count. That charges an intent to provoke resistance to the United States in its war with Germany. Taking the clause in the statute that deals with that in connection with the other elaborate provisions of the Act, I think that resistance to the United States means some forcible act of opposition to some proceeding of the United States in pursuance of the war. I think the intent must be the specific intent that I have described and for the reasons that I have given I think that no such intent was proved or existed in fact. I also think that there is no hint at resistance to the United States as I construe the phrase.

In this case sentences of twenty years imprisonment have been imposed for the publishing of two leaflets that I believe the defendants had as much right to publish as the Government has to publish the Constitution of the United States now vainly invoked by them. Even if I am technically wrong and enough can be squeezed from these poor and puny anonymities to turn the color of legal litmus paper; I will add, even if what I think the necessary intent were shown; the most nominal punishment seems to me all that possible could be inflicted, unless the defendants are to be made to suffer not for what the indictment alleges but for the creed that they avow—a creed that I believe to be the creed of ignorance and immaturity when honestly held, as I see no reason to doubt that it was held here but which, although made the subject of examination at the [250 U.S. 616, 630] trial, no one has a right even to consider in dealing with the charges before the Court.

Persecution for the expression of opinions seems to me perfectly logical. If you have no doubt of your premises or your power and want a certain result with all your heart you naturally express your wishes in law and sweep away all opposition. To allow opposition by speech seems to indicate that you think the speech impotent, as when a man says that he has squared the circle, or that you do not care whole heartedly for the result, or that you doubt either your power or your premises. But when men have realized that time has upset many fighting faiths, they may come to believe even more than they believe the very foundations of their own conduct that the ultimate good desired is better reached by free trade in ideas—that the best test of truth is the power of the thought to get itself accepted in the competition of the market, and that truth is the only ground upon which their wishes safely can be carried out. That at any rate is the theory of our Constitution. It is an experiment, as all life is an experiment. Every year if not every day we have to wager our salvation upon some prophecy based upon imperfect knowledge. While that experiment is part of our system I think that we should be eternally vigilant against attempts to check the expression of opinions that we loathe and believe to be fraught with death, unless they so imminently threaten immediate interference with the lawful and pressing purposes of the law that an immediate check is required to save the country. I wholly disagree with the argument of the Government that the First Amendment left the common law as to seditious libel in force. History seems to me against the notion. I had conceived that the United States through many years had shown its repentance for the Sedition Act of 1798 (Act July 14, 1798, c. 73, 1 Stat. 596), by repaying fines that it imposed. Only the emergency that makes it immediately dangerous to leave the correction of evil counsels to time warrants [250 U.S. 616, 631] making any exception to the sweeping command, 'Congress shall make no law abridging the freedom of speech.' Of course I am speaking only of expressions of opinion and exhortations, which were all that were uttered here, but I regret that I cannot put into more impressive words my belief that in their conviction upon this indictment the defendants were deprived of their rights under the Constitution of the United States.

Mr. Justice BRANDEIS concurs with the foregoing opinion.

Abortion

Chapter Objectives

In this chapter you will learn . . .

- What *Roe v. Wade* determined
- Whether overturning *Roe v. Wade* would render abortions illegal
- How *Roe v. Wade* was expanded by subsequent cases
- What partial-birth abortion is
- How pro-life and pro-choice views are atypical from traditional conservative and liberal views

Introduction

Abortion is one of the most controversial issues affecting American society today. Few issues inspire such heated debates that lead to intense intellectual discussions at best and deadly violence at worst. To inject a little humor into a rather serious topic, let's keep in mind the old joke about the foremost abortion case, *Roe v. Wade*. When asked, "where do you stand on *Roe v. Wade*," the answer is: "if the boat is leaking, you row; if it has a hole in it, you wade." Get it?

Many Americans believe that if the Supreme Court ever overturns *Roe v. Wade*, then abortions will become illegal in all 50 states; women will have to travel out of the country in order to get an abortion, or they will have to go behind some dark alley and have it done in a crude, primitive, and dangerous manner. That is simply not true. For reasons that we have already begun to discuss, it is not difficult to see why.

The Supremacy Clause Revisited

The Supremacy Clause, as we discussed earlier, declares that the Constitution is the supreme law of the land and that no state laws may contradict it. However, state laws that do not conflict with its principles are legitimate. Before *Roe v. Wade* was decided in 1973, each state had the right to create its own laws regarding abortion, because there was no mention of abortion in the Constitution. But *Roe* established that the Constitution, through its right to privacy, always gave women the right to choose whether or not to bring a child they were carrying to term or to abort it. Therefore, if *Roe* were ever to be overturned, it would not render abortions illegal; rather, our nation would return to the days when each state had the right to determine whether or not to permit abortion.

Abortions Have Been Performed for Thousands of Years

Some people may be shocked to learn the abortion is not a relatively modern procedure, but that it has existed for thousands of years! One of the common misconceptions about why abortion was not specifically mentioned in the Constitution is that "abortions did not exist back then." That is utterly false. Unlike airplanes and the Internet, which were invented long after the Constitution was ratified, abortions existed not only during American colonial times, but also during ancient times. It is even mentioned in the Hippocratic Oath, which was established in ancient Greece and named after the person known as the father of medicine, Hippocrates.

Therefore, whatever the reason why the Founders did not refer to abortion in the Constitution has nothing to do with whether or not it existed at the time, because it most certainly did.

What *Roe v. Wade* Actually Determined

Generally, even those who know that the case *Roe v. Wade* is about abortion do not know too much about what it specifically determined. Does it mean that a woman has an absolute legal right to an abortion anyplace, anytime, regardless of what the state in which she wants to have the abortion has to say about it? Not exactly. Let's take a look at *Roe v. Wade* so that we can understand it better as we continue learning about abortion as it pertains to the Constitution.

The easiest way to understand *Roe* is to think of it in terms of months. A woman's pregnancy lasts approximately 9 months: let's consider the first three months the *first trimester*, the next 3 months the *second trimester*, and the final 3 months the *third trimester*. In *Roe*, the Court held that:

1. First Trimester: A woman has an absolute right to abort her child and is not subject to state regulations.

2. Second Trimester: A woman continues to have the right to abort her child, but the state may regulate procedures based on reasonable health concerns.

3. Third Trimester: Once the fetus is viable (i.e., it can live on its own outside the womb), the state has a right to ban abortion.

What If *Roe* Were Overturned?

Accordingly, for roughly the first 3 months of a woman's pregnancy, she has the right to have an abortion anywhere in the United States. That does not mean that the government is obligated to make sure that she gets one. It is not the same as someone having the right to an attorney upon arrest, even if the person cannot afford one.

Taken to the extreme, suppose that every single doctor in the United States refused to perform an abortion: there would be no obligation imposed upon those doctors to perform abortions or lose their license to practice medicine. By contrast, an attorney may be required by the state in which he or she practices law to take on a particular case or risk losing his or her license to practice law (granted, this is unlikely to happen as there always seems to be an attorney ready and willing to take on even the most unpleasant of cases). A woman, then, might have a right to an abortion, but it does not mean that she will necessarily be afforded the opportunity to have one.

There are some states in which abortions are rather common, and abortion clinics are abundant. At the other extreme are states with no abortion clinics at all. If *Roe v. Wade* were to be overturned, then it would seem likely that states in which there is public support for abortion would retain its legality and states in which that support is minimal or nonexistent would render it illegal. In that case, the practical effect on women, whether or not *Roe* remained good law, would be virtually identical.

Roe's Reasoning: Why the Court Decided as It Did

Specifically, the Court in *Roe* examined the Texas statute that prevented the plaintiff (called "Jane *Roe*") from having an abortion. Namely, that no one was permitted to have an abortion in the state of Texas unless the abortion was performed for the purpose of saving the life of the mother. Roe, a single, pregnant woman, was denied the opportunity to obtain a legal abortion in Texas because her life was not in danger and sued on behalf of herself and other similarly situated women.

The Court referred to the common law tradition of abortions not having been indictable offenses before "quickening" (in other words, before the fetus was viable), and concluded that such law must have reflected the philosophical, theological, and civil beliefs about when life begins. The Court also detailed the history of abortion laws, and comments of the American Medical Association and American Bar Association. Ultimately, the Court found that there was no absolute, uniform opinion on the subject.

Next, the Court examined the issue of privacy, acknowledging that the word is not specifically mentioned in the Constitution, but that in other cases, it has been determined a right by the First, Fourth, Fifth, Ninth, and Fourteenth Amendments.

The Court held that the notion of liberty in the Fourteenth Amendment can be applied to a woman's right to privacy in terms of having the right to obtain an abortion. But the Court made it clear that it in no way supported a woman's right to have an abortion in any manner whatsoever. The Court emphasized that the state has an interest to protect the life of the unborn, as well as to maintain medical standards, and those rights must be balanced against the woman's right to privacy.

The Constitutional Amendments in Question

First Amendment   We have already reviewed the First Amendment in earlier chapters. It prohibits Congress from making laws that inhibit religion, speech, the press, peaceful assembly, and the right to petition the government for redress of grievances.

Fourth Amendment   The Fourth Amendment protects against unreasonable searches and seizures, and from search warrants not issued based on probable cause.

Fifth Amendment   The Fifth Amendment protects a person against being deprived of life, liberty, or property without due process of law (for example, a person cannot be thrown in jail, and thus denied liberty, without the due process of a conviction in court).

Ninth Amendment   The rights specifically listed in the Constitution do not mean that the people are denied other rights.

Fourteenth Amendment   No state law may abridge the privileges and immunities of United States citizens, deprive them of life, liberty, or property without due process of law, or deny them equal protection under the law within its jurisdiction.

These amendments were interpreted by the *Roe* majority as protecting a woman's right to privacy by guaranteeing her right to choose to have an abortion based on certain conditions set forth below.

Turning next to the question of whether the unborn fetus is a "person," the Court found that there is no clear Constitutional evidence to support that notion and explicitly refused to answer the question of whether life begins at conception.

The Court concluded that the state has a "legitimate" and "important" interest in every pregnancy at any stage, but that the interest becomes "compelling" only as the date of delivery approaches. Accordingly, *Roe* held that a woman has an absolute right to abort her child during the first trimester, the state may reasonably regulate procedures during the second trimester based on reasonable health concerns, and that the state may ban abortion once the fetus is viable.

Concurring Justices agreed with the Court's notion that liberty under the Fourteenth Amendment covers such a broad range of topics, far too great to be enumerated in the Constitution, and certainly includes a woman's right to have an abortion.

Justice Rehnquist, who would later become the Court's Chief Justice, disagreed with the Court's holding: first, in that the plaintiff lacked standing to sue because she was no longer in her first trimester of pregnancy (which the majority waived, citing that it would thus be impossible for any pregnant woman to sue, as the pregnancy would come to full term before the case even made it to the appeals stage). Second, because the type of privacy that the Court mentions does not rise to the level of a compelling state interest, but only a mere rationality. And third, that the Fourteenth Amendment does not guarantee absolute liberty, it simply denies the taking away of liberty without due process of law.

Other Justices flatly disagreed with the decision, identifying it as the Court's prioritizing of Constitutional rights: namely, that the Court has placed the right of the mother to not carry the child to term ahead of the life of the child.

As much as we have covered *Roe* to this point, it is too important a case not to include in full text. The entire case can be found at the end of this chapter.

Roe Modified: *Planned Parenthood of Southeastern Pennsylvania v. Casey*

Roe is a prime example of a Supreme Court decision that, although a vast majority of Justices (seven out of nine) agreed on certain principles, there was enough uncertainty as to make one wonder how long *Roe* would remain "good law."

In 1992, 19 years after *Roe* was decided, that decision was almost turned on its ear by *Planned Parenthood of Southeastern Pennsylvania v. Casey*. The *Casey* case gives us an opportunity to examine what might happen when a Supreme Court decision is reviewed by a later panel of Justices who might have a different judicial philosophy.

Strict Constructionists Versus Loose Constructionists

Some judges (whether Supreme Court Justices or of other courts) believe that the Constitution should be strictly interpreted, based on the Founders' intent. They are also known as constitutionalists or originalists. Strict constructionists, also referred to as originalists, believe that legislatures, not judges, should make laws, and that if something is not explicitly stated in the Constitution, then the courts have no business altering a statute made by a particular legislature. In terms of abortion, then, strict constructionists would examine the Constitution, determine that there is no mention about abortion, and conclude that the judicial branch has no right to interfere with a particular state's abortion statute.

By contrast, loose constructionists, also known as judicial activists, believe that the Constitution, while an extraordinary document, is not ideally suited for all purposes and, as such, must be interpreted based on society's evolving standards. Unlike strict constructionists, they believe that the judicial branch does indeed have a place in interpreting the Constitution. Although they respect the legislatures, loose constructionists also believe that the Constitution can best be interpreted by the courts. Keeping these two notions in mind, let's take a look at *Casey*.

Justice Antonin Scalia (top) sees little reason to tamper with the Founders' intent, whereas Justice Stephen Breyer (bottom) views the Constitution as an evolving document.

As *Roe* was now the law of the land, albeit a judge-made law, no state could enact a statute that contradicted its holding, as that would be unconstitutional on its face. However, states could regulate various restrictions on abortion, as did the Pennsylvania State Legislature, by requiring the following conditions for women seeking an abortion.

1. Doctors were required to inform patients about the health risks of having an abortion prior to one being performed.
2. Married women were required to notify their husbands prior to having an abortion (though the husbands' actual consent was not necessary).
3. Minors were required to receive consent from a parent or legal guardian before having an abortion.
4. All women seeking an abortion were required to wait 24 hours prior to having one.
5. Public disclosure of various information, such as the woman's age, marital status, and number of prior pregnancies (although the woman's name would not be disclosed).

The nine Justices who decided this case were:

1. Blackmun (who had authored the *Roe* opinion) and Stevens. Both of these Justices voted to reaffirm *Roe* in its entirety. They were the loose constructionists of the *Casey* court, believing that although the Constitution does not specifically mention the right to an abortion, the Court should interpret that it would support that right.
2. Rehnquist (who by that point was Chief Justice), White, Scalia, and Thomas, all of whom voted to overturn *Roe* altogether. As the strict constructionists of the Court, they believed that *Roe* was a bad decision to begin with, as the Court overstepped its Constitutional bounds, and took this opportunity to rule to overturn it.
3. O'Connor, Souter, and Kennedy held the middle ground between the starkly opposing points of views advocated by the Blackmun and Rehnquist contingents. Their joint opinion, a scant plurality of three, reaffirmed a woman's right to have an abortion without interference from the state, unless there are exceptions after the fetus is viable and/or the life or health of the mother is at risk. They also recognized the interest the state has in protecting not only the woman's right to choose but the life of the fetus.

Precedent: *Stare Decisis*

An important point worth mentioning is that the O'Connor block relied on the principle of *stare decisis*, which means that the court in question should respect and apply the decision reached by an earlier court. The three Justices hinted that, had this been the first time the issue of abortion was presented to them, they might not necessarily have ruled as the Justices did in *Roe*. Because *Roe* was settled law, however, the O'Connor block believed that it was most appropriate to let the decision stand.

The Undue Burden Standard Replaces the Trimester Approach

As medical knowledge and technology progressed during the 19 years between *Roe* and *Casey*, the trimester formula in *Roe* was replaced in *Casey* by the "undue burden"

test: the state may regulate abortion to the fullest extent as long as it does not place an undue burden on a woman seeking to abort a *nonviable fetus*. The undue burden would be the presence of a "substantial obstacle" as a result of state law.

As for the Pennsylvania statute, the O'Connor opinion, no longer applying the same level of scrutiny to abortion statutes, determined that of the five requirements, the only one that placed an undue burden upon women seeking an abortion was the obligation of spousal notification. The rationale was that in some physically and psychologically abusive relationships, some women might be terrified to disclose to their spouses that they are having an abortion. The other four provisions were not found to be undue burdens.

Stevens' Opinion

Justice Stevens reasoned that a woman's fundamental right to an abortion is derived from the fundamental right of liberty found in the Constitution, but that the right of the state to protect the life of the unborn fetus does not rise to that same level. His opinion was square with the criteria that had been set forth in *Roe*.

Blackmun's Opinion

Justice Blackmun also insisted that strict scrutiny be applied to abortion, as it was a fundamental right, and believed that none of the requirements in the Pennsylvania statute served a compelling state interest, certainly not one compelling enough to counterbalance a woman's fundamental right to an abortion.

Rehnquist's Dissent

Chief Justice Rehnquist reiterated his position in *Roe*, that abortion is not a fundamental right and thus should be subjected to a rational basis test, which is even lower scrutiny than the undue burden standard: the state may regulate abortion as long as it is rationally related to a legitimate state interest.

Scalia's Dissent

Justice Scalia compared abortion to bigamy, incest, and suicide, in that all have been legally prohibited and such prohibitions are long-standing American traditions. He also admonished the O'Connor block for caving in to popular opinion and implored that changes to laws need to be made by elected representatives, not by the Supreme Court, which he blasted for acting in an imperial manner.

Later Abortion Cases

Cases that followed *Casey*, as of this writing, have not had a profound effect either on the *Casey* or the *Roe* holdings. They involved other state laws regarding some of the same issues addressed in *Casey*, such as spousal notification and parental consent, with no measurable differences. One case, however, merits particular attention because it deals with "partial birth" abortions.

Partial Birth Abortions

In the late 1990s, a term that became a central component of the abortion debate was the so-called "partial birth" abortion. Essentially, that procedure involves a fetus being partially delivered, whereby the doctor then punctures its skull, killing it, and delivers it dead. The procedure has long been part of numerous state abortion statutes as permissible, in order to protect the life of the mother. In *Stenberg v. Carhart*, decided in 2000, the Court struck down a Nebraska statute that did not contain an exception for the mother's health.

The Court determined that partial birth abortions may not only be performed in order to save a pregnant woman's life, but may also be performed if performing a conventional type of abortion or no abortion at all, would endanger the woman's *health* (even if *not* in a *life-threatening* manner).

Contrary to common belief, partial-birth abortions were never considered to be included as an automatic option to conventional ones, nor did they open the doors for unlimited abortion on demand, no matter what stage of the pregnancy.

The Future of Abortions in America

We began this chapter by discussing abortion in terms of *Roe v. Wade* and what would happen if it were overturned. As we have seen, to some extent it has already been modified, though not overturned. Nonetheless, we discussed that even if it were completely overturned, that would not be the end of abortion.

Public policy plays an important role in American law and politics. While there are many who are personally opposed to the concept of abortion, they do not necessarily want to legally prevent others from having one. When lumped into the group with those who do not have any sort of problem with abortion at all, the merger comprises the majority of Americans. On the other hand, as medical technology improves, more and more Americans demand better evidence about when life inside the womb really begins. Before we close this chapter, let's take a look at how abortion has shaped American politics, and some of the contradictions that are quite surprising.

Pro-Life Liberals and Pro-Choice Conservatives

As we discussed earlier in the book, American political labels are very interesting in that they often change with the times. Traditionally, liberals were those who were open-minded to different points of view outside the box, whereas conservatives were largely opposed to change, especially drastic change.

The face of modern-day conservatism changed profoundly in 1980, with the election of President Ronald Reagan. Reagan won in a landslide and revived the conservative movement. But the path back to conservatism was anything but conservative, because conservatives do not make drastic changes! More recently, the presidency of George W. Bush, a self-proclaimed conservative, involved a foreign policy that actively sought to spread democracy in other parts of the world which, again, defies traditional conservative principles of not becoming overly involved in the affairs of other countries.

Liberals and conservatives take opposite points of view regarding abortion: the former regard it to be a fundamental right and absolutely support its continued legality. Conservatives take the opposite view, likening abortion to murder and believing that life begins at conception. Next, there are libertarians, who may not necessarily have a moral problem with abortion, but believe that the government does not have the right to regulate it. They side with the liberals in the result if not the philosophy, or, as we now know to call it, they *concur*.

Interestingly, the traditional conservative principle has been less government is better: don't tax us, don't interfere with our right to own guns, and don't tell us that we don't have the right to smoke cigars or eat fatty foods if that's what we feel like doing. However, you *may* tell us what to do with our bodies if we happen to be carrying a baby!

Liberals fare no better in this hypocrisy: they support government regulation of gun control, corporate profits, smoking, and foods containing trans-fats, but they do not seek government intervention when it comes to saving the lives of unborn children.

Technically, then, the true conservative approach is to be pro-choice. Not because it is a position that many conservatives morally support, but because it is the only anti-government intervention position possible. Conversely, the true liberal/activist position is to be pro-life.

President Ronald Reagan, winner of two landslide elections, revitalized conservatism in America in the 1980s.

Conclusion

This, then, is an overview about the current state of abortion. It remains one of the more unresolved aspects of Constitutional law. Nonetheless, we have made a sizeable dent in understanding its basic principles in this chapter.

In Chapter 7, we will take a look at another controversial issue that is sure to spark debate for years to come: affirmative action.

Questions for Review

1. Does a woman have the right to have an abortion in any state at any point during her pregnancy?
2. Does a woman have the right to have an abortion in any state at least during some part of her pregnancy?
3. Are there any states that absolutely prohibit a woman's right to have an abortion?
4. Are there any states that are required to provide abortions?
5. Is the federal government required to provide abortions?
6. If *Roe v. Wade* were overturned tomorrow, would that make abortion illegal?
7. What criteria did *Roe* establish based on trimesters?
8. How did *Casey* modify *Roe*?
9. What is a partial birth abortion?
10. What is a strict constructionist as opposed to a loose constructionist?

Constitutionally Speaking

When a woman becomes pregnant, should she have the right to determine whether to abort that baby, even though it is alive inside of her? Should the mother's right to terminate that baby's life end at conception, when the fetus becomes viable or when the baby is born? Does the father of the child have as many rights and decision-making authority as the mother regarding the life of the baby?

Constitutional Cases

Here is *Roe v. Wade* in its entirety, and also *Doe v. Bolton*, which was decided by the Court on the same day as *Roe* but has not received as much attention.

Roe v. Wade, 410 U.S. 113 (1973)

A pregnant single woman (Roe) brought a class action challenging the constitutionality of the Texas criminal abortion laws, which proscribe procuring or attempting an abortion except on medical advice for the purpose of saving the mother's life. A licensed physician (Hallford), who had two state abortion prosecutions pending against him, was permitted to intervene. A childless married couple (the Does), the wife not being pregnant, separately attacked the laws, basing alleged injury on the future possibilities of contraceptive failure, pregnancy, unpreparedness for parenthood, and impairment of the wife's health. A three-judge District Court, which consolidated the actions, held that Roe and Hallford, and members of their classes, had standing to sue and presented justiciable controversies. Ruling that declaratory, though not injunctive, relief was warranted, the court declared the abortion statutes void as vague and overbroadly infringing those plaintiffs' Ninth and Fourteenth Amendment rights. The court ruled the Does' complaint not justiciable. Appellants directly appealed to this Court on the injunctive rulings, and appellee cross-appealed from the District Court's grant of declaratory relief to Roe and Hallford. Held:

1. While 28 U.S.C. 1253 authorizes no direct appeal to this Court from the grant or denial of declaratory relief alone, review is not foreclosed when the case is properly before the Court on appeal from specific denial of injunctive relief and the arguments as to both injunctive and declaratory relief are necessarily identical. P. 123.

2. Roe has standing to sue; the Does and Hallford do not. Pp. 123–129.

   (a) Contrary to appellee's contention, the natural termination of Roe's pregnancy did not moot her suit. Litigation involving pregnancy, which is "capable of repetition, yet evading review," is an exception to the usual federal rule that an actual controversy [410 U.S. 113, 114] must exist at review stages and not simply when the action is initiated. Pp. 124–125.

   (b) The District Court correctly refused injunctive, but erred in granting declaratory, relief to Hallford, who alleged no federally protected right not assertable as a defense against the good-faith state prosecutions pending against him. *Samuels v. Mackell*, 401 U.S. 66. Pp. 125–127.

   (c) The Does' complaint, based as it is on contingencies, any one or more of which may not occur, is too speculative to present an actual case or controversy. Pp. 127–129.

3. State criminal abortion laws, like those involved here, that except from criminality only a life-saving procedure on the mother's behalf without regard to the stage of her pregnancy and other interests involved violate the Due Process Clause of the Fourteenth Amendment, which protects against state action the right to privacy, including a woman's qualified right to terminate her pregnancy. Though the State cannot override that right, it has legitimate interests in protecting both the pregnant woman's health and the potentiality of human life, each of which interests grows and reaches a "compelling" point at various stages of the woman's approach to term. Pp. 147–164.

(a) For the stage prior to approximately the end of the first trimester, the abortion decision and its effectuation must be left to the medical judgment of the pregnant woman's attending physician. Pp. 163, 164.

(b) For the stage subsequent to approximately the end of the first trimester, the State, in promoting its interest in the health of the mother, may, if it chooses, regulate the abortion procedure in ways that are reasonably related to maternal health. Pp. 163, 164.

(c) For the stage subsequent to viability the State, in promoting its interest in the potentiality of human life, may, if it chooses, regulate, and even proscribe, abortion except where necessary, in appropriate medical judgment, for the preservation of the life or health of the mother. Pp. 163–164; 165.

4. The State may define the term "physician" to mean only a physician currently licensed by the State, and may proscribe any abortion by a person who is not a physician as so defined. P. 165.

5. It is unnecessary to decide the injunctive relief issue since the Texas authorities will doubtless fully recognize the Court's ruling [410 U.S. 113, 115] that the Texas criminal abortion statutes are unconstitutional. P. 166.

314 F. Supp. 1217, affirmed in part and reversed in part.

BLACKMUN, J., delivered the opinion of the Court, in which BURGER, C. J., and DOUGLAS, BRENNAN, STEWART, MARSHALL, and POWELL, JJ., joined. BURGER, C. J., post, p. 207, DOUGLAS, J., post, p. 209, and STEWART, J., post, p. 167, filed concurring opinions. WHITE, J., filed a dissenting opinion, in which REHNQUIST, J., joined, post, p. 221. REHNQUIST, J., filed a dissenting opinion, post, p. 171.

Sarah Weddington reargued the cause for appellants. With her on the briefs were Roy Lucas, Fred Bruner, Roy L. Merrill, Jr., and Norman Dorsen.

Robert C. Flowers, Assistant Attorney General of Texas, argued the cause for appellee on the reargument. Jay Floyd, Assistant Attorney General, argued the cause for appellee on the original argument. With them on the brief were Crawford C. Martin, Attorney General, Nola White, First Assistant Attorney General, Alfred Walker, Executive Assistant Attorney General, Henry Wade, and John B. Tolle.* [410 U.S. 113, 116]

MR. JUSTICE BLACKMUN delivered the opinion of the Court.

This Texas federal appeal and its Georgia companion, *Doe v. Bolton*, post, p. 179, present constitutional challenges to state criminal abortion legislation. The Texas statutes under attack here are typical of those that have been in effect in many States for approximately a century. The Georgia statutes, in contrast, have a modern cast and are a legislative product that, to an extent at least, obviously reflects the influences of recent attitudinal change, of advancing medical knowledge and techniques, and of new thinking about an old issue.

We forthwith acknowledge our awareness of the sensitive and emotional nature of the abortion controversy, of the vigorous opposing views, even among physicians, and of the deep and seemingly absolute convictions that the subject inspires. One's philosophy, one's experiences, one's exposure to the raw edges of human existence, one's religious training, one's attitudes toward life and family and their values, and the moral standards one establishes and seeks to observe, are all likely to influence and to color one's thinking and conclusions about abortion.

In addition, population growth, pollution, poverty, and racial overtones tend to complicate and not to simplify the problem.

Our task, of course, is to resolve the issue by constitutional measurement, free of emotion and of predilection. We seek earnestly to do this, and, because we do, we [410 U.S. 113, 117] have inquired

---

*Briefs of *amici curiae* were filed by Gary K. Nelson, Attorney General of Arizona; Robert K. Killian, Attorney General of Connecticut; Ed W. Hancock, Attorney General of Kentucky; Clarence A. H. Meyer, Attorney General of Nebraska; and Vernon B. Romney, Attorney General of Utah; by Joseph P. Witherspoon, Jr., for the Association of Texas Diocesan Attorneys; by Charles E. Rice for Americans United for Life; by Eugene J. McMahon for Women for the Unborn et al.; by Carol Ryan for the American College of Obstetricians and Gynecologists et al.; by Dennis J. Horan, Jerome A. Frazel, Jr., Thomas M. Crisham, and Dolores V. Horan for Certain Physicians, Professors and Fellows of the American College of Obstetrics and Gynecology; by Harriet F. Pilpel, Nancy F. Wechsler, and Frederic S. Nathan for Planned Parenthood Federation of America, Inc. et al.; by Alan F. Charles for the National Legal Program on Health Problems of the Poor et al.; by Marttie L. Thompson for State Communities Aid Assn.; by [410 U.S. 113, 116] Alfred L. Scanlan, Martin J. Flynn, and Robert M. Byrn for the National Right to Life Committee; by Helen L. Buttenwieser for the American Ethical Union et al.; by Norma G. Zarky for the American Association of University Women et al.; by Nancy Stearns for New Women Lawyers et al.; by the California Committee to Legalize Abortion et al.; and by Robert E. Dunne for Robert L. Sassone.

(Continues)

into, and in this opinion place some emphasis upon, medical and medical–legal history and what that history reveals about man's attitudes toward the abortion procedure over the centuries. We bear in mind, too, Mr. Justice Holmes' admonition in his now-vindicated dissent in *Lochner v. New York*, 198 U.S. 45, 76 (1905):

"[The Constitution] is made for people of fundamentally differing views, and the accident of our finding certain opinions natural and familiar or novel and even shocking ought not to conclude our judgment upon the question whether statutes embodying them conflict with the Constitution of the United States."

I

The Texas statutes that concern us here are Arts. 1191–1194 and 1196 of the State's Penal Code.[1] These make it a crime to "procure an abortion," as therein [410 U.S. 113, 118] defined, or to attempt one, except with respect to "an abortion procured or attempted by medical advice for the purpose of saving the life of the mother." Similar statutes are in existence in a majority of the States.[2] [410 U.S. 113, 119]

Texas first enacted a criminal abortion statute in 1854. Texas Laws 1854, c. 49, 1, set forth in[3] H. Gammel, *Laws of Texas*, 1502 (1898). This was soon modified into language that has remained substantially unchanged to the present time. See Texas Penal Code of 1857, c. 7, Arts. 531–536; G. Paschal, *Laws of Texas*, Arts. 2192–2197 (1866); Texas Rev. Stat., c. 8, Arts. 536–541 (1879); Texas Rev. Crim. Stat., Arts. 1071–1076 (1911). The final article in each of these compilations provided the same exception, as does the present Article 1196, for an abortion by "medical advice for the purpose of saving the life of the mother."[3] [410 U.S. 113, 120].

II

Jane Roe,[4] a single woman who was residing in Dallas County, Texas, instituted this federal action in March 1970 against the District Attorney of the county. She sought a declaratory judgment that the Texas criminal abortion statutes were unconstitutional on their face, and an injunction restraining the defendant from enforcing the statutes.

Roe alleged that she was unmarried and pregnant; that she wished to terminate her pregnancy by an abortion "performed by a competent, licensed physician, under safe, clinical conditions"; that she was unable to get a "legal" abortion in Texas because her life did not appear to be threatened by the continuation of her pregnancy; and that she could not afford to travel to another jurisdiction in order to secure a legal abortion under safe conditions. She claimed that the Texas statutes were unconstitutionally vague and that they abridged her right of personal privacy, protected by the First, Fourth, Fifth, Ninth, and Fourteenth Amendments. By an amendment to her complaint Roe purported to sue "on behalf of herself and all other women" similarly situated.

James Hubert Hallford, a licensed physician, sought and was granted leave to intervene in Roe's action. In his complaint he alleged that he had been arrested previously for violations of the Texas abortion statutes and [410 U.S. 113, 121] that two such prosecutions were pending against him. He described conditions of patients who came to him seeking abortions, and he claimed that for many cases he, as a physician, was unable to determine whether they fell within or outside the exception recognized by Article 1196. He alleged that, as a consequence, the statutes were vague and uncertain, in violation of the Fourteenth Amendment, and that they violated his own and his patients' rights to privacy in the doctor–patient relationship and his own right to practice medicine, rights he claimed were guaranteed by the First, Fourth, Fifth, Ninth, and Fourteenth Amendments.

John and Mary Doe,[5] a married couple, filed a companion complaint to that of Roe. They also named the District Attorney as defendant, claimed like constitutional deprivations, and sought declaratory and injunctive relief. The Does alleged that they were a childless couple; that Mrs. Doe was suffering from a "neural–chemical" disorder; that her physician had "advised her to avoid pregnancy until such time as her condition has materially improved" (although a pregnancy at the present time would not present "a serious risk" to her life); that, pursuant to medical advice, she had discontinued use of birth control pills; and that if she should become pregnant, she would want to terminate the pregnancy by an abortion performed by a competent, licensed physician under safe, clinical conditions. By an amendment to their complaint, the Does purported to sue "on behalf of themselves and all couples similarly situated."

The two actions were consolidated and heard together by a duly convened three-judge district court. The suits thus presented the situations of the pregnant single woman, the childless couple, with the wife not pregnant, [410 U.S. 113, 122] and the licensed practicing physician, all joining in the attack on the Texas criminal abortion statutes. Upon the filing of affidavits, motions were made for dismissal and for summary judgment. The court held that Roe and members of her class, and Dr. Hallford, had standing to sue and presented justiciable controversies, but that the Does had failed to allege facts sufficient to state a present controversy and did not have standing. It concluded that, with respect to the requests for a declaratory judgment, abstention was not warranted. On the merits, the District Court held that the "fundamental right of single women and married persons to choose whether to have children is protected by the Ninth Amendment, through the Fourteenth Amendment," and that the Texas criminal abortion statutes were void on their face because they were both unconstitutionally vague and constituted an overbroad infringement of the plaintiffs' Ninth Amendment rights. The court then held that abstention was warranted with respect to the requests for an injunction. It therefore dismissed the Does' complaint, declared the abortion statutes void, and dismissed the application for injunctive relief. 314 F. Supp. 1217, 1225 (ND Tex. 1970).

The plaintiffs Roe and Doe and the intervenor Hallford, pursuant to 28 U.S.C. 1253, have appealed to this Court from that part of the District Court's judgment denying the injunction. The defendant District Attorney has purported to cross-appeal, pursuant to the same statute, from the court's grant of declaratory relief to Roe and Hallford. Both sides also have taken protective appeals to the United States Court of Appeals for the Fifth Circuit. That court ordered the appeals held in abeyance pending decision here. We postponed decision on jurisdiction to the hearing on the merits. 402 U.S. 941 (1971). [410 U.S. 113, 123].

III

It might have been preferable if the defendant, pursuant to our Rule 20, had presented to us a petition for *certiorari* before judgment in the Court of Appeals with respect to the granting of the plaintiffs' prayer for declaratory relief. Our decisions in *Mitchell v. Donovan*, 398 U.S. 427 (1970) and *Gunn v. University Committee*, 399 U.S. 383 (1970), are to the effect that 1253 does not authorize an appeal to this Court from the grant or denial of declaratory relief alone. We conclude, nevertheless, that those decisions do not foreclose our review of both the injunctive and the declaratory aspects of a case of this kind when it is properly here, as this one is, on appeal under 1253 from specific denial of injunctive relief, and the arguments as to both aspects are necessarily identical. See *Carter v. Jury Comm'n*, 396 U.S. 320 (1970); *Florida Lime Growers v. Jacobsen*, 362 U.S. 73, 80–81 (1960). It would be destructive of time and energy for all concerned were we to rule otherwise. Cf. *Doe v. Bolton*, post, p. 179.

IV

We are next confronted with issues of justiciability, standing, and abstention. Have Roe and the Does established that "personal stake in the outcome of the controversy," *Baker v. Carr*, 369 U.S. 186, 204 (1962), that insures that "the dispute sought to be adjudicated will be presented in an adversary context and in a form historically viewed as capable of judicial resolution," *Flast v. Cohen*, 392 U.S. 83, 101 (1968), and *Sierra Club v. Morton*, 405 U.S. 727, 732 (1972)? And what effect did the pendency of criminal abortion charges against Dr. Hallford in state court have upon the propriety of the federal court's granting relief to him as a plaintiff–intervenor? [410 U.S. 113, 124].

A. Jane Roe. Despite the use of the pseudonym, no suggestion is made that Roe is a fictitious person. For purposes of her case, we accept as true, and as established, her existence; her pregnant state, as of the inception of her suit in March 1970 and as late as May 21 of that year when she filed an alias affidavit with the District Court; and her inability to obtain a legal abortion in Texas.

Viewing Roe's case as of the time of its filing and thereafter until as late as May, there can be little dispute that it then presented a case or controversy and that, wholly apart from the class aspects, she, as a pregnant single woman thwarted by the Texas criminal abortion laws, had standing to challenge those statutes. *Abele v. Markle*, 452 F.2d 1121, 1125 (CA2 1971); *Crossen v. Breckenridge*, 446 F.2d 833, 838–839 (CA6 1971); *Poe v. Menghini*, 339 F. Supp. 986, 990–991 (Kan. 1972). See *Truax v. Raich*, 239 U.S. 33 (1915). Indeed, we do not read the appellee's brief as really asserting anything to the contrary. The "logical nexus between the status asserted and the claim sought to be adjudicated," *Flast v. Cohen*,

(Continues)

392 U.S., at 102 , and the necessary degree of contentiousness, *Golden v. Zwickler*, 394 U.S. 103 (1969), are both present.

The appellee notes, however, that the record does not disclose that Roe was pregnant at the time of the District Court hearing on May 22, 1970,[6] or on the following June 17 when the court's opinion and judgment were filed. And he suggests that Roe's case must now be moot because she and all other members of her class are no longer subject to any 1970 pregnancy. [410 U.S. 113, 125].

The usual rule in federal cases is that an actual controversy must exist at stages of appellate or *certiorari* review, and not simply at the date the action is initiated. *United States v. Munsingwear, Inc.*, 340 U.S. 36 (1950); *Golden v. Zwickler, supra*; *SEC v. Medical Committee for Human Rights*, 404 U.S. 403 (1972).

But when, as here, pregnancy is a significant fact in the litigation, the normal 266-day human gestation period is so short that the pregnancy will come to term before the usual appellate process is complete. If that termination makes a case moot, pregnancy litigation seldom will survive much beyond the trial stage, and appellate review will be effectively denied. Our law should not be that rigid. Pregnancy often comes more than once to the same woman, and in the general population, if man is to survive, it will always be with us. Pregnancy provides a classic justification for a conclusion of nonmootness. It truly could be "capable of repetition, yet evading review." *Southern Pacific Terminal Co. v. ICC*, 219 U.S. 498, 515 (1911). See *Moore v. Ogilvie*, 394 U.S. 814, 816 (1969); *Carroll v. Princess Anne*, 393 U.S. 175, 178–179 (1968); *United States v. W. T. Grant Co.*, 345 U.S. 629, 632–633 (1953).

We, therefore, agree with the District Court that Jane Roe had standing to undertake this litigation, that she presented a justiciable controversy, and that the termination of her 1970 pregnancy has not rendered her case moot.

B. Dr. Hallford. The doctor's position is different. He entered Roe's litigation as a plaintiff–intervenor, alleging in his complaint that he:

"[I]n the past has been arrested for violating the Texas Abortion Laws and at the present time stands charged by indictment with violating said laws in the Criminal District Court of Dallas County, Texas to-wit: (1) *The State of Texas v.* [410 U.S. 113, 126] *James H. Hallford*, No. C-69-5307-IH, and (2) *The State of Texas v. James H. Hallford*, No. C-69-2524-H. In both cases the defendant is charged with abortion. . . ."

In his application for leave to intervene, the doctor made like representations as to the abortion charges pending in the state court. These representations were also repeated in the affidavit he executed and filed in support of his motion for summary judgment.

Dr. Hallford is, therefore, in the position of seeking, in a federal court, declaratory and injunctive relief with respect to the same statutes under which he stands charged in criminal prosecutions simultaneously pending in state court. Although he stated that he has been arrested in the past for violating the State's abortion laws, he makes no allegation of any substantial and immediate threat to any federally protected right that cannot be asserted in his defense against the state prosecutions. Neither is there any allegation of harassment or bad-faith prosecution. In order to escape the rule articulated in the cases cited in the next paragraph of this opinion that, absent harassment and bad faith, a defendant in a pending state criminal case cannot affirmatively challenge in federal court the statutes under which the State is prosecuting him, Dr. Hallford seeks to distinguish his status as a present state defendant from his status as a "potential future defendant" and to assert only the latter for standing purposes here.

We see no merit in that distinction. Our decision in *Samuels v. Mackell*, 401 U.S. 66 (1971), compels the conclusion that the District Court erred when it granted declaratory relief to Dr. Hallford instead of refraining from so doing. The court, of course, was correct in refusing to grant injunctive relief to the doctor. The reasons supportive of that action, however, are those expressed in *Samuels v. Mackell, supra*, and in *Younger v. Harris* [410 U.S. 113, 127], 401 U.S. 37 (1971); *Boyle v. Landry*, 401 U.S. 77 (1971); *Perez v. Ledesma*, 401 U.S. 82 (1971); and *Byrne v. Karalexis*, 401 U.S. 216 (1971). See also *Dombrowski v. Pfister*, 380 U.S. 479 (1965). We note, in passing, that Younger and its companion cases were decided after the three-judge District Court decision in this case.

Dr. Hallford's complaint in intervention, therefore, is to be dismissed.[7] He is remitted to his defenses in the state criminal proceedings against him. We reverse the judgment of the District Court insofar as it granted Dr. Hallford relief and failed to dismiss his complaint in intervention.

C. The Does. In view of our ruling as to Roe's standing in her case, the issue of the Does' standing in their case has little significance. The claims they assert are essentially the same as those of Roe, and they attack the same statutes. Nevertheless, we briefly note the Does' posture.

Their pleadings present them as a childless married couple, the woman not being pregnant, who have no desire to have children at this time because of their having received medical advice that Mrs. Doe should avoid pregnancy, and for "other highly personal reasons." But they "fear . . . they may face the prospect of becoming [410 U.S. 113, 128] parents." And if pregnancy ensues, they "would want to terminate" it by an abortion. They assert an inability to obtain an abortion legally in Texas and, consequently, the prospect of obtaining an illegal abortion there or of going outside Texas to some place where the procedure could be obtained legally and competently.

We thus have as plaintiffs a married couple who have, as their asserted immediate and present injury, only an alleged "detrimental effect upon [their] marital happiness" because they are forced to "the choice of refraining from normal sexual relations or of endangering Mary Doe's health through a possible pregnancy." Their claim is that sometime in the future Mrs. Doe might become pregnant because of possible failure of contraceptive measures, and at that time in the future she might want an abortion that might then be illegal under the Texas statutes.

This very phrasing of the Does' position reveals its speculative character. Their alleged injury rests on possible future contraceptive failure, possible future pregnancy, possible future unpreparedness for parenthood, and possible future impairment of health. Any one or more of these several possibilities may not take place and all may not combine. In the Does' estimation, these possibilities might have some real or imagined impact upon their marital happiness. But we are not prepared to say that the bare allegation of so indirect an injury is sufficient to present an actual case or controversy. *Younger v. Harris*, 401 U.S., at 41–42; *Golden v. Zwickler*, 394 U.S., at 109–110; *Abele v. Markle*, 452 F.2d, at 1124–1125; *Crossen v. Breckenridge*, 446 F.2d, at 839. The Does' claim falls far short of those resolved otherwise in the cases that the Does urge upon us, namely, *Investment Co. Institute v. Camp*, 401 U.S. 617 (1971); *Data Processing Service v. Camp*, 397 U.S. 150 (1970); [410 U.S. 113, 129] and *Epperson v. Arkansas*, 393 U.S. 97 (1968). See also *Truax v. Raich*, 239 U.S. 33 (1915).

The Does therefore are not appropriate plaintiffs in this litigation. Their complaint was properly dismissed by the District Court, and we affirm that dismissal.

V

The principal thrust of appellant's attack on the Texas statutes is that they improperly invade a right, said to be possessed by the pregnant woman, to choose to terminate her pregnancy. Appellant would discover this right in the concept of personal "liberty" embodied in the Fourteenth Amendment's Due Process Clause; or in personal, marital, familial, and sexual privacy said to be protected by the Bill of Rights or its penumbras, see *Griswold v. Connecticut*, 381 U.S. 479 (1965); *Eisenstadt v. Baird*, 405 U.S. 438 (1972); *id.*, at 460 (WHITE, J., concurring in result); or among those rights reserved to the people by the Ninth Amendment, *Griswold v. Connecticut*, 381 U.S., at 486 (Goldberg, J., concurring). Before addressing this claim, we feel it desirable briefly to survey, in several aspects, the history of abortion, for such insight as that history may afford us, and then to examine the state purposes and interests behind the criminal abortion laws.

VI

It perhaps is not generally appreciated that the restrictive criminal abortion laws in effect in a majority of States today are of relatively recent vintage. Those laws, generally proscribing abortion or its attempt at any time during pregnancy except when necessary to preserve the pregnant woman's life, are not of ancient or even of common-law origin. Instead, they derive from statutory changes effected, for the most part, in the latter half of the 19th century. [410 U.S. 113, 130].

1. Ancient attitudes. These are not capable of precise determination. We are told that at the time of the Persian Empire abortifacients were known and that criminal abortions were severely punished.[8] We are also told, however, that abortion was practiced in Greek times as well as in the Roman Era,[9] and that "it was resorted to without scruple."[10] The Ephesian, Soranos, often described as the greatest of the ancient gynecologists, appears to have been generally opposed to Rome's prevailing free-abortion practices. He found it necessary to think first of the life of the mother, and he resorted to abortion when, upon this standard, he felt the procedure advisable.[11] Greek and Roman law afforded little protection to the unborn. If abortion was prosecuted in some places, it seems to have been based on a concept of a violation of the father's right to his offspring. Ancient religion did not bar abortion.[12]

(Continues)

2. The Hippocratic Oath. What then of the famous Oath that has stood so long as the ethical guide of the medical profession and that bears the name of the great Greek (460[?]–377[?] BC), who has been described [410 U.S. 113, 131] as the Father of Medicine, the "wisest and the greatest practitioner of his art," and the "most important and most complete medical personality of antiquity," who dominated the medical schools of his time, and who typified the sum of the medical knowledge of the past?[13] The Oath varies somewhat according to the particular translation, but in any translation the content is clear: "I will give no deadly medicine to anyone if asked, nor suggest any such counsel; and in like manner I will not give to a woman a pessary to produce abortion,"[14] or "I will neither give a deadly drug to anybody if asked for it, nor will I make a suggestion to this effect. Similarly, I will not give to a woman an abortive remedy."[15]

Although the Oath is not mentioned in any of the principal briefs in this case or in *Doe v. Bolton*, post, p. 179, it represents the apex of the development of strict ethical concepts in medicine, and its influence endures to this day. Why did not the authority of Hippocrates dissuade abortion practice in his time and that of Rome? The late Dr. Edelstein provides us with a theory[16]: The Oath was not uncontested even in Hippocrates' day; only the Pythagorean school of philosophers frowned upon the related act of suicide. Most Greek thinkers, on the other hand, commended abortion, at least prior to viability. See Plato, *Republic*, V, 461; Aristotle, *Politics*, VII, 1335b 25. For the Pythagoreans, however, it was a matter of dogma. For them the embryo was animate from the moment of conception, and abortion meant destruction of a living being. The abortion clause of the Oath, therefore, "echoes Pythagorean doctrines," [410 U.S. 113, 132] and "[i]n no other stratum of Greek opinion were such views held or proposed in the same spirit of uncompromising austerity."[17]

Dr. Edelstein then concludes that the Oath originated in a group representing only a small segment of Greek opinion and that it certainly was not accepted by all ancient physicians. He points out that medical writings down to Galen (AD 130–200) "give evidence of the violation of almost every one of its injunctions."[18] But with the end of antiquity a decided change took place. Resistance against suicide and against abortion became common. The Oath came to be popular. The emerging teachings of Christianity were in agreement with the Pythagorean ethic. The Oath "became the nucleus of all medical ethics" and "was applauded as the embodiment of truth." Thus, suggests Dr. Edelstein, it is "a Pythagorean manifesto and not the expression of an absolute standard of medical conduct."[19]

This, it seems to us, is a satisfactory and acceptable explanation of the Hippocratic Oath's apparent rigidity. It enables us to understand, in historical context, a long-accepted and revered statement of medical ethics.

3. The common law. It is undisputed that at common law, abortion performed before "quickening"—the first recognizable movement of the fetus in utero, appearing usually from the 16th to the 18th week of pregnancy[20]—was not an indictable offense.[21] The absence [410 U.S. 113, 133] of a common-law crime for pre-quickening abortion appears to have developed from a confluence of earlier philosophical, theological, and civil and canon law concepts of when life begins. These disciplines variously approached the question in terms of the point at which the embryo or fetus became "formed" or recognizably human, or in terms of when a "person" came into being, that is, infused with a "soul" or "animated." A loose consensus evolved in early English law that these events occurred at some point between conception and live birth.[22] This was "mediate animation." Although [410 U.S. 113, 134] Christian theology and the canon law came to fix the point of animation at 40 days for a male and 80 days for a female, a view that persisted until the 19th Century, there was otherwise little agreement about the precise time of formation or animation. There was agreement, however, that prior to this point the fetus was to be regarded as part of the mother, and its destruction, therefore, was not homicide. Due to continued uncertainty about the precise time when animation occurred, to the lack of any empirical basis for the 40–80-day view, and perhaps to Aquinas' definition of movement as one of the two first principles of life, Bracton focused upon quickening as the critical point. The significance of quickening was echoed by later common-law scholars and found its way into the received common law in this country.

Whether abortion of a quick fetus was a felony at common law, or even a lesser crime, is still disputed. Bracton, writing early in the 13th Century, thought it homicide.[23] But the later and predominant view, following the great common-law scholars, has been that it was, at most, a lesser offense. In a frequently cited [410 U.S. 113, 135] passage, Coke took the position that abortion of a woman "quick with childe" is "a great misprision, and no murder."[24] Blackstone followed, saying that while abortion after quickening had once been considered manslaughter (though not murder), "modern law" took a less severe view.[25] A recent review of the common-law precedents argues, however, that those precedents contradict Coke and that even post-quickening abortion was never established as a common-law crime.[26] This is of some importance because while most American courts ruled, in holding or dictum, that abortion of an unquickened fetus was not criminal under their received common law,[27] others followed Coke in stating that abortion [410 U.S. 113, 136] of a quick fetus was a "misprision," a term they translated to mean "misdemeanor."[28] That their reliance on Coke on this aspect of the law was uncritical and, apparently in all the reported cases, dictum (due probably to the paucity of common-law prosecutions for post-quickening abortion), makes it now appear doubtful that abortion was ever firmly established as a common-law crime even with respect to the destruction of a quick fetus.

4. The English statutory law. England's first criminal abortion statute, Lord Ellenborough's Act, 43 Geo. 3, c. 58, came in 1803. It made abortion of a quick fetus, 1, a capital crime, but in 2 it provided lesser penalties for the felony of abortion before quickening, and thus preserved the "quickening" distinction. This contrast was continued in the general revision of 1828, 9 Geo. 4, c. 31, 13. It disappeared, however, together with the death penalty, in 1837, 7 Will. 4 & 1 Vict., c. 85. 6, and did not reappear in the Offenses Against the Person Act of 1861, 24 & 25 Vict., c. 100, 59, that formed the core of English anti-abortion law until the liberalizing reforms of 1967. In 1929, the Infant Life (Preservation) Act, 19 & 20 Geo. 5, c. 34, came into being. Its emphasis was upon the destruction of "the life of a child capable of being born alive." It made a willful act performed with the necessary intent a felony. It contained a proviso that one was not to be [410 U.S. 113, 137] found guilty of the offense "unless it is proved that the act which caused the death of the child was not done in good faith for the purpose only of preserving the life of the mother."

A seemingly notable development in the English law was the case of *Rex v. Bourne*, 1939. 1 K. B. 687. This case apparently answered in the affirmative the question whether an abortion necessary to preserve the life of the pregnant woman was excepted from the criminal penalties of the 1861 Act. In his instructions to the jury, Judge Macnaghten referred to the 1929 Act, and observed that that Act related to "the case where a child is killed by a willful act at the time when it is being delivered in the ordinary course of nature." *Id.*, at 691. He concluded that the 1861 Act's use of the word "unlawfully," imported the same meaning expressed by the specific proviso in the 1929 Act, even though there was no mention of preserving the mother's life in the 1861 Act. He then construed the phrase "preserving the life of the mother" broadly, that is, "in a reasonable sense," to include a serious and permanent threat to the mother's health, and instructed the jury to acquit Dr. Bourne if it found he had acted in a good-faith belief that the abortion was necessary for this purpose. *Id.*, at 693–694. The jury did acquit.

Recently, Parliament enacted a new abortion law. This is the Abortion Act of 1967, 15 & 16 Eliz. 2, c. 87. The Act permits a licensed physician to perform an abortion where two other licensed physicians agree (a) "that the continuance of the pregnancy would involve risk to the life of the pregnant woman, or of injury to the physical or mental health of the pregnant woman or any existing children of her family, greater than if the pregnancy were terminated," or (b) "that there is a substantial risk that if the child were born it would suffer from such physical or mental abnormalities as [410 U.S. 113, 138] to be seriously handicapped." The Act also provides that, in making this determination, "account may be taken of the pregnant woman's actual or reasonably foreseeable environment." It also permits a physician, without the concurrence of others, to terminate a pregnancy where he is of the good-faith opinion that the abortion "is immediately necessary to save the life or to prevent grave permanent injury to the physical or mental health of the pregnant woman."

5. The American law. In this country, the law in effect in all but a few States until mid-19th century was the pre-existing English common law. Connecticut, the first State to enact abortion legislation, adopted in 1821 that part of Lord Ellenborough's Act that related to a woman "quick with child."[29] The death penalty was not imposed. Abortion before quickening was made a crime in that State only in 1860.[30] In 1828, New York enacted legislation[31] that, in two respects, was to serve as a model for early anti-abortion statutes. First, while barring destruction of an unquickened fetus as well as a quick fetus, it made the former only a misdemeanor, but the latter second-degree manslaughter. Second, it incorporated a concept of therapeutic abortion by providing that an abortion was excused if it "shall have been necessary to preserve the life of such mother, or shall have been advised by two physicians to be necessary for such purpose." By 1840, when Texas had received the common law,[32] only eight American States [410 U.S. 113, 139] had statutes dealing with abortion.[33] It was not until after the War Between the States that legislation began generally to replace the common law. Most of these initial statutes dealt severely with abortion after quickening but were lenient with it before quickening. Most punished attempts equally with completed abortions.

(Continues)

(Continued)

While many statutes included the exception for an abortion thought by one or more physicians to be necessary to save the mother's life, that provision soon disappeared and the typical law required that the procedure actually be necessary for that purpose.

Gradually, in the middle and late 19th Century the quickening distinction disappeared from the statutory law of most States and the degree of the offense and the penalties were increased. By the end of the 1950s, a large majority of the jurisdictions banned abortion, however and whenever performed, unless done to save or preserve the life of the mother.[34] The exceptions, Alabama and the District of Columbia, permitted abortion to preserve the mother's health.[35] Three States permitted abortions that were not "unlawfully" performed or that were not "without lawful justification," leaving interpretation of those standards to the courts.[36] In [410 U.S. 113, 140] the past several years, however, a trend toward liberalization of abortion statutes has resulted in adoption, by about one-third of the States, of less stringent laws, most of them patterned after the ALI Model Penal Code, 230.3,[37] set forth as Appendix B to the opinion in *Doe v. Bolton, post,* p. 205.

It is thus apparent that at common law, at the time of the adoption of our Constitution, and throughout the major portion of the 19th Century, abortion was viewed with less disfavor than under most American statutes currently in effect. Phrasing it another way, a woman enjoyed a substantially broader right to terminate a pregnancy than she does in most States today. At least with respect to the early stage of pregnancy, and very possibly without such a limitation, the opportunity [410 U.S. 113, 141] to make this choice was present in this country well into the 19th century. Even later, the law continued for some time to treat less punitively an abortion procured in early pregnancy.

6. The position of the American Medical Association. The anti-abortion mood prevalent in this country in the late 19th Century was shared by the medical profession. Indeed, the attitude of the profession may have played a significant role in the enactment of stringent criminal abortion legislation during that period.

An AMA Committee on Criminal Abortion was appointed in May 1857. It presented its report, 12 *Trans. of the Am. Med. Assn.,* 73–78 (1859), to the Twelfth Annual Meeting. That report observed that the Committee had been appointed to investigate criminal abortion "with a view to its general suppression." It deplored abortion and its frequency and it listed three causes of "this general demoralization":

> "The first of these causes is a widespread popular ignorance of the true character of the crime—a belief, even among mothers themselves, that the foetus is not alive till after the period of quickening."
>
> "The second of the agents alluded to is the fact that the profession themselves are frequently supposed careless of foetal life. . . ."
>
> "The third reason of the frightful extent of this crime is found in the grave defects of our laws, both common and statute, as regards the independent and actual existence of the child before birth, as a living being. These errors, which are sufficient in most instances to prevent conviction, are based, and only based, upon mistaken and exploded medical dogmas. With strange inconsistency, the law fully acknowledges the foetus in utero and its inherent rights, for civil purposes; while personally and as criminally affected, it fails to recognize it, [410 U.S. 113, 142] and to its life as yet denies all protection." *Id.,* at 75–76.

The Committee then offered, and the Association adopted, resolutions protesting "against such unwarrantable destruction of human life," calling upon state legislatures to revise their abortion laws, and requesting the cooperation of state medical societies "in pressing the subject." *Id.,* at 28, 78.

In 1871 a long and vivid report was submitted by the Committee on Criminal Abortion. It ended with the observation, "We had to deal with human life. In a matter of less importance we could entertain no compromise. An honest judge on the bench would call things by their proper names. We could do no less." 22 *Trans. of the Am. Med. Assn.,* 258 (1871). It proffered resolutions, adopted by the Association, *id.,* at 38–39, recommending, among other things, that it "be unlawful and unprofessional for any physician to induce abortion or premature labor, without the concurrent opinion of at least one respectable consulting physician, and then always with a view to the safety of the child—if that be possible," and calling "the attention of the clergy of all denominations to the perverted views of morality entertained by a large class of females-aye, and men also, on this important question."

Except for periodic condemnation of the criminal abortionist, no further formal AMA action took place until 1967. In that year, the Committee on Human Reproduction urged the adoption of a stated policy of opposition to induced abortion, except when there is "documented medical evidence" of a threat to the health or life of the mother, or that the child "may be born with incapacitating physical deformity or mental deficiency," or that a pregnancy "resulting from legally established statutory or forcible rape or incest may constitute a threat to the mental or physical health of the [410 U.S. 113, 143] patient," two other physicians "chosen because of their recognized professional competence have examined the patient and have concurred in writing," and the procedure "is performed in a hospital accredited by the Joint Commission on Accreditation of Hospitals." The providing of medical information by physicians to state legislatures in their consideration of legislation regarding therapeutic abortion was "to be considered consistent with the principles of ethics of the American Medical Association." This recommendation was adopted by the House of Delegates. *Proceedings of the AMA House of Delegates 40–51* (June 1967).

In 1970, after the introduction of a variety of proposed resolutions, and of a report from its Board of Trustees, a reference committee noted "polarization of the medical profession on this controversial issue"; division among those who had testified; a difference of opinion among AMA councils and committees; "the remarkable shift in testimony" in 6 months, felt to be influenced "by the rapid changes in state laws and by the judicial decisions which tend to make abortion more freely available;" and a feeling "that this trend will continue." On June 25, 1970, the House of Delegates adopted preambles and most of the resolutions proposed by the reference committee. The preambles emphasized "the best interests of the patient," "sound clinical judgment," and "informed patient consent," in contrast to "mere acquiescence to the patient's demand." The resolutions asserted that abortion is a medical procedure that should be performed by a licensed physician in an accredited hospital only after consultation with two other physicians and in conformity with state law, and that no party to the procedure should be required to violate personally held moral principles.[38] *Proceedings* [410 U.S. 113, 144] *of the AMA House of Delegates* 220 (June 1970). The AMA Judicial Council rendered a complementary opinion.[39]

7. The position of the American Public Health Association. In October 1970, the Executive Board of the APHA adopted Standards for Abortion Services. These were five in number:

   "a. Rapid and simple abortion referral must be readily available through state and local public [410 U.S. 113, 145] health departments, medical societies, or other nonprofit organizations.

   "b. An important function of counselling should be to simplify and expedite the provision of abortion services; it should not delay the obtaining of these services.

   "c. Psychiatric consultation should not be mandatory. As in the case of other specialized medical services, psychiatric consultation should be sought for definite indications and not on a routine basis.

   "d. A wide range of individuals from appropriately trained, sympathetic volunteers to highly skilled physicians may qualify as abortion counselors.

   "e. Contraception and/or sterilization should be discussed with each abortion patient." Recommended Standards for Abortion Services, 61 *Am. J. Pub. Health*, 396 (1971).

Among factors pertinent to life and health risks associated with abortion were three that "are recognized as important":

   "a. the skill of the physician,

   "b. the environment in which the abortion is performed, and above all

   "c. the duration of pregnancy, as determined by uterine size and confirmed by menstrual history." *Id.*, at 397.

It was said that "a well-equipped hospital" offers more protection "to cope with unforeseen difficulties than an office or clinic without such resources. . . . The factor of gestational age is of overriding importance." Thus, it was recommended that abortions in the second trimester and early abortions in the presence of existing medical complications be performed in hospitals as inpatient procedures. For pregnancies in the first trimester, [410 U.S. 113, 146] abortion in the hospital with or without overnight stay "is probably the safest practice." An abortion in an extramural facility, however, is an acceptable alternative "provided arrangements exist in advance to admit patients promptly if unforeseen complications develop." Standards for an abortion facility were listed. It was said that at present abortions should be performed by physicians or osteopaths who are licensed to practice and who have "adequate training." *Id.*, at 398.

8. The position of the American Bar Association. At its meeting in February 1972 the ABA House of Delegates approved, with 17 opposing votes, the Uniform Abortion Act that had been drafted and approved the preceding August by the Conference of Commissioners on Uniform State Laws. 58 A. B. A. J. 380 (1972). We set forth the Act in full in the margin.[40] The [410 U.S. 113, 147] Conference has appended an enlightening Prefatory Note.[41]

(Continues)

VII

Three reasons have been advanced to explain historically the enactment of criminal abortion laws in the 19th century and to justify their continued existence. [410 U.S. 113, 148].

It has been argued occasionally that these laws were the product of a Victorian social concern to discourage illicit sexual conduct. Texas, however, does not advance this justification in the present case, and it appears that no court or commentator has taken the argument seriously.[42] The appellants and *amici* contend, moreover, that this is not a proper state purpose at all and suggest that, if it were, the Texas statutes are overbroad in protecting it since the law fails to distinguish between married and unwed mothers.

A second reason is concerned with abortion as a medical procedure. When most criminal abortion laws were first enacted, the procedure was a hazardous one for the woman.[43] This was particularly true prior to the [410 U.S. 113, 149] development of antisepsis. Antiseptic techniques, of course, were based on discoveries by Lister, Pasteur, and others first announced in 1867, but were not generally accepted and employed until about the turn of the century. Abortion mortality was high. Even after 1900, and perhaps until as late as the development of antibiotics in the 1940s, standard modern techniques such as dilation and curettage were not nearly so safe as they are today. Thus, it has been argued that a State's real concern in enacting a criminal abortion law was to protect the pregnant woman, that is, to restrain her from submitting to a procedure that placed her life in serious jeopardy.

Modern medical techniques have altered this situation. Appellants and various *amici* refer to medical data indicating that abortion in early pregnancy, that is, prior to the end of the first trimester, although not without its risk, is now relatively safe. Mortality rates for women undergoing early abortions, where the procedure is legal, appear to be as low as or lower than the rates for normal childbirth.[44] Consequently, any interest of the State in protecting the woman from an inherently hazardous procedure, except when it would be equally dangerous for her to forgo it, has largely disappeared. Of course, important state interests in the areas of health and medical standards do remain. [410 U.S. 113, 150]. The State has a legitimate interest in seeing to it that abortion, like any other medical procedure, is performed under circumstances that insure maximum safety for the patient. This interest obviously extends at least to the performing physician and his staff, to the facilities involved, to the availability of aftercare, and to adequate provision for any complication or emergency that might arise. The prevalence of high mortality rates at illegal "abortion mills" strengthens, rather than weakens, the State's interest in regulating the conditions under which abortions are performed. Moreover, the risk to the woman increases as her pregnancy continues. Thus, the State retains a definite interest in protecting the woman's own health and safety when an abortion is proposed at a late stage of pregnancy.

The third reason is the State's interest—some phrase it in terms of duty—in protecting prenatal life. Some of the argument for this justification rests on the theory that a new human life is present from the moment of conception.[45] The State's interest and general obligation to protect life then extends, it is argued, to prenatal life. Only when the life of the pregnant mother herself is at stake, balanced against the life she carries within her, should the interest of the embryo or fetus not prevail. Logically, of course, a legitimate state interest in this area need not stand or fall on acceptance of the belief that life begins at conception or at some other point prior to live birth. In assessing the State's interest, recognition may be given to the less rigid claim that as long as at least potential life is involved, the State may assert interests beyond the protection of the pregnant woman alone. [410 U.S. 113, 151].

Parties challenging state abortion laws have sharply disputed in some courts the contention that a purpose of these laws, when enacted, was to protect prenatal life.[46] Pointing to the absence of legislative history to support the contention, they claim that most state laws were designed solely to protect the woman. Because medical advances have lessened this concern, at least with respect to abortion in early pregnancy, they argue that with respect to such abortions the laws can no longer be justified by any state interest. There is some scholarly support for this view of original purpose.[47] The few state courts called upon to interpret their laws in the late 19th and early 20th Centuries did focus on the State's interest in protecting the woman's health rather than in preserving the embryo and fetus.[48] Proponents of this view point out that in many States, including Texas,[49] by statute or judicial interpretation, the pregnant woman herself could not be prosecuted for self-abortion or for cooperating in an abortion performed upon her by another.[50] They claim that adoption of the "quickening" distinction through received common [410 U.S. 113, 152] law and state statutes tacitly recognizes the greater health hazards inherent in late abortion and impliedly repudiates the theory that life begins at conception.

It is with these interests, and the weight to be attached to them, that this case is concerned.

VIII

The Constitution does not explicitly mention any right of privacy. In a line of decisions, however, going back perhaps as far as *Union Pacific R. Co. v. Botsford*, 141 U.S. 250, 251 (1891), the Court has recognized that a right of personal privacy, or a guarantee of certain areas or zones of privacy, does exist under the Constitution. In varying contexts, the Court or individual Justices have, indeed, found at least the roots of that right in the First Amendment, *Stanley v. Georgia*, 394 U.S. 557, 564 (1969); in the Fourth and Fifth Amendments, *Terry v. Ohio*, 392 U.S. 1, 8–9 (1968), *Katz v. United States*, 389 U.S. 347, 350 (1967), *Boyd v. United States*, 116 U.S. 616 (1886), see *Olmstead v. United States*, 277 U.S. 438, 478 (1928) (Brandeis, J., dissenting); in the penumbras of the Bill of Rights, *Griswold v. Connecticut*, 381 U.S., at 484–485; in the Ninth Amendment, *id.*, at 486 (Goldberg, J., concurring); or in the concept of liberty guaranteed by the first section of the Fourteenth Amendment, see *Meyer v. Nebraska*, 262 U.S. 390, 399 (1923). These decisions make it clear that only personal rights that can be deemed "fundamental" or "implicit in the concept of ordered liberty," *Palko v. Connecticut*, 302 U.S. 319, 325 (1937), are included in this guarantee of personal privacy. They also make it clear that the right has some extension to activities relating to marriage, *Loving v. Virginia*, 388 U.S. 1, 12 (1967); procreation, *Skinner v. Oklahoma*, 316 U.S. 535, 541–542 (1942); contraception, *Eisenstadt v. Baird*, 405 U.S., at 453–454; *id.*, at 460, 463–465 [410 U.S. 113, 153] (WHITE, J., concurring in result); family relationships, *Prince v. Massachusetts*, 321 U.S. 158, 166 (1944); and child rearing and education, *Pierce v. Society of Sisters*, 268 U.S. 510, 535 (1925), *Meyer v. Nebraska, supra.*

This right of privacy, whether it be founded in the Fourteenth Amendment's concept of personal liberty and restrictions upon state action, as we feel it is, or, as the District Court determined, in the Ninth Amendment's reservation of rights to the people, is broad enough to encompass a woman's decision whether or not to terminate her pregnancy. The detriment that the State would impose upon the pregnant woman by denying this choice altogether is apparent. Specific and direct harm medically diagnosable even in early pregnancy may be involved. Maternity, or additional offspring, may force upon the woman a distressful life and future. Psychological harm may be imminent. Mental and physical health may be taxed by child care. There is also the distress, for all concerned, associated with the unwanted child, and there is the problem of bringing a child into a family already unable, psychologically and otherwise, to care for it. In other cases, as in this one, the additional difficulties and continuing stigma of unwed motherhood may be involved. All these are factors the woman and her responsible physician necessarily will consider in consultation.

On the basis of elements such as these, appellant and some amici argue that the woman's right is absolute and that she is entitled to terminate her pregnancy at whatever time, in whatever way, and for whatever reason she alone chooses. With this we do not agree. Appellant's arguments that Texas either has no valid interest at all in regulating the abortion decision, or no interest strong enough to support any limitation upon the woman's sole determination, are unpersuasive. The [410 U.S. 113, 154] Court's decisions recognizing a right of privacy also acknowledge that some state regulation in areas protected by that right is appropriate. As noted above, a State may properly assert important interests in safeguarding health, in maintaining medical standards, and in protecting potential life. At some point in pregnancy, these respective interests become sufficiently compelling to sustain regulation of the factors that govern the abortion decision. The privacy right involved, therefore, cannot be said to be absolute. In fact, it is not clear to us that the claim asserted by some *amici* that one has an unlimited right to do with one's body as one pleases bears a close relationship to the right of privacy previously articulated in the Court's decisions. The Court has refused to recognize an unlimited right of this kind in the past. *Jacobson v. Massachusetts*, 197 U.S. 11 (1905) (vaccination); *Buck v. Bell*, 274 U.S. 200 (1927) (sterilization).

We, therefore, conclude that the right of personal privacy includes the abortion decision, but that this right is not unqualified and must be considered against important state interests in regulation.

We note that those federal and state courts that have recently considered abortion law challenges have reached the same conclusion. A majority, in addition to the District Court in the present case, have held state laws unconstitutional, at least in part, because of vagueness or because of overbreadth and abridgment of rights. *Abele v. Markle*, 342 F. Supp. 800 (Conn. 1972), appeal docketed, No. 72-56; *Abele v. Markle*, 351 F. Supp. 224 (Conn. 1972), appeal docketed, No. 72-730; *Doe v. Bolton*, 319 F. Supp. 1048 (ND Ga. 1970), appeal decided today, post, p. 179; *Doe v. Scott*, 321 F. Supp. 1385 (ND Ill. 1971), appeal docketed, No. 70-105; *Poe v. Menghini*, 339 F. Supp. 986 (Kan. 1972); *YWCA v. Kugler*, 342 F. Supp. 1048 (NJ 1972); *Babbitz v. McCann*, [410 U.S. 113, 155] 310 F. Supp. 293 (ED Wis. 1970),

(Continues)

appeal dismissed, 400 U.S. 1 (1970); *People v. Belous*, 71 Cal. 2d 954, 458 P.2d 194 (1969), cert. denied, 397 U.S. 915 (1970); *State v. Barquet*, 262 So.2d 431 (Fla. 1972).

Others have sustained state statutes. *Crossen v. Attorney General*, 344 F. Supp. 587 (ED Ky. 1972), appeal docketed, No. 72-256; *Rosen v. Louisiana State Board of Medical Examiners*, 318 F. Supp. 1217 (ED La. 1970), appeal docketed, No. 70-42; *Corkey v. Edwards*, 322 F. Supp. 1248 (WDNC 1971), appeal docketed, No. 71-92; *Steinberg v. Brown*, 321 F. Supp. 741 (ND Ohio 1970); *Doe v. Rampton* (Utah 1971), appeal docketed, No. 71-5666; *Cheaney v. State*, ___ Ind. ___, 285 N. E. 2d 265 (1972); *Spears v. State*, 257 So.2d 876 (Miss. 1972); *State v. Munson*, 86 S. D. 663, 201 N. W. 2d 123 (1972), appeal docketed, No. 72-631.

Although the results are divided, most of these courts have agreed that the right of privacy, however based, is broad enough to cover the abortion decision; that the right, nonetheless, is not absolute and is subject to some limitations; and that at some point the state interests as to protection of health, medical standards, and prenatal life, become dominant. We agree with this approach.

Where certain "fundamental rights" are involved, the Court has held that regulation limiting these rights may be justified only by a "compelling state interest," *Kramer v. Union Free School District*, 395 U.S. 621, 627 (1969); *Shapiro v. Thompson*, 394 U.S. 618, 634 (1969), *Sherbert v. Verner*, 374 U.S. 398, 406 (1963), and that legislative enactments must be narrowly drawn to express only the legitimate state interests at stake. *Griswold v. Connecticut*, 381 U.S., at 485; *Aptheker v. Secretary of State*, 378 U.S. 500, 508 (1964); *Cantwell v. Connecticut*, 310 U.S. 296, 307–308 (1940); see [410 U.S. 113, 156] *Eisenstadt v. Baird*, 405 U.S., at 460, 463–464 (WHITE, J., concurring in result).

In the recent abortion cases, cited above, courts have recognized these principles. Those striking down state laws have generally scrutinized the State's interests in protecting health and potential life, and have concluded that neither interest justified broad limitations on the reasons for which a physician and his pregnant patient might decide that she should have an abortion in the early stages of pregnancy. Courts sustaining state laws have held that the State's determinations to protect health or prenatal life are dominant and constitutionally justifiable.

IX

The District Court held that the appellee failed to meet his burden of demonstrating that the Texas statute's infringement upon Roe's rights was necessary to support a compelling state interest, and that, although the appellee presented "several compelling justifications for state presence in the area of abortions," the statutes outstripped these justifications and swept "far beyond any areas of compelling state interest." 314 F. Supp., at 1222–1223. Appellant and appellee both contest that holding. Appellant, as has been indicated, claims an absolute right that bars any state imposition of criminal penalties in the area. Appellee argues that the State's determination to recognize and protect prenatal life from and after conception constitutes a compelling state interest. As noted above, we do not agree fully with either formulation.

A. The appellee and certain amici argue that the fetus is a "person" within the language and meaning of the Fourteenth Amendment. In support of this, they outline at length and in detail the well-known facts of fetal development. If this suggestion of personhood is established, the appellant's case, of course, collapses, [410 U.S. 113, 157] for the fetus' right to life would then be guaranteed specifically by the Amendment. The appellant conceded as much on reargument.[51] On the other hand, the appellee conceded on reargument[52] that no case could be cited that holds that a fetus is a person within the meaning of the Fourteenth Amendment.

The Constitution does not define "person" in so many words. Section 1 of the Fourteenth Amendment contains three references to "person." The first, in defining "citizens," speaks of "persons born or naturalized in the United States." The word also appears both in the Due Process Clause and in the Equal Protection Clause. "Person" is used in other places in the Constitution: in the listing of qualifications for Representatives and Senators, Art. I, 2, cl. 2, and 3, cl. 3; in the Apportionment Clause, Art. I, 2, cl. 3[53]; in the Migration and Importation provision, Art. I, 9, cl. 1; in the Emolument Clause, Art. I, 9, cl. 8; in the Electors provisions, Art. II, 1, cl. 2, and the superseded cl. 3; in the provision outlining qualifications for the office of President, Art. II, 1, cl. 5; in the Extradition provisions, Art. IV, 2, cl. 2, and the superseded Fugitive Slave Clause 3; and in the Fifth, Twelfth, and Twenty-Second Amendments, as well as in 2 and 3 of the Fourteenth Amendment. But in nearly all these instances, the use of the word is such that it has application only postnatally. None indicates, with any assurance, that it has any possible prenatal application.[54] [410 U.S. 113, 158].

All this, together with our observation, *supra*, that throughout the major portion of the 19th Century prevailing legal abortion practices were far freer than they are today, persuades us that the word "person," as used in the Fourteenth Amendment, does not include the unborn.[55] This is in accord with the results reached in those few cases where the issue has been squarely presented. *McGarvey v. Magee Womens Hospital*, 340 F. Supp. 751 (WD Pa. 1972); *Byrn v. New York City Health & Hospitals Corp.*, 31 N.Y. 2d 194, 286 N. E. 2d 887 (1972), appeal docketed, No. 72-434; *Abele v. Markle*, 351 F. Supp. 224 (Conn. 1972), appeal docketed, No. 72-730. Cf. *Cheaney v. State*, ___ Ind., at ___, 285 N. E. 2d, at 270; *Montana v. Rogers*, 278 F.2d 68, 72 (CA7 1960), aff'd sub nom. *Montana v. Kennedy*, 366 U.S. 308 (1961); *Keeler v. Superior Court*, 2 Cal. 3d 619, 470 P.2d 617 (1970); *State v. Dickinson*, 28 [410 U.S. 113, 159] Ohio St. 2d 65, 275 N. E. 2d 599 (1971). Indeed, our decision in *United States v. Vuitch*, 402 U.S. 62 (1971), inferentially is to the same effect, for we there would not have indulged in statutory interpretation favorable to abortion in specified circumstances if the necessary consequence was the termination of life entitled to Fourteenth Amendment protection.

This conclusion, however, does not of itself fully answer the contentions raised by Texas, and we pass on to other considerations.

B. The pregnant woman cannot be isolated in her privacy. She carries an embryo and, later, a fetus, if one accepts the medical definitions of the developing young in the human uterus. See *Dorland's Illustrated Medical Dictionary*, 478–479, 547 (24th ed. 1965). The situation therefore is inherently different from marital intimacy, or bedroom possession of obscene material, or marriage, or procreation, or education, with which Eisenstadt and Griswold, Stanley, Loving, Skinner, and Pierce and Meyer were respectively concerned. As we have intimated above, it is reasonable and appropriate for a State to decide that at some point in time another interest, that of health of the mother or that of potential human life, becomes significantly involved. The woman's privacy is no longer sole and any right of privacy she possesses must be measured accordingly.

Texas urges that, apart from the Fourteenth Amendment, life begins at conception and is present throughout pregnancy, and that, therefore, the State has a compelling interest in protecting that life from and after conception. We need not resolve the difficult question of when life begins. When those trained in the respective disciplines of medicine, philosophy, and theology are unable to arrive at any consensus, the judiciary, at this point in the development of man's knowledge, is not in a position to speculate as to the answer. [410 U.S. 113, 160].

It should be sufficient to note briefly the wide divergence of thinking on this most sensitive and difficult question. There has always been strong support for the view that life does not begin until live birth. This was the belief of the Stoics.[56] It appears to be the predominant, though not the unanimous, attitude of the Jewish faith.[57] It may be taken to represent also the position of a large segment of the Protestant community, insofar as that can be ascertained; organized groups that have taken a formal position on the abortion issue have generally regarded abortion as a matter for the conscience of the individual and her family.[58] As we have noted, the common law found greater significance in quickening. Physicians and their scientific colleagues have regarded that event with less interest and have tended to focus either upon conception, upon live birth, or upon the interim point at which the fetus becomes "viable," that is, potentially able to live outside the mother's womb, albeit with artificial aid.[59] Viability is usually placed at about seven months (28 weeks) but may occur earlier, even at 24 weeks.[60] The Aristotelian theory of "mediate animation," that held sway throughout the Middle Ages and the Renaissance in Europe, continued to be official Roman Catholic dogma until the 19th Century, despite opposition to this "ensoulment" theory from those in the Church who would recognize the existence of life from [410 U.S. 113, 161] the moment of conception.[61] The latter is now, of course, the official belief of the Catholic Church. As one brief *amicus* discloses, this is a view strongly held by many non-Catholics as well, and by many physicians. Substantial problems for precise definition of this view are posed, however, by new embryological data that purport to indicate that conception is a "process" over time, rather than an event, and by new medical techniques such as menstrual extraction, the "morning-after" pill, implantation of embryos, artificial insemination, and even artificial wombs.[62]

In areas other than criminal abortion, the law has been reluctant to endorse any theory that life, as we recognize it, begins before live birth or to accord legal rights to the unborn except in narrowly defined situations and except when the rights are contingent upon live birth. For example, the traditional rule of tort law denied recovery for prenatal injuries even though the child was born alive.[63] That rule has been changed in almost every jurisdiction. In most States, recovery is said to be permitted only if the fetus was viable, or at least quick, when the injuries were sustained, though few [410 U.S. 113, 162]

(Continues)

courts have squarely so held.[64] In a recent development, generally opposed by the commentators, some States permit the parents of a stillborn child to maintain an action for wrongful death because of pre-natal injuries.[65] Such an action, however, would appear to be one to vindicate the parents' interest and is thus consistent with the view that the fetus, at most, represents only the potentiality of life. Similarly, unborn children have been recognized as acquiring rights or interests by way of inheritance or other devolution of property, and have been represented by guardians *ad litem*.[66] Perfection of the interests involved, again, has generally been contingent upon live birth. In short, the unborn have never been recognized in the law as persons in the whole sense.

X

In view of all this, we do not agree that, by adopting one theory of life, Texas may override the rights of the pregnant woman that are at stake. We repeat, however, that the State does have an important and legitimate interest in preserving and protecting the health of the pregnant woman, whether she be a resident of the State or a nonresident who seeks medical consultation and treatment there, and that it has still another important and legitimate interest in protecting the potentiality of human life. These interests are separate and distinct. Each grows in substantiality as the woman approaches [410 U.S. 113, 163] term and, at a point during pregnancy, each becomes "compelling."

With respect to the State's important and legitimate interest in the health of the mother, the "compelling" point, in the light of present medical knowledge, is at approximately the end of the first trimester. This is so because of the now-established medical fact, referred to above at 149, that until the end of the first trimester mortality in abortion may be less than mortality in normal childbirth. It follows that, from and after this point, a State may regulate the abortion procedure to the extent that the regulation reasonably relates to the preservation and protection of maternal health. Examples of permissible state regulation in this area are requirements as to the qualifications of the person who is to perform the abortion; as to the licensure of that person; as to the facility in which the procedure is to be performed, that is, whether it must be a hospital or may be a clinic or some other place of less-than-hospital status; as to the licensing of the facility; and the like.

This means, on the other hand, that, for the period of pregnancy prior to this "compelling" point, the attending physician, in consultation with his patient, is free to determine, without regulation by the State, that, in his medical judgment, the patient's pregnancy should be terminated. If that decision is reached, the judgment may be effectuated by an abortion free of interference by the State.

With respect to the State's important and legitimate interest in potential life, the "compelling" point is at viability. This is so because the fetus then presumably has the capability of meaningful life outside the mother's womb. State regulation protective of fetal life after viability thus has both logical and biological justifications. If the State is interested in protecting fetal life after viability, it may go so far as to proscribe abortion [410 U.S. 113, 164] during that period, except when it is necessary to preserve the life or health of the mother.

Measured against these standards, Art. 1196 of the Texas Penal Code, in restricting legal abortions to those "procured or attempted by medical advice for the purpose of saving the life of the mother," sweeps too broadly. The statute makes no distinction between abortions performed early in pregnancy and those performed later, and it limits to a single reason, "saving" the mother's life, the legal justification for the procedure. The statute, therefore, cannot survive the constitutional attack made upon it here.

This conclusion makes it unnecessary for us to consider the additional challenge to the Texas statute asserted on grounds of vagueness. See *United States v. Vuitch*, 402 U.S., at 67–72.

XI

To summarize and to repeat:

1. A state criminal abortion statute of the current Texas type, that excepts from criminality only a life-saving procedure on behalf of the mother, without regard to pregnancy stage and without recognition of the other interests involved, is violative of the Due Process Clause of the Fourteenth Amendment.

    (a) For the stage prior to approximately the end of the first trimester, the abortion decision and its effectuation must be left to the medical judgment of the pregnant woman's attending physician.

    (b) For the stage subsequent to approximately the end of the first trimester, the State, in promoting its interest in the health of the mother, may, if it chooses, regulate the abortion procedure in ways that are reasonably related to maternal health.

(c) For the stage subsequent to viability, the State in promoting its interest in the potentiality of human life [410 U.S. 113, 165] may, if it chooses, regulate, and even proscribe, abortion except where it is necessary, in appropriate medical judgment, for the preservation of the life or health of the mother.

2. The State may define the term "physician," as it has been employed in the preceding paragraphs of this Part XI of this opinion, to mean only a physician currently licensed by the State, and may proscribe any abortion by a person who is not a physician as so defined.

In *Doe v. Bolton, post*, p. 179, procedural requirements contained in one of the modern abortion statutes are considered. That opinion and this one, of course, are to be read together.[67]

This holding, we feel, is consistent with the relative weights of the respective interests involved, with the lessons and examples of medical and legal history, with the lenity of the common law, and with the demands of the profound problems of the present day. The decision leaves the State free to place increasing restrictions on abortion as the period of pregnancy lengthens, so long as those restrictions are tailored to the recognized state interests. The decision vindicates the right of the physician to administer medical treatment according to his professional judgment up to the points where important [410 U.S. 113, 166] state interests provide compelling justifications for intervention. Up to those points, the abortion decision in all its aspects is inherently, and primarily, a medical decision, and basic responsibility for it must rest with the physician. If an individual practitioner abuses the privilege of exercising proper medical judgment, the usual remedies, judicial and intra-professional, are available.

XII

Our conclusion that Art. 1196 is unconstitutional means, of course, that the Texas abortion statutes, as a unit, must fall. The exception of Art. 1196 cannot be struck down separately, for then the State would be left with a statute proscribing all abortion procedures no matter how medically urgent the case.

Although the District Court granted appellant Roe declaratory relief, it stopped short of issuing an injunction against enforcement of the Texas statutes. The Court has recognized that different considerations enter into a federal court's decision as to declaratory relief, on the one hand, and injunctive relief, on the other. *Zwickler v. Koota*, 389 U.S. 241, 252–255 (1967); *Dombrowski v. Pfister*, 380 U.S. 479 (1965). We are not dealing with a statute that, on its face, appears to abridge free expression, an area of particular concern under *Dombrowski* and refined in *Younger v. Harris*, 401 U.S., at 50.

We find it unnecessary to decide whether the District Court erred in withholding injunctive relief, for we assume the Texas prosecutorial authorities will give full credence to this decision that the present criminal abortion statutes of that State are unconstitutional.

The judgment of the District Court as to intervenor Hallford is reversed, and Dr. Hallford's complaint in intervention is dismissed. In all other respects, the judgment [410 U.S. 113, 167] of the District Court is affirmed. Costs are allowed to the appellee.

It is so ordered.

[For concurring opinion of MR. CHIEF JUSTICE BURGER, see post, p. 207.]

[For concurring opinion of MR. JUSTICE DOUGLAS, see post, p. 209.]

[For dissenting opinion of MR. JUSTICE WHITE, see post, p. 221.]

Notes

1. "Article 1191. Abortion

"If any person shall designedly administer to a pregnant woman or knowingly procure to be administered with her consent any drug or medicine, or shall use towards her any violence or means whatever externally or internally applied, and thereby procure an abortion, he shall be confined in the penitentiary not less than two nor more than five years; if it be done without her consent, the punishment shall be doubled. By 'abortion' is meant that the life of the fetus or embryo shall be destroyed in the woman's womb or that a premature birth thereof be caused.

"Art. 1192. Furnishing the means

"Whoever furnishes the means for procuring an abortion knowing the purpose intended is guilty as an accomplice.

"Art. 1193. Attempt at abortion

(Continues)

(Continued)

"If the means used shall fail to produce an abortion, the offender is nevertheless guilty of an attempt to produce abortion, provided [410 U.S. 113, 118] it be shown that such means were calculated to produce that result, and shall be fined not less than one hundred nor more than one thousand dollars.

"Art. 1194. Murder in producing abortion

"If the death of the mother is occasioned by an abortion so produced or by an attempt to effect the same it is murder."

"Art. 1196. By medical advice

"Nothing in this chapter applies to an abortion procured or attempted by medical advice for the purpose of saving the life of the mother."

The foregoing Articles, together with Art. 1195, compose Chapter 9 of Title 15 of the Penal Code. Article 1195, not attacked here, reads:

"Art. 1195. Destroying unborn child

"Whoever shall during parturition of the mother destroy the vitality or life in a child in a state of being born and before actual birth, which child would otherwise have been born alive, shall be confined in the penitentiary for life or for not less than five years."

2. Ariz. Rev. Stat. Ann. 13-211 (1956); Conn. Pub. Act No. 1 (May 1972 special session) (in 4 Conn. Leg. Serv. 677 (1972)), and Conn. Gen. Stat. Rev. 53-29, 53-30 (1968) (or unborn child); Idaho Code 18-601 (1948); Ill. Rev. Stat., c. 38, 23-1 (1971); Ind. Code 35-1-58-1 (1971); Iowa Code 701.1 (1971); Ky. Rev. Stat. 436.020 (1962); La. Rev. Stat. 37:1285 (6) (1964) (loss of medical license) (but see 14:87 (Supp. 1972) containing no exception for the life of the mother under the criminal statute); Me. Rev. Stat. Ann., Tit. 17, 51 (1964); Mass. Gen. Laws Ann., c. 272, 19 (1970) (using the term "unlawfully," construed to exclude an abortion to save the mother's life, *Kudish v. Bd. of Registration*, 356 Mass. 98, 248 N. E. 2d 264 (1969)); Mich. Comp. Laws 750.14 (1948); Minn. Stat. 617.18 (1971); Mo. Rev. Stat. 559.100 (1969); Mont. Rev. Codes Ann. 94-401 (1969); Neb. Rev. Stat. 28-405 (1964); Nev. Rev. Stat. 200.220 (1967); N.H. Rev. Stat. Ann. 585:13 (1955); N.J. Stat. Ann. 2A:87-1 (1969) ("without lawful justification"); N.D. Cent. Code 12-25-01, 12-25-02 (1960); Ohio Rev. Code Ann. 2901.16 (1953); Okla. Stat. Ann., Tit. 21, 861 (1972–1973 Supp.); Pa. Stat. Ann., Tit. 18, [410 U.S. 113, 119] 4718, 4719 (1963) ("unlawful"); R.I. Gen. Laws Ann. 11-3-1 (1969); S.D. Comp. Laws Ann. 22-17-1 (1967); Tenn. Code Ann. 39-301, 39-302 (1956); Utah Code Ann. 76-2-1, 76-2-2 (1953); Vt. Stat. Ann., Tit. 13, 101 (1958); W. Va. Code Ann. 61-2-8 (1966); Wis. Stat. 940.04 (1969); Wyo. Stat. Ann. 6-77, 6-78 (1957).

3. Long ago, a suggestion was made that the Texas statutes were unconstitutionally vague because of definitional deficiencies. The Texas Court of Criminal Appeals disposed of that suggestion peremptorily, saying only,

"It is also insisted in the motion in arrest of judgment that the statute is unconstitutional and void in that it does not sufficiently define or describe the offense of abortion. We do not concur in respect to this question." *Jackson v. State*, 55 Tex. Cr. R. 79, 89, 115 S. W. 262, 268 (1908).

The same court recently has held again that the State's abortion statutes are not unconstitutionally vague or overbroad. *Thompson v. State* (Ct. Crim. App. Tex. 1971), appeal docketed, No. 71-1200. The court held that "the State of Texas has a compelling interest to protect fetal life"; that Art. 1191 "is designed to protect fetal life"; that the Texas homicide statutes, particularly Art. 1205 of the Penal Code, are intended to protect a person "in existence by actual birth" and thereby implicitly recognize other human life that is not "in existence by actual birth"; that the definition of human life is for the legislature and not the courts; that Art. 1196 "is more definite than the District of Columbia statute upheld in [*United States v.*] *Vuitch*" (402 U.S. 62); and that the Texas statute "is [410 U.S. 113, 120] not vague and indefinite or overbroad." A physician's abortion conviction was affirmed.

In Thompson, n. 2, the court observed that any issue as to the burden of proof under the exemption of Art. 1196 "is not before us." But see *Veevers v. State*, 172 Tex. Cr. R. 162, 168–169, 354 S. W. 2d 161, 166–167 (1962). Cf. *United States v. Vuitch*, 402 U.S. 62, 69–71 (1971).

4. The name is a pseudonym.

5. These names are pseudonyms.

6. The appellee twice states in his brief that the hearing before the District Court was held on July 22, 1970. Brief for Appellee 13. The docket entries, App. 2, and the transcript, App. 76,

reveal this to be an error. The July date appears to be the time of the reporter's transcription. See App. 77.

7. We need not consider what different result, if any, would follow if Dr. Hallford's intervention were on behalf of a class. His complaint in intervention does not purport to assert a class suit and makes no reference to any class apart from an allegation that he "and others similarly situated" must necessarily guess at the meaning of Art. 1196. His application for leave to intervene goes somewhat further, for it asserts that plaintiff Roe does not adequately protect the interest of the doctor "and the class of people who are physicians . . . [and] the class of people who are . . . patients. . . . " The leave application, however, is not the complaint. Despite the District Court's statement to the contrary, 314 F. Supp., at 1225, we fail to perceive the essentials of a class suit in the Hallford complaint.

8. A. Castiglioni, *A History of Medicine*, 84 (2d ed. 1947), E. Krumbhaar, translator and editor (hereinafter Castiglioni).

9. J. Ricci, *The Genealogy of Gynaecology*, 52, 84, 113, 149 (2d ed. 1950) (hereinafter Ricci); L. Lader, *Abortion*, 75–77 (1966) (hereinafter Lader); K. Niswander, Medical Abortion Practices in the United States, in *Abortion and the Law*, 37, 38–40 (D. Smith ed. 1967); G. Williams, *The Sanctity of Life and the Criminal Law* 148 (1957) (hereinafter Williams); J. Noonan, An Almost Absolute Value in History, in *The Morality of Abortion*, 1, 3–7 (J. Noonan ed. 1970) (hereinafter Noonan); Quay, *Justifiable Abortion—Medical and Legal Foundations* (pt. 2), 49 Geo. L. J. 395, 406–422 (1961) (hereinafter Quay).

10. L. Edelstein, *The Hippocratic Oath* 10 (1943) (hereinafter Edelstein). But see Castiglioni 227.

11. Edelstein 12; Ricci 113–114, 118–119; Noonan 5.

12. Edelstein 13–14.

13. Castiglioni 148.

14. *Id.*, at 154.

15. Edelstein 3.

16. *Id.*, at 12, 15–18.

17. *Id.*, at 18; Lader 76.

18. Edelstein 63.

19. *Id.*, at 64.

20. *Dorland's Illustrated Medical Dictionary*, 1261 (24th ed. 1965).

21. E. Coke, *Institutes III* *50; 1 W. Hawkins, *Pleas of the Crown*, c. 31, 16 (4th ed. 1762); 1 W. Blackstone, *Commentaries* *129–130; M. Hale, *Pleas of the Crown*, 433 (1st Amer. ed. 1847). For discussions of the role of the quickening concept in English common law, see Lader 78; Noonan 223–226; Means, *The Law of New* [410 U.S. 113, 133] *York Concerning Abortion and the Status of the Foetus, 1664–1968: A Case of Cessation of Constitutionality* (pt. 1), 14 N.Y. L. F. 411, 418–428 (1968) (hereinafter Means I); Stern, Abortion: Reform and the Law, 59 *J. Crim. L. C. & P. S.* 84 (1968) (hereinafter Stern); Quay 430–432; Williams 152.

22. Early philosophers believed that the embryo or fetus did not become formed and begin to live until at least 40 days after conception for a male, and 80 to 90 days for a female. See, for example, Aristotle, *Hist. Anim.*, 7.3.583b; *Gen. Anim.* 2.3.736, 2.5.741; Hippocrates, *Lib. de Nat. Puer.*, No. 10. Aristotle's thinking derived from his three-stage theory of life: vegetable, animal, rational. The vegetable stage was reached at conception, the animal at "animation," and the rational soon after live birth. This theory, together with the 40/80 day view, came to be accepted by early Christian thinkers.

The theological debate was reflected in the writings of St. Augustine, who made a distinction between embryo inanimatus, not yet endowed with a soul, and embryo animatus. He may have drawn upon Exodus 21:22. At one point, however, he expressed the view that human powers cannot determine the point during fetal development at which the critical change occurs. See Augustine, *De Origine Animae* 4.4 (Pub. Law 44.527). See also W. Reany, *The Creation of the Human Soul*, c. 2 and 83–86 (1932); Huser, *The Crime of Abortion in Canon Law* 15 (Catholic Univ. of America, Canon Law Studies No. 162, Washington, D.C., 1942).

Galen, in three treatises related to embryology, accepted the thinking of Aristotle and his followers. Quay 426–427. Later, Augustine on abortion was incorporated by Gratian into the *Decretum*, published about 1140. *Decretum Magistri Gratiani* 2.32.2.7 to 2.32.2.10, [410 U.S. 113, 134] in 1 *Corpus Juris Canonici* 1122, 1123 (A. Friedburg, 2d ed. 1879). This Decretal and the Decretals that followed were recognized as the definitive body of canon law until the new Code of 1917.

(Continues)

(Continued)

For discussions of the canon-law treatment, see Means I, pp. 411–412; Noonan 20–26; Quay 426–430; see also J. Noonan, *Contraception: A History of Its Treatment by the Catholic Theologians and Canonists*, 18–29 (1965).

23. Bracton took the position that abortion by blow or poison was homicide "if the foetus be already formed and animated, and particularly if it be animated." 2 H. Bracton, *De Legibus et Consuetudinibus Angliae*, 279 (T. Twiss ed. 1879), or, as a later translation puts it, "if the foetus is already formed or quickened, especially if it is quickened," 2 H. Bracton, *On the Laws and Customs of England*, 341 (S. Thorne ed. 1968). See Quay 431; see also 2 Fleta 60–61 (Book 1, c. 23) (Selden Society ed. 1955).

24. E. Coke, *Institutes III* *50.

25. 1 W. Blackstone, *Commentaries* *129–130.

26. Means, *The Phoenix of Abortional Freedom: Is a Penumbral or Ninth-Amendment Right About to Arise from the Nineteenth-Century Legislative Ashes of a Fourteenth-Century Common-Law Liberty?* 17 N.Y. L. F. 335 (1971) (hereinafter *Means II*). The author examines the two principal precedents cited marginally by Coke, both contrary to his dictum, and traces the treatment of these and other cases by earlier commentators. He concludes that Coke, who himself participated as an advocate in an abortion case in 1601, may have intentionally misstated the law. The author even suggests a reason: Coke's strong feelings against abortion, coupled with his determination to assert common-law (secular) jurisdiction to assess penalties for an offense that traditionally had been an exclusively ecclesiastical or canon-law crime. See also Lader 78–79, who notes that some scholars doubt that the common law ever was applied to abortion; that the English ecclesiastical courts seem to have lost interest in the problem after 1527; and that the preamble to the English legislation of 1803, 43 Geo. 3, c. 58, 1, referred to in the text, *infra*, at 136, states that "no adequate means have been hitherto provided for the prevention and punishment of such offenses."

27. *Commonwealth v. Bangs*, 9 Mass. 387, 388 (1812); *Commonwealth v. Parker*, 50 Mass. (9 Metc.) 263, 265–266 (1845); *State v. Cooper*, 22 N.J. L. 52, 58 (1849); *Abrams v. Foshee*, 3 Iowa 274, 278–280 (1856); *Smith v. Gaffard*, 31 Ala. 45, 51 (1857); *Mitchell v. Commonwealth*, 78 Ky. 204, 210 (1879); *Eggart v. State*, 40 Fla. [410 U.S. 113, 136] 527, 532, 25 So. 144, 145 (1898); *State v. Alcorn*, 7 Idaho 599, 606, 64 P. 1014, 1016 (1901); *Edwards v. State*, 79 Neb. 251, 252, 112 N. W. 611, 612 (1907); *Gray v. State*, 77 Tex. Cr. R. 221, 224, 178 S. W. 337, 338 (1915); *Miller v. Bennett*, 190 Va. 162, 169, 56 S. E. 2d 217, 221 (1949). *Contra, Mills v. Commonwealth*, 13 Pa. 631, 633 (1850); *State v. Slagle*, 83 N.C. 630, 632 (1880).

28. See *Smith v. State*, 33 Me. 48, 55 (1851); *Evans v. People*, 49 N.Y. 86, 88 (1872); *Lamb v. State*, 67 Md. 524, 533, 10 A. 208 (1887).

29. Conn. Stat., Tit. 20, 14 (1821).

30. Conn. Pub. Acts, c. 71, 1 (1860).

31. N.Y. Rev. Stat., pt. 4, c. 1, Tit. 2, Art. 1, 9, p. 661, and Tit. 6, 21, p. 694 (1829).

32. Act of Jan. 20, 1840, 1, set forth in 2 H. Gammel, *Laws of Texas* 177–178 (1898); see *Grigsby v. Reib*, 105 Tex. 597, 600, 153 S. W. 1124, 1125 (1913).

33. The early statutes are discussed in Quay 435–438. See also Lader 85–88; Stern 85–86; and Means II 375–376.

34. Criminal abortion statutes in effect in the States as of 1961, together with historical statutory development and important judicial interpretations of the state statutes, are cited and quoted in Quay 447–520. See *Comment, A Survey of the Present Statutory and Case Law on Abortion: The Contradictions and the Problems*, 1972 U. Ill. L. F. 177, 179, classifying the abortion statutes and listing 25 States as permitting abortion only if necessary to save or preserve the mother's life.

35. Ala. Code, Tit. 14, 9 (1958); D.C. Code Ann. 22–201 (1967).

36. Mass. Gen. Laws Ann., c. 272, 19 (1970); N.J. Stat. Ann. 2A:87-1 (1969); Pa. Stat. Ann., Tit. 18, 4718, 4719 (1963).

37. Fourteen States have adopted some form of the ALI statute. See Ark. Stat. Ann. 41-303 to 41-310 (Supp. 1971); Calif. Health & Safety Code 25950-25955.5 (Supp. 1972); Colo. Rev. Stat. Ann. 40-2-50 to 40-2-53 (Cum. Supp. 1967); Del. Code Ann., Tit. 24, 1790-1793 (Supp. 1972); Florida Law of Apr. 13, 1972, c. 72-196, 1972 Fla. Sess. Law Serv., pp. 380-382; Ga. Code 26-1201 to 26-1203 (1972); Kan. Stat. Ann. 21-3407 (Supp. 1971); Md. Ann. Code, Art. 43, 137–139 (1971); Miss. Code Ann. 2223 (Supp. 1972); N.M. Stat. Ann. 40A-5-1 to 40A-5-3 (1972); N.C. Gen. Stat. 14-45.1 (Supp. 1971); Ore. Rev. Stat. 435.405 to 435.495 (1971); S.C. Code Ann. 16-82 to 16-89 (1962 and Supp. 1971); Va. Code Ann. 18.1-62 to 18.1-62.3 (Supp. 1972).

Mr. Justice Clark described some of these States as having "led the way." *Religion, Morality, and Abortion: A Constitutional Appraisal*, 2 Loyola U. (L.A.) L. Rev. 1, 11 (1969).

By the end of 1970, four other States had repealed criminal penalties for abortions performed in early pregnancy by a licensed physician, subject to stated procedural and health requirements. Alaska Stat. 11.15.060 (1970); Haw. Rev. Stat. 453-16 (Supp. 1971); N.Y. Penal Code 125.05, subd. 3 (Supp. 1972-1973); Wash. Rev. Code 9.02.060 to 9.02.080 (Supp. 1972). The precise status of criminal abortion laws in some States is made unclear by recent decisions in state and federal courts striking down existing state laws, in whole or in part.

38. "Whereas, Abortion, like any other medical procedure, should not be performed when contrary to the best interests of the patient [410 U.S. 113, 144] since good medical practice requires due consideration for the patient's welfare and not mere acquiescence to the patient's demand; and

"Whereas, The standards of sound clinical judgment, which, together with informed patient consent should be determinative according to the merits of each individual case; therefore be it

"RESOLVED, That abortion is a medical procedure and should be performed only by a duly licensed physician and surgeon in an accredited hospital acting only after consultation with two other physicians chosen because of their professional competency and in conformance with standards of good medical practice and the Medical Practice Act of his State; and be it further

"RESOLVED, That no physician or other professional personnel shall be compelled to perform any act which violates his good medical judgment. Neither physician, hospital, nor hospital personnel shall be required to perform any act violative of personally-held moral principles. In these circumstances good medical practice requires only that the physician or other professional personnel withdraw from the case so long as the withdrawal is consistent with good medical practice." Proceedings of the AMA House of Delegates 220 (June 1970).

39. "The Principles of Medical Ethics of the AMA do not prohibit a physician from performing an abortion that is performed in accordance with good medical practice and under circumstances that do not violate the laws of the community in which he practices.

"In the matter of abortions, as of any other medical procedure, the Judicial Council becomes involved whenever there is alleged violation of the Principles of Medical Ethics as established by the House of Delegates."

40. "UNIFORM ABORTION ACT

"SECTION 1. [Abortion Defined; When Authorized.]

"**(a)** 'Abortion' means the termination of human pregnancy with an intention other than to produce a live birth or to remove a dead fetus.

"**(b)** An abortion may be performed in this state only if it is performed:

"**(1)** by a physician licensed to practice medicine [or osteopathy] in this state or by a physician practicing medicine [or osteopathy] in the employ of the government of the United States or of this state, [and the abortion is performed [in the physician's office or in a medical clinic, or] in a hospital approved by the [Department of Health] or operated by the United States, this state, or any department, agency, or political subdivision of either]; or by a female upon herself upon the advice of the physician; and

"**(2)** within 20. weeks after the commencement of the pregnancy [or after 20. weeks only if the physician has reasonable cause to believe (i) there is a substantial risk that continuance of the pregnancy would endanger the life of the mother or would gravely impair the physical or mental health of the mother, (ii) that the child would be born with grave physical or mental defect, or (iii) that [410 U.S. 113, 147] the pregnancy resulted from rape or incest, or illicit intercourse with a girl under the age of 16 years].

"SECTION 2. [Penalty.] Any person who performs or procures an abortion other than authorized by this Act is guilty of a [felony] and, upon conviction thereof, may be sentenced to pay a fine not exceeding [$1,000] or to imprisonment [in the state penitentiary] not exceeding [5 years], or both.

"SECTION 3. [Uniformity of Interpretation.] This Act shall be construed to effectuate its general purpose to make uniform the law with respect to the subject of this Act among those states which enact it.

"SECTION 4. [Short Title.] This Act may be cited as the Uniform Abortion Act.

(Continues)

"SECTION 5. [Severability.] If any provision of this Act or the application thereof to any person or circumstance is held invalid, the invalidity does not affect other provisions or applications of this Act which can be given effect without the invalid provision or application, and to this end the provisions of this Act are severable.

"SECTION 6. [Repeal.] The following acts and parts of acts are repealed: "(1) "(2) "(3)

"SECTION 7. [Time of Taking Effect.] This Act shall take effect _____."

41. "This Act is based largely upon the New York abortion act following a review of the more recent laws on abortion in several states and upon recognition of a more liberal trend in laws on this subject. Recognition was given also to the several decisions in state and federal courts which show a further trend toward liberalization of abortion laws, especially during the first trimester of pregnancy.

"Recognizing that a number of problems appeared in New York, a shorter time period for 'unlimited' abortions was advisable. The [410 U.S. 113, 148] time period was bracketed to permit the various states to insert a figure more in keeping with the different conditions that might exist among the states. Likewise, the language limiting the place or places in which abortions may be performed was also bracketed to account for different conditions among the states. In addition, limitations on abortions after the initial 'unlimited' period were placed in brackets so that individual states may adopt all or any of these reasons, or place further restrictions upon abortions after the initial period.

"This Act does not contain any provision relating to medical review committees or prohibitions against sanctions imposed upon medical personnel refusing to participate in abortions because of religious or other similar reasons, or the like. Such provisions, while related, do not directly pertain to when, where, or by whom abortions may be performed; however, the Act is not drafted to exclude such a provision by a state wishing to enact the same."

42. See, for example, *YWCA v. Kugler*, 342 F. Supp. 1048, 1074 (N. J. 1972); *Abele v. Markle*, 342 F. Supp. 800, 805–806 (Conn. 1972) (Newman, J., concurring in result), appeal docketed, No. 72-56; *Walsingham v. State*, 250 So.2d 857, 863 (Ervin, J., concurring) (Fla. 1971); *State v. Gedicke*, 43 N. J. L. 86, 90 (1881); Means II 381–382.

43. See C. Haagensen & W. Lloyd, *A Hundred Years of Medicine*, 19 (1943).

44. Potts, Postconceptive Control of Fertility, 8 *Int'l J. of G. & O.* 957, 967 (1970) (England and Wales); Abortion Mortality, 20 *Morbidity and Mortality*, 208, 209 (June 12, 1971) (U.S. Dept. of HEW, Public Health Service) (New York City); Tietze, *United States: Therapeutic Abortions, 1963–1968*, 59 *Studies in Family Planning*, 5, 7 (1970); Tietze, *Mortality with Contraception and Induced Abortion*, 45 *Studies in Family Planning*, 6 (1969) (Japan, Czechoslovakia, Hungary); Tietze & Lehfeldt, *Legal Abortion in Eastern Europe*, 175 *J. A. M. A.* 1149, 1152 (April 1961). Other sources are discussed in Lader 17–23.

45. See Brief of *Amicus* National Right to Life Committee; R. Drinan, The Inviolability of the Right to be Born, in *Abortion and the Law*, 107 (D. Smith ed. 1967); Louisell, Abortion, The Practice of Medicine and the Due Process of Law, 16 *U. C. L. A. L. Rev.*, 233 (1969); Noonan 1.

46. See, e.g., *Abele v. Markle*, 342 F. Supp. 800 (Conn. 1972), appeal docketed, No. 72-56.

47. See discussions in Means I and Means II.

48. See, e.g., *State v. Murphy*, 27 N.J. L. 112, 114 (1858).

49. *Watson v. State*, 9 Tex. App. 237, 244–245 (1880); *Moore v. State*, 37 Tex. Cr. R. 552, 561, 40 S. W. 287, 290 (1897); *Shaw v. State*, 73 Tex. Cr. R. 337, 339, 165 S. W. 930, 931 (1914); *Fondren v. State*, 74 Tex. Cr. R. 552, 557, 169 S. W. 411, 414 (1914); *Gray v. State*, 77 Tex. Cr. R. 221, 229, 178 S. W. 337, 341 (1915). There is no immunity in Texas for the father who is not married to the mother. *Hammett v. State*, 84 Tex. Cr. R. 635, 209 S. W. 661 (1919); *Thompson v. State* (Ct. Crim. App. Tex. 1971), appeal docketed, No. 71-1200.

50. See *Smith v. State*, 33 Me., at 55; In re Vince, 2 N. J. 443, 450, 67 A. 2d 141, 144 (1949). A short discussion of the modern law on this issue is contained in the Comment to the ALI's Model Penal Code 207.11, at 158 and nn. 35–37 (Tent. Draft No. 9, 1959).

51. Tr. of Oral Rearg. 20–21.

52. Tr. of Oral Rearg. 24.

53. We are not aware that in the taking of any census under this clause, a fetus has ever been counted.

54. When Texas urges that a fetus is entitled to Fourteenth Amendment protection as a person, it faces a dilemma. Neither in Texas nor in any other State are all abortions prohibited. Despite broad proscription, an exception always exists. The exception contained [410 U.S. 113, 158] in Art. 1196, for an abortion procured or attempted by medical advice for the purpose of saving the life of the mother, is typical. But if the fetus is a person who is not to be deprived

of life without due process of law, and if the mother's condition is the sole determinant, does not the Texas exception appear to be out of line with the Amendment's command?

There are other inconsistencies between Fourteenth Amendment status and the typical abortion statute. It has already been pointed out, n. 49, *supra*, that in Texas the woman is not a principal or an accomplice with respect to an abortion upon her. If the fetus is a person, why is the woman not a principal or an accomplice? Further, the penalty for criminal abortion specified by Art. 1195 is significantly less than the maximum penalty for murder prescribed by Art. 1257 of the Texas Penal Code. If the fetus is a person, may the penalties be different?

55. Cf. the Wisconsin abortion statute, defining "unborn child" to mean "a human being from the time of conception until it is born alive," Wis. Stat. 940.04 (6) (1969), and the new Connecticut Statute, Pub. Act No. 1 (May 1972 special session), declaring it to be the public policy of the State and the legislative intent "to protect and preserve human life from the moment of conception."

56. Edelstein 16.

57. Lader 97–99; D. Feldman, *Birth Control in Jewish Law* 251–294 (1968). For a stricter view, see I. Jakobovits, Jewish Views on Abortion, in *Abortion and the Law*, 124 (D. Smith ed. 1967).

58. *Amicus* Brief for the American Ethical Union et al. For the position of the National Council of Churches and of other denominations, see Lader 99–101.

59. L. Hellman & J. Pritchard, *Williams Obstetrics*, 493 (14th ed. 1971); *Dorland's Illustrated Medical Dictionary*, 1689 (24th ed. 1965).

60. Hellman & Pritchard, *supra*, n. 59, at 493.

61. For discussions of the development of the Roman Catholic position, see D. Callahan, *Abortion: Law, Choice, and Morality*, 409–447 (1970); Noonan 1.

62. See Brodie, The New Biology and the Prenatal Child, 9 *J. Family L.* 391, 397 (1970); Gorney, The New Biology and the Future of Man, 15 *U. C. L. A. L. Rev.* 273 (1968); Note, Criminal Law—Abortion—The "Morning-After Pill" and Other Pre-Implantation Birth-Control Methods and the Law, 46 *Ore. L. Rev.*, 211 (1967); G. Taylor, *The Biological Time Bomb*, 32 (1968); A. Rosenfeld, *The Second Genesis*, 138–139 (1969); Smith, Through a Test Tube Darkly: Artificial Insemination and the Law, 67 *Mich. L. Rev.*, 127 (1968): Note, Artificial Insemination and the Law, 1968 *U. Ill. L. F.* 203.

63. W. Prosser, *The Law of Torts*, 335–338 (4th ed. 1971); 2 F. Harper & F. James, *The Law of Torts*, 1028–1031 (1956); Note, 63 *Harv. L. Rev.* 173 (1949).

64. See cases cited in Prosser, *supra*, n. 63, at 336-338; Annotation, Action for Death of Unborn Child, 15 *A.L. R.* 3d 992 (1967).

65. Prosser, *supra*, n. 63, at 338; Note, The Law and the Unborn Child: The Legal and Logical Inconsistencies, 46 *Notre Dame Law.*, 349, 354–360 (1971).

66. Louisell, Abortion, The Practice of Medicine and the Due Process of Law, 16 *U. C. L. A. L. Rev.*, 233, 235–238 (1969); Note, 56 *Iowa L. Rev.* 994, 999–1000 (1971); Note, The Law and the Unborn Child, 46 *Notre Dame Law.*, 349, 351–354 (1971).

67. Neither in this opinion nor in *Doe v. Bolton*, *post*, p. 179, do we discuss the father's rights, if any exist in the constitutional context, in the abortion decision. No paternal right has been asserted in either of the cases, and the Texas and the Georgia statutes on their face take no cognizance of the father. We are aware that some statutes recognize the father under certain circumstances. North Carolina, for example, N.C. Gen. Stat. 14-45.1 (Supp. 1971), requires written permission for the abortion from the husband when the woman is a married minor, that is, when she is less than 18 years of age, 41 N. C. A. G. 489 (1971); if the woman is an unmarried minor, written permission from the parents is required. We need not now decide whether provisions of this kind are constitutional.

MR. JUSTICE STEWART, concurring.

In 1963, this Court, in *Ferguson v. Skrupa*, 372 U.S. 726, purported to sound the death knell for the doctrine of substantive due process, a doctrine under which many state laws had in the past been held to violate the Fourteenth Amendment. As Mr. Justice Black's opinion for the Court in Skrupa put it: "We have returned to the original constitutional proposition that courts do not substitute their social and economic beliefs for the judgment of legislative bodies, who are elected to pass laws." *Id.*, at 730.[68]

Barely 2 years later, in *Griswold v. Connecticut*, 381 U.S. 479, the Court held a Connecticut birth control law unconstitutional. In view of what had been so recently said in Skrupa, the Court's opinion in

(Continues)

Griswold understandably did its best to avoid reliance on the Due Process Clause of the Fourteenth Amendment as the ground for decision. Yet, the Connecticut law did not violate any provision of the Bill of Rights, nor any other specific provision of the Constitution.[69] So it was clear [410 U.S. 113, 168] to me then, and it is equally clear to me now, that the Griswold decision can be rationally understood only as a holding that the Connecticut statute substantively invaded the "liberty" that is protected by the Due Process Clause of the Fourteenth Amendment.[70] As so understood, Griswold stands as one in a long line of pre-Skrupa cases decided under the doctrine of substantive due process, and I now accept it as such.

"In a Constitution for a free people, there can be no doubt that the meaning of 'liberty' must be broad indeed." *Board of Regents v. Roth*, 408 U.S. 564, 572. The Constitution nowhere mentions a specific right of personal choice in matters of marriage and family life, but the "liberty" protected by the Due Process Clause of the Fourteenth Amendment covers more than those freedoms explicitly named in the Bill of Rights. See *Schware v. Board of Bar Examiners*, 353 U.S. 232, 238–239; *Pierce v. Society of Sisters*, 268 U.S. 510, 534–535; *Meyer v. Nebraska*, 262 U.S. 390, 399–400. Cf. *Shapiro v. Thompson*, 394 U.S. 618, 629–630; *United States v. Guest*, 383 U.S. 745, 757–758; *Carrington v. Rash*, 380 U.S. 89, 96; *Aptheker v. Secretary of State*, 378 U.S. 500, 505; *Kent v. Dulles*, 357 U.S. 116, 127; *Bolling v. Sharpe*, 347 U.S. 497, 499–500; *Truax v. Raich*, 239 U.S. 33, 41. [410 U.S. 113, 169].

As Mr. Justice Harlan once wrote: "[T]he full scope of the liberty guaranteed by the Due Process Clause cannot be found in or limited by the precise terms of the specific guarantees elsewhere provided in the Constitution. This 'liberty' is not a series of isolated points pricked out in terms of the taking of property; the freedom of speech, press, and religion; the right to keep and bear arms; the freedom from unreasonable searches and seizures; and so on. It is a rational continuum which, broadly speaking, includes a freedom from all substantial arbitrary impositions and purposeless restraints . . . and which also recognizes, what a reasonable and sensitive judgment must, that certain interests require particularly careful scrutiny of the state needs asserted to justify their abridgment." *Poe v. Ullman*, 367 U.S. 497, 543 (opinion dissenting from dismissal of appeal) (citations omitted). In the words of Mr. Justice Frankfurter, "Great concepts like . . . 'liberty' . . . were purposely left to gather meaning from experience. For they relate to the whole domain of social and economic fact, and the statesmen who founded this Nation knew too well that only a stagnant society remains unchanged." *National Mutual Ins. Co. v. Tidewater Transfer Co.*, 337 U.S. 582, 646 (dissenting opinion).

Several decisions of this Court make clear that freedom of personal choice in matters of marriage and family life is one of the liberties protected by the Due Process Clause of the Fourteenth Amendment. *Loving v. Virginia*, 388 U.S. 1, 12; *Griswold v. Connecticut, supra*; *Pierce v. Society of Sisters, supra*; *Meyer v. Nebraska, supra*. See also *Prince v. Massachusetts*, 321 U.S. 158, 166; *Skinner v. Oklahoma*, 316 U.S. 535, 541. As recently as last Term, in *Eisenstadt v. Baird*, 405 U.S. 438, 453, we recognized "the right of the individual, married or single, to be free from unwarranted governmental intrusion into matters so fundamentally affecting a person [410 U.S. 113, 170] as the decision whether to bear or beget a child." That right necessarily includes the right of a woman to decide whether or not to terminate her pregnancy. "Certainly the interests of a woman in giving of her physical and emotional self during pregnancy and the interests that will be affected throughout her life by the birth and raising of a child are of a far greater degree of significance and personal intimacy than the right to send a child to private school protected in *Pierce v. Society of Sisters*, 268 U.S. 510 (1925), or the right to teach a foreign language protected in *Meyer v. Nebraska*, 262 U.S. 390 (1923)." *Abele v. Markle*, 351 F. Supp. 224, 227 (Conn. 1972).

Clearly, therefore, the Court today is correct in holding that the right asserted by Jane Roe is embraced within the personal liberty protected by the Due Process Clause of the Fourteenth Amendment.

It is evident that the Texas abortion statute infringes that right directly. Indeed, it is difficult to imagine a more complete abridgment of a constitutional freedom than that worked by the inflexible criminal statute now in force in Texas. The question then becomes whether the state interests advanced to justify this abridgment can survive the "particularly careful scrutiny" that the Fourteenth Amendment here requires.

The asserted state interests are protection of the health and safety of the pregnant woman, and protection of the potential future human life within her. These are legitimate objectives, amply sufficient to permit a State to regulate abortions as it does other surgical procedures, and perhaps sufficient to permit a State to regulate abortions more stringently or even to prohibit them in the late stages of pregnancy. But such legislation is not before us, and I think the Court today has thoroughly demonstrated that these state interests cannot constitutionally support the broad abridgment of personal [410 U.S. 113, 171] liberty worked by the existing Texas law. Accordingly, I join the Court's opinion holding that that law is invalid under the Due Process Clause of the Fourteenth Amendment.

Notes

68. Only Mr. Justice Harlan failed to join the Court's opinion, 372 U.S., at 733.
69. There is no constitutional right of privacy, as such. "[The Fourth] Amendment protects individual privacy against certain kinds of governmental intrusion, but its protections go further, and often have nothing to do with privacy at all. Other provisions of [410 U.S. 113, 168] the Constitution protect personal privacy from other forms of governmental invasion. But the protection of a person's general right to privacy—his right to be let alone by other people—is, like the protection of his property and of his very life, left largely to the law of the individual States." *Katz v. United States*, 389 U.S. 347, 350–351 (footnotes omitted).
70. This was also clear to Mr. Justice Black, 381 U.S., at 507 (dissenting opinion); to Mr. Justice Harlan, 381 U.S., at 499 (opinion concurring in the judgment); and to MR. JUSTICE WHITE, 381 U.S., at 502 (opinion concurring in the judgment). See also Mr. Justice Harlan's thorough and thoughtful opinion dissenting from dismissal of the appeal in *Poe v. Ullman*, 367 U.S. 497, 522.

MR. JUSTICE REHNQUIST, dissenting.

The Court's opinion brings to the decision of this troubling question both extensive historical fact and a wealth of legal scholarship. While the opinion thus commands my respect, I find myself nonetheless in fundamental disagreement with those parts of it that invalidate the Texas statute in question, and therefore dissent.

I

The Court's opinion decides that a State may impose virtually no restriction on the performance of abortions during the first trimester of pregnancy. Our previous decisions indicate that a necessary predicate for such an opinion is a plaintiff who was in her first trimester of pregnancy at some time during the pendency of her lawsuit. While a party may vindicate his own constitutional rights, he may not seek vindication for the rights of others. *Moose Lodge v. Irvis*, 407 U.S. 163 (1972); *Sierra Club v. Morton*, 405 U.S. 727 (1972). The Court's statement of facts in this case makes clear, however, that the record in no way indicates the presence of such a plaintiff. We know only that plaintiff Roe at the time of filing her complaint was a pregnant woman; for aught that appears in this record, she may have been in her last trimester of pregnancy as of the date the complaint was filed.

Nothing in the Court's opinion indicates that Texas might not constitutionally apply its proscription of abortion as written to a woman in that stage of pregnancy. Nonetheless, the Court uses her complaint against the Texas statute as a fulcrum for deciding that States may [410 U.S. 113, 172] impose virtually no restrictions on medical abortions performed during the first trimester of pregnancy. In deciding such a hypothetical lawsuit, the Court departs from the longstanding admonition that it should never "formulate a rule of constitutional law broader than is required by the precise facts to which it is to be applied." *Liverpool, New York & Philadelphia S.S. Co. v. Commissioners of Emigration*, 113 U.S. 33, 39 (1885). See also *Ashwander v. TVA*, 297 U.S. 288, 345 (1936) (Brandeis, J., concurring).

II

Even if there were a plaintiff in this case capable of litigating the issue which the Court decides, I would reach a conclusion opposite to that reached by the Court. I have difficulty in concluding, as the Court does, that the right of "privacy" is involved in this case. Texas, by the statute here challenged, bars the performance of a medical abortion by a licensed physician on a plaintiff such as Roe. A transaction resulting in an operation such as this is not "private" in the ordinary usage of that word. Nor is the "privacy" that the Court finds here even a distant relative of the freedom from searches and seizures protected by the Fourth Amendment to the Constitution, which the Court has referred to as embodying a right to privacy. *Katz v. United States*, 389 U.S. 347 (1967).

If the Court means by the term "privacy" no more than that the claim of a person to be free from unwanted state regulation of consensual transactions may be a form of "liberty" protected by the Fourteenth Amendment, there is no doubt that similar claims have been upheld in our earlier decisions on the basis of that liberty. I agree with the statement of MR. JUSTICE STEWART in his concurring opinion that the "liberty," against deprivation of which without due process the Fourteenth [410 U.S. 113, 173] Amendment protects, embraces more than the rights found in the Bill of Rights. But that liberty is not guaranteed absolutely against deprivation, only against deprivation without due process of law. The test traditionally applied in the area of social and economic legislation is whether

(Continues)

or not a law such as that challenged has a rational relation to a valid state objective. *Williamson v. Lee Optical Co.*, 348 U.S. 483, 491 (1955). The Due Process Clause of the Fourteenth Amendment undoubtedly does place a limit, albeit a broad one, on legislative power to enact laws such as this. If the Texas statute were to prohibit an abortion even where the mother's life is in jeopardy, I have little doubt that such a statute would lack a rational relation to a valid state objective under the test stated in Williamson, *supra*. But the Court's sweeping invalidation of any restrictions on abortion during the first trimester is impossible to justify under that standard, and the conscious weighing of competing factors that the Court's opinion apparently substitutes for the established test is far more appropriate to a legislative judgment than to a judicial one.

The Court eschews the history of the Fourteenth Amendment in its reliance on the "compelling state interest" test. See *Weber v. Aetna Casualty & Surety Co.*, 406 U.S. 164, 179 (1972) (dissenting opinion). But the Court adds a new wrinkle to this test by transposing it from the legal considerations associated with the Equal Protection Clause of the Fourteenth Amendment to this case arising under the Due Process Clause of the Fourteenth Amendment. Unless I misapprehend the consequences of this transplanting of the "compelling state interest test," the Court's opinion will accomplish the seemingly impossible feat of leaving this area of the law more confused than it found it. [410 U.S. 113, 174].

While the Court's opinion quotes from the dissent of Mr. Justice Holmes in *Lochner v. New York*, 198 U.S. 45, 74 (1905), the result it reaches is more closely attuned to the majority opinion of Mr. Justice Peckham in that case. As in Lochner and similar cases applying substantive due process standards to economic and social welfare legislation, the adoption of the compelling state interest standard will inevitably require this Court to examine the legislative policies and pass on the wisdom of these policies in the very process of deciding whether a particular state interest put forward may or may not be "compelling." The decision here to break pregnancy into three distinct terms and to outline the permissible restrictions the State may impose in each one, for example, partakes more of judicial legislation than it does of a determination of the intent of the drafters of the Fourteenth Amendment.

The fact that a majority of the States reflecting, after all, the majority sentiment in those States, have had restrictions on abortions for at least a century is a strong indication, it seems to me, that the asserted right to an abortion is not "so rooted in the traditions and conscience of our people as to be ranked as fundamental," *Snyder v. Massachusetts*, 291 U.S. 97, 105 (1934). Even today, when society's views on abortion are changing, the very existence of the debate is evidence that the "right" to an abortion is not so universally accepted as the appellant would have us believe.

To reach its result, the Court necessarily has had to find within the scope of the Fourteenth Amendment a right that was apparently completely unknown to the drafters of the Amendment. As early as 1821, the first state law dealing directly with abortion was enacted by the Connecticut Legislature. Conn. Stat., Tit. 22, 14, 16. By the time of the adoption of the Fourteenth [410 U.S. 113, 175] Amendment in 1868, there were at least 36 laws enacted by state or territorial legislatures limiting abortion.[71] While many States have amended or updated [410 U.S. 113, 176] their laws, 21 of the laws on the books in 1868 remain in effect today.[72] Indeed, the Texas statute struck down today was, as the majority notes, first enacted in 1857 [410 U.S. 113, 177] and "has remained substantially unchanged to the present time." *Ante*, at 119.

There apparently was no question concerning the validity of this provision or of any of the other state statutes when the Fourteenth Amendment was adopted. The only conclusion possible from this history is that the drafters did not intend to have the Fourteenth Amendment withdraw from the States the power to legislate with respect to this matter.

III

Even if one were to agree that the case that the Court decides were here, and that the enunciation of the substantive constitutional law in the Court's opinion were proper, the actual disposition of the case by the Court is still difficult to justify. The Texas statute is struck down in toto, even though the Court apparently concedes that at later periods of pregnancy Texas might impose these selfsame statutory limitations on abortion. My understanding of past practice is that a statute found [410 U.S. 113, 178] to be invalid as applied to a particular plaintiff, but not unconstitutional as a whole, is not simply "struck down" but is, instead, declared unconstitutional as applied to the fact situation before the Court. *Yick Wo v. Hopkins*, 118 U.S. 356 (1886); *Street v. New York*, 394 U.S. 576 (1969).

For all of the foregoing reasons, I respectfully dissent.

71. Jurisdictions having enacted abortion laws prior to the adoption of the Fourteenth Amendment in 1868:

1. Alabama—Ala. Acts, c. 6, 2 (1840).
2. Arizona—Howell Code, c. 10, 45 (1865).
3. Arkansas—Ark. Rev. Stat., c. 44, div. III, Art. II, 6 (1838).
4. California—Cal. Sess. Laws, c. 99, 45, p. 233 (1849–1850).
5. Colorado (Terr.)—Colo. Gen. Laws of Terr. of Colo., 1st Sess., 42, pp. 296–297 (1861).
6. Connecticut—Conn. Stat., Tit. 20, 14, 16 (1821). By 1868, this statute had been replaced by another abortion law. Conn. Pub. Acts, c. 71, 1, 2, p. 65 (1860).
7. Florida—Fla. Acts 1st Sess., c. 1637, subc. 3, 10, 11, subc. 8, 9, 10, 11 (1868), as amended, now Fla. Stat. Ann. 782.09, 782.10, 797.01, 797.02, 782.16 (1965).
8. Georgia—Ga. Pen. Code, 4th Div., 20 (1833).
9. Kingdom of Hawaii—Hawaii Pen. Code, c. 12, 1, 2, 3 (1850).
10. Idaho (Terr.)—Idaho (Terr.) Laws, Crimes and Punishments 33, 34, 42, pp. 441, 443 (1863).
11. Illinois—Ill. Rev. Criminal Code 40, 41, 46, pp. 130, 131 (1827). By 1868, this statute had been replaced by a subsequent enactment. Ill. Pub. Laws 1, 2, 3, p. 89 (1867).
12. Indiana—Ind. Rev. Stat. 1, 3, p. 224 (1838). By 1868 this statute had been superseded by a subsequent enactment. Ind. Laws, c. LXXXI, 2 (1859).
13. Iowa (Terr.)—Iowa (Terr.) Stat., 1st Legis., 1st Sess., 18, p. 145 (1838). By 1868, this statute had been superseded by a subsequent enactment. Iowa (Terr.) Rev. Stat., c. 49, 10, 13 (1843).
14. Kansas (Terr.)—Kan. (Terr.) Stat., c. 48, 9, 10, 39 (1855). By 1868, this statute had been superseded by a subsequent enactment. Kan. (Terr.) Laws, c. 28, 9, 10, 37 (1859).
15. Louisiana—La. Rev. Stat., Crimes and Offenses 24, p. 138 (1856).
16. Maine—Me. Rev. Stat., c. 160, 11, 12, 13, 14 (1840).
17. Maryland—Md. Laws, c. 179, 2, p. 315 (1868).
18. Massachusetts—Mass. Acts & Resolves, c. 27 (1845).
19. Michigan—Mich. Rev. Stat., c. 153, 32, 33, 34, p. 662 (1846). [410 U.S. 113, 176].
20. Minnesota (Terr.)—Minn. (Terr.) Rev. Stat., c. 100, 10, 11, p. 493 (1851).
21. Mississippi—Miss. Code, c. 64, 8, 9, p. 958 (1848).
22. Missouri—Mo. Rev. Stat., Art. II, 9, 10, 36, pp. 168, 172 (1835).
23. Montana (Terr.)—Mont. (Terr.) Laws, Criminal Practice Acts 41, p. 184 (1864).
24. Nevada (Terr.)—Nev. (Terr.) Laws, c. 28, 42, p. 63 (1861).
25. New Hampshire—N.H. Laws, c. 743, 1, p. 708 (1848).
26. New Jersey—N.J. Laws, p. 266 (1849).
27. New York—N.Y. Rev. Stat., pt. 4, c. 1, Tit. 2, 8, 9, pp. 12–13 (1828). By 1868, this statute had been superseded. N.Y. Laws, c. 260, 1–6, pp. 285–286 (1845); N.Y. Laws, c. 22, 1, p. 19 (1846).
28. Ohio—Ohio Gen. Stat. 111 (1), 112 (2), p. 252 (1841).
29. Oregon—Ore. Gen. Laws, Crim. Code, c. 43, 509, p. 528 (1845–1864).
30. Pennsylvania—Pa. Laws No. 374, 87, 88, 89 (1860).
31. Texas—Tex. Gen. Stat. Dig., c. VII, Arts. 531–536, p. 524 (Oldham & White 1859).
32. Vermont—Vt. Acts No. 33, 1 (1846). By 1868, this statute had been amended. Vt. Acts No. 57, 1, 3 (1867).
33. Virginia—Va. Acts, Tit. II, c. 3, 9, p. 96 (1848).
34. Washington (Terr.)—Wash. (Terr.) Stats., c. II, 37, 38, p. 81 (1854).
35. West Virginia—See Va. Acts., Tit. II, c. 3, 9, p. 96 (1848); W. Va. Const., Art. XI, par. 8 (1863).
36. Wisconsin—Wis. Rev. Stat., c. 133, 10, 11 (1849). By 1868, this statute had been superseded. Wis. Rev. Stat., c. 164, 10, 11; c. 169, 58, 59 (1858).

72. Abortion laws in effect in 1868 and still applicable as of August 1970:

1. Arizona (1865). 2. Connecticut (1860). 3. Florida (1868). 4. Idaho (1863). 5. Indiana (1838). [410 U.S. 113, 177]. 6. Iowa (1843). 7. Maine (1840). 8. Massachusetts (1845). 9. Michigan (1846). 10. Minnesota (1851). 11. Missouri (1835). 12. Montana (1864). 13. Nevada (1861). 14. New Hampshire (1848). 15. New Jersey (1849). 16. Ohio (1841). 17. Pennsylvania (1860). 18. Texas (1859). 19. Vermont (1867). 20. West Virginia (1863). 21. Wisconsin (1858). [410 U.S. 113, 179].

(Continues)

Doe v. Bolton, 410 U.S. 179 (1973)

Georgia law proscribes an abortion except as performed by a duly licensed Georgia physician when necessary in "his best clinical judgment" because continued pregnancy would endanger a pregnant woman's life or injure her health; the fetus would likely be born with a serious defect; or the pregnancy resulted from rape. 26-1202 (a) of Ga. Criminal Code. In addition to a requirement that the patient be a Georgia resident and certain other requirements, the statutory scheme poses three procedural conditions in 26-1202 (b): (1) that the abortion be performed in a hospital accredited by the Joint Commission on Accreditation of Hospitals (JCAH); (2) that the procedure be approved by the hospital staff abortion committee; and (3) that the performing physician's judgment be confirmed by independent examinations of the patient by two other licensed physicians. Appellant Doe, an indigent married Georgia citizen, who was denied an abortion after eight weeks of pregnancy for failure to meet any of the 26-1202 (a) conditions, sought declaratory and injunctive relief, contending that the Georgia laws were unconstitutional. Others joining in the complaint included Georgia-licensed physicians (who claimed that the Georgia statutes "chilled and deterred" their practices), registered nurses, clergymen, and social workers. Though holding that all the plaintiffs had standing, the District Court ruled that only Doe presented a justiciable controversy. In Doe's case the court gave declaratory, but not injunctive, relief, invalidating as an infringement of privacy and personal liberty the limitation to the three situations specified in 26-1202 (a) and certain other provisions but holding that the State's interest in health protection and the existence of a "potential of independent human existence" justified regulation through 26-1202 (b) of the "manner of performance as well as the quality of the final decision to abort." The appellants, claiming entitlement to broader relief, directly appealed to this Court. Held:

1. Doe's case presents a live, justiciable controversy and she has standing to sue, *Roe v. Wade, ante*, p. 113, as do the physician–appellants [410 U.S. 179, 180] (who, unlike the physician in Wade, were not charged with abortion violations), and it is therefore unnecessary to resolve the issue of the other appellants' standing. Pp. 187–189.

2. A woman's constitutional right to an abortion is not absolute. *Roe v. Wade, supra.* P. 189.

3. The requirement that a physician's decision to perform an abortion must rest upon "his best clinical judgment" of its necessity is not unconstitutionally vague, since that judgment may be made in the light of all the attendant circumstances. *United States v. Vuitch*, 402 U.S. 62, 71–72. Pp. 191–192.

4. The three procedural conditions in 26-1202 (b) violate the Fourteenth Amendment. Pp. 192–200.

    (a) The JCAH-accreditation requirement is invalid, since the State has not shown that only hospitals (let alone those with JCAH accreditation) meet its interest in fully protecting the patient; and a hospital requirement failing to exclude the first trimester of pregnancy would be invalid on that ground alone, see *Roe v. Wade, supra.* Pp. 193–195.

    (b) The interposition of a hospital committee on abortion, a procedure not applicable as a matter of state criminal law to other surgical situations, is unduly restrictive of the patient's rights, which are already safeguarded by her personal physician. Pp. 195–198.

    (c) Required acquiescence by two copractitioners also has no rational connection with a patient's needs and unduly infringes on her physician's right to practice. Pp. 198–200.

5. The Georgia residence requirement violates the Privileges and Immunities Clause by denying protection to persons who enter Georgia for medical services there. P. 200.

6. Appellants' equal protection argument centering on the three procedural conditions in 26-1202 (b), invalidated on other grounds, is without merit. Pp. 200–201.

7. No ruling is made on the question of injunctive relief. Cf. *Roe v. Wade, supra.* P. 201.

319 F. Supp. 1048, modified and affirmed.

BLACKMUN, J., delivered the opinion of the Court, in which BURGER, C. J., and DOUGLAS, BRENNAN, STEWART, MARSHALL, and POWELL, JJ., joined. BURGER, C. J., *post*, p. 207, and DOUGLAS, J., *post*, p. 209, filed concurring opinions. WHITE, J., filed a dissenting opinion, in which REHNQUIST, J., joined, *post*, p. 221. REHNQUIST, J., filed a dissenting opinion, *post*, p. 223. [410 U.S. 179, 181].

Margie Pitts Hames reargued the cause for appellants. With her on the briefs were Reber F. Boult, Jr., Charles Morgan, Jr., Elizabeth Roediger Rindskopf, and Tobiane Schwartz.

Dorothy T. Beasley reargued the cause for appellees. With her on the brief were Arthur K. Bolton, Attorney General of Georgia, Harold N. Hill, Jr., Executive Assistant Attorney General, Courtney Wilder Stanton, Assistant Attorney General, Joel Feldman, Henry L. Bowden, and Ralph H. Witt.*

MR. JUSTICE BLACKMUN delivered the opinion of the Court.

In this appeal, the criminal abortion statutes recently enacted in Georgia are challenged on constitutional grounds. The statutes are 26-1201 through 26-1203 of the State's Criminal Code, formulated by Georgia Laws, 1968 Session, pp. 1249, 1277–1280. In *Roe v. Wade, ante*, p. 113, we today have struck down, as constitutionally defective, the Texas criminal abortion statutes that are representative of provisions long in effect [410 U.S. 179, 182] in a majority of our States. The Georgia legislation, however, is different and merits separate consideration.

I

The statutes in question are reproduced as Appendix A, *post*, p. 202.[73] As the appellants acknowledge,[74] the 1968 statutes are patterned upon the American Law Institute's Model Penal Code, 230.3 (Proposed Official Draft, 1962), reproduced as Appendix B, *post*, p. 205. The ALI proposal has served as the model for recent legislation in approximately one-fourth of our States.[75] The new Georgia provisions replaced statutory law that had been in effect for more than 90 years. Georgia Laws 1876, No. 130, 2, at 113.[76] The predecessor statute paralleled [410 U.S. 179, 183] the Texas legislation considered in *Roe v. Wade, supra*, and made all abortions criminal except those necessary "to preserve the life" of the pregnant woman. The new statutes have not been tested on constitutional grounds in the Georgia state courts.

Section 26-1201, with a referenced exception, makes abortion a crime, and 26-1203 provides that a person convicted of that crime shall be punished by imprisonment for not less than one nor more than 10 years. Section 26-1202 (a) states the exception and removes from 1201's definition of criminal abortion, and thus makes noncriminal, an abortion "performed by a physician duly licensed" in Georgia when, "based upon his best clinical judgment . . . an abortion is necessary because:

"(1) A continuation of the pregnancy would endanger the life of the pregnant woman or would seriously and permanently injure her health; or

"(2) The fetus would very likely be born with a grave, permanent, and irremediable mental or physical defect; or

"(3) The pregnancy resulted from forcible or statutory rape."[77]

Section 26-1202 also requires, by numbered subdivisions of its subsection (b), that, for an abortion to be authorized [410 U.S. 179, 184] or performed as a noncriminal procedure, additional conditions must be fulfilled. These are (1) and (2) residence of the woman in Georgia; (3) reduction to writing of the performing physician's medical judgment that an abortion is justified for one or more of the reasons specified by 26-1202 (a), with written concurrence in that judgment by at least two other Georgia-licensed physicians, based upon their separate personal medical examinations of the woman; (4) performance of the abortion in a hospital licensed by the State Board of Health and also accredited by the Joint Commission on Accreditation of Hospitals; (5) advance approval by an abortion committee of not less than three members of the hospital's staff; (6) certifications in a rape situation; and (7), (8), and (9) maintenance and confidentiality of records. There is a provision (Subsection (c)) for judicial determination of the legality of a proposed abortion on petition of the judicial circuit law officer or of a close relative, as therein defined, of the unborn child, and for expeditious hearing of that petition. There is also a provision (subsection (e)) giving a hospital the right not to admit an abortion patient and giving any physician and any hospital employee or staff member the right, on moral or religious grounds, not to participate in the procedure.

II

On April 16, 1970, Mary Doe,[78] 23 other individuals (nine described as Georgia-licensed physicians, seven as nurses registered in the State, five as clergymen, and two as social workers), and two nonprofit

*Briefs of *amici curiae* were filed by Roy Lucas for the American College of Obstetricians and Gynecologists et al.; by Dennis J. Horan, Jerome A. Frazel, Jr., Thomas M. Crisham, and Delores V. Horan for Certain Physicians, Professors and Fellows of the American College of Obstetrics and Gynecology; by Harriet F. Pilpel, Nancy F. Wechsler, and Frederic S. Nathan for Planned Parenthood Federation of America, Inc., et al.; by Alan F. Charles for the National Legal Program on Health Problems of the Poor et al.; by Marttie L. Thompson for State Communities Aid Assn.; by Alfred L. Scanlan, Martin J. Flynn, and Robert M. Byrn for the National Right to Life Committee; by Helen L. Buttenwieser for the American Ethical Union et al.; by Norma G. Zarky for the American Association of University Women et al.; by Nancy Stearns for New Women Lawyers et al.; by the California Committee to Legalize Abortion et al.; by Robert E. Dunne for Robert L. Sassone; and by Ferdinand Buckley *pro se*.

(Continues)

(Continued)

Georgia corporations that advocate abortion reform instituted this federal action in the Northern District of Georgia against the State's attorney general, the district attorney of [410 U.S. 179, 185] Fulton County, and the chief of police of the city of Atlanta. The plaintiffs sought a declaratory judgment that the Georgia abortion statutes were unconstitutional in their entirety. They also sought injunctive relief restraining the defendants and their successors from enforcing the statutes.

Mary Doe alleged:

1. She was a 22-year-old Georgia citizen, married, and 9 weeks pregnant. She had three living children. The two older ones had been placed in a foster home because of Doe's poverty and inability to care for them. The youngest, born July 19, 1969, had been placed for adoption. Her husband had recently abandoned her and she was forced to live with her indigent parents and their eight children. She and her husband, however, had become reconciled. He was a construction worker employed only sporadically. She had been a mental patient at the State Hospital. She had been advised that an abortion could be performed on her with less danger to her health than if she gave birth to the child she was carrying. She would be unable to care for or support the new child.

2. On March 25, 1970, she applied to the Abortion Committee of Grady Memorial Hospital, Atlanta, for a therapeutic abortion under 26-1202. Her application was denied 16 days later, on April 10, when she was 8 weeks pregnant, on the ground that her situation was not one described in 26-1202 (a).[79]

3. Because her application was denied, she was forced either to relinquish "her right to decide when and how many children she will bear" or to seek an abortion that was illegal under the Georgia statutes. This invaded her [410 U.S. 179, 186] rights of privacy and liberty in matters related to family, marriage, and sex, and deprived her of the right to choose whether to bear children. This was a violation of rights guaranteed her by the First, Fourth, Fifth, Ninth, and Fourteenth Amendments. The statutes also denied her equal protection and procedural due process and, because they were unconstitutionally vague, deterred hospitals and doctors from performing abortions. She sued "on her own behalf and on behalf of all others similarly situated."

The other plaintiffs alleged that the Georgia statutes "chilled and deterred" them from practicing their respective professions and deprived them of rights guaranteed by the First, Fourth, and Fourteenth Amendments. These plaintiffs also purported to sue on their own behalf and on behalf of others similarly situated.

A three-judge district court was convened. An offer of proof as to Doe's identity was made, but the court deemed it unnecessary to receive that proof. The case was then tried on the pleadings and interrogatories.

The District Court, *per curiam*, 319 F. Supp. 1048 (ND Ga. 1970), held that all the plaintiffs had standing but that only Doe presented a justiciable controversy. On the merits, the court concluded that the limitation in the Georgia statute of the "number of reasons for which an abortion may be sought," *id.*, at 1056, improperly restricted Doe's rights of privacy articulated in *Griswold v. Connecticut*, 381 U.S. 479 (1965), and of "personal liberty," both of which it thought "broad enough to include the decision to abort a pregnancy," 319 F. Supp., at 1055. As a consequence, the court held invalid those portions of 26-1202 (a) and (b) (3) limiting legal abortions to the three situations specified; 26-1202 (b) (6) relating to certifications in a rape situation; and 26-1202 (c) authorizing a court test. Declaratory relief was granted accordingly. The court, however, held [410 U.S. 179, 187] that Georgia's interest in protection of health, and the existence of a "potential of independent human existence" (emphasis in original), *id.*, at 1055, justified state regulation of "the manner of performance as well as the quality of the final decision to abort," *id.*, at 1056, and it refused to strike down the other provisions of the statutes. It denied the request for an injunction, *id.*, at 1057.

Claiming that they were entitled to an injunction and to broader relief, the plaintiffs took a direct appeal pursuant to 28 U.S.C. 1253. We postponed decision on jurisdiction to the hearing on the merits. 402 U.S. 941 (1971). The defendants also purported to appeal, pursuant to 1253, but their appeal was dismissed for want of jurisdiction. 402 U.S. 936 (1971). We are advised by the appellees, Brief 42, that an alternative appeal on their part is pending in the United States Court of Appeals for the Fifth Circuit. The extent, therefore, to which the District Court decision was adverse to the defendants, that is, the extent to which portions of the Georgia statutes were held to be unconstitutional, technically is not now before us.[80] *Swarb v. Lennox*, 405 U.S. 191, 201 (1972).

III

Our decision in *Roe v. Wade*, *ante*, p. 113, establishes (1) that, despite her pseudonym, we may accept as true, for this case, Mary Doe's existence and her pregnant state on April 16, 1970; (2) that the constitutional issue is substantial; (3) that the interim termination of Doe's and all other Georgia pregnancies in existence in 1970 has not rendered the case moot; and (4) that Doe presents a justiciable controversy and has standing to maintain the action. [410 U.S. 179, 188].

Inasmuch as Doe and her class are recognized, the question whether the other appellants—physicians, nurses, clergymen, social workers, and corporations—present a justiciable controversy and have standing is perhaps a matter of no great consequence. We conclude, however, that the physician-appellants, who are Georgia-licensed doctors consulted by pregnant women, also present a justiciable controversy and do have standing despite the fact that the record does not disclose that any one of them has been prosecuted, or threatened with prosecution, for violation of the State's abortion statutes. The physician is the one against whom these criminal statutes directly operate in the event he procures an abortion that does not meet the statutory exceptions and conditions. The physician–appellants, therefore, assert a sufficiently direct threat of personal detriment. They should not be required to await and undergo a criminal prosecution as the sole means of seeking relief. *Crossen v. Breckenridge*, 446 F.2d 833, 839–840 (CA6 1971); *Poe v. Menghini*, 339 F. Supp. 986, 990–991 (Kan. 1972).

In holding that the physicians, while theoretically possessed of standing, did not present a justiciable controversy, the District Court seems to have relied primarily on *Poe v. Ullman*, 367 U.S. 497 (1961). There, a sharply divided Court dismissed an appeal from a state court on the ground that it presented no real controversy justifying the adjudication of a constitutional issue. But the challenged Connecticut statute, deemed to prohibit the giving of medical advice on the use of contraceptives, had been enacted in 1879, and, apparently with a single exception, no one had ever been prosecuted under it. Georgia's statute, in contrast, is recent and not moribund. Furthermore, it is the successor to another [410 U.S. 179, 189] Georgia abortion statute under which, we are told,[81] physicians were prosecuted. The present case, therefore, is closer to *Epperson v. Arkansas*, 393 U.S. 97 (1968), where the Court recognized the right of a school teacher, though not yet charged criminally, to challenge her State's anti-evolution statute. See also *Griswold v. Connecticut*, 381 U.S., at 481.

The parallel claims of the nurse, clergy, social worker, and corporation–appellants are another step removed and as to them, the Georgia statutes operate less directly. Not being licensed physicians, the nurses and the others are in no position to render medical advice. They would be reached by the abortion statutes only in their capacity as accessories or as counselor-conspirators. We conclude that we need not pass upon the status of these additional appellants in this suit, for the issues are sufficiently and adequately presented by Doe and the physician–appellants, and nothing is gained or lost by the presence or absence of the nurses, the clergymen, the social workers, and the corporations. See *Roe v. Wade, ante*, at 127.

IV

The appellants attack on several grounds those portions of the Georgia abortion statutes that remain after the District Court decision: undue restriction of a right to personal and marital privacy; vagueness; deprivation of substantive and procedural due process; improper restriction to Georgia residents; and denial of equal protection.

(a) *Roe v. Wade, supra*, sets forth our conclusion that a pregnant woman does not have an absolute constitutional right to an abortion on her demand. What is said there is applicable here and need not be repeated. [410 U.S. 179, 190].

(b) The appellants go on to argue, however, that the present Georgia statutes must be viewed historically, that is, from the fact that prior to the 1968 Act an abortion in Georgia was not criminal if performed to "preserve the life" of the mother. It is suggested that the present statute, as well, has this emphasis on the mother's rights, not on those of the fetus. Appellants contend that it is thus clear that Georgia has given little, and certainly not first, consideration to the unborn child. Yet, it is the unborn child's rights that Georgia asserts in justification of the statute. Appellants assert that this justification cannot be advanced at this late date.

Appellants then argue that the statutes do not adequately protect the woman's right. This is so because it would be physically and emotionally damaging to Doe to bring a child into her poor, "fatherless"[82] family, and because advances in medicine and medical techniques have made it safer for a woman to have a medically induced abortion than for her to bear a child. Thus, "a statute that requires a woman to carry an unwanted pregnancy to term infringes not only on a fundamental right of privacy but on the right to life itself." Brief 27.

The appellants recognize that a century ago medical knowledge was not so advanced as it is today, that the techniques of antisepsis were not known, and that any abortion procedure was dangerous for the woman. To restrict the legality of the abortion to the situation where it was deemed necessary, in

(Continues)

medical judgment, for the preservation of the woman's life was only a natural conclusion in the exercise of the legislative judgment of that time. A State is not to be reproached, however, for a past judgmental determination made in the light of then-existing medical knowledge. It is perhaps unfair to argue, as the appellants do, that because the early focus [410 U.S. 179, 191] was on the preservation of the woman's life, the State's present professed interest in the protection of embryonic and fetal life is to be downgraded. That argument denies the State the right to readjust its views and emphases in the light of the advanced knowledge and techniques of the day.

(c) Appellants argue that 26-1202 (a) of the Georgia statutes, as it has been left by the District Court's decision, is unconstitutionally vague. This argument centers on the proposition that, with the District Court's having struck down the statutorily specified reasons, it still remains a crime for a physician to perform an abortion except when, as 26-1202 (a) reads, it is "based upon his best clinical judgment that an abortion is necessary." The appellants contend that the word "necessary" does not warn the physician of what conduct is proscribed; that the statute is wholly without objective standards and is subject to diverse interpretation; and that doctors will choose to err on the side of caution and will be arbitrary.

The net result of the District Court's decision is that the abortion determination, so far as the physician is concerned, is made in the exercise of his professional, that is, his "best clinical," judgment in the light of all the attendant circumstances. He is not now restricted to the three situations originally specified. Instead, he may range farther afield wherever his medical judgment, properly and professionally exercised, so dictates and directs him.

The vagueness argument is set at rest by the decision in *United States v. Vuitch*, 402 U.S. 62, 71–72 (1971), where the issue was raised with respect to a District of Columbia statute making abortions criminal "unless the same were done as necessary for the preservation of the mother's life or health and under the direction of a competent licensed practitioner of medicine." That statute has been construed to bear upon psychological as [410 U.S. 179, 192] well as physical well-being. This being so, the Court concluded that the term "health" presented no problem of vagueness. "Indeed, whether a particular operation is necessary for a patient's physical or mental health is a judgment that physicians are obviously called upon to make routinely whenever surgery is considered." *Id.*, at 72. This conclusion is equally applicable here. Whether, in the words of the Georgia statute, "an abortion is necessary" is a professional judgment that the Georgia physician will be called upon to make routinely.

We agree with the District Court, 319 F. Supp., at 1058, that the medical judgment may be exercised in the light of all factors—physical, emotional, psychological, familial, and the woman's age—relevant to the well-being of the patient. All these factors may relate to health. This allows the attending physician the room he needs to make his best medical judgment. And it is room that operates for the benefit, not the disadvantage, of the pregnant woman.

(d) The appellants next argue that the District Court should have declared unconstitutional three procedural demands of the Georgia statute: (1) that the abortion be performed in a hospital accredited by the Joint Commission on Accreditation of Hospitals[83]: (2) that the procedure be approved by the hospital staff abortion committee; and (3) that the performing physician's judgment be confirmed by the independent examinations of the patient by two other licensed physicians. The appellants attack these provisions not only on the ground that they unduly restrict the woman's right of privacy, but also on procedural due process and equal protection grounds. The physician–appellants also argue that, by subjecting a doctor's individual medical judgment to [410 U.S. 179, 193] committee approval and to confirming consultations, the statute impermissibly restricts the physician's right to practice his profession and deprives him of due process.

1. JCAH accreditation. The Joint Commission on Accreditation of Hospitals is an organization without governmental sponsorship or overtones. No question whatever is raised concerning the integrity of the organization or the high purpose of the accreditation process.[84] That process, however, has to do with hospital standards generally and has no present particularized concern with abortion as a medical or surgical procedure.[85] In Georgia, there is no restriction on the performance of nonabortion surgery in a hospital not yet accredited by the JCAH so long as other requirements imposed by the State, such as licensing of the hospital and of the operating surgeon, are met. See Georgia Code 88-1901 (a) [410 U.S. 179, 194] and 88-1905 (1971) and 84-907 (Supp. 1971). Furthermore, accreditation by the Commission is not granted until a hospital has been in operation at least one year. The Model Penal Code, 230.3, Appendix B hereto, contains no requirement for JCAH accreditation. And the Uniform Abortion Act (Final Draft, Aug. 1971),[86] approved by the American Bar Association in February 1972, contains no JCAH-accredited hospital specification.[87] Some courts have held that a JCAH-accreditation requirement is an overbroad infringement of fundamental rights because it does not relate to the particular medical problems and dangers of the abortion operation. E.g., *Poe v. Menghini*, 339 F. Supp., at 993–994.

We hold that the JCAH-accreditation requirement does not withstand constitutional scrutiny in the present context. It is a requirement that simply is not "based on differences that are reasonably related to the purposes of the Act in which it is found." *Morey v. Doud*, 354 U.S. 457, 465 (1957).

This is not to say that Georgia may not or should not, from and after the end of the first trimester, adopt [410 U.S. 179, 195] standards for licensing all facilities where abortions may be performed so long as those standards are legitimately related to the objective the State seeks to accomplish. The appellants contend that such a relationship would be lacking even in a lesser requirement that an abortion be performed in a licensed hospital, as opposed to a facility, such as a clinic, that may be required by the State to possess all the staffing and services necessary to perform an abortion safely (including those adequate to handle serious complications or other emergency, or arrangements with a nearby hospital to provide such services). Appellants and various *amici* have presented us with a mass of data purporting to demonstrate that some facilities other than hospitals are entirely adequate to perform abortions if they possess these qualifications. The State, on the other hand, has not presented persuasive data to show that only hospitals meet its acknowledged interest in insuring the quality of the operation and the full protection of the patient. We feel compelled to agree with appellants that the State must show more than it has in order to prove that only the full resources of a licensed hospital, rather than those of some other appropriately licensed institution, satisfy these health interests. We hold that the hospital requirement of the Georgia law, because it fails to exclude the first trimester of pregnancy, see *Roe v. Wade, ante*, at 163, is also invalid. In so holding we naturally express no opinion on the medical judgment involved in any particular case, that is, whether the patient's situation is such that an abortion should be performed in a hospital, rather than in some other facility.

2. Committee approval. The second aspect of the appellants' procedural attack relates to the hospital abortion committee and to the pregnant woman's asserted [410 U.S. 179, 196] lack of access to that committee. Relying primarily on *Goldberg v. Kelly*, 397 U.S. 254 (1970), concerning the termination of welfare benefits, and *Wisconsin v. Constantineau*, 400 U.S. 433 (1971), concerning the posting of an alcoholic's name, Doe first argues that she was denied due process because she could not make a presentation to the committee. It is not clear from the record, however, whether Doe's own consulting physician was or was not a member of the committee or did or did not present her case, or, indeed, whether she herself was or was not there. We see nothing in the Georgia statute that explicitly denies access to the committee by or on behalf of the woman. If the access point alone were involved, we would not be persuaded to strike down the committee provision on the unsupported assumption that access is not provided.

Appellants attack the discretion the statute leaves to the committee. The most concrete argument they advance is their suggestion that it is still a badge of infamy "in many minds" to bear an illegitimate child, and that the Georgia system enables the committee members' personal views as to extramarital sex relations, and punishment therefor, to govern their decisions. This approach obviously is one founded on suspicion and one that discloses a lack of confidence in the integrity of physicians. To say that physicians will be guided in their hospital committee decisions by their predilections on extramarital sex unduly narrows the issue to pregnancy outside marriage. (Doe's own situation did not involve extramarital sex and its product.) The appellants' suggestion is necessarily somewhat degrading to the conscientious physician, particularly the obstetrician, whose professional activity is concerned with the physical and mental welfare, the woes, the emotions, and the concern of his female patients. He, perhaps more than anyone else, is knowledgeable in this area of patient care, and he is aware of human frailty, [410 U.S. 179, 197] so-called "error," and needs. The good physician—despite the presence of rascals in the medical profession, as in all others, we trust that most physicians are "good"—will have sympathy and understanding for the pregnant patient that probably are not exceeded by those who participate in other areas of professional counselling.

It is perhaps worth noting that the abortion committee has a function of its own. It is a committee of the hospital and it is composed of members of the institution's medical staff. The membership usually is a changing one. In this way, its work burden is shared and is more readily accepted. The committee's function is protective. It enables the hospital appropriately to be advised that its posture and activities are in accord with legal requirements. It is to be remembered that the hospital is an entity and that it, too, has legal rights and legal obligations.

(Continues)

Saying all this, however, does not settle the issue of the constitutional propriety of the committee requirement. Viewing the Georgia statute as a whole, we see no constitutionally justifiable pertinence in the structure for the advance approval by the abortion committee. With regard to the protection of potential life, the medical judgment is already completed prior to the committee stage, and review by a committee once removed from diagnosis is basically redundant. We are not cited to any other surgical procedure made subject to committee approval as a matter of state criminal law. The woman's right to receive medical care in accordance with her licensed physician's best judgment and the physician's right to administer it are substantially limited by this statutorily imposed overview. And the hospital itself is otherwise fully protected. Under 26-1202 (e), the hospital is free not to admit a patient for an abortion. It is even free not to have an abortion committee. Further, a physician or any other employee has the right to refrain, [410 U.S. 179, 198] for moral or religious reasons, from participating in the abortion procedure. These provisions obviously are in the statute in order to afford appropriate protection to the individual and to the denominational hospital. Section 26-1202 (e) affords adequate protection to the hospital, and little more is provided by the committee prescribed by 26-1202 (b) (5).

We conclude that the interposition of the hospital abortion committee is unduly restrictive of the patient's rights and needs that, at this point, have already been medically delineated and substantiated by her personal physician. To ask more serves neither the hospital nor the State.

3. Two-doctor concurrence. The third aspect of the appellants' attack centers on the "time and availability of adequate medical facilities and personnel." It is said that the system imposes substantial and irrational roadblocks and "is patently unsuited" to prompt determination of the abortion decision. Time, of course, is critical in abortion. Risks during the first trimester of pregnancy are admittedly lower than during later months.

The appellants purport to show by a local study[88] of Grady Memorial Hospital (serving indigent residents in Fulton and DeKalb Counties) that the "mechanics of the system itself forced . . . discontinuance of the abortion process" because the median time for the workup was 15 days. The same study shows, however, that 27% of the candidates for abortion were already 13 or more weeks pregnant at the time of application, that is, they were at the end of or beyond the first trimester when they made their applications. It is too much to say, as appellants do, that these particular persons "were victims of a system over which they [had] no control." If higher risk was incurred because of abortions in the [410 U.S. 179, 199] second rather than the first trimester, much of that risk was due to delay in application, and not to the alleged cumbersomeness of the system. We note, in passing, that appellant Doe had no delay problem herself; the decision in her case was made well within the first trimester.

It should be manifest that our rejection of the accredited-hospital requirement and, more important, of the abortion committee's advance approval eliminates the major grounds of the attack based on the system's delay and the lack of facilities. There remains, however, the required confirmation by two Georgia-licensed physicians in addition to the recommendation of the pregnant woman's own consultant (making under the statute, a total of six physicians involved, including the three on the hospital's abortion committee). We conclude that this provision, too, must fall.

The statute's emphasis, as has been repetitively noted, is on the attending physician's "best clinical judgment that an abortion is necessary." That should be sufficient. The reasons for the presence of the confirmation step in the statute are perhaps apparent, but they are insufficient to withstand constitutional challenge. Again, no other voluntary medical or surgical procedure for which Georgia requires confirmation by two other physicians has been cited to us. If a physician is licensed by the State, he is recognized by the State as capable of exercising acceptable clinical judgment. If he fails in this, professional censure and deprivation of his license are available remedies. Required acquiescence by co-practitioners has no rational connection with a patient's needs and unduly infringes on the physician's right to practice. The attending physician will know when a consultation is advisable—the doubtful situation, the need for assurance when the medical decision is a delicate one, and the like. Physicians have followed this routine historically and [410 U.S. 179, 200] know its usefulness and benefit for all concerned. It is still true today that "[r]eliance must be placed upon the assurance given by his license, issued by an authority competent to judge in that respect, that he [the physician] possesses the requisite qualifications." *Dent v. West Virginia*, 129 U.S. 114, 122–123 (1889). See *United States v. Vuitch*, 402 U.S., at 71.

(e) The appellants attack the residency requirement of the Georgia law, 26-1202 (b) (1) and (b) (2), as violative of the right to travel stressed in *Shapiro v. Thompson*, 394 U.S. 618, 629–631 (1969), and other cases. A requirement of this kind, of course, could be deemed to have some relationship to the availability of postprocedure medical care for the aborted patient.

Nevertheless, we do not uphold the constitutionality of the residence requirement. It is not based on any policy of preserving state-supported facilities for Georgia residents, for the bar also applies to private hospitals and to privately retained physicians. There is no intimation, either, that Georgia facilities are utilized to capacity in caring for Georgia residents. Just as the Privileges and Immunities Clause, Const. Art. IV, 2, protects persons who enter other States to ply their trade, *Ward v. Maryland*, 12 Wall. 418, 430 (1871); *Blake v. McClung*, 172 U.S. 239, 248–256 (1898), so must it protect persons who enter Georgia seeking the medical services that are available there. See *Toomer v. Witsell*, 334 U.S. 385, 396–397 (1948). A contrary holding would mean that a State could limit to its own residents the general medical care available within its borders. This we could not approve.

(f) The last argument on this phase of the case is one that often is made, namely, that the Georgia system is violative of equal protection because it discriminates against the poor. The appellants do not urge that abortions [410 U.S. 179, 201] should be performed by persons other than licensed physicians, so we have no argument that because the wealthy can better afford physicians, the poor should have nonphysicians made available to them. The appellants acknowledged that the procedures are "nondiscriminatory in . . . express terms" but they suggest that they have produced invidious discriminations. The District Court rejected this approach out of hand. 319 F. Supp., at 1056. It rests primarily on the accreditation and approval and confirmation requirements, discussed above, and on the assertion that most of Georgia's counties have no accredited hospital. We have set aside the accreditation, approval, and confirmation requirements, however, and with that, the discrimination argument collapses in all significant aspects.

V

The appellants complain, finally, of the District Court's denial of injunctive relief. A like claim was made in *Roe v. Wade*, *ante*, p. 113. We declined decision there insofar as injunctive relief was concerned, and we decline it here. We assume that Georgia's prosecutorial authorities will give full recognition to the judgment of this Court.

In summary, we hold that the JCAH-accredited hospital provision and the requirements as to approval by the hospital abortion committee, as to confirmation by two independent physicians, and as to residence in Georgia are all violative of the Fourteenth Amendment. Specifically, the following portions of 26-1202 (b), remaining after the District Court's judgment, are invalid:

1. Subsections (1) and (2).
2. That portion of Subsection (3) following the words "[s]uch physician's judgment is reduced to writing."
3. Subsections (4) and (5). [410 U.S. 179, 202].

The judgment of the District Court is modified accordingly and, as so modified, is affirmed. Costs are allowed to the appellants.

APPENDIX A TO OPINION OF THE COURT

Criminal Code of Georgia

(The italicized portions are those held unconstitutional by the District Court)

CHAPTER 26-12. ABORTION.

26-1201. Criminal Abortion. Except as otherwise provided in Section 26-1202, a person commits criminal abortion when he administers any medicine, drug or other substance whatever to any woman or when he uses any instrument or other means whatever upon any woman with intent to produce a miscarriage or abortion.

26-1202. Exception. (a) Section 26-1201 shall not apply to an abortion performed by a physician duly licensed to practice medicine and surgery pursuant to Chapter 84-9 or 84-12 of the Code of Georgia of 1933, as amended, based upon his best clinical judgment that an abortion is necessary because:

1. A continuation of the pregnancy would endanger the life of the pregnant woman or would seriously and permanently injure her health; or
2. The fetus would very likely be born with a grave, permanent, and irremediable mental or physical defect; or
3. The pregnancy resulted from forcible or statutory rape.

(Continues)

(Continued)

(b) No abortion is authorized or shall be performed under this section unless each of the following conditions are met:

1. The pregnant woman requesting the abortion certifies in writing under oath and subject to the penalties [410 U.S. 179, 203] of false swearing to the physician who proposes to perform the abortion that she is a bona fide legal resident of the State of Georgia.

2. The physician certifies that he believes the woman is a bona fide resident of this State and that he has no information which should lead him to believe otherwise.

3. Such physician's judgment is reduced to writing and concurred in by at least two other physicians duly licensed to practice medicine and surgery pursuant to Chapter 84-9 of the Code of Georgia of 1933, as amended, who certify in writing that based upon their separate personal medical examinations of the pregnant woman, the abortion is, in their judgment, necessary because of one or more of the reasons enumerated above.

4. Such abortion is performed in a hospital licensed by the State Board of Health and accredited by the Joint Commission on Accreditation of Hospitals.

5. The performance of the abortion has been approved in advance by a committee of the medical staff of the hospital in which the operation is to be performed. This committee must be one established and maintained in accordance with the standards promulgated by the Joint Commission on the Accreditation of Hospitals, and its approval must be by a majority vote of a membership of not less than three members of the hospital's staff; the physician proposing to perform the operation may not be counted as a member of the committee for this purpose.

6. If the proposed abortion is considered necessary because the woman has been raped, the woman makes a written statement under oath, and subject to the penalties of false swearing, of the date, time and place of the rape and the name of the rapist, if known. There must be attached to this statement a certified copy of any report of the rape made by any law enforcement officer or agency and a statement by the solicitor general of the [410 U.S. 179, 204] judicial circuit where the rape occurred or allegedly occurred that, according to his best information, there is probable cause to believe that the rape did occur.

7. Such written opinions, statements, certificates, and concurrences are maintained in the permanent files of such hospital and are available at all reasonable times to the solicitor general of the judicial circuit in which the hospital is located.

8. A copy of such written opinions, statements, certificates, and concurrences is filed with the Director of the State Department of Public Health within 10 days after such operation is performed.

9. All written opinions, statements, certificates, and concurrences filed and maintained pursuant to paragraphs (7) and (8) of this subsection shall be confidential records and shall not be made available for public inspection at any time.

(c) Any solicitor general of the judicial circuit in which an abortion is to be performed under this section, or any person who would be a relative of the child within the second degree of consanguinity, may petition the superior court of the county in which the abortion is to be performed for a declaratory judgment whether the performance of such abortion would violate any constitutional or other legal rights of the fetus. Such solicitor general may also petition such court for the purpose of taking issue with compliance with the requirements of this section. The physician who proposes to perform the abortion and the pregnant woman shall be respondents. The petition shall be heard expeditiously and if the court adjudges that such abortion would violate the constitutional or other legal rights of the fetus, the court shall so declare and shall restrain the physician from performing the abortion.

(d) If an abortion is performed in compliance with this section, the death of the fetus shall not give rise to any claim for wrongful death. [410 U.S. 179, 205].

(e) Nothing in this section shall require a hospital to admit any patient under the provisions hereof for the purpose of performing an abortion, nor shall any hospital be required to appoint a committee such as contemplated under Subsection (b) (5). A physician, or any other person who is a member of or associated with the staff of a hospital, or any employee of a hospital in which an abortion has been authorized, who shall state in writing an objection to such abortion on moral or religious grounds shall not be required to participate in the medical procedures which will result in the abortion, and the refusal of any such person to participate therein shall not form the basis of any claim for damages on account of such refusal or for any disciplinary or recriminatory action against such person.

26-1203. Punishment. A person convicted of criminal abortion shall be punished by imprisonment for not less than one nor more than 10 years.

APPENDIX B TO OPINION OF THE COURT

American Law Institute
MODEL PENAL CODE
Section 230.3. Abortion.

1. Unjustified Abortion. A person who purposely and unjustifiably terminates the pregnancy of another otherwise than by a live birth commits a felony of the third degree or, where the pregnancy has continued beyond the 26th week, a felony of the second degree.

2. Justifiable Abortion. A licensed physician is justified in terminating a pregnancy if he believes there is substantial risk that continuance of the pregnancy would gravely impair the physical or mental health of the mother or that the child would be born with grave physical or mental defect, or that the pregnancy resulted from rape, incest, or other felonious intercourse. All [410 U.S. 179, 206] illicit intercourse with a girl below the age of 16 shall be deemed felonious for purposes of this subsection. Justifiable abortions shall be performed only in a licensed hospital except in case of emergency when hospital facilities are unavailable. [Additional exceptions from the requirement of hospitalization may be incorporated here to take account of situations in sparsely settled areas where hospitals are not generally accessible.]

3. Physicians' Certificates; Presumption from Noncompliance. No abortion shall be performed unless two physicians, one of whom may be the person performing the abortion, shall have certified in writing the circumstances which they believe to justify the abortion. Such certificate shall be submitted before the abortion to the hospital where it is to be performed and, in the case of abortion following felonious intercourse, to the prosecuting attorney or the police. Failure to comply with any of the requirements of this Subsection gives rise to a presumption that the abortion was unjustified.

4. Self-Abortion. A woman whose pregnancy has continued beyond the 26th week commits a felony of the third degree if she purposely terminates her own pregnancy otherwise than by a live birth, or if she uses instruments, drugs or violence upon herself for that purpose. Except as justified under Subsection (2), a person who induces or knowingly aids a woman to use instruments, drugs or violence upon herself for the purpose of terminating her pregnancy otherwise than by a live birth commits a felony of the third degree whether or not the pregnancy has continued beyond the 26th week.

5. Pretended Abortion. A person commits a felony of the third degree if, representing that it is his purpose to perform an abortion, he does an act adapted to cause abortion in a pregnant woman although the woman is in fact not pregnant, or the actor does not believe she is. [410 U.S. 179, 207]. A person charged with unjustified abortion under Subsection (1) or an attempt to commit that offense may be convicted thereof upon proof of conduct prohibited by this Subsection.

6. Distribution of Abortifacients. A person who sells, offers to sell, possesses with intent to sell, advertises, or displays for sale anything specially designed to terminate a pregnancy, or held out by the actor as useful for that purpose, commits a misdemeanor, unless:

   (a) the sale, offer or display is to a physician or druggist or to an intermediary in a chain of distribution to physicians or druggists; or
   (b) the sale is made upon prescription or order of a physician; or
   (c) the possession is with intent to sell as authorized in paragraphs (a) and (b); or
   (d) the advertising is addressed to persons named in paragraph (a) and confined to trade or professional channels not likely to reach the general public.

7. Section Inapplicable to Prevention of Pregnancy. Nothing in this section shall be deemed applicable to the prescription, administration or distribution of drugs or other substances for avoiding pregnancy, whether by preventing implantation of a fertilized ovum or by any other method that operates before, at or immediately after fertilization.

Notes

73. The portions italicized in Appendix A are those held unconstitutional by the District Court.
74. Brief for Appellants 25 n. 5; Tr. of Oral Arg. 9.
75. See *Roe v. Wade, ante*, p. 113, at 140 n. 37.
76. The pertinent provisions of the 1876 statute were:

   "Section I. Be it enacted, etc., That from and after the passage of this Act, the willful killing of an unborn child, so far developed as to be ordinarily called 'quick,' by any injury to the mother of such child, which would be murder if it resulted in the death of such mother, shall be guilty of a felony, and punishable by death or imprisonment for life, as the jury trying the case may recommend.

   "Sec. II. Be it further enacted, That every person who shall administer to any woman pregnant with a child, any medicine, drug, or substance whatever, or shall use or employ any instrument or

(Continues)

(*Continued*)

other means, with intent thereby to destroy such child, unless the same shall have been necessary to preserve the life of such mother, or shall have been advised by two physicians to be necessary for such purpose, shall, in case the death of such child or mother be thereby produced, be declared guilty of an assault with intent to murder.

"Sec. III. Be it further enacted, That any person who shall willfully administer to any pregnant woman any medicine, drug or substance, or anything whatever, or shall employ any instrument or means whatever, with intent thereby to procure the miscarriage or abortion of any such woman, unless the same shall have been necessary [410 U.S. 179, 183] to preserve the life of such woman, or shall have been advised by two physicians to be necessary for that purpose, shall, upon conviction, be punished as prescribed in section 4310 of the Revised Code of Georgia."

It should be noted that the second section, in contrast to the first, made no specific reference to quickening. The section was construed, however, to possess this line of demarcation. *Taylor v. State*, 105 Ga. 846, 33 S. E. 190 (1899).

77. In contrast with the ALI model, the Georgia statute makes no specific reference to pregnancy resulting from incest. We were assured by the State at reargument that this was because the statute's reference to "rape" was intended to include incest. Tr. of Oral Rearg. 32.

78. Appellants by their complaint, App. 7, allege that the name is a pseudonym.

79. In answers to interrogatories, Doe stated that her application for an abortion was approved at Georgia Baptist Hospital on May 5, 1970, but that she was not approved as a charity patient there and had no money to pay for an abortion. App. 64.

80. What we decide today obviously has implications for the issues raised in the defendants' appeal pending in the Fifth Circuit.

81. Tr. of Oral Arg. 21–22.

82. Brief for Appellants 25.

83. We were advised at reargument, Tr. of Oral Rearg. 10, that only 54 of Georgia's 159 counties have a JCAH-accredited hospital.

84. Since its founding, JCAH has pursued the "elusive goal" of defining the "optimal setting" for "quality of service in hospitals." JCAH, *Accreditation Manual for Hospitals*, Foreword (Dec. 1970). The Manual's Introduction states the organization's purpose to establish standards and conduct accreditation programs that will afford quality medical care "to give patients the optimal benefits that medical science has to offer." This ambitious and admirable goal is illustrated by JCAH's decision in 1966 "[t]o raise and strengthen the standards from their present level of minimum essential to the level of optimum achievable. . . ." Some of these "optimum achievable" standards required are: disclosure of hospital ownership and control; a dietetic service and written dietetic policies; a written disaster plan for mass emergencies; a nuclear medical services program; facilities for hematology, chemistry, microbiology, clinical microscopy, and sero-immunology; a professional library and document delivery service; a radiology program; a social services plan administered by a qualified social worker; and a special care unit.

85. "The Joint Commission neither advocates nor opposes any particular position with respect to elective abortions." Letter dated July 9, 1971, from John I. Brewer, M.D., Commissioner, JCAH, to the Rockefeller Foundation. Brief for *amici curiae*, American College of Obstetricians and Gynecologists et al., p. A-3.

86. See *Roe v. Wade*, *ante*, at 146–147, n. 40.

87. Some state statutes do not have the JCAH-accreditation requirement. Alaska Stat. 11.15.060 (1970); Hawaii Rev. Stat. 453-16 (Supp. 1971); N.Y. Penal Code 125.05, subd. 3 (Supp. 1972–1973). Washington has the requirement but couples it with the alternative of "a medical facility approved . . . by the state board of health." Wash. Rev. Code 9.02.070 (Supp. 1972). Florida's new statute has a similar provision. Law of Apr. 13, 1972, c. 72-196, 1 (2). Others contain the specification. Ark. Stat. Ann. 41-303 to 41-310 (Supp. 1971); Calif. Health & Safety Code 25950-25955.5 (Supp. 1972); Colo. Rev. Stat. Ann. 40-2-50 to 40-2-53 (Cum. Supp. 1967); Kan. Stat. Ann. 21-3407 (Supp. 1971); Md. Ann. Code, Art. 43, 137-139 (1971). Cf. Del. Code Ann., Tit. 24, 1790-1793 (Supp. 1972), specifying "a nationally recognized medical or hospital accreditation authority," 1790 (a).

88. L. Baker & M. Freeman, Abortion Surveillance at Grady Memorial Hospital Center for Disease Control (June and July 1971) (U.S. Dept. of HEW, Public Health Service).

MR. CHIEF JUSTICE BURGER, concurring*

---

* [This opinion applies also to No. 70-18, *Roe v. Wade*, *ante*, p. 113.] [410 U.S. 179, 209]

I agree that, under the Fourteenth Amendment to the Constitution, the abortion statutes of Georgia and Texas impermissibly limit the performance of abortions necessary to protect the health of pregnant women, using [410 U.S. 179, 208] the term health in its broadest medical context. See *United States v. Vuitch*, 402 U.S. 62, 71–72 (1971). I am somewhat troubled that the Court has taken notice of various scientific and medical data in reaching its conclusion; however, I do not believe that the Court has exceeded the scope of judicial notice accepted in other contexts.

In oral argument, counsel for the State of Texas informed the Court that early abortion procedures were routinely permitted in certain exceptional cases, such as nonconsensual pregnancies resulting from rape and incest. In the face of a rigid and narrow statute, such as that of Texas, no one in these circumstances should be placed in a posture of dependence on a prosecutorial policy or prosecutorial discretion. Of course, States must have broad power, within the limits indicated in the opinions, to regulate the subject of abortions, but where the consequences of state intervention are so severe, uncertainty must be avoided as much as possible. For my part, I would be inclined to allow a State to require the certification of two physicians to support an abortion, but the Court holds otherwise. I do not believe that such a procedure is unduly burdensome, as are the complex steps of the Georgia statute, which require as many as six doctors and the use of a hospital certified by the JCAH.

I do not read the Court's holdings today as having the sweeping consequences attributed to them by the dissenting Justices; the dissenting views discount the reality that the vast majority of physicians observe the standards of their profession, and act only on the basis of carefully deliberated medical judgments relating to life and health. Plainly, the Court today rejects any claim that the Constitution requires abortions on demand.

MR. JUSTICE DOUGLAS, concurring.*

While I join the opinion of the Court,[89] I add a few words.

I

The questions presented in the present cases go far beyond the issues of vagueness, which we considered in *United States v. Vuitch*, 402 U.S. 62. They involve the right of privacy, one aspect of which we considered in *Griswold v. Connecticut*, 381 U.S. 479, 484 , when we held that various guarantees in the Bill of Rights create zones of privacy.[90] [410 U.S. 179, 210].

The Griswold case involved a law forbidding the use of contraceptives. We held that law as applied to married people unconstitutional:

"We deal with a right of privacy older than the Bill of Rights—older than our political parties, older than our school system. Marriage is a coming together for better or for worse, hopefully enduring, and intimate to the degree of being sacred." *Id.*, at 486.

The District Court in Doe held that Griswold and related cases "establish a Constitutional right to privacy broad enough to encompass the right of a woman to terminate an unwanted pregnancy in its early stages, by obtaining an abortion." 319 F. Supp. 1048, 1054.

The Supreme Court of California expressed the same view in *People v. Belous*,[91] 71 Cal. 2d 954, 963, 458 P.2d 194, 199.

The Ninth Amendment obviously does not create federally enforceable rights. It merely says, "The enumeration in the Constitution, of certain rights, shall not be construed to deny or disparage others retained by the people." But a catalogue of these rights includes customary, traditional, and time-honored rights, amenities, privileges, and immunities that come within the sweep of "the Blessings of Liberty" mentioned in the preamble to the Constitution. Many of them, in my view, come [410 U.S. 179, 211] within the meaning of the term "liberty" as used in the Fourteenth Amendment.

First is the autonomous control over the development and expression of one's intellect, interests, tastes, and personality.

These are rights protected by the First Amendment and, in my view, they are absolute, permitting of no exceptions. See *Terminiello v. Chicago*, 337 U.S. 1; *Roth v. United States*, 354 U.S. 476, 508 (dissent); *Kingsley Pictures Corp. v. Regents*, 360 U.S. 684, 697 (concurring); *New York Times Co. v. Sullivan*, 376 U.S. 254, 293 (Black, J., concurring, in which I joined). The Free Exercise Clause of the First Amendment is one facet of this constitutional right. The right to remain silent as respects one's own beliefs, *Watkins v. United States*, 354 U.S. 178, 196–199, is protected by the First and the Fifth. The First Amendment grants the privacy of first-class mail, *United States v. Van Leeuwen*, 397 U.S. 249, 253.

---

*[This opinion applies also to No. 70-18, *Roe v. Wade, ante*, p. 113.]

(Continues)

(Continued)

All of these aspects of the right of privacy are rights "retained by the people" in the meaning of the Ninth Amendment.

Second is freedom of choice in the basic decisions of one's life respecting marriage, divorce, procreation, contraception, and the education and upbringing of children.

These rights, unlike those protected by the First Amendment, are subject to some control by the police power. Thus, the Fourth Amendment speaks only of "unreasonable searches and seizures" and of "probable cause." These rights are "fundamental," and we have held that in order to support legislative action the statute must be narrowly and precisely drawn and that a "compelling state interest" must be shown in support of the limitation. E.g., *Kramer v. Union Free School District*, 395 U.S. 621; *Shapiro v. Thompson*, 394 U.S. 618; [410 U.S. 179, 212] *Carrington v. Rash*, 380 U.S. 89; *Sherbert v. Verner*, 374 U.S. 398; *NAACP v. Alabama*, 357 U.S. 449.

The liberty to marry a person of one's own choosing, *Loving v. Virginia*, 388 U.S. 1; the right of procreation, *Skinner v. Oklahoma*, 316 U.S. 535; the liberty to direct the education of one's children, *Pierce v. Society of Sisters*, 268 U.S. 510, and the privacy of the marital relation, *Griswold v. Connecticut*, *supra*, are in this category.[92] [410 U.S. 179, 213]. Only last Term in *Eisenstadt v. Baird*, 405 U.S. 438, another contraceptive case, we expanded the concept of Griswold by saying:

"It is true that in Griswold the right of privacy in question inhered in the marital relationship. Yet the marital couple is not an independent entity with a mind and heart of its own, but an association of two individuals each with a separate intellectual and emotional makeup. If the right of privacy means anything, it is the right of the individual, married or single, to be free from unwarranted governmental intrusion into matters so fundamentally affecting a person as the decision whether to bear or beget a child." *Id.*, at 453.

This right of privacy was called by Mr. Justice Brandeis the right "to be let alone." *Olmstead v. United States*, 277 U.S. 438, 478 (dissenting opinion). That right includes the privilege of an individual to plan his own affairs, for, "'outside areas of plainly harmful conduct, every American is left to shape his own life as he thinks best, do what he pleases, go where he pleases.'" *Kent v. Dulles*, 357 U.S. 116, 126.

Third is the freedom to care for one's health and person, freedom from bodily restraint or compulsion, freedom to walk, stroll, or loaf.

These rights, though fundamental, are likewise subject to regulation on a showing of "compelling state interest." We stated in *Papachristou v. City of Jacksonville*, 405 U.S. 156, 164, that walking, strolling, and wandering "are historically part of the amenities of life as we have known them." As stated in *Jacobson v. Massachusetts*, 197 U.S. 11, 29:

"There is, of course, a sphere within which the individual may assert the supremacy of his own will [410 U.S. 179, 214] and rightfully dispute the authority of any human government, especially of any free government existing under a written constitution, to interfere with the exercise of that will."

In *Union Pacific R. Co. v. Botsford*, 141 U.S. 250, 252 , the Court said, "The inviolability of the person is as much invaded by a compulsory stripping and exposure as by a blow."

In *Terry v. Ohio*, 392 U.S. 1, 8–9, the Court, in speaking of the Fourth Amendment stated, "This inestimable right of personal security belongs as much to the citizen on the streets of our cities as to the homeowner closeted in his study to dispose of his secret affairs."

Katz v. United States, 389 U.S. 347, 350, emphasizes that the Fourth Amendment "protects individual privacy against certain kinds of governmental intrusion."

In *Meyer v. Nebraska*, 262 U.S. 390, 399, the Court said:

"Without doubt, [liberty] denotes not merely freedom from bodily restraint but also the right of the individual to contract, to engage in any of the common occupations of life, to acquire useful knowledge, to marry, establish a home and bring up children, to worship God according to the dictates of his own conscience, and generally to enjoy those privileges long recognized at common law as essential to the orderly pursuit of happiness by free men."

The Georgia statute is at war with the clear message of these cases—that a woman is free to make the basic decision whether to bear an unwanted child. Elaborate argument is hardly necessary to demonstrate that childbirth may deprive a woman of her preferred lifestyle and force upon her a radically different and undesired future. For example, rejected applicants under the Georgia statute are required to endure the [410 U.S. 179, 215] discomforts of pregnancy; to incur the pain, higher mortality rate, and aftereffects of childbirth; to abandon educational plans; to sustain loss of income; to forgo the satisfactions of careers; to tax further mental and physical health in providing child care; and, in some cases, to bear the lifelong stigma of unwed motherhood, a badge which may haunt, if not deter, later legitimate family relationships.

II

Such reasoning is, however, only the beginning of the problem. The State has interests to protect. Vaccinations to prevent epidemics are one example, as Jacobson, *supra*, holds. The Court held that compulsory sterilization of imbeciles afflicted with hereditary forms of insanity or imbecility is another. *Buck v. Bell*, 274 U.S. 200. Abortion affects another. While childbirth endangers the lives of some women, voluntary abortion at any time and place regardless of medical standards would impinge on a rightful concern of society. The woman's health is part of that concern; as is the life of the fetus after quickening. These concerns justify the State in treating the procedure as a medical one.

One difficulty is that this statute as construed and applied apparently does not give full sweep to the "psychological as well as physical well-being" of women patients which saved the concept "health" from being void for vagueness in *United States v. Vuitch*, 402 U.S., at 72. But, apart from that, Georgia's enactment has a constitutional infirmity because, as stated by the District Court, it "limits the number of reasons for which an abortion may be sought." I agree with the holding of the District Court, "This the State may not do, because such action unduly restricts a decision sheltered by the Constitutional right to privacy." 319 F. Supp., at 1056.

The vicissitudes of life produce pregnancies which may be unwanted, or which may impair "health" in [410 U.S. 179, 216] the broad *Vuitch* sense of the term, or which may imperil the life of the mother, or which in the full setting of the case may create such suffering, dislocations, misery, or tragedy as to make an early abortion the only civilized step to take. These hardships may be properly embraced in the "health" factor of the mother as appraised by a person of insight. Or they may be part of a broader medical judgment based on what is "appropriate" in a given case, though perhaps not "necessary" in a strict sense.

The "liberty" of the mother, though rooted as it is in the Constitution, may be qualified by the State for the reasons we have stated. But where fundamental personal rights and liberties are involved, the corrective legislation must be "narrowly drawn to prevent the supposed evil," *Cantwell v. Connecticut*, 310 U.S. 296, 307, and not be dealt with in an "unlimited and indiscriminate" manner. *Shelton v. Tucker*, 364 U.S. 479, 490. And see *Talley v. California*, 362 U.S. 60. Unless regulatory measures are so confined and are addressed to the specific areas of compelling legislative concern, the police power would become the great leveler of constitutional rights and liberties.

There is no doubt that the State may require abortions to be performed by qualified medical personnel. The legitimate objective of preserving the mother's health clearly supports such laws. Their impact upon the woman's privacy is minimal. But the Georgia statute outlaws virtually all such operations—even in the earliest stages of pregnancy. In light of modern medical evidence suggesting that an early abortion is safer health-wise than childbirth itself,[93] it cannot be seriously [410 U.S. 179, 217] urged that so comprehensive a ban is aimed at protecting the woman's health. Rather, this expansive proscription of all abortions along the temporal spectrum can rest only on a public goal of preserving both embryonic and fetal life.

The present statute has struck the balance between the woman's and the State's interests wholly in favor of the latter. I am not prepared to hold that a State may equate, as Georgia has done, all phases of maturation preceding birth. We held in Griswold that the States may not preclude spouses from attempting to avoid the joinder of sperm and egg. If this is true, it is difficult to perceive any overriding public necessity which might attach precisely at the moment of conception. As Mr. Justice Clark has said[94]:

"To say that life is present at conception is to give recognition to the potential, rather than the actual. The unfertilized egg has life, and if fertilized, it takes on human proportions. But the law deals in reality, not obscurity—the known rather than the unknown. When sperm meets egg life may eventually form, but quite often it does not. The law does not deal in speculation. The phenomenon of [410 U.S. 179, 218] life takes time to develop, and until it is actually present, it cannot be destroyed. Its interruption prior to formation would hardly be homicide, and as we have seen, society does not regard it as such. The rites of Baptism are not performed and death certificates are not required when a miscarriage occurs. No prosecutor has ever returned a murder indictment charging the taking of the life of a fetus.[95] This would not be the case if the fetus constituted human life."

(Continues)

(Continued)

In summary, the enactment is overbroad. It is not closely correlated to the aim of preserving prenatal life. In fact, it permits its destruction in several cases, including pregnancies resulting from sex acts in which unmarried females are below the statutory age of consent. At the same time, however, the measure broadly proscribes aborting other pregnancies which may cause severe mental disorders. Additionally, the statute is overbroad because it equates the value of embryonic life immediately after conception with the worth of life immediately before birth.

III

Under the Georgia Act, the mother's physician is not the sole judge as to whether the abortion should be performed. Two other licensed physicians must concur in his judgment.[96] Moreover, the abortion must be performed in a licensed hospital[97]; and the abortion must be [410 U.S. 179, 219] approved in advance by a committee of the medical staff of that hospital.[98]

Physicians, who speak to us in Doe through an amicus brief, complain of the Georgia Act's interference with their practice of their profession.

The right of privacy has no more conspicuous place than in the physician–patient relationship, unless it be in the priest–penitent relationship.

It is one thing for a patient to agree that her physician may consult with another physician about her case. It is quite a different matter for the State compulsorily to impose on that physician-patient relationship another layer or, as in this case, still a third layer of physicians. The right of privacy—the right to care for one's health and person and to seek out a physician of one's own choice protected by the Fourteenth Amendment—becomes only a matter of theory, not a reality, when a multiple-physician-approval system is mandated by the State.

The State licenses a physician. If he is derelict or faithless, the procedures available to punish him or to deprive him of his license are well known. He is entitled to procedural due process before professional disciplinary sanctions may be imposed. See *In re Ruffalo*, 390 U.S. 544. Crucial here, however, is state-imposed control over the medical decision whether pregnancy should be interrupted. The good-faith decision of the patient's chosen physician is overridden and the final decision passed on to others in whose selection the patient has no part. This is a total destruction of the right of privacy between physician and patient and the intimacy of relation which that entails.

The right to seek advice on one's health and the right to place reliance on the physician of one's choice are [410 U.S. 179, 220] basic to Fourteenth Amendment values. We deal with fundamental rights and liberties, which, as already noted, can be contained or controlled only by discretely drawn legislation that preserves the "liberty" and regulates only those phases of the problem of compelling legislative concern. The imposition by the State of group controls over the physician-patient relationship is not made on any medical procedure apart from abortion, no matter how dangerous the medical step may be. The oversight imposed on the physician and patient in abortion cases denies them their "liberty," viz., their right of privacy, without any compelling, discernible state interest.

Georgia has constitutional warrant in treating abortion as a medical problem. To protect the woman's right of privacy, however, the control must be through the physician of her choice and the standards set for his performance.

The protection of the fetus when it has acquired life is a legitimate concern of the State. Georgia's law makes no rational, discernible decision on that score.[99] For under the Code, the developmental stage of the fetus is irrelevant when pregnancy is the result of rape, when the fetus will very likely be born with a permanent defect, or when a continuation of the pregnancy will endanger the life of the mother or permanently injure her health. When life is present is a question we do not try to resolve. While basically a question for medical experts, as stated by Mr. Justice Clark,[100] it is, of course, caught up in matters of religion and morality.

In short, I agree with the Court that endangering the life of the woman or seriously and permanently injuring [410 U.S. 179, 221] her health are standards too narrow for the right of privacy that is at stake.

I also agree that the superstructure of medical supervision which Georgia has erected violates the patient's right of privacy inherent in her choice of her own physician.

Notes

89. I disagree with the dismissal of Dr. Hallford's complaint in intervention in *Roe v. Wade*, *ante*, p. 113, because my disagreement with *Younger v. Harris*, 401 U.S. 37, revealed in my dissent in that case, still persists and extends to the progeny of that case.

90. There is no mention of privacy in our Bill of Rights but our decisions have recognized it as one of the fundamental values those amendments were designed to protect. The fountainhead case is *Boyd v. United States*, 116 U.S. 616, holding that a federal statute which authorized a court in tax cases to require a taxpayer to produce his records or to concede the Government's allegations offended the Fourth and Fifth Amendments. Mr. Justice Bradley, for the Court, found that the measure unduly intruded into the "sanctity of a man's home and the privacies of life." *Id.*, at 630. Prior to *Boyd*, in *Kilbourn v. Thompson*, 103 U.S. 168, 190, Mr. Justice Miller held for the Court that neither House of Congress "possesses the general power of making inquiry into the private affairs of the citizen." Of *Kilbourn*, Mr. Justice Field later said, "This case will stand for all time as a bulwark against the invasion of the right of the citizen to protection in his private affairs against the unlimited scrutiny of investigation by a congressional committee." In *re Pacific Railway Comm'n*, 32 F. 241, 253 (cited with approval in *Sinclair v. United States*, 279 U.S. 263, 293). Mr. Justice Harlan, also speaking for the Court, in *ICC v. Brimson*, 154 U.S. 447, 478, thought the same was true of [410 U.S. 179, 210] administrative inquiries, saying that the Constitution did not permit a "general power of making inquiry into the private affairs of the citizen." In a similar vein were *Harriman v. ICC*, 211 U.S. 407; *United States v. Louisville & Nashville R. Co.*, 236 U.S. 318, 335; and *FTC v. American Tobacco Co.*, 264 U.S. 298.

91. The California abortion statute, held unconstitutional in the Belous case, made it a crime to perform or help perform an abortion "unless the same is necessary to preserve [the mother's] life." 71 Cal. 2d, at 959, 458 P.2d, at 197.

92. My Brother STEWART, writing in *Roe v. Wade*, *supra*, says that our decision in Griswold reintroduced substantive due process that had been rejected in *Ferguson v. Skrupa*, 372 U.S. 726. *Skrupa* involved legislation governing a business enterprise; and the Court in that case, as had Mr. Justice Holmes on earlier occasions, rejected the idea that "liberty" within the meaning of the Due Process Clause of the Fourteenth Amendment was a vessel to be filled with one's personal choices of values, whether drawn from the laissez faire school, from the socialistic school, or from the technocrats. *Griswold* involved legislation touching on the marital relation and involving the conviction of a licensed physician for giving married people information concerning contraception. There is nothing specific in the Bill of Rights that covers that item. Nor is there anything in the Bill of Rights that in terms protects the right of association or the privacy in one's association. Yet we found those rights in the periphery of the First Amendment. *NAACP v. Alabama*, 357 U.S. 449, 462. Other peripheral rights are the right to educate one's children as one chooses, *Pierce v. Society of Sisters*, 268 U.S. 510, and the right to study the German language, *Meyer v. Nebraska*, 262 U.S. 390. These decisions, with all respect, have nothing to do with substantive due process. One may think they are not peripheral to other rights that are expressed in the Bill of Rights. But that is not enough to bring into play the protection of substantive due process.

   There are, of course, those who have believed that the reach of due process in the Fourteenth Amendment included all of the Bill of Rights but went further. Such was the view of Mr. Justice Murphy and Mr. Justice Rutledge. See *Adamson v. California*, 332 U.S. 46, 123, 124 (dissenting opinion). Perhaps they were right; but it is a bridge that neither I nor those who joined the Court's opinion in *Griswold* crossed.

93. Many studies show that it is safer for a woman to have a medically induced abortion than to bear a child. In the first 11 months of operation of the New York abortion law, the mortality [410 U.S. 179, 217] rate associated with such operations was 6 per 100,000 operations. Abortion Mortality, 20 *Morbidity and Mortality* 208, 209 (June 1971) (U.S. Dept. of HEW, Public Health Service). On the other hand, the maternal mortality rate associated with childbirths other than abortions was 18 per 100,000 live births. Tietze, *Mortality with Contraception and Induced Abortion*, 45 *Studies in Family Planning* 6 (1969). See also Tietze & Lehfeldt, Legal Abortion in Eastern Europe, 175 *J. A. M. A.* 1149, 1152 (Apr. 1961); Kolblova, Legal Abortion in Czechoslovakia, 196 *J. A. M. A.* 371 (Apr. 1966); Mehland, Combating Illegal Abortion in the Socialist Countries of Europe, 13 *World Med. J.* 84 (1966).

94. Religion, Morality, and Abortion: A Constitutional Appraisal, 2 *Loyola U. (L.A.) L. Rev.* 1, 9–10 (1969).

95. In *Keeler v. Superior Court*, 2 Cal. 3d 619, 470 P.2d 617, the California Supreme Court held in 1970 that the California murder statute did not cover the killing of an unborn fetus, even though the fetus be "viable," and that it was beyond judicial power to extend the statute to the killing of an unborn. It held that the child must be "born alive before a charge of homicide can be sustained." *Id.*, at 639, 470 P.2d, at 630.

(Continues)

96. See Ga. Code Ann. 26-1202 (b) (3).

97. See *id.*, 26-1202 (b) (4).

98. *Id.*, 26-1202 (b) (5).

99. See Rochat, Tyler, & Schoenbucher, An Epidemiological Analysis of Abortion in Georgia, 61 *Am. J. of Public Health* 543 (1971).

100. *Supra*, n. 6, at 10.

MR. JUSTICE WHITE, with whom MR. JUSTICE REHNQUIST joins, dissenting.*

At the heart of the controversy in these cases are those recurring pregnancies that pose no danger whatsoever to the life or health of the mother but are, nevertheless, unwanted for any one or more of a variety of reasons—convenience, family planning, economics, dislike of children, the embarrassment of illegitimacy, etc. The common claim before us is that for any one of such reasons, or for no reason at all, and without asserting or claiming any threat to life or health, any woman is entitled to an abortion at her request if she is able to find a medical advisor willing to undertake the procedure.

The Court for the most part sustains this position: During the period prior to the time the fetus becomes viable, the Constitution of the United States values the convenience, whim, or caprice of the putative mother more than the life or potential life of the fetus; the Constitution, therefore, guarantees the right to an abortion as against any state law or policy seeking to protect the fetus from an abortion not prompted by more compelling reasons of the mother.

With all due respect, I dissent. I find nothing in the language or history of the Constitution to support the Court's judgment. The Court simply fashions and announces a new constitutional right for pregnant mothers [410 U.S. 179, 222] and, with scarcely any reason or authority for its action, invests that right with sufficient substance to override most existing state abortion statutes. The upshot is that the people and the legislatures of the 50 States are constitutionally disentitled to weigh the relative importance of the continued existence and development of the fetus, on the one hand, against a spectrum of possible impacts on the mother, on the other hand. As an exercise of raw judicial power, the Court perhaps has authority to do what it does today; but in my view its judgment is an improvident and extravagant exercise of the power of judicial review that the Constitution extends to this Court.

The Court apparently values the convenience of the pregnant mother more than the continued existence and development of the life or potential life that she carries. Whether or not I might agree with that marshaling of values, I can in no event join the Court's judgment because I find no constitutional warrant for imposing such an order of priorities on the people and legislatures of the States. In a sensitive area such as this, involving as it does issues over which reasonable men may easily and heatedly differ, I cannot accept the Court's exercise of its clear power of choice by interposing a constitutional barrier to state efforts to protect human life and by investing mothers and doctors with the constitutionally protected right to exterminate it. This issue, for the most part, should be left with the people and to the political processes the people have devised to govern their affairs.

It is my view, therefore, that the Texas statute is not constitutionally infirm because it denies abortions to those who seek to serve only their convenience rather than to protect their life or health. Nor is this plaintiff, who claims no threat to her mental or physical health, entitled to assert the possible rights of those women [410 U.S. 179, 223] whose pregnancy assertedly implicates their health. This, together with *United States v. Vuitch*, 402 U.S. 62 (1971), dictates reversal of the judgment of the District Court.

Likewise, because Georgia may constitutionally forbid abortions to putative mothers who, like the plaintiff in this case, do not fall within the reach of 26-1202 (a) of its criminal code, I have no occasion, and the District Court had none, to consider the constitutionality of the procedural requirements of the Georgia statute as applied to those pregnancies posing substantial hazards to either life or health. I would reverse the judgment of the District Court in the Georgia case.

MR. JUSTICE REHNQUIST, dissenting.

The holding in *Roe v. Wade, ante*, p. 113, that state abortion laws can withstand constitutional scrutiny only if the State can demonstrate a compelling state interest, apparently compels the Court's close scrutiny of the various provisions in Georgia's abortion statute. Since, as indicated by my dissent in Wade, I view the compelling-state-interest standard as an inappropriate measure of the constitutionality of state abortion laws, I respectfully dissent from the majority's holding. [410 U.S. 179, 224].

---

*[This opinion applies also to No. 70-18, *Roe v. Wade, ante*, p. 113.]

Unjustifiable Discrimination and Affirmative Action

Chapter Objectives

In this chapter you will learn . . .

- The history of slavery in America
- What discrimination really means
- Whether slavery or racism came first
- The history of gender-based discrimination in America
- The role of quotas in affirmative action initiatives

Introduction

Ask many folks nowadays to tell you what "affirmative action" means, and you may get some blank stares. Or ask them to define "discrimination," and they may give you an example that is only the tip of the iceberg. That is troubling, indeed, as the history of unjustifiable discrimination and affirmative action is intertwined with the history of our country as a whole. This chapter will teach you a great deal about both concepts: not only will you never be among those who would give someone a blank stare or incomplete answer when asked that question, but you will be able to enlighten those who know nothing about these very important topics.

Affirmative Action Defined

Affirmative action is a policy designed to remedy unjustifiable discrimination against a historically underrepresented group. Let's take a look at this definition more carefully. We will begin with the word "discrimination."

Discrimination: Most of the Time, It Is a Good Thing

It may shock you to learn that "discrimination" not only can be a *good* thing, but actually *is* a good thing most of the time! That is because we often associate the word discrimination with the bad type of discrimination. Is there a good type, you may ask. Certainly there is. In fact, you have probably discriminated in a good way dozens of times since this morning—maybe even hundreds of times!

You see, in its most basic sense, the word "discriminate" means to *choose*. Therefore, when you woke up this morning and decided (1) what to have for breakfast; (2) what to wear; (3) what time to leave your house, etc., you have made discriminating choices. If you wore a red shirt today, you discriminated against the blue shirt that you chose not to wear. If you had scrambled eggs for breakfast, you discriminated against the bowl of cornflakes you were thinking of having instead.

Unlike other species of the animal kingdom that rely on instinct, we human beings are *thinking* creatures. Every time that we make a choice, we are discriminating in favor of something or someone, and against something or someone. And, most of the time, our decisions are wise. For instance, when we decide to wear a winter coat in freezing weather, we discriminate in favor of the winter coat and against, say, a light jacket. We wear boots in the snow, not sandals. We use a knife and a fork to eat our steak, not a spoon and a straw. These are all among the many discriminating choices that we make, and they are good.

Not all discrimination, however, is good. When a human being is wronged in some manner for no rational or legitimate reason that is an unfortunate circumstance and an embarrassment to our great nation. For instance, if a person applies to become a teacher and is denied *because* of race, gender, nationality, or religion, that is an example of unjustifiable (bad) discrimination. If, however, the person was denied the teaching position because his or her level of education was not sufficient, then that would be justifiable (good) discrimination.

Now that we have covered discrimination, let's return to affirmative action.

Historically Underrepresented Groups

As great a country as the United States might be, it has had its fair share of flaws throughout its illustrious two-plus century history. One of its most unfortunate blemishes, one that deeply scarred and tarnished its very essence, was the unjustifiable discrimination inflicted upon certain persons based on race, gender, nationality, and religion. We will examine some of this history, of which we are not proud, though we are grateful that we have evolved from where we were two hundred years ago, a hundred years ago, and even fifty years ago, and we hope to have evolved even further in another fifty, one hundred, and two hundred years.

Black African Americans

Without question, one of the most shameful actions in American history was the practice of slavery. Actually, it is a fascinating subject, because not many Americans really know the whole history. And though we will not cover the entire history here, we certainly need to discuss at least some of the basics.

Slavery Is as Old and as Vast as the World Itself

Slavery is not something unique to the United States. In fact, slavery existed in virtually every corner of the world, and just about every group of people at one time or another were slaves, or slave owners, and usually both (at different points in time, of course). In olden times, when slavery was common and wars were far more frequent than they are today, the winning side usually would enslave the losing side. A king could easily find himself a slave the next day, or *vice versa*.

When the land on which the United States now sits was discovered by European explorers, predominantly from Great Britain, France, and Spain, the settlers wanted to bring slaves along to work the land (particularly in the South, where agriculture was the primary industry). As absurd and reprehensible as it sounds to us here and now in the 21st Century, slaves were considered little more than any other type of tool, such as a plow or a tractor. Typically, then, the settlers went "shopping" for their slaves at the local "market" in their own native countries. However, by the time they were ready to settle in the New World, slavery had been abolished in Europe.

Not to be dissuaded, the settlers traveled to the next-closest market: Africa. (Asia also conducted a slave trade at the time, though it was not as close a trip from Europe.) The European traders met with African villagers, who sold their fellow Africans to them. The slaves were *predominantly*—though not exclusively—black, as were the Africans who sold them, and the slave owners were *predominantly* white. (We refer to the slaves as "black African Americans" to distinguish them from white Americans of African ancestry who are, technically, "white African Americans.") In any event, the division along racial lines was based far more on practicality than on racism.

Slavery Was Not a Consequence of Racism, Slavery Preceded Racism

As we look back at slavery, which was practiced on this land even before it became the United States and was not abolished until about 150 years ago, we might be tempted to conclude that it was a byproduct of racism: that whites hated blacks and thought of them as inferior, and thereby decided to enslave them. But it is not quite that simple.

Racism certainly existed in the United States during the days of slavery and even though slavery was abolished, racism, unfortunately, still exists. But slavery was not born out of racism. In fact, the opposite is more accurate in terms of what happened.

The British, French, and Spanish who settled in the New World wanted free labor, or more precisely, bought labor, considering they paid to purchase the slaves. Just as today some people will buy a home whereas others will rent one, the settlers chose to buy their labor (that is, the slaves) once, as an investment of free labor for generations to come (because the slaves' descendants would be slaves, too, through the generations). As there was no labor to be bought in Europe, the settlers went to the next-closest place: Africa. It just so happened that Africa was in the midst of a booming slave trade, so there were plenty of slaves for the settlers to buy. That most of them were black added a security advantage in that it would be easy to spot a runaway slave by pure physical appearance.

In other instances, slaves were those who owed a debt and could not pay it, or who were sold into slavery to avoid criminal sentencing in their own countries. Those slaves, not the traditional "merchandise" sold in the African slave trade, were usually not black. Turning to the slave owners, there was one color that spoke clearly: green, as in money. It was quite possible and actually quite real, though also quite rare, that some slave owners were wealthy blacks. However, as we stated earlier, the slave owners were predominantly white and the slaves were black by an overwhelming margin.

Almost as soon as the United States became a nation in 1776, there were apparent contradictions between the principle that "all men are created equal," as set forth in the Declaration of Independence, and that some men, and women, were held captive in chains. Northerners fought to abolish slavery, to which Southerners desperately proclaimed that blacks were inferior to whites and it was their natural disposition to be enslaved by them. Racism, thus, was born out of economic panic. The Southerners certainly could not admit the real reason they were shunning the Declaration of Independence: they did not want to give up the labor force for which they had already paid. And when slavery was finally eradicated in 1865, former slave owners were furious. That is when pure resentment toward former slaves arose, further fueling racism.

Nonetheless, black Americans continued to suffer miserably long after slavery was abolished. Not only did they endure beatings and even lynchings in the South, but they were subjected to disparate treatment in school, in the workplace, and in society in general.

Rosa Parks made national history in 1955, when she refused to give up her seat on the bus to a white passenger. That incident setoff a boycott that propelled Dr. Martin Luther King, Jr. into the national spotlight as a civil rights activist. Parks' ordeal was an example of how black Americans were treated as second-class citizens in their own country: subjected to riding on the back of the bus, giving up their seats to white passengers, and other disparate treatment, like drinking from separate water fountains, not being allowed to enter certain eating or motel establishments, and even being banned from some churches.

Plessy v. Ferguson

Two prominent Supreme Court cases regarding racial segregation were *Plessy v. Ferguson*, decided in 1896, and *Brown v. Board of Education*, decided in 1954.

Plessy addressed the issue of whether separate conditions for blacks and whites was a violation of the Equal

Protection Clause of the Fourteenth Amendment—which guaranteed equal protection under the law—and concluded that it was not.

The Court held that racially segregated railroad cars on a train did not deny either race equal protection under the law, in what famously became known as the Court's "separate but equal" doctrine. For example, if black passengers were denied the right to, say, medical attention while riding the train, whereas white passengers were given medical attention, that could have been construed as unequal protection. However, that the two races were merely kept separate did not amount to inequality in the Court's opinion. In other words, the Court held that the Constitution guarantees equal protection under the law exists even when races are kept separate.

A bitter dissent emphasized that it is clear that the white race is the dominant race in the United States socially, politically, and economically, and that the separation was in fact an expression of superiority versus inferiority. Moreover, there was concern that the majority decision could inspire various new laws resulting in unlimited separation based on other factors, such as religion. In any event, *Plessy* remained a viable law for over 50 years until it was overturned *unanimously* by the Court in *Brown*.

Brown v. Board of Education

All of the Justices in *Brown v. Board of Education* unanimously declared that separate educational facilities based on race do in fact violate the Equal Protection clause.

Arguing along the lines of the dissent in *Plessy*, the Court held that young black children would likely feel inferior by being sent to schools different from their white counterparts.

For advocates of racial equality and colorblindness, *Brown* was a thrilling victory. However, many Constitutionalists were alarmed: not because they disagreed with the notion of black and white children going to school together, but because it would be up to the *legislature*, not the *court* to right that wrong. It is important to note that distinction. When a particular judicial decision is criticized, it is not always based on its substance but often is based on the disagreement that the court had the authority to make that determination in the first place.

Both the *Plessy* and *Brown* cases are found at the end of this chapter, in their entirety.

Women's Rights

Another historically underrepresented group in America has been women of any color. As 21st Century Americans, it is difficult for us to fathom a time when black Americans were denied the right to vote, among other things. In that respect, it is equally unimaginable that more than half of our adult population—the female half—was also denied that right.

In fact, blacks were guaranteed the right to vote by the Fifteenth Amendment, enacted in 1870. But it was not until *50 years later*, in 1920, when women were guaranteed that same right, via the Nineteenth Amendment.

In 2008, Hillary Clinton, then a United States Senator from New York and the wife of President Bill Clinton, ran for president. For awhile, she had been considered the frontrunner, and she mounted a formidable campaign that for a long while challenged the eventual Democratic nominee, Barack Obama. Arguably, her campaign was record setting in terms of her having inched closer to winning the White House than any woman before her, but she was certainly not the first woman to ever run for president.

Quite remarkably, a woman named Victoria Woodhull ran for president in 1872. What is notable about her campaign was that even though she was eligible to be *elected* president, she was not permitted to cast a vote for herself (or for any other candidate)! Her running mate was Frederick Douglass, the famous former slave and abolitionist. An African American, Douglass would have been able to vote for himself, having been guaranteed that right two years earlier by the Fifteenth Amendment.

Woodhull ran on the Equal Rights Party, but did not win; Republican Ulysses S. Grant, the incumbent president at the time, won reelection. Another important distinction to remember regarding the women's right to vote is that, much like abortion, the Constitution was silent on the matter. There was no language in the Constitution expressly granting or forbidding women the right to vote. Accordingly, each state was free to make its own laws regarding that matter. That is why even before the Nineteenth Amendment was ratified, some women had the right to vote. Speaking of abortion, Woodhull was an outspoken pro-life advocate, and was criticized by pro-choice supporters because they felt that as a woman, she should have supported a woman's right to choose. Woodhull maintained that life begins in the womb.

The Nineteenth Amendment was originally written in 1890, but took 30 years to gain ratification. One of its foremost advocates was Susan B. Anthony, a civil rights activist who traveled all over the United States and to various countries speaking about women's *suffrage* (that is, the right to vote). Anthony, who died in 1906, did not live to see the Amendment passed. Nonetheless, her legacy lives on well beyond her years. In 1979, the United States Mint issued a dollar coin bearing her name and likeness. The coin was not very popular, but that was largely because, to date, no dollar coins have been embraced by the American public.

Congress' Equal Pay Act of 1963

Women have been subjected to various types of unjustifiable gender-based discrimination, other than having been denied an absolute right to vote for the first 144 years of our country's history. One such type of discrimination involved pay. Traditionally, women who performed the same jobs as men were paid less money; the rationale was that men are not only physically stronger, but also smarter, more confident, and more capable. In short, men were perceived to be better workers than women and were paid more accordingly.

All of this began to change, particularly with the passage of the Equal Pay Act of 1963, which made it against federal law to pay an employee more or less money based on gender.

Although rights for women and black African Americans were limited in 1872, Victoria Woodhull (left) ran for president of the United States and Frederick Douglass (right) was her running mate.

Legal Effects Help to Remedy, But Do Not Instantly Eliminate the "Isms"

Laws designed to prevent unjustifiable discrimination do not necessarily eliminate the problem, although they might go a long way toward reducing it. Unfortunately, employers who wish to refrain from hiring someone based on race, gender, or other unjustifiable factor may find some loophole by which to do so. Although the law cannot eliminate all such loopholes, it certainly makes finding them more difficult.

The Supreme Court's Level of Scrutiny in Gender-Based Cases

Regarding racial discrimination, the Court has maintained a strict scrutiny standard, one substantially higher than for gender-based discrimination. Why do you suppose that women are not afforded the same protection as, say, persons of color? For one thing, racial discrimination against black Americans far exceeded any type of discrimination to which American women have been subjected. For example, women in America were never enslaved, never forced to attend different schools, or drink out of different water fountains. Nonetheless, gender-based discrimination has not been ignored by the courts.

Generally, the Court maintains that any gender-based discrimination must be *substantially related to an important government interest*. As compared to strict scrutiny, this is midlevel scrutiny: not as rigid as strict scrutiny, but not as flexible as the *rational basis* test. The midlevel standard was established in *Craig v. Boren*, in 1976. Interestingly, this case discriminated against men, not women.

An Oklahoma statute prohibited the sale of a low-alcohol content beer to males under 21, but females under 18. That meant women ages 18 to 20 were permitted to purchase the beer but men in that same age range were not.

The State's Rational Basis for Gender-Based Discrimination

The first question that we ought to consider is: why did the Oklahoma statute differentiate between men and women to begin with? Statistically, 2% of 18- to 20-year-old males in the state had been arrested for drunk driving as compared to only .18% of females. (Note: There is a decimal point before the number 1. That means 0.18%, not 1.8%.) In other words, for every 10,000 18- to 20-year-old Oklahomans, 200 males would get arrested for drunken driving as compared to only 18 females. Because *more than ten times* the number of males would get arrested, the Oklahoma legislature certainly had a rational basis for establishing the gender-based difference.

The majority did not deny that there was a rational basis; rather, it explained that in order to discriminate based on gender, a rational basis was not enough. But, first, it struck down the statute on various grounds.

The Court held that even if ten times more Oklahoman males are likely to drive drunk than Oklahoman females, it only included 2% of them. That means 98% of Oklahoman males were not arrested for driving drunk. Why then, the Court reasoned, should they be negatively affected? Let's consider this point a little bit further. To make it easier to calculate, let's suppose that there were 100,000 Oklahoma males ages 18 to 20, and 100,000 females. If 2% of the males drove drunk, that is 2,000, and .18% of females is 180. Simply examining these two numbers, 2,000 and 180, one could conclude that the statute makes sense. When comparing 98,000 (the number of 18- to 20-year-old male Oklahomans who were not arrested for drunk driving) to 2,000, the question becomes: why penalize 98,000 for the actions of 2,000?

Moreover, the Court emphasized that the statute only prohibited the *purchasing* of the beer by males younger than 21, not the drinking of it (meaning that just as many males under 21 as females were permitted to drink it). Besides, as the Court pointed out, the beer was supposedly nonintoxicating, anyway because of its low alcoholic content.

For these reasons, the majority concluded that the Oklahoma Legislature's objective—to ensure traffic safety—was not sufficiently connected to the statute to justify gender-based discrimination.

Concurring Justices agreed that the statute went too far, but did not completely support the majority's newly-created middle level of scrutiny. Males who are 18 to 20 years old may still drink the beer that someone else purchased for them they reasoned; and also pointed out that men, who are generally heavier than women, are less likely to become intoxicated as a result.

Dissenting Justices favored the lower-level scrutiny standard, declaring that as long as the statute is not irrational, even if it is unwise and foolish, the Court has no place to strike it down.

Interestingly, the Justices did not really address the issue of whether the statute actually did the 18- to 20-year-old males a favor, in that it might have prevented them from driving drunk, or at least reduced that number somewhat. Unlike say, prohibiting someone from drinking from the same water fountain, discrimination against purchasing a product that might make one become injured or killed in an automobile accident actually serves one's own good. But the Court simply looked at it as a right having been taken away, not a life having been saved.

Mid-level Scrutiny That Survived

In *Michael M. v. Superior Court*, decided in 1981, the Court upheld a California statute that would hold adult men liable for sexual intercourse with a minor female partner (under age 18) but did not make such provisions for women. An adult having sexual intercourse with a minor constitutes *statutory rape*, which is different from conventional rape, as follows: rape is sexual intercourse during which the victim is consciously unwilling to have sex, whereas the victim may be willing in statutory rape but is determined by law to be too young to have the capacity to make a decision in his or her best interests.

In any event, when it comes to statutory rape, there are four possibilities:

1. Adult woman and minor boy
2. Adult woman and minor girl
3. Adult man and minor boy
4. Adult man and minor girl

Think for a moment why the law would be interested in protecting against all of these, but *particularly* against number 4. When you are ready, look for the answer in the next paragraph.

Of all of the possible types of statutory rape, number 4 is the only one that might result in a teenage pregnancy (pregnancy can result only when a man and a woman have sexual intercourse, and number 4 is the only example of a minor girl having intercourse with an adult man). Accordingly, that is the logic that the court used in *Michael M.*, in that adult women who had sex with young boys certainly could not impregnate their victims. But what if the adult women were to become pregnant as a result? They were the adults involved, not the minors, and the legislature's main concern was to protect the minors; to avoid teenage pregnancies.

Another case involving differential treatment of men and women, like *Boren* in that it seemed to discriminate against men, was *Rostker v. Goldberg*. The case involved the Military Selective Service Act (MSSA), which required adult males—but not females—to register for the draft. The MSSA clearly protects women from military requirement, though they maintain the option to enlist voluntarily if they so choose. The Court upheld the law, which is clearly gender-based discrimination. Why would the Court rule as it did? Let's take a look.

A six-Justice majority concluded that there is a clear difference between men and women regarding the United States Armed Forces, because women are not eligible for combat. Because the MSSA is designed to prepare the armed forces for combat by recruiting prospective individuals as needed, it was specifically enacted to recruit males, not females.

Moreover, the Court held that when it comes to military matters, Congress is given extremely wide latitude in terms of making decisions. Although the Court's purpose is to oversee the actions of the legislative and executive branches in order to determine that they are proceeding Constitutionally, a particularly high deference is afforded to Congress when making decisions concerning the military.

Dissenting Justices flatly disagreed, contending that there are plenty of vital noncombat roles in the military that could be filled by women just as well as by men. To the extent that it was not established that such roles could be sufficiently filled by women, even during wartime, they clearly viewed the MSSA as unconstitutional.

The MSSA was promulgated in order to ensure the safety and efficiency of the United States Armed Forces and those goals would not be thwarted if women were a part of the military. If the inclusion of women into the armed forces were actually *harmful*, as would be the case if the MSSA recruited, say, known enemies of the United States, then it could be upheld. However, in this case, Marshall found the gender-based discrimination to lack a substantial relationship to an important government objective.

Women in Combat Was Not at Issue

What about the issue of why? By 1981, close to the cusp of the 21st Century, women were still being excluded from combat?

As we discussed much earlier, the Supreme Court acts much like a referee does in a basketball game. If a player *traveled* (moved with the ball improperly without dribbling it), the referee would blow the whistle. What if instead, the player dribbled properly with his left hand and twirled his right hand in the air the entire time? If the referee found that to be distracting, would he be able to blow the whistle and penalize the player? No, because there is nothing in the rule book that prevents such an action.

Similarly, even if the Justices were to wonder why women continued to be excluded from combat, it was not something that the litigants of the case brought forward as an issue. The issue was whether the MSSA discriminated against men by excluding women from the *draft* process; there was no issue about eligibility for *combat*. Accordingly, that made the decision much simpler.

Narrow Rulings: Frustrating, But Prudent

There are those who view decisions made by courts in hope that they will help to resolve many future problems. But rulings such as in *Goldberg*, which are limited to specific issues and do not address others that will likely emerge in the future, often frustrate those who want a "cure-all" answer. Keep in mind, however, that laws are designed to make things better, and laws are created by lawmakers, not by the courts. That is what the Constitution says.

Before we proceed to our discussion about affirmative action, let's take a look at one other type of unjustifiable discrimination: that which is based on nationality.

Nationality and Alienage

The United States is often referred to as "a nation of immigrants" as well as a "melting pot" of various nationalities and cultures. One who has never been to the United States or has never heard much about its people might conclude that it is comprised of about three hundred million people from all over the world, happily working and living together as one friendly nation. To a great extent, that is very true, and is certainly more so the case than that of other nations. However, as there has been racism and sexism in this country, there has also been quite a lot of *xenophobia*, which is a fear of or disdain for persons of other nationalities and cultures.

Immigration

The history of American immigration is older than the United States itself. An *immigrant* is a person who has decided to permanently move to another country. The United States is made up of natural-born American citizens and those who became citizens through the process of *naturalization*. In addition to the natural-born and naturalized citizens, the United States also contains a fairly large number of *aliens*. Anyone living in the United States who is not an American citizen is an alien, and aliens are comprised of immigrants and nonimmigrants. Immigrants are those who intend on permanently settling in the United States, whereas nonimmigrants are only here temporarily, whether for 5 months, 5 years, or some other duration. Aliens who lawfully enter and remain in the United States are legal and those who have unlawfully entered and/or remained after their visa expired are illegal.

When this country was founded, however, the immigration laws were not so complex. In fact, immigration was as simple as physically getting oneself here; that was all there was to it. The immigration door of this nation was completely open. Over time, that door began to close for various reasons.

First, hardened criminals trying to escape prosecution in their own countries would flee to the United States. As one would imagine, some hardened criminals never change; therefore, once they got here, they started committing crimes here as well. That is when aliens with criminal records were prohibited from entering the United States.

Next, there were aliens who were inflicted with dangerous and highly contagious diseases, and they unfortunately spread the diseases once they arrived here. That is when the door closed on them, too.

For a long while, as America was building railroads, bridges, and factories, it needed able-bodied people—Americans and aliens alike—to help. As aliens were more willing to work hard for cheap wages, they became a preferred source of labor. After awhile, Americans became upset that foreign laborers were taking jobs away from them. That is when the immigration door closed even more.

Fear of Foreigners

In addition to economic concerns, many Americans disliked foreigners because of cultural differences. Although America was perceived by some as a melting pot of many cultures, it has never been a nation without its own distinct American culture. English is the primary language, Christianity the primary religion, and, at least for the first two centuries of our country's history, Europe was the continent from which most aliens emigrated. (Note: A person *emigrates from* a country and *immigrates to* another.)

As ethnic groups settled into particular neighborhoods, they often stuck together because they were unwelcome. The popular musical *West Side Story* depicts this cultural war, which, in that case, centers on a group of young, Spanish-speaking Puerto Rican immigrants who moved into a New York City neighborhood, causing the young locals to revolt. The local gang—the Jets—squared off against the Puerto Rican gang—the Sharks—and violence erupted.

A more recent and real example was that of the treatment of Muslims in America, particularly those dressed in traditional religious garb, after September 11, 2001. That day, of course, is one of the most devastating in American history, when Islamic fundamendalist terrorists crashed two commercial airplanes into New York City's World Trade Center Twin Towers and a third plane into the Pentagon in Washington, D.C.; yet another plane (purportedly headed for the White House or U.S. Capitol) crashed in Pennsylvania after passengers on board bravely subdued the hijackers.

Actually, most Muslims neither engage in acts of terrorism nor support them. However, that did not stop many American non-Muslims from being very uneasy when traveling on an airplane with traditionally-dressed Muslims on board. Many Muslim business owners overtly displayed their loyalty to the United States by prominently displaying large American flags in their storefronts, no doubt fearful of backlash against them. President George W. Bush, in the early days after 9/11 when the nation was still in shock, advised that the actions of a few extremists do not represent the beliefs of an entire group of people. As time passed, more and more Americans began to realize that the horrific acts of the 9/11 terrorists no more represented the philosophy of Islam than do acts by Jewish vigilante groups and the Ku Klux Klan represent the beliefs of Judaism or Christianity.

Although the Supreme Court did not have to deal with the issue regarding Muslim–Americans, it issued a landmark ruling regarding Japanese–Americans in *Korematsu v. U.S.* in 1944. On December 7, 1941, the Japanese Empire attacked a U.S. Naval Base at Pearl Harbor on the Hawaiian island of Oahu. The surprise attack, which caused the United States to declare war on Japan and thereby enter World War II, was devastating and caused a great deal of alarm and panic throughout the country. As a result, a military order required persons of Japanese descent living in the Western portion of the United States to move into "relocation camps," which were, effectively, detainment locations. That meant that anyone of Japanese descent, no matter how Americanized and how patriotic, could be required to be quarantined! The list of detainees into these internment camps included various public figures, such as Jack Soo, who played Sergeant Nick Yemana on the long-running television sitcom *Barney Miller* and George Takei, who played Mr. Sulu on the cult classic television show *Star Trek*. Soo and Takei, both born and raised in California, were no less American than anyone else.

Black's Majority Opinion

In *Korematsu*, the Court held that because the United States remained under attack, there was a compelling need to prevent further attacks or espionage, and that it was virtually impossible to rapidly determine which persons of Japanese descent were loyal to the United States and which were not.

The aspect of the Court's opinion that received the most criticism was not that the need to prevent attacks and espionage was compelling, but that the quarantine was necessary to meet that need.

Concurring Justices added that different standards ought to be applied during wartime than during peacetime, and that those entrusted with waging war have no less of an obligation to defend the United States by waging war successfully than do the courts to enforce Constitutional liberties.

Dissenting Justices accused the United States of racism of the ugliest kind, the kind that we went to war to eradicate (referring to Nazi Germany), and noted that the United States did not take similar measures against persons of German or Italian dissent, and attributed that distinction as further evidence of racism toward the Japanese.

Others acknowledged that military decisions are different from civilian ones and not necessarily subject to the same Constitutional scrutiny. Nonetheless, when squarely faced with the question, there was no choice, they believed, but to apply Constitutional principles. In simpler terms, it was a statement that the military is sort of above the law, but if asked whether they broke the law, the answer is yes.

In 1988, President Ronald Reagan officially apologized on behalf of the United States for the interment camps, calling them a result of racism and mass hysteria. Reparations were made by the U.S. government to detainees and their descendants.

Race, nationality, and gender have been the three most notable historical discrimination issues in terms of American Constitutional history. Let's now turn to the concept of affirmative action, particularly as it pertains to groups that have been affected.

Affirmative Action

As we stated earlier in this chapter, affirmative action is a policy designed to remedy unjustifiable discrimination against a historically underrepresented group. Now that we have discussed some examples of historically underrepresented groups; let's take a look at some individuals applying for jobs and see how affirmative action might apply.

Kevin, Linda, and Zaid were all born and raised in the United States and just graduated from college. Kevin is a third generation African-American male, Linda is a third-generation French-Canadian female, and Zaid is a third-generation Iraqi-American male. Kevin majored in accounting, Linda in communications, and Zaid in computer science. Each attempted to obtain jobs with different companies. Suppose that each of these recent graduates has 6 months experience in their respective fields, and each has a Grade Point Average (GPA) of 3.5 from a second-tier university. In each case, they are up against a white male who has 2 years field experience and a 3.85 GPA from a top-tier university.

Suppose that Kevin, Linda, and Zaid, all of whom are qualified, are hired even though their main competitors were even more qualified, because of affirmative action. There are those who might express outrage, labeling affirmative action as "reverse discrimination," and stating that none of the three graduates should be given special consideration because of their membership in a historically underrepresented group. The other side of that argument, however, is that perhaps their competitors enjoyed greater benefits through life, such as:

- Greater financial resources
- Access to better elementary and secondary schools
- Access to tutors
- Influence of college-educated parents or grandparents
- Or other factors

That is not to say that African Americans, women, or descendants of Iraq could not provide all of these privileges to their children, and more, but because there has been historical discrimination against race, gender, and nationality in this country, it is perhaps *more likely* that members of these groups might not have had the same advantages, thereby rendering them eligible for affirmative action.

Another way to look at it is this: Suppose that Sandy and Tammy are about to compete in a 1-mile race, but when the official yells "GO!" someone grabs hold of Sandy and holds her back for a full minute. Now, Tammy is considerably ahead in the race. In order to *compensate* for Sandy's detriment, someone gives Sandy a bicycle so that she can catch up to Tammy, step off the bike, and then run the rest of the way. Affirmative action works in that manner. Those who have been held back get an extra boost.

Nonetheless, important arguments have been made denouncing affirmative action as not choosing the best person for the best job. A common question people ask is: if you need an operation, whom do you want performing the surgery? The person who got the best grades in medical school, or a person with grades not as good, but is from a historically underrepresented group? For all of you sports fans, consider who would you want to be the quarterback of your football team or the starting pitcher for your baseball team? The best player, or a player not quite as good, but from a historically underrepresented group?

As you ponder this difficult notion, for which there are many valid arguments for and against, take a look at how the Supreme Court has ruled.

Quotas

Many opponents of affirmative action falsely believe that it must necessarily involve quotas. *Quotas* in the context of affirmative action means that a certain number of positions must be filled by members of historically underrepresented groups, without a great deal of attention to quality, as long as minimum qualifications are met. In the example with the three graduates, suppose that Kevin, Linda, and Zaid were merely average students. If they were awarded the jobs over outstanding students, then clearly that would appear to be a case involving quotas. That is, the graduates would have been chosen as token representatives of their groups and not based on their merits.

In *Regents of the University of California v. Bakke*, in 1978, the Court ruled against racial quotas, but determined that race could be one of several factors used to determine an applicant's admission to (in that particular case) medical school.

The majority determined that strict scrutiny applies in race-based discrimination even if the subject (in this case, a white male) is not a member of a historically underrepresented group. Accordingly, the Court contended, the State of California, in its admissions policies, did not demonstrate how racial quotas were necessary to achieve its interest of remedying past discrimination and ensuring proper representation in medical education for members of historically underrepresented groups.

Justice Powell was the significant voice in this *Bakke*, because four other Justices (Blackmun, Brennan, Marshall, and White) believed that even racial quotas were Constitutional, and the remaining four Justices (Burger, Rehnquist, Stevens, and Stewart) believed that it was unconstitutional for race to be a factor at all.

Powell thus took sort of a middle ground, ruling against racial quotas but favoring race to be one of several criteria.

In 2003, the Court revisited the issue of race-based affirmative action, in *Grutter v. Bollinger* and *Gratz v. Bollinger*. Those two cases were both brought against the University of Michigan for its discriminatory practices in admitting applicants. The significance of these two cases was that they upheld the notion set forth in *Bakke*, that although racial quotas are unconstitutional, race may be used as a factor to augment representation by members of historically underrepresented groups.

Gender-Based Affirmative Action

A case that appears to be one rooted in gender-based affirmative action, but with a bit of a twist, is *Mississippi University for Women v. Hogan*, decided in 1982. In that case, the university admitted only women to its nursing school, having argued that it is a gender-based affirmative action plan because women in general have been underrepresented in both education and employment as compared to men. The Court, however, not departing from its stance on the topic but distinguishing this case from others, concluded that: because

the restrictions (against male applicants) was specifically to a school of nursing, and because women already dominate the field of nursing, the practice would not help remedy a past wrong done to women. The statute would have had to been *narrowly tailored*, which it was not. If, perhaps, it had been a Truck Driving School for Women, then it might have had a better chance of surviving Constitutional scrutiny.

The Beginning of the End for Affirmative Action?

In Summer 2009, the Supreme Court issued a ruling in *Ricci v. DeStefano* that may very well have set the tone for future opinions that might eliminate affirmative action altogether. The *Ricci* case was about an examination given to firefighters in New Haven, Connecticut. Those who successfully completed the exam would be promoted to lieutenant or captain and enjoy increased salaries and benefits. The results indicated that white firefighters consistently scored higher than their black counterparts, which prompted the latter to charge that the exam was discriminatory. Eighteen candidates who passed the exam—seventeen white and one Hispanic—countered that to discard the examination results would be discriminatory against them.

Faced with this dilemma, the city of New Haven decided to discard the test results, which prompted the plaintiffs to file a lawsuit. In a dramatic five to four decision, the Court sided with the plaintiffs, and held that discarding the test results based on race was unconstitutional.

Kennedy's Majority

In writing for the majority, joined by Chief Justice Roberts, and Justices Scalia, Thomas, and Alito; Justice Kennedy rejected the city's rationale that the test scores had to be thrown out because, otherwise, too many whites and not enough minorities would be promoted. Justice Kennedy identified the rationale as clear racial discrimination, and thus impermissible under the Constitution.

The city claimed that had it certified the exams, it would have been liable under a disparate impact statute, designed to prevent actions whose consequences negatively impact any particular race. Because the exams were job-related and there was no evidence of any racial disparate impact, other than the statistics of the passing scores themselves, the majority concluded that decertifying was Constitutionally unacceptable. Moreover, Kennedy found it insufficient that the city claimed to have been justified in refusing to certify the test results for fear that it would have been bombarded with racial discrimination lawsuits.

Scalia's Concurrence

Justice Scalia, in a concurring opinion, went further than the case at hand. He criticized the disparate impact laws, stating that if they are designed to assist one race over another, they are in violation of the Constitution's Equal Protection Clause. Scalia argued that if the federal government is prohibited from racially discriminating actions, then employers (who might hire or not hire someone based on race) are as well.

Justice Anthony Kennedy's (left) opinion in *Ricci* may have changed the future of affirmative action. Justice Ruth Bader Ginsburg (right) strongly disagreed with the majority.

Alito's Concurrence

In a separate concurring opinion, one joined by Justices Scalia and Thomas; Justice Alito emphasized certain facts that he believed conveyed the real reason why New Haven was so eager to invalidate the test results: namely, that racially-based politics would be problematic otherwise. Alito also focused on the personal stories of the plaintiffs, who studied long and hard for the exams.

Ginsburg's Dissent

Justice Ginsburg, joined by Justices Stevens, Souter, and Breyer, vehemently dissented, maintaining that the refusal to certify the tests was based on the inadequacy of the tests themselves, not because the results would promote a disproportionate number of white firefighters. Ginsburg also took exception to Alito's conclusion that New Haven's decision was politically motivated, in order to appease an angry black constituency.

The *Ricci* decision certainly does not do away with affirmative action, although much of the language by the majority, and by Scalia and Alito in their concurring opinions, hint that the Court is moving in that direction. Nonetheless, the decision was five to four, which is as narrow as it can get. This underscores how affirmative action remains a complex issue with strong arguments on both sides.

Conclusion

We talked a great deal about discrimination and affirmative action. As you can see, we did not achieve a definitive resolution at the end of this chapter. Then again, the Supreme Court has not achieved a resolution either. In other words, there are no absolute "right" or "wrong" answers regarding affirmative action. Only Constitutional interpretations based on those folks wearing the black robes inside the highest Court of our land exist. And now that you have read this chapter, you know a lot more about what goes on in the Court than you did before.

In Chapter 8 we will turn to the issues of civil liberties and security, and decide how much freedom we are willing to give up in order to be kept safe.

Questions for Review

1. What does discrimination mean?
2. What are some examples of how all of us discriminate many times a day, and why it is usually a good thing to do?
3. What is affirmative action?
4. What are some of the major historically underrepresented groups in the United States?
5. How did slavery precede racism in the United States?
6. What is the separate but equal doctrine?
7. Why did *Brown v. Board of Education* invalidate the separate but equal doctrine?
8. Why is gender-based discrimination not held to quite the same standard as race-based discrimination?
9. What are affirmative action quotas?
10. How did the *Ricci v. DeStefano* decision impact affirmative action?

Constitutionally Speaking

The American political landscape has been dominated by white males. Although more women and persons of color have held powerful political positions than ever before, the ratio still overwhelmingly favors white males.

If Congress established a quota system requiring a minimum number of women and persons of color to hold elected seats in Congress, what would be the pros and cons of such a law?

Constitutional Cases

Plessy v. Ferguson and *Brown v. Board of Education* are the two best-known Supreme Court cases regarding racial discrimination and the Constitution. We discussed them earlier in the chapter. They are now presented here in their entirety.

Plessy v. Ferguson, 163 U.S. 537, 538 (1896)

May 18, 1896. This was a petition for writs of prohibition and *certiorari* originally filed in the supreme court of the state by Plessy, the plaintiff in error, against the Hon. John H. Ferguson, judge of the criminal district court for the parish of Orleans, and setting forth, in substance, the following facts:

That petitioner was a citizen of the United States and a resident of the state of Louisiana, of mixed descent, in the proportion of seven-eighths Caucasian and one-eighth African blood; that the mixture of colored blood was not discernible in him, and that he was entitled to every recognition, right, privilege, and immunity secured to the citizens of the United States of the white race by its constitution and laws; that on June 7, 1892, he engaged and paid for a first-class passage on the East Louisiana Railway, from New Orleans to Covington, in the same state, and thereupon entered a passenger train, and took possession of a vacant seat in a coach where passengers of the white race were accommodated; that such railroad company was incorporated by the laws of Louisiana as a common carrier, and was not authorized to distinguish between citizens according to their race, but, notwithstanding this, petitioner was required by the conductor, under penalty of ejection from said train and imprisonment, to vacate said coach, and occupy another seat, in a coach assigned by said company for persons not of the white race, and for no other reason than that petitioner was of the colored race; that, upon petitioner's refusal to comply with such order, he was, with the aid of a police officer, forcibly ejected from said coach, and hurried off to, and imprisoned in, the parish jail of New Orleans, and there held to answer a charge made by such officer to the effect that he was guilty of having criminally violated an act of the general assembly of the state, approved July 10, 1890, in such case made and provided.

The petitioner was subsequently brought before the recorder of the city for preliminary examination, and committed for trial to the criminal district court for the parish of Orleans, where an information was filed against him in the matter above set forth, for a violation of the above act, which act the petitioner affirmed to be null and void, because in conflict with the constitution of the United States; that petitioner interposed a plea to such information, based upon the unconstitutionality of the act of the general assembly, to which the district attorney, on behalf of the state, filed a demurrer; that, upon issue being joined upon such demurrer and plea, the court sustained the demurrer, overruled the plea, and ordered petitioner to plead over to the facts set forth in the information, and that, unless the judge of the said court be enjoined by a writ of prohibition from further proceeding in such case, the court will proceed to fine and sentence petitioner to imprisonment, and thus deprive him of his constitutional rights set forth in his said plea, notwithstanding the unconstitutionality of the act under which he was being prosecuted; that no appeal lay from such sentence, and petitioner was without relief or remedy except by writs of prohibition and *certiorari*. Copies of the information and other proceedings in the criminal district court were annexed to the petition as an exhibit.

Upon the filing of this petition, an order was issued upon the respondent to show cause why a writ of prohibition should not issue, and be made perpetual, and a further order that the record of the proceedings had in the criminal cause be certified and transmitted to the supreme court.

To this order the respondent made answer, transmitting a certified copy of the proceedings, asserting the constitutionality of the law, and averring that, instead of pleading or admitting that he belonged to the colored race, the said Plessy declined and refused, either by pleading or otherwise, to admit that he was in any sense or in any proportion a colored man.

The case coming on for hearing before the supreme court, that court was of opinion that the law under which the prosecution was had was constitutional and denied the relief prayed for by the petitioner (*Ex parte* Plessy, 45 La. Ann. 80, 11 South. 948); whereupon petitioner prayed for a writ of error from this court, which was allowed by the chief justice of the supreme court of Louisiana.

Mr. Justice Harlan dissenting.
A. W. Tourgee and S. F. Phillips, for plaintiff in error.
Alex. Porter Morse, for defendant in error.
Mr. Justice BROWN, after stating the facts in the foregoing language, delivered the opinion of the court.

This case turns upon the constitutionality of an act of the general assembly of the state of Louisiana, passed in 1890, providing for separate railway carriages for the white and colored races. Acts 1890, No. 111, p. 152.

The first section of the statute enacts 'that all railway companies carrying passengers in their coaches in this state, shall provide equal but separate accommodations for the white, and colored races, by providing two or more passenger coaches for each passenger train, or by dividing the passenger coaches by a partition so as to secure separate accommodations: provided, that this section shall not be construed to apply to street railroads. No person or persons shall be permitted to occupy seats in coaches, other than the ones assigned to them, on account of the race they belong to.'

By the second section it was enacted 'that the officers of such passenger trains shall have power and are hereby required to assign each passenger to the coach or compartment used for the race to which such passenger belongs; any passenger insisting on going into a coach or compartment to which by race he does not belong, shall be liable to a fine of twenty-five dollars, or in lieu thereof to imprisonment for a period of not more than twenty days in the parish prison, and any officer of any railroad insisting on assigning a passenger to a coach or compartment other than the one set aside for the race to which said passenger belongs, shall be liable to a fine of twenty-five dollars, or in lieu thereof to imprisonment for a period of not more than twenty days in the parish prison; and should any passenger refuse to occupy the coach or compartment to which he or she is assigned by the officer of such railway, said officer shall have power to refuse to carry such passenger on his train, and for such refusal neither he nor the railway company which he represents shall be liable for damages in any of the courts of this state.'

The third section provides penalties for the refusal or neglect of the officers, directors, conductors, and employees of railway companies to comply with the act, with a proviso that 'nothing in this act shall be construed as applying to nurses attending children of the other race.' The fourth section is immaterial.

The information filed in the criminal district court charged, in substance, that Plessy, being a passenger between two stations within the state of Louisiana, was assigned by officers of the company to the coach used for the race to which he belonged, but he insisted upon going into a coach used by the race to which he did not belong. Neither in the information nor plea was his particular race or color averred.

The petition for the writ of prohibition averred that petitioner was seven-eights Caucasian and one-eighth African blood; that the mixture of colored blood was not discernible in him; and that he was entitled to every right, privilege, and immunity secured to citizens of the United States of the white race; and that, upon such theory, he took possession of a vacant seat in a coach where passengers of the white race were accommodated, and was ordered by the conductor to vacate said coach, and take a seat in another, assigned to persons of the colored race, and, having refused to comply with such demand, he was forcibly ejected, with the aid of a police officer, and imprisoned in the parish jail to answer a charge of having violated the above act.

The constitutionality of this act is attacked upon the ground that it conflicts both with the thirteenth amendment of the constitution, abolishing slavery, and the fourteenth amendment, which prohibits certain restrictive legislation on the part of the states.

1. That it does not conflict with the thirteenth amendment, which abolished slavery and involuntary servitude, except a punishment for crime, is too clear for argument. Slavery implies involuntary servitude,—a state of bondage; the ownership of mankind as a chattel, or, at least, the control of the labor and services of one man for the benefit of another, and the absence of a legal right to the disposal of his own person, property, and services. This amendment was said in the Slaughter-House Cases, 16 Wall. 36, to have been intended primarily to abolish slavery, as it had been previously known in this country, and that it equally forbade Mexican peonage or the Chinese coolie trade, when they amounted to slavery or involuntary servitude, and that the use of the word 'servitude' was intended to prohibit the use of all forms of involuntary slavery, of whatever class or name. It was intimated, however, in that case, that this amendment was regarded by the statesmen of that day as insufficient to protect the colored race from certain laws which had been enacted in the Southern states, imposing upon the colored race onerous disabilities and burdens, and curtailing their rights in the pursuit of life, liberty, and property to such an extent that their freedom was of little value; and that the fourteenth amendment was devised to meet this exigency.

So, too, in the Civil Rights Cases, 109 U.S. 3, 3 Sup. Ct. 18, it was said that the act of a mere individual, the owner of an inn, a public conveyance or place of amusement, refusing accommodations to

(Continues)

(Continued)

colored people, cannot be justly regarded as imposing any badge of slavery or servitude upon the applicant, but only as involving an ordinary civil injury, properly cognizable by the laws of the state, and presumably subject to redress by those laws until the contrary appears. 'It would be running the slavery question into the ground,' said Mr. Justice Bradley, 'to make it apply to every act of discrimination which a person may see fit to make as to the guests he will entertain, or as to the people he will take into his coach or cab or car, or admit to his concert or theater, or deal with in other matters of intercourse or business.'

A statute which implies merely a legal distinction between the white and colored races—a distinction which is founded in the color of the two races, and which must always exist so long as white men are distinguished from the other race by color—has no tendency to destroy the legal equality of the two races, or re-establish a state of involuntary servitude. Indeed, we do not understand that the thirteenth amendment is strenuously relied upon by the plaintiff in error in this connection.

2. By the fourteenth amendment, all persons born or naturalized in the United States, and subject to the jurisdiction thereof, are made citizens of the United States and of the state wherein they reside; and the states are forbidden from making or enforcing any law which shall abridge the privileges or immunities of citizens of the United States, or shall deprive any person of life, liberty, or property without due process of law, or deny to any person within their jurisdiction the equal protection of the laws.

The proper construction of this amendment was first called to the attention of this court in the Slaughter-House Cases, 16 Wall. 36, which involved, however, not a question of race, but one of exclusive privileges. The case did not call for any expression of opinion as to the exact rights it was intended to secure to the colored race, but it was said generally that its main purpose was to establish the citizenship of the negro, to give definitions of citizenship of the United States and of the states, and to protect from the hostile legislation of the states the privileges and immunities of citizens of the United States, as distinguished from those of citizens of the states. The object of the amendment was undoubtedly to enforce the absolute equality of the two races before the law, but, in the nature of things, it could not have been intended to abolish distinctions based upon color, or to enforce social, as distinguished from political, equality, or a commingling of the two races upon terms unsatisfactory to either. Laws permitting, and even requiring, their separation, in places where they are liable to be brought into contact, do not necessarily imply the inferiority of either race to the other, and have been generally, if not universally, recognized as within the competency of the state legislatures in the exercise of their police power. The most common instance of this is connected with the establishment of separate schools for white and colored children, which have been held to be a valid exercise of the legislative power even by courts of states where the political rights of the colored race have been longest and most earnestly enforced.

One of the earliest of these cases is that of *Roberts v. City of Boston*, 5 Cush. 198, in which the supreme judicial court of Massachusetts held that the general school committee of Boston had power to make provision for the instruction of colored children in separate schools established exclusively for them, and to prohibit their attendance upon the other schools. 'The great principle,' said Chief Justice Shaw, 'advanced by the learned and eloquent advocate for the plaintiff [Mr. Charles Sumner], is that, by the constitution and laws of Massachusetts, all persons, without distinction of age or sex, birth or color, origin or condition, are equal before the law. . . . But, when this great principle comes to be applied to the actual and various conditions of persons in society, it will not warrant the assertion that men and women are legally clothed with the same civil and political powers, and that children and adults are legally to have the same functions and be subject to the same treatment; but only that the rights of all, as they are settled and regulated by law, are equally entitled to the paternal consideration and protection of the law for their maintenance and security.' It was held that the powers of the committee extended to the establishment of separate schools for children of different ages, sexes and colors, and that they might also establish special schools for poor and neglected children, who have become too old to attend the primary school, and yet have not acquired the rudiments of learning, to enable them to enter the ordinary schools. Similar laws have been enacted by congress under its general power of legislation over the District of Columbia (sections 281–283, 310, 319, Rev. St. D. C.), as well as by the legislatures of many of the states, and have been generally, if not uniformly, sustained by the courts. *State v. McCann*, 21 Ohio St. 210; *Lehew v. Brummell* (Mo. Sup.) 15 S. W. 765; *Ward v. Flood*, 48 Cal. 36; *Bertonneau v. Directors of City Schools*, 3 Woods, 177, Fed. Cas. No. 1,361; *People v. Gallagher*, 93 N.Y. 438; *Cory v. Carter*, 48 Ind. 337; *Dawson v. Lee*, 83 Ky. 49.

Laws forbidding the intermarriage of the two races may be said in a technical sense to interfere with the freedom of contract, and yet have been universally recognized as within the police power of the state. *State v. Gibson*, 36 Ind. 389.

The distinction between laws interfering with the political equality of the negro and those requiring the separation of the two races in schools, theaters, and railway carriages has been frequently drawn by this court. Thus, in *Strauder v. West Virginia*, 100 U.S. 303, it was held that a law of West Virginia limiting to white male persons 21 years of age, and citizens of the state, the right to sit upon juries, was a discrimination which implied a legal inferiority in civil society, which lessened the security of the right of the colored race, and was a step towards reducing them to a condition of servility. Indeed, the right of a colored man that, in the selection of jurors to pass upon his life, liberty, and property, there shall be no exclusion of his race, and no discrimination against them because of color, has been asserted in a number of cases. *Virginia v. Rivers*, 100 U.S. 313; *Neal v. Delaware*, 103 U.S. 370; *Bush v. Com.*, 107 U.S. 110, 1 Sup. Ct. 625; *Gibson v. Mississippi*, 162 U.S. 565, 16 Sup. Ct. 904. So, where the laws of a particular locality or the charter of a particular railway corporation has provided that no person shall be excluded from the cars on account of color, we have held that this meant that persons of color should travel in the same car as white ones, and that the enactment was not satisfied by the company providing cars assigned exclusively to people of color, though they were as good as those which they assigned exclusively to white persons. *Railroad Co. v. Brown*, 17 Wall. 445.

Upon the other hand, where a statute of Louisiana required those engaged in the transportation of passengers among the states to give to all persons traveling within that state, upon vessels employed in that business, equal rights and privileges in all parts of the vessel, without distinction on account of race or color, and subjected to an action for damages the owner of such a vessel who excluded colored passengers on account of their color from the cabin set aside by him for the use of whites, it was held to be, so far as it applied to interstate commerce, unconstitutional and void. *Hall v. De Cuir*, 95 U.S. 485. The court in this case, however, expressly disclaimed that it had anything whatever to do with the statute as a regulation of internal commerce, or affecting anything else than commerce among the states.

In the Civil Rights Cases, 109 U.S. 3, 3 Sup. Ct. 18, it was held that an act of congress entitling all persons within the jurisdiction of the United States to the full and equal enjoyment of the accommodations, advantages, facilities, and privileges of inns, public conveyances, on land or water, theaters, and other places of public amusement, and made applicable to citizens of every race and color, regardless of any previous condition of servitude, was unconstitutional and void, upon the ground that the fourteenth amendment was prohibitory upon the states only, and the legislation authorized to be adopted by congress for enforcing it was not direct legislation on matters respecting which the states were prohibited from making or enforcing certain laws, or doing certain acts, but was corrective legislation, such as might be necessary or proper for counter-acting and redressing the effect of such laws or acts. In delivering the opinion of the court, Mr. Justice Bradley observed that the fourteenth amendment 'does not invest congress with power to legislate upon subjects that are within the domain of state legislation, but to provide modes of relief against state legislation or state action of the kind referred to. It does not authorize congress to create a code of municipal law for the regulation of private rights, but to provide modes of redress against the operation of state laws, and the action of state officers, executive or judicial, when these are subversive of the fundamental rights specified in the amendment. Positive rights and privileges are undoubtedly secured by the fourteenth amendment; but they are secured by way of prohibition against state laws and state proceedings affecting those rights and privileges, and by power given to congress to legislate for the purpose of carrying such prohibition into effect; and such legislation must necessarily be predicated upon such supposed state laws or state proceedings, and be directed to the correction of their operation and effect.'

Much nearer, and, indeed, almost directly in point, is the case of the *Louisville, N. O. & T. Ry. Co. v. State*, 133 U.S. 587, 10 Sup. Ct. 348, wherein the railway company was indicted for a violation of a statute of Mississippi, enacting that all railroads carrying passengers should provide equal, but separate, accommodations for the white and colored races, by providing two or more passenger cars for each passenger train, or by dividing the passenger cars by a partition, so as to secure separate accommodations. The case was presented in a different aspect from the one under consideration, inasmuch as it was an indictment against the railway company for failing to provide the separate accommodations, but the question considered was the constitutionality of the law. In that case, the supreme court of Mississippi (66 Miss. 662, 6 South. 203) had held that the statute applied solely to commerce within the state, and, that being the construction of the state statute by its highest court, was accepted as conclusive. 'If it be a matter,' said the court (page 591, 133 U.S., and page 348, 10 Sup. Ct.), 'respecting commerce wholly within a state, and not interfering with commerce between the states, then, obviously, there is no violation of the commerce clause of the federal constitution. . . . No question arises under

(*Continues*)

this section as to the power of the state to separate in different compartments interstate passengers, or affect, in any manner, the privileges and rights of such passengers. All that we can consider is whether the state has the power to require that railroad trains within her limits shall have separate accommodations for the two races. That affecting only commerce within the state is no invasion of the power given to congress by the commerce clause.'

A like course of reasoning applies to the case under consideration, since the supreme court of Louisiana, in the case of *State v. Judge*, 44 La. Ann. 770, 11 South. 74, held that the statute in question did not apply to interstate passengers, but was confined in its application to passengers traveling exclusively within the borders of the state. The case was decided largely upon the authority of *Louisville, N. O. & T. Ry. Co. v. State*, 66 Miss. 662, 6 South, 203, and affirmed by this court in 133 U.S. 587, 10 Sup. Ct. 348. In the present case no question of interference with interstate commerce can possibly arise, since the East Louisiana Railway appears to have been purely a local line, with both its termini within the state of Louisiana. Similar statutes for the separation of the two races upon public conveyances were held to be constitutional in *Railroad v. Miles*, 55 Pa. St. 209; *Day v. Owen* 5 Mich. 520; *Railway Co. v. Williams*, 55 Ill. 185; *Railroad Co. v. Wells*, 85 Tenn. 613; 4 S. W. 5; *Railroad Co. v. Benson*, 85 Tenn. 627, 4 S. W. 5; *The Sue*, 22 Fed. 843; *Logwood v. Railroad Co.*, 23 Fed. 318; *McGuinn v. Forbes*, 37 Fed. 639; *People v. King (N. Y. App.)* 18 N. E. 245; *Houck v. Railway Co.*, 38 Fed. 226; *Heard v. Railroad Co.*, 3 Inter St. Commerce Com. R. 111, 1 Inter St. Commerce Com. R. 428.

While we think the enforced separation of the races, as applied to the internal commerce of the state, neither abridges the privileges or immunities of the colored man, deprives him of his property without due process of law, nor denies him the equal protection of the laws, within the meaning of the fourteenth amendment, we are not prepared to say that the conductor, in assigning passengers to the coaches according to their race, does not act at his peril, or that the provision of the second section of the act that denies to the passenger compensation in damages for a refusal to receive him into the coach in which he properly belongs is a valid exercise of the legislative power. Indeed, we understand it to be conceded by the state's attorney that such part of the act as exempts from liability the railway company and its officers is unconstitutional. The power to assign to a particular coach obviously implies the power to determine to which race the passenger belongs, as well as the power to determine who, under the laws of the particular state, is to be deemed a white, and who a colored, person. This question, though indicated in the brief of the plaintiff in error, does not properly arise upon the record in this case, since the only issue made is as to the unconstitutionality of the act, so far as it requires the railway to provide separate accommodations, and the conductor to assign passengers according to their race.

It is claimed by the plaintiff in error that, in an mixed community, the reputation of belonging to the dominant race, in this instance the white race, is 'property,' in the same sense that a right of action or of inheritance is property. Conceding this to be so, for the purposes of this case, we are unable to see how this statute deprives him of, or in any way affects his right to, such property. If he be a white man, and assigned to a colored coach, he may have his action for damages against the company for being deprived of his so-called 'property.' Upon the other hand, if he be a colored man, and be so assigned, he has been deprived of no property, since he is not lawfully entitled to the reputation of being a white man.

In this connection, it is also suggested by the learned counsel for the plaintiff in error that the same argument that will justify the state legislature in requiring railways to provide separate accommodations for the two races will also authorize them to require separate cars to be provided for people whose hair is of a certain color, or who are aliens, or who belong to certain nationalities, or to enact laws requiring colored people to walk upon one side of the street, and white people upon the other, or requiring white men's houses to be painted white, and colored men's black, or their vehicles or business signs to be of different colors, upon the theory that one side of the street is as good as the other, or that a house or vehicle of one color is as good as one of another color. The reply to all this is that every exercise of the police power must be reasonable, and extend only to such laws as are enacted in good faith for the promotion of the public good, and not for the annoyance or oppression of a particular class. Thus, in *Yick Wo v. Hopkins*, 118 U.S. 356, 6 Sup. Ct. 1064, it was held by this court that a municipal ordinance of the city of San Francisco, to regulate the carrying on of public laundries within the limits of the municipality, violated the provisions of the constitution of the United States, if it conferred upon the municipal authorities arbitrary power, at their own will, and without regard to discretion, in the legal sense of the term, to give or withhold consent as to persons or places, without regard to the competency of the persons applying or the propriety of the places selected for the carrying on of the business. It was held to be a covert attempt on the part of the municipality to make an arbitrary and unjust discrimination against the Chinese race. While this was the case of a municipal ordinance, a like principle has been held to apply to acts of a state legislature passed in the exercise of the police power. *Railroad Co. v. Husen*, 95 U.S. 465; *Louisville & N. R. Co. v. Kentucky*, 161 U.S. 677, 16 Sup. Ct. 714, and cases cited on page 700, 161 U. S., and page 714, 16 Sup. Ct.; *Daggett v. Hudson*, 43 Ohio St. 548, 3 N. E. 538; *Capen v. Foster*, 12 Pick. 485; *State v. Baker*, 38 Wis. 71; *Monroe v. Collins*, 17 Ohio St. 665; *Hulseman v. Rems*, 41 Pa. St. 396; *Osman v. Riley*, 15 Cal. 48.

So far, then, as a conflict with the fourteenth amendment is concerned, the case reduces itself to the question whether the statute of Louisiana is a reasonable regulation, and with respect to this there must necessarily be a large discretion on the part of the legislature. In determining the question of reasonableness, it is at liberty to act with reference to the established usages, customs, and traditions of the people, and with a view to the promotion of their comfort, and the preservation of the public peace and good order. Gauged by this standard, we cannot say that a law which authorizes or even requires the separation of the two races in public conveyances is unreasonable, or more obnoxious to the fourteenth amendment than the acts of congress requiring separate schools for colored children in the District of Columbia, the constitutionality of which does not seem to have been questioned, or the corresponding acts of state legislatures.

We consider the underlying fallacy of the plaintiff's argument to consist in the assumption that the enforced separation of the two races stamps the colored race with a badge of inferiority. If this be so, it is not by reason of anything found in the act, but solely because the colored race chooses to put that construction upon it. The argument necessarily assumes that if, as has been more than once the case, and is not unlikely to be so again, the colored race should become the dominant power in the state legislature, and should enact a law in precisely similar terms, it would thereby relegate the white race to an inferior position. We imagine that the white race, at least, would not acquiesce in this assumption. The argument also assumes that social prejudices may be overcome by legislation, and that equal rights cannot be secured to the negro except by an enforced commingling of the two races. We cannot accept this proposition. If the two races are to meet upon terms of social equality, it must be the result of natural affinities, a mutual appreciation of each other's merits, and a voluntary consent of individuals. As was said by the court of appeals of New York in *People v. Gallagher*, 93 N.Y. 438, 448: 'This end can neither be accomplished nor promoted by laws which conflict with the general sentiment of the community upon whom they are designed to operate. When the government, therefore, has secured to each of its citizens equal rights before the law, and equal opportunities for improvement and progress, it has accomplished the end for which it was organized, and performed all of the functions respecting social advantages with which it is endowed.' Legislation is powerless to eradicate racial instincts, or to abolish distinctions based upon physical differences, and the attempt to do so can only result in accentuating the difficulties of the present situation. If the civil and political rights of both races be equal, one cannot be inferior to the other civilly or politically. If one race be inferior to the other socially, the constitution of the United States cannot put them upon the same plane.

It is true that the question of the proportion of colored blood necessary to constitute a colored person, as distinguished from a white person, is one upon which there is a difference of opinion in the different states; some holding that any visible admixture of black blood stamps the person as belonging to the colored race (*State v. Chavers*, 5 Jones [N.C.] 1); others, that it depends upon the preponderance of blood (*Gray v. State*, 4 Ohio, 354; *Monroe v. Collins*, 17 Ohio St. 665); and still others, that the predominance of white blood must only be in the proportion of three-fourths (*People v. Dean*, 14 Mich. 406; *Jones v. Com.*, 80 Va. 544). But these are questions to be determined under the laws of each state, and are not properly put in issue in this case. Under the allegations of his petition, it may undoubtedly become a question of importance whether, under the laws of Louisiana, the petitioner belongs to the white or colored race.

The judgment of the court below is therefore affirmed.

Mr. Justice BREWER did not hear the argument or participate in the decision of this case.

Mr. Justice HARLAN dissenting.

By the Louisiana statute the validity of which is here involved, all railway companies (other than street-railroad companies) carry passengers in that state are required to have separate but equal accommodations for white and colored persons, 'by providing two or more passenger coaches for each passenger train, or by dividing the passenger coaches by a partition so as to secure separate accommodations.'

(Continues)

Under this statute, no colored person is permitted to occupy a seat in a coach assigned to white persons; nor any white person to occupy a seat in a coach assigned to colored persons. The managers of the railroad are not allowed to exercise any discretion in the premises, but are required to assign each passenger to some coach or compartment set apart for the exclusive use of is race. If a passenger insists upon going into a coach or compartment not set apart for persons of his race, he is subject to be fined, or to be imprisoned in the parish jail. Penalties are prescribed for the refusal or neglect of the officers, directors, conductors, and employees of railroad companies to comply with the provisions of the act.

Only 'nurses attending children of the other race' are excepted from the operation of the statute. No exception is made of colored attendants traveling with adults. A white man is not permitted to have his colored servant with him in the same coach, even if his condition of health requires the constant personal assistance of such servant. If a colored maid insists upon riding in the same coach with a white woman whom she has been employed to serve, and who may need her personal attention while traveling, she is subject to be fined or imprisoned for such an exhibition of zeal in the discharge of duty.

While there may be in Louisiana persons of different races who are not citizens of the United States, the words in the act 'white and colored races' necessarily include all citizens of the United States of both races residing in that state. So that we have before us a state enactment that compels, under penalties, the separation of the two races in railroad passenger coaches, and makes it a crime for a citizen of either race to enter a coach that has been assigned to citizens of the other race.

Thus, the state regulates the use of a public highway by citizens of the United States solely upon the basis of race.

However apparent the injustice of such legislation may be, we have only to consider whether it is consistent with the constitution of the United States.

That a railroad is a public highway, and that the corporation which owns or operates it is in the exercise of public functions, is not, at this day, to be disputed. Mr. Justice Nelson, speaking for this court in *New Jersey Steam Nav. Co. v. Merchants' Bank*, 6 How. 344, 382, said that a common carrier was in the exercise 'of a sort of public office, and has public duties to perform, from which he should not be permitted to exonerate himself without the assent of the parties concerned.' Mr. Justice Strong, delivering the judgment of this court in *Olcott v. Supervisors*, 16 Wall. 678, 694, said: 'That railroads, though constructed by private corporations, and owned by them, are public highways, has been the doctrine of nearly all the courts ever since such conveniences for passage and transportation have had any existence. Very early the question arose whether a state's right of eminent domain could be exercised by a private corporation created for the purpose of constructing a railroad. Clearly, it could not, unless taking land for such a purpose by such an agency is taking land for public use. The right of eminent domain nowhere justifies taking property for a private use. Yet it is a doctrine universally accepted that a state legislature may authorize a private corporation to take land for the construction of such a road, making compensation to the owner. What else does this doctrine mean if not that building a railroad, though it be built by a private corporation, is an act done for a public use?' So, in *Township of Pine Grove v. Talcott*, 19 Wall. 666, 676: 'Though the corporation [a railroad company] was private, its work was public, as much so as if it were to be constructed by the state.' So, in *Inhabitants of Worcester v. Western R. Corp.*, 4 Metc. (Mass.) 564: 'The establishment of that great thoroughfare is regarded as a public work, established by public authority, intended for the public use and benefit, the use of which is secured to the whole community, and constitutes, therefore, like a canal, turnpike, or highway, a public easement.' 'It is true that the real and personal property, necessary to the establishment and management of the railroad, is vested in the corporation; but it is in trust for the public.'

In respect of civil rights, common to all citizens, the constitution of the United States does not, I think, permit any public authority to know the race of those entitled to be protected in the enjoyment of such rights. Every true man has pride of race, and under appropriate circumstances, when the rights of others, his equals before the law, are not to be affected, it is his privilege to express such pride and to take such action based upon it as to him seems proper. But I deny that any legislative body or judicial tribunal may have regard to the race of citizens when the civil rights of those citizens are involved. Indeed, such legislation as that here in question is inconsistent not only with that equality of rights which pertains to citizenship, national and state, but with the personal liberty enjoyed by every one within the United States.

The thirteenth amendment does not permit the withholding or the deprivation of any right necessarily inhering in freedom. It not only struck down the institution of slavery as previously existing in the United States, but it prevents the imposition of any burdens or disabilities that constitute badges of slavery or servitude. It decreed universal civil freedom in this country. This court has so adjudged. But, that amendment having been found inadequate to the protection of the rights of those who had been in slavery, it was followed by the fourteenth amendment, which added greatly to the dignity and glory of American citizenship, and to the security of personal liberty, by declaring that 'all persons born or naturalized in the United States, and subject to the jurisdiction thereof, are citizens of the United States and of the state wherein they reside,' and that 'no state shall make or enforce any law which shall abridge the privileges or immunities of citizens of the United States; nor shall any state deprive any person of life, liberty or property without due process of law, nor deny to any person within its jurisdiction the equal protection of the laws.' These two amendments, if enforced according to their true intent and meaning, will protect all the civil rights that pertain to freedom and citizenship. Finally, and to the end that no citizen should be denied, on account of his race, the privilege of participating in the political control of his country, it was declared by the fifteenth amendment that 'the right of citizens of the United States to vote shall not be denied or abridged by the United States or by any state on account of race, color or previous condition of servitude.'

These notable additions to the fundamental law were welcomed by the friends of liberty throughout the world. They removed the race line from our governmental systems. They had, as this court has said, a common purpose, namely, to secure 'to a race recently emancipated, a race that through many generations have been held in slavery, all the civil rights that the superior race enjoy.' They declared, in legal effect, this court has further said, 'that the law in the states shall be the same for the black as for the white; that all persons, whether colored or white, shall stand equal before the laws of the states; and in regard to the colored race, for whose protection the amendment was primarily designed, that no discrimination shall be made against them by law because of their color.' We also said: 'The words of the amendment, it is true, are prohibitory, but they contain a necessary implication of a positive immunity or right, most valuable to the colored race,—the right to exemption from unfriendly legislation against them distinctively as colored; exemption from legal discriminations, implying inferiority in civil society, lessening the security of their enjoyment of the rights which others enjoy; and discriminations which are steps towards reducing them to the condition of a subject race.' It was, consequently, adjudged that a state law that excluded citizens of the colored race from juries, because of their race, however well qualified in other respects to discharge the duties of jurymen, was repugnant to the fourteenth amendment. *Strauder v. West Virginia*, 100 U.S. 303, 306, 307 S.; *Virginia v. Rives, Id.* 313; *Ex parte Virginia, Id.* 339; *Neal v. Delaware*, 103 U.S. 370, 386; *Bush v. Com.*, 107 U.S. 110, 116, 1 S. Sup. Ct. 625. At the present term, referring to the previous adjudications, this court declared that 'underlying all of those decisions is the principle that the constitution of the United States, in its present form, forbids, so far as civil and political rights are concerned, discrimination by the general government or the states against any citizen because of his race. All citizens are equal before the law.' *Gibson v. State*, 162 U.S. 565, 16 Sup. Ct. 904.

The decisions referred to show the scope of the recent amendments of the constitution. They also show that it is not within the power of a state to prohibit colored citizens, because of their race, from participating as jurors in the administration of justice.

It was said in argument that the statute of Louisiana does not discriminate against either race, but prescribes a rule applicable alike to white and colored citizens. But this argument does not meet the difficulty. Every one knows that the statute in question had its origin in the purpose, not so much to exclude white persons from railroad cars occupied by blacks, as to exclude colored people from coaches occupied by or assigned to white persons. Railroad corporations of Louisiana did not make discrimination among whites in the matter of accommodation for travelers. The thing to accomplish was, under the guise of giving equal accommodation for whites and blacks, to compel the latter to keep to themselves while traveling in railroad passenger coaches. No one would be so wanting in candor as to assert the contrary. The fundamental objection, therefore, to the statute, is that it interferes with the personal freedom of citizens. 'Personal liberty,' it has been well said, 'consists in the power of locomotion, of changing situation, or removing one's person to whatsoever places one's own inclination may direct, without imprisonment or restraint, unless by due course of law.' 1 Bl. Comm. *134. If a white man and a black man choose to occupy the same public conveyance on a public highway, it is their right to do so; and no government, proceeding alone on grounds of race, can prevent it without infringing the personal liberty of each.

It is one thing for railroad carriers to furnish, or to be required by law to furnish, equal accommodations for all whom they are under a legal duty to carry. It is quite another thing for government to

(Continues)

forbid citizens of the white and black races from traveling in the same public conveyance, and to punish officers of railroad companies for permitting persons of the two races to occupy the same passenger coach. If a state can prescribe, as a rule of civil conduct, that whites and blacks shall not travel as passengers in the same railroad coach, why may it not so regulate the use of the streets of its cities and towns as to compel white citizens to keep on one side of a street, and black citizens to keep on the other? Why may it not, upon like grounds, punish whites and blacks who ride together in street cars or in open vehicles on a public road or street? Why may it not require sheriffs to assign whites to one side of a court room, and blacks to the other? And why may it not also prohibit the commingling of the two races in the galleries of legislative halls or in public assemblages convened for the consideration of the political questions of the day? Further, if this statute of Louisiana is consistent with the personal liberty of citizens, why may not the state require the separation in railroad coaches of native and naturalized citizens of the United States, or of Protestants and Roman Catholics?

The answer given at the argument to these questions was that regulations of the kind they suggest would be unreasonable, and could not, therefore, stand before the la. Is it meant that the determination of questions of legislative power depends upon the inquiry whether the statute whose validity is questioned is, in the judgment of the courts, a reasonable one, taking all the circumstances into consideration? A statute may be unreasonable merely because a sound public policy forbade its enactment. But I do not understand that the courts have anything to do with the policy or expediency of legislation. A statute may be valid, and yet, upon grounds of public policy, may well be characterized as unreasonable. Mr. Sedgwick correctly states the rule when he says that, the legislative intention being clearly ascertained, 'the courts have no other duty to perform than to execute the legislative will, without any regard to their views as to the wisdom or justice of the particular enactment.' Sedg. St. & Const. Law, 324. There is a dangerous tendency in these latter days to enlarge the functions of the courts, by means of judicial interference with the will of the people as expressed by the legislature. Our institutions have the distinguishing characteristic that the three departments of government are co-ordinate and separate. Each much keep within the limits defined by the constitution. And the courts best discharge their duty by executing the will of the law-making power, constitutionally expressed, leaving the results of legislation to be dealt with by the people through their representatives. Statutes must always have a reasonable construction. Sometimes they are to be construed strictly, sometimes literally, in order to carry out the legislative will. But, however construed, the intent of the legislature is to be respected if the particular statute in question is valid, although the courts, looking at the public interests, may conceive the statute to be both unreasonable and impolitic. If the power exists to enact a statute, that ends the matter so far as the courts are concerned. The adjudged cases in which statutes have been held to be void, because unreasonable, are those in which the means employed by the legislature were not at all germane to the end to which the legislature was competent.

The white race deems itself to be the dominant race in this country. And so it is, in prestige, in achievements, in education, in wealth, and in power. So, I doubt not, it will continue to be for all time, if it remains true to its great heritage, and holds fast to the principles of constitutional liberty. But in view of the constitution, in the eye of the law, there is in this country no superior, dominant, ruling class of citizens. There is no caste here. Our constitution is color-blind, and neither knows nor tolerates classes among citizens. In respect of civil rights, all citizens are equal before the law. The humblest is the peer of the most powerful. The law regards man as man, and takes no account of his surroundings or of his color when his civil rights as guaranteed by the supreme law of the land are involved. It is therefore to be regretted that this high tribunal, the final expositor of the fundamental law of the land, has reached the conclusion that it is competent for a state to regulate the enjoyment by citizens of their civil rights solely upon the basis of race.

In my opinion, the judgment this day rendered will, in time, prove to be quite as pernicious as the decision made by this tribunal in the Dred Scott Case.

It was adjudged in that case that the descendants of Africans who were imported into this country, and sold as slaves, were not included nor intended to be included under the word 'citizens' in the constitution, and could not claim any of the rights and privileges which that instrument provided for and secured to citizens of the United States; that, at time of the adoption of the constitution, they were 'considered as a subordinate and inferior class of beings, who had been subjugated by the dominant race, and, whether emancipated or not, yet remained subject to their authority, and had no rights or privileges but such as those who held the power and the government might choose to grant them.' 17 How. 393, 404. The recent amendments of the constitution, it was supposed, had eradicated these principles from our institutions. But it seems that we have yet, in some of the states, a dominant race,—a superior class of citizens,—which assumes to regulate the enjoyment of civil rights, common to all citizens, upon the basis of race. The present decision, it may well be apprehended, will not only stimulate aggressions, more or less brutal and irritating, upon the admitted rights of colored citizens, but will encourage the belief that it is possible, by means of state enactments, to defeat the beneficent purposes which the people of the United States had in view when they adopted the recent amendments of the constitution, by one of which the blacks of this country were made citizens of the United States and of the states in which they respectively reside, and whose privileges and immunities, as citizens, the states are forbidden to abridge. Sixty millions of whites are in no danger from the presence here of eight millions of blacks. The destinies of the two races, in this country, are indissolubly linked together, and the interests of both require that the common government of all shall not permit the seeds of race hate to be planted under the sanction of law. What can more certainly arouse race hate, what more certainly create and perpetuate a feeling of distrust between these races, than state enactments which, in fact, proceed on the ground that colored citizens are so inferior and degraded that they cannot be allowed to sit in public coaches occupied by white citizens? That, as all will admit, is the real meaning of such legislation as was enacted in Louisiana.

The sure guaranty of the peace and security of each race is the clear, distinct, unconditional recognition by our governments, national and state, of every right that inheres in civil freedom, and of the equality before the law of all citizens of the United States, without regard to race. State enactments regulating the enjoyment of civil rights upon the basis of race, and cunningly devised to defeat legitimate results of the war, under the pretense of recognizing equality of rights, can have no other result than to render permanent peace impossible, and to keep alive a conflict of races, the continuance of which must do harm to all concerned. This question is not met by the suggestion that social equality cannot exist between the white and black races in this country. That argument, if it can be properly regarded as one, is scarcely worthy of consideration; for social equality no more exists between two races when traveling in a passenger coach or a public highway than when members of the same races sit by each other in a street car or in the jury box, or stand or sit with each other in a political assembly, or when they use in common the streets of a city or town, or when they are in the same room for the purpose of having their names placed on the registry of voters, or when they approach the ballot box in order to exercise the high privilege of voting.

There is a race so different from our own that we do not permit those belonging to it to become citizens of the United States. Persons belonging to it are, with few exceptions, absolutely excluded from our country. I allude to the Chinese race. But, by the statute in question, a Chinaman can ride in the same passenger coach with white citizens of the United States, while citizens of the black race in Louisiana, many of whom, perhaps, risked their lives for the preservation of the Union, who are entitled, by law, to participate in the political control of the state and nation, who are not excluded, by law or by reason of their race, from public stations of any kind, and who have all the legal rights that belong to white citizens, are yet declared to be criminals, liable to imprisonment, if they ride in a public coach occupied by citizens of the white race. It is scarcely just to say that a colored citizen should not object to occupying a public coach assigned to his own race. He does not object, nor, perhaps, would he object to separate coaches for his race if his rights under the law were recognized. But he does object, and he ought never to cease objecting, that citizens of the white and black races can be adjudged criminals because they sit, or claim the right to sit, in the same public coach on a public highway. The arbitrary separation of citizens, on the basis of race, while they are on a public highway, is a badge of servitude wholly inconsistent with the civil freedom and the equality before the law established by the constitution. It cannot be justified upon any legal grounds.

If evils will result from the commingling of the two races upon public highways established for the benefit of all, they will be infinitely less than those that will surely come from state legislation regulating the enjoyment of civil rights upon the basis of race. We boast of the freedom enjoyed by our people above all other peoples. But it is difficult to reconcile that boast with a state of the law which, practically, puts the brand of servitude and degradation upon a large class of our fellow citizens,—our equals before the law. The thin disguise of 'equal' accommodations for passengers in railroad coaches will not mislead any one, nor atone for the wrong this day done.

The result of the whole matter is that while this court has frequently adjudged, and at the present term has recognized the doctrine, that a state cannot, consistently with the constitution of the United States, prevent white and black citizens, having the required qualifications for jury service, from sitting in the same jury box, it is now solemnly held that a state may prohibit white and black citizens from

(Continues)

(Continued)

sitting in the same passenger coach on a public highway, or may require that they be separated by a 'partition' when in the same passenger coach. May it not now be reasonably expected that astute men of the dominant race, who affect to be disturbed at the possibility that the integrity of the white race may be corrupted, or that its supremacy will be imperiled, by contact on public highways with black people, will endeavor to procure statutes requiring white and black jurors to be separated in the jury box by a 'partition,' and that, upon retiring from the court room to consult as to their verdict, such partition, if it be a movable one, shall be taken to their consultation room, and set up in such way as to prevent black jurors from coming too close to their brother jurors of the white race. If the 'partition' used in the court room happens to be stationary, provision could be made for screens with openings through which jurors of the two races could confer as to their verdict without coming into personal contact with each other. I cannot see but that, according to the principles this day announced, such state legislation, although conceived in hostility to, and enacted for the purpose of humiliating, citizens of the United States of a particular race, would be held to be consistent with the constitution.

I do not deem it necessary to review the decisions of state courts to which reference was made in argument. Some, and the most important, of them, are wholly inapplicable, because rendered prior to the adoption of the last amendments of the constitution, when colored people had very few rights which the dominant race felt obliged to respect. Others were made at a time when public opinion, in many localities, was dominated by the institution of slavery; when it would not have been safe to do justice to the black man; and when, so far as the rights of blacks were concerned, race prejudice was, practically, the supreme law of the land. Those decisions cannot be guides in the era introduced by the recent amendments of the supreme law, which established universal civil freedom, gave citizenship to all born or naturalized in the United States, and residing ere, obliterated the race line from our systems of governments, national and state, and placed our free institutions upon the broad and sure foundation of the equality of all men before the law.

I am of opinion that the state of Louisiana is inconsistent with the personal liberty of citizens, white and black, in that state, and hostile to both the spirit and letter of the constitution of the United States. If laws of like character should be enacted in the several states of the Union, the effect would be in the highest degree mischievous. Slavery, as an institution tolerated by law, would, it is true, have disappeared from our country; but there would remain a power in the states, by sinister legislation, to interfere with the full enjoyment of the blessings of freedom, to regulate civil rights, common to all citizens, upon the basis of race, and to place in a condition of legal inferiority a large body of American citizens, now constituting a part of the political community, called the 'People of the United States,' for whom, and by whom through representatives, our government is administered. Such a system is inconsistent with the guaranty given by the constitution to each state of a republican form of government, and may be stricken down by congressional action, or by the courts in the discharge of their solemn duty to maintain the supreme law of the land, anything in the constitution or laws of any state to the contrary notwithstanding.

For the reason stated, I am constrained to withhold my assent from the opinion and judgment of the majority.

Brown v. Board of Education, 347 U.S. 483 (1954)

Segregation of white and Negro children in the public schools of a State solely on the basis of race, pursuant to state laws permitting or requiring such segregation, denies to Negro children the equal protection of the laws guaranteed by the Fourteenth Amendment—even though the physical facilities and other "tangible" factors of white and Negro schools may be equal. Pp. 486–496.

(a) The history of the Fourteenth Amendment is inconclusive as to its intended effect on public education. Pp. 489–490.

(b) The question presented in these cases must be determined, not on the basis of conditions existing when the Fourteenth Amendment was adopted, but in the light of the full development of public education and its present place in American life throughout the Nation. Pp. 492–493.

(c) Where a State has undertaken to provide an opportunity for an education in its public schools, such an opportunity is a right which must be made available to all on equal terms. P. 493.

(d) Segregation of children in public schools solely on the basis of race deprives children of the minority group of equal educational opportunities, even though the physical facilities and other "tangible" factors may be equal. Pp. 493–494.

(e) The "separate but equal" doctrine adopted in *Plessy v. Ferguson*, 163 U.S. 537, has no place in the field of public education. P. 495.

(f) The cases are restored to the docket for further argument on specified questions relating to the forms of the decrees. Pp. 495–496.

MR. CHIEF JUSTICE WARREN delivered the opinion of the Court.

These cases come to us from the States of Kansas, South Carolina, Virginia, and Delaware. They are premised on different facts and different local conditions, but a common legal question justifies their consideration together in this consolidated opinion.[1]

In each of the cases, minors of the Negro race, through their legal representatives, seek the aid of the courts in obtaining admission to the public schools of their community on a nonsegregated basis. In each instance, they had been denied admission to schools attended by white children under laws requiring or permitting segregation according to race. This segregation was alleged to deprive the plaintiffs of the equal protection of the laws under the Fourteenth Amendment. In each of the cases other than the Delaware case, a three-judge federal district court denied relief to the plaintiffs on the so-called "separate but equal" doctrine announced by this Court in *Plessy v. Ferguson*, 163 U.S. 537. Under that doctrine, equality of treatment is accorded when the races are provided substantially equal facilities, even though these facilities be separate. In the Delaware case, the Supreme Court of Delaware adhered to that doctrine, but ordered that the plaintiffs be admitted to the white schools because of their superiority to the Negro schools.

The plaintiffs contend that segregated public schools are not "equal" and cannot be made "equal," and that hence they are deprived of the equal protection of the laws. Because of the obvious importance of the question presented, the Court took jurisdiction.[2] Argument was heard in the 1952 Term, and reargument was heard this Term on certain questions propounded by the Court.[3]

Reargument was largely devoted to the circumstances surrounding the adoption of the Fourteenth Amendment in 1868. It covered exhaustively consideration of the Amendment in Congress, ratification by the states, then existing practices in racial segregation, and the views of proponents and opponents of the Amendment. This discussion and our own investigation convince us that, although these sources cast some light, it is not enough to resolve the problem with which we are faced. At best, they are inconclusive. The most avid proponents of the post-War Amendments undoubtedly intended them to remove all legal distinctions among "all persons born or naturalized in the United States." Their opponents, just as certainly, were antagonistic to both the letter and the spirit of the Amendments and wished them to have the most limited effect. What others in Congress and the state legislatures had in mind cannot be determined with any degree of certainty.

An additional reason for the inconclusive nature of the Amendment's history, with respect to segregated schools, is the status of public education at that time.[4] In the South, the movement toward free common schools, supported by general taxation, had not yet taken hold. Education of white children was largely in the hands of private groups. Education of Negroes was almost nonexistent, and practically all of the race were illiterate. In fact, any education of Negroes was forbidden by law in some states. Today, in contrast, many Negroes have achieved outstanding success in the arts and sciences as

---

*Together with No. 2, *Briggs et al. v. Elliott et al.*, on appeal from the United States District Court for the Eastern District of South Carolina, argued December 9–10, 1952, reargued December 7–8, 1953; No. 4, *Davis et al. v. County School Board of Prince Edward County, Virginia, et al.*, on appeal from the United States District Court for the Eastern District of Virginia, argued December 10, 1952, reargued December 7–8, 1953; and No. 10, *Gebhart et al. v. Belton et al.*, on *certiorari* to the Supreme Court of Delaware, argued December 11, 1952, reargued December 9, 1953.

Robert L. Carter argued the cause for appellants in No. 1 on the original argument and on the reargument. Thurgood Marshall argued the cause for appellants in No. 2 on the original argument and Spottswood W. Robinson, III, for appellants in No. 4 on the original argument, and both argued the causes for appellants in Nos. 2 and 4 on the reargument. Louis L. Redding and Jack Greenberg argued the cause for respondents in No. 10 on the original argument and Jack Greenberg and Thurgood Marshall on the reargument.

On the briefs were Robert L. Carter, Thurgood Marshall, Spottswood W. Robinson, III, Louis L. Redding, Jack Greenberg, George E. C. Hayes, William R. Ming, Jr., Constance Baker Motley, James M. Nabrit, Jr., Charles S. Scott, Frank D. Reeves, Harold R. Boulware and Oliver W. Hill for appellants in Nos. 1, 2 and 4 and respondents in No. 10; George M. Johnson for appellants in Nos. 1, 2 and 4; and Loren Miller for appellants in Nos. 2 and 4. Arthur D. Shores and A. T. Walden were on the Statement as to Jurisdiction and a brief opposing a Motion to Dismiss or Affirm in No. 2. (*continued*)

(*Continues*)

well as in the business and professional world. It is true that public school education at the time of the Amendment had advanced further in the North, but the effect of the Amendment on Northern States was generally ignored in the congressional debates. Even in the North, the conditions of public education did not approximate those existing today. The curriculum was usually rudimentary; ungraded schools were common in rural areas; the school term was but three months a year in many states; and compulsory school attendance was virtually unknown. As a consequence, it is not surprising that there should be so little in the history of the Fourteenth Amendment relating to its intended effect on public education.

In the first cases in this Court construing the Fourteenth Amendment, decided shortly after its adoption, the Court interpreted it as proscribing all state-imposed discriminations against the Negro race.[5] The doctrine of "separate but equal" did not make its appearance in this Court until 1896 in the case of *Plessy v. Ferguson*, *supra*, involving not education but transportation.[6] American courts have since labored with the doctrine for over half a century. In this Court, there have been six cases involving the "separate but equal" doctrine in the field of public education.[7] In *Cumming v. County Board of Education*, 175 U.S. 528, and *Gong Lum v. Rice*, 275 U.S. 78, the validity of the doctrine itself was not challenged.[8] In more recent cases, all on the graduate school level, inequality was found in that specific benefits enjoyed by white students were denied to Negro students of the same educational qualifications. *Missouri ex rel. Gaines v. Canada*, 305 U.S. 337; *Sipuel v. Oklahoma*, 332 U.S. 631; *Sweatt v. Painter*, 339 U.S. 629; *McLaurin v. Oklahoma State Regents*, 339 U.S. 637. In none of these cases was it necessary to re-examine the doctrine to grant relief to the Negro plaintiff. And in *Sweatt v. Painter*, *supra*, the Court expressly reserved decision on the question whether *Plessy v. Ferguson* should be held inapplicable to public education.

In the instant cases, that question is directly presented. Here, unlike *Sweatt v. Painter*, there are findings below that the Negro and white schools involved have been equalized, or are being equalized, with respect to buildings, curricula, qualifications and salaries of teachers, and other "tangible" factors.[9] Our decision, therefore, cannot turn on merely a comparison of these tangible factors in the Negro and white schools involved in each of the cases. We must look instead to the effect of segregation itself on public education.

In approaching this problem, we cannot turn the clock back to 1868 when the Amendment was adopted, or even to 1896 when *Plessy v. Ferguson* was written. We must consider public education in the light of its full development and its present place in American life throughout the Nation. Only in this way can it be determined if segregation in public schools deprives these plaintiffs of the equal protection of the laws.

Today, education is perhaps the most important function of state and local governments. Compulsory school attendance laws and the great expenditures for education both demonstrate our recognition of the importance of education to our democratic society. It is required in the performance of our most basic public responsibilities, even service in the armed forces. It is the very foundation of

---

(*continued*) Paul E. Wilson, Assistant Attorney General of Kansas, argued the cause for appellees in No. 1 on the original argument and on the reargument. With him on the briefs was Harold R. Fatzer, Attorney General.

John W. Davis argued the cause for appellees in No. 2 on the original argument and for appellees in Nos. 2 and 4 on the reargument. With him on the briefs in No. 2 were T. C. Callison, Attorney General of South Carolina, Robert McC. Figg, Jr., S. E. Rogers, William R. Meagher, and Taggart Whipple.

J. Lindsay Almond, Jr., Attorney General of Virginia, and T. Justin Moore argued the cause for appellees in No. 4 on the original argument and for appellees in Nos. 2 and 4 on the reargument. On the briefs in No. 4 were J. Lindsay Almond, Jr., Attorney General, and Henry T. Wickham, Special Assistant Attorney General for the State of Virginia, and T. Justin Moore, Archibald G. Robertson, John W. Riely and T. Justin Moore, Jr. for the Prince Edward County School Authorities, appellees.

H. Albert Young, Attorney General of Delaware, argued the cause for petitioners in No. 10 on the original argument and on the reargument. With him on the briefs was Louis J. Finger, Special Deputy Attorney General.

By special leave of Court, Assistant Attorney General Rankin argued the cause for the United States on the reargument, as *amicus curiae*, urging reversal in Nos. 1, 2, and 4 and affirmance in No. 10. With him on the brief were Attorney General Brownell, Philip Elman, Leon Ulman, William J. Lamont, and M. Magdelena Schoch. James P. McGranery, then Attorney General, and Philip Elman filed a brief for the United States on the original argument, as *amicus curiae*, urging reversal in Nos. 1, 2, and 4 and affirmance in No. 10.

Briefs of *amici curiae* supporting appellants in No. 1 were filed by Shad Polier, Will Maslow, and Joseph B. Robison for the American Jewish Congress; by Edwin J. Lukas, Arnold Forster, Arthur Garfield Hays, Frank E. Karelsen, Leonard Haas, Saburo Kido, and Theodore Leskes for the American Civil Liberties Union et al.; and by John Ligtenberg and Selma M. Borchardt for the American Federation of Teachers. Briefs of *amici curiae* supporting appellants in No. 1 and respondents in No. 10 were filed by Arthur J. Goldberg and Thomas E. Harris for the Congress of Industrial Organizations and by Phineas Indritz for the American Veterans Committee, Inc.

good citizenship. Today it is a principal instrument in awakening the child to cultural values, in preparing him for later professional training, and in helping him to adjust normally to his environment. In these days, it is doubtful that any child may reasonably be expected to succeed in life if he is denied the opportunity of an education. Such an opportunity, where the state has undertaken to provide it, is a right which must be made available to all on equal terms.

We come then to the question presented: Does segregation of children in public schools solely on the basis of race, even though the physical facilities and other "tangible" factors may be equal, deprive the children of the minority group of equal educational opportunities? We believe that it does.

In *Sweatt v. Painter, supra,* in finding that a segregated law school for Negroes could not provide them equal educational opportunities, this Court relied in large part on "those qualities which are incapable of objective measurement but which make for greatness in a law school." In *McLaurin v. Oklahoma State Regents, supra,* the Court, in requiring that a Negro admitted to a white graduate school be treated like all other students, again resorted to intangible considerations: ". . . . his ability to study, to engage in discussions and exchange views with other students, and, in general, to learn his profession." Such considerations apply with added force to children in grade and high schools. To separate them from others of similar age and qualifications solely because of their race generates a feeling of inferiority as to their status in the community that may affect their hearts and minds in a way unlikely ever to be undone. The effect of this separation on their educational opportunities was well stated by a finding in the Kansas case by a court which nevertheless felt compelled to rule against the Negro plaintiffs:

"Segregation of white and colored children in public schools has a detrimental effect upon the colored children. The impact is greater when it has the sanction of the law; for the policy of separating the races is usually interpreted as denoting the inferiority of the negro group. A sense of inferiority affects the motivation of a child to learn. Segregation with the sanction of law, therefore, has a tendency to [retard] the educational and mental development of negro children and to deprive them of some of the benefits they would receive in a racial[ly] integrated school system."[10]

Whatever may have been the extent of psychological knowledge at the time of *Plessy v. Ferguson,* this finding is amply supported by modern authority.[11] Any language in *Plessy v. Ferguson* contrary to this finding is rejected.

We conclude that in the field of public education the doctrine of "separate but equal" has no place. Separate educational facilities are inherently unequal. Therefore, we hold that the plaintiffs and others similarly situated for whom the actions have been brought are, by reason of the segregation complained of, deprived of the equal protection of the laws guaranteed by the Fourteenth Amendment. This disposition makes unnecessary any discussion whether such segregation also violates the Due Process Clause of the Fourteenth Amendment.[12]

Because these are class actions, because of the wide applicability of this decision, and because of the great variety of local conditions, the formulation of decrees in these cases presents problems of considerable complexity. On reargument, the consideration of appropriate relief was necessarily subordinated to the primary question—the constitutionality of segregation in public education. We have now announced that such segregation is a denial of the equal protection of the laws. In order that we may have the full assistance of the parties in formulating decrees, the cases will be restored to the docket, and the parties are requested to present further argument on Questions 4 and 5 previously propounded by the Court for the reargument this Term.[13] The Attorney General of the United States is again invited to participate. The Attorneys General of the states requiring or permitting segregation in public education will also be permitted to appear as *amici curiae* upon request to do so by September 15, 1954, and submission of briefs by October 1, 1954.[14]

It is so ordered.

Notes

1. In the Kansas case, *Brown v. Board of Education,* the plaintiffs are Negro children of elementary school age residing in Topeka. They brought this action in the United States District Court for the District of Kansas to enjoin enforcement of a Kansas statute which permits, but does not require, cities of more than 15,000 population to maintain separate school facilities for Negro and white students. Kan. Gen. Stat. 72-1724 (1949). Pursuant to that authority, the Topeka Board of Education elected to establish segregated elementary schools. Other public schools in the community, however, are operated on a nonsegregated basis. The three-judge District Court,

(Continues)

(Continued)

convened under 28 U.S.C. 2281 and 2284, found that segregation in public education has a detrimental effect upon Negro children, but denied relief on the ground that the Negro and white schools were substantially equal with respect to buildings, transportation, curricula, and educational qualifications of teachers. 98 F. Supp. 797. The case is here on direct appeal under 28 U.S.C. 1253. In the South Carolina case, *Briggs v. Elliott*, the plaintiffs are Negro children of both elementary and high school age residing in Clarendon County. They brought this action in the United States District Court for the Eastern District of South Carolina to enjoin enforcement of provisions in the state constitution and statutory code which require the segregation of Negroes and whites in public schools. S.C. Const., Art. XI, 7; S.C. Code 5377 (1942). The three-judge District Court, convened under 28 U.S.C. 2281 and 2284, denied the requested relief. The court found that the Negro schools were inferior to the white schools and ordered the defendants to begin immediately to equalize the facilities. But the court sustained the validity of the contested provisions and denied the plaintiffs admission to the white schools during the equalization program. 98 F. Supp. 529. This Court vacated the District Court's judgment and remanded the case for the purpose of obtaining the court's views on a report filed by the defendants concerning the progress made in the equalization program. 342 U.S. 350. On remand, the District Court found that substantial equality had been achieved except for buildings and that the defendants were proceeding to rectify this inequality as well. 103 F. Supp. 920. The case is again here on direct appeal under 28 U.S.C. 1253. In the Virginia case, *Davis v. County School Board*, the plaintiffs are Negro children of high school age residing in Prince Edward county. They brought this action in the United States District Court for the Eastern District of Virginia to enjoin enforcement of provisions in the state constitution and statutory code which require the segregation of Negroes and whites in public schools. Va. Const., 140; Va. Code 22-221 (1950). The three-judge District Court, convened under 28 U.S.C. 2281 and 2284, denied the requested relief. The court found the Negro school inferior in physical plant, curricula, and transportation, and ordered the defendants forthwith to provide substantially equal curricula and transportation and to "proceed with all reasonable diligence and dispatch to remove" the inequality in physical plant. But, as in the South Carolina case, the court sustained the validity of the contested provisions and denied the plaintiffs admission to the white schools during the equalization program. 103 F. Supp. 337. The case is here on direct appeal under 28 U.S.C. 1253. In the Delaware case, *Gebhart v. Belton*, the plaintiffs are Negro children of both elementary and high school age residing in New Castle County. They brought this action in the Delaware Court of Chancery to enjoin enforcement of provisions in the state constitution and statutory code which require the segregation of Negroes and whites in public schools. Del. Const., Art. X, 2; Del. Rev. Code 2631 (1935). The Chancellor gave judgment for the plaintiffs and ordered their immediate admission to schools previously attended only by white children, on the ground that the Negro schools were inferior with respect to teacher training, pupil-teacher ratio, extracurricular activities, physical plant, and time and distance involved in travel. 87 A. 2d 862. The Chancellor also found that segregation itself results in an inferior education for Negro children (see note 10, *infra*), but did not rest his decision on that ground. *Id.*, at 865. The Chancellor's decree was affirmed by the Supreme Court of Delaware, which intimated, however, that the defendants might be able to obtain a modification of the decree after equalization of the Negro and white schools had been accomplished. 91 A. 2d 137, 152. The defendants, contending only that the Delaware courts had erred in ordering the immediate admission of the Negro plaintiffs to the white schools, applied to this Court for *certiorari*. The writ was granted, 344 U.S. 891. The plaintiffs, who were successful below, did not submit a cross-petition.

2. 344 U.S. 1, 141, 891.

3. 345 U.S. 972. The Attorney General of the United States participated both Terms as *amicus curiae*.

4. For a general study of the development of public education prior to the Amendment, see Butts and Cremin, *A History of Education in American Culture* (1953), Pts. I, II; Cubberley, *Public Education in the United States* (1934 ed.), cc. II–XII. School practices current at the time of the adoption of the Fourteenth Amendment are described in Butts and Cremin, *supra*, at 269–-275; Cubberley, *supra*, at 288–339, 408–431; Knight, *Public Education in the South* (1922), cc. VIII, IX. See also H. Ex. Doc. No. 315, 41st Cong., 2d Sess. (1871). Although the demand for free public schools followed substantially the same pattern in both the North and the South, the development in the South did not begin to gain momentum until about 1850, some twenty years after that in the North. The reasons for the somewhat slower development in the South (e.g., the rural character of the South and the different regional attitudes toward state assistance) are well explained in Cubberley, *supra*, at 408–423. In the country as a whole, but particularly in the South, the War virtually stopped all progress in public education. *Id.*, at 427–428. The low status of Negro education in all sections of the country, both before and immediately after the War, is described in Beale, *A History of Freedom of Teaching in American Schools* (1941), 112–132, 175–195. Compulsory school attendance laws were not generally adopted until after the ratification of the Fourteenth Amendment, and it was not until 1918 that such laws were in force in all the states. Cubberley, *supra*, at 563–565.

5. Slaughter-House Cases, 16 Wall. 36, 67–72 (1873); *Strauder v. West Virginia*, 100 U.S. 303, 307–308 (1880): "It ordains that no State shall deprive any person of life, liberty, or property, without due process of law, or deny to any person within its jurisdiction the equal protection of the laws. What is this but declaring that the law in the States shall be the same for the black as for the white; that all persons, whether colored or white, shall stand equal before the laws of the States, and, in regard to the colored race, for whose protection the amendment was primarily designed, that no discrimination shall be made against them by law because of their color? The words of the amendment, it is true, are prohibitory, but they contain a necessary implication of a positive immunity, or right, most valuable to the colored race,—the right to exemption from unfriendly legislation against them distinctively as colored,—exemption from legal discriminations, implying inferiority in civil society, lessening the security of their enjoyment of the rights which others enjoy, and discriminations which are steps towards reducing them to the condition of a subject race." See also *Virginia v. Rives*, 100 U.S. 313, 318 (1880); *Ex parte* Virginia, 100 U.S. 339, 344–345 (1880).

6. The doctrine apparently originated in *Roberts v. City of Boston*, 59 Mass. 198, 206 (1850), upholding school segregation against attack as being violative of a state constitutional guarantee of equality. Segregation in Boston public schools was eliminated in 1855. Mass. Acts 1855, c. 256. But elsewhere in the North segregation in public education has persisted in some communities until recent years. It is apparent that such segregation has long been a nationwide problem, not merely one of sectional concern.

7. See also *Berea College v. Kentucky*, 211 U.S. 45 (1908).

8. In the *Cumming* case, Negro taxpayers sought an injunction requiring the defendant school board to discontinue the operation of a high school for white children until the board resumed operation of a high school for Negro children. Similarly, in the *Gong Lum* case, the plaintiff, a child of Chinese descent, contended only that state authorities had misapplied the doctrine by classifying him with Negro children and requiring him to attend a Negro school.

9. In the Kansas case, the court below found substantial equality as to all such factors. 98 F. Supp. 797, 798. In the South Carolina case, the court below found that the defendants were proceeding "promptly and in good faith to comply with the court's decree." 103 F. Supp. 920, 921. In the Virginia case, the court below noted that the equalization program was already "afoot and progressing" (103 F. Supp. 337, 341); since then, we have been advised, in the Virginia Attorney General's brief on reargument, that the program has now been completed. In the Delaware case, the court below similarly noted that the state's equalization program was well under way. 91 A. 2d 137, 149.

10. A similar finding was made in the Delaware case: "I conclude from the testimony that in our Delaware society, State-imposed segregation in education itself results in the Negro children, as a class, receiving educational opportunities which are substantially inferior to those available to white children otherwise similarly situated." 87 A. 2d 862, 865.

11. K. B. Clark, *Effect of Prejudice and Discrimination on Personality Development* (Midcentury White House Conference on Children and Youth, 1950); Witmer and Kotinsky, *Personality in the Making* (1952), c. VI; Deutscher and Chein, The Psychological Effects of Enforced Segregation: A Survey of Social Science Opinion, 26 *J. Psychol.* 259 (1948); Chein, What are the Psychological Effects of Segregation Under Conditions of Equal Facilities? 3 *Int. J. Opinion and Attitude Res.*, 229 (1949); Brameld, *Educational Costs, in Discrimination and National Welfare* (MacIver, ed., (1949), 44–48; Frazier, *The Negro in the United States* (1949), 674–681. And see generally Myrdal, *An American Dilemma* (1944).

12. See *Bolling v. Sharpe*, *post*, p. 497, concerning the Due Process Clause of the Fifth Amendment.

13. "4. Assuming it is decided that segregation in public schools violates the Fourteenth Amendment "(a) would a decree necessarily follow providing that, within the limits set by normal geographic school districting, Negro children should forthwith be admitted to schools of their choice, or "(b) may this Court, in the exercise of its equity powers, permit an effective gradual adjustment to be brought about from existing segregated systems to a system not based on color distinctions? "5. On the assumption on which questions 4 (a) and (b) are based, and assuming further that this Court will exercise its equity powers to the end described in question 4 (b), "(a) should this Court formulate detailed decrees in these cases; "(b) if so, what specific issues should the decrees reach;

(Continues)

"(c) should this Court appoint a special master to hear evidence with a view to recommending specific terms for such decrees; "(d) should this Court remand to the courts of first instance with directions to frame decrees in these cases, and if so what general directions should the decrees of this Court include and what procedures should the courts of first instance follow in arriving at the specific terms of more detailed decrees?"

14. See Rule 42, Revised Rules of this Court (effective July 1, 1954).

Civil Liberties and Security

Chapter Objectives

In this chapter you will learn . . .

- The Exclusionary Rule
- The "fruit of the poisonous tree" standard
- The differences between probable cause and reasonable suspicion
- The history of the phrase "you have the right to remain silent"
- The PATRIOT Act's effect on balancing civil liberties and national security

Introduction

Another hotly debated topic regarding the Constitution is the balance of privacy and civil liberties against law enforcement, safety, and national security. How far are you willing to go for your safety? That is what we will ponder in this chapter, as we examine how the Constitution addresses these often-conflicting concerns.

The Fourth Amendment

The Fourth Amendment to the Constitution states that: *The right of the people to be secure in their persons, houses, papers, and effects, against unreasonable searches and seizures, shall not be violated, and no Warrants shall issue, but upon probable cause, supported by Oath or affirmation, and particularly describing the place to be searched, and the persons or things to be seized.*

An example of an unreasonable search and seizure might be the following: if Evelyn took a piece of chewing gum from her purse, put it in her mouth, and threw the wrapper on the ground instead of into a trash can. Howard, a police officer who saw Evelyn litter, ordered her to stand up against the wall, empty her pockets and empty the contents of her purse. Howard's reasoning was that if someone disregards the law against littering, by doing something like throwing a gum wrapper on the ground instead of into a trash can, then that person might have no reservations about breaking other laws, and probably uses illegal drugs. Howard's

logic, however flawed or correct, is nonetheless objectively *unreasonable* when balanced against Evelyn's right to privacy.

Suppose instead, that Evelyn had put on a pair of rubber gloves, opened her purse, removed a blood-stained hammer from inside it, and threw it away in the trash can. In that case, if Howard stopped and searched her, then her behavior certainly would be more suspect and his search would be *reasonable*.

Balancing Privacy and Security

Suppose that you live in a reasonably safe and quiet neighborhood, and you have just learned that terrorist cells have sprouted in another part of the country, far from where you live. Nonetheless, you are concerned that if these terrorists continue to operate undetected, they may do harm not only to your fellow Americans far away from where you live, but they may even do harm to your neighborhood, and even your own home!

Moreover, you have learned that the federal government, in order to stop these terrorists has instituted the Random Terrorist Search Program (RTSP), whereby federal law enforcement agents and military personnel have the right to randomly search any home within 100 miles of any suspected terrorist activity. Therefore, if terrorists were suspected in Manhattan, that would mean that agents can search any home, anyplace, anytime, in all of Manhattan as well as the other four boroughs of New York City (the Bronx, Brooklyn, Queens, and Staten Island), and various parts of Long Island, Westchester, Rockland, parts of Connecticut and New Jersey, and still have more territory to cover!

If you live, say, in Bumble Bee, Arizona (yes, that is a real place!), far from New York City, you might think that it is a good idea to have such random searches. After all, potentially they could save millions of lives. But what if you live in New York and one evening, while sitting in the privacy of your own home having a romantic dinner with your spouse or significant other or perhaps watching television with the entire family, there is a knock on the door. As soon as you answer it, federal agents swarm into your house, turning over furniture, searching behind picture frames, looking through cereal boxes in the kitchen, and rummaging through your dresser drawers in the bedroom. Would you feel that your privacy is somehow being invaded?

Would you feel like an American, or that you are living in some totalitarian nation?

This balance of privacy versus security continues to be debated, so there really are no easy answers. As you develop your own opinion on the topic, let's take a look at some Constitutional history regarding this matter.

Fighting Crime Versus Protecting Privacy: *The Katz Case*

If you are a law enforcement officer whose job is to crush an illegal gambling operation and you know that you have the guilty parties in custody, should they be released based on a Constitutional technicality? A case that decided that very issue in 1967 was *Katz v. United States*. The petitioner, Charles Katz, was convicted in California for illegal gambling. He had used a public telephone booth in Los Angeles to illegally place bets in Boston and Miami. Katz did not know that the Federal Bureau of Investigation (FBI) had installed an electronic eavesdropping device at the booth, which recorded his conversations. Katz was convicted as a result of the evidence from those conversations. Katz appealed, contending that he did not know that the phone booth had been bugged, which was a violation of his Fourth Amendment rights against unreasonable searches and seizures. A seven-Justice majority concluded that the FBI did in fact violate Katz' Fourth Amendment rights.

The Court held that as long as a person would reasonably expect that his or her conversation would remain private, then that conversation is protected by the Fourth Amendment. The majority declared that the importance of the public telephone as a modern communications medium brings with it the expectation that conversations made on it will not be broadcast to the world. Moreover, the Court held that a "physical intrusion" was not necessary to constitute a Fourth Amendment violation.

Concurring Justices established a test for such matters: that the expectation of privacy is both subjective and objective. Simply put, that the individual (in this case, Katz) actually expected privacy (in the phone booth), and that the general public would reasonably expect such privacy (in a phone booth) as well.

The dissenting Justices would agree with holding if they believed that wiretapping fell into the category of "searches and seizures" as described in the Fourth Amendment. As to the issue that electronic wiretapping was a concept unknown to the Fourth Amendment authors, eavesdropping without electronics was not. If the Framers wished to have included eavesdropping as a Fourth Amendment violation, they would have done so; wiretapping, they proclaimed, is nothing more than electronic eavesdropping.

Based on the *Katz* case, then, the FBI could secretly record conversations only if they obtained a warrant in advance. They would have to state their case to a judge, who would be the neutral party to decide objectively whether the cause was in fact probable.

What if you were the FBI agent who wanted to bust the gambling operation? Wouldn't it be much easier if the Court allowed you to continue placing wiretaps wherever you saw fit? Of course it would, but then again, you might be so concerned about making the arrest that you might not even take the time to consider other individuals' privacy that you might invade.

For example, what if Katz had been on the phone with a family member, who disclosed something highly personal and embarrassing to him. Would that family member want to know that an FBI agent was listening to the conversation? Of course not. And that is the balance of security and privacy. Let's read on.

The Exclusionary Rule

More than 50 years before *Katz* was decided, the Supreme Court dealt with the question of whether evidence is admissible depending upon how it was obtained. In *Weeks v. United States* (1914), the Court unanimously declared that evidence obtained by illegal searches and seizures was not admissible in Court. The petitioner, Fremont Weeks, had been convicted for using the U.S. mail for illegal gambling purposes. The evidence was obtained by a warrantless search of his home and papers. The Court reversed the lower court's decision, proclaiming that the very essence of the Fourth Amendment protects against exactly that type of search.

Up until that point, courts were rather generous in admitting incriminating evidence regardless of how it was obtained. The *Weeks* rationale became known as the Exclusionary Rule.

Fruit of the Poisonous Tree

Six years after *Weeks*, in 1920, the Court expanded its Fourth Amendment protection by holding in *Silverthorne Lumber Co. v. United States* that any conviction—whether direct or indirect—based on illegally obtained evidence is unconstitutional. In *Silverthorne*, the government seized records and subsequently returned them as required by a court order, but made copies in the meantime, which were later used in a conviction. The Court's declaration that those photocopies were just as tainted as the originals in terms of admissibility gave rise to the term "fruit of the poisonous tree."

Stop and Frisk

Let's turn back to Howard the police officer and Evelyn, the person whom he searched. Judging from the *Weeks* and *Silverthorne* cases, it would seem that Howard would be powerless to search Evelyn or any other suspect unless Howard had a warrant. Taken to its absurd but logical conclusion that would mean a criminal could shoot someone, conceal the gun, and the police officer would not be able to conduct a warrantless search upon the criminal. Thankfully, the courts do not strip that much power from law enforcement officials! Consider the Supreme Court case *Terry v. Ohio*, decided in 1968, to illustrate.

The petitioner, John W. Terry, and two of his accomplices were spotted "casing" a store by a police officer. That means that they apparently planned to rob the store and would routinely walk by the store, look inside, and then meet away from the store entrance and briefly huddle in conversation. The officer approached Terry and frisked him, discovering that he was armed. Terry was convicted and imprisoned for illegally possessing a concealed weapon.

The Supreme Court upheld the conviction, stating that the officer did not need probable cause for a stop and frisk, but that *reasonable suspicion* was sufficient. Before we look at the Court's decision in greater detail, let's examine the difference between these two standards.

Probable Cause Versus Reasonable Suspicion

It is easier for something to be *reasonable* than to be *probable*. Consider this example. Sally lives in New York City, where it usually snows during the months of December, January, and February, with less chance of snow as early as November or as late as March. On March 28, Sally was doing some spring cleaning in her apartment and wondered whether she should pack her snow boots for the winter. She decided not to, thinking that it was still not "safe" to assume that there would be no more snow for the season. It was *reasonable* for her to assume that it could still snow in New York again after March 28, although it was not *probable*. On the other hand, if Sally expected it to snow in New York on the Fourth of July, that would be downright unreasonable. (Note: Unreasonable, not impossible; after all, anything can happen.)

Another example is closer to the facts of the *Terry* case. A man in his early thirties wearing a blue jacket was spotted trying to break into someone's house. The police were called to the scene, and saw Tom, who fit the description, walking by. If they suspected Tom, that would be reasonable, as he fit the description. Perhaps their beliefs were not probable, but at least they were reasonable. If the description also stated that the suspect was about 6'5" and weighed about 300 pounds, and Tom fit that description, then their suspicion would be more probable. If however, they stopped a woman in her late seventies, thinking she might be the suspect, that would not even be reasonable!

Back to *Terry*: the Court concluded that the police have a great deal of leeway regarding arrests and so the reasonable suspicion standard is appropriate.

Snow in New York on the Fourth of July? Highly unlikely, but not impossible.

The majority did determine that such a "stop and frisk" can be construed as a "seizure," as per the Fourth Amendment's language, but that such seizure was reasonable under the circumstances.

A concurring opinion went further, adding that police officers should not be restricted from asking questions anyplace, anytime. Of course, in most cases, those questioned have the right to refuse to answer and to simply walk away.

Douglas' Dissent

Justice Douglas strongly dissented, arguing that to give police officers broader discretion (reasonable suspicion) than a magistrate (probable cause) is reminiscent of a totalitarian state.

The *Terry* case set the precedent for the "stop and frisk," but other cases expanded on that ruling, as we will now examine.

Michigan v. Long, decided in 1983, dealt with respondent David Long, who was driving his car in an erratic matter, which the police found suspicious. After stopping him and noticing a hunting knife on the floor of his car, they conducted a quick pat down as per *Terry*, but then proceeded to do a weapons search of the car. During that search, they found no weapons, but found a large amount of marijuana; Long was arrested for possession of drugs.

Long argued that his Fourth Amendment rights were violated because the police had no probable cause to search his automobile, and, even if reasonable suspicion would have sufficed, *Terry* limited that to the person, not to the person's automobile. The majority in *Long* disagreed, establishing that the *Terry* search can include a person's car. The dissenting Justices argued that the Court had improperly expanded the *Terry* holding.

Most recently, the Court further expanded the *Terry* and *Long* holdings in *Hiibel v. Sixth Judicial District Court of Nevada*. In *Hiibel*, decided in 2004, the Court held that a police officer during a *Terry* search not only may ask the suspect's name, but that the suspect is compelled to answer. Police in Nevada had received a call that a man had assaulted a woman in a silver and red GMC truck. When police arrived on the scene and found such a truck on the side of the road, along with a man and a woman, and noticed that there were skid marks around where the truck stopped (indicating a sudden stop), the police asked the suspect, Larry Dudley Hiibel, for his name, but Hiibel refused to answer. After asking another ten times, the police arrested Hiibel. The police were acting pursuant to a Nevada statute that compelled suspects to identify themselves, though did not require them to provide any other information to inquiring law enforcement officers.

The majority found that the Nevada statute was Constitutional and that asking suspects to identify themselves is routine practice that, when balanced against individual rights, serves a legitimate government interest.

Dissenting Justices contended that compelling suspects to identify themselves unequivocally violates their Fifth Amendment protection and that such protection is not limited to the confines of criminal court proceedings. Also, that if the Court were to allow compulsory self-identification, it would set a dangerous precedent whereby law enforcement officers might compel suspects to disclose their addresses, driver's license numbers, and other information.

You Have the Right to Remain Silent

Does the *Hiibel* decision make you wonder how it fits into those famous words that we have all heard on police television shows: "You have the right to remain silent." Doesn't that mean that any suspect can refuse to speak? Before we answer that, let's take a look at the case that gave birth to that famous phrase.

The landmark Supreme Court case *Miranda v. Arizona*, decided in 1966, determined that a person who is being placed under arrest must be advised of:

- The right to remain silent
- That anything he or she says may be used against him or her in a court of law
- The right to an attorney
- If unable to afford an attorney, the right to a court-appointed attorney
- That waiver of any of the above rights does not prevent the right to invoke them at any point later in the process

The facts of the case are as follows. Ernesto Arturo Miranda confessed to robbery and rape and was convicted, but was not advised of his rights (as set forth above) prior to his confession. The Court overturned the conviction, which created a great deal of controversy because of its substantial criticism of law enforcement practices, particularly during interrogation. Written by Chief Justice Warren, the seven-Justice majority decision concluded that any suppression of the rights to remain silent and to legal counsel violate the Fifth and Sixth Amendments, respectively.

Dissenting Justices disagreed with the absolute requirement of notifying the accused of a right to an attorney and believed that it should be looked at in the "totality of the circumstances" on a case-by-case basis. They considered the Court's ruling to be "utopian," not designed to prevent police brutality, but to almost frustrate the interrogation process by requiring confessions to be purely voluntary with no pressure whatsoever. Moreover, they did not accept the Court's notion that Fifth Amendment rights are violated if the accused is not made aware of them at a precise moment during the process. Finally, they made a clear distinction between the omission of reading the suspect his rights and an overtly coerced confession.

As one of the most important cases in Constitutional history, *Miranda* deserves even more attention. It appears in its entirety at the end of this chapter.

Ernesto Miranda's Life after the Decision

Ernesto Miranda's life after his name became synonymous with the warnings given by police officers upon arrest—known not only in the legal and criminal justice fields, but by millions of viewers of police crime dramas on television—took various sad and ironic twists. Ultimately, he was convicted of the crimes for which his convictions were overturned in the *Miranda* case, because of different sources of evidence not connected to the unconstitutionally obtained confessions.

After serving 11 years in prison, Miranda worked odd jobs and continued to commit crimes. At times, he would make a few dollars by autographing police officers' Miranda Cards, which had become popular by that point. While playing poker one night in a bar, he was fatally stabbed and died shortly thereafter. In the ultimate of ironies, the police arrested a suspect who, invoking his Miranda rights, decided to remain silent; due to insufficient evidence, he was never prosecuted.

Hiibel and *Miranda* Reconciled

At this point you might be wondering, "weren't Hiibel's Miranda rights violated?" That is a good question, but if you read closely, you will see how the Supreme Court reconciled the two cases. The *Miranda* decision protected against self-incrimination, and *Hiibel* concluded that merely identifying oneself does not amount to actual or even potential self-incrimination.

The Court's reconciliation of these two cases is a prime example of how its interpretation of the Constitution is far from predictable. The best approach then, to understanding the Constitution and its interpreter, the Supreme Court, is to learn more about both. Read on.

PATRIOT Act

Earlier in the chapter we considered some questions about how we might feel if our security was sacrificed for additional liberties, or *vice versa*. One prominent factor in this equation is a law that has been the subject of quite a bit of controversy virtually since its inception: the Patriot Act. The Act is formally known as the USA PATRIOT Act, which is an acronym for Uniting and Strengthening America by Providing Appropriate Tools Required to Intercept and Obstruct Terrorism Act of 2001.

The Act was signed into law by President George W. Bush in October 2001, a mere 6 weeks after the devastating attacks of September 11. Essentially, the Act gives considerably broader power to law enforcement agencies to listen to telephone conversations and intercept e-mails, if there appears to be a connection to terrorism. Let's look at a couple of hypothetical situations that shape the debate.

One the one hand, such enhanced surveillance can help identify and apprehend a terrorist cell in the United States. If a group of terrorists are planning an attack but their every move is being watched, they might inadvertently tip off government officials as to the details of their plan in a phone call or an e-mail communication. In that sense, the PATRIOT Act can save thousands of lives in just a single instance! Think about it. If the government had been spying on the terrorists who executed the attacks on 9/11, then the events of that horrible day might never have happened!

On the other hand, suppose that your coworker, neighbor, or distant relative is suspected of terrorism. You have no idea of that person's alleged connection to terrorism, yet law enforcement agencies have tapped your phones and have intercepted your e-mails. Your most private conversations, however personal and intimate, have been fully disclosed to federal and local agents—and you have no idea that this is going on. Worse yet, the agents might inform you that they have been listening to your private conversations, causing you tremendous embarrassment!

As you can see, like most other Constitutional dilemmas, it is not an easy one to resolve. Let's take a look at what the Supreme Court has had to say about the PATRIOT Act to this point, particularly when dealing with the issue of detainees at Guantanamo Bay. But, before we do that, let's talk a little bit about what Guantanamo Bay is, because far too many Americans know very little about it.

Guantanamo Bay, Cuba

Guantanamo Bay is a U.S. Naval Base located in Cuba. Your immediate question might be: "But don't we have a trade embargo with Cuba? Our two nations aren't friendly, so, how in the world is it possible that we have a naval base over there?" Excellent question. Guantanamo Bay is routinely mentioned in the news as being a U.S. Naval Base in Cuba, but, indeed, not many seem to bother to explain *why*. Here is the short version of why.

In 1898, the United States defeated Spain in the Spanish–American War, and liberated Cuba from Spain in the process. In 1903, the United States and Cuba signed a treaty whereby Guantanamo would become a U.S. Naval Base. In 1959, Cuban communist rebel Fidel Castro seized power from dictator Fulgencio Battista and became Cuba's leader. Battista had been friendly to the United States, whereas Castro was not. In fact, Castro often wanted to oust the United States from Guantanamo, but, under the terms of the treaty, that was not legally possible. The United States and Cuba never quite got to the point of being bitter enemies, although things heated up quite dramatically during the Cuban Missile Crisis of 1962, and President John F. Kennedy imposed a trade embargo afterward, one that endures to this day. (Interestingly, it is said that Kennedy, an avid cigar smoker, made sure to stock up on thousands of Cuban cigars *before* imposing the embargo on all Cuban products. Then again, that's another story and too much of a digression.) Back to Guantanamo.

After 9/11, the U.S. government began detaining terrorist suspects at Guantanamo. In *Rasul v. Bush*, decided in 2004, the Court held that the ultimate authority to determine whether such detainees were rightfully imprisoned rested with the judiciary, not with the president.

In January 2009, almost immediately upon taking office as president of the United States, Barack Obama declared that he would close the prison at Guantanamo Bay. In the aftermath of his decision, questions remain about what to do with Guantanamo's detainees, including how to try them, and where to incarcerate them.

As *Rasul* is a rather recent case, let's take note of how the specific Justices ruled.

President John F. Kennedy (top) imposed a trade embargo on Cuba, which continues a half century later. Dictator Fidel Castro (bottom) ruled Cuba for most of that period.

Stevens' Majority

Justice Stevens, writing for the majority, explained that the judiciary has authority to determine petitioners' claims about whether they were being rightfully detained and that the executive branch did not have the power to hold them indefinitely.

Kennedy's Concurrence

Justice Kennedy concurred with the decision, focusing even more so on the impropriety of the lack of certainty as to when the detainees could expect a trial date, and distinguishing that from other cases in which the detainers provided a more concrete timetable.

Scalia's Dissent

Justice Scalia found it wholly inappropriate for the courts to meddle in such matters, and was concerned that the majority ruling would result in a plethora of lawsuits brought against detainees at U.S. military bases worldwide.

Two years later, the Court decided in *Hamdan v. Rumsfeld*, that President Bush's military tribunals in Guantanamo violated both the Uniform Code of Military Justice and the Geneva Convention. The reasoning was predictably similar to *Rasul*, which had been decided largely by the same Justices. Justice Stevens again wrote the decision, this time a plurality, and Justice Kennedy again cautiously concurred. Justice Scalia dissented largely for the same reasons, believing that the judiciary should not have a role in military matters.

Justice Breyer filed a separate concurring opinion, stating that as long as Congress approved the tribunals, then the Court could not overrule them.

Justice Alito, who was relatively new to the Court at the time, filed a separate dissent as did Justice Thomas. Justice Alito disagreed with the majority and believed that the military commission did in fact amount to a properly constituted court. Justice Thomas bluntly added that the judiciary simply does not have the aptitude to make foreign affairs decisions.

Note that this case is *Hamdan v. Rumsfeld*. A similarly named case is *Hamdi v. Rumsfeld*, which was decided in 2004.

Conclusion

Now that we have thoroughly reviewed the many aspects of law enforcement and military procedure balanced with Constitutional rights, what do you think? Do we live in a safe haven or in a totalitarian state? Where Americans stand on these issues has a lot to do with a gut feeling about law enforcement officials, one that might possibly stem from childhood.

Do you think of the police officer whom you remember from when you were a kid as a friendly hero or a dangerous presence? Do you think of police departments, the FBI, and the Central Intelligence Agency (CIA) as being mostly honorable or being corrupt? Basically, do you believe the government honorably searches to catch the real "bad guys," or are those actions from a bullying, judgmental, dangerously powerful entity that victimizes the "little guy?" The answers to these questions may very well indicate on which

side of the fence you stand regarding personal liberty and national security.

In Chapter 9, we will talk more about criminal justice, punishment, and yet another Constitutional topic that stirs emotions: the death penalty.

Questions for Review

1. What is the exclusionary rule?
2. What does the term "fruit of the poisonous tree" mean?
3. What is the difference between probable cause and reasonable suspicion?
4. What is a "stop and frisk?"
5. What is a Miranda right?
6. How can the *Miranda* and *Hiibel* decisions be reconciled?
7. What is the PATRIOT Act?
8. What is Guantanamo Bay?
9. How is it that the United States operates a military base in Cuba?
10. What did the *Hamdan* case decide regarding military tribunals?

Constitutionally Speaking

If you knew that there was a possibility that government agents are listening to your private telephone conversations, what would be your reaction? Would you feel outraged that such activity can occur in America? Would you not care, because you have nothing to hide or to feel embarrassed about disclosing? Would you simply think that the odds that they are listening to *your* conversation, in a nation of 300 million people, are incredibly slim, and so you would not even waste your time worrying about it?

As you think about your answers, remember that you should consider this issue not only in terms of what you would personally prefer, but also in terms of what the Constitution would permit. The two are not always the same.

Constitutional Cases

First, there is a considerably old case, *Carroll v. United States*, followed by the full text of *Miranda v. Arizona*, which we thoroughly discussed. The *Carroll* opinion was written by Chief Justice William Howard Taft, who became the Court's Chief Justice after he had already served as president of the United States! Most ex-presidents retire from public life, but Taft pursued his greatest professional love—sitting on the United States Supreme Court.

Carroll v. United States, 267 U.S. 132 (1925)

Messrs. Thomas E. Atkinson and Clare J. Hall, both of Grand Rapids, Mich., for plaintiffs in error.
The Attorney General and Mr. James M. Beck, Sol. Gen., of Washington, D.C., for the United States.
Mr. Chief Justice TAFT, after stating the case as above, delivered the opinion of the Court.
The constitutional and statutory provisions involved in this case include the Fourth Amendment and the National Prohibition Act.

The Fourth Amendment is in part as follows:

'The right of the people to be secure in their persons, houses, papers and effects against unreasonable searches and seizures shall not be violated, and no warrants shall issue but upon probable cause, supported by oath or affirmation, and particularly describing the place to be searched, and the persons or things to be seized.'

Section 25, title 2, of the National Prohibition Act, c. 85, 41 Stat. 305, 315, passed to enforce the Eighteenth Amendment, makes it unlawful to have or possess any liquor intended for use in violating the act, or which has been so used, and provides that no property rights shall exist in such *inquor*. A search warrant may issue and such liquor, with the containers thereof, may be seized under the warrant and be ultimately destroyed. The section further provides:

'No search warrant shall issue to search any private dwelling occupied as such unless it is being used for the unlawful sale of intoxicating liquor, or unless it is in part used for some business purpose such as a store, shop, saloon, restaurant, hotel, or boaring house. The term 'private dwelling' shall be construed to include the room or rooms used and occupied not transiently but solely as a residence in an apartment house, hotel, or boarding house.'

Section 26, title 2, under which the seizure herein was made, provides in part as follows:

'When the commissioner, his assistants, inspectors, or any officer of the law shall discover any person in the act of transporting in violation of the law, intoxicating liquors in any wagon, buggy, automobile, water or air craft, or other vehicle, it shall be his duty to seize any and all intoxicating liquors found therein being transported contrary to law. Whenever intoxicating liquors transported or possessed illegally shall be seized by an officer he shall take possession of the vehicle and team or automobile, boat, air or water craft, or any other conveyance, and shall arrest any person in charge thereof.'

The section then provides that the court upon conviction of the person so arrested shall order the liquor destroyed, and except for good cause shown shall order a sale by public auction of the other property seized, and that the proceeds shall be paid into the Treasury of the United States.

By section 6 of an act supplemental to the National Prohibition Act (42 Stat. 222, 223, c. 134 [Comp. St. Ann. Supp. 1923, 10184a]) it is provided that if any officer or agent or employee of the United States engaged in the enforcement of the Prohibition Act or this Amendment, 'shall search any private dwelling,' as defined in that act, 'without a warrant directing such search,' or 'shall without a search warrant maliciously and without reasonable cause search any other building or property,' he shall be guilty of a misdemeanor and subject to fine or imprisonment or both.

In the passage of the supplemental act through the Senate, amendment No. 32, known as the Stanley Amendment, was adopted, the relevant part of which was as follows:

'Sec. 6. That any officer, agent or employee of the United States engaged in the enforcement of this act or the National Prohibition Act, or any other law of the United States, who shall search or attempt to search the property or premises of any person without previously securing a search warrant, as provided by law, shall be guilty of a misdemeanor and upon conviction thereof shall be fined not to exceed $1,000, or imprisoned not to exceed one year, or both so fined and imprisoned in the discretion of the court.'

This amendment was objected to in the House, and the judiciary committee, to whom it was referred, reported to the House of Representatives the following as a substitute:

'Sec. 6. That no officer, agent or employee of the United States, while engaged in the enforcement of this act, the National Prohibition Act, or any law in reference to the manufacture or taxation of, or traffic in, intoxicating liquor, shall search any private dwelling without a warrant directing such search, and no such warrant shall issue unless there is reason to believe such dwelling is used as a place in which liquor is manufactured for sale or sold. The term 'private dwelling' shall be construed to include the room or rooms occupied not transiently, but solely as a residence in an apartment, house, hotel, or boarding house. Any violation of any provision of this paragraph shall be punished by a fine of not to exceed $1,000 or imprisonment not to exceed one year, or both such fine and imprisonment, in the discretion of the court.'

(Continues)

(Continued)

In its report the committee spoke in part as follows:

'It appeared to the committee that the effect of the Senate amendment No. 32, if agreed to by the House, would greatly cripple the enforcement of the National Prohibition Act and would otherwise seriously interfere with the government in the enforcement of many other laws, as its scope is not limited to the prohibition law, but applies equally to all laws where prompt action is necessary. There are on the statute books of the United States a number of laws authorizing search without a search warrant. Under the common law and agreeable to the Constitution search may in many cases be legally made without a warrant. The Constitution does not forbid search, as some parties contend, but it does forbid unreasonable search. This provision in regard to search is as a rule contained in the various state Constitutions, but notwithstanding that fact search without a warrant is permitted in many cases, and especially is that true in the enforcement of liquor legislation.

'The Senate amendment prohibits all search or attempt to search any property or premises without a search warrant. The effect of that would necessarily be to prohibit all search, as no search can take place if it is not on some property or premises.

'Not only does this amendment prohibit search of any lands but it prohibits the search of all property. It will prevent the search of the common bootlegger and his stock in trade, though caught and arrested in the act of violating the law. But what is perhaps more serious, it will make it impossible to stop the rum-running automobiles engaged in like illegal traffic. It would take from the officers the power that they absolutely must have to be of any service, for if they cannot search for liquor without a warrant they might as well be discharged. It is impossible to get a warrant to stop an automobile. Before a warrant could be secured the automobile would be beyond the reach of the officer with its load of illegal liquor disposed of.'

The conference report resulted, so far as the difference between the two houses was concerned, in providing for the punishment of any officer, agent, or employee of the government who searches a 'private dwelling' without a warrant, and for the punishment of any such officer, etc., who searches any 'other building or property' where, and only where, he makes the search without a warrant 'maliciously and without probable cause.' In other words, it left the way open for searching an automobile or vehicle of transportation without a warrant, if the search was not malicious or without probable cause.

The intent of Congress to make a distinction between the necessity for a search warrant in the searching of private dwellings and in that of automobiles and other road vehicles in the enforcement of the Prohibition Act is thus clearly established by the legislative history of the Stanley Amendment. Is such a distinction consistent with the Fourth Amendment? We think that it is, The Fourth Amendment does not denounce all searches or seizures, but only such as are unreasonable.

The leading case on the subject of search and seizure is *Boyd v. United States*, 116 U.S. 616, 6 S. Ct. 524. An Act of Congress of June 22, 1874 (18 Stat. 187), authorized a court of the United States in revenue cases, on motion of the government attorney, to require the defendant to produce in court his private books, invoices, and papers on pain in case of refusal of having the allegations of the attorney in his motion taken as confessed. This was held to be unconstitutional and void as applied to suits for penalties or to establish a forfeiture of goods, on the ground that under the Fourth Amendment the compulsory production of invoices to furnish evidence for forfeiture of goods constituted an unreasonable search even where made upon a search warrant, and was also a violation of the Fifth Amendment, in that it compelled the defendant in a criminal case to produce evidence against himself or be in the attitude of confessing his guilt.

In *Weeks v. United States*, 232 U.S. 383, 34 S. Ct. 341, L.R.A. 1915B, 834, Ann. Cas. 1915C, 1177, it was held that a court in a criminal prosecution could not retain letters of the accused seized in his house, in his absence and without his authority, by a United States marshal holding no warrant for his arrest and none for the search of his premises, to be used as evidence against him, the accused having made timely application to the court for an order for the return of the letters.

In *Silverthorne Lumber Co. v. United States*, 251 U.S. 385, 40 S. Ct. 182, a writ of error was brought to reverse a judgment of contempt of the District Court, fining the company and imprisoning one Silverthorne, its president, until he should purge himself of contempt in not producing books and documents of the company before the grand jury to prove violation of the statutes of the United States by the company and Silverthorne. Silverthorne had been arrested, and while under arrest the marshal had gone to the office of the company without a warrant and made a clean sweep of all books, papers, and documents found there and had taken copies and photographs of the papers. The District Court ordered the return of the originals, but impounded the photographs and copies. This was held to be an unreasonable search of the property and possessions of the corporation and a violation of the Fourth Amendment and the judgment for contempt was reversed.

In *Gouled v. United States*, 255 U.S. 298, 41 S. Ct. 261, the obtaining through stealth by a representative of the government from the office of one suspected of defrauding the government of a paper which had no pecuniary value in itself, but was only to be used as evidence against its owner, was held to be a violation of the Fourth Amendment. It was further held that when the paper was offered in evidence and duly objected to it must be ruled inadmissible because obtained through an unreasonable search and seizure and also in violation of the Fifth Amendment because working compulsory incrimination.

In *Amos v. United States*, 255 U.S. 313, 41 S. Ct. 266, it was held that where concealed liquor was found by government officers without a search warrant in the home of the defendant, in his absence, and after a demand made upon his wife, it was inadmissible as evidence against the defendant, because acquired by an unreasonable seizure.

In none of the cases cited is there any ruling as to the validity under the Fourth Amendment of a seizure without a warrant of contraband goods in the course of transportation and subject to forfeiture or destruction.

On reason and authority the true rule is that if the search and seizure without a warrant are made upon probable cause, that is, upon a belief, reasonably arising out of circumstances known to the seizing officer, that an automobile or other vehicle contains that which by law is subject to seizure and destruction, the search and seizure are valid. The Fourth Amendment is to be construed in the light of what was deemed an unreasonable search and seizure when it was adopted, and in a manner which will conserve public interests as well as the interests and rights of individual citizens.

In *Boyd v. United States*, 116 U.S. 616, 6 S. Ct. 524, as already said, the decision did not turn on whether a reasonable search might be made without a warrant; but for the purpose of showing the principle on which the Fourth Amendment proceeds, and to avoid any misapprehension of what was decided, the court, speaking through Mr. Justice Bradley, used language which is of particular significance and applicability here. It was there said (page 623 [6 S. Ct. 528]):

'The search for and seizure of stolen or forfeited goods, or goods liable to duties and concealed to avoid the payment thereof, are totally different things from a search for and seizure of a man's private books and papers for the purpose of obtaining information therein contained, or of using them as evidence against him. The two things differ *toto coelo*. In the one case, the government is entitled to the possession of the property; in the other it is not. The seizure of stolen goods is authorized by the common law; and the seizure of goods forfeited for a breach of the revenue laws, or concealed to avoid the duties payable on them, has been authorized by English statutes for at least two centuries past; and the like seizures have been authorized by our own revenue acts from the commencement of the government. The first statute passed by Congress to regulate the collection of duties, the Act of July 31, 1789, 1 Stat. 29, 43, contains provisions to this effect. As this act was passed by the same Congress which proposed for adoption the original amendments to the Constitution, it is clear that the members of that body did not regard searches and seizures of this kind as 'unreasonable,' and they are not embraced within the prohibition of the amendment. So, also, the supervision authorized to be exercised by officers of the revenue over the manufacture or custody of excisable articles, and the entries thereof in books required by law to be kept for their inspection, are necessarily excepted out of the category of unreasonable searches and seizures. So, also, the laws which provide for the search and seizure of articles and things which it is unlawful for a person to have in his possession for the purpose of issue or disposition, such as counterfeit coin, lottery tickets, implements of gambling, etc., are not within this category. *Commonwealth v. Dana*, 2 Metc. (Mass.) 329. Many other things of this character might be enumerated.'

It is noteworthy that the twenty-fourth section of the act of 1789 to which the court there refers provides:

'That every collector, naval officer and surveyor, or other person specially appointed by either of them for that purpose, shall have full power and authority, to enter any ship or vessel, in which they shall have reason to suspect any goods, wares or merchandise subject to duty shall be concealed; and therein to search for, seize, and secure any such goods, wares or merchandise; and if they shall have cause to suspect a concealment thereof, in any particular dwelling house, store, building, or other place, they or either of them shall, upon application on oath or affirmation to any justice of the peace, be entitled to a warrant to enter such house, store, or other place (in the daytime only) and there to search for such goods, and if any shall be found, to seize and secure the same for trial; and all such goods, wares and merchandise, on which the duties shall not have been paid or secured, shall be forfeited.' 1 Stat. 43.

(Continues)

(Continued)

Like provisions were contained in the Act of August 4, 1790, c. 35, 48–51, 1 Stat. 145, 170; in section 27 of the Act of February 18, 1793, c. 8, 1 Stat. 305, 315; and in sections 68–71 of the Act of March 2, 1799, c. 22, 1 Stat. 627, 677, 678.

Thus contemporaneously with the adoption of the Fourth Amendment we find in the First Congress, and in the following Second and Fourth Congresses, a difference made as to the necessity for a search warrant between goods subject to forfeiture, when concealed in a dwelling house or similar place, and like goods in course of transportation and concealed in a movable vessel where they readily could be put out of reach of a search warrant. Compare *Hester v. United States*, 265 U.S. 57, 44 S. Ct. 445.

Again, by the second section of the Act of March 3, 1815, 3 Stat. 231, 232, it was made lawful for customs officers, not only to board and search vessels within their own and adjoining districts, but also to stop, search, and examine any vehicle, beast, or person on which or whom they should suspect there was merchandise which was subject to duty or had been introduced into the United States in any manner contrary to law, whether by the person in charge of the vehicle or beast or otherwise, and if they should find any goods, wares or merchandise thereon, which they had probable cause to believe had been so unlawfully brought into the country, to seize and secure the same, and the vehicle or beast as well, for trial and forfeiture. This act was renewed April 27, 1816 (3 Stat. 315), for a year and expired. The Act of February 28, 1865, revived section 2 of the Act of 1815, above described, 13 Stat. 441, c. 67. The substance of this section was re-enacted in the third section of the Act of July 18, 1866, c. 201, 14 Stat. 178, and was thereafter embodied in the Revised Statutes as section 3061 (Comp. St. 5763). Neither section 3061 nor any of its earlier counterparts has ever been attacked as unconstitutional. Indeed, that section was referred to and treated as operative by this court in *Cotzhausen v. Nazro*, 107 U.S. 215, 219, 2 S. Ct. 503. See, also, *United States v. One Black Horse (D.C.)* 129 F. 167.

Again by section 2140 of the Revised Statutes (Comp. St. 4141) any Indian agent, subagent or commander of a military post in the Indian country, having reason to suspect or being informed that any white person or Indian is about to introduce, or has introduced, any spirituous liquor or wine into the Indian country, in violation of law, may cause the boats, stores, packages, wagons, sleds and places of deposit of such person to be searched and if any liquor is found therein, then it, together with the vehicles, shall be seized and proceeded against by libel in the proper court and forfeited. Section 2140 was the outgrowth of the Act of May 6, 1822, c. 58, 3 Stat. 682, authorizing Indian agents to cause the goods of traders in the Indian country to be searched upon suspicion or information that ardent spirits were being introduced into the Indian country to be seized and forfeited if found, and of the Act of June 30, 1834, 20, c. 161, 4 Stat. 729, 732, enabling an Indian agent having reason to suspect any person of having introduced or being about to introduce liquors into the Indian country to cause the boat, stores or places of deposit of such person to be searched and the liquor found forfeited. This court recognized the statute of 1822 as justifying such a search and seizure in *American Fur Co. v. United States*, 2 Pet. 358. By the Indian Appropriation Act of March 2, 1917, c. 146, 39 Stat. 969, 970, automobiles used in introducing or attempting to introduce intoxicants into the Indian territory may be seized, libeled, and forfeited as provided in the Revised Statutes, 2140.

And again in Alaska, by section 174 of the Act of March 3, 1899, c. 429, 30 Stat. 1253, 1280, it is provided that collectors and deputy collectors or any person authorized by them in writing shall be given power to arrest persons and seize vessels and merchandise in Alaska liable to fine, penalties, or forfeiture under the act and to keep and deliver the same, and the Attorney General, in construing the act, advised the government:

> 'If your agents reasonably suspect that a violation of law has occurred, in my opinion they have power to search any vessel within the three-mile limit according to the practice of customs officers when acting under section 3059 of the Revised Statutes [Comp. St. 5761], and to seize such vessels.' 26 Op. Attys. Gen. 243.

We have made a somewhat extended reference to these statutes to show that the guaranty of freedom from unreasonable searches and seizures by the Fourth Amendment has been construed, practically since the beginning of the government, as recognizing a necessary difference between a search of a store, dwelling house, or other structure in respect of which a proper official warrant readily may be obtained and a search of a ship, motor boat, wagon, or automobile for contraband goods, where it is not practicable to secure a warrant, because the vehicle can be quickly moved out of the locality or jurisdiction in which the warrant must be sought.

Having thus established that contraband goods concealed and illegally transported in an automobile or other vehicle may be searched for without a warrant, we come now to consider under what circumstances such search may be made. It would be intolerable and unreasonable if a prohibition agent were authorized to stop every automobile on the chance of finding liquor, and thus subject all persons lawfully using the highways to the inconvenience and indignity of such a search. Travelers may be so stopped in crossing an international boundary because of national self-protection reasonably requiring one entering the country to identify himself as entitled to come in, and his belongings as effects which may be lawfully brought in. But those lawfully within the country, entitled to use the public highways, have a right to free passage without interruption or search unless there is known to a competent official, authorized to search, probable cause for believing that their vehicles are carrying contraband or illegal merchandise. Section 26, title 2, of the National Prohibition Act, like the second section of the act of 1789, for the searching of vessels, like the provisions of the act of 1815, and section 3601, Revised Statutes, for searching vehicles for smuggled goods, and like the act of 1822, and that of 1834 and section 2140, R.S., and the Act of 1917 for the search of vehicles and automobiles for liquor smuggled into the Indian country, was enacted primarily to accomplish the seizure and destruction of contraband goods; secondly, the automobile was to be forfeited; and, thirdly, the driver was to be arrested. Under section 29, title 2, of the act the latter might be punished by not more than $500 fine for the first offense, not more than $1,000 fine and 90 days' imprisonment for the second offense, and by a fine of $500 or more and by not more than 2 years' imprisonment for the third offense. Thus he is to be arrested for a misdemeanor for his first and second offenses, and for a felony if he offends the third time.

The main purpose of the act obviously was to deal with the liquor and its transportation, and to destroy it. The mere manufacture of liquor can do little to defeat the policy of the Eighteenth Amendment and the Prohibition Act, unless the forbidden product can be distributed for illegal sale and use. Section 26 was intended to reach and destroy the forbidden liquor in transportation and the provisions for forfeiture of the vehicle and the arrest of the transporter were incidental. The rule for determining what may be required before a seizure may be made by a competent seizing official is not to be determined by the character of the penalty to which the transporter may be subjected. Under section 28, title 2, of the Prohibition Act, the Commissioner of Internal Revenue, his assistants, agents and inspectors are to have the power and protection in the enforcement of the act conferred by the existing laws relating to the manufacture or sale of intoxicating liquors. Officers who seize under section 26 of the Prohibition Act are therefore protected by section 970 of the Revised Statutes (Comp. St. 1611), providing that:

'When, in any prosecution commenced on account of the seizure of any vessel, goods, wares, or merchandise, made by any collector or other officer, under any act of Congress authorizing such seizure, judgment is rendered for the claimant, but it appears to the court that there was reasonable cause of seizure, the court shall cause a proper certificate thereof to be entered, and the claimant shall not, in such case, be entitled to costs, nor shall the person who made the seizure, nor the prosecutor, be liable to suit or judgment on account of such suit or prosecution: Provided, that the vessel, goods, wares, or merchandise be, after judgment, forthwith returned to such claimant or his agent.'

It follows from this that, if an officer seizes an automobile or the liquor in it without a warrant, and the facts as subsequently developed do not justify a judgment of condemnation and forfeiture, the officer may escape costs or a suit for damages by a showing that he had reasonable or probable cause for the seizure. *Stacey v. Emery*, 97 U.S. 642. The measure of legality of such a seizure is, therefore, that the seizing officer shall have reasonable or probable cause for believing that the automobile which he stops and seizes has contraband liquor therein which is being illegally transported.

We here find the line of distinction between legal and illegal seizures of liquor in transport in vehicles. It is certainly a reasonable distinction. It gives the owner of an automobile or other vehicle seized under section 26, in absence of probable cause, a right to have restored to him the automobile, it protects him under the *Weeks* and *Amos* cases from use of the liquor as evidence against him, and it subjects the officer making the seizures to damages. On the other hand, in a case showing probable cause, the government and its officials are given the opportunity which they should have, to make the investigation necessary to trace reasonably suspected contraband goods and to seize them.

(Continues)

(Continued)

Such a rule fulfills the guaranty of the Fourth Amendment. In cases where the securing of a warrant is reasonably practicable, it must be used and when properly supported by affidavit and issued after judicial approval protects the seizing officer against a suit for damages. In cases where seizure is impossible except without warrant, the seizing officer acts unlawfully and at his peril unless he can show the court probable cause. *United States v. Kaplan (D.C.)* 286 F. 963, 972.

But we are pressed with the argument that if the search of the automobile discloses the presence of liquor and leads under the statue to the arrest of the person in charge of the automobile, the right of seizure should be limited by the common-law rule as to the circumstances justifying an arrest without a warrant for a misdemeanor. The usual rule is that a police officer may arrest without warrant one believed by the officer upon reasonable cause to have been guilty of a felony, and that he may only arrest without a warrant one guilty of a misdemeanor if committed in his presence. *Kurtz v. Moffitt*, 115 U.S. 487, 6 S. Ct. 148; *John Bad Elk v. United States*, 177 U.S. 529, 20 S. Ct. 729. The rule is sometimes expressed as follows:

> 'In cases of misdemeanor, a peace officer like a private person has at common law no power of arresting without a warrant except when a breach of the peace has been committed in his presence or there is reasonable ground for supposing that a breach of peace is about to be committed or renewed in his presence.' *Halsbury's Laws of England*, vol. 9, part III, 612.

The reason for arrest for misdemeanors without warrant at common law was promptly to suppress breaches of the peace (1 Stephen, *History of Criminal Law*, 193), while the reason for arrest without warrant on a reliable report of a felony was because the public safety and the due apprehension of criminals charged with heinous offenses required that such arrests should be made at once without warrant (*Rohan v. Sawin*, 5 Cush. [Mass.] 281). The argument for defendants is that, as the misdemeanor to justify arrest without warrant must be committed in the presence of the police officer, the offense is not committed in his presence unless he can by his senses detect that the liquor is being transported, no matter how reliable his previous information by which he can identify the automobile as loaded with it. *Elrod v. Moss* (C.C.A.) 278 F. 123; *Hughes v. State*, 145 Tenn. 544, 238 S.W. 588, 20 A. L. R. 639.

So it is that under the rule contended for by defendants the liquor if carried by one who has been already twice convicted of the same offense may be seized on information other than the senses, while if he has been only once convicted it may not be seized unless the presence of the liquor is detected by the senses as the automobile concealing it rushes by. This is certainly a very unsatisfactory line of difference when the main object of the section is to forfeit and suppress the liquor, the arrest of the individual being only incidental as shown by the lightness of the penalty. See *Commonwealth v. Street*, 3 Pa. Dist. and Co. Ct. Rep. 783. In England at the common law the difference in punishment between felonies and misdemeanors was very great. Under our present federal statutes, it is much less important and Congress may exercise a relatively wide discretion in classing particular offenses as felonies or misdemeanors. As the main purpose of section 26 was seizure and forfeiture, it is not so much the owner as the property that offends. *Agnew v. Haymes*, 141 F. 631, 641, 72 C.C.A. 325. The language of the section provides for seizure when the officer of the law 'discovers' any one in the act of transporting the liquor by automobile or other vehicle. Certainly it is a very narrow and technical construction of this word which would limit it to what the officer sees, hears or smells as the automobile rolls by and excludes therefrom when he identifies the car the convincing information that he may previously have received as to the use being made of it.

We do not think such a nice distinction is applicable in the present case. When a man is legally arrested for an offense, whatever is found upon his person or in his control which it is unlawful for him to have and which may be used to prove the offense may be seized and held as evidence in the prosecution. *Weeks v. United States*, 232 U.S. 383, 392, 34 S. Ct. 341, L.R.A. 1915B, 834, Ann. Cas. 1915C, 1177; *Dillon v. O'Brien and Davis*, 16 Cox, C.C. 245; *Getchell v. Page*, 103 Me. 387, 69 A. 624, 18 L.R.A. (N.S.) 253, 125 Am. St. Rep. 307; *Kneeland v. Connally*, 70 Ga. 424; 1 Bishop, *Criminal Procedure*, 211; 1 Wharton, *Criminal Procedure* (10th ed.) 97. The argument of defendants is based on the theory that the seizure in this case can only be thus justified. If their theory were sound, their conclusion would be. The validity of the seizure then would turn wholly on the validity of the arrest without a seizure. But the theory is unsound. The right to search and the validity of the seizure are not dependent on the right to arrest. They are dependent on the reasonable cause the seizing officer has for belief that the contents of the automobile offend against the law. The seizure in such a proceeding comes before the arrest as section 26 indicates. It is true that section 26, title 2, provides for immediate proceedings against the person arrested and that upon conviction the liquor is to be destroyed and the automobile or other vehicle is to be sold, with the saving of the interest of a lienor who does not know of its unlawful use; but it is evident that if the person arrested is ignorant of the contents of the vehicle, or if he escapes, proceedings can be had against the liquor for destruction or other disposition under section 25 of the same title. The character of the offense for which, after the contraband liquor is found and seized, the driver can be prosecuted does not affect the validity of the seizure.

This conclusion is in keeping with the requirements of the Fourth Amendment and the principles of search and seizure of contraband forfeitable property; and it is a wise one because it leaves the rule one which is easily applied and understood and is uniform. *Houck v. State*, 106 Ohio St. 195, 140 N.E. 112, accords with this conclusion. *Ash v. United States* (C.C.A.) 299 F. 277, and *Milam v. United States* (C.C.A.) 296 F. 629, decisions by the Circuit Court of Appeals for the Fourth Circuit take the same view. The *Ash* case is very similar in its facts to the case at bar, and both were by the same court which decided *Snyder v. United States* (C.C.A.) 285 F. 1, cited for the defendants. See, also, *Park v. United States* (1st C.C.A.) 294 F. 776, 783, and *Lambert v. United States* (9th C.C.A.) 282 F. 413.

Finally, was there probable cause? In The Apollon, 9 Wheat. 362, the question was whether the seizure of a French vessel at a particular place was upon probable cause that she was there for the purpose of smuggling. In this discussion Mr. Justice Story, who delivered the judgment of the court, said (page 374):

'It has been very justly observed at the bar that the court is bound to take notice of public facts and geographical positions, and that this remote part of the country has been infested, at different periods, by smugglers, is matter of general notoriety, and may be gathered from the public documents of the government.'

We know in this way that Grand Rapids is about 152 miles from Detroit, and that Detroit and its neighborhood along the Detroit River, which is the international boundary, is one of the most active centers for introducing illegally into this country spirituous liquors for distribution into the interior. It is obvious from the evidence that the prohibition agents were engaged in a regular patrol along the important highways from Detroit to Grand Rapids to stop and seize liquor carried in automobiles. They knew or had convincing evidence to make them believe that the Carroll boys, as they called them, were so-called 'bootleggers' in Grand Rapids; i.e., that they were engaged in plying the unlawful trade of selling such liquor in that city. The officers had soon after noted their going from Grand Rapids half way to Detroit, and attempted to follow them to that city to see where they went, but they escaped observation. Two months later these officers suddenly met the same men on their way westward presumably from Detroit. The partners in the original combination to sell liquor in Grand Rapids were together in the same automobile they had been in the night when they tried to furnish the whisky to the officers, which was thus identified as part of the firm equipment. They were coming from the direction of the great source of supply for their stock to Grand Rapids, where they plied their trade. That the officers, when they saw the defendants, believed that they were carrying liquor, we can have no doubt, and we think it is equally clear that they had reasonable cause for thinking so. Emphasis is put by defendants' counsel on the statement made by one of the officers that they were not looking for defendants at the particular time when they appeared. We do not perceive that it has any weight. As soon as they did appear, the officers were entitled to use their reasoning faculties upon all the facts of which they had previous knowledge in respect to the defendants.

The necessity for probable cause in justifying seizures on land or sea, in making arrests without warrant for past felonies, and in malicious prosecution and false imprisonment cases has led to frequent definition of the phrase. In *Stacey v. Emery*, 97 U.S. 642, 645 (24 L. Ed. 1035), a suit for damages for seizure by a collector, this court defined probable cause as follows:

'If the facts and circumstances before the officer are such as to warrant a man of prudence and caution in believing that the offense has been committed, it is sufficient.'

See *Locke v. United States*, 7 Cranch, 339; The George, 1 Mason, 24, Fed. Cas. No. 5328; The Thompson, 3 Wall. 155.

(Continues)

(Continued)

It was laid down by Chief Justice Shaw, in Commonwealth v. Carey, 12 Cush. 246, 251, that:

'If a constable or other peace officer arrest a person without a warrant, he is not bound to show in his justification a felony actually committed, to render the arrest lawful; but if he suspects one on his own knowledge of facts, or on facts communicated to him by others, and thereupon he has reasonable ground to believe that the accused has been guilty of felony, the arrest is not unlawful.' *Commonwealth v. Phelps*, 209 Mass. 396, 95 N.E. 868, Ann. Cas. 1912B, 566; *Rohan v. Sawin*, 5 Cush. 281, 285.

In *McCarthy v. De Armit*, 99 Pa. 63, the Supreme Court of Pennsylvania sums up the definition of probable cause in this way (page 69):

'The substance of all the definitions is a reasonable ground for belief of guilt.'

In the case of the *Director General v. Kastenbaum*, 263 U.S. 25, 44 S. Ct. 52, which was a suit for false imprisonment, it was said by this court (page 28 [44 S. Ct. 53]):

'But, as we have seen, good faith is not enough to constitute probable cause. That faith must be grounded on facts within knowledge of the Director General's agent, which in the judgment of the court would make his faith reasonable.'

See, also, *Munn v. De Nemours*, 3 Wash. C.C. 37, Fed. Cas. No. 9926.

In the light of these authorities, and what is shown by this record, it is clear the officers here had justification for the search and seizure. This is to say that the facts and circumstances within their knowledge and of which they had reasonably trustworthy information were sufficient in themselves to warrant a man of reasonable caution in the belief that intoxicating liquor was being transported in the automobile which they stopped and searched.

Counsel finally argue that the defendants should be permitted to escape the effect of the conviction because the court refused on motion to deliver them the liquor when, as they say, the evidence adduced on the motion was much less than that shown on the trial, and did not show probable cause. The record does not make it clear what evidence was produced in support of or against the motion. But, apart from this, we think the point is without substance here. If the evidence given on the trial was sufficient, as we think it was, to sustain the introduction of the liquor as evidence, it is immaterial that there was an inadequacy of evidence when application was made for its return. A conviction on adequate and admissible evidence should not be set aside on such a ground. The whole matter was gone into at the trial, so no right of the defendants was infringed.

Counsel for the government contend that Kiro, the defendant who did not own the automobile, could not complain of the violation of the Fourth Amendment in the use of the liquor as evidence against him, whatever the view taken as to Carroll's rights. Our conclusion as to the whole case makes it unnecessary for us to discuss this aspect of it.

The judgment is affirmed. Mr. Justice McKENNA, before his retirement, concurred in this opinion.

The separate opinion of Mr. Justice McREYNOLDS.

1. The damnable character of the 'bootlegger's' business should not close our eyes to the mischief which will surely follow any attempt to destroy it by unwarranted methods. 'To press forward to a great principle by breaking through every other great principle that stands in the way of its establishment; . . . in short, to procure an eminent good by means that are unlawful, is as little consonant to private morality as to public justice.' Sir William Scott, *The Le Louis*, 2 Dodson, 210, 257.

While quietly driving an ordinary automobile along a much frequented public road, plaintiffs in error were arrested by federal officers without a warrant and upon mere suspicion-ill-founded, as I think. The officers then searched the machine and discovered carefully secreted whisky, which was seized and thereafter used as evidence against plaintiffs in error when on trial for transporting intoxicating liquor contrary to the Volstead Act. 41 Stat. 305, c. 85. They maintain that both arrest and seizure were unlawful and that use of the liquor as evidence violated their constitutional rights.

This is not a proceeding to forfeit seized goods; nor is it an action against the seizing officer for a tort. Cases like the following are not controlling: *Crowell v. McFadon*. 8 Cranch, 94, 98; *United States v. 1960 Bags of Coffee*, 8 Cranch, 398, 403, 405; *Otis v. Watkins*, 9 Cranch, 339; *Gelston v. Hoyt*, 3 Wheat. 246, 310, 318; *Wood v. United States*, 16 Pet. 342; *Taylor v. United States*, 3 How. 197, 205. They turned upon express provisions of applicable acts of Congress; they did not involve the point now presented and afford little, if any, assistance toward its proper solution. The Volstead Act does not, in terms, authorize arrest or seizure upon mere suspicion. Whether the officers are shielded from prosecution or action by Rev. Stat. 970, is not important. That section does not undertake to deprive the citizen of any constitutional right or to permit the use of evidence unlawfully obtained. It does, however, indicate the clear understanding of Congress that probable cause is not always enough to justify a seizure.

Nor are we now concerned with the question whether by apt words Congress might have authorized the arrest without a warrant. It has not attempted to do this. On the contrary, the whole history of the legislation indicates a fixed purpose not so to do. First and second violations are declared to be misdemeanors—nothing more—and Congress, of course, understood the rule concerning arrests for such offenses. Whether different penalties should have been prescribed or other provisions added is not for us to inquire; nor do difficulties attending enforcement give us power to supplement the legislation.

2. As the Volstead Act contains no definite grant of authority to arrest upon suspicion and without warrant for a first offense, we come to inquire whether such authority can be inferred from its provisions.

Unless the statute which creates a misdemeanor contains some clear provision to the contrary, suspicion that it is being violated will not justify an arrest. Criminal statutes must be strictly construed and applied, in harmony with rules of the common law. *United States v. Harris*, 177 U.S. 305, 310, 20 S. Ct. 609. And the well-settled doctrine is that an arrest for a misdemeanor may not be made without a warrant unless the offense is committed in the officer's presence.

Kurtz v. Moffitt, 115 U.S. 487, 498, 6 S. Ct. 148, 152 (29 L. Ed. 458):

'By the common law of England, neither a civil officer nor a private citizen had the right without a warrant to make an arrest for a crime not committed in his presence, except in the case of felony, and then only for the purpose of bringing the offender before a civil magistrate.'

John Bad Elk v. United States, 177 U.S. 529, 534, 20 S. Ct. 729, 731 (44 L. Ed. 874):

'An officer, at common law, was not authorized to make an arrest without a warrant, for a mere misdemeanor not committed in his presence.'

Commonwealth v. Wright, 158 Mass. 149, 158, 33 N.E. 82, 85 (19 L.R.A. 206, 35 Am. St. Rep. 475):

'It is suggested that the statutory misdemeanor of having in one's possession short lobsters with intent to sell them is a continuing offence, which is being committed while such possession continues, and that therefore an officer who sees any person in possession of such lobsters with intent to sell them can arrest such person without a warrant, as for a misdemeanor committed in his presence. We are of opinion, however, that for statutory misdemeanors of this kind, not amounting to a breach of the peace, there is no authority in an officer to arrest without a warrant, unless it is given by statute...The Legislature has often empowered officers to arrest without a warrant for similar offenses, which perhaps tends to show that, in its opinion, no such right exists at common law.'

Pinkerton v. Verberg, 78 Mich. 573, 584, 44 N.W. 579, 582 (7 L.R.A. 507, 18 Am. St. Rep. 473):

'Any law which would place the keeping and safe-conduct of another in the hands of even a conservator of the peace, unless for some breach of the peace committed in his presence, or upon suspicion of felony, would be most oppressive and unjust, and destroy all the rights which our Constitution guarantees. These are rights which existed long before our Constitution, and we have taken just pride in their maintenance, making them a part of the fundamental law of the land.' 'If persons can be restrained of their liberty, and assaulted and imprisoned, under such circumstances, without complaint or warrant, then there is no limit to the power of a police officer.'

3. The Volstead Act contains no provision which annuls the accepted common-law rule or discloses definite intent to authorize arrests without warrant for misdemeanors not committed in the officer's presence.

To support the contrary view section 26 is relied upon.

'When . . . any officer of the law shall discover any person in the act of transporting in violation of the law, intoxicating liquors in any wagon, buggy, automobile, water or air craft, or other vehicle, it shall be his duty to seize any and all intoxicating liquors found therein being transported contrary to law. Whenever

(Continues)

intoxicating liquors transported or possessed illegally shall be seized by an officer he shall take possession of the vehicle and team or automobile, boat, air or water craft, or any other conveyance, and shall arrest any person in charge thereof.'

Let it be observed that this section has no special application to automobiles; it includes any vehicle-buggy, wagon, boat, or air craft. Certainly, in a criminal statute, always to be strictly construed, the words 'shall discover . . . in the act of transporting in violation of the law' cannot mean shall have reasonable cause to suspect or believe that such transportation is being carried on. To discover and to suspect are wholly different things. Since the beginning apt words have been used when Congress intended that arrests for misdemeanors or seizures might be made upon suspicion. It has studiously refrained from making a felony of the offense here charged; and it did not undertake by any apt words to enlarge the power to arrest. It was not ignorant of the established rule on the subject, and well understood how this could be abrogated, as plainly appears from statutes like the following:

'An act to regulate the collection of duties on imports and tonnage,' approved March 2, 1789, 1 Stat. 627, 677, 678, c. 22; 'An act to provide more effectually for the collection of the duties imposed by law on goods, wares and merchandise imported into the United States, and on the tonnage of ships or vessels,' approved August 4, 1790, 1 Stat. 145, 170, c. 35; 'An act further to provide for the collection of duties on imports and tonnage,' approved March 3, 1815, 3 Stat. 231, 232, c. 94.

These and similar acts definitely empowered officers to seize upon suspicion and therein radically differ from the Volstead Act, which authorized no such thing.

'An act supplemental to the National Prohibition Act,' approved November 23, 1921, 42 Stat. 222, 223, c. 134, provides:

'That any officer, agent, or employee of the United States engaged in the enforcement of this act, or the National Prohibition Act, or any other law of the United States, who shall search any private dwelling as defined in the National Prohibition Act, and occupied as such dwelling, without a warrant directing such search, or who while so engaged shall without a search warrant maliciously and without reasonable cause search any other building or property, shall be guilty of a misdemeanor and upon conviction thereof shall be fined for a first offense not more than $1,000, and for a subsequent offense not more than $1,000 or imprisoned not more than one year, or both such fine and imprisonment.'

And it is argued that the words and history of this section indicate the intent of Congress to distinguish between the necessity for warrants in order to search private dwelling and the right to search automobiles without one. Evidently Congress regarded the searching of private dwellings as matter of much graver consequence than some other searches and distinguished between them by declaring the former criminal. But the connection between this distinction and the legality of plaintiffs in error's arrest is not apparent. Nor can I find reason for inquiring concerning the validity of the distinction under the Fourth Amendment. Of course, the distinction is valid, and so are some seizures. But what of it? The act made nothing legal which theretofore was unlawful, and to conclude that by declaring the unauthorized search of a private dwelling criminal Congress intended to remove ancient restrictions from other searches and from arrests as well, would seem impossible.

While the Fourth Amendment denounces only unreasonable seizures unreasonableness often depends upon the means adopted. Here the seizure followed an unlawful arrest, and therefore became itself unlawful-as plainly unlawful as the seizure within the home so vigorously denounced in *Weeks v. United States*, 232 U.S. 383, 391, 392 S., 393, 34 S. Ct. 341, L.R.A. 1915B, 834, Ann. Cas. 1915C, 1177.

In *Snyder v. United States*, 285 F. 1, 2, the Court of Appeals, Fourth Circuit, rejected evidence obtained by an unwarranted arrest, and clearly announced some very wholesome doctrine:

'That an officer may not make an arrest for a misdemeanor not committed in his presence, without a warrant, has been so frequently decided as not to require citation of authority. It is equally fundamental that a citizen may not be arrested on suspicion of having committed a misdemeanor and have his person searched by force, without a warrant of arrest. If, therefore, the arresting officer in this case had no other justification for the arrest than the mere suspicion that a bottle, only the neck of which he could see protruding from the pocket of defendant's coat, contained intoxicating liquor, then it would seem to follow without much question that the arrest and search, without first having secured a warrant, were illegal. And that his only justification was his suspicion is admitted by the evidence of the arresting officer himself. If the bottle had been empty or if it had contained any one of a dozen innoxious liquids, the act of the officer would, admittedly, have been an unlawful invasion of the personal liberty of the defendant. That it happened in this instance to contain whisky, we think, neither justifies the assault nor condemns the principle which makes such an act unlawful.'

The validity of the seizure under consideration depends on the legality of the arrest. This did not follow the seizure, but the reverse is true. Plaintiffs in error were first brought within the officers' power, and, while therein, the seizure took place. If an officer, upon mere suspicion of a misdemeanor, may stop one on the public highway, take articles away from him and thereafter use them as evidence to convict him of crime, what becomes of the Fourth and Fifth Amendments?

In *Weeks v. United States, supra*, through Mr. Justice Day, this court said:

The effect of the Fourth Amendment is to put the courts of the United States and federal officials, in the exercise of their power and authority, under limitations and restraints as to the exercise of such power and authority, and to forever secure the people, their persons, houses, papers and effects against all unreasonable searches and seizures under the guise of law. This protection reaches all alike, whether accused of crime or not, and the duty of giving to it force and effect is obligatory upon all entrusted under our federal system with the enforcement of the laws. The tendency of those who execute the criminal laws of the country to obtain conviction by means of unlawful seizures and enforced confessions, the latter often obtained after subjecting accused persons to unwarranted practices destructive of rights secured by the federal Constitution, should find no sanction in the judgments of the courts which are charged at all times with the support of the Constitution and to which people of all conditions have a right to appeal for the maintenance of such fundamental rights. . . . The efforts of the courts and their officials to bring the guilty to punishment, praiseworthy as they are, are not to be aided by the sacrifice of those great principles established by years of endeavor and suffering which have resulted in their embodiment in the fundamental law of the land.'

Silverthorne Lumber Co. v. United States, 251 U.S. 385, 391, 40 S. Ct. 182:

'The proposition could not be presented more nakedly. It is that although of course its seizure was an outrage which the government now regrets, it may study the papers before it returns them, copy them, and then may use the knowledge that it has gained to call upon the owners in a more regular form to produce them; that the protection of the Constitution covers the physical possession but not any advantages that the government can gain over the object of its pursuit by doing the forbidden act. *Weeks v. United States*, 232 U.S. 383, to be sure, had established that laying the papers directly before the grand jury was unwarranted, but it is taken to mean only that two steps are required instead of one. In our opinion such is not the law. It reduces the Fourth Amendment to a form of words. 232 U.S. 393. The essence of a provision forbidding the acquisition of evidence in a certain way is that not merely evidence so acquired shall not be used before the court but that it shall not be used at all. Of course this does not mean that the facts thus obtained become sacred and inaccessible. If knowledge of them is gained from an independent source they may be proved like any others, but the knowledge gained by the government's own wrong cannot be used by it in the way proposed.'

Gouled v. United States, 255 U.S. 298, 41 S. Ct. 261, and *Amos v. United States*, 255 U.S. 313, 41 S. Ct. 266, distinctly point out that property procured by unlawful action of federal officers cannot be introduced as evidence.

The arrest of plaintiffs in error was unauthorized, illegal, and violated the guaranty of due process given by the Fifth Amendment. The liquor offered in evidence was obtained by the search which followed this arrest and was therefore obtained in violation of their constitutional rights. Articles found upon or in the control of one lawfully arrested may be used as evidence for certain purposes, but not at all when secured by the unlawful action of a federal officer.

4. The facts known by the officers who arrested plaintiffs in error were wholly insufficient to create a reasonable belief that they were transporting liquor contrary to law. These facts were detailed by Fred Cronenwett, chief prohibition officer. His entire testimony as given at the trial follows:

'I am in charge of the federal prohibition department in this district. I am acquainted with these two respondents, and first saw them on September 29, 1921, in Mr. Scully's apartment on Oakes Street, Grand Rapids. There were three of them that came to Mr. Scully's apartment, one by the name of Kruska, George Krio, and John Carroll. I was introduced to them under the name of Stafford, and told them I was working for the Michigan Chair Company, and wanted to buy three cases of whisky, and the price was agreed upon.

(Continues)

(Continued)

After they thought I was all right, they said they would be back in half or three-quarters of an hour; that they had to go out to the east end of Grand Rapids to get this liquor. They went away and came back in a short time, and Mr. Kruska came upstairs and said they couldn't get it that night; that a fellow by the name of Irving, where they were going to get it, wasn't in, but they were going to deliver it the next day, about ten. They didn't deliver it the next day. I am not positive about the price. It seems to me it was around $130 a case. It might be $135. Both respondents took part in this conversation. When they came to Mr. Scully's apartment they had this same car. While it was dark and I wasn't able to get a good look at this car, later, on the 6th day of October, when I was out on the road with Mr. Scully, I was waiting on the highway while he went to Reed's Lake to get a light lunch, and they drove by, and I had their license number and the appearance of their car, and knowing the two boys, seeing them on the 29th day of September, I was satisfied when I seen the car on December 15th it was the same car I had seen on the 6th day of October. On the 6th day of October it was probably twenty minutes before Scully got back to where I was. I told him the Carroll boys had just gone toward Detroit and we were trying to catch up with them and see where they were going. We did catch up with them somewhere along by Ada, just before we got to Ada, and followed them to East Lansing. We gave up the chase at East Lansing.

'On the 15th of December, when Peterson and Scully and I overhauled this car on the road, it was in the country, on Pike 16, the road leading between Grand Rapids and Detroit. When we passed the car we were going toward Ionia, or Detroit, and the Kiro and Carroll boys were coming towards Grand Rapids when Mr. Scully and I recognized them and said, 'There goes the Carroll brothers,' and we went on still further in the same direction we were going and turned around and went back to them—drove up to the side of them. Mr. Scully was driving the car; I was sitting in the front seat, and I stepped out on the running board and held out my hand and said, 'Carroll, stop that car,' and they did stop it. John Kiro was driving the car. After we got them stopped, we asked them to get out of the car, which they did. Carroll referred to me, and called me by the name of 'Fred,' just as soon as I got up to him. Raised up the back part of the roadster; didn't find any liquor there; then raised up the cushion; then I struck at the lazyback of the seat and it was hard. I then started to open it up, and I did tear the cushion some, and Carroll said, 'Don't tear the cushion; we have only got six cases in there;' and I took out two bottles and found out it was liquor; satisfied it was liquor. Mr. Peterson and a fellow by the name of Gerald Donker came in with the two Carroll boys and the liquor and the car to Grand Rapids. They brought the two defendants and the car and the liquor to Grand Rapids. I and the other men besides Peterson stayed out on the road, looking for other cars that we had information were coming in. There was conversation between me and Carroll before Peterson started for town with the defendants. Mr. Carroll said, 'Take the liquor, and give us one more chance, and I will make it right with you.' At the same time he reached in one of his trousers pockets and pulled out money; the amount of it I don't know. I wouldn't say it was a whole lot. I saw a $10 bill and there was some other bills; I don't know how much there was; it wasn't a large amount.

'As I understand, Mr. Hanley helped carry the liquor from the car. On the next day afterwards, we put this liquor in boxes, steel boxes, and left it in the marshal's vault, and it is still there now. Mr. Hanley and Chief Deputy Johnson, some of the agents and myself were there. Mr. Peterson was there the next day that the labels were signed by the different officers; those two bottles, Exhibits A and B.

'Q. Now, those two bottles, Exhibits A and B, were those the two bottles you took out of the car out there, or were those two bottles taken out of the liquor after it got up here? A. We didn't label them out on the road; simply found it was liquor and sent it in; and this liquor was in Mr. Hanley's custody that evening and during the middle of the next day when we checked it over to see the amount of liquor that was there. Mr. Johnson and I sealed the bottles, and Mr. Johnson's name is on the label that goes over the bottle with mine, and this liquor was taken out of the case to-day. It was taken out for the purpose of analyzation. The others were not broken until today.

'Q. And are you able to tell us, from the label and from the bottles, whether it is part of the same liquor taken out of that car? A. It has the appearance of it; yes, sir. Those are the bottles that were in there that Mr. Hanley said was gotten out of the Carroll car.'

Cross-examination:

'I think I was the first one to get back to the Carroll car after it was stopped. I had a gun in my pocket; I didn't present it. I was the first one to the car and raised up the back of the car, but the others were there shortly afterward. We assembled right around the car immediately.

'Q. And whatever examination and what investigation you made you went right ahead and did it in your own way? A. Yes, sir.

'Q. And took possession of it, arrested them, and brought them in? A. Yes, sir.

'Q. And at that time, of course, you had no search warrant? A. No, sir. We had no knowledge that this car was coming through at that particular time.'

Redirect examination:

'The lazyback was awfully hard when I struck it with my fist. It was harder than upholstery ordinarily is in those backs; a great deal harder. It was practically solid. Sixty-nine quarts of whisky in one lazyback.'

The negotiation concerning three cases of whisky on September 29th was the only circumstance which could have subjected plaintiffs in error to any reasonable suspicion. No whisky was delivered, and it is not certain that they ever intended to deliver any. The arrest came 2 1/2 months after the negotiation. Every act in the meantime is consistent with complete innocence. Has it come about that merely because a man once agreed to deliver whisky, but did not, he may be arrested whenever thereafter he ventures to drive an automobile on the road to Detroit!

5. When Congress has intended that seizures or arrests might be made upon suspicion it has been careful to say so. The history and terms of the Volstead Act are not consistent with the suggestion that it was the purpose of Congress to grant the power here claimed for enforcement officers. The facts known when the arrest occurred were wholly insufficient to engender reasonable belief that plaintiffs in error were committing a misdemeanor, and the legality of the arrest cannot be supported by facts ascertained through the search which followed.

To me it seems clear enough that the judgment should be reversed.

I am authorized to say that Mr. Justice SUTHERLAND concurs in this opinion.

Miranda v. Arizona, 384 U.S. 436 (1966)

In each of these cases the defendant while in police custody was questioned by police officers, detectives, or a prosecuting attorney in a room in which he was cut off from the outside world. None of the defendants was given a full and effective warning of his rights at the outset of the interrogation process. In all four cases the questioning elicited oral admissions, and in three of them signed statements as well, which were admitted at their trials. All defendants were convicted and all convictions, except in No. 584, were affirmed on appeal. Held:

1. The prosecution may not use statements, whether exculpatory or inculpatory, stemming from questioning initiated by law enforcement officers after a person has been taken into custody or otherwise deprived of his freedom of action in any significant way, unless it demonstrates the use of procedural safeguards effective to secure the Fifth Amendment's privilege against self-incrimination. Pp. 444–491.

    (a) The atmosphere and environment of incommunicado interrogation as it exists today is inherently intimidating and works to undermine the privilege against self-incrimination. Unless adequate preventive measures are taken to dispel the compulsion inherent in custodial surroundings, no statement obtained from the defendant can truly be the product of his free choice. Pp. 445–458.

    (b) The privilege against self-incrimination, which has had a long and expansive historical development, is the essential mainstay of our adversary system and guarantees to the individual the "right to remain silent unless he chooses to speak in the unfettered exercise of his own will," during a period of custodial interrogation as well as in the courts or during the course of other official investigations. Pp. 458–465.

    (c) The decision in *Escobedo v. Illinois*, 378 U.S. 478, stressed the need for protective devices to make the process of police interrogation conform to the dictates of the privilege. Pp. 465–466.

    (d) In the absence of other effective measures the following procedures to safeguard the Fifth Amendment privilege must be observed: The person in custody must, prior to interrogation, be clearly informed that he has the right to remain silent, and that anything he says will be used against him in court; he must be clearly informed that he has the right to consult with a lawyer and to have the lawyer with him during interrogation, and that, if he is indigent, a lawyer will be appointed to represent him. Pp. 467–473.

    (e) If the individual indicates, prior to or during questioning, that he wishes to remain silent, the interrogation must cease; if he states that he wants an attorney, the questioning must cease until an attorney is present. Pp. 473–474.

    (f) Where an interrogation is conducted without the presence of an attorney and a statement is taken, a heavy burden rests on the Government to demonstrate that the defendant knowingly and intelligently waived his right to counsel. P. 475.

    (g) Where the individual answers some questions during in-custody interrogation he has not waived his privilege and may invoke his right to remain silent thereafter. Pp. 475–476.

(Continues)

(h) The warnings required and the waiver needed are, in the absence of a fully effective equivalent, prerequisites to the admissibility of any statement, inculpatory or exculpatory, made by a defendant. Pp. 476–477.

2. The limitations on the interrogation process required for the protection of the individual's constitutional rights should not cause an undue interference with a proper system of law enforcement, as demonstrated by the procedures of the FBI and the safeguards afforded in other jurisdictions. Pp. 479–491.

3. In each of these cases the statements were obtained under circumstances that did not meet constitutional standards for protection of the privilege against self-incrimination. Pp. 491–499.

98 Ariz. 18, 401 P.2d 721; 15 N.Y. 2d 970, 207 N.E. 2d 527; 16 N.Y. 2d 614, 209 N.E. 2d 110; 342 F.2d 684, reversed; 62 Cal. 2d 571, 400 P.2d 97, affirmed.

John J. Flynn argued the cause for petitioner in No. 759. With him on the brief was John P. Frank. Victor M. Earle III argued the cause and filed a brief for petitioner in No. 760. F. Conger Fawcett argued the cause and filed a brief for petitioner in No. 761. Gordon Ringer, Deputy Attorney General of California, argued the cause for petitioner in No. 584. With him on the briefs were Thomas C. Lynch, Attorney General, and William E. James, Assistant Attorney General.

Gary K. Nelson, Assistant Attorney General of Arizona, argued the cause for respondent in No. 759. With him on the brief was Darrell F. Smith, Attorney General. William I. Siegel argued the cause for respondent in No. 760. With him on the brief was Aaron E. Koota. Solicitor General Marshall argued the cause for the United States in No. 761. With him on the brief were Assistant Attorney General Vinson, Ralph S. Spritzer, Nathan Lewin, Beatrice Rosenberg and Ronald L. Gainer. William A. Norris, by appointment of the Court, 382 U.S. 952, argued the cause and filed a brief for respondent in No. 584.

Telford Taylor, by special leave of Court, argued the cause for the State of New York, as *amicus curiae*, in all cases. With him on the brief were Louis J. Lefkowitz, Attorney General of New York, Samuel A. Hirshowitz, First Assistant Attorney General, and Barry Mahoney and George D. Zuckerman, Assistant Attorneys General, joined by the Attorneys General for their respective States and jurisdictions as follows: Richmond M. Flowers of Alabama, Darrell F. Smith of Arizona, Bruce Bennett of Arkansas, Duke W. Dunbar of Colorado, David P. Buckson of Delaware, Earl Faircloth of Florida, Arthur K. Bolton of Georgia, Allan G. Shepard of Idaho, William G. Clark of Illinois, Robert C. Londerholm of Kansas, Robert Matthews of Kentucky, Jack P. F. Gremillion of Louisiana, Richard J. Dubord of Maine, Thomas B. Finan of Maryland, Norman H. Anderson of Missouri, Forrest H. Anderson of Montana, Clarence A. H. Meyer of Nebraska, T. Wade Bruton of North Carolina, Helgi Johanneson of North Dakota, Robert Y. Thornton of Oregon, Walter E. Alessandroni of Pennsylvania, J. Joseph Nugent of Rhode Island, Daniel R. McLeod of South Carolina, Waggoner Carr of Texas, Robert Y. Button of Virginia, John J. O'Connell of Washington, C. Donald Robertson of West Virginia, John F. Raper of Wyoming, Rafael Hernandez Colon of Puerto Rico and Francisco Corneiro of the Virgin Islands.

Duane R. Nedrud, by special leave of Court, argued the cause for the National District Attorneys Association, as *amicus curiae*, urging affirmance in Nos. 759 and 760, and reversal in No. 584. With him on the brief was Marguerite D. Oberto.

Anthony G. Amsterdam, Paul J. Mishkin, Raymond L. Bradley, Peter Hearn, and Melvin L. Wulf filed a brief for the American Civil Liberties Union, as *amicus curiae*, in all cases.

MR. CHIEF JUSTICE WARREN delivered the opinion of the Court.

The cases before us raise questions which go to the roots of our concepts of American criminal jurisprudence: the restraints society must observe consistent with the Federal Constitution in prosecuting individuals for crime. More specifically, we deal with the admissibility of statements obtained from an individual who is subjected to custodial police interrogation and the necessity for procedures which assure that the individual is accorded his privilege under the Fifth Amendment to the Constitution not to be compelled to incriminate himself.

We dealt with certain phases of this problem recently in *Escobedo v. Illinois*, 378 U.S. 478 (1964). There, as in the four cases before us, law enforcement officials took the defendant into custody and interrogated him in a police station for the purpose of obtaining a confession. The police did not effectively advise him of his right to remain silent or of his right to consult with his attorney. Rather, they confronted him with an alleged accomplice who accused him of having perpetrated a murder. When the defendant denied the accusation and said "I didn't shoot Manuel, you did it," they handcuffed him and took him to an interrogation room. There, while handcuffed and standing, he was questioned for four hours until he confessed. During this interrogation, the police denied his request to speak to his attorney, and they prevented his retained attorney, who had come to the police station, from consulting with him. At his trial, the State, over his objection, introduced the confession against him. We held that the statements thus made were constitutionally inadmissible.

This case has been the subject of judicial interpretation and spirited legal debate since it was decided two years ago. Both state and federal courts, in assessing its implications, have arrived at varying conclusions.[1] A wealth of scholarly material has been written tracing its ramifications and underpinnings.[2] Police and prosecutor [384 U.S. 436, 441] have speculated on its range and desirability.[3] We granted certiorari in these cases, 382 U.S. 924, 925, 937, in order further to explore some facets of the problems, thus exposed, of applying the privilege against self-incrimination to in-custody interrogation, and to give [384 U.S. 436, 442] concrete constitutional guidelines for law enforcement agencies and courts to follow.

We start here, as we did in Escobedo, with the premise that our holding is not an innovation in our jurisprudence, but is an application of principles long recognized and applied in other settings. We have undertaken a thorough re-examination of the Escobedo decision and the principles it announced, and we reaffirm it. That case was but an explication of basic rights that are enshrined in our Constitution—that "No person . . . shall be compelled in any criminal case to be a witness against himself," and that "the accused shall . . . have the Assistance of Counsel"—rights which were put in jeopardy in that case through official overbearing. These precious rights were fixed in our Constitution only after centuries of persecution and struggle. And in the words of Chief Justice Marshall, they were secured "for ages to come, and . . . designed to approach immortality as nearly as human institutions can approach it," *Cohens v. Virginia*, 6 Wheat. 264, 387 (1821).

Over 70 years ago, our predecessors on this Court eloquently stated:

"The maxim *nemo tenetur seipsum accusare* had its origin in a protest against the inquisitorial and manifestly unjust methods of interrogating accused persons, which [have] long obtained in the continental system, and, until the expulsion of the Stuarts from the British throne in 1688, and the erection of additional barriers for the protection of the people against the exercise of arbitrary power, [were] not uncommon even in England. While the admissions or confessions of the prisoner, when voluntarily and freely made, have always ranked high in the scale of incriminating evidence, if an accused person be asked to explain his apparent connection with a crime under investigation, the ease with which the [384 U.S. 436, 443] questions put to him may assume an inquisitorial character, the temptation to press the witness unduly, to browbeat him if he be timid or reluctant, to push him into a corner, and to entrap him into fatal contradictions, which is so painfully evident in many of the earlier state trials, notably in those of Sir Nicholas Throckmorton, and Udal, the Puritan minister, made the system so odious as to give rise to a demand for its total abolition. The change in the English criminal procedure in that particular seems to be founded upon no statute and no judicial opinion, but upon a general and silent acquiescence of the courts in a popular demand. But, however adopted, it has become firmly embedded in English, as well as in American jurisprudence. So deeply did the iniquities of the ancient system impress themselves upon the minds of the American colonists that the States, with one accord, made a denial of the right to question an accused person a part of their fundamental law, so that a maxim, which in England was a mere rule of evidence, became clothed in this country with the impregnability of a constitutional enactment." *Brown v. Walker*, 161 U.S. 591, 596–597 (1896).

In stating the obligation of the judiciary to apply these constitutional rights, this Court declared in *Weems v. United States*, 217 U.S. 349, 373 (1910):

". . . our contemplation cannot be only of what has been but of what may be. Under any other rule a constitution would indeed be as easy of application as it would be deficient in efficacy and power. Its general principles would have little value and be converted by precedent into impotent and lifeless formulas. Rights declared in words might be lost in reality. And this has been recognized. The [384 U.S. 436, 444] meaning and vitality of the Constitution have developed against narrow and restrictive construction."

This was the spirit in which we delineated, in meaningful language, the manner in which the constitutional rights of the individual could be enforced against overzealous police practices. It was necessary in Escobedo, as here, to insure that what was proclaimed in the Constitution had not become but a "form of words," *Silverthorne Lumber Co. v. United States*, 251 U.S. 385, 392 (1920), in the hands of government officials. And it is in this spirit, consistent with our role as judges, that we adhere to the principles of Escobedo today.

(Continues)

(Continued)

Our holding will be spelled out with some specificity in the pages which follow but briefly stated it is this: the prosecution may not use statements, whether exculpatory or inculpatory, stemming from custodial interrogation of the defendant unless it demonstrates the use of procedural safeguards effective to secure the privilege against self-incrimination. By custodial interrogation, we mean questioning initiated by law enforcement officers after a person has been taken into custody or otherwise deprived of his freedom of action in any significant way.[4] As for the procedural safeguards to be employed, unless other fully effective means are devised to inform accused persons of their right of silence and to assure a continuous opportunity to exercise it, the following measures are required. Prior to any questioning, the person must be warned that he has a right to remain silent, that any statement he does make may be used as evidence against him, and that he has a right to the presence of an attorney, either retained or appointed. The defendant may waive effectuation of these rights, provided the waiver is made voluntarily, knowingly and intelligently. If, however, he indicates in any manner and at any stage of the [384 U.S. 436, 445] process that he wishes to consult with an attorney before speaking there can be no questioning. Likewise, if the individual is alone and indicates in any manner that he does not wish to be interrogated, the police may not question him. The mere fact that he may have answered some questions or volunteered some statements on his own does not deprive him of the right to refrain from answering any further inquiries until he has consulted with an attorney and thereafter consents to be questioned.

I

The constitutional issue we decide in each of these cases is the admissibility of statements obtained from a defendant questioned while in custody or otherwise deprived of his freedom of action in any significant liberty way. In each, the defendant was questioned by police officers, detectives, or a prosecuting attorney in a room in which he was cut off from the outside world. In none of these cases was the defendant given a full and effective warning of his rights at the outset of the interrogation process. In all the cases, the questioning elicited oral admissions, and in three of them, signed statements as well which were admitted at their trials. They all thus share salient features—incommunicado interrogation of individuals in a police-dominated atmosphere, resulting in self-incriminating statements without full warnings of constitutional rights.

An understanding of the nature and setting of this in-custody interrogation is essential to our decisions today. The difficulty in depicting what transpires at such interrogations stems from the fact that in this country they have largely taken place incommunicado. From extensive factual studies undertaken in the early 1930's, including the famous Wickersham Report to Congress by a Presidential Commission, it is clear that police violence and the "third degree" flourished at that time.[5] [384 U.S. 436, 446]. In a series of cases decided by this Court long after these studies, the police resorted to physical brutality—beating, hanging, whipping—and to sustained and protracted questioning incommunicado in order to extort confessions.[6] The Commission on Civil Rights in 1961 found much evidence to indicate that "some policemen still resort to physical force to obtain confessions," 1961 Comm'n on Civil Rights Rep., Justice, pt. 5, 17. The use of physical brutality and violence is not, unfortunately, relegated to the past or to any part of the country. Only recently in Kings County, New York, the police brutally beat, kicked and placed lighted cigarette butts on the back of a potential witness under interrogation for the purpose of securing a statement incriminating a third party. *People v. Portelli*, 15 N.Y. 2d 235, 205 N.E. 2d 857, 257 N.Y.S. 2d 931 (1965).[7] [384 U.S. 436, 447].

The examples given above are undoubtedly the exception now, but they are sufficiently widespread to be the object of concern. Unless a proper limitation upon custodial interrogation is achieved—such as these decisions will advance—there can be no assurance that practices of this nature will be eradicated in the foreseeable future. The conclusion of the Wickersham Commission Report, made over 30 years ago, is still pertinent:

> "To the contention that the third degree is necessary to get the facts, the reporters aptly reply in the language of the present Lord Chancellor of England (Lord Sankey): 'It is not admissible to do a great right by doing a little wrong. . . . It is not sufficient to do justice by obtaining a proper result by irregular or improper means.' Not only does the use of the third degree involve a flagrant violation of law by the officers of the law, but it involves also the dangers of false confessions, and it tends to make police and prosecutors less zealous in the search for objective evidence. As the New York prosecutor quoted in the report said, 'It is a short cut and makes the police lazy and unenterprising.' Or, as another official quoted remarked:

'If you use your fists, you are not so likely to use your wits.' We agree with the conclusion expressed in the report, that 'The third degree brutalizes the police, hardens the prisoner against society, and lowers the esteem in which the administration of justice is held by the public.'" IV National Commission on Law Observance and Enforcement, *Report on Lawlessness in Law Enforcement*[5] (1931).

Again we stress that the modern practice of in-custody interrogation is psychologically rather than physically oriented. As we have stated before, "Since *Chambers v. Florida*, 309 U.S. 227, this Court has recognized that coercion can be mental as well as physical, and that the blood of the accused is not the only hallmark of an unconstitutional inquisition." *Blackburn v. Alabama*, 361 U.S. 199, 206 (1960). Interrogation still takes place in privacy. Privacy results in secrecy and this in turn results in a gap in our knowledge as to what in fact goes on in the interrogation rooms. A valuable source of information about present police practices, however, may be found in various police manuals and texts which document procedures employed with success in the past, and which recommend various other effective tactics.[8] These [384 U.S. 436, 449] texts are used by law enforcement agencies themselves as guides.[9] It should be noted that these texts professedly present the most enlightened and effective means presently used to obtain statements through custodial interrogation. By considering these texts and other data, it is possible to describe procedures observed and noted around the country.

The officers are told by the manuals that the "principal psychological factor contributing to a successful interrogation is privacy—being alone with the person under interrogation."[10] The efficacy of this tactic has been explained as follows:

"If at all practicable, the interrogation should take place in the investigator's office or at least in a room of his own choice. The subject should be deprived of every psychological advantage. In his own home he may be confident, indignant, or recalcitrant. He is more keenly aware of his rights and [384 U.S. 436, 450] more reluctant to tell of his indiscretions or criminal behavior within the walls of his home. Moreover his family and other friends are nearby, their presence lending moral support. In his own office, the investigator possesses all the advantages. The atmosphere suggests the invincibility of the forces of the law."[11]

To highlight the isolation and unfamiliar surroundings, the manuals instruct the police to display an air of confidence in the suspect's guilt and from outward appearance to maintain only an interest in confirming certain details. The guilt of the subject is to be posited as a fact. The interrogator should direct his comments toward the reasons why the subject committed the act, rather than court failure by asking the subject whether he did it. Like other men, perhaps the subject has had a bad family life, had an unhappy childhood, had too much to drink, had an unrequited desire for women. The officers are instructed to minimize the moral seriousness of the offense,[12] to cast blame on the victim or on society.[13] These tactics are designed to put the subject in a psychological state where his story is but an elaboration of what the police purport to know already—that he is guilty. Explanations to the contrary are dismissed and discouraged.

The texts thus stress that the major qualities an interrogator should possess are patience and perseverance. [384 U.S. 436, 451]. One writer describes the efficacy of these characteristics in this manner:

"In the preceding paragraphs emphasis has been placed on kindness and stratagems. The investigator will, however, encounter many situations where the sheer weight of his personality will be the deciding factor. Where emotional appeals and tricks are employed to no avail, he must rely on an oppressive atmosphere of dogged persistence. He must interrogate steadily and without relent, leaving the subject no prospect of surcease. He must dominate his subject and overwhelm him with his inexorable will to obtain the truth. He should interrogate for a spell of several hours pausing only for the subject's necessities in acknowledgment of the need to avoid a charge of duress that can be technically substantiated. In a serious case, the interrogation may continue for days, with the required intervals for food and sleep, but with no respite from the atmosphere of domination. It is possible in this way to induce the subject to talk without resorting to duress or coercion. The method should be used only when the guilt of the subject appears highly probable."[14]

The manuals suggest that the suspect be offered legal excuses for his actions in order to obtain an initial admission of guilt. Where there is a suspected revenge-killing, for example, the interrogator may say:

"Joe, you probably didn't go out looking for this fellow with the purpose of shooting him. My guess is, however, that you expected something from him and that's why you carried a gun—for your own

(Continues)

protection. You knew him for what he was, no good. Then when you met him he probably started using foul, abusive language and he gave some indication [384 U.S. 436, 452] that he was about to pull a gun on you, and that's when you had to act to save your own life. That's about it, isn't it, Joe?"[15]

Having then obtained the admission of shooting, the interrogator is advised to refer to circumstantial evidence which negates the self-defense explanation. This should enable him to secure the entire story. One text notes that "Even if he fails to do so, the inconsistency between the subject's original denial of the shooting and his present admission of at least doing the shooting will serve to deprive him of a self-defense 'out' at the time of trial."[16]

When the techniques described above prove unavailing, the texts recommend they be alternated with a show of some hostility. One ploy often used has been termed the "friendly–unfriendly" or the "Mutt and Jeff" act:

". . . In this technique, two agents are employed. Mutt, the relentless investigator, who knows the subject is guilty and is not going to waste any time. He's sent a dozen men away for this crime and he's going to send the subject away for the full term. Jeff, on the other hand, is obviously a kindhearted man. He has a family himself. He has a brother who was involved in a little scrape like this. He disapproves of Mutt and his tactics and will arrange to get him off the case if the subject will cooperate. He can't hold Mutt off for very long. The subject would be wise to make a quick decision. The technique is applied by having both investigators present while Mutt acts out his role. Jeff may stand by quietly and demur at some of Mutt's tactics. When Jeff makes his plea for cooperation, Mutt is not present in the room."[17] [384 U.S. 436, 453].

The interrogators sometimes are instructed to induce a confession out of trickery. The technique here is quite effective in crimes which require identification or which run in series. In the identification situation, the interrogator may take a break in his questioning to place the subject among a group of men in a line-up. "The witness or complainant (previously coached, if necessary) studies the line-up and confidently points out the subject as the guilty party."[18] Then the questioning resumes "as though there were now no doubt about the guilt of the subject." A variation on this technique is called the "reverse line-up":

"The accused is placed in a line-up, but this time he is identified by several fictitious witnesses or victims who associated him with different offenses. It is expected that the subject will become desperate and confess to the offense under investigation in order to escape from the false accusations."[19]

The manuals also contain instructions for police on how to handle the individual who refuses to discuss the matter entirely, or who asks for an attorney or relatives. The examiner is to concede him the right to remain silent. "This usually has a very undermining effect. First of all, he is disappointed in his expectation of an unfavorable reaction on the part of the interrogator. Secondly, a concession of this right to remain silent impresses [384 U.S. 436, 454] the subject with the apparent fairness of his interrogator."[20] After this psychological conditioning, however, the officer is told to point out the incriminating significance of the suspect's refusal to talk:

"Joe, you have a right to remain silent. That's your privilege and I'm the last person in the world who'll try to take it away from you. If that's the way you want to leave this, O. K. But let me ask you this. Suppose you were in my shoes and I were in yours and you called me in to ask me about this and I told you, 'I don't want to answer any of your questions.' You'd think I had something to hide, and you'd probably be right in thinking that. That's exactly what I'll have to think about you, and so will everybody else. So let's sit here and talk this whole thing over."[21]

Few will persist in their initial refusal to talk, it is said, if this monologue is employed correctly. In the event that the subject wishes to speak to a relative or an attorney, the following advice is tendered:

"[T]he interrogator should respond by suggesting that the subject first tell the truth to the interrogator himself rather than get anyone else involved in the matter. If the request is for an attorney, the interrogator may suggest that the subject save himself or his family the expense of any such professional service, particularly if he is innocent of the offense under investigation. The interrogator may also add, 'Joe, I'm only looking for the truth, and if you're telling the truth, that's it. You can handle this by yourself.'"[22]

From these representative samples of interrogation techniques, the setting prescribed by the manuals and observed in practice becomes clear. In essence, it is this: To be alone with the subject is essential to prevent distraction and to deprive him of any outside support. The aura of confidence in his guilt undermines his will to resist. He merely confirms the preconceived story the police seek to have him describe. Patience and persistence, at times relentless questioning, are employed. To obtain a confession, the interrogator must "patiently maneuver himself or his quarry into a position from which the desired objective may be attained."[23] When normal procedures fail to produce the needed result, the police may resort to deceptive stratagems such as giving false legal advice. It is important to keep the subject off balance, for example, by trading on his insecurity about himself or his surroundings. The police then persuade, trick, or cajole him out of exercising his constitutional rights.

Even without employing brutality, the "third degree" or the specific stratagems described above, the very fact of custodial interrogation exacts a heavy toll on individual liberty and trades on the weakness of individuals.[24] [384 U.S. 436, 456]. This fact may be illustrated simply by referring to three confession cases decided by this Court in the Term immediately preceding our Escobedo decision. In *Townsend v. Sain*, 372 U.S. 293 (1963), the defendant was a 19-year-old heroin addict, described as a "near mental defective," *id.*, at 307–310. The defendant in *Lynumn v. Illinois*, 372 U.S. 528 (1963), was a woman who confessed to the arresting officer after being importuned to "cooperate" in order to prevent her children from being taken by relief authorities. This Court as in those cases reversed the conviction of a defendant in *Haynes v. Washington*, 373 U.S. 503 (1963), whose persistent request during his interrogation was to phone his wife or attorney.[25] In other settings, these individuals might have exercised their constitutional rights. In the incommunicado police-dominated atmosphere, they succumbed.

In the cases before us today, given this background, we concern ourselves primarily with this interrogation atmosphere and the evils it can bring. In No. 759, *Miranda v. Arizona*, the police arrested the defendant and took him to a special interrogation room where they secured a confession. In No. 760, *Vignera v. New York*, the defendant made oral admissions to the police after interrogation in the afternoon, and then signed an inculpatory statement upon being questioned by an assistant district attorney later the same evening. In No. 761, *Westover v. United States*, the defendant was handed over to the Federal Bureau of Investigation by local authorities after they had detained and interrogated him for a lengthy period, both at night and the following morning. After some two hours of questioning, the federal officers had obtained signed statements from the defendant. Lastly, in No. 584, *California v. Stewart*, the local police held the defendant five days in the station and interrogated him on nine separate occasions before they secured his inculpatory statement.

In these cases, we might not find the defendants' statements to have been involuntary in traditional terms. Our concern for adequate safeguards to protect precious Fifth Amendment rights is, of course, not lessened in the slightest. In each of the cases, the defendant was thrust into an unfamiliar atmosphere and run through menacing police interrogation procedures. The potentiality for compulsion is forcefully apparent, for example, in Miranda, where the indigent Mexican defendant was a seriously disturbed individual with pronounced sexual fantasies, and in Stewart, in which the defendant was an indigent Los Angeles Negro who had dropped out of school in the sixth grade. To be sure, the records do not evince overt physical coercion or patent psychological ploys. The fact remains that in none of these cases did the officers undertake to afford appropriate safeguards at the outset of the interrogation to insure that the statements were truly the product of free choice.

It is obvious that such an interrogation environment is created for no purpose other than to subjugate the individual to the will of his examiner. This atmosphere carries its own badge of intimidation. To be sure, this is not physical intimidation, but it is equally destructive of human dignity.[26] The current practice of incommunicado interrogation is at odds with one of our Nation's most cherished principles—that the individual may not be compelled to incriminate himself. Unless adequate protective devices are employed to dispel the compulsion inherent in custodial surroundings, no statement obtained from the defendant can truly be the product of his free choice.

From the foregoing, we can readily perceive an intimate connection between the privilege against self-incrimination and police custodial questioning. It is fitting to turn to history and precedent underlying the Self-Incrimination Clause to determine its applicability in this situation.

II

We sometimes forget how long it has taken to establish the privilege against self-incrimination, the sources from which it came and the fervor with which it was defended. Its roots go back into ancient times.[27]

(Continues)

(Continued)

Perhaps [384 U.S. 436, 459] the critical historical event shedding light on its origins and evolution was the trial of one John Lilburn, a vocal anti-Stuart Leveller, who was made to take the Star Chamber Oath in 1637. The oath would have bound him to answer to all questions posed to him on any subject. The Trial of John Lilburn and John Wharton, 3 How. St. Tr. 1315 (1637). He resisted the oath and declaimed the proceedings, stating:

> "Another fundamental right I then contended for, was, that no man's conscience ought to be racked by oaths imposed, to answer to questions concerning himself in matters criminal, or pretended to be so." Haller & Davies, *The Leveller Tracts 1647–1653*, p. 454 (1944).

On account of the Lilburn Trial, Parliament abolished the inquisitorial Court of Star Chamber and went further in giving him generous reparation. The lofty principles to which Lilburn had appealed during his trial gained popular acceptance in England.[28] These sentiments worked their way over to the Colonies and were implanted after great struggle into the Bill of Rights.[29] Those who framed our Constitution and the Bill of Rights were ever aware of subtle encroachments on individual liberty. They knew that "illegitimate and unconstitutional practices get their first footing . . . by silent approaches and slight deviations from legal modes of procedure." *Boyd v. United States*, 116 U.S. 616, 635 (1886). The privilege was elevated to constitutional status and has always been "as broad as the mischief [384 U.S. 436, 460] against which it seeks to guard." *Counselman v. Hitchcock*, 142 U.S. 547, 562 (1892). We cannot depart from this noble heritage.

Thus we may view the historical development of the privilege as one which groped for the proper scope of governmental power over the citizen. As a "noble principle often transcends its origins," the privilege has come rightfully to be recognized in part as an individual's substantive right, a "right to a private enclave where he may lead a private life. That right is the hallmark of our democracy." *United States v. Grunewald*, 233 F.2d 556, 579, 581–582 (Frank, J., dissenting), rev'd, 353 U.S. 391 (1957). We have recently noted that the privilege against self-incrimination–the essential mainstay of our adversary system—is founded on a complex of values, *Murphy v. Waterfront Comm'n*, 378 U.S. 52, 55–57, n. 5 (1964); *Tehan v. Shott*, 382 U.S. 406, 414–415, n. 12 (1966). All these policies point to one overriding thought: the constitutional foundation underlying the privilege is the respect a government—state or federal—must accord to the dignity and integrity of its citizens. To maintain a "fair state–individual balance," to require the government "to shoulder the entire load," 8 Wigmore, *Evidence* 317 (McNaughton rev. 1961), to respect the inviolability of the human personality, our accusatory system of criminal justice demands that the government seeking to punish an individual produce the evidence against him by its own independent labors, rather than by the cruel, simple expedient of compelling it from his own mouth. *Chambers v. Florida*, 309 U.S. 227, 235–238 (1940). In sum, the privilege is fulfilled only when the person is guaranteed the right "to remain silent unless he chooses to speak in the unfettered exercise of his own will." *Malloy v. Hogan*, 378 U.S. 1, 8 (1964).

The question in these cases is whether the privilege is fully applicable during a period of custodial interrogation. In this Court, the privilege has consistently been accorded a liberal construction. *Albertson v. SACB*, 382 U.S. 70, 81 (1965); *Hoffman v. United States*, 341 U.S. 479, 486 (1951); *Arndstein v. McCarthy*, 254 U.S. 71, 72–73 (1920); *Counselman v. Hitchcock*, 142 U.S. 547, 562 (1892). We are satisfied that all the principles embodied in the privilege apply to informal compulsion exerted by law-enforcement officers during in-custody questioning. An individual swept from familiar surroundings into police custody, surrounded by antagonistic forces, and subjected to the techniques of persuasion described above cannot be otherwise than under compulsion to speak. As a practical matter, the compulsion to speak in the isolated setting of the police station may well be greater than in courts or other official investigations, where there are often impartial observers to guard against intimidation or trickery.[30]

This question, in fact, could have been taken as settled in federal courts almost 70 years ago, when, in *Bram v. United States*, 168 U.S. 532, 542 (1897), this Court held:

> "In criminal trials, in the courts of the United States, wherever a question arises whether a confession is incompetent because not voluntary, the issue is controlled by that portion of the Fifth Amendment . . . commanding that no person 'shall be compelled in any criminal case to be a witness against himself.'"

In *Bram*, the Court reviewed the British and American history and case law and set down the Fifth Amendment standard for compulsion which we implement today:

> "Much of the confusion which has resulted from the effort to deduce from the adjudged cases what would be a sufficient quantum of proof to show that a confession was or was not voluntary, has arisen from a

misconception of the subject to which the proof must address itself. The rule is not that in order to render a statement admissible the proof must be adequate to establish that the particular communications contained in a statement were voluntarily made, but it must be sufficient to establish that the making of the statement was voluntary; that is to say, that from the causes, which the law treats as legally sufficient to engender in the mind of the accused hope or fear in respect to the crime charged, the accused was not involuntarily impelled to make a statement, when but for the improper influences he would have remained silent . . ." 168 U.S., at 549. And see, *id.*, at 542.

The Court has adhered to this reasoning. In 1924, Mr. Justice Brandeis wrote for a unanimous Court in reversing a conviction resting on a compelled confession, *Wan v. United States*, 266 U.S. 1. He stated:

"In the federal courts, the requisite of voluntariness is not satisfied by establishing merely that the confession was not induced by a promise or a threat. A confession is voluntary in law if, and only if, it was, in fact, voluntarily made. A confession may have been given voluntarily, although it was made to police officers, while in custody, and in answer to an examination conducted by them. But a confession obtained by compulsion must be excluded whatever may have been the character of the compulsion, and whether the compulsion was applied in a judicial proceeding or otherwise." *Bram v. United States*, 168 U.S. 532. 266 U.S., at 14–15.

In addition to the expansive historical development of the privilege and the sound policies which have nurtured [384 U.S. 436, 463] its evolution, judicial precedent thus clearly establishes its application to incommunicado interrogation. In fact, the Government concedes this point as well established in No. 761, *Westover v. United States*, stating: "We have no doubt...that it is possible for a suspect's Fifth Amendment right to be violated during in-custody questioning by a law-enforcement officer."[31]

Because of the adoption by Congress of Rule 5 (a) of the Federal Rules of Criminal Procedure, and this Court's effectuation of that Rule in *McNabb v. United States*, 318 U.S. 332 (1943), and *Mallory v. United States*, 354 U.S. 449 (1957), we have had little occasion in the past quarter century to reach the constitutional issues in dealing with federal interrogations. These supervisory rules, requiring production of an arrested person before a commissioner "without unnecessary delay" and excluding evidence obtained in default of that statutory obligation, were nonetheless responsive to the same considerations of Fifth Amendment policy that unavoidably face us now as to the States. In *McNabb*, 318 U.S., at 343–344, and in *Mallory*, 354 U.S., at 455–456, we recognized both the dangers of interrogation and the appropriateness of prophylaxis stemming from the very fact of interrogation itself.[32]

Our decision in *Malloy v. Hogan*, 378 U.S. 1 (1964), necessitates an examination of the scope of the privilege in state cases as well. In *Malloy*, we squarely held the privilege applicable to the States, and held that the substantive standards underlying the privilege applied with full force to state court proceedings. There, as in *Murphy v. Waterfront Comm'n*, 378 U.S. 52 (1964), and *Griffin v. California*, 380 U.S. 609 (1965), we applied the existing Fifth Amendment standards to the case before us. Aside from the holding itself, the reasoning in *Malloy* made clear what had already become apparent—that the substantive and procedural safeguards surrounding admissibility of confessions in state cases had become exceedingly exacting, reflecting all the policies embedded in the privilege, 378 U.S., at 7–8.[33] The voluntariness doctrine in the state cases, as *Malloy* indicates, encompasses all interrogation practices which are likely to exert such pressure upon an individual as to disable him from making a free and rational choice.[34] The implications of this proposition were elaborated in our decision in *Escobedo v. Illinois*, 378 U.S. 478, decided one week after Malloy applied the privilege to the States.

Our holding there stressed the fact that the police had not advised the defendant of his constitutional privilege to remain silent at the outset of the interrogation, and we drew attention to that fact at several points in the decision, 378 U.S., at 483, 485, 491. This was no isolated factor, but an essential ingredient in our decision. The entire thrust of police interrogation there, as in all the cases today, was to put the defendant in such an emotional state as to impair his capacity for rational judgment. The abdication of the constitutional privilege—the choice on his part to speak to the police—was not made knowingly or competently because of the failure to apprise him of his rights; the compelling atmosphere of the in-custody interrogation, and not an independent decision on his part, caused the defendant to speak.

A different phase of the Escobedo decision was significant in its attention to the absence of counsel during the questioning. There, as in the cases today, we sought a protective device to dispel the compelling

(Continues)

atmosphere of the interrogation. In Escobedo, however, the police did not relieve the defendant of the anxieties which they had created in the interrogation rooms. Rather, they denied his request for the assistance of counsel, 378 U.S., at 481, 488, 491.[35] This heightened his dilemma, and made his later statements the product of this compulsion. Cf. *Haynes v. Washington*, 373 U.S. 503, 514 (1963). The denial of the defendant's request for his attorney thus undermined his ability to exercise the privilege—to remain silent if he chose or to speak without any intimidation, blatant or subtle. The presence of counsel, in all the cases before us today, would be the adequate protective device necessary to make the process of police interrogation conform to the dictates of the privilege. His presence would insure that statements made in the government-established atmosphere are not the product of compulsion.

It was in this manner that Escobedo explicated another facet of the pre-trial privilege, noted in many of the Court's prior decisions: the protection of rights at trial.[36] That counsel is present when statements are taken from an individual during interrogation obviously enhances the integrity of the fact-finding processes in court. The presence of an attorney, and the warnings delivered to the individual, enable the defendant under otherwise compelling circumstances to tell his story without fear, effectively, and in a way that eliminates the evils in the interrogation process. Without the protections flowing from adequate warnings and the rights of counsel, "all the careful safeguards erected around the giving of testimony, whether by an accused or any other witness, would become empty formalities in a procedure where the most compelling possible evidence of guilt, a confession, would have already been obtained at the unsupervised pleasure of the police." *Mapp v. Ohio*, 367 U.S. 643, 685 (1961) (HARLAN, J., dissenting). Cf. *Pointer v. Texas*, 380 U.S. 400 (1965).

III

Today, then, there can be no doubt that the Fifth Amendment privilege is available outside of criminal court proceedings and serves to protect persons in all settings in which their freedom of action is curtailed in any significant way from being compelled to incriminate themselves. We have concluded that without proper safeguards the process of in-custody interrogation of persons suspected or accused of crime contains inherently compelling pressures which work to undermine the individual's will to resist and to compel him to speak where he would not otherwise do so freely. In order to combat these pressures and to permit a full opportunity to exercise the privilege against self-incrimination, the accused must be adequately and effectively apprised of his rights and the exercise of those rights must be fully honored.

It is impossible for us to foresee the potential alternatives for protecting the privilege which might be devised by Congress or the States in the exercise of their creative rule-making capacities. Therefore we cannot say that the Constitution necessarily requires adherence to any particular solution for the inherent compulsions of the interrogation process as it is presently conducted. Our decision in no way creates a constitutional straitjacket which will handicap sound efforts at reform, nor is it intended to have this effect. We encourage Congress and the States to continue their laudable search for increasingly effective ways of protecting the rights of the individual while promoting efficient enforcement of our criminal laws. However, unless we are shown other procedures which are at least as effective in apprising accused persons of their right of silence and in assuring a continuous opportunity to exercise it, the following safeguards must be observed.

At the outset, if a person in custody is to be subjected to interrogation, he must first be informed in clear and unequivocal terms that he has the right to remain silent. For those unaware of the privilege, the warning is needed simply to make them aware of it—the threshold requirement for an intelligent decision as to its exercise. More important, such a warning is an absolute prerequisite in overcoming the inherent pressures of the interrogation atmosphere. It is not just the subnormal or woefully ignorant who succumb to an interrogator's imprecations, whether implied or expressly stated, that the interrogation will continue until a confession is obtained or that silence in the face of accusation is itself damning and will bode ill when presented to a jury.[37] Further, the warning will show the individual that his interrogators are prepared to recognize his privilege should he choose to exercise it.

The Fifth Amendment privilege is so fundamental to our system of constitutional rule and the expedient of giving an adequate warning as to the availability of the privilege so simple, we will not pause to inquire in individual cases whether the defendant was aware of his rights without a warning being given. Assessments of the knowledge the defendant possessed, based on information [384 U.S. 436, 469] as to his age, education, intelligence, or prior contact with authorities, can never be more than speculation[38]; a warning is a clearcut fact. More important, whatever the background of the person interrogated, a warning at the time of the interrogation is indispensable to overcome its pressures and to insure that the individual knows he is free to exercise the privilege at that point in time.

The warning of the right to remain silent must be accompanied by the explanation that anything said can and will be used against the individual in court. This warning is needed in order to make him aware not only of the privilege, but also of the consequences of forgoing it. It is only through an awareness of these consequences that there can be any assurance of real understanding and intelligent exercise of the privilege. Moreover, this warning may serve to make the individual more acutely aware that he is faced with a phase of the adversary system—that he is not in the presence of persons acting solely in his interest.

The circumstances surrounding in-custody interrogation can operate very quickly to overbear the will of one merely made aware of his privilege by his interrogators. Therefore, the right to have counsel present at the interrogation is indispensable to the protection of the Fifth Amendment privilege under the system we delineate today. Our aim is to assure that the individual's right to choose between silence and speech remains unfettered throughout the interrogation process. A once-stated warning, delivered by those who will conduct the interrogation, cannot itself suffice to that end among those who most require knowledge of their rights. A mere [384 U.S. 436, 470] warning given by the interrogators is not alone sufficient to accomplish that end. Prosecutors themselves claim that the admonishment of the right to remain silent without more "will benefit only the recidivist and the professional." Brief for the National District Attorneys Association as *amicus curiae*, p. 14. Even preliminary advice given to the accused by his own attorney can be swiftly overcome by the secret interrogation process. Cf. *Escobedo v. Illinois*, 378 U.S. 478, 485, n. 5. Thus, the need for counsel to protect the Fifth Amendment privilege comprehends not merely a right to consult with counsel prior to questioning, but also to have counsel present during any questioning if the defendant so desires.

The presence of counsel at the interrogation may serve several significant subsidiary functions as well. If the accused decides to talk to his interrogators, the assistance of counsel can mitigate the dangers of untrustworthiness. With a lawyer present the likelihood that the police will practice coercion is reduced, and if coercion is nevertheless exercised the lawyer can testify to it in court. The presence of a lawyer can also help to guarantee that the accused gives a fully accurate statement to the police and that the statement is rightly reported by the prosecution at trial. See *Crooker v. California*, 357 U.S. 433, 443–448 (1958) (DOUGLAS, J., dissenting).

An individual need not make a pre-interrogation request for a lawyer. While such request affirmatively secures his right to have one, his failure to ask for a lawyer does not constitute a waiver. No effective waiver of the right to counsel during interrogation can be recognized unless specifically made after the warnings we here delineate have been given. The accused who does not know his rights and therefore does not make a request [384 U.S. 436, 471] may be the person who most needs counsel. As the California Supreme Court has aptly put it:

"Finally, we must recognize that the imposition of the requirement for the request would discriminate against the defendant who does not know his rights. The defendant who does not ask for counsel is the very defendant who most needs counsel. We cannot penalize a defendant who, not understanding his constitutional rights, does not make the formal request and by such failure demonstrates his helplessness. To require the request would be to favor the defendant whose sophistication or status had fortuitously prompted him to make it." *People v. Dorado*, 62 Cal. 2d 338, 351, 398 P .2d 361, 369–370, 42 Cal. Rptr. 169, 177–178 (1965) (Tobriner, J.).

In *Carnley v. Cochran*, 369 U.S. 506, 513 (1962), we stated: "[I]t is settled that where the assistance of counsel is a constitutional requisite, the right to be furnished counsel does not depend on a request." This proposition applies with equal force in the context of providing counsel to protect an accused's Fifth Amendment privilege in the face of interrogation.[39] Although the role of counsel at trial differs from the role during interrogation, the differences are not relevant to the question whether a request is a prerequisite.

Accordingly we hold that an individual held for interrogation must be clearly informed that he has the right to consult with a lawyer and to have the lawyer with him during interrogation under the system for protecting the privilege we delineate today. As with the warnings of the right to remain silent and that anything stated can be used in evidence against him, this warning is an absolute prerequisite to interrogation. No amount of circumstantial evidence that the person may have been aware of this right will suffice to stand in its stead: Only through such a warning is there ascertainable assurance that the accused was aware of this right.

(Continues)

(*Continued*)

If an individual indicates that he wishes the assistance of counsel before any interrogation occurs, the authorities cannot rationally ignore or deny his request on the basis that the individual does not have or cannot afford a retained attorney. The financial ability of the individual has no relationship to the scope of the rights involved here. The privilege against self-incrimination secured by the Constitution applies to all individuals. The need for counsel in order to protect the privilege exists for the indigent as well as the affluent. In fact, were we to limit these constitutional rights to those who can retain an attorney, our decisions today would be of little significance. The cases before us as well as the vast majority of confession cases with which we have dealt in the past involve those unable to retain counsel.[40] While authorities are not required to relieve the accused of his poverty, they have the obligation not to take advantage of indigence in the administration of justice.[41] Denial of counsel to the indigent at the time of interrogation while allowing an attorney to those who can afford one would be no more supportable by reason or logic than the similar situation at trial and on appeal struck down in *Gideon v. Wainwright*, 372 U.S. 335 (1963), and *Douglas v. California*, 372 U.S. 353 (1963).

In order fully to apprise a person interrogated of the extent of his rights under this system then, it is necessary to warn him not only that he has the right to consult with an attorney, but also that if he is indigent a lawyer will be appointed to represent him. Without this additional warning, the admonition of the right to consult with counsel would often be understood as meaning only that he can consult with a lawyer if he has one or has the funds to obtain one. The warning of a right to counsel would be hollow if not couched in terms that would convey to the indigent—the person most often subjected to interrogation—the knowledge that he too has a right to have counsel present.[42] As with the warnings of the right to remain silent and of the general right to counsel, only by effective and express explanation to the indigent of this right can there be assurance that he was truly in a position to exercise it.[43]

Once warnings have been given, the subsequent procedure is clear. If the individual indicates in any manner, at any time prior to or during questioning, that he wishes to remain silent, the interrogation must cease.[44] At this point he has shown that he intends to exercise his Fifth Amendment privilege; any statement taken after the person invokes his privilege cannot be other than the product of compulsion, subtle or otherwise. Without the right to cut off questioning, the setting of in-custody interrogation operates on the individual to overcome free choice in producing a statement after the privilege has been once invoked. If the individual states that he wants an attorney, the interrogation must cease until an attorney is present. At that time, the individual must have an opportunity to confer with the attorney and to have him present during any subsequent questioning. If the individual cannot obtain an attorney and he indicates that he wants one before speaking to police, they must respect his decision to remain silent.

This does not mean, as some have suggested, that each police station must have a "station house lawyer" present at all times to advise prisoners. It does mean, however, that if police propose to interrogate a person they must make known to him that he is entitled to a lawyer and that if he cannot afford one, a lawyer will be provided for him prior to any interrogation. If authorities conclude that they will not provide counsel during a reasonable period of time in which investigation in the field is carried out, they may refrain from doing so without violating the person's Fifth Amendment privilege so long as they do not question him during that time. [384 U.S. 436, 475].

If the interrogation continues without the presence of an attorney and a statement is taken, a heavy burden rests on the government to demonstrate that the defendant knowingly and intelligently waived his privilege against self-incrimination and his right to retained or appointed counsel. *Escobedo v. Illinois*, 378 U.S. 478, 490, n. 14. This Court has always set high standards of proof for the waiver of constitutional rights, *Johnson v. Zerbst*, 304 U.S. 458 (1938), and we re-assert these standards as applied to in-custody interrogation. Since the State is responsible for establishing the isolated circumstances under which the interrogation takes place and has the only means of making available corroborated evidence of warnings given during incommunicado interrogation, the burden is rightly on its shoulders.

An express statement that the individual is willing to make a statement and does not want an attorney followed closely by a statement could constitute a waiver. But a valid waiver will not be presumed simply from the silence of the accused after warnings are given or simply from the fact that a confession was in fact eventually obtained. A statement we made in *Carnley v. Cochran*, 369 U.S. 506, 516 (1962), is applicable here:

> "Presuming waiver from a silent record is impermissible. The record must show, or there must be an allegation and evidence which show, that an accused was offered counsel but intelligently and understandingly rejected the offer. Anything less is not waiver."

See also *Glasser v. United States*, 315 U.S. 60 (1942). Moreover, where in-custody interrogation is involved, there is no room for the contention that the privilege is waived if the individual answers some questions or gives some information on his own prior to invoking his right to remain silent when interrogated.[45]

Whatever the testimony of the authorities as to waiver of rights by an accused, the fact of lengthy interrogation or incommunicado incarceration before a statement is made is strong evidence that the accused did not validly waive his rights. In these circumstances the fact that the individual eventually made a statement is consistent with the conclusion that the compelling influence of the interrogation finally forced him to do so. It is inconsistent with any notion of a voluntary relinquishment of the privilege. Moreover, any evidence that the accused was threatened, tricked, or cajoled into a waiver will, of course, show that the defendant did not voluntarily waive his privilege. The requirement of warnings and waiver of rights is a fundamental with respect to the Fifth Amendment privilege and not simply a preliminary ritual to existing methods of interrogation.

The warnings required and the waiver necessary in accordance with our opinion today are, in the absence of a fully effective equivalent, prerequisites to the admissibility of any statement made by a defendant. No distinction can be drawn between statements which are direct confessions and statements which amount to "admissions" of part or all of an offense. The privilege against self-incrimination protects the individual from being compelled to incriminate himself in any manner; it does not distinguish degrees of incrimination. Similarly, [384 U.S. 436, 477] for precisely the same reason, no distinction may be drawn between inculpatory statements and statements alleged to be merely "exculpatory." If a statement made were in fact truly exculpatory it would, of course, never be used by the prosecution. In fact, statements merely intended to be exculpatory by the defendant are often used to impeach his testimony at trial or to demonstrate untruths in the statement given under interrogation and thus to prove guilt by implication. These statements are incriminating in any meaningful sense of the word and may not be used without the full warnings and effective waiver required for any other statement. In Escobedo itself, the defendant fully intended his accusation of another as the slayer to be exculpatory as to himself.

The principles announced today deal with the protection which must be given to the privilege against self-incrimination when the individual is first subjected to police interrogation while in custody at the station or otherwise deprived of his freedom of action in any significant way. It is at this point that our adversary system of criminal proceedings commences, distinguishing itself at the outset from the inquisitorial system recognized in some countries. Under the system of warnings we delineate today or under any other system which may be devised and found effective, the safeguards to be erected about the privilege must come into play at this point.

Our decision is not intended to hamper the traditional function of police officers in investigating crime. See *Escobedo v. Illinois*, 378 U.S. 478, 492 . When an individual is in custody on probable cause, the police may, of course, seek out evidence in the field to be used at trial against him. Such investigation may include inquiry of persons not under restraint. General on-the-scene questioning as to facts surrounding a crime or other general questioning of citizens in the fact-finding process is not affected by our holding. It is an act of responsible citizenship for individuals to give whatever information they may have to aid in law enforcement. In such situations the compelling atmosphere inherent in the process of in-custody interrogation is not necessarily present.[46]

In dealing with statements obtained through interrogation, we do not purport to find all confessions inadmissible. Confessions remain a proper element in law enforcement. Any statement given freely and voluntarily without any compelling influences is, of course, admissible in evidence. The fundamental import of the privilege while an individual is in custody is not whether he is allowed to talk to the police without the benefit of warnings and counsel, but whether he can be interrogated. There is no requirement that police stop a person who enters a police station and states that he wishes to confess to a crime,[47] or a person who calls the police to offer a confession or any other statement he desires to make. Volunteered statements of any kind are not barred by the Fifth Amendment and their admissibility is not affected by our holding today.

To summarize, we hold that when an individual is taken into custody or otherwise deprived of his freedom by the authorities in any significant way and is subjected to questioning, the privilege against self-incrimination is jeopardized. Procedural safeguards must be employed to [384 U.S. 436, 479] protect the privilege, and unless other fully effective means are adopted to notify the person of his right of silence and to assure that the exercise of the right will be scrupulously honored, the following

(Continues)

measures are required. He must be warned prior to any questioning that he has the right to remain silent, that anything he says can be used against him in a court of law, that he has the right to the presence of an attorney, and that if he cannot afford an attorney one will be appointed for him prior to any questioning if he so desires. Opportunity to exercise these rights must be afforded to him throughout the interrogation. After such warnings have been given, and such opportunity afforded him, the individual may knowingly and intelligently waive these rights and agree to answer questions or make a statement. But unless and until such warnings and waiver are demonstrated by the prosecution at trial, no evidence obtained as a result of interrogation can be used against him.[48]

IV

A recurrent argument made in these cases is that society's need for interrogation outweighs the privilege. This argument is not unfamiliar to this Court. See, e.g., *Chambers v. Florida*, 309 U.S. 227, 240–241 (1940). The whole thrust of our foregoing discussion demonstrates that the Constitution has prescribed the rights of the individual when confronted with the power of government when it provided in the Fifth Amendment that an individual cannot be compelled to be a witness against himself. That right cannot be abridged. As Mr. Justice Brandeis once observed:

"Decency, security and liberty alike demand that government officials shall be subjected to the same [384 U.S. 436, 480] rules of conduct that are commands to the citizen. In a government of laws, existence of the government will be imperilled if it fails to observe the law scrupulously. Our Government is the potent, the omnipresent teacher. For good or for ill, it teaches the whole people by its example. Crime is contagious. If the Government becomes a lawbreaker, it breeds contempt for law; it invites every man to become a law unto himself; it invites anarchy. To declare that in the administration of the criminal law the end justifies the means . . . would bring terrible retribution. Against that pernicious doctrine this Court should resolutely set its face." *Olmstead v. United States*, 277 U.S. 438, 485 (1928) (dissenting opinion).[49]

In this connection, one of our country's distinguished jurists has pointed out: "The quality of a nation's civilization can be largely measured by the methods it uses in the enforcement of its criminal law."[50]

If the individual desires to exercise his privilege, he has the right to do so. This is not for the authorities to decide. An attorney may advise his client not to talk to police until he has had an opportunity to investigate the case, or he may wish to be present with his client during any police questioning. In doing so an attorney is merely exercising the good professional judgment he has been taught. This is not cause for considering the attorney a menace to law enforcement. He is merely carrying out what he is sworn to do under his oath—to protect to the extent of his ability the rights of his [384 U.S. 436, 481] client. In fulfilling this responsibility the attorney plays a vital role in the administration of criminal justice under our Constitution.

In announcing these principles, we are not unmindful of the burdens which law enforcement officials must bear, often under trying circumstances. We also fully recognize the obligation of all citizens to aid in enforcing the criminal laws. This Court, while protecting individual rights, has always given ample latitude to law enforcement agencies in the legitimate exercise of their duties. The limits we have placed on the interrogation process should not constitute an undue interference with a proper system of law enforcement. As we have noted, our decision does not in any way preclude police from carrying out their traditional investigatory functions. Although confessions may play an important role in some convictions, the cases before us present graphic examples of the overstatement of the "need" for confessions. In each case authorities conducted interrogations ranging up to five days in duration despite the presence, through standard investigating practices, of considerable evidence against each defendant.[51] Further examples are chronicled in our prior cases. See, e.g., *Haynes v. Washington*, 373 U.S. 503, 518–519 (1963); *Rogers v. Richmond*, 365 U.S. 534, 541 (1961); *Malinski v. New York*, 324 U.S. 401, 402 (1945).[52]

It is also urged that an unfettered right to detention for interrogation should be allowed because it will often redound to the benefit of the person questioned. When police inquiry determines that there is no reason to believe that the person has committed any crime, it is said, he will be released without need for further formal procedures. The person who has committed no offense, however, will be better able to clear himself after warnings with counsel present than without. It can be assumed that in such circumstances a lawyer would advise his client to talk freely to police in order to clear himself.

Custodial interrogation, by contrast, does not necessarily afford the innocent an opportunity to clear themselves. A serious consequence of the present practice of the interrogation alleged to be beneficial for the innocent is that many arrests "for investigation" subject large numbers of innocent persons to detention and interrogation. In one of the cases before us, No. 584, *California v. Stewart*, police held four persons, who were in the defendant's house at the time of the arrest, in jail for five days until defendant confessed. At that time they were finally released. Police stated that there was "no evidence to connect them with any crime." Available statistics on the extent of this practice where it is condoned indicate that these four are far from alone in being subjected to arrest, prolonged detention, and interrogation without the requisite probable cause.[53] [384 U.S. 436, 483].

Over the years the Federal Bureau of Investigation has compiled an exemplary record of effective law enforcement while advising any suspect or arrested person, at the outset of an interview, that he is not required to make a statement, that any statement may be used against him in court, that the individual may obtain the services of an attorney of his own choice and, more recently, that he has a right to free counsel if he is unable to pay.[54] A letter received from the Solicitor General in response to a question from the Bench makes it clear that the present pattern of warnings and respect for the [384 U.S. 436, 484] rights of the individual followed as a practice by the FBI is consistent with the procedure which we delineate today. It states:

"At the oral argument of the above cause, Mr. Justice Fortas asked whether I could provide certain information as to the practices followed by the Federal Bureau of Investigation. I have directed these questions to the attention of the Director of the Federal Bureau of Investigation and am submitting herewith a statement of the questions and of the answers which we have received.

"'(1) When an individual is interviewed by agents of the Bureau, what warning is given to him?

"'The standard warning long given by Special Agents of the FBI to both suspects and persons under arrest is that the person has a right to say nothing and a right to counsel, and that any statement he does make may be used against him in court. Examples of this warning are to be found in the *Westover* case at 342 F.2d 684 (1965), and *Jackson v. U.S.*, 337 F.2d 136 (1964), *cert. den.* 380 U.S. 935.

"'After passage of the Criminal Justice Act of 1964, which provides free counsel for Federal defendants unable to pay, we added to our instructions to Special Agents the requirement that any person who is under arrest for an offense under FBI jurisdiction, or whose arrest is contemplated following the interview, must also be advised of his right to free counsel if he is unable to pay, and the fact that such counsel will be assigned by the Judge. At the same time, we broadened the right to counsel warning [384 U.S. 436, 485] to read counsel of his own choice, or anyone else with whom he might wish to speak.

"'(2) When is the warning given?

"'The FBI warning is given to a suspect at the very outset of the interview, as shown in the Westover case, cited above. The warning may be given to a person arrested as soon as practicable after the arrest, as shown in the Jackson case, also cited above, and in *U.S. v. Konigsberg*, 336 F.2d 844 (1964), *cert. den.* 379 U.S. 933, but in any event it must precede the interview with the person for a confession or admission of his own guilt.

"'(3) What is the Bureau's practice in the event that (a) the individual requests counsel and (b) counsel appears?

"'When the person who has been warned of his right to counsel decides that he wishes to consult with counsel before making a statement, the interview is terminated at that point, *Shultz v. U.S.*, 351 F.2d 287 (1965). It may be continued, however, as to all matters other than the person's own guilt or innocence. If he is indecisive in his request for counsel, there may be some question on whether he did or did not waive counsel. Situations of this kind must necessarily be left to the judgment of the interviewing Agent. For example, in *Hiram v. U.S.*, 354 F.2d 4 (1965), the Agent's conclusion that the person arrested had waived his right to counsel was upheld by the courts.

"'A person being interviewed and desiring to consult counsel by telephone must be permitted to do so, as shown in *Caldwell v. U.S.*, 351 F.2d 459 (1965). When counsel appears in person, he is permitted to confer with his client in private. [384 U.S. 436, 486].

"'(4) What is the Bureau's practice if the individual requests counsel, but cannot afford to retain an attorney?

"'If any person being interviewed after warning of counsel decides that he wishes to consult with counsel before proceeding further the interview is terminated, as shown above. FBI Agents do not pass judgment on the ability of the person to pay for counsel. They do, however, advise those who have been arrested for an offense under FBI jurisdiction, or whose arrest is contemplated following the interview, of a right to free counsel if they are unable to pay, and the availability of such counsel from the Judge.'"[55]

The practice of the FBI can readily be emulated by state and local enforcement agencies. The argument that the FBI deals with different crimes than are dealt with by state authorities does not mitigate the significance of the FBI experience.[56]

(Continues)

(Continued)

The experience in some other countries also suggests that the danger to law enforcement in curbs on interrogation is overplayed. The English procedure since 1912 under the Judges' Rules is significant. As recently strengthened, the Rules require that a cautionary warning be given an accused by a police officer as soon as he has evidence that affords reasonable grounds for suspicion; they also require that any statement made be given by the accused without questioning by police.[57] The right of the individual to consult with an attorney during this period is expressly recognized.[58]

The safeguards present under Scottish law may be even greater than in England. Scottish judicial decisions bar use in evidence of most confessions obtained through police interrogation.[59] In India, confessions made to police not in the presence of a magistrate have been excluded by rule of evidence since 1872, at a time when it operated under British law.[60] Identical provisions appear in the Evidence Ordinance of Ceylon, enacted in 1895.[61] Similarly, in our country the Uniform Code of Military Justice has long provided that no suspect may be interrogated without first being warned of his right not to make a statement and that any statement he makes may be used against him.[62] Denial of the right to consult counsel during interrogation has also been proscribed by military tribunals.[63] There appears to have been no marked detrimental effect on criminal law enforcement in these jurisdictions as a result of these rules. Conditions of law enforcement in our country are sufficiently similar to permit reference to this experience as assurance that lawlessness will not result from warning an individual of his rights or allowing him to exercise them. Moreover, it is consistent with our legal system that we give at least as much protection to these rights as is given in the jurisdictions described. We deal in our country with rights grounded in a specific requirement of the Fifth Amendment of the Constitution, [384 U.S. 436, 490] whereas other jurisdictions arrived at their conclusions on the basis of principles of justice not so specifically defined.[64]

It is also urged upon us that we withhold decision on this issue until state legislative bodies and advisory groups have had an opportunity to deal with these problems by rule making.[65] We have already pointed out that the Constitution does not require any specific code of procedures for protecting the privilege against self-incrimination during custodial interrogation. Congress and the States are free to develop their own safeguards for the privilege, so long as they are fully as effective as those described above in informing accused persons of their right of silence and in affording a continuous opportunity to exercise it. In any event, however, the issues presented are of constitutional dimensions and must be determined by the courts. The admissibility of a statement in the face of a claim that it was obtained in violation of the defendant's constitutional rights is an issue the resolution of which has long since been undertaken by this Court. See *Hopt v. Utah*, 110 U.S. 574 (1884). Judicial solutions to problems of constitutional dimension have evolved decade by decade. As courts have been presented with the need to enforce constitutional rights, they have found means of doing so. That was our responsibility when Escobedo was before us and it is our responsibility today. Where rights secured by the Constitution are involved, there can be no rule making or legislation which would abrogate them.

V

Because of the nature of the problem and because of its recurrent significance in numerous cases, we have to this point discussed the relationship of the Fifth Amendment privilege to police interrogation without specific concentration on the facts of the cases before us. We turn now to these facts to consider the application to these cases of the constitutional principles discussed above. In each instance, we have concluded that statements were obtained from the defendant under circumstances that did not meet constitutional standards for protection of the privilege.

No. 759. *Miranda v. Arizona.*

On March 13, 1963, petitioner, Ernesto Miranda, was arrested at his home and taken in custody to a Phoenix police station. He was there identified by the complaining witness. The police then took him to "Interrogation Room No. 2" of the detective bureau. There he was questioned by two police officers. The officers admitted at trial that Miranda was not advised that he had a right to have an attorney present.[66] Two hours later, the officers emerged from the interrogation room with a written confession signed by Miranda. At the top of the statement was a typed paragraph stating that the confession was made voluntarily, without threats or promises of immunity and "with full knowledge of my legal rights, understanding any statement I make may be used against me."[67]

At his trial before a jury, the written confession was admitted into evidence over the objection of defense counsel, and the officers testified to the prior oral confession made by Miranda during the interrogation. Miranda was found guilty of kidnapping and rape. He was sentenced to 20 to 30 years' imprisonment on each count, the sentences to run concurrently. On appeal, the Supreme Court of Arizona held that Miranda's constitutional rights were not violated in obtaining the confession and affirmed the conviction. 98 Ariz. 18, 401 P.2d 721. In reaching its decision, the court emphasized heavily the fact that Miranda did not specifically request counsel.

We reverse. From the testimony of the officers and by the admission of respondent, it is clear that Miranda was not in any way apprised of his right to consult with an attorney and to have one present during the interrogation, nor was his right not to be compelled to incriminate himself effectively protected in any other manner. Without these warnings the statements were inadmissible. The mere fact that he signed a statement which contained a typed-in clause stating that he had "full knowledge" of his "legal rights" does not approach the knowing and intelligent waiver required to relinquish constitutional rights. Cf. *Haynes v. Washington*, 373 U.S. 503, 512–513 (1963); *Haley v. Ohio*, 332 U.S. 596, 601 (1948) (opinion of MR. JUSTICE DOUGLAS).

No. 760. *Vignera v. New York*.

Petitioner, Michael Vignera, was picked up by New York police on October 14, 1960, in connection with the robbery three days earlier of a Brooklyn dress shop. They took him to the 17th Detective Squad headquarters in Manhattan. Sometime thereafter he was taken to the 66th Detective Squad. There a detective questioned Vignera with respect to the robbery. Vignera orally admitted the robbery to the detective. The detective was asked on cross-examination at trial by defense counsel whether Vignera was warned of his right to counsel before being interrogated. The prosecution objected to the question and the trial judge sustained the objection. Thus, the defense was precluded from making any showing that warnings had not been given. While at the 66th Detective Squad, Vignera was identified by the store owner and a saleslady as the man who robbed the dress shop. At about 3 P.M. he was formally arrested. The police then transported him to still another station, the 70th Precinct in Brooklyn, "for detention." At 11 P.M. Vignera was questioned by an assistant district attorney in the presence of a hearing reporter who transcribed the questions and Vignera's answers. This verbatim account of these proceedings contains no statement of any warnings given by the assistant district attorney. At Vignera's trial on a charge of first degree robbery, the detective testified as to the oral confession. The transcription of the statement taken was also introduced in evidence. At the conclusion of the testimony, the trial judge charged the jury in part as follows:

> "The law doesn't say that the confession is void or invalidated because the police officer didn't advise the defendant as to his rights. Did you hear what [384 U.S. 436, 494] I said? I am telling you what the law of the State of New York is."

Vignera was found guilty of first degree robbery. He was subsequently adjudged a third-felony offender and sentenced to 30 to 60 years' imprisonment.[68] The conviction was affirmed without opinion by the Appellate Division, Second Department, 21 App. Div. 2d 752, 252 N.Y.S. 2d 19, and by the Court of Appeals, also without opinion, 15 N.Y. 2d 970, 207 N.E. 2d 527, 259 N.Y.S. 2d 857, *remittitur* amended, 16 N.Y. 2d 614, 209 N.E. 2d 110, 261 N.Y.S. 2d 65. In argument to the Court of Appeals, the State contended that Vignera had no constitutional right to be advised of his right to counsel or his privilege against self-incrimination.

We reverse. The foregoing indicates that Vignera was not warned of any of his rights before the questioning by the detective and by the assistant district attorney. No other steps were taken to protect these rights. Thus he was not effectively apprised of his Fifth Amendment privilege or of his right to have counsel present and his statements are inadmissible.

No. 761. *Westover v. United States*.

At approximately 9:45 P.M. on March 20, 1963, petitioner, Carl Calvin Westover, was arrested by local police in Kansas City as a suspect in two Kansas City robberies. A report was also received from the FBI that he was wanted on a felony charge in California. The local authorities took him to a police station and placed him in a line-up on the local charges, and at about 11:45 P.M. he was booked. Kansas City police interrogated Westover [384 U.S. 436, 495] on the night of his arrest. He denied any knowledge of criminal activities. The next day local officers interrogated him again throughout the morning. Shortly before noon they informed the FBI that they were through interrogating Westover and that the FBI could proceed to interrogate him. There is nothing in the record to indicate that Westover was

(Continues)

ever given any warning as to his rights by local police. At noon, three special agents of the FBI continued the interrogation in a private interview room of the Kansas City Police Department, this time with respect to the robbery of a savings and loan association and a bank in Sacramento, California. After two or two and one-half hours, Westover signed separate confessions to each of these two robberies which had been prepared by one of the agents during the interrogation. At trial one of the agents testified, and a paragraph on each of the statements states, that the agents advised Westover that he did not have to make a statement, that any statement he made could be used against him, and that he had the right to see an attorney.

Westover was tried by a jury in federal court and convicted of the California robberies. His statements were introduced at trial. He was sentenced to 15 years' imprisonment on each count, the sentences to run consecutively. On appeal, the conviction was affirmed by the Court of Appeals for the Ninth Circuit. 342 F.2d 684.

We reverse. On the facts of this case we cannot find that Westover knowingly and intelligently waived his right to remain silent and his right to consult with counsel prior to the time he made the statement.[69] At the [384 U.S. 436, 496] time the FBI Agents began questioning Westover, he had been in custody for over 14 hours and had been interrogated at length during that period. The FBI interrogation began immediately upon the conclusion of the interrogation by Kansas City police and was conducted in local police headquarters. Although the two law enforcement authorities are legally distinct and the crimes for which they interrogated Westover were different, the impact on him was that of a continuous period of questioning. There is no evidence of any warning given prior to the FBI interrogation nor is there any evidence of an articulated waiver of rights after the FBI commenced its interrogation. The record simply shows that the defendant did in fact confess a short time after being turned over to the FBI following interrogation by local police. Despite the fact that the FBI Agents gave warnings at the outset of their interview, from Westover's point of view the warnings came at the end of the interrogation process. In these circumstances an intelligent waiver of constitutional rights cannot be assumed.

We do not suggest that law enforcement authorities are precluded from questioning any individual who has been held for a period of time by other authorities and interrogated by them without appropriate warnings. A different case would be presented if an accused were taken into custody by the second authority, removed both in time and place from his original surroundings, and then adequately advised of his rights and given an opportunity to exercise them. But here the FBI interrogation was conducted immediately following the state interrogation in the same police station—in the same compelling surroundings. Thus, in obtaining a confession from Westover [384 U.S. 436, 497] the federal authorities were the beneficiaries of the pressure applied by the local in-custody interrogation. In these circumstances the giving of warnings alone was not sufficient to protect the privilege.

No. 584. *California v. Stewart.*

In the course of investigating a series of purse-snatch robberies in which one of the victims had died of injuries inflicted by her assailant, respondent, Roy Allen Stewart, was pointed out to Los Angeles police as the endorser of dividend checks taken in one of the robberies. At about 7:15 P.M., January 31, 1963, police officers went to Stewart's house and arrested him. One of the officers asked Stewart if they could search the house, to which he replied, "Go ahead." The search turned up various items taken from the five robbery victims. At the time of Stewart's arrest, police also arrested Stewart's wife and three other persons who were visiting him. These four were jailed along with Stewart and were interrogated. Stewart was taken to the University Station of the Los Angeles Police Department where he was placed in a cell. During the next five days, police interrogated Stewart on nine different occasions. Except during the first interrogation session, when he was confronted with an accusing witness, Stewart was isolated with his interrogators.

During the ninth interrogation session, Stewart admitted that he had robbed the deceased and stated that he had not meant to hurt her. Police then brought Stewart before a magistrate for the first time. Since there was no evidence to connect them with any crime, the police then released the other four persons arrested with him.

Nothing in the record specifically indicates whether Stewart was or was not advised of his right to remain silent or his right to counsel. In a number of instances, [384 U.S. 436, 498] however, the interrogating officers were asked to recount everything that was said during the interrogations. None indicated that Stewart was ever advised of his rights.

Stewart was charged with kidnapping to commit robbery, rape, and murder. At his trial, transcripts of the first interrogation and the confession at the last interrogation were introduced in evidence.

The jury found Stewart guilty of robbery and first degree murder and fixed the penalty as death. On appeal, the Supreme Court of California reversed. 62 Cal. 2d 571, 400 P.2d 97, 43 Cal. Rptr. 201. It held that under this Court's decision in Escobedo, Stewart should have been advised of his right to remain silent and of his right to counsel and that it would not presume in the face of a silent record that the police advised Stewart of his rights.[70]

We affirm.[71] In dealing with custodial interrogation, we will not presume that a defendant has been effectively apprised of his rights and that his privilege against self-incrimination has been adequately safeguarded on a record that does not show that any warnings have been given or that any effective alternative has been employed. Nor can a knowing and intelligent waiver of [384 U.S. 436, 499] these rights be assumed on a silent record. Furthermore, Stewart's steadfast denial of the alleged offenses through eight of the nine interrogations over a period of five days is subject to no other construction than that he was compelled by persistent interrogation to forgo his Fifth Amendment privilege.

Therefore, in accordance with the foregoing, the judgments of the Supreme Court of Arizona in No. 759, of the New York Court of Appeals in No. 760, and of the Court of Appeals for the Ninth Circuit in No. 761 are reversed. The judgment of the Supreme Court of California in No. 584 is affirmed.

It is so ordered.

Notes

1. Compare *United States v. Childress*, 347 F.2d 448 (C.A. 7th Cir. 1965), with *Collins v. Beto*, 348 F.2d 823 (C.A. 5th Cir. 1965). Compare *People v. Dorado*, 62 Cal. 2d 338, 398 P.2d 361, 42 Cal. Rptr. 169 (1964) with *People v. Hartgraves*, 31 Ill. 2d 375, 202 N.E. 2d 33 (1964).

2. See, e.g., Enker & Elsen, Counsel for the Suspect: *Massiah v. United States* and *Escobedo v. Illinois*, 49 Minn. L. Rev. 47 (1964); Herman, *The Supreme Court and Restrictions on Police Interrogation*, 25 Ohio St. L. J. 449 (1964); Kamisar, Equal Justice in the Gatehouses and Mansions of American Criminal Procedure, in *Criminal Justice in Our Time*, 1 (1965); Dowling, Escobedo and Beyond: The Need for a Fourteenth Amendment Code of Criminal Procedure, 56 *J. Crim. L., C. & P. S.* 143, 156 (1965).

   The complex problems also prompted discussions by jurists. Compare Bazelon, Law, Morality, and Civil Liberties, 12 *U.C.L.A.L. Rev.*, 13 (1964), with Friendly, The Bill of Rights as a Code of Criminal Procedure, 53 *Calif. L. Rev.* 929 (1965).

3. For example, the Los Angeles Police Chief stated that "If the police are required . . . to . . . establish that the defendant was apprised of his constitutional guarantees of silence and legal counsel prior to the uttering of any admission or confession, and that he intelligently waived these guarantees . . . a whole Pandora's box is opened as to under what circumstances . . . can a defendant intelligently waive these rights . . . Allegations that modern criminal investigation can compensate for the lack of a confession or admission in every criminal case is totally absurd!" Parker, 40 *L.A. Bar Bull.* 603, 607, 642 (1965). His prosecutorial counterpart, District Attorney Younger, stated that "[I]t begins to appear that many of these seemingly restrictive decisions are going to contribute directly to a more effective, efficient and professional level of law enforcement." *L.A. Times*, Oct. 2, 1965, p. 1. The former Police Commissioner of New York, Michael J. Murphy, stated of Escobedo: "What the Court is doing is akin to requiring one boxer to fight by Marquis of Queensbury rules while permitting the other to butt, gouge and bite." *N.Y. Times*, May 14, 1965, p. 39. The former United States Attorney for the District of Columbia, David C. Acheson, who is presently Special Assistant to the Secretary of the Treasury (for Enforcement), and directly in charge of the Secret Service and the Bureau of Narcotics, observed that "Prosecution procedure has, at most, only the most remote causal connection with crime. Changes in court decisions and prosecution procedure would have about the same effect on the crime rate as an aspirin would have on a tumor of the brain." Quoted in Herman, *supra*, n. 2, at 500, n. 270. Other views on the subject in general are collected in Weisberg, Police Interrogation of Arrested Persons: A Skeptical View, 52 *J. Crim. L., C. & P. S.* 21 (1961).

4. This is what we meant in *Escobedo* when we spoke of an investigation which had focused on an accused.

5. See, for example, IV National Commission on Law Observance and Enforcement, *Report on Lawlessness in Law Enforcement* (1931) [*Wickersham Report*]; Booth, Confessions, and Methods Employed in Procuring Them, 4 *So. Calif. L. Rev.* 83 (1930); Kauper, Judicial Examination of the Accused—A Remedy for the Third Degree, 30 *Mich. L. Rev.* 1224 (1932). It is significant that instances of third-degree treatment of prisoners almost invariably took place during the period between arrest and preliminary examination. *Wickersham Report*, at 169; Hall, The Law of Arrest

(Continues)

(*Continued*)

in Relation to Contemporary Social Problems, 3 *U. Chi. L. Rev.* 345, 357 (1936). See also Foote, Law and Police Practice: Safeguards in the Law of Arrest, 52 *Nw. U. L. Rev.* 16 (1957).

6. *Brown v. Mississippi*, 297 U.S. 278 (1936); *Chambers v. Florida*, 309 U.S. 227 (1940); *Canty v. Alabama*, 309 U.S. 629 (1940); *White v. Texas*, 310 U.S. 530 (1940); *Vernon v. Alabama*, 313 U.S. 547 (1941); *Ward v. Texas*, 316 U.S. 547 (1942); *Ashcraft v. Tennessee*, 322 U.S. 143 (1944); *Malinski v. New York*, 324 U.S. 401 (1945); *Leyra v. Denno*, 347 U.S. 556 (1954). See also *Williams v. United States*, 341 U.S. 97 (1951).

7. In addition, see *People v. Wakat*, 415 Ill. 610, 114 N.E. 2d 706 (1953); *Wakat v. Harlib*, 253 F.2d 59 (C.A. 7th Cir. 1958) (defendant suffering from broken bones, multiple bruises and injuries sufficiently serious to require eight months' medical treatment after being manhandled by five policemen); *Kier v. State*, 213 Md. 556, 132 A. 2d 494 (1957) (police doctor told accused, who was strapped to a chair completely nude, that he proposed to take hair and skin scrapings from anything that looked like blood or sperm from various parts of his body); *Bruner v. People*, 113 Colo. 194, 156 P.2d 111 (1945) (defendant held in custody over two months, deprived of food for 15 hours, forced to submit to a lie detector test when he wanted to go to the toilet); *People v. Matlock*, 51 Cal. 2d 682, 336 P.2d 505 (1959) (defendant questioned incessantly over an evening's time, made to lie on cold board and to answer questions whenever it appeared he was getting sleepy). Other cases are documented in American Civil Liberties Union, Illinois Division, *Secret Detention by the Chicago Police* (1959); Potts, The Preliminary Examination and "The Third Degree," 2 *Baylor L. Rev.* 131 (1950); Sterling, Police Interrogation and the Psychology of Confession, 14 *J. Pub. L.* 25 (1965).

8. The manuals quoted in the text following are the most recent and representative of the texts currently available. Material of the same nature appears in Kidd, *Police Interrogation* (1940); Mulbar, *Interrogation* (1951); Dienstein, *Technics for the Crime Investigator*, 97–115 (1952). Studies concerning the observed practices of the police appear in LaFave, *Arrest: The Decision To Take a Suspect Into Custody*, 244–437, 490–521 (1965); LaFave, Detention for Investigation by the Police: An Analysis of Current Practices, 1962 *Wash. U.L.Q.* 331; Barrett, Police Practices and the Law— From Arrest to Release or Charge, 50 *Calif. L. Rev.* 11 (1962); Sterling, *supra*, n. 7, at 47–65.

9. The methods described in Inbau & Reid, *Criminal Interrogation and Confessions* (1962), are a revision and enlargement of material presented in three prior editions of a predecessor text, *Lie Detection and Criminal Interrogation* (3d ed. 1953). The authors and their associates are officers of the Chicago Police Scientific Crime Detection Laboratory and have had extensive experience in writing, lecturing and speaking to law enforcement authorities over a 20-year period. They say that the techniques portrayed in their manuals reflect their experiences and are the most effective psychological stratagems to employ during interrogations. Similarly, the techniques described in O'Hara, *Fundamentals of Criminal Investigation* (1956), were gleaned from long service as observer, lecturer in police science, and work as a federal criminal investigator. All these texts have had rather extensive use among law enforcement agencies and among students of police science, with total sales and circulation of over 44,000.

10. Inbau & Reid, *Criminal Interrogation and Confessions* (1962), at 1.

11. O'Hara, *supra*, at 99.

12. Inbau & Reid, *supra*, at 34–43, 87. For example, in *Leyra v. Denno*, 347 U.S. 556 (1954), the interrogator–psychiatrist told the accused, "We do sometimes things that are not right, but in a fit of temper or anger we sometimes do things we aren't really responsible for," *id.*, at 562, and again, "We know that morally you were just in anger. Morally, you are not to be condemned," *id.*, at 582.

13. Inbau & Reid, *supra*, at 43–55.

14. O'Hara, *supra*, at 112.

15. Inbau & Reid, *supra*, at 40.

16. Ibid.

17. O'Hara, *supra*, at 104, Inbau & Reid, *supra*, at 58–59. See *Spano v. New York*, 360 U.S. 315 (1959). A variant on the technique of creating hostility is one of engendering fear. This is perhaps best described by the prosecuting attorney in *Malinski v. New York*, 324 U.S. 401, 407 (1945): "Why this talk about being undressed? Of course, they had a right to undress him to look for bullet scars, and keep the clothes off him. That was quite proper police procedure. That is some more psychology— let him sit around with a blanket on him, humiliate him there for a while; let him sit in the corner, let him think he is going to get a shellacking."

18. O'Hara, *supra*, at 105–106.

19. *Id.*, at 106.

20. Inbau & Reid, *supra*, at 111.

21. Ibid.

22. Inbau & Reid, *supra*, at 112.

23. Inbau & Reid, *Lie Detection and Criminal Interrogation* 185 (3d ed. 1953).

24. Interrogation procedures may even give rise to a false confession. The most recent conspicuous example occurred in New York, in 1964, when a Negro of limited intelligence confessed to two brutal murders and a rape which he had not committed. When this was discovered, the prosecutor was reported as saying: "Call it what you want—brain-washing, hypnosis, fright. They made him give an untrue confession. The only thing I don't believe is that Whitmore was beaten." *N.Y. Times*, Jan. 28, 1965, p. 1, col. 5. In two other instances, similar events had occurred. *N.Y. Times*, Oct. 20, 1964, p. 22, col. 1; *N.Y. Times*, Aug. 25, 1965, p. 1, col. 1. In general, see Borchard, *Convicting the Innocent* (1932); Frank & Frank, *Not Guilty* (1957).

25. In the fourth confession case decided by the Court in the 1962 Term, *Fay v. Noia*, 372 U.S. 391 (1963), our disposition made it unnecessary to delve at length into the facts. The facts of the defendant's case there, however, paralleled those of his co-defendants, whose confessions were found to have resulted from continuous and coercive interrogation for 27 hours, with denial of requests for friends or attorney. See *United States v. Murphy*, 222 F.2d 698 (C.A. 2d Cir. 1955) (Frank, J.); *People v. Bonino*, 1 N.Y. 2d 752, 135 N.E. 2d 51 (1956).

26. The absurdity of denying that a confession obtained under these circumstances is compelled is aptly portrayed by an example in Professor Sutherland's recent article, Crime and Confession, 79 *Harv. L. Rev.* 21, 37 (1965):

> "Suppose a well-to-do testatrix says she intends to will her property to Elizabeth. John and James want her to bequeath it to them instead. They capture the testatrix, put her in a carefully designed room, out of touch with everyone but themselves and their convenient 'witnesses,' keep her secluded there for hours while they make insistent demands, weary her with contradictions of her assertions that she wants to leave her money to Elizabeth, and finally induce her to execute the will in their favor. Assume that John and James are deeply and correctly convinced that Elizabeth is unworthy and will make base use of the property if she gets her hands on it, whereas John and James have the noblest and most righteous intentions. Would any judge of probate accept the will so procured as the 'voluntary' act of the testatrix?"

27. Thirteenth century commentators found an analogue to the privilege grounded in the Bible. "To sum up the matter, the principle that no man is to be declared guilty on his own admission is a divine decree." Maimonides, Mishneh Torah (Code of Jewish Law), Book of Judges, Laws of the Sanhedrin, c. 18, 6, III *Yale Judaica Series* 52–53. See also Lamm, The Fifth Amendment and Its Equivalent in the Halakhah, 5 *Judaism* 53 (Winter 1956).

28. See Morgan, The Privilege Against Self-Incrimination, 34 *Minn. L. Rev.* 1, 9–11 (1949); 8 Wigmore, *Evidence* 289–295 (McNaughton rev. 1961). See also Lowell, The Judicial Use of Torture, Parts I and II, 11 *Harv. L. Rev.* 220, 290 (1897).

29. See Pittman, The Colonial and Constitutional History of the Privilege Against Self-Incrimination in America, 21 *Va. L. Rev.* 763 (1935); *Ullmann v. United States*, 350 U.S. 422, 445–449 (1956) (DOUGLAS, J., dissenting).

30. Compare *Brown v. Walker*, 161 U.S. 591 (1896); *Quinn v. United States*, 349 U.S. 155 (1955).

31. Brief for the United States, p. 28. To the same effect, see Brief for the United States, pp. 40–49, n. 44, *Anderson v. United States*, 318 U.S. 350 (1943); Brief for the United States, pp. 17–18, *McNabb v. United States*, 318 U.S. 332 (1943).

32. Our decision today does not indicate in any manner, of course, that these rules can be disregarded. When federal officials arrest an individual, they must as always comply with the dictates of the congressional legislation and cases thereunder. See generally, Hogan & Snee, The McNabb-Mallory Rule: Its Rise, Rationale and Rescue, 47 *Geo. L. J.* 1 (1958).

33. The decisions of this Court have guaranteed the same procedural protection for the defendant whether his confession was used in a federal or state court. It is now axiomatic that the defendant's constitutional rights have been violated if his conviction is based, in whole or in part, on an involuntary confession, regardless of its truth or falsity. *Rogers v. Richmond*, 365 U.S. 534, 544 (1961); *Wan v. United States*, 266 U.S. 1 (1924). This is so even if there is ample evidence aside from the confession to support the conviction, e.g., *Malinski v. New York*, 324 U.S. 401, 404 (1945); *Bram v. United States*, 168 U.S. 532, 540–542 (1897). Both state and federal courts now adhere to trial procedures which seek to assure a reliable and clear-cut determination of the voluntariness of the confession offered at trial, *Jackson v. Denno*, 378 U.S. 368 (1964); *United States v. Carignan*, 342 U.S. 36, 38 (1951); see also *Wilson v. United States*, 162 U.S. 613, 624 (1896). Appellate review is exacting,

(Continues)

see *Haynes v. Washington*, 373 U.S. 503 (1963); *Blackburn v. Alabama*, 361 U.S. 199 (1960). Whether his conviction was in a federal or state court, the defendant may secure a post-conviction hearing based on the alleged involuntary character of his confession, provided he meets the procedural requirements, *Fay v. Noia*, 372 U.S. 391 (1963); *Townsend v. Sain*, 372 U.S. 293 (1963). In addition, see *Murphy v. Waterfront Comm'n*, 378 U.S. 52 (1964).

34. See *Lisenba v. California*, 314 U.S. 219, 241 (1941); *Ashcraft v. Tennessee*, 322 U.S. 143 (1944); *Malinski v. New York*, 324 U.S. 401 (1945); *Spano v. New York*, 360 U.S. 315 (1959); *Lynumn v. Illinois*, 372 U.S. 528 (1963); *Haynes v. Washington*, 373 U.S. 503 (1963).

35. The police also prevented the attorney from consulting with his client. Independent of any other constitutional proscription, this action constitutes a violation of the Sixth Amendment right to the assistance of counsel and excludes any statement obtained in its wake. See *People v. Donovan*, 13 N.Y. 2d 148, 193 N.E. 2d 628, 243 N.Y.S. 2d 841 (1963) (Fuld, J.).

36. *In re Groban*, 352 U.S. 330, 340–352 (1957) (BLACK, J., dissenting); Note, 73 *Yale L. J.* 1000, 1048–1051 (1964); Comment, 31 *U. Chi. L. Rev.* 313, 320 (1964) and authorities cited.

37. See p. 454, *supra*. Lord Devlin has commented:

> "It is probable that even today, when there is much less ignorance about these matters than formerly, there is still a general belief that you must answer all questions put to you by a policeman, or at least that it will be the worse for you if you do not." Devlin, *The Criminal Prosecution in England*, 32 (1958).

In accord with our decision today, it is impermissible to penalize an individual for exercising his Fifth Amendment privilege when he is under police custodial interrogation. The prosecution may not, therefore, use at trial the fact that he stood mute or claimed his privilege in the face of accusation. Cf. *Griffin v. California*, 380 U.S. 609 (1965); *Malloy v. Hogan*, 378 U.S. 1, 8 (1964); Comment, 31 *U. Chi. L. Rev.* 556 (1964); Developments in the Law—Confessions, 79 *Harv. L. Rev.* 935, 1041–1044 (1966). See also *Bram v. United States*, 168 U.S. 532, 562 (1897).

38. Cf. *Betts v. Brady*, 316 U.S. 455 (1942), and the recurrent inquiry into special circumstances it necessitated. See generally, Kamisar, *Betts v. Brady* Twenty Years Later: The Right to Counsel and Due Process Values, 61 *Mich. L. Rev.* 219 (1962).

39. See Herman, The Supreme Court and Restrictions on Police Interrogation, 25 *Ohio St. L. J.* 449, 480 (1964).

40. Estimates of 50–90% indigency among felony defendants have been reported. Pollock, Equal Justice in Practice, 45 *Minn. L. Rev.* 737, 738–739 (1961); Birzon, Kasanof & Forma, The Right to Counsel and the Indigent Accused in Courts of Criminal Jurisdiction in New York State, 14 *Buffalo L. Rev.* 428, 433 (1965).

41. See Kamisar, Equal Justice in the Gatehouses and Mansions of American Criminal Procedure, in *Criminal Justice in Our Time* 1, 64–81 (1965). As was stated in the *Report of the Attorney General's Committee on Poverty and the Administration of Federal Criminal Justice* 9 (1963):

> "When government chooses to exert its powers in the criminal area, its obligation is surely no less than that of taking reasonable measures to eliminate those factors that are irrelevant to just administration of the law but which, nevertheless, may occasionally affect determinations of the accused's liability or penalty. While government may not be required to relieve the accused of his poverty, it may properly be required to minimize the influence of poverty on its administration of justice."

42. Cf. *United States ex rel. Brown v. Fay*, 242 F. Supp. 273, 277 (D.C. S.D. N.Y. 1965); *People v. Witenski*, 15 N.Y. 2d 392, 207 N.E. 2d 358, 259 N.Y.S. 2d 413 (1965).

43. While a warning that the indigent may have counsel appointed need not be given to the person who is known to have an attorney or is known to have ample funds to secure one, the expedient of giving a warning is too simple and the rights involved too important to engage in *ex post facto* inquiries into financial ability when there is any doubt at all on that score.

44. If an individual indicates his desire to remain silent, but has an attorney present, there may be some circumstances in which further questioning would be permissible. In the absence of evidence of overbearing, statements then made in the presence of counsel might be free of the compelling influence of the interrogation process and might fairly be construed as a waiver of the privilege for purposes of these statements.

45. Although this Court held in *Rogers v. United States*, 340 U.S. 367 (1951), over strong dissent, that a witness before a grand jury may not in certain circumstances decide to answer some questions and then refuse to answer others, that decision has no application to the interrogation situation we deal with today. No legislative or judicial fact-finding authority is involved here, nor is there a possibility that the individual might make self-serving statements of which he could make use at trial while refusing to answer incriminating statements.

46. The distinction and its significance has been aptly described in the opinion of a Scottish court:

"In former times such questioning, if undertaken, would be conducted by police officers visiting the house or place of business of the suspect and there questioning him, probably in the presence of a relation or friend. However convenient the modern practice may be, it must normally create a situation very unfavorable to the suspect." *Chalmers v. H. M. Advocate*, 1954. Sess. Cas. 66, 78 (J.C.).

47. See *People v. Dorado*, 62 Cal. 2d 338, 354, 398 P.2d 361, 371, 42 Cal. Rptr. 169, 179 (1965).

48. In accordance with our holdings today and in *Escobedo v. Illinois*, 378 U.S. 478, 492, *Crooker v. California*, 357 U.S. 433 (1958) and *Cicenia v. Lagay*, 357 U.S. 504 (1958) are not to be followed.

49. In quoting the above from the dissenting opinion of Mr. Justice Brandeis we, of course, do not intend to pass on the constitutional questions involved in the Olmstead case.

50. Schaefer, Federalism and State Criminal Procedure, 70 *Harv. L. Rev.* 1, 26 (1956).

51. Miranda, Vignera, and Westover were identified by eyewitnesses. Marked bills from the bank robbed were found in Westover's car. Articles stolen from the victim as well as from several other robbery victims were found in Stewart's home at the outset of the investigation.

52. Dealing as we do here with constitutional standards in relation to statements made, the existence of independent corroborating evidence produced at trial is, of course, irrelevant to our decisions. *Haynes v. Washington*, 373 U.S. 503, 518–519 (1963); *Lynumn v. Illinois*, 372 U.S. 528, 537–538 (1963); *Rogers v. Richmond*, 365 U.S. 534, 541 (1961); *Blackburn v. Alabama*, 361 U.S. 199, 206 (1960).

53. See, e.g., *Report and Recommendations of the [District of Columbia] Commissioners' Committee on Police Arrests for Investigation* (1962); American Civil Liberties Union, *Secret Detention by the Chicago Police* (1959). An extreme example of this practice occurred in the District of Columbia in 1958. Seeking three "stocky" young Negroes who had robbed a restaurant, police rounded up 90 persons of that general description. Sixty-three were held overnight before being released for lack of evidence. A man not among the 90 arrested was ultimately charged with the crime. *Washington Daily News*, January 21, 1958, p. 5, col. 1; Hearings before a Subcommittee of the Senate Judiciary Committee on H. R. 11477, S. 2970, S. 3325, and S. 3355, 85th Cong., 2d Sess. (July 1958), pp. 40, 78.

54. In 1952, J. Edgar Hoover, Director of the Federal Bureau of Investigation, stated:

"Law enforcement, however, in defeating the criminal, must maintain inviolate the historic liberties of the individual. To turn back the criminal, yet, by so doing, destroy the dignity of the individual, would be a hollow victory.

. . .

"We can have the Constitution, the best laws in the land, and the most honest reviews by courts—but unless the law enforcement profession is steeped in the democratic tradition, maintains the highest in ethics, and makes its work a career of honor, civil liberties will continually—and without end—be violated. . . . The best protection of civil liberties is an alert, intelligent and honest law enforcement agency. There can be no alternative.

. . .

". . . Special Agents are taught that any suspect or arrested person, at the outset of an interview, must be advised that he is not required to make a statement and that any statement given can be used against him in court. Moreover, the individual must be informed that, if he desires, he may obtain the services of an attorney of his own choice."

Hoover, Civil Liberties and Law Enforcement: The Role of the FBI, 37 *Iowa L. Rev.* 175, 177–182 (1952).

55. We agree that the interviewing agent must exercise his judgment in determining whether the individual waives his right to counsel. Because of the constitutional basis of the right, however, the standard for waiver is necessarily high. And, of course, the ultimate responsibility for resolving this constitutional question lies with the courts.

56. Among the crimes within the enforcement jurisdiction of the FBI are kidnapping, 18 U.S.C. 1201 (1964 ed.), white slavery, 18 U.S.C. 2421–2423 (1964 ed.), bank robbery, 18 U.S.C. 2113 (1964 ed.), interstate transportation and sale of stolen property, 18 U.S.C. 2311–2317 (1964 ed.), all manner of conspiracies, 18 U.S.C. 371 (1964 ed.), and violations of civil rights, 18 U.S.C. 241–242 (1964 ed.). See also 18 U.S.C. 1114 (1964 ed.) (murder of officer or employee of the United States).

(Continues)

57. 1964. *Crim. L. Rev.*, at 166–170. These Rules provide in part:

"II. As soon as a police officer has evidence which would afford reasonable grounds for suspecting that a person has committed an offence, he shall caution that person or cause him to be cautioned before putting to him any questions, or further questions, relating to that offence.

"The caution shall be in the following terms:

"'You are not obliged to say anything unless you wish to do so but what you say may be put into writing and given in evidence.'

"When after being cautioned a person is being questioned, or elects to make a statement, a record shall be kept of the time and place at which any such questioning or statement began and ended and of the persons present.

. . .

"III. . . .

. . .

"(b) It is only in exceptional cases that questions relating to the offence should be put to the accused person after he has been charged or informed that he may be prosecuted.

. . .

"IV. All written statements made after caution shall be taken in the following manner:

"(a) If a person says that he wants to make a statement he shall be told that it is intended to make a written record of what he says.

"He shall always be asked whether he wishes to write down himself what he wants to say; if he says that he cannot write or that he would like someone to write it for him, a police officer may offer to write the statement for him.

. . .

"(b) Any person writing his own statement shall be allowed to do so without any prompting as distinct from indicating to him what matters are material.

. . .

"(d) Whenever a police officer writes the statement, he shall take down the exact words spoken by the person making the statement, without putting any questions other than such as may be needed to [384 U.S. 436, 488] make the statement coherent, intelligible and relevant to the material matters: he shall not prompt him."

The prior Rules appear in Devlin, *The Criminal Prosecution in England*, 137–141 (1958).

Despite suggestions of some laxity in enforcement of the Rules and despite the fact some discretion as to admissibility is invested in the trial judge, the Rules are a significant influence in the English criminal law enforcement system. See, e.g., 1964. *Crim. L. Rev.*, at 182; and articles collected in 1960. *Crim. L. Rev.*, at 298–356.

58. The introduction to the Judges' Rules states in part:

"These Rules do not affect the principles

. . .

"(c) That every person at any stage of an investigation should be able to communicate and to consult privately with a solicitor. This is so even if he is in custody provided that in such a case no unreasonable delay or hindrance is caused to the processes of investigation or the administration of justice by his doing so ..." 1964. *Crim. L. Rev.*, at 166–167.

59. As stated by the Lord Justice General in *Chalmers v. H. M. Advocate*, 1954. Sess. Cas. 66, 78 (J.C.):

"The theory of our law is that at the stage of initial investigation the police may question anyone with a view to acquiring information which may lead to the detection of the criminal; but that, when the stage has been reached at which suspicion, or more than suspicion, has in their view centered upon some person as the likely perpetrator of the crime, further interrogation of that person becomes very dangerous, and, if carried too far, e.g., to the point of extracting a confession by what amounts to cross-examination, the evidence of that confession will almost certainly be excluded. Once the accused has been apprehended and charged he has the statutory right to a private interview with a solicitor and to be brought before a magistrate with all convenient speed so that he may, if so advised, emit a declaration in presence of his solicitor under conditions which safeguard him against prejudice."

60. "No confession made to a police officer shall be proved as against a person accused of any offence." Indian Evidence Act 25.

"No confession made by any person whilst he is in the custody of a police officer unless it be made in the immediate presence of a Magistrate, shall be proved as against such person." Indian Evidence Act 26. See 1 Ramaswami & Rajagopalan, *Law of Evidence in India*, 553–569 (1962). To avoid any continuing effect of police pressure or inducement, the Indian Supreme Court has invalidated a confession made shortly after police brought a suspect before a magistrate, suggesting: "[I]t would, we think, be reasonable to insist upon giving an accused person at least 24 hours to decide whether or not he should make a confession." *Sarwan Singh v. State of Punjab*, 44 All India Rep. 1957, Sup. Ct. 637, 644.

61. I *Legislative Enactments of Ceylon*, 211 (1958).

62. 10 U.S.C. 831 (b) (1964 ed.).

63. *United States v. Rose*, 24 CMR 251 (1957); *United States v. Gunnels*, 23 CMR 354 (1957).

64. Although no constitution existed at the time confessions were excluded by rule of evidence in 1872, India now has a written constitution which includes the provision that "No person accused of any offence shall be compelled to be a witness against himself." Constitution of India, Article 20 (3). See Tope, *The Constitution of India*, 63–67 (1960).

65. Brief for United States in No. 761, *Westover v. United States*, pp. 44–47; Brief for the State of New York as *amicus curiae*, pp. 35–39. See also Brief for the National District Attorneys Association as *amicus curiae*, pp. 23–26.

66. Miranda was also convicted in a separate trial on an unrelated robbery charge not presented here for review. A statement introduced at that trial was obtained from Miranda during the same interrogation which resulted in the confession involved here. At the robbery trial, one officer testified that during the interrogation he did not tell Miranda that anything he said would be held against him or that he could consult with an attorney. The other officer stated that they had both told Miranda that anything he said would be used against him and that he was not required by law to tell them anything.

67. One of the officers testified that he read this paragraph to Miranda. Apparently, however, he did not do so until after Miranda had confessed orally.

68. Vignera thereafter successfully attacked the validity of one of the prior convictions, *Vignera v. Wilkins*, Civ. 9901 (D.C. W.D. N.Y. Dec. 31, 1961) (unreported), but was then resentenced as a second-felony offender to the same term of imprisonment as the original sentence. R. 31–33.

69. The failure of defense counsel to object to the introduction of the confession at trial, noted by the Court of Appeals and emphasized by the Solicitor General, does not preclude our consideration of the issue. Since the trial was held prior to our decision in Escobedo and, of course, prior to our decision today making the objection available, the failure to object at trial does not constitute a waiver of the claim. See, e.g., United States *ex rel. Angelet v. Fay*, 333 F.2d 12, 16 (C.A. 2d Cir. 1964), aff'd, 381 U.S. 654 (1965). Cf. *Ziffrin, Inc. v. United States*, 318 U.S. 73, 78 (1943).

70. Because of this disposition of the case, the California Supreme Court did not reach the claims that the confession was coerced by police threats to hold his ailing wife in custody until he confessed, that there was no hearing as required by *Jackson v. Denno*, 378 U.S. 368 (1964), and that the trial judge gave an instruction condemned by the California Supreme Court's decision in *People v. Morse*, 60 Cal. 2d 631, 388 P.2d 33, 36 Cal. Rptr. 201 (1964).

71. After *certiorari* was granted in this case, respondent moved to dismiss on the ground that there was no final judgment from which the State could appeal since the judgment below directed that he be retried. In the event respondent was successful in obtaining an acquittal on retrial, however, under California law the State would have no appeal. Satisfied that in these circumstances the decision below constituted a final judgment under 28 U.S.C. 1257 (3) (1964 ed.), we denied the motion. 383 U.S. 903.

MR. JUSTICE CLARK, dissenting in Nos. 759, 760, and 761, and concurring in the result in No. 584.

It is with regret that I find it necessary to write in these cases. However, I am unable to join the majority because its opinion goes too far on too little, while my dissenting brethren do not go quite far enough. Nor can I join in the Court's criticism of the present practices of police and investigatory agencies as to custodial interrogation. The materials it refers to as "police manuals"[72] are, as I read them, merely writings in this field by professors and some police officers. Not one is shown by the record here to be the official manual of any police department, much less in universal use in crime detection. Moreover, the examples of police brutality mentioned by the Court[73] are rare exceptions to the thousands of cases that appear every year in the law reports. The police agencies—all the way from municipal and state forces to the federal bureaus—are responsible for law enforcement and public

(Continues)

safety in this country. I am proud of their efforts, which in my view are not fairly characterized by the Court's opinion.

I

The *ipse dixit* of the majority has no support in our cases. Indeed, the Court admits that "we might not find the defendants' statements [here] to have been involuntary in traditional terms." *Ante*, p. 457. In short, the Court has added more to the requirements that the accused is entitled to consult with his lawyer and that he must be given the traditional warning that he may remain silent and that anything that he says may be used against him. *Escobedo v. Illinois*, 378 U.S. 478, 490–491 (1964). Now, the Court fashions a constitutional rule that the police may engage in no custodial interrogation without additionally advising the accused that he has a right under the Fifth Amendment to the presence of counsel during interrogation and that, if he is without funds, counsel will be furnished him. When at any point during an interrogation the accused seeks affirmatively or impliedly to invoke his rights to silence or counsel, interrogation must be forgone or postponed. The Court further holds that failure to follow the new procedures requires inexorably the exclusion of any statement by the accused, as well as the fruits thereof. Such a strict constitutional specific inserted at the nerve center of crime detection may well kill the patient.[74] Since there is at this time a paucity of information and an almost total lack of empirical knowledge on the practical operation of requirements truly comparable to those announced by the majority, I would be more restrained lest we go too far too fast.

II

Custodial interrogation has long been recognized as "undoubtedly an essential tool in effective law enforcement." *Haynes v. Washington*, 373 U.S. 503, 515 (1963). Recognition of this fact should put us on guard against the promulgation of doctrinaire rules. Especially is this true where the Court finds that "the Constitution has prescribed" its holding and where the light of our past cases, from *Hopt v. Utah*, 110 U.S. 574, (1884), down to *Haynes v. Washington*, *supra*, is to the contrary. Indeed, even in *Escobedo* the Court never hinted that an affirmative "waiver" was a prerequisite to questioning; that the burden of proof as to waiver was on the prosecution; that the presence of counsel—absent a waiver—during interrogation was required; that a waiver can be withdrawn at the will of the accused; that counsel must be furnished during an accusatory stage to those unable to pay; nor that admissions and exculpatory statements are "confessions." To require all those things at one gulp should cause the Court to choke over more cases than *Crooker v. California*, 357 U.S. 433 (1958), and *Cicenia v. Lagay*, 357 U.S. 504 (1958), which it expressly overrules today.

The rule prior to today—as Mr. Justice Goldberg, the author of the Court's opinion in *Escobedo*, stated it in *Haynes v. Washington*—depended upon "a totality of circumstances evidencing an involuntary . . . admission of guilt." 373 U.S., at 514. And he concluded:

> "Of course, detection and solution of crime is, at best, a difficult and arduous task requiring determination and persistence on the part of all responsible officers charged with the duty of law enforcement. And, certainly, we do not mean to suggest that all interrogation of witnesses and suspects is impermissible. Such questioning is undoubtedly an essential tool in effective law enforcement. The line between proper and permissible police conduct and techniques and methods offensive to due process is, at best, a difficult one to draw, particularly in cases such as this where it is necessary to make fine judgments as to the effect of psychologically coercive pressures and inducements on the mind and will of an accused. . . . We are here impelled to the conclusion, from all of the facts presented, that the bounds of due process have been exceeded." *Id.*, at 514–515.

III

I would continue to follow that rule. Under the "totality of circumstances" rule of which my Brother Goldberg spoke in *Haynes*, I would consider in each case whether the police officer prior to custodial interrogation added the warning that the suspect might have counsel present at the interrogation and, further, that a court would appoint one at his request if he was too poor to employ counsel. In the absence of warnings, the burden would be on the State to prove that counsel was knowingly and intelligently waived or that in the totality of the circumstances, including the failure to give the necessary warnings, the confession was clearly voluntary.

Rather than employing the arbitrary Fifth Amendment rule[75] which the Court lays down I would follow the more pliable dictates of the Due Process Clauses of the Fifth and Fourteenth Amendments which we are accustomed to administering and which we know from our cases are effective instruments in protecting persons in police custody. In this way we would not be acting in the dark nor in one full sweep changing the traditional rules of custodial interrogation which this Court has for so long recognized as a justifiable and proper tool in balancing individual rights against the rights of society. It will be soon enough to go further when we are able to appraise with somewhat better accuracy the effect of such a holding.

I would affirm the convictions in *Miranda v. Arizona*, No. 759; *Vignera v. New York*, No. 760; and *Westover v. United States*, No. 761. In each of those cases I find from the circumstances no warrant for reversal. In *California v. Stewart*, No. 584, I would dismiss the writ of *certiorari* for want of a final judgment, 28 U.S.C. 1257 (3) (1964 ed.); but if the merits are to be reached I would affirm on the ground that the State failed to fulfill its burden, in the absence of a showing that appropriate warnings were given, of proving a waiver or a totality of circumstances showing voluntariness. Should there be a retrial, I would leave the State free to attempt to prove these elements.

Notes

72. E.g., Inbau & Reid, *Criminal Interrogation and Confessions* (1962); O'Hara, *Fundamentals of Criminal Investigation* (1956); Dienstein, *Technics for the Crime Investigator* (1952); Mulbar, *Interrogation* (1951); Kidd, *Police Interrogation* (1940).

73. As developed by my Brother HARLAN, *post*, pp. 506–514, such cases, with the exception of the long-discredited decision in *Bram v. United States*, 168 U.S. 532 (1897), were adequately treated in terms of due process.

74. The Court points to England, Scotland, Ceylon and India as having equally rigid rules. As my Brother HARLAN points out, *post*, pp. 521–523, the Court is mistaken in this regard, for it overlooks counterbalancing prosecutorial advantages. Moreover, the requirements of the Federal Bureau of Investigation do not appear from the Solicitor General's letter, *ante*, pp. 484–486, to be as strict as those imposed today in at least two respects: (1) The offer of counsel is articulated only as "a right to counsel"; nothing is said about a right to have counsel present at the custodial interrogation. (See also the examples cited by the Solicitor General, *Westover v. United States*, 342 F.2d 684, 685 (1965) ("right to consult counsel"); *Jackson v. United States*, 337 F.2d 136, 138 (1964) (accused "entitled to an attorney").) Indeed, the practice is that whenever the suspect "decides that he wishes to consult with counsel before making a statement, the interview is terminated at that point . . . When counsel appears in person, he is permitted to confer with his client in private." This clearly indicates that the FBI does not warn that counsel may be present during custodial interrogation. (2) The Solicitor General's letter states: "[T]hose who have been arrested for an offense under FBI jurisdiction, or whose arrest is contemplated following the interview, [are advised] of a right to free counsel if they are unable to pay, and the availability of such counsel from the Judge." So phrased, this warning does not indicate that the agent will secure counsel. Rather, the statement may well be interpreted by the suspect to mean that the burden is placed upon himself and that he may have counsel appointed only when brought before the judge or at trial—but not at custodial interrogation. As I view the FBI practice, it is not as broad as the one laid down today by the Court.

75. In my view there is "no significant support" in our cases for the holding of the Court today that the Fifth Amendment privilege, in effect, forbids custodial interrogation. For a discussion of this point see the dissenting opinion of my Brother WHITE, *post*, pp. 526–531.

MR. JUSTICE HARLAN, whom MR. JUSTICE STEWART and MR. JUSTICE WHITE join, dissenting.

I believe the decision of the Court represents poor constitutional law and entails harmful consequences for the country at large. How serious these consequences may prove to be only time can tell. But the basic flaws in the Court's justification seem to me readily apparent now once all sides of the problem are considered.

I. INTRODUCTION

At the outset, it is well to note exactly what is required by the Court's new constitutional code of rules for confessions. The foremost requirement, upon which later admissibility of a confession depends, is

(Continues)

(Continued)

that a fourfold warning be given to a person in custody before he is questioned, namely, that he has a right to remain silent, that anything he says may be used against him, that he has a right to have present an attorney during the questioning, and that if indigent he has a right to a lawyer without charge. To forgo these rights, some affirmative statement of rejection is seemingly required, and threats, tricks, or cajolings to obtain this waiver are forbidden. If before or during questioning the suspect seeks to invoke his right to remain silent, interrogation must be forgone or cease; a request for counsel brings about the same result until a lawyer is procured. Finally, there are a miscellany of minor directives, for example, the burden of proof of waiver is on the State, admissions and exculpatory statements are treated just like confessions, withdrawal of a waiver is always permitted, and so forth.[76]

While the fine points of this scheme are far less clear than the Court admits, the tenor is quite apparent. The new rules are not designed to guard against police brutality or other unmistakably banned forms of coercion. Those who use third-degree tactics and deny them in court are equally able and destined to lie as skillfully about warnings and waivers. Rather, the thrust of the new rules is to negate all pressures, to reinforce the nervous or ignorant suspect, and ultimately to discourage any confession at all. The aim in short is toward "voluntariness" in a utopian sense, or to view it from a different angle, voluntariness with a vengeance.

To incorporate this notion into the Constitution requires a strained reading of history and precedent and a disregard of the very pragmatic concerns that alone may on occasion justify such strains. I believe that reasoned examination will show that the Due Process Clauses provide an adequate tool for coping with confessions and that, even if the Fifth Amendment privilege against self-incrimination be invoked, its precedents taken as a whole do not sustain the present rules. Viewed as a choice based on pure policy, these new rules prove to be a highly debatable, if not one-sided, appraisal of the competing interests, imposed over widespread objection, at the very time when judicial restraint is most called for by the circumstances.

II. CONSTITUTIONAL PREMISES

It is most fitting to begin an inquiry into the constitutional precedents by surveying the limits on confessions the Court has evolved under the Due Process Clause of the Fourteenth Amendment. This is so because these cases show that there exists a workable and effective means of dealing with confessions in a judicial manner; because the cases are the baseline from which the Court now departs and so serve to measure the actual as opposed to the professed distance it travels; and because examination of them helps reveal how the Court has coasted into its present position.

The earliest confession cases in this Court emerged from federal prosecutions and were settled on a nonconstitutional basis, the Court adopting the common-law rule that the absence of inducements, promises, and threats made a confession voluntary and admissible. *Hopt v. Utah*, 110 U.S. 574; *Pierce v. United States*, 160 U.S. 355. While a later case said the Fifth Amendment privilege controlled admissibility, this proposition was not itself developed in subsequent decisions.[77] The Court did, however, heighten the test of admissibility in federal trials to one of voluntariness "in fact," *Wan v. United States*, 266 U.S. 1, 14 (quoted, *ante*, p. 462), and then by and large left federal judges to apply the same standards the Court began to derive in a string of state court cases.

This new line of decisions, testing admissibility by the Due Process Clause, began in 1936 with *Brown v. Mississippi*, 297 U.S. 278, and must now embrace somewhat more than 30 full opinions of the Court.[78] While the voluntariness rubric was repeated in many instances, e.g., *Lyons v. Oklahoma*, 322 U.S. 596, the Court never pinned it down to a single meaning but on the contrary infused it with a number of different values. To travel quickly over the main themes, there was an initial emphasis on reliability, e.g., *Ward v. Texas*, 316 U.S. 547, supplemented by concern over the legality and fairness of the police practices, e.g., *Ashcraft v. Tennessee*, 322 U.S. 143, in an "accusatorial" system of law enforcement, *Watts v. Indiana*, 338 U.S. 49, 54, and eventually by close attention to the individual's state of mind and capacity for effective choice, e.g., *Gallegos v. Colorado*, 370 U.S. 49. The outcome was a continuing re-evaluation on the facts of each case of how much pressure on the suspect was permissible.[79]

Among the criteria often taken into account were threats or imminent danger, e.g., *Payne v. Arkansas*, 356 U.S. 560, physical deprivations such as lack of sleep or food, e.g., *Reck v. Pate*, 367 U.S. 433, repeated or extended interrogation, e.g., *Chambers v. Florida*, 309 U.S. 227, limits on access to counsel or friends, *Crooker v. California*, 357 U.S. 433; *Cicenia v. Lagay*, 357 U.S. 504, length and illegality of detention under state law, e.g., *Haynes v. Washington*, 373 U.S. 503, and individual weakness or incapacities, *Lynumn v. Illinois*, 372 U.S. 528. Apart from direct physical coercion, however, no single default or fixed combination of defaults guaranteed exclusion, and synopses of the cases would serve little use because the overall gauge has been steadily changing, usually in the direction of restricting admissibility. But to mark just what point had been reached before the Court jumped the rails in *Escobedo v. Illinois*, 378 U.S. 478, it is worth capsulizing the then-recent case of *Haynes v. Washington*, 373 U.S. 503. There, Haynes had been held some 16 or more hours in violation of state law before signing the disputed confession, had received no warnings of any kind, and despite requests had been refused access to his wife or to counsel, the police indicating that access would be allowed after a confession. Emphasizing especially this last inducement and rejecting some contrary indicia of voluntariness, the Court in a 5-to-4 decision held the confession inadmissible.

There are several relevant lessons to be drawn from this constitutional history. The first is that with over 25 years of precedent the Court has developed an elaborate, sophisticated, and sensitive approach to admissibility of confessions. It is "judicial" in its treatment of one case at a time, see *Culombe v. Connecticut*, 367 U.S. 568, 635 (concurring opinion of THE CHIEF JUSTICE), flexible in its ability to respond to the endless mutations of fact presented, and ever more familiar to the lower courts. Of course, strict certainty is not obtained in this developing process, but this is often so with constitutional principles, and disagreement is usually confined to that borderland of close cases where it matters least.

The second point is that in practice and from time to time in principle, the Court has given ample recognition to society's interest in suspect questioning as an instrument of law enforcement. Cases countenancing quite significant pressures can be cited without difficulty,[80] and the lower courts may often have been yet more tolerant. Of course the limitations imposed today were rejected by necessary implication in case after case, the right to warnings having been explicitly rebuffed in this Court many years ago. *Powers v. United States*, 223 U.S. 303; *Wilson v. United States*, 162 U.S. 613. As recently as *Haynes v. Washington*, 373 U.S. 503, 515, the Court openly acknowledged that questioning of witnesses and suspects "is undoubtedly an essential tool in effective law enforcement." Accord, *Crooker v. California*, 357 U.S. 433, 441.

Finally, the cases disclose that the language in many of the opinions overstates the actual course of decision. It has been said, for example, that an admissible confession must be made by the suspect "in the unfettered exercise of his own will," *Malloy v. Hogan*, 378 U.S. 1, 8 , and that "a prisoner is not 'to be made the deluded instrument of his own conviction,'" *Culombe v. Connecticut*, 367 U.S. 568, 581 (Frankfurter, J., announcing the Court's judgment and an opinion). Though often repeated, such principles are rarely observed in full measure. Even the word "voluntary" may be deemed somewhat misleading, especially when one considers many of the confessions that have been brought under its umbrella. See, e.g., *supra*, n. 5. The tendency to overstate may be laid in part to the flagrant facts often before the Court; but in any event one must recognize how it has tempered attitudes and lent some color of authority to the approach now taken by the Court.

I turn now to the Court's asserted reliance on the Fifth Amendment, an approach which I frankly regard as a *trompe l'oeil*. The Court's opinion in my view reveals no adequate basis for extending the Fifth Amendment's privilege against self-incrimination to the police station. Far more important, it fails to show that the Court's new rules are well supported, let alone compelled, by Fifth Amendment precedents. Instead, the new rules actually derive from quotation and analogy drawn from precedents under the Sixth Amendment, which should properly have no bearing on police interrogation.

The Court's opening contention, that the Fifth Amendment governs police station confessions, is perhaps not an impermissible extension of the law but it has little to commend itself in the present circumstances. Historically, the privilege against self-incrimination did not bear at all on the use of extra-legal confessions, for which distinct standards evolved; indeed, "the history of the two principles is wide apart, differing by one hundred years in origin, and derived through separate lines of precedents . . ." 8 Wigmore, *Evidence* 2266, at 401 (McNaughton rev. 1961). Practice under the two doctrines has also differed in a number of important respects.[81] Even those who would readily enlarge the privilege must concede some linguistic difficulties since the Fifth Amendment in terms proscribes only compelling any person "in any criminal case to be a witness against himself." Cf. Kamisar, *Equal Justice in the Gatehouses and Mansions of American Criminal Procedure, in Criminal Justice in Our Time* 1, 25–26 (1965).

Though weighty, I do not say these points and similar ones are conclusive, for, as the Court reiterates, the privilege embodies basic principles always capable of expansion.[82] Certainly the privilege does represent a protective concern for the accused and an emphasis upon accusatorial rather than inquisitorial values in law enforcement, although this is similarly true of other limitations such as the

(Continues)

(Continued)

grand jury requirement and the reasonable doubt standard. Accusatorial values, however, have openly been absorbed into the due process standard governing confessions; this indeed is why at present "the kinship of the two rules [governing confessions and self-incrimination] is too apparent for denial." McCormick, *Evidence*, 155 (1954). Since extension of the general principle has already occurred, to insist that the privilege applies as such serves only to carry over inapposite historical details and engaging rhetoric and to obscure the policy choices to be made in regulating confessions.

Having decided that the Fifth Amendment privilege does apply in the police station, the Court reveals that the privilege imposes more exacting restrictions than does the Fourteenth Amendment's voluntariness test.[83] It then emerges from a discussion of *Escobedo* that the Fifth Amendment requires for an admissible confession that it be given by one distinctly aware of his right not to speak and shielded from "the compelling atmosphere" of interrogation. See *ante*, pp. 465–466. From these key premises, the Court finally develops the safeguards of warning, counsel, and so forth. I do not believe these premises are sustained by precedents under the Fifth Amendment.[84]

The more important premise is that pressure on the suspect must be eliminated though it be only the subtle influence of the atmosphere and surroundings. The Fifth Amendment, however, has never been thought to forbid all pressure to incriminate one's self in the situations covered by it. On the contrary, it has been held that failure to incriminate one's self can result in denial of removal of one's case from state to federal court, *Maryland v. Soper*, 270 U.S. 9; in refusal of a military commission, *Orloff v. Willoughby*, 345 U.S. 83; in denial of a discharge in bankruptcy, *Kaufman v. Hurwitz*, 176 F.2d 210; and in numerous other adverse consequences. See 8 Wigmore, *Evidence* 2272, at 441–444, n. 18 (McNaughton rev. 1961); Maguire, *Evidence of Guilt*, 2.062 (1959). This is not to say that short of jail or torture any sanction is permissible in any case; policy and history alike may impose sharp limits. See, e.g., *Griffin v. California*, 380 U.S. 609. However, the Court's unspoken assumption that any pressure violates the privilege is not supported by the precedents and it has failed to show why the Fifth Amendment prohibits that relatively mild pressure the Due Process Clause permits.

The Court appears similarly wrong in thinking that precise knowledge of one's rights is a settled prerequisite under the Fifth Amendment to the loss of its protections. A number of lower federal court cases have held that grand jury witnesses need not always be warned of their privilege, e.g., *United States v. Scully*, 225 F.2d 113, 116, and Wigmore states this to be the better rule for trial witnesses. See 8 Wigmore, *Evidence* 2269 (McNaughton rev. 1961). Cf. *Henry v. Mississippi*, 379 U.S. 443, 451–452 (waiver of constitutional rights by counsel despite defendant's ignorance held allowable). No Fifth Amendment precedent is cited for the Court's contrary view. There might of course be reasons apart from Fifth Amendment precedent for requiring warning or any other safeguard on questioning but that is a different matter entirely. See *infra*, pp. 516–517.

A closing word must be said about the Assistance of Counsel Clause of the Sixth Amendment, which is never expressly relied on by the Court but whose judicial precedents turn out to be linchpins of the confession rules announced today. To support its requirement of a knowing and intelligent waiver, the Court cites *Johnson v. Zerbst*, 304 U.S. 458, *ante*, p. 475; appointment of counsel for the indigent suspect is tied to *Gideon v. Wainwright*, 372 U.S. 335, and *Douglas v. California*, 372 U.S. 353, *ante*, p. 473; the silent-record doctrine is borrowed from *Carnley v. Cochran*, 369 U.S. 506, *ante*, p. 475, as is the right to an express offer of counsel, *ante*, p. 471. All these cases imparting glosses to the Sixth Amendment concerned counsel at trial or on appeal. While the Court finds no pertinent difference between judicial proceedings and police interrogation, I believe the differences are so vast as to disqualify wholly the Sixth Amendment precedents as suitable analogies in the present cases.[85]

The only attempt in this Court to carry the right to counsel into the station house occurred in *Escobedo*, the Court repeating several times that that stage was no less "critical" than trial itself. See 378 U.S., 485–488. This is hardly persuasive when we consider that a grand jury inquiry, the filing of a certiorari petition, and certainly the purchase of narcotics by an undercover agent from a prospective defendant may all be equally "critical" yet provision of counsel and advice on that score have never been thought compelled by the Constitution in such cases. The sound reason why this right is so freely extended for a criminal trial is the severe injustice risked by confronting an untrained defendant with a range of technical points of law, evidence, and tactics familiar to the prosecutor but not to himself. This danger shrinks markedly in the police station where indeed the lawyer in fulfilling his professional responsibilities of necessity may become an obstacle to truthfinding. See *infra*, n. 12. The Court's summary citation of the Sixth Amendment cases here seems to me best described as "the domino method of constitutional adjudication . . . wherein every explanatory statement in a previous opinion is made the basis for extension to a wholly different situation." Friendly, *supra*, n. 10, at 950.

III. POLICY CONSIDERATIONS

Examined as an expression of public policy, the Court's new regime proves so dubious that there can be no due compensation for its weakness in constitutional law. The foregoing discussion has shown, I think, how mistaken is the Court in implying that the Constitution has struck the balance in favor of the approach the Court takes. *Ante*, p. 479. Rather, precedent reveals that the Fourteenth Amendment in practice has been construed to strike a different balance, that the Fifth Amendment gives the Court little solid support in this context, and that the Sixth Amendment should have no bearing at all. Legal history has been stretched before to satisfy deep needs of society. In this instance, however, the Court has not and cannot make the powerful showing that its new rules are plainly desirable in the context of our society, something which is surely demanded before those rules are engrafted onto the Constitution and imposed on every State and county in the land.

Without at all subscribing to the generally black picture of police conduct painted by the Court, I think it must be frankly recognized at the outset that police questioning allowable under due process precedents may inherently entail some pressure on the suspect and may seek advantage in his ignorance or weaknesses. The atmosphere and questioning techniques, proper and fair though they be, can in themselves exert a tug on the suspect to confess, and in this light "[t]o speak of any confessions of crime made after arrest as being 'voluntary' or 'uncoerced' is somewhat inaccurate, although traditional. A confession is wholly and incontestably voluntary only if a guilty person gives himself up to the law and becomes his own accuser." *Ashcraft v. Tennessee*, 322 U.S. 143, 161 (Jackson, J., dissenting). Until today, the role of the Constitution has been only to sift out undue pressure, not to assure spontaneous confessions.[86]

The Court's new rules aim to offset these minor pressures and disadvantages intrinsic to any kind of police interrogation. The rules do not serve due process interests in preventing blatant coercion since, as I noted earlier, they do nothing to contain the policeman who is prepared to lie from the start. The rules work for reliability in confessions almost only in the Pickwickian sense that they can prevent some from being given at all.[87] In short, the benefit of this new regime is simply to lessen or wipe out the inherent compulsion and inequalities to which the Court devotes some nine pages of description. *Ante*, pp. 448–456.

What the Court largely ignores is that its rules impair, if they will not eventually serve wholly to frustrate, an instrument of law enforcement that has long and quite reasonably been thought worth the price paid for it.[88] There can be little doubt that the Court's new code would markedly decrease the number of confessions. To warn the suspect that he may remain silent and remind him that his confession may be used in court are minor obstructions. To require also an express waiver by the suspect and an end to questioning whenever he demurs must heavily handicap questioning. And to suggest or provide counsel for the suspect simply invites the end of the interrogation. See, *supra*, n. 12.

How much harm this decision will inflict on law enforcement cannot fairly be predicted with accuracy. Evidence on the role of confessions is notoriously incomplete, see *Developments*, *supra*, n. 2, at 941–944, and little is added by the Court's reference to the FBI experience and the resources believed wasted in interrogation. See *infra*, n. 19, and text. We do know that some crimes cannot be solved without confessions, that ample expert testimony attests to their importance in crime control,[89] and that the Court is taking a real risk with society's welfare in imposing its new regime on the country. The social costs of crime are too great to call the new rules anything but a hazardous experimentation.

While passing over the costs and risks of its experiment, the Court portrays the evils of normal police questioning in terms which I think are exaggerated. Albeit stringently confined by the due process standards interrogation is no doubt often inconvenient and unpleasant for the suspect. However, it is no less so for a man to be arrested and jailed, to have his house searched, or to stand trial in court, yet all this may properly happen to the most innocent given probable cause, a warrant, or an indictment. Society has always paid a stiff price for law and order, and peaceful interrogation is not one of the dark moments of the law.

This brief statement of the competing considerations seems to me ample proof that the Court's preference is highly debatable at best and therefore not to be read into the Constitution. However, it may make the analysis more graphic to consider the actual facts of one of the four cases reversed by the Court. *Miranda v. Arizona* serves best, being neither the hardest nor easiest of the four under the Court's standards.[90]

On March 3, 1963, an 18-year-old girl was kidnapped and forcibly raped near Phoenix, Arizona. Ten days later, on the morning of March 13, petitioner Miranda was arrested and taken to the police station.

(Continues)

Constitutional Cases   271

(Continued)

At this time Miranda was 23 years old, indigent, and educated to the extent of completing half the ninth grade. He had "an emotional illness" of the schizophrenic type, according to the doctor who eventually examined him; the doctor's report also stated that Miranda was "alert and oriented as to time, place, and person," intelligent within normal limits, competent to stand trial, and sane within the legal definition. At the police station, the victim picked Miranda out of a lineup, and two officers then took him into a separate room to interrogate him, starting about 11:30 A.M. Though at first denying his guilt, within a short time Miranda gave a detailed oral confession and then wrote out in his own hand and signed a brief statement admitting and describing the crime. All this was accomplished in two hours or less without any force, threats or promises and—I will assume this though the record is uncertain, *ante*, 491–492 and nn. 66–67—without any effective warnings at all.

Miranda's oral and written confessions are now held inadmissible under the Court's new rules. One is entitled to feel astonished that the Constitution can be read to produce this result. These confessions were obtained during brief, daytime questioning conducted by two officers and unmarked by any of the traditional indicia of coercion. They assured a conviction for a brutal and unsettling crime, for which the police had and quite possibly could obtain little evidence other than the victim's identifications, evidence which is frequently unreliable. There was, in sum, a legitimate purpose, no perceptible unfairness, and certainly little risk of injustice in the interrogation. Yet the resulting confessions, and the responsible course of police practice they represent, are to be sacrificed to the Court's own finespun conception of fairness which I seriously doubt is shared by many thinking citizens in this country.[91]

The tenor of judicial opinion also falls well short of supporting the Court's new approach. Although *Escobedo* has widely been interpreted as an open invitation to lower courts to rewrite the law of confessions, a significant heavy majority of the state and federal decisions in point have sought quite narrow interpretations.[92] Of the courts that have accepted the invitation, it is hard to know how many have felt compelled by their best guess as to this Court's likely construction; but none of the state decisions saw fit to rely on the state privilege against self-incrimination, and no decision at all has gone as far as this Court goes today.[93]

It is also instructive to compare the attitude in this case of those responsible for law enforcement with the official views that existed when the Court undertook three major revisions of prosecutorial practice prior to this case, *Johnson v. Zerbst*, 304 U.S. 458, *Mapp v. Ohio*, 367 U.S. 643, and *Gideon v. Wainwright*, 372 U.S. 335. In *Johnson*, which established that appointed counsel must be offered the indigent in federal criminal trials, the Federal Government all but conceded the basic issue, which had in fact been recently fixed as Department of Justice policy. See Beaney, *Right to Counsel*, 29–30, 36–42 (1955). In *Mapp*, which imposed the exclusionary rule on the States for Fourth Amendment violations, more than half of the States had themselves already adopted some such rule. See 367 U.S., at 651. In Gideon, which extended *Johnson v. Zerbst* to the States, an *amicus* brief was filed by 22 States and Commonwealths urging that course; only two States besides that of the respondent came forward to protest. See 372 U.S., at 345. By contrast, in this case new restrictions on police questioning have been opposed by the United States and in an *amicus* brief signed by 27 States and Commonwealths, not including the three other States which are parties. No State in the country has urged this Court to impose the newly announced rules, nor has any State chosen to go nearly so far on its own.

The Court in closing its general discussion invokes the practice in federal and foreign jurisdictions as lending weight to its new curbs on confessions for all the States. A brief resume will suffice to show that none of these jurisdictions has struck so one-sided a balance as the Court does today. Heaviest reliance is placed on the FBI practice. Differing circumstances may make this comparison quite untrustworthy,[94] but in any event the FBI falls sensibly short of the Court's formalistic rules. For example, there is no indication that FBI agents must obtain an affirmative "waiver" before they pursue their questioning. Nor is it clear that one invoking his right to silence may not be prevailed upon to change his mind. And the warning as to appointed counsel apparently indicates only that one will be assigned by the judge when the suspect appears before him; the thrust of the Court's rules is to induce the suspect to obtain appointed counsel before continuing the interview. See *ante*, pp. 484–486. Apparently American military practice, briefly mentioned by the Court, has these same limits and is still less favorable to the suspect than the FBI warning, making no mention of appointed counsel. *Developments*, *supra*, n. 2, at 1084–1089.

The law of the foreign countries described by the Court also reflects a more moderate conception of the rights of the accused as against those of society when other data are considered. Concededly, the English experience is most relevant. In that country, a caution as to silence but not counsel has long been mandated by the "Judges' Rules," which also place other somewhat imprecise limits on police cross-examination of suspects. However, in the court's discretion confessions can be and apparently quite frequently are admitted in evidence despite disregard of the Judges' Rules, so long as they are found voluntary under the common-law test. Moreover, the check that exists on the use of pretrial statements is counterbalanced by the evident admissibility of fruits of an illegal confession and by the judge's often-used authority to comment adversely on the defendant's failure to testify.[95]

India, Ceylon and Scotland are the other examples chosen by the Court. In India and Ceylon the general ban on police-adduced confessions cited by the Court is subject to a major exception: if evidence is uncovered by police questioning, it is fully admissible at trial along with the confession itself, so far as it relates to the evidence and is not blatantly coerced. See *Developments, supra*, n. 2, at 1106–1110; *Reg. v. Ramasamy* 1965. A.C. 1 (P.C.). Scotland's limits on interrogation do measure up to the Court's; however, restrained comment at trial on the defendant's failure to take the stand is allowed the judge, and in many other respects Scotch law redresses the prosecutor's disadvantage in ways not permitted in this country.[96] The Court ends its survey by imputing added strength to our privilege against self-incrimination since, by contrast to other countries, it is embodied in a written Constitution. Considering the liberties the Court has today taken with constitutional history and precedent, few will find this emphasis persuasive.

In closing this necessarily truncated discussion of policy considerations attending the new confession rules, some reference must be made to their ironic untimeliness. There is now in progress in this country a massive re-examination of criminal law enforcement procedures on a scale never before witnessed. Participants in this undertaking include a Special Committee of the American Bar Association, under the chairmanship of Chief Judge Lumbard of the Court of Appeals for the Second Circuit; a distinguished study group of the American Law Institute, headed by Professors Vorenberg and Bator of the Harvard Law School; and the President's Commission on Law Enforcement and Administration of Justice, under the leadership of the Attorney General of the United States.[97] Studies are also being conducted by the District of Columbia Crime Commission, the Georgetown Law Center, and by others equipped to do practical research.[98] There are also signs that legislatures in some of the States may be preparing to re-examine the problem before us.[99]

It is no secret that concern has been expressed lest long-range and lasting reforms be frustrated by this Court's too rapid departure from existing constitutional standards. Despite the Court's disclaimer, the practical effect of the decision made today must inevitably be to handicap seriously sound efforts at reform, not least by removing options necessary to a just compromise of competing interests. Of course legislative reform is rarely speedy or unanimous, though this Court has been more patient in the past.[100] But the legislative reforms when they come would have the vast advantage of empirical data and comprehensive study, they would allow experimentation and use of solutions not open to the courts, and they would restore the initiative in criminal law reform to those forums where it truly belongs.

IV. CONCLUSIONS

All four of the cases involved here present express claims that confessions were inadmissible, not because of coercion in the traditional due process sense, but solely because of lack of counsel or lack of warnings concerning counsel and silence. For the reasons stated in this opinion, I would adhere to the due process test and reject the new requirements inaugurated by the Court. On this premise my disposition of each of these cases can be stated briefly.

In two of the three cases coming from state courts, *Miranda v. Arizona* (No. 759) and *Vignera v. New York* (No. 760), the confessions were held admissible and no other errors worth comment are alleged by petitioners. I would affirm in these two cases. The other state case is *California v. Stewart* (No. 584), where the state supreme court held the confession inadmissible and reversed the conviction. In that case I would dismiss the writ of *certiorari* on the ground that no final judgment is before us, 28 U.S.C. 1257 (1964 ed.); putting aside the new trial open to the State in any event, the confession itself has not even been finally excluded since the California Supreme Court left the State free to show proof of a waiver. If the merits of the decision in Stewart be reached, then I believe it should be reversed and the case remanded so the state supreme court may pass on the other claims available to respondent.

In the federal case, *Westover v. United States* (No. 761), a number of issues are raised by petitioner apart from the one already dealt with in this dissent. None of these other claims appears to me tenable, nor in this context to warrant extended discussion. It is urged that the confession was also inadmissible because not voluntary even measured by due process standards and because federal–state cooperation

(Continues)

brought the McNabb-Mallory rule into play under *Anderson v. United States*, 318 U.S. 350. However, the facts alleged fall well short of coercion in my view, and I believe the involvement of federal agents in petitioner's arrest and detention by the State too slight to invoke Anderson. I agree with the Government that the admission of the evidence now protested by petitioner was at most harmless error, and two final contentions—one involving weight of the evidence and another improper prosecutor comment—seem to me without merit. I would therefore affirm Westover's conviction.

In conclusion: Nothing in the letter or the spirit of the Constitution or in the precedents squares with the heavy-handed and one-sided action that is so precipitously taken by the Court in the name of fulfilling its constitutional responsibilities. The foray which the Court makes today brings to mind the wise and farsighted words of Mr. Justice Jackson in *Douglas v. Jeannette*, 319 U.S. 157, 181 (separate opinion): "This Court is forever adding new stories to the temples of constitutional law, and the temples have a way of collapsing when one story too many is added."

Notes

76. My discussion in this opinion is directed to the main questions decided by the Court and necessary to its decision; in ignoring some of the collateral points, I do not mean to imply agreement.

77. The case was *Bram v. United States*, 168 U.S. 532 (quoted, *ante*, p. 461). Its historical premises were afterwards disproved by Wigmore, who concluded "that no assertions could be more unfounded." 3 Wigmore, *Evidence* 823, at 250, n. 5 (3d ed. 1940). The Court in *United States v. Carignan*, 342 U.S. 36, 41, declined to choose between *Bram* and Wigmore, and *Stein v. New York*, 346 U.S. 156, 191, n. 35, cast further doubt on *Bram*. There are, however, several Court opinions which assume in dicta the relevance of the Fifth Amendment privilege to confessions. *Burdeau v. McDowell*, 256 U.S. 465, 475; see *Shotwell Mfg. Co. v. United States*, 371 U.S. 341, 347 . On *Bram* and the federal confession cases generally, see Developments in the Law—Confessions, 79 *Harv. L. Rev.* 935, 959–961 (1966).

78. Comment, 31 *U. Chi. L. Rev.* 313 & n. 1 (1964), states that by the 1963 Term 33 state coerced-confession cases had been decided by this Court, apart from per *curiams*. *Spano v. New York*, 360 U.S. 315, 321, n. 2, collects 28 cases.

79. Bator & Vorenberg, Arrest, Detention, Interrogation and the Right to Counsel, 66 *Col. L. Rev.* 62, 73 (1966): "In fact, the concept of involuntariness seems to be used by the courts as a shorthand to refer to practices which are repellent to civilized standards of decency or which, under the circumstances, are thought to apply a degree of pressure to an individual which unfairly impairs his capacity to make a rational choice." See Herman, The Supreme Court and Restrictions on Police Interrogation, 25 *Ohio St. L. J.* 449, 452–458 (1964); *Developments*, *supra*, n. 2, at 964–984.

80. See the cases synopsized in Herman, *supra*, n. 4, at 456, nn. 36–39. One not too distant example is *Stroble v. California*, 343 U.S. 181, in which the suspect was kicked and threatened after his arrest, questioned a little later for two hours, and isolated from a lawyer trying to see him; the resulting confession was held admissible.

81. Among the examples given in 8 Wigmore, *Evidence* 2266, at 401 (McNaughton rev. 1961), are these: the privilege applies to any witness, civil or criminal, but the confession rule protects only criminal defendants; the privilege deals only with compulsion, while the confession rule may exclude statements obtained by trick or promise; and where the privilege has been nullified—as by the English Bankruptcy Act—the confession rule may still operate.

82. Additionally, there are precedents and even historical arguments that can be arrayed in favor of bringing extra-legal questioning within the privilege. See generally Maguire, *Evidence of Guilt* 2.03, at 15–16 (1959).

83. This, of course, is implicit in the Court's introductory announcement that "[o]ur decision in *Malloy v. Hogan*, 378 U.S. 1 (1964) [extending the Fifth Amendment privilege to the States] necessitates an examination of the scope of the privilege in state cases as well." *Ante*, p. 463. It is also inconsistent with Malloy itself, in which extension of the Fifth Amendment to the States rested in part on the view that the Due Process Clause restriction on state confessions has in recent years been "the same standard" as that imposed in federal prosecutions assertedly by the Fifth Amendment. 378 U.S., at 7.

84. I lay aside *Escobedo* itself; it contains no reasoning or even general conclusions addressed to the Fifth Amendment and indeed its citation in this regard seems surprising in view of *Escobedo's* primary reliance on the Sixth Amendment.

85. Since the Court conspicuously does not assert that the Sixth Amendment itself warrants its new police-interrogation rules, there is no reason now to draw out the extremely powerful historical and precedential evidence that the Amendment will bear no such meaning. See generally Friendly, The Bill of Rights as a Code of Criminal Procedure, 53 *Calif. L. Rev.* 929, 943–948 (1965).

86. See *supra*, n. 4, and text. Of course, the use of terms like voluntariness involves questions of law and terminology quite as much as questions of fact. See *Collins v. Beto*, 348 F.2d 823, 832 (concurring opinion); *Bator & Vorenberg, supra*, n. 4, at 72–73.

87. The Court's vision of a lawyer "mitigat[ing] the dangers of untrustworthiness" (*ante*, p. 470) by witnessing coercion and assisting accuracy in the confession is largely a fancy; for if counsel arrives, there is rarely going to be a police station confession. *Watts v. Indiana*, 338 U.S. 49, 59 (separate opinion of Jackson, J.): "[A]ny lawyer worth his salt will tell the suspect in no uncertain terms to make no statement to police under any circumstances." See Enker & Elsen, Counsel for the Suspect, 49 *Minn. L. Rev.* 47, 66–68 (1964).

88. This need is, of course, what makes so misleading the Court's comparison of a probate judge readily setting aside as involuntary the will of an old lady badgered and beleaguered by the new heirs. *Ante*, pp. 457-458, n. 26. With wills, there is no public interest save in a totally free choice; with confessions, the solution of crime is a countervailing gain, however the balance is resolved.

89. See, e.g., the voluminous citations to congressional committee testimony and other sources collected in *Culombe v. Connecticut*, 367 U.S. 568, 578–579 (Frankfurter, J., announcing the Court's judgment and an opinion).

90. In *Westover*, a seasoned criminal was practically given the Court's full complement of warnings and did not heed them. The *Stewart* case, on the other hand, involves long detention and successive questioning. In *Vignera*, the facts are complicated and the record somewhat incomplete.

91. "[J]ustice, though due to the accused, is due to the accuser also. The concept of fairness must not be strained till it is narrowed to a filament. We are to keep the balance true." *Snyder v. Massachusetts*, 291 U.S. 97, 122 (Cardozo, J.).

92. A narrow reading is given in: *United States v. Robinson*, 354 F.2d 109 (C.A. 2d Cir.); *Davis v. North Carolina*, 339 F.2d 770 (C.A. 4th Cir.); *Edwards v. Holman*, 342 F.2d 679 (C.A. 5th Cir.); *United States ex rel. Townsend v. Ogilvie*, 334 F.2d 837 (C.A. 7th Cir.); *People v. Hartgraves*, 31 Ill. 2d 375, 202 N. E. 2d 33; *State v. Fox*, ___ Iowa ___, 131 N. W. 2d 684; *Rowe v. Commonwealth*, 394 S.W. 2d 751 (Ky.); *Parker v. Warden*, 236 Md. 236, 203 A. 2d 418; *State v. Howard*, 383 S. W. 2d 701 (Mo.); *Bean v. State*, ___ Nev. ___, 398 P.2d 251; *State v. Hodgson*, 44 N.J. 151, 207 A. 2d 542; *People v. Gunner*, 15 N.Y. 2d 226, 205 N.E. 2d 852; *Commonwealth ex rel. Linde v. Maroney*, 416 Pa. 331, 206 A. 2d 288; *Browne v. State*, 24 Wis. 2d 491, 131 N.W. 2d 169.

    An ample reading is given in: *United States ex rel. Russo v. New Jersey*, 351 F.2d 429 (C.A. 3d Cir.); *Wright v. Dickson*, 336 F.2d 878 (C.A. 9th Cir.); *People v. Dorado*, 62 Cal. 2d 338, 398 P.2d 361; *State v. Dufour*, ___ R.I. ___, 206 A. 2d 82; *State v. Neely*, 239 Ore. 487, 395 P.2d 557, modified, 398 P.2d 482.

    The cases in both categories are those readily available; there are certainly many others.

93. For instance, compare the requirements of the catalytic case of *People v. Dorado*, 62 Cal. 2d 338, 398 P.2d 361, with those laid down today. See also Traynor, The Devils of Due Process in Criminal Detection, Detention, and Trial, 33 *U. Chi. L. Rev.* 657, 670.

94. The Court's obiter dictum notwithstanding, *ante*, p. 486, there is some basis for believing that the staple of FBI criminal work differs importantly from much crime within the ken of local police. The skill and resources of the FBI may also be unusual.

95. For citations and discussion covering each of these points, see Developments, *supra*, n. 2, at 1091–1097 and Enker & Elsen, *supra*, n. 12, at 80 & n. 94.

96. On comment, see Hardin, Other Answers: Search and Seizure, Coerced Confession, and Criminal Trial in Scotland, 113 *U. Pa. L. Rev.* 165, 181 and nn. 96–97 (1964). Other examples are less stringent search and seizure rules and no automatic exclusion for violation of them, *id.*, at 167–169; guilt based on majority jury verdicts, *id.*, at 185; and pre-trial discovery of evidence on both sides, *id.*, at 175.

97. Of particular relevance is the ALI's drafting of a Model Code of Pre-Arraignment Procedure, now in its first tentative draft. While the ABA and National Commission studies have wider scope, the former is lending its advice to the ALI project and the executive director of the latter is one of the reporters for the Model Code.

98. See Brief for the United States in *Westover*, p. 45. *The N.Y. Times*, June 3, 1966, p. 41 (late city ed.) reported that the Ford Foundation has awarded $1,100,000 for a five-year study of arrests and confessions in New York.

(Continues)

(Continued)

99. The New York Assembly recently passed a bill to require certain warnings before an admissible confession is taken, though the rules are less strict than are the Court's. *N.Y. Times*, May 24, 1966, p. 35 (late city ed.).

100. The Court waited 12 years after *Wolf v. Colorado*, 338 U.S. 25, declared privacy against improper state intrusions to be constitutionally safeguarded before it concluded in *Mapp v. Ohio*, 367 U.S. 643, that adequate state remedies had not been provided to protect this interest so the exclusionary rule was necessary.

MR. JUSTICE WHITE, with whom MR. JUSTICE HARLAN and MR. JUSTICE STEWART join, dissenting.

I

The proposition that the privilege against self-incrimination forbids in-custody interrogation without the warnings specified in the majority opinion and without a clear waiver of counsel has no significant support in the history of the privilege or in the language of the Fifth Amendment. As for the English authorities and the common-law history, the privilege, firmly established in the second half of the seventeenth century, was never applied except to prohibit compelled judicial interrogations. The rule excluding coerced confessions matured about 100 years later, "[b]ut there is nothing in the reports to suggest that the theory has its roots in the privilege against self-incrimination. And so far as the cases reveal, the privilege, as such, seems to have been given effect only in judicial proceedings, including the preliminary examinations by authorized magistrates." Morgan, The Privilege Against Self-Incrimination, 34 *Minn. L. Rev.* 1, 18 (1949).

Our own constitutional provision provides that no person "shall be compelled in any criminal case to be a witness against himself." These words, when "[c]onsidered in the light to be shed by grammar and the dictionary . . . appear to signify simply that nobody shall be compelled to give oral testimony against himself in a criminal proceeding under way in which he is defendant." Corwin, The Supreme Court's Construction of the Self-Incrimination Clause, 29 *Mich. L. Rev.* 1, 2. And there is very little in the surrounding circumstances of the adoption of the Fifth Amendment or in the provisions of the then existing state constitutions or in state practice which would give the constitutional provision any broader meaning. Mayers, The Federal Witness' Privilege Against Self-Incrimination: Constitutional or Common-Law? 4 *American Journal of Legal History* 107 (1960). Such a construction, however, was considerably narrower than the privilege at common law, and when eventually faced with the issues, the Court extended the constitutional privilege to the compulsory production of books and papers, to the ordinary witness before the grand jury and to witnesses generally. *Boyd v. United States*, 116 U.S. 616, and *Counselman v. Hitchcock*, 142 U.S. 547. Both rules had solid support in common-law history, if not in the history of our own constitutional provision.

A few years later the Fifth Amendment privilege was similarly extended to encompass the then well-established rule against coerced confessions: "In criminal trials, in the courts of the United States, wherever a question arises whether a confession is incompetent because not voluntary, the issue is controlled by that portion of the Fifth Amendment to the Constitution of the United States, commanding that no person 'shall be compelled in any criminal case to be a witness against himself.'" *Bram v. United States*, 168 U.S. 532, 542. Although this view has found approval in other cases, *Burdeau v. McDowell*, 256 U.S. 465, 475; *Powers v. United States*, 223 U.S. 303, 313; *Shotwell v. United States*, 371 U.S. 341, 347, it has also been questioned, see *Brown v. Mississippi*, 297 U.S. 278, 285; *United States v. Carignan*, 342 U.S. 36, 41; *Stein v. New York*, 346 U.S. 156, 191, n. 35, and finds scant support in either the English or American authorities, see generally *Regina v. Scott, Dears. & Bell* 47; 3 Wigmore, *Evidence* 823 (3d ed. 1940), at 249 ("a confession is not rejected because of any connection with the privilege against self-crimination"), and 250, n. 5 (particularly criticizing *Bram*); 8 Wigmore, *Evidence* 2266, at 400–401 (McNaughton rev. 1961). Whatever the source of the rule excluding coerced confessions, it is clear that prior to the application of the privilege itself to state courts, *Malloy v. Hogan*, 378 U.S. 1, the admissibility of a confession in a state criminal prosecution was tested by the same standards as were applied in federal prosecutions. *Id.*, at 6–7, 10.

Bram, however, itself rejected the proposition which the Court now espouses. The question in *Bram* was whether a confession, obtained during custodial interrogation, had been compelled, and if such interrogation was to be deemed inherently vulnerable the Court's inquiry could have ended there. After examining the English and American authorities, however, the Court declared that:

"In this court also it has been settled that the mere fact that the confession is made to a police officer, while the accused was under arrest in or out of prison, or was drawn out by his questions, does not necessarily render the confession involuntary, but, as one of the circumstances, such imprisonment or interrogation may be taken into account in determining whether or not the statements of the prisoner were voluntary." 168 U.S., at 558.

In this respect the Court was wholly consistent with prior and subsequent pronouncements in this Court.

Thus prior to *Bram* the Court, in *Hopt v. Utah*, 110 U.S. 574, 583–587, had upheld the admissibility of a confession made to police officers following arrest, the record being silent concerning what conversation had occurred between the officers and the defendant in the short period preceding the confession. Relying on *Hopt*, the Court ruled squarely on the issue in *Sparf and Hansen v. United States*, 156 U.S. 51, 55:

"Counsel for the accused insist that there cannot be a voluntary statement, a free open confession, while a defendant is confined and in irons under an accusation of having committed a capital offence. We have not been referred to any authority in support of that position. It is true that the fact of a prisoner being in custody at the time he makes a confession is a circumstance not to be overlooked, because it bears upon the inquiry whether the confession was voluntarily made or was extorted by threats or violence or made under the influence of fear. But confinement or imprisonment is not in itself sufficient to justify the exclusion of a confession, if it appears to have been voluntary, and was not obtained by putting the prisoner in fear or by promises." *Wharton's Cr. Ev.* 9th ed. 661, 663, and authorities cited.

Accord, *Pierce v. United States*, 160 U.S. 355, 357.

And in *Wilson v. United States*, 162 U.S. 613, 623, the Court had considered the significance of custodial interrogation without any antecedent warnings regarding the right to remain silent or the right to counsel. There the defendant had answered questions posed by a Commissioner, who had failed to advise him of his rights, and his answers were held admissible over his claim of involuntariness. "The fact that [a defendant] is in custody and manacled does not necessarily render his statement involuntary, nor is that necessarily the effect of popular excitement shortly preceding. . . . And it is laid down that it is not essential to the admissibility of a confession that it should appear that the person was warned that what he said would be used against him, but on the contrary, if the confession was voluntary, it is sufficient though it appear that he was not so warned."

Since *Bram*, the admissibility of statements made during custodial interrogation has been frequently reiterated. *Powers v. United States*, 223 U.S. 303, cited Wilson approvingly and held admissible as voluntary statements the accused's testimony at a preliminary hearing even though he was not warned that what he said might be used against him. Without any discussion of the presence or absence of warnings, presumably because such discussion was deemed unnecessary, numerous other cases have declared that "[t]he mere fact that a confession was made while in the custody of the police does not render it inadmissible," *McNabb v. United States*, 318 U.S. 332, 346; accord, *United States v. Mitchell*, 322 U.S. 65, despite its having been elicited by police examination, *Wan v. United States*, 266 U.S. 1, 14 ; *United States v. Carignan*, 342 U.S. 36, 39. Likewise, in *Crooker v. California*, 357 U.S. 433, 437, the Court said that "the bare fact of police 'detention and police examination in private of one in official state custody' does not render involuntary a confession by the one so detained." And finally, in *Cicenia v. Lagay*, 357 U.S. 504, a confession obtained by police interrogation after arrest was held voluntary even though the authorities refused to permit the defendant to consult with his attorney. See generally *Culombe v. Connecticut*, 367 U.S. 568, 587–602 (opinion of Frankfurter, J.); 3 Wigmore, *Evidence* 851, at 313 (3d ed. 1940); see also Joy, *Admissibility of Confessions* 38, 46 (1842).

Only a tiny minority of our judges who have dealt with the question, including today's majority, have considered in-custody interrogation, without more, to be a violation of the Fifth Amendment. And this Court, as every member knows, has left standing literally thousands of criminal convictions that rested at least in part on confessions taken in the course of interrogation by the police after arrest.

II

That the Court's holding today is neither compelled nor even strongly suggested by the language of the Fifth Amendment, is at odds with American and English legal history, and involves a departure

(Continues)

from a long line of precedent does not prove either that the Court has exceeded its powers or that the Court is wrong or unwise in its present reinterpretation of the Fifth Amendment. It does, however, underscore the obvious—that the Court has not discovered or found the law in making today's decision, nor has it derived it from some irrefutable sources; what it has done is to make new law and new public policy in much the same way that it has in the course of interpreting other great clauses of the Constitution.[101] This is what the Court historically has done. Indeed, it is what it must do and will continue to do until and unless there is some fundamental change in the constitutional distribution of governmental powers.

But if the Court is here and now to announce new and fundamental policy to govern certain aspects of our affairs, it is wholly legitimate to examine the mode of this or any other constitutional decision in this Court and to inquire into the advisability of its end product in terms of the long-range interest of the country. At the very least the Court's text and reasoning should withstand analysis and be a fair exposition of the constitutional provision which its opinion interprets. Decisions like these cannot rest alone on syllogism, metaphysics or some ill-defined notions of natural justice, although each will perhaps play its part. In proceeding to such constructions as it now announces, the Court should also duly consider all the factors and interests bearing upon the cases, at least insofar as the relevant materials are available; and if the necessary considerations are not treated in the record or obtainable from some other reliable source, the Court should not proceed to formulate fundamental policies based on speculation alone.

III

First, we may inquire what are the textual and factual bases of this new fundamental rule. To reach the result announced on the grounds it does, the Court must stay within the confines of the Fifth Amendment, which forbids self-incrimination only if compelled. Hence the core of the Court's opinion is that because of the "compulsion inherent in custodial surroundings, no statement obtained from [a] defendant [in custody] can truly be the product of his free choice," *ante*, at 458, absent the use of adequate protective devices as described by the Court. However, the Court does not point to any sudden inrush of new knowledge requiring the rejection of 70 years' experience. Nor does it assert that its novel conclusion reflects a changing consensus among state courts, see *Mapp v. Ohio*, 367 U.S. 643, or that a succession of cases had steadily eroded the old rule and proved it unworkable, see *Gideon v. Wainwright*, 372 U.S. 335. Rather than asserting new knowledge, the Court concedes that it cannot truly know what occurs during custodial questioning, because of the innate secrecy of such proceedings. It extrapolates a picture of what it conceives to be the norm from police investigatorial manuals, published in 1959 and 1962 or earlier, without any attempt to allow for adjustments in police practices that may have occurred in the wake of more recent decisions of state appellate tribunals or this Court. But even if the relentless application of the described procedures could lead to involuntary confessions, it most assuredly does not follow that each and every case will disclose this kind of interrogation or this kind of consequence.[102] Insofar as appears from the Court's opinion, it has not examined a single transcript of any police interrogation, let alone the interrogation that took place in any one of these cases which it decides today. Judged by any of the standards for empirical investigation utilized in the social sciences the factual basis for the Court's premise is patently inadequate.

Although in the Court's view in-custody interrogation is inherently coercive, the Court says that the spontaneous product of the coercion of arrest and detention is still to be deemed voluntary. An accused, arrested on probable cause, may blurt out a confession which will be admissible despite the fact that he is alone and in custody, without any showing that he had any notion of his right to remain silent or of the consequences of his admission. Yet, under the Court's rule, if the police ask him a single question such as "Do you have anything to say?" or "Did you kill your wife?" his response, if there is one, has somehow been compelled, even if the accused has been clearly warned of his right to remain silent. Common sense informs us to the contrary. While one may say that the response was "involuntary" in the sense the question provoked or was the occasion for the response and thus the defendant was induced to speak out when he might have remained silent if not arrested and not questioned, it is patently unsound to say the response is compelled.

Today's result would not follow even if it were agreed that to some extent custodial interrogation is inherently coercive. See *Ashcraft v. Tennessee*, 322 U.S. 143, 161 (Jackson, J., dissenting). The test has been whether the totality of circumstances deprived the defendant of a "free choice to admit, to deny, or to refuse to answer," *Lisenba v. California*, 314 U.S. 219, 241, and whether physical or psychological coercion was of such a degree that "the defendant's will was overborne at the time he confessed," *Haynes v. Washington*, 373 U.S. 503, 513; *Lynumn v. Illinois*, 372 U.S. 528, 534. The duration and nature of incommunicado custody, the presence or absence of advice concerning the defendant's constitutional rights, and the granting or refusal of requests to communicate with lawyers, relatives or friends have all been rightly regarded as important data bearing on the basic inquiry. See, e.g., *Ashcraft v. Tennessee*, 322 U.S. 143; *Haynes v. Washington*, 373 U.S. 503.[103] But it has never been suggested, until today, that such questioning was so coercive and accused persons so lacking in hardihood that the very first response to the very first question following the commencement of custody must be conclusively presumed to be the product of an overborne will.

If the rule announced today were truly based on a conclusion that all confessions resulting from custodial interrogation are coerced, then it would simply have no rational foundation. Compare *Tot v. United States*, 319 U.S. 463, 466; *United States v. Romano*, 382 U.S. 136. A *fortiori* that would be true of the extension of the rule to exculpatory statements, which the Court effects after a brief discussion of why, in the Court's view, they must be deemed incriminatory but without any discussion of why they must be deemed coerced. See *Wilson v. United States*, 162 U.S. 613, 624. Even if one were to postulate that the Court's concern is not that all confessions induced by police interrogation are coerced but rather that some such confessions are coerced and present judicial procedures are believed to be inadequate to identify the confessions that are coerced and those that are not, it would still not be essential to impose the rule that the Court has now fashioned. Transcripts or observers could be required, specific time limits, tailored to fit the cause, could be imposed, or other devices could be utilized to reduce the chances that otherwise indiscernible coercion will produce an inadmissible confession.

On the other hand, even if one assumed that there was an adequate factual basis for the conclusion that all confessions obtained during in-custody interrogation are the product of compulsion, the rule propounded by the Court would still be irrational, for, apparently, it is only if the accused is also warned of his right to counsel and waives both that right and the right against self-incrimination that the inherent compulsiveness of interrogation disappears. But if the defendant may not answer without a warning a question such as "Where were you last night?" without having his answer be a compelled one, how can the Court ever accept his negative answer to the question of whether he wants to consult his retained counsel or counsel whom the court will appoint? And why if counsel is present and the accused nevertheless confesses, or counsel tells the accused to tell the truth, and that is what the accused does, is the situation any less coercive insofar as the accused is concerned? The Court apparently realizes its dilemma of foreclosing questioning without the necessary warnings but at the same time permitting the accused, sitting in the same chair in front of the same policemen, to waive his right to consult an attorney. It expects, however, that the accused will not often waive the right; and if it is claimed that he has, the State faces a severe, if not impossible burden of proof.

All of this makes very little sense in terms of the compulsion which the Fifth Amendment proscribes. That amendment deals with compelling the accused himself. It is his free will that is involved. Confessions and incriminating admissions, as such, are not forbidden evidence; only those which are compelled are banned. I doubt that the Court observes these distinctions today. By considering any answers to any interrogation to be compelled regardless of the content and course of examination and by escalating the requirements to prove waiver, the Court not only prevents the use of compelled confessions but for all practical purposes forbids interrogation except in the presence of counsel. That is, instead of confining itself to protection of the right against compelled self-incrimination the Court has created a limited Fifth Amendment right to counsel—or, as the Court expresses it, a "need for counsel to protect the Fifth Amendment privilege . . ." *Ante*, at 470. The focus then is not on the will of the accused but on the will of counsel and how much influence he can have on the accused. Obviously there is no warrant in the Fifth Amendment for thus installing counsel as the arbiter of the privilege.

In sum, for all the Court's expounding on the menacing atmosphere of police interrogation procedures, it has failed to supply any foundation for the conclusions it draws or the measures it adopts.

IV

Criticism of the Court's opinion, however, cannot stop with a demonstration that the factual and textual bases for the rule it propounds are, at best, less than compelling. Equally relevant is an assessment of the rule's consequences measured against community values. The Court's duty to assess the consequences of its action is not satisfied by the utterance of the truth that a value of our system of criminal justice is

(Continues)

"to respect the inviolability of the human personality" and to require government to produce the evidence against the accused by its own independent labors. *Ante*, at 460. More than the human dignity of the accused is involved; the human personality of others in the society must also be preserved. Thus the values reflected by the privilege are not the sole desideratum; society's interest in the general security is of equal weight.

The obvious underpinning of the Court's decision is a deep-seated distrust of all confessions. As the Court declares that the accused may not be interrogated without counsel present, absent a waiver of the right to counsel, and as the Court all but admonishes the lawyer to advise the accused to remain silent, the result adds up to a judicial judgment that evidence from the accused should not be used against him in any way, whether compelled or not. This is the not so subtle overtone of the opinion—that it is inherently wrong for the police to gather evidence from the accused himself. And this is precisely the nub of this dissent. I see nothing wrong or immoral, and certainly nothing unconstitutional, in the police's asking a suspect whom they have reasonable cause to arrest whether or not he killed his wife or in confronting him with the evidence on which the arrest was based, at least where he has been plainly advised that he may remain completely silent, see *Escobedo v. Illinois*, 378 U.S. 478, 499 (dissenting opinion). Until today, "the admissions or confessions of the prisoner, when voluntarily and freely made, have always ranked high in the scale of incriminating evidence." *Brown v. Walker*, 161 U.S. 591, 596; see also *Hopt v. Utah*, 110 U.S. 574, 584–585. Particularly when corroborated, as where the police have confirmed the accused's disclosure of the hiding place of implements or fruits of the crime, such confessions have the highest reliability and significantly contribute to the certitude with which we may believe the accused is guilty. Moreover, it is by no means certain that the process of confessing is injurious to the accused. To the contrary it may provide psychological relief and enhance the prospects for rehabilitation.

This is not to say that the value of respect for the inviolability of the accused's individual personality should be accorded no weight or that all confessions should be indiscriminately admitted. This Court has long read the Constitution to proscribe compelled confessions, a salutary rule from which there should be no retreat. But I see no sound basis, factual or otherwise, and the Court gives none, for concluding that the present rule against the receipt of coerced confessions is inadequate for the task of sorting out inadmissible evidence and must be replaced by the per se rule which is now imposed. Even if the new concept can be said to have advantages of some sort over the present law, they are far outweighed by its likely undesirable impact on other very relevant and important interests.

The most basic function of any government is to provide for the security of the individual and of his property. *Lanzetta v. New Jersey*, 306 U.S. 451, 455. These ends of society are served by the criminal laws which for the most part are aimed at the prevention of crime. Without the reasonably effective performance of the task of preventing private violence and retaliation, it is idle to talk about human dignity and civilized values.

The modes by which the criminal laws serve the interest in general security are many. First the murderer who has taken the life of another is removed from the streets, deprived of his liberty and thereby prevented from repeating his offense. In view of the statistics on recidivism in this country[104] and of the number of instances in which apprehension occurs only after repeated offenses, no one can sensibly claim that this aspect of the criminal law does not prevent crime or contribute significantly to the personal security of the ordinary citizen.

Secondly, the swift and sure apprehension of those who refuse to respect the personal security and dignity of their neighbor unquestionably has its impact on others who might be similarly tempted. That the criminal law is wholly or partly ineffective with a segment of the population or with many of those who have been apprehended and convicted is a very faulty basis for concluding that it is not effective with respect to the great bulk of our citizens or for thinking that without the criminal laws, or in the absence of their enforcement, there would be no increase in crime. Arguments of this nature are not borne out by any kind of reliable evidence that I have seen to this date.

Thirdly, the law concerns itself with those whom it has confined. The hope and aim of modern penology, fortunately, is as soon as possible to return the convict to society a better and more law-abiding man than when he left. Sometimes there is success, sometimes failure. But at least the effort is made, and it should be made to the very maximum extent of our present and future capabilities.

The rule announced today will measurably weaken the ability of the criminal law to perform these tasks. It is a deliberate calculus to prevent interrogations, to reduce the incidence of confessions and pleas of guilty and to increase the number of trials.[105] Criminal trials, no matter how efficient the police are, are not sure bets for the prosecution, nor should they be if the evidence is not forthcoming. Under the present law, the prosecution fails to prove its case in about 30% of the criminal cases actually tried in the federal courts. See Federal Offenders: 1964, *supra*, note 4, at 6 (Table 4), 59 (Table 1); Federal Offenders: 1963, *supra*, note 4, at 5 (Table 3); District of Columbia Offenders: 1963, *supra*, note 4, at 2 (Table 1). But it is something else again to remove from the ordinary criminal case all those confessions which heretofore have been held to be free and voluntary acts of the accused and to thus establish a new constitutional barrier to the ascertainment of truth by the judicial process. There is, in my view, every reason to believe that a good many criminal defendants who otherwise would have been convicted on what this Court has previously thought to be the most satisfactory kind of evidence will now, under this new version of the Fifth Amendment, either not be tried at all or will be acquitted if the State's evidence, minus the confession, is put to the test of litigation.

I have no desire whatsoever to share the responsibility for any such impact on the present criminal process.

In some unknown number of cases the Court's rule will return a killer, a rapist or other criminal to the streets and to the environment which produced him, to repeat his crime whenever it pleases him. As a consequence, there will not be a gain, but a loss, in human dignity. The real concern is not the unfortunate consequences of this new decision on the criminal law as an abstract, disembodied series of authoritative proscriptions, but the impact on those who rely on the public authority for protection and who without it can only engage in violent self-help with guns, knives and the help of their neighbors similarly inclined. There is, of course, a saving factor: the next victims are uncertain, unnamed and unrepresented in this case.

Nor can this decision do other than have a corrosive effect on the criminal law as an effective device to prevent crime. A major component in its effectiveness in this regard is its swift and sure enforcement. The easier it is to get away with rape and murder, the less the deterrent effect on those who are inclined to attempt it. This is still good common sense. If it were not, we should posthaste liquidate the whole law enforcement establishment as a useless, misguided effort to control human conduct.

And what about the accused who has confessed or would confess in response to simple, noncoercive questioning and whose guilt could not otherwise be proved? Is it so clear that release is the best thing for him in every case? Has it so unquestionably been resolved that in each and every case it would be better for him not to confess and to return to his environment with no attempt whatsoever to help him? I think not. It may well be that in many cases it will be no less than a callous disregard for his own welfare as well as for the interests of his next victim.

There is another aspect to the effect of the Court's rule on the person whom the police have arrested on probable cause. The fact is that he may not be guilty at all and may be able to extricate himself quickly and simply if he were told the circumstances of his arrest and were asked to explain. This effort, and his release, must now await the hiring of a lawyer or his appointment by the court, consultation with counsel and then a session with the police or the prosecutor. Similarly, where probable cause exists to arrest several suspects, as where the body of the victim is discovered in a house having several residents, compare *Johnson v. State*, 238 Md. 140, 207 A. 2d 643 (1965), *cert. denied*, 382 U.S. 1013, it will often be true that a suspect may be cleared only through the results of interrogation of other suspects. Here too the release of the innocent may be delayed by the Court's rule.

Much of the trouble with the Court's new rule is that it will operate indiscriminately in all criminal cases, regardless of the severity of the crime or the circumstances involved. It applies to every defendant, whether the professional criminal or one committing a crime of momentary passion who is not part and parcel of organized crime. It will slow down the investigation and the apprehension of confederates in those cases where time is of the essence, such as kidnapping, see *Brinegar v. United States*, 338 U.S. 160, 183 (Jackson, J., dissenting); *People v. Modesto*, 62 Cal. 2d 436, 446, 398 P.2d 753, 759 (1965), those involving the national security, see *United States v. Drummond*, 354 F.2d 132, 147 (C.A. 2d Cir. 1965) (*en banc*) (espionage case), pet. for *cert.* pending, No. 1203, Misc., O.T. 1965; cf. *Gessner v. United States*, 354 F.2d 726, 730, n. 10 (C.A. 10th Cir. 1965) (upholding, in espionage case, trial ruling that Government need not submit classified portions of interrogation transcript), and some of those involving organized crime. In the latter context the lawyer who arrives may also be the lawyer for the defendant's colleagues and can be relied upon to insure that no breach of the organization's security takes place even though the accused may feel that the best thing he can do is to cooperate.

At the same time, the Court's per se approach may not be justified on the ground that it provides a "bright line" permitting the authorities to judge in advance whether interrogation may safely be pursued

(Continues)

(*Continued*)

without jeopardizing the admissibility of any information obtained as a consequence. Nor can it be claimed that judicial time and effort, assuming that is a relevant consideration, will be conserved because of the ease of application of the new rule. Today's decision leaves open such questions as whether the accused was in custody, whether his statements were spontaneous or the product of interrogation, whether the accused has effectively waived his rights, and whether nontestimonial evidence introduced at trial is the fruit of statements made during a prohibited interrogation, all of which are certain to prove productive of uncertainty during investigation and litigation during prosecution. For all these reasons, if further restrictions on police interrogation are desirable at this time, a more flexible approach makes much more sense than the Court's constitutional straitjacket which forecloses more discriminating treatment by legislative or rule-making pronouncements.

Applying the traditional standards to the cases before the Court, I would hold these confessions voluntary. I would therefore affirm in Nos. 759, 760, and 761, and reverse in No. 584.

Notes

101. Of course the Court does not deny that it is departing from prior precedent; it expressly overrules *Crooker and Cicenia, ante,* at 479, n. 48, and it acknowledges that in the instant "cases we might not find the defendants' statements to have been involuntary in traditional terms," *ante,* at 457.

102. In fact, the type of sustained interrogation described by the Court appears to be the exception rather than the rule. A survey of 399 cases in one city found that in almost half of the cases the interrogation lasted less than 30 minutes. Barrett, Police Practices and the Law—From Arrest to Release or Charge, 50 *Calif. L. Rev.* 11, 41–45 (1962). Questioning tends to be confused and sporadic and is usually concentrated on confrontations with witnesses or new items of evidence, as these are obtained by officers conducting the investigation. See generally LaFave, *Arrest: The Decision to Take a Suspect into Custody* 386 (1965); *ALI, A Model Code of Pre-Arraignment Procedure, Commentary* 5.01, at 170, n. 4 (Tent. Draft No. 1, 1966).

103. By contrast, the Court indicates that in applying this new rule it "will not pause to inquire in individual cases whether the defendant was aware of his rights without a warning being given." *Ante,* at 468. The reason given is that assessment of the knowledge of the defendant based on information as to age, education, intelligence, or prior contact with authorities can never be more than speculation, while a warning is a clear-cut fact. But the officers' claim that they gave the requisite warnings may be disputed, and facts respecting the defendant's prior experience may be undisputed and be of such a nature as to virtually preclude any doubt that the defendant knew of his rights. See *United States v. Bolden,* 355 F.2d 453 (C.A. 7th Cir. 1965), petition for cert. pending No. 1146, O.T. 1965 (Secret Service Agent); *People v. Du Bont,* 235 Cal. App. 2d 844, 45 Cal. Rptr. 717, pet. for *cert.* pending No. 1053, Misc., O.T. 1965 (former police officer).

104. Precise statistics on the extent of recidivism are unavailable, in part because not all crimes are solved and in part because criminal records of convictions in different jurisdictions are not brought together by a central data collection agency. Beginning in 1963, however, the Federal Bureau of Investigation began collating data on "Careers in Crime," which it publishes in its *Uniform Crime Reports.* Of 92,869 offenders processed in 1963 and 1964, 76% had a prior arrest record on some charge. Over a period of 10 years the group had accumulated 434,000 charges. FBI, *Uniform Crime Reports—1964,* 27–28. In 1963 and 1964 between 23% and 25% of all offenders sentenced in 88 federal district courts (excluding the District Court for the District of Columbia) whose criminal records were reported had previously been sentenced to a term of imprisonment of 13 months or more. Approximately an additional 40% had a prior record less than prison (juvenile record, probation record, etc.). Administrative Office of the United States Courts, *Federal Offenders in the United States District Courts: 1964,* x, 36 (hereinafter cited as *Federal Offenders: 1964*); Administrative Office of the United States Courts, *Federal Offenders in the United States District Courts: 1963,* 25–27 (hereinafter cited as *Federal Offenders: 1963*). During the same two years in the District Court for the District of Columbia between 28% and 35% of those sentenced had prior prison records and from 37% to 40% had a prior record less than prison. Federal Offenders: 1964, xii, 64, 66; Administrative Office of the United States Courts, *Federal Offenders in the United States District Court for the District of Columbia: 1963,* 8, 10 (hereinafter cited as *District of Columbia Offenders: 1963*).

A similar picture is obtained if one looks at the subsequent records of those released from confinement. In 1964, 12.3% of persons on federal probation had their probation revoked because of the commission of major violations (defined as one in which the probationer has been committed to imprisonment for a period of 90 days or more, been placed on probation for over one year on a new offense, or has absconded with felony charges outstanding). Twenty-three and two-tenths percent of parolees and 16.9% of those who had been mandatorily released after service of a portion of their sentence likewise committed major violations. *Reports of the Proceedings of the Judicial Conference of the United States* and *Annual Report of the Director of the Administrative Office of the United States Courts: 1965*, 138. See also Mandel et al., Recidivism Studied and Defined, 56 *J. Crim. L., C. & P. S.* 59 (1965) (within five years of release 62.33% of sample had committed offenses placing them in recidivist category).

105. Eighty-eight federal district courts (excluding the District Court for the District of Columbia) disposed of the cases of 33,381 criminal defendants in 1964. Only 12.5% of those cases were actually tried. Of the remaining cases, 89.9% were terminated by convictions upon pleas of guilty and 10.1% were dismissed. Stated differently, approximately 90% of all convictions resulted from guilty pleas. *Federal Offenders: 1964, supra*, note 4, 3–6. In the District Court for the District of Columbia a higher percentage, 27%, went to trial, and the defendant pleaded guilty in approximately 78% of the cases terminated prior to trial. *Id.*, at 58–59. No reliable statistics are available concerning the percentage of cases in which guilty pleas are induced because of the existence of a confession or of physical evidence unearthed as a result of a confession. Undoubtedly the number of such cases is substantial.

Perhaps of equal significance is the number of instances of known crimes which are not solved. In 1964, only 388,946, or 23.9% of 1,626,574 serious known offenses were cleared. The clearance rate ranged from 89.8% for homicides to 18.7% for larceny. FBI, *Uniform Crime Reports—1964*, 20–22, 101. Those who would replace interrogation as an investigatorial tool by modern scientific investigation techniques significantly overestimate the effectiveness of present procedures, even when interrogation is included.

Crime, Punishment, and the Death Penalty

Chapter Objectives

In this chapter you will learn . . .

- The two main types of crimes
- The three main criminal mental states
- The types and purposes of criminal punishment
- Why the death penalty is legal, but caning is not
- The history of capital punishment in the United States

Introduction

In this chapter we examine crimes in detail and attempt to understand the criminal mind to some extent. We also try to understand why society reacts to crimes as it does, and where punishment fits into the equation. Finally, we look at the ultimate form of punishment—the death penalty—and consider whether it is even permissible under the Constitution; many say that it is, while many others vehemently disagree. Read on.

Introduction of Crime into Society

Let us go back in time to the very first group of people here on earth. Suppose that you were one of them, and you lived happily among the rest of the group. Everyone worked together, ate together, socialized together, and generally helped one another. But the great sense of community suffered a major setback one day, when two of these early human beings got into an argument. One of them then picked up a big rock, hit the other one over the head, and killed him! You, along with the rest of the community, looked on in horror. It was not only the very first murder that you *witnessed*, but it was actually the very first murder ever to take place! In fact, up until that point, none of you had fathomed the possibility of one human being intentionally taking the life of another.

To follow along more easily, let's call this killer caveman Mur (as in mur-derer), and we will call the dead fellow Vic (as in vic-tim). As you and the others gather around poor Vic, you begin to wonder, "what do we do about Mur?" As the shock of the murder begins to sink in, it turns into anger, and the anger then turns into reasoned thinking. Some of you might even feel sorry for Mur, wondering what must

have gone through his mind to get him to the point of killing Vic. As you all continue to think about it, you draw the conclusion that it is a bad thing and that it must never happen again. Accordingly, you inform Mur that what he did was wrong, and that he can never do it again, and that no one else would be allowed to do it, either.

So, after some months had passed, everything settled down again, and everyone happily went about their ways—until Mur struck again, that is. You see, the problem with the directive that all of you gave to Mur, "you cannot do this ever again," was that there were no consequences if he disobeyed. And so, as is the case for various reasons, people often tend to repeat their actions, whether the habits are good ones or bad ones. Mur got into another argument with someone else, a woman named Su, and killed her, too!

At that point the community realized that imposing laws without consequences was ineffective. They picked up some rocks themselves and stoned Mur to death. This time, however, they were not so naïve as to think that just because they killed Mur, murder would forever be extinguished; they realized that other human beings could become capable of murder.

A few years later, Sam killed his neighbor, Jak, because of a dispute over property: Jak always loaded his logs on Sam's property line, very close to the entrance of his cave. Sam found this to be inconsiderate, and clubbed Jak to death. This time, the community was prepared: Murder was already against the law, and now the question was what to do with Sam. Should they stone him to death, as with Mur, or perhaps impose a different type of punishment?

Types of Crimes

Before we go any further, let's take a look at the two main types of crimes: *malum in se* and *malum prohibitum*. Those are Latin phrases; typically, if you come across words in the law that look foreign, chances are that they are Latin. *Malum in se* crimes are considered evil, or otherwise morally wrong; whereas *malum prohibitum* crimes are against the law because they are likely to bring about harm or disorder. Here are some examples.

Murder, rape, assault, arson, kidnapping, and burglary are considered to be *malum in se* crimes, because they are, by society's measure, "bad" things. Even though most criminal laws are state laws and thus vary from state to state, all of those acts are crimes, *malum in se* ones, in all 50 states.

Examples of *malum prohibitum* crimes include: riding a motorcycle without a helmet, driving a car without a license, driving through a red light, and operating a school that does not have a fire exit. None of those activities are considered evil or morally wrong, but they could lead to disorder and, even worse, harm.

Malum in se crimes are typically considered more serious than *malum prohibitum* ones, thereby warranting a more severe punishment. In every state, then, the penalty for, say, robbing a bank will be greater than the penalty for keeping a pet goat in your backyard if you live in a nonagricultural residential zone.

Criminal Mental States

Now that we have talked about the two main types of crimes, let's focus on the criminal. There are three basic criminal mental states: intent, recklessness, and negligence. Let's take a look at each of them.

Intent

Intent is when a person willfully does something; he or she *means* to do it. If you are done drinking a can of soda and find a garbage can in which to throw it away, then your having thrown the soda in the garbage is an intentional act. However, if you *accidentally* also throw away your house keys, that is most certainly not an intentional act.

In terms of crimes, if a person means to commit a certain act, then that act is intentional, *even if the person is not aware that the act is a crime* (more about that later).

Recklessness

Recklessness is the second-most severe criminal mental state, behind intent, which is why we mention it next in order. However, to truly understand recklessness, you need to understand negligence first.

Negligence

Negligence, in its simplest definition, is the failure to use reasonable care. For instance, suppose that Owen is a sports fan and he drives to the store to buy the newspaper to find out whether his favorite team won last night's game. He rushes back to his car and begins to drive because he is late for an appointment. Because he is so impatient to find out the score of the game, he begins to look through the newspaper while driving. Unfortunately, he smashes his car into a storefront window because he was not paying attention.

Along with any civil penalties that Owen might incur, he is also criminally liable for negligence. Naturally, Owen did not *intend* to drive his car into the storefront window. Certainly, he did not wish to cause injury or property damage to either anyone, including himself. Owen caused an accident, but he is still liable, because he still should have been more careful. Because Owen failed to use reasonable care in driving, he is negligent.

Technically, a person would be liable for negligence if he or she failed to use reasonable care *when a duty of care was* owed. For the purposes of our discussion, that condition will not be an issue, because we all generally owe a duty not to cause harm to one another, whether the harm would be physical, economic, or damaging to one's reputation.

Back to Recklessness

A great example of recklessness can be found in the 1992 movie, *Scent of a Woman*, starring Al Pacino. Pacino, who won the Academy Award for Best Actor for his role, portrayed a retired army colonel named Frank Slade, who had gone blind and had become quite outrageous in his behavior.

In one scene, Slade drives a Ferarri through the busy streets of New York City, guided only by a college student who was hired to take care of him, who periodically yells out to him when it is time to turn. Slade's act, a blind man driving a sports car at high speeds in the world's largest city, would be considered reckless. Now that you know the example, here is the best way to define recklessness: it is negligence that has a high degree of probability of occurring.

Consider the difference between the examples involving Owen and Slade. Owen, while rifling through a newspaper but fully sighted and driving at a reasonable speed, *might* wind up causing an accident. Slade, blind and driving at excessively high speeds, *probably will* cause an accident. A good way to remember the standard for recklessness is to think of it as: "super-duper" negligence.

Proceeding further with our examples, let's look at a situation where that storefront window is smashed into by cars driven by.

1. A man named Palmer, who *deliberately* drove his car into the store window, because he wanted to cause damage to it;
2. Slade, who was blind and took a sports car for a joyride; and
3. Owen, who was thumbing through a newspaper while driving.

In terms of any criminal liability, their actions would be considered intentional, reckless, and negligent, respectively. Generally, the closer an act is to being intentional, the more severe it is considered, and the more likely it is that the criminal will be punished. For instance, if a person had been killed on each instance when the cars smashed through the storefront window, Palmer would probably be punished most severely, because he *meant* to cause the accident; Slade would be punished almost as severely—he did not *mean* to cause the accident but his actions were highly irresponsible—and Owen would be punished least severely of the three; his actions, though not as awful, still fell short of the standard of reasonable care.

Now that we have covered the basic criminal mental states and how they relate to punishment, let us return to our example of the murdering cavemen and discuss the main types and purposes of punishment.

Types and Purposes of Punishment

Punishment is a consequence of a crime. If a person commits a crime, then he or she is likely to be punished. But, *why*? What is the purpose of punishing a criminal? The answer to that question may not be as simple as it sounds. Think about it for a while. As you are thinking, let us consider the five main theories of punishment, and see what you think about each of them.

Retribution

Retribution is perhaps the type of punishment most rooted in emotion; it is based on revenge: an eye for an eye. In its most extreme form, it imposes the death penalty on murderers because if they took a life, they deserve their lives to be taken as well.

General Deterrence

For some people, the reason to punish is to make someone suffer, or otherwise pay, for his or her criminal act. That puts all of the focus on the criminal. For others, however, the second-worst part about a crime (other than the harm inflicted upon the victim), is that there might be a likelihood of a similar crime occurring at some point in the future. Those folks are more concerned with inflicting a punishment that would prevent others from occurring. The more severe the punishment, they believe, the less likely another person would commit a similar or identical crime. For instance, imposing the death penalty for murder might cause someone else to think twice about killing someone, for fear of facing the death penalty.

Specific Deterrence

Closely linked to general deterrence is specific deterrence, which is a reason to punish with a focus on preventing the criminal from ever committing a crime (particularly the one for which he or she is punished) ever again. In that case, the death penalty would be the ultimate form of specific deterrence, because if a person is dead, then, obviously, he or she cannot commit any more crimes.

Incarceration

Here is where some folks might get a bit confused, because *incarceration* means to be imprisoned, but it is also a theory of punishment. You see, the actual *act* of incarceration, such as sentencing someone to 20 years in prison, may be done for any number of punishment theories, including retribution, general deterrence, or specific deterrence. But the *theory* of incarceration is probably the least emotional of all; it is all about removing the danger from society.

If a man robs a bank, starts a fire, or steals a car, what is the best way to keep him from doing that again, short of executing him? Locking him up, of course. The theory of incarceration does not focus on making him suffer, nor is it concerned about how his punishment will affect him, or others, in the future. The incarceration theory is chiefly concerned with removing the danger from society.

Rehabilitation

The punishment theory of rehabilitation does not seem like much of a punishment at all. Actually, it sounds more like a treatment. Then again, we identified punishment as a *consequence*; under that definition, then, rehabilitation most certainly is a type of punishment.

Rehabilitation is entirely different from the other four punishment types insofar as it is the most hopeful in the criminal's ability to change his or her ways. Rehabilitationists begin with the premise that it is normal to be good and law abiding, and that committing crimes is an aberration that is often attributable to some type of behavior deficiency that can be remedied. Instead of treating the criminal with anger (retribution), hopelessness (incarceration), intimidation (specific deterrence), or entirely dismissing his or her significance (general deterrence), rehabilitation seeks to reeducate the individual, preparing him or her to reenter society as a moral, upstanding, law-abiding citizen.

Where do you stand on punishment? Are you a retributionist or are you more focused on deterrence? Do you concentrate on removing the danger from society or removing the criminal propensity from the person? As you continue to reflect on your answer, let us look at the issue in terms of the Constitution.

The Eighth Amendment and Capital Punishment

The Eighth Amendment of the Constitution states: *Excessive bail shall not be required, nor excessive fines imposed, nor cruel and unusual punishments inflicted.* Though that amendment is only 16 words in length, it is yet another Constitutional provision over which legal scholars have disagreed for many years, and the debate continues to this day.

Specifically, 3 of the 16 words are the controversial ones: *excessive, cruel,* and *unusual.* Actually, the word *excessive* deals mostly with bails and fines, and pales in comparison to frequency of debate generated by the other two words, which often go hand in hand: *cruel* and *unusual.* Before we deal with what might constitute cruel and unusual punishment, let's quickly touch upon what an excessive bail or fine might be.

Bail is the process by which a criminal suspect posts a specific amount of money as security in order to be released prior to trial. To illustrate, suppose that Angela was suspected of burglarizing a convenience store and was being held in prison prior to trial. Her bail would be the amount of money left as a deposit with the court for her release while awaiting trial. If Angela returns for trial on time, then the overwhelming majority of the money will be refunded to her. The amount at which bail would be set, if bail would be granted at all, depends on the judge's discretion.

Suppose, then, that Angela's bail was set at ten million dollars. A bail that high would certainly be considered excessive! Even one million dollars, a hundred thousand, or fifty thousand dollar bail would be considered excessive for a relatively small crime of stealing a few hundred dollars' worth of cash and other items from a grocery store. That type of bail, then, would be considered excessive.

Similarly, leaving a car in front of a parking meter after the time on the meter has expired will result in a fine. If that fine is, say, ten thousand dollars, undoubtedly it would be considered excessive! In most cases, that might be far more than what the entire car is worth! Even one thousand dollars would be excessive, as would a hundred dollars, although in my home town of Manhattan, a hundred dollars for an overtime meter is par for the course. Nowadays, just about everything in Manhattan is excessively priced, but that is a whole other story.

The main focus of our discussion, then, is cruel and unusual punishment. What exactly does that mean? What type of punishment would be cruel and unusual? Let's take a look at a news event that made front-page headlines a few years ago to find out more.

Singapore Caning

Caning is the act by which a convicted criminal is lashed by use of a wooden cane, usually to the palms of the hands, the soles of the feet, and other body parts. Caning is prohibited in the United States and many other countries but permitted in some other ones.

In 1994, American-born Michael Fay was 19 years old and living in Singapore, where he attended the Singapore American School. Fay was convicted of vandalizing various automobiles and, as part of his punishment, which included four months in prison and a fine, he was sentenced to six lashes by cane.

U.S. President Bill Clinton condemned the practice and asked the Sinagporian government for clemency on Fay's behalf. The sentence was not commuted, but as a gesture of respect to the president, it was reduced from six lashes to four. The caning received extensive coverage by the American media, as the American public was exposed to a form of punishment not permitted in the United States because it is a prime example of what would be considered cruel and unusual under the Eighth Amendment.

President Bill Clinton condemned the practice of caning, but the Singaporean government caned an American vandal, anyway.

Other types of punishment that would be considered cruel and unusual include denying basic needs to prisoners (such as food, clothing, medical attention), or causing them mental or physical harm based on sleep deprivation or physical attack. Let's take a look at how the Supreme Court has ruled regarding cruel and unusual punishment.

Excessive Punishment

Most cases with which the Supreme Court has dealt regarding cruel and unusual punishment focused less on the *type* of punishment than on the degree. If you recall, a case reaches the Supreme Court on appeal, which means that the federal courts would have had to rule that certain types of punishment were permitted. Such was not the case. It was not as if the lower courts permitted physical abuse, deprivation of basic needs, or other such constitutional violations. Rather, the Court has mostly examined cases dealing with whether or not the type of punishment used was excessive.

In *Robinson v. California*, decided in 1962, the Court held that a 90-day prison term for the misdemeanor of having used narcotics, amounts to cruel and unusual punishment, and added that narcotic addiction is an illness and should be treated as such. But two dissenting Justices, Clark and White, determined that the petitioner, Robinson, had not lost his faculties because of his drug use and that drug addiction is different from disease insofar as the former can cause potential future harm to others in a more prevalent manner.

In *Hammelin v. Michigan*, however, decided in 1991, the Court established that cruel and unusual punishment applies to excessive sentencing only where there is a "gross disproportionality."

A plurality also determined that the Eighth Amendment does not establish a proportionality standard, and Justice Scalia pointed out that had the Founding Fathers wanted to comment about sentencing disproportionality, they certainly would have done so, considering that state constitutions at the time contained similar language. That comment underscores that the Founders had not overlooked that concept.

Let us now move onto the type of punishment that would seem to be the most cruel and unusual of all: the death penalty. Or, is it? Read on.

Capital Punishment: The Death Penalty

The death penalty has been used for centuries in countries around the world, among them, the United States. Although many other advanced industrialized nations have eliminated the death penalty, it remains legal in many states throughout America.

Convicted criminals had been sentenced to death in the United States since the early 1600s, long before this territory had even become the United States. The first official execution on record once our nation was founded took place in February 1777, when convicted murderer John Mecom was hanged.

Note: If you noticed, the past tense of hang is *hanged* when dealing with the hanging of a human being, but is *hung* when dealing with other types of hanging. For instance, you would say: I *hung* the laundry, or I *hung* out at the mall yesterday afternoon. However, you would say, three convicted criminals were *hanged* this morning.

Many other executions did not involve murder convictions. Some examples include:

- John Jacobs, who was hanged for counterfeiting 11 days after Mecom.
- James Fitzpatrick, who was hanged for burglary in 1788.
- John Vann, who was hanged for horse stealing in 1782.
- Tom Hood, who was hanged for arson in 1787.
- John White, who was hanged for piracy in 1788.
- Henry Hombeck, who was hanged for forgery in 1789.
- Polly Barclay, who was hanged for conspiracy to murder in 1806.
- William Smith, who was hanged for assisting a runaway slave in 1810.
- Timothy Webster, who was hanged for espionage in 1862.
- David Jones, who was hanged for desertion from the military in 1864.
- Amos Johnson, who was hanged for rape in 1887.
- Sam Wright, who, in one of the first executions of the 20th Century, was hanged for attempted rape in 1900.

Most executions until the 20th Century were for murder, and most were conducted by hanging. There were some exceptions, though:

- Many deserting soldiers were shot to death.
- Many black slaves convicted of murder were burned to death.
- Some convicted of treason were bludgeoned to death.

By the late 19th Century, electrocution was introduced as a method of execution, and eventually surpassed hanging as the most common form of capital punishment by the early 1920s. In 1930, Robert White was executed via the gas chamber, introducing yet another form capital punishment. In 1984, Autry James was executed via lethal injection, which has since become the most popular method of choice. As of this writing, only New Hampshire and Washington continue to permit execution by hanging, and only Idaho and Oklahoma permit a firing squad.

Currently, the death penalty is legal in over three-quarters of the states, but a little over a generation ago, it was illegal throughout the country. Let us take a look at how the death penalty was outlawed, made a legal comeback, and now experiences new challenges.

Death Penalty Cases

In the case *Furman v. Georgia*, decided in 1972, the Supreme Court directly questioned the Constitutionality of capital punishment. The Justices were in such disagreement—their views ranging along various points of whether capital punishment is cruel and unusual *per se* to whether it is not— they ultimately concluded that the existing death penalty statutes, as written, were unconstitutional. The *Furman* decision established a brief era of confusion, and no executions took place until after the Court decided in *Gregg v. Georgia*,

in 1977, that Georgia's new death penalty laws now passed Constitutional muster. At that point, executions resumed.

The Court reconciled *Furman* and *Gregg* as follows: the previous Georgia death penalty statutes were found to be arbitrary and capricious, whereas the rewritten versions set forth objective criteria that would be reviewed at the appellate level, and allowed the sentencing judge to take the defendant's character into account.

Minors Who Murder

The death penalty was restored by *Gregg* in 1977. What about imposing a death sentence on convicted criminals who were under 18 years of age when they committed murder?

The Court addressed that issue in *Roper v. Simmons* in 2005. Petitioner Christopher Simmons was 17-years old when he planned and carried out the murder of Shirley Crook. The evidence against Simmons was overwhelming and included his own videotaped confession and reenactment of the crime. Simmons was convicted of murder and sentenced to death. Again, because this is a rather recent case, it is valuable to consider which specific Justices decided this case, and why they decided as they did.

Kennedy's Majority

Justice Kennedy wrote the majority opinion in *Roper*, determining that capital punishment for anyone who was under age 18 when having committed the crime in question is cruel and unusual *per se*.

Stevens' Concurrence

Justice Stevens emphasized that it is important for the Court to rule based on society's "evolving standards of decency." Otherwise, he said, the Eighth Amendment, as originally written, might allow the execution of a 7-year old. The Court referred to a national consensus prohibiting the execution of minors, as well as an international consensus, citing only a very small group of nations where such practice is allowed.

O'Connor's Dissent

Justice O'Connor did not ascribe to the majority's theory that there was a national consensus against the execution of persons under age 18. Rather, she identified it as a moral decision taken by the Court, and one directly contradicting that of the state legislature in *Roper* (which was in the state of Missouri). The thrust of O'Connor's dissent was on those grounds, that the decision was based less on a national consensus than on the Court's personal moral stance. O'Connor disagreed, however, with Justice Scalia, who in his dissent wrote that foreign and international laws have no place in the Court's decision-making process.

Scalia's Dissent

Justice Scalia bitterly dissented with the majority's holding, calling it a mockery of the judicial system and that by imposing decisions based on societal changes, the Court is proclaiming itself to be the sole arbiter of our nation's moral standards.

Scalia's points of view are particularly important to our understanding the Constitution because he was not legally opposed to society's standards changing, but believed that such changes must stem from the legislature, not the judiciary.

In examining the reasons by which convicted criminals were executed in the early days of our nation's history, we noticed several instances in which the crime was not murder. In later years—certainly in the 20th Century and beyond—executions for other crimes became virtually extinct.

Types of Crimes for Which Capital Punishment Is Imposed

In 1977, the Court held in *Coker v. Georgia* that a person cannot be punished by death for the rape of an adult woman. Erlich Anthony Coker was a convicted murderer who escaped from prison, broke into a couple's home, raped the woman, and stole their vehicle. Because of Coker's prior convictions and the rape committed along with armed robbery, the Georgia courts sentenced him to death.

The Supreme Court reversed the decision, determining that death sentences are *largely* reserved for crimes that result in the death of a human being. Because that is the predominant but not absolute standard, state legislatures have enacted subsequent laws sentencing child rapists to death.

Chief Justice Burger dissented, stating that the Court used a proportionality test to determine that the punishment did not fit the crime, with which he disagreed because he concluded that such a test undermined the Georgia legislature. His reasoning is similar to Justice Scalia's in *Roper*.

Most recently, the Supreme Court in *Kennedy v. Louisiana* held that the Eighth Amendment prohibits imposing the death penalty for the rape of a minor child if the act did not result in the death of the child. Although the Court acknowledged that the crime of raping a small child is extremely horrific, it stopped short of recognizing that it rose to the level of crimes that could be punishable by death; those would have to, at the very least, result in the death of the victim. Justice Kennedy wrote the decision for the majority of five, which also included Justices Stevens, Souter, Ginsburg, and Breyer. (Again, we include the names of the specific Justices as this is such a recent case and you should be familiar with them.)

The four-Justice dissenting opinion, written by Justice Alito and joined by Chief Justice Roberts and Justices Scalia and Thomas, argued that the Court had inappropriately usurped the power of the Louisiana State Legislature, and that the Eighth Amendment deals with protecting the rights of the accused but does not extend to repealing state criminal statutes.

As the most recent Constitutional interpretation of the death penalty as of this writing, *Kennedy* was a narrow five-to-four decision, which means that it would not be as difficult to overturn in the future as if, say, it were a unanimous decision or even a seven-to-two decision.

How Is the Death Penalty Not Cruel and Unusual?

Of all of the Supreme Court cases regarding the death penalty that we have examined, you will notice that there were none in which the Court decided that the death penalty is unconstitutional *per se*. How can that be, you might ask. If you give a convicted criminal the option of being executed or, say, receiving 10 lashes from a cane, wouldn't the criminal happily take his lashes rather than lose his or her life? How, then, is caning forbidden because it is cruel and unusual, but death by electrocution, the gas chamber, and lethal injection are not?

Cruel and unusual punishment does not mean that the punishment is more severe, just that it is more lingering and painful. The death penalty is supposed to be swift and almost instantaneous. Torture is what is sought to be prevented.

Because some execution methods have failed and have caused severe pain to those being executed, and because the mistake of executing the wrong person is irreversible, many states have repealed their death penalty legislation, and the debate about the propriety of capital punishment continues.

Conclusion

These then, are the theories of punishment and some applications of them that the Supreme Court has examined.

Quite often the United States' judicial system is described as imperfect, and it certainly is. Then again, it is also described by many as the least imperfect in the world, which is another way of saying it remains the greatest.

The cases and issues set forth in this chapter are designed to help you develop your own well-informed opinion on crime and punishment with regard to the Constitution.

In Chapter 10, we will take a look at a Constitutional term that is commonly used but less often understood: double jeopardy.

Questions for Review

1. What are *malum in se* and *malum prohibitum* crimes?
2. What are the three criminal mental states?
3. What is the punishment theory of retribution?
4. What is the punishment theory of general deterrence?
5. What is the punishment theory of specific deterrence?
6. What is the punishment theory of incarceration?
7. What is the punishment theory of rehabilitation?
8. What does the Eighth Amendment state about punishment?
9. What effect did *Furman v. Georgia* have on the death penalty?
10. What effect did *Gregg v. Georgia* have on the death penalty?

Constitutionally Speaking

What are your personal and legal positions about the death penalty? Do you think it is ever justifiable, such as in the most extreme and horrific types of murders? Do you think that it is ever justifiable in cases other than murder? Is the death penalty unconstitutional in any sense, under certain circumstances, or never?

Constitutional Cases

Here are a couple of old and interesting cases regarding punishment and the Eighth Amendment: *Wilkerson v. Utah*, and *Weems v. United States*.

Wilkerson v. Utah, 99 U.S. 130 (1878)

ERROR to the Supreme Court of the Territory of Utah.

The facts are stated in the opinion of the court.

Submitted by Mr. E. D. Hoge and Mr. P. L. Williams for the plaintiff in error, and by The Solicitor-General for the defendant in error.

MR. JUSTICE CLIFFORD delivered the opinion of the court.

Duly organized Territories are invested with legislative power, which extends to all rightful subjects of legislation not inconsistent with the Constitution and laws of the United States. Rev. Stats., sect. 1851.

Congress organized the Territory of Utah on the 9th of September, 1850, and provided that the legislative power and authority of the Territory shall be vested in the governor and legislative assembly. 9 Stat. 454.

Sufficient appears to show that the prisoner named in the record was legally charged with the wilful, malicious, and premeditated murder of William Baxter, with malice aforethought, by indictment of the grand jury in due form of law, as fully set forth in the transcript; and that he, upon his arraignment, pleaded that he was not guilty of the alleged offence. Pursuant to the order of the court, a jury for the trial of the prisoner was duly impanelled and sworn; and it appears that the jury, after a full and fair trial, found, by their verdict, that the prisoner was guilty of murder in the first degree.

Regular proceedings followed, and the record also shows that the presiding justice in open court sentenced the prisoner as follows: That 'you be taken from hence to some place in this Territory, where you shall be safely kept until Friday, the fourteenth day of December next; that between the hours of ten o'clock in the forenoon and three o'clock in the afternoon of the last-named day you be taken from your place of confinement to some place within this district, and that you there be publicly shot until you are dead.'

Proceedings in the court of original jurisdiction being ended, the prisoner sued out a writ of error and removed the cause into the Supreme Court of the Territory, where the judgment of the subordinate court was affirmed. Final judgment having been rendered in the Supreme Court of the Territory, the prisoner sued out the present writ of error, the act of Congress providing that such a writ from this court to the Supreme Court of the Territory will lie in criminal cases where the accused is sentenced to capital punishment or is convicted of bigamy or polygamy. 18 Stat. 254.

Appended to the proceedings is the assignment of error imputed to the court below, which is repeated in the same words in the brief of his counsel filed since the case was removed into this court. No exception was taken to the proceedings in either court prior to the sentence, the assignment of error being that the court below erred in affirming the judgment of the court of original jurisdiction and in adjudging and sentencing the prisoner to be shot to death.

Murder, as defined by the Compiled Laws of the Territory, is the unlawful killing of a human being with malice aforethought, and the provision is that such malice may be express or implied. Comp. Laws Utah, 1876, 585. Express malice is when there is manifested a deliberate intention unlawfully to take away the life of a fellow-creature, and it may be implied when there is no considerable provocation, or when the circumstances attending the killing show an abandoned or malignant heart.

Criminal homicide, when perpetrated by a person lying in wait, or by any other kind of wilful, deliberate, malicious, and premediated killing, or which is committed in the perpetration or attempt to perpetrate any one of the offences therein enumerated, and evidencing a depraved mind, regardless of human life, is murder in the first degree. *Id.* 586.

Provision is also made that every person guilty of murder in the first degree shall suffer death, or, upon the recommendation of the jury, may be imprisoned at hard labor in the penitentiary for life, at the discretion of the court; and that every person guilty of murder in the second degree shall be imprisoned at hard labor in the penitentiary for not less than five nor more than fifteen years. Comp. Laws Utah, 1876, 586.

Duly convicted of murder in the first degree as the prisoner was by the verdict of the jury, it is conceded that the existing law of the Territory provides that he 'shall suffer death;' nor is it denied that the antecedent law of the Territory which was in force from March 6, 1852, to March 4, 1876, provided that 'when any person shall be convicted of any crime the punishment of which is death, . . . he shall suffer death by being shot, hung, or beheaded, as the court may direct,' or as the convicted person may choose. Sess. Laws Utah, 1852, p. 61; Comp. Laws Utah, 1876, 564.

When the Revised Penal Code went into operation, it is doubtless true that it repealed that provision, as sect. 400 provides that 'all acts and parts of acts' heretofore passed 'inconsistent with the provisions of this act be and the same are hereby repealed.' Comp. Laws Utah, 651.

Assume that sect. 124 of the prior law is repealed by the Revised Penal Code, and it follows that the existing law of the Territory provides that every person guilty of murder in the first degree shall suffer death, without any other statutory regulation as to the mode of executing the sentence than what is found in the following enactment of the Revised Penal Code. Sect. 10 provides that 'the several sections of this code, which declare certain crimes to be punishable as therein mentioned, devolve a duty upon the court authorized to pass sentence to determine and impose the punishment prescribed.' Comp. Laws Utah, 1876, 567.

Construed as that provision must be in connection with the enactment that every person guilty of murder in the first degree shall suffer death, and in view of the fact that the laws of the Territory contain no other specific regulation as to the mode of executing such a sentence, the court here is of the opinion that the assignment of error shows no legal ground for reversing the judgment of the court below. Authority to pass such a sentence is certainly not possessed by the circuit courts of the United States, as the act of Congress provides that the manner of inflicting the punishment of death shall be by hanging. Rev. Stat., sect. 5325.

Punishments of the kind are always directed by the circuit courts to be inflicted in that manner, but organized Territories are invested with legislative power which extends to all rightful subjects of legislation not inconsistent with the Constitution and laws of the United States. By virtue of that power the legislative branch of the Territory may define offences and prescribe the punishment of the offenders, subject to the prohibition of the Constitution that cruel and unusual punishments shall not be inflicted. Story, Const. (3d ed.), sect. 1903.

Good reasons exist for supposing that Congress never intended that the provision referred to, that the punishment of death shall be by hanging, should supersede the power of the Territories to legislate upon the subject, as the congressional provision is a part of the first crimes act ever passed by the national legislature. 1 Stat. 114. Different statutory regulations existed in the Territory for nearly a quarter of a century, and the usages of the army to the present day are that sentences of the kind may in certain cases be executed by shooting, and in others by hanging.

Offences of various kinds are defined in the rules and articles of war where the offender, if duly convicted, may be sentenced to the death penalty. In some of those cases the provision is that the accused, if convicted, shall suffer death, and in others the punishment to be awarded depends upon the finding of the court-martial; but in none of those cases is the mode of putting to death prescribed in the articles of war or the military regulations. Art. 96 provides that no person shall be sentenced to suffer death except by the concurrence of two-thirds of the members of a general court-martial, and in the cases specified in the rules and articles enacted by Congress. Rev. Stat., p. 238.

Repeated instances occur where the death penalty is prescribed in those articles; but the invariable enactment is that the person guilty of the offence shall suffer death, without any specification as to the mode in which the sentence shall be executed, and the regulations of the army are as silent in that respect as the rules and articles of war. Congress having made no regulations in that regard, the custom of war, says a learned writer upon the subject, has, in the absence of statutory law, determined that capital punishment be inflicted by shooting or hanging; and the same author adds to the effect that mutiny, meaning mutiny not resulting in loss of life, desertion, or other military crime, if a capital offence, is commonly punished by shooting; that a spy is always hanged, and that mutiny, if accompanied by loss of life, is punished in the same manner,—that is, by hanging. Benet, *Courts-Martial* (5th ed.), 163.

Military laws, says another learned author, do not say how a criminal offending against such laws shall be put to death, but leave it entirely to the custom of war; and his statement is that shooting or hanging is the method determined by such custom. DeHart, *Courts-Martial*, 196. Like the preceding author, he also proceeds to state that a spy is generally hanged, and that mutiny unaccompanied with loss of life is punished by the same means; and he also concurs with Benet, that desertion, disobedience of orders, or other capital crimes are usually punished by shooting, adding, that the mode in all cases, that is, either shooting or hanging, may be declared in the sentence.

Corresponding rules prevail in other countries, of which the following authorities will afford sufficient proof: Simmons, *Courts-Martial* (5th ed.), sect. 645; Griffith, *Military Law*, 86.

Capital punishment, says the author first named, may be either by shooting or hanging. For mutiny, desertion, or other military crime it is commonly by shooting; for murder not combined with mutiny, for treason, and piracy accompanied with wounding or attempt to murder, by hanging, as the sentence in England must accord with the law of the country in regard to the punishment of offenders. Exactly the same views are expressed by the other writer, which need not be reproduced.

(Continues)

(Continued)

Cruel and unusual punishments are forbidden by the Constitution, but the authorities referred to are quite sufficient to show that the punishment of shooting as a mode of executing the death penalty for the crime of murder in the first degree is not included in that category, within the meaning of the eighth amendment. Soldiers convicted of desertion or other capital military offences are in the great majority of cases sentenced to be shot, and the ceremony for such occasions is given in great fulness by the writers upon the subject of courts-martial. Simmons, sects. 759, 760; DeHart, pp. 247–248.

Where the conviction is in the civil tribunals, the rule of the common law was that the sentence or judgment must be pronounced or rendered by the court in which the prisoner was tried or finally condemned, and the rule was universal that it must be such as is annexed to the crime by law. Of these, says Blackstone, some are capital, which extend to the life of the offender, and consist generally in being hanged by the neck till dead. 4 Bl. Com. 377.

Such is the general statement of that commentator, but he admits that in very atrocious crimes other circumstances of terror, pain, or disgrace were sometimes superadded. Cases mentioned by the author are, where the prisoner was drawn or dragged to the place of execution, in treason; or where he was embowelled alive, beheaded, and quartered, in high treason. Mention is also made of public dissection in murder, and burning alive in treason committed by a female. History confirms the truth of these atrocities, but the commentator states that the humanity of the nation by tacit consent allowed the mitigation of such parts of those judgments as savored of torture or cruelty, and he states that they were seldom strictly carried into effect. Examples of such legislation in the early history of the parent country are given by the annotator of the last edition of *Archbold's Treatise. Arch. Crim. Pr. and Pl.* (8th ed.) 584.

Many instances, says Chitty, have arisen in which the ignominious or more painful parts of the punishment of high treason have been remitted, until the result appears to be that the king, though he cannot vary the sentence so as to aggravate the punishment, may mitigate or remit a part of its severity. 1 Chitt. *Cr. L.* 787; 1 Hale, *P. C.* 370.

Difficulty would attend the effort to define with exactness the extent of the constitutional provision which provides that cruel and unusual punishments shall not be inflicted; but it is safe to affirm that punishments of torture, such as those mentioned by the commentator referred to, and all others in the same line of unnecessary cruelty, are forbidden by that emendment to the Constitution. Cooley, *Const. Lim.* (4th ed.) 408; Wharton, *Cr. L.* (7th ed.), sect. 3405.

Concede all that, and still it by no means follows that the sentence of the court in this case falls within that category, or that the Supreme Court of the Territory erred in affirming the judgment of the court of original jurisdiction. Antecedent to the enactment of the code which went into operation March 4, 1876, the statute of the Territory passed March 6, 1852, provided that when any person was convicted of any capital offence he shall suffer death by being shot, hanged, or beheaded, as the court may direct, subject to the qualification therein expressed, to the effect that the person condemned might have his option as to the manner of his execution, the meaning of which qualification, as construed, was that the option was limited to the modes prescribed in the statute, and that if it was not exercised, the direction must be given by the court passing the sentence.

Nothing of the kind is contained in the existing code, and the legislature in dropping the provision as to the option failed to enact any specific regulation as to the mode of executing the death penalty. Instead of that, the explicit enactment is that every person guilty of murder in the first degree shall suffer death, or, upon the recommendation of the jury, may be imprisoned at hard labor in the penitentiary for life, at the discretion of the court.

Beyond all question, the first clause of the provision is applicable in this case, as the jury gave no such recommendation as that recited in the second clause, the record showing that their verdict was unconditional and absolute, from which it follows that the sentence that the prisoner shall suffer death is legally correct. Comp. Laws Utah, 1876, p. 586.

Had the statute prescribed the mode of executing the sentence, it would have been the duty of the court to follow it, unless the punishment to be inflicted was cruel and unusual, within the meaning of the eighth amendment to the Constitution, which is not pretended by the counsel of the prisoner. Statutory directions being given that the prisoner when duly convicted shall suffer death, without any statutory regulation specifically pointing out the mode of executing the command of the law, it must be that the duty is devolved upon the court authorized to pass the sentence to determine the mode of execution and to impose the sentence prescribed. *Id.*, p. 567.

Persons guilty of murder in the first degree 'shall suffer death,' are the words of the territorial statute; and when that provision is construed in connection with sect. 10 of the code previously referred to, it is clear that it is made obligatory upon the court to prescribe the mode of executing the sentence of death which the code imposes where the conviction is for murder in the first degree, subject, of course, to the constitutional prohibition, that cruel and unusual punishment shall not be inflicted.

Other modes besides hanging were sometimes resorted to at common law, nor did the common law in terms require the court in passing the sentence either to prescribe the mode of execution or to fix the time or place for carrying it into effect, as is frequently if not always done in the Federal circuit courts. At common law, neither the mode of executing the prisoner nor the time or place of execution was necessarily embodied in the sentence. Directions in regard to the former were usually given by the judge in the calendar of capital cases prepared by the clerk at the close of the term; as, for example, in the case of murder, the direction was 'let him be hanged by the neck,' which calendar was signed by the judge and clerk, and constituted in many cases the only authority of the officer as to the mode of execution. 4 Bl. Com. 404; Bishop, (*Cr. Proc.* (2d ed.), sects. 1146–1148; Bishop, *Cr. L.* (6th ed.), sect. 935.

Reference is made to the cases of *Hartung v. The People* (22 N.Y. 95), *The People v. Hartung* (23 How. Pr. (N.Y.) 314), *Same v. Same* (26 *id.* 154), and *Same v. Same* (28 *id.* 400), as supporting the theory of the prisoner that the court possessed no authority to prescribe the mode of execution; but the court here is entirely of a different opinion, for the reasons already given.

Judgment affirmed.

Weems v. United States, 217 U.S. 349 (1910)

Mr. A. S. Worthington for plaintiff in error.

Assistant Attorney General Fowler and Solicitor General Hoyt for defendant in error.

Mr. Justice McKenna delivered the opinion of the court:

This writ of error brings up for review the judgment of the supreme court of the Philippine Islands, affirming the conviction of plaintiff in error for falsifying a 'public and official document.'

In the 'complaint,' by which the prosecution was begun, it was charged that the plaintiff in error, 'a duly appointed, qualified, and acting disbursing officer of the Bureau of Coast Guard and Transportation of the United States Government of the Philippine Islands,' did, as such, 'corruptly, and with intent then and there to deceive and defraud the United States government of the Philippine Islands and its officials, falsify a public and official document, namely, a cash book of the captain of the port of Manilla, Philippine Islands, and the Bureau of Coast Guard and Transportation of the United States Government of the Philippine Islands,' kept by him as disbursing officer of that bureau. The falsification, which is alleged with much particularity, was committed by entering as paid out, 'as wages of employees of the lighthouse service of the United States government of the Philippine Islands,' at the Capul lighthouse, of 204 pesos, and for like service at the Matabriga lighthouse of 408 pesos, Philippine currency. A demurrer was filed to the 'complaint,' which was overruled.

He was convicted, and the following sentence was imposed upon him: 'To the penalty of fifteen years of *cadena*, together with the accessories of 56 of the Penal Code, and to pay a fine of 4,000 pesetas, but not to serve imprisonment as a subsidiary punishment in case of his insolvency, on account of the nature of the main penalty, and to pay the costs of this cause.'

The judgment and sentence were affirmed by the supreme court of the Islands.

It is conceded by plaintiff in error that some of the questions presented to the supreme court of the Philippine Islands cannot be raised in this court, as the record does not contain the evidence. Indeed, plaintiff in error confines his discussion to one point raised in the court below and to three other questions, which, though not brought to the attention of the supreme court of the islands, and not included in the assignment of errors, are of such importance, it is said, that this court will consider them under the right reserved in rule 35. These questions are as follows:

'I. The court below erred in overruling the demurrer to the complaint, this assignment being based upon the fact that, in the complaint, the plaintiff in error is described as the 'disbursing officer of the Bureau of Coast Guard and Transportation of the United States Government of the Philippine Islands,' and the cash book referred to in the complaint is described as a book 'of the captain of the port of Manila, Philippine Islands,' whereas there is no such body politic as the 'United States government of the Philippine Island.'

(Continues)

(Continued)

'**2.** The record does not disclose that the plaintiff in error was arraigned, or that he pleaded to the complaint after his demurrer was overruled and he was 'ordered to plead to the complaint.''

'**3.** The record does not show that the plaintiff in error was present when he was tried, or, indeed, that he was present in court at any time.

'**4.** The punishment of fifteen years' imprisonment was a cruel and unusual punishment, and, to the extent of the sentence, the judgment below should be reversed on this ground.'

The second assignment of error was based upon a misapprehension of the fact, and has been abandoned.

The argument to support the first assignment of error is based upon certain acts of Congress and certain acts of the Philippine Commission in which the government of the United States and the government of the Islands are distinguished. And it is urged that in one of the acts (3396 of the acts of the commission) it is recognized that there may be allegiance to or treason against both or 'either of them,' and (3397) that there may be 'rebellion or insurrection against the authority' of either, and (3398) that there may be a conspiracy to overthrow either, or to 'prevent, hinder, or delay the execution of any law of either.' Other sections are cited, in which it is contended that the insular government is spoken of as an 'entity,' and distinguished from that of the United States. Section 1366, which defines the duty of the attorney general, it is pointed out, especially distinguishes between 'causes, civil or criminal, to which the United States or any officer thereof in his official capacity is a party,' and causes, civil or criminal, to which the 'government of the Philippine Islands or any officer thereof in his official capacity is a party.' And still more decisively, it is urged, by subdivision 'C' of 1366, in which it is recognized that the cause of action may be for money, and that the judgment may be for money, 'belonging to the government of the United States and that of the Philippine Islands or some other province.' It is therefore contended that the government of the United States and that of the Philippine Islands are distinct legal entities, and that there may be civil obligations to one, and not to the other; that there may be governmental liability to the one, and not to the other; and that proceedings, civil or criminal, against either, must recognize the distinction to be either, must recognize the distinction to be these principles, let us see what the information charges. It describes Weems, plaintiff in error, as 'a public official of the United States government of the Philippine Islands; to wit, a duly appointed and qualified acting disbursing official of the Bureau of Coast Guard and Transportation of the United States Government of the Philippine Islands;' and it is charged that, by taking advantage of his official position, with intent to 'deceive and defraud the United States government of the Philippine Islands,' he falsified a public and official document. In the same manner the government is designated throughout the information. It is contended that 'there is no such body politic as the 'United States government of the Philippine Islands,'' and it is urged that the objection does not relate to a matter of form. 'It is as substantial,' it is said, as the point involved in *Carrington v. United States*, 208 U.S. 1, 52 L. ed. 367, 28 Sup. Ct. Rep. 203, where a military officer of the United States was prosecuted as a civil officer of the government of the Philippines. His conviction was reversed, this court holding that, 'as a soldier, he was not an official of the Philippines, but of the United States.'

It is true that the distinctions raised are expressed in the statutes, and necessarily so. It would be difficult otherwise to provide for government where there is a paramount authority making use of subordinate instrumentalities. We have examples in the states of the Union and their lesser municipal divisions, and rights may flow from and to such lesser divisions. And the distinction in the Philippine statutes means no more than that, and, conforming to that, a distinction is clearly made in the information. Weems's official position is described as 'disbursing officer of the Bureau of Coast Guard and Transportation of the United States Government of the Philippine Islands.' There is no real uncertainty in this description, and whatever technical nicety of discrimination might have been insisted on at one time cannot now be, in view of the provisions of the Philippine Criminal Code of Procedure, which requires a public offense to be described in 'ordinary and concise language,' not necessarily in the words of the statute, 'but in such form as to enable a person of common understanding to know what is intended, and the court to pronounce indgment according to the right.' And it is further provided that 'no information or complaint is insufficient, nor can the trial, judgment, or other proceeding be affected, by reason of a defect in matter of form which does not tend to prejudice a substantial right of the defendant upon the merits' (10).

Carrington v. United States, 208 U.S. 1, 52 L. ed. 367, 28 Sup. Ct. Rep. 203, is not in point. In that case it was attempted to hold Carrington guilty of an offense as a civil officer for what he had done as a military officer. As he was the latter, he had not committed any offense under the statute. The first assignment of error is therefore not sustained.

It is admitted, as we have seen, that the questions presented by the third and fourth assignments of error were not made in the courts below, but a consideration of them is invoked under rule 35, which provides that this court, 'at its option, may notice a plain error not assigned.'

It is objected on the other side that *Paraiso v. United States*, 207 U.S. 368, 52 L. ed. 249, 28 Sup. Ct. Rep. 127, stands in the way. But the rule is not altogether controlled by precedent. It confers a discretion that may be exercised at any time, no matter what may have been done at some other time. It is true we declined to exercise it in *Paraiso v. United States*, but we exercised it in *Wiborg v. United States*, 163 U.S. 632, 658, 41 S. L. ed. 289, 298, 16 Sup. Ct. Rep. 1127, 1197; *Clyatt v. United States*, 197 U.S. 207, 221, 49 S. L. ed. 726, 731, 25 Sup. Ct. Rep. 429, and *Crawford v. United States*, 212 U.S. 183, 53 L. ed. 465, 29 Sup. Ct. Rep. 260, 15 A. & E. Ann. Cas. 392. It may be said, however, that *Paraiso v. United States* is more directly applicable, as it was concerned with the same kind of a crime as that in the case at bar, and that it was contended there, as here, that the amount of fine and imprisonment imposed inflicted a cruel and unusual punishment. It may be that we were not sufficiently impressed with the importance of those contentions, or saw in the circumstances of the case no reason to exercise our right of review under rule 35. As we have already said, the rule is not a rigid one, and we have less reluctance to disregard prior examples in criminal cases than in civil cases, and less reluctance to act under it when rights are asserted which are of such high character as to find expression and sanction in the Constitution or Bill of Rights. And such rights are asserted in this case.

The assignment of error is that 'a punishment of fifteen years' imprisonment was a cruel and unusual punishment, and, to the extent of the sentence, the judgment below should be reversed on this ground.' Weems was convicted, as we have seen, for the falsification of a public and official document, by entering therein, as paid out, the sums of 208 and 408 pesos, respectively, as wages to certain employees of the lighthouse service. In other words, in entering upon his cash book those sums as having been paid out when they were not paid out; and the 'truth,' to use the language of the statue, was thereby perverted 'in the narration of facts.'

A false entry is all that is necessary to constitute the offense. Whether an offender against the statute injures anyone by his act, or intended to injure anyone, is not material, the trial court held. The court said: 'It is not necessary that there be any fraud nor even the desire to defraud, nor intention of personal gain on the part of the person committing it, that a falsification of a public document be punishable; it is sufficient that the one who committed it had the intention to pervert the truth and to falsify the document, and that by it damage might result to a third party.' The court further, in the definition of the nature of the offense and the purpose of the law, said: 'In public documents, the law takes into consideration not only private interests, but also the interests of the community;' and it is its endeavor (and for this a decision of the Supreme Court of Spain, delivered in 1873, was quoted) 'to protect the interest of society by the most strict faithfulness on the part of a public official in the administration of the office intrusted to him,' and thereby fulfil the 'responsibility of the state to the community for the official or public documents under the safeguard of the state.' And this was attempted to be secured through the law in controversy. It is found in 1 of chapter 4 of the Penal Code of Spain. The caption of the section is, 'Falsification of Official and Commercial Documents and Telegraphic Despatches.' Article 300 provides as follows: 'The penalties of *cadena temporal* and a fine of from 1,250 to 12,500 pesetas shall be imposed on a public official who, taking advantage of his authority, shall commit a falsification . . . By perverting the truth in the narration of facts . . .'

By other provisions of the Code we find that there are only two degrees of punishment higher in scale than *cadena temporal*,—death, and *cadena perpetua*. The punishment of *cadena temporal* is from twelve years and one day to twenty years (arts. 28 and 96), which 'shall be served' in certain 'penal institutions.' And it is provided that 'those sentenced to *cadena temporal* and *cadena perpetua* shall labor for the benefit of the state. They shall always carry a chain at the ankle, hanging from the wrists; they shall be employed at hard and painful labor, and shall receive no assistance whatsoever from without the institution.' Arts. 105, 106. There are, besides, certain accessory penalties imposed, which are defined to be (1) civil interdiction; (2) perpetual absolute disqualification; (3) subjection to surveillance during life. These penalties are defined as follows:

'Art. 42. Civil interdiction shall deprive the person punished, as long as he suffers it, of the rights of parental authority, guardianship of person or property, participation in the family council, marital authority, it, of the rights of parental authority, the right to dispose of his own property by acts *inter vivos*. Those cases are excepted in which the laws explicitly limit its effects.

(Continues)

'Art. 43. Subjection to the surveillance of the authorities imposes the following obligations on the persons punished:

'**1.** That of fixing his domicil and giving notice thereof to the authority immediately in charge of his surveillance, not being allowed to change it without the knowledge and permission of said authority, in writing.
'**2.** To observe the rules of inspection prescribed.
'**3.** To adopt some trade, art, industry, or profession should he not have known means of subsistence of his own.

'Whenever a person punished is placed under the surveillance of the authorities, notice thereof shall be given to the government and to the governor general.'

The penalty of perpetual absolute disqualification is the deprivation of office, even though it be held by popular election, the deprivation of the right to vote or to be elected to public office, the disqualification to acquire honors, etc., and the loss of retirement pay, etc.

These provisions are attacked as infringing that provision of the Bill of Rights of the islands which forbids the infliction of cruel and unusual punishment. It must be confessed that they, and the sentence in this case, excite wonder in minds accustomed to a more considerate adaptation of punishment to the degree of crime. In a sense the law in controversy seems to be independent of degrees. One may be an offender against it, as we have seen, though he gain nothing and injure nobody. It has, however, some human indulgence,—it is not exactly Draconian in uniformity. Though it starts with a severe penalty, between that and the maximum penalty it yields something to extenuating circumstances. Indeed, by article 96 of the Penal Code the penalty is declared to be 'divisible,' and the legal term of its 'duration is understood as distributed into three parts, forming the three degrees,—that is, the minimum, medium, and maximum,'—being respectively twelve years and one day to fourteen years and eight months; from fourteen years, eight months, and one day to seventeen years and four months; from seventeen years, four months, and one day to twenty years. The law therefore allows a range from twelve years and a day to twenty years, and the government, in its brief, ventures to say that 'the sentence of fifteen years is well within the law.' But the sentence is attacked as well as the law, and what it is to be well within the law a few words will exhibit. The mimimum term of imprisonment is twelve years, and that, therefore, must be imposed for 'perverting the truth' in a single item of a public record, though there be no one injured, though there be no fraud or purpose of it, no gain or desire of it. Twenty years is the maximum imprisonment, and that only can be imposed for the perversion of truth in every item of an officer's accounts, whatever be the time covered and whatever fraud it conceals or tends to conceal. Between these two possible sentences, which seem to have no adaptable relation, or rather in the difference of eight years for the lowest possible offense and the highest possible, the courts below selected three years to add to the minimum of twelve years and a day for the falsification of two items of expenditure, amounting to the sums of 408 and 204 pesos. And the fine and 'accessories' must be brought into view. The fine was 4,000 pesetas,-an excess also over the minimum. The 'accessories' we have already defined. We can now give graphic description of Weems' sentence and of the law under which it was imposed. Let us confine it to the minimum degree of the law, for it is with the law that we are most concerned. Its minimum degree is confinement in a penal institution for twelve years and one day, a chain at the ankle and wrist of the offender, hard and painful labor, no assistance from friend or relative, no marital authority or parental rights or rights of property, no participation even in the family council. These parts of his penalty endure for the term of imprisonment. From other parts there is no intermission. His prison bars and chains are removed, it is true, after twelve years, but he goes from them to a perpetual limitation of his liberty. He is forever kept under the shadow of his crime, forever kept within voice and view of the criminal magistrate, not being able to change his domicil without giving notice to the 'authority immediately in charge of his surveillance,' and without permission in writing. He may not seek, even in other scenes and among other people, to retrieve his fall from rectitude. Even that hope is taken from him, and he is subject to tormenting regulations that, if not so tangible as iron bars and stone walls, oppress as much by their continuity, and deprive of essential liberty. No circumstance of degradation is omitted. It may be that even the cruelty of pain is not omitted. He must bear a chain night and day. He is condemned to painful as well as hard labor. What painful labor may mean we have no exact measure. It must be something more than hard labor. It may be hard labor pressed to the point of pain. Such penalties for such offenses amaze those who have formed their conception of the relation of a state to even its offending citizens from the practice of the American commonwealths, and believe that it is a precept of justice that punishment for crime should be graduated and proportioned to offense.

Is this also a precept of the fundamental law? We say fundamental law, for the provision of the Philippine Bill of Rights, prohibiting the infliction of cruel and unusual punishment, was taken from the Constitution of the United States, and must have the same meaning. This was decided in *Kepner v. United States*, 195 U.S. 100, 49 L. ed. 114, 24 Sup. Ct. Rep. 797, 1 A. & E. Ann. Cas. 655, and *Serra v. Mortiga*, 204 U.S. 477, 51 L. ed. 574, 27 Sup. Ct. Rep. 343. in *Kepner v. United States* this court considered the instructions of the President to the Philippine Commission, and quoted from them the admonition to the commission that the government that we were establishing was not designed 'for our satisfaction or for the expression of our theoretical views, but for the happiness . . . of the people of the Philippine Island; and the measures adopted should be made to conform to their customs, their habits, and even their prejudices, to the fullest extent consistent with the accomplishment of the indispensable requisites of just and effective government.' But, it was pointed out, a qualification accompanied the admonition, and the commission was instructed 'to bear in mind' and the people of the islands 'made plainly to understand' that certain great principles of government had been made the basis of our governmental system, which were deemed 'essential to the rule of law and the maintenance of individual freedom.' And the president further declared that there were 'certain practical rules of government which we have found to be essential to the preservation of those great principles of liberty and law.' These he admonished the commission to establish and maintain in the islands 'for the sake of their liberty and happiness,' however they might conflict with the customs or laws of procedure with which they were familiar. In view of the importance of these principles and rules, which the President said the 'enlightened thought of the Philippine Islands' would come to appreciate, he imposed their observance 'upon every division and branch of the government of the Philippines.'

Among those rules was that which prohibited the infliction of cruel and unusual punishment. It was repeated in the act of July 1, 1902 [32 Stat. at L. 691, chap. 1369], providing for the administration of the affairs of the civil government in the islands, and this court said of it and of the instructions of the President that they were 'intended to carry to the Philippine Islands those principles of our government which the President declared to be established as rules of law for the maintenance of individual freedom.' The instructions of the President and the act of Congress found in nominal existence in the islands the Penal Code of Spain, its continuance having been declared by military order. It may be there was not and could not be a careful consideration of its provisions and a determination to what extent they accorded with or were repugnant to the 'great principles of liberty and law' which had been 'made the basis of our governmental system.' Upon the institution of the government of the commission, if not before, that consideration and determination necessarily came to the courts and are presented by this record.

What constitutes a cruel and unusual punishment has not been exactly decided. It has been said that ordinarily the terms imply something inhuman and barbarous,—torture and the like. *McDonald v. Com.* 173 Mass. 322, 73 Am. St. Rep. 293, 53 N.E. 874. The court, however, in that case, conceded the possibility 'that punishment in the state prison for a long term of years might be so disproportionate to the offense as to constitute a cruel and unusual punishment.' Other cases have selected certain tyrannical acts of the English monarchs as illustrating the meaning of the clause and the extent of its prohibition.

The provision received very little debate in Congress. We find from the Congressional Register, p. 225, that Mr. Smith, of South Carolina, 'objected to the words 'nor cruel and unusual punishment,' the import of them being too indefinite.' Mr. Livermore opposed the adoption of the clause saying:

'The clause seems to express a great deal of humanity, on which account I have no objection to it; but, as it seems to have no meaning in it, I do not think it necessary. What is meant by the terms 'excessive bail?' Who are to be the judges? What is understood by 'excessive fines?' It lays with the court to determine. No cruel and unusual punishment is to be inflicted; it is sometimes necessary to hang a man, villains often deserve whipping, and perhaps having their ears cut off; but are we, in future, to be prevented from inflicting these punishments because they are cruel? If a more lenient mode of correcting vice and deterring others from the commission of it could be invented, it would be very prudent in the legislature to adopt it; but until we have some security that this will be done, we ought not to be restrained from making necessary laws by any declaration of this kind.'

The question was put on the clause, and it was agreed to by a considerable majority.

No case has occurred in this court which has called for an exhaustive definition. In *Pervear v. Massachusetts*, 5 Wall. 475, 18 L. ed. 608, it was decided that the clause did not apply to state but to

(Continues)

national legislation. But we went further, and said that we perceive nothing excessive, or cruel, or unusual in a fine of $50 and imprisonment at hard labor in the house of correction for three months, which was imposed for keeping and maintaining, without a license, a tenement for the illegal sale and illegal keeping of intoxicating liquors. A decision from which no one will dissent.

In *Wilkerson v. Utah*, 99 U.S. 130, 25 L. ed. 345, the clause came up again for consideration. A statute of Utah provided that 'a person convicted of a capital offense should suffer death by being shot, hanged, or beheaded,' as the court might direct, or he should 'have his option as to the manner of his execution.' The statute was sustained. The court pointed out that death was an usual punishment for murder, that it prevailed in the territory for many years, and was inflicted by shooting; also that that mode of execution was usual under military law. It was hence concluded that it was not forbidden by the Constitution of the United States as cruel or unusual. The court quoted Blackstone as saying that the sentence of death was generally executed by hanging, but also that circumstances of terror, pain, or disgrace were sometimes superadded. 'Cases mentioned by the author,' the court said, 'are where the person was drawn or dragged to the place of execution, in treason; or where he was disemboweled alive, beheaded, and quartered, in high treason. Mention is also made of public dissection in murder and burning alive in treason committed by a female.' And it was further said: 'Examples of such legislation in the early history of the parent country are given by the annotator of the last edition of Archbold's treatise. Archbold, *Crim. Pr. & Pl.* 8th ed. 584.'

This court's final commentary was that 'difficulty would attend the effort to define with exactness the extent of the constitutional provision which provides that cruel and unusual punishments shall not be inflicted; but it is safe to affirm that punishments of torture, such as those mentioned by the commentator referred to, and all others in the same line of unnecessary cruelty, are forbidden by that Amendment to the Constitution. Cooley, *Const. Lim.* 4th ed. 408; Wharton, *Crim. Law*, 7th ed. 3405.'

That passage was quoted in *Re Kemmler*, 136 U.S. 436, 447, 34 S. L. ed. 519, 524, 10 Sup. Ct. Rep. 930 and this comment was made: 'Punishments are cruel when they involve torture or a lingering death; but the punishment of death is not cruel, within the meaning of that word as used in the Constitution. It implies there something inhuman and barbarous, and something more than the mere extinguishment of life.' The case was an application for habeas corpus, and went off on a question of jurisdiction, this court holding that the 8th Amendment did not apply to state legislation. It was not meant in the language we have quoted to give a comprehensive definition of cruel and unusual punishment, but only to explain the application of the provision to the punishment of death. In other words, to describe what might make the punishment of death cruel and unusual, though of itself it is not so. It was found as a fact by the state court that death by electricity was more humane than death by hanging.

In *O'Neil v. Vermont*, 144 U.S. 323, 36 L. ed. 450, 12 Sup. Ct. Rep. 693, the question was raised, but not decided. The reasons given for this were that because it was not as a Federal question assigned as error, and, so far as it arose under the Constitution of Vermont, it was not within the province of the court to decide. Moreover, it was said, as a Federal question, it had always been ruled that the 8th Amendment of the Constitution of the United States did not apply to the states. Mr. Justice Field, Mr. Justice Harlan, and Mr. Justice Brewer were of opinion that the question was presented, and Mr. Justice Field, construing the clause of the Constitution prohibiting the infliction of cruel and unusual punishment, said, the other two justices concurring, that the inhibition was directed not only against punishments which inflict torture, 'but against all punishments which, by their execssive length or severity, are greatly disproportioned to the offenses charged.' He said further: 'The whole inhibition is against that which is excessive in the bail required or fine imposed or punishment inflicted.'

The law writers are indefinite. Story, in his work on the Constitution, vol. 2, 5th ed. 1903, says that the provision 'is an exact transcript of a clause in the Bill of Rights framed at the revolution of 1688.' He expressed the view that the provision 'would seem to be wholly unnecessary in a free government, since it is scarcely possible that any department of such a government should authorize or justify such atrocious conduct.' He, however, observed that it was 'adopted as an admonition to all departments of the national department, to warn them against such violent proceedings as had taken place in England in the arbitrary reigns of some of the Stuarts.' For this he cites 2 *Elliott's Debates*, 345, and refers to 2 *Lloyd's Debates*, 225, 226; 3 *Elliott's Debates*, 345. If the learned author meant by this to confine the prohibition of the provision to such penalties and punishment as were inflicted by the Stuarts, his citations do not sustain him. Indeed, the provision is not mentioned except in 2 *Elliott's Debates*, from which we have already quoted. The other citations are of the remarks of Patrick Henry in the Virginia convention, and of Mr. Wilson in the Pennsylvania convention. Patrick Henry said that there was danger in the adoption of the Constitution without a Bill of Rights. Mr. Wilson considered that it was unnecessary, and had been purposely omitted from the Constitution. Both, indeed, referred to the tyranny of the Stuarts. Henry said that the people of England, in the Bill of Rights, prescribed to William, Prince of Orange, upon what terms he should reign. Wilson said that 'the doctrine and practice of a declaration of rights have been borrowed from the conduct of the people of England on some remarkable occasions; but the principles and maxims on which their government is constituted are widely different from those of ours.' It appears, therefore, that Wilson, and those who thought like Wilson, felt sure that the spirit of liberty could be trusted, and that its ideals would be represented, not debased, by legislation. Henry and those who believed as he did would take no chances. Their predominant political impulse was distrust of power, and they insisted on constitutional limitations against its abuse. But surely they intended more than to register a fear of the forms of abuse that went out of practice with the Stuarts. Surely, their jealousy of power had a saner justification than that. They were men of action, practical and sagacious, not beset with vain imagining, and it must have come to them that there could be exercises of cruelty by laws other than those which inflicted bodily pain or mutilation. With power in a legislature great, if not unlimited, to give criminal character to the actions of men, with power unlimited to fix terms of imprisonment with what accompaniments they might, what more potent instrument of cruelty could be put into the hands of power? And it was believed that power might be tempted to cruelty. This was the motive of the clause, and if we are to attribute an intelligent providence to its advocates we cannot think that it was intended to prohibit only practices like the Stuarts', or to prevent only an exact repetition of history. We cannot think that the possibility of a coercive cruelty being exercised through other forms of punishment was overlooked. We say 'coercive cruelty,' because there was more to be considered than the ordinary criminal laws. Cruelty might become an instrument of tyranny; of zeal for a purpose, either honest or sinister.

Legislation, both statutory and constitutional, is enacted, it is true, from an experience of evils but its general language should not, therefore, be necessarily confined to the form that evil had theretofore taken. Time works changes, brings into existence new conditions and purposes. Therefore a principle, to be vital, must be capable of wider application than the mischief which gave it birth. This is peculiarly true of constitutions. They are not ephemeral enactments, designed to meet passing occasions. They are, to use the words of Chief Justice Marshall, 'designed to approach immortality as nearly as human institutions can approach it.' The future is their care, and provision for events of good and bad tendencies of which no prophecy can be made. In the application of a constitution, therefore, our contemplation cannot be only of what has been, but of what may be. Under any other rule a constitution would indeed be as easy of application as it would be deficient in efficacy and power. Its general principles would have little value, and be converted by precedent into impotent and lifeless formulas. Rights declared in words might be lost in reality. And this has been recognized. The meaning and vitality of the Constitution have developed against narrow and restrictive construction. There is an example of this in *Cummings v. Missouri*, 4 Wall. 277, 18 L. ed. 356, where the prohibition against *ex post facto* laws was given a more extensive application than what a minority of this court thought had been given in *Calder v. Bull*, 3 Dall. 386, 1 L. ed. 648. See also *Ex parte Garland*, 4 Wall. 333, 18 L. ed. 366. The construction of the 14th Amendment is also an example, for it is one of the limitations of the Constitution. In a not unthoughtful opinion, Mr. Justice Miller expressed great doubt whether that Amendment would ever be held as being directed against any action of a state which did not discriminate 'against the negroes as a class, or on account of their race.' *Slaughter House Cases*, 16 Wall. 36, 81, 21 L. ed. 394, 410. To what extent the Amendment has expanded beyond that limitation need not be instanced.

There are many illustrations of resistance to narrow constructions of the grants of power to the national government. One only need be noticed, and we select it because it was made against a power which, more than any other, is kept present to our minds in visible and effective action. We mean the power over interstate commerce. This power was deduced from the eleven simple words,—'to regulate commerce with foreign nations and among the several states.' The judgment which established it was pronounced by Chief Justice Marshall (*Gibbons v. Ogden*, 9 Wheat. 1, 6 L. ed. 23), and reversed a judgment of Chancellor Kent, justified, as that celebrated jurist supposed, by a legislative practice of fourteen years, and fortified by the opinions of men familiar with the discussions which had attended the adoption of the Constitution. Persuaded by such considerations the learned chancellor confidently decided that the congressional power related to 'external, not to internal, commerce,' and adjudged that, under an act of the state of New York, Livingston and Fulton had the exclusive right of using steamboats upon all of the navigable waters of the state. The strength of the reasoning was not

(Continues)

underrated. It was supported, it was said, 'by great names, by names which have all the titles to consideration that virtue, intelligence, and office can bestow.' The narrow construction, however, did not prevail, and the propriety of the arguments upon which it was based was questioned. It was said, in effect, that they supported a construction which 'would cripple the government and render it unequal to the objects for which it was declared to be instituted, and to which the powers given, as fairly understood, render it competent.'

But general discussion we need not farther pursue. We may rely on the conditions which existed when the Constitution was adopted. As we have seen, it was the thought of Story, indeed, it must come to a less trained reflection than his, that government by the people, instituted by the Constitution, would no imitate the conduct of arbitrary monarchs. The abuse of power might, indeed, be apprehended, but not that it would be manifested in provisions or practices which would shock the sensibilities of men.

Cooley, in his 'Constitutional Limitations,' apparently in a struggle between the effect to be given to ancient examples and the inconsequence of a dread of them in these enlightened times, is not very clear or decisive. He hesitates to advance definite views, and expresses the 'difficulty of determining precisely what is meant by cruel and unusual punishment.' It was probable, however, he says, that 'any punishment declared by statute for an offense which was punishable in the same way at common law could not be regarded as cruel or unusual, in a constitutional sense.' And he says further that 'probably any new statutory offense may be punished to the extent [italics ours] and in the mode permitted by the common law for offenses of a similar nature.'

In the cases in the state courts, different views of the provision are taken. In *State v. Driver*, 78 N.C. 423, 427, it was said that criminal legislation and its administration are so uniformly humane that there is seldom occasion for complaint. In that case, a sentence of the defendant for assault and battery upon his wife was imprisonment in the county jail for five years, and at the expiration thereof to give security to keep the peace for five, in the sum of $500, with sureties, was held to be cruel and unusual. To sustain its judgment, the court said that the prohibition against cruel and unusual punishment was not 'intended to warn against merely erratic modes of punishment or torture, but applied expressly to 'bail,' 'fines' and 'punishments.'' It was also said that 'the earliest application of the provision in England was in 1689, the first year after the adoption of the Bill of Rights in 1688, to avoid an excessive pecuniary fine imposed upon Lord Devonshire by the court of King's bench. 11 How. St. Tr. 1354.' Lord Devonshire was fined $30,000 for an assault and battery upon Colonel Culpepper, and the House of Lords, in reviewing the case, took the opinion of the law Lords, and decided that the fine 'was excessive and exorbitant, against Magna Charta, the common right of the subject, and the law of the land.' Other cases have given a narrower construction, feeling constrained thereto by the incidences of history.

In *Hobbs v. State*, 133 Ind. 404, 18 L.R.A. 774, 32 N.E. 1019, the supreme court of Indiana expressed the opinion that the provision did not apply to punishment by 'fine or imprisonment or both, but such as that inflicted at the whipping post, in the pillory, burning at the stake, breaking on the wheel,' etc.

It was further said: 'The word, according to modern interpretation, does not affect legislation providing imprisonment for life or for years, or the death penalty by hanging or electrocution. If it did, our laws for the punishment of crime would give no security to the citizen.' That conclusion certainly would not follow, and its expression can only be explained by the impatience the court exhibited at the contention in that case, which attacked a sentence of two years' imprisonment in the state prison for combining to assault, beat, and bruise a man in the nighttime. Indeed, in court ventured the inquiry 'whether, in this country, at the close of the nineteenth century,' the provision was 'not obsolete,' except as an admonition to the courts 'against the infliction of punishment so severe as not to 'fit the crime.'' In other words, that it had ceased to be a restraint upon legislatures, and had become an admonition only to the courts not to abuse the discretion which might be intrusted to them. Other cases might be cited in illustration, some looking backwards for examples by which to fix the meaning of the clause; others giving a more expansive and vital character to the provision, such as the President of the United States thought it possessed, and admonished the Philippine Commission that it possessed as 'essential [with other rights] to the rule of law and the maintenance of individual freedom.'

An extended review of the cases in the state courts, interpreting their respective constitutions, we will not make. It may be said of all of them that there was not such challenge to the import and consequence of the inhibition of cruel and unusual punishments as the law under consideration presents. It has no fellow in American legislation. Let us remember that it has come to us from a government of a different form and genius from ours. It is cruel in its excess of imprisonment and that which accompanies and follows imprisonment. It is unusual in its character. Its punishments come under the condemnation of the Bill of Rights, both on account of their degree and kind. And they would have those bad attributes even if they were found in a Federal enactment, and not taken from an alien source.

Many of the state cases which have been brought to our attention require no comment. They are based upon sentences of courts, not upon the constitutional validity of laws. The contentions in other cases vary in merit and in their justification of serious consideration. We have seen what the contention was in *Hobbs v. State*, *supra*. In others, however, there was more inducement to an historical inquiry. In *Com. v. Wyatt*, 6 Rand. (Va.) 694, the whipping post had to be justified and was justified. In comparison with the 'barbarities of quartering, hanging in chains, castration, etc.,' it was easily reduced to insignificance. The court in the latter case pronounced it 'odious, but not unusual.' Other cases have seen something more than odiousness in it, and have regarded it as one of the forbidden punishments. It is certainly as odious as the pillory, and the latter has been pronounced to be within the prohibitory clause. Whipping was also sustained in *Foote v. State* (1882) 59 Md. 264, as a punishment for wife beating. And, it may be, in *Aldridge v. Com.* 2 Va. Cas. 447. The law considered was one punishing free negroes and mulattoes for grand larceny. Under the law, a free person of color could be condemned to be sold as a slave, and transported and banished beyond the limits of the United States. Such was the judgment pronounced on the defendant by the trial court, and, in addition, thirty-nine stripes on his bare back. The judgment was held valid on the ground that the Bill of Rights of the state was 'never designed to control the legislative right to determine *ad libitum* upon the adequacy of punishment, but is merely applicable to the modes of punishment.' Cooley, in his Constitutional Limitations, says that it may be well doubted if the right exist 'to establish the whipping post and the pillory in states where they were never recognized as instruments of punishment, or in states whose constitutions, revised since public opinion had banished them, have forbidden cruel and unusual punishment.' [7th ed. p. 472.] The clause of the Constitution, in the opinion of the learned commentators, may be therefore progressive, and is not fastened to the obsolete, but may acquire meaning as public opinion becomes enlightened by a humane justice. See *Ex parte Wilson*, 114 U.S. 417, 427, 29 S. L. ed. 89, 92, 5 Sup. Ct. Rep. 935; *Mackin v. United States*, 117 U.S. 348, 350, 29 S. L. ed. 909, 910, 6 Sup. Ct. Rep. 777.

In *Hobbs v. State*, *supra*, and in other cases, prominence is given to the power of the legislature to define crimes and their punishment. We concede the power in most of its exercises. We disclaim the right to assert a judgment against that of the legislature, of the expediency of the laws, or the right to oppose the judicial power to the legislative power to define crimes and fix their punishment, unless that power encounters in its exercise a constitutional prohibition. In such case, not our discretion, but our legal duty, strictly defined and imperative in its direction, is invoked. Then the legislative power is brought to the judgment of a power superior to it for the instant. And for the proper exercise of such power there must be a comprehension of all that the legislature did or could take into account,—that is, a consideration of the mischief and the remedy. However, there is a certain subordination of the judiciary to the legislature. The function of the legislature is primary, its exercise fortified by presumptions of right and legality, and is not to be interfered with lightly, nor by any judicial conception of its wisdom or propriety. They have no limitation, we repeat, but constitutional ones, and what those are the judiciary must judge. We have expressed these elementary truths to avoid the misapprehension that we do not recognize to the fullest the wide range of power that the legislature possesses to adapt its penal laws to conditions as they may exist, and punish the crimes of men according to their forms and frequency. We do not intend in this opinion to express anything that contravenes those propositions.

Our meaning may be illustrated. For instance, in *Territory v. Ketchum*, 10 N.M. 718, 55 L.R.A. 90, 65 Pac. 169, a case that has been brought to our attention as antagonistic to our views of cruel and unusual punishments, a statute was sustained which imposed the penalty of death upon any person who should make an assault upon any railroad train, car, or locomotive, for the purpose and with the intent to commit murder, robbery, or other felony upon a passenger or employee, express messenger or mail agent. The supreme court of the territory discussed the purpose of the 8th Amendment, and expressed views opposed to those we announce in this opinion, but finally rested its decision upon the conditions which existed in the territory, and the circumstances of terror and danger which accompanied the crime denounced. So, also, may we mention the legislation of some of the states, enlarging the common-law definition of burglary, and dividing it into degrees, fixing a severer punishment for that committed in the nighttime from that committed in the daytime, and for arson of buildings in which human beings may be from arson of buildings which may be vacant. In all such cases there is something more to give character and degree to the crimes then the seeking of a felonious gain, and it may properly become an element in the measure of their punishment.

(Continues)

From this comment we turn back to the law in controversy. Its character and the contence in this case may be illustrated by examples even better than it can be represented by words. There are degrees of homicide that are not punished so severely, nor are the following crimes: misprision of treason, inciting rebellion, conspiracy to destroy the government by force, recruiting soldiers in the United States to fight against the United States, forgery of letters patent, forgery of bonds and other instruments for the purpose of defrauding the United States, robbery, larceny, and other crimes. Section 86 of the Penal Laws of the United States, as revised and amended by the act of Congress of March 4, 1909 (35 Stat. at L. 1088, chap. 321, U.S. Comp. Stat. Supp. 1909, p. 1391), provides that any person charged with the payment of any appropriation made by Congress, who shall pay to any clerk or other employee of the United States a sum less than that provided by law, and require a receipt for a sum greater than that paid to and received by him, shall be guilty of embezzlement, and shall be fined in double the amount so withheld, and imprisoned not more than two years. The offense described has similarity to the offense for which Weems was convicted, but the punishment provided for it is in great contrast to the penalties of *cadena temporal* and its 'accessories.' If we turn to the legislation of the Philippine Commission we find that instead of the penalties of *cadena temporal*, medium degree (fourteen years, eight months, and one day, to seventeen years and four months, with fine and 'accessories'), to *cadena perpetua*, fixed by the Spanish Penal Code for the falsification of bank notes and other instruments authorized by the law of the kingdom, it is provided that the forgery of or counterfeiting the obligations or securities of the United States or of the Philippine Islands shall be punished by a fine of not more than 10,000 pesos and by imprisonment of not more than fifteen years. In other words, the highest punishment possible for a crime which may cause the loss of many thousand of dollars, and to prevent which the duty of the state should be as eager as to prevent the perversion of truth in a public document, is not greater than that which may be imposed for falsifying a single item of a public account. And this contrast shows more than different exercises of legislative judgment. It is greater than that. It condemns the sentence in this case as cruel and unusual. It exhibits a difference between unrestrained power and that which is exercised under the spirit of constitutional limitations formed to establish justice. The state thereby suffers nothing and loses no power. The purpose of punishment is fulfilled, crime is repressed by penalties of just, not tormenting, severity, its repetition is prevented, and hope is given for the reformation of the criminal.

It is suggested that the provision for imprisonment in the Philippine Code is separable from the accessory punishment, and that the latter may be declared illegal, leaving the former to have application. *United States v. Pridgeon*, 153 U.S. 48, 38 L. ed. 631, 14 Sup. Ct. Rep. 746, is referred to. The proposition decided in that case was that 'where a court has jurisdiction of the person and of the offense, the imposition of a sentence in excess of what the law permits does not render the legal or authorized portion of the sentence void, but only leaves such portion of the sentence as may be in excess open to question and attack.' This proposition is not applicable to the case at bar. The imprisonment and the accessories were in accordance with the law. They were not in excess of it, but were positively required by it. It is provided in article 106, as we have seen, that those sentenced to *cadena temporal* shall labor for the benefit of the state; shall always carry a chain at the ankle, hanging from the wrist; shall be employed at hard and painful labor; shall receive no assistance whatsoever from without the penal institutions. And it is provided in article 56 that the penalty of *cadena temporal* shall include the accessory penalties.

In *Re Graham*, 138 U.S. 461, 34 L. ed. 1051, 11 Sup. Ct. Rep. 363, it was recognized to be 'the general rule that a judgment rendered by a court in a criminal case must conform strictly to the statute, and that any variation from its provisions, either in the character or the extent of punishment inflicted, renders the judgment absolutely void.' In *Ex parte Karstendick*, 93 U.S. 396, 399, 23 S. L. ed. 889, 890, it was said: 'In cases where the statute makes hard labor a part of the punishment, it is imperative upon the court to include that in its sentence.' A similar view was expressed in *Re Mills*, 135 U.S. 263, 266, 34 S. L. ed. 107, 108, 10 Sup. Ct. Rep. 762. It was recognized in *United States v. Pridgeon* and the cases quoted which sustained it.

The Philippine Code unites the penalties of *cadena temporal*, principal and accessory, and it is not in our power to separate them, even if they are separable, unless their independence is such that we can say that their union was not made imperative by the legislature. Employers' Liability Cases (*Howard v. Illinois C. R. Co.*) 207 U.S. 463, 52 L. ed. 297, 28 Sup. Ct. Rep. 141. This certainly cannot be said of the Philippine Code, as a Spanish enactment, and the order putting it into effect in the Islands did not attempt to destroy the unity of its provisions or the effect of that unity. In other words, it was put into force as it existed, with all its provisions dependent. We cannot, therefore, declare them separable.

It follows from these views that, even if the minimum penalty of *cadena temporal* had been imposed, it would have been repugnant to the Bill of Rights. In other words, the fault is in the law; and, as we are pointed to no other under which a sentence can be imposed, the judgment must be reversed, with directions to dismiss the proceedings.

So ordered.

Mr. Justice Lurton, not being a member of the court when this case was argued, took no part in its decision.

Mr. Justice White, dissenting:

The Philippine law made criminal the entry in a public record by a public official of a knowingly false statement. The punishment prescribed for violating this law was fine and imprisonment in a penal institution at hard and painful labor for a period ranging from twelve years and a day to twenty years, the prisoner being subjected, as accessories to the main punishment, to carrying during his imprisonment a chain at the ankle, hanging from the wrist, deprivation during the term of imprisonment of civil rights, and subjection, besides, to perpetual disqualification to enjoy political rights, hold office, etc., and, after discharge, to the surveillance of the authorities. The plaintiff in error, having been convicted of a violation of this law, was sentenced to pay a small fine and to undergo imprisonment for fifteen years, with the resulting accessory punishments above referred to. Neither at the trial in the court of first instance nor in the supreme court of the Philippine Islands was any question raised concerning the repugnancy of the statute defining the crime and fixing its punishment to the provision of the Philippine Bill of Rights, forbidding cruel and unusual punishment. Indeed, no question on that subject was even indirectly referred to in the assignments of error filed in the court below for the purpose of this writ of error. In the brief of counsel, however, in this court, the contention was made that the sentence was void, because the term of imprisonment was a cruel and unusual one, and therefore repugnant to the Bill of Rights. Deeming this contention to be of such supreme importance as to require it to be passed upon, although not raised below, the court now holds that the statute, because of the punishment which it prescribes, was repugnant to the Bill of Rights, and therefore void, and for this reason alone reverses and remands with directions to discharge.

The Philippine Bill of Rights, which is construed and applied, is identical with the cruel and unusual punishment clause of the 8th Amendment. Because of this identity it is now decided that it is necessary to give to the Philippine Bill of Rights the meaning properly attributable to the provision on the same subject found in the 8th Amendment, as, in using the language of that Amendment in the statute, it is to be presumed that Congress intended to give to the words their constitutional significance. The ruling now made, therefore, is an interpretation of the 8th Amendment, and announces the limitation which that Amendment imposes on Congress when exercising its legislative authority to define and punish crime. The great importance of the decision is hence obvious.

Of course, in every case where punishment is inflicted for the commission of crime, if the suffering of the punishment by the wrongdoer be alone regarded, the sense of compassion aroused would mislead and render the performance of judicial duty impossible. And it is to be conceded that this natural conflict between the sense of commiseration and the commands of duty is augmented when the nature of the crime defined by the Philippine law and the punishment which that law prescribes are only abstractly considered, since the impression is at once produced that the legislative authority has been severely exerted. I say only abstractly considered, because the first impression produced by the merely abstract view of the subject is met by the admonition that the duty of defining and punishing crime has never, in any civilized country, been exerted upon mere abstract considerations of the inherent nature of the crime punished, but has always involved the most practical consideration of the tendency at a particular time to commit certain crimes, of the difficulty of repressing the same, and of how far it is necessary to impose stern remedies to prevent the commission of such crimes. And, of course, as these considerations involve the necessity for a familiarity with local conditions in the Philippine Islands which I do not possess, such want of knowledge at once additionally admonishes me of the wrong to arise from forming a judgment upon insufficient data, or without a knowledge of the subject-matter upon which the judgment is to be exerted. Strength, indeed, is added to this last suggestion by the fact that no question concerning the subject was raised in the courts below or there considered; and therefore no opportunity was afforded those courts, presumably, at least, relatively familiar with the local conditions, to express their views as to the considerations which may have led to the prescribing of the punishment in question. Turning aside, therefore, from mere emotional tendencies, and

(Continues)

guiding my judgment alone by the aid of the reason at my command, I am unable to agree with the ruling of the court. As, in my opinion, that ruling rests upon an interpretation of the cruel and unusual punishment clause of the 8th Amendment, naver before announced, which is repugnant to the natural import of the language employed in the clause, and which interpretation curtails the legislative power of Congress to defind and punish crime by asserting a right of judicial supervision over the exertion of that power, in disregard of the distinction between the legislative and judicial department of the government, I deem it my duty to dissent and state my reasons.

To perform this duty requires at the outset a precise statement of the construction given by the ruling now made to the provision of the 8th Amendment. My inability to do this must, however, be confessed, because I find it impossible to fix with precision the meaning which the court gives to that provision. Not for the purpose of criticizing, but solely in order to indicate my perplexity on the subject, the reasons for my doubt are briefly given. Thus, to my mind, it appears as follows: First. That the court interprets the inhibition against cruel and unusual punishment as imposing upon Congress the duty of proportioning punishment according to the nature of the crime, and casts upon the judiciary the duty of determining whether punishments have been properly apportioned in a particular statute, and if not, to decline to enforce it. This seems to me to be the case, because of the reference made by the court to the harshness of the principal punishment (imprisonment), and its comments as to what it deems to be the severity, if not inhumanity, of the accessories which result from or accompany it, and the declaration in substance that these things offend against the just principle of proportioning punishment to the nature of the crime punished, stated to be a fundamental precept of justice and of American criminal law. That this is the view now upheld, it seems to me, is additionally demonstrated by the fact that the punishment for the crime in question, as imposed by the Philippine law, is compared with other Philippine punishments for crimes deemed to be less heinous, and the conclusion is deduced that this fact, in and of itself, serves to establish that the punishment imposed in this case is an exertion of unrestrained power, condemned by the cruel and unusual punishment clause.

Second. That this duty of apportionment compels not only that the lawmaking power should adequately apportion punishment for the crimes as to which it legislates, but also further exacts that the performance of the duty of apportionment must be discharged by taking into view the standards, whether lenient or severe, existing in other and distinct jurisdictions; and that a failure to do so authorizes the courts to consider such standards in their discretion, and judge of the validity of the law accordingly. I say this because, although the court expressly declares in the opinion, when considering a case decided by the highest court of one of the territories of the United States, that the legislative power to define and punish crime committed in a territory, for the purpose of the 8th Amendment, is separate and distinct from the legislation of Congress, yet, in testing the validity of the punishment affixed by the law here in question, proceeds to measure it not alone by the Philippine legislation, but by the provisions of several acts of Congress punishing crime, and in substance declares such congressional laws to be a proper standard, and in effect holds that the greater proportionate punishment inflicted by the Philippine law over the more lenient punishments prescribed in the laws of Congress establishes that the Philippine law is repugnant to the 8th Amendment.

Third. That the cruel and unusual punishment clause of the 8th Amendment controls not only the exertion of legislative power as to modes of punishment, proportionate or otherwise, but addresses itself also to the mainspring of the legislative motives in enacting legislation punishing crime in a particular case, and therefore confers upon courts the power to refuse to enforce a particular law defining and punishing crime, if, in their opinion, such law does not manifest that the lawmaking power, in fixing the punishment, was sufficiently impelled by a purpose to effect a frformation of the criminal. This is said because of the statements contained in the opinion of the court as to the legislative duty to shape legislation not only with a view to punish, but to reform the criminal, and the inferences which I deduce that it is conceived that the failure to do so is a violation of constitutional duty.

Fourth. That the cruel and unusual punishment clause does not merely limit the legislative power to fix the punishment for crime by excepting out of that authority the right to impose bodily punishments of a cruel kind, in the strict acceptation of those terms, but limits the legislative discretion in determining to what degree of severity an appropriate and usual mode of punishment may, in a particular case, be inflicted; and therefore endows the courts with the right to supervise the exercise of legislative discretion as to the adequacy of punishment, even although resort is had only to authorized kinds of punishment, thereby endowing the courts with the power to refuse to enforce laws punishing crime, if, in the judicial judgment, the legislative branch of the government has prescribed a too severe punishment.

Not being able to assent to these, as it to me seems, in some respects conflicting, or, at all events, widely divergent, propositions, I shall consider them all as sanctioned by the interpretation now given to the prohibition of the 8th Amendment, and with this conception in mind shall consider the subject.

Before approaching the text of the 8th Amendment to determine its true meaning, let me briefly point out why, in my opinion, it cannot have the significance which it must receive to sustain the propositions rested upon it. In the first place, if it be that the lawmaker, in defining and punishing crime, is imperatively restrained by constitutional provisions to apportion punishment by a consideration alone of the abstract heinousness of the offenses punished, it must result that the power is so circumscribed as to be impossible of execution; or, at all events, is so restricted as to exclude the possibility of taking into account, in defining and punishing crime, all those considerations concerning the condition of society, the tendency to commit the particular crime, the difficulty of detecting the same, the necessity for resorting to stern measures of repression, and various other subjects which have, at all times, been deemed essential to be weighed in defining and punishing crime. And certainly the paralysis of the discretion vested in the lawmaking authority which the propositions accomplish is immeasurably magnified when it is considered that this duty of proportioning punishment requires the taking into account of the standards prevailing in other or different countries or jurisdictions, thereby at once exacting that legislation on the subject of crime must be proportioned not to the conditions to which it is intended to apply, but must be based upon conditions with which the legislation, when enacted, will have no relation or concern whatever. And when it is considered that the propositions go further, and insist that, if the legislation seems to the judicial mind not to have been sufficiently impelled by motives of reformation of the criminal, such legislation defining and punishing crime is to be held repugnant to constitutional limitations, the impotency of the legislative power to define and punish crime is made manifest. When to this result is added the consideration that the interpretation, by its necessary effect, does not simply cause the cruel and unusual punishment clause to carve out of the domain of legislative authority the power to resort to prohibited kinds of punishments, but subjects to judicial control the degree of severity with which authorized modes of punishment may be inflicted, it seems to me that the demonstration is conclusive that nothing will be left of the independent legislative power to punish and define crime, if the interpretation now made be pushed in future application to its logical conclusion. But let me come to the 8th Amendment, for the purpose of stating why the clause in question does not, in my opinion, authorize the deductions drawn from it, and therefore does not sanction the ruling now made.

I shall consider the Amendment (a) as to its origin in the mother country, and the meaning there given to it prior to the American Revolution; (b) its migration and existence in the states after the Revolution, and prior to the adoption of the Constitution; (c) its incorporation into the Constitution, and the construction given to it in practice from the beginning to this time; and (d) the judicial interpretation which it has received, associated with the construction affixed, both in practice and judicially, to the same provision found in various state constitutions or Bills of Rights.

Without going into unnecessary historical detail, it is sufficient to point out, as did the court in *Re Kemmler*, 136 U.S. 436, 446, 34 S. L. ed. 519, 524, 10 Sup. Ct. Rep. 930, 933, that 'the provision in reference to cruel and unusual punishments was taken from the well-known act of Parliament of 1688 [1689?], entitled 'An Act Declaring the Rights and Liberties of the Subject, and Settling the Succession of the Crown.'' And this act, it is to be observed, was but in regular form a crystallization of the Declaration of Rights of the same year. 3 Hallam, *Const. Hist.* p. 106. It is also certain, as declared in the Kemmler Case, that 'this Declaration of Rights had reference to the acts of the executive and judicial departments of the government of England,' since it but embodied the grievances which it was deemed had been suffered by the usurpations of the Crown and transgressions of authority by the courts. In the recitals both of the Declaration of Rights and the Bill of Rights, the grievances complained of were that illegal and cruel punishments had been inflicted, 'which are utterly and directly contrary to the known laws and statutes and freedom of this realm;' while in both the Declaration and the Bill of Rights the remedy formulated was a declaration against the infliction of cruel and unusual punishments.

Whatever may be the difficulty, if any, in fixing the meaning of the prohibition at its origin, it may not be doubted, and indeed is not questioned by anyone, that the cruel punishments against which the Bill of Rights provided were the atrocious, sanguinary, and inhuman punishments which had been inflicted in the past upon the persons of criminals. This being certain, the difficulty of interpretation, if any, is involved in determining what was intended by the unusual punishments referred to and which were provided against. Light, however, on this subject, is at once afforded by observing that the

(*Continues*)

unusual punishments provided against were responsive to and obviously considered to be the illegal punishments complained of. These complaints were, first, that customary modes of bodily punishments, such as whipping and the pillory, had, under the exercise of judicial discretion, been applied to so unusual a degree as to cause them to be illegal; and, second, that in some cases an authority to sentence to perpetual imprisonment had been exerted under the assumption that power to do so resulted from the existence of judicial discretion to sentence to imprisonment, when it was unusual, and therefore illegal, to inflict life imprisonment in the absence of express legislative authority. In other words, the prohibitions, although conjunctively stated, were really disjunctive, and embraced braced as follows: (a) Prohibitions against a resort to the inhuman bodily punishments of the past; (b) or, where certain bodily punishments were customary, a prohibition against their infliction to such an extent as to be unusual and consequently illegal; (c) or the infliction, under the assumption of the exercise of judicial discretion, of unusual punishments not bodily, which could not be imposed except by express statute, or which were wholly beyond the jurisdiction of the court to impose.

The scope and power of the guaranty as we have thus stated it will be found portrayed in the reasons assigned by the members of the House of Lords who dissented against two judgments for perjury entered in the King's bench against Titus Oates. 10 How. St. Tr. col. 1325. The judgments and the dissenting reasons are copied in the margin.

As well the dissent feferred to as the report of the conferees Judgment against Titus Oates upon conviction upon two indictments for perjury, as announced by the court (10 How. St. Tr. cols. 1316, 1317):

'First, The court does order for a fine that you pay 1,000 marks upon each Indictment.

"Secondly, That you be stript of all your Canonical Habits.

"Thirdly, The Court does award, That you do stand upon the Pillory, and in the Pillory, here before Westminster-hall gate, upon Monday next, for an hour's time, between the hours of 10 and 12; with a paper over your head (which you must first walk with round about to all the Courts in Westminster-hall) declaring your crime.' And that is upon the first indictment.

"Fourthly (on the Second Indictment), upon Tuesday, you shall stand upon, and in the Pillory, at the Royal Exchange in London, for the space of an hour, between the hours of 12 and 2; with the same inscription.

"You shall upon the next Wednesday be whipped from Aldgate to Newgate.

"Upon Friday, you shall be whipped from Newgate to Tyburn, by the hands of the common hangman.'

'But, Mr. Oates, we cannot but remember, there were several particular times you swore false about; and therefore, as annual commemorations, that it may be known to all people as long as you live, we have taken special care of you for an annual punishment.

"Upon the 24th of April every year, as long as you live, you are to stand upon the Pillory and in the Pillory, at Tyburn, just opposite to the gallows, for the space of an hour, between the hours of 10 and 12.

"You are to stand upon, and in the Pillory, here at Westminster-hall gate, every 9th of August, in every year, so long as you live. And that it may be known what we mean by it, 'tis to remember, what he swore about Mr. Ireland's being in town between the 8th and 12th of August.

"You are to stand upon, and in the Pillory, at Charing-cross, on the 10th of August, every year, during your life, for an hour, between 10 and 12.

"The like over against the Temple gate, upon the 11th.

"And upon the 2d of September (which is another notorious time, which you cannot but be remember'd of) you are to stand upon, and in the Pillory, for the space of one hour, between 12 and 2, at the Royal Exchange; and all this you are to do every year, during your life; and to be committed close prisoner, as long as you live."

Dissenting statement of a minority of the House of Lords: on the part of the House of Commons, made to that body concerning a bill to set aside the judgments against Oates above referred to (5 *Cobbett's Parl. History*, col. 386), proceeded upon the identity of what was deemed to be the illegal practices complained of, and which were intended to be rectified by the prohibition against cruel and unusual punishments, made in the Declaration of Rights, and treated that prohibition, as already stated, as substantially disjunctive, and as forbidding the doing of the things we have above enumerated. See, for the disjunctive character of the provision, Stephen, *Com. Law Eng.* 15th ed. p. 379.

When the origin and purpose of the Declaration and the Bill of Rights is thus fixed it becomes clear that that Declaration is not susceptible of the meaning now attributed to the same language found in the Constitution of the United States. That in England it was nowhere deemed that any theory of proportional punishment was suggested by the Bill of Rights, or that a protest was thereby intended against the severity of punishments, speaking generally, is demonstrated by the practice which prevailed in

England as to punishing crime from the time of the Bill of Rights to the time of the American Revolution. Speaking on this subject, Stephen, in his history of the criminal law of England, vol. 1, pp. 470, 471, says:

'The severity of the criminal law was greatly increased all through the eighteenth century by the creation of new felonies without benefit of clergy . . . However, after making all deductions on these grounds, there can be no doubt that the legislation of the eighteenth century in criminal matters was severe to the highest degree, and destitute of any sort of principal or system.'

For the sake of brevity a review of the practises which prevailed in the colonial period will not be referred to. Therefore, attention is at once directed to the express guaranties in certain of the state constitutions adopted after the Declaration of Independence, and prior to the formation of the Constitution of the United States, and the circumstances connected with the subsequent adoption of the 8th Amendment.

In 1776, Maryland, in a Bill of Rights, declared (1 Charters and Constitutions, pp. 818, 819):

'14. That sanguinary laws ought to be avoided, as far as is consistent with the safety of the state; and no law to inflict cruel and unusual pains and penalties ought to be made in any case, or at any time hereafter.'
  '22. That excessive bail ought not to be required, nor excessive fines imposed, nor cruel or unusual punishments inflicted, by the courts of law.'

The Constitution of North Carolina of 1776, in general terms prohibited the infliction of 'cruel or unusual punishments.'

Virginia, by 9 of the Bill of Rights adopted in 1776, provided as follows:

'That excessive bail ought not to be required, nor excessive fines imposed, nor cruel and unusual punishments inflicted.'

In the Massachusetts Declaration of Rights of 1780, a direct prohibition was placed upon the infliction by magistrates or courts of cruel or unusual punishments, the provision being as follows:

'Art. 26. No magistrate or court of law shall demand excessive bail or sureties, impose excessive fines, or inflict cruel or unusual punishments.'

The Declaration of Rights of New Hampshire, of 1784, was as follows:

'18. All penalties ought to be proportioned to the nature of the offense. No wise legislature will affix the same punishment to the crimes of theft, forgery, and the like, which they do to those of murder and treason; where the same undistinguishing severity is exerted against all offense the people are led to forget the real distinction in the crimes themselves, and to commit the most flagrant with as little compunction as they do those of the lightest dye. For the same reason a multitude of sanguinary laws is both impolitic and unjust. The true design of all punishments being to reform, not to exterminate, mankind.'
  '33. No magistrate or court of law shall demand excessive bail or sureties, impose excessive fines, or inflict cruel or unusual punishments.'

The substantial identity between the provisions of these several constitutions or Bills of Rights shows beyond doubt that their meaning was understood; that is to say, that the significance attributed to them in the mother country as the result of the Bill of Rights of 1689 was appreciated, and that it was intended, in using the identical words, to give them the same well-understood meaning. It is to be observed that the New Hampshire Bill of Rights contains a clause admonishing as to the wisdom of the apportionment of punishment of crime according to the nature of the offense, but in marked contrast to the re-enactment, in express and positive terms, of the cruel and unusual punishment clause of the English Bill of Rights, the provision as to apportionment is merely advisory, additionally demonstrating the precise and accurate conception then entertained of the nature and character of the prohibition adopted from the English Bill of Rights.

Undoubtedly, in the American states, prior to the formation of the Constitution, the necessity for the protection afforded by the cruel and unusual punishment guaranty of the English Bill of Rights

(Continues)

had ceased to be a matter of concern, because, as a rule, the cruel bodily punishments of former times were no longer imposed, and judges, where moderate bodily punishment was usual, had not, under the guise of discretion, directed the infliction of such punishments to so unusual a degree as to transcend the limits of discretion and cause the punishment to he illegal, and had also not attempted, in virtue of mere discretion, to inflict such unusual and extreme punishments as had always been deemed proper to be inflicted only as the result of express statutory authority. Despite these considerations, it is true that some of the solicitude which arose after the submission of the Constitution for ratification, and which threatened to delay or prevent such ratification, in part, at least, was occasioned by the failure to guarantee against the infliction of cruel and unusual punishments. Thus, in the Massachusetts convention, Mr. Holmes, discussing the general result of the judicial powers conferred by the Constitution, and referring to the right of Congress to define and fix the punishment for crime, said (2 Elliot, *Debates*, 111): 'They are nowhere restrained from inventing the most cruel and unheared-of punishments, and annexing them to crimes; and there is no constitutional check on them, but that racks and gibbets may be amongst the most mild instruments of their discipline.'

That the opposition to the ratification in the Virginia convention was earnestly and eloquently voiced by Patrick Henry is too well known to require anything but statement. That the absence of a guaranty against cruel and unusual punishment was one of the causes of the solicitude by which Henry was possessed is shown by the debates in that convention. Thus Patrick Henry said (3 Elliot, *Debates*, 447):

'In this business of legislation, your members of Congress will lose the restriction of not imposing excessive fines, demanding excessive bail, and inflicting cruel and unusual punishments. These are prohibited by your Declaration of Rights. What has distinguished our ancestors? That they would not admit of tortures, or cruel and barbarous punishment. But Congress may introduce the practice of the civil law, in preference to that of the common law. They may introduce the practice of France, Spain, and Germany,-of torturing to extort a confession of the crime. They will say that they might as well draw examples from those countries as from Great Britain, and they will tell you that there is such a necessity of strengthening the arm of government that they must have a criminal equity, and extort confession by torture, in order to punish with still more relentless severity. We are then lost and undone. And can any man think it troublesome when he can, by a small interference, prevent our rights from being lost? If you will, like the Virginian government, give them knowledge of the extent of the rights retained by the people, and the powers of themselves, they will, if they be honest men, thank you for it. Will they not wish to go on sure grounds? But, if you leave them otherwise, they will not know how to proceed; and, being in a state of uncertainty, they will assume rather than give up powers by implication.' These observations, it is plainly to be seen, were addressed to the fear of the repetition, either by the sanction of law or by the practice of courts, of the barbarous modes of bodily punishment or torture, the protest against which was embodied in the Bill of Rights in 1689.

The ultimate recognition by Henry of the patriotic duty to ratify the Constitution and trust to the subsequent adoption of a Bill of Rights, the submission and adoption of the first ten Amendments as a Bill of Rights, which followed ratification, the connection of Mr. Madison with the drafting of the amendments, and the fact that the 8th Amendment is in the precise words of the guaranty on that subject in the Virginia Bill of Rights, would seem to make it perfectly clear that it was only intended by that Amendment to remedy the wrongs which had been provided against in the English Bill of Rights, and which were likewise provided against in the Virginia provision, and therefore was intended to guard against the evils so vividly portrayed by Henry in the debate which we have quoted. That this was the common understanding which must have existed on the subject is plainly to be inferred from the fact that the 8th Amendment was substantially submitted by Congress without any debate on the subject. 2 *Lloyd's Debates*, 225. Of course, in view of the nature and character of the government which the Constitution called into being, the incorporation of the 8th Amendment caused its provisions to operate a direct and controlling prohibition upon the legislative branch (as well as all other departments), restraining it from authorizing or directing the infliction of the cruel bodily punishments of the past, which was one of the evils sought to be prevented for the future by the English Bill of Rights, and also restrained the courts from exerting and Congress from empowering them, to select and exert by way of discretion modes of punishment which were not usual, or usual modes of punishment to a degree not usual, and which could alone be imposed by express authority of law. But this obvious result lends no support to the theory that the adoption of the Amendment operated or was intended to prevent the legislative branch of the government from prescribing, according to its conception of what public policy required, such punishments, severe or otherwise, as it deemed necessary for the prevention of crime, provided, only, resort was not had to the infliction of bodily punishments of a cruel and barbarous character, against which the Amendment expressly provided. Not to so conclude is to hold that because the Amendment, in addition to depriving the lawmaking power of the right to authorize the infliction of cruel bodily punishments, had restricted the courts, where discretion was possessed by them, from exerting the power to punish by a mode or in a manner so unusual as to require legislative sanction, it thereby deprived Congress of the power to sanction the punishments which the Amendment forbade being imposed, merely because they were not sanctioned. In other words, that because the power was denied to the judiciary to do certain things without legislative authority, thereby the right on the part of the legislature to confer the authority was taken away. And this impossible conclusion would lead to the equally impossible result that the effect of the Amendment was to deprive Congress of its legitimate authority to punish crime, by prescribing such modes of punishment, even although not before employed, as were appropriate for the purpose.

That no such meaning as is now ascribed to the Amendment was attributed to it at the time of its adoption is shown by the fact that not a single suggestion that it had such a meaning is pointed to, and that, on the other hand, the practice from the very beginning shows directly to the contrary, and demonstrates that the very Congress that adopted the Amendment construed it in practice as I have construed it. This is so, since the first crimes act of the United States prescribed punishments for crime utterly without reference to any assumed rule of proportion, or of a conception of a right in the judiciary to supervise the action of Congress in respect to the severity of punishment, excluding, always, the right to impose as a punishment the cruel bodily punishments which were prohibited. What clearer demonstration can there be of this than the statement made by this court in *Ex parte Wilson*, 114 U.S. 427, 29 L. ed. 92, 5 Sup. Ct. Rep. 935, of the nature of the first crimes act, as follows:

> 'By the first crimes act of the United States, forgery of public securities, or knowingly uttering forged public securities with intent to defraud, as well as treason, murder, piracy, mutiny, robbery, or rescue of a person convicted of a capital crime, was punishable with death; most other offenses were punished by fine and imprisonment; whipping was part of the punishment of stealing or falsifying records, fraudulently acknowledging bail, larceny of goods, or receiving stolen goods; disqualification to hold office was part of the punishment of bribery; and those convicted of perjury or subornation of perjury, besides being fined and imprisoned, were to stand in the pillory for one hour, and rendered incapable of testifying in any court of the United States. Act of April 30, 1790, chap. 9, 1 Stat. at L. 112–117; Mr. Justice Wilson's Charge to the Grand Jury in 1791, 3 *Wilson's Works*, 380, 381.'

And it is, I think, beyond power even of question that the legislation of Congress, from the date of the first crimes act to the present time, but exemplifies the truth of what has been said, since that legislation from time to time altered modes of punishment, increasing or diminishing the amount of punishment, as was deemed necessary for the public good, prescribing punishments of a new character, without reference to any assumed rule of apportionment, or the conception that a right of judicial supervision was deemed to obtain. It is impossible with any regard for brevity to demonstrate these statements by many illustrations. But let me give a sample from legislation enacted by Congress of the change of punishment. By 14 of the first crimes act (Act April 30, 1790, chap. 9, 1 Stat. at L. 115), forgery, etc., of the public securities of the United States, or the knowingly uttering and offering for sale of forged or counterfeited securities of the United States with intent to defraud, was made punishable by death. The punishment now is a fine of not more than $5,000, and imprisonment at hard labor for not more than fifteen years. Rev. Stat. 5414, U.S. Comp. Stat. 1901, p. 3662.

By the first crimes act, also, as in numerous others since that time, various additional punishments for the commission of crime were imposed, prescribing disqualification to hold office, to be a witness in the courts, etc., and as late as 1865 a law was enacted by Congress which prescribed as a punishment for crime the disqualification to enjoy rights of citizenship. Rev. Stat. 1996–1998, U.S. Comp. Stat. 1901, p. 1269.

Comprehensively looking at the rulings of this court, it may be conceded that hitherto they have not definitely interpreted the precise meaning of the clause in question, because in most of the cases in which the protection of the Amendment has been invoked, the cases came from courts of last resorts of states, and the opinions leave room for the contention that they proceeded upon the implied assumption that the 8th Amendment did not govern the states, by virtue of the adoption of the 14th Amendment.

(Continues)

(*Continued*)

However, in *Wilkerson v. Utah*, 99 U.S. 130, 25 L. ed. 345, a case coming to this court from the territory of Utah, the meaning of the clause of the 8th Amendment in question came directly under review. The question for decision was whether a sentence to death by shooting, which had been imposed by the court under the assumed exercise of a discretionary power to fix the mode of execution of the sentence, was repugnant to the clause. While the court, in deciding that it was not, did not undertake to fully interpret the meaning of the clause, it nevertheless, reasoning by exclusion, expressly negatived the construction now placed upon it. It was said (pp. 135, 136):

> *Pervear v. Massachusetts*, 5 Wall. 475, 18 L. ed. 608; *Wilkerson v. Utah*, 99 U.S. 130, 25 L. ed. 345; *Re Kemmler*, 136 U.S. 436, 34 L. ed. 519, 10 Sup. Ct. Rep. 930; *McElvaine v. Brush*, 142 U.S. 155, 35 L. ed. 971, 12 Sup. Ct. Rep. 156; *Howard v. Fleming*, 191 U.S. 126, 48 L. ed. 121, 24 Sup. Ct. Rep. 49. 'Difficulty would attend the effort to define with exactness the extent of the constitutional provision which provides that cruel and unusual punishments shall not be inflicted; but it is safe to affirm that punishments of torture, such as those mentioned by the commentator referred to, and all others in the same line of unnecessary cruelty, are forbidden by that Amendment to the Constitution. Cooley, *Const. Lim.* 4th ed. 408; Wharton, *Crim. Law*, 7th ed. 3405.'

And it was doubtless this ruling which caused the court subsequently to say in *Re Kemmler*, 136 U.S. 436, 447, 34 S.L. ed. 519, 524, 10 Sup. Ct. Rep. 930, 933:

> 'Punishments are cruel when they involve torture or a lingering death; but the punishment of death is not cruel, within the meaning of that word as used in the Constitution. It implies there something inhuman and barbarous, something more than the mere extinguishment of life.'

Generally viewing the action of the states in their Bills of Rights as to the prohibition against inhuman or cruel and unusual punishments, it is true to say that those provisions substantially conform to the English Bill of Rights and to the provision of the 8th Amendment we are considering, some using the expression 'cruel and unusual,' others the more accurate expression 'cruel or unusual,' and some 'cruel' only; and in a few instances a provision requiring punishments to be proportioned to the nature of the offense is added to the inhibition against cruel and unusual punishments. In one (Illinois) the prohibition against cruel and unusual punishments is not expressed, although proportional punishment is commanded; yet in *Kelly v. State*, 115 Ill. 583, 56 Am. Rep. 184, 4 N.E. 644, discussing the extent of punishment inflicted by a criminal statute, the supreme court of Illinois declared that 'it would not be for the court to say the penalty was not proportioned to the nature of the offense.' In another state (Ohio), where, in the early constitution of the state, proportionate punishment was conjoined with the cruel and unusual punishment provision, the proportionate provision was omitted in a later constitution. Here, again, it is true to say, time forbidding my indulging in a review of the statutes, that the legislation of all the states is absolutely in conflict with and repugnant to the construction now given to the clause, since that legislation but exemplifies the exertion of legislative power to define and punish crime according to the legislative conception of the necessities of the situation, without the slightest indication of the assumed duty to proportion punishments, and without the suggestion of the existence of judicial power to control the legislative discretion, provided only that the cruel bodily punishments forbidden were not resorted to. And the decisions of the state courts of last resort, it seems to me, with absolute uniformity, and without a single exception from the beginning, proceed upon this conception. It is true that when the reasoning employed in the various cases in critically examined, a difference of conception will be manifested as to the occasion for the adoption of the English Bill of Rights and of the remedy which it provided. Generally speaking, when carefully analyzed, it will be seen that this difference was occasioned by treating the provision against cruel and unusual punishment as conjunctive instead of disjunctive, thereby overlooking the fact, which I think has been previously demonstrated to be the case, that the term 'unusual,' as used in the clause, was not a qualification of the provision against cruel punishments, but was simply synonymous with illegal, and was mainly intended to restrain the courts, under the guise of discretion, from indulging in an unusual and consequently illegal exertion of power. Certain it is, however, whatever may be these differences of reasoning, there stands out in bold relief in the state cases, as it is given to me to understand them, without a single exception, the clear and certain exclusion of any prohibition upon the lawmaking power to determine the adequacy with which crime shall be punished, provided only the cruel bodily punishments of the past are not resorted to. Let me briefly refer to some of the cases. In *Aldridge v. Com.* 2 Va. Cas. 447, decided about twenty years after the ratification of the 8th Amendment, speaking concerning the evils to which the guaranty of the Virginia Bill of Rights against cruel and unusual punishments was addressed, the court, after referring to the punishments usually applicable in that state to crime at the time of the adoption of the Bill of Rights of Virginia, said (p. 450):

'We consider these sanctions as sufficiently rigorous, and we knew that the best heads and hearts of the land of our ancestors had long and loudly declaimed against the wanton cruelty of many of the punishments practised in other countries; and this section in the Bill of Rights was framed effectually to exclude these, so that no future legislature, in a moment, perhaps, of great and general excitement, should be tempted to disgrace our Code by the introduction of any of those odious modes of punishment.'

And, four years later, in 1828, applying the same doctrine in *Com. v. Wyatt*, 6 Rand. (Va.) 694, where a punishment by whipping was challenged as contrary to the Virginia Bill of Rights, the court said (p. 700): 'The punishment of offenses by stripes is certainly odius, but cannot be said to be unusual.'

Until 1865 there was no provision in the Constitution of Georgia expressly guaranteeing against cruel and unusual punishments. The Constitution of that year, however, contained a clause identical in terms with the 8th Amendment, and the scope of the guaranty arose for decision in 1872 in *Whitten v. State*, 47 Ga. 297. The case was this: Upon a conviction for assault and battery, Whitten had been sentenced to imprisonment or the payment of a fine of $250 and costs. The contention was that this sentence was so disproportionate to the offense committed as to be cruel and unusual and repugnant to the guaranty. In one of its immediate aspects the case involved the guaranty against excessive fines; but, as the imprisonment was the coercive means for the payment of the fine, in that aspect the case involved the cruel and unusual punishment clause, and the court so considered; and, in coming to interpret the clause, said (p. 301):

'Whether the law is unconstitutional, a violation of that article of the Constitution which declares excessive fines shall not be imposed nor cruel and unusual punishments inflicted, is another question. The latter clause was, doubtless, intended to prohibit the barbarities of quartering, hanging in chains, castration, etc. When adopted by the framers of the Constitution of the United States, larceny was generally punished by hanging; forgeries, burglaries, etc., in the same way; for, be it remembered, penitentiaries are of modern origin, and I doubt if it ever entered into the mind of men of that day that a crime such as this witness makes the defendant guilty of deserved a less penalty than the judge has inflicted. It would be an interference with matters left by the Constitution to the legislative department of the government for us to undertake to weigh the propriety of this or that penalty fixed by the legislature for specific offenses. So long as they do not provide cruel and unusual punishments, such as disgraced the civilization of former ages, and made one shudder with horror to read of them, as drawing, quartering, burning, etc., the Constitution does not put any limit upon legislative discretion.'

In *State v. White* (1890) 44 Kan. 514, 25 Pac. 33, it was sought to reverse a sentence of five years' imprisonment in the penitentiary, imposed upon a boy of sixteen for statutory rape. The girl was aged sixteen, and had consented. It was contended that if the statute applied, it was unconstitutional and void, 'for the reason that it conflicts with 9 of the Bill of Rights, because it inflicts cruel and unusual punishment, and is in conflict with the spirit of the Bill of Rights generally, and is in violation of common sense, common reason, and common justice.'

The court severely criticized the statute. After deciding that the offense was embraced in the statute, the court said: 'With respect to the severity of the punishment, while we think it is true that is a severer one than has ever before been provided for in any other state or country for such an offense, yet we cannot say that the statute is void for that reason. Imprisonment in the penitentiary at hard labor is not of itself a cruel or unusual punishment, within the meaning of 9 of the Bill of Rights of the Constitution, for it is a kind of punishment which has been resorted to ever since Kansas has had any existence, and is a kind of punishment common in all civilized countries. That section of the Constitution probably, however, relates to the kind of punishment to be inflicted, and not to its duration. Although the punishment in this case may be considered severe, and much severer, indeed, than the punishment for offenses of much greater magnitude, as adultery, or sexual intercourse coupled with seduction, yet we cannot say that the act providing for it is unconstitutional or void.'

In *State v. Hogan* (1900) 63 Ohio St. 218, 52 L.R.A. 863, 81 Am. St. Rep. 626, 58 N.E. 572, the court sustained a 'tramp law,' which prescribed as the punishment to be imposed on a tramp for threatening

(Continues)

to do injury to the person of another, imprisonment in the penintentiary not more than three years nor less than one year. In the course of the opinion the court said:

'The objection that the act prescribes a cruel and unusual punishment we think not well taken. Imprisonment at hard labor is neither cruel nor unusual. It may be severe in the given instance, but that is a question for the law-making power. *Re Kemmler*, 136 U.S. 436, 34 L. ed. 519, 10 Sup. Ct. Rep. 930; *Cornelison v. Com.* 84 Ky. 583, 2 S. W. 235. The punishment, to be effective, should be such as will prove a deterrent. The tramp cares nothing for a jail sentence. Often he courts it. A workhouse sentence is less welcome, but there are but few workhouses in the state. A penitentiary sentence is a real punishment. There he has to work, and cannot shirk.'

In Minnesota a register of deeds was convicted of misappropriating the sum of $62.50, which should have been turned over by him to the county treasurer. He was sentenced to pay a fine of $500 and be imprisoned at hard labor for one year. The contention that the sentence was repugnant to the state constitutional guaranty against cruel and unusual punishment was considered and disposed of by the court in *State v. Borgstrom*, 69 Minn. 508, 72 N.W. 799, 975. Among other things the court said:

'It is claimed that the sentence imposed was altogether disproportionate to the offense charged, and of which the defendant was convicted, and comes within the inhibition of Const. art. 1, 5, that no cruel or unusual punishments be inflicted. . . . We are not unmindful of the importance of this question, and have given to it that serious and thorough examination which such importance demands . . . In England there was a time when punishment was by torture, by loading him with weights to make him confess. Traitors were condemned to be drowned, disemboweled, or burned. It was the law 'that the offender shall be drawn, or rather dragged, to the gallows; he shall be hanged and cut down alive; his entrails shall be removed and burned while he yet lives; his head shall be decapitated; his body divided into four parts.' Browne, Bl. Com. 617. For certain other offenses the offender was punished by cutting off the hands or ears, or boiling in oil, or putting in the pillory. By the Roman law a parricide was punished by being sewed up in a leather sack with a live dog, a cock, a viper, and an ape, and cast into the sea. These punishments may properly be termed cruel, but happily the more humane spirit of this nation does not permit such punishments to be inflicted upon criminals. Such punishments are not warranted by the laws of nature or society, and we find that they are prohibited by our Constitution. But, within this limitation or restriction, the legislature is ordinarily the judge of the expediency of creating new crimes and of prescribing the penalty. . . . While the amount of money misappropriated in this instance was not great, the legislature evidently had in mind the fact that the misappropriation by a public official of the public money was destructive of the public rights and the stability of our government. But fine and imprisonment are not ordinarily cruel and unusual punishments.'

In *Territory v. Ketchum*, 10 N.M. 721, 55 L.R.A. 90, 65 Pac. 169, the court considered whether a statute which had recently been put in force, and which imposed the death penalty instead of a former punishment of imprisonment, for an attempt at train robbery, was cruel and unusual. In sustaining the validity of the law, the court pointed out the conditions of society which presumably had led the law-making power to fix the stern penalty, and after a lengthy discussion of the subject it was held that the law did not impose punishment which was cruel or unusual.

The cases just reviewed are typical, and I therefore content myself with noting in the margin many others to the same general effect.[3]

In stating, as I have done, that, in my opinion, no case could be found sustaining the proposition which the court now holds, I am, of course, not unmindful that a North Carolina case (*State v. Driver*, 78 N.C. 423) is cited by the court as authority, and that a Louisiana case (*State ex rel. Garvey v. Whitaker*, 48 La. Ann. 527, 35 L.R.A. 561, 19 So. 457) is sometimes referred to as of the same general tenor. A brief analysis of the Driver Case will indicate why, in my opinion, it does not support the contention based upon it. In that case the accused was convicted of assault and battery, and sentenced to imprisonment for five years in the county jail. The offense was a common-law misdemeanor, and the punishment not being fixed by statute, as observed by the court (page 429), was left to the discretion of the judge. In testing whether the term of the sentence was unusual and therefore illegal, the court held that a long term of imprisonment in the county jail was unlawful because unusual, and was a gross abuse by the lower court of its discretion. Although the court made reference to the constitutional guaranty, there is not the slightest indication in its opinion that it was deemed there would have been power to set aside the sentence had it been inflicted by virtue of an express statutory command.

But this aside, it seems to me, as the test applied in the Driver Case to determine what was an unusual punishment in North Carolina was necessarily so local in character, that it affords no possible ground here for giving an erroneous meaning to the 8th Amendment. I say this because an examination of the opinion will disclose that it proceeded upon a consideration of the disadvantages peculiar to an imprisonment in a county jail in North Carolina, as compared with the greater advantages to arise from the imprisonment for a like term in the penitentiary, the court saying:

> 'Now, it is true, our terms of imprisonment are much longer, but they are in the penitentiary, where a man may live and be made useful; but a county jail is a close prison, where life is soon in jeopardy, and where the prisoner is not only useless, but a heavy public expense.'

As to the Louisiana case, I content myself with saying that it, in substance, involved merely the question of error committed by a magistrate in imposing punishment for many offenses when, under the law, the offense was a continuing and single one.

From all the considerations which have been stated, I can deduce no ground whatever which, to my mind, sustains the interpretation now given to the cruel and unusual punishment clause. On the contrary, in my opinion, the review which has been made demonstrates that the word 'cruel,' as used in the Amendment, forbids only the lawmaking power, in prescribing punishment for crime, and the courts in imposing punishment, from inflicting unnecessary bodily suffering through a resort to inhuman methods for causing bodily torture, like or which are of the nature of the cruel methods of bodily torture which had been made use of prior to the Bill of Rights of 1689, and against the recurrence of which the word 'cruel' was used in that instrument. To illustrate. Death was a well-known method of punishment, prescribed by law, and it was, of course, painful, and in that sense was cruel. But the infliction of this punishment was clearly not prohibited by the word 'cruel,' although that word manifestly was intended to forbid the resort to barbarous and unnecessary methods of bodily torture in executing even the penalty of death.

In my opinion, the previous considerations also establish that the word 'unusual' accomplished only three results: First, it primarily restrains the courts when acting under the authority of a general discretionary power to impose punishment, such as was possessed at common law, from inflicting lawful modes of punishment to so unusual a degree as to cause the punishment to be illegal, because to that degree it cannot be inflicted without express statutory authority; second, it restrains the courts in the exercise of the same discretion from inflicting a mode of punishment so unusual as to be impliedly not within its discretion, and to be consequently illegal in the absence of express statutory authority; and, third, as to both the foregoing, it operated to restrain the lawmaking power from endowing the judiciary with the right to exert an illegal discretion as to the kind and extent of punishment to be inflicted.

Nor is it given to me to see in what respect the construction thus stated minimizes the constitutional guaranty by causing it to become obsolete or ineffective in securing the purposes which led to its adoption. Of course, it may not be doubted that the provision against cruel bodily punishment is not restricted to the mere means used in the past to accomplish the prohibited result. The prohibition, being generic, embraces all methods within its intendment. Thus, if it could be conceived that tomorrow the lawmaking power, instead of providing for the infliction of the death penalty by hanging, should command its infliction by burying alive, who could doubt that the law would be repugnant to the constitutional inhibition against cruel punishment? But while this consideration is obvious, it must be equally apparent that the prohibition against the infliction of cruel bodily torture cannot be extended so as to limit legislative discretion in prescribing punishment for crime by modes and methods which are not embraced within the prohibition against cruel bodily punishment, considered even in their most generic sense, without disregarding the elementary rules of construction which have prevailed from the beginning. Of course, the beneficent application of the Constitution to the ever-changing requirements of our national life has, in a great measure, resulted from the simple and general terms by which the powers created by the Constitution are conferred, or in which the limitations which it provides are expressed. But this beneficent result has also essentially depended upon the fact that this court, while never hasitating to bring within the powers granted or to restrain by the limitations created all things generically within their embrace, has also incessantly declined to allow general words to be construed so as to include subjects not within their intendment. That these great results have been accomplished through the application by the court of the familiar rule that what is generically included in the words employed in the Constitution is to be ascertained by considering their

(Continues)

(Continued)

origin and their significance at the time of their adoption in the instrument may not be denied,—*Boyd v. United States,* 116 U.S. 616, 624 , 29 S.L. ed. 746, 748, 6 Sup. Ct. Rep. 524; *Kepner v. United States,* 195 U.S. 100, 124, 125 S., 49 L. ed. 114, 122, 123, 24 Sup. Ct. Rep. 797, 1 A. & E. Ann. Cas. 655,—rulings which are directly repugnant to the conception that by judicial construction constitutional limitations may be made to progress so as to ultimately include that which they were not intended to embrace,—a principle with which it seems to me the ruling now made is in direct conflict, since, by the interpretation now adopted, two results are accomplished: (a) the clause against cruel punishments, which was intended to prohibit inhumane and barbarous bodily punishments, is so construed as to limit the discretion of the lawmaking power in determining the mere severity with which punishments not of the prohibited character may be prescribed, and (b) by interpreting the word 'unusual,' adopted for the sole purpose of limiting judicial discretion in order thereby to maintain the supremacy of the lawmaking power, so as to cause the prohibition to bring about the directly contrary result; that is, to expand the judicial power by endowing it with a vast authority to control the legislative department in the exercise of its discretion to define and punish crime.

But further than this, assuming, for the sake of argument, that I am wrong in my view of the 8th Amendment, and that it endows the courts with the power to review the discretion of the lawmaking body in prescribing sentence of imprisonment for crime, I yet cannot agree with the conclusion reached in this case, that, because of the mere term of imprisonment, it is within the rule. True, the imprisonment is at hard and painful labor. But certainly the mere qualification of painful in addition to hard cannot be the basis upon which it is now decided that the legislative discretion was abused, since to understand the meaning of the term requires a knowledge of the discipline prevailing in the prisons in the Philippine Islands. The division of hard labor into classes, one more irksome, and, it may be said, more painful than the other in the sense of severity, is well known. English prisons act of 1865, Pub. Gen. Stat. 19, p. 835. I do not assume that the mere fact that a chain is to be carried by the prisoner causes the punishment to be repugnant to the Bill of Rights, since, while the chain may be irksome, it is evidently not intended to prevent the performance of the penalty of hard labor. Such a provision may well be part of the ordinary prison discipline, particularly in communities where the jails are insecure, and it may be a precaution applied, as it is commonly applied in this country, as a means of preventing the escape of prisoners; for instance, where the sentence imposed is to work on the roads or other work where escape might be likely. I am brought, then, to the conclusion that the accessory punishments are the basis of the ruling now made, that the legislative discretion was so abused as to cause it to be necessary to declare the law prescribing the punishment for the crime invalid. But I can see no foundation for this ruling, as, to my mind, these accessory punishments, even under the assumption, for the sake of argument, that they amounted to an abuse of legislative discretion, are clearly separable from the main punishment,-imprisonment. Where a sentence is legal in one part and illegal in another, it is not open to controversy that the illegal, if separable, may be disregarded and the legal enforced. *United States v. Pridgeon,* 153 U.S. 48, 38 L. ed. 631, 14 Sup. Ct. Rep. 746. But it is said here the illegality is not merely in the sentence, but in the law which authorizes the sentence. Grant the premise. The illegal is capable of separation from the legal in the law as well as in the sentence; and because this is a criminal case, it is none the less subject to the rule that where a statute is unconstitutional in part and in part not, the unconstitutional part, if separable, may be rejected and the constitutional part maintained. Of course it is true that that can only be done provided it can be assumed that the legislature would have enacted the legal part separate from the illegal. The ruling now made must therefore rest upon the proposition that because the law has provided an illegal in addition to a legal punishment, it must be assumed that the legislature would not have defined and punished the crime to the legal extent, because to some extent the legislature was mistaken as to its powers. But this I contend is to indulge in an assumption which is unwarranted and has been directly decided to the contrary at this term in *United States v. Union Supply Co.,* 215 U.S. 50, 54 L. ed.–30 Sup. Ct. Rep. 15. In that case a corporation was proceeded against criminally for an offense punishable by imprisonment and fine. The corporation clearly could not be subjected to the imprisonment, and the contention was that the lawmaker must be presumed to have intended that both the punishments should be inflicted upon the person violating the law, and therefore it could not be intended to include a corporation within its terms. In overruling the contention, it was said:

'And if we free our minds from the notion that criminal statutes must be construed by some artificial and conventional rule, the natural inference, when a statute prescribes two independent penalties, is that it means to inflict them so far as it can, and that if one of them is impossible, it does not mean, on that account, to let the defendant escape.'

I am authorized to say that Mr. Justice Holmes concurs in this dissent.

Notes

1. For that the King's bench, being a temporal court, made it part of the judgment, that Titus Oates, being a clerk, should, for his said perjuries, be devested of his canonical and priestly habit, and to continue devested all his life; which is a matter wholly out of their power, belonging to the ecclesiastical courts only.
2. For that the said judgments are barbarous, inhuman, and unchristian; and there is no precedents to warrant the punishments of whipping and committing to prison for life, for the crime of perjury; which yet were but part of the punishments inflicted upon him.
3. For that the particular matters upon which the indictments were found were the points objected against Mr. Titus Oates' testimony in several of the trials, in which he was allowed to be a good and credible witness, though testified against him by most of the same persons, who witnessed against him upon those indictments.*
4. For that this will be an encouragement and allowance for giving the like cruel, barbarous, and illegal judgments hereafter, unless this judgment be reversed.
5. Because Sir John Holt, Sir Henry Pollexfen, the two chief justices, and Sir Robert Atkins, chief baron, with six judges more (being all that were then present), for these and many other reasons, did, before us, solemnly deliver their opinions, and unanimously declare, That the said judgments were contrary to law and ancient practice, and therefore erroneous, and ought to be reversed.
6. Because it is contrary to the declaration on the 12th of February last, which was ordered by the Lords Spiritual and Temporal and Commons then assembled, and by their declaration engrossed in parchment, and enrolled among the records of Parliament, and recorded in chancery; whereby it doth appear, that excessive bail ought not to be required, nor excessive fines imposed, nor cruel nor unusual punishments inflicted.'

---

*Cases decided in state and territorial courts of last resort, involving the question whether particular punishments were cruel and unusual: *Ex parte Mitchell*, 70 Cal. 1. 11 Pac. 488; *People v. Clark*, 106 Cal. 32, 39 Pac. 53; *Fogarty v. State*, 80 Ga. 450, 5 S.E. 782; *Kelly v. State*, 115 Ill. 683, 56 Am. Rep. 184, 4 N.E. 644; *Hobbs v. State*, 133 Ind. 404, 18 L.R.A. 774, 32 N.E. 1019; *State v. Teeters*, 97 Iowa, 458, 66 N.W. 754; *Re Tutt*, 55 Kan. 705, 41 Pac. 957; *Cornelison v. Com.* 84 Ky. 583, 608, 2 S.W. 235; *Harper v. Com.* 93 Ky. 290, 19 S.W. 737; *State ex rel. Hohn v. Baker*, 105 La. 378, 29 So. 940; *Foote v. State*, 59 Md. 264, 267; *Com. v. Hitchings*, 5 Gray, 482; *McDonald v. Com.* 173 Mass. 322, 73 Am. St. Rep. 293, 53 N.E. 874; *Lurton v. Circuit Judge*, 69 Mich. 610, 37 N.W. 701; *People v. Morris*, 80 Mich. 637, 8 L.R.A. 685, 45 N.W. 591; *People v. Smith*, 94 Mich. 644, 54 N.W. 487; *People v. Whitney*, 105 Mich. 622, 63 N.W. 765; *Dummer v. Nungesser*, 107 Mich. 481, 65 N.W. 564; *People v. Huntley*, 112 Mich. 569, 71 N.W. 178; *State v. Williams*, 77 Mo. 310; *Ex parte Swann*, 96 Mo. 44, 9 S.W. 10; *State v Moore*, 121 Mo. 514, 42 Am. St. Rep. 542, 26 S.W. 345; *State v. Van Wye*, 136 Mo. 227, 58 Am. St. Rep. 627, 37 S.W. 938; *State v. Gedicke*, 43 N.J.L. 86; *Garcie v. Territory*, 1 N.M. 415; *State v. Apple*, 121 N.C. 585, 28 S.E. 469; *State ex rel. Larabee v. Barnes*, 3 N.D. 319, 55 N.W. 883; *State v. Becker*, 3 S.D. 29, 51 N.W. 1018; *State v. Hodgson*, 66 Vt. 134, 28 Atl. 1089; *State v. De Lano*, 80 Wis. 259, 49 N.W. 808; *State v. Fackler*, 91 Wis. 418, 64 N.W. 1029; *Re McDonald*, 4 Wyo. 150, 33 Pac. 18.

10 Double Jeopardy

Chapter Objectives

In this chapter you will learn . . .

- Why O. J. Simpson was tried twice for the same act
- Whether prosecutors get a second chance to correct their mistakes
- Whether new trials may be ordered to remedy court errors
- What constitutes "same offense"
- Underlying sentiment in the double jeopardy debate

Introduction

To many game show fans across America, the term "double jeopardy" immediately brings to mind the portion of the popular game show *Jeopardy* when a correct response is worth twice as much. Television aside, the term is a legal one whose roots can be traced to the Constitution.

The Fifth Amendment's clause pertinent to double jeopardy states that: "nor shall any person be subject to the same offense to be twice put in jeopardy of life or limb . . ." A simple, modern translation of that clause might be that "you cannot be put on trial twice for the same act." As we have learned, however, definitions that are not carefully explained can often be incomplete, and thereby incorrect.

In this chapter, we learn about the meaning of double jeopardy and we analyze how it has been interpreted by the Supreme Court over the years.

O. J. Simpson and the "Trial of the Century"

A good way to learn about double jeopardy is to take a look at one of the most famous trials in recent memory: the O. J. Simpson trial. The defendant was found not guilty of murder but, 2 years later, had to pay over $33 million in damages for the same act. Let us take a look at how something like that is even legally possible.

Orenthal James Simpson, better known as "O. J." was already one of the most recognizable professional athletes of all time. In 1973, Simpson became the first National Football League player to rush for more than 2,000 yards in a single season, which among other feats, assured his election into the Pro Football Hall of Fame. He starred in various movies and television shows throughout the 1970s and 1980s, and he is well-remembered for his commercials for the Hertz car-rental company, during which he would sprint through the airport as if he was on the football field.

In 1994, Simpson would become even more famous, but not for something positive. In stark contrast to his charming all-American image, Simpson was accused of murdering his ex-wife Nicole Brown, and her friend Ronald Goldman, in Los Angeles on June 12 of that year. In an incredible sequence of events, Simpson was suspected of the murders, and on June 17, rather than turning himself into the authorities as had been expected, he led police on a multihour low-speed chase on Interstate 405 in California.

As America watched the drama unfold on national news channels, Simpson finally surrendered to the police but maintained his innocence. In what became known as the "Trial of the Century," the nation watched as Simpson's star-studded legal team, including F. Lee Bailey, Johnnie Cochran, and Robert Shapiro, defended their high-profile client. In the end, Simpson was acquitted of the murders, triggering intense debate about the outcome. Many based their opinion on the matter at heart, whether or not Simpson killed Brown and Goldman. Other reactions were based on ideological reasons: some supported the outcome as a vindication for all black defendants who were oppressed by a white judicial system, while others saw Simpson not as a disadvantaged black man but as a multimillionaire celebrity who bought his freedom through high-priced attorneys, a purchase unaffordable to the average American.

In any event, the jury had rendered its verdict and O. J. was a free man. But 2 years later, in 1997, another jury found Simpson liable for battery of Brown and Goldman and the wrongful death of Goldman, and ordered him to pay Brown's and Goldman's families $33,500,000 in damages.

The question, then, on the minds of many casual observers was, "O. J. was acquitted in 1995. Why was he on trial again? Isn't that double jeopardy?" The answer, in this particular situation, is "no." As we stated earlier, double jeopardy does not mean that a person cannot possibly stand trial for the same offense under any circumstances. There are some exceptions.

Football great O. J. Simpson, during his murder "trial of the century."

Civil Versus Criminal Trial

We have already learned that a crime is different from a civil offense. A crime is a wrong that is committed against society as a whole. When Nicole Brown and Ronald Goldman were murdered, the crime was not only against them but against the people as a whole. That is why Simpson's criminal trial was brought by the people of the state of California, through their representatives, the prosecuting attorneys.

The trial that took place 2 years later, however, was a civil trial. If Simpson were found liable, he would not be punished; rather, he would be held liable for a civil offense, and would have to pay damages. In fact, that is exactly what happened. The damages were awarded to the plaintiffs, who were the families of Brown and Goldman, as compensation for the deaths of their loved ones.

Accordingly, the criminal and civil trials surrounding the murders of Brown and Goldman teach us that double jeopardy does not apply when a person is tried *for a different offense*, even if it was based on the same act. In that case, Simpson was suspected of having murdered Brown and Goldman. In one court, he was tried for the crime of murder and in the other, for the civil offenses of wrongful death and battery.

Unrelated Trial

To be clear, Simpson's legal battles did not end with the trials surrounding Brown's and Goldman's murders. He has had other incidents with the law, most recently having been convicted of armed robbery. In 2008, a Nevada court convicted Simpson for taking sports memorabilia at gunpoint, which he said were his items that had been stolen from him. Simpson was sentenced to 33 years in jail. His attorneys are planning to appeal the conviction. Some believe that the sentencing was harsh and see it as retribution for the Brown and Goldman murders, for which he never served jail time.

Simpson's guilt remains a topic of debate, with many convinced one way or the other. In any event, the Nevada trial is not connected to the ones in California over a decade earlier.

Different Criminal Elements Within a Single Act

The reason that O. J. Simpson was eligible to stand trial for wrongful death and battery after having been acquitted of murder was that the latter was a civil trial whereas the former was a criminal one. What if both had been criminal trials, however? Could Simpson have been acquitted of murder and then tried for a lesser charge—again in criminal court?

The case of *Blockburger v. United States*, decided in 1932, sheds light on this important question. Harry Blockburger was convicted of violating various sections of the Harrison Anti-Narcotic Act. Specifically, on 1 day he sold 10 grains of morphine not in or from the original stamped package; on the following day he sold 8 grains of morphine, also not in or from the original stamped package; and regarding the second sale, it was made without a written order from the purchaser.

Blockburger was sentenced to 5 years in prison and a $2,000 fine for each offense. He appealed the decision, arguing that the offenses amounted to one, not three. Blockburger argued that because both transactions involved the same purchaser and were made on consecutive days, they really amounted to one offense. Moreover, Blockburger claimed that the lack of written request to purchase the morphine on the second day should not have been required for the same reason: because it was all part of one big sale.

Accordingly, Blockburger's lawyer contended, he could not be convicted more than once for the same offense. The Supreme Court agreed with Blockburger's definition of double jeopardy—that he could not be convicted twice of the same offense. The Court disagreed, however, with Blockburger's definition of "offense." The Court held that each of the sales was a separate act in itself, regardless of whether the sales were made to the same purchaser. Moreover, the Court concluded that one provision of the statute pertained to the original stamped package, while another concerned the purchaser's written request. The Court reasoned that, because it would be possible for one condition to have been met but not the other, that they were two separate offenses.

In other words, if Blockburger had in fact sold the morphine in the original stamped package, but absent a written request, then he would have violated the statute on one count. If, however, he had sold morphine not in or from the package, but pursuant to a written request, he would have violated another count. That he actually violated both counts, and three in all, does not mean that the counts can be combined into one offense. For those reasons, the Court denied Blockburger's appeal, and established that a person can be convicted for *separate elements of a crime* that were committed within a single act.

The Court challenged its own *Blockburger* holding in *Grady v. Corbin*, decided in 1990. In *Grady*, the defendant,

Corbin, had struck another car with his own and was convicted of two misdemeanors: driving while intoxicated, and driving on the wrong side of the road. The local judge had not been aware that there was a pending homicide investigation, and that a person had died in the automobile accident. New charges were brought against Corbin, this time, for reckless manslaughter and criminally negligent homicide.

Holding

The Court found that a new trial would constitute double jeopardy, because the prosecution would have to establish certain conduct for which Corbin had already been prosecuted.

Scalia's Dissent

In a vigorous dissent, Justice Scalia criticized the holding, insisting that it departed from the standard set forth in *Blockburger*. He maintained that the Constitution's double jeopardy clause bars prosecution for the same *offense*, not for the same *conduct*.

Conspiracy Not Protected by Double Jeopardy

The Supreme Court took a different position, one more along the lines of Scalia's *Grady* dissent, in *United States v. Felix*, decided in 1992. The defendant, Felix, was in the process of manufacturing illegal drugs in Oklahoma, when the federal Drug Enforcement Administration (DEA) shut down the facility. Felix then made arrangements to begin processing the drugs in Missouri. He was convicted in Missouri for manufacturing illegal drugs, but then was also indicted in Oklahoma for conspiracy to manufacture illegal drugs. The Court held that, for the purposes of double jeopardy, a particular crime and the conspiracy to commit that crime are two separate offenses. Accordingly, the Court did not bar Felix' prosecution in Oklahoma.

The *Felix* decision was unanimous, however, not because the Justices who ruled in Corbin's favor in *Grady* had a change of heart. Rather, they were swayed by the *Felix* majority's language, that an offense and its conspiracy are two distinct offenses.

State and Federal Levels

Blockburger dealt with the Harrison Anti-Narcotic Act, which was a federal law. There was no question that double jeopardy applied to federal laws, but did it extend to state laws as well? Let's take a look at the 1969 Supreme Court case *Benton v. Maryland* for the answer.

Benton was an interesting case that involved numerous issues, but the one most relevant to our discussion is whether double jeopardy protections apply to state laws as well as to federal ones. Benton had been charged with burglary and larceny. He was convicted of burglary but acquitted of larceny. Benton was convicted by jurors who had been required to affirm their belief in God in order to serve on the jury. That requirement, which had been part of Maryland's constitution, was declared unconstitutional

by the Maryland Court of Appeals. Accordingly, Benton was asked whether he wanted a new trial. As one might imagine, because he serving a jail sentence at the time, Benton said yes to a new trial.

Benton was convicted of both burglary and larceny at the new trial, and argued that because he had already been acquitted of larceny in the original trial, he should not have been retried on that issue, because it constituted double jeopardy.

The Supreme Court agreed with Benton's argument. The Court held that double jeopardy is not limited to federal laws but applies to state laws as well. Although there were other procedural points on which some of the Justices disagreed, it became well-established that double jeopardy would apply to state laws as well as federal laws from that point forward.

Prevention of Multiple Prosecutions

We learned from the *Blockburger* case that a defendant may be put on trial for a different element of a crime resulting from the same offense. That is different, however, from having been tried for a lesser crime and then being tried for a greater crime that includes the lesser offense within it.

Consider the following, to illustrate: the crime of robbery is a combination of the crimes of larceny and assault. Larceny, which is the taking of another person's property, by assault, which is force or threat of force, amounts to robbery. Therefore, forcing someone at gunpoint to hand over his or her wallet is committing robbery. The threat at gunpoint is the assault, and the taking of the wallet is larceny. Together, they are robbery.

On the other hand, the crimes of larceny and arson are entirely different. Larceny, as we just mentioned, is the taking of another person's property. Arson is burning another person's home or other structure. Suppose that James went to Chester's house when Chester was not home, and stole much of Chester's property. Then, in order to avoid any evidence of his having been there, James burned Chester's house to the ground. In that case, James would have committed two entirely different crimes, independent from one another, even though they were part of the same activity at Chester's house.

That then, is the difference between completely independent crimes as part of the same act, and a lesser crime that becomes part of a greater crime. In *Brown v. Ohio*, decided in 1977, the Supreme Court made that distinction as well. The defendant stole a car and was convicted of joyriding, but was then indicted for automobile theft. As the two Ohio laws were written, both crimes entailed the taking and driving away of another person's automobile without that person's consent. The difference with auto theft, which made it a greater crime than joyriding, was that there had to have been an intent to deprive the owner permanently of the car, whereas in a joyride, the criminal could have abandoned the car once the joyride was over.

Because the Court reasoned that auto theft contained the entire crime of joyriding within it, it reversed the lower court's holding that the defendant could stand trial for the greater crime, although he had already been convicted of the lesser one. The Court concluded that laws are made by legislatures, and prosecutors may decide to what extent to pursue them. But prosecutors, according to the Court, only get one chance to do so. If they opt to prosecute on a lesser charge, they cannot decide later to retry the defendant on a greater charge that contains the lesser one within it.

Multiple Crimes Within a Single Trial

In *Missouri v. Hunter*, decided in 1983, the appellant argued that his conviction of more than one crime based on a single act was a violation of the Constitution's double jeopardy clause. The Supreme Court saw it differently, however. The Court emphasized that regardless of the cumulative sentencing based on more than one crime having been committed, the appellant was subjected to a single trial.

In other words, a defendant may be convicted of numerous crimes as a result of a single act, and that does not constitute double jeopardy, if the convictions are imposed within a single trial. It is another trial, the Court reasoned, that creates double jeopardy, not conviction on another crime within the same trial.

Dissent: Multiple Punishments Are No Different Than Multiple Trials

The dissenting Justices concluded otherwise, citing *Brown* as the case that established what constitutes an offense. If a lesser crime that fits into a greater crime does not justify multiple prosecutions, they argued, why should it justify multiple punishments? Nonetheless, the majority saw it differently, and *Hunter* clarified double jeopardy as applying to multiple trials.

No Second Chance for Court's Mistake

We learned in *Brown* that prosecutors get one chance to get things right, and cannot appeal an acquittal without violating a defendant's Constitutional right not to be subjected to double jeopardy. The same "one chance" standard applies to courts as well.

In *Fong Foo v. United States*, decided in 1962, the Supreme Court recognized that a trial court judge had made an error in securing the defendants' acquittal, but nonetheless, denied the prosecution's appeal for a new trial. In *Fong Foo*, the defendant corporation and two of its employees were on trial for conspiracy and concealment of material facts. Although the government was not done calling witnesses, the judge dismissed the case based on the prosecuting attorney's improper conduct and the lack of credibility of the government's witnesses.

Subsequently, the prosecution moved for a new trial, contending that the trial judge did not have the authority to grant a dismissal based on that ground. It is important to emphasize that the Supreme Court, in upholding the defendants' acquittal and not subjecting them to a new trial, agreed that the trial judge's dismissal was improper.

Essentially, the *Fong Foo* holding is a message to the lower courts, to get things right the first time, because there will be no second chance.

The Defendant May Appeal, But the Prosecution May Not

The Supreme Court rulings set forth herein all point to a common procedural rule, which we should note here for emphasis: although the defendant may appeal a criminal conviction, the prosecution may not appeal a criminal acquittal. Let us return to the O. J. Simpson criminal trial, to illustrate.

Simpson was acquitted of murdering Nicole Brown and Ronald Goldman. He would have had the right to appeal had he been convicted, of course. He would have gotten that second chance. If the appeal was unsuccessful, perhaps there would have been a Constitutional issue for the United States Supreme Court to decide (although those instances are comparatively rare), and Simpson would have had yet another opportunity to overturn his conviction. The prosecution, however, does not get a second chance. If the defendant is found not guilty, then he or she is entitled to Constitutional protection against double jeopardy.

Although it is possible for the prosecution to reopen a case, for instance, based on new evidence, once a defendant has been acquitted, it is highly unlikely that he or she would have to face another trial for the same offense.

Judge's Reversal in the Middle of the Trial

One of the more interesting Supreme Court cases regarding double jeopardy, which is also quite a recent one, is *Smith v. Massachusetts*, decided in 2005. Because the case is fairly new and involves most of the Court's current Justices, it is worth examining closely, as it may help us to contemplate how the Court might rule on double jeopardy cases in the years to come.

Melvin Smith was brought to trial in Massachusetts on charges pertaining to the shooting of his girlfriend's cousin. He was charged with: (1) armed assault with intent to murder; (2) assault and battery by means of a dangerous weapon; and (3) unlawful possession of a firearm. Massachusetts law required that the third count, unlawful possession of a firearm must be proven insofar as the weapon must have a barrel less than 16 inches long. The victim had testified that Smith had shot him with a "revolver pistol," although there was no specific mention of the barrel's length.

At the conclusion of the prosecution's case, Smith made a motion that he could not possibly be guilty on the firearm count, because the prosecution had not proved that the gun barrel was less than 16 inches long. During that exchange, which was in a sidebar conference, the judge granted Smith's motion but did not inform the jury. Smith, the defendant, then proceeded with his case.

The prosecution then informed the court that a legal precedent had been established in Massachusetts, which automatically rendered the type of gun that Smith used, as per the victim's testimony, as having a barrel shorter than 16 inches. In other words, Smith had moved to dismiss the third count, stating that the prosecution had not proven that the barrel was shorter than 16 inches, and there would be no way of proving that, because the prosecution's case was over. The prosecution, however, then retorted that by definition, a "revolver pistol" in Massachusetts has a barrel of less than 16 inches. Of course, it would still be up to the jury to determine whether Smith had shot the victim—but the judge had already dismissed the count.

Upon the prosecution's explanation, the judge reversed herself and allowed the jury to consider the unlawful firearm possession count.

Smith was convicted on all three counts, and the unlawful firearm possession count, when considering that he was a repeat offender, lengthened his prison sentence by at least 10 years. Smith appealed the conviction, arguing that the judge's granting of his motion about the unlawful firearm count amounted to an acquittal, and that her reversal violated his double jeopardy rights.

Justice Scalia, the Court's most vocal strict constructionist, wrote for the majority. If you were to guess how Scalia ruled, would you think that he was in favor of Smith's conviction on the third count or that he would consider it a double jeopardy violation? If you guessed that Scalia would be a tough law-and-order Justice, who would never waste an opportunity to rule for a stiffer sentence, you will be surprised! Scalia, in fact, upheld the defendant's double jeopardy violation claim.

Majority

The majority, which, along with Scalia, included Justices Stevens, O'Connor, Souter, and Thomas, concluded that the Double Jeopardy Clause prohibits reexamination of an acquittal that the court had already decreed, even if the reexamination were to take place within the same trial. Scalia focused his determination on the fact that the prosecution had rested its case. As we learned in *Brown* and *Fong Foo*, mistakes made in one trial cannot be corrected in a new one if it would subject the defendant to double jeopardy. The *Smith* holding extends that "one chance to get it right" principle to actions *within* a trial. Once the prosecution had rested, they no longer reserved the right to bring additional information to the judge's attention, even if that information was highly relevant and extremely likely to have changed the judge's mind—had it been brought up *during* the prosecution's case.

The majority emphasized that double jeopardy must remain reliable, and cannot be ignored, even when necessary to make a legal correction after the fact.

Dissent

Four Justices dissented in an opinion written by Justice Ginsburg, with whom Chief Justice Rehnquist, and Justices Kennedy and Breyer joined. Ginsburg emphasized that the trial court judge had not disclosed her having granted the motion to the jury and reversed herself on that same day. As a matter of law, Ginsburg continued, courts historically have revisited their midtrial rulings. Moreover, the dissenting Justices underscored that the trial judge's reversal did not mean that the jury would have to engage in new fact finding, because Smith had never been acquitted or convicted of that count. The motion simply rejected the unlawful firearm possession count, and the reversal merely restored it. There was no additional fact finding to determine whether or not Smith was guilty of that count, prior to its restoration.

The *Smith* case is a great one on which to conclude this chapter for many reasons. First, it gives us a glimpse into the nuance that often determines Supreme Court decisions. Second, it is a relatively recent case, which allows us to ponder how the Court might rule no double jeopardy in the near future, if such a case rises to that level.

Finally, and, perhaps most importantly, it is a classic example of the complexities of the Court and its Justices. Contrary to the simple view that certain Justices will always vote certain ways, perceived conservatives Antonin Scalia and William Rehnquist were on opposite sides. Sharing Scalia's view was noted liberal David Souter; sharing Rehnquist's view was renowned liberal Ruth Bader Ginsburg. Justices Sandra Day O'Connor and Anthony Kennedy, considered the moderates of the group, were in the Scalia and Ginsburg camps, respectively.

Supreme Court Justices are not always predictable. In *Smith v. Massachusetts*, Chief Justice William Rehnquist (top) and Justice Antonin Scalia (bottom), traditional allies, ruled differently from each other.

Smith provides hope that the outcome of a Supreme Court case is not a foregone conclusion. After all, if it were, then why would we even need a Supreme Court?

Defining Double Jeopardy

Now that we have examined numerous Supreme Court cases, we can create a more accurate definition of double jeopardy: Subjecting a person to an offense for which he or she has already been acquitted. You might wonder, "isn't that the same as saying 'you cannot be placed on trial twice for the same act,'" which we discussed earlier in the chapter and concluded that it is an oversimplification?

Note that "act" and "offense" are two different things. An act may be blowing up a bridge. The "offenses" involved may range from murder (of people who are killed in the explosion) to pollution of the river below it from the falling debris. Also, as we have seen, different courts have defined offense in different ways. Some have limited the definition to a trial's outcome, others have narrowed it further, to motions granted or denied within a trial.

Some judges have considered a particular crime an offense, while others have classified each element, or even subelement, as a separate offense.

Similarly, some courts have defined an acquittal as a final verdict, usually decided by a jury, whereas others have considered a judge's midtrial ruling to suffice as an acquittal.

Our general definition of double jeopardy, then, covers all of those aspects, as long as one keeps in mind that "offense" and "acquittal" have been, and likely will continue to be, subject to a particular court's interpretation.

Conclusion: The Root of Double Jeopardy Sentiment

Aside from the legal reasoning conveyed by the courts, examples of which we have discussed in this chapter, there is strong public policy sentiment at the root of the double jeopardy debate. Quite often, it boils down to a sense of priorities.

When considering the following statements, which one comes to mind first, and most prominently?

1. Crime is a major problem in society and the best way to fight it is to make sure the courts impose tough sentences on criminals. Criminals should not be able to walk free because of a legal technicality.
2. Our system of justice is based on civil liberties, which are guaranteed by the Constitution. Overly ambitious prosecutors should not be permitted to use courtroom trials as witch hunts by which to perpetuate their crime fighting aspirations. Sometimes, in order to preserve the integrity of the Constitution, even heinous criminals have to walk away on a technicality.

Essentially, then, the argument can be reduced to this: which is the number one goal? Fighting crime or respecting the Constitution? Obviously, both are extremely important. When you ask different people to choose one over the other, though, you might get some very different answers.

"Respecting the Constitution is all well and good, but I want to see murderers behind bars!"

"Putting dangerous criminals behind bars is a priority, but never at the expense of compromising the Constitution."

More often than not, the argument boils down to those two strongly held but conflicting principles. They are worth considering as you examine future cases involving double jeopardy.

In Chapter 11, we will discuss one of the least-known Constitutional topics, but one that gives us great insight into how the Supreme Court interprets the Constitution: eminent domain.

Questions for Review

1. What is double jeopardy?
2. What are some ways in which "offense" has been interpreted by the courts?
3. What are some ways in which "acquittal" has been interpreted by the courts?
4. Describe the facts and outcome of the O. J. Simpson murder trial.
5. Why was O. J. Simpson tried again for the same deaths of his earlier murder trial?
6. What did *Blockburger v. United States* determine about double jeopardy?
7. How did *Grady v. Corbin* differ from *Blockburger* regarding double jeopardy?
8. What did the Court, in unison, decide in *Felix*?
9. What did *Fong Foo v. United States* establish regarding double jeopardy?
10. Why is *Smith v. Massachusetts* a particularly important case to review when learning about double jeopardy?

Constitutionally Speaking

How do you feel about double jeopardy? Where do you stand on the issue of crime fighting versus the Constitution? Assuming that a line has to be drawn at some point, where do you draw it? Would you limit double jeopardy to full trial decisions, or would you extend it to midtrial motions? Would you limit it to specific acts, specific crimes, or specific elements within a crime?

Constitutional Cases

Three additional cases presented here, *United States v. Martin Linen Supply Company*, *Sanabria v. United States*, and *Smalis v. Pennsylvania*, also provide some interesting legal reasoning that help us to understand double jeopardy even more thoroughly.

United States v. Martin Linen Supply Co., 430 U.S. 564 (1977)

After a deadlocked jury was discharged when unable to agree upon a verdict at the criminal contempt trial of respondent corporations, the District Judge granted respondents' timely motions for judgments of acquittal under Fed. Rule Crim. Proc. 29 (c), which provides that "a motion for judgment of acquittal may be made . . . within 7 days after the jury is discharged [and] the court may enter judgment of acquittal. . . ." The Government appealed pursuant to 18 U.S.C. 3731, which allows an appeal by the United States in a criminal case "to a court of appeals from a . . . judgment . . . of a district court dismissing an indictment . . ., except that no appeal shall lie where the double jeopardy clause of the United States Constitution prohibits further prosecution." The Court of Appeals dismissed the appeal. Held: The Double Jeopardy Clause bars appellate review and retrial following a judgment of acquittal entered under Rule 29 (c). Pp. 568–576.

(a) The "controlling constitutional principle" of the Double Jeopardy Clause focuses on prohibitions against multiple trials, *United States v. Wilson*, 420 U.S. 332, 346, and where an appeal by the Government presents no threat of successive prosecutions, the Clause is not offended. Pp. 568–570.

(b) The normal policy granting the Government the right to retry a defendant after a mistrial that does not determine the outcome of a trial does not apply here since valid judgments of acquittal were entered on the express authority of and in strict compliance with Rule 29 (c), and a successful governmental appeal reversing the judgments of acquittal would necessitate another trial or further proceedings to resolve factual issues going to the elements of the offense charged. Pp. 570–571.

(c) The judgments of acquittal here were "acquittals" in substance as well as form, since the District Court plainly granted the Rule 29 (c) motion on the express view that the Government had not proved facts constituting criminal contempt. Pp. 571–572.

(d) Rule 29 recognizes no legal distinction between judge and jury with respect to the invocation of the protections of the Double Jeopardy Clause. P. 573.

(e) Rule 29 contemplated no artificial distinctions between situations where the judge enters a judgment of acquittal prior to submission of the case to the jury under Rule 29 (a), or after submission but prior to the jury's return of a verdict under Rule 29 (b), and the jury is thereafter discharged, and the situation involved here, where the judge chose to await the outcome of the jury's deliberations and, upon its failure to reach a verdict, acted on a timely motion for acquittal after the jury's discharge. *United States v. Sanford*, 429 U.S. 14, distinguished. Pp. 573–575.

534 F.2d 585, affirmed.

BRENNAN, J., delivered the opinion of the Court, in which STEWART, WHITE, MARSHALL, BLACKMUN, and POWELL, J. J., joined. STEVENS, J., filed an opinion concurring in the judgment, *post*, p. 576. BURGER, C. J., filed a dissenting opinion, *post*, p. 581. REHNQUIST, J., took no part in the consideration or decision of the case.

Frank H. Easterbrook argued the cause for the United States *pro hac vice*. With him on the brief was Solicitor General Bork.

J. Burleson Smith argued the cause and filed a brief for respondents.

MR. JUSTICE BRENNAN delivered the opinion of the Court.

A "hopelessly deadlocked" jury was discharged when unable to agree upon a verdict at the criminal contempt trial of respondent corporations in the District Court for the Western District of Texas.[1] Federal Rule Crim. Proc. 29 (c) provides that in such case "a motion for judgment of acquittal may be made . . . within 7 days after the jury is discharged [and] the court may enter judgment of acquittal. . . ."[2] Timely motions for judgments of acquittal under the Rule made by respondents six days after the discharge of the jury resulted two months later in the entry by the District Court of judgments of acquittal.[3] The sole question presented for our decision is whether these judgments of acquittal under Rule 29 (c) are appealable by the United States pursuant to 18 U.S.C. 3731. Section 3731 provides that an appeal by the United States in a criminal case "shall lie to a court of appeals from a . . . judgment . . . of a district court dismissing an indictment . . ., except that no appeal shall lie where the double jeopardy clause of the United States Constitution prohibits further prosecution."[4] The Court of Appeals for the Fifth Circuit held that no appeal lay under 3731 from the judgments of acquittal entered by the District Court under Rule 29 (c). 534 F.2d 585 (1976). The Court of Appeals reasoned that, since reversal of the acquittals would enable the United States to try respondents a second time, the bar of the Double Jeopardy Clause "leads inescapably to the conclusion that no appeal lies from the directed verdict ordered by the court below." *Id.*, at 589.[5] We granted *certiorari*. 429 U.S. 917 (1976). We affirm.

I

It has long been established that the United States cannot appeal in a criminal case without express congressional authorization. *United States v. Wilson*, 420 U.S. 332, 336 (1975); *United States v. Sanges*, 144 U.S. 310 (1892). Only two Terms ago Wilson traced the uneven course of such statutory authority until 1970 when Congress amended the Criminal Appeals Act, 420 U.S., at 336–339, and that history need not be repeated here. See also *United States v. Sisson*, 399 U.S. 267, 307–308 (1970). It suffices for present purposes that this Court in Wilson found that in enacting 3731 as Title III of the Omnibus Crime Control Act of 1970, 84 Stat. 1890, "Congress intended to remove all statutory barriers to Government appeals and to allow appeals whenever the Constitution would permit." 420 U.S., at 337. Therefore, unless barred by the Double Jeopardy Clause of the Constitution, appeals by the Government from the judgments of acquittal entered by the District Court under Rule 29 (c) are authorized by 3731.

Consideration of the reach of the constitutional limitations inhibiting governmental appeals was largely unnecessary during the prior regime of statutory restrictions. But see *Fong Foo v. United States*, 369 U.S. 141 (1962); *Kepner v. United States*, 195 U.S. 100 (1904). However, now that Congress has removed the statutory limitations to appeal and the relevant inquiry turns on the reach of the Double Jeopardy Clause itself, it has become "necessary to take a closer look at the policies underlying the Clause in order to determine more precisely the boundaries of the Government's appeal rights in criminal cases." *United States v. Wilson, supra*, at 339. In the few cases decided since 1970 that have taken this "closer look," many of the policies shaping restrictions on governmental appeal rights have been brought into sharper focus.

"The development of the Double Jeopardy Clause from its common-law origins . . . suggests that it was directed at the threat of multiple prosecutions, not at Government appeals, at least where those appeals would not require a new trial." *Id.*, at 342. Thus Wilson held that the "controlling constitutional principle" focuses on prohibitions against multiple trials. *Id.*, at 346. At the heart of this policy is the concern that permitting the sovereign freely to subject the citizen to a second trial for the same offense would arm Government with a potent instrument of oppression. The Clause, therefore, guarantees that the State shall not be permitted to make repeated attempts to convict the accused, "thereby subjecting him to embarrassment, expense and ordeal and compelling him to live in a continuing state of anxiety and insecurity, as well as enhancing the possibility that even though innocent he may be found guilty." *Green v. United States*, 355 U.S. 184, 187–188 (1957); see also *Downum v. United States*, 372 U.S. 734, 736 (1963). "[S]ociety's awareness of the heavy personal strain which a criminal trial represents for the individual defendant is manifested in the willingness to limit the Government to a single criminal proceeding to vindicate its very vital interest in enforcement of criminal laws." *United States v. Jorn*, 400 U.S. 470, 479 (1971) (Harlan, J.).[6]

In animating this prohibition against multiple prosecutions, the Double Jeopardy Clause rests upon two threshold conditions. The protections afforded by the Clause are implicated only when the accused has actually been placed in jeopardy. *Serfass v. United States*, 420 U.S. 377 (1975). This state of jeopardy attaches when a jury is empaneled and sworn, or, in a bench trial, when the judge begins to receive evidence. *Illinois v. Somerville*, 410 U.S. 458, 471 (1973) (WHITE, J., dissenting); *Downum v. United States, supra*. Further, where a Government appeal presents no threat of successive prosecutions, the Double Jeopardy Clause is not offended. Thus a postverdict dismissal of an indictment after a jury rendered a guilty verdict has been held to be appealable by the United States because restoration of the guilty verdict, and not a new trial, would necessarily result if the Government prevailed. *United States v. Wilson, supra*.[7]

II

None of the considerations favoring appealability is present in the case of a Government appeal from the District Court's judgments of acquittal under Rule 29 (c) where the jury failed to agree on a verdict. The normal policy granting the Government the right to retry a defendant after a mistrial that does not determine the outcome of a trial, *United States v. Perez*, 9 Wheat. 579, 580 (1824), is not applicable since valid judgments of acquittal were entered on the express authority of, and strictly in compliance with, Rule 29 (c). Those judgments, according to the very wording of the Rule, act to terminate a trial in which jeopardy has long since attached.[8] And a successful governmental appeal reversing the judgments of acquittal would necessitate another trial, or, at least, "further proceedings of some sort, devoted to the resolution of factual issues going to the elements of the offense charged. . . ."

(Continues)

(*Continued*)

United States v. Jenkins, 420 U.S. 358, 370 (1975). Therefore, the present case is not one where the double jeopardy bar to appealability is automatically averted. Rather, we must inquire further into the constitutional significance of a Rule 29 (c) acquittal.

Perhaps the most fundamental rule in the history of double jeopardy jurisprudence has been that "[a] verdict of acquittal . . . could not be reviewed, on error or otherwise, without putting [a defendant] twice in jeopardy, and thereby violating the Constitution." *United States v. Ball*, 163 U.S. 662, 671 (1896). In *Fong Foo v. United States, supra*, for example, a District Court directed jury verdicts of acquittal and subsequently entered formal judgments of acquittal. The Court of Appeals entertained the appeal of the United States and reversed the District Court's ruling on the ground that the trial judge was without power to direct acquittals under the circumstances disclosed by the record. We reversed, holding that, although the Court of Appeals may correctly have believed "that the acquittal was based upon an egregiously erroneous foundation, . . . [n]evertheless, '[t]he verdict of acquittal was final, and could not be reviewed . . . without putting [the defendants] twice in jeopardy, and thereby violating the Constitution.'" 369 U.S., at 143. See also *Kepner v. United States, supra*; *United States v. Sisson*, 399 U.S., at 289–290; *Serfass v. United States, supra*, at 392. In applying this teaching of *Ball*, *Fong Foo*, and like cases, we have emphasized that what constitutes an "acquittal" is not to be controlled by the form of the judge's action. *United States v. Sisson, supra*, at 270; cf. *United States v. Wilson*, 420 U.S., at 336.[9] Rather, we must determine whether the ruling of the judge, whatever its label, actually represents a resolution, correct or not, of some or all of the factual elements of the offense charged.

There can be no question that the judgments of acquittal entered here by the District Court were "acquittals" in substance as well as form. The District Court plainly granted the Rule 29 (c) motion on the view that the Government had not proved facts constituting criminal contempt.[10] The court made only too clear its belief that the prosecution was "'the weakest [contempt case that] I've ever seen.'" 534 F.2d, at 587. In entering the judgments of acquittal, the court also recorded its view that "'the Government has failed to prove the material allegations beyond a reasonable doubt'" and that "'defendant should be found "not guilty."'"

Thus, it is plain that the District Court in this case evaluated the Government's evidence and determined that it was legally insufficient to sustain a conviction. The Court of Appeals concluded that this determination of insufficiency of the evidence triggered double jeopardy protection.[11] The Government, however, disputes the constitutional significance of the District Court's action. It submits that only a verdict of acquittal formally returned by the jury should absolutely bar further proceedings and that "[o]nce the district court declared a mistrial and dismissed the jury, any double jeopardy bar to a second trial dissolved." Brief for United States 21. We cannot agree.

Of course, as the Government argues, in a jury trial the primary finders of fact are the jurors. Their overriding responsibility is to stand between the accused and a potentially arbitrary or abusive Government that is in command of the criminal sanction. For this reason, a trial judge is prohibited from entering a judgment of conviction or directing the jury to come forward with such a verdict, see *Sparf & Hansen v. United States*, 156 U.S. 51, 105 (1895); *Carpenters v. United States*, 330 U.S. 395, 408 (1947), regardless of how overwhelmingly the evidence may point in that direction. The trial judge is thereby barred from attempting to override or interfere with the jurors' independent judgment in a manner contrary to the interests of the accused.

Such a limitation on the role of a trial judge, however, has never inhibited his ruling in favor of a criminal defendant. *Fong Foo v. United States*, 369 U.S. 141 (1962), establishing the binding nature of a directed verdict, is dispositive on that point. Since Rule 29 merely replaces the directed-verdict mechanism employed in *Fong Foo*, and accords the federal trial judge greater flexibility in timing his judgment of acquittal, no persuasive basis exists for construing the Rule as weakening the trial court's binding authority for purposes of double jeopardy.[12] Rather, the Notes of the Advisory Committee have confirmed that Rule 29 intends no substantive alteration in the role of judge or jury, but creates a purely formal modification of the directed-verdict device in order "to make the nomenclature accord with the realities." 18 U.S.C. App., p. 4504. Accordingly, *United States v. Sisson, supra*, at 290, held that Rule 29 recognizes no "legal distinction" between judge and jury with respect to the invocation of the protections of the Double Jeopardy Clause.

The Government, however, would read *Fong Foo* and, by implication, Rule 29 differently. It argues that the judge's directed verdict in *Fong Foo* was binding for double jeopardy purposes because the formal verdict of acquittal, though on direction, was rendered not by the judge, but by the jury, which then was discharged. This in effect turns the constitutional significance of a Rule 29 judgment of acquittal on a matter of timing. Thus, if the judge orders entry of judgment of acquittal on his own or on defendant's motion prior to submission of the case to the jury, as he may under Rule 29 (a), or after submission but prior to the jury's return of a verdict, as authorized by Rule 29 (b)—and the jury thereafter is discharged—the Government's argument necessarily concedes that the Double Jeopardy Clause would preclude both appeal and retrial. If, however, the judge chooses to await the outcome of the jury's deliberations and, upon its failure to reach a verdict, acts on a timely motion for acquittal filed under Rule 29 (c) within 7 days of its discharge, the Government submits that the Double Jeopardy Clause should not bar an appeal.

We are not persuaded. Rule 29 contemplated no such artificial distinctions. Rather the differentiations in timing were intentionally incorporated into the Rule to afford a trial judge the maximum opportunity to consider with care a pending acquittal motion. Insofar as the Government desires an appeal to correct error, irrational behavior, or prejudice on the part of the trial judge, its interest is not dependent on the point of trial when the judge enters his Rule 29 judgment, and suffers no special prejudice by a judge's acquittal after the jury disagrees and is discharged.[13] And to the extent that the judge's authority under Rule 29 is designed to provide additional protection to a defendant by filtering out deficient prosecutions, the defendant's interest in such protection is essentially identical both before the jury is allowed to come to a verdict and after the jury is unable to reach a verdict: In either case, the defendant has neither been condemned nor exculpated by a panel of his peers and, in the absence of intervention by the trial judge, his vindication must await further action by a jury.

We thus conclude that judgments under Rule 29 are to be treated uniformly and, accordingly, the Double Jeopardy Clause bars appeal from an acquittal entered under Rule 29 (c) after a jury mistrial no less than under Rule 29 (a) or (b). *United States v. Sanford*, 429 U.S. 14 (1976), does not dictate a contrary result. In Sanford, a jury trial ended in the declaration of a mistrial. A judgment of acquittal was never entered. Some four months later, with the second trial well into the preparatory stage, the trial court dismissed the prosecution's indictment. Because the dismissal "occurred several months after the first trial had ended in a mistrial, but before the retrial of respondents had begun," *id.*, at 16, the Court characterized the judge's dismissal as "a pretrial order," *ibid.*, and concluded that its appealability was governed by *Serfass v. United States*, 420 U.S. 377 (1975). The Court's linking of *Sanford* with *Serfass* highlights the distinctiveness of an acquittal under Rule 29 (c). In *Serfass* the Court carefully distinguished between appeal of a pretrial order and appeal of "'a legal determination on the basis of facts adduced at the trial relating to the general issue of the case.'" 420 U.S., at 393, quoting *United States v. Sisson*, 399 U.S., at 290 n. 19. A Rule 29 acquittal, however, falls squarely within the latter category: By the very language of the Rule, such a judgment of acquittal plainly concludes a pending prosecution in which jeopardy has attached, following the introduction at trial of evidence on the general issue. In that circumstance we hold that "although retrial is sometimes permissible after a mistrial is declared but no verdict or judgment has been entered, the verdict of acquittal foreclosed retrial and thus barred appellate review." *United States v. Wilson*, 420 U.S., at 348.

Affirmed.

MR. JUSTICE REHNQUIST took no part in the consideration or decision of this case.

Notes

1. The criminal contempt proceeding was filed in 1971 and charged respondents, two commonly owned linen supply companies, and their president, William B. Troy, with violation of a consent decree entered in 1969 as the final judgment in an antitrust suit. The petitions were originally dismissed by the District Court but the dismissal was reversed by the Court of Appeals, 485 F.2d 1143 (1973). The Government filed a supplemental criminal contempt petition on which trial was had in February 1975. On February 21, 1975, the jury was discharged after returning the not-guilty verdict as to Troy and announcing that it was "hopelessly deadlocked" as to respondent corporations. Six days later, on February 27, 1975, respondents filed their motions for judgments of acquittal under Rule 29 (c). On April 24, 1975, the District Court granted the motions and entered judgments of acquittal.

2. Rule 29 provides: "Motion for Judgment of Acquittal "(a) MOTION BEFORE SUBMISSION TO JURY. Motions for directed verdict are abolished and motions for judgment of acquittal shall be used in their place. The court on motion of a defendant or of its own motion shall order the entry of judgment of acquittal of one or more offenses charged in the indictment or information after the evidence on either side is closed if the evidence is insufficient to sustain a conviction of such offense or offenses. If a defendant's motion for judgment of acquittal at the close of the evidence offered by the government is not granted, the defendant may offer evidence without having reserved the right.

(Continues)

"(b) RESERVATION OF DECISION ON MOTION. If a motion for judgment of acquittal is made at the close of all the evidence, the court may reserve decision on the motion, submit the case to the jury and decide the motion either before the jury returns a verdict or after it returns a verdict of guilty or is discharged without having returned a verdict. "(c) MOTION AFTER DISCHARGE OF JURY. If the jury returns a verdict of guilty or is discharged without having returned a verdict, a motion for judgment of acquittal may be made or renewed within 7 days after the jury is discharged or within such further time as the court may fix during the 7-day period. If a verdict of guilty is returned the court may on such motion set aside the verdict and enter judgment of acquittal. If no verdict is returned the court may enter judgment of acquittal. It shall not be necessary to the making of such a motion that a similar motion has been made prior to the submission of the case to the jury."

3. After dismissal of the jury, the District Judge advised counsel for all parties that he would be inclined "to enter a judgment of acquittal as to [respondents] if an appropriate motion was made." App. 31. He said that he had "almost instructed a verdict for all Defendants" because the Government's case "is without a doubt the weakest [contempt case that] I've ever seen." *Id.*, at 30.

4. In pertinent part, 3731 provides: "3731. Appeal by United States "In a criminal case an appeal by the United States shall lie to a court of appeals from a decision, judgment, or order of a district court dismissing an indictment or information as to any one or more counts, except that no appeal shall lie where the double jeopardy clause of the United States Constitution prohibits further prosecution." Although this provision authorizes appeal from a district court "dismiss[al]" rather than "acquittal," it is now established that the form of the ruling is not dispositive of appealability in a statutory sense, see *infra*, at 568.

5. In characterizing the trial court's action as a "directed verdict," the Court of Appeals erred in terminology, for Rule 29 (a) expressly substitutes "judgment of acquittal" for "directed verdict." As shall be seen, however, see *infra*, at 573, the purely formal nature of the change in federal criminal procedure marked by Rule 29 speaks strongly in favor of treating Rule 29 judgments of acquittal the same as their predecessor directed verdicts for purposes of invoking double jeopardy. See *Fong Foo v. United States*, 369 U.S. 141 (1962).

6. The Double Jeopardy Clause also accords nonappealable finality to a verdict of guilty entered by judge or jury, disabling the Government from seeking to punish a defendant more than once for the same offense. See *Ex parte Lange*, 18 Wall. 163 (1874).

7. The absence of a threatened second trial mitigates the possibility of governmental jury shopping and substantially reduces the expense and anxiety to be borne by the defendant. In addition, the Government's interest in preserving a conviction fairly attained obviously is far greater than its interest in investing additional time and resources in reprosecuting a defendant following a jury's failure to reach a verdict and a trial court's judgment of acquittal.

8. A motion under Rule 29 for a judgment of acquittal can be entertained, at the earliest, "after the evidence on either side is closed. . . ." This stage of the trial obviously arises well after jeopardy has attached.

9. The Court must inquire whether "the ruling in [defendant's] favor was actually an 'acquittal' even though the District Court characterized it otherwise." *United States v. Wilson*, 420 U.S. 332, 336 (1975).

10. Rule 29 (a) in terms authorizes a judgment of acquittal "if the evidence is insufficient to sustain a conviction of such offense or offenses."

11. The only other Court of Appeals specifically to address this issue reached the same conclusion. *United States v. Suarez*, 505 F.2d 166 (CA2 1974) (*per curiam*).

12. In the situation where a criminal prosecution is tried to a judge alone, there is no question that the Double Jeopardy Clause accords his determination in favor of a defendant full constitutional effect. See *United States v. Jenkins*, 420 U.S. 358, 365–367 (1975). Even though, as proposed here by the Government with respect to a Rule 29 judgment of acquittal, it can be argued that the prosecution has a legitimate interest in correcting the possibility of error by a judge sitting without a jury, the Court in Jenkins refused to accept theories of double jeopardy that would permit reconsideration of a trial judge's ruling discharging a criminal defendant.

13. The Advisory Committee that framed Rule 29 explicitly noted that subdivision (c), permitting the entry of a judgment of acquittal after the jury's discharge, works no undue prejudice on the Government because the prosecution has no constitutionally sanctioned interest in receiving a verdict from the jury: "The constitutional requirement of a jury trial in criminal cases is primarily a right accorded to the defendant." 18 U.S.C. App., p. 4505. Cf. *Singer v. United States*, 380 U.S. 24 (1965). Any Government right to demand a jury verdict is limited to that afforded by Fed. Rule Crim. Proc. 23 (a) (jury trial waivable with the consent of the Government) and, of course, can be qualified by authority granted the trial judge under Rule 29.

MR. JUSTICE STEVENS, concurring in the judgment.

There is no statutory authority for a Government appeal from a judgment of acquittal in a criminal case. The plain language of 18 U.S.C. 3731, together with its unambiguous legislative history, makes it perfectly clear that Congress did not authorize—and did not intend to authorize—appeals from acquittals.[14]

Prior to its most recent amendment in 1970, the Criminal Appeals Act had been a source of great confusion, "a most unruly child that has not improved with age," *United States v. Sisson*, 399 U.S. 267, 307. The Act had been construed to incorporate obscure distinctions between various types of dismissals, some of which were appealable directly to this Court, some to the court of appeals, and some that could not be appealed to either court.[15] However, the one thing that had always been clear was that "no appeal [could] be taken by the Government from an acquittal no matter how erroneous the legal theory underlying the decision," *id.*, at 299.

The 1970 amendment changed the law by eliminating all distinctions between different kinds of dismissals, but neither the present statute nor any of its predecessors has ever authorized an appeal from an acquittal. The statute, in relevant part, now reads:

"In a criminal case an appeal by the United States shall lie to a court of appeals from a decision, judgment, or order of a district court dismissing an indictment or information as to any one or more counts, except that no appeal shall lie where the double jeopardy clause of the United States Constitution prohibits further prosecution." 18 U.S.C. 3731 (emphasis added).

There is nothing in this statutory language to suggest that a judgment of acquittal, as opposed to a dismissal, is appealable.

The legislative history demonstrates that Congress intended to eliminate nonconstitutional barriers to appeals from dismissals, but did not intend to allow appeals from acquittals. As this Court has recognized, the Senate Report is the key to the legislative history.[16] The Report opens by describing the purpose of the bill as being "to resolve serious problems which frequently have arisen with respect to the right of the United States to appeal rulings which terminate prosecutions other than by judgments of acquittal . . ." S. Rep. No. 91-1296, p. 2 (1970) (emphasis added). Apart from the problem of direct Supreme Court review, the Report states that the "major problem that has arisen under the present statute concerns the total lack of appealability of certain kinds of dismissals and suppressions." *Id.*, at 4 (emphasis added). The Report then discusses at length the then-existing limitations on appeals from dismissals.[17] The Committee believed that the Constitution allowed the Government to appeal any dismissal, *id.*, at 7–12, and stated that the bill was "intended to be liberally construed so as to effectuate its purpose of permitting the Government to appeal from dismissals of criminal prosecutions by district courts in all cases where the Constitution permits . . ." *Id.*, at 18 (emphasis added). On the other hand, the Committee believed that the Constitution barred any appeal from an acquittal or from a dismissal amounting to an acquittal; "[a] true acquittal is based upon the insufficiency of the evidence to prove an element of the offense." *Id.*, at 11.

The same understanding was demonstrated by the bill's sponsor when he presented the Senate Report on the floor. He summarized the bill as providing that "the Government has the right to appeal any ruling by a district court in a criminal case which dismisses a prosecution in favor of a defendant except where the ruling is an acquittal"; he also presented a letter from the Solicitor General explaining that the bill would allow "an appeal from any dismissal except one amounting to a 'judgment of acquittal,' i.e., a factual judgment that the defendant is not guilty of the crime charged and is thereby entitled to protection against double jeopardy." 116 Cong. Rec. 35659 (1970) (remarks of Sen. Hruska).

As the Court explained in Wilson, the Conference Committee made a minor change in the wording of the bill. See *Wilson*, 420 U.S., at 338. That change narrowed the bill in two respects. The Senate bill had allowed appeals from dismissals and also from any order "terminating a prosecution in favor of a defendant," and had expressly barred appeals from a judgment of acquittal.[18] In short, as the Conference Committee stated, the Senate bill authorized an appeal from "any decision or order terminating a prosecution except an acquittal," H.R. Conf. Rep. No. 91-1768, p. 21 (1970). The Conference Committee's change narrowed the bill by deleting the reference to orders "terminating a prosecution in favor of a defendant," leaving only dismissals appealable. (This deletion rendered superfluous the exception for acquittals, which was also deleted.) The Committee's change also narrowed the bill by barring any appeal, even from a dismissal, when further prosecution would violate double jeopardy.

(Continues)

(Continued)

An attempt to authorize the Government to appeal from acquittals would have represented a radical change in the law. The sponsor of the bill apparently did not understand the legislation to have such far-reaching effects; he described it as "noncontroversial legislation which would do away with unnecessary and perplexing jurisdictional problems in appeals by the Government in criminal cases . . ." 116 Cong. Rec. 35659 (1970) (remarks of Sen. Hruska). Similarly, the Conference Report describes the Senate bill as merely eliminating "[t]echnical distinctions . . . on appeals by the United States," H. R. Conf. Rep. No. 91-1768, *supra*, at 21.[19]

Interpreting legislative history is sometimes a perplexing and uncertain task. In this instance, however, the legislative history is absolutely clear: Congress was interested solely in expanding the Government's right to appeal from the dismissal of an indictment; it had no desire to allow appeals from acquittals and believed such appeals would be unconstitutional.

Since I am satisfied that Congress has not authorized the Government to appeal from a judgment of acquittal, the only question presented is whether such a judgment was entered in this case. The answer to that question, as the Court demonstrates, is perfectly clear. By virtue of Fed. Rule Crim. Proc. 29 (c), the mistrial did not terminate the judge's power to make a decision on the merits. His ruling, in substance as well as form, was therefore an acquittal.[20] For this reason, I concur in the Court's judgment.

Notes

14. The contrary dictum in *United States v. Wilson*, 420 U.S. 332, 336–339; *United States v. Jenkins*, 420 U.S. 358, 363–364; *Serfass v. United States*, 420 U.S. 377, 383–387, is not controlling for these reasons: First, the statutory issue was not in dispute in any of those cases. Two of the defendants expressly conceded the applicability of the statute in their cases, Brief for Respondent in *United States v. Wilson*, O.T. 1974, No. 73-1395, p. 2; Brief for Respondent in *United States v. Jenkins*, O. T. 1974, No. 73-1513, p. 10. The third defendant simply failed to address the statutory issue, see Brief for Petitioner in *Serfass v. United States*, O.T. 1974, No. 73-1424, probably because his case involved a pretrial dismissal of the indictment. Hence, the Court was unaided by an adversary presentation of the issue. Moreover, re-examination of the language used in the decisions would not undermine their holdings. The two cases in which the Court upheld the Government appeal clearly did not involve acquittals on the merits. (*Serfass* was a pretrial dismissal; *Wilson* was a dismissal on speedy trial grounds.) The third case, Jenkins, arguably involved an acquittal, but the Court held on constitutional grounds that the appeal was barred. Second, as I indicate in the text, *infra*, at 581, it is perfectly clear that the dictum is incorrect. In view of our special responsibility for supervising the proper functioning of the federal criminal justice system, we should not hesitate to correct a plain mistake involving a technical problem of procedure when there has been no prejudicial reliance on that mistake.

15. The difficulty of the problems presented by the statute is illustrated by the sharply divided conclusions reached in the various opinions in cases such as *United States v. Sisson*, 399 U.S. 267; *United States v. Ponto*, 454 F.2d 657 (CA7 1971) (*en banc*); *United States v. Apex Distributing Co.*, 270 F.2d 747 (CA9 1959) (*en banc*).

16. The significance of this Senate Report in understanding the Act was well expressed in *Serfass v. United States*, *supra*, at 387 n. 10: "The relevance and significance of the 'well considered and carefully prepared' report of the Senate Judiciary Committee, see *Schwegmann Bros. v. Calvert Distillers Corp.*, 341 U.S. 384, 395 (1951) (Jackson, J., concurring), is not affected by the fact that the amendments proposed by the Committee and adopted without change by the Senate were modified by the House–Senate Conference Committee. See H.R. Conf. Rep. No. 91-1768, p. 21 (1970). The latter report contains no explanation of the changes made, and the changes themselves are consistent with the intent expressed in the Senate Report. See *United States v. Wilson*, *ante*, at 337–339."

17. Subsection A is entitled "The Nature of the District Court Decision as a Limitation on Appeals from Dismissals," and begins with the statement that "[t]he now-archaic terminology employed in the original statute . . . unnecessarily precludes the Government from appealing many dismissals of prosecutions." S. Rep. No. 91-1296, at 5. The Report then states that the current Act "does not provide for an appeal by the United States to any court in a large variety of cases where the dismissal is based on grounds having nothing to do with any defect in the indictment, or the construction or invalidity of the underlying statute." *Ibid.* The Report gives as examples dismissals for failure of the prosecution to comply with discovery or for lack of timely prosecution. The Report then refers to the use of old common-law terms like "'judgment sustaining a motion in bar,'" giving rise to problems like that which the Court confronted in *United States v. Sisson*, *supra*. S. Rep. No. 91-1296, p. 6. Subpart B of the Senate Report deals with "The Attachment of Jeopardy as a Limitation on Appeals from Dismissals."

This section was concerned with appeal of "a decision sustaining a motion in bar after jeopardy has attached," *ibid.* Congress was concerned that a defendant could reserve issues of law until the trial and then preclude any possible review. *Id.,* at 7. An example was a case in which the trial judge ruled the Selective Service Act unconstitutional during the trial. *Id.,* at 11.

18. The bill provided that an appeal would lie "from a decision, judgment or order of a district court dismissing an indictment or information or terminating a prosecution in favor of a defendant as to one or more counts, except that no appeal shall lie from a judgment of acquittal." S. 3132.

19. When the Conference bill was reported back to both Houses, its provision on appeals was described in cautious terms hardly appropriate to a proposal to go to the constitutional limits: in the Senate, as "authoriz[ing] appeals in certain classes of criminal cases," 116 Cong. Rec. 42147 (1970) (remarks of Sen. McClellan) (emphasis added); in the House, as an amendment "to broaden and clarify the right of the Government to appeal dismissals of criminal cases," *id.,* at 42197 (remarks of Rep. Celler).

20. As we pointed out in *United States v. Sanford,* 429 U.S. 14, the mistrial in that case was entirely different because the proceedings in the trial court terminated without any decision on the merits. "The trial of respondents on the indictment terminated, not in their favor, but in a mistrial declared, *sua sponte,* by the District Court. Where the trial is terminated in this manner, the classical test for determining whether the defendants may be retried without violating the Double Jeopardy Clause is stated in Mr. Justice Story's opinion for this Court in *United States v. Perez,* 9 Wheat. 579, 580 (1824): "'We are of opinion, that the facts constitute no legal bar to a future trial. The prisoner has not been convicted or acquitted, and may again be put upon his defense . . .'" *Id.,* at 15.

MR. CHIEF JUSTICE BURGER, dissenting.

The order of acquittal in favor of respondents was entered by the District Judge after a mistrial had been declared due to a jury deadlock. Once the jury was dismissed, respondents ceased to be in jeopardy in that proceeding; they could no longer be convicted except after undergoing a new trial. For a century and a half it has been accepted that a defendant may properly be reprosecuted after the declaration of such a mistrial, *United States v. Perez,* 9 Wheat. 579 (1824). Therefore the District Judge's ruling here was made "prior to a trial that the Government had a right to prosecute and that the defendant was required to defend." *United States v. Sanford,* 429 U.S. 14, 16(1976).[21]

The present case cannot be distinguished from Sanford in constitutionally material respects. It is true that the District Judge here phrased his order as an acquittal rather than as a dismissal, and that the order was entered pursuant to a timely Rule 29 (c) motion. However, such mechanical niceties are not dispositive of whether retrial would expose defendants to double jeopardy; our Fifth Amendment inquiry should focus on the substance rather than the form of the proceedings below. In ruling on a motion for acquittal the District Judge must pass on the sufficiency, not on the weight, of the Government's case, *United States v. Isaacs,* 516 F.2d 409, 410 (CA5), *cert. denied,* 423 U.S. 936 (1975); *United States v. Wooten,* 503 F.2d 65, 66 (CA4 1974). "[T]he applicable standard is whether [the District Judge as a trier of fact] could, not whether he would, find the accused guilty on the Government's evidence." *United States v. Consolidated Laundries Corp.,* 291 F.2d 563, 574 (CA2 1961) (emphasis in original).

The District Judge's ruling is thus plainly one of law, not of fact; it could only exonerate, not convict, the defendant. No legitimate interest of the defendant requires that this ruling be insulated from appellate review. On the other hand, barring the appeal jeopardizes the Government's substantial interest in presenting a legally sufficient case to the jury. The Court's holding today is thus wholly inconsistent with the intent of Rule 29 (c) as described by the drafters in the Advisory Committee Notes. In explaining the 1966 amendments to the Rule, the Notes expressly state: "No legitimate interest of the government is intended to be prejudiced by permitting the court to direct an acquittal on a post-verdict motion." 18 U.S.C. App., p. 4505. Surely the well-recognized right to reprosecute is such a "legitimate interest of the government," and should remain unaffected by the District Judge's order of acquittal.

Nor will the interest of clarity and consistency in the administration of the criminal justice system be served by today's holding. By hinging the outcome of this case on the timing of the post-trial motion and the label on the order, the Court is elevating form over substance and undermining the theoretical framework established by the *Wilson-Jenkins-Serfass* trilogy[22] of two Terms ago and the Sanford and *United States v. Morrison,* 429 U.S. 1 (1976), decisions earlier this Term. All litigants in our criminal courts—Government and defendants alike—are harmed by the uncertainty thus created. For these reasons, I cannot join the Court's holding and I respectfully dissent.

(Continues)

(*Continued*)

Notes

21. *Fong Foo v. United States*, 369 U.S. 141 (1962), on which the Court relies so heavily, is not in point. There the District Judge directed a verdict while the original trial was still in progress. Unlike the case before us, the jury there was still properly empaneled, and had not yet even begun to deliberate. Where the District Judge interrupts the trial process, important rights of the defendant may be jeopardized. The opportunity to try the case is frustrated so that the possibility of an acquittal from the originally empaneled jury is lost. No such rights are implicated where, as here, the original trial has ended when the jury cannot agree; at that point the defendant is already subject to a second trial. Thus, the timing of the District Court's order is not, as the Court suggests, an irrelevant technicality. A midtrial judgment of acquittal interrupts the trial process at a time when the defendant is constitutionally entitled to have it proceed to verdict.

22. *United States v. Wilson*, 420 U.S. 332 (1975); *United States v. Jenkins*, 420 U.S. 358 (1975); *Serfass v. United States*, 420 U.S. 377 (1975).

Sanabria v. United States, 437 U.S. 54 (1978)

Title 18 U.S.C. 1955 (1976 ed.) makes it a federal offense for five or more persons to conduct an "illegal gambling business" in violation of the law of the place where the business is located. Petitioner, along with several others, was indicted for violating 1955 in a single count charging that the defendants' gambling business involved numbers betting and betting on horse races in violation of a specified Massachusetts statute. The Government's evidence at trial in the District Court showed that the defendants had been engaged in both horse betting and numbers betting. At the close of the Government's case defense counsel argued that the Government had failed to prove a violation of the Massachusetts statute because that statute did not prohibit numbers betting but only horse betting. After the defendants had rested, the trial judge granted their motion to exclude all evidence of numbers betting and then granted a motion to acquit petitioner because of lack of evidence of his connection with the horse-betting business. The case against the remaining defendants went to the jury, and they were all convicted. The Government appealed under 18 U.S.C. 3731 (1976 ed.) from the order excluding the numbers-betting evidence and from the judgment acquitting petitioner, and sought a new trial on the portion of the indictment relating to numbers betting. The Court of Appeals held that it had jurisdiction of the appeal, taking the view that, although 3731, by its terms, authorizes the Government to appeal only from orders "dismissing an indictment . . . as to any one or more counts," the word "counts" refers to any discrete basis for imposing criminal liability, that since the horse-betting and numbers allegations were discrete bases for liability duplicitously joined in a single count, the District Court's action constituted a "dismissal" of the numbers "charge" and an acquittal for insufficient evidence on the horse-betting charge, and that therefore 3731 authorized an appeal from the "dismissal" of the numbers charge. The court went on to hold that the Double Jeopardy Clause of the Fifth Amendment did not bar a retrial, because petitioner had voluntarily terminated the proceedings on the numbers portion of the count by moving, in effect, to dismiss it. The court vacated the judgment of acquittal, and remanded for a new trial on the numbers charge. *Held:*

1. A retrial on the numbers theory of liability is barred by the Double Jeopardy Clause. Pp. 63–74.

   (a) The Court of Appeals erroneously characterized the District Court's action as a "dismissal" of the numbers theory. There was only one count charged, the District Court did not order language in the indictment stricken, and the indictment was not amended, but the judgment of acquittal was entered on the entire count and found petitioner not guilty of violating 1955 without specifying that it did so only with respect to one theory of liability. Pp. 65–68.

   (b) To the extent that the District Court found the indictment's description of the offense too narrow to warrant admission of certain evidence, the court's ruling was an erroneous evidentiary ruling, which led to an acquittal for insufficient evidence, and that judgment of acquittal, however erroneous, bars further prosecution on any aspect of the count and hence bars appellate review of the trial court's error. Pp. 68–69.

   (c) Even if it could be said that the District Court "dismissed" the numbers allegation, a retrial on that theory would subject petitioner to a second trial on the "same offense" of which he was acquitted. Under 1955 participation in a single gambling business is but a single offense, no matter how many state statutes the enterprise violated, and with regard to this single gambling business petitioner was acquitted. The Government having charged only a single gambling business, the discrete violations of state law that that business may have committed are not severable in order to avoid the Double Jeopardy Clause's bar of retrials for the "same offense." Pp. 69–74.

2. Once the defendant has been acquitted, no matter how "egregiously erroneous" the legal rulings leading to the judgment of acquittal might be, there is no exception to the constitutional rule forbidding successive trials for the same offense. *Fong Foo v. United States*, 369 U.S. 141. Thus here, while the numbers evidence was erroneously excluded, the judgment of acquittal produced thereby is final and unreviewable. *Lee v. United States*, 432 U.S. 23; *Jeffers v. United States*, 432 U.S. 137, distinguished. Pp. 75–78.

548 F.2d 1, reversed.

MARSHALL, J., delivered the opinion of the Court, in which BURGER, C. J., and BRENNAN, STEWART, and POWELL, J. J., joined; in all but n. 23 of which STEVENS, J., joined; and in Parts I, II-A, and III of which WHITE, J., joined. STEVENS, J., filed a concurring opinion, *post*, p. 78. BLACKMUN, J., filed a dissenting opinion, in which REHNQUIST, J., joined, *post*, p. 80.

Francis J. DiMento argued the cause and filed briefs for petitioner.

Frank H. Easterbrook argued the cause for the United States *pro hac vice*. With him on the brief were Solicitor General McCree, Assistant Attorney General Civiletti, and Sidney M. Glazer.

MR. JUSTICE MARSHALL delivered the opinion of the Court.*

The issue presented is whether the United States may appeal in a criminal case from a midtrial ruling resulting in the exclusion of certain evidence and from a subsequently entered judgment of acquittal. Resolution of this issue depends on the application of the Double Jeopardy Clause of the Fifth Amendment to the somewhat unusual facts of this case.

I

Petitioner was indicted, along with several others, for violating 18 U.S.C. 1955 (1976 ed.), which makes it a federal offense to conduct, finance, manage, supervise, direct, or own all or part of an "illegal gambling business." 1955 (a). Such a business is defined as one that is conducted by five or more persons in violation of the law of the place where the business is located and that operates for at least 30 days or earns at least $2,000 in any one day. 1955 (b) (1).[23] The single-count indictment here charged in relevant part that the defendants' gambling business involved "accepting, recording and registering bets and wagers on a parimutual [sic] number pool and on the result of a trial and contest of skill, speed, and endurance of beast," and that the business "was a violation of the laws of the Commonwealth of Massachusetts, to wit, M. G. L. A. Chapter 271, Section 17."[24]

The Government's evidence at trial showed the defendants to have been engaged primarily in horse betting and numbers betting. At the close of the Government's case, petitioner's counsel, who represented 8 of the 11 defendants, moved for a judgment of acquittal as to all of his clients. Joined by counsel for other defendants, he argued, *inter alia*, that the Government had failed to prove that there was a violation of the state statutory section as alleged in the indictment, since Mass. Gen. Laws Ann., ch. 271, 17 (West 1970), as construed by the state courts, did not prohibit numbers betting but applied only to betting on "games of competition" such as horse races. The Government responded that "violation of the State law is a jurisdictional element of [the federal] statute" and that "not every [defendant] must be found to be violating this State law." The District Court accepted the Government's theory and denied the defendants' motion, stating that "a defendant to be convicted must [only] be found to have joined in [the illegal] enterprise in some way."

Petitioner's counsel then sought clarification of whether "the numbers pool allegation [was] still in the case." The court indicated that it was, because counsel had not presented any state-court authority for the proposition that 17 did not include numbers betting. The court also expressed the view, however, that if petitioner's counsel were correct, "we would have to exclude . . . all of the evidence that has to do with bets o[n] numbers." The Government demurred, arguing that exclusion of the numbers evidence would "not necessarily follow" from acceptance of petitioner's theory.[25] Taking his lead from the court, petitioner's counsel next moved "to strike or limit the evidence." The motion was denied.

---

*MR. JUSTICE WHITE joins Parts I, II-A, and III of this opinion.

(Continues)

(Continued)

After the defendants had rested, the trial judge announced that he was reversing his earlier ruling on the motion to exclude evidence, because he had discovered a Massachusetts case holding that numbers betting was not prohibited by 17, but only by 7 of ch. 271.[26] The court then struck all evidence of numbers betting, apparently because it believed such action to be required by the indictment's failure to set forth the proper section.[27]

At this point counsel moved for a judgment of acquittal as to petitioner alone, arguing that there was no evidence of his connection with horse-betting activities. The Government did not disagree that the evidence was insufficient to show petitioner's involvement with a horse-betting operation, but repeated its earlier argument relating to the "jurisdictional" nature of the state-law violation. The court rejected this contention, stating that the offense had "to be established in the terms that you [the Government] charged it, which was as a violation of 17" and that petitioner had to be "connected with this operation, and by that I mean a horse operation." The court concluded: "I don't think you've done it." It then granted petitioner's motion for a judgment of acquittal[28] and entered an order embodying this ruling later that day.[29]

The next day the Government moved the court to reconsider both "its ruling . . . striking . . . evidence concerning the operation of an illegal . . . numbers pool" and "its decision granting defendant Thomas Sanabria's motion for judgement [sic] of acquittal."[30] Prompted by the Government's arguments in support of reconsideration, the court asked defense counsel why he had not raised the objection to the indictment's citation of 17 earlier and what prejudice resulted to petitioner from the failure to cite the proper section. Counsel responded that the objection had not "ripened" until, at the end of the Government's case, the court was asked to take judicial notice of 17, and that he need not and did not allege actual prejudice. The court denied the motions to reconsider, but indicated that, had it granted the motion to restore the numbers evidence, it also would have vacated the judgment of acquittal.[31] The case against the remaining 10 defendants went to the jury on a theory that the gambling business was engaged in horse betting; all were convicted.

The Government filed a timely appeal "from [the] decision and order . . . excluding evidence and entering a judgment of acquittal . . . and . . . denying the Motion for Reconsideration." Conceding that there could be no review of the District Court's ruling that there was insufficient evidence of petitioner's involvement with horse betting, the Government sought a new trial on the portion of the indictment relating to numbers betting.

The Court of Appeals for the First Circuit held first that it had jurisdiction of the appeal. Although the jurisdictional statute, 18 U.S.C. 3731 (1976 ed.), by its terms authorizes the Government to appeal only from orders "dismissing an indictment . . . as to any one or more counts,"[32] the word "count" was "interpret[ed] . . . to refer to any discrete basis for the imposition of criminal liability." 548 F.2d 1, 5 (1976). Viewing the horse-betting and numbers allegations as "discrete bas[es] of criminal liability" duplicitously joined in a single count, the court characterized the District Court's action as a "dismissal" of the numbers "charge" and an acquittal for insufficient evidence on the horse-betting charge. *Id.*, at 4–5, and n. 4. It concluded that 3731 authorized an appeal from the "dismissal" of the numbers charge, "if the double jeopardy clause does not bar a future prosecution on this charge." 548 F.2d, at 5.

Consistent with its above analysis, the court found that petitioner had voluntarily terminated the proceedings on the numbers portion of the count by moving, in effect, to dismiss it. Since the "dismissal" imported no ruling on petitioner's "criminal liability as such," and since petitioner's motion was not attributable to "prosecutorial or judicial overreaching," the court applied the rule permitting retrials after a prosecution is terminated by a defendant's request for a mistrial. *Id.*, at 7–8, citing *United States v. Dinitz*, 424 U.S. 600 (1976). There being no double jeopardy bar to a new trial, the court went on to resolve the merits of the appeal in the Government's favor. It held, based on an intervening First Circuit decision,[33] that the District Court had erred in "dismissing" the numbers theory. Accordingly, the judgment of acquittal was "vacated" and the case "remanded so that the government may try defendant on that portion of the indictment that charges a violation of 1955 based upon numbering [sic] activities." 548 F.2d, at 8.

We granted *certiorari*, 433 U.S. 907 (1977),[34] limiting our review to the related issues of appealability and double jeopardy.[35] We now reverse.

II

In *United States v. Wilson*, 420 U.S. 332 (1975), we found that the primary purpose of the Double Jeopardy Clause was to prevent successive trials, and not Government appeals *per se*. Thus we held that, where an indictment is dismissed after a guilty verdict is rendered, the Double Jeopardy Clause did not bar an appeal since the verdict could simply be reinstated without a new trial if the Government were successful.[36] That a new trial will follow upon a Government appeal does not necessarily forbid it, however, because in limited circumstances a second trial on the same offense is constitutionally permissible.[37] Appealability in this case therefore turns on whether the new trial ordered by the court below would violate the command of the Fifth Amendment that no "person [shall] be subject for the same offence to be twice put in jeopardy of life or limb."[38]

In deciding whether a second trial is permissible here, we must immediately confront the fact that petitioner was acquitted on the indictment. That "'[a] verdict of acquittal . . . [may] not be reviewed . . . without putting [the defendant] twice in jeopardy, and thereby violating the Constitution,'" has recently been described as "the most fundamental rule in the history of double jeopardy jurisprudence." *United States v. Martin Linen Supply Co.*, 430 U.S. 564, 571 (1977), quoting *United States v. Ball*, 163 U.S. 662, 671 (1896). The fundamental nature of this rule is manifested by its explicit extension to situations where an acquittal is "based upon an egregiously erroneous foundation." *Fong Foo v. United States*, 369 U.S. 141, 143 (1962); see *Green v. United States*, 355 U.S. 184, 188 (1957). In *Fong Foo* the Court of Appeals held that the District Court had erred in various rulings and lacked power to direct a verdict of acquittal before the Government rested its case.[39] We accepted the Court of Appeals' holding that the District Court had erred, but nevertheless found that the Double Jeopardy Clause was "violated when the Court of Appeals set aside the judgment of acquittal and directed that petitioners be tried again for the same offense." 369 U.S., at 143. Thus when a defendant has been acquitted at trial he may not be retried on the same offense, even if the legal rulings underlying the acquittal were erroneous.

The Government does not take issue with these basic principles. Indeed, it concedes that the acquittal for insufficient evidence on what it refers to as the horse-betting theory of liability is unreviewable and bars a second trial on that charge.[40] The disputed question, however, is whether a retrial on the numbers theory of liability would be on the "same offense" as that on which petitioner has been acquitted.

The Government contends, in accordance with the reasoning of the Court of Appeals, that the numbers theory was dismissed from the count before the judgment of acquittal was entered and therefore that petitioner was not acquitted of the numbers theory. Petitioner responds that the District Court did not "dismiss" anything but rather struck evidence and acquitted petitioner on the entire count; further, assuming *arguendo* that there was a "dismissal" of the numbers theory, he urges that a retrial on this theory would nevertheless be barred as a second trial on the same statutory offense. We first consider whether the Court of Appeals correctly characterized the District Court's action as a "dismissal" of the numbers theory.

A

In the Government's view, the numbers theory was "dismissed" from the case as effectively as if the Government had actually charged the crime in two counts and the District Court had dismissed the numbers count. The first difficulty this argument encounters is that the Government did not in fact charge this offense in two counts. Legal consequences ordinarily flow from what has actually happened, not from what a party might have done from the vantage of hindsight. See *Central Tablet Mfg. Co. v. United States*, 417 U.S. 673, 690 (1974).[41] The precise manner in which an indictment is drawn cannot be ignored, because an important function of the indictment is to ensure that, "in case any other proceedings are taken against [the defendant] for a similar offence, . . . the record [will] sho[w] with accuracy to what extent he may plead a former acquittal or conviction." *Cochran v. United States*, 157 U.S. 286, 290 (1895), quoted with approval in *Russell v. United States*, 369 U.S. 749, 764 (1962); *Hanger v. United States*, 285 U.S. 427, 431 (1932).[42]

With regard to the one count that was in fact charged, as to which petitioner has been at least formally acquitted, we are not persuaded that it is correct to characterize the trial court's action as a "dismissal" of a discrete portion of the count. While form is not to be exalted over substance in determining the double jeopardy consequences of a ruling terminating a prosecution, *Serfass v. United States*, 420 U.S. 377, 392–393 (1975); *United States v. Jorn*, 400 U.S. 470, 478 n. 7 (1971); *United States v. Goldman*, 277 U.S. 229, 236 (1928), neither is it appropriate entirely to ignore the form of order entered by the trial court, see *United States v. Barber*, 219 U.S. 72, 78 (1911). Here the District Court issued only two orders, one excluding certain evidence and the other entering a judgment of acquittal on the single count charged. No language in the indictment was ordered to be stricken, compare *United States v. Alberti,*

(Continues)

568 F.2d 617, 621 (CA2 1977), nor was the indictment amended. The judgment of acquittal was entered on the entire count and found petitioner not guilty of the crime of violating 18 U.S.C. 1955 (1976 ed.), without specifying that it did so only with respect to one theory of liability:

"The defendant having been set to the bar to be tried for the offense of unlawfully engaging in an illegal gambling business, in violation of Title 18, United States Code, Sections 1955 and 2, and the Court having allowed defendant's motion for judgment of acquittal at the close of government's evidence,

"It is hereby ORDERED that the defendant Thomas Sanabria be, and he hereby is, acquitted of the offense charged, and it is further ORDERED that the defendant Thomas Sanabria is hereby discharged to go without day."

The Government itself characterized the District Court's ruling from which it sought to appeal as "a decision and order . . . excluding evidence and entering a judgment of acquittal." Notice of Appeal.[43] Similar language appears in its motion for reconsideration filed in the District Court. Indeed, the view that the trial court "dismissed" as to one "discrete basis of liability" appears to have originated in the opinion below. Thus, not only defense counsel and the trial court but the Government as well seemed in agreement that the trial court had made an evidentiary ruling based on its interpretation of the indictment.

We must assume that the trial court's interpretation of the indictment was erroneous. See n. 13, *supra*. But not every erroneous interpretation of an indictment for purposes of deciding what evidence is admissible can be regarded as a "dismissal." Here the District Court did not find that the count failed to charge a necessary element of the offense, *cf. Lee v. United States*, 432 U.S. 23 (1977); rather, it found the indictment's description of the offense too narrow to warrant the admission of certain evidence. To this extent, we believe the ruling below is properly to be characterized as an erroneous evidentiary ruling,[44] which led to an acquittal for insufficient evidence. That judgment of acquittal, however erroneous, bars further prosecution on any aspect of the count and hence bars appellate review of the trial court's error. *United States v. Martin Linen Supply Co.*, 430 U.S., at 571; *Fong Foo v. United States*, 369 U.S. 141 (1962); *Green v. United States*, 355 U.S., at 188; *United States v. Ball*, 163 U.S., at 671.

B

Even if the Government were correct that the District Court "dismissed" the numbers allegation, in our view a retrial on that theory would subject petitioner to a second trial on the "same offense" of which he has been acquitted.[45]

It is Congress, and not the prosecution, which establishes and defines offenses. Few, if any, limitations are imposed by the Double Jeopardy Clause on the legislative power to define offenses. *Brown v. Ohio*, 432 U.S. 161, 165 (1977). But once Congress has defined a statutory offense by its prescription of the "allowable unit of prosecution," *United States v. Universal C. I. T. Credit Corp.*, 344 U.S. 218, 221 (1952); *Bell v. United States*, 349 U.S. 81 (1955); *Braverman v. United States*, 317 U.S. 49 (1942); *In re Nielsen*, 131 U.S. 176 (1889), that prescription determines the scope of protection afforded by a prior conviction or acquittal. Whether a particular course of conduct involves one or more distinct "offenses" under the statute depends on this congressional choice.[46]

The allowable unit of prosecution under 1955 is defined as participation in a single "illegal gambling business." Congress did not assimilate state gambling laws per se into the federal penal code, nor did it define discrete acts of gambling as independent federal offenses. See H.R. Rep. No. 91-1549, p. 53 (1970). See also *Iannelli v. United States*, 420 U.S. 770, 784–790 (1975). The Government need not prove that the defendant himself performed any act of gambling prohibited by state law.[47] It is participation in the gambling business that is a federal offense, and it is only the gambling business that must violate state law.[48] And, as the Government recognizes, under 1955 participation in a single gambling business is but a single offense, "no matter how many state statutes the enterprise violated." Brief for United States 31.

The Government's undisputed theory of this case is that there was a single gambling business, which engaged in both horse betting and numbers betting. With regard to this single business, participation in which is concededly only a single offense, we have no doubt that petitioner was truly acquitted.

We have recently defined an acquittal as "'a resolution, correct or not, of some or all of the factual elements of the offense charged.'" *Lee v. United States*, 432 U.S., at 30 n. 8, quoting *United States v.*

Martin Linen Supply Co., supra, at 571. Petitioner was found not guilty for a failure of proof on a key "factual element of the offense charged": that he was "connected with" the illegal gambling business. See *supra,* at 59.[49] Had the Government charged only that the business was engaged in horse betting and had petitioner been acquitted, his acquittal would bar any further prosecution for participating in the same gambling business during the same time period on a numbers theory.[50] That the trial court disregarded the Government's allegation of numbers betting does not render its acquittal on the horse-betting theory any less an acquittal on the "offense" charged. "The Double Jeopardy Clause is not such a fragile guarantee that . . . its limitations [can be avoided] by the simple expedient of dividing a single crime into a series of temporal or spatial units," *Brown v. Ohio,* 432 U.S., at 169, or, as we hold today, into "discrete bases of liability" not defined as such by the legislature. See *id.,* at 169 n. 8.[51]

While recognizing that only a single violation of the statute is alleged under either theory,[52] the Government nevertheless contends that separate counts would have been proper, and that an acquittal of petitioner on a horse-betting count would not bar another prosecution on a numbers count. Brief for United States 33. Although there may be circumstances in which this is true, petitioner here was acquitted for insufficient proof of an element of the crime which both such counts would share— that he was "connected with" the single gambling business. See *supra,* at 59. This finding of fact stands as an absolute bar to any further prosecution for participation in that business.[53]

The Government having charged only a single gambling business, the discrete violations of state law which that business may have committed are not severable in order to avoid the Double Jeopardy Clause's bar on retrials for the "same offense."[54] Indeed, the Government's argument that these are discrete bases of liability warranting reprosecution following a final judgment of acquittal on one such "discrete basis" is quite similar to an unsuccessful argument that it presented in *Braverman v. United States,* 317 U.S. 49 (1942). *Braverman* had been convicted of and received consecutive sentences on four separate counts of conspiracy, each count alleging a conspiracy to violate a separate substantive provision of the federal narcotics laws. The Government conceded that only a single conspiracy existed, as it concedes here that only a single gambling business existed; nonetheless, it urged that separate punishments were appropriate because the single conspiracy had several discrete objects. We firmly rejected that argument:

> "[T]he precise nature and extent of the conspiracy must be determined by reference to the agreement which embraces and defines its objects. Whether the object of a single agreement is to commit one or many crimes, it is in either case that agreement which constitutes the conspiracy which the statute punishes. The one agreement cannot be taken to be several agreements and hence several conspiracies because it envisages the violation of several statutes rather than one." *Id.,* at 53.

The same reasoning must also apply where the essence of the crime created by Congress is participation in a "business," rather than participation in an "agreement."[55]

The Double Jeopardy Clause is no less offended because the Government here seeks to try petitioner twice for this single offense, instead of seeking to punish him twice as it did in Braverman.[56] "If two offenses are the same . . . for purposes of barring consecutive sentences at a single trial, they necessarily will be the same for purposes of barring successive prosecutions." *Brown v. Ohio, supra,* at 166. Accordingly, even if the numbers allegation were "dismissed," we conclude that a subsequent trial of petitioner for conducting the same illegal gambling business as that at issue in the first trial would subject him to a second trial on the "same offense" of which he was acquitted.

III

The only question remaining is whether any of the exceptions to the constitutional rule forbidding successive trials on the same offense, see n. 15, *supra,* apply here. The short answer to this question is that there is no exception permitting retrial once the defendant has been acquitted, no matter how "egregiously erroneous," *Fong Foo v. United States,* 369 U.S., at 143, the legal rulings leading to that judgment might be. The Government nevertheless argues, relying principally on *Lee v. United States,* 432 U.S. 23 (1977), and *Jeffers v. United States,* 432 U.S. 137 (1977), that petitioner waived his double jeopardy rights by moving to "dismiss" the numbers allegation and by not objecting to the form of the allegation prior to trial.

(Continues)

In *Lee* we held a retrial permissible because the District Court's midtrial decision granting the defendant's motion to dismiss the indictment for failure to state an offense was "functionally indistinguishable from a declaration of mistrial" at the defendant's request. 432 U.S., at 31. The mistrial analogy relied on in Lee is manifestly inapposite here. Although jeopardy had attached in Lee, no verdict had been rendered; indeed, petitioner conceded that "the District Court's termination of the first trial was not an acquittal," *id.*, at 30 n. 8. Here, by contrast, the trial proceeded to verdict, and petitioner was acquitted. While in Lee the trial court clearly did contemplate a reprosecution when it granted defendant's motion, *id.*, at 30–31, neither petitioner's motion here nor the trial court's rulings contemplated a second trial— nor could they have, since only a single offense was involved and petitioner went to judgment on that offense. Where a trial terminates with a judgment of acquittal, as here, "double jeopardy principles governing the permissibility of retrial after a declaration of mistrial," *Lee v. United States*, 432 U.S., at 31, have no bearing.

Nor does Jeffers support the Government's position. The defendant there was first tried and convicted of conspiring to distribute narcotics in violation of 21 U.S.C. 846. Eight Members of the Court agreed that his subsequent trial for conducting a continuing criminal enterprise in violation of 21 U.S.C. 848 during the same time period was on the "same offense," since the 846 violation was a lesser included offense to the 848 violation. Prior to the first trial, however, Jeffers had specifically opposed the Government's effort to try both indictments together, in part on the ground that they involved distinct offenses. 432 U.S., at 144 n. 8. Reasoning that Jeffers necessarily contemplated a second trial, four Members of the Court found that he had "elect[ed] to have the two offenses tried separately," *id.*, at 152, and, by not raising the potential double jeopardy problem, had waived any objection on that ground to successive trials, *id.*, at 152–154.[57] The instant case presents quite a different situation. Petitioner's counsel never argued that horse betting and numbers were distinct offenses,[58] a fortiori did not argue for or contemplate separate trials on each theory, and a *multo fortiori* did not "elect" to undergo successive trials.

Finally, we agree with the Court of Appeals that this case does not present the hypothetical situation on which we reserved judgment in *Serfass v. United States*, of "'a defendant who is afforded an opportunity to obtain a determination of a legal defense prior to trial and nevertheless knowingly allows himself to be placed in jeopardy before raising the defense.'" 420 U.S., at 394, quoting Solicitor General; see 548 F.2d, at 7. Petitioner did not have a "legal defense" to the single offense charged: participating in an illegal gambling business in violation of 1955. Unlike questions of whether an indictment states an offense, a statute is unconstitutional, or conduct set forth in an indictment violates the statute, what proof may be presented in support of a valid indictment and the sufficiency of that proof are not "legal defenses" required to be or even capable of being resolved before trial. In all of the former instances, a ruling in the defendant's favor completely precludes conviction, at least on that indictment. Here, even if the numbers language had been struck before trial, there was no "legal" reason why petitioner could not have been convicted on this indictment, as were his 10 codefendants. The acquittal resulted from the insufficiency of the Government's proof at trial to establish petitioner's connection with the gambling business, as the trial judge erroneously understood it to have been charged.

The Government's real quarrel is with the judgment of acquittal. While the numbers evidence was erroneously excluded, the judgment of acquittal produced thereby is final and unreviewable. Neither 18 U.S.C. 3731 (1976 ed.) nor the Double Jeopardy Clause permits the Government to obtain relief from all of the adverse rulings—most of which result from defense motions—that lead to the termination of a criminal trial in the defendant's favor. See *United States v. Wilson*, 420 U.S., at 351–352; S. Rep. No. 91-1296, p. 2 (1970). To hold that a defendant waives his double jeopardy protection whenever a trial court error in his favor on a midtrial motion leads to an acquittal would undercut the adversary assumption on which our system of criminal justice rests, see *Jeffers v. United States*, 432 U.S., at 159–160 (STEVENS, J., dissenting in part and concurring in judgment in part), and would vitiate one of the fundamental rights established by the Fifth Amendment.

The trial court's rulings here led to an erroneous resolution in the defendant's favor on the merits of the charge. As *Fong Foo v. United States* makes clear, the Double Jeopardy Clause absolutely bars a second trial in such circumstances. The Court of Appeals thus lacked jurisdiction of the Government's appeal.

Accordingly, the judgment of the Court of Appeals is

Reversed.

Notes

23. Title 18 U.S.C. 1955 (1976 ed.) provides in relevant part:

"Prohibition of illegal gambling businesses.

"(a) Whoever conducts, finances, manages, supervises, directs, or owns all or part of an illegal gambling business shall be fined not more than $20,000 or imprisoned not more than five years, or both.

"(b) As used in this section—
"(1) 'illegal gambling business' means a gambling business which—
"(i) is a violation of the law of a State or political subdivision in which it is conducted;
"(ii) involves five or more persons who conduct, finance, manage, supervise, direct, or own all or part of such business; and
"(iii) has been or remains in substantially continuous operation for a period in excess of thirty days or has a gross revenue of $2,000 in any single day.
"(2) 'gambling' includes but is not limited to pool-selling, bookmaking, maintaining slot machines, roulette wheels or dice tables, and conducting lotteries, policy, bolita or numbers games, or selling chances therein.
"(3) 'State' means any State of the United States, the District of Columbia, the Commonwealth of Puerto Rico, and any territory or possession of the United States."

24. The indictment alleged in full:

"From on or about June 1, 1971 and continuing thereafter up to and including November 13, 1971 at Revere, Massachusetts within the District of Massachusetts, [the defendants] did unlawfully, knowingly, and wilfully conduct, finance, manage, supervise, direct and own all and a part of an illegal gambling business, to wit, accepting, recording and registering bets and wagers on a parimutuel [sic] number pool and on the result of a trial and contest of skill, speed, and endurance of beast, said illegal gambling business; (i) was a violation of the laws of the Commonwealth of Massachusetts, to wit, M. G. L.A. Chapter 271, Section 17, in which place said gambling business was being conducted; (ii) involved five and more persons who conducted, financed, managed, supervised, directed and owned all and a part of said business; (iii) had been in substantially continuous operation for a period in excess of thirty days and had a gross revenue of two thousand dollars ($2,000) in any single day; all in violation of Title 18, United States Code, Sections 1955 and 2."

25. When the District Judge asked why exclusion of the numbers evidence "would not necessarily follow," the Government responded:

"Because the Defendants have been charged with operating a gambling business, which is in violation of State law. Now, there's no question that the horse race aspect of it is in violation of State law. There are other aspects to the bets as well, but the violation of State law is merely a jurisdictional element which must be satisfied prior to the initiation of Federal prosecution."

26. *Commonwealth v. Boyle*, 346 Mass. 1, 189 N.E. 2d 844 (1963).

27. The Government did not at this time argue, as it had previously, see n. 3, *supra*, that the numbers evidence was relevant to show "other aspects" of the bets even if it could not be used to prove that the business violated state law. Instead, it urged that the numbers evidence was admissible as proof of "similar acts."

28. Petitioner has consistently maintained that he properly moved to exclude the numbers evidence as irrelevant to the indictment's characterization of the gambling business; that the District Court properly granted the evidentiary motion, see Tr. of Oral Arg. 12; and that the District Court properly granted petitioner's motion for a judgment of acquittal after excluding the numbers evidence on the grounds of insufficient evidence.

29. The text of the judgment is quoted *infra*, at 67.

30. In support of these motions, the Government argued that the failure to cite Mass. Gen. Laws Ann., ch. 271, 7 (West 1970), in the indictment was a technical defect causing no prejudice to the defendants and subject to correction during trial under Fed. Rule Crim. Proc. 7. See n. 11, *infra*. If the numbers evidence were restored to the case, the Government argued, vacating the judgment of acquittal would be proper, since it had resulted solely from the erroneous exclusion of evidence and since no new trial would be necessary in view of the fact that the jury had not been discharged.

31. The trial court explained its reasoning as follows:

"If the other motion had been granted, I think, probably, the Motion to Reconsider the Acquittal of Sanabria would be allowed under these new decisions: *Wilson*, which is in 420 U.S. 332; *Jenkins*, 420

(Continues)

(*Continued*)

U.S. 358; and *Serfass* at 420 U.S. 377, all decided the last term. All of those seem to say if a judgment of acquittal or judgment of dismissal is entered on legal grounds as opposed to containing or importing a finding of fact and the reversal of that decision would not require a new trial, then it may be reversed.

. . . .

"In *Fong Foo* [v. *United States*, 369 U.S. 141 (1962)] the jury had been discharged, and it would have been necessary to draw a new jury and start a new trial, and in *Jenkins* they specifically distinguished *Fong Foo* from the *Wilson-Jenkins-Serfass* group. . . ."

32. Another provision of 3731 authorizes the Government to appeal from orders "suppressing or excluding evidence . . . not made after the defendant has been put in jeopardy and before the verdict or finding on [the] indictment." The Government does not contend that the ruling excluding numbers evidence was appealable under this provision. By its plain terms, moreover, this second paragraph of 3731 does not authorize this appeal, since the ruling excluding evidence occurred after the defendant had been put in jeopardy and before verdict. *Cf. United States v. Morrison*, 429 U.S. 1 (1976).

33. *United States v. Morrison*, 531 F.2d 1089, 1094, *cert. denied*, 429 U.S. 837 (1976). Morrison held a failure to cite Mass. Gen. Laws Ann., ch. 271, 7 (West 1970), in a similarly worded indictment to be harmless error. Based on Morrison, the court below concluded that the indictment was sufficient to give "notice that numbers activity was a basis upon which the government sought to establish criminal liability under 1955." 548 F.2d, at 4.

34. The petition for *certiorari* was filed one day out of time. The time requirement of this Court's Rule 22 (2) is not jurisdictional, *Schacht v. United States*, 398 U.S. 58, 63–65 (1970), and petitioner has filed a motion, supported by affidavits, seeking waiver of this requirement. We now grant petitioner's motion.

35. The petition for certiorari presented four questions for review, the first three relating to whether the Government's appeal was authorized by statute and not barred by the Double Jeopardy Clause. The fourth question sought review of the Court of Appeals' ruling that the indictment gave sufficient notice of the Government's intent to rely on evidence of numbers betting. Our order limited the grant of *certiorari* to the first three questions. 433 U.S. 907 (1977). Accordingly, we must assume that the District Court erred in ruling that the indictment did not encompass the numbers allegation because of its failure to cite Mass. Gen. Laws Ann., ch. 271, 7 (West 1970).

36. *United States v. Jenkins*, 420 U.S. 358 (1975), by contrast, held that appeal of an order dismissing an indictment after jeopardy had attached, but before verdict, was barred because a successful appeal would require "further proceedings . . . devoted to the resolution of factual issues going to the elements of the offense charged." *Id.*, at 370. See *Lee v. United States*, 432 U.S. 23, 29–30 (1977).

37. A new trial is permitted, e. g., where the defendant successfully appeals his conviction, *United States v. Ball*, 163 U.S. 662, 672 (1896); where a mistrial is declared for a "manifest necessity," *Wade v. Hunter*, 336 U.S. 684 (1949); where the defendant requests a mistrial in the absence of prosecutorial or judicial overreaching, *United States v. Dinitz*, 424 U.S. 600 (1976); or where an indictment is dismissed at the defendant's request in circumstances functionally equivalent to a mistrial, *Lee v. United States*, supra. See also *Jeffers v. United States*, 432 U.S. 137 (1977).

38. We have on several occasions observed that the jurisdictional statute authorizing Government appeals, 18 U.S.C. 3731 (1976 ed.), was "'intended to remove all statutory barriers'" to appeals from orders terminating prosecutions. *United States v. Martin Linen Supply Co.*, 430 U.S. 564, 568 (1977), quoting *United States v. Wilson*, 420 U.S. 332, 337 (1975). We therefore turn immediately to the constitutional issues.

39. In *re United States*, 286 F.2d 556 (CA1 1961).

40. It is without constitutional significance that the court entered a judgment of acquittal rather than directing the jury to bring in a verdict of acquittal or giving it erroneous instructions that resulted in an acquittal. *United States v. Martin Linen Supply Co.*, *supra*, at 567 n. 5, 573; *United States v. Sisson*, 399 U.S. 267, 290 (1970).

41. The difficulty in allowing a defendant's rights to turn on what the Government might have done is illustrated by considering that, had the Government alleged each "theory of liability" in a separate count, the indictment would have been subject to objection on grounds of multiplicity, the charging of a single offense in separate counts. See n. 20, *infra*. The Government might then have been forced to elect on which count it would proceed against petitioner, *United States v. Universal C. I. T. Credit Corp.*, 344 U.S. 218 (1952), and probably would have chosen to proceed on the numbers theory as to which its evidence was apparently stronger. In that event, however, petitioner could not have been acquitted of the horse-betting count, and the instant problem would not have arisen.

42. The Court of Appeals erred in its apparent view that the Government should have drawn the indictment in two counts because the single count was duplicitous. 548 F.2d, at 5 n. 4. Only a single gambling business was alleged, and hence only a single offense. See *infra*, at 70–71. A single offense should normally be charged in one count rather than several, even if different means of committing the offense are alleged. See Fed. Rule Crim. Proc. 7(c) (1); Advisory Committee's Notes on Fed. Rule Crim. Proc. 7, 18 U.S.C. App., p. 1413 (1976 ed.); n. 19, *supra*.

43. The Court of Appeals might have been warranted in dismissing the appeal for failure of the notice to specify the only arguably appealable ruling rendered below. The court believed that "[t]he critical ruling by the district court was that the indictment failed to charge a violation of 1955 on a numbers theory." 548 F.2d, at 5 n. 5. But this "critical ruling," which the court below concluded was a "dismissal," is not set forth in the notice of appeal. Since the Government is not authorized to appeal from all adverse rulings in criminal cases, it is especially important that it specify precisely what it claims to have been the appealable ruling.

The Court of Appeals, however, must have concluded that the notice was sufficient to bring up for review the legal ruling preceding the order excluding evidence. A mistake in designating the judgment appealed from is not always fatal, so long as the intent to appeal from a specific ruling can fairly be inferred by probing the notice and the other party was not misled or prejudiced. *Daily Mirror, Inc. v. New York News, Inc.*, 533 F.2d 53 (CA2 1976) (*per curiam*); *Jones v. Nelson*, 484 F.2d 1165 (CA10 1973). The Government's "Designation of Issue [sic] on Appeal," apparently filed after the notice, did set forth that "[t]he trial judge erred in ruling that M.G.L.A. Chapter 271, Section 17 does not encompass an illegal numbers operation and as a result erred in granting the Motion to Strike and the Motion for Judgment of Acquittal."

44. The District Court's interpretation of the indictment as not encompassing a charge that the gambling business engaged in numbers betting in violation of state law did not by itself require that numbers evidence be excluded. Even if the indictment had charged only that the defendants had conducted an illegal gambling business engaged in horse-betting activities in violation of state law, evidence relating to numbers betting would have been admissible, absent actual surprise or prejudice, to show the defendants' connection with "all or part of [that] illegal gambling business." 18 U.S.C. 1955 (a) (1976 ed.). As the Government repeatedly argued to the District Court, the violation of state law is a jurisdictional element which need only be proved with respect to the business.

The District Court's erroneous assumption that the numbers evidence had to be excluded may have resulted in part from the Government's failure to repeat in full its earlier argument, see *supra*, at 58, when the judge ruled that 17 did not encompass numbers betting, see *supra*, at 58–59. See n. 5, *supra*. Had the numbers evidence not been excluded, the judgment of acquittal would not have been entered, even if the court adhered to its ruling on the scope of the indictment, and the case would have gone to the jury, presumably with instructions that the jurors had to find the gambling business to have engaged in horse betting, and the defendants to have conducted "all or part" of that gambling business.

45. We agree with the Court of Appeals, see *supra*, at 61, that there is no statutory barrier to an appeal from an order dismissing only a portion of a count. One express purpose of 18 U.S.C. 3731 (1976 ed.) is to permit appeals from orders dismissing indictments "as to any one or more counts." A "count" is the usual organizational subunit of an indictment, and it would therefore appear that Congress intended to authorize appeals from any order dismissing an indictment in whole or in part. Congress could hardly have meant appealability to depend on the initial decision of a prosecutor to charge in one count what could also have been charged in two, a decision frequently fortuitous for purposes of the interests served by 3731. To so rule would import an empty formalism into a statute expressly designed to eliminate "[t]echnical distinctions in pleadings as limitations on appeals by the United States." H.R. Conf. Rep. No. 91-1768, p. 21 (1970); accord, S. Rep. No. 91-1296, p. 5 (1970). We note that the only Court of Appeals other than the court below that has considered this question reached a similar result. *United States v. Alberti*, 568 F.2d 617 (CA2 1977).

46. See Note, Twice in Jeopardy, 75 *Yale L. J.* 262, 268, 302–310 (1965). Because only a single violation of a single statute is at issue here, we do not analyze this case under the so-called "same evidence" test, which is frequently used to determine whether a single transaction may give rise to separate prosecutions, convictions, and/or punishments under separate statutes. See, e.g., *Gavieres v. United States*, 220 U.S. 338, 342 (1911); *Blockburger v. United States*, 284 U.S. 299 (1932); *Gore v. United States*, 357 U.S. 386 (1958); *Iannelli v. United States*, 420 U.S. 770 (1975). See also *Brown v. Ohio*, 432 U.S. 161, 166–167, n. 6 (1977); *United States v. Jones*, 533 F.2d 1387 (CA6 1976), *cert. denied*, 431 U.S. 964 (1977). Nor is the case controlled by decisions permitting prosecution under statutes defining as the criminal offense a discrete act, after a prior conviction or acquittal of a distinguishable discrete act that is a separate violation of the statute. See, e.g., *Ebeling v. Morgan*, 237 U.S. 625 (1915); *Burton v. United States*, 202 U.S. 344 (1906). Cf. *Ladner v. United States*, 358 U.S. 169 (1958); *Bell v. United States*, 349 U.S. 81 (1955).

(Continues)

(*Continued*)

47. *United States v. Hawes*, 529 F.2d 472, 478 (CA5 1976).

48. Numerous cases have recognized that 18 U.S.C. 1955 (1976 ed.) proscribes any degree of participation in an illegal gambling business, except participation as a mere bettor. See, e.g., *United States v. DiMuro*, 540 F.2d 503, 507–508 (CA1 1976), cert. denied, 429 U.S. 1038 (1977); *United States v. Leon*, 534 F.2d 667, 676 (CA6 1976); *United States v. Brick*, 502 F.2d 219, 225 n. 17 (CA8 1974); *United States v. Smaldone*, 485 F.2d 1333, 1351 (CA10 1973), *cert. denied*, 416 U.S. 936 (1974); *United States v. Hunter*, 478 F.2d 1019, 1021–1022 (CA7), *cert. denied*, 414 U.S. 857 (1973); *United States v. Ceraso*, 467 F.2d 653, 656 (CA3 1972); *United States v. Becker*, 461 F.2d 230, 232–233 (CA2 1972), vacated on other grounds, 417 U.S. 903 (1974). Similarly, the Government need not prove that each defendant participated in an illegal gambling business for more than 30 days (or grossed more than $2,000 in a single day), but only that the business itself existed for more than 30 days (or met the earnings criteria). *United States v. Graham*, 534 F.2d 1357, 1359 (CA9 1976) (*per curiam*); *United States v. Marrifield*, 515 F.2d 877, 880–881 (CA5 1975); *United States v. Schaefer*, 510 F.2d 1307, 1312 (CA8), *cert. denied sub nom. Del Pietro v. United States*, 421 U.S. 975 (1975); *United States v. Smaldone, supra*, at 1351; see *United States v. DiMario*, 473 F.2d 1046, 1048 (CA6), *cert. denied*, 412 U.S. 907 (1973).

49. The court's finding that petitioner was not "connected with" the gambling business necessarily meant that he was found not to conduct, finance, manage, supervise, direct, or own it. See 18 U.S.C. 1955 (a) (1976 ed.).

50. See 1 C. Wright, *Federal Practice and Procedure* 125, p. 241 (1969). See also *United States v. Sabella*, 272 F.2d 206, 211 (CA2 1959) (Friendly, J.); *Hanf v. United States*, 235 F.2d 710, 715 (CA8), *cert. denied*, 352 U.S. 880 (1956).

51. See also *United States v. Jackson*, 560 F.2d 112, 121 n. 9 (CA2 1977) (Government may not, under Double Jeopardy Clause, "fragment what is in fact a single crime into its components").

52. The Government concedes that it was required to bring all "theories of liability" in a single trial, and that only a single punishment could be imposed upon conviction on more than one such theory. Brief for United States 31, 33.

53. It is true that no factual determination was made that petitioner had not engaged in numbers betting. Thus, there would be no collateral–estoppel bar to a prosecution of petitioner for a different offense in which his liability would depend on proof of that fact. Cf. *Ashe v. Swenson*, 397 U.S. 436 (1970).

54. A single gambling business theoretically may violate as many laws as a State has prohibiting gambling, and 1955 specifies six means by which a defendant may illegally participate in such a business, i.e., by conducting, financing, managing, supervising, directing, or owning it. If we were to accept the Government's theory, each of these could be varied, one at a time, to charge a separate count on which a defendant could be reprosecuted following acquittals on any of the others.

55. If two different gambling businesses were alleged and proved, separate convictions and punishments would be proper. See *American Tobacco Co. v. United States*, 328 U.S. 781, 787–788 (1946) (holding Braverman inapplicable where two distinct conspiracies alleged). It is not always easy to ascertain whether one or more gambling businesses have been proved under 1955. See, e.g., *United States v. DiMuro*, 540 F.2d, at 508–509; *United States v. Bobo*, 477 F.2d 974, 988 (CA4 1973). No such difficulties are presented here because both sides agree that only a single gambling business existed.

56. *United States v. Tanner*, 471 F.2d 128, 141 n. 21 (CA7), *cert. denied*, 409 U.S. 949 (1972); see *United States v. Mayes*, 512 F.2d 637, 652 (CA6), cert. denied, 422 U.S. 1008 (1975); *United States v. Young*, 503 F.2d 1072, 1075 (CA3 1974); *United States v. Cohen*, 197 F.2d 26 (CA3 1952). See also *Short v. United States*, 91 F.2d 614 (CA4 1937); *Powe v. United States*, 11 F.2d 598 (CA5 1926); *United States v. Weiss*, 293 F. 992 (ND Ill. 1923).

57. While holding that Jeffers could be subjected to a second trial, these four Justices were of the view that the total punishment imposed on Jeffers could not be in excess of that authorized for a single violation of 21 U.S.C. 848. They relied in part on the fact that Jeffers, who had argued in the District Court that the two statutes involved distinct offenses, had "never affirmatively argued that the difference in the two statutes was so great as to authorize separate punishments . . ." 432 U.S., at 154 n. 23. They were joined in voting to vacate the excess punishment by the four Justices who believed that Jeffers could not be constitutionally subjected to another trial. MR. JUSTICE WHITE believed that Jeffers could be subjected to both a second trial and separate punishments.

58. That no such argument was made as to the numbers and horse-betting allegations is highlighted by the fact that petitioner's counsel did argue on behalf of another defendant that evidence relating to that defendant's betting on dog races should be excluded because

> "the theory of the Government's case is that this is a horse and numbers business. . . . [The dog betting] stands by itself as a separate business, and . . . the Government [must] prove one business here. It's like having multiple conspiracy." Record 28–29.

The motion for exclusion was denied because the District Court found that dog betting was part of the single gambling business shown to have been conducted from the office at 63 Bickford Avenue. *Id.*, at 29–30.

MR. JUSTICE STEVENS, concurring.

Although I join the text of the Court's opinion, I cannot agree with the dictum in footnote 23 [45]. It is true "that there is no statutory barrier to an appeal from an order dismissing only a portion of a count," *ante*, at 69 n. 23, but it is equally true that there is no statutory authority for such an appeal. It necessarily follows—at least if we are faithful to the concept that federal courts have only such jurisdiction as is conferred by Congress—that the Court of Appeals had no jurisdiction of this appeal.

The Criminal Appeals Act, 18 U.S.C. 3731 (1976 ed.), authorizes the United States to appeal an order of a district court "dismissing an indictment or information as to any one or more counts, except that no appeal shall lie where the double jeopardy clause of the United States Constitution prohibits further prosecution." (Emphasis added.) By its plain terms, this statute does not encompass the present case.

Putting to one side the question whether an acquittal may properly be regarded as an order "dismissing an indictment" within the meaning of the statute, see *United States v. Martin Linen Supply Co.*, 430 U.S. 564, 576 (STEVENS, J., concurring), the statutory grant of appellate jurisdiction is still unequivocally limited to review of a dismissal "as to any one or more counts." The statute does not refer to "subunit[s] of an indictment" or "portion[s] of a count," *ante*, at 69 n. 23, but only to "counts," a well-known and unambiguous term of art.

Prior to the amendment of 3731 in 1971, this Court's rule of statutory interpretation was that "the Criminal Appeals Act [should be] strictly construed against the Government's right of appeal, *Carroll v. United States*, 354 U.S. 394, 399–400 (1957)." *Will v. United States*, 389 U.S. 90, 96–97. The Court's present pattern of interpretation of 3731, as exemplified by *Martin Linen*, *supra*, does more than simply abandon this approach; it reverses direction entirely and reads the statute in whatever manner would favor a Government appeal. It is, of course, true that the legislative history of the Act indicates that Congress intended 3731 "to be liberally construed," S. Rep. No. 91-1296, p. 18 (1970), but this expression of legislative intent does not give us a license to ignore the words of the statute. In fact, the Court does not even suggest that the language "one or more counts" is ambiguous; instead it argues that the words cannot be given their proper meaning because the Act was intended "to eliminate '[t]echnical distinctions in pleadings . . .'" *Ante*, at 69 n. 23. This argument has a hollow ring in light of the Court's prior assertion that "[t]he precise manner in which an indictment is drawn cannot be ignored, because an important function of the indictment is to ensure that, 'in case any other proceedings are taken against [the defendant] for a similar offense, . . . the record [will] show with accuracy to what extent he may plead a former acquittal or conviction.'" *Ante*, at 65–66. Furthermore, in my judgment, a rule that the Government may appeal from the "dismissal" of a portion of a count, provided that the portion establishes a "discrete basis of liability," fosters rather than eliminates technical distinctions and encourages exactly the sort of nearsighted parsing of indictments that the amendment was intended to discourage.

I cannot, therefore, join that portion of the Court's decision which states that the Criminal Appeals Act permits an appeal from only a portion of a count. It clearly does not, and for that reason, as well as for the reasons stated in the text of the Court's opinion, the Court of Appeals' decision must be reversed.

MR. JUSTICE BLACKMUN, with whom MR. JUSTICE REHNQUIST joins, dissenting.

This case, of course, is an odd and an unusual one, factually and procedurally. Because it is, the case will afford little guidance as precedent in the Court's continuing struggle to create order and understanding out of the confusion of the lengthening list of its decisions on the Double Jeopardy Clause. I would have thought, however, that the principles enunciated late last Term in *Lee v. United States*, 432 U.S. 23 (1977)—which I deem a more difficult case for the Government than this one—had application to the facts here. I do not share the Court's distinction of *Lee*, *ante*, at 75, and I do not agree that Lee is "manifestly inapposite." Here, as in *Lee*, there is misdescription by the trial court of the nature of its order, and, as in *Lee*, the defendant–petitioner's maneuvers should result in a surrender of his right to receive a verdict by the jury that had been drawn. Further, it appears to me that petitioner has succeeded in having the indictment read one way in the trial court, and another way here, as the situation required.

I would affirm the judgment of the Court of Appeals.

(Continues)

Smalis v. Pennsylvania, 476 U.S. 140 (1986)

Petitioners, husband and wife, who owned a building housing a restaurant and apartments, were charged with various crimes in connection with a fire in the building that resulted in the killing of two tenants. At the close of the prosecution's case in chief at their bench trial in a Pennsylvania state court, petitioners challenged the sufficiency of the evidence by filling a demurrer pursuant to a Pennsylvania Rule of Criminal Procedure. The trial court sustained the demurrer, and the Pennsylvania Superior Court quashed the Commonwealth's appeal on the ground that it was barred by the Double Jeopardy Clause. The Pennsylvania Supreme Court reversed, holding that the granting of a demurrer is not the functional equivalent of an acquittal and that, for purposes of considering a plea of double jeopardy, a defendant who demurs at the close of the prosecution's case in chief "elects to seek dismissal on grounds unrelated to his factual guilt or innocence."

Held:

The trial judge's granting of petitioners' demurrer was an acquittal under the Double Jeopardy Clause, and the Commonwealth's appeal was barred because reversal would have led to further trial proceedings. Whether the trial is to a jury or, as here, to the bench, subjecting the defendant to postacquittal factfinding proceedings going to guilt or innocence violates the Double Jeopardy Clause. Pp. 144–146.

507 Pa. 344, 490 A. 2d 394, reversed.

WHITE, J., delivered the opinion for a unanimous Court.

Norma Chase argued the cause for petitioners. With her on the briefs was Thomas A. Livingston.

Robert L. Eberhardt argued the cause and filed a brief for respondent.

Deputy Solicitor General Frey argued the cause for the United States as *amicus curiae* urging affirmance. With him on the brief was Solicitor General Fried, Assistant Attorney General Trott, and Alan I. Horowitz.*

JUSTICE WHITE delivered the opinion of the Court.

At the close of the prosecution's case in chief, the trial court dismissed certain charges against petitioners on the ground that the evidence presented was legally insufficient to support a conviction. The question presented is whether the Double Jeopardy Clause bars the prosecution from appealing this ruling.

I

Petitioners, husband and wife, owned a building housing a restaurant and some apartments that burned under suspicious circumstances, killing two of the tenants. Petitioners were charged with various crimes in connection with this fire, including criminal homicide, reckless endangerment, and causing a catastrophe.[59] They opted for a bench trial, and at the close of the prosecution's case in chief challenged the sufficiency of the evidence by filing a demurrer pursuant to Pennsylvania Rule of Criminal Procedure 1124(a)(1).[60] The trial court sustained petitioners' demurrer to charges of murder, voluntary manslaughter, and causing a catastrophe, stating:

> "As the trier of fact and law, the court was not satisfied, after considering all of the facts together with all reasonable inferences which the Commonwealth's evidence tended to prove, that there was sufficient evidence from which it could be concluded that either of the defendants was guilty beyond a reasonable doubt of setting or causing to be set the fire in question." App. to Pet. for Cert. 101a–102a.

The Commonwealth sought review of this ruling in the Superior Court of Pennsylvania, but a panel of that court quashed the appeal, holding it barred by the Double Jeopardy Clause. The Superior Court granted review *en banc* and affirmed. 331 Pa. Super. 307, 480 A. 2d 1046 (1984). Citing a number of our decisions as controlling authority, the court set out two relevant principles of law. First, a judgment that the evidence is legally insufficient to sustain a guilty verdict constitutes an acquittal for purposes of the Double Jeopardy Clause. See, e.g., *United States v. Martin Linen Supply Co.*, 430 U.S. 564 (1977); *Burks v. United States*, 437 U.S. 1 (1978); *Sanabria v. United States*, 437 U.S. 54 (1978); *United States v. Scott*, 437 U.S. 82, 91 (1978) (*dicta*); *Hudson v. Louisiana*, 450 U.S. 40 (1981). Second, when a trial court enters such a judgment, the Double Jeopardy Clause bars an appeal by the prosecution not only when it might result in a second trial, but also if reversal would translate into further proceedings devoted to the resolution of factual issues going to the elements of the offense charged. The Superior Court concluded

---

*Charles S. Sims filed a brief for the American Civil Liberties Union et al. as *amici curiae* urging reversal.

that because reversal of the trial court's granting of petitioners' demurrer would necessitate further trial proceedings, the Commonwealth's appeal was improper under *Martin Linen*.

The Commonwealth appealed to the Supreme Court of Pennsylvania, which reversed. *Commonwealth v. Zoller*, 507 Pa. 344, 490 A. 2d 394 (1985).[61] The court relied heavily on the statement in *United States v. Scott, supra*, that a trial judge's ruling in a defendant's favor constitutes an acquittal "only when 'the ruling of the judge, whatever its label, actually represents a resolution [in the defendant's favor], correct or not, of some or all of the factual elements of the offense charged.'" *Id.*, at 97 (quoting *Martin Linen, supra*, at 571). The court gave the following explanation of why the trial court's ruling on petitioners' demurrer is not within this definition of an acquittal:

> "In deciding whether to grant a demurrer, the court does not determine whether or not the defendant is guilty on such evidence, but determines whether the evidence, if credited by the jury, is legally sufficient to warrant the conclusion that the defendant is guilty beyond a reasonable doubt. . . .
>
> "Hence, by definition, a demurrer is not a factual determination. . . . [T]he question before the trial judge in ruling on a demurrer remains purely one of law.
>
> "We conclude, therefore, that a demurrer is not the functional equivalent of an acquittal, and that the Commonwealth has the right to appeal from an order sustaining defendant's demurrer to its case-in-chief. In such a situation, the defendant himself elects to seek dismissal on grounds unrelated to his factual guilt or innocence." *Commonwealth v. Zoller, supra*, at 357–358, 490 A. 2d, at 401.

Accordingly, the Pennsylvania Supreme Court remanded the case to the Superior Court for a determination on the merits of the appeal. We granted *certiorari*, 474 U.S. 944 (1985), and now reverse.[62]

II

The Pennsylvania Supreme Court erred in holding that, for purposes of considering a plea of double jeopardy, a defendant who demurs at the close of the prosecution's case in chief "elects to seek dismissal on grounds unrelated to his factual guilt or innocence." *Commonwealth v. Zoller, supra*, at 358, 490 A. 2d, at 401. What the demurring defendant seeks is a ruling that as a matter of law the State's evidence is insufficient to establish his factual guilt.[63] Our past decisions, which we are not inclined to reconsider at this time, hold that such a ruling is an acquittal under the Double Jeopardy Clause. See, e.g., *United States v. Martin Linen Supply Co., supra; Sanabria v. United States, supra*.[64] *United States v. Scott* does not overturn these precedents; indeed, it plainly indicates that the category of acquittals includes "judgment[s] . . . by the court that the evidence is insufficient to convict." 437 U.S., at 91.[65]

The Commonwealth argues that its appeal is nonetheless permissible under *Justices of Boston Municipal Court v. Lydon*, 466 U.S. 294 (1984), because resumption of petitioners' bench trial following a reversal on appeal would simply constitute "continuing jeopardy." Brief for Respondent 87–88. But *Lydon* teaches that "[a]cquittals, unlike convictions, terminate the initial jeopardy." 466 U.S., at 308. Thus, whether the trial is to a jury or to the bench, subjecting the defendant to postacquittal factfinding proceedings going to guilt or innocence violates the Double Jeopardy Clause. *Arizona v. Rumsey*, 467 U.S. 203, 211–212 (1984).[66]

When a successful postacquittal appeal by the prosecution would lead to proceedings that violate the Double Jeopardy Clause, the appeal itself has no proper purpose. Allowing such an appeal would frustrate the interest of the accused in having an end to the proceedings against him. The Superior Court was correct, therefore, in holding that the Double Jeopardy Clause bars a postacquittal appeal by the prosecution not only when it might result in a second trial, but also if reversal would translate into "'further proceedings of some sort, devoted to the resolution of factual issues going to the elements of the offense charged.'" *Martin Linen*, 430 U.S., at 570.[67]

We hold, therefore, that the trial judge's granting of petitioners' demurrer was an acquittal under the Double Jeopardy Clause, and that the Commonwealth's appeal was barred because reversal would have led to further trial proceedings.

The judgment of the Pennsylvania Supreme Court is
Reversed.

Notes

59. Various misdemeanor charges were also filed against petitioners, as well as charges relating to a previous fire in another building that they owned. These other charges are not relevant to this petition.

(Continues)

(*Continued*)

60. Pennsylvania Rule of Criminal Procedure 1124, 42 Pa. Cons. Stat. (1985 Pamphlet), provides in relevant part:

"Challenges to Sufficiency of Evidence

"(a) A defendant may challenge the sufficiency of the evidence to sustain a conviction of one or more of the offenses charged by a:
"(1) demurrer to the evidence presented by the Commonwealth at the close of the Commonwealth's case-in-chief;

. . . . .

"(b) A demurrer to the evidence shall not constitute an admission of any facts or inferences except for the purpose of deciding the demurrer. If the demurrer is not sustained, the defendant may present evidence and the case shall proceed."

61. Before the Pennsylvania Supreme Court, petitioners' case was consolidated with another case presenting the same double jeopardy issue, *Commonwealth v. Zoller*, 318 Pa. Super. 402, 465 A. 2d 16 (1983).

62. For purposes of our jurisdiction, the judgment of the Pennsylvania Supreme Court was final and subject to review at this time under 28 U.S.C. 1257(3). *Harris v. Washington*, 404 U.S. 55 (1971). As explained in *Abney v. United States*, 431 U.S. 651 (1977):

"[T]he guarantee against double jeopardy assures an individual that, among other things, he will not be forced, with certain exceptions, to endure the personal strain, public embarrassment, and expense of a criminal trial more than once for the same offense . . .Obviously, these aspects of the guarantee's protections would be lost if the accused were forced to 'run the gauntlet' a second time before an appeal could be taken; even if the accused is acquitted, or, if convicted, has his conviction ultimately reversed on double jeopardy grounds, he has still been forced to endure a trial that the Double Jeopardy Clause was designed to prohibit." *Id.*, at 661–662 (footnote omitted).

63. We of course accept the Pennsylvania Supreme Court's definition of what the trial judge must consider in ruling on a defendant's demurrer. But just as "the trial judge's characterization of his own action cannot control the classification of the action [under the Double Jeopardy Clause]," *United States v. Scott*, 437 U.S. 82, 96 (1978) (citation omitted), so too the Pennsylvania Supreme Court's characterization, as a matter of double jeopardy law, of an order granting a demurrer is not binding on us.

64. See also *Burks v. United States*, 437 U.S. 1 (1978), where a Court of Appeals' reversal of the defendant's conviction on the ground that the evidence was insufficient to sustain the jury verdict "unquestionably . . . 'represente[d] a resolution, correct or not, of some or all of the factual elements of the offense charged.'" *Id.* at 10 (quoting *Martin Linen*, 430 U.S., at 571).

65. The status of the trial court's judgment as an acquittal is not affected by the Commonwealth's allegation that the court "erred in deciding what degree of recklessness was . . . required to be shown under Pennsylvania's definition of [third-degree] murder." Tr. of Oral Arg. 24. "[T]he fact that 'the acquittal may result from erroneous evidentiary rulings or erroneous interpretations of governing legal principles' . . . affects the accuracy of that determination but it does not alter its essential character." *United States v. Scott*, 437 U.S., at 98 (quoting *id.*, at 106 (BRENNAN, J., dissenting)). Accord, *Sanabria v. United States*, 437 U.S. 54 (1978); *Arizona v. Rumsey*, 467 U.S. 203 (1984).

66. In Rumsey, a trial judge sitting as a sentencer in a death-penalty proceeding entered an "acquittal," i.e., a life sentence, based on an erroneous construction of the law governing a particular aggravating circumstance. The Court held that the Double Jeopardy Clause barred a second sentencing hearing. It distinguished *United States v. Wilson*, 420 U.S. 332 (1975), which holds that the prosecution may appeal when the trial court enters judgment n.o.v. following a jury verdict of guilty. Rumsey explains that "[n]o double jeopardy problem was presented in Wilson because the appellate court, upon reviewing asserted legal errors of the trial judge, could simply order the jury's guilty verdict reinstated; no new factfinding would be necessary, and the defendant therefore would not be twice placed in jeopardy." 467 U.S., at 211–212.

67. The fact that the "further proceedings" standard which the Superior Court quoted from *Martin Linen* was first articulated in *United States v. Jenkins*, 420 U.S. 358, 370 (1975), does not detract from its authority. *United States v. Scott, supra*, overrules Jenkins only insofar as Jenkins bars an appeal by the government when a defendant successfully moves for dismissal on a ground "unrelated to factual guilt or innocence. . . ." *Scott, supra*, at 99. The issue before us in Scott was what constitutes an acquittal under the Double Jeopardy Clause; the question of the circumstances under which an acquittal is appealable was not presented.

Property Rights and Eminent Domain

Chapter Objectives

In this chapter you will learn . . .

- Why the government has the right to take over people's homes
- How the Supreme Court has interpreted "public use"
- How the Supreme Court has interpreted "just compensation"
- President Bush's Executive Order regarding private property rights
- The history of big versus small government in the United States

Introduction

We have all heard the famous adage, "a man's home is his castle." Is there anything wrong with it? An obvious answer might be, what about women? They are homeowners, too. In this case, if we also add, "a woman's home is her castle," or if we simply say, "persons' homes are their castles," is there anything wrong with that sentence now?

Let us focus on the word "castle." It implies that the homeowner is like a king or queen. The owner fully and absolutely owns the home and no one has a right to take it away. When describing America's virtues, people often will describe how the government cannot take over another person's house. But actually that is not entirely true. Under certain circumstances, the government has a right to take over our homes—and the Constitution says so!

In this chapter, we will discuss how and why.

Eminent Domain

The term "eminent domain" is not a particularly common one as compared to other Constitutional issues such as "freedom of speech," "equal protection," and "cruel and unusual punishment." One reason for it being comparatively uncommon is because the words "eminent domain" are not actually found in the Constitution. Another reason is that eminent domain affects a rather small percentage of the overall population.

Eminent domain is when the government takes private property for public use. In other words, there are circumstances under which the government has the right to take

a person's home or business, for the good of the public. Many people do not even know that this is possible, or even legal. Consider the following example, to illustrate.

Suppose that you live on the outskirts of a mountain, in a town with a population of about 50,000 residents. There is a much larger city on the other side of the mountain, in which you and most of your neighbors work. Job opportunities are much better in the city than in the town where you live, and the salaries are much higher. The only drawback is that you have to drive 80 miles to get to work every day. That takes you well over an hour, and you spend a lot of money filling your gas tank, not to mention the wear and tear on your car driving to and from work each day.

In an effort to improve the commute for both you and your neighbors, the government has decided to build a new highway that would cut your commuting time and expenses by more than half. The new highway will be a shortcut and will provide multiple lanes, allowing you to breeze to work in about 20 minutes. That will save you time, money, and the aggravation of sitting in traffic. In order to build the road, however, the government has to tear down a house that is in the path of where the new highway will be constructed. The house is owned by Sam, who is furious that the government has the right to take him out and claim it as its own!

Fifth Amendment Protection

Fortunately for Sam, the government does not have the right to take away his property without being compensated fairly. The Fifth Amendment clearly states: ". . . nor shall private property be taken for public use, without just compensation." Therefore, if Sam's house is worth, say $150,000, and the government pays him $200,000 for it, Sam might consider the deal quite fair. If he is able to buy a similar house for $150,000 on another street, he will have made a $50,000 profit.

In that case, Sam might be very pleased with the arrangement, and you and your neighbors certainly will be, because your commute to and from work will be much easier. Of course, the $200,000 is taxpayer money, but if the rest of your neighbors are willing to share the bill (which only averages to four dollars a person, considering there are 50,000 people living in your town), they will have paid a very small price for a much easier commute. It seems like a good situation for everyone concerned.

What if, however, Sam was attached to his house because it was in his family for 100 years, and he does not want to sell it? He and his siblings all grew up in that house, he inherited it from his parents, and his wife and children have lived there for many years. There is a lot of history in that house for Sam, a lot of emotion. The house evokes priceless memories for Sam that are worth far more than a $50,000 profit to him. Accordingly, Sam insists that the government either pay him one million dollars for the house, or leave him alone.

As the government struggles to obtain the property from Sam, you and your neighbors consider him to be the villain. Because he is holding up progress, the highway cannot be built, and you all have to suffer with the long and tiring commute to work every day. Can Sam ask for whatever price he wants or can the government require Sam to accept whatever price they give him?

Just Compensation

What if the government only gave Sam $160,000? That would be $150,000 for fair market value of the house, and an extra $10,000 for moving expenses. In that case, Sam would think that for all the time and trouble of moving out of his beloved house he would barely break even.

The question of "just compensation" ("just" meaning "fair"), is one that is arguable. What Sam might consider just, the government might consider extravagant. What the government might consider just, Sam might consider insufficient. That might lead to a lawsuit and delay the construction of the highway for months, even years.

Public Use

The next question to consider is: what constitutes "public use?" A highway would be a classic example of public use, but what about a shopping mall owned by a private developer?

Suppose that Chester is a wealthy land developer who wants to open a new shopping mall in your neighborhood. The government thinks that it is a great idea because it will revitalize your town's economy. It will create new jobs, and everyone in town can save money by shopping at the new mall instead of the next-closest mall, which is 100 miles away. The only catch is that Sam's house is in the way. Does the government have the right to take Sam's house? It all depends on whether they offer him "just compensation," and whether the shopping mall is considered "public use."

As with all of the other Constitutional issues that we have examined to this point, the United States Supreme Court has issued rulings on eminent domain as well. Let's take a look at a few cases, which will help us to understand this important topic more clearly.

Case Law

Although eminent domain has gained more attention over the past few years, the Supreme Court has ruled on the issue long before that. One such case, *Barron v. City of Baltimore*, is particularly important for two reasons: first, it was decided in 1833, which demonstrates that the

manifest destiny controversy traces far back into American history. Second, it set a precedent that the Court would follow for many years to come, until it finally reversed itself: that the Bill of Rights does not apply to state laws.

In that case, Barron's property was damaged as a result of construction that the city of Baltimore was doing. Barron sued the city for damages, claiming that the damage they did constituted a "taking," and that pursuant to the Fifth Amendment, he was entitled to "just compensation." The Court rejected Barron's argument, declaring that the Fifth Amendment right did not apply to state governments. In other words, had the construction been done by the federal government, then the Fifth Amendment would apply and Barron would be entitled to just compensation. Because the construction was done by the Baltimore government, which is part of the state of Maryland, the Fifth Amendment would not apply.

The *Barron* holding was significant because it reached far beyond establishing a precedent for eminent domain. It declared the Bill of Rights inapplicable to state laws. Based on that rationale, one could argue that freedom of speech, of the press, and of religion—all guaranteed by the First Amendment—would not apply to state laws. That type of reasoning reminds us of the Founders' concern about a tyrannical federal government. As long as they had protection from the national government, they were not overly concerned about the states. Nowadays, however, when we are all far removed from the dictatorial rulings of King George III, we might be cautious about state governments that are not required to follow the federal Bill of Rights.

Once the Fourteenth Amendment was ratified in 1868, the Court began to apply the Bill of Rights to state laws as well. Effectively, the rationale in *Barron* was overturned. The case that overruled *Barron*, specifically pertaining to eminent domain, was *Chicago B. & Q. Railroad Company v. Chicago*, decided in 1897. In that case, the Chicago City Council passed an ordinance that would widen two streets within the city, which included some land owned by the railroad company. As compensation, they offered to pay the railroad company one dollar. The Supreme Court determined that the Fourteenth Amendment ensured that the property rights secured by the Fifth Amendment applied to state laws as well. Moreover, the Court held that state laws would include any ordinances or regulations passed by a local government within a state. Therefore, the City Council of Chicago, as much as the State Government of Illinois, was bound by the Fourteenth Amendment.

Another case involving eminent domain, also over 100 years old, is *Clark v. Nash*, which was decided in 1905. In that case, Clark and Nash were neighboring farmers in Utah. Under eminent domain, the government compelled Nash to give up a portion of his property for a ditch that Clark would use to provide water for his own land. Nash objected, questioning how the land, which would be used by Clark exclusively, amounted to "public use."

The Supreme Court ruled in Clark's favor, though it limited its decision to the specific circumstances at hand. The Court maintained that opportunities to obtain water in a dry, Western state such as Utah were far more scarce than say, on the East Coast. Accordingly, if Clark could not irrigate his property, the land would be virtually useless. Because it was not a matter of maximizing land value, but rather a case of saving the land or rendering it obsolete for farming purposes, the Court reasoned that eminent domain did apply, and that it was for the "public good," even though the "public" was a private beneficiary.

The *Nash* decision hardly rendered the issue of eminent domain well-settled, because the Court acknowledged that future decisions would be made on a case-by-case basis, and that its holding was not designed to encourage the government to seize private land for whatever purpose it saw fit.

A somewhat more modern case, albeit over 50 years old, that involved eminent domain is *Berman v. Parker*, which was decided in 1954. In *Berman*, the issue was whether the plaintiff's department store, which was in a severely deteriorated neighborhood but not itself in poor condition, could be subjected to the District of Columbia's development plan to improve the neighborhood.

In a unanimous decision, the Court ruled in favor of the compulsory development. Even though the department store itself was not beyond repair, several other structures in the vicinity were in such poor condition, that if the department store were allowed to stand, it would impede the entire development project. Essentially, *Berman* was an example of how justice does not always provide a perfect solution, and it often has to decide to allow the least amount of harm for the benefit of the greatest amount of good. Specifically, the department store wanted to stay in business. Why should a structure that is in perfectly good shape have to be torn down, just because the government says so? Because, when weighed against the salvaging of an entire community, the community's interest overrides the individuals, said the Court.

Thirty years later, the Court handed down another interesting and rather bold decision. In *Hawaii Housing Authority v. Midkiff*. In *Midkiff*, the Hawaiian government was concerned that a mere 72 people owned 47% of Hawaii's land. The government believed that for virtually half of an entire state to be owned by so few was contrary to Hawaii's history, and not in the Hawaiian people's best interests. As the Court did in *Berman*, it ruled unanimously in *Midkiff*, extending the *Berman* holding in terms of what the government can do to improve its citizens' quality of life. The Court concluded that eminent domain did not mean that the land would have to be used by the public at large. That it would become available for the public to purchase it and then use it privately would suffice.

Actually, the Court's rationale was not much different from ensuring that companies do not have a monopoly on a particular product. For instance, if one company owned all of the corn produced in the United States, the Court would strike that down as an unlawful monopoly. Granted, the United States is a capitalist system, where individuals and companies are permitted to grow as big and as wealthy as they can. If such growth and wealth prevents competition, however, then the government may step in and impose limitations on it. Similarly, because the proportion of landowners in Hawaii to the state's overall population was extremely small, the Court believed that legal intervention was necessary to correct it.

The *Kelo* Controversy

The most significant Supreme Court case about eminent domain, and as of 2005, the year of its decision, the most controversial, is *Kelo v. City of New London*. *Kelo* sparked a tirade of protests from conservatives and libertarians alike, who were outraged that the Court had supported a new level of government interventionism.

Kelo and her neighbors owned homes in the city of New London, Connecticut. For years, New London had been considered a "distressed municipality" because of its weak economy. In an effort to revitalize the city's economic troubles, the New London Development Corporation, a private entity, planned to create a sizeable commercial complex along the city's waterfront, including shops, restaurants, and a $300 million research facility for Pfizer, the pharmaceutical conglomerate. The government wanted to include Kelo's and her neighbors' properties as part of the complex, but the landowners objected.

As we have done before, we will analyze the various opinions rendered in this decision, as it is a very recent one, and most of the Justices still sit on the High Court.

Stevens' Majority

The majority opinion, written by Justice Stevens, favored New London. Justices Kennedy, Souter, Ginsburg, and Breyer, along with Stevens, formed a five-Justice majority, and held that when the government wants to take land for public use and public good, the land itself does not have to be public. Specifically, the Court reasoned that the complex would create new jobs and rejuvenate the troubled city, which would be a benefit to the public at large. That the New London Development Corporation was a private entity did not bar the City of New London from exercising eminent domain, in the Court's view.

Kennedy's Concurrence

Justice Kennedy, who sided with the majority, wrote a separate concurring opinion, emphasizing that transfers of property that primarily benefit private individuals or corporations, with only a minimal benefit to the public, do not fall under the eminent domain purview. As Kennedy did not believe such was the case in New London, he did not reject that city's right to transfer the property from Kelo and her neighbors to the developers.

O'Connor's Dissent

In a strongly worded dissent, Justice O'Connor, joined by Chief Justice Rehnquist, Justice Scalia, and Justice Thomas, warned that as a result of the Court's decision, all private property was now vulnerable. As long as there was a promise to upgrade the property, the dissenting Justices wrote, there would be no stopping the government from exercising eminent domain, even if the transferee were a private entity.

O'Connor elaborated on the dissenting Justices reasoning, explaining that it might have been a different matter if Kelo and her neighbors had not kept their homes in good condition. If the homes had been badly deteriorated, as had been the case in *Berman*, then there might have been more of a dire need for government interference for the community's behalf as a whole. There was no evidence, however, that any of the homes that were being subjected to eminent domain were in deteriorating or otherwise subpar condition. O'Connor likened this taking to a plan to maximize productivity, which she found to be clearly unconstitutional.

Kelo's Effect

Essentially, the *Kelo* Court raises a series of new questions. For example, what would happen if Bob owned a coffee shop that was not doing particularly well, but he managed to keep it running, and the government forced him to sell them his property so that they could allow McDonald's to take over the property and put one of its restaurants there? Arguably, McDonald's has an impressive track record of profitability, but does that give the government the right to replace Bob's coffee shop with a McDonald's restaurant, just because the people of the town might enjoy a McDonald's restaurant instead?

Consider another possibility: you keep your house in relatively good shape, but a wealthy developer wants to tear down your house in order to build a more beautiful house on your property. Should the government be permitted to force you to give up your house because the neighborhood might look nicer with a different house on the block?

Granted, the *Kelo* Court never went so far as to insinuate that it would support either of these possibilities. However, its decision went far enough as to cause many to worry about such a possibility.

President Bush's Executive Order

In a response to the seemingly unlimited power of government regarding eminent domain that the *Kelo* Court guaranteed, President George W. Bush issued an executive order in June 2006, regarding property rights. President Bush reiterated the fundamentals of eminent domain: to protect private property by limiting eminent domain to public use and for the purpose of benefiting the general public, not advancing the economic interests of private individuals. The Order also referred to just compensation as a necessary condition.

Moreover, President Bush's Order cited some examples of public use, such as a medical facility, roadway, park, forest, government building, or military base. The Order also required that the use of the land is subject to government regulation.

It is important to note, however, that the Order specifically applied to the federal government. State governments would not be bound by it. As we discussed earlier in the chapter, the Supreme Court in *Barron* held that, pursuant to the Fourteenth Amendment, state and local governments may exercise their rights to eminent domain as well.

Accordingly, though President Bush's Executive Order somewhat curbed the federal government's eminent domain power, governments on the state and local levels, where much of the taking of private property takes place, were not affected.

Subsequent State Law

The *Kelo* decision generated outrage across the nation, prompting the Executive Order issued by President Bush

After the *Kelo* decision, President Bush issued an Executive Order protecting private property rights.

on the federal level and several state legislatures, in turn, passed their own restrictions to eminent domain.

Alabama, for example, retained an exception for deteriorated property, known as *blight*, but otherwise banned the use of eminent domain for commercial or residential development. Colorado prohibited eminent domain for the purposes of economic development or additional tax revenue but did not specifically contain a blight exception. Delaware permitted eminent domain for "recognized public use."

Florida's legislation is interesting in that it explicitly does not make a blight exemption, as was the case in *Barron*, but does support taking of property when it is necessary to further a public project, consistent with the reasoning in *Midkiff*.

Georgia, Indiana, and Wisconsin made blight exceptions, but defined blight as a condition detrimental to public health and safety. In other words, run-down buildings that might be an eyesore, but are not unsafe or a health hazard, do not fall within the exception.

Idaho and Illinois both emphasized that public use must be clearly demonstrated and not be a pretext for economic development.

Maine's law focuses on environmental preservation, and specifically prohibits land used for agriculture, fishing, or forestry to be transferred for commercial, industrial, or residential purposes.

Minnesota and West Virginia focus on ensuring the compensation paid to landowners is fair and requires good-faith negotiations as a condition. Utah requires extensive procedural notifications and independent approvals before eminent domain can be exercised.

How Much Government Intervention Is Acceptable?

At the onset of this chapter, we discussed how eminent domain is not exactly at the top of the list when one ponders Constitutional issues. Now that we have seen some examples of the controversy, however, it might become more apparent just how important a topic it is. Not only because of its own substance, but because it is an excellent example of the debate about what type of role the government should play in our society.

Big Versus Small Government

Since our nation's founding, there has always been a debate about what the role of government ought to be. The Federalists believed in a strong central government, whereas the anti-Federalists wanted the national government to be very limited. As we discussed earlier in the book, the Constitution was a compromise of both principles, and gave rise to our two-tier (federal and state) system of government.

Through the years, the debate continued over the type of role that government should play in our society. One of the most notable examples of big government was the New Deal legislation, advocated by President Franklin Roosevelt. Roosevelt was elected in 1932, and promised to lift the United States out of the Great Depression. Roosevelt's plan was to create government programs that would put people back to work again. The plan took much longer to materialize than expected, and it was not until the United States entered World War II that the economy bounced back in full force. Nonetheless, Roosevelt's New Deal helped restore the American people's confidence in their government, and confidence is an essential element to economic recovery.

By the 1960s, President Lyndon Johnson envisioned a country without poverty, with affordable housing and a good education for everyone. Johnson planned to structure this Great Society by using the federal government as the architect of the plan. After more than a decade of the Great Society, which was essentially an outgrowth of the New Deal, it became clear that some of the problems that had been targeted, such as poverty and lack of education, had not been solved. Moreover, the 1970s brought an unwelcome combination of inflation and unemployment.

Accordingly, in 1980, the country elected Ronald Reagan as president largely on his promise to restore America to its former greatness. Reagan wanted to solve the nation's problems just as much as Roosevelt and Johnson did, but his approach was radically different. Reagan famously said that government is not the solution to the problem, government is the problem. Reagan cut taxes across the board, which helped to stimulate the economy, create jobs, and shift the source of prosperity from the government to the free market.

The 1980s, often referred to as the "Reagan Revolution," had changed the American people's thinking once again. Just as they had turned to government in the 1930s for answers, they turned away from government a half century later. Another of Reagan's famous quotes was that the nine most dangerous words in the English language are: "I'm from the government and I'm here to help." For a generation to follow, Americans turned their backs on government, no longer considering it a beneficial force in driving the country's engine.

After almost 30 years of post-New Deal, post-Great Society Reaganism, the United States faced more economic troubles at the end of 2008. As Americans began to panic with the collapse of industry after industry, they

President Franklin Roosevelt (top) believed in using the government to solve the nation's problems, whereas President Reagan (bottom) believed that the problem was too much government.

began to realize that problems are not always caused by too much government, they are sometimes caused by too little government as well.

Accordingly, Americans went to the polls in 2008 and unequivocally sent a message denouncing the *status quo*. They elected Barack Obama as president of the United States in a near-landslide, largely based on his promise to improve conditions *through* bigger government.

Bailouts

One of the centerpieces of Obama's first few months in office was his policy to use taxpayer money to bailout troubled companies. One industry that suffered a great deal during the economic downturn was the American auto industry. All three American automobile manufacturers, Chrysler, Ford, and General Motors, experienced dismal sales. Consumers began to sour on sport utility vehicles (SUVs). Perceived as shining examples of American luxury and power, SUVs were now considered extravagant gas-guzzlers.

Rather than sit by while the entire American auto industry collapsed, which inevitably would impose a damaging rippling effect on the rest of the economy and vastly increase the ranks of the unemployed, President Obama vowed to lend the automakers enough money to rebound from their downfall. Most Americans begrudgingly stood by the decision. They were not happy that the government bailout would add billions to an already record-high national deficit, but they accepted that if nothing was done, things would be worse yet. Others condemned the act as an act of socialism. Why should General Motors get a bailout, they argued, while a corner grocery store did not?

The question remains: to what extent should government get involved in private lives in order to try to improve them? Are the government's bailout policies, like its eminent domain policies, overreaching social engineering, or beneficial steps toward improving the lives of the people as a whole?

Eminent domain is analogous to the government bailouts, because in both cases private citizens are often swept up, and many times against their will, in the government's grandiose improvement plans. Critics of government intervention either chastise the government for being corrupt, favoring those who make large contributions to political campaigns, or at least, criticize the government for being incompetent even if it is well-intentioned. On the other hand, those who support government intervention trust elected officials who are accountable to the people, far more so than they trust wealthy businesspersons who are often accountable to no one.

In any event, the question of eminent domain often boils down to political ideology: does the government know what is best for us, or not. Beyond that, it is an issue of Constitutional authority. What are the true definitions of the Fifth Amendment's "public use" and "just compensation" clauses? The answer may depend on which Supreme Court Justice you ask.

Conclusion

As has been the case with every other Constitutional topic that we have addressed thus far, eminent domain is another one that is not absolute. It is true that Americans are free to own property, thus giving rise to the term that a home is one's "castle." We also have learned, however, that such ownership is not absolute. Although the conditions are rather restrictive, the government nonetheless has the opportunity to take the people's property if it deems such taking as necessary for public use.

It is highly unlikely that the government, on a whim, would decide that it would like to create a new office building for its employees, with a waterfront view and thereby force residents who own homes along the waterfront to evacuate their properties. On the other hand, suppose that the government discovered a particular area of the U.S. border, whether adjacent to Canada or Mexico, or

to both, from which a large number of illegal aliens would enter our country. If the government compelled homeowners in that area to evacuate, so that the government could tear down their homes and erect a protective fence there, then that would probably be a permissible public use.

The sizeable gray area in between will most likely continued to be determined by the three branches of government, most notably, by the Supreme Court, which has expanded the government's eminent domain powers as of late. Perhaps the executive and legislative branches will continue to respond to the Court's rulings, as they did following the *Kelo* decision. In any event, although it is unlikely that the majority of Americans will ever be affected by eminent domain personally, students of the Constitution may continue to rely on the topic as one firmly in line with the continuing debate about the government's role in American society.

In Chapter 12, we will examine a Constitutional issue that is as furiously debated as any: the right to bear arms.

Questions for Review

1. To what extent is the concept that a home is one's castle not entirely applicable to life in the United States?
2. Where in the Constitution is the government's right to take private property mentioned?
3. What does "just compensation" mean?
4. What did *Barron v. City of Baltimore* establish regarding state governments and eminent domain?
5. How did the Fourteenth Amendment change the type of reasoning found in *Barron v. City of Baltimore?*
6. Which Supreme Court case overturned *Barron v. City of Baltimore?*
7. How did the Court in *Berman v. Parker* rule regarding blighted property?
8. How did the Court's holding in *Hawaii Housing Authority v. Midkiff* expand the *Berman v. Parker* holding?
9. What did the Supreme Court decide in *Kelo v. City of New London*, and why was the decision so controversial?
10. How did President Bush's Executive Order protect private property owners from the *Kelo* decision?

Constitutionally Speaking

Suppose that federal government wanted to build a maximum security military prison complex in order to detain terrorists, and the plan was to build it in your neighborhood. You and eight other of your friends and neighbors were required to turn over your homes to the government for fair market value. Would you comply or would you demand that the government look elsewhere to build its facility? If the case went to court, what do you think the outcome would be, and why?

Constitutional Cases

Ruckelshaus v. Monsanto is a case that we did not discuss in the body of the chapter, but it provides interesting information about a less traditional type of "taking." Also, *Kelo v. City of New London* appears in its entirety. As it is currently in the forefront of the eminent domain debate, it is worth reading word-for-word.

Ruckelshaus v. Monsanto Co., 467 U.S. 986 (1984)

The Federal Insecticide, Fungicide, and Rodenticide Act (FIFRA) authorizes the Environmental Protection Agency (EPA) to use data submitted by an applicant for registration of a covered product (hereinafter pesticide) in evaluating the application of a subsequent applicant, and to disclose publicly some of the submitted data. Under the data-consideration provisions of 3, as amended in 1978, applicants now are granted a 10-year period of exclusive use for data on new active ingredients contained in pesticides registered after September 30, 1978, while all other data submitted after December 31, 1969, may be cited and considered in support of another application for 15 years after the original submission if the applicant offers to compensate the original submitter. If the parties cannot agree on the amount of compensation, either may initiate a binding arbitration proceeding, and if an original submitter refuses to participate in negotiations or arbitration, he forfeits his claim for compensation. Data that do not qualify for either the 10-year period of exclusive use or the 15-year period of compensation may be considered by EPA without limitation. Section 10, as amended in 1978, authorizes, in general, public disclosure of all health, safety, and environmental data even though it may result in disclosure of trade secrets. Appellee, a company headquartered in Missouri, is an inventor, producer, and seller of pesticides, and invests substantial sums in developing active ingredients for pesticides and in producing end-use products that combine such ingredients with inert ingredients. Appellee brought suit in Federal District Court for injunctive and declaratory relief, alleging, *inter alia*, that the data-consideration and data-disclosure provisions of FIFRA effected a "taking" of property without just compensation, in violation of the Fifth Amendment, and that the data-consideration provisions violated the Amendment because they effected a taking of property for a private, rather than a public, purpose. The District Court held that the challenged provisions of FIFRA are unconstitutional, and permanently enjoined EPA from implementing or enforcing those provisions.
Held:

1. To the extent that appellee has an interest in its health, safety, and environmental data cognizable as a trade-secret property right under Missouri law, that property right is protected by the Taking Clause of the Fifth Amendment. Despite their intangible nature, trade secrets have many of the characteristics of more traditional forms of property. Moreover, this Court has found other kinds of intangible interests to be property for purposes of the Clause. Pp. 1000–1004.

2. EPA's consideration or disclosure of data submitted by appellee prior to October 22, 1972, or after September 30, 1978, does not effect a taking, but EPA's consideration or disclosure of certain health, safety, and environmental data constituting a trade secret under state law and submitted by appellee between those two dates may constitute a taking under certain conditions. Pp. 1004–1014.

   (a) A factor for consideration in determining whether a governmental action short of acquisition or destruction of property has gone beyond proper "regulation" and effects a "taking" is whether the action interferes with reasonable investment-backed expectations. With respect to any health, safety, and environmental data that appellee submitted to EPA after the effective date of the 1978 FIFRA amendments (October 1, 1978), appellee could not have had a reasonable, investment-backed expectation that EPA would keep the data confidential beyond the limits prescribed in the amended statute itself. As long as appellee is aware of the conditions under which the data are submitted, and the conditions are rationally related to a legitimate Government interest, a voluntary submission of data in exchange for the economic advantages of a registration can hardly be called a taking. Pp. 1005–1008.

   (b) Prior to its amendment in 1972 (effective October 22, 1972), FIFRA was silent with respect to EPA's authorized use and disclosure of data submitted to it in connection with an application for registration. Although the Trade Secrets Act provides a criminal penalty for a Government employee who discloses, in a manner not authorized by law, any trade-secret information revealed to him during the course of his official duties, it is not a guarantee of confidentiality to submitters of data, and, absent an express promise, appellee had no reasonable, investment-backed expectation that its information submitted to EPA before October 22, 1972, would remain inviolate in the EPA's hands. The possibility was substantial that the Federal Government at some future time would find disclosure to be in the public interest. A fortiori, the Trade Secrets Act, which penalizes only unauthorized disclosure, cannot be construed as any sort of assurance against internal agency use of submitted data during consideration of the application of a subsequent applicant for registration. Pp. 1008–1010.

(*Continues*)

(*Continued*)

(c) However, under the statutory scheme in effect between October 22, 1972, and September 30, 1978, a submitter was given an opportunity to protect its trade secrets from disclosure by designating them as trade secrets at the time of submission. The explicit governmental guarantee to registration applicants of confidentiality and exclusive use with respect to trade secrets during this period formed the basis of a reasonable investment-backed expectation. If EPA, consistent with current provisions of FIFRA, were now to disclose such trade-secret data or consider those data in evaluating the application of a subsequent applicant in a manner not authorized by the version of FIFRA in effect between 1972 and 1978, its actions would frustrate appellee's reasonable investment-backed expectation. If, however, arbitration pursuant to FIFRA were to yield just compensation for the loss in the market value of appellee's trade-secret data suffered because of EPA's consideration of the data in connection with another application (no arbitration having yet occurred), then appellee would have no claim against the Government for a taking. Pp. 1010–1014.

3. Any taking of private property that may occur in connection with EPA's use of data submitted to it by appellee between October 22, 1972, and September 30, 1978, is a taking for a "public use," rather than for a "private use," even though subsequent applicants may be the most direct beneficiaries. So long as a taking has a conceivable public character, the means by which it will be attained is for Congress to determine. Congress believed that the data-consideration provisions would eliminate costly duplication of research and streamline the registration process, making new end-use products available to consumers more quickly. Such a procompetitive purpose is within Congress' police power. With regard to FIFRA's data-disclosure provisions, the optimum amount of disclosure to assure the public that a product is safe and effective is to be determined by Congress, not the courts. Pp. 1014–1016.

4. A Tucker Act remedy is available to provide appellee with just compensation for any taking of property that may occur as a result of FIFRA's data-consideration and data-disclosure provisions, and thus the District Court erred in enjoining EPA from acting under those provisions. Neither FIFRA nor its legislative history discusses the interaction between FIFRA and the Tucker Act, and inferring a withdrawal of Tucker Act jurisdiction would amount to a disfavored partial repeal by implication of the Tucker Act. FIFRA's provision that an original submitter of data forfeits his right to compensation from a later submitter for the use of the original submitter's data if he fails to participate in, or comply with the terms of, a negotiated or arbitrated compensation settlement merely requires a claimant to first seek satisfaction through FIFRA's procedure before asserting a Tucker Act claim. Pp. 1016–1019.

5. Because the Tucker Act is available as a remedy for any uncompensated taking appellee may suffer as a result of the operation of the challenged provisions of FIFRA, appellee's challenges to the constitutionality of the arbitration and compensation scheme of FIFRA are not ripe for resolution. Pp. 1019–1020.

564 F. Supp. 552, vacated and remanded.

BLACKMUN, J., delivered the opinion of the Court, in which BURGER, C. J., and BRENNAN, MARSHALL, POWELL, REHNQUIST, and STEVENS, JJ., joined, and in which O'CONNOR, J., joined, except for Part IV-B and a statement on p. 1013. O'CONNOR, J., filed an opinion concurring in part and dissenting in part, post, p. 1021. WHITE, J., took no part in the consideration or decision of the case.

Deputy Solicitor General Wallace argued the cause for appellant. With him on the briefs were Solicitor General Lee, Acting Assistant Attorney General Liotta, Deputy Assistant Attorney General Walker, Jerrold J. Ganzfried, Raymond N. Zagone, Anne S. Almy, and John A. Bryson.

A. Raymond Randolph, Jr., argued the cause for appellee. With him on the briefs were David G. Norrell, Thomas O. Kuhns, W. Wayne Withers, Frederick A. Provorny, Gary S. Dyer, C. David Barrier, and Kenneth R. Heineman.*

---

* Briefs of *amici curiae* urging reversal were filed for the American Association for the Advancement of Science et al. by Thomas O. McGarity; for the American Federation of Labor and Congress of Industrial Organizations et al. by Marsha S. Berzon, Michael Rubin, Laurence Gold, Albert H. Meyerhoff, and J. Albert Woll; for the Pesticide Producers Association et al. by David B. Weinberg and William R. Weissman; and for PPG Industries, Inc., by Thomas H. Truitt, David R. Berz, and Jeffrey F. Liss.

Briefs of *amici curiae* urging affirmance were filed for Abbott Laboratories et al. by Kenneth W. Weinstein and Lawrence S. Ebner; for the American Chemical Society et al. by William J. Butler, Jr., and Arthur D. McKey; for the American Patent Law Association, Inc., by Donald S. Chisum; for Avco Corp. by Alvin D. Shapiro; for Sathon, Inc., by Ralph E. Brown and Mark E. Singer; for SDS Biotech Corp. et al. by Harold Himmelman and Cynthia A. Lewis; and for Stauffer Chemical Co. by Lawrence S. Ebner, John T. Ronan III, and John W. Behan.

JUSTICE BLACKMUN delivered the opinion of the Court.

In this case, we are asked to review a United States District Court's determination that several provisions of the Federal Insecticide, Fungicide, and Rodenticide Act (FIFRA), 61 Stat. 163, as amended, 7 U.S.C. 136 et seq., are unconstitutional. The provisions at issue authorize the Environmental Protection Agency (EPA) to use data submitted by an applicant for registration of a pesticide[1] in evaluating the application of a subsequent applicant, and to disclose publicly some of the submitted data.

I

Over the past century, the use of pesticides to control weeds and minimize crop damage caused by insects, disease, and animals has become increasingly more important for American agriculture. See S. Rep. No. 95-334, p. 32 (1977); S. Rep. No. 92-838, pp. 3–4, 6–7 (1972); H. R. Rep. No. 92-511, pp. 3–7 (1971). While pesticide use has led to improvements in productivity, it has also led to increased risk of harm to humans and the environment. See S. Rep. No. 92-838, at 3–4, 6–7; H. R. Rep. No. 92-511, at 3–7. Although the Federal Government has regulated pesticide use for nearly 75 years,[2] FIFRA was first adopted in 1947. 61 Stat. 163.

As first enacted, FIFRA was primarily a licensing and labeling statute. It required that all pesticides be registered with the Secretary of Agriculture prior to their sale in interstate or foreign commerce. 3(a) and 4(a) of the 1947 Act, 61 Stat. 166–167. The 1947 legislation also contained general standards setting forth the types of information necessary for proper labeling of a registered pesticide, including directions for use; warnings to prevent harm to people, animals, and plants; and claims made about the efficacy of the product. 2(u)(2) and 3(a)(3).

Upon request of the Secretary, an applicant was required to submit test data supporting the claims on the label, including the formula for the pesticide. 4(a) and (b). The 1947 version of FIFRA specifically prohibited disclosure of "any information relative to formulas of products," 3(c)(4) and 8(c), but was silent with respect to the disclosure of any of the health and safety data submitted with an application.[3]

In 1970, the Department of Agriculture's FIFRA responsibilities were transferred to the then newly created Environmental Protection Agency, whose Administrator is the appellant in this case. See Reorganization Plan No. 3 of 1970, 35 Fed. Reg. 15623 (1970), 5 U.S.C. App., p. 1132.

Because of mounting public concern about the safety of pesticides and their effect on the environment and because of a growing perception that the existing legislation was not equal to the task of safeguarding the public interest, see S. Rep. No. 92-838, at 3–9; S. Rep. No. 92-970, p. 9 (1972); H. R. Rep. No. 92-511, at 5–13, Congress undertook a comprehensive revision of FIFRA through the adoption of the Federal Environmental Pesticide Control Act of 1972, 86 Stat. 973. The amendments transformed FIFRA from a labeling law into a comprehensive regulatory statute. H. R. Rep. No. 92-511, at 1. As amended, FIFRA regulated the use, as well as the sale and labeling, of pesticides; regulated pesticides produced and sold in both intrastate and interstate commerce; provided for review, cancellation, and suspension of registration; and gave EPA greater enforcement authority. Congress also added a new criterion for registration: that EPA determine that the pesticide will not cause "unreasonable adverse effects on the environment." 3(c)(5)(C) and (D), 86 Stat. 980–981.

For purposes of this litigation, the most significant of the 1972 amendments pertained to the pesticide-registration procedure and the public disclosure of information learned through that procedure. Congress added to FIFRA a new section governing public disclosure of data submitted in support of an application for registration. Under that section, the submitter of data could designate any portions of the submitted material it believed to be "trade secrets or commercial or financial information." 10(a), 86 Stat. 989. Another section prohibited EPA from publicly disclosing information which, in its judgment, contained or related to "trade secrets or commercial or financial information." 10(b). In the event that EPA disagreed with a submitter's designation of certain information as "trade secrets or commercial or financial information" and proposed to disclose that information, the original submitter could institute a declaratory judgment action in federal district court. 10(c).

The 1972 amendments also included a provision that allowed EPA to consider data submitted by one applicant for registration in support of another application pertaining to a similar chemical, provided the subsequent applicant offered to compensate the applicant who originally submitted the data. 3(c)(1)(D). In effect, the provision instituted a mandatory data-licensing scheme. The amount of compensation was to be negotiated by the parties, or, in the event negotiations failed, was to be determined by EPA, subject to judicial review upon the instigation of the original data submitter. The scope of the

(Continues)

(*Continued*)

1972 data-consideration provision, however, was limited, for any data designated as "trade secrets or commercial or financial information" exempt from disclosure under 10 could not be considered at all by EPA to support another registration application unless the original submitter consented. *Ibid*.

The 1972 amendments did not specify standards for the designation of submitted data as "trade secrets or commercial or financial information." In addition, Congress failed to designate an effective date for the data-consideration and disclosure schemes. In 1975, Congress amended 3(c)(1)(D) to provide that the data-consideration and data-disclosure provisions applied only to data submitted on or after January 1, 1970, 89 Stat. 755, but left the definitional question unanswered.

Much litigation centered around the definition of "trade secrets or commercial or financial information" for the purposes of the data-consideration and data-disclosure provisions of FIFRA. EPA maintained that the exemption from consideration or disclosure applied only to a narrow range of information, principally statements of formulae and manufacturing processes. In a series of lawsuits, however, data-submitting firms challenged EPA's interpretation and obtained several decisions to the effect that the term "trade secrets" applied to any data, including health, safety, and environmental data, that met the definition of trade secrets set forth in Restatement of Torts 757 (1939). See, e.g., *Mobay Chemical Corp. v. Castle*, 447 F. Supp. 811 (WD Mo. 1978); *Chevron Chemical Co. v. Castle*, 443 F. Supp. 1024 (ND Cal. 1978). These decisions prevented EPA from disclosing much of the data on which it based its decision to register pesticides and from considering the data submitted by one applicant in reviewing the application of a later applicant. See S. Rep. No. 95-334, at 7; H. R. Rep. No. 95-663, p. 18 (1977).

Because of these and other problems with the regulatory scheme embodied in FIFRA as amended in 1972, see S. Rep. No. 95–334, at 2–5; H. R. Rep. No. 95-663, at 15–21; see generally EPA Office of Pesticide Programs, *FIFRA: Impact on the Industry* (1977), reprinted in S. Rep. No. 95-334, at 34–68, Congress enacted other amendments to FIFRA in 1978. These were effected by the Federal Pesticide Act of 1978, 92 Stat. 819. The new amendments included a series of revisions in the data-consideration and data-disclosure provisions of FIFRA's 3 and 10, 7 U.S.C. 136a and 136h.

Under FIFRA, as amended in 1978, applicants are granted a 10-year period of exclusive use for data on new active ingredients contained in pesticides registered after September 30, 1978. 3(c)(1)(D)(i). All other data submitted after December 31, 1969, may be cited and considered in support of another application for 15 years after the original submission if the applicant offers to compensate the original submitter. 3(c)(1)(D)(ii).[4] If the parties cannot agree on the amount of compensation, either may initiate a binding arbitration proceeding. The results of the arbitration proceeding are not subject to judicial review, absent fraud or misrepresentation. The same statute provides that an original submitter who refuses to participate in negotiations or in the arbitration proceeding forfeits his claim for compensation. Data that do not qualify for either the 10-year period of exclusive use or the 15-year period of compensation may be considered by EPA without limitation. 3(c)(1)(D)(iii).

Also in 1978, Congress added a new subsection, 10(d), 7 U.S.C. 136h(d), that provides for disclosure of all health, safety, and environmental data to qualified requesters, notwithstanding the prohibition against disclosure of trade secrets contained in 10(b). The provision, however, does not authorize disclosure of information that would reveal "manufacturing or quality control processes" or certain details about deliberately added inert ingredients unless "the Administrator has first determined that the disclosure is necessary to protect against an unreasonable risk of injury to health or the environment." 10(d)(1)(A) to (C).[5] EPA may not disclose data to representatives of foreign or multinational pesticide companies unless the original submitter of the data consents to the disclosure. 10(g). Another subsection establishes a criminal penalty for wrongful disclosure by a Government employee or contractor of confidential or trade secret data. 10(f).

II

Appellee Monsanto Company (Monsanto) is an inventor, developer, and producer of various kinds of chemical products, including pesticides. Monsanto, headquartered in St. Louis County, Mo., sells in both domestic and foreign markets. It is one of a relatively small group of companies that invent and develop new active ingredients for pesticides and conduct most of the research and testing with respect to those ingredients.[6]

These active ingredients are sometimes referred to as "manufacturing-use products" because they are not generally sold directly to users of pesticides. Rather, they must first be combined with "inert ingredients"—chemicals that dissolve, dilute, or stabilize the active components. The results of this process are sometimes called "end-use products," and the firms that produce end-use products are called "formulators." See the opinion of the District Court in this case, *Monsanto Co. v. Acting Administrator, United States Environmental Protection Agency*, 564 F. Supp. 552, 554 (ED Mo. 1983). A firm that produces an active ingredient may use it for incorporation into its own end-use products, may sell it to formulators, or may do both. Monsanto produces both active ingredients and end-use products. *Ibid.*

The District Court found that development of a potential commercial pesticide candidate typically requires the expenditure of $5 million to $15 million annually for several years. The development process may take between 14 and 22 years, and it is usually that long before a company can expect any return on its investment. *Id.*, at 555. For every manufacturing-use pesticide the average company finally markets, it will have screened and tested 20,000 others. Monsanto has a significantly better-than-average success rate; it successfully markets 1 out of every 10,000 chemicals tested. *Ibid.*

Monsanto, like any other applicant for registration of a pesticide, must present research and test data supporting its application. The District Court found that Monsanto had incurred costs in excess of $23.6 million in developing the health, safety, and environmental data submitted by it under FIFRA. *Id.*, at 560. The information submitted with an application usually has value to Monsanto beyond its instrumentality in gaining that particular application. Monsanto uses this information to develop additional end-use products and to expand the uses of its registered products. The information would also be valuable to Monsanto's competitors. For that reason, Monsanto has instituted stringent security measures to ensure the secrecy of the data. *Ibid.*

It is this health, safety, and environmental data that Monsanto sought to protect by bringing this suit. The District Court found that much of these data "contai[n] or relat[e] to trade secrets as defined by the Restatement of Torts and Confidential, commercial information." *Id.*, at 562.

Monsanto brought suit in District Court, seeking injunctive and declaratory relief from the operation of the data-consideration provisions of FIFRA's 3(c)(1)(D), and the data-disclosure provisions of FIFRA's 10 and the related 3(c)(2)(A). Monsanto alleged that all of the challenged provisions effected a "taking" of property without just compensation, in violation of the Fifth Amendment. In addition, Monsanto alleged that the data-consideration provisions violated the Amendment because they effected a taking of property for a private, rather than a public, purpose. Finally, Monsanto alleged that the arbitration scheme provided by 3(c)(1)(D)(ii) violates the original submitter's due process rights and constitutes an unconstitutional delegation of judicial power.

After a bench trial, the District Court concluded that Monsanto possessed property rights in its submitted data, specifically including the right to exclude others from the enjoyment of such data by preventing their unauthorized use and by prohibiting their disclosure. 564 F. Supp., at 566. The court found that the challenged data-consideration provisions "give Monsanto's competitors a free ride at Monsanto's expense." *Ibid.* The District Court reasoned that 3(c)(1)(D) appropriated Monsanto's fundamental right to exclude, and that the effect of that appropriation is substantial. The court further found that Monsanto's property was being appropriated for a private purpose and that this interference was much more significant than the public good that the appropriation might serve. 564 F. Supp., at 566–567.

The District Court also found that operation of the disclosure provisions of FIFRA constituted a taking of Monsanto's property. The cost incurred by Monsanto when its property is "permanently committed to the public domain and thus effectively destroyed" was viewed by the District Court as significantly outweighing any benefit to the general public from having the ability to scrutinize the data, for the court seemed to believe that the general public could derive all the assurance it needed about the safety and effectiveness of a pesticide from EPA's decision to register the product and to approve the label. *Id.*, at 567, and n. 4.

After finding that the data-consideration provisions operated to effect a taking of property, the District Court found that the compulsory binding-arbitration scheme set forth in 3(c)(1)(D)(ii) did not adequately provide compensation for the property taken. The court found the arbitration provision to be arbitrary and vague, reasoning that the statute does not give arbitrators guidance as to the factors that enter into the concept of just compensation, and that judicial review is foreclosed except in cases of fraud. 564 F. Supp., at 567. The District Court also found that the arbitration scheme was infirm because it did not meet the requirements of Art. III of the Constitution. *Ibid.* Finally, the court found that a remedy under the Tucker Act was not available for the deprivations of property effected by 3 and 10. 564 F. Supp., at 567–568.

(Continues)

(Continued)

The District Court therefore declared 3(c)(1)(D), 3(c)(2)(A), 10(b), and 10(d) of FIFRA, as amended by the Federal Pesticide Act of 1978, to be unconstitutional, and permanently enjoined EPA from implementing or enforcing those sections. See Amended Judgment, App. to Juris. Statement 41a.[7]

We noted probable jurisdiction. 464 U.S. 890 (1983).

III

In deciding this case, we are faced with four questions: (1) Does Monsanto have a property interest protected by the Fifth Amendment's Taking Clause in the health, safety, and environmental data it has submitted to EPA? (2) If so, does EPA's use of the data to evaluate the applications of others or EPA's disclosure of the data to qualified members of the public effect a taking of that property interest? (3) If there is a taking, is it a taking for a public use? (4) If there is a taking for a public use, does the statute adequately provide for just compensation?

For purposes of this case, EPA has stipulated that "Monsanto has certain property rights in its information, research and test data that it has submitted under FIFRA to EPA and its predecessor agencies which may be protected by the Fifth Amendment to the Constitution of the United States." App. 36. Since the exact import of that stipulation is not clear, we address the question whether the data at issue here can be considered property for the purposes of the Taking Clause of the Fifth Amendment.

This Court never has squarely addressed the applicability of the protections of the Taking Clause of the Fifth Amendment to commercial data of the kind involved in this case. In answering the question now, we are mindful of the basic axiom that "'[p]roperty interests . . . are not created by the Constitution. Rather, they are created and their dimensions are defined by existing rules or understandings that stem from an independent source such as state law.'" *Webb's Fabulous Pharmacies, Inc. v. Beckwith*, 449 U.S. 155, 161 (1980), quoting *Board of Regents v. Roth*, 408 U.S. 564, 577 (1972). Monsanto asserts that the health, safety, and environmental data it has submitted to EPA are property under Missouri law, which recognizes trade secrets, as defined in 757, Comment b, of the Restatement of Torts, as property. See *Reddi-Wip, Inc. v. Lemay Valve Co.*, 354 S. W. 2d 913, 917 (Mo. App. 1962); *Harrington v. National Outdoor Advertising Co.*, 355 Mo. 524, 532, 196 S. W. 2d 786, 791 (1946); *Luckett v. Orange Julep Co.*, 271 Mo. 289, 302–304, 196 S. W. 740, 743 (1917). The Restatement defines a trade secret as "any formula, pattern, device or compilation of information which is used in one's business, and which gives him an opportunity to obtain an advantage over competitors who do not know or use it." 757, Comment b. And the parties have stipulated that much of the information, research, and test data that Monsanto has submitted under FIFRA to EPA "contains or relates to trade secrets as defined by the Restatement of Torts." App. 36.

Because of the intangible nature of a trade secret, the extent of the property right therein is defined by the extent to which the owner of the secret protects his interest from disclosure to others. See *Harrington, supra*; *Reddi-Wip, supra*; Restatement of Torts, *supra*; see also *Kewanee Oil Co. v. Bicron Corp.*, 416 U.S. 470, 474–476 (1974). Information that is public knowledge or that is generally known in an industry cannot be a trade secret. Restatement of Torts, *supra*. If an individual discloses his trade secret to others who are under no obligation to protect the confidentiality of the information, or otherwise publicly discloses the secret, his property right is extinguished. See *Harrington, supra*; 1 R. Milgrim, *Trade Secrets* 1.012. (1983).

Trade secrets have many of the characteristics of more tangible forms of property. A trade secret is assignable. See, e.g., *Dr. Miles Medical Co. v. John D. Park & Sons Co.*, 220 U.S. 373, 401–402 (1911); *Painton & Co. v. Bourns, Inc.*, 442 F.2d 216, 225 (CA2 1971). A trade secret can form the res of a trust, Restatement (Second) of Trusts 82, Comment e (1959); 1 A. Scott, *Law of Trusts* 82.5, p. 703 (3d ed. 1967), and it passes to a trustee in bankruptcy. See In re Uniservices, Inc., 517 F.2d 492, 496–497 (CA7 1975).

Even the manner in which Congress referred to trade secrets in the legislative history of FIFRA supports the general perception of their property-like nature. In discussing the 1978 amendments to FIFRA, Congress recognized that data developers like Monsanto have a "proprietary interest" in their data. S. Rep. No. 95-334, at 31. Further, Congress reasoned that submitters of data are "entitled" to "compensation" because they "have legal ownership of the data." H. R. Conf. Rep. No. 95-1560, p. 29 (1978).[8] This general perception of trade secrets as property is consonant with a notion of "property" that extends beyond land and tangible goods and includes the products of an individual's "labour and invention." 2 W. Blackstone, *Commentaries* *405; see generally J. Locke, *The Second Treatise of Civil Government*, ch. 5 (J. Gough ed. 1947).

Although this Court never has squarely addressed the question whether a person can have a property interest in a trade secret, which is admittedly intangible, the Court has found other kinds of intangible interests to be property for purposes of the Fifth Amendment's Taking Clause. See, e.g., *Armstrong v. United States*, 364 U.S. 40, 44, 46 (1960) (materialman's lien provided for under Maine law protected by Taking Clause); *Louisville Joint Stock Land Bank v. Radford*, 295 U.S. 555, 596–602 (1935) (real estate lien protected); *Lynch v. United States*, 292 U.S. 571, 579 (1934) (valid contracts are property within meaning of the Taking Clause). That intangible property rights protected by state law are deserving of the protection of the Taking Clause has long been implicit in the thinking of this Court:

> "It is conceivable that [the term 'property' in the Taking Clause] was used in its vulgar and untechnical sense of the physical thing with respect to which the citizen exercises rights recognized by law. On the other hand, it may have been employed in a more accurate sense to denote the group of rights inhering in the citizen's relation to the physical thing, as the right to possess, use and dispose of it. In point of fact, the construction given the phrase has been the latter." *United States v. General Motors Corp.*, 323 U.S. 373, 377–378 (1945).

We therefore hold that to the extent that Monsanto has an interest in its health, safety, and environmental data cognizable as a trade-secret property right under Missouri law, that property right is protected by the Taking Clause of the Fifth Amendment.[9]

IV

Having determined that Monsanto has a property interest in the data it has submitted to EPA, we confront the difficult question whether a "taking" will occur when EPA discloses those data or considers the data in evaluating another application for registration. The question of what constitutes a "taking" is one with which this Court has wrestled on many occasions. It has never been the rule that only governmental acquisition or destruction of the property of an individual constitutes a taking, for

> "courts have held that the deprivation of the former owner rather than the accretion of a right or interest to the sovereign constitutes the taking. Governmental action short of acquisition of title or occupancy has been held, if its effects are so complete as to deprive the owner of all or most of his interest in the subject matter, to amount to a taking." *United States v. General Motors Corp.*, 323 U.S., at 378.

See also *PruneYard Shopping Center v. Robins*, 447 U.S. 74 (1980); *Pennsylvania Coal Co. v. Mahon*, 260 U.S. 393, 415 (1922).

As has been admitted on numerous occasions, "this Court has generally 'been unable to develop any "set formula" for determining when "justice and fairness" require that economic injuries caused by public action'" must be deemed a compensable taking. *Kaiser Aetna v. United States*, 444 U.S. 164, 175 (1979), quoting *Penn Central Transportation Co. v. New York City*, 438 U.S. 104, 124 (1978); accord, *Hodel v. Virginia Surface Mining & Reclamation Assn., Inc.*, 452 U.S. 264, 295 (1981). The inquiry into whether a taking has occurred is essentially an "ad hoc, factual" inquiry. *Kaiser Aetna*, 444 U.S., at 175. The Court, however, has identified several factors that should be taken into account when determining whether a governmental action has gone beyond "regulation" and effects a "taking." Among those factors are: "the character of the governmental action, its economic impact, and its interference with reasonable investment-backed expectations." *PruneYard Shopping Center v. Robins*, 447 U.S., at 83; see *Kaiser Aetna*, 444 U.S., at 175; *Penn Central*, 438 U.S., at 124. It is to the last of these three factors that we now direct our attention, for we find that the force of this factor is so overwhelming, at least with respect to certain of the data submitted by Monsanto to EPA, that it disposes of the taking question regarding those data.

A

A "reasonable investment-backed expectation" must be more than a "unilateral expectation or an abstract need." *Webb's Fabulous Pharmacies*, 449 U.S., at 161. We find that with respect to any health, safety, and environmental data that Monsanto submitted to EPA after the effective date of the 1978 FIFRA amendments—that is, on or after October 1, 1978[10] Monsanto could not have had a reasonable, investment-backed expectation that EPA would keep the data confidential beyond the limits

(Continues)

prescribed in the amended statute itself. Monsanto was on notice of the manner in which EPA was authorized to use and disclose any data turned over to it by an applicant for registration.

Thus, with respect to any data submitted to EPA on or after October 1, 1978, Monsanto knew that, for a period of 10 years from the date of submission, EPA would not consider those data in evaluating the application of another without Monsanto's permission. 3(c)(1)(D)(i). It was also aware, however, that once the 10-year period had expired, EPA could use the data without Monsanto's permission. 3(c)(1)(D)(ii) and (iii). Monsanto was further aware that it was entitled to an offer of compensation from the subsequent applicant only until the end of the 15th year from the date of submission. 3(c)(1)(D)(iii). In addition, Monsanto was aware that information relating to formulae of products could be revealed by EPA to "any Federal agency consulted and [could] be revealed at a public hearing or in findings of fact" issued by EPA "when necessary to carry out" EPA's duties under FIFRA. 10(b). The statute also gave Monsanto notice that much of the health, safety, and efficacy data provided by it could be disclosed to the general public at any time. 10(d). If, despite the data-consideration and data-disclosure provisions in the statute, Monsanto chose to submit the requisite data in order to receive a registration, it can hardly argue that its reasonable investment-backed expectations are disturbed when EPA acts to use or disclose the data in a manner that was authorized by law at the time of the submission.

Monsanto argues that the statute's requirement that a submitter give up its property interest in the data constitutes placing an unconstitutional condition on the right to a valuable Government benefit. See Brief for Appellee 29. But Monsanto has not challenged the ability of the Federal Government to regulate the marketing and use of pesticides. Nor could Monsanto successfully make such a challenge, for such restrictions are the burdens we all must bear in exchange for "'the advantage of living and doing business in a civilized community.'" *Andrus v. Allard*, 444 U.S. 51, 67 (1979), quoting *Pennsylvania Coal Co. v. Mahon*, 260 U.S., at 422 (Brandeis, J., dissenting); see *Day-Brite Lighting, Inc. v. Missouri*, 342 U.S. 421, 424 (1952). This is particularly true in an area, such as pesticide sale and use, that has long been the source of public concern and the subject of government regulation. That Monsanto is willing to bear this burden in exchange for the ability to market pesticides in this country is evidenced by the fact that it has continued to expand its research and development and to submit data to EPA despite the enactment of the 1978 amendments to FIFRA.[11] 564 F. Supp., at 561.

Thus, as long as Monsanto is aware of the conditions under which the data are submitted, and the conditions are rationally related to a legitimate Government interest, a voluntary submission of data by an applicant in exchange for the economic advantages of a registration can hardly be called a taking. See *Corn Products Refining Co. v. Eddy*, 249 U.S. 427, 431–432 (1919) ("The right of a manufacturer to maintain secrecy as to his compounds and processes must be held subject to the right of the State, in the exercise of its police power and in promotion of fair dealing, to require that the nature of the product be fairly set forth"); see also *Westinghouse Electric Corp. v. United States Nuclear Regulatory Comm'n*, 555 F.2d 82, 95 (CA3 1977).

B

Prior to the 1972 amendments, FIFRA was silent with respect to EPA's authorized use and disclosure of data submitted to it in connection with an application for registration. Another statute, the Trade Secrets Act, 18 U.S.C. 1905, however, arguably is relevant. That Act is a general criminal statute that provides a penalty for any employee of the United States Government who discloses, in a manner not authorized by law, any trade-secret information that is revealed to him during the course of his official duties. This Court has determined that 1905 is more than an "antileak" statute aimed at deterring Government employees from profiting by information they receive in their official capacities. See *Chrysler Corp. v. Brown*, 441 U.S. 281, 298–301 (1979). Rather, 1905 also applies to formal agency action, i.e., action approved by the agency or department head. *Ibid.*

It is true that, prior to the 1972 amendments, neither FIFRA nor any other provision of law gave EPA authority to disclose data obtained from Monsanto. But the Trade Secrets Act is not a guarantee of confidentiality to submitters of data, and, absent an express promise, Monsanto had no reasonable, investment-backed expectation that its information would remain inviolate in the hands of EPA. In an industry that long has been the focus of great public concern and significant government regulation, the possibility was substantial that the Federal Government, which had thus far taken no position on disclosure of health, safety, and environmental data concerning pesticides, upon focusing on the issue, would find disclosure to be in the public interest. Thus, with respect to data submitted to EPA in connection with an application for registration prior to October 22, 1972,[12] the Trade Secrets Act provided no basis for a reasonable investment-backed expectation that data submitted to EPA would remain confidential.

A fortiori, the Trade Secrets Act cannot be construed as any sort of assurance against internal agency use of submitted data during consideration of the application of a subsequent applicant for registration.[13] Indeed, there is some evidence that the practice of using data submitted by one company during consideration of the application of a subsequent applicant was widespread and well known.[14] Thus, with respect to any data that Monsanto submitted to EPA prior to the effective date of the 1972 amendments to FIFRA, we hold that Monsanto could not have had a "reasonable investment-backed expectation" that EPA would maintain those data in strictest confidence and would use them exclusively for the purpose of considering the Monsanto application in connection with which the data were submitted.

C

The situation may be different, however, with respect to data submitted by Monsanto to EPA during the period from October 22, 1972, through September 30, 1978. Under the statutory scheme then in effect, a submitter was given an opportunity to protect its trade secrets from disclosure by designating them as trade secrets at the time of submission. When Monsanto provided data to EPA during this period, it was with the understanding, embodied in FIFRA, that EPA was free to use any of the submitted data that were not trade secrets in considering the application of another, provided that EPA required the subsequent applicant to pay "reasonable compensation" to the original submitter. 3(c)(1)(D), 86 Stat. 979. But the statute also gave Monsanto explicit assurance that EPA was prohibited from disclosing publicly, or considering in connection with the application of another, any data submitted by an applicant if both the applicant and EPA determined the data to constitute trade secrets. 10, 86 Stat. 989. Thus, with respect to trade secrets submitted under the statutory regime in force between the time of the adoption of the 1972 amendments and the adoption of the 1978 amendments, the Federal Government had explicitly guaranteed to Monsanto and other registration applicants an extensive measure of confidentiality and exclusive use. This explicit governmental guarantee formed the basis of a reasonable investment-backed expectation. If EPA, consistent with the authority granted it by the 1978 FIFRA amendments, were now to disclose trade-secret data or consider those data in evaluating the application of a subsequent applicant in a manner not authorized by the version of FIFRA in effect between 1972 and 1978, EPA's actions would frustrate Monsanto's reasonable investment-backed expectation with respect to its control over the use and dissemination of the data it had submitted.

The right to exclude others is generally "one of the most essential sticks in the bundle of rights that are commonly characterized as property." *Kaiser Aetna*, 444 U.S., at 176. With respect to a trade secret, the right to exclude others is central to the very definition of the property interest. Once the data that constitute a trade secret are disclosed to others, or others are allowed to use those data, the holder of the trade secret has lost his property interest in the data.[15] That the data retain usefulness for Monsanto even after they are disclosed—for example, as bases from which to develop new products or refine old products, as marketing and advertising tools, or as information necessary to obtain registration in foreign countries—is irrelevant to the determination of the economic impact of the EPA action on Monsanto's property right. The economic value of that property right lies in the competitive advantage over others that Monsanto enjoys by virtue of its exclusive access to the data, and disclosure or use by others of the data would destroy that competitive edge.

EPA encourages us to view the situation not as a taking of Monsanto's property interest in the trade secrets, but as a "pre-emption" of whatever property rights Monsanto may have had in those trade secrets. Brief for Appellant 27–28. The agency argues that the proper functioning of the comprehensive FIFRA registration scheme depends upon its uniform application to all data. Thus, it is said, the Supremacy Clause dictates that the scheme not vary depending on the property law of the State in which the submitter is located. *Id.*, at 28. This argument proves too much. If Congress can "pre-empt" state property law in the manner advocated by EPA, then the Taking Clause has lost all vitality. This Court has stated that a sovereign, "by *ipse dixit*, may not transform private property into public property without compensation . . . This is the very kind of thing that the Taking Clause of the Fifth Amendment was meant to prevent." *Webb's Fabulous Pharmacies, Inc. v. Beckwith*, 449 U.S., at 164.

If a negotiation or arbitration pursuant to 3(c)(1)(D)(ii) were to yield just compensation to Monsanto for the loss in the market value of its trade-secret data suffered because of EPA's consideration

(Continues)

(Continued)

of the data in connection with another application, then Monsanto would have no claim against the Government for a taking. Since no arbitration has yet occurred with respect to any use of Monsanto's data, any finding that there has been an actual taking would be premature. See *infra*, at 1019–1020.[16]

In summary, we hold that EPA's consideration or disclosure of data submitted by Monsanto to the agency prior to October 22, 1972, or after September 30, 1978, does not effect a taking. We further hold that EPA consideration or disclosure of health, safety, and environmental data will constitute a taking if Monsanto submitted the data to EPA between October 22, 1972, and September 30, 1978;[17] the data constituted trade secrets under Missouri law; Monsanto had designated the data as trade secrets at the time of its submission; the use or disclosure conflicts with the explicit assurance of confidentiality or exclusive use contained in the statute during that period; and the operation of the arbitration provision does not adequately compensate for the loss in market value of the data that Monsanto suffers because of EPA's use or disclosure of the trade secrets.

V

We must next consider whether any taking of private property that may occur by operation of the data-disclosure and data-consideration provisions of FIFRA is a taking for a "public use." We have recently stated that the scope of the "public use" requirement of the Taking Clause is "coterminous with the scope of a sovereign's police powers." *Hawaii Housing Authority v. Midkiff, ante,* at 240; see *Berman v. Parker,* 348 U.S. 26, 33 (1954). The role of the courts in second-guessing the legislature's judgment of what constitutes a public use is extremely narrow. *Midkiff, supra; Berman, supra,* at 32.

The District Court found that EPA's action pursuant to the data-consideration provisions of FIFRA would effect a taking for a private use, rather than a public use, because such action benefits subsequent applicants by forcing original submitters to share their data with later applicants. 564 F. Supp., at 566. It is true that the most direct beneficiaries of EPA actions under the data-consideration provisions of FIFRA will be the later applicants who will support their applications by citation to data submitted by Monsanto or some other original submitter. Because of the data-consideration provisions, later applicants will not have to replicate the sometimes intensive and complex research necessary to produce the requisite data. This Court, however, has rejected the notion that a use is a public use only if the property taken is put to use for the general public. *Midkiff, ante,* at 243–244; *Rindge Co. v. Los Angeles,* 262 U.S. 700, 707 (1923); *Block v. Hirsh,* 256 U.S. 135, 155 (1921).

So long as the taking has a conceivable public character, "the means by which it will be attained is . . . for Congress to determine." *Berman,* 348 U.S., at 33. Here, the public purpose behind the data-consideration provisions is clear from the legislative history. Congress believed that the provisions would eliminate costly duplication of research and streamline the registration process, making new end-use products available to consumers more quickly. Allowing applicants for registration, upon payment of compensation, to use data already accumulated by others, rather than forcing them to go through the time-consuming process of repeating the research, would eliminate a significant barrier to entry into the pesticide market, thereby allowing greater competition among producers of end-use products. S. Rep. No. 95-334, at 30–31, 40–41; 124 Cong. Rec. 29756–29757 (1978) (remarks of Sen. Leahy). Such a procompetitive purpose is well within the police power of Congress. See *Midkiff, ante,* at 241–242.[18]

Because the data-disclosure provisions of FIFRA provide for disclosure to the general public, the District Court did not find that those provisions constituted a taking for a private use. Instead, the court found that the data-disclosure provisions served no use. It reasoned that because EPA, before registration, must determine that a product is safe and effective, and because the label on a pesticide, by statute, must set forth the nature, contents, and purpose of the pesticide, the label provided the public with all the assurance it needed that the product is safe and effective. 564 F. Supp., at 567, and n. 4. It is enough for us to state that the optimum amount of disclosure to the public is for Congress, not the courts, to decide, and that the statute embodies Congress' judgment on that question. See 123 Cong. Rec., at 25706 (remarks of Sen. Leahy). We further observe, however, that public disclosure can provide an effective check on the decisionmaking processes of EPA and allows members of the public to determine the likelihood of individualized risks peculiar to their use of the product. See H. R. Rep. No. 95-343, p. 8 (1977) (remarks of Douglas M. Costle); S. Rep. No. 95-334, at 13.

We therefore hold that any taking of private property that may occur in connection with EPA's use or disclosure of data submitted to it by Monsanto between October 22, 1972, and September 30, 1978, is a taking for a public use.

VI

Equitable relief is not available to enjoin an alleged taking of private property for a public use, duly authorized by law,[19] when a suit for compensation can be brought against the sovereign subsequent to the taking. *Larson v. Domestic & Foreign Commerce Corp.*, 337 U.S. 682, 697, n. 18 (1949). The Fifth Amendment does not require that compensation precede the taking. *Hurley v. Kincaid*, 285 U.S. 95, 104 (1932). Generally, an individual claiming that the United States has taken his property can seek just compensation under the Tucker Act, 28 U.S.C. 1491.[20] *United States v. Causby*, 328 U.S. 256, 267 (1946) ("If there is a taking, the claim is 'founded upon the Constitution' and within the jurisdiction of the Court of Claims to hear and determine"); *Yearsley v. Ross Construction Co.*, 309 U.S. 18, 21 (1940).

In this case, however, the District Court enjoined EPA action under the data-consideration and data-disclosure provisions of FIFRA, finding that a Tucker Act remedy is not available for any taking of property that may occur as a result of the operation of those provisions. We do not agree with the District Court's assessment that no Tucker Act remedy will lie for whatever taking may occur due to EPA activity pursuant to FIFRA.

In determining whether a Tucker Act remedy is available for claims arising out of a taking pursuant to a federal statute, the proper inquiry is not whether the statute "expresses an affirmative showing of congressional intent to permit recourse to a Tucker Act remedy," but "whether Congress has in the [statute] withdrawn the Tucker Act grant of jurisdiction to the Court of Claims to hear a suit involving the [statute] 'founded . . . upon the Constitution.'" Regional Rail Reorganization Act Cases, 419 U.S. 102, 126 (1974) (emphasis in original).

Nowhere in FIFRA or in its legislative history is there discussion of the interaction between FIFRA and the Tucker Act. Since the Tucker Act grants what is now the Claims Court "jurisdiction to render judgment upon any claim against the United States founded . . . upon the Constitution," we would have to infer a withdrawal of jurisdiction with respect to takings under FIFRA from the structure of the statute or from its legislative history. A withdrawal of jurisdiction would amount to a partial repeal of the Tucker Act. This Court has recognized, however, that "repeals by implication are disfavored." Regional Rail Reorganization Act Cases, 419 U.S., at 133. See, e.g., *Amell v. United States*, 384 U.S. 158, 165–166 (1966); *Mercantile National Bank v. Langdeau*, 371 U.S. 555, 565 (1963); *United States v. Borden Co.*, 308 U.S. 188, 198–199 (1939).

Monsanto argues that FIFRA's provision that an original submitter of data who fails to participate in a procedure for reaching an agreement or in an arbitration proceeding, or fails to comply with the terms of an agreement or arbitration decision, "shall forfeit the right to compensation for the use of the data in support of the application," 3(c)(1)(D)(ii), indicates Congress' intent that there be no Tucker Act remedy. But where two statutes are "'capable of co-existence, it is the duty of the courts, absent a clearly expressed congressional intention to the contrary, to regard each as effective.'" Regional Rail Reorganization Act Cases, 419 U.S., at 133–134, quoting *Morton v. Mancari*, 417 U.S. 535, 551 (1974). Here, contrary to Monsanto's claim, it is entirely possible for the Tucker Act and FIFRA to co-exist. The better interpretation, therefore, of the FIFRA language on forfeiture, which gives force to both the Tucker Act and the FIFRA provision, is to read FIFRA as implementing an exhaustion requirement as a precondition to a Tucker Act claim. That is, FIFRA does not withdraw the possibility of a Tucker Act remedy, but merely requires that a claimant first seek satisfaction through the statutory procedure. Cf. Regional Rail Reorganization Act Cases, 419 U.S., at 154–156 (viewing Tucker Act remedy as covering any shortfall between statutory remedy and just compensation).[21]

With respect to data disclosure to the general public, FIFRA provides for no compensation whatsoever. Thus, Monsanto's argument that Congress intended the compensation scheme provided in FIFRA to be exclusive has no relevance to the data-disclosure provisions of 10.

Congress in FIFRA did not address the liability of the Government to pay just compensation should a taking occur. Congress' failure specifically to mention or provide for recourse against the Government may reflect a congressional belief that use of data by EPA in the ways authorized by FIFRA effects no Fifth Amendment taking or it may reflect Congress' assumption that the general grant of jurisdiction under the Tucker Act would provide the necessary remedy for any taking that may occur. In any event, the failure cannot be construed to reflect an unambiguous intention to withdraw the Tucker Act remedy. "[W]hether or not the United States so intended," any taking claim under FIFRA is one "founded . . . upon the Constitution," and is thus remediable under the Tucker Act. Regional Rail Reorganization Act Cases, 419 U.S., at 126. Therefore, where the operation of the

(Continues)

(Continued)

data-consideration and data-disclosure provisions of FIFRA effect a taking of property belonging to Monsanto, an adequate remedy for the taking exists under the Tucker Act. The District Court erred in enjoining the taking.

VII

Because we hold that the Tucker Act is available as a remedy for any uncompensated taking Monsanto may suffer as a result of the operation of the challenged provisions of FIFRA, we conclude that Monsanto's challenges to the constitutionality of the arbitration and compensation scheme are not ripe for our resolution. Because of the availability of the Tucker Act, Monsanto's ability to obtain just compensation does not depend solely on the validity of the statutory compensation scheme. The operation of the arbitration procedure affects only Monsanto's ability to vindicate its statutory right to obtain compensation from a subsequent applicant whose registration application relies on data originally submitted by Monsanto, not its ability to vindicate its constitutional right to just compensation.

Monsanto did not allege or establish that it had been injured by actual arbitration under the statute. While the District Court acknowledged that Monsanto had received several offers of compensation from applicants for registration, 564 F. Supp., at 561, it did not find that EPA had considered Monsanto's data in considering another application. Further, Monsanto and any subsequent applicant may negotiate and reach agreement concerning an outstanding offer. If they do not reach agreement, then the controversy must go to arbitration. Only after EPA has considered data submitted by Monsanto in evaluating another application and an arbitrator has made an award will Monsanto's claims with respect to the constitutionality of the arbitration scheme become ripe. See *Duke Power Co. v. Carolina Environmental Study Group, Inc.*, 438 U.S. 59, 81 (1978); Regional Rail Reorganization Act Cases, 419 U.S., at 138.

VIII

We find no constitutional infirmity in the challenged provisions of FIFRA. Operation of the provisions may effect a taking with respect to certain health, safety, and environmental data constituting trade secrets under state law and designated by Monsanto as trade secrets upon submission to EPA between October 22, 1972, and September 30, 1978.[22] But whatever taking may occur is one for a public use, and a Tucker Act remedy is available to provide Monsanto with just compensation. Once a taking has occurred, the proper forum for Monsanto's claim is the Claims Court. Monsanto's challenges to the constitutionality of the arbitration procedure are not yet ripe for review. The judgment of the District Court is therefore vacated, and the case is remanded for further proceedings consistent with this opinion.

It is so ordered.

JUSTICE WHITE took no part in the consideration or decision of this case.

Notes

1. For purposes of our discussion of FIFRA, the term "pesticides" includes herbicides, insecticides, fungicides, rodenticides, and plant regulators. See 2(t) and (u) of FIFRA, as amended, 7 U.S.C. 136(t) and (u).

2. The first federal legislation in this area was the Insecticide Act of 1910, 36 Stat. 331, which made it unlawful to manufacture and sell insecticides that were adulterated or misbranded. In 1947, the 1910 legislation was repealed and replaced with FIFRA. 61 Stat. 172.

   Some States had undertaken to regulate pesticide use before there was federal legislation, and many more continued to do so after federal legislation was enacted. In 1946, the Council of State Governments recommended for adoption a model state statute, the Uniform State Insecticide, Fungicide, and Rodenticide Act. See S. Rep. No. 92-838, p. 7 (1972); H. R. Rep. No. 313, 80th Cong., 1st Sess., 3 (1947).

3. Appellant here concedes, however, that as a matter of practice, the Department of Agriculture did not publicly disclose the health and safety information. Brief for Appellant 5, n. 5.

4. Section 3(c)(1)(D), 92 Stat. 820-822, 7 U.S.C. 136a(c)(1)(D), reads in relevant part:

   "(i) With respect to pesticides containing active ingredients that are initially registered under this Act after [September 30, 1978], data submitted to support the application for the original registration of the pesticide, or an application for an amendment adding any new use to the registration and that pertain solely to such new use, shall not, without the written permission of the original data submitter, be considered by the Administrator to support an application by another person during a period of ten years following the date the Administrator first registers the pesticide . . .;

"(ii) except as otherwise provided in subparagraph (D)(i) of this paragraph, with respect to data submitted after December 31, 1969, by an applicant or registrant to support an application for registration, experimental use permit, or amendment adding a new use to an existing registration, to support or maintain in effect an existing registration, or for reregistration, the Administrator may, without the permission of the original data submitter, consider any such item of data in support of an application by any other person . . . within the fifteen-year period following the date the data were originally submitted only if the applicant has made an offer to compensate the original data submitter and submitted such offer to the Administrator accompanied by evidence of delivery to the original data submitter of the offer. The terms and amount of compensation may be fixed by agreement between the original data submitter and the applicant, or, failing such agreement, binding arbitration under this subparagraph. If, at the end of ninety days after the date of delivery to the original data submitter of the offer to compensate, the original data submitter and the applicant have neither agreed on the amount and terms of compensation nor on a procedure for reaching an agreement on the amount and terms of compensation, either person may initiate binding arbitration proceedings by requesting the Federal Mediation and Conciliation Service to appoint an arbitrator from the roster of arbitrators maintained by such Service . . . [T]he findings and determination of the arbitrator shall be final and conclusive, and no official or court of the United States shall have power or jurisdiction to review any such findings and determination, except for fraud, misrepresentation, or other misconduct by one of the parties to the arbitration or the arbitrator where there is a verified complaint with supporting affidavits attesting to specific instances of such fraud, misrepresentation, or other misconduct. . . . If the Administrator determines that an original data submitter has failed to participate in a procedure for reaching an agreement or in an arbitration proceeding as required by this subparagraph, or failed to comply with the terms of an agreement or arbitration decision concerning compensation under this subparagraph, the original data submitter shall forfeit the right to compensation for the use of the data in support of the application. . . . Registration action by the Administrator shall not be delayed pending the fixing of compensation;

"(iii) after expiration of any period of exclusive use and any period for which compensation is required for the use of an item of data under subparagraphs (D)(i) and (D)(ii) of this paragraph, the Administrator may consider such item of data in support of an application by any other applicant without the permission of the original data submitter and without an offer having been received to compensate the original data submitter for the use of such item of data."

5. Section 10(d), 92 Stat. 830, reads in relevant part:

"(1) All information concerning the objectives, methodology, results, or significance of any test or experiment performed on or with a registered or previously registered pesticide or its separate ingredients, impurities, or degradation products and any information concerning the effects of such pesticide on any organism or the behavior of such pesticide in the environment, including, but not limited to, data on safety to fish and wildlife, humans, and other mammals, plants, animals, and soil, and studies on persistence, translocation and fate in the environment, and metabolism, shall be available for disclosure to the public: Provided, That the use of such data for any registration purpose shall be governed by section 3 of this Act: Provided further, That this paragraph does not authorize the disclosure of any information that—

"(A) discloses manufacturing or quality control processes,

"(B) discloses the details of any methods for testing, detecting, or measuring the quantity of any deliberately added inert ingredients of a pesticide, or

"(C) discloses the identity or percentage quantity of any deliberately added inert ingredient of a pesticide, unless the Administrator has first determined that disclosure is necessary to protect against an unreasonable risk of injury to health or the environment.

"(2) Information concerning production, distribution, sale, or inventories of a pesticide that is otherwise entitled to confidential treatment under subsection (b) of this section may be publicly disclosed in connection with a public proceeding to determine whether a pesticide, or any ingredient of a pesticide, causes unreasonable adverse effects on health or the environment, if the Administrator determines that such disclosure is necessary in the public interest."

6. A study by the Office of Pesticide Programs of the EPA showed that in 1977 approximately 400 firms were registered to produce manufacturing-use products. S. Rep. No. 95-334, p. 34 (1977). It was estimated that the 10 largest firms account for 75% of this country's pesticide production. *Id.*, at 60. A correspondingly small number of new pesticides are marketed each year. In 1974, only 10

(Continues)

(*Continued*)

new pesticides were introduced. See Goring, The Costs of Commercializing Pesticides, International Conference of Entomology, Aug. 20, 1976, reprinted in Hearings on Extension of the Federal Insecticide, Fungicide, and Rodenticide Act before the Subcommittee on Agricultural Research and General Legislation of the Senate Committee on Agriculture, Nutrition, and Forestry, 95th Cong., 1st Sess., 250, 254 (1977).

7. The District Court's judgment in this case is in conflict with the holdings of other federal courts. See, e.g., *Petrolite Corp. v. United States Environmental Protection Agency*, 519 F. Supp. 966 (DC 1981); *Mobay Chemical Corp. v. Costle*, 517 F. Supp. 252, and 517 F. Supp. 254 (WD Pa. 1981), aff'd *sub nom. Mobay Chemical Co. v. Gorsuch*, 682 F.2d 419 (CA3), *cert. denied*, 459 U.S. 988 (1982); *Chevron Chemical Co. v. Costle*, 499 F. Supp. 732 (Del. 1980), aff'd, 641 F.2d 104 (CA3), *cert. denied*, 452 U.S. 961 (1981).

8. Of course, it was not necessary that Congress recognize the data at issue here as property in order for the data to be protected by the Taking Clause. We mention the legislative history merely as one more illustration of the general perception of the property-like nature of trade secrets.

9. Contrary to EPA's contention, Brief for Appellant 29, Justice Holmes' dictum in *E. I. du Pont de Nemours Powder Co. v. Masland*, 244 U.S. 100 (1917), does not undermine our holding that a trade secret is property protected by the Fifth Amendment Taking Clause. *Masland* arose from a dispute about the disclosure of trade secrets during preparation for a trial. In his opinion for the Court, the Justice stated:

"The case has been considered as presenting a conflict between a right of property and a right to make a full defence, and it is said that if the disclosure is forbidden to one who denies that there is a trade secret, the merits of his defence are adjudged against him before he has a chance to be heard or to prove his case. We approach the question somewhat differently. The word property as applied to trade-marks and trade secrets is an unanalyzed expression of certain secondary consequences of the primary fact that the law makes some rudimentary requirements of good faith. Whether the plaintiffs have any valuable secret or not the defendant knows the facts, whatever they are, through a special confidence that he accepted. The property may be denied but the confidence cannot be. Therefore the starting point for the present matter is not property or due process of law, but that the defendant stood in confidential relations with the plaintiffs." *Id.*, at 102.

Justice Holmes did not deny the existence of a property interest; he simply deemed determination of the existence of that interest irrelevant to resolution of the case. In a case decided prior to *Masland*, the Court had spoken of trade secrets in property terms. *Board of Trade v. Christie Grain & Stock Co.*, 198 U.S. 236, 250–253 (1905) (Holmes, J., for the Court). See generally 1 R. Milgrim, *Trade Secrets* 1.011. (1983).

10. The Federal Pesticide Act of 1978 was approved on September 30, 1978. 92 Stat. 842. The new data-consideration and data-disclosure provisions applied with full force to all data submitted after that date.

11. Because the market for Monsanto's pesticide products is an international one, Monsanto could decide to forgo registration in the United States and sell a pesticide only in foreign markets. Presumably, it will do so in those situations where it deems the data to be protected from disclosure more valuable than the right to sell in the United States.

12. The 1972 amendments to FIFRA became effective at the close of the business day on October 21, 1972. 86 Stat. 998.

13. The Trade Secrets Act prohibits a Government employee from "publish[ing], divulg[ing], disclos[ing] or mak[ing] known" confidential information received in his official capacity. 18 U.S.C. 1905. In considering the data of one applicant in connection with the application of another, EPA does not violate any of these prohibitions.

14. The District Court found: "During the period that USDA administered FIFRA, it was also its policy that the data developed and submitted by companies such as [Monsanto] could not be used to support the registration of another's product without the permission of the data submitter." *Monsanto Co. v. Acting Administrator, United States Environmental Protection Agency*, 564 F. Supp. 552, 564 (ED Mo. 1983) (emphasis in original). The District Court apparently based this finding on the testimony of two former Directors of the Pesticide Regulation Division, who testified that they knew of no instance in which data submitted by one applicant were subsequently considered in evaluating another application. *Ibid.*

This finding is in marked conflict with the statement of the National Agricultural Chemicals Association, presented before a Senate Subcommittee in 1972, which advocated that the 1972 amendments to FIFRA should contain an exclusive-use provision:

"Under the present law registration information submitted to the Administrator has not routinely been made available for public inspection. Such information has, however, as a matter of practice but without statutory authority, been considered by the Administrator to support the registration of the same or a similar product by another registrant." Federal Environmental Pesticide Control Act: Hearings before the Subcommittee on Agricultural Research and General Legislation of the Senate Committee on Agriculture and Forestry, 92d Cong., 2d Sess., pt. 2, p. 245 (1972).

In addition, EPA points to the Department of Agriculture's Interpretation with Respect to Warning, Caution and Antidote Statements Required to Appear on Labels of Economic Poisons, 27 Fed. Reg. 2267 (1962), which presents a list of pesticides that would require no additional toxicological data for registration. The clear implication from the Interpretation is that the Department determined that the data already submitted with respect to those chemicals would be sufficient for purposes of evaluating any future applications for registration of those chemicals.

Although the evidence against the District Court's finding seems overwhelming, we need not determine that the finding was clearly erroneous in order to find that a submitter had no reasonable expectation that the Department or EPA would not use the data it had submitted when evaluating the application of another. The District Court did not find that the policy of the Department was publicly known at the time or that there was any explicit guarantee of exclusive use.

15. We emphasize that the value of a trade secret lies in the competitive advantage it gives its owner over competitors. Thus, it is the fact that operation of the data-consideration or data-disclosure provisions will allow a competitor to register more easily its product or to use the disclosed data to improve its own technology that may constitute a taking. If, however, a public disclosure of data reveals, for example, the harmful side effects of the submitter's product and causes the submitter to suffer a decline in the potential profits from sales of the product, that decline in profits stems from a decrease in the value of the pesticide to consumers, rather than from the destruction of an edge the submitter had over its competitors, and cannot constitute the taking of a trade secret.

16. Because the record contains no findings with respect to the value of the trade-secret data at issue and because no arbitration proceeding has yet been held to determine the amount of recovery to be paid by a subsequent applicant to Monsanto, we cannot preclude the possibility that the arbitration award will be sufficient to provide Monsanto with just compensation, thus nullifying any claim against the Government for a taking when EPA uses Monsanto's data in considering another application. The statutory arbitration scheme, of course, provides for compensation only in cases where the data are considered in connection with a subsequent application, not in cases of disclosure of the data.

17. While the 1975 amendments to FIFRA purported to carry backward the protections against data consideration and data disclosure to submissions of data made on or after January 1, 1970, 89 Stat. 751, the relevant consideration for our purposes is the nature of the expectations of the submitter at the time the data were submitted. We therefore do not extend our ruling as to a possible taking to data submitted prior to October 22, 1972.

18. Monsanto argues that EPA and, by implication, Congress misapprehended the true "barriers to entry" in the pesticide industry and that the challenged provisions of the law create, rather than reduce, barriers to entry. Brief for Appellee 35, n. 48. Such economic arguments are better directed to Congress. The proper inquiry before this Court is not whether the provisions in fact will accomplish their stated objectives. Our review is limited to determining that the purpose is legitimate and that Congress rationally could have believed that the provisions would promote that objective. *Midkiff, ante*, at 242–243; *Western & Southern Life Ins. Co. v. State Bd. of Equalization*, 451 U.S. 648, 671–672 (1981).

19. Any taking of private property that would occur as a result of EPA disclosure or consideration of data submitted by Monsanto between October 22, 1972, and September 30, 1978, is, of course, duly authorized by FIFRA as amended in 1978.

20. The Tucker Act, 28 U.S.C. 1491, reads, in relevant part:

"The United States Claims Court shall have jurisdiction to render judgment upon any claim against the United States founded either upon the Constitution, or any Act of Congress or any regulation of

(Continues)

an executive department, or upon any express or implied contract with the United States, or for liquidated or unliquidated damages in cases not sounding in tort."

21. Exhaustion of the statutory remedy is necessary to determine the extent of the taking that has occurred. To the extent that the operation of the statute provides compensation, no taking has occurred and the original submitter of data has no claim against the Government.
22. We emphasize that nothing in our opinion prohibits EPA's consideration or disclosure, in a manner authorized by FIFRA, of data submitted to it by Monsanto. Our decision merely holds that, with respect to a certain limited class of data submitted by Monsanto to EPA, EPA actions under the data-disclosure and data-consideration provisions of the statute may give Monsanto a claim for just compensation.

JUSTICE O'CONNOR, concurring in part and dissenting in part.

I join all of the Court's opinion except for part IV-B and the Court's conclusion, *ante*, at 1013, that "EPA's consideration or disclosure of data submitted by Monsanto to the agency prior to October 22, 1972 . . . does not effect a taking." In my view public disclosure of pre-1972 data would effect a taking. As to consideration of this information within EPA in connection with other license applications not submitted by Monsanto, I believe we should remand to the District Court for further factual findings concerning Monsanto's expectations regarding interagency uses of trade secret information prior to 1972.

It is important to distinguish at the outset public disclosure of trade secrets from use of those secrets entirely within EPA. Internal use may undermine Monsanto's competitive position within the United States, but it leaves Monsanto's position in foreign markets undisturbed. As the Court notes, *ante*, at 1007, n. 11, the likely impact on foreign market position is one that Monsanto would weigh when deciding whether to submit trade secrets to EPA. Thus a submission of trade secrets to EPA that implicitly consented to further use of the information within the agency is not necessarily the same as one that implicitly consented to public disclosure.

It seems quite clear—indeed the Court scarcely disputes—that public disclosure of trade secrets submitted to the Federal Government before 1972 was neither permitted by law, nor customary agency practice before 1972, nor expected by applicants for pesticide registrations. The Court correctly notes that the Trade Secrets Act, 18 U.S.C. 1905, flatly proscribed such disclosures. The District Court expressly found that until 1970 it was Government "policy that the data developed and submitted by companies such as [Monsanto] be maintained confidentially by the [administrative agency] and was not to be disclosed without the permission of the data submitter." *Monsanto Co. v. Acting Administrator, EPA*, 564 F. Supp. 552, 564 (1983). Finally, the Court, *ante*, at 1009, n. 14, quotes from a 1972 statement by the National Agricultural Chemicals Association that "registration information submitted to the Administrator has not routinely been made available for public inspection." It is hard to imagine how a pre-1972 applicant for a pesticide license would not, under these circumstances, have formed a very firm expectation that its trade secrets submitted in connection with a pesticide registration would not be disclosed to the public.

The Court's analysis of this question appears in a single sentence: an "industry that long has been the focus of great public concern and significant government regulation" can have no reasonable expectation that the Government will not later find public disclosure of trade secrets to be in the public interest. *Ante*, at 1008. I am frankly puzzled to read this statement in the broader context of the Court's otherwise convincing opinion. If the degree of Government regulation determines the reasonableness of an expectation of confidentiality, Monsanto had as little reason to expect confidentiality after 1972 as before, since the 1972 amendments were not deregulatory in intent or effect. And the Court entirely fails to explain why the nondisclosure provision of the 1972 Act, 10, 86 Stat. 989, created any greater expectation of confidentiality than the Trade Secrets Act. Section 10 prohibited EPA from disclosing "trade secrets or commercial or financial information." No penalty for disclosure was prescribed, unless disclosure was with the intent to defraud. The Trade Secrets Act, 18 U.S.C. 1905, prohibited and still prohibits Government disclosure of trade secrets and other commercial or financial information revealed during the course of official duties, on pain of substantial criminal sanctions. The Court acknowledges that this prohibition has always extended to formal and official agency action. *Chrysler Corp. v. Brown*, 441 U.S. 281, 298–301 (1979). It seems to me that the criminal sanctions in the Trade Secrets Act therefore created at least as strong an expectation of privacy before 1972 as the precatory language of 10 created after 1972.

The Court's tacit analysis seems to be this: an expectation of confidentiality can be grounded only on a statutory nondisclosure provision situated in close physical proximity, in the pages of the United States Code, to the provisions pursuant to which information is submitted to the Government. For my part, I see no reason why Congress should not be able to give effective protection to all trade secrets submitted to the Federal Government by means of a single, overarching, trade secrets provision. We routinely assume that wrongdoers are put on notice of the entire contents of the Code, though in all likelihood most of them have never owned a copy or opened a single page of it. It seems strange to assume, on the other hand, that a company like Monsanto, well served by lawyers who undoubtedly do read the Code, could build an expectation of privacy in pesticide trade secrets only if the assurance of confidentiality appeared in Title 7 itself.

The question of interagency use of trade secrets before 1972 is more difficult because the Trade Secrets Act most likely does not extend to such uses. The District Court found that prior to October 1972 only two competitors' registrations were granted on the basis of data submitted by Monsanto, and that Monsanto had no knowledge of either of these registrations prior to their being granted. 564 F. Supp., at 564. The District Court also found that before 1970 it was agency policy "that the data developed and submitted by companies such as [Monsanto] could not be used to support the registration of another's product without the permission of the data submitter." *Ibid.* This Court, however, concludes on the basis of two cited fragments of evidence that "the evidence against the District Court's finding seems overwhelming." *Ante*, at 1010, n. 14. The Court nevertheless wisely declines to label the District Court's findings of fact on this matter clearly erroneous. Instead, the Court notes that the "District Court did not find that the policy of the Department [of Agriculture] was publicly known at the time [before 1970] or that there was any explicit guarantee of exclusive use." *Ibid.* This begs exactly the right question, but the Court firmly declines to answer it. The Court simply states that "there is some evidence that the practice of using data submitted by one company during consideration of the application of a subsequent applicant was widespread and well known." *Ante*, at 1009 (footnote omitted). And then, without more ado, the Court declares that with respect to pre-1972 data Monsanto "could not have had a 'reasonable investment-backed expectation' that EPA would . . . use [the data] exclusively for the purpose of considering the Monsanto application in connection with which the data were submitted." *Ante*, at 1010.

If one thing is quite clear it is that the extent of Monsanto's pre-1972 expectations, whether reasonable and investment-backed or otherwise, is a heavily factual question. It is fairly clear that the District Court found that those expectations existed as a matter of fact and were reasonable as a matter of law. But if the factual findings of the District Court on this precise question were not as explicit as they might have been, the appropriate disposition is to remand to the District Court for further factfinding. That is the course I would follow with respect to interagency use of trade secrets submitted by Monsanto before 1972.

Kelo et al. v. City of New London et al., 545 U.S. 469 (2005)

After approving an integrated development plan designed to revitalize its ailing economy, respondent city, through its development agent, purchased most of the property earmarked for the project from willing sellers, but initiated condemnation proceedings when petitioners, the owners of the rest of the property, refused to sell. Petitioners brought this state–court action claiming, *inter alia*, that the taking of their properties would violate the "public use" restriction in the Fifth Amendment's Takings Clause. The trial court granted a permanent restraining order prohibiting the taking of the some of the properties, but denying relief as to others. Relying on cases such as *Hawaii Housing Authority v. Midkiff*, 467 U.S. 229, and *Berman v. Parker*, 348 U.S. 26, the Connecticut Supreme Court affirmed in part and reversed in part, upholding all of the proposed takings.

Held: The city's proposed disposition of petitioners' property qualifies as a "public use" within the meaning of the Takings Clause. Pp. 6–20.

(a) Though the city could not take petitioners' land simply to confer a private benefit on a particular private party, see, *e.g.*, *Midkiff*, 467 U.S., at 245, the takings at issue here would be executed pursuant to a carefully considered development plan, which was not adopted "to benefit a particular class of identifiable individuals," *ibid.* Moreover, while the city is not

(*Continues*)

(*Continued*)

planning to open the condemned land—at least not in its entirety—to use by the general public, this "Court long ago rejected any literal requirement that condemned property be put into use for the . . . public." *Id.*, at 244. Rather, it has embraced the broader and more natural interpretation of public use as "public purpose." See, *e.g., Fallbrook Irrigation Dist. v. Bradley*, 164 U.S. 112, 158–164. Without exception, the Court has defined that concept broadly, reflecting its longstanding policy of deference to legislative judgments as to what public needs justify the use of the takings power. *Berman*, 348 U.S. 26; *Midkiff*, 467 U.S. 229; *Ruckelshaus v. Monsanto Co.*, 467 U.S. 986. Pp. 6–13.

(b) The city's determination that the area at issue was sufficiently distressed to justify a program of economic rejuvenation is entitled to deference. The city has carefully formulated a development plan that it believes will provide appreciable benefits to the community, including, but not limited to, new jobs and increased tax revenue. As with other exercises in urban planning and development, the city is trying to coordinate a variety of commercial, residential, and recreational land uses, with the hope that they will form a whole greater than the sum of its parts. To effectuate this plan, the city has invoked a state statute that specifically authorizes the use of eminent domain to promote economic development. Given the plan's comprehensive character, the thorough deliberation that preceded its adoption, and the limited scope of this Court's review in such cases, it is appropriate here, as it was in *Berman*, to resolve the challenges of the individual owners, not on a piecemeal basis, but rather in light of the entire plan. Because that plan unquestionably serves a public purpose, the takings challenged here satisfy the Fifth Amendment. P. 13.

(c) Petitioners' proposal that the Court adopt a new bright-line rule that economic development does not qualify as a public use is supported by neither precedent nor logic. Promoting economic development is a traditional and long accepted governmental function, and there is no principled way of distinguishing it from the other public purposes the Court has recognized. See, *e.g., Berman*, 348 U.S., at 24. Also rejected is petitioners' argument that for takings of this kind the Court should require a "reasonable certainty" that the expected public benefits will actually accrue. Such a rule would represent an even greater departure from the Court's precedent. *E.g., Midkiff*, 467 U.S., at 242. The disadvantages of a heightened form of review are especially pronounced in this type of case, where orderly implementation of a comprehensive plan requires all interested parties' legal rights to be established before new construction can commence. The Court declines to second-guess the wisdom of the means the city has selected to effectuate its plan. *Berman*, 348 U.S., at 26. Pp. 13–20.

268 Conn. 1, 843 A. 2d 500, affirmed.

Stevens, J., delivered the opinion of the Court, in which *Kennedy, Souter, Ginsburg,* and *Breyer, JJ.,* joined. *Kennedy, J.,* filed a concurring opinion. *O'Connor, J.,* filed a dissenting opinion, in which *Rehnquist, C. J.,* and *Scalia* and *Thomas, JJ.,* joined. *Thomas, J.,* filed a dissenting opinion.

Justice Stevens delivered the opinion of the Court.

In 2000, the city of New London approved a development plan that, in the words of the Supreme Court of Connecticut, was "projected to create in excess of 1,000 jobs, to increase tax and other revenues, and to revitalize an economically distressed city, including its downtown and waterfront areas." 268 Conn. 1, 5, 843 A. 2d 500, 507 (2004). In assembling the land needed for this project, the city's development agent has purchased property from willing sellers and proposes to use the power of eminent domain to acquire the remainder of the property from unwilling owners in exchange for just compensation. The question presented is whether the city's proposed disposition of this property qualifies as a "public use" within the meaning of the Takings Clause of the Fifth Amendment to the Constitution.[23]

I

The city of New London (hereinafter City) sits at the junction of the Thames River and the Long Island Sound in southeastern Connecticut. Decades of economic decline led a state agency in 1990 to designate the City a "distressed municipality." In 1996, the Federal Government closed the Naval Undersea Warfare Center, which had been located in the Fort Trumbull area of the City and had employed over 1,500 people. In 1998, the City's unemployment rate was nearly double that of the State, and its population of just under 24,000 residents was at its lowest since 1920.

These conditions prompted state and local officials to target New London, and particularly its Fort Trumbull area, for economic revitalization. To this end, respondent New London Development

Corporation (NLDC), a private nonprofit entity established some years earlier to assist the City in planning economic development, was reactivated. In January 1998, the State authorized a $5.35 million bond issue to support the NLDC's planning activities and a $10 million bond issue toward the creation of a Fort Trumbull State Park. In February, the pharmaceutical company Pfizer Inc. announced that it would build a $300 million research facility on a site immediately adjacent to Fort Trumbull; local planners hoped that Pfizer would draw new business to the area, thereby serving as a catalyst to the area's rejuvenation. After receiving initial approval from the city council, the NLDC continued its planning activities and held a series of neighborhood meetings to educate the public about the process. In May, the city council authorized the NLDC to formally submit its plans to the relevant state agencies for review.[24] Upon obtaining state-level approval, the NLDC finalized an integrated development plan focused on 90 acres of the Fort Trumbull area.

The Fort Trumbull area is situated on a peninsula that juts into the Thames River. The area comprises approximately 115 privately owned properties, as well as the 32 acres of land formerly occupied by the naval facility (Trumbull State Park now occupies 18 of those 32 acres). The development plan encompasses seven parcels. Parcel 1 is designated for a waterfront conference hotel at the center of a "small urban village" that will include restaurants and shopping. This parcel will also have marinas for both recreational and commercial uses. A pedestrian "riverwalk" will originate here and continue down the coast, connecting the waterfront areas of the development. Parcel 2 will be the site of approximately 80 new residences organized into an urban neighborhood and linked by public walkway to the remainder of the development, including the state park. This parcel also includes space reserved for a new U.S. Coast Guard Museum. Parcel 3, which is located immediately north of the Pfizer facility, will contain at least 90,000 square feet of research and development office space. Parcel 4A is a 2.4-acre site that will be used either to support the adjacent state park, by providing parking or retail services for visitors, or to support the nearby marina. Parcel 4B will include a renovated marina, as well as the final stretch of the riverwalk. Parcels 5, 6, and 7 will provide land for office and retail space, parking, and water-dependent commercial uses. 1 App. 109–113.

The NLDC intended the development plan to capitalize on the arrival of the Pfizer facility and the new commerce it was expected to attract. In addition to creating jobs, generating tax revenue, and helping to "build momentum for the revitalization of downtown New London," id., at 92, the plan was also designed to make the City more attractive and to create leisure and recreational opportunities on the waterfront and in the park.

The city council approved the plan in January 2000, and designated the NLDC as its development agent in charge of implementation. See Conn. Gen. Stat. §8-188 (2005). The city council also authorized the NLDC to purchase property or to acquire property by exercising eminent domain in the City's name. §8-193. The NLDC successfully negotiated the purchase of most of the real estate in the 90-acre area, but its negotiations with petitioners failed. As a consequence, in November 2000, the NLDC initiated the condemnation proceedings that gave rise to this case.[25]

II

Petitioner Susette Kelo has lived in the Fort Trumbull area since 1997. She has made extensive improvements to her house, which she prizes for its water view. Petitioner Wilhelmina Dery was born in her Fort Trumbull house in 1918 and has lived there her entire life. Her husband Charles (also a petitioner) has lived in the house since they married some 60 years ago. In all, the nine petitioners own 15 properties in Fort Trumbull—4 in parcel 3 of the development plan and 11 in parcel 4A. Ten of the parcels are occupied by the owner or a family member; the other five are held as investment properties. There is no allegation that any of these properties is blighted or otherwise in poor condition; rather, they were condemned only because they happen to be located in the development area.

In December 2000, petitioners brought this action in the New London Superior Court. They claimed, among other things, that the taking of their properties would violate the "public use" restriction in the Fifth Amendment. After a 7-day bench trial, the Superior Court granted a permanent restraining order prohibiting the taking of the properties located in parcel 4A (park or marina support). It, however, denied petitioners relief as to the properties located in parcel 3 (office space). 2 App. to Pet. for Cert. 343–350.[26]

After the Superior Court ruled, both sides took appeals to the Supreme Court of Connecticut. That court held, over a dissent, that all of the City's proposed takings were valid. It began by upholding the lower court's determination that the takings were authorized by chapter 132, the State's municipal

(Continues)

development statute. See Conn. Gen. Stat. §8-186 *et seq.* (2005). That statute expresses a legislative determination that the taking of land, even developed land, as part of an economic development project is a "public use" and in the "public interest." 268 Conn., at 18–28, 843 A. 2d, at 515–521. Next, relying on cases such as *Hawaii Housing Authority v. Midkiff*, 467 U.S. 229 (1984), and *Berman v. Parker*, 348 U.S. 26 (1954), the court held that such economic development qualified as a valid public use under both the Federal and State Constitutions. 268 Conn., at 40, 843 A. 2d, at 527.

Finally, adhering to its precedents, the court went on to determine, first, whether the takings of the particular properties at issue were "reasonably necessary" to achieving the City's intended public use, *id.*, at 82, 843 A. 2d, at 552–553, and, second, whether the takings were for "reasonably foreseeable needs," *id.*, at 93, 843 A. 2d, at 558–559. The court upheld the trial court's factual findings as to parcel 3, but reversed the trial court as to parcel 4A, agreeing with the City that the intended use of this land was sufficiently definite and had been given "reasonable attention" during the planning process. *Id.*, at 120–121, 843 A. 2d, at 574.

The three dissenting justices would have imposed a "heightened" standard of judicial review for takings justified by economic development. Although they agreed that the plan was intended to serve a valid public use, they would have found all the takings unconstitutional because the City had failed to adduce "clear and convincing evidence" that the economic benefits of the plan would in fact come to pass. *Id.*, at 144, 146, 843 A. 2d, at 587, 588 (Zarella, J., joined by Sullivan, C. J., and Katz, J., concurring in part and dissenting in part).

We granted *certiorari* to determine whether a city's decision to take property for the purpose of economic development satisfies the "public use" requirement of the Fifth Amendment. 542 U.S. ___ (2004).

III

Two polar propositions are perfectly clear. On the one hand, it has long been accepted that the sovereign may not take the property of *A* for the sole purpose of transferring it to another private party *B*, even though *A* is paid just compensation. On the other hand, it is equally clear that a State may transfer property from one private party to another if future "use by the public" is the purpose of the taking; the condemnation of land for a railroad with common-carrier duties is a familiar example. Neither of these propositions, however, determines the disposition of this case.

As for the first proposition, the City would no doubt be forbidden from taking petitioners' land for the purpose of conferring a private benefit on a particular private party. See *Midkiff*, 467 U.S., at 245 ("A purely private taking could not withstand the scrutiny of the public use requirement; it would serve no legitimate purpose of government and would thus be void"); *Missouri Pacific R. Co. v. Nebraska*, 164 U.S. 403 (1896).[27] Nor would the City be allowed to take property under the mere pretext of a public purpose, when its actual purpose was to bestow a private benefit. The takings before us, however, would be executed pursuant to a "carefully considered" development plan. 268 Conn., at 54, 843 A. 2d, at 536. The trial judge and all the members of the Supreme Court of Connecticut agreed that there was no evidence of an illegitimate purpose in this case.[28] Therefore, as was true of the statute challenged in *Midkiff*, 467 U.S., at 245, the City's development plan was not adopted "to benefit a particular class of identifiable individuals."

On the other hand, this is not a case in which the City is planning to open the condemned land—at least not in its entirety—to use by the general public. Nor will the private lessees of the land in any sense be required to operate like common carriers, making their services available to all comers. But although such a projected use would be sufficient to satisfy the public use requirement, this "Court long ago rejected any literal requirement that condemned property be put into use for the general public." *Id.*, at 244. Indeed, while many state courts in the mid-19th century endorsed "use by the public" as the proper definition of public use, that narrow view steadily eroded over time. Not only was the "use by the public" test difficult to administer (*e.g.*, what proportion of the public need have access to the property? at what price?),[29] but it proved to be impractical given the diverse and always evolving needs of society.[30] Accordingly, when this Court began applying the Fifth Amendment to the States at the close of the 19th century, it embraced the broader and more natural interpretation of public use as "public purpose." See, *e.g.*, *Fallbrook Irrigation Dist. v. Bradley*, 164 U.S. 112, 158–164 (1896). Thus, in a case upholding a mining company's use of an aerial bucket line to transport ore over property it did not own, Justice Holmes' opinion for the Court stressed "the inadequacy of use by the general public as a universal test." *Strickley v. Highland Boy Gold Mining Co.*, 200 U.S. 527, 531 (1906).[31] We have repeatedly and consistently rejected that narrow test ever since.[32]

The disposition of this case therefore turns on the question whether the City's development plan serves a "public purpose." Without exception, our cases have defined that concept broadly, reflecting our longstanding policy of deference to legislative judgments in this field.

In *Berman v. Parker*, 348 U.S. 26 (1954), this Court upheld a redevelopment plan targeting a blighted area of Washington, D. C., in which most of the housing for the area's 5,000 inhabitants was beyond repair. Under the plan, the area would be condemned and part of it utilized for the construction of streets, schools, and other public facilities. The remainder of the land would be leased or sold to private parties for the purpose of redevelopment, including the construction of low-cost housing.

The owner of a department store located in the area challenged the condemnation, pointing out that his store was not itself blighted and arguing that the creation of a "better balanced, more attractive community" was not a valid public use. *Id.*, at 31. Writing for a unanimous Court, Justice Douglas refused to evaluate this claim in isolation, deferring instead to the legislative and agency judgment that the area "must be planned as a whole" for the plan to be successful. *Id.*, at 34. The Court explained that "community redevelopment programs need not, by force of the Constitution, be on a piecemeal basis—lot by lot, building by building." *Id.*, at 35. The public use underlying the taking was unequivocally affirmed:

> "We do not sit to determine whether a particular housing project is or is not desirable. The concept of the public welfare is broad and inclusive. . . . The values it represents are spiritual as well as physical, aesthetic as well as monetary. It is within the power of the legislature to determine that the community should be beautiful as well as healthy, spacious as well as clean, well-balanced as well as carefully patrolled. In the present case, the Congress and its authorized agencies have made determinations that take into account a wide variety of values. It is not for us to reappraise them. If those who govern the District of Columbia decide that the Nation's Capital should be beautiful as well as sanitary, there is nothing in the Fifth Amendment that stands in the way." *Id.*, at 33.

In *Hawaii Housing Authority v. Midkiff*, 467 U.S. 229 (1984), the Court considered a Hawaii statute whereby fee title was taken from lessors and transferred to lessees (for just compensation) in order to reduce the concentration of land ownership. We unanimously upheld the statute and rejected the Ninth Circuit's view that it was "a naked attempt on the part of the state of Hawaii to take the property of *A* and transfer it to *B* solely for *B*'s private use and benefit." *Id.*, at 235 (internal quotation marks omitted). Reaffirming *Berman*'s deferential approach to legislative judgments in this field, we concluded that the State's purpose of eliminating the "social and economic evils of a land oligopoly" qualified as a valid public use. 467 U.S., at 241–242. Our opinion also rejected the contention that the mere fact that the State immediately transferred the properties to private individuals upon condemnation somehow diminished the public character of the taking. "[I]t is only the taking's purpose, and not its mechanics," we explained, that matters in determining public use. *Id.*, at 244.

In that same Term we decided another public use case that arose in a purely economic context. In *Ruckelshaus v. Monsanto, Co.*, 467 U.S. 986 (1984), the Court dealt with provisions of the Federal Insecticide, Fungicide, and Rodenticide Act under which the Environmental Protection Agency could consider the data (including trade secrets) submitted by a prior pesticide applicant in evaluating a subsequent application, so long as the second applicant paid just compensation for the data. We acknowledged that the "most direct beneficiaries" of these provisions were the subsequent applicants, *id.*, at 1014, but we nevertheless upheld the statute under *Berman* and *Midkiff*. We found sufficient Congress' belief that sparing applicants the cost of time-consuming research eliminated a significant barrier to entry in the pesticide market and thereby enhanced competition. 467 U.S., at 1015.

Viewed as a whole, our jurisprudence has recognized that the needs of society have varied between different parts of the Nation, just as they have evolved over time in response to changed circumstances. Our earliest cases in particular embodied a strong theme of federalism, emphasizing the "great respect" that we owe to state legislatures and state courts in discerning local public needs. See *Hairston v. Danville & Western R. Co.*, 208 U.S. 598, 606–607 (1908) (noting that these needs were likely to vary depending on a State's "resources, the capacity of the soil, the relative importance of industries to the general public welfare, and the long-established methods and habits of the people").[33] For more than a century, our public use jurisprudence has wisely eschewed rigid formulas and intrusive scrutiny in favor of affording legislatures broad latitude in determining what public needs justify the use of the takings power.

(Continues)

IV

Those who govern the City were not confronted with the need to remove blight in the Fort Trumbull area, but their determination that the area was sufficiently distressed to justify a program of economic rejuvenation is entitled to our deference. The City has carefully formulated an economic development plan that it believes will provide appreciable benefits to the community, including—but by no means limited to—new jobs and increased tax revenue. As with other exercises in urban planning and development,[34] the City is endeavoring to coordinate a variety of commercial, residential, and recreational uses of land, with the hope that they will form a whole greater than the sum of its parts. To effectuate this plan, the City has invoked a state statute that specifically authorizes the use of eminent domain to promote economic development. Given the comprehensive character of the plan, the thorough deliberation that preceded its adoption, and the limited scope of our review, it is appropriate for us, as it was in *Berman*, to resolve the challenges of the individual owners, not on a piecemeal basis, but rather in light of the entire plan. Because that plan unquestionably serves a public purpose, the takings challenged here satisfy the public use requirement of the Fifth Amendment.

To avoid this result, petitioners urge us to adopt a new bright-line rule that economic development does not qualify as a public use. Putting aside the unpersuasive suggestion that the City's plan will provide only purely economic benefits, neither precedent nor logic supports petitioners' proposal. Promoting economic development is a traditional and long accepted function of government. There is, moreover, no principled way of distinguishing economic development from the other public purposes that we have recognized. In our cases upholding takings that facilitated agriculture and mining, for example, we emphasized the importance of those industries to the welfare of the States in question, see, *e.g.*, *Strickley*, 200 U.S. 527; in *Berman*, we endorsed the purpose of transforming a blighted area into a "well-balanced" community through redevelopment, 348 U.S., at 33[35]; in *Midkiff*, we upheld the interest in breaking up a land oligopoly that "created artificial deterrents to the normal functioning of the State's residential land market," 467 U.S., at 242; and in *Monsanto*, we accepted Congress' purpose of eliminating a "significant barrier to entry in the pesticide market," 467 U.S., at 1014–1015. It would be incongruous to hold that the City's interest in the economic benefits to be derived from the development of the Fort Trumbull area has less of a public character than any of those other interests. Clearly, there is no basis for exempting economic development from our traditionally broad understanding of public purpose.

Petitioners contend that using eminent domain for economic development impermissibly blurs the boundary between public and private takings. Again, our cases foreclose this objection. Quite simply, the government's pursuit of a public purpose will often benefit individual private parties. For example, in *Midkiff*, the forced transfer of property conferred a direct and significant benefit on those lessees who were previously unable to purchase their homes. In *Monsanto*, we recognized that the "most direct beneficiaries" of the data-sharing provisions were the subsequent pesticide applicants, but benefiting them in this way was necessary to promoting competition in the pesticide market. 467 U.S., at 1014.[36] The owner of the department store in *Berman* objected to "taking from one businessman for the benefit of another businessman," 348 U.S., at 33, referring to the fact that under the redevelopment plan land would be leased or sold to private developers for redevelopment.[37] Our rejection of that contention has particular relevance to the instant case: "The public end may be as well or better served through an agency of private enterprise than through a department of government—or so the Congress might conclude. We cannot say that public ownership is the sole method of promoting the public purposes of community redevelopment projects." *Id.*, at 34.[38]

It is further argued that without a bright-line rule nothing would stop a city from transferring citizen *A*'s property to citizen *B* for the sole reason that citizen *B* will put the property to a more productive use and thus pay more taxes. Such a one-to-one transfer of property, executed outside the confines of an integrated development plan, is not presented in this case. While such an unusual exercise of government power would certainly raise a suspicion that a private purpose was afoot,[39] the hypothetical cases posited by petitioners can be confronted if and when they arise.[40] They do not warrant the crafting of an artificial restriction on the concept of public use.[41]

Alternatively, petitioners maintain that for takings of this kind we should require a "reasonable certainty" that the expected public benefits will actually accrue. Such a rule, however, would represent an even greater departure from our precedent. "When the legislature's purpose is legitimate and its means are not irrational, our cases make clear that empirical debates over the wisdom of takings—no less than debates over the wisdom of other kinds of socioeconomic legislation—are not to be carried out in the federal courts." *Midkiff*, 467 U.S., at 242.[42] Indeed, earlier this Term we explained why similar practical concerns (among others) undermined the use of the "substantially advances" formula in our regulatory takings doctrine. See *Lingle v. Chevron U.S.A. Inc.*, 544 U.S. ___, ___ (2005) (slip op., at 14–15) (noting that this formula "would empower—and might often require—courts to substitute their predictive judgments for those of elected legislatures and expert agencies"). The disadvantages of a heightened form of review are especially pronounced in this type of case. Orderly implementation of a comprehensive redevelopment plan obviously requires that the legal rights of all interested parties be established before new construction can be commenced. A constitutional rule that required postponement of the judicial approval of every condemnation until the likelihood of success of the plan had been assured would unquestionably impose a significant impediment to the successful consummation of many such plans.

Just as we decline to second-guess the City's considered judgments about the efficacy of its development plan, we also decline to second-guess the City's determinations as to what lands it needs to acquire in order to effectuate the project. "It is not for the courts to oversee the choice of the boundary line nor to sit in review on the size of a particular project area. Once the question of the public purpose has been decided, the amount and character of land to be taken for the project and the need for a particular tract to complete the integrated plan rests in the discretion of the legislative branch." *Berman*, 348 U.S., at 35–36.

In affirming the City's authority to take petitioners' properties, we do not minimize the hardship that condemnations may entail, notwithstanding the payment of just compensation.[43] We emphasize that nothing in our opinion precludes any State from placing further restrictions on its exercise of the takings power. Indeed, many States already impose "public use" requirements that are stricter than the federal baseline. Some of these requirements have been established as a matter of state constitutional law,[44] while others are expressed in state eminent domain statutes that carefully limit the grounds upon which takings may be exercised.[45] As the submissions of the parties and their *amici* make clear, the necessity and wisdom of using eminent domain to promote economic development are certainly matters of legitimate public debate.[46] This Court's authority, however, extends only to determining whether the City's proposed condemnations are for a "public use" within the meaning of the Fifth Amendment to the Federal Constitution. Because over a century of our case law interpreting that provision dictates an affirmative answer to that question, we may not grant petitioners the relief that they seek.

The judgment of the Supreme Court of Connecticut is affirmed.

It is so ordered.

Justice Kennedy, concurring.

I join the opinion for the Court and add these further observations.

This Court has declared that a taking should be upheld as consistent with the Public Use Clause, U.S. Const., Amdt. 5., as long as it is "rationally related to a conceivable public purpose." *Hawaii Housing Authority v. Midkiff*, 467 U.S. 229, 241 1984); see also *Berman v. Parker*, 348 U.S. 26 (1954). This deferential standard of review echoes the rational-basis test used to review economic regulation under the Due Process and Equal Protection Clauses, see, *e.g.*, *FCC v. Beach Communications, Inc.*, 508 U.S. 307, 313–314 (1993); *Williamson v. Lee Optical of Okla., Inc.*, 348 U.S. 483 (1955). The determination that a rational-basis standard of review is appropriate does not, however, alter the fact that transfers intended to confer benefits on particular, favored private entities, and with only incidental or pretextual public benefits, are forbidden by the Public Use Clause.

A court applying rational-basis review under the Public Use Clause should strike down a taking that, by a clear showing, is intended to favor a particular private party, with only incidental or pretextual public benefits, just as a court applying rational-basis review under the Equal Protection Clause must strike down a government classification that is clearly intended to injure a particular class of private parties, with only incidental or pretextual public justifications. See *Cleburne v. Cleburne Living Center, Inc.*, 473 U.S. 432, 446–447, 450 (1985); *Department of Agriculture v. Moreno*, 413 U.S. 528, 533–536 (1973). As the trial court in this case was correct to observe, "Where the purpose [of a taking] is economic development and that development is to be carried out by private parties or private parties will be benefited, the court must decide if the stated public purpose—economic advantage to a city sorely in need of it—is only incidental to the benefits that will be confined on private parties of a development plan." 2 App. to Pet. for Cert. 263. See also *ante*, at 7.

(Continues)

A court confronted with a plausible accusation of impermissible favoritism to private parties should treat the objection as a serious one and review the record to see if it has merit, though with the presumption that the government's actions were reasonable and intended to serve a public purpose. Here, the trial court conducted a careful and extensive inquiry into "whether, in fact, the development plan is of primary benefit to . . . the developer [*i.e.*, Corcoran Jennison], and private businesses which may eventually locate in the plan area [*e.g.*, Pfizer], and in that regard, only of incidental benefit to the city." 2 App. to Pet. for Cert. 261. The trial court considered testimony from government officials and corporate officers; *id.*, at 266–271; documentary evidence of communications between these parties, *ibid.*; respondents' awareness of New London's depressed economic condition and evidence corroborating the validity of this concern, *id.*, at 272–273, 278–279; the substantial commitment of public funds by the State to the development project before most of the private beneficiaries were known, *id.*, at 276; evidence that respondents reviewed a variety of development plans and chose a private developer from a group of applicants rather than picking out a particular transferee beforehand, *id.*, at 273, 278; and the fact that the other private beneficiaries of the project are still unknown because the office space proposed to be built has not yet been rented, *id.*, at 278.

The trial court concluded, based on these findings, that benefiting Pfizer was not "the primary motivation or effect of this development plan"; instead, "the primary motivation for [respondents] was to take advantage of Pfizer's presence." *Id.*, at 276. Likewise, the trial court concluded that "[t]here is nothing in the record to indicate that . . . [respondents] were motivated by a desire to aid [other] particular private entities." *Id.*, at 278. See also *ante*, at 7–8. Even the dissenting justices on the Connecticut Supreme Court agreed that respondents' development plan was intended to revitalize the local economy, not to serve the interests of Pfizer, Corcoran Jennison, or any other private party. 268 Conn. 1, 159, 843 A. 2d 500, 595 (2004) (Zarella, J., concurring in part and dissenting in part). This case, then, survives the meaningful rational basis review that in my view is required under the Public Use Clause.

Petitioners and their *amici* argue that any taking justified by the promotion of economic development must be treated by the courts as *per se* invalid, or at least presumptively invalid. Petitioners overstate the need for such a rule, however, by making the incorrect assumption that review under *Berman* and *Midkiff* imposes no meaningful judicial limits on the government's power to condemn any property it likes. A broad *per se* rule or a strong presumption of invalidity, furthermore, would prohibit a large number of government takings that have the purpose and expected effect of conferring substantial benefits on the public at large and so do not offend the Public Use Clause.

My agreement with the Court that a presumption of invalidity is not warranted for economic development takings in general, or for the particular takings at issue in this case, does not foreclose the possibility that a more stringent standard of review than that announced in *Berman* and *Midkiff* might be appropriate for a more narrowly drawn category of takings. There may be private transfers in which the risk of undetected impermissible favoritism of private parties is so acute that a presumption (rebuttable or otherwise) of invalidity is warranted under the Public Use Clause. Cf. *Eastern Enterprises v. Apfel*, 524 U.S. 498, 549–550 (1998) (*Kennedy, J.*, concurring in judgment and dissenting in part) (heightened scrutiny for retroactive legislation under the Due Process Clause). This demanding level of scrutiny, however, is not required simply because the purpose of the taking is economic development.

This is not the occasion for conjecture as to what sort of cases might justify a more demanding standard, but it is appropriate to underscore aspects of the instant case that convince me no departure from *Berman* and *Midkiff* is appropriate here. This taking occurred in the context of a comprehensive development plan meant to address a serious city-wide depression, and the projected economic benefits of the project cannot be characterized as *de minimus*. The identity of most of the private beneficiaries were unknown at the time the city formulated its plans. The city complied with elaborate procedural requirements that facilitate review of the record and inquiry into the city's purposes. In sum, while there may be categories of cases in which the transfers are so suspicious, or the procedures employed so prone to abuse, or the purported benefits are so trivial or implausible, that courts should presume an impermissible private purpose, no such circumstances are present in this case.

***

For the foregoing reasons, I join in the Court's opinion.

Justice O'Connor, with whom *The Chief Justice, Justice Scalia*, and *Justice Thomas* join, dissenting.

Over two centuries ago, just after the Bill of Rights was ratified, Justice Chase wrote:

"An *act* of the Legislature (for I cannot call it a law) contrary to the great first principles of the social compact, cannot be considered a rightful exercise of legislative authority. . . . A few instances will suffice to explain what I mean. . . . [A] law that takes property from A. and gives it to B: It is against all reason and justice, for a people to entrust a Legislature with *such* powers; and, therefore, it cannot be presumed that they have done it." *Calder v. Bull*, 3 Dall. 386, 388 (1798) (emphasis deleted).

Today the Court abandons this long-held, basic limitation on government power. Under the banner of economic development, all private property is now vulnerable to being taken and transferred to another private owner, so long as it might be upgraded—*i.e.*, given to an owner who will use it in a way that the legislature deems more beneficial to the public—in the process. To reason, as the Court does, that the incidental public benefits resulting from the subsequent ordinary use of private property render economic development takings "for public use" is to wash out any distinction between private and public use of property—and thereby effectively to delete the words "for public use" from the Takings Clause of the Fifth Amendment. Accordingly I respectfully dissent.

I

Petitioners are nine resident or investment owners of 15 homes in the Fort Trumbull neighborhood of New London, Connecticut. Petitioner Wilhelmina Dery, for example, lives in a house on Walbach Street that has been in her family for over 100 years. She was born in the house in 1918; her husband, petitioner Charles Dery, moved into the house when they married in 1946. Their son lives next door with his family in the house he received as a wedding gift, and joins his parents in this suit. Two petitioners keep rental properties in the neighborhood.

In February 1998, Pfizer Inc., the pharmaceuticals manufacturer, announced that it would build a global research facility near the Fort Trumbull neighborhood. Two months later, New London's city council gave initial approval for the New London Development Corporation (NLDC) to prepare the development plan at issue here. The NLDC is a private, nonprofit corporation whose mission is to assist the city council in economic development planning. It is not elected by popular vote, and its directors and employees are privately appointed. Consistent with its mandate, the NLDC generated an ambitious plan for redeveloping 90 acres of Fort Trumbull in order to "complement the facility that Pfizer was planning to build, create jobs, increase tax and other revenues, encourage public access to and use of the city's waterfront, and eventually 'build momentum' for the revitalization of the rest of the city." App. to Pet. for Cert. 5.

Petitioners own properties in two of the plan's seven parcels—Parcel 3 and Parcel 4A. Under the plan, Parcel 3 is slated for the construction of research and office space as a market develops for such space. It will also retain the existing Italian Dramatic Club (a private cultural organization) though the homes of three plaintiffs in that parcel are to be demolished. Parcel 4A is slated, mysteriously, for "'park support.'" *Id.*, at 345–346. At oral argument, counsel for respondents conceded the vagueness of this proposed use, and offered that the parcel might eventually be used for parking. Tr. of Oral Arg. 36.

To save their homes, petitioners sued New London and the NLDC, to whom New London has delegated eminent domain power. Petitioners maintain that the Fifth Amendment prohibits the NLDC from condemning their properties for the sake of an economic development plan. Petitioners are not hold-outs; they do not seek increased compensation, and none is opposed to new development in the area. Theirs is an objection in principle: They claim that the NLDC's proposed use for their confiscated property is not a "public" one for purposes of the Fifth Amendment. While the government may take their homes to build a road or a railroad or to eliminate a property use that harms the public, say petitioners, it cannot take their property for the private use of other owners simply because the new owners may make more productive use of the property.

II

The Fifth Amendment to the Constitution, made applicable to the States by the Fourteenth Amendment, provides that "private property [shall not] be taken for public use, without just compensation." When interpreting the Constitution, we begin with the unremarkable presumption that every word in the document has independent meaning, "that no word was unnecessarily used, or needlessly added." *Wright v. United States*, 302 U.S. 583, 588 (1938). In keeping with that presumption, we have read the Fifth Amendment's language to impose two distinct conditions on the exercise of eminent domain: "the taking must be for a 'public use' and 'just compensation' must be paid to the owner." *Brown v. Legal Foundation of Wash.*, 538 U.S. 216, 231–232 (2003).

(Continues)

(Continued)

These two limitations serve to protect "the security of Property," which Alexander Hamilton described to the Philadelphia Convention as one of the "great obj[ects] of Gov[ernment]." 1 Records of the Federal Convention of 1787, p. 302 (M. Farrand ed. 1934). Together they ensure stable property ownership by providing safeguards against excessive, unpredictable, or unfair use of the government's eminent domain power—particularly against those owners who, for whatever reasons, may be unable to protect themselves in the political process against the majority's will.

While the Takings Clause presupposes that government can take private property without the owner's consent, the just compensation requirement spreads the cost of condemnations and thus "prevents the public from loading upon one individual more than his just share of the burdens of government." *Monongahela Nav. Co. v. United States*, 148 U.S. 312, 325 (1893); see also *Armstrong v. United States*, 364 U.S. 40, 49 (1960). The public-use requirement, in turn, imposes a more basic limitation, circumscribing the very scope of the eminent domain power: Government may compel an individual to forfeit her property for the *public's* use, but not for the benefit of another private person. This requirement promotes fairness as well as security. Cf. *Tahoe-Sierra Preservation Council, Inc. v. Tahoe Regional Planning Agency*, 535 U.S. 302, 336 (2002) ("The concepts of 'fairness and justice' . . . underlie the Takings Clause").

Where is the line between "public" and "private" property use? We give considerable deference to legislatures' determinations about what governmental activities will advantage the public. But were the political branches the sole arbiters of the public–private distinction, the Public Use Clause would amount to little more than hortatory fluff. An external, judicial check on how the public use requirement is interpreted, however limited, is necessary if this constraint on government power is to retain any meaning. See *Cincinnati v. Vester*, 281 U.S. 439, 446 (1930) ("It is well established that . . . the question [of] what is a public use is a judicial one").

Our cases have generally identified three categories of takings that comply with the public use requirement, though it is in the nature of things that the boundaries between these categories are not always firm. Two are relatively straightforward and uncontroversial. First, the sovereign may transfer private property to public ownership—such as for a road, a hospital, or a military base. See, *e.g., Old Dominion Land Co. v. United States*, 269 U.S. 55 (1925); *Rindge Co. v. County of Los Angeles*, 262 U.S. 700 (1923). Second, the sovereign may transfer private property to private parties, often common carriers, who make the property available for the public's use—such as with a railroad, a public utility, or a stadium. See, *e.g., National Railroad Passenger Corporation v. Boston & Maine Corp.*, 503 U.S. 407 (1992); *Mt. Vernon-Woodberry Cotton Duck Co. v. Alabama Interstate Power Co.*, 240 U.S. 30 (1916). But "public ownership" and "use-by-the-public" are sometimes too constricting and impractical ways to define the scope of the Public Use Clause. Thus we have allowed that, in certain circumstances and to meet certain exigencies, takings that serve a public purpose also satisfy the Constitution even if the property is destined for subsequent private use. See, *e.g., Berman v. Parker*, 348 U.S. 26 (1954); *Hawaii Housing Authority v. Midkiff*, 467 U.S. 229 (1984).

This case returns us for the first time in over 20 years to the hard question of when a purportedly "public purpose" taking meets the public use requirement. It presents an issue of first impression: Are economic development takings constitutional? I would hold that they are not. We are guided by two precedents about the taking of real property by eminent domain. In *Berman*, we upheld takings within a blighted neighborhood of Washington, D.C. The neighborhood had so deteriorated that, for example, 64.3% of its dwellings were beyond repair. 348 U.S., at 30. It had become burdened with "overcrowding of dwellings," "lack of adequate streets and alleys," and "lack of light and air." *Id.*, at 34. Congress had determined that the neighborhood had become "injurious to the public health, safety, morals, and welfare" and that it was necessary to "eliminat[e] all such injurious conditions by employing all means necessary and appropriate for the purpose," including eminent domain. *Id.*, at 28. Mr. Berman's department store was not itself blighted. Having approved of Congress' decision to eliminate the harm to the public emanating from the blighted neighborhood, however, we did not second-guess its decision to treat the neighborhood as a whole rather than lot-by-lot. *Id.*, at 34–35; see also *Midkiff*, 467 U.S., at 244 ("it is only the taking's purpose, and not its mechanics, that must pass scrutiny").

In *Midkiff*, we upheld a land condemnation scheme in Hawaii whereby title in real property was taken from lessors and transferred to lessees. At that time, the State and Federal Governments owned nearly 49% of the State's land, and another 47% was in the hands of only 72 private landowners. Concentration of land ownership was so dramatic that on the State's most urbanized island, Oahu, 22 landowners owned 72.5% of the fee simple titles. *Id.*, at 232. The Hawaii Legislature had concluded that the oligopoly in land ownership was "skewing the State's residential fee simple market, inflating land prices, and injuring the public tranquility and welfare," and therefore enacted a condemnation scheme for redistributing title. *Ibid.*

In those decisions, we emphasized the importance of deferring to legislative judgments about public purpose. Because courts are ill-equipped to evaluate the efficacy of proposed legislative initiatives, we rejected as unworkable the idea of courts' "'deciding on what is and is not a governmental function and . . . invalidating legislation on the basis of their view on that question at the moment of decision, a practice which has proved impracticable in other fields.'" *Id.*, at 240–241 (quoting *United States ex rel. TVA v. Welch*, 327 U.S. 546, 552 (1946)); see *Berman, supra*, at 32 ("[T]he legislature, not the judiciary, is the main guardian of the public needs to be served by social legislation"); see also *Lingle v. Chevron U.S.A., Inc.*, 544 U.S. __ (2005). Likewise, we recognized our inability to evaluate whether, in a given case, eminent domain is a necessary means by which to pursue the legislature's ends. *Midkiff, supra*, at 242; *Berman, supra*, at 103.

Yet for all the emphasis on deference, *Berman* and *Midkiff* hewed to a bedrock principle without which our public use jurisprudence would collapse: "A purely private taking could not withstand the scrutiny of the public use requirement; it would serve no legitimate purpose of government and would thus be void." *Midkiff*, 467 U.S., at 245; *id.*, at 241 ("[T]he Court's cases have repeatedly stated that 'one person's property may not be taken for the benefit of another private person without a justifying public purpose, even though compensation be paid'" (quoting *Thompson v. Consolidated Gas Util. Corp.*, 300 U.S. 55, 80 (1937))); see also *Missouri Pacific R. Co. v. Nebraska*, 164 U.S. 403, 417 (1896). To protect that principle, those decisions reserved "a role for courts to play in reviewing a legislature's judgment of what constitutes a public use . . . [though] the Court in *Berman* made clear that it is 'an extremely narrow' one." *Midkiff, supra*, at 240 (quoting *Berman, supra*, at 32).

The Court's holdings in *Berman* and *Midkiff* were true to the principle underlying the Public Use Clause. In both those cases, the extraordinary, precondemnation use of the targeted property inflicted affirmative harm on society—in *Berman* through blight resulting from extreme poverty and in *Midkiff* through oligopoly resulting from extreme wealth. And in both cases, the relevant legislative body had found that eliminating the existing property use was necessary to remedy the harm. *Berman, supra*, at 28–29; *Midkiff, supra*, at 232. Thus a public purpose was realized when the harmful use was eliminated. Because each taking *directly* achieved a public benefit, it did not matter that the property was turned over to private use. Here, in contrast, New London does not claim that Susette Kelo's and Wilhelmina Dery's well-maintained homes are the source of any social harm. Indeed, it could not so claim without adopting the absurd argument that any single-family home that might be razed to make way for an apartment building, or any church that might be replaced with a retail store, or any small business that might be more lucrative if it were instead part of a national franchise, is inherently harmful to society and thus within the government's power to condemn.

In moving away from our decisions sanctioning the condemnation of harmful property use, the Court today significantly expands the meaning of public use. It holds that the sovereign may take private property currently put to ordinary private use, and give it over for new, ordinary private use, so long as the new use is predicted to generate some secondary benefit for the public—such as increased tax revenue, more jobs, maybe even aesthetic pleasure. But nearly any lawful use of real private property can be said to generate some incidental benefit to the public. Thus, if predicted (or even guaranteed) positive side effects are enough to render transfer from one private party to another constitutional, then the words "for public use" do not realistically exclude *any* takings, and thus do not exert any constraint on the eminent domain power.

There is a sense in which this troubling result follows from errant language in *Berman* and *Midkiff*. In discussing whether takings within a blighted neighborhood were for a public use, *Berman* began by observing: "We deal, in other words, with what traditionally has been known as the police power." 348 U.S., at 32. From there it declared that "[o]nce the object is within the authority of Congress, the right to realize it through the exercise of eminent domain is clear." *Id.*, at 33. Following up, we said in *Midkiff* that "[t]he 'public use' requirement is coterminous with the scope of a sovereign's police powers." 467 U.S., at 240. This language was unnecessary to the specific holdings of those decisions. *Berman* and *Midkiff* simply did not put such language to the constitutional test, because the takings in those cases were within the police power but also for "public use" for the reasons I have described. The case before us now demonstrates why, when deciding if a taking's purpose is constitutional, the police power and "public use" cannot always be equated. The Court protests that it does not sanction

(Continues)

the bare transfer from *A* to *B* for *B*'s benefit. It suggests two limitations on what can be taken after today's decision. First, it maintains a role for courts in ferreting out takings whose sole purpose is to bestow a benefit on the private transferee—without detailing how courts are to conduct that complicated inquiry. *Ante*, at 7. For his part, *Justice Kennedy* suggests that courts may divine illicit purpose by a careful review of the record and the process by which a legislature arrived at the decision to take—without specifying what courts should look for in a case with different facts, how they will know if they have found it, and what to do if they do not. *Ante*, at 2–3 (concurring opinion). Whatever the details of *Justice Kennedy*'s as-yet-undisclosed test, it is difficult to envision anyone but the "stupid staff[er]" failing it. See *Lucas v. South Carolina Coastal Council*, 505 U.S. 1003, 1025–1026, n. 12 (1992). The trouble with economic development takings is that private benefit and incidental public benefit are, by definition, merged and mutually reinforcing. In this case, for example, any boon for Pfizer or the plan's developer is difficult to disaggregate from the promised public gains in taxes and jobs. See App. to Pet. for Cert. 275–277.

Even if there were a practical way to isolate the motives behind a given taking, the gesture toward a purpose test is theoretically flawed. If it is true that incidental public benefits from new private use are enough to ensure the "public purpose" in a taking, why should it matter, as far as the Fifth Amendment is concerned, what inspired the taking in the first place? How much the government does or does not desire to benefit a favored private party has no bearing on whether an economic development taking will or will not generate secondary benefit for the public. And whatever the reason for a given condemnation, the effect is the same from the constitutional perspective—private property is forcibly relinquished to new private ownership.

A second proposed limitation is implicit in the Court's opinion. The logic of today's decision is that eminent domain may only be used to upgrade—not downgrade—property. At best this makes the Public Use Clause redundant with the Due Process Clause, which already prohibits irrational government action. See *Lingle*, 544 U.S. __. The Court rightfully admits, however, that the judiciary cannot get bogged down in predictive judgments about whether the public will actually be better off after a property transfer. In any event, this constraint has no realistic import. For who among us can say she already makes the most productive or attractive possible use of her property? The specter of condemnation hangs over all property. Nothing is to prevent the State from replacing any Motel 6 with a Ritz-Carlton, any home with a shopping mall, or any farm with a factory. Cf. *Bugryn v. Bristol*, 63 Conn. App. 98, 774 A. 2d 1042 (2001) (taking the homes and farm of four owners in their 70's and 80's and giving it to an "industrial park"); *99 Cents Only Stores v. Lancaster Redevelopment Authority*, 237 F. Supp. 2d 1123 (CD Cal. 2001) (attempted taking of 99 Cents store to replace with a Costco); *Poletown Neighborhood Council v. Detroit*, 410 Mich. 616, 304 N. W. 2d 455 (1981) (taking a working-class, immigrant community in Detroit and giving it to a General Motors assembly plant), overruled by *County of Wayne v. Hathcock*, 471 Mich. 415, 684 N. W. 2d 765 (2004); Brief for the Becket Fund for Religious Liberty as *Amicus Curiae* 4-11 (describing takings of religious institutions' properties); Institute for Justice, D. Berliner, *Public Power, Private Gain: A Five-Year, State-by-State Report Examining the Abuse of Eminent Domain* (2003) (collecting accounts of economic development takings).

The Court also puts special emphasis on facts peculiar to this case: The NLDC's plan is the product of a relatively careful deliberative process; it proposes to use eminent domain for a multipart, integrated plan rather than for isolated property transfer; it promises an array of incidental benefits (even aesthetic ones), not just increased tax revenue; it comes on the heels of a legislative determination that New London is a depressed municipality. See, *e.g.*, *ante*, at 16 ("[A] one-to-one transfer of property, executed outside the confines of an integrated development plan, is not presented in this case"). *Justice Kennedy*, too, takes great comfort in these facts. *Ante*, at 4 (concurring opinion). But none has legal significance to blunt the force of today's holding. If legislative prognostications about the secondary public benefits of a new use can legitimate a taking, there is nothing in the Court's rule or in *Justice Kennedy*'s gloss on that rule to prohibit property transfers generated with less care, that are less comprehensive, that happen to result from less elaborate process, whose only projected advantage is the incidence of higher taxes, or that hope to transform an already prosperous city into an even more prosperous one.

Finally, in a coda, the Court suggests that property owners should turn to the States, who may or may not choose to impose appropriate limits on economic development takings. *Ante*, at 19. This is an abdication of our responsibility. States play many important functions in our system of dual sovereignty, but compensating for our refusal to enforce properly the Federal Constitution (and a provision meant to curtail state action, no less) is not among them.

***

It was possible after *Berman* and *Midkiff* to imagine unconstitutional transfers from *A* to *B*. Those decisions endorsed government intervention when private property use had veered to such an extreme that the public was suffering as a consequence. Today nearly all real property is susceptible to condemnation on the Court's theory. In the prescient words of a dissenter from the infamous decision in *Poletown*, "[n]ow that we have authorized local legislative bodies to decide that a different commercial or industrial use of property will produce greater public benefits than its present use, no homeowner's, merchant's or manufacturer's property, however productive or valuable to its owner, is immune from condemnation for the benefit of other private interests that will put it to a 'higher' use." 410 Mich., at 644–645, 304 N. W. 2d, at 464 (opinion of Fitzgerald, J.). This is why economic development takings "seriously jeopardiz[e] the security of all private property ownership." *Id.*, at 645, 304 N. W. 2d, at 465 (Ryan, J., dissenting).

Any property may now be taken for the benefit of another private party, but the fallout from this decision will not be random. The beneficiaries are likely to be those citizens with disproportionate influence and power in the political process, including large corporations and development firms. As for the victims, the government now has license to transfer property from those with fewer resources to those with more. The Founders cannot have intended this perverse result. "[T]hat alone is a *just* government," wrote James Madison, "which *impartially* secures to every man, whatever is his *own*." For the *National Gazette*, Property, (Mar. 29, 1792), reprinted in *14 Papers of James Madison* 266 (R. Rutland et al. eds. 1983).

I would hold that the takings in both Parcel 3 and Parcel 4A are unconstitutional, reverse the judgment of the Supreme Court of Connecticut, and remand for further proceedings.

Justice Thomas, dissenting.

Long ago, William Blackstone wrote that "the law of the land ... postpone[s] even public necessity to the sacred and inviolable rights of private property."[47] *Commentaries on the Laws of England* 134–135 (1765) (hereinafter Blackstone). The Framers embodied that principle in the Constitution, allowing the government to take property not for "public necessity," but instead for "public use." Amdt. 5. Defying this understanding, the Court replaces the Public Use Clause with a "'[P]ublic [P]urpose'" Clause, *ante*, at 9–10 (or perhaps the "Diverse and Always Evolving Needs of Society" Clause, *ante*, at 8 (capitalization added)), a restriction that is satisfied, the Court instructs, so long as the purpose is "legitimate" and the means "not irrational," *ante*, at 17 (internal quotation marks omitted). This deferential shift in phraseology enables the Court to hold, against all common sense, that a costly urban-renewal project whose stated purpose is a vague promise of new jobs and increased tax revenue, but which is also suspiciously agreeable to the Pfizer Corporation, is for a "public use."

I cannot agree. If such "economic development" takings are for a "public use," any taking is, and the Court has erased the Public Use Clause from our Constitution, as *Justice O'Connor* powerfully argues in dissent. *Ante*, at 1–2, 8–13. I do not believe that this Court can eliminate liberties expressly enumerated in the Constitution and therefore join her dissenting opinion. Regrettably, however, the Court's error runs deeper than this. Today's decision is simply the latest in a string of our cases construing the Public Use Clause to be a virtual nullity, without the slightest nod to its original meaning. In my view, the Public Use Clause, originally understood, is a meaningful limit on the government's eminent domain power. Our cases have strayed from the Clause's original meaning, and I would reconsider them.

I

The Fifth Amendment provides:

"No person shall be held to answer for a capital, or otherwise infamous crime, unless on a presentment or indictment of a Grand Jury, except in cases arising in the land or naval forces, or in the Militia, when in actual service in time of War or public danger; nor shall any person be subject for the same offence to be twice put in jeopardy of life or limb, nor shall be compelled in any criminal case to be a witness against himself, nor be deprived of life, liberty, or property, without due process, of law; *nor shall private property be taken for public use, without just compensation*." (Emphasis added.)

It is the last of these liberties, the Takings Clause, that is at issue in this case. In my view, it is "imperative that the Court maintain absolute fidelity to" the Clause's express limit on the power of the

(Continues)

(*Continued*)

government over the individual, no less than with every other liberty expressly enumerated in the Fifth Amendment or the Bill of Rights more generally. *Shepard v. United States*, 544 U.S. ___, ___ (2005) (slip op., at 2) (*Thomas, J.*, concurring in part and concurring in judgment) (internal quotation marks omitted).

Though one component of the protection provided by the Takings Clause is that the government can take private property only if it provides "just compensation" for the taking, the Takings Clause also prohibits the government from taking property except "for public use." Were it otherwise, the Takings Clause would either be meaningless or empty. If the Public Use Clause served no function other than to state that the government may take property through its eminent domain power—for public or private uses—then it would be surplusage. See *ante*, at 3–4 (*O'Connor, J.*, dissenting); see also *Marbury v. Madison*, 1 Cranch 137, 174 (1803) ("It cannot be presumed that any clause in the constitution is intended to be without effect"); *Myers v. United States*, 272 U.S. 52, 151 (1926). Alternatively, the Clause could distinguish those takings that require compensation from those that do not. That interpretation, however, "would permit private property to be taken or appropriated for private use without any compensation whatever." *Cole v. La Grange*, 113 U.S. 1, 8 (1885) (interpreting same language in the Missouri Public Use Clause). In other words, the Clause would require the government to compensate for takings done "for public use," leaving it free to take property for purely private uses without the payment of compensation. This would contradict a bedrock principle well established by the time of the founding: that all takings required the payment of compensation. 1 Blackstone 135; 2 J. Kent, *Commentaries on American Law* 275 (1827) (hereinafter Kent); J. Madison, for the National Property Gazette, (Mar. 27, 1792), in *14 Papers of James Madison* 266, 267 (R. Rutland et al. eds. 1983) (arguing that no property "shall be taken *directly* even for public use without indemnification to the owner").[47] The Public Use Clause, like the Just Compensation Clause, is therefore an express limit on the government's power of eminent domain.

The most natural reading of the Clause is that it allows the government to take property only if the government owns, or the public has a legal right to use, the property, as opposed to taking it for any public purpose or necessity whatsoever. At the time of the founding, dictionaries primarily defined the noun "use" as "[t]he act of employing any thing to any purpose." 2 S. Johnson, *A Dictionary of the English Language* 2194 (4th ed. 1773) (hereinafter Johnson). The term "use," moreover, "is from the Latin *utor*, which means 'to use, make use of, avail one's self of, employ, apply, enjoy, etc." J. Lewis, *Law of Eminent Domain* §165, p. 224, n. 4 (1888) (hereinafter Lewis). When the government takes property and gives it to a private individual, and the public has no right to use the property, it strains language to say that the public is "employing" the property, regardless of the incidental benefits that might accrue to the public from the private use. The term "public use," then, means that either the government or its citizens as a whole must actually "employ" the taken property. See *id.*, at 223 (reviewing founding-era dictionaries).

Granted, another sense of the word "use" was broader in meaning, extending to "[c]onvenience" or "help," or "[q]ualities that make a thing proper for any purpose." 2 Johnson 2194. Nevertheless, read in context, the term "public use" possesses the narrower meaning. Elsewhere, the Constitution twice employs the word "use," both times in its narrower sense. Claeys, *Public-Use Limitations and Natural Property Rights*, 2004 Mich. St. L. Rev. 877, 897 (hereinafter Public Use Limitations). Article 1, §10 provides that "the net Produce of all Duties and Imposts, laid by any State on Imports or Exports, shall be for the Use of the Treasury of the United States," meaning the Treasury itself will control the taxes, not use it to any beneficial end. And Article I, §8 grants Congress power "[t]o raise and support Armies, but no Appropriation of Money to that Use shall be for a longer Term than two Years." Here again, "use" means "employed to raise and support Armies," not anything directed to achieving any military end. The same word in the Public Use Clause should be interpreted to have the same meaning.

Tellingly, the phrase "public use" contrasts with the very different phrase "general Welfare" used elsewhere in the Constitution. See *ibid.* ("Congress shall have Power To . . . provide for the common Defence and general Welfare of the United States"); preamble (Constitution established "to promote the general Welfare"). The Framers would have used some such broader term if they had meant the Public Use Clause to have a similarly sweeping scope. Other founding-era documents made the contrast between these two usages still more explicit. See Sales, Classical Republicanism and the Fifth Amendment's "Public Use" Requirement, 49 *Duke L. J.* 339, 368 (2000) (hereinafter Sales) (noting contrast between, on the one hand, the term "public use" used by 6 of the first 13 States and, on the other, the terms "public exigencies" employed in the Massachusetts Bill of Rights and the Northwest Ordinance, and the term "public necessity" used in the Vermont Constitution of 1786).

The Constitution's text, in short, suggests that the Takings Clause authorizes the taking of property only if the public has a right to employ it, not if the public realizes any conceivable benefit from the taking.

The Constitution's common-law background reinforces this understanding. The common law provided an express method of eliminating uses of land that adversely impacted the public welfare: nuisance law. Blackstone and Kent, for instance, both carefully distinguished the law of nuisance from the power of eminent domain. Compare 1 Blackstone 135 (noting government's power to take private property with compensation), with 3 *id.*, at 216 (noting action to remedy "*public . . .* nuisances, which affect the public and are an annoyance to *all* the king's subjects"); see also 2 Kent 274–276 (distinguishing the two). Blackstone rejected the idea that private property could be taken solely for purposes of any public benefit. "So great . . . is the regard of the law for private property," he explained, "that it will not authorize the least violation of it; no, not even for the general good of the whole community." 1 Blackstone 135. He continued: "If a new road . . . were to be made through the grounds of a private person, it might perhaps be extensively beneficial to the public; but the law permits no man, or set of men, to do this without the consent of the owner of the land." *Ibid.* Only "by giving [the landowner] full indemnification" could the government take property, and even then "[t]he public [was] now considered as an individual, treating with an individual for an exchange." *Ibid.* When the public took property, in other words, it took it as an individual buying property from another typically would: for one's own use. The Public Use Clause, in short, embodied the Framers' understanding that property is a natural, fundamental right, prohibiting the government from "tak[ing] *property* from A. and giv[ing] it to B." *Calder v. Bull,* 3 Dall. 386, 388 (1798); see also *Wilkinson v. Leland,* 2 Pet. 627, 658 (1829); *Vanhorne's Lessee v. Dorrance,* 2 Dall. 304, 311 (CC Pa. 1795).

The public purpose interpretation of the Public Use Clause also unnecessarily duplicates a similar inquiry required by the Necessary and Proper Clause. The Takings Clause is a prohibition, not a grant of power: The Constitution does not expressly grant the Federal Government the power to take property for any public purpose whatsoever. Instead, the Government may take property only when necessary and proper to the exercise of an expressly enumerated power. See *Kohl v. United States,* 91 U.S. 367, 371–372 (1876) (noting Federal Government's power under the Necessary and Proper Clause to take property "needed for forts, armories, and arsenals, for navy-yards and lighthouses, for custom-houses, post-offices, and court-houses, and for other public uses"). For a law to be within the Necessary and Proper Clause, as I have elsewhere explained, it must bear an "obvious, simple, and direct relation" to an exercise of Congress' enumerated powers, *Sabri v. United States,* 541 U.S. 600, 613 (2004) (*Thomas, J.,* concurring in judgment), and it must not "subvert basic principles of" constitutional design, *Gonzales v. Raich, ante,* at __ (*Thomas, J.,* dissenting). In other words, a taking is permissible under the Necessary and Proper Clause only if it serves a valid public purpose. Interpreting the Public Use Clause likewise to limit the government to take property only for sufficiently public purposes replicates this inquiry. If this is all the Clause means, it is, once again, surplusage. See *supra,* at 3. The Clause is thus most naturally read to concern whether the property is used by the public or the government, not whether the purpose of the taking is legitimately public.

II

Early American eminent domain practice largely bears out this understanding of the Public Use Clause. This practice concerns state limits on eminent domain power, not the Fifth Amendment, since it was not until the late 19th century that the Federal Government began to use the power of eminent domain, and since the Takings Clause did not even arguably limit state power until after the passage of the Fourteenth Amendment. See Note, The Public Use Limitation on Eminent Domain: An Advance Requiem, 58 *Yale L. J.* 599, 599-600, and nn. 3–4 (1949); *Barron ex rel. Tiernan v. Mayor of Baltimore,* 7 Pet. 243, 250–251 (1833) (holding the Takings Clause inapplicable to the States of its own force). Nevertheless, several early state constitutions at the time of the founding likewise limited the power of eminent domain to "public uses." See Sales 367–369, and n. 137 (emphasis deleted). Their practices therefore shed light on the original meaning of the same words contained in the Public Use Clause.

States employed the eminent domain power to provide quintessentially public goods, such as public roads, toll roads, ferries, canals, railroads, and public parks. Lewis §§166, 168–171, 175, at 227–228, 234–241, 243. Though use of the eminent domain power was sparse at the time of the founding, many States did have so-called Mill Acts, which authorized the owners of grist mills operated by water power to flood upstream lands with the payment of compensation to the upstream landowner.

(Continues)

(*Continued*)

See, *e.g., id.*, §178, at 245–246; *Head v. Amoskeag Mfg. Co.*, 113 U.S. 9, 16–19, and n. (1885). Those early grist mills "were regulated by law and compelled to serve the public for a stipulated toll and in regular order," and therefore were actually used by the public. Lewis §178, at 246, and n. 3; see also *Head, supra,* at 18–19. They were common carriers—quasi-public entities. These were "public uses" in the fullest sense of the word, because the public could legally use and benefit from them equally. See Public Use Limitations 903 (common-carrier status traditionally afforded to "private beneficiaries of a state franchise or another form of state monopoly, or to companies that operated in conditions of natural monopoly").

To be sure, some early state legislatures tested the limits of their state-law eminent domain power. Some States enacted statutes allowing the taking of property for the purpose of building private roads. See Lewis §167, at 230. These statutes were mixed; some required the private landowner to keep the road open to the public, and others did not. See *id.*, §167, at 230–234. Later in the 19th century, moreover, the Mill Acts were employed to grant rights to private manufacturing plants, in addition to grist mills that had common-carrier duties. See, *e.g.*, M. Horwitz, *The Transformation of American Law 1780–1860*, pp. 51–52 (1977).

These early uses of the eminent domain power are often cited as evidence for the broad "public purpose" interpretation of the Public Use Clause, see, *e.g., ante*, at 8, n. 8 (majority opinion); Brief for Respondents 30; Brief for American Planning Assn. et al. as *Amici Curiae* at 6–7, but in fact the constitutionality of these exercises of eminent domain power under state public use restrictions was a hotly contested question in state courts throughout the 19th and into the 20th century. Some courts construed those clauses to authorize takings for public purposes, but others adhered to the natural meaning of "public use."[48] As noted above, the earliest Mill Acts were applied to entities with duties to remain open to the public, and their later extension is not deeply probative of whether that subsequent practice is consistent with the original meaning of the Public Use Clause. See *McIntyre v. Ohio Elections Comm'n*, 514 U.S. 334, 370 (1995) (*Thomas, J.*, concurring in judgment). At the time of the founding, "[b]usiness corporations were only beginning to upset the old corporate model, in which the raison d'être of chartered associations was their service to the public," Horwitz, *supra*, at 49–50, so it was natural to those who framed the first Public Use Clauses to think of mills as inherently public entities. The disagreement among state courts, and state legislatures' attempts to circumvent public use limits on their eminent domain power, cannot obscure that the Public Use Clause is most naturally read to authorize takings for public use only if the government or the public actually uses the taken property.

III

Our current Public Use Clause jurisprudence, as the Court notes, has rejected this natural reading of the Clause. *Ante*, at 8–10. The Court adopted its modern reading blindly, with little discussion of the Clause's history and original meaning, in two distinct lines of cases: first, in cases adopting the "public purpose" interpretation of the Clause, and second, in cases deferring to legislatures' judgments regarding what constitutes a valid public purpose. Those questionable cases converged in the boundlessly broad and deferential conception of "public use" adopted by this Court in *Berman v. Parker*, 348 U.S. 26 (1954), and *Hawaii Housing Authority v. Midkiff*, 467 U.S. 229 (1984), cases that take center stage in the Court's opinion. See *ante*, 10–12. The weakness of those two lines of cases, and consequently *Berman* and *Midkiff*, fatally undermines the doctrinal foundations of the Court's decision. Today's questionable application of these cases is further proof that the "public purpose" standard is not susceptible of principled application. This Court's reliance by rote on this standard is ill advised and should be reconsidered.

A

As the Court notes, the "public purpose" interpretation of the Public Use Clause stems from *Fallbrook Irrigation Dist. v. Bradley*, 164 U.S. 112, 161–162 (1896). *Ante*, at 11. The issue in *Bradley* was whether a condemnation for purposes of constructing an irrigation ditch was for a public use. 164 U.S., at 161. This was a public use, Justice Peckham declared for the Court, because "[t]o irrigate and thus to bring into possible cultivation these large masses of otherwise worthless lands would seem to be a public purpose and a matter of public interest, not confined to landowners, or even to any one section of the State." *Ibid.* That broad statement was dictum, for the law under review also provided that "[a]ll landowners in the district have the right to a proportionate share of the water." *Id.*, at 162. Thus, the "public" did have the right to use the irrigation ditch because all similarly situated members of the public—those who owned lands irrigated by the ditch-had a right to use it. The Court cited no authority for its dictum, and did not discuss either the Public Use Clause's original meaning or the numerous authorities that had adopted the "actual use" test (though it at least acknowledged the conflict of authority in state courts, see *id.*, at 158; *supra*, at 9, and n. 2). Instead, the Court reasoned that "[t]he use must be regarded as a public use, or else it would seem to follow that no general scheme of irrigation can be formed or carried into effect." *Bradley, supra*, at 160–161. This is no statement of constitutional principle: Whatever the utility of irrigation districts or the merits of the Court's view that another rule would be "impractical given the diverse and always evolving needs of society," *ante*, at 8, the Constitution does not embody those policy preferences any more than it "enact[s] Mr. Herbert Spencer's Social Statics." *Lochner v. New York*, 198 U.S. 45, 75 (1905) (Holmes, J., dissenting); but see *id.*, at 58–62 (Peckham, J., for the Court).

This Court's cases followed *Bradley*'s test with little analysis. In *Clark v. Nash*, 198 U.S. 361 (1905) (Peckham, J., for the Court), this Court relied on little more than a citation to *Bradley* in upholding another condemnation for the purpose of laying an irrigation ditch. 198 U.S., at 369–370. As in *Bradley*, use of the "public purpose" test was unnecessary to the result the Court reached. The government condemned the irrigation ditch for the purpose of ensuring access to water in which "[o]ther land owners adjoining the defendant in error . . . might share," 198 U.S., at 370, and therefore *Clark* also involved a condemnation for the purpose of ensuring access to a resource to which similarly situated members of the public had a legal right of access. Likewise, in *Strickley v. Highland Boy Gold Mining Co.*, 200 U.S. 527 (1906), the Court upheld a condemnation establishing an aerial right-of-way for a bucket line operated by a mining company, relying on little more than *Clark*, see *Strickley, supra*, at 531. This case, too, could have been disposed of on the narrower ground that "the plaintiff [was] a carrier for itself and others," 200 U.S., at 531–532, and therefore that the bucket line was legally open to the public. Instead, the Court unnecessarily rested its decision on the "inadequacy of use by the general public as a universal test." *Id.*, at 531. This Court's cases quickly incorporated the public purpose standard set forth in *Clark* and *Strickley* by barren citation. See, *e.g.*, *Rindge Co. v. County of Los Angeles*, 262 U.S. 700, 707 (1923); *Block v. Hirsh*, 256 U.S. 135, 155 (1921); *Mt. Vernon-Woodberry Cotton Duck Co. v. Alabama Interstate Power Co.*, 240 U.S. 30, 32 (1916); *O'Neill v. Leamer*, 239 U.S. 244, 253 (1915).

B

A second line of this Court's cases also deviated from the Public Use Clause's original meaning by allowing legislatures to define the scope of valid "public uses." *United States v. Gettysburg Electric R. Co.*, 160 U.S. 668 (1896), involved the question whether Congress' decision to condemn certain private land for the purpose of building battlefield memorials at Gettysburg, Pennsylvania, was for a public use. *Id.*, at 679–680. Since the Federal Government was to use the lands in question, *id.*, at 682, there is no doubt that it was a public use under any reasonable standard. Nonetheless, the Court, speaking through Justice Peckham, declared that "when the legislature has declared the use or purpose to be a public one, its judgment will be respected by the courts, unless the use be palpably without reasonable foundation." *Id.*, at 680. As it had with the "public purpose" dictum in *Bradley, supra*, the Court quickly incorporated this dictum into its Public Use Clause cases with little discussion. See, *e.g.*, *United States ex rel. TVA v. Welch*, 327 U.S. 546, 552 (1946); *Old Dominion Land Co. v. United States*, 269 U.S. 55, 66 (1925).

There is no justification, however, for affording almost insurmountable deference to legislative conclusions that a use serves a "public use." To begin with, a court owes no deference to a legislature's judgment concerning the quintessentially legal question of whether the government owns, or the public has a legal right to use, the taken property. Even under the "public purpose" interpretation, moreover, it is most implausible that the Framers intended to defer to legislatures as to what satisfies the Public Use Clause, uniquely among all the express provisions of the Bill of Rights. We would not defer to a legislature's determination of the various circumstances that establish, for example, when a search of a home would be reasonable, see, *e.g.*, *Payton v. New York*, 445 U.S. 573, 589–590 (1980), or when a convicted double-murderer may be shackled during a sentencing proceeding without on-the-record findings, see *Deck v. Missouri*, 544 U.S. ___ (2005), or when state law creates a property interest protected by the Due Process Clause, see, *e.g.*, *Castle Rock v. Gonzales, post*, at __; *Board of Regents of State Colleges v. Roth*, 408 U.S. 564, 576 (1972); *Goldberg v. Kelly*, 397 U.S. 254, 262–263 (1970).

(Continues)

(Continued)

Still worse, it is backwards to adopt a searching standard of constitutional review for nontraditional property interests, such as welfare benefits, see, *e.g., Goldberg, supra,* while deferring to the legislature's determination as to what constitutes a public use when it exercises the power of eminent domain, and thereby invades individuals' traditional rights in real property. The Court has elsewhere recognized "the overriding respect for the sanctity of the home that has been embedded in our traditions since the origins of the Republic," *Payton, supra,* at 601, when the issue is only whether the government may search a home. Yet today the Court tells us that we are not to "second-guess the City's considered judgments," *ante,* at 18, when the issue is, instead, whether the government may take the infinitely more intrusive step of tearing down petitioners' homes. Something has gone seriously awry with this Court's interpretation of the Constitution. Though citizens are safe from the government in their homes, the homes themselves are not. Once one accepts, as the Court at least nominally does, *ante,* at 6, that the Public Use Clause is a limit on the eminent domain power of the Federal Government and the States, there is no justification for the almost complete deference it grants to legislatures as to what satisfies it.

C

These two misguided lines of precedent converged in *Berman v. Parker,* 348 U.S. 26 (1954), and *Hawaii Housing Authority v. Midkiff,* 467 U.S. 229 (1984). Relying on those lines of cases, the Court in *Berman* and *Midkiff* upheld condemnations for the purposes of slum clearance and land redistribution, respectively. "Subject to specific constitutional limitations," *Berman* proclaimed, "when the legislature has spoken, the public interest has been declared in terms well-nigh conclusive. In such cases the legislature, not the judiciary, is the main guardian of the public needs to be served by social legislation." 348 U.S., at 32. That reasoning was question begging, since the question to be decided was whether the "specific constitutional limitation" of the Public Use Clause prevented the taking of the appellant's (concededly "nonblighted") department store. *Id.,* at 31, 34. *Berman* also appeared to reason that any exercise by Congress of an enumerated power (in this case, its plenary power over the District of Columbia) was *per se* a "public use" under the Fifth Amendment. *Id.,* at 33. But the very point of the Public Use Clause is to limit that power. See *supra,* at 3–4.

More fundamentally, *Berman* and *Midkiff* erred by equating the eminent domain power with the police power of States. See *Midkiff,* 467 U.S., at 240 ("The 'public use' requirement is . . . coterminous with the scope of a sovereign's police powers"); *Berman,* 348 U.S., at 32. Traditional uses of that regulatory power, such as the power to abate a nuisance, required no compensation whatsoever, see *Mugler v. Kansas,* 123 U.S. 623, 668–669 (1887), in sharp contrast to the takings power, which has always required compensation, see *supra,* at 3, and n. 1. The question whether the State can take property using the power of eminent domain is therefore distinct from the question whether it can regulate property pursuant to the police power. See, *e.g., Lucas v. South Carolina Coastal Council,* 505 U.S. 1003, 1014 (1992); *Mugler, supra,* at 668–669. In *Berman,* for example, if the slums at issue were truly "blighted," then state nuisance law, see, *e.g. supra,* at 5–6; *Lucas, supra,* at 1029, not the power of eminent domain, would provide the appropriate remedy. To construe the Public Use Clause to overlap with the States' police power conflates these two categories.[49]

The "public purpose" test applied by *Berman* and *Midkiff* also cannot be applied in principled manner. "When we depart from the natural import of the term 'public use,' and substitute for the simple idea of a public possession and occupation, that of public utility, public interest, common benefit, general advantage or convenience . . . we are afloat without any certain principle to guide us." *Bloodgood v. Mohawk & Hudson R. Co.,* 18 Wend. 9, 60–61 (NY 1837) (opinion of Tracy, Sen.). Once one permits takings for public purposes in addition to public uses, no coherent principle limits what could constitute a valid public use—at least, none beyond *Justice O'Connor's* (entirely proper) appeal to the text of the Constitution itself. See *ante,* at 1–2, 8–13 (dissenting opinion). I share the Court's skepticism about a public use standard that requires courts to second-guess the policy wisdom of public works projects. *Ante,* at 16–19. The "public purpose" standard this Court has adopted, however, demands the use of such judgment, for the Court concedes that the Public Use Clause would forbid a purely private taking. *Ante,* at 7–8. It is difficult to imagine how a court could find that a taking was purely private except by determining that the taking did not, in fact, rationally advance the public interest. Cf. *ante,* at 9–10 (*O'Connor, J.,* dissenting) (noting the complicated inquiry the Court's test requires). The Court is therefore wrong to criticize the "actual use" test as "difficult to administer." *Ante,* at 8. It is far easier to analyze whether the government owns or the public has a legal right to use the taken property than to ask whether the taking has a "purely private purpose"—unless the Court means to eliminate public use scrutiny of takings entirely. *Ante*, at 7–8, 16–17. Obliterating a provision of the Constitution, of course, guarantees that it will not be misapplied.

For all these reasons, I would revisit our Public Use Clause cases and consider returning to the original meaning of the Public Use Clause: that the government may take property only if it actually uses or gives the public a legal right to use the property.

IV

The consequences of today's decision are not difficult to predict, and promise to be harmful. So-called "urban renewal" programs provide some compensation for the properties they take, but no compensation is possible for the subjective value of these lands to the individuals displaced and the indignity inflicted by uprooting them from their homes. Allowing the government to take property solely for public purposes is bad enough, but extending the concept of public purpose to encompass any economically beneficial goal guarantees that these losses will fall disproportionately on poor communities. Those communities are not only systematically less likely to put their lands to the highest and best social use, but are also the least politically powerful. If ever there were justification for intrusive judicial review of constitutional provisions that protect "discrete and insular minorities," *United States v. Carolene Products Co.*, 304 U.S. 144, 152, n. 4 (1938), surely that principle would apply with great force to the powerless groups and individuals the Public Use Clause protects. The deferential standard this Court has adopted for the Public Use Clause is therefore deeply perverse. It encourages "those citizens with disproportionate influence and power in the political process, including large corporations and development firms" to victimize the weak. *Ante*, at 11 (*O'Connor, J.,* dissenting).

Those incentives have made the legacy of this Court's "public purpose" test an unhappy one. In the 1950's, no doubt emboldened in part by the expansive understanding of "public use" this Court adopted in *Berman*, cities "rushed to draw plans" for downtown development. B. Frieden & L. Sagalayn, Downtown, Inc. *How America Rebuilds Cities* 17 (1989). "Of all the families displaced by urban renewal from 1949 through 1963, 63 percent of those whose race was known were nonwhite, and of these families, 56 percent of nonwhites and 38 percent of whites had incomes low enough to qualify for public housing, which, however, was seldom available to them." *Id.*, at 28. Public works projects in the 1950s and 1960s destroyed predominantly minority communities in St. Paul, Minnesota, and Baltimore, Maryland. *Id.*, at 28–29. In 1981, urban planners in Detroit, Michigan, uprooted the largely "lower-income and elderly" Poletown neighborhood for the benefit of the General Motors Corporation. J. Wylie, *Poletown: Community Betrayed* 58 (1989). Urban renewal projects have long been associated with the displacement of blacks; "[i]n cities across the country, urban renewal came to be known as 'Negro removal.'" Pritchett, The "Public Menace" of Blight: Urban Renewal and the Private Uses of Eminent Domain, 21 *Yale L. & Pol'y Rev.* 1, 47 (2003). Over 97 percent of the individuals forcibly removed from their homes by the "slum-clearance" project upheld by this Court in *Berman* were black. 348 U.S., at 30. Regrettably, the predictable consequence of the Court's decision will be to exacerbate these effects.

***

The Court relies almost exclusively on this Court's prior cases to derive today's far-reaching, and dangerous, result. See *ante*, at 8–12. But the principles this Court should employ to dispose of this case are found in the Public Use Clause itself, not in Justice Peckham's high opinion of reclamation laws, see *supra*, at 11. When faced with a clash of constitutional principle and a line of unreasoned cases wholly divorced from the text, history, and structure of our founding document, we should not hesitate to resolve the tension in favor of the Constitution's original meaning. For the reasons I have given, and for the reasons given in *Justice O'Connor*'s dissent, the conflict of principle raised by this boundless use of the eminent domain power should be resolved in petitioners' favor. I would reverse the judgment of the Connecticut Supreme Court.

Notes

23. "[N]or shall private property be taken for public use, without just compensation." U.S. Const., Amdt. 5. That Clause is made applicable to the States by the Fourteenth Amendment. See *Chicago, B. & Q. R. Co. v. Chicago*, 166 U.S. 226 (1897).
24. Various state agencies studied the project's economic, environmental, and social ramifications. As part of this process, a team of consultants evaluated six alternative development proposals for the area, which varied in extensiveness and emphasis. The Office of Planning and Management, one of

(Continues)

the primary state agencies undertaking the review, made findings that the project was consistent with relevant state and municipal development policies. See 1 App. 89–95.

25. In the remainder of the opinion we will differentiate between the City and the NLDC only where necessary.

26. While this litigation was pending before the Superior Court, the NLDC announced that it would lease some of the parcels to private developers in exchange for their agreement to develop the land according to the terms of the development plan. Specifically, the NLDC was negotiating a 99-year ground lease with Corcoran Jennison, a developer selected from a group of applicants. The negotiations contemplated a nominal rent of $1 per year, but no agreement had yet been signed. See 268 Conn. 1, 9, 61, 843 A. 2d 500, 509–510, 540 (2004).

27. See also *Calder v. Bull*, 3 Dall. 386, 388 (1798) ("An *act* of the Legislature (for I cannot call it a law) contrary to the great first principles of the social compact, cannot be considered a rightful exercise of legislative authority. . . . A few instances will suffice to explain what I mean . . . [A] law that takes property from *A.* and gives it to *B:* It is against all reason and justice, for a people to entrust a Legislature with *such* powers; and, therefore, it cannot be presumed that they have done it. The genius, the nature, and the spirit, of our State Governments, amount to a prohibition of such acts of legislation; and the general principles of law and reason forbid them" (emphasis deleted)).

28. See 268 Conn., at 159, 843 A. 2d, at 595 (Zarella, J., concurring in part and dissenting in part) ("The record clearly demonstrates that the development plan was not intended to serve the interests of Pfizer, Inc., or any other private entity, but rather, to revitalize the local economy by creating temporary and permanent jobs, generating a significant increase in tax revenue, encouraging spin-off economic activities and maximizing public access to the waterfront"). And while the City intends to transfer certain of the parcels to a private developer in a long-term lease—which developer, in turn, is expected to lease the office space and so forth to other private tenants—the identities of those private parties were not known when the plan was adopted. It is, of course, difficult to accuse the government of having taken *A*'s property to benefit the private interests of *B* when the identity of *B* was unknown.

29. See, *e.g., Dayton Gold & Silver Mining Co. v. Seawell*, 11 Nev. 394, 410, 1876 WL 4573, *11 (1876) ("If public occupation and enjoyment of the object for which land is to be condemned furnishes the only and true test for the right of eminent domain, then the legislature would certainly have the constitutional authority to condemn the lands of any private citizen for the purpose of building hotels and theaters. Why not? A hotel is used by the public as much as a railroad. The public have the same right, upon payment of a fixed compensation, to seek rest and refreshment at a public inn as they have to travel upon a railroad").

30. From upholding the Mill Acts (which authorized manufacturers dependent on power-producing dams to flood upstream lands in exchange for just compensation), to approving takings necessary for the economic development of the West through mining and irrigation, many state courts either circumvented the "use by the public" test when necessary or abandoned it completely. See Nichols, The Meaning of Public Use in the Law of Eminent Domain, 20 B. *U.L. Rev.* 615, 619–624 (1940) (tracing this development and collecting cases). For example, in rejecting the "use by the public" test as overly restrictive, the Nevada Supreme Court stressed that "[m]ining is the greatest of the industrial pursuits in this state. All other interests are subservient to it. Our mountains are almost barren of timber, and our valleys could never be made profitable for agricultural purposes except for the fact of a home market having been created by the mining developments in different sections of the state. The mining and milling interests give employment to many men, and the benefits derived from this business are distributed as much, and sometimes more, among the laboring classes than with the owners of the mines and mills. . . . The present prosperity of the state is entirely due to the mining developments already made, and the entire people of the state are directly interested in having the future developments unobstructed by the obstinate action of any individual or individuals." *Dayton Gold & Silver Mining Co.*, 11 Nev., at 409–410, 1876 WL, at *11.

31. See also *Clark v. Nash*, 198 U.S. 361 (1905) (upholding a statute that authorized the owner of arid land to widen a ditch on his neighbor's property so as to permit a nearby stream to irrigate his land).

32. See, *e.g., Mt. Vernon-Woodberry Cotton Duck Co. v. Alabama Interstate Power Co.*, 240 U.S. 30, 32(1916) ("The inadequacy of use by the general public as a universal test is established"); *Ruckelshaus v. Monsanto Co.*, 467 U.S. 986, 1014-1015 (1984) ("This Court, however, has rejected the notion that a use is a public use only if the property taken is put to use for the general public").

33. See also *Clark*, 198 U.S., at 367–368; *Strickley v. Highland Boy Gold Mining Co.*, 200 U.S. 527, 531(1906) ("In the opinion of the legislature and the Supreme Court of Utah the public welfare of that State demands that aerial lines between the mines upon its mountain sides and railways in the valleys below should not be made impossible by the refusal of a private owner to sell the right to cross his land. The Constitution of the United States does not require us to say that they are wrong"); *O'Neill v. Leamer*, 239 U.S. 244, 253 (1915) ("States may take account of their special exigencies, and when the extent of their arid or wet lands is such that a plan for irrigation or reclamation according to districts may fairly be regarded as one which promotes the public interest, there is nothing in the Federal Constitution which denies to them the right to formulate this policy or to exercise the power of eminent domain in carrying it into effect. With the local situation the state court is peculiarly familiar and its judgment is entitled to the highest respect").

34. Cf. *Village of Euclid v. Ambler Realty Co.*, 272 U.S. 365 (1926).

35. It is a misreading of *Berman* to suggest that the only public use upheld in that case was the initial removal of blight. See Reply Brief for Petitioners 8. The public use described in *Berman* extended beyond that to encompass the purpose of *developing* that area to create conditions that would prevent a reversion to blight in the future. See 348 U.S., at 34–35 ("It was not enough, [the experts] believed, to remove existing buildings that were insanitary or unsightly. It was important to redesign the whole area so as to eliminate the conditions that cause slums. . . . The entire area needed redesigning so that a balanced, integrated plan could be developed for the region, including not only new homes, but also schools, churches, parks, streets, and shopping centers. In this way it was hoped that the cycle of decay of the area could be controlled and the birth of future slums prevented"). Had the public use in *Berman* been defined more narrowly, it would have been difficult to justify the taking of the plaintiff's nonblighted department store.

36. Any number of cases illustrate that the achievement of a public good often coincides with the immediate benefiting of private parties. See, *e.g.*, *National Railroad Passenger Corporation v. Boston & Maine Corp.*, 503 U.S. 407, 422 (1992) (public purpose of "facilitating Amtrak's rail service" served by taking rail track from one private company and transferring it to another private company); *Brown v. Legal Foundation of Wash.*, 538 U.S. 216 (2003) (provision of legal services to the poor is a valid public purpose). It is worth noting that in *Hawaii Housing Authority v. Midkiff,* 467 U.S. 229 (1984), *Monsanto*, and *Boston & Maine Corp.*, the property in question retained the same use even after the change of ownership.

37. Notably, as in the instant case, the private developers in *Berman* were required by contract to use the property to carry out the redevelopment plan. See 348 U.S., at 30.

38. Nor do our cases support *Justice O'Connor's* novel theory that the government may only take property and transfer it to private parties when the initial taking eliminates some "harmful property use." *Post*, at 8 (dissenting opinion). There was nothing "harmful" about the nonblighted department store at issue in *Berman*, 348 U.S. 26; see also n. 13, *supra*; nothing "harmful" about the lands at issue in the mining and agriculture cases, see, *e.g.*, *Strickley*, 200 U.S. 527; see also nn. 9, 11, *supra*; and certainly nothing "harmful" about the trade secrets owned by the pesticide manufacturers in *Monsanto*, 467 U.S. 986. In each case, the public purpose we upheld depended on a private party's *future* use of the concededly nonharmful property that was taken. By focusing on a property's future use, as opposed to its past use, our cases are faithful to the text of the Takings Clause. See U.S. Const., Amdt. 5. ("[N]or shall private property be taken for public use, without just compensation"). *Justice O'Connor's* intimation that a "public purpose" may not be achieved by the action of private parties, see *post*, at 8, confuses the *purpose* of a taking with its *mechanics*, a mistake we warned of in *Midkiff*, 467 U.S., at 244. See also *Berman*, 348 U.S., at 33–34 ("The public end may be as well or better served through an agency of private enterprise than through a department of government").

39. Courts have viewed such aberrations with a skeptical eye. See, *e.g.*, *99 Cents Only Stores v. Lancaster Redevelopment Agency*, 237 F. Supp. 2d 1123 (CD Cal. 2001); cf. *Cincinnati v. Vester*, 281 U.S. 439, 448 (1930) (taking invalid under state eminent domain statute for lack of a reasoned explanation). These types of takings may also implicate other constitutional guarantees. See *Village of Willowbrook v. Olech*, 528 U.S. 562 (2000) *(per curiam)*.

40. Cf. *Panhandle Oil Co. v. Mississippi ex rel. Knox*, 277 U.S. 218, 223 (1928) (Holmes, J., dissenting) ("The power to tax is not the power to destroy while this Court sits").

41. A parade of horribles is especially unpersuasive in this context, since the Takings Clause largely "operates as a conditional limitation, permitting the government to do what it wants so long as it pays the charge." *Eastern Enterprises v. Apfel*, 524 U.S. 498, 545 (1998) *(Kennedy, J., concurring in judgment and dissenting in part)*. Speaking of the takings power, Justice Iredell observed that "[i]t is not sufficient to urge, that the power may be abused, for, such is the nature of all power— such is the tendency of every human institution: and, it might as fairly be said, that the power of

(Continues)

taxation, which is only circumscribed by the discretion of the Body, in which it is vested, ought not to be granted, because the Legislature, disregarding its true objects, might, for visionary and useless projects, impose a tax to the amount of nineteen shillings in the pound. We must be content to limit power where we can, and where we cannot, consistently with its use, we must be content to repose a salutory confidence." *Calder*, 3 Dall., at 400 (opinion concurring in result).

42. See also *Boston & Maine Corp.*, 503 U.S., at 422–423 ("[W]e need not make a specific factual determination whether the condemnation will accomplish its objectives"); *Monsanto*, 467 U.S., at 1015, n. 18 ("Monsanto argues that EPA and, by implication, Congress, misapprehended the true 'barriers to entry' in the pesticide industry and that the challenged provisions of the law create, rather than reduce, barriers to entry. . . . Such economic arguments are better directed to Congress. The proper inquiry before this Court is not whether the provisions in fact will accomplish their stated objectives. Our review is limited to determining that the purpose is legitimate and that Congress rationally could have believed that the provisions would promote that objective").

43. The *amici* raise questions about the fairness of the measure of just compensation. See, *e.g.*, Brief for American Planning Association et al. as *Amici Curiae* 26–30. While important, these questions are not before us in this litigation.

44. See, *e.g.*, *County of Wayne v. Hathcock*, 471 Mich. 445, 684 N. W. 2d 765 (2004).

45. Under California law, for instance, a city may only take land for economic development purposes in blighted areas. Cal. Health & Safety Code Ann. §§33030–33037 (West 1997). See, *e.g.*, *Redevelopment Agency of Chula Vista v. Rados Bros.*, 95 Cal. App. 4th 309 (2002).

46. For example, some argue that the need for eminent domain has been greatly exaggerated because private developers can use numerous techniques, including secret negotiations or precommitment strategies, to overcome holdout problems and assemble lands for genuinely profitable projects. See Brief for Jane Jacobs as *Amicus Curiae* 13–15; see also Brief for John Norquist as *Amicus Curiae*. Others argue to the contrary, urging that the need for eminent domain is especially great with regard to older, small cities like New London, where centuries of development have created an extreme overdivision of land and thus a real market impediment to land assembly. See Brief for Connecticut Conference for Municipalities et al. as *Amici Curiae* 13, 21; see also Brief for National League of Cities et al. as *Amici Curiae*.

47. Some state constitutions at the time of the founding lacked just compensation clauses and took property even without providing compensation. See *Lucas v. South Carolina Coastal Council*, 505 U.S. 1003, 1056–1057 (1992) (Blackmun, J., dissenting). The Framers of the Fifth Amendment apparently disagreed, for they expressly prohibited uncompensated takings, and the Fifth Amendment was not incorporated against the States until much later. See *id.*, at 1028, n. 15.

48. Compare *ante*, at 8, and n. 8 (majority opinion) (noting that some state courts upheld the validity of applying the Mill Acts to private purposes and arguing that the "'use by the public' test" "eroded over time"), with, *e.g.*, *Ryerson v. Brown*, 35 Mich. 333, 338–339 (1877) (holding it "essential" to the constitutionality of a Mill Act "that the statute should require the use to be public in fact; in other words, that it should contain provisions entitling the public to accommodations"); *Gaylord v. Sanitary Dist. of Chicago*, 204 Ill. 576, 581–584, 68 N. E. 522, 524 (1903) (same); *Tyler v. Beacher*, 44 Vt. 648, 652–656 (1871) (same); *Sadler v. Langham*, 34 Ala. 311, 332–334 (1859) (striking down taking for purely private road and grist mill); *Varner v. Martin*, 21 W. Va. 534, 546–548, 556–557, 566–567 (1883) (grist mill and private road had to be open to public for them to constitute public use); *Harding v. Goodlett*, 3 Yerg. 41, 53 (1832); *Jacobs v. Clearview Water Supply Co.*, 220 Pa. 388, 393–395, 69 A. 870, 872 (1908) (endorsing actual public use standard); *Minnesota Canal & Power Co. v. Koochiching Co.*, 97 Minn. 429, 449–451, 107 N. W. 405, 413 (1906) (same); *Chesapeake Stone Co. v. Moreland*, 126 Ky. 656, 663–667, 104 S. W. 762, 765 (Ct. App. 1907) (same); Note, Public Use in Eminent Domain, 21 *N.Y. U. L. Q. Rev.* 285, 286, and n. 11 (1946) (calling the actual public use standard the "majority view" and citing other cases).

49. Some States also promoted the alienability of property by abolishing the feudal "quit rent" system, *i.e.*, long-term leases under which the proprietor reserved to himself the right to perpetual payment of rents from his tenant. See Vance, The Quest for Tenure in the United States, 33 *Yale L. J.* 248, 256–257, 260–263 (1923). In *Hawaii Housing Authority v. Midkiff*, 467 U.S. 229 (1984), the Court cited those state policies favoring the alienability of land as evidence that the government's eminent domain power was similarly expansive, see *id.*, at 241–242, and n. 5. But they were uses of the States' regulatory power, not the takings power, and therefore were irrelevant to the issue in *Midkiff*. This mismatch underscores the error of conflating a State's regulatory power with its taking power.

The Right to Bear Arms

Chapter Objectives

In this chapter you will learn . . .

- The history of gun ownership in America
- The history of the American militia
- Who is responsible for calling the National Guard into action during hurricanes and other natural disasters
- The "obvious appositive" reading of the Second Amendment
- The deep-rooted sentiment behind the right to bear arms debate

Introduction

Having gone through most of our journey of understanding the Constitution by examining various controversial Constitutional issues, we now turn to one that continues to spark as much furious debate as any: the right to bear arms.

A man who had recently moved to the United States from another country was watching an exhibit of grizzly bears at a local museum. Some of the bears, which were artificial, were being put together. He thought that the color and texture was so lifelike that he wanted one as a souvenir. But the entire bear was too big, so he picked up a couple of loose arms and headed for the door. The security guard stopped him and yelled at him for taking property that was not his. He answered, "this is America, I have the right to bear arms!"

That was a joke, much like the one in Chapter 6 about rowing versus wading. But the passions that run very deeply about the issue of whether Americans have the right to arm themselves are anything but humorous and lighthearted. In this chapter, we learn about the history of our laws regarding guns, as well as take a look at what the Constitution has to say about the subject.

The Second Amendment

The Second Amendment has baffled historians, Constitutional lawyers, and English grammarians for centuries! It states: **A well-regulated Militia, being necessary to the security of a free State, the right of the people to keep and bear Arms, shall not be infringed.**

Many questions arise about what the Second Amendment really means. In fact, it is difficult to think of any Amendment that is more difficult to define, and precious few that even approach the same level of vagueness.

Essentially, there are two prevailing points of view that, at odds with one another, dominate the debate today. A third view, though a distinct minority, has also generated some attention.

One View: An Individual Right to Bear Arms

One major interpretation of the Second Amendment is rooted in the Amendment's final 14 words: **the right of the people to keep and bear Arms, shall not be infringed.** These words, taken alone, seem to indicate that the Founding Fathers specifically included that provision to establish that individuals had the right to own guns and protect themselves.

Absolute v. Limited Right

Even if we were to accept that the Second Amendment guarantees the individual right to bear arms, we could not conclude that such a right is absolute, just like none of the other Constitutional rights are absolute. If the right to bear arms were absolute, then the police would not have a right to take a gun away from a captured criminal. Virtually everyone would agree that criminals sent to jail do not have the right to bear arms (except maybe the criminals themselves), which makes the point that the right is not absolute. Questions remain, however, as to how limited the right is, as well as which tier of government (federal or state) has the right to limit it. We will examine those issues a little later, but first, let's take a look at some of the other interpretations of the Second Amendment.

Another View: Arms for a Well-Regulated Militia

Those who oppose the notion that there is a Constitutionally guaranteed individual right to bear arms emphasize the Second Amendment's first four words: **A well-regulated Militia.** A militia is an armed group of individuals, typically under some sort of government control, but often distinct from a country's actual military. In the United States and territories (remember, many of our states were U.S. territories first), militias were under state control and, as the Constitution provides, the president only has the right to command the militia when its capacity would be *in the actual service of the United States.*

Keep in mind that the United States was founded because of the colonists' intolerance of an all-powerful and controlling government. Distrustful of the government's control of all firearms and skeptical that the military might become tyrannical, they established state militias, thereby arming the people as a defense against a military that might potentially spiral out of control.

Another reason militias were necessary was because the United States, even before it expanded coast to coast, was situated on a vast mass of land that was sparsely populated. Many settlers and farmers could live in an area without seeing another soul for hundreds of miles. Accordingly, that made such individuals very vulnerable to attack by another American, by a Native American Indian, or by anyone else who would wish to do them harm. Militias then, were useful in patrolling potentially dangerous territory.

Proponents of gun control initiatives usually point out that nowadays almost every city and town has its own police department, and each state has its own law enforcement agencies as well. They argue that it is no longer necessary for individuals to keep their own guns, because we no longer live in the Wild West.

President Bush and Hurricane Katrina

In the fall of 2005, a devastating hurricane struck the city of New Orleans and many other cities along America's Gulf Coast. The hurricane, named Katrina, caused a massive uprooting of people who lost their homes and businesses. President George W. Bush was subjected to a barrage of criticism for not having called upon the National Guard immediately to rush to the scene. In retrospect, there were many factors involved that caused the horror and devastation to thousands of residents along the Gulf Coast. A great deal of the problem was just a large dose of bad luck, coupled with poor planning by local, state, and federal agencies. Technically, the president was not authorized to call upon the National Guard; that task was the responsibility of the governors of the states in question.

Response to natural disasters does not qualify as an activity that is "in the service of the United States," as would say, being called upon to assist the military during wartime. Granted, the president certainly may take the lead and call upon the governors to command the National Guard into action, but technically speaking, it is the governors who are authorized to issue that order.

A Third View: A Well-Regulated Militia Shall Not Be Infringed

A quick review of English grammar brings us to the *appositive*, which is a noun or pronoun that is often found next to another noun or pronoun that it describes, and is set off on either side by commas. Sound confusing? Don't worry, here are some examples of appositives (the appositives are in **bold**).

1. Florida, **a state in the American South**, is my favorite place to vacation.
2. Skiing, **which is racing down a snowy mountain**, is typically done during the winter months.

3. Bob, **who is my best friend**, is going to be the best man at my wedding.
4. The American people, **whose right to express their views must not be infringed**, are free to write letters to newspapers criticizing their elected officials.
5. Public schools, **necessary to a well-educated population, the right of children to learn**, shall not be infringed.

The first four appositives are fairly simple to understand: In the first one, **a state in the American South** describes Florida. In the second, **racing down a snowy mountain** describes skiing. In the third, **best friend** describes Bob, and in the fourth, the **right to express their views** describes a characteristic of the American people.

What about the fifth appositive? Well, we see that there are two of them, which is a bit awkward, to say the least. Reading that sentence, the following conclusions can be drawn: (1) public schools are necessary to a well-educated population; and (2) schools shall not be infringed. Some might argue that the right of children to learn shall not be infringed is also a conclusion that can be drawn. While that may be true, another way to look at it is an *obvious appositive.*

In other words, it is obvious that children have a right to learn, and it is also obvious that a well-educated population is a desired goal. Therefore, the sentence really teaches us two things: (1) Schools are necessary to a well-educated population; and (2) therefore, they shall not be infringed.

Following that logic, let's take a look at the Second Amendment again, this time bolding only the appositives: A well-regulated Militia, **being necessary to the security of a free State, the right of the people to keep and bear Arms**, shall not be infringed. We can conclude that the obvious appositives are that the people have the right to keep and bear arms, and that the security of a free state is a desired goal. And the two things that we learn from the Second Amendment are: (1) A well-regulated militia is necessary to the security of a free state; and (2) therefore, it shall not be infringed.

In reading the Second Amendment in that manner, it seems that the absolute right is that individuals have the right to bear arms, a right that by its very placement in the sentence is obvious. As that right is apparent, the Amendment proceeds to declare that in order to maintain the security of a free state, which again is an obvious goal, the right of the people to keep and bear arms must be *extended* to guarantee that a well-regulated militia shall not be infringed.

To summarize, the three interpretations of the Second Amendment that we have discussed are listed below.

1. The Second Amendment guarantees individuals' right to bear arms.
2. The Second Amendment guarantees the right to bear arms only as part of a well-regulated militia.
3. The Second Amendment guarantees the protection of a well-regulated militia, an extension of the obvious right of individuals to keep and bear arms.

Basic Feelings About Guns

At first glance, it would seem that any one of those interpretations seems plausible. Why, then, all the furor about which reading is correct? The answer lies in the role of guns in America, and that feelings about guns run the gamut of emotions.

A great deal of the passion stems from Americans' varied feelings about guns. Take a look at *The Gun Test* (below), and for each of the five statements, answer either A or B. Then, we will take a look at the results together.

Statement 1:
  A. I think of a gun as a dangerous instrument used for killing and other sorts of violent and criminal activities.
  B. I think of a gun as a tool, much like a hammer or a screwdriver that is used to accomplish tasks.

Statement 2:
  A. I have never handled a gun in my life and I have never seen anyone handle one, either. We did not grow up with any guns in the house.
  B. My dad taught us how to shoot when we were kids. He taught us the responsibility of handling a gun, and it helped us learn its value. My mom also shot for target practice and we went shooting as a family.

Statement 3:
  A. I have never gone hunting in my life and never plan to. It is an awful activity and I would never do it.
  B. I have been going hunting since I was a kid. If you eat meat, you might as well learn to hunt it yourself. Either way, you are causing an animal to lose its life—might as well be a part of the process.

Statement 4:
  A. I think people who own guns are either criminals or gun nuts.
  B. People who own guns are good, decent, responsible people. It's people who *don't* own guns that cause the crime rate to be as high as it is.

Statement 5:
  A. If we make guns illegal, that will save many lives. Too many people own handguns, and then their kids steal the guns and go into schools killing their fellow students.
  B. If we make guns illegal, the criminals will have them anyway, and it will be even easier for them to use them against law-abiding citizens.

If you answered "A" to most or all of these questions, you are the classic example of someone who does not believe that guns should be part of every individual's and family's lives, and are best left to law enforcement officials. If you answered "B" to most or all of the questions, then you view guns differently: more as essential household tools, like a hammer or a drill, perhaps like a hunting tool, such as a fishing rod and even a sporting tool, such as a baseball bat.

The reason that the alternative view of the right to bear arms, as an obvious appositive, is plausible is that at the time that the Constitution was drafted, it was extremely common for individuals to own guns. Nowadays, if you live in New York City, it is quite possible that neither you nor any of your friends own guns. If you live in Texarkana, Arkansas, however, where hunting is quite common, then not only is it likely that you own a gun, but you might have to think long and hard to determine if you know anyone who *doesn't* own one.

The Originalists' View

Another view regarding the Second Amendment is the originalist concept: Rather than being based on a personal point of view, as might be the case depending on the answers to *The Gun Test* (above), it is based on what the Founding Fathers intended. Therefore, an Originalist who personally detests guns might nonetheless agree that individuals have the right to own and carry them because the Constitution says so. That person might hope for a Constitutional Amendment to repeal the Second Amendment, but vows that, short of such action, the Second Amendment is the law of the land.

President Reagan and the Brady Bill

Ronald Reagan was elected president of the United States on November 4, 1980 and took office on January 20, 1981. A popular and charismatic politician, Reagan won an easy victory over the incumbent president, Jimmy Carter. But on March 30, 1981, just a little over 2 months into his presidency, Reagan was shot and almost killed by John Hinckley, Jr.

Hinckley, who was declared legally insane, was obsessed with the actress Jodie Foster, and in an attempt to impress her a la the plot in the film *Taxi Driver*, in which Foster starred opposite Robert De Niro, Hinckley planned to assassinate Reagan.

Reagan survived the assassination attempt, suffering a punctured lung in the process. Had the bullet lodged in a different spot, Reagan might have died. Fortunately, Reagan made a rather speedy recovery, particularly impressive due to his age (he was 70 years old at the time). Reagan's press secretary, James Brady, did not fare quite as well. Brady suffered a very serious head wound and was permanently disabled. Throughout the rest of Reagan's presidency, Brady remained the ceremonial press secretary, though he was unable to undertake the daily rigors of that job.

As a measure to prevent future gun violence, Brady and his wife, Sarah, became active in procuring legislation that became known as the Brady Handgun Violence Prevention Act, commonly known as the Brady Bill. Essentially, the Bill required a background check for prospective buyers of firearms. If, after 5 days, the check had not been completed, then it was waived. States were free to process the checks as they saw fit; in some instances, they were merely 5-day waiting periods. In others, previous documentation, such as previous permits granted, satisfied the requirement.

The Bill was signed into law by President Bill Clinton in 1993, and throughout the process of becoming a law, was supported by Reagan himself. Reagan's support of the Bill was surprising to many because, as the icon of the modern-day conservative movement, it was stunning that he would adopt any position that would in any way hamper or even momentarily inconvenience individuals' rights to own guns. Then again, perhaps his personal experience in the assassination attempt, and his affection for Brady, tempered to influenced.

Taxi Driver, **starring Robert De Niro (top) and Jodie Foster (bottom), was what John Hinckley Jr., claimed to have influenced him to attempt to assassinate President Reagan.**

By 1998, the waiting period became virtually obsolete, as the National Instant Check System (NICS) was implemented and monitored by the Federal Bureau of Investigation (FBI). The NICS facilitates background checks within minutes. Extreme proponents of gun control do not think that the NICS does enough, whereas extreme opponents of gun control think it goes too far.

As we continue to examine the debate about gun control and the Second Amendment, let's take a look at what the Supreme Court has had to say about it.

Case Law and the Second Amendment

Dred Scott and the Second Amendment

The famous case *Dred Scott v. Sanford*, decided in 1856, is best known for the Court's declaration that black slaves were not considered American citizens. A lesser-known point, but one more relevant to our Second Amendment discussion, is that the Court held that *if* black slaves were

in fact on par with citizens, then they would be entitled to a host of rights, including the right to bear arms. By implication, then, the Court confirmed that citizens were guaranteed that right.

United States v. Cruikshank

In 1875, the Supreme Court commented about the Second Amendment in *United States v. Cruikshank*, declaring it to be a measure that prevents Congress from denying individuals the right to bear arms, but disagreeing that such a right extends to individuals against state laws. If you recall our discussion in Chapter 2, the counterargument would be that if that were the case, then why was the Second Amendment not written as was the First, beginning with Congress shall make no law? A counterargument to that might be that the Second Amendment is merely a continuation of the first, and the second in a series of the ten-Amendment Bill of Rights; accordingly, the phrase "Congress shall make no law" applied to all of them. And, so, the debate continues.

United States v. Miller

In 1934, the Supreme Court had the opportunity to comment about the Second Amendment in a unanimous decision (eight of nine Justices; one did not participate) in *United States v. Miller*. *Miller* was about the Constitutionality of the National Firearms Act of 1934 (NFA), which had been passed as a measure amidst the public outcry following the infamous St. Valentine's Day Massacre. The Massacre itself was not at issue in the case, but is important to note in context, so as to provide the backdrop of the public mood regarding firearms and violence.

The St. Valentine's Day Massacre

On St. Valentine's Day (February 14) 1929, seven members of Chicago gangster Bugs Moran's North Side gang were brutally murdered by men who were reportedly members of or hired by the South Side gang, headed by Moran's rival, Al Capone. Capone's men dressed up as police officers and stormed into a warehouse where Moran's men had already arrived. Capone's men ordered Moran's men to stand against the wall, their backs turned to Capone's men, which Moran's men continued to believe were police officers. Once their backs were turned to them, Capone's men opened fire, killing all of the men in a barrage of over 70 machine gun bullets.

Violence was rampant in Chicago, particularly during the reign of Capone and Moran, as well as in other parts of the country, and the public demanded that Congress put a stop to it. Largely based on public outcry, Congress passed the NFA, which imposed a $200 tax on machine guns and various other types of firearms. A tax of $200 may seem even excessive today, but back in 1934, $200 had approximately the same value as $3,000 does today. How many people do you know who would pay a $3,000 tax to buy a gun? Some might say that would be a good thing, because it would keep people, including criminals, from buying guns. Others say that it is wrong, because it would be too expensive for many honest, law-abiding citizens to afford, and they would be even more helpless if confronted by gun-toting criminals.

In any event, the *Miller* case dealt with criminals Jack Miller and Frank Layton, who were convicted for possessing such guns without having paid the required tax. The Court ruled that the NFA did not violate the Second Amendment because neither the guns nor their owners were connected to the maintenance of a well-regulated militia. Many view *Miller* as confirmation that the Second Amendment provided for the preservation of a well-regulated militia, and that individuals, expected to be ready and available to be called for militia duty and to provide their own firearms, had the right to carry firearms accordingly. In the absence of such demands in this day and age, they argue, the right cannot be extended to bear those arms for their own individual purposes.

Gun rights proponents argue differently, explaining that the *Miller* Court, by commenting solely on the Second Amendment's guarantee to preserve a well-regulated militia, in no way declared that there is no similar guarantee for individuals.

District of Columbia v. Heller

The most recent decision involving the Second Amendment was handed down by the Supreme Court in June 2008, in *District of Columbia v. Heller*. It has been stated, falsely, that this is the first case in which the Supreme Court discussed the Second Amendment. That is simply not so, as evidenced by some of the cases we have just discussed. Nonetheless, gun rights and gun control advocates alike anxiously awaited the results, as the case promised to bring considerable clarity to the Second Amendment debate, which, arguably, is the most hotly disputed of all of the Amendments.

Heller was about a Washington D.C. law that generally prohibited civilians to carry firearms or to own them unless they were disassembled or their triggers were locked. The five-Justice majority opinion, written by Justice Scalia and joined by Chief Justice Roberts and Justices Kennedy, Thomas, and Alito, held that the Second Amendment protects an individual's right to bear arms, and that even though there is a reference to a well-regulated militia, that militia virtually consisted of every adult male. That, by implication, necessitated the right and responsibility of all adult males to bear arms.

Although the Court determined that a *ban* on the right to bear arms may not be absolute, as was the case with the D.C. law, the right is not absolute, either. For instance, the Court mentioned as reasonable restrictions, among others, that felons and the mentally ill may be prohibited from owning and carrying guns.

The four-Justice dissent, written by Justice Stevens and joined by Justices Souter, Ginsburg, and Breyer, questioned the majority's conclusion that the Second Amendment clearly protected individuals' rights to own guns, arguing that if that were the case, the language would have been clearer. They also found the majority's argument to be inconsistent: on the one hand, arguing that all of the people had the right to bear arms, and on the other hand, limiting that right only to law-abiding ones who are not mentally ill.

Justice Breyer also dissented and was joined by Justices Stevens, Souter, and Ginsburg. Justice Breyer's argument emphasized that even if the Second Amendment was designed to protect an individual's right to self-defense, the D.C. law fulfilled that goal by taking guns out of high-crime urban areas.

The essence then, of the argument reverts to our original questions about guns in *The Gun Test*: do anti-gun laws protect society by keeping guns out of the hands of criminals or do they harm society by keeping guns out of the hands of law-abiding citizens who want to defend themselves against criminals?

The Supreme Court's Current Political Landscape

As of this writing, the nine men and women in black robes, the Supreme Court Justices, who are the stewards of our Constitution, typically can be classified into two camps: the Originalists, and the Progressives.

The Originalists, those most resistant to changing the intent of our Founding Fathers, tend to be Chief Justice Roberts and Justices Scalia, Thomas, and Alito. The Progressives (some call them Activists) are those who emphasize society's "evolving standards of decency" and are thereby less apt to retain the Founders traditions if a more progressive Constitutional interpretation is warranted. They are Justices Stevens, Breyer, Ginsburg, and Sotomayor.

That leaves Justice Kennedy in a category all his own. For years, Justice Sandra Day O'Connor, the first woman Supreme Court Justice, was considered the Court's most moderate voice, the proverbial "swing vote." Upon Justice O'Connor's retirement, Justice Kennedy became the one most likely to jump into either camp, depending on the issue. For instance, in *Heller*, Kennedy sided with the Originalists, whereas, in a decision handed down exactly 1 day earlier (and which we discussed in Chapter 9), *Kennedy v. Louisiana*, he sided with the Progressives.

The immediate future of the Constitution, then, in great part rests on Kennedy's shoulders. Of course, the political climate often changes, as do the men and women who sit on the Supreme Court.

Early in his presidency, Barack Obama appointed Sonia Sotomayor to the Supreme Court. She became the first person of Latino descent to serve in that capacity.

Conclusion

Despite the *Heller* decision, the debate about the right to keep and bear arms remains unresolved. The essential questions are: (1) Did the Founding Fathers intend for the Constitution to protect individuals' rights to keep and bear arms in the same manner that it protects freedoms of speech, press, and religion? (2) If so, then have times changed so drastically that such a fundamental right ought to be overturned? Along these lines, can you ever envision American society to change to such a drastic extent that the freedom of speech, the press, or religion should be overturned?

Questions for Review

1. What is the essence of the Second Amendment interpretation of an individual's right to bear arms?
2. What is the essence of the Second Amendment interpretation of arms only for a well-regulated militia?
3. What is the essence of the Second Amendment interpretation of the obvious appositive?
4. Was President Bush technically responsible for commanding the National Guard into action regarding Hurricane Katrina?
5. What might an Originalist's view be regarding the Second Amendment?
6. What is the story behind the Brady Bill?
7. What is the NICS and how did it make some of the Brady Bill provisions obsolete?
8. How is the *Dred Scott* decision helpful in interpreting the Second Amendment?
9. Why was the NFA considered excessive?
10. What was the St. Valentine's Day Massacre?

Constitutionally Speaking

What are your personal reactions to the following two laws: (1) that all American citizens would be required to own and know how to use a firearm; and (2) that no American citizen, other than an officer of the law, member of the United States Armed Forces, or of the National Guard, will be permitted to own a firearm.

In addition to your personal reactions to these laws, do you think that one, neither, or both of them are Constitutional?

Constitutional Cases

As the only two Supreme Court cases to date that directly address the Second Amendment, *United States v. Miller* and *District of Columbia v. Heller* appear here in their entirety.

United States v. Miller, 307 U.S. 174 (1939)

Appeal from the District Court of the United States for the Western District of Arkansas. [307 U.S. 174, 175] Mr. Gordon Dean, of Washington, D.C., for the United States.

No appearance for appellees.

Mr. Justice McREYNOLDS delivered the opinion of the Court.

An indictment in the District Court Western District Arkansas, charged that Jack Miller and Frank Layton 'did unlawfully, knowingly, wilfully, and feloniously transport in interstate commerce from the town of Claremore in the State of Oklahoma to the town of Siloam Springs in the State of Arkansas a certain firearm, to-wit, a double barrel 12-gauge Stevens shotgun having a barrel less than 18 inches in length, bearing identification number 76230, said defendants, at the time of so transporting said firearm in interstate commerce as aforesaid, not having registered said firearm as required by Section 1132d of Title 26, United States Code, 26 U.S.C.A. 1132d (Act of June 26, 1934, c. 757, Sec. 5, 48 Stat. 1237), and not having in their possession a stamp-affixed written order for said firearm as provided by Section 1132c, Title 26, United States Code, 26 U.S.C.A. 1132c (June 26, 1934, c. 757, Sec. 4, 48 Stat. 1237) and the regulations issued under authority of the said Act of Congress known as the 'National Firearms Act' approved June 26, 1934, contrary to the form of the statute in such case made and provided, and against the peace and dignity of the United States.'[1] A duly interposed demurrer alleged: The National Firearms Act is not a revenue measure but an attempt to usurp police power reserved to the States, and is therefore unconstitutional. Also, it offends the inhibition of the Second Amendment to the Constitution, U.S.C.A.—'A well regulated Militia, being necessary to the security of a free State, the right of the people to keep and bear Arms, shall not be infringed.' The District Court held that section 11 of the Act violates the Second Amendment. It accordingly sustained the demurrer and quashed the indictment.

The cause is here by direct appeal.

Considering *Sonzinsky v. United States*, 1937, 300 U.S. 506, 513, 57 S. Ct. 554, and what was ruled in sundry causes arising under the Harrison Narcotic Act[2]—*United States v. Jin Fuey Moy*, 1916, 241 U.S. 394, 36 S.Ct. 658, Ann.Cas.1917D, 854; *United States v. Doremus*, 1919, 249 U.S. 86, 94, 39 S.Ct. 214; *Linder v. United States*, 1925, 268 U.S. 5, 45 S.Ct. 446, 39 A.L.R. 229; *Alston v. United States*, 1927, 274 U.S. 289, 47 S.Ct. 634; *Nigro v. United States*, 1928, 276 U.S. 332, 48 S.Ct. 388—the objection that the Act usurps police power reserved to the States is plainly untenable.

In the absence of any evidence tending to show that possession or use of a 'shotgun having a barrel of less than eighteen inches in length' at this time has some reasonable relationship to the preservation or efficiency of a well regulated militia, we cannot say that the Second Amendment guarantees the right to keep and bear such an instrument. Certainly it is not within judicial notice that this weapon is any part of the ordinary military equipment or that its use could contribute to the common defense. *Aymette v. State of Tennessee*, 2 Humph., Tenn., 154, 158.

The Constitution as originally adopted granted to the Congress power—'To provide for calling forth the Militia to execute the Laws of the Union, suppress Insurrections and repel Invasions; To provide for organizing, arming, and disciplining, the Militia, and for governing such Part of them as may be employed in the Service of the United States, reserving to the States respectively, the Appointment of the Officers, and the Authority of training the Militia according to the discipline prescribed by Congress.' U.S.C.A.Const. art. 1, 8. With obvious purpose to assure the continuation and render possible the effectiveness of such forces the declaration and guarantee of the Second Amendment were made. It must be interpreted and applied with that end in view.

The Militia which the States were expected to maintain and train is set in contrast with Troops which they were forbidden to keep without the consent of Congress. The sentiment of the time strongly disfavored standing armies; the common view was that adequate defense of country and laws could be secured through the Militia—civilians primarily, soldiers on occasion.

The signification attributed to the term Militia appears from the debates in the Convention, the history and legislation of Colonies and States, and the writings of approved commentators. These show plainly enough that the Militia comprised all males physically capable of acting in concert for the common defense. 'A body of citizens enrolled for military discipline.' And further, that ordinarily when called for service these men were expected to appear bearing arms supplied by themselves and of the kind in common use at the time.

Blackstone's *Commentaries*, Vol. 2, Ch. 13, p. 409 points out 'that king Alfred first settled a national militia in this kingdom' and traces the subsequent development and use of such forces.

Adam Smith's *Wealth of Nations*, Book V. Ch. 1, contains an extended account of the Militia. It is there said: 'Men of republican principles have been jealous of a standing army as dangerous to liberty.' 'In a militia, the character of the labourer, artificer, or tradesman, predominates over that of the soldier: in a standing army, that of the soldier predominates over every other character; and in this distinction seems to consist the essential difference between those two different species of military force.'

'*The American Colonies In The 17th Century*', Osgood, Vol. 1, ch. XIII, affirms in reference to the early system of defense in New England—

'In all the colonies, as in England, the militia system was based on the principle of the assize of arms. This implied the general obligation of all adult male inhabitants to possess arms, and, with certain exceptions, to cooperate in the work of defence.' 'The possession of arms also implied the possession of ammunition, and the authorities paid quite as much attention to the latter as to the former.' 'A year later (1632) it was ordered that any single man who had not furnished himself with arms might be put out to service, and this became a permanent part of the legislation of the colony (Massachusetts).'

Also 'Clauses intended to insure the possession of arms and ammunition by all who were subject to military service appear in all the important enactments concerning military affairs. Fines were the penalty for delinquency, whether of towns or individuals. According to the usage of the times, the infantry of Massachusetts consisted of pikemen and musketeers. The law, as enacted in 1649 and thereafter, provided that each of the former should be armed with a pike, corselet, head-piece, sword, and knapsack. The musketeer should carry a 'good fixed musket,' not under bastard musket bore, not less than three feet, nine inches, nor more than four feet three inches in length, a priming wire, scourer, and mould, a sword, rest, bandoleers, one pound of powder, twenty bullets, and two fathoms of match. The law also required that two-thirds of each company should be musketeers.'

The General Court of Massachusetts, January Session 1784 (Laws and Resolves 1784, c. 55, pp. 140, 142), provided for the organization and government of the Militia. It directed that the Train Band should 'contain all able bodied men, from sixteen to forty years of age, and the Alarm List, all other men under sixty years of age,. . . .' Also, 'That every non-commissioned officer and private soldier of the said militia not under the controul of parents, masters or guardians, and being of sufficient ability therefor in the judgment of the Selectmen of the town in which he shall dwell, shall equip himself, and be constantly provided with a good fire arm, &c.'

(Continues)

(Continued)

By an Act passed April 4, 1786 (Laws 1786, c. 25), the New York Legislature directed: 'That every able-bodied Male Person, being a Citizen of this State, or of any of the United States, and residing in this State, (except such Persons as are herein after excepted) and who are of the Age of Sixteen, and under the Age of Forty-five Years, shall, by the Captain or commanding Officer of the Beat in which such Citizens shall reside, within four Months after the passing of this Act, be enrolled in the Company of such Beat.... That every Citizen so enrolled and notified, shall, within three Months thereafter, provide himself, at his own Expense, with a good Musket or Firelock, a sufficient Bayonet and Belt, a Pouch with a Box therein to contain not less than Twenty-four Cartridges suited to the Bore of his Musket or Firelock, each Cartridge containing a proper Quantity of Powder and Ball, two spare Flints, a Blanket and Knapsack;....'

The General Assembly of Virginia, October, 1785 (12 Hening's Statutes c. 1, p. 9 et seq.), declared: 'The defense and safety of the commonwealth depend upon having its citizens properly armed and taught the knowledge of military duty.'

It further provided for organization and control of the Militia and directed that 'All free male persons between the ages of eighteen and fifty years,' with certain exceptions, 'shall be inrolled or formed into companies.' 'There shall be a private muster of every company once in two months.'

Also that 'Every officer and soldier shall appear at his respective muster-field on the day appointed, by eleven o'clock in the forenoon, armed, equipped, and accoutred, as follows: ... every non-commissioned officer and private with a good, clean musket carrying an ounce ball, and three feet eight inches long in the barrel, with a good bayonet and iron ramrod well fitted thereto, a cartridge box properly made, to contain and secure twenty cartridges fitted to his musket, a good knapsack and canteen, and moreover, each non-commissioned officer and private shall have at every muster one pound of good powder, and four pounds of lead, including twenty blind cartridges; and each serjeant shall have a pair of moulds fit to cast balls for their respective companies, to be purchased by the commanding officer out of the monies arising on delinquencies. Provided, That the militia of the counties westward of the Blue Ridge, and the counties below adjoining thereto, shall not be obliged to be armed with muskets, but may have good rifles with proper accoutrements, in lieu thereof. And every of the said officers, non-commissioned officers, and privates, shall constantly keep the aforesaid arms, accoutrements, and ammunition, ready to be produced whenever called for by his commanding officer. If any private shall make it appear to the satisfaction of the court hereafter to be appointed for trying delinquencies under this act that he is so poor that he cannot purchase the arms herein required, such court shall cause them to be purchased out of the money arising from delinquents.'

Most if not all of the States have adopted provisions touching the right to keep and bear arms. Differences in the language employed in these have naturally led to somewhat variant conclusions concerning the scope of the right guaranteed. But none of them seem to afford any material support for the challenged ruling of the court below.

In the margin some of the more important opinions and comments by writers are cited.[3] We are unable to accept the conclusion of the court below and the challenged judgment must be reversed. The cause will be remanded for further proceedings.

Reversed and remanded.

Mr. Justice DOUGLAS took no part in the consideration or decision of this cause.

Notes

1. Act of June 26, 1934, c. 757, 48 Stat. 1236–1240, 26 U.S.C.A. 1132 et seq.:

'That for the purposes of (sections 1132 to 1132q) this Act—

'Sec. 1 (Section 1132). (a) The term 'firearm' means a shotgun or rifle having a barrel of less than eighteen inches in length, or any other weapon, except a pistol or revolver, from which a shot is discharged by an explosive if such weapon is capable of being concealed on the person, or a machine gun, and includes a muffler or silencer for any firearm whether or not such firearm is included within the foregoing definition, (The Act of April 10, 1936, c. 169, 49 Stat. 1192, 26 U.S.C.A. 1132, added the words) but does not include any rifle which is within the foregoing provisions solely by reason of the length of its barrel if the caliber of such rifle is .22 or smaller and if its barrel is sixteen inches or more in length.

'Sec. 3 (1132b). (a) There shall be levied, collected, and paid upon firearms transferred in the continental United States a tax at the rate of $200 for each firearm, such tax to be paid by the transferor, and to be represented by appropriate stamps to be provided by the Commissioner, with the approval of the Secretary; and the stamps herein provided shall be affixed to the order for such firearm, hereinafter provided for. The tax imposed by this section shall be in addition to any import duty imposed on such firearm.

'Sec. 4 (1132c). (a) It shall be unlawful for any person to transfer a firearm except in pursuance of a written order from the person seeking to obtain such article, on an application form issued in blank in duplicate for that purpose by the Commissioner. Such order shall identify the applicant by such means of identification as may be prescribed by regulations under (sections 1132 to 1132q) this Act: Provided, That, if the applicant is an individual, such identification shall include fingerprints and a photograph thereof.

'(c) Every person so transferring a firearm shall set forth in each copy of such order the manufacturer's number or other mark identifying such firearm, and shall forward a copy of such order to the Commissioner. The original thereof with stamps affixed, shall be returned to the applicant.

'(d) No person shall transfer a firearm which has previously been transferred on or after the (thirtieth day after June 26, 1934), effective date of this Act, unless such person, in addition to complying with subsection (c), transfers therewith the stamp-affixed order provided for in this section for each such prior transfer, in compliance with such regulations as may be prescribed under (sections 1132 to 1132q) this Act for proof of payment of all taxes on such firearms.

'Sec. 5 (1132d). (a) Within sixty days after the (thirtieth day after June 26, 1934) effective date of this Act every person possessing a firearm shall register, with the collector of the district in which he resides, the number or other mark identifying such firearm, together with his name, address, place where such firearm is usually kept, and place of business or employment, and, if such person is other than a natural person, the name and home address of an executive officer thereof: Provided, That no person shall be required to register under this section with respect to any firearm acquired after the (thirtieth day after June 26, 1934) effective date of, and in conformity with the provisions of, (sections 1132 to 1132q) this Act.

'Sec. 6 (1132e). It shall be unlawful for any person to receive or possess any firearm which has at any time been transferred in violation of section (1132b or 1132c) 3 or 4 of this Act.

'Sec. 11 (1132j). It shall be unlawful for any person who is required to register as provided in section (1132d) 5 hereof and who shall not have so registered, or any other person who has not in his possession a stamp-affixed order as provided in section (1132c of this title) 4 hereof, to ship, carry, or deliver any firearm in interstate commerce.

'Sec. 12 (1132k). The Commissioner, with the approval of the Secretary, shall prescribe such rules and regulations as may be necessary for carrying the provisions of (sections 1132 to 1132q) this Act into effect.

'Sec. 14 (1132m). Any person who violates or fails to comply with any of the requirements of (sections 1132 to 1132q) this Act shall, upon conviction, be fined not more than $2,000 or be imprisoned for not more than five years, or both, in the discretion of the court.

'Sec. 16 (1132o). If any provision of (sections 1132 to 1132q) this Act, or the application thereof to any person or circumstance, is held invalid, the remainder of (sections 1132 to 1132q) the Act, and the application of such provision to other persons or circumstances, shall not be affected thereby.

'Sec. 18 (1132q). This (chapter (1132 to 1132q)) Act may be cited as the 'National Firearms Act."

2. Act December 17, 1914, c. 1, 38 Stat. 785, February 24, 1919, c. 18, 40 Stat. 1057, 1130, 26 U.S.C.A. 1040–1054, 1383–1391.

3. Concerning *The Militia-Presser v. Illinois*, 116 U.S. 252, 6 S.Ct. 580; *Robertson v. Baldwin*, 165 U.S. 275, 17 S.Ct. 326; *Fife v. State*, 31 Ark. 455, 25 Am.Rep. 556; *Jeffers v. Fair*, 33 Ga. 347; *Salina v. Blaksley*, 72 Kan. 230, 83 P. 619, 3 L.R.A., N.S., 168, 115 Am.St.Rep. 196, 7 Ann.Cas. 925; *People v. Brown*, 253 Mich. 537, 235 N. W. 245, 82 A.L.R. 341; *Aymette v. State*, 2 Humph., Tenn., 154; *State v. Duke*, 42 Tex. 455; *State v. Workman*, 35 W. Va. 367, 14 S.E. 9, 14 L.R.A. 600; *Cooley's Constitutional Limitations*, Vol. 1, p. 729; *Story on The Constitution*, 5th Ed., Vol. 2, p. 646; *Encyclopaedia of the Social Sciences*, Vol. X, p. 471, 474.

District of Columbia et al. v. Heller, 554 U.S. (2008)

Argued March 18, 2008—Decided June 26,_No. 07-290. 2008

District of Columbia law bans handgun possession by making it a crime to carry an unregistered firearm and prohibiting the registration of handguns; provides separately that no person may carry an unlicensed handgun, but authorizes the police chief to issue 1-year licenses; and requires residents to keep lawfully owned firearms unloaded and dissembled or bound by a trigger lock or similar device. Respondent Heller, a D.C. special policeman, applied to register a handgun he wished to keep at home, but the District refused. He filed this suit seeking, on Second Amendment grounds, to enjoin the city from enforcing the bar on handgun registration, the licensing requirement insofar as it prohibits carrying an

(Continues)

(Continued)

unlicensed firearm in the home, and the trigger-lock requirement insofar as it prohibits the use of functional firearms in the home. The District Court dismissed the suit, but the D.C. Circuit reversed, holding that the Second Amendment protects an individual's right to possess firearms and that the city's total ban on handguns, as well as its requirement that firearms in the home be kept nonfunctional even when necessary for self-defense, violated that right.

Held:

1. The Second Amendment protects an individual right to possess a firearm unconnected with service in a militia, and to use that arm for traditionally lawful purposes, such as self-defense within the home. Pp. 2–53.

   (a) The Amendment's prefatory clause announces a purpose, but does not limit or expand the scope of the second part, the operative clause. The operative clause's text and history demonstrate that it connotes an individual right to keep and bear arms. Pp. 2–22.

   (b) The prefatory clause comports with the Court's interpretation of the operative clause. The "militia" comprised all males physically capable of acting in concert for the common defense. The Antifederalists feared that the Federal Government would disarm the people in order to disable this citizens' militia, enabling a politicized standing army or a select militia to rule. The response was to deny Congress power to abridge the ancient right of individuals to keep and bear arms, so that the ideal of a citizens' militia would be preserved. Pp. 22–28.

   (c) The Court's interpretation is confirmed by analogous arms-bearing rights in state constitutions that preceded and immediately followed the Second Amendment. Pp. 28–30.

   (d) The Second Amendment's drafting history, while of dubious interpretive worth, reveals three state Second Amendment proposals that unequivocally referred to an individual right to bear arms. Pp. 30–32.

   (e) Interpretation of the Second Amendment by scholars, courts and legislators, from immediately after its ratification through the late 19th century also supports the Court's conclusion. Pp. 32–47.

   (f) None of the Court's precedents forecloses the Court's interpretation. Neither *United States v. Cruikshank*, 92 U.S. 542, 553, nor *Presser v. Illinois*, 116 U.S. 252, 264–265, refutes the individual-rights interpretation. *United States v. Miller*, 307 U.S. 174, does not limit the right to keep and bear arms to militia purposes, but rather limits the type of weapon to which the right applies to those used by the militia, *i.e.*, those in common use for lawful purposes. Pp. 47–54.

2. Like most rights, the Second Amendment right is not unlimited. It is not a right to keep and carry any weapon whatsoever in any manner whatsoever and for whatever purpose: For example, concealed weapons prohibitions have been upheld under the Amendment or state analogues. The Court's opinion should not be taken to cast doubt on longstanding prohibitions on the possession of firearms by felons and the mentally ill, or laws forbidding the carrying of firearms in sensitive places such as schools and government buildings, or laws imposing conditions and qualifications on the commercial sale of arms. *Miller's* holding that the sorts of weapons protected are those "in common use at the time" finds support in the historical tradition of prohibiting the carrying of dangerous and unusual weapons. Pp. 54–56.

3. The handgun ban and the trigger-lock requirement (as applied to self-defense) violate the Second Amendment. The District's total ban on handgun possession in the home amounts to a prohibition on an entire class of "arms" that Americans overwhelmingly choose for the lawful purpose of self-defense. Under any of the standards of scrutiny the Court has applied to enumerated constitutional rights, this prohibition—in the place where the importance of the lawful defense of self, family, and property is most acute—would fail constitutional muster. Similarly, the requirement that any lawful firearm in the home be disassembled or bound by a trigger lock makes it impossible for citizens to use arms for the core lawful purpose of self-defense and is hence unconstitutional. Because Heller conceded at oral argument that the D.C. licensing law is permissible if it is not enforced arbitrarily and capriciously, the Court assumes that a license will satisfy his prayer for relief and does not address the licensing requirement. Assuming he is not disqualified from exercising Second Amendment rights, the District must permit Heller to register his handgun and must issue him a license to carry it in the home. Pp. 56–64.

478 F. 3d 370, affirmed.

Scalia, J., delivered the opinion of the Court, in which *Roberts, C.J.*, and *Kennedy, Thomas*, and *Alito, JJ.*, joined. *Stevens, J.*, filed a dissenting opinion, in which *Souter, Ginsburg*, and *Breyer, JJ.*, joined. *Breyer, J.*, filed a dissenting opinion, in which *Stevens, Souter*, and *Ginsburg, JJ.*, joined.

DISTRICT OF COLUMBIA, *et al.*, PETITIONERS *v.* DICK ANTHONY HELLER

on writ of certiorari to the united states court of appeals for the district of columbia circuit
[June 26, 2008]
Justice Scalia delivered the opinion of the Court.

We consider whether a District of Columbia prohibition on the possession of usable handguns in the home violates the Second Amendment to the Constitution.

I

The District of Columbia generally prohibits the possession of handguns. It is a crime to carry an unregistered firearm, and the registration of handguns is prohibited. See D.C. Code §§7-2501.01(12), 7-2502.01(a), 7-2502.02(a)(4) (2001). Wholly apart from that prohibition, no person may carry a handgun without a license, but the chief of police may issue licenses for 1-year periods. See §§22-4504(a), 22-4506. District of Columbia law also requires residents to keep their lawfully owned firearms, such as registered long guns, "unloaded and dissembled or bound by a trigger lock or similar device" unless they are located in a place of business or are being used for lawful recreational activities. See §7-2507.02.[4]

Respondent Dick Heller is a D.C. special police officer authorized to carry a handgun while on duty at the Federal Judicial Center. He applied for a registration certificate for a handgun that he wished to keep at home, but the District refused. He thereafter filed a lawsuit in the Federal District Court for the District of Columbia seeking, on Second Amendment grounds, to enjoin the city from enforcing the bar on the registration of handguns, the licensing requirement insofar as it prohibits the carrying of a firearm in the home without a license, and the trigger-lock requirement insofar as it prohibits the use of "functional firearms within the home." App. 59a. The District Court dismissed respondent's complaint, see *Parker v. District of Columbia*, 311 F. Supp. 2d 103, 109 (2004). The Court of Appeals for the District of Columbia Circuit, construing his complaint as seeking the right to render a firearm operable and carry it about his home in that condition only when necessary for self-defense,[5] reversed, see *Parker v. District of Columbia*, 478 F. 3d 370, 401 (2007). It held that the Second Amendment protects an individual right to possess firearms and that the city's total ban on handguns, as well as its requirement that firearms in the home be kept nonfunctional even when necessary for self-defense, violated that right. See *id.*, at 395, 399–401. The Court of Appeals directed the District Court to enter summary judgment for respondent.

We granted *certiorari*. 552 U.S. ___ (2007).

II

We turn first to the meaning of the Second Amendment.

A

The Second Amendment provides: "A well-regulated Militia, being necessary to the security of a free State, the right of the people to keep and bear Arms, shall not be infringed." In interpreting this text, we are guided by the principle that "[t]he Constitution was written to be understood by the voters; its words and phrases were used in their normal and ordinary as distinguished from technical meaning." *United States v. Sprague*, 282 U.S. 716, 731 (1931); see also *Gibbons v. Ogden*, 9 Wheat. 1, 188 (1824). Normal meaning may of course include an idiomatic meaning, but it excludes secret or technical meanings that would not have been known to ordinary citizens in the founding generation.

The two sides in this case have set out very different interpretations of the Amendment. Petitioners and today's dissenting Justices believe that it protects only the right to possess and carry a firearm in connection with militia service. See Brief for Petitioners 11–12; *post*, at 1 (Stevens, J., dissenting). Respondent argues that it protects an individual right to possess a firearm unconnected with service in a militia, and to use that arm for traditionally lawful purposes, such as self-defense within the home. See Brief for Respondent 2–4.

The Second Amendment is naturally divided into two parts: its prefatory clause and its operative clause. The former does not limit the latter grammatically, but rather announces a purpose. The Amendment could be rephrased, "Because a well regulated Militia is necessary to the security of a free State, the right of the people to keep and bear Arms shall not be infringed." See J. Tiffany, *A Treatise on Government and Constitutional Law* §585, p. 394 (1867); Brief for Professors of Linguistics and English as *Amici Curiae* 3 (hereinafter Linguists' Brief). Although this structure of the Second

(*Continues*)

(*Continued*)

Amendment is unique in our Constitution, other legal documents of the founding era, particularly individual-rights provisions of state constitutions, commonly included a prefatory statement of purpose. See generally Volokh, *The Commonplace Second Amendment*, 73 *N.Y. U. L. Rev.* 793, 814–821 (1998).

Logic demands that there be a link between the stated purpose and the command. The Second Amendment would be nonsensical if it read, "A well regulated Militia, being necessary to the security of a free State, the right of the people to petition for redress of grievances shall not be infringed." That requirement of logical connection may cause a prefatory clause to resolve an ambiguity in the operative clause ("The separation of church and state being an important objective, the teachings of canons shall have no place in our jurisprudence." The preface makes clear that the operative clause refers not to canons of interpretation but to clergymen.) But apart from that clarifying function, a prefatory clause does not limit or expand the scope of the operative clause. See F. Dwarris, *A General Treatise on Statutes* 268–269 (P. Potter ed. 1871) (hereinafter Dwarris); T. Sedgwick, *The Interpretation and Construction of Statutory and Constitutional Law* 42–45 (2d ed. 1874).[6] "It is nothing unusual in acts . . . for the enacting part to go beyond the preamble; the remedy often extends beyond the particular act or mischief which first suggested the necessity of the law.'" J. Bishop, *Commentaries on Written Laws and Their Interpretation* §51, p. 49 (1882) (quoting *Rex v. Marks*, 3 East, 157, 165 (K. B. 1802)). Therefore, while we will begin our textual analysis with the operative clause, we will return to the prefatory clause to ensure that our reading of the operative clause is consistent with the announced purpose.[7]

1. Operative Clause

a. "Right of the People."   The first salient feature of the operative clause is that it codifies a "right of the people." The unamended Constitution and the Bill of Rights use the phrase "right of the people" two other times, in the First Amendment's Assembly-and-Petition Clause and in the Fourth Amendment's Search-and-Seizure Clause. The Ninth Amendment uses very similar terminology ("The enumeration in the Constitution, of certain rights, shall not be construed to deny or disparage others retained by the people"). All three of these instances unambiguously refer to individual rights, not "collective" rights, or rights that may be exercised only through participation in some corporate body.[8]

Three provisions of the Constitution refer to "the people" in a context other than "rights"—the famous preamble ("We the people"), §2 of Article I (providing that "the people" will choose members of the House), and the Tenth Amendment (providing that those powers not given the Federal Government remain with "the States" or "the people"). Those provisions arguably refer to "the people" acting collectively—but they deal with the exercise or reservation of powers, not rights. Nowhere else in the Constitution does a "right" attributed to "the people" refer to anything other than an individual right.[9]

What is more, in all six other provisions of the Constitution that mention "the people," the term unambiguously refers to all members of the political community, not an unspecified subset. As we said in *United States v. Verdugo-Urquidez*, 494 U.S. 259, 265 (1990):

"'[T]he people' seems to have been a term of art employed in select parts of the Constitution. . . . [Its uses] sugges[t] that 'the people' protected by the Fourth Amendment, and by the First and Second Amendments, and to whom rights and powers are reserved in the Ninth and Tenth Amendments, refers to a class of persons who are part of a national community or who have otherwise developed sufficient connection with this country to be considered part of that community."

This contrasts markedly with the phrase "the militia" in the prefatory clause. As we will describe below, the "militia" in colonial America consisted of a subset of "the people"—those who were male, able bodied, and within a certain age range. Reading the Second Amendment as protecting only the right to "keep and bear Arms" in an organized militia therefore fits poorly with the operative clause's description of the holder of that right as "the people."

We start therefore with a strong presumption that the Second Amendment right is exercised individually and belongs to all Americans.

b. "Keep and bear Arms."   We move now from the holder of the right—"the people"—to the substance of the right: "to keep and bear Arms."

Before addressing the verbs "keep" and "bear," we interpret their object: "Arms." The 18th-century meaning is no different from the meaning today. The 1773 edition of Samuel Johnson's dictionary defined "arms" as "weapons of offence, or armour of defence." 1 *Dictionary of the English Language* 107 (4th ed.) (hereinafter Johnson). Timothy Cunningham's important 1771 legal dictionary defined "arms" as "any thing that a man wears for his defence, or takes into his hands, or useth in wrath to cast at or strike another." 1 *A New and Complete Law Dictionary* (1771); see also N. Webster, *American Dictionary of the English Language* (1828) (reprinted 1989) (hereinafter Webster) (similar).

The term was applied, then as now, to weapons that were not specifically designed for military use and were not employed in a military capacity. For instance, Cunningham's legal dictionary gave as an example of usage: "Servants and labourers shall use bows and arrows on *Sundays*, &c. and not bear other arms." See also, *e.g.*, An Act for the trial of Negroes, 1797 Del. Laws ch. XLIII, §6, p. 104, in 1 *First Laws of the State of Delaware* 102, 104 (J. Cushing ed. 1981 (pt. 1)); see generally *State v. Duke*, 42 Tex. 455, 458 (1874) (citing decisions of state courts construing "arms"). Although one founding-era thesaurus limited "arms" (as opposed to "weapons") to "instruments of offence *generally* made use of in war," even that source stated that all firearms constituted "arms." 1 J. Trusler, *The Distinction Between Words Esteemed Synonymous in the English Language* 37 (1794) (emphasis added).

Some have made the argument, bordering on the frivolous, that only those arms in existence in the 18th century are protected by the Second Amendment. We do not interpret constitutional rights that way. Just as the First Amendment protects modern forms of communications, *e.g.*, *Reno v. American Civil Liberties Union*, 521 U.S. 844, 849 (1997), and the Fourth Amendment applies to modern forms of search, *e.g.*, *Kyllo v. United States*, 533 U.S. 27, 35–36 (2001), the Second Amendment extends, prima facie, to all instruments that constitute bearable arms, even those that were not in existence at the time of the founding.

We turn to the phrases "keep arms" and "bear arms." Johnson defined "keep" as, most relevantly, "[t]o retain; not to lose," and "[t]o have in custody." Johnson 1095. Webster defined it as "[t]o hold; to retain in one's power or possession." No party has apprised us of an idiomatic meaning of "keep Arms." Thus, the most natural reading of "keep Arms" in the Second Amendment is to "have weapons."

The phrase "keep arms" was not prevalent in the written documents of the founding period that we have found, but there are a few examples, all of which favor viewing the right to "keep Arms" as an individual right unconnected with militia service. William Blackstone, for example, wrote that Catholics convicted of not attending service in the Church of England suffered certain penalties, one of which was that they were not permitted to "keep arms in their houses." 4 *Commentaries on the Laws of England* 55 (1769) (hereinafter Blackstone); see also 1 W. & M., c. 15, §4, in 3 Eng. Stat. at Large 422 (1689) ("[N]o Papist . . . shall or may have or keep in his House . . . any Arms . . ."); 1 Hawkins, *Treatise on the Pleas of the Crown* 26 (1771) (similar). Petitioners point to militia laws of the founding period that required militia members to "keep" arms in connection with militia service, and they conclude from this that the phrase "keep Arms" has a militia-related connotation. See Brief for Petitioners 16–17 (citing laws of Delaware, New Jersey, and Virginia). This is rather like saying that, since there are many statutes that authorize aggrieved employees to "file complaints" with federal agencies, the phrase "file complaints" has an employment-related connotation. "Keep arms" was simply a common way of referring to possessing arms, for militiamen *and everyone else*.[10]

At the time of the founding, as now, to "bear" meant to "carry." See Johnson 161; Webster; T. Sheridan, *A Complete Dictionary of the English Language* (1796); 2 *Oxford English Dictionary* 20 (2d ed. 1989) (hereinafter Oxford). When used with "arms," however, the term has a meaning that refers to carrying for a particular purpose—confrontation. In *Muscarello v. United States*, 524 U.S. 125 (1998), in the course of analyzing the meaning of "carries a firearm" in a federal criminal statute, *Justice Ginsburg* wrote that "[s]urely a most familiar meaning is, as the Constitution's Second Amendment . . . indicate[s]: 'wear, bear, or carry . . . upon the person or in the clothing or in a pocket, for the purpose . . . of being armed and ready for offensive or defensive action in a case of conflict with another person.' " *Id.*, at 143 (dissenting opinion) (quoting *Black's Law Dictionary* 214 (6th ed. 1998)). We think that *Justice Ginsburg* accurately captured the natural meaning of "bear arms." Although the phrase implies that the carrying of the weapon is for the purpose of "offensive or defensive action," it in no way connotes participation in a structured military organization.

From our review of founding-era sources, we conclude that this natural meaning was also the meaning that "bear arms" had in the 18th century. In numerous instances, "bear arms" was unambiguously used to refer to the carrying of weapons outside of an organized militia. The most prominent examples are those most relevant to the Second Amendment: Nine state constitutional provisions written in the 18th century or the first two decades of the 19th, which enshrined a right of citizens to "bear arms in defense of themselves and the state" or "bear arms in defense of himself and the state."[11] It is clear from those formulations that "bear arms" did not refer only to carrying a weapon in an organized military unit. Justice James Wilson interpreted the Pennsylvania Constitution's arms-bearing right, for example,

(Continues)

as a recognition of the natural right of defense "of one's person or house"—what he called the law of "self preservation." 2 *Collected Works of James Wilson* 1142, and n. x (K. Hall & M. Hall eds. 2007) (citing Pa. Const., Art. IX, §21 (1790)); see also T. Walker, *Introduction to American Law* 198 (1837) ("Thus the right of self-defence [is] guaranteed by the [Ohio] constitution"); see also *id.*, at 157 (equating Second Amendment with that provision of the Ohio Constitution). That was also the interpretation of those state constitutional provisions adopted by pre-Civil War state courts.[12] These provisions demonstrate—again, in the most analogous linguistic context—that "bear arms" was not limited to the carrying of arms in a militia.

The phrase "bear Arms" also had at the time of the founding an idiomatic meaning that was significantly different from its natural meaning: "to serve as a soldier, do military service, fight" or "to wage war." See Linguists' Brief 18; *post*, at 11 (Stevens, J., dissenting). But it *unequivocally* bore that idiomatic meaning only when followed by the preposition "against," which was in turn followed by the target of the hostilities. See 2 Oxford 21. (That is how, for example, our Declaration of Independence ¶28, used the phrase: "He has constrained our fellow Citizens taken Captive on the high Seas to bear Arms against their Country. . . .") Every example given by petitioners' *amici* for the idiomatic meaning of "bear arms" from the founding period either includes the preposition "against" or is not clearly idiomatic. See Linguists' Brief 18–23. Without the preposition, "bear arms" normally meant (as it continues to mean today) what *Justice Ginsburg*'s opinion in *Muscarello* said.

In any event, the meaning of "bear arms" that petitioners and *Justice Stevens* propose is *not even* the (sometimes) idiomatic meaning. Rather, they manufacture a hybrid definition, whereby "bear arms" connotes the actual carrying of arms (and therefore is not really an idiom) but only in the service of an organized militia. No dictionary has ever adopted that definition, and we have been apprised of no source that indicates that it carried that meaning at the time of the founding. But it is easy to see why petitioners and the dissent are driven to the hybrid definition. Giving "bear Arms" its idiomatic meaning would cause the protected right to consist of the right to be a soldier or to wage war—an absurdity that no commentator has ever endorsed. See L. Levy, *Origins of the Bill of Rights* 135 (1999). Worse still, the phrase "keep and bear Arms" would be incoherent. The word "Arms" would have two different meanings at once: "weapons" (as the object of "keep") and (as the object of "bear") one-half of an idiom. It would be rather like saying "He filled and kicked the bucket" to mean "He filled the bucket and died." Grotesque.

Petitioners justify their limitation of "bear arms" to the military context by pointing out the unremarkable fact that it was often used in that context—the same mistake they made with respect to "keep arms." It is especially unremarkable that the phrase was often used in a military context in the federal legal sources (such as records of congressional debate) that have been the focus of petitioners' inquiry. Those sources would have had little occasion to use it *except* in discussions about the standing army and the militia. And the phrases used primarily in those military discussions include not only "bear arms" but also "carry arms," "possess arms," and "have arms"—though no one thinks that those *other* phrases also had special military meanings. See Barnett, Was the Right to Keep and Bear Arms Conditioned on Service in an Organized Militia?, 83 *Tex. L. Rev.* 237, 261 (2004). The common references to those "fit to bear arms" in congressional discussions about the militia are matched by use of the same phrase in the few nonmilitary federal contexts where the concept would be relevant. See, *e.g.*, 30 *Journals of Continental Congress* 349–351 (J. Fitzpatrick ed. 1934). Other legal sources frequently used "bear arms" in nonmilitary contexts.[13] Cunningham's legal dictionary, cited above, gave as an example of its usage a sentence unrelated to military affairs ("Servants and labourers shall use bows and arrows on *Sundays*, &c. and not bear other arms"). And if one looks beyond legal sources, "bear arms" was frequently used in nonmilitary contexts. See Cramer & Olson, What Did "Bear Arms" Mean in the Second Amendment?, 6 *Georgetown J. L. & Pub. Pol'y* (forthcoming Sept. 2008), online at http://papers.ssrn.com/abstract=1086176 (as visited June 24, 2008, and available in Clerk of Court's case file) (identifying numerous nonmilitary uses of "bear arms" from the founding period).

Justice Stevens points to a study by *amici* supposedly showing that the phrase "bear arms" was most frequently used in the military context. See *post*, at 12–13, n. 9; Linguists' Brief 24. Of course, as we have said, the fact that the phrase was commonly used in a particular context does not show that it is limited to that context, and, in any event, we have given many sources where the phrase was used in nonmilitary contexts. Moreover, the study's collection appears to include (who knows how many times) the idiomatic phrase "bear arms against," which is irrelevant. The *amici* also dismiss examples such as " 'bear arms . . . for the purpose of killing game' " because those uses are "expressly qualified." Linguists' Brief 24. (*Justice Stevens* uses the same excuse for dismissing the state constitutional provisions analogous to the Second Amendment that identify private-use purposes for which the individual right can be asserted. See *post*, at 12.) That analysis is faulty. A purposive qualifying phrase that contradicts the word or phrase it modifies is unknown this side of the looking glass (except, apparently, in some courses on Linguistics). If "bear arms" means, as we think, simply the carrying of arms, a modifier can limit the purpose of the carriage ("for the purpose of self-defense" or "to make war against the King"). But if "bear arms" means, as the petitioners and the dissent think, the carrying of arms only for military purposes, one simply cannot add "for the purpose of killing game." The right "to carry arms in the militia for the purpose of killing game" is worthy of the mad hatter. Thus, these purposive qualifying phrases positively establish that "to bear arms" is not limited to military use.[14]

Justice Stevens places great weight on James Madison's inclusion of a conscientious-objector clause in his original draft of the Second Amendment: "but no person religiously scrupulous of bearing arms, shall be compelled to render military service in person." *Creating the Bill of Rights* 12 (H. Veit, K. Bowling, & C. Bickford eds. 1991) (hereinafter Veit). He argues that this clause establishes that the drafters of the Second Amendment intended "bear Arms" to refer only to military service. See *post*, at 26. It is always perilous to derive the meaning of an adopted provision from another provision deleted in the drafting process.[15] In any case, what *Justice Stevens* would conclude from the deleted provision does not follow. It was not meant to exempt from military service those who objected to going to war but had no scruples about personal gunfights. Quakers opposed the use of arms not just for militia service, but for any violent purpose whatsoever—so much so that Quaker frontiersmen were forbidden to use arms to defend their families, even though "[i]n such circumstances the temptation to seize a hunting rifle or knife in self-defense . . . must sometimes have been almost overwhelming." P. Brock, *Pacifism in the United States* 359 (1968); see M. Hirst, *The Quakers in Peace and War* 336–339 (1923); 3 T. Clarkson, *Portraiture of Quakerism* 103–104 (3d ed. 1807). The Pennsylvania Militia Act of 1757 exempted from service those "*scrupling the use of arms*"—a phrase that no one contends had an idiomatic meaning. See 5 Stat. at Large of Pa. 613 (J. Mitchell & H. Flanders eds. 1898) (emphasis added). Thus, the most natural interpretation of Madison's deleted text is that those opposed to carrying weapons for potential violent confrontation would not be "compelled to render military service," in which such carrying would be required.[16]

Finally, *Justice Stevens* suggests that "keep and bear Arms" was some sort of term of art, presumably akin to "hue and cry" or "cease and desist." (This suggestion usefully evades the problem that there is no evidence whatsoever to support a military reading of "keep arms.") *Justice Stevens* believes that the unitary meaning of "keep and bear Arms" is established by the Second Amendment's calling it a "right" (singular) rather than "rights" (plural). See *post*, at 16. There is nothing to this. State constitutions of the founding period routinely grouped multiple (related) guarantees under a singular "right," and the First Amendment protects the "right [singular] of the people peaceably to assemble, and to petition the Government for a redress of grievances." See, *e.g.*, Pa. Declaration of Rights §§IX, XII, XVI, in 5 Thorpe 3083–3084; Ohio Const., Arts. VIII, §§11, 19 (1802), in *id.*, at 2910–2911.[17] And even if "keep and bear Arms" were a unitary phrase, we find no evidence that it bore a military meaning. Although the phrase was not at all common (which would be unusual for a term of art), we have found instances of its use with a clearly nonmilitary connotation. In a 1780 debate in the House of Lords, for example, Lord Richmond described an order to disarm private citizens (not militia members) as "a violation of the constitutional right of Protestant subjects to keep and bear arms for their own defense." 49 *The London Magazine or Gentleman's Monthly Intelligencer* 467 (1780). In response, another member of Parliament referred to "the right of bearing arms for personal defence," making clear that no special military meaning for "keep and bear arms" was intended in the discussion. *Id.*, at 467–468.[18]

c. Meaning of the Operative Clause. Putting all of these textual elements together, we find that they guarantee the individual right to possess and carry weapons in case of confrontation. This meaning is strongly confirmed by the historical background of the Second Amendment. We look to this because it has always been widely understood that the Second Amendment, like the First and Fourth Amendments, codified a *pre-existing* right. The very text of the Second Amendment implicitly recognizes the pre-existence of the right and declares only that it "shall not be infringed." As we said in *United States v. Cruikshank*, 92 U.S. 542, 553 (1876), "[t]his is not a right granted by the Constitution. Neither is it in any manner dependent upon that instrument for its existence. The Second amendment declares that it shall not be infringed. . . ."[19]

Between the Restoration and the Glorious Revolution, the Stuart Kings Charles II and James II succeeded in using select militias loyal to them to suppress political dissidents, in part by disarming their

(Continues)

(Continued)

opponents. See J. Malcolm, *To Keep and Bear Arms* 31–53 (1994) (hereinafter Malcolm); L. Schwoerer, *The Declaration of Rights, 1689*, p. 76 (1981). Under the auspices of the 1671 Game Act, for example, the Catholic James II had ordered general disarmaments of regions home to his Protestant enemies. See Malcolm 103–106. These experiences caused Englishmen to be extremely wary of concentrated military forces run by the state and to be jealous of their arms. They accordingly obtained an assurance from William and Mary, in the Declaration of Right (which was codified as the English Bill of Rights), that Protestants would never be disarmed: "That the subjects which are Protestants may have arms for their defense suitable to their conditions and as allowed by law." 1 W. & M., c. 2, §7, in 3 Eng. Stat. at Large 441 (1689). This right has long been understood to be the predecessor to our Second Amendment. See E. Dumbauld, *The Bill of Rights and What It Means Today* 51 (1957); W. Rawle, *A View of the Constitution of the United States of America* 122 (1825) (hereinafter Rawle). It was clearly an individual right, having nothing whatever to do with service in a militia. To be sure, it was an individual right not available to the whole population, given that it was restricted to Protestants, and like all written English rights it was held only against the Crown, not Parliament. See Schwoerer, *To Hold and Bear Arms: The English Perspective*, in Bogus 207, 218; but see 3 J. Story, *Commentaries on the Constitution of the United States* §1858 (1833) (hereinafter Story) (contending that the "right to bear arms" is a "limitatio[n] upon the power of parliament" as well). But it was secured to them as individuals, according to "libertarian political principles," not as members of a fighting force. Schwoerer, *Declaration of Rights*, at 283; see also *id.*, at 78; G. Jellinek, *The Declaration of the Rights of Man and of Citizens* 49, and n. 7 (1901) (reprinted 1979).

By the time of the founding, the right to have arms had become fundamental for English subjects. See Malcolm 122–134. Blackstone, whose works, we have said, "constituted the preeminent authority on English law for the founding generation," *Alden v. Maine*, 527 U.S. 706, 715 (1999), cited the arms provision of the Bill of Rights as one of the fundamental rights of Englishmen. See 1 Blackstone 136, 139–140 (1765). His description of it cannot possibly be thought to tie it to militia or military service. It was, he said, "the natural right of resistance and self-preservation," *id.*, at 139, and "the right of having and using arms for self-preservation and defence," *id.*, at 140; see also 3 *id.*, at 2–4 (1768). Other contemporary authorities concurred. See G. Sharp, *Tracts, Concerning the Ancient and Only True Legal Means of National Defence, by a Free Militia* 17–18, 27 (3d ed. 1782); 2 J. de Lolme, *The Rise and Progress of the English Constitution* 886–887 (1784) (A. Stephens ed. 1838); W. Blizard, *Desultory Reflections on Police* 59–60 (1785). Thus, the right secured in 1689 as a result of the Stuarts' abuses was by the time of the founding understood to be an individual right protecting against both public and private violence.

And, of course, what the Stuarts had tried to do to their political enemies, George III had tried to do to the colonists. In the tumultuous decades of the 1760's and 1770's, the Crown began to disarm the inhabitants of the most rebellious areas. That provoked polemical reactions by Americans invoking their rights as Englishmen to keep arms. A New York article of April 1769 said that "[i]t is a natural right which the people have reserved to themselves, confirmed by the Bill of Rights, to keep arms for their own defence." A Journal of the Times: Mar. 17, *New York Journal*, Supp. 1, Apr. 13, 1769, in Boston Under Military Rule 79 (O. Dickerson ed. 1936); see also, *e.g.*, Shippen, *Boston Gazette*, Jan. 30, 1769, in 1 *The Writings of Samuel Adams* 299 (H. Cushing ed. 1968). They understood the right to enable individuals to defend themselves. As the most important early American edition of *Blackstone's Commentaries* (by the law professor and former Antifederalist St. George Tucker) made clear in the notes to the description of the arms right, Americans understood the "right of self-preservation" as permitting a citizen to "repe[l] force by force" when "the intervention of society in his behalf, may be too late to prevent an injury." 1 *Blackstone's Commentaries* 145–146, n. 42 (1803) (hereinafter Tucker's Blackstone). See also W. Duer, *Outlines of the Constitutional Jurisprudence of the United States* 31–32 (1833).

There seems to us no doubt, on the basis of both text and history, that the Second Amendment conferred an individual right to keep and bear arms. Of course the right was not unlimited, just as the First Amendment's right of free speech was not, see, *e.g.*, *United States v. Williams*, 553 U.S. ___ (2008). Thus, we do not read the Second Amendment to protect the right of citizens to carry arms for *any sort* of confrontation, just as we do not read the First Amendment to protect the right of citizens to speak for *any purpose*. Before turning to limitations upon the individual right, however, we must determine whether the prefatory clause of the Second Amendment comports with our interpretation of the operative clause.

2. Prefatory Clause

The prefatory clause reads: "A well-regulated Militia, being necessary to the security of a free State. . . ."

a. "Well-Regulated Militia." In *United States v. Miller*, 307 U.S. 174, 179 (1939), we explained that "the Militia comprised all males physically capable of acting in concert for the common defense." That definition comports with founding-era sources. See, *e.g.*, Webster ("The militia of a country are the able bodied men organized into companies, regiments and brigades . . . and required by law to attend military exercises on certain days only, but at other times left to pursue their usual occupations"); The Federalist No. 46, pp. 329, 334 (B. Wright ed. 1961) (J. Madison) ("near half a million of citizens with arms in their hands"); Letter to Destutt de Tracy (Jan. 26, 1811), in *The Portable Thomas Jefferson* 520, 524 (M. Peterson ed. 1975) ("[T]he militia of the State, that is to say, of every man in it able to bear arms").

Petitioners take a seemingly narrower view of the militia, stating that "[m]ilitias are the state- and congressionally-regulated military forces described in the Militia Clauses (art. I, §8, cls. 15–16)." Brief for Petitioners 12. Although we agree with petitioners' interpretive assumption that "militia" means the same thing in Article I and the Second Amendment, we believe that petitioners identify the wrong thing, namely, the organized militia. Unlike armies and navies, which Congress is given the power to create ("to raise . . . Armies"; "to provide . . . a Navy," Art. I, §8, cls. 12–13), the militia is assumed by Article I already to be *in existence*. Congress is given the power to "provide for calling forth the militia," §8, cl. 15; and the power not to create, but to "organiz[e]" it—and not to organize "a" militia, which is what one would expect if the militia were to be a federal creation, but to organize "the" militia, connoting a body already in existence, *ibid.*, cl. 16. This is fully consistent with the ordinary definition of the militia as all able-bodied men. From that pool, Congress has plenary power to organize the units that will make up an effective fighting force. That is what Congress did in the first militia Act, which specified that "each and every free able-bodied white male citizen of the respective states, resident therein, who is or shall be of the age of eighteen years, and under the age of forty-five years (except as is herein after excepted) shall severally and respectively be enrolled in the militia." Act of May 8, 1792, 1 Stat. 271. To be sure, Congress need not conscript every able-bodied man into the militia, because nothing in Article I suggests that in exercising its power to organize, discipline, and arm the militia, Congress must focus upon the entire body. Although the militia consists of all able-bodied men, the federally organized militia may consist of a subset of them.

Finally, the adjective "well-regulated" implies nothing more than the imposition of proper discipline and training. See Johnson 1619 ("Regulate": "To adjust by rule or method"); Rawle 121–122; cf. Va. Declaration of Rights §13 (1776), in 7 Thorpe 3812, 3814 (referring to "a well-regulated militia, composed of the body of the people, trained to arms").

b. "Security of a Free State." The phrase "security of a free state" meant "security of a free polity," not security of each of the several States as the dissent below argued, see 478 F. 3d, at 405, and n. 10. Joseph Story wrote in his treatise on the Constitution that "the word 'state' is used in various senses [and in] its most enlarged sense, it means the people composing a particular nation or community." 1 Story §208; see also 3 *id.*, §1890 (in reference to the Second Amendment's prefatory clause: "The militia is the natural defence of a free country"). It is true that the term "State" elsewhere in the Constitution refers to individual States, but the phrase "security of a free state" and close variations seem to have been terms of art in 18th-century political discourse, meaning a " 'free country' " or free polity. See Volokh, "Necessary to the Security of a Free State," 83 *Notre Dame L. Rev.* 1, 5 (2007); see, *e.g.*, 4 Blackstone 151 (1769); Brutus Essay III (Nov. 15, 1787), in *The Essential Antifederalist* 251, 253 (W. Allen & G. Lloyd eds., 2d ed. 2002). Moreover, the other instances of "state" in the Constitution are typically accompanied by modifiers making clear that the reference is to the several States—"each state," "several states," "any state," "that state," "particular states," "one state," "no state." And the presence of the term "foreign state" in Article I and Article III shows that the word "state" did not have a single meaning in the Constitution.

There are many reasons why the militia was thought to be "necessary to the security of a free state." See 3 Story §1890. First, of course, it is useful in repelling invasions and suppressing insurrections. Second, it renders large standing armies unnecessary—an argument that Alexander Hamilton made in favor of federal control over the militia. *The Federalist* No. 29, pp. 226, 227 (B. Wright, ed. 1961) (A. Hamilton). Third, when the able-bodied men of a nation are trained in arms and organized, they are better able to resist tyranny.

(Continues)

3. Relationship Between Prefatory Clause and Operative Clause

We reach the question, then: Does the preface fit with an operative clause that creates an individual right to keep and bear arms? It fits perfectly, once one knows the history that the founding generation knew and that we have described above. That history showed that the way tyrants had eliminated a militia consisting of all the able-bodied men was not by banning the militia but simply by taking away the people's arms, enabling a select militia or standing army to suppress political opponents. This is what had occurred in England that prompted codification of the right to have arms in the English Bill of Rights.

The debate with respect to the right to keep and bear arms, as with other guarantees in the Bill of Rights, was not over whether it was desirable (all agreed that it was) but over whether it needed to be codified in the Constitution. During the 1788 ratification debates, the fear that the federal government would disarm the people in order to impose rule through a standing army or select militia was pervasive in Antifederalist rhetoric. See, *e.g.*, Letters from The Federal Farmer III (Oct. 10, 1787), in 2 *The Complete Anti-Federalist* 234, 242 (H. Storing ed. 1981). John Smilie, for example, worried not only that Congress's "command of the militia" could be used to create a "select militia," or to have "no militia at all," but also, as a separate concern, that "[w]hen a select militia is formed; the people in general may be disarmed." 2 *Documentary History of the Ratification of the Constitution* 508–509 (M. Jensen ed. 1976) (hereinafter Documentary Hist.). Federalists responded that because Congress was given no power to abridge the ancient right of individuals to keep and bear arms, such a force could never oppress the people. See, *e.g.*, A Pennsylvanian III (Feb. 20, 1788), in *The Origin of the Second Amendment* 275, 276 (D. Young ed., 2d ed. 2001) (hereinafter Young); White, *To the Citizens of Virginia*, Feb. 22, 1788, in *id.*, at 280, 281; *A Citizen of America*, (Oct. 10, 1787) in *id.*, at 38, 40; Remarks on the Amendments to the federal Constitution, Nov. 7, 1788, in *id.*, at 556. It was understood across the political spectrum that the right helped to secure the ideal of a citizen militia, which might be necessary to oppose an oppressive military force if the constitutional order broke down.

It is therefore entirely sensible that the Second Amendment's prefatory clause announces the purpose for which the right was codified: to prevent elimination of the militia. The prefatory clause does not suggest that preserving the militia was the only reason Americans valued the ancient right; most undoubtedly thought it even more important for self-defense and hunting. But the threat that the new Federal Government would destroy the citizens' militia by taking away their arms was the reason that right—unlike some other English rights—was codified in a written Constitution. *Justice Breyer*'s assertion that individual self-defense is merely a "subsidiary interest" of the right to keep and bear arms, see *post*, at 36, is profoundly mistaken. He bases that assertion solely upon the prologue—but that can only show that self-defense had little to do with the right's *codification*; it was the *central component* of the right itself.

Besides ignoring the historical reality that the Second Amendment was not intended to lay down a "novel principl[e]" but rather codified a right "inherited from our English ancestors," *Robertson v. Baldwin*, 165 U.S. 275, 281 (1897), petitioners' interpretation does not even achieve the narrower purpose that prompted codification of the right. If, as they believe, the Second Amendment right is no more than the right to keep and use weapons as a member of an organized militia, see Brief for Petititioners 8—if, that is, the *organized* militia is the sole institutional beneficiary of the Second Amendment's guarantee—it does not assure the existence of a "citizens' militia" as a safeguard against tyranny. For Congress retains plenary authority to organize the militia, which must include the authority to say who will belong to the organized force.[20] That is why the first Militia Act's requirement that only whites enroll caused States to amend their militia laws to exclude free blacks. See Siegel, The Federal Government's Power to Enact Color-Conscious Laws, 92 *Nw. U. L. Rev.* 477, 521–525 (1998). Thus, if petitioners are correct, the Second Amendment protects citizens' right to use a gun in an organization from which Congress has plenary authority to exclude them. It guarantees a select militia of the sort the Stuart kings found useful, but not the people's militia that was the concern of the founding generation.

B

Our interpretation is confirmed by analogous arms-bearing rights in state constitutions that preceded and immediately followed adoption of the Second Amendment. Four States adopted analogues to the Federal Second Amendment in the period between independence and the ratification of the Bill of Rights.

Two of them—Pennsylvania and Vermont—clearly adopted individual rights unconnected to militia service. Pennsylvania's Declaration of Rights of 1776 said: "That the people have a right to bear arms *for the defence of themselves*, and the state. . . ." §XIII, in 5 Thorpe 3082, 3083 (emphasis added). In 1777, Vermont adopted the identical provision, except for inconsequential differences in punctuation and capitalization. See Vt. Const., ch. 1, §15, in 6 *id.*, at 3741.

North Carolina also codified a right to bear arms in 1776: "That the people have a right to bear arms, for the defence of the State. . . ." Declaration of Rights §XVII, in *id.*, at 2787, 2788. This could plausibly be read to support only a right to bear arms in a militia—but that is a peculiar way to make the point in a constitution that elsewhere repeatedly mentions the militia explicitly. See §§14, 18, 35, in 5 *id.*, 2789, 2791, 2793. Many colonial statutes required individual arms-bearing for public-safety reasons—such as the 1770 Georgia law that "for the security and *defence of this province* from internal dangers and insurrections" required those men who qualified for militia duty individually "to carry fire arms" "to places of public worship." 19 *Colonial Records of the State of Georgia* 137–139 (A. Candler ed. 1911 (pt. 2)) (emphasis added). That broad public-safety understanding was the connotation given to the North Carolina right by that State's Supreme Court in 1843. See *State v. Huntly*, 3 Ired. 418, 422–423.

The 1780 Massachusetts Constitution presented another variation on the theme: "The people have a right to keep and to bear arms for the common defence. . . ." Pt. First, Art. XVII, in 3 Thorpe 1888, 1892. Once again, if one gives narrow meaning to the phrase "common defence" this can be thought to limit the right to the bearing of arms in a state-organized military force. But once again the State's highest court thought otherwise. Writing for the court in an 1825 libel case, Chief Justice Parker wrote: "The liberty of the press was to be unrestrained, but he who used it was to be responsible in cases of its abuse; like the right to keep fire arms, which does not protect him who uses them for annoyance or destruction." *Commonwealth v. Blanding*, 20 Mass. 304, 313–314. The analogy makes no sense if firearms could not be used for any individual purpose at all. See also Kates, Handgun Prohibition and the Original Meaning of the Second Amendment, 82 *Mich. L. Rev.* 204, 244 (1983) (19th-century courts never read "common defence" to limit the use of weapons to militia service).

We therefore believe that the most likely reading of all four of these pre-Second Amendment state constitutional provisions is that they secured an individual right to bear arms for defensive purposes. Other States did not include rights to bear arms in their pre-1789 constitutions—although in Virginia a Second Amendment analogue was proposed (unsuccessfully) by Thomas Jefferson. (It read: "No freeman shall ever be debarred the use of arms [within his own lands or tenements].")[21] 1 *The Papers of Thomas Jefferson* 344 (J. Boyd ed. 1950)).

Between 1789 and 1820, nine States adopted Second Amendment analogues. Four of them—Kentucky, Ohio, Indiana, and Missouri—referred to the right of the people to "bear arms in defence of themselves and the State." See n. 8, *supra*. Another three States—Mississippi, Connecticut, and Alabama—used the even more individualistic phrasing that each citizen has the "right to bear arms in defence of himself and the State." See *ibid.* Finally, two States—Tennessee and Maine—used the "common defence" language of Massachusetts. See Tenn. Const., Art. XI, §26 (1796), in 6 Thorpe 3414, 3424; Me. Const., Art. I, §16 (1819), in 3 *id.*, at 1646, 1648. That of the nine state constitutional protections for the right to bear arms enacted immediately after 1789 at least seven unequivocally protected an individual citizen's right to self-defense is strong evidence that that is how the founding generation conceived of the right. And with one possible exception that we discuss in Part II-D-2, 19th-century courts and commentators interpreted these state constitutional provisions to protect an individual right to use arms for self-defense. See n. 9, *supra*; *Simpson v. State*, 5 Yer. 356, 360 (Tenn. 1833).

The historical narrative that petitioners must endorse would thus treat the Federal Second Amendment as an odd outlier, protecting a right unknown in state constitutions or at English common law, based on little more than an overreading of the prefatory clause.

C

Justice Stevens relies on the drafting history of the Second Amendment—the various proposals in the state conventions and the debates in Congress. It is dubious to rely on such history to interpret a text that was widely understood to codify a pre-existing right, rather than to fashion a new one. But even assuming that this legislative history is relevant, *Justice Stevens* flatly misreads the historical record.

It is true, as *Justice Stevens* says, that there was concern that the Federal Government would abolish the institution of the state militia. See *post*, at 20. That concern found expression, however, *not* in the

(Continues)

(Continued)

various Second Amendment precursors proposed in the State conventions, but in separate structural provisions that would have given the States concurrent and seemingly nonpre-emptible authority to organize, discipline, and arm the militia when the Federal Government failed to do so. See Veit 17, 20 (Virginia proposal); 4 J. Eliot, *The Debates in the Several State Conventions on the Adoption of the Federal Constitution* 244, 245 (2d ed. 1836) (reprinted 1941) (North Carolina proposal); see also 2 Documentary Hist. 624 (Pennsylvania minority's proposal). The Second Amendment precursors, by contrast, referred to the individual English right already codified in two (and probably four) State constitutions. The Federalist-dominated first Congress chose to reject virtually all major structural revisions favored by the Antifederalists, including the proposed militia amendments. Rather, it adopted primarily the popular and uncontroversial (though, in the Federalists' view, unnecessary) individual-rights amendments. The Second Amendment right, protecting only individuals' liberty to keep and carry arms, did nothing to assuage Antifederalists' concerns about federal control of the militia. See, *e.g.*, Centinel, Revived, No. XXIX, *Philadelphia Independent Gazetteer*, Sept. 9, 1789, in Young 711, 712.

Justice Stevens thinks it significant that the Virginia, New York, and North Carolina Second Amendment proposals were "embedded . . . within a group of principles that are distinctly military in meaning," such as statements about the danger of standing armies. *Post*, at 22. But so was the highly influential minority proposal in Pennsylvania, yet that proposal, with its reference to hunting, plainly referred to an individual right. See 2 Documentary Hist. 624. Other than that erroneous point, *Justice Stevens* has brought forward absolutely no evidence that those proposals conferred only a right to carry arms in a militia. By contrast, New Hampshire's proposal, the Pennsylvania minority's proposal, and Samuel Adams' proposal in Massachusetts unequivocally referred to individual rights, as did two state constitutional provisions at the time. See Veit 16, 17 (New Hampshire proposal); 6 *Documentary Hist.* 1452, 1453 (J. Kaminski & G. Saladino eds. 2000) (Samuel Adams' proposal). *Justice Stevens*' view thus relies on the proposition, unsupported by any evidence, that different people of the founding period had vastly different conceptions of the right to keep and bear arms. That simply does not comport with our longstanding view that the Bill of Rights codified venerable, widely understood liberties.

D

We now address how the Second Amendment was interpreted from immediately after its ratification through the end of the 19th century. Before proceeding, however, we take issue with *Justice Stevens*' equating of these sources with postenactment legislative history, a comparison that betrays a fundamental misunderstanding of a court's interpretive task. See *post*, at 27, n. 28. "Legislative history," of course, refers to the pre-enactment statements of those who drafted or voted for a law; it is considered persuasive by some, not because they reflect the general understanding of the disputed terms, but because the legislators who heard or read those statements presumably voted with that understanding. *Ibid.* "Postenactment legislative history," *ibid.*, a deprecatory contradiction in terms, refers to statements of those who drafted or voted for the law that are made after its enactment and hence could have had no effect on the congressional vote. It most certainly does not refer to the examination of a variety of legal and other sources to determine *the public understanding* of a legal text in the period after its enactment or ratification. That sort of inquiry is a critical tool of constitutional interpretation. As we will show, virtually all interpreters of the Second Amendment in the century after its enactment interpreted the amendment as we do.

1. Post-Ratification Commentary

Three important founding-era legal scholars interpreted the Second Amendment in published writings. All three understood it to protect an individual right unconnected with militia service.

St. George Tucker's version of Blackstone's *Commentaries*, as we explained above, conceived of the Blackstonian arms right as necessary for self-defense. He equated that right, absent the religious and class-based restrictions, with the Second Amendment. See 2 Tucker's Blackstone 143. In Note D, entitled, "View of the Constitution of the United States," Tucker elaborated on the Second Amendment: "This may be considered as the true palladium of liberty. . . . The right to self-defence is the first law of nature: in most governments it has been the study of rulers to confine the right within the narrowest limits possible. Wherever standing armies are kept up, and the right of the people to keep and bear arms is, under any colour or pretext whatsoever, prohibited, liberty, if not already annihilated, is on the brink of destruction." 1 *id.*, at App. 300 (ellipsis in original). He believed that the English game laws had abridged the right by prohibiting "keeping a gun or other engine for the destruction of game." *Ibid*; see also 2 *id.*, at 143, and nn. 40 and 41. He later grouped the right with some of the individual rights included in the First Amendment and said that if "a law be passed by congress, prohibiting" any of those rights, it would "be the province of the judiciary to pronounce whether any such act were constitutional, or not; and if not, to acquit the accused. . . ." 1 *id.*, at App. 357. It is unlikely that Tucker was referring to a person's being "accused" of violating a law making it a crime to bear arms in a state militia.[22]

In 1825, William Rawle, a prominent lawyer who had been a member of the Pennsylvania Assembly that ratified the Bill of Rights, published an influential treatise, which analyzed the Second Amendment as follows:

> "The first [principle] is a declaration that a well regulated militia is necessary to the security of a free state; a proposition from which few will dissent. . . .
>
> "The corollary, from the first position is, that the right of the people to keep and bear arms shall not be infringed.
>
> "The prohibition is general. No clause in the constitution could by any rule of construction be conceived to give to congress a power to disarm the people. Such a flagitious attempt could only be made under some general pretence by a state legislature. But if in any blind pursuit of inordinate power, either should attempt it, this amendment may be appealed to as a restraint on both." Rawle 121–122.[23]

Like Tucker, Rawle regarded the English game laws as violating the right codified in the Second Amendment. See *id.*, 122–123. Rawle clearly differentiated between the people's right to bear arms and their service in a militia: "In a people permitted and accustomed to bear arms, we have the rudiments of a militia, which properly consists of armed citizens, divided into military bands, and instructed at least in part, in the use of arms for the purposes of war." *Id.*, at 140. Rawle further said that the Second Amendment right ought not "be abused to the disturbance of the public peace," such as by assembling with other armed individuals "for an unlawful purpose"—statements that make no sense if the right does not extend to *any* individual purpose.

Joseph Story published his famous *Commentaries on the Constitution of the United States* in 1833. *Justice Stevens* suggests that "[t]here is not so much as a whisper" in Story's explanation of the Second Amendment that favors the individual-rights view. *Post*, at 34. That is wrong. Story explained that the English Bill of Rights had also included a "right to bear arms," a right that, as we have discussed, had nothing to do with militia service. 3 Story §1858. He then equated the English right with the Second Amendment:

> "§1891. A similar provision [to the Second Amendment] in favour of protestants (for to them it is confined) is to be found in the bill of rights of 1688, it being declared, 'that the subjects, which are protestants, may have arms for their defence suitable to their condition, and as allowed by law.' But under various pretences the effect of this provision has been greatly narrowed; and it is at present in England more nominal than real, as a defensive privilege." (Footnotes omitted.)

This comparison to the Declaration of Right would not make sense if the Second Amendment right was the right to use a gun in a militia, which was plainly not what the English right protected. As the Tennessee Supreme Court recognized 38 years after Story wrote his *Commentaries*, "[t]he passage from Story, shows clearly that this right was intended . . . and was guaranteed to, and to be exercised and enjoyed by the citizen as such, and not by him as a soldier, or in defense solely of his political rights." *Andrews v. State*, 50 Tenn. 165, 183 (1871). Story's Commentaries also cite as support Tucker and Rawle, both of whom clearly viewed the right as unconnected to militia service. See 3 Story §1890, n. 2; §1891, n. 3. In addition, in a shorter 1840 work Story wrote: "One of the ordinary modes, by which tyrants accomplish their purposes without resistance, is, by disarming the people, and making it an offence to keep arms, and by substituting a regular army in the stead of a resort to the militia." *A Familiar Exposition of the Constitution of the United States* §450 (reprinted in 1986).

Antislavery advocates routinely invoked the right to bear arms for self-defense. Joel Tiffany, for example, citing Blackstone's description of the right, wrote that "the right to keep and bear arms, also implies the right to use them if necessary in self defence; without this right to use the guaranty would have hardly been worth the paper it consumed." *A Treatise on the Unconstitutionality of American Slavery* 117–118 (1849); see also L. Spooner, *The Unconstitutionality of Slavery* 116 (1845) (right enables

(Continues)

"personal defence"). In his famous Senate speech about the 1856 "Bleeding Kansas" conflict, Charles Sumner proclaimed:

> "The rifle has ever been the companion of the pioneer and, under God, his tutelary protector against the red man and the beast of the forest. Never was this efficient weapon more needed in just self-defence, than now in Kansas, and at least one article in our National Constitution must be blotted out, before the complete right to it can in any way be impeached. And yet such is the madness of the hour, that, in defiance of the solemn guarantee, embodied in the Amendments to the Constitution, that 'the right of the people to keep and bear arms shall not be infringed,' the people of Kansas have been arraigned for keeping and bearing them, and the Senator from South Carolina has had the face to say openly, on this floor, that they should be disarmed—of course, that the fanatics of Slavery, his allies and constituents, may meet no impediment." The Crime Against Kansas, May 19–20, 1856, in *American Speeches: Political Oratory from the Revolution to the Civil War* 553, 606–607 (2006).

We have found only one early 19th-century commentator who clearly conditioned the right to keep and bear arms upon service in the militia—and he recognized that the prevailing view was to the contrary. "The provision of the constitution, declaring the right of the people to keep and bear arms, &c. was probably intended to apply to the right of the people to bear arms for such [militia-related] purposes only, and not to prevent congress or the legislatures of the different states from enacting laws to prevent the citizens from always going armed. A different construction however has been given to it." B. Oliver, *The Rights of an American Citizen* 177 (1832).

2. Pre-Civil War Case Law

The 19th-century cases that interpreted the Second Amendment universally support an individual right unconnected to militia service. In *Houston v. Moore*, 5 Wheat. 1, 24 (1820), this Court held that States have concurrent power over the militia, at least where not pre-empted by Congress. Agreeing in dissent that States could "organize, discipline, and arm" the militia in the absence of conflicting federal regulation, Justice Story said that the Second Amendment "may not, perhaps, be thought to have any important bearing on this point. If it have, it confirms and illustrates, rather than impugns the reasoning already suggested." *Id.*, at 51–53. Of course, if the Amendment simply "protect[ed] the right of the people of each of the several States to maintain a well-regulated militia," *post*, at 1 (*Stevens*, J., dissenting), it would have enormous and obvious bearing on the point. But the Court and Story derived the States' power over the militia from the nonexclusive nature of federal power, not from the Second Amendment, whose preamble merely "confirms and illustrates" the importance of the militia. Even clearer was Justice Baldwin. In the famous fugitive-slave case of *Johnson v. Tompkins*, 13 F. Cas. 840, 850, 852 (CC Pa. 1833), Baldwin, sitting as a circuit judge, cited both the Second Amendment and the Pennsylvania analogue for his conclusion that a citizen has "a right to carry arms in defence of his property or person, and to use them, if either were assailed with such force, numbers or violence as made it necessary for the protection or safety of either."

Many early 19th-century state cases indicated that the Second Amendment right to bear arms was an individual right unconnected to militia service, though subject to certain restrictions. A Virginia case in 1824 holding that the Constitution did not extend to free blacks explained that "numerous restrictions imposed on [blacks] in our Statute Book, many of which are inconsistent with the letter and spirit of the Constitution, both of this State and of the United States as respects the free whites, demonstrate, that, here, those instruments have not been considered to extend equally to both classes of our population. We will only instance the restriction upon the migration of free blacks into this State, and upon their right to bear arms." *Aldridge v. Commonwealth*, 2 Va. Cas. 447, 449 (Gen. Ct.). The claim was obviously not that blacks were prevented from carrying guns in the militia.[24] See also *Waters v. State*, 1 Gill 302, 309 (Md. 1843) (because free blacks were treated as a "dangerous population," "laws have been passed to prevent their migration into this State; to make it unlawful for them to bear arms; to guard even their religious assemblages with peculiar watchfulness"). An 1829 decision by the Supreme Court of Michigan said: "The constitution of the United States also grants to the citizen the right to keep and bear arms. But the grant of this privilege cannot be construed into the right in him who keeps a gun to destroy his neighbor. No rights are intended to be granted by the constitution for an unlawful or unjustifiable purpose." *United States v. Sheldon*, in 5 Transactions of the Supreme Court of the Territory of Michigan 337, 346 (W. Blume ed. 1940) (hereinafter Blume). It is not possible to read this as discussing anything other than an individual right unconnected to militia service. If it did have to do with militia service, the limitation upon it would not be any "unlawful or unjustifiable purpose," but any nonmilitary purpose whatsoever.

In *Nunn v. State*, 1 Ga. 243, 251 (1846), the Georgia Supreme Court construed the Second Amendment as protecting the "*natural* right of self-defence" and therefore struck down a ban on carrying pistols openly. Its opinion perfectly captured the way in which the operative clause of the Second Amendment furthers the purpose announced in the prefatory clause, in continuity with the English right:

> "The right of the whole people, old and young, men, women and boys, and not militia only, to keep and bear *arms* of every description, and not *such* merely as are used by the *militia*, shall not be *infringed*, curtailed, or broken in upon, in the smallest degree; and all this for the important end to be attained: the rearing up and qualifying a well-regulated militia, so vitally necessary to the security of a free State. Our opinion is, that any law, State or Federal, is repugnant to the Constitution, and void, which contravenes this *right*, originally belonging to our forefathers, trampled under foot by Charles 1. and his two wicked sons and successors, re-established by the revolution of 1688, conveyed to this land of liberty by the colonists, and finally incorporated conspicuously in our own Magna Charta!"

Likewise, in *State v. Chandler*, 5 La. Ann. 489, 490 (1850), the Louisiana Supreme Court held that citizens had a right to carry arms openly: "This is the right guaranteed by the Constitution of the United States, and which is calculated to incite men to a manly and noble defence of themselves, if necessary, and of their country, without any tendency to secret advantages and unmanly assassinations."

Those who believe that the Second Amendment preserves only a militia-centered right place great reliance on the Tennessee Supreme Court's 1840 decision in *Aymette v. State*, 21 Tenn. 154. The case does not stand for that broad proposition; in fact, the case does not mention the word "militia" at all, except in its quoting of the Second Amendment. *Aymette* held that the state constitutional guarantee of the right to "bear" arms did not prohibit the banning of concealed weapons. The opinion first recognized that both the state right and the federal right were descendents of the 1689 English right, but (erroneously, and contrary to virtually all other authorities) read that right to refer only to "protect[ion of] the public liberty" and "keep[ing] in awe those in power," *id.*, at 158. The court then adopted a sort of middle position, whereby citizens were permitted to carry arms openly, unconnected with any service in a formal militia, but were given the right to use them only for the military purpose of banding together to oppose tyranny. This odd reading of the right is, to be sure, not the one we adopt—but it is not petitioners' reading either. More importantly, seven years earlier the Tennessee Supreme Court had treated the state constitutional provision as conferring a right "of all the free citizens of the State to keep and bear arms for their defence," *Simpson*, 5 Yer., at 360; and 21 years later the court held that the "keep" portion of the state constitutional right included the right to personal self-defense: "[T]he right to keep arms involves, necessarily, the right to use such arms for all the ordinary purposes, and in all the ordinary modes usual in the country, and to which arms are adapted, limited by the duties of a good citizen in times of peace." *Andrews*, 50 Tenn., at 178; see also *ibid.* (equating state provision with Second Amendment).

3. Post-Civil War Legislation

In the aftermath of the Civil War, there was an outpouring of discussion of the Second Amendment in Congress and in public discourse, as people debated whether and how to secure constitutional rights for newly free slaves. See generally S. Halbrook, Freedmen, *the Fourteenth Amendment, and the Right to Bear Arms, 1866–1876* (1998) (hereinafter Halbrook); Brief for Institute for Justice as *Amicus Curiae*. Since those discussions took place 75 years after the ratification of the Second Amendment, they do not provide as much insight into its original meaning as earlier sources. Yet those born and educated in the early 19th century faced a widespread effort to limit arms ownership by a large number of citizens; their understanding of the origins and continuing significance of the Amendment is instructive.

Blacks were routinely disarmed by Southern States after the Civil War. Those who opposed these injustices frequently stated that they infringed blacks' constitutional right to keep and bear arms. Needless to say, the claim was not that blacks were being prohibited from carrying arms in an organized state militia. A Report of the Commission of the Freedmen's Bureau in 1866 stated plainly: "[T]he civil law [of Kentucky] prohibits the colored man from bearing arms . . . Their arms are taken from

(Continues)

(Continued)

them by the civil authorities. . . . Thus, the right of the people to keep and bear arms as provided in the Constitution is *infringed*." H. R. Exec. Doc. No. 70, 39th Cong., 1st Sess., 233, 236. A joint congressional Report decried:

> "in some parts of [South Carolina], armed parties are, without proper authority, engaged in seizing all firearms found in the hands of the freemen. Such conduct is in clear and direct violation of their personal rights as guaranteed by the Constitution of the United States, which declares that 'the right of the people to keep and bear arms shall not be infringed.' The freedmen of South Carolina have shown by their peaceful and orderly conduct that they can safely be trusted with fire-arms, and they need them to kill game for subsistence, and to protect their crops from destruction by birds and animals." Joint Comm. on Reconstruction, H. R. Rep. No. 30, 39th Cong., 1st Sess., pt. 2, p. 229 (1866) (Proposed Circular of Brigadier General R. Saxton).

The view expressed in these statements was widely reported and was apparently widely held. For example, an editorial in The Loyal Georgian (Augusta) on February 3, 1866, assured blacks that "[a]ll men, without distinction of color, have the right to keep and bear arms to defend their homes, families or themselves." Halbrook 19.

Congress enacted the Freedmen's Bureau Act on July 16, 1866. Section 14 stated:

> "[T]he right . . . to have full and equal benefit of all laws and proceedings concerning personal liberty, personal security, and the acquisition, enjoyment, and disposition of estate, real and personal, including the constitutional right to bear arms, shall be secured to and enjoyed by all the citizens . . . without respect to race or color, or previous condition of slavery. . . ." 14 Stat. 176–177.

The understanding that the Second Amendment gave freed blacks the right to keep and bear arms was reflected in congressional discussion of the bill, with even an opponent of it saying that the founding generation "were for every man bearing his arms about him and keeping them in his house, his castle, for his own defense." Cong. Globe, 39th Cong., 1st Sess., 362, 371 (1866) (Sen. Davis).

Similar discussion attended the passage of the Civil Rights Act of 1871 and the Fourteenth Amendment. For example, Representative Butler said of the Act: "Section eight is intended to enforce the well-known constitutional provision guaranteeing the right of the citizen to 'keep and bear arms,' and provides that whoever shall take away, by force or violence, or by threats and intimidation, the arms and weapons which any person may have for his defense, shall be deemed guilty of larceny of the same." H. R. Rep. No. 37, 41st Cong., 3d Sess., pp. 7–8 (1871). With respect to the proposed Amendment, Senator Pomeroy described as one of the three "indispensable" "safeguards of liberty . . . under the Constitution" a man's "right to bear arms for the defense of himself and family and his homestead." Cong. Globe, 39th Cong., 1st Sess., 1182 (1866). Representative Nye thought the Fourteenth Amendment unnecessary because "[a]s citizens of the United States [blacks] have equal right to protection, and to keep and bear arms for self-defense." *Id.*, at 1073 (1866).

It was plainly the understanding in the post-Civil War Congress that the Second Amendment protected an individual right to use arms for self-defense.

4. Post-Civil War Commentators

Every late-19th-century legal scholar that we have read interpreted the Second Amendment to secure an individual right unconnected with militia service. The most famous was the judge and professor Thomas Cooley, who wrote a massively popular 1868 Treatise on Constitutional Limitations. Concerning the Second Amendment it said:

> "Among the other defences to personal liberty should be mentioned the right of the people to keep and bear arms. . . . The alternative to a standing army is 'a well-regulated militia,' but this cannot exist unless the people are trained to bearing arms. How far it is in the power of the legislature to regulate this right, we shall not undertake to say, as happily there has been very little occasion to discuss that subject by the courts." *Id.*, at 350.

That Cooley understood the right not as connected to militia service, but as securing the militia by ensuring a populace familiar with arms, is made even clearer in his 1880 work, *General Principles of Constitutional Law*. The Second Amendment, he said, "was adopted with some modification and enlargement from the English Bill of Rights of 1688, where it stood as a protest against arbitrary action of the overturned dynasty in disarming the people." *Id.*, at 270. In a section entitled "The Right in General," he continued:

"It might be supposed from the phraseology of this provision that the right to keep and bear arms was only guaranteed to the militia; but this would be an interpretation not warranted by the intent. The militia, as has been elsewhere explained, consists of those persons who, under the law, are liable to the performance of military duty, and are officered and enrolled for service when called upon. But the law may make provision for the enrolment of all who are fit to perform military duty, or of a small number only, or it may wholly omit to make any provision at all; and if the right were limited to those enrolled, the purpose of this guaranty might be defeated altogether by the action or neglect to act of the government it was meant to hold in check. The meaning of the provision undoubtedly is, that the people, from whom the militia must be taken, shall have the right to keep and bear arms; and they need no permission or regulation of law for the purpose. But this enables government to have a well-regulated militia; for to bear arms implies something more than the mere keeping; it implies the learning to handle and use them in a way that makes those who keep them ready for their efficient use; in other words, it implies the right to meet for voluntary discipline in arms, observing in doing so the laws of public order." *Id.*, at 271.

All other post-Civil War 19th-century sources we have found concurred with Cooley. One example from each decade will convey the general flavor:

"[The purpose of the Second Amendment is] to secure a well-armed militia. . . . But a militia would be useless unless the citizens were enabled to exercise themselves in the use of warlike weapons. To preserve this privilege, and to secure to the people the ability to oppose themselves in military force against the usurpations of government, as well as against enemies from without, that government is forbidden by any law or proceeding to invade or destroy the right to keep and bear arms. . . . The clause is analogous to the one securing the freedom of speech and of the press. Freedom, not license, is secured; the fair use, not the libellous abuse, is protected." J. Pomeroy, *An Introduction to the Constitutional Law of the United States* 152–153 (1868) (hereinafter Pomeroy).

"As the Constitution of the United States, and the constitutions of several of the states, in terms more or less comprehensive, declare the right of the people to keep and bear arms, it has been a subject of grave discussion, in some of the state courts, whether a statute prohibiting persons, when not on a journey, or as travellers, from *wearing or carrying concealed weapons*, be constitutional. There has been a great difference of opinion on the question." 2 J. Kent, *Commentaries on American Law* *340, n. 2 (O. Holmes ed., 12th ed. 1873) (hereinafter Kent).

"Some general knowledge of firearms is important to the public welfare; because it would be impossible, in case of war, to organize promptly an efficient force of volunteers unless the people had some familiarity with weapons of war. The Constitution secures the right of the people to keep and bear arms. No doubt, a citizen who keeps a gun or pistol under judicious precautions, practices in safe places the use of it, and in due time teaches his sons to do the same, exercises his individual right. No doubt, a person whose residence or duties involve peculiar peril may keep a pistol for prudent self-defence." B. Abbott, *Judge and Jury: A Popular Explanation of the Leading Topics in the Law of the Land* 333 (1880) (hereinafter Abbott).

"The right to bear arms has always been the distinctive privilege of freemen. Aside from any necessity of self-protection to the person, it represents among all nations power coupled with the exercise of a certain jurisdiction. . . . [I]t was not necessary that the right to bear arms should be granted in the Constitution, for it had always existed." J. Ordronaux, *Constitutional Legislation in the United States* 241–242 (1891).

E

We now ask whether any of our precedents forecloses the conclusions we have reached about the meaning of the Second Amendment.

United States v. Cruikshank, 92 U.S. 542, in the course of vacating the convictions of members of a white mob for depriving blacks of their right to keep and bear arms, held that the Second Amendment does not by its own force apply to anyone other than the Federal Government. The opinion explained that the right "is not a right granted by the Constitution [or] in any manner dependent upon that instrument for its existence. The second amendment . . . means no more than that it shall not be infringed by Congress." 92 U.S., at 553. States, we said, were free to restrict or protect the right under their police powers. The limited discussion of the Second Amendment in *Cruikshank* supports, if anything, the

(Continues)

(*Continued*)

individual-rights interpretation. There was no claim in *Cruikshank* that the victims had been deprived of their right to carry arms in a militia; indeed, the Governor had disbanded the local militia unit the year before the mob's attack, see C. Lane, The Day Freedom Died 62 (2008). We described the right protected by the Second Amendment as "'bearing arms for a lawful purpose'"[25] and said that "the people [must] look for their protection against any violation by their fellow-citizens of the rights it recognizes" to the States' police power. 92 U.S., at 553. That discussion makes little sense if it is only a right to bear arms in a state militia.[26]

Presser v. Illinois, 116 U.S. 252 (1886), held that the right to keep and bear arms was not violated by a law that forbade "bodies of men to associate together as military organizations, or to drill or parade with arms in cities and towns unless authorized by law." *Id.*, at 264–265. This does not refute the individual-rights interpretation of the Amendment; no one supporting that interpretation has contended that States may not ban such groups. *Justice Stevens* presses *Presser* into service to support his view that the right to bear arms is limited to service in the militia by joining *Presser*'s brief discussion of the Second Amendment with a later portion of the opinion making the seemingly relevant (to the Second Amendment) point that the plaintiff was not a member of the state militia. Unfortunately for *Justice Stevens*' argument, that later portion deals with the *Fourteenth Amendment*; it was the *Fourteenth Amendment* to which the plaintiff's nonmembership in the militia was relevant. Thus, *Justice Stevens*' statement that *Presser* "suggested that . . . nothing in the Constitution protected the use of arms outside the context of a militia," *post*, at 40, is simply wrong. *Presser* said nothing about the Second Amendment's meaning or scope, beyond the fact that it does not prevent the prohibition of private paramilitary organizations.

Justice Stevens places overwhelming reliance upon this Court's decision in *United States v. Miller*, 307 U.S. 174 (1939). "[H]undreds of judges," we are told, "have relied on the view of the amendment we endorsed there," *post*, at 2, and "[e]ven if the textual and historical arguments on both side of the issue were evenly balanced, respect for the well-settled views of all of our predecessors on this Court, and for the rule of law itself . . . would prevent most jurists from endorsing such a dramatic upheaval in the law," *post*, at 4. And what is, according to *Justice Stevens*, the holding of *Miller* that demands such obeisance? That the Second Amendment "protects the right to keep and bear arms for certain military purposes, but that it does not curtail the legislature's power to regulate the nonmilitary use and ownership of weapons." *Post*, at 2.

Nothing so clearly demonstrates the weakness of *Justice Stevens*' case. *Miller* did not hold that and cannot possibly be read to have held that. The judgment in the case upheld against a Second Amendment challenge two men's federal convictions for transporting an unregistered short-barreled shotgun in interstate commerce, in violation of the National Firearms Act, 48 Stat. 1236. It is entirely clear that the Court's basis for saying that the Second Amendment did not apply was *not* that the defendants were "bear[ing] arms" not "for . . . military purposes" but for "nonmilitary use," *post*, at 2. Rather, it was that the *type of weapon at issue* was not eligible for Second Amendment protection: "In the absence of any evidence tending to show that the possession or use of a [short-barreled shotgun] at this time has some reasonable relationship to the preservation or efficiency of a well regulated militia, we cannot say that the Second Amendment guarantees the right to keep and bear *such an instrument*." 307 U.S., at 178 (emphasis added). "Certainly," the Court continued, "it is not within judicial notice that this weapon is any part of the ordinary military equipment or that its use could contribute to the common defense." *Ibid.* Beyond that, the opinion provided no explanation of the content of the right.

This holding is not only consistent with, but positively suggests, that the Second Amendment confers an individual right to keep and bear arms (though only arms that "have some reasonable relationship to the preservation or efficiency of a well regulated militia"). Had the Court believed that the Second Amendment protects only those serving in the militia, it would have been odd to examine the character of the weapon rather than simply note that the two crooks were not militiamen. *Justice Stevens* can say again and again that *Miller* did "not turn on the difference between muskets and sawed-off shotguns, it turned, rather, on the basic difference between the military and nonmilitary use and possession of guns," *post*, at 42–43, but the words of the opinion prove otherwise. The most *Justice Stevens* can plausibly claim for *Miller* is that it declined to decide the nature of the Second Amendment right, despite the Solicitor General's argument (made in the alternative) that the right was collective, see Brief for United States, O. T. 1938, No. 696, pp. 4–5. *Miller* stands only for the proposition that the Second Amendment right, whatever its nature, extends only to certain types of weapons.

It is particularly wrongheaded to read *Miller* for more than what it said, because the case did not even purport to be a thorough examination of the Second Amendment. *Justice Stevens* claims, *post*, at 42, that the opinion reached its conclusion "[a]fter reviewing many of the same sources that are discussed at greater length by the Court today." Not many, which was not entirely the Court's fault. The respondent made no appearance in the case, neither filing a brief nor appearing at oral argument; the Court heard from no one but the Government (reason enough, one would think, not to make that case the beginning and the end of this Court's consideration of the Second Amendment). See Frye, The Peculiar Story of *United States v. Miller*, 3 *N.Y. U. J. L. & Liberty* 48, 65–68 (2008). The Government's brief spent two pages discussing English legal sources, concluding "that at least the carrying of weapons without lawful occasion or excuse was always a crime" and that (because of the class-based restrictions and the prohibition on terrorizing people with dangerous or unusual weapons) "the early English law did not guarantee an unrestricted right to bear arms." Brief for United States, O. T. 1938, No. 696, at 9–11. It then went on to rely primarily on the discussion of the English right to bear arms in *Aymette v. State*, 21 Tenn. 154, for the proposition that the only uses of arms protected by the Second Amendment are those that relate to the militia, not self-defense. See Brief for United States, O. T. 1938, No. 696, at 12–18. The final section of the brief recognized that "some courts have said that the right to bear arms includes the right of the individual to have them for the protection of his person and property," and launched an alternative argument that "weapons which are commonly used by criminals," such as sawed-off shotguns, are not protected. See *id.*, at 18–21. The Government's *Miller* brief thus provided scant discussion of the history of the Second Amendment—and the Court was presented with no counterdiscussion. As for the text of the Court's opinion itself, that discusses *none* of the history of the Second Amendment. It assumes from the prologue that the Amendment was designed to preserve the militia, 307 U.S., at 178 (which we do not dispute), and then reviews some historical materials dealing with the nature of the militia, and in particular with the nature of the arms their members were expected to possess, *id.*, at 178–182. Not a word (*not a word*) about the history of the Second Amendment. This is the mighty rock upon which the dissent rests its case.[27]

We may as well consider at this point (for we will have to consider eventually) *what* types of weapons *Miller* permits. Read in isolation, *Miller*'s phrase "part of ordinary military equipment" could mean that only those weapons useful in warfare are protected. That would be a startling reading of the opinion, since it would mean that the National Firearms Act's restrictions on machineguns (not challenged in *Miller*) might be unconstitutional, machineguns being useful in warfare in 1939. We think that *Miller*'s "ordinary military equipment" language must be read in tandem with what comes after: "[O]rdinarily when called for [militia] service [able-bodied] men were expected to appear bearing arms supplied by themselves and of the kind in common use at the time." 307 U.S., at 179. The traditional militia was formed from a pool of men bringing arms "in common use at the time" for lawful purposes like self-defense. "In the colonial and revolutionary war era, [small-arms] weapons used by militiamen and weapons used in defense of person and home were one and the same." *State v. Kessler*, 289 Ore. 359, 368, 614 P. 2d 94, 98 (1980) (citing G. Neumann, *Swords and Blades of the American Revolution* 6–15, 252–254 (1973)). Indeed, that is precisely the way in which the Second Amendment's operative clause furthers the purpose announced in its preface. We therefore read *Miller* to say only that the Second Amendment does not protect those weapons not typically possessed by law-abiding citizens for lawful purposes, such as short-barreled shotguns. That accords with the historical understanding of the scope of the right, see Part III, *infra*.[28]

We conclude that nothing in our precedents forecloses our adoption of the original understanding of the Second Amendment. It should be unsurprising that such a significant matter has been for so long judicially unresolved. For most of our history, the Bill of Rights was not thought applicable to the States, and the Federal Government did not significantly regulate the possession of firearms by law-abiding citizens. Other provisions of the Bill of Rights have similarly remained unilluminated for lengthy periods. This Court first held a law to violate the First Amendment's guarantee of freedom of speech in 1931, almost 150 years after the Amendment was ratified, see *Near v. Minnesota ex rel. Olson*, 283 U.S. 697 (1931), and it was not until after World War II that we held a law invalid under the Establishment Clause, see *Illinois ex rel. McCollum v. Board of Ed. of School Dist. No. 71, Champaign Cty.*, 333 U.S. 203 (1948). Even a question as basic as the scope of proscribable libel was not addressed by this Court until 1964, nearly two centuries after the founding. See *New York Times Co. v. Sullivan*, 376 U.S. 254 (1964). It is demonstrably not true that, as *Justice Stevens* claims, *post*, at 41–42,

(Continues)

(*Continued*)

"for most of our history, the invalidity of Second-Amendment-based objections to firearms regulations has been well settled and uncontroversial." For most of our history the question did not present itself.

III

Like most rights, the right secured by the Second Amendment is not unlimited. From Blackstone through the 19th-century cases, commentators and courts routinely explained that the right was not a right to keep and carry any weapon whatsoever in any manner whatsoever and for whatever purpose. See, *e.g.*, *Sheldon*, in 5 Blume 346; Rawle 123; Pomeroy 152–153; Abbott 333. For example, the majority of the 19th-century courts to consider the question held that prohibitions on carrying concealed weapons were lawful under the Second Amendment or state analogues. See, *e.g.*, *State v. Chandler*, 5 La. Ann., at 489–490; *Nunn v. State*, 1 Ga., at 251; see generally 2 Kent *340, n. 2; *The American Students' Blackstone* 84, n. 11 (G. Chase ed. 1884). Although we do not undertake an exhaustive historical analysis today of the full scope of the Second Amendment, nothing in our opinion should be taken to cast doubt on longstanding prohibitions on the possession of firearms by felons and the mentally ill, or laws forbidding the carrying of firearms in sensitive places such as schools and government buildings, or laws imposing conditions and qualifications on the commercial sale of arms.[29]

We also recognize another important limitation on the right to keep and carry arms. *Miller* said, as we have explained, that the sorts of weapons protected were those "in common use at the time." 307 U.S., at 179. We think that limitation is fairly supported by the historical tradition of prohibiting the carrying of "dangerous and unusual weapons." See 4 Blackstone 148–149 (1769); 3 B. Wilson, *Works of the Honourable James Wilson* 79 (1804); J. Dunlap, *The New York Justice* 8 (1815); C. Humphreys, *A Compendium of the Common Law in Force in Kentucky* 482 (1822); 1 W. Russell, *A Treatise on Crimes and Indictable Misdemeanors* 271–272 (1831); H. Stephen, *Summary of the Criminal Law* 48 (1840); E. Lewis, *An Abridgment of the Criminal Law of the United States* 64 (1847); F. Wharton, *A Treatise on the Criminal Law of the United States* 726 (1852). See also *State v. Langford*, 10 N.C. 381, 383–384 (1824); *O'Neill v. State*, 16 Ala. 65, 67 (1849); *English v. State*, 35 Tex. 473, 476 (1871); *State v. Lanier*, 71 N.C. 288, 289 (1874).

It may be objected that if weapons that are most useful in military service—M-16 rifles and the like—may be banned, then the Second Amendment right is completely detached from the prefatory clause. But as we have said, the conception of the militia at the time of the Second Amendment's ratification was the body of all citizens capable of military service, who would bring the sorts of lawful weapons that they possessed at home to militia duty. It may well be true today that a militia, to be as effective as militias in the 18th century, would require sophisticated arms that are highly unusual in society at large. Indeed, it may be true that no amount of small arms could be useful against modern-day bombers and tanks. But the fact that modern developments have limited the degree of fit between the prefatory clause and the protected right cannot change our interpretation of the right.

IV

We turn finally to the law at issue here. As we have said, the law totally bans handgun possession in the home. It also requires that any lawful firearm in the home be disassembled or bound by a trigger lock at all times, rendering it inoperable.

As the quotations earlier in this opinion demonstrate, the inherent right of self-defense has been central to the Second Amendment right. The handgun ban amounts to a prohibition of an entire class of "arms" that is overwhelmingly chosen by American society for that lawful purpose. The prohibition extends, moreover, to the home, where the need for defense of self, family, and property is most acute. Under any of the standards of scrutiny that we have applied to enumerated constitutional rights,[30] banning from the home "the most preferred firearm in the nation to 'keep' and use for protection of one's home and family," 478 F. 3d, at 400, would fail constitutional muster.

Few laws in the history of our Nation have come close to the severe restriction of the District's handgun ban. And some of those few have been struck down. In *Nunn v. State*, the Georgia Supreme Court struck down a prohibition on carrying pistols openly (even though it upheld a prohibition on carrying concealed weapons). See 1 Ga., at 251. In *Andrews v. State*, the Tennessee Supreme Court likewise held that a statute that forbade openly carrying a pistol "publicly or privately, without regard to time or place, or circumstances," 50 Tenn., at 187, violated the state constitutional provision (which the court equated with the Second Amendment). That was so even though the statute did not restrict the carrying of long guns. *Ibid.* See also *State v. Reid*, 1 Ala. 612, 616–617 (1840) ("A statute which, under the pretence of regulating, amounts to a destruction of the right, or which requires arms to be so borne as to render them wholly useless for the purpose of defence, would be clearly unconstitutional").

It is no answer to say, as petitioners do, that it is permissible to ban the possession of handguns so long as the possession of other firearms (*i.e.*, long guns) is allowed. It is enough to note, as we have observed, that the American people have considered the handgun to be the quintessential self-defense weapon. There are many reasons that a citizen may prefer a handgun for home defense: It is easier to store in a location that is readily accessible in an emergency; it cannot easily be redirected or wrestled away by an attacker; it is easier to use for those without the upper-body strength to lift and aim a long gun; it can be pointed at a burglar with one hand while the other hand dials the police. Whatever the reason, handguns are the most popular weapon chosen by Americans for self-defense in the home, and a complete prohibition of their use is invalid.

We must also address the District's requirement (as applied to respondent's handgun) that firearms in the home be rendered and kept inoperable at all times. This makes it impossible for citizens to use them for the core lawful purpose of self-defense and is hence unconstitutional. The District argues that we should interpret this element of the statute to contain an exception for self-defense. See Brief for Petitioners 56–57. But we think that is precluded by the unequivocal text, and by the presence of certain other enumerated exceptions: "Except for law enforcement personnel . . ., each registrant shall keep any firearm in his possession unloaded and disassembled or bound by a trigger lock or similar device unless such firearm is kept at his place of business, or while being used for lawful recreational purposes within the District of Columbia." D.C. Code §7-2507.02. The nonexistence of a self-defense exception is also suggested by the D.C. Court of Appeals' statement that the statute forbids residents to use firearms to stop intruders, see *McIntosh v. Washington*, 395 A. 2d 744, 755–756 (1978).[31]

Apart from his challenge to the handgun ban and the trigger-lock requirement respondent asked the District Court to enjoin petitioners from enforcing the separate licensing requirement "in such a manner as to forbid the carrying of a firearm within one's home or possessed land without a license." App. 59a. The Court of Appeals did not invalidate the licensing requirement, but held only that the District "may not prevent [a handgun] from being moved throughout one's house." 478 F. 3d, at 400. It then ordered the District Court to enter summary judgment "consistent with [respondent's] prayer for relief." *Id.*, at 401. Before this Court petitioners have stated that "if the handgun ban is struck down and respondent registers a handgun, he could obtain a license, assuming he is not otherwise disqualified," by which they apparently mean if he is not a felon and is not insane. Brief for Petitioners 58. Respondent conceded at oral argument that he does not "have a problem with . . . licensing" and that the District's law is permissible so long as it is "not enforced in an arbitrary and capricious manner." Tr. of Oral Arg. 74–75. We therefore assume that petitioners' issuance of a license will satisfy respondent's prayer for relief and do not address the licensing requirement.

Justice Breyer has devoted most of his separate dissent to the handgun ban. He says that, even assuming the Second Amendment is a personal guarantee of the right to bear arms, the District's prohibition is valid. He first tries to establish this by founding-era historical precedent, pointing to various restrictive laws in the colonial period. These demonstrate, in his view, that the District's law "imposes a burden upon gun owners that seems proportionately no greater than restrictions in existence at the time the Second Amendment was adopted." *Post*, at 2. Of the laws he cites, only one offers even marginal support for his assertion. A 1783 Massachusetts law forbade the residents of Boston to "take into" or "receive into" "any Dwelling House, Stable, Barn, Out-house, Ware-house, Store, Shop or other Building" loaded firearms, and permitted the seizure of any loaded firearms that "shall be found" there. Act of Mar. 1, 1783, ch. 13, 1783 Mass. Acts p. 218. That statute's text and its prologue, which makes clear that the purpose of the prohibition was to eliminate the danger to firefighters posed by the "depositing of loaded Arms" in buildings, give reason to doubt that colonial Boston authorities would have enforced that general prohibition against someone who temporarily loaded a firearm to confront an intruder (despite the law's application in that case). In any case, we would not stake our interpretation of the Second Amendment upon a single law, in effect in a single city, that contradicts the overwhelming weight of other evidence regarding the right to keep and bear arms for defense of the home. The other laws *Justice Breyer* cites are gunpowder-storage laws that he concedes did not clearly prohibit loaded weapons, but required only that excess gunpowder be kept in a special container or on the top floor of the home. *Post*, at 6–7. Nothing about those fire-safety laws undermines our analysis; they do not remotely burden the right of self-defense as much as an absolute ban on handguns. Nor, correspondingly, does our analysis suggest the invalidity of laws regulating the storage of firearms to prevent accidents.

(Continues)

(Continued)

Justice Breyer points to other founding-era laws that he says "restricted the firing of guns within the city limits to at least some degree" in Boston, Philadelphia and New York. *Post*, at 4 (citing Churchill, Gun Regulation, the Police Power, and the Right to Keep Arms in Early America, 25 *Law & Hist. Rev.* 139, 162 (2007)). Those laws provide no support for the severe restriction in the present case. The New York law levied a fine of 20 shillings on anyone who fired a gun in certain places (including houses) on New Year's Eve and the first two days of January, and was aimed at preventing the "great Damages . . . frequently done on [those days] by persons going House to House, with Guns and other Firearms and being often intoxicated with Liquor." 5 *Colonial Laws of New York* 244–246 (1894). It is inconceivable that this law would have been enforced against a person exercising his right to self-defense on New Year's Day against such drunken hooligans. The Pennsylvania law to which *Justice Breyer* refers levied a fine of 5 shillings on one who fired a gun or set off fireworks in Philadelphia without first obtaining a license from the governor. See Act of Aug. 26, 1721, §4, in 3 Stat. at Large 253–254. Given Justice Wilson's explanation that the right to self-defense with arms was protected by the Pennsylvania Constitution, it is unlikely that this law (which in any event amounted to at most a licensing regime) would have been enforced against a person who used firearms for self-defense. *Justice Breyer* cites a Rhode Island law that simply levied a 5-shilling fine on those who fired guns in *streets* and *taverns*, a law obviously inapplicable to this case. See An Act for preventing Mischief being done in the town of Newport, or in any other town in this Government, 1731, Rhode Island Session Laws. Finally, *Justice Breyer* points to a Massachusetts law similar to the Pennsylvania law, prohibiting "discharg[ing] any Gun or Pistol charged with Shot or Ball in the Town of *Boston*." Act of May 28, 1746, ch. X, Acts and Laws of Mass. Bay 208. It is again implausible that this would have been enforced against a citizen acting in self-defense, particularly given its preambulatory reference to "the *indiscreet* firing of Guns." *Ibid.* (preamble) (emphasis added).

A broader point about the laws that *Justice Breyer* cites: All of them punished the discharge (or loading) of guns with a small fine and forfeiture of the weapon (or in a few cases a very brief stay in the local jail), not with significant criminal penalties.[32] They are akin to modern penalties for minor public-safety infractions like speeding or jaywalking. And although such public-safety laws may not contain exceptions for self-defense, it is inconceivable that the threat of a jaywalking ticket would deter someone from disregarding a "Do Not Walk" sign in order to flee an attacker, or that the Government would enforce those laws under such circumstances. Likewise, we do not think that a law imposing a 5-shilling fine and forfeiture of the gun would have prevented a person in the founding era from using a gun to protect himself or his family from violence, or that if he did so the law would be enforced against him. The District law, by contrast, far from imposing a minor fine, threatens citizens with a year in prison (five years for a second violation) for even obtaining a gun in the first place. See D.C. Code §7-2507.06.

Justice Breyer moves on to make a broad jurisprudential point: He criticizes us for declining to establish a level of scrutiny for evaluating Second Amendment restrictions. He proposes, explicitly at least, none of the traditionally expressed levels (strict scrutiny, intermediate scrutiny, rational basis), but rather a judge-empowering "interest-balancing inquiry" that "asks whether the statute burdens a protected interest in a way or to an extent that is out of proportion to the statute's salutary effects upon other important governmental interests." *Post*, at 10. After an exhaustive discussion of the arguments for and against gun control, *Justice Breyer* arrives at his interest-balanced answer: because handgun violence is a problem, because the law is limited to an urban area, and because there were somewhat similar restrictions in the founding period (a false proposition that we have already discussed), the interest-balancing inquiry results in the constitutionality of the handgun ban. QED.

We know of no other enumerated constitutional right whose core protection has been subjected to a freestanding "interest-balancing" approach. The very enumeration of the right takes out of the hands of government—even the Third Branch of Government—the power to decide on a case-by-case basis whether the right is *really worth* insisting upon. A constitutional guarantee subject to future judges' assessments of its usefulness is no constitutional guarantee at all. Constitutional rights are enshrined with the scope they were understood to have when the people adopted them, whether or not future legislatures or (yes) even future judges think that scope too broad. We would not apply an "interest-balancing" approach to the prohibition of a peaceful neo-Nazi march through Skokie. See *National Socialist Party of America v. Skokie*, 432 U.S. 43 (1977) (*per curiam*). The First Amendment contains the freedom-of-speech guarantee that the people ratified, which included exceptions for obscenity, libel, and disclosure of state secrets, but not for the expression of extremely unpopular and wrong-headed views. The Second Amendment is no different. Like the First, it is the very *product* of an interest-balancing by the people—which *Justice Breyer* would now conduct for them anew. And whatever else it leaves to future evaluation, it surely elevates above all other interests the right of law-abiding, responsible citizens to use arms in defense of hearth and home.

Justice Breyer chides us for leaving so many applications of the right to keep and bear arms in doubt, and for not providing extensive historical justification for those regulations of the right that we describe as permissible. See *post*, at 42–43. But since this case represents this Court's first in-depth examination of the Second Amendment, one should not expect it to clarify the entire field, any more than *Reynolds v. United States*, 98 U.S. 145 (1879), our first in-depth Free Exercise Clause case, left that area in a state of utter certainty. And there will be time enough to expound upon the historical justifications for the exceptions we have mentioned if and when those exceptions come before us.

In sum, we hold that the District's ban on handgun possession in the home violates the Second Amendment, as does its prohibition against rendering any lawful firearm in the home operable for the purpose of immediate self-defense. Assuming that Heller is not disqualified from the exercise of Second Amendment rights, the District must permit him to register his handgun and must issue him a license to carry it in the home.

* * *

We are aware of the problem of handgun violence in this country, and we take seriously the concerns raised by the many *amici* who believe that prohibition of handgun ownership is a solution. The Constitution leaves the District of Columbia a variety of tools for combating that problem, including some measures regulating handguns, see *supra*, at 54–55, and n. 26. But the enshrinement of constitutional rights necessarily takes certain policy choices off the table. These include the absolute prohibition of handguns held and used for self-defense in the home. Undoubtedly some think that the Second Amendment is outmoded in a society where our standing army is the pride of our Nation, where well-trained police forces provide personal security, and where gun violence is a serious problem. That is perhaps debatable, but what is not debatable is that it is not the role of this Court to pronounce the Second Amendment extinct.

We affirm the judgment of the Court of Appeals.

It is so ordered.

DISTRICT OF COLUMBIA, *et al.*, PETITIONERS *v.* DICK ANTHONY HELLER

on writ of certiorari to the united states court of appeals for the district of columbia circuit

[June 26, 2008]

Justice Stevens, with whom *Justice Souter*, *Justice Ginsburg*, and *Justice Breyer* join, dissenting.

The question presented by this case is not whether the Second Amendment protects a "collective right" or an "individual right." Surely it protects a right that can be enforced by individuals. But a conclusion that the Second Amendment protects an individual right does not tell us anything about the scope of that right.

Guns are used to hunt, for self-defense, to commit crimes, for sporting activities, and to perform military duties. The Second Amendment plainly does not protect the right to use a gun to rob a bank; it is equally clear that it *does* encompass the right to use weapons for certain military purposes. Whether it also protects the right to possess and use guns for nonmilitary purposes like hunting and personal self-defense is the question presented by this case. The text of the Amendment, its history, and our decision in *United States v. Miller*, 307 U.S. 174 (1939), provide a clear answer to that question.

The Second Amendment was adopted to protect the right of the people of each of the several States to maintain a well-regulated militia. It was a response to concerns raised during the ratification of the Constitution that the power of Congress to disarm the state militias and create a national standing army posed an intolerable threat to the sovereignty of the several States. Neither the text of the Amendment nor the arguments advanced by its proponents evidenced the slightest interest in limiting any legislature's authority to regulate private civilian uses of firearms. Specifically, there is no indication that the Framers of the Amendment intended to enshrine the common-law right of self-defense in the Constitution.

In 1934, Congress enacted the National Firearms Act, the first major federal firearms law.[33] Upholding a conviction under that Act, this Court held that, "[i]n the absence of any evidence tending to show

(*Continues*)

(*Continued*)

that possession or use of a 'shotgun having a barrel of less than eighteen inches in length' at this time has some reasonable relationship to the preservation or efficiency of a well regulated militia, we cannot say that the Second Amendment guarantees the right to keep and bear such an instrument." *Miller*, 307 U.S., at 178. The view of the Amendment we took in *Miller*—that it protects the right to keep and bear arms for certain military purposes, but that it does not curtail the Legislature's power to regulate the nonmilitary use and ownership of weapons—is both the most natural reading of the Amendment's text and the interpretation most faithful to the history of its adoption.

Since our decision in *Miller*, hundreds of judges have relied on the view of the Amendment we endorsed there[34]; we ourselves affirmed it in 1980. See *Lewis v. United States*, 445 U.S. 55, 65–66, n. 8 (1980).[35] No new evidence has surfaced since 1980 supporting the view that the Amendment was intended to curtail the power of Congress to regulate civilian use or misuse of weapons. Indeed, a review of the drafting history of the Amendment demonstrates that its Framers *rejected* proposals that would have broadened its coverage to include such uses.

The opinion the Court announces today fails to identify any new evidence supporting the view that the Amendment was intended to limit the power of Congress to regulate civilian uses of weapons. Unable to point to any such evidence, the Court stakes its holding on a strained and unpersuasive reading of the Amendment's text; significantly different provisions in the 1689 English Bill of Rights, and in various 19th-century State Constitutions; postenactment commentary that was available to the Court when it decided *Miller*; and, ultimately, a feeble attempt to distinguish *Miller* that places more emphasis on the Court's decisional process than on the reasoning in the opinion itself.

Even if the textual and historical arguments on both sides of the issue were evenly balanced, respect for the well-settled views of all of our predecessors on this Court, and for the rule of law itself, see *Mitchell v. W. T. Grant Co.*, 416 U.S. 600, 636 (1974) (Stewart, J., dissenting), would prevent most jurists from endorsing such a dramatic upheaval in the law.[36] As Justice Cardozo observed years ago, the "labor of judges would be increased almost to the breaking point if every past decision could be reopened in every case, and one could not lay one's own course of bricks on the secure foundation of the courses laid by others who had gone before him." *The Nature of the Judicial Process* 149 (1921).

In this dissent I shall first explain why our decision in *Miller* was faithful to the text of the Second Amendment and the purposes revealed in its drafting history. I shall then comment on the postratification history of the Amendment, which makes abundantly clear that the Amendment should not be interpreted as limiting the authority of Congress to regulate the use or possession of firearms for purely civilian purposes.

I

The text of the Second Amendment is brief. It provides: "A well regulated Militia, being necessary to the security of a free State, the right of the people to keep and bear Arms, shall not be infringed."

Three portions of that text merit special focus: the introductory language defining the Amendment's purpose, the class of persons encompassed within its reach, and the unitary nature of the right that it protects.

"A well regulated Militia, being necessary to the security of a free State"

The preamble to the Second Amendment makes three important points. It identifies the preservation of the militia as the Amendment's purpose; it explains that the militia is necessary to the security of a free State; and it recognizes that the militia must be "well regulated." In all three respects it is comparable to provisions in several State Declarations of Rights that were adopted roughly contemporaneously with the Declaration of Independence.[37] Those state provisions highlight the importance members of the founding generation attached to the maintenance of state militias; they also underscore the profound fear shared by many in that era of the dangers posed by standing armies.[38] While the need for state militias has not been a matter of significant public interest for almost two centuries, that fact should not obscure the contemporary concerns that animated the Framers.

The parallels between the Second Amendment and these state declarations, and the Second Amendment's omission of any statement of purpose related to the right to use firearms for hunting or personal self-defense, is especially striking in light of the fact that the Declarations of Rights of Pennsylvania and Vermont *did* expressly protect such civilian uses at the time. Article XIII of Pennsylvania's 1776 Declaration of Rights announced that "the people have a right to bear arms for the defence *of themselves* and the state," 1 Schwartz 266 (emphasis added); §43 of the Declaration assured that "the inhabitants of this state shall have the liberty to fowl and hunt in seasonable times on the lands they hold, and on all other lands therein not inclosed," *id.*, at 274. And Article XV of the 1777 Vermont Declaration of Rights guaranteed "[t]hat the people have a right to bear arms for the defence *of themselves* and the State." *Id.*, at 324 (emphasis added). The contrast between those two declarations and the Second Amendment reinforces the clear statement of purpose announced in the Amendment's preamble. It confirms that the Framers' single-minded focus in crafting the constitutional guarantee "to keep and bear arms" was on military uses of firearms, which they viewed in the context of service in state militias.

The preamble thus both sets forth the object of the Amendment and informs the meaning of the remainder of its text. Such text should not be treated as mere surplusage, for "[i]t cannot be presumed that any clause in the constitution is intended to be without effect." *Marbury v. Madison*, 1 Cranch 137, 174 (1803).

The Court today tries to denigrate the importance of this clause of the Amendment by beginning its analysis with the Amendment's operative provision and returning to the preamble merely "to ensure that our reading of the operative clause is consistent with the announced purpose." *Ante*, at 5. That is not how this Court ordinarily reads such texts, and it is not how the preamble would have been viewed at the time the Amendment was adopted. While the Court makes the novel suggestion that it need only find some "logical connection" between the preamble and the operative provision, it does acknowledge that a prefatory clause may resolve an ambiguity in the text. *Ante*, at 4.[39] Without identifying any language in the text that even mentions civilian uses of firearms, the Court proceeds to "find" its preferred reading in what is at best an ambiguous text, and then concludes that its reading is not foreclosed by the preamble. Perhaps the Court's approach to the text is acceptable advocacy, but it is surely an unusual approach for judges to follow.

"The right of the people"

The centerpiece of the Court's textual argument is its insistence that the words "the people" as used in the Second Amendment must have the same meaning, and protect the same class of individuals, as when they are used in the First and Fourth Amendments. According to the Court, in all three provisions— as well as the Constitution's preamble, section 2 of Article I, and the Tenth Amendment—"the term unambiguously refers to all members of the political community, not an unspecified subset." *Ante,* at 6. But the Court *itself* reads the Second Amendment to protect a "subset" significantly narrower than the class of persons protected by the First and Fourth Amendments; when it finally drills down on the substantive meaning of the Second Amendment, the Court limits the protected class to "law-abiding, responsible citizens," *ante*, at 63. But the class of persons protected by the First and Fourth Amendments is *not* so limited; for even felons (and presumably irresponsible citizens as well) may invoke the protections of those constitutional provisions. The Court offers no way to harmonize its conflicting pronouncements.

The Court also overlooks the significance of the way the Framers used the phrase "the people" in these constitutional provisions. In the First Amendment, no words define the class of individuals entitled to speak, to publish, or to worship; in that Amendment it is only the right peaceably to assemble, and to petition the Government for a redress of grievances, that is described as a right of "the people." These rights contemplate collective action. While the right peaceably to assemble protects the individual rights of those persons participating in the assembly, its concern is with action engaged in by members of a group, rather than any single individual. Likewise, although the act of petitioning the Government is a right that can be exercised by individuals, it is primarily collective in nature. For if they are to be effective, petitions must involve groups of individuals acting in concert.

Similarly, the words "the people" in the Second Amendment refer back to the object announced in the Amendment's preamble. They remind us that it is the collective action of individuals having a duty to serve in the militia that the text directly protects and, perhaps more importantly, that the ultimate purpose of the Amendment was to protect the States' share of the divided sovereignty created by the Constitution.

As used in the Fourth Amendment, "the people" describes the class of persons protected from unreasonable searches and seizures by Government officials. It is true that the Fourth Amendment describes a right that need not be exercised in any collective sense. But that observation does not settle the meaning of the phrase "the people" when used in the Second Amendment. For, as we have seen, the

(Continues)

phrase means something quite different in the Petition and Assembly Clauses of the First Amendment. Although the abstract definition of the phrase "the people" could carry the same meaning in the Second Amendment as in the Fourth Amendment, the preamble of the Second Amendment suggests that the uses of the phrase in the First and Second Amendments are the same in referring to a collective activity. By way of contrast, the Fourth Amendment describes a right *against* governmental interference rather than an affirmative right *to* engage in protected conduct, and so refers to a right to protect a purely individual interest. As used in the Second Amendment, the words "the people" do not enlarge the right to keep and bear arms to encompass use or ownership of weapons outside the context of service in a well-regulated militia.

"To keep and bear Arms"

Although the Court's discussion of these words treats them as two "phrases"—as if they read "to keep" and "to bear"—they describe a unitary right: to possess arms if needed for military purposes and to use them in conjunction with military activities.

As a threshold matter, it is worth pausing to note an oddity in the Court's interpretation of "to keep and bear arms." Unlike the Court of Appeals, the Court does not read that phrase to create a right to possess arms for "lawful, private purposes." *Parker v. District of Columbia*, 478 F. 3d 370, 382 (CADC 2007). Instead, the Court limits the Amendment's protection to the right "to possess and carry weapons in case of confrontation." *Ante*, at 19. No party or *amicus* urged this interpretation; the Court appears to have fashioned it out of whole cloth. But although this novel limitation lacks support in the text of the Amendment, the Amendment's text *does* justify a different limitation: the "right to keep and bear arms" protects only a right to possess and use firearms in connection with service in a state-organized militia.

The term "bear arms" is a familiar idiom; when used unadorned by any additional words, its meaning is "to serve as a soldier, do military service, fight." 1 *Oxford English Dictionary* 634 (2d ed. 1989). It is derived from the Latin *arma ferre*, which, translated literally, means "to bear [*ferre*] war equipment [*arma*]." Brief for Professors of Linguistics and English as *Amici Curiae* 19. One 18th-century dictionary defined "arms" as "weapons of offence, or armour of defence," 1 S. Johnson, *A Dictionary of the English Language* (1755), and another contemporaneous source explained that "[b]y *arms*, we understand those instruments of offence generally made use of in war; such as firearms, swords, & c. By *weapons*, we more particularly mean instruments of other kinds (exclusive of fire-arms), made use of as offensive, on special occasions." 1 J. Trusler, *The Distinction Between Words Esteemed Synonymous in the English Language* 37 (1794).[40] Had the Framers wished to expand the meaning of the phrase "bear arms" to encompass civilian possession and use, they could have done so by the addition of phrases such as "for the defense of themselves," as was done in the Pennsylvania and Vermont Declarations of Rights. The *unmodified* use of "bear arms," by contrast, refers most naturally to a military purpose, as evidenced by its use in literally dozens of contemporary texts.[41] The absence of any reference to civilian uses of weapons tailors the text of the Amendment to the purpose identified in its preamble.[42] But when discussing these words, the Court simply ignores the preamble.

The Court argues that a "qualifying phrase that contradicts the word or phrase it modifies is unknown this side of the looking glass." *Ante*, at 15. But this fundamentally fails to grasp the point. The stand-alone phrase "bear arms" most naturally conveys a military meaning *unless* the addition of a qualifying phrase signals that a different meaning is intended. When, as in this case, there is no such qualifier, the most natural meaning is the military one; and, in the absence of any qualifier, it is all the more appropriate to look to the preamble to confirm the natural meaning of the text.[43] The Court's objection is particularly puzzling in light of its own contention that the addition of the modifier "against" changes the meaning of "bear arms." Compare *ante*, at 10 (defining "bear arms" to mean "carrying [a weapon] for a particular purpose—confrontation"), with *ante*, at 12 ("The phrase 'bear Arms' also had at the time of the founding an idiomatic meaning that was significantly different from its natural meaning: to serve as a soldier, do military service, fight or to wage war. But it unequivocally bore that idiomatic meaning only when followed by the preposition 'against.'" (citations and some internal quotation marks omitted)).

The Amendment's use of the term "keep" in no way contradicts the military meaning conveyed by the phrase "bear arms" and the Amendment's preamble. To the contrary, a number of state militia laws in effect at the time of the Second Amendment's drafting used the term "keep" to describe the requirement that militia members store their arms at their homes, ready to be used for service when necessary.

The Virginia military law, for example, ordered that "every one of the said officers, non-commissioned officers, and privates, shall constantly *keep* the aforesaid arms, accoutrements, and ammunition, ready to be produced whenever called for by his commanding officer." Act for Regulating and Disciplining the Militia, 1785 Va. Acts ch. 1, §3, p. 2 (emphasis added).[44] "[K]eep and bear arms" thus perfectly describes the responsibilities of a framing-era militia member.

This reading is confirmed by the fact that the clause protects only one right, rather than two. It does not describe a right "to keep arms" and a separate right "to bear arms." Rather, the single right that it does describe is both a duty and a right to have arms available and ready for military service, and to use them for military purposes when necessary.[45] Different language surely would have been used to protect nonmilitary use and possession of weapons from regulation if such an intent had played any role in the drafting of the Amendment.

* * *

When each word in the text is given full effect, the Amendment is most naturally read to secure to the people a right to use and possess arms in conjunction with service in a well-regulated militia. So far as appears, no more than that was contemplated by its drafters or is encompassed within its terms. Even if the meaning of the text were genuinely susceptible to more than one interpretation, the burden would remain on those advocating a departure from the purpose identified in the preamble and from settled law to come forward with persuasive new arguments or evidence. The textual analysis offered by respondent and embraced by the Court falls far short of sustaining that heavy burden.[46] And the Court's emphatic reliance on the claim "that the Second Amendment . . . codified a *pre-existing* right," *ante*, at 19, is of course beside the point because the right to keep and bear arms for service in a state militia was also a pre-existing right.

Indeed, not a word in the constitutional text even arguably supports the Court's overwrought and novel description of the Second Amendment as "elevat[ing] above all other interests" "the right of law-abiding, responsible citizens to use arms in defense of hearth and home." *Ante*, at 63.

II

The proper allocation of military power in the new Nation was an issue of central concern for the Framers. The compromises they ultimately reached, reflected in Article I's Militia Clauses and the Second Amendment, represent quintessential examples of the Framers' "splitting the atom of sovereignty."[47]

Two themes relevant to our current interpretive task ran through the debates on the original Constitution. "On the one hand, there was a widespread fear that a national standing Army posed an intolerable threat to individual liberty and to the sovereignty of the separate States." *Perpich v. Department of Defense*, 496 U.S. 334, 340 (1990).[48] Governor Edmund Randolph, reporting on the Constitutional Convention to the Virginia Ratification Convention, explained: "With respect to a standing army, I believe there was not a member in the federal Convention, who did not feel indignation at such an institution." 3 J. Elliot, *Debates in the Several State Conventions on the Adoption of the Federal Constitution* 401 (2d ed. 1863) (hereinafter Elliot). On the other hand, the Framers recognized the dangers inherent in relying on inadequately trained militia members "as the primary means of providing for the common defense," *Perpich*, 496 U.S., at 340; during the Revolutionary War, "[t]his force, though armed, was largely untrained, and its deficiencies were the subject of bitter complaint." Wiener, The Militia Clause of the Constitution, 54 *Harv. L. Rev.* 181, 182 (1940).[49] In order to respond to those twin concerns, a compromise was reached: Congress would be authorized to raise and support a national Army[50] and Navy, and also to organize, arm, discipline, and provide for the calling forth of "the Militia." U.S. Const., Art. I, §8, cls. 12–16. The President, at the same time, was empowered as the "Commander in Chief of the Army and Navy of the United States, and of the Militia of the several States, when called into the actual Service of the United States." Art. II, §2. But, with respect to the militia, a significant reservation was made to the States: Although Congress would have the power to call forth,[51] organize, arm, and discipline the militia, as well as to govern "such Part of them as may be employed in the Service of the United States," the States respectively would retain the right to appoint the officers and to train the militia in accordance with the discipline prescribed by Congress. Art. I, §8, cl. 16.[52]

But the original Constitution's retention of the militia and its creation of divided authority over that body did not prove sufficient to allay fears about the dangers posed by a standing army. For it was perceived by some that Article I contained a significant gap: While it empowered Congress to organize, arm, and discipline the militia, it did not prevent Congress from providing for the militia's *disarmament*.

(Continues)

(Continued)

As George Mason argued during the debates in Virginia on the ratification of the original Constitution:

> "The militia may be here destroyed by that method which has been practiced in other parts of the world before; that is, by rendering them useless—by disarming them. Under various pretences, Congress may neglect to provide for arming and disciplining the militia; and the state governments cannot do it, for Congress has the exclusive right to arm them." Elliot 379.

This sentiment was echoed at a number of state ratification conventions; indeed, it was one of the primary objections to the original Constitution voiced by its opponents. The Anti-Federalists were ultimately unsuccessful in persuading state ratification conventions to condition their approval of the Constitution upon the eventual inclusion of any particular amendment. But a number of States did propose to the first Federal Congress amendments reflecting a desire to ensure that the institution of the militia would remain protected under the new Government. The proposed amendments sent by the States of Virginia, North Carolina, and New York focused on the importance of preserving the state militias and reiterated the dangers posed by standing armies. New Hampshire sent a proposal that differed significantly from the others; while also invoking the dangers of a standing army, it suggested that the Constitution should more broadly protect the use and possession of weapons, without tying such a guarantee expressly to the maintenance of the militia. The States of Maryland, Pennsylvania, and Massachusetts sent no relevant proposed amendments to Congress, but in each of those States a minority of the delegates advocated related amendments. While the Maryland minority proposals were exclusively concerned with standing armies and conscientious objectors, the unsuccessful proposals in both Massachusetts and Pennsylvania would have protected a more broadly worded right, less clearly tied to service in a state militia. Faced with all of these options, it is telling that James Madison chose to craft the Second Amendment as he did.

The relevant proposals sent by the Virginia Ratifying Convention read as follows:

> "17th, That the people have a right to keep and bear arms; that a well regulated Militia composed of the body of the people trained to arms is the proper, natural and safe defence of a free State. That standing armies are dangerous to liberty, and therefore ought to be avoided, as far as the circumstances and protection of the Community will admit; and that in all cases the military should be under strict subordination to and be governed by the civil power." Elliot 659.
>
> "19th. That any person religiously scrupulous of bearing arms ought to be exempted, upon payment of an equivalent to employ another to bear arms in his stead." *Ibid.*

North Carolina adopted Virginia's proposals and sent them to Congress as its own, although it did not actually ratify the original Constitution until Congress had sent the proposed Bill of Rights to the States for ratification. 2 Schwartz 932–933; see *The Complete Bill of Rights* 182–183 (N. Cogan ed. 1997) (hereinafter Cogan).

New York produced a proposal with nearly identical language. It read:

> "That the people have a right to keep and bear Arms; that a well regulated Militia, including the body of the People capable of bearing Arms, is the proper, natural, and safe defence of a free State. . . . That standing Armies, in time of Peace, are dangerous to Liberty, and ought not to be kept up, except in Cases of necessity; and that at all times, the Military should be kept under strict Subordination to the civil Power." 2 Schwartz 912.

Notably, each of these proposals used the phrase "keep and bear arms," which was eventually adopted by Madison. And each proposal embedded the phrase within a group of principles that are distinctly military in meaning.[53]

By contrast, New Hampshire's proposal, although it followed another proposed amendment that echoed the familiar concern about standing armies,[54] described the protection involved in more clearly personal terms. Its proposal read:

> "*Twelfth*, Congress shall never disarm any Citizen unless such as are or have been in Actual Rebellion." *Id.*, at 758, 761.

The proposals considered in the other three States, although ultimately rejected by their respective ratification conventions, are also relevant to our historical inquiry. First, the Maryland proposal, endorsed by a minority of the delegates and later circulated in pamphlet form, read:

"4. That no standing army shall be kept up in time of peace, unless with the consent of two thirds of the members present of each branch of Congress.

. . . .

"10. That no person conscientiously scrupulous of bearing arms in any case, shall be compelled personally to serve as a soldier." *Id.,* at 729, 735.

The rejected Pennsylvania proposal, which was later incorporated into a critique of the Constitution titled "The Address and Reasons of Dissent of the Pennsylvania Minority of the Convention of the State of Pennsylvania to Their Constituents (1787)," signed by a minority of the State's delegates (those who had voted against ratification of the Constitution), *id.,* at 628, 662, read:

7. "That the people have a right to bear arms for the defense of themselves and their own State, or the United States, or for the purpose of killing game; and no law shall be passed for disarming the people or any of them unless for crimes committed, or real danger of public injury from individuals; and as standing armies in the time of peace are dangerous to liberty, they ought not to be kept up; and that the military shall be kept under strict subordination to, and be governed by the civil powers." *Id.,* at 665.

Finally, after the delegates at the Massachusetts Ratification Convention had compiled a list of proposed amendments and alterations, a motion was made to add to the list the following language: "[T]hat the said Constitution never be construed to authorize Congress to . . . prevent the people of the United States, who are peaceable citizens, from keeping their own arms." Cogan 181. This motion, however, failed to achieve the necessary support, and the proposal was excluded from the list of amendments the State sent to Congress. 2 Schwartz 674–675.

Madison, charged with the task of assembling the proposals for amendments sent by the ratifying States, was the principal draftsman of the Second Amendment.[55] He had before him, or at the very least would have been aware of, all of these proposed formulations. In addition, Madison had been a member, some years earlier, of the committee tasked with drafting the Virginia Declaration of Rights. That committee considered a proposal by Thomas Jefferson that would have included within the Virginia Declaration the following language: "No freeman shall ever be debarred the use of arms [within his own lands or tenements]." 1 *Papers of Thomas Jefferson* 363 (J. Boyd ed. 1950). But the committee rejected that language, adopting instead the provision drafted by George Mason.[56]

With all of these sources upon which to draw, it is strikingly significant that Madison's first draft omitted any mention of nonmilitary use or possession of weapons. Rather, his original draft repeated the essence of the two proposed amendments sent by Virginia, combining the substance of the two provisions succinctly into one, which read: "The right of the people to keep and bear arms shall not be infringed; a well armed, and well regulated militia being the best security of a free country; but no person religiously scrupulous of bearing arms, shall be compelled to render military service in person." Cogan 169.

Madison's decision to model the Second Amendment on the distinctly military Virginia proposal is therefore revealing, since it is clear that he considered and rejected formulations that would have unambiguously protected civilian uses of firearms. When Madison prepared his first draft, and when that draft was debated and modified, it is reasonable to assume that all participants in the drafting process were fully aware of the other formulations that would have protected civilian use and possession of weapons and that their choice to craft the Amendment as they did represented a rejection of those alternative formulations.

Madison's initial inclusion of an exemption for conscientious objectors sheds revelatory light on the purpose of the Amendment. It confirms an intent to describe a duty as well as a right, and it unequivocally identifies the military character of both. The objections voiced to the conscientious-objector clause only confirm the central meaning of the text. Although records of the debate in the Senate, which is where the conscientious-objector clause was removed, do not survive, the arguments raised in the House illuminate the perceived problems with the clause: Specifically, there was concern that Congress "can declare who are those religiously scrupulous, and prevent them from bearing arms."[57] The ultimate removal of the clause, therefore, only serves to confirm the purpose of the Amendment—to protect against congressional disarmament, by whatever means, of the States' militias.

The Court also contends that because "Quakers opposed the use of arms not just for militia service, but for any violent purpose whatsoever," *ante,* at 17, the inclusion of a conscientious-objector clause in the original draft of the Amendment does not support the conclusion that the phrase "bear arms" was

(Continues)

(Continued)

military in meaning. But that claim cannot be squared with the record. In the proposals cited *supra*, at 21–22, both Virginia and North Carolina included the following language: "That any person religiously scrupulous of bearing arms ought to be exempted, upon payment of an equivalent *to employ another to bear arms in his stead*" (emphasis added).[58] There is no plausible argument that the use of "bear arms" in those provisions was not unequivocally and exclusively military: The State simply does not compel its citizens to carry arms for the purpose of private "confrontation," *ante*, at 10, or for self-defense.

The history of the adoption of the Amendment thus describes an overriding concern about the potential threat to state sovereignty that a federal standing army would pose, and a desire to protect the States' militias as the means by which to guard against that danger. But state militias could not effectively check the prospect of a federal standing army so long as Congress retained the power to disarm them, and so a guarantee against such disarmament was needed.[59] As we explained in *Miller*: "With obvious purpose to assure the continuation and render possible the effectiveness of such forces the declaration and guarantee of the Second Amendment were made. It must be interpreted and applied with that end in view." 307 U.S., at 178. The evidence plainly refutes the claim that the Amendment was motivated by the Framers' fears that Congress might act to regulate any civilian uses of weapons. And even if the historical record were genuinely ambiguous, the burden would remain on the parties advocating a change in the law to introduce facts or arguments "'newly ascertained,'" *Vasquez,* 474 U.S., at 266; the Court is unable to identify any such facts or arguments.

III

Although it gives short shrift to the drafting history of the Second Amendment, the Court dwells at length on four other sources: the 17th-century English Bill of Rights; Blackstone's Commentaries on the Laws of England; postenactment commentary on the Second Amendment; and post-Civil War legislative history.[60] All of these sources shed only indirect light on the question before us, and in any event offer little support for the Court's conclusion.[61]

The English Bill of Rights

The Court's reliance on Article VII of the 1689 English Bill of Rights—which, like most of the evidence offered by the Court today, was considered in *Miller*[62]—is misguided both because Article VII was enacted in response to different concerns from those that motivated the Framers of the Second Amendment, and because the guarantees of the two provisions were by no means coextensive. Moreover, the English text contained no preamble or other provision identifying a narrow, militia-related purpose.

The English Bill of Rights responded to abuses by the Stuart monarchs; among the grievances set forth in the Bill of Rights was that the King had violated the law "[b]y causing several good Subjects being Protestants to be disarmed at the same time when Papists were both armed and Employed contrary to Law." Article VII of the Bill of Rights was a response to that selective disarmament; it guaranteed that "the Subjects which are Protestants may have Armes for their defence, Suitable to their condition and as allowed by Law." L. Schwoerer, *The Declaration of Rights, 1689* (App. 1, pp. 295, 297) (1981). This grant did not establish a general right of all persons, or even of all Protestants, to possess weapons. Rather, the right was qualified in two distinct ways: First, it was restricted to those of adequate social and economic status ("suitable to their Condition"); second, it was only available subject to regulation by Parliament ("as allowed by Law").[63]

The Court may well be correct that the English Bill of Rights protected the right of *some* English subjects to use *some* arms for personal self-defense free from restrictions by the Crown (but not Parliament). But that right—adopted in a different historical and political context and framed in markedly different language—tells us little about the meaning of the Second Amendment.

Blackstone's Commentaries

The Court's reliance on Blackstone's *Commentaries on the Laws of England* is unpersuasive for the same reason as its reliance on the English Bill of Rights. Blackstone's invocation of "'the natural right of resistance and self-preservation,'" *ante*, at 20, and "'the right of having and using arms for self-preservation and defence'" *ibid.,* referred specifically to Article VII in the English Bill of Rights. The excerpt from Blackstone offered by the Court, therefore, is, like Article VII itself, of limited use in interpreting the very differently worded, and differently historically situated, Second Amendment.

What *is* important about Blackstone is the instruction he provided on reading the sort of text before us today. Blackstone described an interpretive approach that gave far more weight to preambles than the Court allows. Counseling that "[t]he fairest and most rational method to interpret the will of the legislator, is by exploring his intentions at the time when the law was made, by *signs* the most natural and probable," Blackstone explained that "[i]f words happen to be still dubious, we may establish their meaning from the context; with which it may be of singular use to compare a word, or a sentence, whenever they are ambiguous, equivocal, or intricate. Thus, the proeme, or preamble, is often called in to help the construction of an act of parliament." 1 *Commentaries on the Laws of England* 59–60 (1765) (hereinafter Blackstone). In light of the Court's invocation of Blackstone as "'the preeminent authority on English law for the founding generation,'" *ante*, at 20 (quoting *Alden v. Maine*, 527 U.S. 706, 715 (1999)), its disregard for his guidance on matters of interpretation is striking.

Postenactment Commentary

The Court also excerpts, without any real analysis, commentary by a number of additional scholars, some near in time to the framing and others post-dating it by close to a century. Those scholars are for the most part of limited relevance in construing the guarantee of the Second Amendment: Their views are not altogether clear,[64] they tended to collapse the Second Amendment with Article VII of the English Bill of Rights, and they appear to have been unfamiliar with the drafting history of the Second Amendment.[65]

The most significant of these commentators was Joseph Story. Contrary to the Court's assertions, however, Story actually supports the view that the Amendment was designed to protect the right of each of the States to maintain a well-regulated militia. When Story used the term "palladium" in discussions of the Second Amendment, he merely echoed the concerns that animated the Framers of the Amendment and led to its adoption. An excerpt from his 1833 *Commentaries on the Constitution of the United States*—the same passage cited by the Court in *Miller*[66]—merits reproducing at some length:

"The importance of [the Second Amendment] will scarcely be doubted by any persons who have duly reflected upon the subject. The militia is the natural defence of a free country against sudden foreign invasions, domestic insurrections, and domestic usurpations of power by rulers. It is against sound policy for a free people to keep up large military establishments and standing armies in time of peace, both from the enormous expenses with which they are attended and the facile means which they afford to ambitious and unprincipled rulers to subvert the government, or trample upon the rights of the people. The right of the citizens to keep and bear arms has justly been considered as the palladium of the liberties of a republic, since it offers a strong moral check against the usurpation and arbitrary power of rulers, and will generally, even if these are successful in the first instance, enable the people to resist and triumph over them. And yet, though this truth would seem so clear, and the importance of a well-regulated militia would seem so undeniable, it cannot be disguised that, among the American people, there is a growing indifference to any system of militia discipline, and a strong disposition, from a sense of its burdens, to be rid of all regulations. How it is practicable to keep the people duly armed without some organization, it is difficult to see. There is certainly no small danger that indifference may lead to disgust, and disgust to contempt; and thus gradually undermine all the protection intended by the clause of our national bill of rights." 2 J. Story, *Commentaries on the Constitution of the United States* §1897, pp. 620–621 (4th ed. 1873) (footnote omitted).

Story thus began by tying the significance of the Amendment directly to the paramount importance of the militia. He then invoked the fear that drove the Framers of the Second Amendment—specifically, the threat to liberty posed by a standing army. An important check on that danger, he suggested, was a "well-regulated militia," *id.*, at 621, for which he assumed that arms would have to be kept and, when necessary, borne. There is not so much as a whisper in the passage above that Story believed that the right secured by the Amendment bore any relation to private use or possession of weapons for activities like hunting or personal self-defense.

After extolling the virtues of the militia as a bulwark against tyranny, Story went on to decry the "growing indifference to any system of militia discipline." *Ibid.* When he wrote, "[h]ow it is practicable to keep the people duly armed without some organization it is difficult to see," *ibid.*, he underscored the degree to which he viewed the arming of the people and the militia as indissolubly linked. Story warned that the "growing indifference" he perceived would "gradually undermine all the protection intended by this clause of our national bill of rights," *ibid.* In his view, the importance of the Amendment was directly related to the continuing vitality of an institution in the process of apparently becoming obsolete.

(Continues)

In an attempt to downplay the absence of any reference to nonmilitary uses of weapons in Story's commentary, the Court relies on the fact that Story characterized Article VII of the English Declaration of Rights as a "'similar provision,'" *ante,* at 36. The two provisions were indeed similar, in that both protected some uses of firearms. But Story's characterization in no way suggests that he believed that the provisions had the same scope. To the contrary, Story's exclusive focus on the militia in his discussion of the Second Amendment confirms his understanding of the right protected by the Second Amendment as limited to military uses of arms.

Story's writings as a Justice of this Court, to the extent that they shed light on this question, only confirm that Justice Story did not view the Amendment as conferring upon individuals any "self-defense" right disconnected from service in a state militia. Justice Story dissented from the Court's decision in *Houston v. Moore,* 5 Wheat. 1, 24 (1820), which held that a state court "had a concurrent jurisdiction" with the federal courts "to try a militia man who had disobeyed the call of the President, and to enforce the laws of Congress against such delinquent." *Id.,* at 31–32. Justice Story believed that Congress' power to provide for the organizing, arming, and disciplining of the militia was, when Congress acted, plenary; but he explained that in the absence of congressional action, "I am certainly not prepared to deny the legitimacy of such an exercise of [state] authority." *Id.,* at 52. As to the Second Amendment, he wrote that it "may not, perhaps, be thought to have any important bearing on this point. If it have, it confirms and illustrates, rather than impugns the reasoning already suggested." *Id.,* at 52–53. The Court contends that had Justice Story understood the Amendment to have a militia purpose, the Amendment would have had "enormous and obvious bearing on the point." *Ante,* at 38. But the Court has it quite backwards: If Story had believed that the purpose of the Amendment was to permit civilians to keep firearms for activities like personal self-defense, what "confirm[ation] and illustrat[ion]," *Houston,* 5 Wheat., at 53, could the Amendment possibly have provided for the point that States retained the power to organize, arm, and discipline their own militias?

Post-Civil War Legislative History

The Court suggests that by the post-Civil War period, the Second Amendment was understood to secure a right to firearm use and ownership for purely private purposes like personal self-defense. While it is true that some of the legislative history on which the Court relies supports that contention, see *ante,* at 41–44, such sources are entitled to limited, if any, weight. All of the statements the Court cites were made long after the framing of the Amendment and cannot possibly supply any insight into the intent of the Framers; and all were made during pitched political debates, so that they are better characterized as advocacy than good-faith attempts at constitutional interpretation.

What is more, much of the evidence the Court offers is decidedly less clear than its discussion allows. The Court notes that "[b]lacks were routinely disarmed by Southern States after the Civil War. Those who opposed these injustices frequently stated that they infringed blacks' constitutional right to keep and bear arms." *Ante,* at 42. The Court hastily concludes that "[n]eedless to say, the claim was not that blacks were being prohibited from carrying arms in an organized state militia," *ibid.* But some of the claims of the sort the Court cites may have been just that. In some Southern States, Reconstruction-era Republican governments created state militias in which both blacks and whites were permitted to serve. Because "[t]he decision to allow blacks to serve alongside whites meant that most southerners refused to join the new militia," the bodies were dubbed "Negro militia[s]." S. Cornell, *A Well-Regulated Militia* 176–177 (2006). The "arming of the Negro militias met with especially fierce resistance in South Carolina. . . . The sight of organized, armed freedmen incensed opponents of Reconstruction and led to an intensified campaign of Klan terror. Leading members of the Negro militia were beaten or lynched and their weapons stolen." *Id.,* at 177.

One particularly chilling account of Reconstruction-era Klan violence directed at a black militia member is recounted in the memoir of Louis F. Post, A "Carpetbagger" in South Carolina, 10 *Journal of Negro History* 10 (1925). Post describes the murder by local Klan members of Jim Williams, the captain of a "Negro militia company," *id.,* at 59, this way:

> "[A] cavalcade of sixty cowardly white men, completely disguised with face masks and body gowns, rode up one night in March, 1871, to the house of Captain Williams . . . in the wood [they] hanged [and shot] him . . . [and on his body they] then pinned a slip of paper inscribed, as I remember it, with these grim words: 'Jim Williams gone to his last muster.'" *Id.,* at 61.

In light of this evidence, it is quite possible that at least some of the statements on which the Court relies actually did mean to refer to the disarmament of black militia members.

IV

The brilliance of the debates that resulted in the Second Amendment faded into oblivion during the ensuing years, for the concerns about Article I's Militia Clauses that generated such pitched debate during the ratification process and led to the adoption of the Second Amendment were short lived.

In 1792, the year after the Amendment was ratified, Congress passed a statute that purported to establish "an Uniform Militia throughout the United States." 1 Stat. 271. The statute commanded every able-bodied white male citizen between the ages of 18 and 45 to be enrolled therein and to "provide himself with a good musket or firelock" and other specified weaponry.[67] *Ibid.* The statute is significant, for it confirmed the way those in the founding generation viewed firearm ownership: as a duty linked to military service. The statute they enacted, however, "was virtually ignored for more than a century," and was finally repealed in 1901. See *Perpich*, 496 U.S., at 341.

The postratification history of the Second Amendment is strikingly similar. The Amendment played little role in any legislative debate about the civilian use of firearms for most of the 19th century, and it made few appearances in the decisions of this Court. Two 19th-century cases, however, bear mentioning.

In *United States v. Cruikshank*, 92 U.S. 542 (1876), the Court sustained a challenge to respondents' convictions under the Enforcement Act of 1870 for conspiring to deprive any individual of "'any right or privilege granted or secured to him by the constitution or laws of the United States.'" *Id.*, at 548. The Court wrote, as to counts 2 and 10 of respondents' indictment:

"The right there specified is that of 'bearing arms for a lawful purpose.' This is not a right granted by the Constitution. Neither is it in any manner dependent on that instrument for its existence. The second amendment declares that it shall not be infringed; but this, as has been seen, means no more than that it shall not be infringed by Congress. This is one of the amendments that has no other effect than to restrict the powers of the national government." *Id.*, at 553.

The majority's assertion that the Court in *Cruikshank* "described the right protected by the Second Amendment as '"bearing arms for a lawful purpose,"'" *ante*, at 47 (quoting *Cruikshank*, 92 U.S., at 553), is not accurate. The *Cruikshank* Court explained that the defective *indictment* contained such language, but the Court did not itself describe the right, or endorse the indictment's description of the right.

Moreover, it is entirely possible that the basis for the indictment's counts 2 and 10, which charged respondents with depriving the victims of rights secured by the Second Amendment, was the prosecutor's belief that the victims—members of a group of citizens, mostly black but also white, who were rounded up by the Sheriff, sworn in as a posse to defend the local courthouse, and attacked by a white mob—bore sufficient resemblance to members of a state militia that they were brought within the reach of the Second Amendment. See generally C. Lane, *The Day Freedom Died: The Colfax Massacre, The Supreme Court, and the Betrayal of Reconstruction* (2008).

Only one other 19th-century case in this Court, *Presser v. Illinois,* 116 U.S. 252 (1886), engaged in any significant discussion of the Second Amendment. The petitioner in *Presser* was convicted of violating a state statute that prohibited organizations other than the Illinois National Guard from associating together as military companies or parading with arms. Presser challenged his conviction, asserting, as relevant, that the statute violated both the Second and the Fourteenth Amendments. With respect to the Second Amendment, the Court wrote:

"We think it clear that the sections under consideration, which only forbid bodies of men to associate together as military organizations, or to drill or parade with arms in cities and towns unless authorized by law, do not infringe the right of the people to keep and bear arms. But a conclusive answer to the contention that this amendment prohibits the legislation in question lies in the fact that the amendment is a limitation only upon the power of Congress and the National government, and not upon that of the States." *Id.*, at 264–265.

And in discussing the Fourteenth Amendment, the Court explained:

"The plaintiff in error was not a member of the organized volunteer militia of the State of Illinois, nor did he belong to the troops of the United States or to any organization under the militia law of the United States.

(Continues)

On the contrary, the fact that he did not belong to the organized militia or the troops of the United States was an ingredient in the offence for which he was convicted and sentenced. The question is, therefore, had he a right as a citizen of the United States, in disobedience of the State law, to associate with others as a military company, and to drill and parade with arms in the towns and cities of the State? If the plaintiff in error has any such privilege he must be able to point to the provision of the Constitution or statutes of the United States by which it is conferred." *Id.,* at 266.

Presser, therefore, both affirmed *Cruikshank's* holding that the Second Amendment posed no obstacle to regulation by state governments, and suggested that in any event nothing in the Constitution protected the use of arms outside the context of a militia "authorized by law" and organized by the State or Federal Government.[68]

In 1901 the President revitalized the militia by creating "'the National Guard of the several States,'" *Perpich,* 496 U.S., at 341, and nn. 9–10; meanwhile, the dominant understanding of the Second Amendment's inapplicability to private gun ownership continued well into the 20th century. The first two federal laws directly restricting civilian use and possession of firearms—the 1927 Act prohibiting mail delivery of "pistols, revolvers, and other firearms capable of being concealed on the person," Ch. 75, 44 Stat. 1059, and the 1934 Act prohibiting the possession of sawed-off shotguns and machine guns—were enacted over minor Second Amendment objections dismissed by the vast majority of the legislators who participated in the debates.[69] Members of Congress clashed over the wisdom and efficacy of such laws as crime-control measures. But since the statutes did not infringe upon the military use or possession of weapons, for most legislators they did not even raise the specter of possible conflict with the Second Amendment.

Thus, for most of our history, the invalidity of Second-Amendment-based objections to firearms regulations has been well settled and uncontroversial.[70] Indeed, the Second Amendment was not even mentioned in either full House of Congress during the legislative proceedings that led to the passage of the 1934 Act. Yet enforcement of that law produced the judicial decision that confirmed the status of the Amendment as limited in reach to military usage. After reviewing many of the same sources that are discussed at greater length by the Court today, the *Miller* Court unanimously concluded that the Second Amendment did not apply to the possession of a firearm that did not have "some reasonable relationship to the preservation or efficiency of a well regulated militia." 307 U.S., at 178.

The key to that decision did not, as the Court belatedly suggests, *ante,* at 49–51, turn on the difference between muskets and sawed-off shotguns; it turned, rather, on the basic difference between the military and nonmilitary use and possession of guns. Indeed, if the Second Amendment were not limited in its coverage to military uses of weapons, why should the Court in *Miller* have suggested that some weapons but not others were eligible for Second Amendment protection? If use for self-defense were the relevant standard, why did the Court not inquire into the suitability of a particular weapon for self-defense purposes?

Perhaps in recognition of the weakness of its attempt to distinguish *Miller,* the Court argues in the alternative that *Miller* should be discounted because of its decisional history. It is true that the appellee in *Miller* did not file a brief or make an appearance, although the court below had held that the relevant provision of the National Firearms Act violated the Second Amendment (albeit without any reasoned opinion). But, as our decision in *Marbury v. Madison,* 1 Cranch 137, in which only one side appeared and presented arguments, demonstrates, the absence of adversarial presentation alone is not a basis for refusing to accord *stare decisis* effect to a decision of this Court. See Bloch, *Marbury* Redux, in Arguing *Marbury v. Madison* 59, 63 (M. Tushnet ed. 2005). Of course, if it can be demonstrated that new evidence or arguments were genuinely not available to an earlier Court, that fact should be given special weight as we consider whether to overrule a prior case. But the Court does not make that claim, because it cannot. Although it is true that the drafting history of the Amendment was not discussed in the Government's brief, see *ante,* at 51, it is certainly not the drafting history that the Court's decision today turns on. And those sources upon which the Court today relies most heavily *were* available to the *Miller* Court. The Government cited the English Bill of Rights and quoted a lengthy passage from *Aymette* detailing the history leading to the English guarantee, Brief for United States in *United States v. Miller,* O. T. 1938, No. 696, pp 12–13; it also cited Blackstone, *id.,* at 9, n. 2, Cooley, *id.,* at 12, 15, and Story, *id.,* at 15. The Court is reduced to critiquing the number of *pages* the Government devoted to exploring the English legal sources. Only two (in a brief 21 pages in length)! Would the Court be satisfied with four? Ten?

The Court is simply wrong when it intones that *Miller* contained "*not a word*" about the Amendment's history. *Ante,* at 52. The Court plainly looked to history to construe the term "Militia," and, on the best reading of *Miller*, the entire guarantee of the Second Amendment. After noting the original Constitution's grant of power to Congress and to the States over the militia, the Court explained:

"With obvious purpose to assure the continuation and render possible the effectiveness of such forces the declaration and guarantee of the Second Amendment were made. It must be interpreted and applied with that end in view."

"The Militia which the States were expected to maintain and train is set in contrast with Troops which they were forbidden to keep without the consent of Congress. The sentiment of the time strongly disfavored standing armies; the common view was that adequate defense of country and laws could be secured through the Militia—civilians primarily, soldiers on occasion.

"The signification attributed to the term Militia appears from the debates in the Convention, the history and legislation of Colonies and States, and the writings of approved commentators." *Miller*, 307 U.S., at 178–179.

The majority cannot seriously believe that the *Miller* Court did not consider any relevant evidence; the majority simply does not approve of the conclusion the *Miller* Court reached on that evidence. Standing alone, that is insufficient reason to disregard a unanimous opinion of this Court, upon which substantial reliance has been placed by legislators and citizens for nearly 70 years.

V

The Court concludes its opinion by declaring that it is not the proper role of this Court to change the meaning of rights "enshrine[d]" in the Constitution. *Ante*, at 64. But the right the Court announces was not "enshrined" in the Second Amendment by the Framers; it is the product of today's law-changing decision. The majority's exegesis has utterly failed to establish that as a matter of text or history, "the right of law-abiding, responsible citizens to use arms in defense of hearth and home" is "elevate[d] above all other interests" by the Second Amendment. *Ante*, at 64.

Until today, it has been understood that legislatures may regulate the civilian use and misuse of firearms so long as they do not interfere with the preservation of a well-regulated militia. The Court's announcement of a new constitutional right to own and use firearms for private purposes upsets that settled understanding, but leaves for future cases the formidable task of defining the scope of permissible regulations. Today judicial craftsmen have confidently asserted that a policy choice that denies a "law-abiding, responsible citize[n]" the right to keep and use weapons in the home for self-defense is "off the table." *Ante*, at 64. Given the presumption that most citizens are law abiding, and the reality that the need to defend oneself may suddenly arise in a host of locations outside the home, I fear that the District's policy choice may well be just the first of an unknown number of dominoes to be knocked off the table.[71]

I do not know whether today's decision will increase the labor of federal judges to the "breaking point" envisioned by Justice Cardozo, but it will surely give rise to a far more active judicial role in making vitally important national policy decisions than was envisioned at any time in the 18th, 19th, or 20th centuries.

The Court properly disclaims any interest in evaluating the wisdom of the specific policy choice challenged in this case, but it fails to pay heed to a far more important policy choice—the choice made by the Framers themselves. The Court would have us believe that over 200 years ago, the Framers made a choice to limit the tools available to elected officials wishing to regulate civilian uses of weapons, and to authorize this Court to use the common-law process of case-by-case judicial lawmaking to define the contours of acceptable gun control policy. Absent compelling evidence that is nowhere to be found in the Court's opinion, I could not possibly conclude that the Framers made such a choice.

For these reasons, I respectfully dissent.

DISTRICT OF COLUMBIA, *et al.*, PETITIONERS *v.* DICK ANTHONY HELLER

on writ of certiorari to the united states court of appeals for the district of columbia circuit

[June 26, 2008]

Justice Breyer, with whom *Justice Stevens, Justice Souter,* and *Justice Ginsburg* join, dissenting.

We must decide whether a District of Columbia law that prohibits the possession of handguns in the home violates the Second Amendment. The majority, relying upon its view that the Second Amendment

(Continues)

(Continued)

seeks to protect a right of personal self-defense, holds that this law violates that Amendment. In my view, it does not.

I

The majority's conclusion is wrong for two independent reasons. The first reason is that set forth by *Justice Stevens*—namely, that the Second Amendment protects militia-related, not self-defense-related, interests. These two interests are sometimes intertwined. To assure 18th-century citizens that they could keep arms for militia purposes would necessarily have allowed them to keep arms that they could have used for self-defense as well. But self-defense alone, detached from any militia-related objective, is not the Amendment's concern.

The second independent reason is that the protection the Amendment provides is not absolute. The Amendment permits government to regulate the interests that it serves. Thus, irrespective of what those interests are—whether they do or do not include an independent interest in self-defense—the majority's view cannot be correct unless it can show that the District's regulation is unreasonable or inappropriate in Second Amendment terms. This the majority cannot do.

In respect to the first independent reason, I agree with *Justice Stevens*, and I join his opinion. In this opinion I shall focus upon the second reason. I shall show that the District's law is consistent with the Second Amendment even if that Amendment is interpreted as protecting a wholly separate interest in individual self-defense. That is so because the District's regulation, which focuses upon the presence of handguns in high-crime urban areas, represents a permissible legislative response to a serious, indeed life-threatening, problem.

Thus I here assume that one objective (but, as the majority concedes, *ante*, at 26, not the *primary* objective) of those who wrote the Second Amendment was to help assure citizens that they would have arms available for purposes of self-defense. Even so, a legislature could reasonably conclude that the law will advance goals of great public importance, namely, saving lives, preventing injury, and reducing crime. The law is tailored to the urban crime problem in that it is local in scope and thus affects only a geographic area both limited in size and entirely urban; the law concerns handguns, which are specially linked to urban gun deaths and injuries, and which are the overwhelmingly favorite weapon of armed criminals; and at the same time, the law imposes a burden upon gun owners that seems proportionately no greater than restrictions in existence at the time the Second Amendment was adopted. In these circumstances, the District's law falls within the zone that the Second Amendment leaves open to regulation by legislatures.

II

The Second Amendment says that: "A well regulated Militia, being necessary to the security of a free State, the right of the people to keep and bear Arms, shall not be infringed." In interpreting and applying this Amendment, I take as a starting point the following four propositions, based on our precedent and today's opinions, to which I believe the entire Court subscribes:

> The Amendment protects an "individual" right— (1) *i.e.*, one that is separately possessed, and may be separately enforced, by each person on whom it is conferred. See, *e.g.*, *ante*, at 22 (opinion of the Court); *ante*, at 1 (*Stevens, J.*, dissenting).
>
> As evidenced by its preamble, the Amendment was adopted "[w]ith (2) obvious purpose to assure the continuation and render possible the effectiveness of [militia] forces." *United States v. Miller*, 307 U.S. 174, 178 (1939); see *ante*, at 26 (opinion of the Court); *ante*, at 1 (*Stevens, J.*, dissenting).
>
> The Amendment "must be interpreted and applied with that end in (3) view." *Miller, supra*, at 178.
>
> The right protected by the Second Amendment is not absolute, but (4) instead is subject to government regulation. See *Robertson v. Baldwin*, 165 U.S. 275, 281–282 (1897); *ante*, at 22, 54 (opinion of the Court).

My approach to this case, while involving the first three points, primarily concerns the fourth. I shall, as I said, assume with the majority that the Amendment, in addition to furthering a militia-related purpose, also furthers an interest in possessing guns for purposes of self-defense, at least to some degree. And I shall then ask whether the Amendment nevertheless permits the District handgun restriction at issue here.

Although I adopt for present purposes the majority's position that the Second Amendment embodies a general concern about self-defense, I shall not assume that the Amendment contains a specific untouchable right to keep guns in the house to shoot burglars. The majority, which presents evidence in favor of the former proposition, does not, because it cannot, convincingly show that the Second Amendment seeks to maintain the latter in pristine, unregulated form.

To the contrary, colonial history itself offers important examples of the kinds of gun regulation that citizens would then have thought compatible with the "right to keep and bear arms," whether embodied in Federal or State Constitutions, or the background common law. And those examples include substantial regulation of firearms in urban areas, including regulations that imposed obstacles to the use of firearms for the protection of the home.

Boston, Philadelphia, and New York City, the three largest cities in America during that period, all restricted the firing of guns within city limits to at least some degree. See Churchill, Gun Regulation, the Police Power, and the Right to Keep Arms in Early America, 25 *Law & Hist. Rev.* 139, 162 (2007); Dept. of Commerce, Bureau of Census, C. Gibson, Population of the 100 Largest Cities and Other Urban Places in the United States: 1790 to 1990 (1998) (Table 2), online at http://www.census.gov/population/documentation/twps0027/tab02.txt (all Internet materials as visited June 19, 2008, and available in Clerk of Court's case file). Boston in 1746 had a law prohibiting the "discharge" of "any Gun or Pistol charged with Shot or Ball in the Town" on penalty of 40 shillings, a law that was later revived in 1778. See Act of May 28, 1746, ch. 10; An Act for Reviving and Continuing Sundry Laws that are Expired, and Near Expiring, 1778 Massachusetts Session Laws, ch. 5, pp. 193, 194. Philadelphia prohibited, on penalty of 5 shillings (or two days in jail if the fine were not paid), firing a gun or setting off fireworks in Philadelphia without a "governor's special license." See Act of Aug. 26, 1721, §4, in 3 Mitchell, *Statutes at Large of Pennsylvania* 253–254. And New York City banned, on penalty of a 20-shilling fine, the firing of guns (even in houses) for the three days surrounding New Year's Day. 5 *Colonial Laws of New York*, ch. 1501, pp. 244–246 (1894); see also An Act to Suppress the Disorderly Practice of Firing Guns, & c., on the Times Therein Mentioned, 8 *Statutes at Large of Pennsylvania 1770–1776*, pp. 410–412 (1902) (similar law for all "inhabited parts" of Pennsylvania). See also An Act for preventing Mischief being done in the Town of *Newport*, or in any other Town in this Government, 1731, Rhode Island Session Laws (prohibiting, on penalty of 5 shillings for a first offense and more for subsequent offenses, the firing of "any Gun or Pistol . . . in the Streets of any of the Towns of this Government, or in any Tavern of the same, after dark, on any Night whatsoever").

Furthermore, several towns and cities (including Philadelphia, New York, and Boston) regulated, for fire-safety reasons, the storage of gunpowder, a necessary component of an operational firearm. See Cornell & DeDino, A Well Regulated Right, 73 *Fordham L. Rev.* 487, 510–512 (2004). Boston's law in particular impacted the use of firearms in the home very much as the District's law does today. Boston's gunpowder law imposed a 10 fine upon "any Person" who "shall take into any Dwelling-House, Stable, Barn, Out-house, Ware-house, Store, Shop, or other Building, within the Town of Boston, any . . . Fire-Arm, loaded with, or having Gun-Powder." An Act in Addition to the several Acts already made for the prudent Storage of Gun-Powder within the Town of Boston, ch. XIII, 1783 Mass. Acts 218–219; see also 1 S. Johnson, *A Dictionary of the English Language* 751 (4th ed. 1773) (defining "firearms" as "[a]rms which owe their efficacy to fire; guns"). Even assuming, as the majority does, see *ante*, at 59–60, that this law included an implicit self-defense exception, it would nevertheless have prevented a homeowner from keeping in his home a gun that he could immediately pick up and use against an intruder. Rather, the homeowner would have had to get the gunpowder and load it into the gun, an operation that would have taken a fair amount of time to perform. See Hicks, *United States Military Shoulder Arms, 1795–1935*, 1 Am. Military Hist. Foundation 23, 30 (1937) (experienced soldier could, with specially prepared cartridges as opposed to plain gunpowder and ball, load and fire musket 3-to-4 times per minute); *id.*, at 26–30 (describing the loading process); see also Grancsay, The Craft of the Early American Gunsmith, 6 *Metropolitan Museum of Art Bulletin* 54, 60 (1947) (noting that rifles were slower to load and fire than muskets).

Moreover, the law would, as a practical matter, have prohibited the carrying of loaded firearms anywhere in the city, unless the carrier had no plans to enter any building or was willing to unload or discard his weapons before going inside. And Massachusetts residents must have believed this kind of law compatible with the provision in the Massachusetts Constitution that granted "the people . . . a right to keep and to bear arms for the common defence"—a provision that the majority says was interpreted as "secur[ing] an individual right to bear arms for defensive purposes." Art. XVII (1780), in 3 *The Federal and State Constitutions, Colonial Charters, and Other Organic Laws 1888, 1892* (F. Thorpe ed. 1909) (hereinafter Thorpe); *ante*, at 28–29 (opinion of the Court).

(Continues)

(Continued)

The New York City law, which required that gunpowder in the home be stored in certain sorts of containers, and laws in certain Pennsylvania towns, which required that gunpowder be stored on the highest story of the home, could well have presented similar obstacles to in-home use of firearms. See Act of April 13, 1784, ch. 28, 1784 N.Y. Laws p. 627; An Act for Erecting the Town of Carlisle, in the County of Cumberland, into a Borough, ch. XIV, §XLII, 1782 Pa. Laws p. 49; An Act for Erecting the Town of Reading, in the County of Berks, into a Borough, ch. LXXVI, §XLII, 1783 Pa. Laws p. 211. Although it is unclear whether these laws, like the Boston law, would have prohibited the storage of gunpowder inside a firearm, they would at the very least have made it difficult to reload the gun to fire a second shot unless the homeowner happened to be in the portion of the house where the extra gunpowder was required to be kept. See 7 *United States Encyclopedia of History* 1297 (P. Oehser ed. 1967) ("Until 1835 all small arms [were] single-shot weapons, requiring reloading by hand after every shot"). And Pennsylvania, like Massachusetts, had at the time one of the self-defense-guaranteeing state constitutional provisions on which the majority relies. See *ante*, at 28 (citing Pa. Declaration of Rights, Art. XIII (1776), in 5 Thorpe 3083).

The majority criticizes my citation of these colonial laws. See *ante*, at 59–62. But, as much as it tries, it cannot ignore their existence. I suppose it is possible that, as the majority suggests, see *ante*, at 59–61, they all in practice contained self-defense exceptions. But none of them expressly provided one, and the majority's assumption that such exceptions existed relies largely on the preambles to these acts—an interpretive methodology that it elsewhere roundly derides. Compare *ibid.* (interpreting 18th-century statutes in light of their preambles), with *ante*, at 4–5, and n. 3 (contending that the operative language of an 18th-century enactment may extend beyond its preamble). And in any event, as I have shown, the gunpowder-storage laws would have *burdened* armed self-defense, even if they did not completely *prohibit* it.

This historical evidence demonstrates that a self-defense assumption is the *beginning*, rather than the *end*, of any constitutional inquiry. That the District law impacts self-defense merely raises *questions* about the law's constitutionality. But to answer the questions that are raised (that is, to see whether the statute is unconstitutional) requires us to focus on practicalities, the statute's rationale, the problems that called it into being, its relation to those objectives—in a word, the details. There are no purely logical or conceptual answers to such questions. All of which to say that to raise a self-defense question is not to answer it.

III

I therefore begin by asking a process-based question: How is a court to determine whether a particular firearm regulation (here, the District's restriction on handguns) is consistent with the Second Amendment? What kind of constitutional standard should the court use? How high a protective hurdle does the Amendment erect?

The question matters. The majority is wrong when it says that the District's law is unconstitutional "[u]nder any of the standards of scrutiny that we have applied to enumerated constitutional rights." *Ante*, at 56. How could that be? It certainly would not be unconstitutional under, for example, a "rational basis" standard, which requires a court to uphold regulation so long as it bears a "rational relationship" to a "legitimate governmental purpose." *Heller v. Doe*, 509 U.S. 312, 320 (1993). The law at issue here, which in part seeks to prevent gun-related accidents, at least bears a "rational relationship" to that "legitimate" life-saving objective. And nothing in the three 19th-century state cases to which the majority turns for support mandates the conclusion that the present District law must fall. See *Andrews v. State*, 50 Tenn. 165, 177, 186–187, 192 (1871) (striking down, as violating a *state* constitutional provision adopted in 1870, a *statewide* ban on a carrying a broad class of weapons, insofar as it applied to revolvers); *Nunn v. State*, 1 Ga. 243, 246, 250–251 (1846) (striking down similarly broad ban on openly carrying weapons, based on erroneous view that the Federal Second Amendment applied to the States); *State v. Reid*, 1 Ala. 612, 614–615, 622 (1840) (*upholding* a concealed-weapon ban against a *state* constitutional challenge). These cases were decided well (80, 55, and 49 years, respectively) after the framing; they neither claim nor provide any special insight into the intent of the Framers; they involve laws much less narrowly tailored that the one before us; and state cases in any event are not determinative of federal constitutional questions, see, *e.g.*, *Garcia v. San Antonio Metropolitan Transit Authority*, 469 U.S. 528, 549 (1985) (citing *Martin v. Hunter's Lessee*, 1 Wheat. 304 (1816)).

Respondent proposes that the Court adopt a "strict scrutiny" test, which would require reviewing with care each gun law to determine whether it is "narrowly tailored to achieve a compelling governmental interest." *Abrams v. Johnson*, 521 U.S. 74, 82 (1997); see Brief for Respondent 54–62. But the majority implicitly, and appropriately, rejects that suggestion by broadly approving a set of laws—prohibitions on concealed weapons, forfeiture by criminals of the Second Amendment right, prohibitions on firearms in certain locales, and governmental regulation of commercial firearm sales—whose constitutionality under a strict scrutiny standard would be far from clear. See *ante*, at 54.

Indeed, adoption of a true strict-scrutiny standard for evaluating gun regulations would be impossible. That is because almost every gun-control regulation will seek to advance (as the one here does) a "primary concern of every government—a concern for the safety and indeed the lives of its citizens." *United States v. Salerno*, 481 U.S. 739, 755 (1987). The Court has deemed that interest, as well as "the Government's general interest in preventing crime," to be "compelling," see *id.*, at 750, 754, and the Court has in a wide variety of constitutional contexts found such public-safety concerns sufficiently forceful to justify restrictions on individual liberties, see *e.g., Brandenburg v. Ohio*, 395 U.S. 444, 447 (1969) *(per curiam)* (First Amendment free speech rights); *Sherbert v. Verner*, 374 U.S. 398, 403 (1963) (First Amendment religious rights); *Brigham City v. Stuart*, 547 U.S. 398, 403–404 (2006) (Fourth Amendment protection of the home); *New York v. Quarles*, 467 U.S. 649, 655 (1984) (Fifth Amendment rights under *Miranda v. Arizona*, 384 U.S. 436 (1966)); *Salerno, supra*, at 755 (Eighth Amendment bail rights). Thus, any attempt *in theory* to apply strict scrutiny to gun regulations will *in practice* turn into an interest-balancing inquiry, with the interests protected by the Second Amendment on one side and the governmental public-safety concerns on the other, the only question being whether the regulation at issue impermissibly burdens the former in the course of advancing the latter.

I would simply adopt such an interest-balancing inquiry explicitly. The fact that important interests lie on both sides of the constitutional equation suggests that review of gun-control regulation is not a context in which a court should effectively presume either constitutionality (as in rational-basis review) or unconstitutionality (as in strict scrutiny). Rather, "where a law significantly implicates competing constitutionally protected interests in complex ways," the Court generally asks whether the statute burdens a protected interest in a way or to an extent that is out of proportion to the statute's salutary effects upon other important governmental interests. See *Nixon v. Shrink Missouri Government PAC*, 528 U.S. 377, 402 (2000) *(Breyer*, J., concurring). Any answer would take account both of the statute's effects upon the competing interests and the existence of any clearly superior less restrictive alternative. See *ibid.* Contrary to the majority's unsupported suggestion that this sort of "proportionality" approach is unprecedented, see *ante*, at 62, the Court has applied it in various constitutional contexts, including election-law cases, speech cases, and due process cases. See 528 U.S., at 403 (citing examples where the Court has taken such an approach); see also, *e.g., Thompson v. Western States Medical Center*, 535 U.S. 357, 388 (2002) *(Breyer*, J., dissenting) (commercial speech); *Burdick v. Takushi*, 504 U.S. 428, 433 (1992) (election regulation); *Mathews v. Eldridge*, 424 U.S. 319, 339–349 (1976) (procedural due process); *Pickering v. Board of Ed. of Township High School Dist. 205, Will Cty.*, 391 U.S. 563, 568 (1968) (government employee speech).

In applying this kind of standard the Court normally defers to a legislature's empirical judgment in matters where a legislature is likely to have greater expertise and greater institutional factfinding capacity. See *Turner Broadcasting System, Inc. v. FCC*, 520 U.S. 180, 195–196 (1997); see also *Nixon, supra*, at 403 *(Breyer, J.*, concurring). Nonetheless, a court, not a legislature, must make the ultimate constitutional conclusion, exercising its "independent judicial judgment" in light of the whole record to determine whether a law exceeds constitutional boundaries. *Randall v. Sorrell*, 548 U.S. 230, 249 (2006) (opinion of *Breyer, J.*) (citing *Bose Corp. v. Consumers Union of United States, Inc.*, 466 U.S. 485, 499 (1984)).

The above-described approach seems preferable to a more rigid approach here for a further reason. Experience as much as logic has led the Court to decide that in one area of constitutional law or another the interests are likely to prove stronger on one side of a typical constitutional case than on the other. See, *e.g., United States v. Virginia*, 518 U.S. 515, 531–534 (1996) (applying heightened scrutiny to gender-based classifications, based upon experience with prior cases); *Williamson v. Lee Optical of Okla., Inc.*, 348 U.S. 483, 488 (1955) (applying rational-basis scrutiny to economic legislation, based upon experience with prior cases). Here, we have little prior experience. Courts that *do* have experience in these matters have uniformly taken an approach that treats empirically-based legislative judgment with a degree of deference. See Winkler, Scrutinizing the Second Amendment, 105 *Mich. L. Rev.* 683, 687, 716–718 (2007) (describing hundreds of gun-law decisions issued in the last half-century by Supreme Courts in 42 States, which courts with "surprisingly little variation," have adopted a standard more deferential than strict scrutiny). While these state cases obviously are not controlling, they

(Continues)

(*Continued*)

are instructive. Cf., *e.g.*, *Bartkus v. Illinois*, 359 U.S. 121, 134 (1959) (looking to the "experience of state courts" as informative of a constitutional question). And they thus provide some comfort regarding the practical wisdom of following the approach that I believe our constitutional precedent would in any event suggest.

IV

The present suit involves challenges to three separate District firearm restrictions. The first requires a license from the District's Chief of Police in order to carry a "pistol," *i.e.*, a handgun, anywhere in the District. See D. C. Code §22-4504(a) (2001); see also §§22-4501(a), 22-4506. Because the District assures us that respondent could obtain such a license so long as he meets the statutory eligibility criteria, and because respondent concedes that those criteria are facially constitutional, I, like the majority, see no need to address the constitutionality of the licensing requirement. See *ante*, at 58–59.

The second District restriction requires that the lawful owner of a firearm keep his weapon "unloaded and disassembled or bound by a trigger lock or similar device" unless it is kept at his place of business or being used for lawful recreational purposes. See §7-2507.02. The only dispute regarding this provision appears to be whether the Constitution requires an exception that would allow someone to render a firearm operational when necessary for self-defense (*i.e.*, that the firearm may be operated under circumstances where the common law would normally permit a self-defense justification in defense against a criminal charge). See *Parker v. District of Columbia*, 478 F. 3d 370, 401 (2007) (case below); *ante*, at 57–58 (opinion of the Court); Brief for Respondent 52–54. The District concedes that such an exception exists. See Brief for Petitioners 56–57. This Court has final authority (albeit not often used) to definitively interpret District law, which is, after all, simply a species of federal law. See, *e.g.*, *Whalen v. United States*, 445 U.S. 684, 687–688 (1980); see also *Griffin v. United States*, 336 U.S. 704, 716–718 (1949). And because I see nothing in the District law that would *preclude* the existence of a background common-law self-defense exception, I would avoid the constitutional question by interpreting the statute to include it. See *Ashwander v. TVA*, 297 U.S. 288, 348 (1936) (Brandeis, J., concurring).

I am puzzled by the majority's unwillingness to adopt a similar approach. It readily reads unspoken self-defense exceptions into every colonial law, but it refuses to accept the District's concession that this law has one. Compare *ante*, at 59–61, with *ante*, at 57–58. The one District case it cites to support that refusal, *McIntosh v. Washington*, 395 A. 2d 744, 755–756 (1978), merely concludes that the District Legislature had a rational basis for applying the trigger-lock law in homes but not in places of business. Nowhere does that case say that the statute precludes a self-defense exception of the sort that I have just described. And even if it did, we are not bound by a lower court's interpretation of federal law.

The third District restriction prohibits (in most cases) the registration of a handgun within the District. See §7-2502.02(a)(4). Because registration is a prerequisite to firearm possession, see §7-2502.01(a), the effect of this provision is generally to prevent people in the District from possessing handguns. In determining whether this regulation violates the Second Amendment, I shall ask how the statute seeks to further the governmental interests that it serves, how the statute burdens the interests that the Second Amendment seeks to protect, and whether there are practical less burdensome ways of furthering those interests. The ultimate question is whether the statute imposes burdens that, when viewed in light of the statute's legitimate objectives, are disproportionate. See *Nixon*, 528 U.S., at 402 (*Breyer, J.*, concurring).

A

No one doubts the constitutional importance of the statute's basic objective, saving lives. See, *e.g.*, *Salerno*, 481 U.S., at 755. But there is considerable debate about whether the District's statute helps to achieve that objective. I begin by reviewing the statute's tendency to secure that objective from the perspective of (1) the legislature (namely, the Council of the District of Columbia) that enacted the statute in 1976, and (2) a court that seeks to evaluate the Council's decision today.

1

First, consider the facts as the legislature saw them when it adopted the District statute. As stated by the local council committee that recommended its adoption, the major substantive goal of the District's handgun restriction is "to reduce the potentiality for gun-related crimes and gun-related deaths from occurring within the District of Columbia." Hearing and Disposition before the House

Committee on the District of Columbia, 94th Cong., 2d Sess., on H. Con. Res. 694, Ser. No. 94-24, p. 25 (1976) (herinafter DC Rep.) (reproducing, *inter alia*, the Council committee report). The committee concluded, on the basis of "extensive public hearings" and "lengthy research," that "[t]he easy availability of firearms in the United States has been a major factor contributing to the drastic increase in gun-related violence and crime over the past 40 years." *Id.*, at 24, 25. It reported to the Council "startling statistics," *id.*, at 26, regarding gun-related crime, accidents, and deaths, focusing particularly on the relation between handguns and crime and the proliferation of handguns within the District. See *id.*, at 25–26.

The committee informed the Council that guns were "responsible for 69 deaths in this country each day," for a total of "[a]pproximately 25,000 gun-deaths . . . each year," along with an additional 200,000 gun-related injuries. *Id.*, at 25. Three thousand of these deaths, the report stated, were accidental. *Ibid.* A quarter of the victims in those accidental deaths were children under the age of 14. *Ibid.* And according to the committee, "[f]or every intruder stopped by a homeowner with a firearm, there are 4 gun-related accidents within the home." *Ibid.*

In respect to local crime, the committee observed that there were 285 murders in the District during 1974—a record number. *Id.*, at 26. The committee also stated that, "[c]ontrary to popular opinion on the subject, firearms are more frequently involved in deaths and violence among relatives and friends than in premeditated criminal activities." *Ibid.* Citing an article from the American Journal of Psychiatry, the committee reported that "[m]ost murders are committed by previously law-abiding citizens, in situations where spontaneous violence is generated by anger, passion or intoxication, and where the killer and victim are acquainted." *Ibid.* "Twenty-five percent of these murders," the committee informed the Council, "occur within families." *Ibid.*

The committee report furthermore presented statistics strongly correlating handguns with crime. Of the 285 murders in the District in 1974, 155 were committed with handguns. *Ibid.* This did not appear to be an aberration, as the report revealed that "handguns [had been] used in roughly 54% of all murders" (and 87% of murders of law enforcement officers) nationwide over the preceding several years. *Ibid.* Nor were handguns only linked to murders, as statistics showed that they were used in roughly 60% of robberies and 26% of assaults. *Ibid.* "A crime committed with a pistol," the committee reported, "is 7 times more likely to be lethal than a crime committed with any other weapon." *Id.*, at 25. The committee furthermore presented statistics regarding the availability of handguns in the United States, *ibid.*, and noted that they had "become easy for juveniles to obtain," even despite then-current District laws prohibiting juveniles from possessing them, *id.*, at 26.

In the committee's view, the current District firearms laws were unable "to reduce the potentiality for gun-related violence," or to "cope with the problems of gun control in the District" more generally. *Ibid.* In the absence of adequate federal gun legislation, the committee concluded, it "becomes necessary for local governments to act to protect their citizens, and certainly the District of Columbia as the only totally urban statelike jurisdiction should be strong in its approach." *Id.*, at 27. It recommended that the Council adopt a restriction on handgun registration to reflect "a legislative decision that, at this point in time and due to the gun-control tragedies and horrors enumerated previously" in the committee report, "pistols . . . are no longer justified in this jurisdiction." *Id.*, at 31; see also *ibid.* (handgun restriction "denotes a policy decision that handguns . . . have no legitimate use in the purely urban environment of the District").

The District's special focus on handguns thus reflects the fact that the committee report found them to have a particularly strong link to undesirable activities in the District's exclusively urban environment. See *id.*, at 25–26. The District did not seek to prohibit possession of other sorts of weapons deemed more suitable for an "urban area." See *id.*, at 25. Indeed, an original draft of the bill, and the original committee recommendations, had sought to prohibit registration of shotguns as well as handguns, but the Council as a whole decided to narrow the prohibition. Compare *id.*, at 30 (describing early version of the bill), with D.C. Code §7-2502.02).

2

Next, consider the facts as a court must consider them looking at the matter as of today. See, *e.g.*, *Turner*, 520 U.S., at 195 (discussing role of court as factfinder in a constitutional case). Petitioners, and their *amici*, have presented us with more recent statistics that tell much the same story that the committee report told 30 years ago. At the least, they present nothing that would permit us to second-guess the Council in respect to the numbers of gun crimes, injuries, and deaths, or the role of handguns.

(Continues)

(Continued)

From 1993 to 1997, there were 180,533 firearm-related deaths in the United States, an average of over 36,000 per year. Dept. of Justice, Bureau of Justice Statistics, M. Zawitz & K. Strom, *Firearm Injury and Death from Crime, 1993-97*, p. 2 (Oct. 2000), online at http://www.ojp.usdoj.gov/bjs/pub/pdf/fidc9397.pdf (hereinafter Firearm Injury and Death from Crime). Fifty-one percent were suicides, 44% were homicides, 1% were legal interventions, 3% were unintentional accidents, and 1% were of undetermined causes. See *ibid.* Over that same period there were an additional 411,800 nonfatal firearm-related injuries treated in U. S. hospitals, an average of over 82,000 per year. *Ibid.* Of these, 62% resulted from assaults, 17% were unintentional, 6% were suicide attempts, 1% were legal interventions, and 13% were of unknown causes. *Ibid.*

The statistics are particularly striking in respect to children and adolescents. In over one in every eight firearm-related deaths in 1997, the victim was someone under the age of 20. American Academy of Pediatrics, Firearm-Related Injuries Affecting the Pediatric Population, 105 Pediatrics 888 (2000) (hereinafter Firearm-Related Injuries). Firearm-related deaths account for 22.5% of all injury deaths between the ages of 1 and 19. *Ibid.* More male teenagers die from firearms than from all natural causes combined. Dresang, Gun Deaths in Rural and Urban Settings, 14 *J. Am. Bd. Family Practice* 107 (2001). Persons under 25 accounted for 47% of hospital-treated firearm injuries between June 1, 1992 and May 31, 1993. Firearm-Related Injuries 891.

Handguns are involved in a majority of firearm deaths and injuries in the United States. *Id.*, at 888. From 1993 to 1997, 81% of firearm-homicide victims were killed by handgun. Firearm Injury and Death from Crime 4; see also Dept. of Justice, Bureau of Justice Statistics, C. Perkins, *Weapon Use and Violent Crime*, p. 8 (Sept. 2003), (Table 10), http://www.ojp.usdoj.gov/bjs/pub/pdf/wuvc01.pdf (hereinafter Weapon Use and Violent Crime) (statistics indicating roughly the same rate for 1993–2001). In the same period, for the 41% of firearm injuries for which the weapon type is known, 82% of them were from handguns. Firearm Injury and Death From Crime 4. And among children under the age of 20, handguns account for approximately 70% of all unintentional firearm-related injuries and deaths. Firearm-Related Injuries 890. In particular, 70% of all firearm-related teenage suicides in 1996 involved a handgun. *Id.*, at 889; see also Zwerling, Lynch, Burmeister, & Goertz, The Choice of Weapons in Firearm Suicides in Iowa, 83 *Am. J. Public Health* 1630, 1631 (1993) (Table 1) (handguns used in 36.6% of all firearm suicides in Iowa from 1980–1984 and 43.8% from 1990–1991).

Handguns also appear to be a very popular weapon among criminals. In a 1997 survey of inmates who were armed during the crime for which they were incarcerated, 83.2% of state inmates and 86.7% of federal inmates said that they were armed with a handgun. See Dept. of Justice, Bureau of Justice Statistics, C. Harlow, *Firearm Use by Offenders*, p. 3 (Nov. 2001), online at http://www.ojp.usdoj.gov/bjs/pub/pdf/fuo.pdf; see also Weapon Use and Violent Crime 2 (Table 2) (statistics indicating that handguns were used in over 84% of nonlethal violent crimes involving firearms from 1993 to 2001). And handguns are not only popular tools for crime, but popular objects of it as well: the FBI received on average over 274,000 reports of stolen guns for each year between 1985 and 1994, and almost 60% of stolen guns are handguns. Dept. of Justice, Bureau of Justice Statistics, M. Zawitz, *Guns Used in Crime*, p. 3 (July 1995), online at http://www.ojp.usdoj.gov/bjs/pub/pdf/guic.pdf. Department of Justice studies have concluded that stolen handguns in particular are an important source of weapons for both adult and juvenile offenders. *Ibid.*

Statistics further suggest that urban areas, such as the District, have different experiences with gun-related death, injury, and crime, than do less densely populated rural areas. A disproportionate amount of violent and property crimes occur in urban areas, and urban criminals are more likely than other offenders to use a firearm during the commission of a violent crime. See Dept. of Justice, Bureau of Justice Statistics, D. Duhart, *Urban, Suburban, and Rural Victimization, 1993–98*, pp. 1, 9 (Oct. 2000), online at http://www.ojp.usdoj.gov/bjs/pub/pdf/usrv98.pdf. Homicide appears to be a much greater issue in urban areas; from 1985 to 1993, for example, "half of all homicides occurred in 63 cities with 16% of the nation's population." Wintemute, The Future of Firearm Violence Prevention, 282 *JAMA* 475 (1999). One study concluded that although the overall rate of gun death between 1989 and 1999 was roughly the same in urban than rural areas, the urban homicide rate was three times as high; even after adjusting for other variables, it was still twice as high. Branas, Nance, Elliott, Richmond, & Schwab, Urban-Rural Shifts in Intentional Firearm Death, 94 *Am. J. Public Health* 1750, 1752 (2004); see also *ibid.* (noting that rural areas appear to have a higher rate of firearm suicide). And a study of firearm injuries to children and adolescents in Pennsylvania between 1987 and 2000 showed an injury rate in urban counties 10 times higher than in nonurban counties. Nance & Branas, The Rural-Urban Continuum, 156 *Archives of Pediatrics & Adolescent Medicine* 781, 782 (2002).

Finally, the linkage of handguns to firearms deaths and injuries appears to be much stronger in urban than in rural areas. "[S]tudies to date generally support the hypothesis that the greater number of rural gun deaths are from rifles or shotguns, whereas the greater number of urban gun deaths are from handguns." Dresang, *supra*, at 108. And the Pennsylvania study reached a similar conclusion with respect to firearm injuries—they are much more likely to be caused by handguns in urban areas than in rural areas. See Nance & Branas, *supra*, at 784.

3

Respondent and his many *amici* for the most part do not disagree about the *figures* set forth in the preceding subsection, but they do disagree strongly with the District's *predictive judgment* that a ban on handguns will help solve the crime and accident problems that those figures disclose. In particular, they disagree with the District Council's assessment that "freezing the pistol . . . population within the District," DC Rep., at 26, will reduce crime, accidents, and deaths related to guns. And they provide facts and figures designed to show that it has not done so in the past, and hence will not do so in the future.

First, they point out that, since the ban took effect, violent crime in the District has increased, not decreased. See Brief for Criminologists et al. as *Amici Curiae* 4–8, 3a (hereinafter Criminologists' Brief); Brief for Congress of Racial Equality as *Amicus Curiae* 35–36; Brief for National Rifle Assn. et al. as *Amici Curiae* 28–30 (hereinafter NRA Brief). Indeed, a comparison with 49 other major cities reveals that the District's homicide rate is actually substantially *higher* relative to these other cities than it was before the handgun restriction went into effect. See Brief for Academics as *Amici Curiae* 7-10 (hereinafter Academics' Brief); see also Criminologists' Brief 6–9, 3a–4a, 7a. Respondent's *amici* report similar results in comparing the District's homicide rates during that period to that of the neighboring States of Maryland and Virginia (neither of which restricts handguns to the same degree), and to the homicide rate of the Nation as a whole. See Academics' Brief 11–17; Criminologists' Brief 6a, 8a.

Second, respondent's *amici* point to a statistical analysis that regresses murder rates against the presence or absence of strict gun laws in 20 European nations. See Criminologists' Brief 23 (citing Kates & Mauser, Would Banning Firearms Reduce Murder and Suicide? 30 *Harv. J. L. & Pub. Pol'y* 649, 651–694 (2007)). That analysis concludes that strict gun laws are correlated with *more* murders, not fewer. See Criminologists' Brief 23; see also *id.*, at 25–28. They also cite domestic studies, based on data from various cities, States, and the Nation as a whole, suggesting that a reduction in the number of guns does not lead to a reduction in the amount of violent crime. See *id.*, at 17–20. They further argue that handgun bans do not reduce suicide rates, see *id.*, at 28–31, 9a, or rates of accidents, even those involving children, see Brief for International Law Enforcement Educators and Trainers Assn. et al. as *Amici Curiae* App. 7–15 (hereinafter ILEETA Brief).

Third, they point to evidence indicating that firearm ownership does have a beneficial self-defense effect. Based on a 1993 survey, the authors of one study estimated that there were 2.2-to-2.5 million defensive uses of guns (mostly brandishing, about a quarter involving the actual firing of a gun) annually. See Kleck & Gertz, Armed Resistance to Crime, 86 *J. Crim. L. & C.* 150, 164 (1995); see also ILEETA Brief App. 1-6 (summarizing studies regarding defensive uses of guns). Another study estimated that for a period of 12 months ending in 1994, there were 503, 481 incidents in which a burglar found himself confronted by an armed homeowner, and that in 497,646 (98.8%) of them, the intruder was successfully scared away. See Ikida, Dahlberg, Sacks, Mercy, & Powell, *Estimating Intruder-Related Firearms Retrievals in U.S. Households, 12 Violence & Victims* 363 (1997). A third study suggests that gun-armed victims are substantially less likely than non-gun-armed victims to be injured in resisting robbery or assault. Barnett & Kates, Under Fire, 45 *Emory L. J.* 1139, 1243–1244, n. 478 (1996). And additional evidence suggests that criminals are likely to be deterred from burglary and other crimes if they know the victim is likely to have a gun. See Kleck, Crime Control Through the Private Use of Armed Force, 35 *Social Problems* 1, 15 (1988) (reporting a substantial drop in the burglary rate in an Atlanta suburb that required heads of households to own guns); see also ILEETA Brief 17–18 (describing decrease in sexual assaults in Orlando when women were trained in the use of guns).

Fourth, respondent's *amici* argue that laws criminalizing gun possession are self-defeating, as evidence suggests that they will have the effect only of restricting law-abiding citizens, but not criminals, from acquiring guns. See, *e.g.*, Brief for President *Pro Tempore* of Senate of Pennsylvania as *Amicus Curiae* 35, 36, and n. 15. That effect, they argue, will be especially pronounced in the District, whose proximity to Virginia and Maryland will provide criminals with a steady supply of guns. See Brief for Heartland Institute as *Amicus Curiae* 20.

(Continues)

(Continued)

In the view of respondent's *amici*, this evidence shows that other remedies—such as *less* restriction on gun ownership, or liberal authorization of law-abiding citizens to carry concealed weapons—better fit the problem. See, *e.g.*, Criminologists' Brief 35–37 (advocating easily obtainable gun licenses); Brief for Southeastern Legal Foundation, Inc. et al. as *Amici Curiae* 15 (hereinafter SLF Brief) (advocating "widespread gun ownership" as a deterrent to crime); see also J. Lott, *More Guns, Less Crime* (2d ed. 2000). They further suggest that at a minimum the District fails to show that its *remedy*, the gun ban, bears a reasonable relation to the crime and accident *problems* that the District seeks to solve. See, *e.g.*, Brief for Respondent 59–61.

These empirically based arguments may have proved strong enough to convince many legislatures, as a matter of legislative policy, not to adopt total handgun bans. But the question here is whether they are strong enough to destroy judicial confidence in the reasonableness of a legislature that rejects them. And that they are not. For one thing, they can lead us more deeply into the uncertainties that surround any effort to reduce crime, but they cannot prove either that handgun possession diminishes crime or that handgun bans are ineffective. The statistics do show a soaring District crime rate. And the District's crime rate went up after the District adopted its handgun ban. But, as students of elementary logic know, *after it* does not mean *because of it*. What would the District's crime rate have looked like without the ban? Higher? Lower? The same? Experts differ; and we, as judges, cannot say.

What about the fact that foreign nations with strict gun laws have higher crime rates? Which is the cause and which the effect? The proposition that strict gun laws *cause* crime is harder to accept than the proposition that strict gun laws in part grow out of the fact that a nation already has a higher crime rate. And we are then left with the same question as before: What would have happened to crime without the gun laws—a question that respondent and his *amici* do not convincingly answer.

Further, suppose that respondent's *amici* are right when they say that householders' possession of loaded handguns help to frighten away intruders. On that assumption, one must still ask whether that benefit is worth the potential death-related cost. And that is a question without a directly provable answer.

Finally, consider the claim of respondent's *amici* that handgun bans *cannot* work; there are simply too many illegal guns already in existence for a ban on legal guns to make a difference. In a word, they claim that, given the urban sea of pre-existing legal guns, criminals can readily find arms regardless. Nonetheless, a legislature might respond, we want to make an effort to try to dry up that urban sea, drop by drop. And none of the studies can show that effort is not worthwhile.

In a word, the studies to which respondent's *amici* point raise policy-related questions. They succeed in proving that the District's predictive judgments are controversial. But they do not by themselves show that those judgments are incorrect; nor do they demonstrate a consensus, academic or otherwise, supporting that conclusion.

Thus, it is not surprising that the District and its *amici* support the District's handgun restriction with studies of their own. One in particular suggests that, statistically speaking, the District's law has indeed had positive life-saving effects. See Loftin, McDowall, Weirsema, & Cottey, Effects of Restrictive Licensing of Handguns on Homicide and Suicide in the District of Columbia, 325 *New England J. Med.* 1615 (1991) (hereinafter Loftin study). Others suggest that firearm restrictions as a general matter reduce homicides, suicides, and accidents in the home. See, *e.g.*, Duggan, More Guns, More Crime, 109 *J. Pol. Econ.* 1086 (2001); Kellerman, Somes, Rivara, Lee, & Banton, Injuries and Deaths Due to Firearms in the Home, 45 *J. Trauma, Infection & Critical Care* 263 (1998); Miller, Azrael, & Hemenway, Household Firearm Ownership and Suicide Rates in the United States, 13 *Epidemiology* 517 (2002). Still others suggest that the defensive uses of handguns are not as great in number as respondent's *amici* claim. See, *e.g.*, Brief for American Public Health Assn. et al. as *Amici Curiae* 17–19 (hereinafter APHA Brief) (citing studies).

Respondent and his *amici* reply to these responses; and in doing so, they seek to discredit as methodologically flawed the studies and evidence relied upon by the District. See, *e.g.*, Criminologists' Brief 9–17, 20–24; Brief for Assn. Am. Physicians and Surgeons, Inc. as *Amicus Curiae* 12–18; SLF Brief 17–22; Britt, Kleck, & Bordua, A Reassessment of the D.C. Gun Law, 30 *Law & Soc. Rev.* 361 (1996) (criticizing the Loftin study). And, of course, the District's *amici* produce counter-rejoinders, referring to articles that defend their studies. See, *e.g.*, APHA Brief 23, n. 5 (citing McDowall, Loftin, & Wiersema et al., Using Quasi-Experiments to Evaluate Firearm Laws, 30 *Law & Soc. Rev.* 381 (1996)).

The upshot is a set of studies and counterstudies that, at most, could leave a judge uncertain about the proper policy conclusion. But from respondent's perspective any such uncertainty is not good enough. That is because legislators, not judges, have primary responsibility for drawing policy conclusions from empirical fact. And, given that constitutional allocation of decision making responsibility, the empirical evidence presented here is sufficient to allow a judge to reach a firm *legal* conclusion.

In particular this Court, in First Amendment cases applying intermediate scrutiny, has said that our "sole obligation" in reviewing a legislature's "predictive judgments" is "to assure that, in formulating its judgments," the legislature "has drawn reasonable inferences based on substantial evidence." *Turner*, 520 U.S., at 195 (internal quotation marks omitted). And judges, looking at the evidence before us, should agree that the District legislature's predictive judgments satisfy that legal standard. That is to say, the District's judgment, while open to question, is nevertheless supported by "substantial evidence."

There is no cause here to depart from the standard set forth in *Turner*, for the District's decision represents the kind of empirically based judgment that legislatures, not courts, are best suited to make. See *Nixon*, 528 U.S., at 402 (*Breyer, J.,* concurring). In fact, deference to legislative judgment seems particularly appropriate here, where the judgment has been made by a local legislature, with particular knowledge of local problems and insight into appropriate local solutions. See *Los Angeles v. Alameda Books, Inc.*, 535 U.S. 425, 440 (2002) (plurality opinion) ("[W]e must acknowledge that the Los Angeles City Council is in a better position than the Judiciary to gather an evaluate data on local problems"); cf. DC Rep., at 67 (statement of Rep. Gude) (describing District's law as "a decision made on the local level after extensive debate and deliberations"). Different localities may seek to solve similar problems in different ways, and a "city must be allowed a reasonable opportunity to experiment with solutions to admittedly serious problems." *Renton v. Playtime Theatres, Inc.*, 475 U.S. 41, 52 (1986) (internal quotation marks omitted). "The Framers recognized that the most effective democracy occurs at local levels of government, where people with firsthand knowledge of local problems have more ready access to public officials responsible for dealing with them." *Garcia v. San Antonio Metropolitan Transit Authority*, 469 U.S. 528, 575, n. 18 (1985) (Powell, J., dissenting) (citing *The Federalist* No. 17, p. 107 (J. Cooke ed. 1961) (A. Hamilton)). We owe that democratic process some substantial weight in the constitutional calculus.

For these reasons, I conclude that the District's statute properly seeks to further the sort of life-preserving and public-safety interests that the Court has called "compelling." *Salerno*, 481 U.S., at 750, 754.

B

I next assess the extent to which the District's law burdens the interests that the Second Amendment seeks to protect. Respondent and his *amici*, as well as the majority, suggest that those interests include: (1) the preservation of a "well regulated Militia"; (2) safeguarding the use of firearms for sporting purposes, *e.g.*, hunting and marksmanship; and (3) assuring the use of firearms for self-defense. For argument's sake, I shall consider all three of those interests here.

1

The District's statute burdens the Amendment's first and primary objective hardly at all. As previously noted, there is general agreement among the Members of the Court that the principal (if not the only) purpose of the Second Amendment is found in the Amendment's text: the preservation of a "well regulated Militia." See *supra*, at 3. What scant Court precedent there is on the Second Amendment teaches that the Amendment was adopted "[w]ith obvious purpose to assure the continuation and render possible the effectiveness of [militia] forces" and "must be interpreted and applied with that end in view." *Miller*, 307 U.S., at 178. Where that end is implicated only minimally (or not at all), there is substantially less reason for constitutional concern. Compare *ibid.* ("In the absence of any evidence tending to show that possession or use of a 'shotgun having a barrel of less than eighteen inches in length' at this time has some reasonable relationship to the preservation or efficiency of a well regulated militia, we cannot say that the Second Amendment guarantees the right to keep and bear such an instrument").

To begin with, the present case has nothing to do with *actual* military service. The question presented presumes that respondent is "*not* affiliated with any state-regulated militia." 552 U.S. __ (2007) (emphasis added). I am aware of no indication that the District either now or in the recent past has called up its citizenry to serve in a militia, that it has any inkling of doing so anytime in the foreseeable future, or that this law must be construed to prevent the use of handguns during legitimate militia activities. Moreover, even if the District were to call up its militia, respondent would not be among the citizens whose service would be requested. The District does not consider him, at 66 years of age, to be a member of its militia. See D.C. Code §49-401 (2001) (militia includes only male residents ages 18 to 45); App. to Pet. for Cert. 120a (indicating respondent's date of birth).

(Continues)

Nonetheless, as some *amici* claim, the statute might interfere with training in the use of weapons, training useful for military purposes. The 19th-century constitutional scholar, Thomas Cooley, wrote that the Second Amendment protects "learning to handle and use [arms] in a way that makes those who keep them ready for their efficient use" during militia service. *General Principles of Constitutional Law* 271 (1880); *ante*, at 45 (opinion of the Court); see also *ante*, at 45–46 (citing other scholars agreeing with Cooley on that point). And former military officers tell us that "private ownership of firearms makes for a more effective fighting force" because "[m]ilitary recruits with previous firearms experience and training are generally better marksmen, and accordingly, better soldiers." Brief for Retired Military Officers as *Amici Curiae* 1–2 (hereinafter Military Officers' Brief). An *amicus* brief filed by retired Army generals adds that a "well-regulated militia—whether *ad hoc* or as part of our organized military—depends on recruits who have familiarity and training with firearms—rifles, pistols, and shotguns." Brief for Major General John D. Altenburg, Jr., et al. as *Amici Curiae* 4 (hereinafter Generals' Brief). Both briefs point out the importance of handgun training. Military Officers' Brief 26–28; Generals' Brief 4. Handguns are used in military service, see *id.*, at 26, and "civilians who are familiar with handgun marksmanship and safety are much more likely to be able to safely and accurately fire a rifle or other firearm with minimal training upon entering military service," *id.*, at 28.

Regardless, to consider the military-training objective a modern counterpart to a similar militia-related colonial objective and to treat that objective as falling within the Amendment's primary purposes makes no difference here. That is because the District's law does not seriously affect military training interests. The law permits residents to engage in activities that will increase their familiarity with firearms. They may register (and thus possess in their homes) weapons other than handguns, such as rifles and shotguns. See D.C. Code §§7-2502.01, 7-2502.02(a) (only weapons that cannot be registered are sawed-off shotguns, machine guns, short-barreled rifles, and pistols not registered before 1976); compare Generals' Brief 4 (listing "*rifles*, pistols, and *shotguns*" as useful military weapons; emphasis added). And they may operate those weapons within the District "for lawful recreational purposes." §7-2507.02; see also §7-2502.01(b)(3) (nonresidents "participating in any lawful recreational firearm-related activity in the District, or on his way to or from such activity in another jurisdiction" may carry even weapons not registered in the District). These permissible recreations plainly include actually using and firing the weapons, as evidenced by a specific D.C. Code provision contemplating the existence of local firing ranges. See §7-2507.03.

And while the District law prevents citizens from training with handguns *within the District*, the District consists of only 61.4 square miles of urban area. See Dept. of Commerce, Bureau of Census, United States: 2000 (pt. 1), p. 11 (2002) (Table 8). The adjacent States do permit the use of handguns for target practice, and those States are only a brief subway ride away. See Md. Crim. Law Code Ann. §4-203(b)(4) (Lexis Supp. 2007) (general handgun restriction does not apply to "the wearing, carrying, or transporting by a person of a handgun used in connection with," *inter alia*, "a target shoot, formal or informal target practice, sport shooting event, hunting, [or] a Department of Natural Resources-sponsored firearms and hunter safety class"); Va. Code Ann. §18.2-287.4 (Lexis Supp. 2007) (general restriction on carrying certain loaded pistols in certain public areas does not apply "to any person actually engaged in lawful hunting or lawful recreational shooting activities at an established shooting range or shooting contest"); Washington Metropolitan Area Transit Authority, Metrorail System Map, http://www.wmata.com/metrorail/systemmmap.cfm.

Of course, a subway rider must buy a ticket, and the ride takes time. It also costs money to store a pistol, say, at a target range, outside the District. But given the costs already associated with gun ownership and firearms training, I cannot say that a subway ticket and a short subway ride (and storage costs) create more than a minimal burden. Compare *Crawford v. Marion County Election Bd.*, 553 U.S. ___, ___ (2008) (slip op., at 3) (*Breyer, J.*, dissenting) (acknowledging travel burdens on indigent persons in the context of voting where public transportation options were limited). Indeed, respondent and two of his coplaintiffs below may well use handguns outside the District on a regular basis, as their declarations indicate that they keep such weapons stored there. See App. to Pet. for Cert. 77a (respondent); see also *id.*, at 78a, 84a (coplaintiffs). I conclude that the District's law burdens the Second Amendment's primary objective little, or not at all.

2

The majority briefly suggests that the "right to keep and bear Arms" might encompass an interest in hunting. See, *e.g.*, *ante*, at 26. But in enacting the present provisions, the District sought "to take nothing away from sportsmen." DC Rep., at 33. And any inability of District residents to hunt near where they live has much to do with the jurisdiction's exclusively urban character and little to do with the District's firearm laws. For reasons similar to those I discussed in the preceding subsection—that the District's law does not prohibit possession of rifles or shotguns, and the presence of opportunities for sporting activities in nearby States—I reach a similar conclusion, namely, that the District's law burdens any sports-related or hunting-related objectives that the Amendment may protect little, or not at all.

3

The District's law does prevent a resident from keeping a loaded handgun in his home. And it consequently makes it more difficult for the householder to use the handgun for self-defense in the home against intruders, such as burglars. As the Court of Appeals noted, statistics suggest that handguns are the most popular weapon for self defense. See 478 F. 3d, at 400 (citing Kleck & Gertz, 86 *J. Crim. L. & C.*, at 182–183). And there are some legitimate reasons why that would be the case: *Amici* suggest (with some empirical support) that handguns are easier to hold and control (particularly for persons with physical infirmities), easier to carry, easier to maneuver in enclosed spaces, and that a person using one will still have a hand free to dial 911. See ILEETA Brief 37–39; NRA Brief 32–33; see also *ante*, at 57. But see Brief for Petitioners 54–55 (citing sources preferring shotguns and rifles to handguns for purposes of self-defense). To that extent the law burdens to some degree an interest in self-defense that for present purposes I have assumed the Amendment seeks to further.

C

In weighing needs and burdens, we must take account of the possibility that there are reasonable, but less restrictive alternatives. Are there *other* potential measures that might similarly promote the same goals while imposing lesser restrictions? See *Nixon*, 528 U.S., at 402 (*Breyer, J.*, concurring) ("existence of a clearly superior, less restrictive alternative" can be a factor in determining whether a law is constitutionally proportionate). Here I see none.

The reason there is no clearly superior, less restrictive alternative to the District's handgun ban is that the ban's very objective is to reduce significantly the number of handguns in the District, say, for example, by allowing a law enforcement officer immediately to assume that *any* handgun he sees is an *illegal* handgun. And there is no plausible way to achieve that objective other than to ban the guns.

It does not help respondent's case to describe the District's objective more generally as an "effort to diminish the dangers associated with guns." That is because the very attributes that make handguns particularly useful for self-defense are also what make them particularly dangerous. That they are easy to hold and control means that they are easier for children to use. See Brief for American Academy of Pediatrics et al. as *Amici Curiae* 19 ("[C]hildren as young as three are able to pull the trigger of most handguns"). That they are maneuverable and permit a free hand likely contributes to the fact that they are by far the firearm of choice for crimes such as rape and robbery. See *Weapon Use and Violent Crime* 2 (Table 2). That they are small and light makes them easy to steal, see *supra*, at 19, and concealable, cf. *ante*, at 54 (opinion of the Court) (suggesting that concealed-weapon bans are constitutional).

This symmetry suggests that any measure less restrictive in respect to the use of handguns for self-defense will, to that same extent, prove less effective in preventing the use of handguns for illicit purposes. If a resident has a handgun in the home that he can use for self-defense, then he has a handgun in the home that he can use to commit suicide or engage in acts of domestic violence. See *supra*, at 18 (handguns prevalent in suicides); Brief for National Network to End Domestic Violence et al. as *Amici Curiae* 27 (handguns prevalent in domestic violence). If it is indeed the case, as the District believes, that the number of guns contributes to the number of gun-related crimes, accidents, and deaths, then, although there may be less restrictive, *less effective* substitutes for an outright ban, there is no less restrictive *equivalent* of an outright ban.

Licensing restrictions would not similarly reduce the handgun population, and the District may reasonably fear that even if guns are initially restricted to law-abiding citizens, they might be stolen and thereby placed in the hands of criminals. See *supra*, at 19. Permitting certain types of handguns, but not others, would affect the commercial market for handguns, but not their availability. And requiring safety devices such as trigger locks, or imposing safe-storage requirements would interfere with any self-defense interest while simultaneously leaving operable weapons in the hands of owners (or others capable of acquiring the weapon and disabling the safety device) who might use them for domestic violence or other crimes.

(Continues)

(*Continued*)

The absence of equally effective alternatives to a complete prohibition finds support in the empirical fact that other States and urban centers prohibit particular types of weapons. Chicago has a law very similar to the District's, and many of its suburbs also ban handgun possession under most circumstances. See Chicago, Ill., Municipal Code §§8-20-030(k), 8-20-40, 8-20-50(c) (2008); Evanston, Ill., City Code §9-8-2 (2007); Morton Grove, Ill., Village Code §6-2-3(C) (2008); Oak Park, Ill., Village Code §27-2-1 (2007); Winnetka, Ill., Village Ordinance §9.12.020(B) (2008); Wilmette, Ill., Ordinance §12-24(b) (2008). Toledo bans certain types of handguns. Toledo, Ohio, Municipal Code, ch. 549.25 (2007). And San Francisco in 2005 enacted by popular referendum a ban on most handgun possession by city residents; it has been precluded from enforcing that prohibition, however, by state–court decisions deeming it pre-empted by state law. See *Fiscal v. City and County of San Francisco*, 158 Cal. App. 4th 895, 900–901, 70 Cal. Rptr. 3d 324, 326–328 (2008). (Indeed, the fact that as many as 41 States may pre-empt local gun regulation suggests that the absence of more regulation like the District's may perhaps have more to do with state law than with a lack of locally perceived need for them. See Legal Community Against Violence, Regulating Guns in America 14 (2006), http://www.lcav.org/Library/reports_analyses/National_Audit_Total_8.16.06.pdf.

In addition, at least six States and Puerto Rico impose general bans on certain types of weapons, in particular assault weapons or semiautomatic weapons. See Cal. Penal Code §12280(b) (West Supp. 2008); Conn. Gen. Stat. §§53-202c (2007); Haw. Rev. Stat. §134-8 (1993); Md. Crim. Law Code Ann. §4-303(a) (Lexis 2002); Mass. Gen. Laws, ch. 140, §131M (West 2006); N.Y. Penal Law Ann. §265.02(7) (West Supp. 2008); 25 Laws P. R. Ann. §456m (Supp. 2006); see also 18 U. S. C. §922(o) (federal machine gun ban). And at least 14 municipalities do the same. See Albany, N.Y., Municipal Code §193-16(A) (2005); Aurora, Ill., Ordinance §29-49(a) (2007); Buffalo, N.Y., City Code §180-1(F) (2000); Chicago, Ill., Municipal Code §8-24-025(a), 8-20-030(h); Cincinnati, Ohio, Admin. Code §708-37(a) (Supp. 2008); Cleveland, Ohio, Ordinance §628.03(a) (2008); Columbus, Ohio, City Code §2323.31 (2007); Denver, Colo., Municipal Code §38-130(e) (2008); Morton Grove, Ill., Village Code §6-2-3(B); N. Y. C. Admin. Code §10-303.1 (2007); Oak Park, Ill., Village Code §27-2-1; Rochester, N.Y., Code §47-5(f) (2008); South Bend, Ind., Ordinance §§13-97(b), 13–98 (2008); Toledo, Ohio, Municipal Code §549.23(a). These bans, too, suggest that there may be no substitute to an outright prohibition in cases where a governmental body has deemed a particular type of weapon especially dangerous.

D

The upshot is that the District's objectives are compelling; its predictive judgments as to its law's tendency to achieve those objectives are adequately supported; the law does impose a burden upon any self-defense interest that the Amendment seeks to secure; and there is no clear less restrictive alternative. I turn now to the final portion of the "permissible regulation" question: Does the District's law *disproportionately* burden Amendment-protected interests? Several considerations, taken together, convince me that it does not.

First, the District law is tailored to the life-threatening problems it attempts to address. The law concerns one class of weapons, handguns, leaving residents free to possess shotguns and rifles, along with ammunition. The area that falls within its scope is totally urban. Cf. *Lorillard Tobacco Co. v. Reilly*, 533 U.S. 525, 563 (2001) (varied effect of statewide speech restriction in "rural, urban, or suburban" locales "demonstrates a lack of narrow tailoring"). That urban area suffers from a serious handgun-fatality problem. The District's law directly aims at that compelling problem. And there is no less restrictive way to achieve the problem-related benefits that it seeks.

Second, the self-defense interest in maintaining loaded handguns in the home to shoot intruders is not the *primary* interest, but at most a subsidiary interest, that the Second Amendment seeks to serve. The Second Amendment's language, while speaking of a "Militia," says nothing of "self-defense." As *Justice Stevens* points out, the Second Amendment's drafting history shows that the language reflects the Framers' primary, if not exclusive, objective. See *ante*, at 17–28 (dissenting opinion). And the majority itself says that "the threat that the new Federal Government would destroy the citizens' militia by taking away their arms was *the* reason that right . . . was codified in a written Constitution." *Ante*, at 26 (emphasis added). The *way* in which the Amendment's operative clause seeks to promote that interest—by protecting a right "to keep and bear Arms"—may *in fact* help further an interest in self-defense. But a factual connection falls far short of a primary objective. The Amendment itself tells us that militia preservation was first and foremost in the Framers' minds. See *Miller*, 307 U.S., at 178

("With obvious purpose to assure the continuation and render possible the effectiveness of [militia] forces the declaration and guarantee of the Second Amendment were made," and the amendment "must be interpreted and applied with that end in view").

Further, any self-defense interest at the time of the Framing could not have focused exclusively upon urban-crime related dangers. Two hundred years ago, most Americans, many living on the frontier, would likely have thought of self-defense primarily in terms of outbreaks of fighting with Indian tribes, rebellions such as Shays' Rebellion, marauders, and crime-related dangers to travelers on the roads, on footpaths, or along waterways. See Dept. of Commerce, Bureau of Census, Population: 1790 to 1990 (1998) (Table 4), online at http://www.census.gov/population/censusdata/table-4.pdf (of the 3,929,214 Americans in 1790, only 201,655—about 5%—lived in urban areas). Insofar as the Framers focused at all on the tiny fraction of the population living in large cities, they would have been aware that these city dwellers were subject to firearm restrictions that their rural counterparts were not. See *supra*, at 4–7. They are unlikely then to have thought of a right to keep loaded handguns in homes to confront intruders in urban settings as *central*. And the subsequent development of modern urban police departments, by diminishing the need to keep loaded guns nearby in case of intruders, would have moved any such right even further away from the heart of the amendment's more basic protective ends. See, *e.g.*, Sklansky, The Private Police, 46 *UCLA L. Rev.* 1165, 1206–1207 (1999) (professional urban police departments did not develop until roughly the mid-19th century).

Nor, for that matter, am I aware of any evidence that *handguns* in particular were central to the Framers' conception of the Second Amendment. The lists of militia-related weapons in the late 18th-century state statutes appear primarily to refer to other sorts of weapons, muskets in particular. See *Miller*, 307 U.S., at 180–182 (reproducing colonial militia laws). Respondent points out in his brief that the Federal Government and two States at the time of the founding had enacted statutes that listed handguns as "acceptable" militia weapons. Brief for Respondent 47. But these statutes apparently found them "acceptable" only for certain special militiamen (generally, certain soldiers on horseback), while requiring muskets or rifles for the general infantry. See Act of May 8, 1792, ch. XXXIII, 1 Stat. 271; Laws of the State of North Carolina 592 (1791); First Laws of the State of Connecticut 150 (1784); see also 25 Journals of the Continental Congress, pp. 1774–1789 741–742 (1922).

Third, irrespective of what the Framers *could have thought,* we know what they *did think.* Samuel Adams, who lived in Boston, advocated a constitutional amendment that would have precluded the Constitution from ever being "construed" to "prevent the people of the United States, who are peaceable citizens, from keeping their own arms." 6 *Documentary History of the Ratification of the Constitution* 1453 (J. Kaminski & G. Saladino eds. 2000). Samuel Adams doubtless knew that the Massachusetts Constitution contained somewhat similar protection. And he doubtless knew that Massachusetts law prohibited Bostonians from keeping loaded guns in the house. So how could Samuel Adams have advocated such protection *unless* he thought that the protection was *consistent* with local regulation that seriously impeded urban residents from using their arms against intruders? It seems unlikely that he meant to deprive the Federal Government of power (to enact Boston-type weapons regulation) that he know Boston had and (as far as we know) he would have thought constitutional under the Massachusetts Constitution. Indeed, since the District of Columbia (the subject of the Seat of Government Clause, U.S. Const., Art. I, §8, cl. 17) was the only *urban* area under direct federal control, it seems unlikely that the Framers thought about *urban* gun control at all. Cf. *Palmore v. United States*, 411 U.S. 389, 397–398 (1973) (Congress can "legislate for the District in a manner with respect to subjects that would exceed its powers, or at least would be very unusual, in the context of national legislation enacted under other powers delegated to it").

Of course the District's law and the colonial Boston law are not identical. But the Boston law disabled an even wider class of weapons (indeed, all firearms). And its existence shows at the least that local legislatures could impose (as here) serious restrictions on the right to use firearms. Moreover, as I have said, Boston's law, though highly analogous to the District's, was not the *only* colonial law that could have impeded a homeowner's ability to shoot a burglar. Pennsylvania's and New York's laws could well have had a similar effect. See *supra*, at 6–7. And the Massachusetts and Pennsylvania laws were not only thought consistent with an *unwritten* common-law gun-possession right, but also consistent with *written* state constitutional provisions providing protections similar to those provided by the Federal Second Amendment. See *supra*, at 6–7. I cannot agree with the majority that these laws are largely uninformative because the penalty for violating them was civil, rather than criminal. *Ante*, at 61–62. The Court has long recognized that the exercise of a constitutional right can be burdened by penalties far short of jail time. See, *e.g.*, *Murdock v. Pennsylvania*, 319 U.S. 105 (1943) (invalidating

(Continues)

(Continued)

$7 per week solicitation fee as applied to religious group); see also *Forsyth County v. Nationalist Movement*, 505 U.S. 123, 136 (1992) ("A tax based on the content of speech does not become more constitutional because it is a small tax").

Regardless, why would the majority require a precise colonial regulatory analogue in order to save a modern gun regulation from constitutional challenge? After all, insofar as we look to history to discover how we can constitutionally regulate a right to self-defense, we must look, not to what 18th-century legislatures actually *did* enact, but to what they would have thought they *could* enact. There are innumerable policy-related reasons why a legislature might not act on a particular matter, despite having the power to do so. This Court has "frequently cautioned that it is at best treacherous to find in congressional silence alone the adoption of a controlling rule of law." *United States v. Wells*, 519 U.S. 482, 496 (1997). It is similarly "treacherous" to reason from the fact that colonial legislatures *did not* enact certain kinds of legislation an unalterable constitutional limitation on the power of a modern legislature *cannot* do so. The question should not be whether a modern restriction on a right to self-defense *duplicates* a past one, but whether that restriction, when compared with restrictions originally thought possible, enjoys a similarly strong justification. At a minimum that similarly strong justification is what the District's modern law, compared with Boston's colonial law, reveals.

Fourth, a contrary view, as embodied in today's decision, will have unfortunate consequences. The decision will encourage legal challenges to gun regulation throughout the Nation. Because it says little about the standards used to evaluate regulatory decisions, it will leave the Nation without clear standards for resolving those challenges. See *ante*, at 54, and n. 26. And litigation over the course of many years, or the mere specter of such litigation, threatens to leave cities without effective protection against gun violence and accidents during that time.

As important, the majority's decision threatens severely to limit the ability of more knowledgeable, democratically elected officials to deal with gun-related problems. The majority says that it leaves the District "a variety of tools for combating" such problems. *Ante*, at 64. It fails to list even one seemingly adequate replacement for the law it strikes down. I can understand how reasonable individuals can disagree about the merits of strict gun control as a crime-control measure, even in a totally urbanized area. But I cannot understand how one can take from the elected branches of government the right to decide whether to insist upon a handgun-free urban populace in a city now facing a serious crime problem and which, in the future, could well face environmental or other emergencies that threaten the breakdown of law and order.

V

The majority derides my approach as "judge-empowering." *Ante*, at 62. I take this criticism seriously, but I do not think it accurate. As I have previously explained, this is an approach that the Court has taken in other areas of constitutional law. See *supra*, at 10–11. Application of such an approach, of course, requires judgment, but the very nature of the approach—requiring careful identification of the relevant interests and evaluating the law's effect upon them—limits the judge's choices; and the method's necessary transparency lays bare the judge's reasoning for all to see and to criticize.

The majority's methodology is, in my view, substantially less transparent than mine. At a minimum, I find it difficult to understand the reasoning that seems to underlie certain conclusions that it reaches.

The majority spends the first 54 pages of its opinion attempting to rebut *Justice Stevens*' evidence that the Amendment was enacted with a purely militia-related purpose. In the majority's view, the Amendment also protects an interest in armed personal self-defense, at least to some degree. But the majority does not tell us precisely what that interest is. "Putting all of [the Second Amendment's] textual elements together," the majority says, "we find that they guarantee the individual right to possess and carry weapons in case of confrontation." *Ante*, at 19. Then, three pages later, it says that "we do not read the Second Amendment to permit citizens to carry arms for *any sort* of confrontation." *Ante*, at 22. Yet, with one critical exception, it does not explain which confrontations count. It simply leaves that question unanswered.

The majority does, however, point to one type of confrontation that counts, for it describes the Amendment as "elevat[ing] above all other interests the right of law-abiding, responsible citizens to use arms in defense of hearth and home." *Ante*, at 63. What is its basis for finding that to be the core of the Second Amendment right? The only historical sources identified by the majority that even appear to touch upon that specific matter consist of an 1866 newspaper editorial discussing the Freedmen's Bureau Act, see *ante*, at 43, two quotations from that 1866 Act's legislative history, see *ante*, at 43–44, and a 1980 state court opinion saying that in colonial times the same were used to defend the home as to maintain the militia, see *ante*, at 52. How can citations such as these support the far-reaching proposition that the Second Amendment's primary concern is not its stated concern about the militia, but rather a right to keep loaded weapons at one's bedside to shoot intruders?

Nor is it at all clear to me how the majority decides *which* loaded "arms" a homeowner may keep. The majority says that that Amendment protects those weapons "typically possessed by law-abiding citizens for lawful purposes." *Ante*, at 53. This definition conveniently excludes machineguns, but permits handguns, which the majority describes as "the most popular weapon chosen by Americans for self-defense in the home." *Ante*, at 57; see also *ante*, at 54–55. But what sense does this approach make? According to the majority's reasoning, if Congress and the States lift restrictions on the possession and use of machineguns, and people buy machineguns to protect their homes, the Court will have to reverse course and find that the Second Amendment *does*, in fact, protect the individual self-defense-related right to possess a machinegun. On the majority's reasoning, if tomorrow someone invents a particularly useful, highly dangerous self-defense weapon, Congress and the States had better ban it immediately, for once it becomes popular Congress will no longer possess the constitutional authority to do so. In essence, the majority determines what regulations are permissible by looking to see what existing regulations permit. There is no basis for believing that the Framers intended such circular reasoning.

I am similarly puzzled by the majority's list, in Part III of its opinion, of provisions that in its view would survive Second Amendment scrutiny. These consist of (1) "prohibitions on carrying concealed weapons"; (2) "prohibitions on the possession of firearms by felons"; (3) "prohibitions on the possession of firearms by . . . the mentally ill"; (4) "laws forbidding the carrying of firearms in sensitive places such as schools and government buildings"; and (5) government "conditions and qualifications" attached "to the commercial sale of arms." *Ante*, at 54. Why these? Is it that similar restrictions existed in the late 18th century? The majority fails to cite any colonial analogues. And even were it possible to find analogous colonial laws in respect to all these restrictions, why should these colonial laws count, while the Boston loaded-gun restriction (along with the other laws I have identified) apparently does not count? See *supra*, at 5–6, 38–39.

At the same time the majority ignores a more important question: Given the purposes for which the Framers enacted the Second Amendment, how should it be applied to modern-day circumstances that they could not have anticipated? Assume, for argument's sake, that the Framers did intend the Amendment to offer a degree of self-defense protection. Does that mean that the Framers also intended to guarantee a right to possess a loaded gun near swimming pools, parks, and playgrounds? That they would not have cared about the children who might pick up a loaded gun on their parents' bedside table? That they (who certainly showed concern for the risk of fire, see *supra*, at 5–7) would have lacked concern for the risk of accidental deaths or suicides that readily accessible loaded handguns in urban areas might bring? Unless we believe that they intended future generations to ignore such matters, answering questions such as the questions in this case requires judgment—judicial judgment exercised within a framework for constitutional analysis that guides that judgment and which makes its exercise transparent. One cannot answer those questions by combining inconclusive historical research with judicial *ipse dixit*.

The argument about method, however, is by far the less important argument surrounding today's decision. Far more important are the unfortunate consequences that today's decision is likely to spawn. Not least of these, as I have said, is the fact that the decision threatens to throw into doubt the constitutionality of gun laws throughout the United States. I can find no sound legal basis for launching the courts on so formidable and potentially dangerous a mission. In my view, there simply is no untouchable constitutional right guaranteed by the Second Amendment to keep loaded handguns in the house in crime-ridden urban areas.

VI

For these reasons, I conclude that the District's measure is a proportionate, not a disproportionate, response to the compelling concerns that led the District to adopt it. And, for these reasons as well as the independently sufficient reasons set forth by *Justice Stevens*, I would find the District's measure consistent with the Second Amendment's demands.

With respect, I dissent.

(Continues)

(Continued)

Notes

4. There are minor exceptions to all of these prohibitions, none of which is relevant here.

5. That construction has not been challenged here.

6. As Sutherland explains, the key 18th-century English case on the effect of preambles, *Copeman v. Gallant*, 1 P. Wms. 314, 24 Eng. Rep. 404 (1716), stated that "the preamble could not be used to restrict the effect of the words of the purview." J. Sutherland, *Statutes and Statutory Construction*, 47.04 (N. Singer ed. 5th ed. 1992). This rule was modified in England in an 1826 case to give more importance to the preamble, but in America "the settled principle of law is that the preamble cannot control the enacting part of the statute in cases where the enacting part is expressed in clear, unambiguous terms." *Ibid.*

   Justice Stevens says that we violate the general rule that every clause in a statute must have effect. *Post*, at 8. But where the text of a clause itself indicates that it does not have operative effect, such as "whereas" clauses in federal legislation or the Constitution's preamble, a court has no license to make it do what it was not designed to do. Or to put the point differently, operative provisions should be given effect as operative provisions, and prologues as prologues.

7. *Justice Stevens* criticizes us for discussing the prologue last. *Post*, at 8. But if a prologue can be used only to clarify an ambiguous operative provision, surely the first step must be to determine whether the operative provision is ambiguous. It might be argued, we suppose, that the prologue itself should be one of the factors that go into the determination of whether the operative provision is ambiguous—but that would cause the prologue to be used to produce ambiguity rather than just to resolve it. In any event, even if we considered the prologue *along with* the operative provision we would reach the same result we do today, since (as we explain) our interpretation of "the right of the people to keep and bear arms" furthers the purpose of an effective militia no less than (indeed, more than) the dissent's interpretation. See *infra*, at 26–27.

8. *Justice Stevens* is of course correct, *post*, at 10, that the right to assemble cannot be exercised alone, but it is still an individual right, and not one conditioned upon membership in some defined "assembly," as he contends the right to bear arms is conditioned upon membership in a defined militia. And *Justice Stevens* is dead wrong to think that the right to petition is "primarily collective in nature." *Ibid.* See *McDonald v. Smith*, 472 U.S. 479, 482–484 (1985) (describing historical origins of right to petition).

9. If we look to other founding-era documents, we find that some state constitutions used the term "the people" to refer to the people collectively, in contrast to "citizen," which was used to invoke individual rights. See Heyman, Natural Rights and the Second Amendment, in *The Second Amendment in Law and History* 179, 193–195 (C. Bogus ed. 2000) (hereinafter Bogus). But that usage was not remotely uniform. See, *e.g.*, N.C. Declaration of Rights §XIV (1776), in 5 *The Federal and State Constitutions, Colonial Charters, and Other Organic Laws* 2787, 2788 (F. Thorpe ed. 1909) (hereinafter Thorpe) (jury trial); Md. Declaration of Rights §XVIII (1776), in 3 *id.*, at 1686, 1688 (vicinage requirement); Vt. Declaration of Rights ch. 1, §XI (1777), in 6 *id.*, at 3737, 3741 (searches and seizures); Pa. Declaration of Rights §XII (1776), in 5 *id.*, at 3081, 3083 (free speech). And, most importantly, it was clearly not the terminology used in the Federal Constitution, given the First, Fourth, and Ninth Amendments.

10. See, *e.g.*, 3 *A Compleat Collection of State-Tryals* 185 (1719) ("Hath not every Subject power to keep Arms, as well as Servants in his House for defence of his Person?"); T. Wood, A New Institute of the Imperial or Civil Law 282 (1730) ("Those are guilty of *publick* Force, who keep Arms in their Houses, and make use of them otherwise than upon Journeys or Hunting, or for Sale . . ."); A Collection of All the Acts of Assembly, Now in Force, in the Colony of Virginia 596 (1733) ("Free Negros, Mulattos, or Indians, and Owners of Slaves, seated at Frontier Plantations, may obtain Licence from a Justice of Peace, for keeping Arms, &c."); J. Ayliffe, *A New Pandect of Roman Civil Law* 195 (1734) ("Yet a Person might keep Arms in his House, or on his Estate, on the Account of Hunting, Navigation, Travelling, and on the Score of Selling them in the way of Trade or Commerce, or such Arms as accrued to him by way of Inheritance"); J. Trusler, *A Concise View of the Common Law and Statute Law of England* 270 (1781) ("if [papists] keep arms in their houses, such arms may be seized by a justice of the peace"); *Some Considerations on the Game Laws* 54 (1796) ("Who has been deprived by [the law] of keeping arms for his own defence? What law forbids the veriest pauper, if he can raise a sum sufficient for the purchase of it, from mounting his Gun on his Chimney Piece . . . ?"); 3 B. Wilson, *The Works of the Honourable James Wilson* 84 (1804) (with reference to state constitutional right: "This is one of our many renewals of the Saxon regulations. 'They were bound,' says Mr. Selden, 'to keep arms for the preservation of the kingdom, and of their own person'"); W. Duer, *Outlines of the Constitutional Jurisprudence of the United States* 31–32 (1833) (with reference to colonists' English rights: "The right of every individual to keep arms for his defence,

suitable to his condition and degree; which was the public allowance, under due restrictions of the natural right of resistance and self-preservation"); 3 R. Burn, *Justice of the Peace and the Parish Officer* 88 (1815) ("It is, however, laid down by Serjeant Hawkins, . . . that if a lessee, after the end of the term, keep arms in his house to oppose the entry of the lessor, . . ."); *State v. Dempsey*, 31 N.C. 384, 385 (1849) (citing 1840 state law making it a misdemeanor for a member of certain racial groups "to carry about his person or keep in his house any shot gun or other arms").

11. See Pa. Declaration of Rights §XIII, in 5 Thorpe 3083 ("That the people have a right to bear arms for the defence of themselves and the state . . ."); Vt. Declaration of Rights §XV, in 6 *id.*, at 3741 ("That the people have a right to bear arms for the defence of themselves and the State . . ."); Ky. Const., Art. XII, cl. 23 (1792), in 3 *id.*, at 1264, 1275 ("That the right of the citizens to bear arms in defence of themselves and the State shall not be questioned"); Ohio Const., Art. VIII, §20 (1802), in 5 *id.*, at 2901, 2911 ("That the people have a right to bear arms for the defence of themselves and the State . . ."); Ind. Const., Art. I, §20 (1816), in 2 *id.*, at 1057, 1059 ("That the people have a right to bear arms for the defense of themselves and the State . . ."); Miss. Const., Art. I, §23 (1817), in 4 *id.*, at 2032, 2034 ("Every citizen has a right to bear arms, in defence of himself and the State"); Conn. Const., Art. I, §17 (1818), in 1 *id.*, at 536, 538 ("Every citizen has a right to bear arms in defence of himself and the state"); Ala. Const., Art. I, §23 (1819), in 1 *id.*, at 96, 98 ("Every citizen has a right to bear arms in defence of himself and the State"); Mo. Const., Art. XIII, §3 (1820), in 4 *id.*, at 2150, 2163 ("[T]hat their right to bear arms in defence of themselves and of the State cannot be questioned"). See generally Volokh, State Constitutional Rights to Keep and Bear Arms, 11 *Tex. Rev. L. & Politics* 191 (2006).

12. See *Bliss v. Commonwealth*, 2 Litt. 90, 91-92 (Ky. 1822); *State v. Reid*, 1 Ala. 612, 616–617 (1840); *State v. Schoultz*, 25 Mo. 128, 155 (1857); see also *Simpson v. State*, 5 Yer. 356, 360 (Tenn. 1833) (interpreting similar provision with "common defence" purpose); *State v. Huntly*, 25 N. C. 418, 422–423 (1843) (same); cf. *Nunn v. State*, 1 Ga. 243, 250-251 (1846) (construing Second Amendment); *State v. Chandler*, 5 La. Ann. 489, 489–490 (1850) (same).

13. See J. Brydall, *Privilegia Magnatud apud Anglos* 14 (1704) (Privilege XXXIII) ("In the 21st Year of King Edward the Third, a Proclamation Issued, that no Person should bear any Arms within London, and the Suburbs"); J. Bond, *A Compleat Guide to Justices of the Peace* 43 (1707) ("Sheriffs, and all other Officers in executing their Offices, and all other persons pursuing Hu[e] and Cry may lawfully bear arms"); 1 *An Abridgment of the Public Statutes in Force and Use Relative to Scotland* (1755) (entry for "Arms": "And if any person above described shall have in his custody, use, or bear arms, being thereof convicted before one justice of peace, or other judge competent, summarily, he shall for the first offense forfeit all such arms" (quoting 1 Geo. 1, c. 54, §1)); Statute Law of Scotland Abridged 132–133 (2d ed. 1769) ("Acts for disarming the highlands" but "exempting those who have particular licenses to bear arms"); E. de Vattel, *The Law of Nations, or, Principles of the Law of Nature* 144 (1792) ("Since custom has allowed persons of rank and gentlemen of the army to bear arms in time of peace, strict care should be taken that none but these should be allowed to wear swords"); E. Roche, *Proceedings of a Court-Martial, Held at the Council-Chamber, in the City of Cork* 3 (1798) (charge VI: "With having held traitorous conferences, and with having conspired, with the like intent, for the purpose of attacking and despoiling of the arms of several of the King's subjects, qualified by law to bear arms"); C. Humphreys, *A Compendium of the Common Law in force in Kentucky* 482 (1822) ("[I]n this country the constitution guaranties to all persons the right to bear arms; then it can only be a crime to exercise this right in such a manner, as to terrify people unnecessarily").

14. *Justice Stevens* contends, *post*, at 15, that since we assert that adding "against" to "bear arms" gives it a military meaning we must concede that adding a purposive qualifying phrase to "bear arms" can alter its meaning. But the difference is that we do not maintain that "against *alters* the meaning of "bear arms" but merely that it *clarifies* which of various meanings (one of which is military) is intended. *Justice Stevens*, however, argues that "[t]he term 'bear arms' is a familiar idiom; when used unadorned by any additional words, its meaning is 'to serve as a soldier, do military service, fight.'" *Post*, at 11. He therefore must establish that adding a contradictory purposive phrase can *alter* a word's meaning.

15. *Justice Stevens* finds support for his legislative history inference from the recorded views of one Antifederalist member of the House. *Post*, at 26 n. 25. "The claim that the best or most representative reading of the [language of the] amendments would conform to the understanding and concerns of [the Antifederalists] is . . . highly problematic." Rakove, *The Second Amendment: The Highest Stage of Originalism*, Bogus 74, 81.

16. The same applies to the conscientious-objector amendments proposed by Virginia and North Carolina, which said: "That any person religiously scrupulous of bearing arms ought to be exempted upon payment of an equivalent to employ another to bear arms in his stead." See Veit 19; 4 J. Eliot, *The Debates in the Several State Constitutions on the Adoption of the Federal Constitution* 243, 244 (2d ed. 1836)

(Continues)

(reprinted 1941). Certainly their second use of the phrase ("bear arms in his stead") refers, by reason of context, to compulsory bearing of arms for military duty. But their first use of the phrase ("any person religiously scrupulous of bearing arms") assuredly did not refer to people whose God allowed them to bear arms for defense of themselves but not for defense of their country.

17. Faced with this clear historical usage, *Justice Stevens* resorts to the bizarre argument that because the word "to" is not included before "bear" (whereas it is included before "petition" in the First Amendment), the unitary meaning of "to keep and bear" is established. *Post*, at 16, n. 13. We have never heard of the proposition that omitting repetition of the "to" causes two verbs with different meanings to become one. A promise "to support and to defend the Constitution of the United States" is not a whit different from a promise "to support and defend the Constitution of the United States."

18. Cf. 3 Geo., 34, §3, in 7 Eng. Stat. at Large 126 (1748) ("That the Prohibition contained . . . in this Act, of having, keeping, bearing, or wearing any Arms or Warlike Weapons . . . shall not extend . . . to any Officers or their Assistants, employed in the Execution of Justice . . .").

19. Contrary to *Justice Stevens'* wholly unsupported assertion, *post*, at 17, there was no pre-existing right in English law "to use weapons for certain military purposes" or to use arms in an organized militia.

20. Article I, §8, cl. 16 of the Constitution gives Congress the power

> "[t]o provide for organizing, arming, and disciplining, the Militia, and for governing such Part of them as may be employed in the Service of the United States, reserving to the States respectively, the Appointment of the Officers, and the Authority of training the Militia according to the discipline prescribed by Congress."

It could not be clearer that Congress's "organizing" power, unlike its "governing" power, can be invoked even for that part of the militia not "employed in the Service of the United States." *Justice Stevens* provides no support whatever for his contrary view, see *post*, at 19 n. 20. Both the Federalists and Anti-Federalists read the provision as it was written, to permit the creation of a "select" militia. See *The Federalist* No. 29, pp. 226, 227 (B. Wright ed. 1961); Centinel, Revived, No. XXIX, *Philadelphia Independent Gazetteer*, Sept. 9, 1789, in Young 711, 712.

21. *Justice Stevens* says that the drafters of the Virginia Declaration of Rights rejected this proposal and adopted "instead" a provision written by George Mason stressing the importance of the militia. See *post*, at 24, and n. 24. There is no evidence that the drafters regarded the Mason proposal as a substitute for the Jefferson proposal.

22. *Justice Stevens* quotes some of Tucker's unpublished notes, which he claims show that Tucker had ambiguous views about the Second Amendment. See *post*, at 31, and n. 32. But it is clear from the notes that Tucker located the power of States to arm their militias in the *Tenth* Amendment, and that he cited the Second Amendment for the proposition that such armament could not run afoul of any power of the federal government (since the amendment prohibits Congress from ordering disarmament). Nothing in the passage implies that the Second Amendment pertains only to the carrying of arms in the organized militia.

23. Rawle, writing before our decision in *Barron ex rel. Tiernan v. Mayor of Baltimore*, 7 Pet. 243 (1833), believed that the Second Amendment could be applied against the States. Such a belief would of course be nonsensical on petitioners' view that it protected only a right to possess and carry arms when conscripted by the State itself into militia service.

24. *Justice Stevens* suggests that this is not obvious because free blacks in Virginia had been required to muster without arms. See *post*, at 28, n. 29 (citing Siegel, The Federal Government's Power to Enact Color-Conscious Laws, 92 *Nw. U. L. Rev.* 477, 497 (1998)). But that could not have been the type of law referred to in *Aldridge*, because that practice had stopped 30 years earlier when blacks were excluded entirely from the militia by the First Militia Act. See Siegel, *supra*, at 498, n. 120. *Justice Stevens* further suggests that laws barring blacks from militia service could have been said to violate the "right to bear arms." But under *Justice Stevens'* reading of the Second Amendment (we think), the protected right is the right to carry arms to the extent one is enrolled in the militia, not the right *to be in the militia*. Perhaps *Justice Stevens* really does adopt the full-blown idiomatic meaning of "bear arms," in which case every man and woman in this country has a right "to be a soldier" or even "to wage war." In any case, it is clear to us that *Aldridge*'s allusion to the existing Virginia "restriction" upon the right of free blacks "to bear arms" could only have referred to "laws prohibiting blacks from keeping weapons," Siegel, *supra*, at 497–498.

25. *Justice Stevens'* accusation that this is "not accurate," *post*, at 39, is wrong. It is true it was the indictment that described the right as "bearing arms for a lawful purpose." But, in explicit reference to the right described in the indictment, the Court stated that "The second amendment declares that it [*i.e.*, the right of bearing arms for a lawful purpose] shall not be infringed." 92 U.S., at 553.

26. With respect to *Cruikshank*'s continuing validity on incorporation, a question not presented by this case, we note that *Cruikshank* also said that the First Amendment did not apply against the States and did not engage in the sort of Fourteenth Amendment inquiry required by our later cases. Our later decisions in *Presser v. Illinois*, 116 U.S. 252, 265 (1886) and *Miller v. Texas*, 153 U.S. 535, 538 (1894), reaffirmed that the Second Amendment applies only to the Federal Government.

27. As for the "hundreds of judges," *post*, at 2, who have relied on the view of the Second Amendment *Justice Stevens* claims we endorsed in *Miller*: If so, they overread *Miller*. And their erroneous reliance upon an uncontested and virtually unreasoned case cannot nullify the reliance of millions of Americans (as our historical analysis has shown) upon the true meaning of the right to keep and bear arms. In any event, it should not be thought that the cases decided by these judges would necessarily have come out differently under a proper interpretation of the right.

28. *Miller* was briefly mentioned in our decision in *Lewis v. United States*, 445 U.S. 55 (1980), an appeal from a conviction for being a felon in possession of a firearm. The challenge was based on the contention that the prior felony conviction had been unconstitutional. No Second Amendment claim was raised or briefed by any party. In the course of rejecting the asserted challenge, the Court commented gratuitously, in a footnote, that "[t]hese legislative restrictions on the use of firearms are neither based upon constitutionally suspect criteria, nor do they trench upon any constitutionally protected liberties. See *United States v. Miller* . . . (the Second Amendment guarantees no right to keep and bear a firearm that does not have 'some reasonable relationship to the preservation or efficiency of a well regulated militia')." *Id.*, at 65–66, n. 8. The footnote then cites several Court of Appeals cases to the same effect. It is inconceivable that we would rest our interpretation of the basic meaning of any guarantee of the Bill of Rights upon such a footnoted dictum in a case where the point was not at issue and was not argued.

29. We identify these presumptively lawful regulatory measures only as examples; our list does not purport to be exhaustive.

30. *Justice Breyer* correctly notes that this law, like almost all laws, would pass rational-basis scrutiny. *Post*, at 8. But rational-basis scrutiny is a mode of analysis we have used when evaluating laws under constitutional commands that are themselves prohibitions on irrational laws. See, *e.g.*, *Engquist v. Oregon Dept. of Agriculture*, 553 U.S. ___, ___ (2008) (slip op., at 9–10). In those cases, "rational basis" is not just the standard of scrutiny, but the very substance of the constitutional guarantee. Obviously, the same test could not be used to evaluate the extent to which a legislature may regulate a specific, enumerated right, be it the freedom of speech, the guarantee against double jeopardy, the right to counsel, or the right to keep and bear arms. See *United States v. Carolene Products Co.*, 304 U.S. 144, 152, n. 4 (1938) ("There may be narrower scope for operation of the presumption of constitutionality [*i.e.*, narrower than that provided by rational-basis review] when legislation appears on its face to be within a specific prohibition of the Constitution, such as those of the first ten amendments . . ."). If all that was required to overcome the right to keep and bear arms was a rational basis, the Second Amendment would be redundant with the separate constitutional prohibitions on irrational laws, and would have no effect.

31. *McIntosh* upheld the law against a claim that it violated the Equal Protection Clause by arbitrarily distinguishing between residences and businesses. See 395 A. 2d, at 755. One of the rational bases listed for that distinction was the legislative finding "that for each intruder stopped by a firearm there are four gun-related accidents within the home." *Ibid.* That tradeoff would not bear mention if the statute did not prevent stopping intruders by firearms.

32. The Supreme Court of Pennsylvania described the amount of five shillings in a contract matter in 1792 as "nominal consideration." *Morris's Lessee v. Smith*, 4 Dall. 119, 120 (Pa. 1792). Many of the laws cited punished violation with fine in a similar amount; the 1783 Massachusetts gunpowder-storage law carried a somewhat larger fine of 10 (200 shillings) and forfeiture of the weapon.

33. There was some limited congressional activity earlier: A 10% federal excise tax on firearms was passed as part of the Revenue Act of 1918, 40 Stat. 1057, and in 1927 a statute was enacted prohibiting the shipment of handguns, revolvers, and other concealable weapons through the United States mails. Ch. 75, 44 Stat. 1059–1060 (hereinafter 1927 Act).

34. Until the Fifth Circuit's decision in *United States v. Emerson*, 270 F. 3d 203 (2001), every Court of Appeals to consider the question had understood *Miller* to hold that the Second Amendment does not protect the right to possess and use guns for purely private, civilian purposes. See, *e.g.*, *United States v. Haney*, 264 F. 3d 1161, 1164–1166 (CA10 2001); *United States v. Napier*, 233 F. 3d 394, 402–404 (CA6 2000); *Gillespie v. Indianapolis*, 185 F. 3d 693, 710-711 (CA7 1999); *United States v. Scanio*, No. 97–1584, 1998 WL 802060, *2 (CA2, Nov. 12, 1998) (unpublished opinion); *United States v. Wright*, 117 F. 3d 1265, 1271–1274 (CA11 1997); *United States v. Rybar*, 103 F. 3d 273, 285–286 (CA3 1996); *Hickman v. Block*, 81 F. 3d 98, 100–103 (CA9 1996); *United States v. Hale*, 978 F. 2d 1016, 1018–1020 (CA8 1992); *Thomas v. City Council of Portland*, 730 F. 2d 41, 42 (CA1 1984) (*per curiam*);

(Continues)

United States v. Johnson, 497 F. 2d 548, 550 (CA4 1974) (*per curiam*); *United States v. Johnson,* 441 F. 2d 1134, 1136 (CA5 1971); see also *Sandidge v. United States,* 520 A. 2d 1057, 1058–1059 (DC App. 1987). And a number of courts have remained firm in their prior positions, even after considering *Emerson.* See, *e.g., United States v. Lippman,* 369 F. 3d 1039, 1043–1045 (CA8 2004); *United States v. Parker,* 362 F. 3d 1279, 1282–1284 (CA10 2004); *United States v. Jackubowski,* 63 Fed. Appx. 959, 961 (CA7 2003) (unpublished opinion); *Silveira v. Lockyer,* 312 F. 3d 1052, 1060–1066 (CA9 2002); *United States v. Milheron,* 231 F. Supp. 2d 376, 378 (Me. 2002); *Bach v. Pataki,* 289 F. Supp. 2d 217, 224–226 (NDNY 2003); *United States v. Smith,* 56 M. J. 711, 716 (C. A. Armed Forces 2001).

35. Our discussion in *Lewis* was brief but significant. Upholding a conviction for receipt of a firearm by a felon, we wrote: "These legislative restrictions on the use of firearms are neither based upon constitutionally suspect criteria, nor do they entrench upon any constitutionally protected liberties. See *United States v. Miller,* 307 U.S. 174, 178 (1939) (the Second Amendment guarantees no right to keep and bear a firearm that does not have 'some reasonable relationship to the preservation or efficiency of a well regulated militia')." 445 U.S., at 65, n. 8.

36. See *Vasquez v. Hillery,* 474 U.S. 254, 265, 266 (1986) ("[*Stare decisis*] permits society to presume that bedrock principles are founded in the law rather than in the proclivities of individuals, and thereby contributes to the integrity of our constitutional system of government, both in appearance and in fact. While *stare decisis* is not an inexorable command, the careful observer will discern that any detours from the straight path of *stare decisis* in our past have occurred for articulable reasons, and only when the Court has felt obliged 'to bring its opinions into agreement with experience and with facts newly ascertained.' *Burnet v. Coronado Oil & Gas Co.,* 285 U.S. 393, 412 (1932) (Brandeis, J., dissenting)"); *Pollock v. Farmers' Loan & Trust Co.,* 157 U.S. 429, 652 (1895) (White, J., dissenting) ("The fundamental conception of a judicial body is that of one hedged about by precedents which are binding on the court without regard to the personality of its members. Break down this belief in judicial continuity and let it be felt that on great constitutional questions this Court is to depart from the settled conclusions of its predecessors, and to determine them all according to the mere opinion of those who temporarily fill its bench, and our Constitution will, in my judgment, be bereft of value and become a most dangerous instrument to the rights and liberties of the people").

37. The Virginia Declaration of Rights ¶13 (1776), provided: "That a well-regulated militia, composed of the body of the people, trained to arms, is the proper, natural, and safe defence of a free State; that Standing Armies, in time of peace, should be avoided, as dangerous to liberty; and that, in all cases, the military should be under strict subordination to, and governed by, the civil power." 1 B. Schwartz, The Bill of Rights 235 (1971) (hereinafter Schwartz).

Maryland's Declaration of Rights, Arts. XXV-XXVII (1776), provided: "That a well-regulated militia is the proper and natural defence of a free government"; "That standing armies are dangerous to liberty, and ought not to be raised or kept up, without consent of the Legislature"; "That in all cases, and at all times, the military ought to be under strict subordination to and control of the civil power." 1 Schwartz 282.

Delaware's Declaration of Rights, §§18-20 (1776), provided: "That a well regulated militia is the proper, natural, and safe defence of a free government"; "That standing armies are dangerous to liberty, and ought not to be raised or kept up without the consent of the Legislature"; "That in all cases and at all times the military ought to be under strict subordination to and governed by the civil power." 1 Schwartz 278.

Finally, New Hampshire's Bill of Rights, Arts. XXIV-XXVI (1783), read: "A well regulated militia is the proper, natural, and sure defence of a state"; "Standing armies are dangerous to liberty, and ought not to be raised or kept up without consent of the legislature"; "In all cases, and at all times, the military ought to be under strict subordination to, and governed by the civil power." 1 Schwartz 378. It elsewhere provided: "No person who is conscientiously scrupulous about the lawfulness of bearing arms, shall be compelled thereto, provided he will pay an equivalent." *Id.,* at 377 (Art. XIII).

38. The language of the Amendment's preamble also closely tracks the language of a number of contemporaneous state militia statutes, many of which began with nearly identical statements. Georgia's 1778 militia statute, for example, began, "[w]hereas a well ordered and disciplined Militia, is essentially necessary, to the Safety, peace and prosperity, of this State." Act of Nov. 15, 1778, 19 *Colonial Records of the State of Georgia* 103 (Candler ed. 1911 (pt. 2)). North Carolina's 1777 militia statute started with this language: "Whereas a well regulated Militia is absolutely necessary for the defending and securing the Liberties of a free State." N.C. Sess. Laws ch. 1, §I, p. 1. And Connecticut's 1782 "Acts and Laws Regulating the Militia" began, "Whereas the Defence and Security of all free States depends (under God) upon the Exertions of a well regulated Militia, and the Laws heretofore enacted have proved inadequate to the End designed." Conn. Acts and Laws p. 585 (hereinafter 1782 Conn. Acts).

These state militia statutes give content to the notion of a "well-regulated militia." They identify those persons who compose the State's militia; they create regiments, brigades, and divisions; they set forth command structures and provide for the appointment of officers; they describe how the militia will be assembled when necessary and provide for training; and they prescribe penalties for nonappearance, delinquency, and failure to keep the required weapons, ammunition, and other necessary equipment. The obligation of militia members to "keep" certain specified arms is detailed further, n. 14, *infra*, and accompanying text.

39. The sources the Court cites simply do not support the proposition that some "logical connection" between the two clauses is all that is required. The Dwarris treatise, for example, merely explains that "[t]he general purview of a statute is not . . . *necessarily* to be restrained by any words introductory to the enacting clauses." F. Dwarris, *A General Treatise on Statutes* 268 (P. Potter ed. 1871) (emphasis added). The treatise proceeds to caution that "the preamble cannot control the enacting part of a statute, which is expressed in clear and unambiguous terms, yet, if any doubt arise on the words of the enacting part, the preamble may be resorted to, to explain it." *Id.*, at 269. Sutherland makes the same point. Explaining that "[i]n the United States preambles are not as important as they are in England," the treatise notes that in the United States "the settled principle of law is that the preamble cannot control the enacting part of the statute *in cases where the enacting part is expressed in clear, unambiguous terms.*" 2A N. Singer, *Sutherland on Statutory Construction* §47.04, p. 146 (rev. 5th ed. 1992) (emphasis added). Surely not even the Court believes that the Amendment's operative provision, which, though only 14 words in length, takes the Court the better part of 18 pages to parse, is perfectly "clear and unambiguous."

40. The Court's repeated citation to the dissenting opinion in *Muscarello v. United States,* 524 U.S. 125 (1998), *ante,* at 10, 13, as illuminating the meaning of "bear arms," borders on the risible. At issue in *Muscarello* was the proper construction of the word "carries" in 18 U. S. C. §924(c) (2000 ed. and Supp. V); the dissent in that case made passing reference to the Second Amendment only in the course of observing that both the Constitution and Black's Law Dictionary suggested that something more active than placement of a gun in a glove compartment might be meant by the phrase " 'carries a firearm.' " 524 U.S., at 143.

41. *Amici* professors of Linguistics and English reviewed uses of the term "bear arms" in a compilation of books, pamphlets, and other sources disseminated in the period between the Declaration of Independence and the adoption of the Second Amendment. See Brief for Professors of Linguistics and English as *Amici Curiae* 23–25. *Amici* determined that of 115 texts that employed the term, all but five usages were in a clearly military context, and in four of the remaining five instances, further qualifying language conveyed a different meaning.

    The Court allows that the phrase "bear Arms" did have as an idiomatic meaning, "'to serve as a soldier, do military service, fight,'" *ante,* at 12, but asserts that it "*unequivocally* bore that idiomatic meaning only when followed by the preposition 'against,' which was in turn followed by the target of the hostilities," *ante,* at 12–13. But contemporary sources make clear that the phrase "bear arms" was often used to convey a military meaning without those additional words. See, *e.g.,* To The Printer, Providence Gazette, (May 27, 1775) ("By the common estimate of three millions of people in America, allowing one in five to bear arms, there will be found 600,000 fighting men"); Letter of Henry Laurens to the Mass. Council (Jan. 21, 1778), in *Letters of Delegates to Congress 1774–1789,* p. 622 (P. Smith ed. 1981) ("Congress were yesterday informed . . . that those Canadians who returned from Saratoga . . . had been compelled by Sir Guy Carleton to bear Arms"); Of the Manner of Making War among the Indians of North-America, Connecticut Courant (May 23, 1785) ("The Indians begin to bear arms at the age of fifteen, and lay them aside when they arrive at the age of sixty. Some nations to the southward, I have been informed, do not continue their military exercises after they are fifty"); 28 *Journals of the Continental Congress* 1030 (G. Hunt ed. 1910) ("That hostages be mutually given as a security that the Convention troops and those received in exchange for them do not bear arms prior to the first day of May next"); H. R. J., 9th Cong., 1st Sess., 217 (Feb. 12, 1806) ("Whereas the commanders of British armed vessels have impressed many American seamen, and compelled them to bear arms on board said vessels, and assist in fighting their battles with nations in amity and peace with the United States"); H. R. J., 15th Cong., 2d Sess., 182–183 (Jan. 14, 1819) ("[The petitioners] state that they were residing in the British province of Canada, at the commencement of the late war, and that owing to their attachment to the United States, they refused to bear arms, when called upon by the British authorities . . .").

42. *Aymette v. State,* 21 Tenn. 154, 156 (1840), a case we cited in *Miller,* further confirms this reading of the phrase. In *Aymette,* the Tennessee Supreme Court construed the guarantee in Tennessee's 1834 Constitution that "'the free white men of this State, have a right to keep and bear arms for their common defence.'" Explaining that the provision was adopted with the same goals as the Federal

(Continues)

Constitution's Second Amendment, the court wrote: "The words 'bear arms' . . . have reference to their military use, and were not employed to mean wearing them about the person as part of the dress. As the object for which the right to keep and bear arms is secured, is of general and public nature, to be exercised by the people in a body, for their *common defence*, so the *arms*, the right to keep which is secured, are such as are usually employed in civilized warfare, and that constitute the ordinary military equipment." 21 Tenn., at 158. The court elaborated: "[W]e may remark, that the phrase '*bear arms*' is used in the Kentucky Constitution as well as our own, and implies, as has already been suggested, their military use. . . . A man in the pursuit of deer, elk, and buffaloes, might carry his rifle every day, for forty years, and, yet, it would never be said of him, that he had *borne arms*, much less could it be said, that a private citizen *bears arms*, because he has a dirk or pistol concealed under his clothes, or a spear in a cane." *Id.*, at 161.

43. As lucidly explained in the context of a statute mandating a sentencing enhancement for any person who "uses" a firearm during a crime of violence or drug trafficking crime:

> "To use an instrumentality ordinarily means to use it for its intended purpose. When someone asks, 'Do you use a cane?,' he is not inquiring whether you have your grandfather's silver-handled walking stick on display in the hall; he wants to know whether you *walk* with a cane. Similarly, to speak of 'using a firearm' is to speak of using it for its distinctive purpose, *i.e.*, as a weapon. To be sure, one can use a firearm in a number of ways, including as an article of exchange, just as one can 'use' a cane as a hall decoration—but that is not the ordinary meaning of 'using' the one or the other. The Court does not appear to grasp the distinction between how a word *can be* used and how it *ordinarily* is used." *Smith v. United States*, 508 U.S. 223, 242 (1993) (*Scalia, J.*, dissenting) (some internal marks, footnotes, and citations omitted).

44. See also Act for the regulating, training, and arraying of the Militia, . . . of the State, 1781 N.J. Laws, ch. XIII, §12, p. 43 ("And be it Enacted, That each Person enrolled as aforesaid, shall also *keep* at his Place of Abode one Pound of good merchantable Gunpowder and three Pounds of Ball sized to his Musket or Rifle" (emphasis added)); An Act for establishing a Militia, 1785 Del. Laws §7, p. 59 ("*And be it enacted*, That every person between the ages of eighteen and fifty . . . shall at his own expense, provide himself . . . with a musket or firelock, with a bayonet, a cartouch box to contain twenty three cartridges, a priming wire, a brush and six flints, all in good order, on or before the first day of April next, under the penalty of forty shillings, and shall *keep* the same by him at all times, ready and fit for service, under the penalty of two shillings and six pence for each neglect or default thereof on every muster day" (second emphasis added)); 1782 Conn. Acts 590 ("And it shall be the duty of the Regional Quarter-Master to provide and *keep* a sufficient quantity of Ammunition and warlike stores for the use of their respective regiments, to be *kept* in such place or places as shall be ordered by the Field Officers" (emphasis added)).

45. The Court notes that the First Amendment protects two separate rights with the phrase "the 'right [singular] of the people peaceably to assemble, and to petition the Government for a redress of grievances.'" *Ante*, at 18. But this only proves the point: In contrast to the language quoted by the Court, the Second Amendment does not protect a "right to keep *and to* bear arms," but rather a "right to keep and bear arms." The state constitutions cited by the Court are distinguishable on the same ground.

46. The Court's atomistic, word-by-word approach to construing the Amendment calls to mind the parable of the six blind men and the elephant, famously set in verse by John Godfrey Saxe. *The Poems of John Godfrey Saxe* 135–136 (1873). In the parable, each blind man approaches a single elephant; touching a different part of the elephant's body in isolation, each concludes that he has learned its true nature. One touches the animal's leg, and concludes that the elephant is like a tree; another touches the trunk and decides that the elephant is like a snake; and so on. Each of them, of course, has fundamentally failed to grasp the nature of the creature.

47. By "'split[ting] the atom of sovereignty,'" the Framers created "'two political capacities, one state and one federal, each protected from incursion by the other. The resulting Constitution created a legal system unprecedented in form and design, establishing two orders of government, each with its own direct relationship, its own privity, its own set of mutual rights and obligations to the people who sustain it and are governed by it.'" *Saenz v. Roe*, 526 U.S. 489, 504, n. 17 (1999) (quoting *U.S. Term Limits, Inc. v. Thornton*, 514 U.S. 779, 838 (1995) (*Kennedy, J.*, concurring)).

48. Indeed, this was one of the grievances voiced by the colonists: Paragraph 13 of the Declaration of Independence charged of King George, "He has kept among us, in times of peace, Standing Armies without the Consent of our legislatures."

49. George Washington, writing to Congress on September 24, 1776, warned that for Congress "[t]o place any dependance upon Militia, is, assuredly, resting upon a broken staff." 6 *Writings of George Washington* 106, 110 (J. Fitzpatrick ed. 1932). Several years later he reiterated this view in another letter to Congress: "Regular Troops alone are equal to the exigencies of modern war, as well for defence as offence. . . . *No Militia* will ever acquire the habits necessary to resist a regular force. . . . The firmness requisite for the real business of fighting is only to be attained by a constant course of discipline and service." 20 *id.,* at 49, 49–50 (Sept. 15, 1780). And Alexander Hamilton argued this view in many debates. In 1787, he wrote:

> "Here I expect we shall be told that the militia of the country is its natural bulwark, and would be at all times equal to the national defense. This doctrine, in substance, had like to have lost us our independence. . . . . War, like most other things, is a science to be acquired and perfected by diligence, by perseverance, by time, and by practice." *The Federalist* No. 25, p. 166 (C. Rossiter ed. 1961).

50. "[B]ut no Appropriation of Money to that Use [raising and supporting Armies] shall be for a longer Term than two Years." U.S. Const., Art I, §8, cl. 12

51. This "calling forth" power was only permitted in order for the militia "to execute the Laws of the Union, suppress Insurrections and repel Invasions." *Id.,* Art. I, §8, cl. 15.

52. The Court assumes—incorrectly, in my view—that even when a state militia was not called into service, Congress would have had the power to exclude individuals from enlistment in that state militia. See *ante,* at 27. That assumption is not supported by the text of the Militia Clauses of the original Constitution, which confer upon Congress the power to "organiz[e], ar[m], and discipl[in[e], the Militia," Art. I, §8, cl. 16, but not the power to say who will be members of a state militia. It is also flatly inconsistent with the Second Amendment. The States' power to create their own militias provides an easy answer to the Court's complaint that the right as I have described it is empty because it merely guarantees "citizens' right to use a gun in an organization from which Congress has plenary authority to exclude them." *Ante,* at 28.

53. In addition to the cautionary references to standing armies and to the importance of civil authority over the military, each of the proposals contained a guarantee that closely resembled the language of what later became the Third Amendment. The 18th proposal from Virginia and North Carolina read "That no soldier in time of peace ought to be quartered in any house without the consent of the owner, and in time of war in such manner only as the law directs." Elliott 659. And New York's language read: "That in time of Peace no Soldier ought to be quartered in any House without the consent of the Owner, and in time of War only by the Civil Magistrate in such manner as the Laws may direct." 2 Schwartz 912.

54. *"Tenth,* That no standing Army shall be Kept up in time of Peace unless with the consent of three fourths of the Members of each branch of Congress, nor shall Soldiers in Time of Peace be quartered upon private Houses with out the consent of the Owners."

55. Madison explained in a letter to Richard Peters, Aug. 19, 1789, the paramount importance of preparing a list of amendments to placate those States that had ratified the Constitution in reliance on a commitment that amendments would follow: "In many States the [Constitution] was adopted under a tacit compact in [favor] of some subsequent provisions on this head. In [Virginia]. It would have been *certainly* rejected, had no assurances been given by its advocates that such provisions would be pursued. As an honest man *I feel* my self bound by this consideration." *Creating the Bill of Rights* 281, 282 (H. Veit, K. Bowling, & C. Bickford eds. 1991) (hereinafter Veit).

56. The adopted language, Virginia Declaration of Rights ¶13 (1776), read as follows: "That a well-regulated Militia, composed of the body of the people, trained to arms, is the proper, natural, and safe defence of a free State; that Standing Armies, in time of peace, should be avoided as dangerous to liberty; and that, in all cases, the military should be under strict subordination to, and governed by, the civil power." 1 Schwartz 234.

57. Veit 182. This was the objection voiced by Elbridge Gerry, who went on to remark, in the next breath: "What, sir, is the use of a militia? It is to prevent the establishment of a standing army, the bane of liberty. . . . Whenever government mean to invade the rights and liberties of the people, they always attempt to destroy the militia, in order to raise an army upon their ruins." *Ibid.*

58. The failed Maryland proposals contained similar language. See *supra,* at 23.

59. The Court suggests that this historical analysis casts the Second Amendment as an "odd outlier," *ante,* at 30; if by "outlier," the Court means that the Second Amendment was enacted in a unique and novel context, and responded to the particular challenges presented by the Framers' federalism experiment, I have no quarrel with the Court's characterization.

60. The Court's fixation on the last two types of sources is particularly puzzling, since both have the same characteristics as postenactment legislative history, which is generally viewed as the least reliable source of authority for ascertaining the intent of any provision's drafters. As has been explained:

> "The legislative history of a statute is the history of its consideration and enactment. 'Subsequent legislative history'—which presumably means the *post*-enactment history of a statute's consideration and enactment—is a contradiction in terms. The phrase is used to smuggle into judicial consideration legislators' expression *not* of what a bill currently under consideration means (which, the theory goes, reflects what their colleagues understood they were voting for), but of what a law *previously enacted* means. . . . In my opinion, the views of a legislator concerning a statute already enacted are entitled to no more weight than the views of a judge concerning a statute not yet passed." *Sullivan v. Finkelstein*, 496 U.S. 617, 631–632 (1990) (*Scalia, J.,* concurring in part).

61. The Court stretches to derive additional support from scattered state-court cases primarily concerned with state constitutional provisions. See *ante,* at 38–41. To the extent that those state courts assumed that the Second Amendment was coterminous with their differently worded state constitutional arms provisions, their discussions were of course dicta. Moreover, the cases on which the Court relies were decided between 30 and 60 years after the ratification of the Second Amendment, and there is no indication that any of them engaged in a careful textual or historical analysis of the federal constitutional provision. Finally, the interpretation of the Second Amendment advanced in those cases is not as clear as the Court apparently believes. In *Aldridge v. Commonwealth*, 2 Va. Cas. 447 (Gen. Ct. 1824), for example, a Virginia court pointed to the restriction on free blacks' "right to bear arms" as evidence that the protections of the State and Federal Constitutions did not extend to free blacks. The Court asserts that "[t]he claim was obviously not that blacks were prevented from carrying guns in the militia." *Ante*, at 39. But it is not obvious at all. For in many States, including Virginia, free blacks during the colonial period were prohibited from carrying guns in the militia, instead being required to "muste[r] without arms"; they were later barred from serving in the militia altogether. See Siegel, The Federal Government's Power to Enact Color-Conscious Laws: An Originalist Inquiry, 92 *Nw. U. L. Rev.* 477, 497–498, and n. 120 (1998). But my point is not that the *Aldridge* court endorsed my view of the Amendment—plainly it did not, as the premise of the relevant passage was that the Second Amendment applied to the States. Rather, my point is simply that the court could have understood the Second Amendment to protect a militia-focused right, and thus that its passing mention of the right to bear arms provides scant support for the Court's position.

62. The Government argued in its brief that:

> "[I]t would seem that the early English law did not guarantee an unrestricted right to bear arms. Such recognition as existed of a right in the people to keep and bear arms appears to have resulted from oppression by rulers who disarmed their political opponents and who organized large standing armies which were obnoxious and burdensome to the people. This right, however, it is clear, gave sanction only to the arming of the people as a body to defend their rights against tyrannical and unprincipled rulers. It did not permit the keeping of arms for purposes of private defense." Brief for United States in *United States v. Miller*, O. T. 1938, No. 696, pp. 11–12 (citations omitted). The Government then cited at length the Tennessee Supreme Court's opinion in *Aymette,* 21 Tenn. 154, which further situated the English Bill of Rights in its historical context. See n. 10, *supra.*

63. Moreover, it was the Crown, not Parliament, that was bound by the English provision; indeed, according to some prominent historians, Article VII is best understood not as announcing any individual right to unregulated firearm ownership (after all, such a reading would fly in the face of the text), but as an assertion of the concept of parliamentary supremacy. See Brief for Jack N. Rakove et al. as *Amici Curiae* 6–9.

64. For example, St. George Tucker, on whom the Court relies heavily, did not consistently adhere to the position that the Amendment was designed to protect the "Blackstonian" self-defense right, *ante,* at 33. In a series of unpublished lectures, Tucker suggested that the Amendment should be understood in the context of the compromise over military power represented by the original Constitution and the Second and Tenth Amendments:

> "If a State chooses to incur the expense of putting arms into the Hands of its own Citizens for their defense, it would require no small ingenuity to prove that they have no right to do it, or that it could by any means contravene the Authority of the federal Govt. It may be alleged indeed that this might be done for the purpose of resisting the laws of the federal Government, or of shaking off the

union: to which the plainest answer seems to be, that whenever the States think proper to adopt either of these measures, they will not be with-held by the fear of infringing any of the powers of the federal Government. But to contend that such a power would be dangerous for the reasons above maintained would be subversive of every principle of Freedom in our Government; of which the first Congress appears to have been sensible by proposing an Amendment to the Constitution, which has since been ratified and has become part of it, viz., 'That a well regulated militia being necessary to the Security of a free State, the right of the people to keep and bear arms shall not be infringed.' To this we may add that this power of arming the militia, is not one of those prohibited to the States by the Constitution, and, consequently, is reserved to them under the twelfth Article of the ratified aments." S. Tucker, *Ten Notebooks of Law Lectures, 1790's, Tucker-Coleman Papers*, pp. 127–128 (College of William and Mary).

See also Cornell, St. George Tucker and the Second Amendment: Original Understandings and Modern Misunderstandings, 47 *Wm. & Mary L. Rev.* 1123 (2006).

65. The Court does acknowledge that at least one early commentator described the Second Amendment as creating a right conditioned upon service in a state militia. See *ante,* at 37–38 (citing B. Oliver, *The Rights of an American Citizen* (1832)). Apart from the fact that Oliver is the *only* commentator in the Court's exhaustive survey who appears to have inquired into the intent of the drafters of the Amendment, what is striking about the Court's discussion is its failure to refute Oliver's description of the meaning of the Amendment or the intent of its drafters; rather, the Court adverts to simple nose-counting to dismiss his view.

66. *Miller,* 307 U.S., at 182, n. 3.

67. The additional specified weaponry included: "a sufficient bayonet and belt, two spare flints, and a knapsack, a pouch with a box therein to contain not less than twenty-four cartridges, suited to the bore of his musket or firelock, each cartridge to contain a proper quantity of powder and ball: or with a good rifle, knapsack, shot-pouch and powder-horn, twenty balls suited to the bore of his rifle and a quarter of a pound of powder." 1 Stat. 271.

68. In another case the Court endorsed, albeit indirectly, the reading of *Miller* that has been well settled until today. In *Burton v. Sills,* 394 U.S. 812 (1969) (*per curiam*), the Court dismissed for want of a substantial federal question an appeal from a decision of the New Jersey Supreme Court upholding, against a Second Amendment challenge, New Jersey's gun control law. Although much of the analysis in the New Jersey court's opinion turned on the inapplicability of the Second Amendment as a constraint on the States, the court also quite correctly read *Miller* to hold that "Congress, though admittedly governed by the second amendment, may regulate interstate firearms so long as the regulation does not impair the maintenance of the active, organized militia of the states." *Burton v. Sills,* 53 N.J. 86, 98, 248 A. 2d 521, 527 (1968).

69. The 1927 statute was enacted with no mention of the Second Amendment as a potential obstacle, although an earlier version of the bill had generated some limited objections on Second Amendment grounds; see 66 Cong. Rec. 725–735 (1924). And the 1934 Act featured just one colloquy, during the course of lengthy Committee debates, on whether the Second Amendment constrained Congress' ability to legislate in this sphere; see Hearings on House Committee on Ways and Means H. R. 9006, before the 73d Cong., 2d Sess., p. 19 (1934).

70. The majority appears to suggest that even if the meaning of the Second Amendment has been considered settled by courts and legislatures for over two centuries, that settled meaning is overcome by the "reliance of millions of Americans" "upon the true meaning of the right to keep and bear arms." *Ante,* at 52, n. 24. Presumably by this the Court means that many Americans own guns for self-defense, recreation, and other lawful purposes, and object to government interference with their gun ownership. I do not dispute the correctness of this observation. But it is hard to see how Americans have "relied," in the usual sense of the word, on the existence of a constitutional right that, until 2001, had been rejected by every federal court to take up the question. Rather, gun owners have "relied" on the laws passed by democratically elected legislatures, which have generally adopted only limited gun-control measures.

Indeed, reliance interests surely cut the other way: Even apart from the reliance of judges and legislators who properly believed, until today, that the Second Amendment did not reach possession of firearms for purely private activities, "millions of Americans," have relied on the power of government to protect their safety and well-being, and that of their families. With respect to the case before us, the legislature of the District of Columbia has relied on its ability to act to "reduce the potentiality for gun-related crimes and gun-related deaths from occurring within the District of Columbia," H. Con. Res. 694, 94th Cong., 2d Sess., 25 (1976); see *post,* at 14–17 (*Breyer, J.,* dissenting); so, too have the residents of the District.

(Continues)

(*Continued*)

71. It was just a few years after the decision in *Miller* that Justice Frankfurter (by any measure a true judicial conservative) warned of the perils that would attend this Court's entry into the "political thicket" of legislative districting. *Colegrove v. Green*, 328 U.S. 549, 556 (1946) (plurality opinion). The equally controversial political thicket that the Court has decided to enter today is qualitatively different from the one that concerned Justice Frankfurter: While our entry into that thicket was justified because the political process was manifestly unable to solve the problem of unequal districts, no one has suggested that the political process is not working exactly as it should in mediating the debate between the advocates and opponents of gun control. What impact the Court's unjustified entry into *this* thicket will have on that ongoing debate—or indeed on the Court itself—is a matter that future historians will no doubt discuss at length. It is, however, clear to me that adherence to a policy of judicial restraint would be far wiser than the bold decision announced today.

Afterword

Well, we have come to the end of our wonderful adventure in understanding the Constitution!

Having thoroughly discussed the true brilliance and wonder of the United States Constitution, it is also essential to realize that it is a document written over 200 years ago by a group of men wearing white wigs who are now all dead. Because they are not around to explain to us exactly what they meant by every word they wrote, this very special document is now interpreted by nine men and women wearing black robes.

It is possible that the nine Supreme Court Justices can accurately determine what the Founding Fathers meant by everything they wrote? Of course not! But this is our system of government and, despite its imperfections, it is what we have, what we have fought for, and what most Americans would not trade for anything. Nonetheless, that does not negate the fact that Supreme Court Justices make mistakes at best, or inject their political agenda into the mix at worst. How then, can we stop them from doing either?

Think about it this way: there are computer techies who take 3 hours to fix a problem they could have fixed in 20 minutes; they spend the 20 minutes fixing your computer, and then take a two and a half hour lunch, but tell you they are still looking into the problem. Also, there are plumbers who will charge you $1,000 to install a five dollar part that takes 10 minutes to install, and they will spend another 3 hours screwing the same piece on and off your pipes just to kill time. Why do they do this? To take advantage of you. How do they get away with it? Easy: if we do not know very much about computers or plumbing, the techies and plumbers can get away with just about anything. If we *do* know a thing or two about computers and plumbing, however, then it becomes difficult for them to get one over on us.

Similarly, the more we, the American people, understand about our Constitution, the less likely it will be for the Justices to make mistakes or intentionally inject their personal agendas into their decisions. The more we learn, the more powerful we become, and the less likely we are to be removed from the government that belongs to us in the first place.

Therefore, in conclusion, I congratulate you on having finished this book, and advise you not to throw it away, sell it, or even give it away. Keep it with you always: it will be your permanent reference to the law on which our great nation was founded, on which it runs today, and on which it will continue to operate in the days, months, and years to come.

Did I say this is the *end* of our adventure? Actually, it is just the beginning.

Appendix

The following lists contain all of the United States Presidents, Vice Presidents, Supreme Court Chief Justices, and Speakers of the House of Representatives.

Presidents of the United States

President	Years Served	Political Party	Vice President(s)
George Washington	1789–1787	None (Federalist ideology)	John Adams
John Adams	1797–1801	Federalist	Thomas Jefferson
Thomas Jefferson	1801–1809	Democratic–Republican	Aaron Burr
			George Clinton
James Madison	1809–1817	Democratic–Republican	George Clinton
			Elbridge Gerry
James Monroe	1817–1825	Democratic–Republican	Daniel Tompkins
John Quincy Adams	1825–1829	Democratic–Republican	John C. Calhoun
Andrew Jackson	1829–1837	Democratic	John C. Calhoun
			Marin Van Buren
Martin Van Buren	1837–1841	Democratic	Richard Johnson
William Henry Harrison	1841	Whig	John Tyler
John Tyler	1841–1845	Whig	None
James Polk	1845–1849	Democratic	George Dallas
Zachary Taylor	1849–1850	Whig	Millard Fillmore
Millard Fillmore	1850–1853	Whig	None
Franklin Pierce	1853–1857	Democratic	William R. King
James Buchanan	1857–1861	Democratic	John Breckinridge
Abraham Lincoln	1861–1865	Republican	Hannibal Hamlin
			Andrew Johnson
Andrew Johnson	1865–1869	Democratic	None
Ulysses S. Grant	1869–1877	Republican	Schuyler Colfax
			Henry Wilson
Rutherford B. Hayes	1877–1881	Republican	William Wheeler
James A. Garfield	1881	Republican	Chester Alan Arthur
Chester Alan Arthur	1881–1885	Republican	None
Grover Cleveland	1885–1889	Democratic	Thomas Hendricks
Benjamin Harrison	1889–1893	Republican	Levi P. Morton
Grover Cleveland	1893–1897	Democratic	Adlai E. Stevenson I
William McKinley	1897–1901	Republican	Garret Hobart
			Theodore Roosevelt

Presents of the United States (*Continued*)

President	Years Served	Political Party	Vice President(s)
Theodore Roosevelt	1901–1909	Republican	Charles W. Fairbanks
William Howard Taft	1909–1913	Republican	James S. Sherman
Woodrow Wilson	1913–1921	Democratic	Thomas Marshall
Warren G. Harding	1921–1923	Republican	Calvin Coolidge
Calvin Coolidge	1923–1929	Republican	Charles Dawes
Herbert Hoover	1929–1933	Republican	Charles Curtis
Franklin D. Roosevelt	1933–1945	Democratic	John Garner
			Henry Wallace
			Harry S. Truman
Harry S. Truman	1945–1953	Democratic	Alben Barkley
Dwight D. Eisenhower	1953–1961	Republican	Richard Nixon
John F. Kennedy	1961–1963	Democratic	Lyndon B. Johnson
Lyndon B. Johnson	1963–1969	Democratic	Hubert Humphrey
Richard Nixon	1969–1974	Republican	Spiro Agnew
			Gerald Ford
Gerald Ford	1974–1977	Republican	Nelson Rockefeller
Jimmy Carter	1977–1981	Democratic	Walter Mondale
Ronald Reagan	1981–1989	Republican	George Bush
George Bush	1989–1993	Republican	Dan Quayle
Bill Clinton	1993–2001	Democratic	Al Gore
George W. Bush	2001–2009	Republican	Dick Cheney
Barack Obama	2009–0000	Democratic	Joe Biden

Chief Justices of the United States Supreme Court

Chief Justice	Years Served	Nominated by President
John Jay	1789–1795	George Washington
John Rutledge	1795	George Washington
Oliver Ellsworth	1796–1800	George Washington
John Marshall	1801–1835	John Adams
Roger Brooke Taney	1836–1864	Andrew Jackson
Salmon Portland Chase	1864–1873	Abraham Lincoln
Morrison Remick Waite	1874–1888	Ulysses S. Grant
Melville Weston Fuller	1888–1910	Grover Cleveland
Edward Douglas White	1910–1921	William Howard Taft
William Howard Taft	1921–1930	Warren G. Harding
Charles Evans Hughes	1930–1941	Herbert Hoover
Harlan Fiske Stone	1941–1946	Franklin D. Roosevelt
Frederick Moore Vinson	1946–1953	Harry S. Truman
Earl Warren	1953–1969	Dwight D. Eisenhower
Warren E. Burger	1969–1986	Richard Nixon
William H. Rehnquist	1986–2005	Ronald Reagan
John Roberts	2005–0000	George W. Bush

Speakers of the United States House of Representatives

Speaker	Years Served	Political Party
Frederic Muhelenberg	1789–1791	None (Federalist ideology)
Jonathan Trumbull, Jr.	1791–1793	None (Federalist ideology)
Frederic Muhelenberg	1793–1795	None (Anti-Federalist ideology)
Jonathan Dayton	1795–1799	Federalist
Theodore Sedwick	1799–1801	Federalist
Nathaniel Macon	1801–1807	Democratic–Republican
Joseph Bradley Varnum	1807–1811	Democratic–Republican
Henry Clay	1811–1814	Democratic–Republican
Langdon Cheves	1814–1815	Democratic–Republican
Henry Clay	1815–1820	Democratic–Republican
John W. Taylor	1820	Democratic–Republican
Philip Barbour	1821–1823	Democratic–Republican
Henry Clay	1823–1825	Democratic–Republican
John W. Taylor	1825–1827	Democratic–Republican
Andrew Stevenson	1827–1834	Democratic
John Bell	1834-1835	Democratic
James Polk	1835–1839	Democratic
Robert Hunter	1839–1841	Whig
John White	1841–1843	Whig
John Winston Jones	1843–1845	Democratic
John Wesley Davis	1845–1847	Democratic
Robert Charles Winthrop	1847–1849	Whig
Howell Cobb	1849–1851	Democratic
Limm Boyd	1851–1855	Democratic
Nathaniel Banks	1856–1857	Republican
James Orr	1857–1859	Democratic
William Pennington	1860–1861	Republican
Galusha Grow	1861–1863	Republican
Schuyler Colfax	1863–1869	Republican
Theodore Pomeroy	1869	Republican
James Blaine	1869–1875	Republican
Michael Kerr	1875–1876	Democratic
Samuel Randall	1876–1881	Democratic
Joseph Warren Keifer	1881–1883	Republican
John Carlisle	1883–1889	Democratic
Thomas Reed	1889–1891	Republican
Charles Crisp	1891–1895	Democratic
Thomas Reed	1895–1899	Republican
David Henderson	1899–1903	Republican
Joseph Cannon	1903–1911	Republican
Champ Clark	1911–1919	Democratic
Frederick Gillet	1919–1925	Republican
Nicholas Longworth	1925–1931	Republican
John Garner	1931–1933	Democratic
Henry Rainey	1933–1934	Democratic
Joseph Byrns	1935–1936	Democratic
William Bankead	1936–1940	Democratic
Samuel Rayburn	1941–1947	Democratic
Joseph W. Martin, Jr.	1947–1949	Republican
Samuel T. Rayburn	1949–1953	Democratic
Joseph W. Martin, Jr.	1953–1955	Republican
Samuel T. Rayburn	1955–1961	Democratic
John W. McCormack	1962–1971	Democratic
Carl Albert	1971–1977	Democratic
Thomas P. O'Neill, Jr.	1977–1987	Democratic
James C. Wright, Jr.	1987–1989	Democratic
Thomas Foley	1989–1995	Democratic
Newt Gingrich	1995–1999	Republican
Dennis Hastert	1999–2007	Republican
Nancy Pelosi	2007–0000	Democratic

CASE INDEX

A

Abrams v. United States, 116–117, 118, 143–148
ACLU v. Reno, 119
Allegheny County v. American Civil Liberties Union, 82

B

Barron v. City of Baltimore, 346, 348
Benton v. Maryland, 318
Berman v. Parker, 347
Blockburger v. United States, 317, 318
Bob Jones University v. United States, 82, 83
Brandenburg v. Ohio, 118
Brown v. Board of Education, 198, 199, 206, 216–222
Brown v. Ohio, 318–319, 320
Bush v. Gore, 7–31, 59

C

Capitol Square Review Board v. Pinette, 82
Carroll v. United States, 228–241
Chicago B. & Q. Railroad Company v. Chicago, 346
Church of the Lukumi Babalu Aye, Inc. v. Hialeah, 82, 83
Clark v. Nash, 346–347
Coker v. Georgia, 289
Craig v. Boren, 200–201

D

District of Columbia v. Heller, 393, 394, 397–458
Doe v. Bolton, 154, 180–196
Dred Scott v. Sanford, 392

E

Engel v. Vitale, 80

F

FCC v. Pacifica Foundation, 119
Fong Foo v. United States, 319, 320
Furman v. Georgia, 288

G

Gerard v. La Coste, 51–52
Grady v. Corbin, 317–318
Gratz v. Bollinger, 204
Gregg v. Georgia, 288
Grutter v. Bollinger, 204

H

Hamdan v. Rumsfeld, 227
Hamdi v. Rumsfeld, 228
Hammelin v. Michigan, 287
Hawaii Housing Authority v. Midkiff, 347, 348
Hiibel v. Sixth District Court of Nevada, 225–226
Hollingsworth v. Leiper, 50–51

J

Jacobellis v. Ohio, 118

K

Katz v. United States, 223–224
Kelo v. City of New London, 347–348, 350, 367–388
Kennedy v. Fury, 49
Kennedy v. Louisiana, 289, 393
Korematsu v. U.S., 202–203

L

Leib v. Bolton, 49
Lemon v. Kurtzman, 80–81
Lynch v. Donnely, 81–82

M

Marbury v. Madison, 60, 67–78
Marsh v. Chambers, 84, 95–114
Michael v. Superior Court, 200
Michigan v. Long, 225
Miller v. California, 118–119
Miranda v. Arizona, 226, 241–283
Mississippi University for Women v. Hogan, 204
Missouri v. Hunter, 319

N

NAACP v. Claiborne Hardware Co., 118
New York Times v. Sullivan, 116, 121–142

P

Planned Parenthood of Southeastern Pennsylvania v. Casey, 151–152
Plessy v. Ferguson, 198–199, 206–216

R

Rasul v. Bush, 227–228
Regents of the University of California v. Bakke, 204
Reynolds v. United States, 84–95
Ricci v. DeStefano, 204–205
Robinson v. California, 287
Roe v. Wade, 59, 149–179
Roper v. Simmons, 288, 289
Rostker v. Goldberg, 201–202
Ruckelshaus v. Monsanto, 350, 351–367

S

Sanabria v. United States, 321, 330–341
Santa Fe Independent School District v. Doe, 81
Schenck v. United States, 115
Sherbert v. Verner, 82, 83
Shrider's Lessee v. Morgan, 48–49
Silverthorne Lumber Co. v. United States, 224
Smalis v. Pennsylvania, 321, 342–344

INDEX

A

Constitutional Amendment(s); *See also* Bill of Rights; *specific amendments*
  Bill of Rights as first ten, 79
  process, 5
Constitutional Convention, 40–41, 42
  Madison's Preface to the, 42–48
constitutionalists, 151; *See also* constructionists, strict; originalists
  Brown v. Board of Education and, 199
  legislative *vs.* judicial authority and, 199
constructionists, loose, 151–152; *See also* judicial activists
constructionists, strict, 152; *See also* constitutionalists; originalists
  Founders' intent and, 151
Continental Congress; *See also* Congress
  First, 38
  Second, 38
court
  cases under Articles of Confederation, 48–52
  opinion (decision), 5
crime; *See also* double jeopardy; *malum in se* crime; *malum prohibitum* crime; trial(s)
  cases and jury trials, 3
  civil offense *vs.*, 317
  civil rights and, 321
  definition of, 317
  fighting *vs.* privacy protection, 224
  introduction into society, 284
  punishment and, 284–289
crime types, 284–285
  for death penalty, 287–288, 289
criminal mental states
  intent, 285
  negligence, 285
  punishment and, 285
  recklessness, 285
  three basic, 285
Crook, Shirley, 288
cruel and unusual punishment. *See* punishment, cruel and unusual
Cuba, and U.S./Guantanamo Bay, 227
Cuban Missile Crisis (1962), 227

D

DEA. *See* Drug Enforcement Administration
death penalty
  cases, 288–289
  Coker v. Georgia and, 289
  crime types for imposition of, 287–288, 289
  cruel and unusual punishment and, 287, 288, 289
  electrocution, 288, 289
  Furman v. Georgia and, 288
  Gregg v. Georgia and, 288
  hanging, 287, 288
  justifiability, 289
  Kennedy v. Louisiana and, 289
  for minors, 288
  for murder, 286, 287, 288, 289
  rape and, 289
  recipients of, 287–288
  Roper v. Simmons and, 288, 289
  states and, 289
  Supreme Court and, 288–289
  U.S. history of, 286–287
Declaration of Independence, 38
  "all men are created equal" contradiction with slavery, 198
defamation, 116
defendant, 5
democracy
  definition of, 1
  Electoral College and, 4
  the masses and, 4–5
  minority rights *vs.*, 41
  people and, 4–5, 7
  pure *vs.* representative, 1

republic *vs.*, 1, 7, 41
  U.S. and, 1, 6
  voting in, 1
Democratic Party, 7; *See also* Democrats; political parties
  history of, 55–56
democratic republic
  republican democracy *vs.*, 2
  U.S. as, 1, 2
Democratic-Republican Party, 56
Democrats; *See also* Democratic Party
  Antifederalists and, 55, 56
  big government and, 56
De Niro, Robert, 391, 392
Depression. *See* Great Depression
detainment, terrorist suspects
  Guantanamo Bay and, 227–228
  Rasul v. Bush and, 227–228
  Supreme Court and, 227–228
  trials and, 227–228
deterrence punishment theory
  general, 286
  specific, 286
discrimination, 205
  definition of, 197
  good *vs.* bad, 197
discrimination, unjustifiable; *See also* affirmative action; gender-based discrimination; nationality-based discrimination; racial discrimination
  affirmative action and, 197, 203–205
  black African Americans, 198–199, 200
  definition of, 197
  gender-based, 197, 199–202
  legal remedies *vs.* elimination of, 200
  nationality-based, 197, 202–203
  racial, 197, 198–199, 200, 202–203
  religious, 197
dissenting opinion, 6
double jeopardy, 317, 318
  act/offense/acquittal and, 321
  Benton v. Maryland and, 318
  Blockburger v. United States and, 317, 318
  Brown v. Ohio and, 318–319, 320
  civil liberties and, 321
  civil *vs.* criminal trials and, 317
  conspiracy unprotected by, 318
  defendant appeal *vs.* prosecution appeal and, 319
  defining, 321
  exceptions, 316–317
  federal/state levels and, 318
  Fifth Amendment and, 316
  Fong Foo v. United States and, 319, 320
  Grady v. Corbin and, 317–318
  judge's reversal midtrial and, 319–321
  lesser crime within greater crime and, 318–319
  meaning/interpretations of, 316, 317
  Missouri v. Hunter and, 319
  multiple crimes within single trial, 319
  multiple prosecutions prevention and, 318–319
  multiple trials and, 319
  multiple trials *vs.* multiple punishments, 319
  no second chance for court's mistake, 319, 320
  Sanabria v. United States and, 321, 330–341
  sentiment root, 321
  separate elements of a crime and, 317–318
  Smalis v. Pennsylvania and, 321, 342–344
  Smith v. Massachusetts and, 319–321
  Supreme Court and, 316, 317–318, 319–321
  "Trial of the Century" and, 316–317
  United States v. Felix and, 318
  United States v. Martin Linen Supply Company and, 321, 322–330
Douglass, Frederick, 199, 200, 225
Drug Enforcement Administration (DEA), 318
drugs, 225, 287, 317, 318

government intervention; *See also* big government; small government
    bailouts and, 349–350
    big *vs.* small government and, 349–350
    critics/supporters of, 350
    eminent domain and acceptable, 348–349, 350
Grant, Ulysses S., 199
Great Britain, and colonies, 38
Great Depression, 349
Great Society, 349
Green Party, 7
Griffin, Cyrus, 37
Guantanamo Bay, Cuba
    detainment, terrorist suspects and, 227–228
    military tribunals, 228
    PATRIOT Act and, 227
    U.S./Cuba and, 227
gun(s)
    Second Amendment interpretations, and feelings about, 390–391
    test, 391, 393
gun control, 394
    Brady Bill, 391–392
    firearm unlawful possession, 319–320
    NICS, 392
    no longer Wild West argument for, 390
    right to bear arms and, 390, 391–392, 393
    Second Amendment and, 390, 391–392, 393
Gun Test, 391, 393

H

Hamilton, Alexander
    biography, 41
    The Federalist Papers of, 4, 41–42
    voting and, 4
Hancock, John, 37
hanging, 287, 288
Hanson, John, 37, 40
Harrison, Benjamin, 81
Harrison, William Henry, 57
Harrison Anti-Narcotic Act, 317, 318
hate speech, 118
Hiibel, Larry Dudley, 225
Hinckley, John, Jr., 391, 392
Holmes, Oliver Wendell, 117, 118
Hombeck, Henry, 288
Hood, Tom, 288
Hoover, Herbert, 57
House of Representatives, 54; *See also* Congress
housing, affordable, 349
Hurricane Katrina
    Bush, George W. and, 390
    National Guard and, 58, 390

I

immigrants; *See also* nonimmigrants
    alien, 202
    definition, 202
    illegal, 350
immigration history, 202
impeachment. *See* Presidential impeachment
incarceration punishment theory, 286
indecency
    FCC v. Pacifica Foundation/"Seven Dirty Words" case, 119
    obscenity *vs.*, 119
    "Seven Dirty Words" case, 119
intent, 285
Internet
    Congress/pornography and, 119
    First Amendment and, 119
Iraq, 56–57

J

Jackson, Andrew, 56
Jacobs, John, 288
James, Autry, 288
Japanese–Americans
    Korematsu v. U.S., 202–203
    nationality-based discrimination, 202–203
Jay, John
    The Federalist Papers of, 41
    as first Supreme Court justice, 41
Jefferson, Thomas, 37, 41, 56, 59
Johnson, Amos, 288
Johnson, Andrew, 58, 59
Johnson, Lyndon Baines, 349
Jones, David, 288
joy riding, 318
judgment, 6
judicial activists, 151, 393; *See also* constructionists, loose; Progressives
judicial authority, *vs.* legislative authority, 60, 199, 289
judicial branch, 54; *See also* Supreme Court
    Article III and, 59
judicial philosophy; *See also* constitutionalists; originalists
    loose constructionist, 151–152
    strict constructionist, 151–152
jury trials
    criminal cases and, 3
    Fourth Amendment and, 3
    Seventh Amendment and, 53–54
just compensation, eminent domain, 345, 348
    arguability/true definitions of, 346, 350
Justice(s), 59; *See also* Supreme Court
    complexities of, 320
    Jay as first, 41
    Presidents as, 228
justice, requesting government for legal, 79

K

Katz, Charles, 224
Kennedy, Anthony, 152, 204, 205, 227, 228, 288, 289, 320, 347, 393
Kennedy, John F., 227
Kerry, John, 55–56
kidnapping, 284
King, Martin Luther, Jr., 198
Ku Klux Klan, 82, 118

L

larceny, 318
law(s); *See also* case law; state law
    Congress and "necessary and proper" clause, 55, 56
    court, 5
    enforcement, 228
    First Amendment and "Congress shall make no . . .", 79–80, 82
    legislative, 5
    Supreme Court and, 5
lawsuit, 5
Layton, Frank, 392–393
Lee, Richard Henry, 37
legislative authority
    judicial authority *vs.*, 60, 199, 289
    Supreme Court *vs.*, 60, 199
legislative branch; *See also* Congress
    Article I and, 54–56
    bicameral compromise, 54
    Congress as, 54–56
    elections/terms, 54
    powers/obligations, 55
    qualifications, 54
    term limits, 54–55
legislative intent, Founders, 80
lethal injection, 289

voting; *See also* Presidential election(s)
  in democracy, 1
  does count, 6, 7
  Electoral College and, 4, 5
  Founding Fathers and, 4
  Hamilton and, 4
  individual, 7
  the masses and, 4, 5
  people and, 4, 5, 7
  Presidential election (2000) and, 4, 7
  states and, 5
  Twenty-Sixth Amendment and, 1
voting right(s)
  black Americans Fifteenth Amendment, 2, 199
  Constitution and, 2–3, 5, 6, 199
  Fifteenth Amendment and, 2
  Fourteenth Amendment and, 2–3
  Nineteenth Amendment and, 2
  race and, 2
  Seventeenth Amendment and, 54
  states and, 3, 5, 53, 199
  technical *vs.* practical reality of, 3
  Twenty-Sixth Amendment and, 2, 53
  Williams v. Mississippi and, 31–36
  women's Nineteenth Amendment, 2, 3, 199

W

war
  governmental criticism during time of, 115, 116–117
  protests, 117
  Supreme Court and, 115, 116–117, 202–203
War for Independence. *See* Revolutionary War
warrants, and searches, 224
Warren, Earl, 226
Washington, D.C., 54

Washington, George, 41, 55, 59
  as eighth President, 37, 40
  Farewell Address, 56, 60–67
  warning about political parties, 56
Watergate scandal, 59
Webster, Timothy, 288
West Side Story, 202
Whig Party, 56, 57
White, Byron R., 152, 204, 287
White, John, 288
White, Robert, 288
Whitten, Jamie L., 54–55
Wilson, Woodrow, 116, 117
wiretapping; *See also* surveillance
  Constitution and, 228
  eavesdropping and, 224
  PATRIOT Act and, 226–227
  searches/seizures and, 224
women
  gender-based discrimination and, 197, 199–202
  in military/combat, 201
  in Presidential elections, 199, 200
  in underrepresented groups history, 199–202
  unjustifiable gender-based discrimination and, 197, 199–202
women's rights; *See also* gender-based discrimination
  to abortion, 152
  Congress' Equal Pay Act (1963) and, 199–200
  Nineteenth Amendment voting rights, 2, 3, 199
  suffrage, 199
Woodhull, Victoria, 199, 200
World War II, 202–203, 349
Wright, Sam, 288

X

xenophobia, 202

Photo Credits

Introduction

Page xvii © Anna Frajtova/ShutterStock, Inc.

Chapter 1

Page 3 (top) © Amanda Haddox/ShutterStock, Inc.; page 3 (bottom) © stocklight/ShutterStock, Inc.; page 6 (top) © Bert Reisfield/dpa/Landov; page 6 (bottom) © NBCU Photo Bank/AP Photos

Chapter 2

Page 38 Courtesy of Library of Congress, Prints & Photographs Division [reproduction number pga 01390]; page 40 Courtesy of Library of Congress, Prints & Photographs Division [reproduction number pga 03226]

Chapter 3

Page 54 © VisualField/ShutterStock, Inc.; page 57 Courtesy of the National Library of Medicine; page 58 Courtesy of Library of Congress, Prints & Photographs Division [reproduction number pga 02636]

Chapter 4

Page 81 Courtesy of Library of Congress, Prints & Photographs Division [reproduction number cph 3c04961]; page 83 © Jakub Wiechetek/Dreamstime.com

Chapter 5

Page 117 (top) © Warpress/Dreamstime.com; page 117 (bottom) Courtesy of Library of Congress, Prints & Photographs Division [reproduction number cph 3c28385]; page 120 © iconex/ShutterStock, Inc.

Chapter 6

Page 151 (top) Courtesy of Mollie Isaacs, Collection of the Supreme Court of the United States; page 151 (bottom) Courtesy of Steve Petteway, Collection of the Supreme Court of the United States; page 153 Courtesy of Ronald Reagan Presidential Library and Museum

Chapter 7

Page 200 (left) Courtesy of Library of Congress, Prints & Photographs Division [reproduction number LC-USZ62-2023]; page 200 (right) Courtesy of National Archives; page 205 (left) Courtesy of Robin Reid, Collection of the Supreme Court of the United States; page 205 (right) Courtesy of Steve Petteway, Collection of the Supreme Court of the United States

Chapter 8

Page 225 © Zina Seletskaya/ShutterStock, Inc.; page 227 (top) Courtesy of John F. Kennedy Presidential Library and Museum, Boston; page 227 (bottom) Courtesy of Library of Congress, Prints & Photographs Division [reproduction number ppmsc 03256]

Chapter 9

Page 287 Courtesy of Mass Communication Specialist 1st Class Chad J. McNeeley/U.S. Navy

Chapter 10

Page 317 © Sam Mircovich/Reuters/Landov; page 320 (top) Courtesy of Dane Pennland, Collection of the Supreme Court of the United States; page 320 (bottom) © Dennis Brack/Landov

Chapter 11

Page 348 Courtesy of Helene C. Stikkel/U.S. Department of Defense; page 349 (top) Courtesy of the Franklin D. Roosevelt Presidential Library & Museum, Hyde Park, New York; page 349 (bottom) Courtesy of Ronald Reagan Presidential Library and Museum

Chapter 12

Page 392 (top) © AP Photos; page 392 (bottom) © HO/AP Photos; page 393 Courtesy of Steve Petteway, Collection of the Supreme Court of the United States